Praise for Samuel Johnson

'A solidly constructed literary biography that makes judicious use of sources sidelined by Boswell, as well as later academic findings'
Guardian

'Well-researched, fully annotated and judiciously expressed . . . Peter Martin's volume is a worthy addition to everyone's shelf of Johnsoniana' *The Literary Review*

'Martin tells the familiar story well' *Observer*

'[*Samuel Johnson*] is a brisk and readable introduction to the great man's life. And if it encourages people to seek out Johnson's works, it will have performed a great service . . . He was a great critic, a great wit, a great writer; above all, as this book remind us, he was a great Englishman' *Daily Telegraph*

'Martin is industrious and engaging . . . Martin's virtue is his focus on his subject's humanity: less on the public man, more on his strange character, his depression and physical awkwardness, his piety and generosity – his brave tussles for happiness. And for Johnson that was the recipe of good, accessible biography'
Sunday Times

'A vivid, sensitively observed narrative of the life of Samuel Johnson' *New York Times*

'Modern biographers are aware of the competition. They have to write a first-rate book about Johnson or hear from critics that they've foolishly entered the wrong league. And a number of scholars . . . have given us remarkable portraits. They're now joined by Peter Martin, whose *Samuel Johnson: A Biography* is a model of its kind: a deeply felt, beautifully written account of a personality about whom we cannot know enough' *Wall Street Journal*

'A fetching new version of the life of Samuel Johnson'
Chicago Tribune

Peter Martin was born in Argentina of English parents and educated there and in America. He has taught English literature in both England and America and has written extensively on eighteenth-century British and American literature and culture. His books include a biography of Edmond Malone, *A Life of James Boswell* and (as editor) *The Essential Boswell: Selections from the Writings of James Boswell*. He spends some of the year in southern Spain and the rest of the year in West Sussex.

By Peter Martin

Pursuing Innocent Pleasures:
The Gardening World of Alexander Pope

British and American Gardens in the Eighteenth Century
(as editor)

From Jamestown to Jefferson: The Pleasure Gardens of Virginia

Edmond Malone, Shakespearean Scholar

A Life of James Boswell

The Essential Boswell *(as editor)*

Samuel Johnson: Selected Writings *(as editor)*

Samuel Johnson: A Biography

A Dog Called Perth

SAMUEL JOHNSON

A Biography

PETER MARTIN

PHOENIX

A PHOENIX PAPERBACK

First published in Great Britain in 2008
by Weidenfeld & Nicolson
This paperback edition published in 2009
by Phoenix,
an imprint of Orion Books Ltd,
Orion House, 5 Upper Saint Martin's Lane,
London WC2H 9EA

An Hachette UK company

1 3 5 7 9 10 8 6 4 2

A CIP catalogue record for this book
is available from the British Library.

ISBN 978-0-7538-2592-1

Typeset by Input Data Services Ltd, Bridgwater, Somerset

Printed and bound in the UK by
CPI Mackays, Chatham ME5 8TD

The Orion Publishing Group's policy is to use papers that
are natural, renewable and recyclable products and
made from wood grown in sustainable forests. The logging
and manufacturing processes are expected to conform to
the environmental regulations of the country of origin.

www.orionbooks.co.uk

For Maureen,
and in memory of Cindy

To strive with difficulties, and to conquer them, is the highest human felicity; the next, is to strive and deserve to conquer.

Ye who listen with credulity to the whispers of fancy, and pursue with eagerness the phantoms of hope; who expect that age will perform the promises of youth, and that the deficiencies of the present day will be supplied by the morrow; attend to the history of Rasselas, Prince of Abissinia.

SAMUEL JOHNSON

CONTENTS

LIST OF ILLUSTRATIONS

SECTION ONE

Michael Johnson (*engraving by E. Finden; Hyde Collection, Houghton Library, Harvard University*)

Edial School (*watercolour by Maureen Pier, after an engraving by C.J. Smith; Private Collection*)

Elizabeth Porter Johnson (*artist unknown, eighteenth century; Hyde Collection, Houghton Library, Harvard University*)

Letter from Johnson to his wife (*Hyde Collection, Houghton Library, Harvard University*)

Johnson's tea service (*The Samuel Johnson Birthplace Museum, Lichfield*)

Molly Aston (*frontispiece to Aleyn Reade*, Johnsonian Gleanings, *part VI*)

St John's Gate (*by John Chessel Buckler, 1809; Museum of the Order of St John, St John's Gate, London*)

Dr Johnson at Cave's the Publisher by Henry Wallis, 1854 (*Bridgeman Art Library*)

Elizabeth Carter by Joseph Highmore (*Dover Museum, Dover*)

Samuel Johnson by Reynolds (*National Portrait Gallery, London*)

Sir Joshua Reynolds, self-portrait (*National Portrait Gallery, London*)

Giuseppe Baretti after Reynolds, 1774 (*National Portrait Gallery, London*)

James Boswell (*Scottish National Portrait Gallery, Edinburgh*)

SECTION TWO

Mrs Thrale and her daughter Queeney (*The Beaverbrook Art Gallery, Fredericton, New Brunswick, Canada*)

Streatham Place in the late eighteenth century (*Hyde Collection, Houghton Library, Harvard University*)

Samuel Johnson by Reynolds (*Tate Britain*)

Oliver Goldsmith (*National Portrait Gallery, London*)

James Boswell, sketch by Lawrence (*National Portrait Gallery, London*)

Turk's Head Tavern (*watercolour by Maureen Pier, after an eighteenth-century engraving; Private Collection*)

Samuel Johnson, Oliver Goldsmith and Mrs Thrale (*probably by Nathaniel Dance, early 1770s; Private collection of Sir William Rees-Mogg*)

Charlotte Lennox (*engraving by Francesco Bartolozzi, after portrait by Reynolds; National Portrait Gallery, London*)

Anna Williams by Frances Reynolds (*Dr Johnson's House, Gough Square, London*)

The Nine Living Muses of Great Britain (National Portrait Gallery, London)

Mr and Mrs Garrick at Hampton, by Johann Zoffany (*Collection of the Earl of Durham*)

Samuel Johnson by Reynolds (*Tate Britain*)

SECTION THREE

Samuel Johnson by Reynolds (*The Huntington Art Collections, San Marino, California*)

Samuel Johnson by Barry (*National Portrait Gallery, London*)

A Young Black by Reynolds (*The Menil Foundation Collection, Houston, Texas*)

Page from Johnson's 'Diary' (*Hyde Collection, Houghton Library, Harvard University*)

Fanny Burney by Edward Francisco Burney, 1784–5 (*National Portrait Gallery, London*)

Hannah More by Frances Reynolds (*City of Bristol Museum and Art Gallery*)

Frances Reynolds (*mezzotint by Samuel William Reynolds, published in 1824, after portrait by Joshua Reynolds; National Portrait Gallery, London*)

Edmund Burke by James Barry, c.1774–5 (*National Portrait Gallery, London*)

A plaster cast of the bust of Johnson by Cruikshank and Hoskins (*National Portrait Gallery, London*)

PART-TITLE ILLUSTRATIONS

The watercolours of Market Square, Lichfield; Pembroke College, Oxford; Johnson's house in Gough Square and Thomas Davies's house are by Maureen Pier (Private Collection). Engraving of Edward Cave (Hyde Collection, Houghton Library, Harvard University). Eighteenth-century token of Johnson (Beinecke Rare Book and Manuscript Library, Yale University)

MAPS

London (by M. Pier, based on R. and J. Dodsley's map of 1761)   xx–xxi

Johnson's travels in Scotland   376

PREFACE

I came to write a biography of Samuel Johnson for the tercentenary of his birth in 2009 through writing biographies of Edmond Malone and James Boswell, two good friends devoted to the great man who between them did the most to create a post-Johnson Johnsonian world. The leading Shakespearean of the eighteenth century, Malone quickly joined the Johnson circle after he moved to London from Ireland in the late 1770s to devote himself to literature. Boswell called him 'Johnsonianissimus'. By then Johnson had already been Boswell's dear friend and hero for fifteen years. When Boswell and Malone first met shortly before Johnson's death, Malone saw clearly that if Boswell was going to fulfil his long-time ambition of writing Johnson's life, he would need all the help and encouragement he could give him. He dedicated himself to that end, prodding and cajoling, lifting Boswell out of his wearying melancholia, and spending hundreds of hours with him reading out loud and correcting the manuscripts of both his *Tour to the Hebrides* and monumental *Life of Johnson* (1791), which has often been called the greatest biography in the English language. Without Malone's help, Boswell would probably never have published his *Life*.

But there are problems with Boswell's biography. Although it preserves the vast majority of Johnson's conversation that has come down to us – a huge artistic achievement of narrative skill, memory and persistence – and presents him dynamically in scenes among friends and in all sorts of social situations which make him come alive in ways that none of his other biographers have ever equalled, it perpetuates a popular perception of Johnson, which flourished in his own lifetime, chiefly as a personality and truculent conversationalist. This is only part of the picture.

After Johnson published his brilliant moral essays in the 1740s and his great *Dictionary* in 1755, he became the voice of the age, the rationalist epitome and sage of the Enlightenment. His reputation was enormous.

Bewigged, muscular and, for his day, unusually tall at six feet, his massive frame famously dressed in crumpled and soiled clothes, beset by involuntary tics and erratic movements that startled many, opinionated, deferred to, feared for his strong rebuttals, powered in his inimitable and legendary conversation by a prodigious memory, Johnson became a literary and social icon such as no other man of letters in that age ever achieved. 'I believe there is hardly a day in which there is not something about me in the newspapers,' he remarked to Boswell a few years before he died. In his *Life*, Boswell celebrated these personality stereotypes and helped create a cult featuring Johnson as the Great Cham and the Great Clubman through a portrait so large and aggressive that for over a century and a half after Johnson's death the man dominated the writer. While in the nineteenth and early twentieth centuries Boswell's biography of Johnson became one of the best-known books in the English language, Johnson's own extensive and remarkable works became relatively unpopular. Johnson has been frozen in the minds of people who have never read him into a firm image of a man always in company talking and living up to the public's caricature of him: the great literary dictator and arbiter, the rigid neo-classical critic, the lexicographer and editor lacking poetic imagination, one who spent the better part of his waking hours acting out his role as the great 'club' man, the conservative spokesman for the Tory cause – indeed, the defender of tradition from language to politics to social behaviour. Virtually all of these tags are inaccurate and misleading. It was not until well into the twentieth century that, in a reaction against this lopsided view, critics and biographers began to direct attention to Johnson's writings, but the popular image refuses to fade away.

There are other problems with Boswell's *Life*. It presents a man essentially at peace in his own mind. Boswell did not want his portrait to be of a man wracked with self-doubt, guilt, fear and depression. He rarely cited from Johnson's writings, did not make sensational use of Johnson's diary extracts to which he had access, and was not privy to his friend's deepest secrets and worries as was Mrs Hester Thrale, Johnson's most intimate female friend who later after remarriage wrote his biography, with something of a bias against him, under her new name 'Piozzi', but whom for the sake of clarity I will always refer to as Mrs Thrale. She turned out to be, in Boswell's mind, his greatest rival as Johnson's biographer. Except for mentioning it, neither did he explore the manifestations of his subject's melancholia even though an assortment of fears connected to that 'vile melancholy' afflicted Johnson's entire life and deeply shaped much of his thought and behaviour. A horrible act about three weeks before he died throws a retrospective light on what he once called 'the general disease of my life'.

One cold day in late November or early December, dying and very likely in a depressed state of acute guilt for a life he felt had not lived up to God's and his own expectations, and accompanied by his faithful black servant Frank Barber, Johnson began rounding up his personal papers and taking them in arm-loads out into his garden at Bolt Court, just off Fleet Street. There for more than a week he did 'little else' than set fire to them in a conflagration or holocaust that has to be numbered as one of the greatest literary tragedies of all time. Letters and manuscripts of all kinds went up in flames. Hour after hour Johnson fed the fire, hoping it would help consume his guilt and prepare his soul for death. He burned his mother's letters with tears streaming from his eyes. Few letters written to him survived. We would have fewer still if Boswell earlier had not preserved many of his own to Johnson and if Johnson himself had not, as it appears, spared Hester Thrale's from the blaze. Even two of his large quarto diaries fed the flames. Only fragments of these have survived, again partly due to Boswell's enterprise. For a man who repeatedly urged Boswell and several others to keep journals, such an act seems recklessly contradictory. It surprised and horrified his friends.

How did such a literary calamity come to pass? Johnson's surviving prayers, meditations and diaries – most of which Boswell never saw – as well as his letters, abound with warning signs. Poised dangerously between control and madness, between doubt, fear and faith, tormented by the dread of loneliness and death and lacerated by physical as well as mental sickness, he often feared he would fall into madness. In his recent book, *Shakespeare: The Invention of the Human*, Harold Bloom wrote, 'I worship Johnson, particularly on Shakespeare, and suspect that his own perilous balance, the fear of madness, made him seek rational design where none exists.'[1] Shakespeare scholarship, the classics, lexicography, essay writing, biography, journalism, travel writing, sermons, allegorical fables, and a host of other forms of prose and poetry in which Johnson relentlessly probed himself and the world around him, not to mention his passion for conversation, all constituted rational triumphs against despair and depression. Ironically, his extraordinary religious faith deepened his fears. His growing certainty that he would not go to heaven, that he had let God down and not used his talents fully enough, and that he had wasted time through indolence and idle thoughts all conspired against him. The holocaust was a final, desperate effort to wipe the slate clean before death.

Who really was this man who his own and later ages have celebrated, even venerated, so thoroughly? There is a portrait by his friend Sir Joshua Reynolds painted in the 1760s, when Johnson was in his late fifties, which speaks volumes about the private Johnson. In it Johnson does not hide under the wig in which men were conventionally painted in the eighteenth century and which could blur the persona with an appearance of social respectability. He looks less cloaked and protected, vulnerable yet courageous, even defiantly introspective. The energy of the profile seems almost agonised, focused on troubled thoughts, wrestling with difficult ideas that lie deep within – a mind seemingly preying on itself. Instead of resting inert on a table or chair, Johnson's hands are held up prominently, gesticulating oddly, his fingers bent tensely, 'as if he had been seized with the cramp'.[2] The side view also accentuates Johnson's vitality and force, his physicality and great strength: a large, muscular frame with broad shoulders, large facial features and a massive neck. This is my favourite portrait of the several Reynolds painted of him because it cuts through the clichés about Johnson which prevailed during his lifetime and have persisted ever since. It helps make him accessible to us not as a relic of the eighteenth century but as a man beset by problems common to us all, with important things to say about the human condition. The portrait invites us to confront tragic realities about Johnson's life and character which Boswell and other early biographers more or less underplayed. His life was a journey of agony and courage, a struggle to survive. It was never a level playing field for him. When his wife died early in their marriage, he fell into a despondency and grief from which he really never recovered and which almost drowned him in recurring guilt for the rest of his life. And yet, the portrait also projects Johnson's bravery and determination to overcome such fearful odds.

The best way to get the measure of Johnson is to read him. I have often thought that if I were stranded on a desert island, in addition to the Bible and the complete works of Shakespeare I would wish to have with me a complete run of Johnson's moral essays, especially those from the *Rambler* – almost 450 of them in all. John Ruskin wrote that on their foreign travels his father would carefully pack the *Rambler* and *Idler* in their luggage because they contained 'more substantial literary nourishment than could be, from any other author, packed into so portable compass ... I at once and for ever recognised in him a man entirely sincere, and infallibly wise in the view and estimate he gave of the common questions, business, and ways of the world ... No other writer could have secured me, as he did, against all chance of being misled by my own sanguine and metaphysical temperament. He taught me carefully to measure life, and distrust fortune.'[3] Ruskin hit a nerve there. What makes Johnson such a great character is that in all his writing he combines enormous intelligence with frank personal weakness. He is able to unfold for us endless shades of morality at the same time as guiding us into the labyrinths of human nature itself as an open book – making his own human nature the greatest text. That was very empirical and English of him. That was what the Argentinian writer Jorge Luis Borges, a rabid Anglophile for whom Johnson was a literary hero, had in mind when, on a visit to England, he surprised an audience by stating that Johnson was more English than Shakespeare.

Johnson was something of a hero of Jane Austen's, too. She showed a vigorous keenness for his moral essays especially and how they attacked social pretentiousness and prideful self-delusion. When one reads Johnson, one is struck by how modern he is. Far from being rigidly conservative, backward-looking and authoritarian, he was one of the most advanced liberals of his time. Author of some of the greatest critical writing ever written, his natural instinct was to prick bubbles of pretension and nonsense – what he called 'cant', 'a whining pretension to goodness' – under whatever labels or in whatever institutions they flourished. The anger and defiance in his writing often make one wince – a feature of his persona which has not been sufficiently stressed by biographers. He had a sharp tongue when he detected humbug, flimflam, smugness and insincerity, and sent many home licking their wounds. Interlopers, pompous hypocrites, people in power, the chattering aristocracy and irresponsible newspapers were certain to provoke his indignation and mockery. He was empirical, downright, willing to argue, brave, and deftly and sometimes severely humorous. He could be every bit as funny as modern humourists, savouring a comic thought like Oliver Goldsmith's vanity over his new purple coat for hours afterwards, his laughter filling a room and echoing along the streets. His directness and impatience with what today we call political correctness would have made him a popular guest for television interviews and talk shows. He was also unorthodox, which he felt was the only way to be a critic, judging not by conventional rules but according to his reading of human nature. On behalf of native populations, he hit hard against colonial expansion and imperialism, especially in the Americas. While the Government and people were strongly behind it, he was stridently opposed to the Seven Years' War. Far from being a spokesman for the Establishment and Tory cause, he was one of the strongest advocates for the abolition of slavery, treating his own black servant Frank Barber like a son, 'freeing' and educating him, and leaving most of his estate to him in his will.

Far in advance of his time, Johnson's encouragement of women writers and his respect for their works was legendary. 'Always fly at the eagle,' he implored his shy but witty young friend and admirer Fanny Burney. He treated women as intellectual equals and promoted their literary careers – a theme mostly untouched by Boswell. 'I dined yesterday at Mrs Garrick's with Mrs [Elizabeth] Carter, Miss Hannah More, and Miss Fanny Burney,' he wrote. 'Three such women are not to be found'.[4] His tireless charity and Christian benevolence towards the underprivileged, oppressed and poor were well known in his lifetime. All these themes I pursue in this book, benefiting hugely from the large body of recent critical scholarship that has explored new attitudes towards Johnson and his world.

How well known is Johnson today? He is a pervasive presence in the English-speaking world, the second most quoted literary figure in Britain (after Shakespeare). Sometimes it seems as if scarcely a day passes without his being cited in a travel guide, sports article, philosophical tract, sermon, newspaper report or advertisement (as recently for an Arab airline). The 2005 fifty-pence coin bears his name on it as the author of the *Dictionary*. And he was even the target of a hammer attack in August 2007 at the National Portrait Gallery when a man apparently furious over the plight of the English language and somehow blaming Johnson for it smashed through the glass and damaged the canvas of Reynolds's portrait of him, known as 'Dictionary Johnson' and valued at almost £2 million. A more positive event occurred in 2001 when I picked up the American biographer David McCullough at the St Louis airport for a talk he was delivering at the college where I was then teaching. He was nearing the final stages of his best-selling biography of John Adams and as we drove across the flat Illinois landscape he told me he had read Johnson's *Dictionary* to help him tune into the eighteenth-century English that Adams knew. Paradoxically, in spite of Johnson's iconic status and occasional programmes about him on television and on the radio, I have been surprised from spot interviews in the high streets of several English towns that only about a quarter of the people I spoke to could identify him. Some wondered whether he was a boxer, or a contemporary of Shakespeare's, or a Canadian sprinter convicted of drug-taking, or a leading Conservative MP. One might have thought that the featuring of Johnson and his *Dictionary* in a hilarious episode of the British television sitcom *Blackadder* would have lodged his name somewhat more permanently in the general public's memory. With a little help several people did at last recall something about a dictionary. The problem is partly that few people read Johnson today. His works are rarely assigned in schools and scarcely ever appear in school examinations. As a great thinker and writer Johnson must be read, otherwise, even after decades of penetrating scholarship and biographical illumination, he will continue to take a back seat in the popular mind to his worshipper, Boswell.

My debts to Johnsonian research are obvious in my notes, but here I would like to express particular gratitude to a number of people who have made Johnson their life's work. The late Paul Korshin, a friend and founder and editor of *The Age of Johnson*, encouraged me in this enterprise and read several chapters before his tragic death. Robert Folkenflik has read the entire manuscript and provided minute and insightful criticism, drawing on his encyclopedic grasp of Johnson's life and writings; my debt to him is considerable. Jack Lynch has also read the manuscript and corrected a few errors, as has John Kulka. Thomas Kaminski also took time out from his busy schedule to carefully read several chapters and give me helpful suggestions on Johnson's early career in London. In an endless number of ways numerous other critics and Johnsonians have helped me find my way through this huge project.

No biography exists in a critical vacuum, and mine is no exception in being heavily indebted to the following biographical scholarship on Johnson over the past thirty years: Thomas Kaminski, *The Early Career of Samuel Johnson*; Robert DeMaria, *The Life of Samuel Johnson: A Critical Biography* and *Samuel Johnson and the Life of Reading*; John Wain's *Samuel Johnson*; Robert Folkenflik, *Samuel Johnson, Biographer*; Walter Jackson Bate, *Samuel Johnson*; and Lawrence Lipking, *Samuel Johnson: The Life of an Author*. Also extremely valuable and useful have been Bruce Redford's edition of Johnson's *Letters*, Roger Lonsdale's edition of *The Lives of the Poets*, Alvin Kernan's *Samuel Johnson and the Impact of Print*, Allen Reddick's *The Making of Johnson's Dictionary*, John Wiltshire's *Samuel Johnson in the Medical World*, Pat Rogers's *The Samuel Johnson Encyclopedia*, several recent 'companion' volumes of Johnson criticism with a plethora of fresh insights into Johnson's life and works, and a host of essays that have appeared for almost twenty years now in Paul Korshin and Jack Lynch's splendid annual publication, *The Age of Johnson: A Scholarly Annual*. I should also mention Henry Hitchings's vivid and perceptive *Dr Johnson's Dictionary: The Extraordinary Story of the Book that Defined the World*.

The Johnsonian world of societies and clubs on both sides of the

Atlantic still thrives, and it is a measure of Johnson's continuing strong influence that their members continue to maintain 'clubbability' and support each other in their efforts to make Johnson and his humanitarian contributions more widely known throughout the world. When I laid the wreath on Johnson's tomb in Westminster Abbey a few years ago as part of the annual Johnson Society of London's commemoration of his death, I palpably felt that I was one member of a world community expressing gratitude to this extraordinary man. It is hoped that the tercentenary events in 2009 commemorating Johnson's birth will do much to extend that world and especially make his writings more widely read.

I should also like to thank the Leverhulme Trust for granting me an Emeritus Fellowship in 2003 that enabled me to spend several months working at the Beinecke Rare Book and Manuscript Library at Yale University and with the Hyde Collection, now in the Houghton Library, Harvard University, but then at Four Oaks Farm, Princeton, New Jersey. My thanks, too, to Robinson College, University of Cambridge, for a Bye-Fellowship in the spring of 2003.

A word of remembrance for my former agent, the late Giles Gordon, whose friendship and help in the early stages of writing this book were critical. Thanks, too, to my agent David Godwin, my editor at Weidenfeld and Nicolson, Benjamin Buchan, who provided valuable detailed commentary on the manuscript and skilfully steered it through the press, and to Ion Trewin for his encouragement and many lunches at the Garrick. My late wife Cindy was at the heart of this project in its early days, a radiant support, while Andrew, Claire, Adele, and Iain have, as always, been as anchors in rough waters. Finally, Maureen Pier has been here to help me with editing, proofreading and collecting illustrations, as well as in a host of other ways that have smoothed the way and kept me, in Johnson's words, from being 'deranged through solitude and intense study'.

Peter Martin
West Sussex and Spain
January 2008

LONDON

Based on R. and J. Dodsley's
map of 1761

Gray's Inn — 15

Gray's Inn Lane

Holborn

High Holborn

Lincoln's Inn Fields — 14

Fetter Lane

Oxford Street

Drury Lane

1

2   3

Fleet Street

Covent Garden Market — 9   8

7

4

5

The Temple

10

St Martin's Lane

Leicester Fields

The Strand

Temple Stairs

12

6

Piccadilly

11

River Thames

St James's Square

Whitehall

St James's Park

Buckingham House

Westminster Bridge

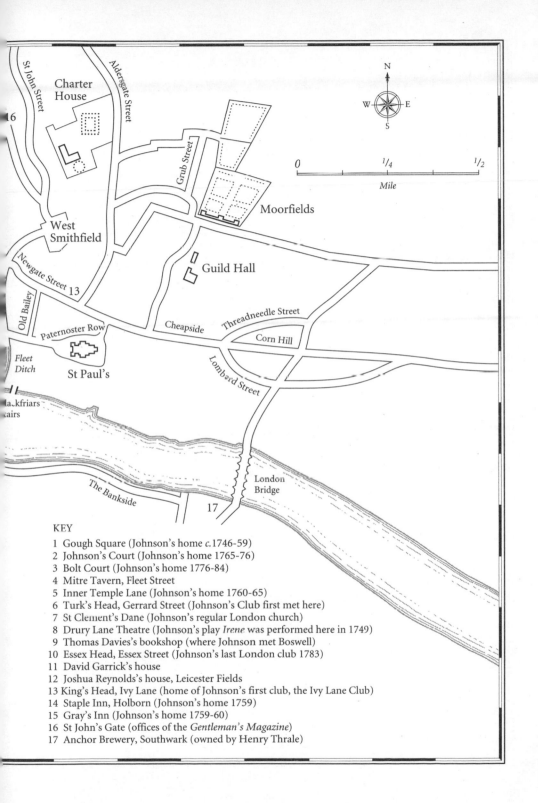

KEY

1 Gough Square (Johnson's home c.1746-59)
2 Johnson's Court (Johnson's home 1765-76)
3 Bolt Court (Johnson's home 1776-84)
4 Mitre Tavern, Fleet Street
5 Inner Temple Lane (Johnson's home 1760-65)
6 Turk's Head, Gerrard Street (Johnson's Club first met here)
7 St Clement's Dane (Johnson's regular London church)
8 Drury Lane Theatre (Johnson's play *Irene* was performed here in 1749)
9 Thomas Davies's bookshop (where Johnson met Boswell)
10 Essex Head, Essex Street (Johnson's last London club 1783)
11 David Garrick's house
12 Joshua Reynolds's house, Leicester Fields
13 King's Head, Ivy Lane (home of Johnson's first club, the Ivy Lane Club)
14 Staple Inn, Holborn (Johnson's home 1759)
15 Gray's Inn (Johnson's home 1759-60)
16 St John's Gate (offices of the *Gentleman's Magazine*)
17 Anchor Brewery, Southwark (owned by Henry Thrale)

PART I

Staffordshire Youth

Market Square, Lichfield

CHAPTER I

Anecdotes of Beggary

[1]

'I was born at Lichfield.' These are the first words Johnson, in his mid-fifties, writes about himself in his *Diaries, Prayers, and Annals*. When he wrote the *Annals* he had somewhat resolved the uncomfortable ambivalence he had felt towards his birthplace ever since leaving it with David Garrick in 1737 at the age of twenty-seven for London, the vast scene of his eventual fame. He was to return three months later, then again two years later for several months. But after that he would not be back for twenty-two long years, three years after the death of his mother.

When he finally returned in the winter of 1761–2, a famous man and subsidised by a government pension, he wrote the following about his visit:

> I went down to my native town, where I found the streets much narrower and shorter than I thought I had left them ... My play-fellows were grown old, and forced me to suspect, that I was no longer young ... I wandered about for five days, and took the first convenient opportunity of returning to a place, where, if there is not much happiness, there is at least such a diversity of good and evil, that slight vexations do not fix upon a heart.

It is understandable, though not for that reason less surprising, that Johnson should wipe so much about Lichfield, family and friends off his mental landscape for almost a quarter of a century. Relative poverty, health problems from infancy, depression, disappointments and family strife all conspired to deprive him of a happy Lichfield youth. It would not be until he was in his mid-fifties that the foundations of his affection for his Staffordshire roots would begin to surface and claim his attention and heart. When in 1767 he made his first lengthy visit 'home' since the winter of 1739–40, for about five months, the bookseller Thomas Davies, who famously first introduced Johnson to

Boswell, thought it was significant enough to report it to Boswell: 'Dr Johnson is still at his beloved Lichfield, the place of his birth. I had a letter from him very lately ... [he] is at last become sick of the place for want of proper amusement, and yet cannot assume resolution enough to break his fetters and come away to his friends.' 'Beloved' Lichfield certainly, but Davies touches on the fact that in later years Johnson tended to get bored there and long to return to the excitement of London. Not until his last fifteen years did he feel a pull strong enough to draw him to Lichfield almost every year until he died, which impelled him to think about and visit old friends and schoolmates, and even inspired him to come to the rescue of a few of them who were in dire personal and financial circumstances.[1]

Lichfield was no out-of-the-way place. By the middle of the eighteenth century England's notoriously miserable roads, largely unchanged since the Middle Ages and very dangerous, had begun to give way to comprehensive road improvements. As a result, the country developed a network of fast, convenient and relatively comfortable coaching routes far in advance of any other country in the world. Lichfield was helped prominently on to the map because it sat strategically at the crossroads of two major trunk routes: from London up to Liverpool, Manchester and the North-West, and from Bristol to Sheffield, Leeds and the North-East.[2] In spite of its energy as one of the most important coaching cities in the Midlands, however – and it was commonly referred to as a city – Lichfield looked and felt more like a close-knit market town. It had a village atmosphere to it, and people knew and gossiped about each other and luxuriated in the personal and beautiful character of the town's layout. Though Johnson remarked how altered it seemed to him, Lichfield had, in fact, changed relatively little for over a century, except for the establishment of several coaching inns. In Johnson's later years something stirred within him for the old place and for his vanished youth among the small lanes, leafy groves and watery ways. He lamented the deaths of old friends and his local attachment to particular scenes. Every time he returned, there were fewer old faces to see and therefore there was more boredom. 'This place grows more and more barren of entertainment,' he wrote in the summer of 1777. He also was vexed when Lichfield's Corporation clouded his evaporating memories with 'improvements' here and there, such as on the occasion he dined with the Corporation and 'talked against a workhouse which they have in *contemplation*'; or when one of his favourite haunts, Stowe Mill, lay 'much degenerated'; or when in the summer of 1769, after wandering by the streams and along the familiar lanes in a Virgilian fantasy, he discovered to his horror that 'they have cut down the trees in George Lane'. Lichfield's small-town atmosphere was valuable to him – in the last year of his life he returned to it in a tender Latin poem for his boyhood friend and classmate Edmund Hector – but he also found it disturbing because it revived memories of neighbours he had known in his boyhood who had died and been replaced by strangers. His roots were in these streets, but there seemed little there to afford him a feeling of stability or permanence.[3]

[2]

In his *Dictionary of the English Language*, Johnson defined 'lich' as 'a dead carcase', from which lichgate, a covered gateway to a churchyard through which the dead are carried to be buried, takes its name. He then elaborates: '*Lichfield*, the field of the dead, a city in Staffordshire, so named from martyred Christians.'[4] '*Salve magna parens*,' or 'Hail, great mother,' he added, saluting his place of birth. To have one's town described as 'the field of the dead' may not have entirely pleased Lichfield residents in the mid-eighteenth century, but there were grounds for believing that the 'lich' in Lichfield meant death instead of marsh, as had been more commonly believed at the time. Johnson was alluding to the massacre of early Christian Britons in the fourth century by Roman soldiers who, according to legend, massacred them all in an area where the town now sits. It was not until AD 669 that a Christian settlement was established there by St Chad, the Bishop of Mercia, who was a principal force in spreading Christianity in the Midlands. The story goes that he chose this spot for his see because St Augustine is supposed to have visited the site of the massacre and pronounced it hallowed ground. A primitive Christian church already existed there and St Chad quickly turned Lichfield into the ecclesiastical centre of Middle England. His cell was to the east of the centre of the modern town, at the east end of which was the hamlet of Stowe (Saxon for 'holy place'), now Stowe Pool, dear to Johnson's heart because it was where Molly Aston lived, one of the great loves of his life. The little twelfth-century church of St Chad, the oldest building in Staffordshire, sits peacefully there today next to Stowe Pool. The well where St Chad is thought to have baptised members of his flock is still known as St Chad's Well. According to 'The Venerable Bede' in his *Ecclesiastical History* (731), St Chad at his death in 672 was accompanied to heaven by a flight of angels, whereupon this religious settlement became known as a type of Fatima or Lourdes. For centuries until the Reformation pilgrims came to worship and be cured there.[5]

There was plenty of water on the site of the town from the start, a swampy or marshy valley cutting east-west through which streams glided peacefully and from which in the twelfth century two beautiful ponds were created, Minster Pool and Stowe Pool. It was on the north side of this valley, just above Minster Pool, that a Saxon church was first built in the seventh century, supplanted by a Norman church begun in 1085, which in turn was replaced by the present triumph of English cathedrals (built between 1195 and the 1330s), described by Daniel Defoe as 'one of the finest and most beautiful in England', with three spires known as 'The Ladies of the Vale'. To the south of the little valley and Minster Pool is where the modern town was laid out and where, a short walk across a little bridge from the cathedral and its close, Johnson was born and went to school next to the Market Place. By the time he was born, Lichfield had emerged as an important cultural centre in the Midlands, an increasingly urbane semi-rural community of about three thousand inhabitants for whom the vortex of ecclesiastical life and influence had diminished considerably.[6]

[3]

When Defoe passed through Lichfield, mostly in the 1720s, he was undoubtedly aware of a couple of the recent famous 'sons' of the town. One was Elias Ashmole, the seventeenth-century antiquarian and astrologer, who was born in Breadmarket Street in 1617 and attended Lichfield Grammar School. In 1682 he founded the Ashmolean Museum at Oxford University by giving the university his large collection of curiosities, many of them bequeathed to him by the famous naturalist and plant collector John Tradescant. Joseph Addison, the most famous English essayist in the eighteenth century, was also brought up in Lichfield. He was still an infant when his father was appointed Dean of Lichfield and the family moved into the cathedral close. But Defoe (who died in 1731) would have been impressed, even amazed, had he been told something of what lay ahead for this little Midlands market town by way of intellectual, literary and scientific

achievements during the rest of the century. 'We are a city of philosophers,' Johnson once boasted. Apart from Johnson, Lichfield's
greatest gift to English culture in the eighteenth century was David
Garrick, whose meteoric career as an actor in London began soon
after he and Johnson arrived there together. Born in Hereford, brought
up in Lichfield, and also a pupil at the grammar school, Garrick was
always a faithful friend to Johnson although his spectacular success
and considerable wealth provoked Johnson's jealousy.[7]

On the scientific side, Erasmus Darwin, the literary botanist,
poet and grandfather of Charles Darwin, was born in 1731, moved
to Lichfield in 1756, and practised medicine there for many years.
He established a famous botanical garden at his large house by the
West Gate entrance to the Close in Beacon Street, where he did
much of the botanical research leading to, among other things,
ideas on the sexual behaviour of plants and on evolution which
influenced his grandson. After he left Lichfield in 1781, he turned
literary and published his famous poem in heroic couplets, *The
Botanic Garden* (1791), which left its mark on Shelley, Coleridge and
other Romantic poets. As it happened, Darwin's radical and free-
thinking religious and political views were such that he and Johnson
took a dislike to one another, though that did not stop Johnson
from taking Hester Thrale and her husband to visit him and his
eight-acre botanical garden in 1774, where Mrs Thrale was particularly struck by Darwin's one hundred varieties of roses. Darwin
contributed his radical and political views as well as his scientific
insights to the proceedings of the famous Lunar Society in Birmingham which, with great entrepreneurs, inventors and industrialists such as Josiah Wedgwood, James Watt, Joseph Priestley
and Matthew Boulton (whom Boswell called the 'iron chieftain')
among its members, was one of the forces that kick-started the
Industrial Revolution. The society, which took its name from its
meetings at each full moon, occasionally convened in Lichfield.
Johnson may have had no truck with the radical philosophies that
permeated the proceedings of the society, nor with the newer
generation of Lichfield personalities such as the educational moralist
Thomas Day (who was inspired by Rousseau) or the socialist
philosopher Richard Lovell Edgeworth (the father of the novelist
Maria Edgeworth) who had links to it, but he had an instinctive
sympathy with the remarkable industrial innovations its members
were offering the country from that part of his world.

[4]

It was in the cathedral close that the best conversation and manners were to be found as Samuel was growing up. The town itself offered a few old Lichfield families and fine homes, but as the Johnsons had lived in the town for only two generations and were still regarded as newcomers, and as they were always stifled by lack of money, they did not move easily or naturally in those social orbits. His bookseller father and mother 'had not much happiness from each other,' Johnson wrote in his *Annals*. 'They seldom conversed; for my father could not bear to talk of his affairs; and my mother, being unacquainted with books, cared not to talk of any thing else. Had my mother been more literate, they had been better companions.' Apparently he confided in Mrs Thrale his unhappiness with his family in his youth, for later she wrote that he 'did not delight in talking much of his family – "one has (says he) *so* little pleasure in reciting the anecdotes of beggary".' Unable to leave the matter alone, a few pages later he added, 'My father considered tea as very expensive, and discouraged my mother from keeping company with the neighbours, and from paying visits or receiving them. She lived to say, many years after, that, if the time were to pass again, she would not comply with such unsocial injunctions.' It is unlikely, however, that if his mother had been more literate the marriage would have been significantly happier, for the seeds of its aridity lay in the starkly different backgrounds of Sarah Ford and Michael Johnson.[8]

Mrs Thrale remarked that he, clearly alluding to his mother's lack of learning, once told her, 'I did not respect my own mother, though I loved her.' In Johnson's autobiographical snatches there are precious few 'little memorials' of tender moments in his childhood home, but after recollecting a handful involving his mother he admitted that they 'soothe my mind'. By that he meant that they softened his memory of her and lessened his guilt about her. The guilt can be traced partly to his behaviour, perhaps an adolescent type of intellectual arrogance, which sprang from a lack of respect or regard for her ignorance of books, not from any lack of love or regard for her motherliness and practical wisdom, although he never once in later years referred to her as his *dearest* mother, as he did to several female friends. Johnson confided to Mrs Thrale one example of his arrogance towards his mother which is shocking in its disrespect. 'Poor people's children, dear Lady,' he told her, 'never respect them . . . one day, when in anger she called me a puppy, I asked her if she knew what they called a puppy's mother.' When she died in 1759, he wrote a heartfelt prayer for her petitioning God: 'Forgive me whatever I have done unkindly to my mother, and whatever I have omitted to do kindly. Make me to remember her good precepts, and good example.'[9]

Although Boswell maintained that Sarah Ford was 'a woman of distinguished understanding', there is no evidence to back this up, unless he meant simply that she was a sensible and practical home-maker. Indeed, Johnson stressed the opposite about his mother during his boyhood, 'My mother ... lived in a narrow sphere ... affected by little things ... Her mind, I think, was afterwards much enlarged, or greater evils wore out the care of less.' Her great leverage in her marriage was that she came of a good yeoman family, even affluent, from the Birmingham area. Of this social status the Fords were fully conscious and naturally proud, as was Johnson who, in the epitaph he wrote for his mother, highlighted that she was 'of the ancient family of Ford'. In his *Annals* he also played up this assumed superiority and the ill-feeling it generated, urging it as a prevalent theme of contention between his mother and father: 'My mother had no value for his relations; those indeed whom we knew of were much lower than hers. This contempt began, I know not on which side, very early: but, as my father was little at home, it had not much effect.' It is a pretty dismal picture, one that Johnson painted for Mrs Thrale clearly and insistently enough to elicit this passage she wrote on the marriage in her *Anecdotes of the Late Samuel Johnson*, published a couple of years after Johnson's death:

> Mr Johnson's mother was daughter to a gentleman in the country, such as there were many of in those days, who possessing, perhaps, one or two hundred pounds a year in land, lived on the profits, and sought not to increase their income: she was therefore inclined to think higher of herself than of her husband, whose conduct in money matters being but indifferent, she had a trick of teasing him about it, and was, by her son's account, very importunate with regard to her fears of spending more than they could afford, though she never arrived at knowing how much that was; a fault common, as he said, to most women who pride themselves on their economy.

Johnson allowed that, as far as he could tell, his parents did not 'live ill together on the whole', but sadly that was because 'my father could always take his horse and ride away for orders when things went badly'.[10]

Johnson's great-grandfather Henry Ford was a substantial yeoman and miller at the start of the seventeenth century living in the parish of Aston, just north of Birmingham, and then later in West Bromwich, to the west of the city. After his death in 1648 his widow Mary Ford and their son Cornelius moved to the bucolic village of King's Norton, Worcestershire, five miles south of Birmingham, where they purchased a large property picturesquely called Haunch Hall for a substantial sum. Mary Ford's other son, Henry, became a highly successful London lawyer with a big house and lots of property also very near Birmingham. Cornelius married around 1661 and had eight children at Haunch Hall, which must have made it an energetic and lively place to grow up. But it was more than that, for Cornelius was far better educated than most of his village neighbours, appreciated books, and owned something of a library which uniquely nourished his children in their village setting and opened up opportunities and promising futures for them. The whole family had moved to another big house not far away in Curdworth, Warwickshire by 1688, and then to Packwood in the same county about thirteen years later. All of the boys either married well or became highly successful professionals in medicine, law and education. It was at Packwood that, after all her brothers and sisters had left, Johnson's mother stayed with her father in their new home following the death of her mother in 1701, entirely devoting herself (as she had previously) to the running of her father's household. This was her lot and as the years rolled by she was content with it.[11]

In 1706 she was thirty-seven. Unmarried at that advanced age and prepared for little except the routines of housekeeping, she was in a poor position to find a good husband except that she came from a good family. Her destiny seemed to be to live out her life as a spinster until her elder sister Phoebe came to her rescue. Phoebe had married a saddler named John Harrison of Lichfield whose father had been Sheriff of the city and claimed some murky aristocratic lineage. It was probably through the Harrisons, who lived in Lichfield, that Sarah was fatefully introduced to the 49-year-old Lichfield bookseller Michael Johnson and married him on 19 June 1706. Phoebe's marriage to Harrison, therefore, may be seen as a supreme gift to English literature and culture, but it was not an ideal marriage for her. Harrison was a widower and had moved to Birmingham by 1719, when his nephew Samuel at the age of nine and his younger brother stayed in his house for a few days during the Whitsuntide holidays. 'Why such boys were sent to trouble other houses, I cannot tell,' Johnson wrote, but 'my mother had some opinion that much improvement was to be had by changing the mode of life', and also by exposing him to her side of the family. His uncle disgusted him: 'My uncle Harrison did not much like us, nor did we like him. He was a very mean and vulgar man, drunk every night, but drunk with little drink, very peevish, very proud, very ostentatious, but, luckily, not rich.' Actually, his drunkenness may not have been that unusual in Lichfield, Johnson told Boswell with some exaggeration, because people of that generation drank mostly ale instead of wine, so that 'all the decent people in Lichfield got drunk every night, and were not the worse thought of it.' However, Sarah had other more cultured relatives to whom she could turn to broaden her children's horizons and who a few years later would prove to be a distinctly positive, if risky, influence.[12]

Mrs Thrale described Michael Johnson as 'a man of still larger size and greater strength than his son; who was reckoned very like him'. Boswell added the word 'robust'. There is a sense about him that he was attractive to women, for there are at least two stories, one true and the other probably not, of women who were ready and willing to marry him when he was a young man. He was licensed to marry the daughter of a prominent tradesman when he was twenty-nine but the wedding never came off. His son may not have known this romantic fact about him, for it is the sort of detail of family history that he surely would have mentioned in his *Annals*. Boswell tells another, certainly apocryphal, tale of a woman named Elizabeth Blaney who conceived such a desire for the brawny Michael that she in effect stalked him, taking lodgings across from his house in Lichfield and indulging her 'hopeless flame' for months on end. As Boswell tells it, Michael's 'generous humanity' eventually took pity on her and he offered to marry her, but 'it was then too late: her vital power was exhausted; and she actually exhibited one of the very rare instances of dying for love'. The details of the story were a fabrication, perpetuated probably by the poetess Anna Seward, known as 'the swan of Lichfield', who did not like Johnson, but it was one way to evoke a romantic early manhood for a man who, by the time he married and fathered his famous son, was an unromantic, late middle-aged, tired bookseller, financially burdened, desperate for someone like Sarah Ford to keep his house in order, and impressed by her family connections. For Sarah, eager to escape the fate of spinsterhood, marriage to Michael Johnson was nonetheless a good idea even if she felt she was marrying beneath her. A life full of books did nothing to make him more attractive to her, but at least he seemed to be selling them and coming up in the world.[13]

Samuel Johnson made the remarkable admission to Boswell that the Johnson family history was so obscure that 'I can hardly tell who was my grandfather'. He could squeeze out 'some pretensions to blood' from his mother's background, but for his father's family he mustered mostly bitterness and disdain because of the huge economic and social disadvantages in which its relative poverty placed him. Either he never had any interest in learning about his father's parentage and ancestors, or he was too ashamed of them to admit he knew very much. He did know that his grandfather William Johnson eked out a living of some sort, probably as a farm labourer, in Cubley, Derbyshire, on the road to Ashbourne about twenty miles north of Lichfield, where three sons and a daughter were born to him and his wife Catherine: Michael in 1657, Benjamin in 1659, Andrew in 1660 and Margaret in 1663. Soon after Margaret's birth the family made the dramatic and courageous move from sleepy Cubley to bustling Lichfield, hoping to enhance its economic prospects and the children's educational opportunities. What William did for a living in Lichfield is as much of a blank to us as, apparently, it was to his grandson, but we know he moved his home from street to street in the next few years and did not do well with whatever line of work he chose. The parish assessed his worth at almost the lowest in town. He died in 1672 and was buried at St Michael's Church in Lichfield, leaving behind an impoverished widow and four hungry young mouths.[14]

Various parish charities saved the widow and children from serious poverty and possibly even homelessness. The children very likely were also able to attend the superb Lichfield Grammar School. When Michael was five, he received a grant to defray school fees from the Lichfield Conduit Lands Trust, and then in 1673, when he was sixteen and just after his father died, the Trust paid his mother £4 (about £400 today),[15] including travel expenses, to have him apprenticed for eight years to a bookseller called Richard Simpson in London. This of course was a huge turning point in the boy's life, so off he went to London to be bound to Simpson in the bookshop the latter had just set up at the sign of The Harp in St Paul's Churchyard. Simpson turned out to be prominent in the London book trade and eventually Master of the Stationers' Company, so Michael was in good hands. Later his two brothers were also apprenticed to Simpson. Michael did not dally in London once his apprenticeship ended in 1681. He hastened back to Lichfield to set up a bookselling and bookbinding business at a prime commercial location in Sadler Street (later Market Street). So the families of both of Samuel's parents turned out to have books as an important part of their lives. The chief difference was that Cornelius Ford collected them while the Johnsons sold them.

Twenty-five years in the business would elapse before Michael Johnson married, but they were years which he appears to have put to good use if his reputation and civic role in the town are reliable clues. In three years he was elected Warden of the Conduit Lands Trust, which involved him, among other things, in a scheme for building a house for the headmaster of the grammar school – a headmaster, ironically, whom his son came to despise. Three years after that he became Overseer of the Poor and then a churchwarden of St Mary's Church, just around the corner from his shop. These were notable responsibilities, not likely to be given to someone who had not impressed the town's leaders as successful and reliable. Still, it remains a puzzle how a man who launched himself as a bookseller with no capital so quickly began to make a mark, and why he failed to translate this early success and his considerable industry and energy into sustainable prosperity in later years.

In the *Annals* Samuel Johnson gives us his take on this. He wrote impatiently of his parents that 'neither of them ever tried to calculate the profits of trade, or the expenses of living'. Presumably, this was Michael's problem before he was married as well. Johnson continues that his nagging mother 'concluded that we were poor, because we lost by some of our trades [business transactions]; but the truth was, that my father, having in the early part of his life contracted debts, never had trade sufficient to enable him to pay them, and maintain his family; he got something, but not enough.' Other diversifying enterprises for which he had to borrow included several costly forays into publishing, from which he made little profit, and in the late 1690s a bold move into the manufacture of vellum and parchment. He set up a little workshop or parchment factory on the marshy perimeter of Stowe Pool, in an area known as the Moggs halfway along the picturesque path to St Chad's Church. This 'factory' plodded along as a drain on his resources until 1717 when he was charged by the Lichfield Quarter Sessions for practising the trade without the required seven-year apprenticeship. Add to this his bad bookkeeping and the recipe for financial frustration is complete. As for his wife, she appears to have been no help with any aspect of the business and may even have demoralised her husband. 'Of business,' Johnson writes, 'she had no distinct conception; and therefore her discourse was composed only of complaint, fear, and suspicion.' Exasperated, Johnson adds that in about 1768 he picked up some family papers and computed his father's profits. 'This, I believe, my parents never did.' He does not tell us what he discovered, though in 1774 he still meant to but did not 'note down my father's stock, expenses, and profit'.[16]

There would be more borrowing. Michael Johnson was determined that as a newly married man he would have a book business and home befitting his new wife's social background. The costs of the effort conspired to render his family household perpetually poor in later years, although at first it must have felt prosperous enough owing to his wife's dowry of almost five hundred pounds and the carefully arranged marriage settlement by Sarah's father, who doubted Michael's ability to provide properly for his daughter and a future family.[17]

Michael started to spend heavily right away. In 1706, the year of his marriage, he threw himself off the deep end financially in an effort to advance to a higher league in the bookselling business. He borrowed to buy the entire library of no fewer than 2,900 volumes belonging to the Earl of Derby (who had died in 1702) at Knowsley, near Liverpool. This was supposed to expand his business dramatically, for which he must have thought he had encouragement from wealthy customers and the cathedral close's ecclesiastical population, but the unhappy reality was he had trouble selling the books. Many volumes from the collection hung around his shop unsold for decades. The next year he did something even more audacious. He purchased a seventeenth-century property on the corner of Market and Breadmarket streets, virtually across from St Mary's Church and commandingly facing Market Place with all its hustle and bustle of twice-weekly markets. He paid £80 for it and surely caused a stir in town by proceeding immediately to reduce the building to rubble. He leased extra land along the street from the Lichfield Corporation and in the place of the old building raised the tall, respectable residence where Samuel was born and which served as both home and shop. The imposing new home had a basement and four lovely storeys supported on outside pillars and cantilevered prettily on Breadmarket Street, the main entrance facing the market square. The house looked much as it does today, with the kitchen in the basement, a large bookshop on the ground floor, two parlours, and perhaps as many as ten or eleven bedrooms. The four bedrooms at the top were for servants and apprentices. All of this initially would have delighted Sarah Johnson, of course, but none of it was inexpensive and the reckoning would inevitably come, much of it to Samuel's conspicuous disadvantage.[18]

Given Sarah's age when they married, if the Johnsons were going to have a family they could not afford to wait. Childbearing was fraught with dangers. Yet more than two years elapsed before Sarah's first pregnancy, and it did not help that four months before she gave birth her father died, leaving them a meagre legacy. It also disturbed their domestic peace that a few weeks before the birth Michael was elected Sheriff of Lichfield, one of the town's highest offices. It was an honour (without financial benefits) but there was so much more to think about as a result, at a time when fewer distractions and demands on the family may have been desirable.

[5]

An important legacy of Michael Johnson's should be mentioned. It had nothing to do with money and it is unlikely that either Cornelius Ford or his daughter knew anything about it. He was born with a serious constitutional melancholy, 'a morbid disposition of both body and mind', which was aggravated by his family's money troubles and a wife who harped on them. Samuel was to inherit this disease in large measure. Referring to Michael's sturdy, large body, Boswell wrote in his *Life of Johnson*, 'as in the most solid rocks veins of unsound substance are often discovered, there was in him a mixture of that disease, the nature of which eludes the most minute enquiry, though the effects are well known to be a weariness of life, an unconcern about those things which agitate the greater part of mankind, and a general sensation of gloomy wretchedness'. This 'wrong-headed, positive ... melancholy' was almost the first fact Mrs Thrale chose to mention in her *Anecdotes*, obviously convinced (as was Boswell) that Michael Johnson's morbidity was of enormous importance in understanding the character, attitudes and life of the son. The latter told her that his father, unlike him, was fortunate to be able to cope with the affliction through physical exercise and the demands of his job, 'leading him to be much on horseback [which] contributed to the preservation of his bodily health and sanity'. But there were periods of inertia at home oppressed with alarming danger signals of 'imagination' and 'madness':

> Mr Johnson said, that when his [parchment] workshop, a detached building, had fallen half down for want of money to repair it, his father was not less diligent to lock the door every night, though he saw that anybody might walk in at the back part and knew that there was no security obtained by barring the front door. '*This* (says his son) was madness, you may see, and would have been discoverable in other instances of the prevalence of imagination, but that poverty prevented it from playing such tricks as riches and leisure encourage.'

It was such incidents and irrational habits that sank deep into the son's psyche as he grew up and terrified him that he would one day inherit his father's melancholy and lapse into an even worse kind of madness.[19]

CHAPTER 2

Stepping on the Duckling

[1]

Michael and Sarah Johnson's eldest son, Samuel, was born in the large bedroom over the bookshop in the new house on Wednesday, 18 September 1709. It was an auspicious year in English literary history: the first Copyright Act was passed in Great Britain; Alexander Pope launched his poetic career with the publication of his *Pastorals*; Nicholas Rowe published his famous edition of Shakespeare's plays, the first important editorial instalment in a century of sometimes frenetic Shakespeareana; and Joseph Addison and Sir Richard Steele published the original issue of *The Tatler*, the first major British periodical. If Michael Johnson the bookseller was at all aware of these far off stirrings in the nation's literature, he had little leisure to appreciate them.

The overwhelming theme of the first few pages of Johnson's *Annals* is his terrible health in the first hours, months and years of his life. The appalling condition of his birth and the travails of his parents' efforts to keep him alive made a profound impression on his self-identity for the rest of his life, although growing up he had heard so many horror stories about his first days that he admitted, 'confusions of memory I suspect to be common'. He did not exactly spring from the womb: 'My mother had a very difficult and dangerous labour, and was assisted by George Hector, a man-midwife of great reputation. I was born almost dead, and could not cry for some time. When he had me in his arms, he said, "Here is a brave boy."' Fearing he would die, the parents lost no time baptising him on the same day. The baby's condition did not improve right away but it clung to life: 'In a few weeks an inflammation was discovered on my buttock, which was at first, I think, taken for a burn; but soon appeared to be a natural disorder. It swelled, broke, and healed.'[1]

Soon after the birth, Michael persuaded Sarah to have the baby sent out to a wet nurse and chose for the purpose Joan Marclew, whose brick-maker husband worked for him in some capacity or who herself had been one of his servants. They lived a few hundred metres away on George Lane. Johnson recollects with some pastoral nostalgia that when he was 'a bigger boy' he used to visit the Marclew orchard and 'eat fruit in the garden, which was full of trees'. It was common practice to use the services of a wet nurse, but that did not stop Sarah Johnson from missing her baby terribly. Johnson must have heard from her or his father that she contrived to visit him every day on George Lane, an unusual practice that neighbours could easily have read as a sign of maternal sentimentality or weakness. It was something she was embarrassed to admit and 'used to go different ways, that her assiduity might not expose her to ridicule; and often left her fan or glove behind her, that she might have a pretence to come back unexpected'. She 'never discovered any token of neglect' at the Marclews, however, in the way her baby was being cared for.

There were other, more serious problems: 'Here it was discovered that my eyes were bad; and an issue was cut in my left arm, of which I took no great notice, as I think my mother has told me, having my little hand in a custard. How long this issue was continued I do not remember. I believe it was suffered to dry when I was about six years old.' It turns the stomach to contemplate that for the first six years of his life in order to purge an infection that was thought to be affecting his eyesight the boy was burdened with an incision kept open with threads or horsehairs. It was the first in a lifetime of incisions and blood-letting to which Johnson, according to barbaric medical practices of that age, was subjected in efforts to relieve this or that malady.

Worse was to come: 'scrofulous sores' began to appear on the little body. The respected physician Samuel Swynfen, the baby's godfather, who had taken lodgings in the Johnsons' new spacious house as a convenient place to carry on his practice, remarked (according to Johnson), 'he never knew any child reared with so much difficulty'; the scrofula passed to the infant from the infected milk or 'bad humours of the nurse, whose son had the same distemper, and was likewise short-sighted, but both in a less degree'. Dr Swynfen was right, though Johnson added that his mother thought 'my diseases derived from her family'. The scrofula, a tubercular infection in the lymph glands, may have been the direct cause of the baby's damaged eyesight, leading to almost complete blindness in the left eye and partial vision in the right one. 'Now had I been an Indian, I must have died early', he confided to Boswell; 'my eyes would not have served me to get food'. Mrs Thrale noted, however, that one could not tell by looking at Johnson which eye was the blind one, and his friends in later years seemed unaware of this blindness, and aware only of his short-sightedness. His hearing also was affected by this tubercular disease. After ten weeks at the Marclews, he was brought home, 'a poor, diseased infant, almost blind'. Johnson recalls that his otherwise sweet-tempered aunt Jane told him harshly she 'would not have picked such a poor creature up in the street'. Mrs Thrale's take on his condition was that the 'scrofulous evil' so afflicted his childhood that it 'left such marks as greatly disfigured a countenance naturally harsh and rugged, besides doing irreparable damage to the auricular organs, which never could perform their functions since I knew him.'[2]

Even if he could not recall those ten weeks himself, Johnson knew from what others and his body told him that during that period the die was cast for much of his personal and emotional life. On his visit to Lichfield in 1767, he could not escape the psychological need to translate the imagined nightmare of those early months into the reality of an actual place. He wrote in the *Annals* that he 'went to look for my nurse's house; and, enquiring somewhat obscurely, was told "this is the house in which you were nursed"'. There was an unexpected shock waiting for him there, one that was nonetheless liberating in that it objectified for him the tragedy of his own physical history: 'I saw my nurse's son, to whose milk I succeeded, reading a large Bible, which my nurse had bought ... some time before her death.' He was apparently unable to earn a living because of his eyesight, and was pitifully poring over a Bible in large print that his mother had bought him for solace and comfort.[3] Johnson's advantage over this man, and the reason the scrofula and its effects as well as other ailments did not debilitate him, was that in spite of suffering more severely he was endowed, like his father, with a strong, robust, large physical frame, not to mention a tenacity and a courage that showed themselves very early in his life and enabled him to overcome or minimise his handicaps.

Johnson was scarred by the enlarged lymph glands that scrofula causes, in his case chiefly around the neck, though whether or not the scars showed themselves dramatically in infancy is not clear. It is certain that his eyesight showed no improvement as the months passed. Increasingly desperate, Sarah Johnson decided to take things into her own hands. Johnson's impression was that one day in the second year of his thus far diseased existence on earth his mother gathered him up and rushed off to Trysul near Wolverhampton, the manor house of her wealthy first cousin Mrs Harriotts, where she could more conveniently consult the reputable oculist Dr Thomas Attwood of Worcester. Apparently there was no eye specialist in Lichfield. Nothing useful came of the visit except that Michael Johnson conceived from it a still greater dislike for his wife's relatives to whom she was wont to turn for help in emergencies and need. The visit rubbed salt into the tender wounds of his relative poverty. His injured pride, aggravated by his wife's lording her family over him, forced him over the years to retaliate by mischievously teasing and annoying Mrs Harriotts. His son wrote that he could do no more than that because his financial 'adversity' made him and his vanity powerless. Such behaviour, however, did not prevent Mrs Harriotts in 1728 from bequeathing to Sarah £40 along with 'a pair of her best flaxen sheets and pillow cases, as well as a large pewter dish and a dozen pewter plates'. She and Dr Attwood had been unable to help the infant in 1710, but this legacy at least, as we shall see, turned out to be hugely important in Samuel's education and unpromising young career.[4]

[2]

Desperate to find some other way of helping her baby overcome the plague of scrofula, Sarah made a dramatic decision. On the advice of the respected Lichfield physician Dr John Floyer, who must have felt as helpless as she did, she decided to take her baby to London to be 'touched' by Queen Anne. For centuries in England and France monarchs were believed to have the ability to heal scrofula by simply touching the sufferer in a healing ritual known as 'touching for the King's evil'. Thousands of people had been allegedly healed by this royal touch ever since the custom began during the reign of Edward the Confessor as the result of the legendary dream of a young woman. Evidence exists that this popular superstition still persisted in the Midlands itself. That year the Catholic King James II actually came to Lichfield and in the cathedral 'touched' a number of locals suffering from scrofula. Queen Anne went so far as to proclaim her own powers to heal in this way. In 1714 she 'touched' as many as two hundred people at one time who, like Sarah Johnson, were willing to try anything to conquer the disease. The practice died suddenly in the reign of George I, partly because of its Roman Catholic overtones. In March 1712 Sarah Ford cared little about ecclesiastical or monarchical niceties. She wanted her baby to be healed. In order to keep people from receiving the 'touch piece' unwarrantedly, applicants had to prove that the disease in question really was the King's Evil, so before leaving she had to obtain from a physician a statement that the child was in fact suffering from it, and that it had not had the royal 'touch' before. For her to take her ailing, probably noisy, thirty-month-old son on an uncomfortable, jolting two- or three-day journey via stagecoach all the way to London on such a blind mission of hope was a large undertaking and suggests, in addition to her desperation, a strongly religious and superstitious nature.

The family could ill afford the expense. Furthermore, Sarah was obliged to conceal that she was now two months pregnant with her second son Nathaniel, fearing she would not be allowed on the stagecoach if it became known. Johnson writes about this journey in his *Annals* from his own faint, dreamlike recall of images, people, and events: 'I always retained some memory of this journey,' he wrote, 'though I was then but thirty months old.' Such journeys, not-withstanding Christmas cards and coaching prints showing gaily painted stagecoaches flying along rolling green or snowy countryside with joy and expectation written across the faces of coachman and passengers, were exercises in stamina, even without a toddler like Samuel in tow. Inside, the passengers were squeezed together while the rest of the passengers braved the elements outside, hoping they would not freeze or be thrown off the coach by a sudden bump or turn in the road. Half remembering, half reporting what he had been told, Johnson wrote: 'We were troublesome to the passengers; but to suffer such inconveniences in the stagecoach was common in those days to persons in much higher rank. I was sick; one woman fondled me, the other was disgusted.' From a shop at one of the stopping places along the route, perhaps Coleshill, Coventry, Daventry or Stony Stratford, the kind woman 'bought me a small silver cup and spoon, marked SAM. J. lest if they had been marked S.J. which was her [his mother's] name, they should, upon her death, have been taken from me'. She did not stop there but also bought him a speckled linen frock which 'I knew afterwards by the name of my London frock'. He kept the cup into his manhood until, sadly, the 'distress' of poverty early in his marriage forced his wife to sell it − 'one of the last pieces of plate' −

though he still had the spoon when he wrote these lines.[5]

Johnson dimly recollected – 'I know not whether I remember the thing, or the talk of it' – that in London he and his mother stayed near a relative of hers in a bookseller's shop in Little Britain, a favourite haunt of booksellers and prostitutes near St Paul's Cathedral where 'the booksellers ... were knowing and conversible men, with whom, for the sake of bookish knowledge, the greatest wits were pleased to converse'. It is probable that Nicholson, the bookseller with whom mother and son stayed, was a contact of Michael Johnson's from his days of apprenticeship. He remembered a jack weight at Nicholson's for turning a spit (into which he stumbled once), a string and bell given to him to play with by his cousin, the shop counter, a cat with a white collar, and a dog called Chops 'that leaped over a stick'. All this lingered in his mind as part of the ineradicable imagery of this desperate quest for a healing. He wrote nothing of seeing the Queen, only of hearing a boy cry at the palace, though he did tell Mrs Thrale 'he had a confused, but somehow a sort of solemn recollection of a lady in diamonds, and a long black hood'. The ceremony was quite religious, with the Queen flanked by chaplains who recited prayers. Nothing miraculous for Samuel immediately resulted from the royal touch, although the received wisdom was that the healing could occur anytime within the next six months and still be regarded as a miracle. It did not, however. Sarah and the baby then had to make their way back to Lichfield, taking with them a gold coin or 'touch piece' specially minted for such pilgrims and threaded on a white ribbon that the Queen hung around Samuel's neck. Johnson wore his under his shirt for the rest of his life.[6]

Their return journey was misery. To save 'a few shillings' Sarah booked passage this time on a stage-wagon, taking care also to sew two guineas into her petticoat 'lest she should be robbed'. These rumbling wagons, covered by canvas and pulled by a team of eight or more horses led by a waggoner on foot, were intended really for transporting goods but they also carried a handful of passengers. Travelling at three or four miles per hour, it took them about five days to get home, which would have seemed like an eternity even to someone without an infirm toddler in tow. Apart from some regular praying at St Chad's Well or at the shrine in the cathedral, as well as at home, the parents do not appear to have sought out any more miracle or superstitious cures.[7]

[3]

If Sarah and Michael concluded they could do no more to repair their son's damaged body, they could still address his spiritual needs. Michael apparently thought that a little religious preaching might do young Samuel some good. There is a story, probably spurious in some or possibly all of its details, that Boswell picked up from Mary Adey, Johnson's young Lichfield friend, describing how when the child was three his father took him to hear the famous preacher and author Dr Henry Sacheverell preach in Lichfield Cathedral. Boswell was sceptical of such stories 'which the credulous relate with eager satisfaction', but he included this anecdote in the *Life* because it suggested to him rather romantically Johnson's characteristic precociousness and fierce concentration even as a toddler. According to Mary Adey, her grandfather saw Johnson sitting on his father's shoulders during the sermon, 'listening and gaping at the much celebrated preacher'. The iconic story makes Johnson out to be a type of saintly visitant to the temple, eagerly taking in the scholarly and spiritual wisdom of the church elders. According to Boswell, Michael Johnson is supposed to have defended his bringing his infant son to church by explaining 'it was impossible to keep him at home; for, young as he was, he believed he had caught the public spirit and zeal for Sacheverell'. Like many fathers who have to drag their children to certain events because they cannot at the moment do anything else with them, Michael may well have listened while his son gaped in boredom from above. It is more plausible that the boy was gaping at other gaping children.[8]

It was Sarah, not Michael, however, who took in hand Samuel's spiritual education. She did what most mothers usually did to promote their children's religious education, although his physical problems gave her efforts a special urgency. Johnson described her earliest efforts to tell him about heaven and hell, what seems like, but was not, a Calvinist type of indoctrination about original sin and damnation, future reward and punishment. It was a normal, if to us severe, brand of Protestant fundamentalism to which most children were subjected. Johnson was only three and in bed at the time: 'I suppose that in this year I was first informed of a future state. I remember, that being in bed with my mother one morning, I was told by her of the two places to which the inhabitants of this world were received after death; one a fine place filled with happiness, called Heaven; the other a *sad* place, called Hell. That this account much affected my imagination, I do not remember.' Nevertheless, his mother's assiduous piety introduced a strong theme in his youth. She was so insistent that this lesson should sink in that she had him get out of bed immediately and repeat it to their servant Thomas Jackson, but his take on that, at least when he talked to Mrs Thrale about it, had to do more with the general education of children than with religion: 'Little people should be encouraged always to tell whatever they hear particularly striking, to some brother, sister, servant, immediately before the impression is erased by the intervention of newer occurrences.' In later years, when Johnson reminded his mother of their talk, she was surprised she had waited until he was three to lay out this scenario of hell and heaven for him.[9]

He did not say that his mother's religious instruction had any darker effect on him than weariness, such as cultivating a fear of damnation, but Boswell did think it damaged his 'tender imagination' and sowed the seeds of what he called Johnson's 'diseased imagination'. All Johnson allowed was that the whole business was hard going:

> Sunday [said he] was a heavy day to me when I was a boy. My mother confined me on that day, and made me read 'The Whole Duty of Man', from a great part of which I could derive no instruction. When, for instance, I had read the chapter on theft, which from my infancy I had been taught was wrong, I was no more convinced that theft was wrong than before; so there was no accession of knowledge.

If his mother had possessed the ability and knowledge, he added, to sweeten this religious teaching with observations on style and other 'excellencies of composition', so that his mind could have been uplifted by 'an amusing variety of objects' and 'not grow weary', it might have benefited him more.[10]

Sarah Johnson probably was no gloomier than the average mother in the way she explained religion and committed no greater sin in her son's eyes than that of being dull and unimaginative. She was disciplined in the way she kept his attention on various forms of religion, especially on learning passages by heart. One day in Lichfield in 1776, Johnson's stepdaughter Lucy Porter told Boswell, in Johnson's presence, that Sarah Johnson once boasted about her son's precociousness: 'When he was a child in petticoats,' Boswell writes, 'and had learned to read, Mrs Johnson one morning put the common prayer-book [*The Book of Common Prayer*] into his hands, pointed to the collect for the day, and said, "Sam, you must get this by heart."

She went upstairs, leaving him to study it: But by the time she had reached the second floor, she heard him following her. "What's the matter?" said she. "I can say it," he replied; and repeated it distinctly, though he could not have read it over more than twice.' While this sounds a bit like one of those stories that get embellished in the telling, the piety and discipline of the mother nonetheless ring true in it. *The Whole Duty of Man*, from which she required him to read regularly as soon as he was able to read, was the enormously popular Protestant manual by Richard Allestree, chaplain in ordinary to the King and Provost of Eton, published in 1658. For over a century in edition after edition it was obligatory fare for children. Written for even 'the meanest reader', it was little Samuel's earliest exposure to moral writing, divided into seventeen chapters which mostly addressed moral qualities such as temperance, obedience, and contentment and secular duties such as marriage. This stern regimen of reading and instruction laid the foundations of his lifelong piety and Christian discipline, the core of his morality.[11]

[4]

The religious recitations he was made to perform for family and friends both angered and saddened Johnson as he looked back on his childhood. In later years, he felt strongly that children should not be treated as exhibitions by their parents, remembering with acute displeasure how his parents would trot him out for performances. He told Mrs Thrale that a few days after his brother Nathaniel was born in October 1712, whose christening he remembered 'with all its circumstances', his mother made him learn how to spell and pronounce 'the words *little Natty*, syllable by syllable, making him say it over in the evening to her husband and his guests'. According to her, the 'trick which most parents play with their children, of showing off their newly-acquired accomplishments, disgusted Mr Johnson beyond expression'. His parents had treated him this way 'till he absolutely loathed his father's caresses, because he knew they were sure to precede some unpleasing display of his early abilities; and he used, when neighbours came visiting, to run up a tree that he might not be found and exhibited, such, as no doubt he was, a prodigy of early understanding'.[12]

In conversation with Boswell and Lucy Porter, Johnson also remembered another day when he and his father were out walking in

Lichfield, perhaps along the green banks of Stowe Pool, and he accidentally stepped on a duckling, 'the eleventh of a brood', and killed it. His mother circulated the story many years later that on his father's urging him to write an epitaph for the duck's burial he quickly composed these verses and repeated them to her:

> Under this stone lyes Mr Duck
> Whom Samuel Johnson trode on
> He might have liv'd if he had luck;
> But then he'd been an odd one.

Mrs Thrale cites the poem in her *Anecdotes* as a sign of the boy's 'early expansion of mind, and knowledge of language'. Boswell, too, quotes it in his *Life*. Whether or not Michael Johnson wrote half of the verses, as Johnson maintained, or all of them, Johnson's exasperated complaint was that with them his father yet again proved himself 'a foolish old man – that is to say, foolish in talking of his children'. Johnson 'always seemed more mortified at the recollection of the bustle his parents made with his wit', Mrs Thrale added, 'than pleased with the thoughts of possessing it. "That (said he to me one day) is the great misery of late marriages, the unhappy produce of them becomes the plaything of dotage."' Sentimental about neither children, ducks, dogs, nor his own childhood, he often hurt or offended parents by going out of his way to avoid hearing their children recite verses or sing songs, particularly one father who asked him to listen to his two sons repeat separately Thomas Gray's 'Elegy Written in a Country Churchyard' so that he could judge which one had the 'happier cadence'. 'No, pray Sir', Johnson replied instantly, 'let the dears both speak it at once; more noise will by that means be made, and the noise will be sooner over.'[13]

[5]

With Nathaniel's birth in October 1712 life changed dramatically for young Samuel. He suddenly diminished as the anxious focus of his parents. There is virtually no record of the brothers' relationship as toddlers up through adolescence, but what there is reveals a mood of rivalry, if not a sad deficiency of brotherly love. Johnson spoke positively once to Mrs Thrale about Nathaniel's 'manly spirit' in later years with 'pride and pleasure', but this is almost the only surviving fond remark on the part of the elder brother. From him Mrs Thrale clearly received the impression that 'the two brothers did not . . . much delight in each other's company, being always rivals for the mother's fondness'. In fact, the severity of Johnson's observations on domestic life in his fable, *Rasselas*, she thinks, can be clearly traced to domestic friction in his childhood, much of it apparently between the two boys and much of it of his own making. Since he admitted to Mrs Thrale that as a boy he was of 'a sullen temper and reserved disposition', Nathaniel must have had a rough time of it. Whatever the causes, this domestic friction remained a soreness in Johnson's psyche for most of his life, likely to pain him whenever he witnessed family harmony, such as in his musical friend Dr Charles Burney's London home: 'Of this consanguineous unanimity I have had never much experience; but it appears to me one of the great lenitives of life.' He had almost nothing to say about his brother in any of his surviving writings, which in its own way is remarkable.[14]

[6]

Sarah Johnson did not have, in her son's eyes, knowledge enough to be able to 'sweeten' her religious teaching, but she began to teach him to read with the adventures of St George and the Dragon, which made a deep impression: 'The recollection of such reading as had delighted him in his infancy, made him always persist in fancying that it was the only reading which could please an infant.' What he relished most was robust romantic adventure stories about 'giants and castles, and of somewhat which can stretch and stimulate . . . little minds.' In 1780, at his dear friend Bennet Langton's home in Rochester, Johnson once fell into conversation about what children should and should not read. John Longley, the Recorder of that city and eventual father of an archbishop of Canterbury, happened to be there and noticed the vigour with which Johnson attacked their hostess's then fashionable notion that children benefited most from 'little books published purposely for their instruction'. He rounded on her, 'asserting that at an early age it was better to gratify curiosity with wonders than to attempt planting truth, before the mind was prepared to receive it and that therefore, *Jack the Giant-Killer, Parisenus and Parismenus*, and *The Seven Champions of Christendom* were fitter for them than Mrs [Anna Letitia] Barbauld and Mrs [Sarah] Trimmer'. On another occasion he was impatient with Mrs Thrale for giving her own children trifling and trendy stories with moral agendas. 'Babies do not want to hear about babies,' he told her bluntly, thinking of the diet of his publisher friend John Newbery's instructional books such as *Goody Two Shoes* and *Tommy Prudent* to which she was subjecting them. He deplored this fad for spoiling the innocence of children with stories that made them self-conscious about morality, convinced that 'endeavouring to make children prematurely wise is useless labour'. 'One may write things to a child without being childish,' he urged in his *Life of Milton*. When Mrs Thrale defended herself, he reminded her that 'the parents *buy* the books, and the children never read them'.[15]

The great thing was to provoke the child's imagination. One adventure story which he must certainly have heard of and grabbed quickly after it came out in 1719 was Defoe's *Robinson Crusoe*. Along with Bunyan's *Pilgrim's Progress* and *Don Quixote*, it was one of the very few books he later singled out as an exception to his notion that very few books were 'ever ... written by mere man that was wished longer by its readers'. As for the imagination, a child could do no better than Shakespeare – 'he that peruses Shakespeare, looks round alarmed, and starts to find himself alone,' he once wrote. *Hamlet*, which he plucked off his father's shelves at the tender age of nine, certainly was not urged on him for instructional purposes. Reading it one day at home in the stillness of the basement kitchen and looking up, he was terrified to find himself in the company of the Ghost on the ramparts of Elsinore Castle. Throwing down the book, 'he suddenly hurried upstairs to the street door that he might see people about him'. He frequently told this story by way of celebrating Shakespeare's imaginative power but also because he liked to stress proudly that at a very young age he did not go in for 'small beer' and was already diving into Shakespeare and loved to read poetry. His strong imagination as a boy was repelled by little frivolous, tidy stories and had to be fed by more expansive adventures and romances set in strange lands with exotic characters. It was a taste that as he grew up merged into an unquenchable thirst for travel stories and accounts, especially ones informing readers about far-off lands, societies, cultures and manners.[16]

CHAPTER 3

Leaping over the Rail

[1]

Johnson always held the profession of a teacher to be sacred, easily abused with tragic consequences. In his *Life of Joseph Addison* he remarked that in biography 'not to name the school or the masters of men illustrious for literature, is a kind of historical fraud, by which honest fame is injuriously diminished'.[1] Nonetheless, he thought his teachers were definitely a mixed bunch. He either revered or despised them for the rest of his life.

About one hundred metres from the Johnson house, along the Market Place and then left into Dam Street, lived Dame Ann Oliver, the sufficiently educated widow of a simple shoemaker who decided to open a school in her home when her husband died, leaving her with one or more children to bring up. Dame Oliver's home classroom was in the middle of Lichfield, and she seems to have had a confectionery business in her home as well by the time she began her school. It was most likely here when he was four or five, not at home, that Samuel first learned to read properly. Dame Oliver took a liking to this odd, disfigured little boy, which was reciprocated, for he remembered fondly how 'in the simplicity of her kindness' she proudly gave him one of her gingerbread biscuits as a going-away present when he went off to university and told him he was 'the best scholar she had ever had'.

Nothing more is known about his year or two with Dame Oliver except an account of an incident which Boswell picked up from Johnson in Bath in 1776. Johnson himself did not recollect what happened, having heard it only from his mother, but he thought it was important enough to mention to Boswell. One day after school when his mother was late coming to fetch him he started for home on his own, which was just around the corner, 'though he was then so near-sighted, that he was obliged to stoop down on his hands and knees to take a view of the kennel before he ventured to step over it'. Apprehensive, the schoolmistress followed him but did it 'slyly', hoping to stay out of sight apparently out of a healthy respect for his already evident independent and impetuous spirit. As he turned the corner, however, he caught sight of her and 'was so angry at being tended that he went back and beat her'. Dr Thomas Percy, the cranky literary historian and cleric, told Boswell that in a fury the boy actually kicked his teacher, 'an early proof of his irritable and violent temper'. Nobody knows where the priggish Percy got this kicking detail, but it is believable and conveys essentially the boy's defiant trigger-like challenge to anyone who was foolish enough to feel sorry for him on account of any of his physical handicaps.[2]

After a couple of years Dame Oliver, opting to dedicate her time to shaping gingerbread instead of children, passed Samuel on to Thomas Browne, a friend of hers a few doors down in Dam Street, another lapsed shoemaker of about sixty who decided to open a school. The boy's health probably was the reason he went there instead of directly on to Lichfield School at the age of five. A desk and chair it seems were the only furniture in the schoolroom, so the children spent most of the time sitting on the floor when they were not standing for recitation. The only thing Johnson thought memorable about his two years with this man was that he published a spelling book of which, although he dedicated it rather confidently to the universe, he feared, 'no copy of it can now be had'. Browne died within a year of Samuel's leaving the school.

[2]

At the age of seven, Samuel's education finally began in earnest at Lichfield Grammar School. Several months before, however, an accident at St Mary's Church upset his life and had a knock-on effect on his religious behaviour and outlook. This Gothic-style church (rebuilt in 1721) was where the Johnsons worshipped and rented a pew, and conceivably they were in it on Easter Sunday 1716 when parts of its stone spire fell away and landed on the roof and in one of the aisles, causing a panic that was reported as far away as London in the *Weekly Journal*: 'The people (being a numerous congregation) crowded so fast that they tumbled upon one another, and lay crawling in heaps ... Hats, books, hoods, scarfs, cover-sluts or long riding-hoods, head-dresses, spectacles, gloves, clogs, snuff-boxes, fans, etc. were left in abundance.' They had to break windows to get out. Johnson recalled the consequences of the calamity on him:

> I fell into an inattention to religion, or an indifference about it ... The church at Lichfield, in which we had a seat, wanted reparation, so I was to go and find a scat in other churches; and having bad eyes, and being awkward about this, I used to go and read in the fields on Sunday. This habit continued till my fourteenth year; and still I find a great reluctance to go to church. I then became a lax *talker* against religion, for I did not much *think* against it.

It is a pleasant image he calls up: with books in hand, presumably including the Bible and *Book of Common Prayer*, taking to the fields around Lichfield as a substitute for public worship at St Michael's on the south side of town where his parents began to attend. In the fields he felt no awkwardness about his eyesight and other physical infirmities. There was a delicious sense of freedom.[3]

He became a 'lax talker' against religion but is careful to say he did not '*think*' against it. On the contrary, he sought to know more about it. It was a pursuit he never abandoned, one that became the centre of his imaginative life, although he once admitted, 'I myself was for some years totally regardless of religion. It had dropped out of my mind. It was at an early part of my life.' What seems to have occurred was the first known crisis in his mental state at the early age of ten if we are to believe – Boswell did not – what after his death Mrs Thrale said he had told her:

> At the age of ten years his mind was disturbed by scruples of infidelity [doubts of Christian faith], which preyed upon his spirits, and made him very uneasy; the more so, as he revealed his uneasiness to no one, being naturally (as he said) 'of a sullen temper and reserved disposition'. He searched, however, diligently but fruitlessly, for evidences of the truth of revelation; and at length recollecting a book he had once seen in his father's shop, intitled, *De Veritate Religionis, &c.* he began to think himself highly culpable for neglecting such a means of information, and took himself severely to task for this sin, adding many acts of voluntary, and to others unknown, penance.

Once he found the book and realised he was too young to understand it anyway, his guilt subsided, 'and not thinking to enquire whether there were any English books written on the subject, followed his usual amusements'. Boswell indignantly described Thrale's reading of this early crisis as a 'strange fantastical account', 'childish, irrational, and ridiculous' because of its superficiality and trivialisation. What is important is that Johnson himself acknowledged the religious doubts and guilt he experienced at this early age.[4]

[3]

Lichfield Grammar School[5] was one of the major reasons Lichfield rose to such eminence in the seventeenth and eighteenth centuries. Situated a quarter of a mile south-west of the town centre, the school was established in 1495, by William Smith, the Bishop of Lichfield and co-founder of Brasenose College, Oxford. Originally serving the church as an institution for the teaching of Latin grammar as part of St John's Hospital, it was as a free school in St John's Street run by the town corporation that it left its mark in the beginning of the seventeenth century. Under the forceful and fearful headmastership of the Revd John Hunter from 1704 to 1741, it became nationally famous. While grammar schools were established long before the Reformation, the teaching of Latin as the basis of their system of education – 'the good old waie of teaching', 'clogged with much labour, wearinesse and difficulty' – clinging to the same textbooks and methods, and resistance to change and the introduction of more modern subjects (like English, for example) pushed them into decline in the seventeenth century. In the North, however, they thrived, where a good master could become famous and be a magnet for good pupils, most of whom boarded.

At the time Samuel was in the school, Hunter was responsible for and presided over a period of prosperity for the school. With over one hundred boarders, he cast a wide net that drew in the sons of gentlemen from Leicestershire and Derbyshire as well as Staffordshire. He educated a surprising number of nationally known and professionally distinguished men, including several judges who ended up sitting in the superior courts at Westminster, John Wyatt the inventor of the cotton spinning-machine, and David Garrick. With stern discipline and extensive learning, Hunter turned the school into a going enterprise, so that eventually he had to rent property nearby to house boarders in addition to local day pupils. The school still thrives today.

Samuel's career as a day scholar began well enough. He entered the lower school under the intelligent care of the usher or undermaster, Humphrey Hawkins, whom he described as 'very skillful in his little way'. Johnson recalled the almost two and a half years with Hawkins with unreserved pleasure, 'for I was indulged and caressed by my master, and, I think, really excelled the rest'. Hawkins's gentle encouragement was crucial because at the age of seven the boy's large frame, scrofula-scarred features, severely limited eyesight and increasingly odd gesticulations and movements, not to mention what Mrs Thrale described as his sullen and reserved disposition, were at first surely likely to make him the butt of his classmates's jokes. The two and a half years in the lower class flew by: 'The time, till I had computed it, appeared much longer by the multitude of novelties which it supplied, and of incidents, then in my thoughts important, it produced. Perhaps it is not possible that any other period can make the same impression on the memory.'[6]

The curriculum at grammar schools had remained virtually unchanged for two hundred years. Writing and arithmetic were no part of it, nor of course was science as we know it. There was some Greek grammar based on a study of Euripides, Sophocles, Xenophon and Homer, among others, but Latin grammar and translation were what it was mostly all about. The standard texts were Aesop's *Fables*, Cicero's letters, Ovid, Virgil, Horace, Pliny, Juvenal, Plautus and Livy. The books Johnson remembered reading in those first years of school were easy and mostly a pleasure for him. Most agreeable, of course, were the literary texts, Aesop's *Fables* in an edition by Charles Hoole (1687) with English and Latin on facing pages, and other classical fables and dialogues appealing to a boy's imagination and tending to make learning fun. Every Thursday there were examinations consisting mainly of recitation, but they posed no problems or challenges for anyone. According to Johnson, everybody looked forward to Thursday, in fact, because there was no need to prepare any lessons for that day and the questions were always ones the boys had been asked before and 'could regularly answer'. The boys learned Aesop by heart on Thursday nights and were examined lightly the next morning. The entertaining Latin dialogues or *Colloquies* of Mathurin Corderius, a friend of Calvin's, presented side by side with English translations in an edition also by Charles Hoole (1657), pleased the pupils because many of them involved the mischief of little boys their own age.

Johnson kept several of his schoolboy Latin grammar books on his shelves for the rest of his life, especially William Lily's *Short Introduction of Grammar*, used widely in schools all over the country since 1542 and (in a revised state) into the nineteenth century as the Eton

Grammar. Lily, who became the first high master of St Paul's School in London, presented the parts of speech, conjugations, and other rules of Latin usage in little jingles to aid memorisation, calculated to appeal to children. Shakespeare based his hilarious Latin lesson in Act IV of *The Merry Wives of Windsor* on Lily's *Grammar*. The first section on 'accidence' or parts of speech, part of which at least he appears to have learned at home before he started school, appealed to him so much that he could repeat 141 lines of it 'without any effort of recollection'. Another more difficult section in Lily that deals with verb conjugations, however, he found 'disgusting'. With verbs, though, his mother was a great support in preparing for examinations, for which ever after he was tenderly grateful: 'This was very difficult to me; and I was once very anxious about the next day, when this exercise was to be performed, in which I had failed till I was discouraged. My mother encouraged me, and I proceeded better. When I told her of my good escape, "We often", said she, dear mother! "come off best, when we are most afraid."' 'I did not form them in ugly shapes,' he proudly announced to his mother on another occasion when she asked about his progress with verbs at school. She told him years later how she had delighted in having a boy who 'was forming verbs'. 'These little memorials sooth my mind', he recalled tenderly.[7]

During the Whitsun holidays of 1719 Sarah Johnson packed off her two boys to Birmingham sixteen miles away to be improved culturally and socially by spending a fortnight with her relatives there. At one uncle's house, possibly Samuel Ford's, he was 'much caressed' by his gossipy aunt, 'a good-natured, coarse woman, easy of converse'. His mother was appalled to hear, though, that at one sitting he devoured a huge portion of a boiled leg of mutton. She interpreted it as an early sign of her boy's coarse manners and warned that 'it would hardly ever be forgotten' – not by her, at any rate. Johnson's comment on this was simply that she lived in 'a narrow sphere' and that greater evils eventually replaced her worry over such small annoyances. When the boys moved on to stay with their alcoholic uncle John Harrison the widower, life was not as pleasant but at least there they were centrally located in Birmingham's High Street, next to the Castle Inn which Johnson briefly used as a forwarding address in the early 1730s. The best thing about the Harrison household, though, was his sweet-tempered cousin Sally Ford, his Uncle Cornelius Ford's eldest daughter, who was living there as a housekeeper. It sounds as if he contracted a puppy love for her – 'I used to say she had no fault.'

Apparently, soon after the boys returned home, she visited them there and provided Samuel with the first illustration of how sustained concentration could defeat both her and time: 'I was writing at the kitchen windows, as I thought, alone, and turning my head saw Sally dancing. I went on without notice, and had finished almost without perceiving that any time had elapsed. This close attention I have seldom in my whole life obtained.' Sally may have been the reason why Samuel delayed his return home. He wrote to his mother (the letter is lost) with characteristic imperiousness asking for the horses that would fetch him to be delayed until Thursday of the first school week, 'and then, and not till then, they should be welcome to go'. He also mentioned his delight over a new 'rattle' for his whip. His father duly appeared with horses to fetch him and Nathaniel on that Thursday but the main thing he remembered about that was being offended by his father, who insulted his pride by casually telling the ostler within his earshot that he was burdened by having to travel with 'two boys under his care'. 'This offended me,' Johnson remembered. It was not the first or last time Michael Johnson underestimated his eldest son's kindling independence.[8]

More serious was what Samuel found waiting for him back at school. In his absence his comfortable world there had been turned upside down. In one fell swoop his class of eleven – all but one of whose names he remembered in later life – was moved up to the upper school and put under the tutelage of an assistant schoolmaster, the twenty-three-year-old Revd Edward Holbrooke, a recent graduate of Cambridge. Suddenly Samuel and his classmates found themselves in a less friendly, stricter, more demanding environment. Johnson remained sore about the move for the rest of his life, calling Holbrooke 'a peevish and ill-tempered man' when, in fact, others like Dr John Taylor, a classmate and one of Johnson's most intimate lifelong friends, called him 'one of the most ingenious men, best scholars, and best preachers of his age'. Johnson could not agree less, and for him the shift was tantamount to a loss of innocence – 'At this removal I cried.'[9]

Immediately he had to work harder. He found the new regimen of exercises with gerunds and syntax 'very troublesome', but promptly he began to excel. One typical day when his classmates completed the assigned sixteen exercises, he completed twenty-five. With a tact that his genius and drive for superiority had already told him were crucial if he was to remain liked by his classmates, he never showed Holbrooke all of his – 'five lay long after in a drawer in the shop,' he confessed.

By then he had discovered his ability to read and work at a tremendous speed when he put his mind to it. His chief adversary, however, was not the exercises but dilatoriness, a lack of concentration, and an inability to sustain work for long. His mother understood this, saying to him once, 'though you could make an exercise in so short a time, I thought you would find it difficult to make them all as soon as you should'.[10]

Holbrooke right away 'raised' the boys from Aesop to Phaedrus (first century AD), who translated many of the Greek fables into Latin. The sheer volume of work Holbrooke set of translating, parsing and memorising from Phaedrus was onerous: 'It was the only book which we learned to the end. In the latter part thirty lines were expected for a lesson.' The resulting lessons in which the boys had to recite lengthily from this work surely were as painful to Holbrooke as to the boys, but still he piled on the work. 'What reconciles masters to long lessons is the pleasure of tasking,' Johnson observed dryly in his *Annals*. After hours of study they made 'little progress'. As Johnson saw it, one of the reasons for that may have been Holbrooke's incompetence, for he made the point of mentioning in his *Annals* that he and a few of the others noticed one day that their schoolmaster had no idea of the meaning of a particular passage in an exercise. The stakes were high because if the boys failed to master a passage they were sent up to the Hunter to be punished. Samuel tolerated this the first time, but 'the second time we complained that we could not get the passage. Being told that we should ask, we informed him that we had asked, and that the assistant would not tell us.' Johnson says 'we' informed the headmaster, but there is a very good chance that he was the only one who defended himself in front of the menacing Hunter, with the very real possibility of a flogging as his reward.[11]

Samuel had little enough respect for his new schoolmaster, but worse was to come when he and others were promoted to Hunter's class at the top of the school either this or early in the next term. His recollections about this stage of his schooling turn deeply negative. In his *Annals* he is surprisingly silent about Hunter; elsewhere he is scathing. Nothing could be plainer about Johnson's Lichfield Grammar School years than that he and Hunter did not, to put it mildly, get on well together. It was a classic case of personality clash: the harsh disciplinarian pitted against a brilliant and ripening rebel of a boy. Hunter was not about to be deterred or defeated by a town boy of ten. On the other hand, he cannot have had anyone like Samuel in his class before: proud, defiant, sullen, reserved, physically handi-capped, scarred by disease, prone to strange convulsive movements, and possessed of an amazing memory and quick intelligence. As the battle lines had already been drawn over Holbrooke's alleged incompetence, Hunter could not have been surprised by this boy's independent spirit. Samuel knew that in his new class he was involved in a steep learning curve, but his chief grievance was Hunter's brutality, as he protested to Boswell: 'He used to beat us unmercifully; and he did not distinguish between ignorance and negligence; for he would beat a boy equally for not knowing a thing, as for neglecting to know it.' Particularly galling was Hunter's savage tyranny in asking a boy a question, such as the Latin for a candlestick 'which the boy could not expect to be asked', and then beating him if he could not answer correctly. 'Now, Sir,' Johnson put it to Boswell, 'if a boy could answer every question, there would be no need of a master to teach him.'[12]

Still, the question of how severe a schoolmaster could reasonably and usefully be with his scholars was one that troubled Johnson in later years in a psychological confusion involving painful memories of Hunter and his own conviction that without the threat of corporal punishment of some sort a boy would learn much less. 'Severity must be continued until obstinacy be subdued, and negligence be cured,' he once said. Moreover, in the classroom Samuel knew he was learning more from Hunter than he had ever learned from anyone else. He rejected Boswell's notion that he was prejudiced against Hunter because he was a Scot. Hunter was not a Scot, Johnson shot back, and 'abating his brutality, he was a very good master'. 'My master whipped me very well,' he told a friend, but 'without that, Sir, I should have done nothing.' While Hunter was thrashing the boys 'unmercifully', he added, he would proclaim, 'and this I do to save you from the gallows'. But the flogging had to be just, not vindictive or cruel, and the boys must always understand the reasons for it, which in Hunter's class (according to Johnson) many did not.[13]

The force of Samuel's personality, his large uncouth presence in the classroom, and his academic brilliance made a lasting impression on his classmates as well as on Hunter: 'His favourites used to receive very liberal assistance from him.' His capacity to hear verses and recite them immediately had already become legendary at school. One of his classmates recalls how he once recited eighteen verses to his friend, 'which, after a little pause, he repeated verbatim, varying only one epithet, by which he improved the line'. Apart from academics, there was something of a magnetic influence that he exerted on classmates. Of the handful of schoolfellows cropping up in Johnson's letters years later were the two Congreve brothers, Charles and Richard, sons of the first cousin of the dramatist William Congreve, both of whom went up to Oxford from Lichfield. Charles became a clergyman but ruined his life with drink. In the oppressive and dirty London room where in 1774 Johnson found him 'a man much broken' and tried to revive him with questions of their past, he had 'the appearance of a man wholly sunk into that sordid self-indulgence which disease, real or imaginary, is apt to dictate'. Although Johnson was eager to see him after more than fifty years, he found it hard to believe that this man had no interest whatever in recollecting their precious school years together. Worse than that, in his reclusive 'sullen sensuality' he seemed to have forgotten everything about schooldays. Another visit a few days later to the same grubby room was again deeply disappointing for him. The younger Richard Congreve was another matter. In one of his earliest surviving letters when he was twenty-six, Johnson remembered their 'former familiarity' in school in which they were 'content to love without complimenting each other'. Their friendship's honest simplicity, he added, was exactly in tune with 'our rural retreats, shades unpolluted by flattery and falsehood, thickets where interest and artifice never lay concealed!'[14]

Another of the boys in the class whom Hunter flogged and who eventually rose to Lord Chief Justice, Sir John Wilmot, had a vivid image of Samuel, 'a long, lank, lounging boy' especially targeted by Hunter for idleness. It was his classmate and lifelong steadfast friend Edmund Hector, however, who provided Boswell with a windfall of information about his schooldays. Hector's sister Ann was his first love, for whom he said love 'imperceptibly' dropped out of his head although he saw her again in later years when she was living in Birmingham with her brother and always felt a 'kindness' towards her. Probably Samuel's best friend in school, Hector became a surgeon and lived most of his life in Birmingham, so they had the chance to see each other occasionally after Johnson began annual visits to Lichfield in the 1770s. 'Hector is . . . an old friend,' Johnson wrote just three years before his death, 'the only companion of my childhood that passed through the school with me. We have always loved one another.' In Hector's words, they took pleasure 'sauntering away the hours of vacation in the fields, during which Johnson was more engaged in talking to himself than to his companion.' In a stream of anecdotes for both Boswell and Sir John Hawkins, Johnson's early friend and other major biographer after he died, Hector stressed the effects of Samuel's prodigious academic ability on his classmates: 'As his uncommon abilities for learning far exceeded us, we endeavoured by every boyish piece of flattery to gain his assistance, and three of us, by turns, used to call on him in a morning, on one of whose backs, supported by the other two, he rode triumphantly to school.' There was only one rival for academic supremacy, Theophilus Lowe, eighteen months older and the son of a local plumber, who went on to win a fellowship at St John's College, Cambridge. But Samuel knew his superiority: 'They never thought to raise me by comparing me to any one; they never said, Johnson is as good a scholar as such a one; but such a one is as good a scholar as Johnson; and this was said but of one, but of Lowe; and I do not think he was as good a scholar'.[15]

Even the senior boys looked upon him as 'the head and leader' in the class, who 'acquiesced in whatever he proposed or did'. His only trouble was with Hunter who, according to Hector, took it out on him not only for his 'indolence and procrastination' but also for his 'talking and diverting other boys from their business, by which, perhaps he might hope to keep his ascendancy'. His difficulty in rousing himself to work steadily and systematically was already so acute that Hector remembered his friend's returning to school after long vacations an hour earlier than everyone else to 'begin one of his exercises, in which he purposely left some faults, in order to gain time to finish the rest'. Such dexterity and isolated power of concentration made him a classroom champion in the eyes of the boys but infuriated Hunter. Apart from flogging this Hercules among the boys with apparent regularity, Hunter, as we shall see, was biding his time for a serious slip from this impertinent boy that would enable him to take his revenge. What outraged him was the implied insult to the academic establishment and his own authority by this boy's treating the regimen of school studies in this way and getting away with it through the force of intellect. That the other boys celebrated Samuel could hardly have helped his relationship with the headmaster.[16]

Another classmate, John Taylor, deserves mention. He was second only to Mrs Thrale and Boswell as a correspondent, receiving one hundred known letters from Johnson and, over several decades, developing a unique intimacy with him. They turned out to be an odd couple, given Taylor's unintellectual, rural, inattentive clerical way of life and his fairly obtuse tactlessness at critical times – not to mention that as a strong Whig he was politically a polar opposite to Johnson although, as we shall see, Johnson was far from subscribing to the blind Toryism with which he has traditionally been identified – but Johnson did tell Mrs Thrale that Taylor was 'better acquainted with my *heart* than any man or woman now alive'. It was chiefly to Taylor that Johnson wrote about old classmates not seen for decades: 'How few does the man who has lived sixty years now know of the friends of his youth?' Yet Taylor maddeningly proved to be a relatively arid source for Boswell or any other biographer of Johnson. Another classmate who regrettably never provided any facts about Johnson's years in school (he died in 1776 before Boswell could get to him) but who figures in his life later on was Robert James. James practised medicine and became famous for his widely used fever-reducing James's Powder, a pharmacological compound of antimony and calcium phosphate. Oliver Goldsmith was said by some to have been poisoned by it.[17]

While Samuel was popular with his classmates, he found it difficult to take part in 'ordinary diversions' with them. Hector remembered, though, that 'he used to go upon Stowpool and make a boy pull off his stockings and shoes and put a garter round him and draw him on the ice'. This seems at least as likely, given his size, than the way Boswell told it: 'He took a pleasure in being drawn upon the ice by a boy barefooted, who pulled him along by a garter fixed round him.' During the summers he swam regularly in either Stowe Pool or in the leafy loneliness of the pure Curborough Brook not far from St Chad's Church and below Stowe Mill, where, with great insistence, his father taught him to swim. With a tenderness for these innocent boyhood days, in that nostalgic Latin poem that in the last year of his life he wrote for his old chum Hector, his mind floated back to the 'daytime darkness' of his favourite swimming haunt. Here they are in a translation from the Latin by the poet John Wain:

> Clear as glass the stream still wanders through green fields.
>   Here, as a boy, I bathed
> my tender limbs, unskilled, frustrated, while
> with gentle voice my father from the bank
> taught me to swim.
>   The branches made
> a hiding-place; the bending trees concealed
> the water in a daytime darkness.
>   Now

hard axes have destroyed those ancient shades:
the pool lies naked, even to distant eyes.
But the water, never tiring, still runs on
in the same channel: once hidden, now overt,
always flowing.[18]

His father's swimming lessons provided him with one of the essential ways he got exercise and learned to coordinate his large and awkward limbs. He remained a strong and fearless swimmer for the rest of his life, whether in dangerous pools by Oxford or in the cold sea at Brighton (then called Brighthelmstone). Dancing lessons were also laid on to improve his coordination, but his eyesight was not up to them. What apparently his eyesight did not frustrate was a relish for running races and jumping over walls in reckless acts of bravado, especially to impress schoolmates. He remembered all this physical activity with undiluted joy, maintaining that 'a boy at school was the happiest of human beings'. A touching sign of this was his nostalgic return three years before his death to see Levett's Field behind the school. What happened was told by an anonymous writer:

> He had gone round Mr Levett's field (the place where the scholars play) in search of a rail that he used to jump over when a boy, 'and,' says the Doctor in a transport of joy, 'I have been so fortunate as to find it: I stood, said he, 'gazing upon it some time with a degree of rapture, for it brought to my mind all my juvenile sports and pastimes, and at length I determined to try my skill and dexterity; I laid aside my hat and wig, pulled off my coat, and leapt over it twice.' Thus the great Dr Johnson, only three years before his death, was, without hat, wig or coat, jumping over a rail that he had used to fly over when a school-boy.[19]

Only one schoolfellow seems to have become a poet and perhaps been good at making verses in school, Isaac Hawkins Browne the elder, about five years older than Samuel. On the basis of their friendship in school Johnson praised him as a person of great conversational powers, 'the most delightful with whom I ever was in company', with talk 'at once so elegant, so apparently artless, so pure, and so pleasing, it seemed a perpetual stream of sentiment, enlivened by gaiety, and sparkling with images'. Vast praise indeed. But Johnson remembered him also because of his odd behaviour. Late in life in a letter to Susanna Thrale, Mrs Thrale's thirteen-year-old daughter, he illustrated gluttony by describing how Browne, 'of great eminence in the learned and the witty world', disgustingly used to hang pots on his wall as nests in which to catch sparrows which he would then eat. 'I never heard any man speak of any future enjoyment with such contortions of delight as he exhibited when he talked of eating the young ones.' This eccentricity stuck in Johnson's mind perhaps because he thought it hinted at a streak of madness or at least some social maladjustment that typically fascinated him.[20]

In his solitary periods Samuel was certainly busying himself writing poetry by the time he was fifteen or sixteen. A few of his earliest poems and exercises in translation of Horace, Homer and Virgil (often for his own amusement) have come to light – the exercises appear to have been the first poems he attempted. On at least one occasion while he was at this school he won the prize of a guinea for a Latin poem he composed. Hector kept a number of these poems and sent them to Boswell the year after Johnson's death. The earliest were composed after Samuel was in his next school at the age of sixteen, but one, 'On a Daffodil', may well date from towards the end of his time at Lichfield Grammar School. It consists of six quatrains of alternating lilting rhymes conventionally full of allusions to stock pastoral forms celebrating the flower with such lines as 'May the morn's earliest tears on thee be shed,/And thou impearl'd with dew appear more gay.' The last eight lines about time's ravages and the fleeting joys of beauty in nature, woman and poetry are precociously philosophical for a boy of fifteen, three of which read: 'And ah! behold the shriveling blossoms die,/So late admir'd and prais'd, alas! In vain!' ... Alike must fall the poet and his theme.' Apart from little Sally Ford back in Birmingham and Ann Hector in Lichfield, we know of no other girls in this stage of his life who may have inspired such verses.[21]

[4]

By the time Samuel was fifteen the seeds had been sown for many of his ideas about children and how they should be educated and treated. Several of them are angry and contentious, in which one may detect bitterness stirring, a distaste for the unquestioned authority of a parent. Often in his comments about education he took the side of children, urging that what adults and educational institutions think is best for them is not always in their best interests. 'Mr Johnson was himself exceedingly disposed to the general indulgence of children' without spoiling them, Mrs Thrale observed, 'and was even scrupulously and ceremoniously attentive not to offend them: he had strongly persuaded himself of the difficulty people always find to erase early impressions either of kindness or resentment, and said, "he should never have so loved his mother when a man, had she not given him coffee she could ill afford, to gratify his appetite as a boy".' The important thing, he felt, was to avoid the cold, negative, even neutral approach in bringing up children: "'My mother ... was always telling me that I did not *behave* myself properly; that I should endeavour to learn *behaviour*, and such cant: but when I replied, that she ought to tell me what to do, and what to avoid, her admonitions were commonly ... at an end."' Musing over what he would have done as a parent, he added, 'I would not have set their future friendship to hazard for the sake of thrusting into their heads knowledge of things for which they might not perhaps have either taste or necessity.' 'You teach your daughters the diameters of the planets,' he told Mrs Thrale, 'and wonder when you have done that they do not delight in your company.' With schooling more specifically in mind, he could easily shift into a strident tone. He was 'very solicitous to preserve the felicity of children' and once persuaded Dr Robert Sumner, Headmaster of Harrow, to ease up on the burden of study 'usually given to fill up boys' time during the holidays'.[22]

CHAPTER 4

Two Benefactors

[1]

In the autumn of 1725 Samuel's mother got it in her mind again to send him (this time apparently without Nathaniel) to spend some time with her flamboyant nephew Cornelius Ford, the son of her brother Joseph. She may simply have wanted to get him out of the house at a time when serious family financial problems had begun to surface. There were also signs of family strife, suggesting that Michael Johnson was undergoing some sort of emotional crisis, aggravated by attacks of melancholia, and that all was not well between him and his wife. In any case, if ever young Samuel had a watershed life-changing experience, this visit to Cornelius was it, the full effects of which his distracted mother could not have anticipated.

One sign that Sarah Johnson was finding things too much at home is that she hired a fifteen-year-old girl, Catherine Chambers, known as 'Kitty', to live with them as a household maid. Mrs Thrale got it wrong that Samuel had learned to read while sitting in Kitty's lap and hearing her tell the story of George and the Dragon, as he was sixteen by the time Kitty arrived. But he quickly conceived a great affection for her and spoke of her over the years with unfailing tenderness. She remained in the house long after his mother and father died, keeping the house and his father's bookshop running as well as taking in lodgers until her death in 1767.[1]

'Kitty' freed Sarah from some of the household drudgery so that she could spend more time in the bookshop organising her husband's affairs, but ultimately she could do little either about Michael's hypochondria or his chaotic way of running his business. This year he was in trouble again over the payment of taxes on his parchment business, an experience embittering his son enough to have fired his vicious definition of 'excise' in the *Dictionary* as 'a hateful tax levied upon commodities, and adjudged not by the common judges of property, but wretches hired by those to whom excise is paid'. Through thick and thin, Michael ended up keeping the business for a total of about thirty years in the course of which much of the moderate wealth he earned from books he lost in parchment. Parchment also distracted him from bookselling, printing, publishing, and selling prints, pocketbooks and other stationery-type items, which alone kept him extremely busy, especially as he had to sell his books at auctions at markets in the region. Scarred by the memories of his father's constant struggle as a country bookseller, Johnson wrote on one occasion that with meagre profits such a bookseller 'cannot live; for his receipts are small, and his debts sometimes bad'. As the years wore on the family finances steadily deteriorated and, according to what Johnson told Hawkins, his father eventually 'in the course of his trade of a book-seller, had become bankrupt', or at least insolvent, so that he had to be bailed out with money or credit by fellow bookseller William Innys, well known for his trade in St Paul's Churchyard in London. It was an act of charity that deeply and lastingly affected Samuel.[2]

[2]

Johnson's cousin Cornelius has become something of a legendary figure in the life of Samuel Johnson. The son of Sarah's brother Joseph from his first marriage, Cornelius was fifteen years older than his cousin, and was a Cambridge graduate and Fellow of Peterhouse in the early 1720s. He had a lot going for him as a first-class classical scholar, sparkling wit and conversationalist, and heir of a decent family estate when his father died in 1721. He inherited a house in Pedmore, close to Stourbridge, to which he moved from Cambridge, lured to exchange the stimulating but simple life of a Peterhouse don for a more genteel lifestyle in rural Worcestershire. Cornelius imprudently gave up his fellowship when he was thirty, married the wealthy spinster Judith Crowley thirteen years older than he, and settled down to a reasonably prosperous life, a universe away from his privileged Cambridge existence.

Neither he nor his father by then knew the Lichfield Johnsons well. It was a fresh breeze of energy and intelligence that blew through the dull, troubled household of Michael Johnson when Cornelius travelled to Lichfield one day to talk to Michael about certain financially unfulfilled provisions of his 1706 marriage settlement – Cornelius's father was a trustee of the settlement. Michael Johnson may have dreaded his visit as he knew he owed the trustees £100, but Cornelius surprised them all with a creative piece of financial management that ended up instead with his giving Michael £100.

While he was there Cornelius was impressed with this strange, intellectual, curious, well-read, strong-minded prodigy of sixteen hidden within the household and boundaries of Lichfield. Samuel had potential. Why not invite him to Pedmore to learn a thing or two about a more worldly life? It would be amusing. He could also help him with his classical studies. This may well have been arranged at the time of Cornelius's visit, to Lichfield. Cornelius's polish and brilliance had thrilled Samuel during his brief visit and the boy was eager to fly to him at Pedmore. Whether Cornelius took him with him on the spot or he followed soon after, he felt his luck had turned. In a matter of days he found himself delightfully settled in Cornelius's pleasant house in an entirely different environment among his mother's prosperous relatives, removed for a while from the financial worries and bickering of his own family. He arrived in September or October 1725.

Fairly wealthy, aged forty-three, and unexciting, Cornelius's wife had succeeded in making her husband comfortable and prosperous. He found amusement elsewhere, in reading and an intense social life of witty conversation and merriment. He cultivated an epicurean existence for which there had been little scope at Cambridge. In the months just before Samuel's visit he was also awaiting preferment in the Church, which he eventually received at the hands of Philip Stanhope, the fourth Earl of Chesterfield, a friend from his Cambridge days whom almost thirty years later Johnson would majestically snub on the eve of the publication of his *Dictionary*. Cornelius would soon enough become a prototype of the debauched parson, however, well known as 'Parson Ford', conscientious in many respects about his clerical calling but unable to control his profligacy in a turbulent London world of letters, wit, high society and dissipation. According to one unverifiable claim, made by both Hawkins (who rather blackened his name) and Mrs Thrale, among others, Cornelius even became the model for the presiding drunk parson in Hogarth's satiric painting, *Midnight Modern Conversation* (1731–2). He was also an acquaintance of Alexander Pope. Johnson's own view of his young mentor half a century later was that his abilities, 'instead of furnishing convivial merriment to the voluptuous and dissolute, might have enabled him to excel among the virtuous and the wise'. He told Boswell, 'I never saw him but in the country. I have been told he was a man of great parts; very profligate, but I never heard he was impious.' When the expectant Samuel walked into his house for what Sarah and Michael intended as a few days' visit, Cornelius was conscientious, discreet, lively and charming. There was no stain of profligacy about him.[3]

What happened to Samuel during his idyll with Cornelius and his wife? Nothing less than an expanded view of life's possibilities. Known as 'Neely', Cornelius instructed him in the classics, but that was only part of it. Whenever Johnson spoke of him to Mrs Thrale, she said it was 'always with tenderness, praising his acquaintance with life and manners'. The boy felt flattered, honoured by the flow of advice from a man fifteen years older who sketched out for him images of the way of the world and probably also the current far-off London literary scene. As Pope's translation of the first half of the *Odyssey* had just been published and was a general literary talking point, it is likely that Cornelius thrilled Samuel with first-hand accounts of Pope and his Homeric collaborators, William Broome and Elijah Fenton. Then there was Pope's new edition of Shakespeare, a hugely important publishing event of even more immediate interest to Samuel. Daniel Defoe was also continuing his success with novels, narratives and journals.

There was endless literary and social gossip, too, to which Cornelius was attentive. One thing he could not abide was pedantry, of which he had seen much at Cambridge. Mrs Thrale wrote in her diary: 'Neely Ford, his relation, the profligate parson immortalised by Hogarth, was he told me the man who advised him to study the principles of everything, that a general acquaintance with life might be the consequence of his enquiries. Learn said he the leading Precognita of all things – no need perhaps to turn over leaf by leaf; but grasp the trunk hard only, and you will shake all the branches.' A person who can talk about only one subject or perform in only one area 'is seldom wanted, and perhaps never wished for; while the man of general knowledge can often benefit, and always please'. This would become a code of social and scholastic conduct for Samuel. According to Mrs Thrale, Johnson also cited Cornelius's lecture to him about conversation: avoid questioning another man's excellence in conversation and your 'pretensions as a writer' will be more readily acknowledged. Whether he practised this remains to be seen.[4]

Neither of them left a record of their time together but before they knew it days had passed into seven or eight months. There were excursions to be taken, such as to the Lyttelton estate at Hagley Park where he may have met members of the family, especially the Whig first Baron (George Lyttelton) – a close friend of Pope and later an eminent political figure whose controversial biography Johnson wrote more than half a century later. Johnson's friend of later years, Thomas Percy, wrote of 'colloquial disputes' the boy is supposed to have had at Hagley with Lyttelton, his exact contemporary, from which he allegedly conceived a prejudice against him – a doubtful assertion considering the generally Whiggish Stourbridge-Pedmore-Hagley environment he was enjoying at the time with Cornelius. Contemplating a visit to Hagley in 1771, Johnson mused that the experience would give him 'the opportunity of recollecting past times' wandering through the cooling shades and sacred springs of Hagley Park and 'recalling the images of sixteen, and reviewing my conversations with poor Ford'. Here he would have been not the tradesman's son but the guest of a respected member of Worcestershire society. A native of the area, years later Percy wrote that Samuel was 'admitted into the best company of the place, and had no common attention paid to his conversation; of which remarkable instances were long remembered'. He stayed for the autumn and winter and through the spring, no fewer than nine months, not returning to Lichfield until Whitsuntide, an expectant and dramatically altered young man.[5]

Unknown to him and his parents, though, throughout all those months there was a ticking bomb in the person of the ominous Hunter. Hunter greeted Johnson on his return to Lichfield in early June 1726 with the news that after more than half a year of truancy he was not about to let him back into the school as if nothing had happened. Hunter apparently took his absence as an insult to his teaching and a flouting of the school's authority. It is tempting to read his defiance as a repayment for the irritation and frustration this precocious, stubborn day pupil had caused him. The end result was that the Johnsons had to scramble quickly to find another school. They failed to get him in at Newport Grammar School in Shropshire, but with Cornelius (who probably felt responsible for Samuel's dismissal from Lichfield Grammar School) and his half-brother Gregory Hickman's timely intervention – he was a former governor of the school – Samuel was quickly admitted as a boarder at the Stourbridge Grammar School. It was not a bad turn of events for the boy. Now he could be near Pedmore and his new mentor for months on end. After only a few days in Lichfield, he returned to Stourbridge to enroll in his new school. He began there after the Whitsuntide holidays in 1726.

The headmaster of Stourbridge Grammar School was the Revd John Wentworth, a bachelor, who had been in charge there since 1704. A good scholar, he was a far cry from the highly disciplined, organised taskmaster Samuel was used to in Hunter. The agreement, according to Thomas Percy, was that the sixteen-year-old would take on some teaching of the younger boys as a type of pupil-teacher. Wentworth was not kind to him, however. 'Mr Wentworth was a very able man, but an idle man, and to me very severe,' Johnson told Boswell, 'but I cannot blame him much. I was then a big boy; he saw I did not reverence him; and that he should get no honour by me. I had brought enough with me, to carry me through; and all I should get at his school would be ascribed to my own labour, or to my former master. Yet he taught me a great deal.' All in all, the educational value of his months at the school was minimal, although he was surprised to find there a good collection of folios of Greek and Latin classics, divinity, geography and history that occupied much of his time. He summed up his education at Stourbridge and Lichfield schools by remarking to Percy that at one he had learned much in the school but nothing from the master, at the other much from the master and nothing in the school.[6]

[3]

Whatever Johnson may have gained or wasted from his months at school in Stourbridge, he made some good use of his time there to write verses. Among the earliest of his attempts at poetry, they reveal that from the start he showed a good ear for the music of verse, readiness to experiment with English poetic forms, and sensitivity to rhythmic smoothness. Most of the eleven poems that have survived from this period are school exercises in translating Homer, Horace and Virgil, written presumably more under the watchful eye of Wentworth than in the privacy of his room, and they must have been thought impressive enough to merit keeping by his schoolmaster whose nephew sent them to Boswell after Johnson's death. Most of the poetry being published at the time by Pope and others was in heroic couplets, satirical or pastoral, focused on society, and was full of classical allusions and elegant diction. Johnson's verses were conventional enough in their elegance, rhythm and imagery, largely unaffected by private impulses, but on the whole unspectacular.

Johnson himself did not think well enough of them to merit revision and publication, but they offer a sprinkling of biographical glimpses.

While the poems are stocked with pastoral references, emotions and other traditional devices of song, they also reveal his lyrical appreciation for the lusciousness of nature and landscape – what one would expect from a boy who has grown up walking solitarily through the shades and meadows of Staffordshire and reading Virgil, Theocritus and Ovid amid the cooling midsummer breezes. And Wentworth showed insight into his character – as an impetuous boy in speech who had to slow down and consider where his behaviour was leading him – by asking him to translate a short poem, '*Festina Lente*' with its ethical, moral impulse 'to make haste slowly': 'Observe your steps; be carefull to command/Your passions; guide the reins with steady hand/ ... Rashness! thou spring from whence misfortunes flow!' It is not known how physically big he was at this time but his large frame must already have filled out with a heftiness resembling his father, and his awkwardness have been aggravated by gauche movements: 'Observe your steps ... Nor down steep cliffs precipitately move.'[7]

One poem he wrote for himself was a love poem, an 'amorous lay', to an eighteen-year-old Quaker girl named Olivia Lloyd whom he met in Stourbridge, probably at Cornelius's house since she was his niece. She stirred Johnson's fancy with her own love of the classics. Alas, the poem has been lost. Nothing came of that young love and, in any case, after six months he was expelled from school. Hector recalled mysteriously that Samuel left precipitously, 'a difference arising between his Master and him about the purity of a phrase in his exercise'. Was the offending passage an overly erotic piece of translation? Whatever it was, it had to be a stiff, heated disagreement to conclude in Samuel being sent packing in November 1726. This was the second school to dismiss him in the space of six months. His independent spirit and contentiousness were bearing fruit in a way that were seriously beginning to threaten his education and life-prospects. He was now fed up with school and disinclined to think about it after he left Stourbridge – a disinclination that stayed with him for years. 'As we come forward into life,' he confessed to Hector in 1756, 'we naturally turn back now and then upon the past. I now think more upon my schooldays than I did when I had just broken loose from a Master. Happy is he that can look back upon the past with pleasure'.[8]

[4]

Samuel was suddenly trapped again in his dull family life in anti-climactic Lichfield, wrenched from the heady social environment Cornelius had opened up for him. Nothing much had changed at home except for the welcome presence of the young housekeeper Kitty Chambers. His father's finances continued to deteriorate. His brother was still at school, though even if he had not been the two had so little in common that it is doubtful they would have been good company for each other. John Taylor was finishing up at the Grammar School and soon to go off to university. Edmund Hector was purposefully studying and not as available as in former times. Samuel was now seventeen and too old to start at another school. He knew too much and was too argumentative for the average schoolmaster. Sending him to university was financially out of the question and he showed little urge to do anything in particular except read. It was time for him to earn some money and help with the family finances. Such an energetic, powerfully built young man even with defective eyesight could certainly pull his weight.

The obvious answer was to help his father in the book business, and perhaps even in the parchment factory. His father 'took him home, probably with a view to bring him up to his own trade', Hawkins reasons, 'for I have heard Johnson say, that he himself was able to bind a book.'[9] Many years later, when he was an old man, Johnson actually spotted a book on the bookshop shelves that he had bound during this period. This was a skill he seemed not to have forgotten when he bound a book or two for the Thrales fifty years later in their summer house. He also worked in the bookshop itself, but the problem was that he found selling books or anything else in the shop, from children's toys to sundry types of stationery, excruciatingly boring. He preferred reading the books to selling them, disinclined to have anything to do with the retail side of the business either in the shop or at any of the several markets in nearby towns where his father kept a stall on market days.

One of the more famous episodes in Johnson's life may have its source around this time. When his father asked him to assist him at his stall in Uttoxeter, twelve miles north of Lichfield, he refused. If this did not anger his exasperated father, it certainly increased tension in the household. Everyone was busy trying to make ends meet and here was the eldest son lying about day after day at home, not doing much of anything useful to anyone. As it turned out, not going to Uttoxeter was a teenage decision and moment that rooted itself in his accumulating guilt. The year he died he told a young clergyman that while 'he could not in general accuse himself of having been an undutiful son', his pride on this occasion pained him so much that (according to one source) on the fiftieth anniversary of his disobedience he forced himself to perform an action of contrition: 'A few years ago, I desired to atone for this fault; I went to Uttoxeter in very bad weather, and stood for a considerable time bareheaded in the rain, on the spot where my father's stall used to stand. In contrition I stood, and I hope the penance was expiatory.'[10] The scene has been pictorially represented and cited so many times that it has become certified as one of the great images of Johnson's troubled soul.

Johnson admitted to Boswell that he was idle, scolded by his father for 'his want of steady application' and not having a 'settled plan of life', but later he backtracked, 'I would not have you think I was doing nothing then.' His father may have been happier if his reading had been more systematic, pragmatically leading to something, but he was reading omnivorously and impulsively. William Shaw, one of Johnson's best early biographers and a young clerical friend and scholar from the 1770s, tracked down boyhood friends and acquaintances who had seen Samuel reading either in school or his father's shop. He wrote this about young Samuel's eccentric tenacity as a reader which rendered him oblivious to everything around him, almost as if he had lapsed into a hypnotic or drug-induced state:

> Even in the act of devouring the sublimest passages of ancient literature ... his perseverance was so singular and exemplary that all attempts to divert him from the task assigned, or which he assigned to himself, were uniformly without effect. [There was] a rapacity with which he commenced his primary pursuit [reading], and grasped at every object of classical intelligence ...
>
> He is said, when a mere school-boy, to have read indefatigably, and probably picked up no despicable acquaintance with books, by occasionally attending his father's shop. Here he was, not infrequently, so absorbed by his predilection for the classical lore of antiquity, as entirely to neglect the business he had in trust. Being often chid for disobliging some of his father's customers and friends, in this manner, he replied with great shrewdness, *that to supersede the pleasures of reading, by the attentions of traffic, was a task he never could master.*[11]

The bookshop was like a huge biblio-cabinet of curiosities, a bookish bower of bliss tempting him into divergent and crisscrossing intellectual, cultural, historical, literary, religious, scientific and geographic paths. His reading took him everywhere but at the same time (in his father's eyes) nowhere. 'Sir,' he said to Boswell, 'in my early years I read very hard. It is a sad reflection, but a true one, that I knew almost as much at eighteen as I do now. My judgement, to be sure, was not so good; but, I had all the facts.' From twelve to eighteen, he told his friend Bennet Langton, was his 'great period of *study*'. He read not merely entertaining works, 'not [only] voyages and travels, but all literature, Sir, all ancient writers, all manly: though but little Greek, only some Anacreon and Hesiod; but in this irregular manner ... I had looked into a great many books, which were not commonly known at the universities, where they seldom read any books but what are put into their hands by their tutors.' His sweeping imagination did not exclude books on metaphysics either. And if he hunted, as he did once, through the upper shelves of the shop for an apple his brother had hidden there, he might happen on a large folio of Petrarch or some other classic to pull down and devour pretty much on the spot. With a vivid imagination and mounting intellectual curiosity he went on turning the pages through the following year, 'roaming at large in the fields of literature' to his father's irritation and doubtless to customers' occasional annoyance.[12]

Thomas Percy's psychological take on what seemed to him (from Johnson's description) an immoderate amount of isolation while he read 'romances of chivalry' and 'extravagant fictions' was that it sowed the seeds of Johnson's restlessness and overactive imagination, bearing fruit shortly in severe melancholia. On top of this was the emptiness of Lichfield, at least compared to Stourbridge life, and the gnawing frustration of seeing school friends less able than he go on to Oxford and Cambridge. He was unhappy and standing still, a dangerous physical condition and state of mind for him. There was, however, a vital lifeline, the second in his life after Cornelius, at close hand over in the cathedral close, a bachelor almost thirty years older than he, Gilbert Walmesley.

A lawyer by training, Walmesley was one of the richest and most distinguished citizens of Lichfield, then Registrar (Judge) of the ecclesiastical court, whose father had been chancellor of the diocese. He lived in the most imposing house in town, the spacious Bishop's Palace, one of a series of beautiful ecclesiastic buildings on Dean's Walk next to the Deanery on the north side of the small cathedral close, which he had the opportunity to rent because up to 1868 the bishops of Coventry and Lichfield chose to live instead at Eccleshall in Staffordshire. Like Cornelius he was urbane and sophisticated, with access to the best society in the area. The palace allowed him graciously to entertain men and women of significance, people who could be counted on to generate sparkling conversation of a high order, much of it literary and political. He was also an enthusiastic book-collector and in the palace had the perfect place to house his fine library. Indeed, he bought many of his books at Michael Johnson's bookshop to which he could quickly walk, past Minster Pool, down Dam Street, and around a couple of corners to Market Place.

At the shop in the closing months of 1726, Walmesley noticed Samuel, really noticed him, for the first time. What particularly caught his attention is unknown – perhaps he caught the drift of his comments on certain books and simply liked the boy and became concerned that he was wasting time, going nowhere – but before long he invited him to the palace. It was a fateful act of social patronage. Johnson spoke for himself regarding Walmesley in an uncharacteristically celebrative passage from his *Life of Edmund Smith* more than fifty years later:

> Of Gilbert Walmesley, thus presented to my mind, let me indulge myself in the remembrance. I knew him very early; he was one of the first friends that literature procured me, and I hope that at least my gratitude made me worthy of his notice.
>
> He was of an advanced age, and I was only not a boy; yet he never received my notions with contempt . . . His studies had been so various that I am not able to name a man of equal knowledge. His acquaintance with books was great; and what he did not immediately know he could at least tell where to find. Such was his amplitude of learning and such his copiousness of communication that it may be doubted whether a day now passes in which I have not some advantage from his friendship.[13]

This is dramatic praise, a gesture of gratitude deeply felt. For the seventeen-year-old the Bishop's Palace may as well have been the pot at the end of a rainbow, so close yet so elusive; to be invited there was for him an unimaginable privilege. The fact that to some extent he made it into that society in town was especially sweet because for all his life it had been denied to him and his family.

What made Walmesley, in addition to his learning, encouragement, and patience, so appealing and valuable to the young man was that in his younger years he had 'mingled with the world without exemption from its vices or its follies'. He differed from Cornelius, however, in that he 'had never neglected the cultivation of his mind; his belief in Revelation was unshaken; his learning preserved his principles: he grew first regular, and then pious'. Walmesley was a perfect mentor for the young protégé: lively, open, 'copious in communication', and worldly, yet his breadth of scholarship kept him open-minded and true to his Christian principles. It could have been an irrecoverable problem, however, that politically and socially Walmesley was also a Whig, which in his *Dictionary* Johnson briskly defined as a radical 'faction' and illustrated with passages suggesting that Whigs were threats to Church, Crown, and the order of the state. Johnson acknowledged Walmesley was one, 'with all the virulence and malevolence of his party', but neither he nor Walmesley allowed it to get in the way: 'Difference of opinion did not keep us apart. I honoured him, and he endured me,' Johnson wrote.[14]

Samuel may have been disappointed that Walmesley was a Whig but that would not have been a party-political disappointment. Walmesley was part of a powerful social and intellectual Whig world that, in fact, Samuel would have respected. All his life he admired this kind of company, people who were fashionable, well-informed, amicable, intelligent and forward-looking. The Whigs were the party of power and wealth, and had been since 1688, associated equally with innovative business as well as with inherited aristocratic privilege. The Whig and Tory parties were not then, as now, divided by the politics of right and left, of an industrial society that pitches labouring classes against the money-makers and affluent, but rather by attitudes to the past. The Whigs were linked with irreverence for the past while the Tories treasured it culturally, artistically, poetically and institutionally. That is why Johnson thought of himself as a Tory, not unhesitatingly sympathetic to the mighty and wealthy as much as attuned to the practices and sentiments of simpler townspeople and their worlds, to Christian virtues and associations, and to the beauties and solidity of a rural market town like Lichfield. The high and mighty Whigs were breathtaking to the teenager who, with Cornelius's help, had begun to shed his provinciality. Furthermore, Johnson as a boy and adolescent did not live in a closed and sheltered world of Tories. As Donald Greene, the historian of Johnson's politics, has urged, 'There was little of the starry-eyed about eighteenth-century politics in Staffordshire; Lichfield was far from being a Tory stronghold; and from his earliest days Johnson seems to have had at least as many and as opinionated Whig friends, acquaintances, and relations as Tory.'[15]

Johnson's father's Toryism was of little or no importance or influence on him. Greene frames Johnson's position in this society perfectly in these balanced words: 'Had he been a lesser person, he might have succumbed to their attraction and to the comfortable security of a ready-made intellectual pattern, accustoming himself to mouth their facile clichés ... Something like this is, after all, what does happen to the majority of "bright young men". But as it was, Johnson could never stifle the acute awareness that he was not as they were, and never could be.' He knew poverty and deprivation as they had not, and he would give Walmesley's Bishop's Palace circle a run for their money just as he had the Stourbridge-Pedmore, Hagley circle. He drew the urgency and strength of his arguments, just as in the future he would his political ideas in general, from 'the world of small, ordinary, suffering, inarticulate people', from the disadvantaged to whom he was always drawn. He was not then, nor would be in maturity, a blind and retrogressive Tory. Walmesley became a model to Samuel of how an older man can nurture and assist a younger person struggling to develop self-respect and a clear persona. 'At this man's table,' Johnson remembered with pleasure, 'I enjoyed many cheerful and instructive hours, with companions such as are not often found.' Walmesley was a gracious, learned, worthy debating partner and friend. That was enough for him.[16]

One of the companions whom Walmesley welcomed to the palace was Samuel's schoolfellow Robert James, already mentioned as the inventor of the notorious James powder, but there was another, David Garrick, a boy eight years younger than Samuel who would become the most famous actor in eighteenth-century England and one of the greatest entertainers in all of Europe. 'Davy' had grown up in Lichfield, attended the Grammar School, and had already been 'taken on' by Walmesley when Samuel first made his appearance at the Bishop's Palace. The son of an army captain, his family was poor but genteel and, unlike Samuel's family, had social access to the finer citizens of Lichfield, including Walmesley. There is no evidence that he and Samuel knew each other before meeting at the palace because Davy began at the school two years after Samuel left. The contrast between them could scarcely have been greater. Davy was friendly, amazingly vivacious, and small for his age, with something of a tendency to be cheeky, while Samuel was 'long, lank, and lounging', awkward,

melancholic and argumentative. Garrick endeared himself to just
about everyone. Walmesley saw the promise in him even at the age of
nine, delighting in his 'smart repartees and frolicsome actions'. At
some point during this period when he had the run of the palace,
Davy previewed his early thespian inclinations by precociously staging
George Farquhar's rollicking *The Recruiting Officer*, most probably in
the large drawing room of the palace. It is possible that Samuel was
in the audience and near enough the action so that his poor eyesight
and hearing did not prejudice him against the play, as it tended to do
later towards the stage generally – there is no evidence of his ever
wearing eyeglasses. What we do know is that the two young men
became friends for life though it was an uneasy relationship, with
Walmesley as a common, warm, secure point of reference in their
youth to which they both looked back with gratitude and warmth.

Anna Seward, the spirited poetess who was more than thirty years
younger than Johnson and turned against him partly because of what
she felt was his rough rudeness, put a different spin on his tutelage
under Walmesley. She came to live in the Bishop's Palace when her
father Thomas Seward, Canon of Lichfield, had moved into the house
with his family after Walmesley's death in 1751. Indeed, Johnson on
several visits to Lichfield in later years made a point of visiting the
Sewards in the palace, from which she gradually formed her opinion
of him as liberal and compassionate but conversationally abusive.
After a point, nothing she said about Johnson was ever likely to be
offered without a dash of venom – a great shame since she was so well
placed to learn about Johnson's youth and must have had a huge fund
of anecdotes picked up through the years. Boswell's eventual hostility
towards her and her prejudice for the most part ruled her out of his
biography of Johnson as a credible witness. But it is interesting to place
her reading of Samuel's introduction to the palace society alongside the
dominant biographies that appeared shortly after his death. In spite
of her bias against Johnson – which may also incidentally have had
something to do with the fact that her mother was the daughter of
Samuel's headmaster John Hunter and that she may have heard of
her grandfather's irritation with this 'huge, over-grown, misshapen,
probably dirty stripling' – she wrote:

> Within the walls which my father's family inhabits, in this very dining-
> room, the munificent Mr Walmesley, with the taste, the learning and the

liberality of Maecenas, administered to rising genius the kind nutriment of attention and praise . . .

Two or three evenings every week Mr Walmesley called the stupendous stripling and his livelier companion David Garrick, who was a few years younger, to his own plentiful board. There, in the hours of convivial gaiety, did he delight to wave every restraint of superiority formed by rank, afflu-ence, polished manners and the dignity of advanced life; and there, 'as man to man, as friend to friend', he drew forth the different powers of each expanding spirit, by the vivid interchange of sentiment and opinion, and by the cheering influence of generous applause.

This was magnanimous of Walmesley the Whig, she added, because Samuel came to the palace with a baggage of 'furious' pro-Jacobitism imbibed from 'his master's [Hunter's] absurd zeal for the forfeit rights of the house of Stuart'. This specific claim was not, so far as we know, made by anyone else who knew Samuel in Lichfield, including the communicative Hector, but she used it to construct her portrait of both his argumentative insolence and Walmesley's infinite patience within the palace walls. 'I am told [that] even at that early period of life,' she continued, Johnson 'maintained his opinions, on every subject, with the same sturdy, dogmatical and arrogant fierceness with which he now overbears all opposition to them in company'. How amazing therefore, she concluded, that Walmesley's love of genius 'induced him to suffer insolent sallies from the son of an indigent bookseller' concerning the risky topic of the legitimacy of the Han-overian succession.[17]

Notwithstanding Johnson's apparent failure in his maturity to impress Anna Seward favourably on visits to the palace, Boswell makes the point that it was the company of women in particular at the palace which proved to be of huge importance to young Samuel. At Stourbridge he had recently been exposed to genteel women but at the palace he had a more sustained opportunity to talk to them and observe their grace and 'good breeding'. Boswell's point is that exposure to this class of women courtesy of Walmesley even as early as 1726 must be weighed against the contemporary reputation of Johnson as painfully awkward in society and of 'coarse and ferocious manners' and temper as well as appearance. Walmesley plucked him out of a relatively isolated existence in his father's bookshop and exposed him to the softening influences of happy female society, and for the rest of his life in all kinds of polite society he was both attracted to women and found attractive by them because of the flattering notice he took of them. Mrs Thrale noticed his keen interest in and awareness of what women wore. On entering a crowded room he invariably would make for the women first. The great Shakespearean editor George Steevens observed that he 'delighted in the company of women' and Boswell added, 'Some of the ladies have assured me, they recollected him well when a young man, as distinguished for his complaisance' or desire of pleasing. This urge sprang partly from a highly scxed nature, about which there will be more later, but more characteristically it was due to his capacity, learned early, to understand and enjoy female company. Frances Reynolds, sister of the painter Sir Joshua Reynolds, stated flatly that he placed 'a higher value upon female friendship than perhaps men'. There were several women in Lichfield alone who appreciated this in him and whom he made a point of visiting on his several trips there over the last twenty-five years of his life.[18]

Walmesley and the Bishop's Palace, debate, extensive reading, labour in his father's bookshop, and no small amount of frustration as he waited – for what he did not know – comprised the pattern of his days during these fallow years of 1726–8. Jonathan Swift published his caustic ironic romance satire *Gulliver's Travels* in 1726; in 1727 George I died (succeeded by his son George II), as did Sir Isaac Newton, and Spanish forces laid siege to the English garrison at Gibraltar; and in 1728 John Gay came out with his triumphant satiric-comic ballad opera *The Beggar's Opera* and Pope, already Samuel's great model of the professional author, published his scathing bombshell *The Dunciad*, a comprehensive mock-heroic satire of literary 'Dulness'. The world was moving ahead excitingly and England's great age of satire had dawned, but for Samuel the future did not look so bright.

PART II

Despondency and Hope

Pembroke College, Oxford

CHAPTER 5

Oxford: Wielding a Scholar's Weapon

[1]

S uddenly another light appeared unexpectedly on Johnson's con-
stricted horizon that had nothing to do with Walmesley. Sarah
Johnson's rich cousin Elizabeth Harriotts, to whom in desperation
she had taken Samuel for medical advice regarding his eyesight, died
in February 1728 and left her a legacy. Mrs Harriotts specified that
Michael Johnson was not to get his hands on any of it. In addition to
sheets, pillow cases, and pewter dishes and plates, the joyful surprise
was £40 (about £4000 today) she received 'for her own separate use'.
The legacy was generous enough to make Michael in 'the humility of
distress' change his mind about 'our good cousin Harriotts'. He could
have plowed the money into the black hole of his faltering business,
but since this was not possible they decided to use it to send their
brilliant and restless son to university and hope that a scholarship or
some other source of money would materialise in the course of his
first year to enable him to remain there for the remaining two. With
some prudence the money would surely pay for a year. They decided
on Oxford partly because one of Samuel's school chums at Lichfield,
Andrew Corbet, was already there and offered vaguely to help pay for
his friend's expenses in order to have him there as a companion. As it
happened, Corbet left Oxford only a few weeks after Johnson arrived,
and with him disappeared his promise of help. Another likely reason
for choosing Oxford was that Johnson's godfather, Dr Swynfen, who
had recently moved his medical practice from Lichfield to Birmingham, was a Pembroke College graduate and possibly urged that
college on the Johnsons. Pembroke it was to be.

The scene was set for the first great chapter in the life of the
nineteen-year-old, one the family hoped would determine his career
and unlock all the prosperity and distinction that promised to flow
from it. On the morning in late October 1728 when he and his father

mounted horses for the long ride to Oxford, there may well have been a small gathering to see him off: his two mentors Dr Swynfen and Walmesley cheering him on, his brother eager to have him out of the house again, his mother beaming with pride, interested neighbours struck by the uniqueness or novelty of having this unusual young man of limited means, who had not even completed his formal schooling, going off to study at a major centre of learning, and, not least, Dame Oliver with an offering of gingerbread in hand telling him he was the best pupil she ever had. He never forgot her remark at that memorable moment, as Boswell recalls: 'He delighted in mentioning this early compliment: adding, with a smile, that "this was as high a proof of his merit as he could conceive".[1] With the trunk of books he had selected following later by wagon, he and his proud father set off for the academic Promised Land.

[2]

As a Catholic, Alexander Pope could not matriculate at Oxford, but in the autumn of 1717 at the age of twenty-five he caught the magic of the place as he rode up to it for a short visit with a friend. There is a romantic exultation about his description, in his case vicarious, which Johnson may well himself have felt as he and his father first caught sight of the approaching horizon of dreaming ancient spires:

> About a mile before I reached Oxford, all the bells toll'd, in different notes; the clocks of every college answered one another; and told me in a deeper, some in a softer voice, that it was eleven a clock. All this was no ill preparation to the life I have led since; among these old walls, venerable galleries, stone porticos, studious walks and solitary scenes of the university, I wanted nothing but a black gown and a salary, to be as mere a bookworm as any there.[2]

The Gothic medieval beauty and mystery of Oxford that Pope was so acutely attuned to on this visit, especially in the evening or by moon-light, was something that Johnson would have plenty of time later to explore. Now the business at hand was to make for Pembroke College, take possession of his room, meet his tutor, and seek out one of the pro-Vice-Chancellors in order to matriculate and pay his fees. He entered the university on 31 October, though for some reason he did not formally matriculate until 16 December, apparently 'a delay unusual and against the University statutes'. He did have to hand over seven pounds immediately to the Bursar, John Radcliffe, as a 'caution' or deposit.

On their first night he and his father met both his appointed tutor Revd William Jorden and William Adams, then a young fellow at the college who became Johnson's intimate and lifelong friend and a fertile source of anecdotes about him. Adams, who was also educated at Pembroke and its Master from 1775, told Boswell about this first encounter. 'On that evening', Boswell wrote, Johnson's father 'who had anxiously accompanied him, found means to have him introduced to Mr Jorden, who was to be his tutor in Classics. His father seemed very full of the merits of his son, and told the company he was a good scholar, and a poet, and wrote Latin verses.' At first both Adams and Jorden were taken aback by the physical appearance of this large, muscular, scarred, short-sighted young man subject to odd, abrupt movements, but they recovered when they heard him speak: 'His figure and manner appeared strange to them; but he behaved modestly, and sat silent, till upon something which occurred in the course of conversation, he suddenly struck in and quoted the Roman grammarian Macrobius; and thus he gave the first impression of that more extensive reading in which he had indulged himself.' Over the past two lonely years he had foraged in the fields of literature and added to his mental storehouse; now was the time to reap the harvest. He felt his powers: 'When I came to Oxford, Dr Adams, now Master of Pembroke College, told me, I was the best qualified for the University that he had ever known come there.'[3]

[3]

There was never much chance that he would fit into Oxford academic and social life quietly. Right away he disturbed some of the equanimity and tempo of Pembroke. At his first morning tutorial he quickly discovered that his tutor Jorden could not teach him much. He once remarked rudely that his tutor's lecture on logic was not worth half the twopence fine he incurred for missing it. 'He was a very worthy man, but a heavy man, and I did not profit much by his instructions. Indeed, I did not attend him much. The first day after I came to college, I waited upon him, and then stayed away four.' This was insolent enough in an undergraduate who had barely had time to unpack, especially as Jorden was a senior fellow, having been appointed

Viceregent of the College just a few weeks before Johnson arrived. The Viceregent was nominated by the Master to act as his deputy and perform with all his authority when he was absent from college. When Jorden mildly confronted Johnson about his repeated absences after he finally reappeared, instead of backing off he rubbed it in with an arrogance of which he seemed unaware: 'I answered I had been sliding [skating] in Christ-Church meadow. And this I said with as much *nonchalance* as I am now talking to you. I had no notion that I was wrong or irreverent to my tutor.' Mrs Thrale noted that 'he laughed very heartily at the recollection of his own insolence'. Boswell was impressed. 'Fortitude of mind,' he called it. No, Johnson replied, it was 'stark insensibility', the words of a self-centred, arrogant youth.[4]

According to Thomas Warton, who heard it from Johnson himself twenty-six years later, Jorden summoned him ominously to his chambers. By then the truant had had time to reflect a little on his cheekiness. 'I expected a sharp rebuke for my idleness, and went with a beating heart', but he found Jorden offering only warmth and understanding, probably conscious of the limitations as a scholar that his new charge had spotted so speedily: 'When we were seated, he told me he had sent for me to drink a glass of wine with him, and to tell me, he was *not* angry with me for missing his lecture.' 'This was, in fact, a most severe reprimand,' Johnson recalled uncomfortably almost thirty years later. 'Some more of the boys were then sent for, and we spent a very pleasant afternoon.' While that evening salvaged Johnson's regard for Jorden's character, it appears not to have had any effect on his attendance, although in a letter to Boswell on 12 July 1786, Adams denied Mrs Thrale's assertion that Johnson ignored most of Jorden's lectures.[5]

Jorden stayed at Oxford until mid-December 1729 when he was inducted to a clerical living about one hundred miles away. His students then seem to have been passed on to the young Fellow William Adams who humbly called himself his 'nominal' tutor and admitted to Boswell that this wilful prodigy they had allowed into their midst 'was above my mark' – a compliment which, when Johnson heard it, made his eyes flash 'with grateful satisfaction'.[6] 'That was liberal and noble,' he exclaimed. Adams explained that Johnson maintained a warm feeling the rest of his life for Jorden's paternal care, whose death in 1739 he 'much regretted' and 'for whom he seemed to retain the greatest regard'. 'Whenever a young man becomes Jorden's pupil,'

Johnson said, 'he becomes his son', though one less charitable observer called him 'a noted pupil monger'. To Mrs Thrale he expressed a similar affection for Jorden: 'That creature would defend his pupils to the last: no young lad under his care should suffer for committing slight improprieties, while he had breath to defend, or power to protect them. If I had sons to send to college, Jorden should have been their tutor.' As we shall see, Adams never taught Johnson anything as a tutor. Had he done so, Boswell wrote, 'his equal temper, mild disposition, and politeness of manners, might have insensibly softened the harshness of Johnson, and infused into him, those more delicate charities, those *petites morales*, in which, it must be confessed, our great moralist was more deficient than his best friends could fully justify'.[7]

[4]

Johnson soon realised he had not landed in the lap of a golden age of learning and scholarship. There were able, even brilliant, tutors but glaringly lacking were rules governing the degree of involvement of a tutor with a student, so students could easily go astray and tutors readily become lazy about their teaching and scholarship. Another flaw in the system was that many tutors were biding their time for clerical preferment, like Jorden himself, and could not generate much enthusiasm for the academic or even pastoral imperatives in their appointments. One historian has called the eighteenth century at Oxford 'The Great Depression', although others have maintained that the university was not as moribund as has often been maintained, with significant pieces of scholarship being published and a few colleges sustaining high standards of teaching. Certain scholars and dons like Thomas Warton were remarkably productive, but they were the exception, and even Warton had little taste for lecturing, sequestered as he was at either Trinity College or the Bodleian and preferring his 'ale and tobacco, and the riverside watermen and his cronies in the taverns'. He even wrote a poem, *Panegyric on Oxford Ale*, celebrating the libation as 'Sweet Helicon of logic'. On entering Warton's 'very elegant apartment' at Trinity College with Johnson in 1776, Boswell was surprised because he 'had heard that Tom kept low drunken company, and I expected to see a confused dusty room and a little, fat, laughing fellow. In place of which I found a good, sizable man, with most decent clothes and darkish periwig, one who might figure as a canon.' Richard West, a friend of the poet Thomas Gray who found himself at Christ Church in 1735, described Oxford as 'a country flowing with syllogisms and ale, where Horace and Virgil are equally unknown.'[8]

Students contracted their own peculiar brand of 'brisk intemperance' from the way the university ran itself. To begin with, they were admitted in a rigidly hierarchical manner that tended to foster its own breed of class consciousness and stifle creativity. Johnson entered Pembroke as a commoner, the largest group of students, ostensibly under the greatest supervision by assigned tutors and, led by the heads or scholars of their colleges who received special grants, likely to do the most serious academic work. They had to pay their own way and as sons of relatively poor families had severely limited budgets with which they had to cover their fees and expenses such as battels (college bills for food and other services), all of which were modest enough so that Johnson's forty pounds potentially could last him for a year. Commoners had to toe the line in all sorts of ways. They were required to attend lectures as well as chapel. If they were caught absenting themselves from academic duties with any kind of regularity they were punished with 'impositions' (written exercises). They had to eat dinner in hall, keep certain hours in college instead of whiling away the hours in ale or coffee houses where they were in danger of being hunted down by roving proctors, and dress appropriately for various occasions. Their compulsory daily dress in college and out in town was a simple ankle-length, sleeveless black gown of stuff decorated plainly with braided black streamers. Simple as it was and very soon looking grubby and worn, one wonders whether young Johnson fresh from Lichfield nevertheless became infected with 'the strong contagion of the gown', one of the destructive vanities he identifies in his poem *The Vanity of Human Wishes* twenty years later. It would appear he was mildly infected on a visit to Oxford in 1759 when he donned his Master's gown and was loath to take it off – 'It was at my first coming quite new and handsome' – but as a student it is more likely he was grateful for the gown as a way to conceal his increasingly threadbare clothes.

Finer, more embellished gowns were worn by the two socially more elevated ranks of students, the noblemen at the top and the gentlemen commoners next down. The noblemen were a small aristocratic group who enjoyed almost unlimited privileges with no need to have a tutor or take a degree. They often dined with the dons, could have pets, luxuriated in splendid private rooms, and generally indulged in a life of debauchery. Gentlemen commoners, the sons of wealthy families, were indulged almost as much and, with dangerously large amounts of money to spend, proved to be even more notorious in their idleness, drinking, eating and whoring – much of the latter in their rooms, an audacious breach of university rules. Gentlemen commoners considered commoners 'very *low* company (chiefly on account of the liquor they drank),' wrote the poet William Shenstone. With port and claret to oil the proceedings, 'they kept late hours, drank their favourite toasts on their knees; and, in short, were what we called "bucks of the first head".' Gentlemen commoners often left without taking a degree, and a few did not even bother to matriculate.[9]

Johnson was acutely conscious of his social inferiority and would never have attached himself as Shenstone did to an orgy of gentleman commoners. Nonetheless, in this rigid academic-social pecking order he was above the 'battelers', who had to feed and take care of themselves in return for a reduction of fees, and the lowest class of student, the servitor, whom he would describe in his *Dictionary* as 'one of the lowest order in the university'. The parents of servitors were so poor they could spare no money at all for their sons at the university. Servitors were assigned tutors and had free board and tuition, in exchange for which they had to perform certain duties in college, many of them quite menial and degrading, such as waiting on the gentlemen commoners and commoners in hall. One of the annoying tasks with which servitors were saddled, annoying to themselves as well as to others, was to knock periodically on their superiors' chamber doors to verify that they were in their rooms when they were supposed to be, reporting them if they were not. Fretting over this 'big brother' type of surveillance, which injured his pride and bred his resentment, Johnson contemptuously went out of his way to mislead the servitors and confound the system by deliberately ignoring the knocking at the door, scoffing at the regulations. He got himself reported and shrugged in indifference.[10]

Oxford's decline in the eighteenth century included a decline in student enrolment with the result that many colleges including Pembroke had rooms to spare. There was a good choice of rooms at Pembroke though chiefly for the more affluent students. Commoners and servitors had to put up with inexpensive small rooms high up near the roof line, reached through dark, bare, twisting stairways. Johnson had one of these for about £4 per year on the second floor above the

Porters Lodge in the Gatehouse, a three-storey building in classical style and, as it turned out, rather prominently located next to the Master's House which extended out at right angles to the north or Gatehouse wing of the Old Quadrangle. The location of the room was potentially awkward for him since with his window open he could be, and at least once was, overheard mumbling to himself by the Master, Matthew Panting (Master from 1714 to 1738 and admired by Johnson as 'a fine Jacobite'). The stairway to his room today is not much different in its starkness and dinginess from what he was obliged to climb every day, except for the fire extinguisher halfway up. If he stuck his head out of his window and looked not left into the Master's rooms but to the right (east), he took in the high walls of Christ Church and a good view of Tom Tower a short distance away on the other side of Carfax. He also looked squarely out at St Aldgate's Church, a few feet away, where in the south aisle the college held its services and in the upper chamber accommodated its library.

Pembroke was a small and self-contained academic and social world but of course the town and countryside offered an abundance of both salubrious and nefarious amusements by day and night. Against rules enforced by roving proctors, Johnson seems to have known one or two of the no fewer than three hundred alehouses in town, many of them scenes of drunkenness and riot. If not at an alehouse, he could lose himself in conversation – even then his antidote to tedium – at one or other of the innumerable coffee houses, many of which catered to the members of particular colleges. With several intense conversations or 'bull-sessions' with Johnson in-coffee houses, alehouses, or their rooms resonating in his memory, a fellow commoner at Pembroke, Oliver Edwards, told Johnson and Boswell half a century later, 'Sir, I remember you would not let us say *prodigious* at College.' Turning to Boswell, Edwards added, 'even then, Sir ... he was delicate in language, and we all feared him'. Then with astonishing recall Johnson reminded Edwards of an Oxford alehouse conversation: 'O! Mr Edwards! I'll convince you that I recollect you. Do you remember our dining together at an alehouse near Pembroke gate?' At this old alehouse very near the college, probably late into the night, they had exchanged some Latin verses, and now all these years later he cited the lines and one of Edwards's anecdotes from memory.[11]

Ice-skating on the Isis or in Christ Church Meadow, as we have seen, was another popular pastime at Oxford which Johnson enjoyed, as was swimming in the Isis or some nearby pond, although the authorities were perpetually alarmed that the river had claimed by drowning many undergraduates neither as strong nor as good a swimmer as he was. There were many pleasant walks outside Oxford. A particularly convenient one for him just across the street from Pembroke was Christ Church Meadow, which one foreign traveller thought was a peaceful garden-paradise with its Broad Walk planted on each side with elm; another not far away was the sheltered walk beneath the south walls of Merton. There was also the Physic Garden (now known as the Botanic Garden), of course, opposite Magdalen, a bit messy, perhaps, early in the century but replete with topiary of yew reflecting the French and Dutch tastes of the day. But perhaps most appealing of all in town for Johnson who in his boyhood was fond of rural walks, were the grounds behind Magdalen, including the extensive Deer Park. On his visit to Oxford in August 1754 – his first since leaving the university – Johnson took a walk with Warton such as he might well have taken as a student at a quicker pace than the one he now adopted. Warton described it: 'Johnson and I walked, three or four times, to Ellsfield, a village beautifully situated about three miles from Oxford, to see Mr [Revd Francis] Wise, Radclivian librarian ... As we returned to Oxford in the evening, I out-walked Johnson, and he cried out *Sufflamina*, a Latin word which came from his mouth with peculiar grace, and was as much as to say, *Put on your drag chain* ... In an evening, we frequently took long walks from Oxford into the country, returning to supper.'[12]

[5]

Poverty, defiant pride, academic arrogance, the declining fortunes of his family back home and resurgent melancholia were all responsible for Johnson's mental distress at Oxford. The keynote to much of it was bitterness. He had been bitter for some time. When things for some reason went wrong at Stourbridge Grammar School and he was forced to return to Lichfield, his friend Hector, who knew him well, noticed something especially wrong: 'After a long absence from Lichfield, when he returned I was apprehensive of something wrong in his constitution, which might either impair his intellect or endanger his life ...'[13] It was very likely a higher level than normal of despondency and bitterness. Johnson's robustness, strength of character, intellectual precociousness and detachment, and sense of humour for the most part enabled him to transcend the bitterness, but he co-existed with it. His good fortune in the small legacy that sent him to Oxford, one might suppose, could or should have dissolved or at least attenuated that bitterness, lifting him up to new ways of seeing himself. And possibly it would have, had it not been for the malevolent partnership of poverty and melancholia, and had he had more time.

William Adams told Boswell that Johnson could scarcely have been happier at Pembroke, that he 'was caressed and loved by all about him, was a gay and frolicsome fellow, and passed there the happiest part of his life'. 'Gay and frolicksome', however, is not the way Johnson remembered himself there. When Boswell shared Adams's remark with him, he instantly shot back, 'Ah, Sir, I was rude and violent. It was bitterness which they mistook for frolic.' Was it a mode of cynicism and irony, a 'violent' or reckless sort of satiric banter, that Adams mistook for an upbeat participation in college life? Percy added this: 'I have heard from some of his contemporaries that he was generally seen lounging at the College gate, with a circle of young students round him, whom he was entertaining with wit, and keeping from their studies, if not spiriting them up to rebellion against the College discipline, which in his maturer years he so much extolled.' 'How little any of us know of the real internal state even of those whom we see most frequently,' Boswell moralised, 'for the truth is, that he was then depressed by poverty, and irritated by disease.'[14]

The disease was melancholia. The poverty was his own meagre daily budget compounded by the regular spectacle in college of undergraduates with money to burn and his own stark realisation that his family was never going to help him economically. 'I was miserably poor, and I thought to fight my way by my literature and my wit; so I disregarded all power and all authority.' And if he were not successful there, he would go elsewhere to study, as the Master Matthew Panting once heard him through an open window declaiming to himself in a strong emphatic voice: 'Well, I have a mind to see what is done in other places of learning. I'll go and visit the universities abroad. I'll go to France and Italy. I'll go to Padua. And I'll mind my business.' Some day he would show these '*Athenian* blockheads'.[15]

For his entire life Johnson's mind would dwell on the debilitating effects of poverty. 'He could not, at this early period of his life, divest. himself of an opinion, that poverty was disgraceful,' Hawkins wrote, 'and was very severe in his censures of economy in both our universities, which exacted at meals the attendance of poor scholars, under the several denominations of servitors in the one, and sizers in the other

[Cambridge]: he thought that the scholar's, like the Christian life, [should have] levelled all distinctions of rank and worldly pre-eminence.' But class discrimination was what made the Oxford world go round, Johnson understood, ugly as it was:

> What is it but opinion, by which we have a respect for authority, that prevents us, who are the rabble, from rising up and pulling down you who are gentlemen from your places, and saying 'We will be gentlemen in our turn'? Now, Sir, that respect for authority is much more easily granted to a man whose father has had it, than to an upstart, and so society is more easily supported.

The system was distasteful, even a scandal. Johnson's friend, Oliver Goldsmith, put the case starkly many years later in a way that Johnson the student-rebel would have applauded: 'It implies a contradiction, for men to be at once learning the *liberal* arts, and at the same time treated as *slaves*; at once studying freedom, and practising servitude.'[16]

How poor exactly was Johnson at Oxford? Did his bitterness, roused by the spectacle of students enacting the class system amid the ancient spires, make him think his poverty was worse than it really was? The Battels (or 'buttery') books which record individual items charged daily and weekly to everyone in residence reveal an average commons expense of eight and a half shillings per week charged to him, or a total of just over twenty-four pounds for forty-two weeks – a little below the average among commoners and two or three shillings more than the average servitor. Like others, he tended to spend three or four shillings more per week during the period of a feast or 'gaudy' such as Gunpowder Plot week, but that was neither unusual nor especially extravagant. The fact was, he had very little money to spend on entertainment such as at alehouses or coffee houses, a huge constraint for a young man who loved to hold forth in front of his peers. Instead he opted for draughts in the Pembroke common room. Visiting William Adams, then Master, at the College with Boswell in 1776, as they walked into the Common Room, Johnson suddenly was transported into 'a reverie of meditation' after which equally suddenly he exclaimed, 'Ay! Here I used to play at draughts with Phil. Jones and [John] Fludyer.' Both were Scholars so, presumably, he was in good intellectual as well as inexpensive company. Jones loved beer, said Johnson, but Fludyer 'turned out a scoundrel, a [violent] Whig, and said he was ashamed of having been bred at Oxford'. Was he a scoundrel in any other way than political, asked Boswell, cheating at draughts, for example? 'Sir, we never played for *money*,' Johnson replied quickly.[17]

There is other testimony of his financial extremity at Pembroke. Humphrey Hawkins, the undermaster at Lichfield Grammar School, gives a general picture of his wardrobe:

> The want of that assistance, which scholars in general derive from their parents, relations, and friends, soon became visible in the garb and appearance of Johnson, which, though in some degree concealed by a scholar's gown, and that we know is never deemed the less honourable for being old, was so apparent as to excite pity in some that saw and noticed him.

His deteriorating clothes and shoes were an acute embarrassment, especially outside the college, to which he responded with disdain and wounded pride.[18]

It was about this time that John Taylor 'was taken by his father ... with the intention to enter him at Pembroke that he might be with Johnson as had been agreed between the two friends on account of their great intimacy which had been kept up by a constant correspondence by letters'. Taylor was dropped off at the Crown Inn, where Johnson met him. They walked to Pembroke together where Johnson closed his door and immediately announced: 'I cannot in conscience suffer you to enter here. For the tutor under whom you must be [Jorden] is such a blockhead that you will not be five minutes at his lectures till you find out what a fool he is and upbraid me with your looks for recommending you to him.' Taylor's friendship in college would have been an emotional lift, but he had done some scouting around the university and, discovering that the name of Revd Edmund Bateman of Christ Church was on everybody's lips as one of the most celebrated tutors, recommended that his friend matriculate there. Taylor did just that and Johnson in a sense followed him by crossing the street to Christ Church frequently after that to feast hungrily on Taylor's summaries of what Bateman had to say on the classics, logic and ethics, as well as on mathematics, which he taught as preparation for algebra. His threadbare clothes let him down, though. He began to notice the way people there looked at his dilapidated shoes. After that he came no more. Instead, Taylor came to Pembroke and repeated the lectures there for his friend. Johnson's shoes were noticed at Pembroke, too. Leaving his room one morning, he discovered a new pair on the landing outside his door. Hawkins relates that 'with all the indignation of an insulted man, he threw them away'. Whoever had made the gesture, a combination of generosity and bad judgement or taste, would have been amazed the next day to see the indigent student still shuffling around in his old shoes, still embarrassed but also angry. As is common with such anecdotes, we are never told by anyone what came next: how long he continued wearing those shoes, or if he ever discarded them while he remained at Oxford. Unless a pair were forthcoming from home, it is possible he stuck with them as a proud and sullen act of defiance.[19]

He appeared to be in debt when he left Oxford, as none of his caution money (seven pounds) was refunded afterwards. This suggests that without some supplement to the forty-pound legacy that brought him to Pembroke, he could not afford to stay. There was no other recourse in plain sight such as a scholarship – open scholarships were not available. He could not request a demotion to batteler or servitor because downgrading of students in that rigid social climate was for the most part out of the question. In any case, after a year as a commoner he would have looked upon life as a servitor as heinous and humiliating. His pride could not have borne it. As the weeks passed, he could only hope that somebody somewhere, perhaps Walmesley or his godfather Swynfen, would come forward with a loan or gift that would enable to him stay.

[6]

He pursued his studies in an unconventional manner partly because of his habit – to which he would adhere for the rest of his life – of devouring a book quickly without ever finishing it. 'He read by fits and starts,' Hawkins states, 'and, in the intervals, digested his reading by meditation, to which he was ever prone. Neither did he regard the hours of study, farther than the discipline of the college compelled him.' His melancholia also made his study habits erratic. It was while he and Boswell were talking in 1763 about his Oxford days that he brought it up: 'He mentioned to me now, for the first time, that he had been distressed by melancholy, and for that reason had been obliged to fly from study and meditation, to the dissipating variety of life.' Adams had taken over as his 'nominal' tutor after Jorden left, but Johnson was pretty much on his own and that was the way he needed and wanted it.[20]

Johnson would also have us believe that he was 'very idle and neglectful of his studies'. The remark seems disingenuous. Boswell

insisted that 'idleness and reading hard were with him relative terms':
'I always thought that he did himself injustice in his account of what
he had read, and that he must have been speaking with reference to
the vast portion of study which is possible, and to which a few scholars
in the whole history of literature have attained.' In fact, that he read
hard at Oxford is the point of his comment in 1763 that while there
an 'old gentleman' said to him, 'Young man, ply your book diligently
now, and acquire a stock of knowledge; for when years come upon
you, you will find that poring over books will be but an irksome
task.' What he 'read *solidly*' at Oxford was Greek, 'not the Grecian
historians, but Homer and Euripides, and now and then a little
Epigram'. He was especially fond of metaphysics and ethics since it
helped him 'compose' his mind. What else he read at Oxford besides
classical literature, theology and ethics is unknown but the close to one
hundred volumes he left behind after leaving the university (hoping he
would return), chiefly works of theology and classical literature as well
as some modern literature by such as Shakespeare, Spenser, Milton,
Waller, Dryden, Prior, Addison and Pope, provide some clues,
although it is difficult to distinguish those he brought with him from
Lichfield from ones acquired at Oxford.[21]

On his own terms, he nurtured an intense desire to compete and
excel as a compensation for his poverty. Out of envy or a sense of
superiority he could not bear a rival. John Meeke, a brilliant Scholar
then at Pembroke who later become a Fellow of the College, was one
whom he could not bring himself to hear when he 'declaimed or
disputed in the hall', retreating 'to the farthest corner thereof, that he
might be out of the reach of his voice'. 'I used to think Meeke
had excellent parts, when we were boys together at the College,' he
remarked to Warton just after they dropped in on him at Pembroke
in the summer of 1754, 'but alas ... I could not bear Meeke's superiority,' he added; 'about the same time of life, Meeke was left behind
at Oxford to feed on a Fellowship, and I went to London to get my
living: now, Sir, see the difference of our literary characters!'[22]

Still, it is clear that what he regarded as laziness was proving to be
one of his personal devils. Under October 1729, after twelve months
at Oxford, he wrote in his 1729–34 'Diary' a Latin line which Boswell
translated as, 'I bid farewell to sloth, being resolved henceforth not to
listen to her syren strains.' Hector confirmed that Johnson was drifting, listless and unable to do what was expected of him, much to the
annoyance of the Master who 'seeing him frequently idling about had

twice [fines] imposed him, without effect, and he called him up, and once more charged [that] if he did not comply with his request, he should take no farther notice of him. The Dr promised, and performed.' On 21 November 1729, in an effort to get down to study, he made a self-disciplining table of how much reading he could get done in a week, month and year if he read ten pages per day: 60, 240 and 2880 respectively. To begin with a meagre ten pages per day may suggest just how indolent he thought he had become. He soon realised that ten pages per day would get him nowhere, so he tabulated what he could achieve based on 30, 50, 60, 150, 300, 400 and 600 per day, though he did not take the last four as far as computing annual totals, realising the stark fantasy in such an exercise. Sixty would yield 17,280 for a year, and apparently he thought that was as much as he could realistically read. Such computations would become almost chronic with him as he struggled to impose order on a sense of disorder, 'as it fixed his attention steadily upon something without, and prevented his mind from preying upon itself'. He even counted the number of lines to be read in *The Aeneid* and other works by Virgil, as well as in works by Euripides, Horace, Ovid, Theocritus and Juvenal.[23]

This impulse to tabulate and count, incidentally, which later became compulsive, appears also to account for the appearance of a cryptic 'M' under 22 October in his 1729–34 'Diary'. If the Latin that follows is translated as 'Remember what I did on 9, 12, 17, 19, 22, 26 and 28 September', this would simply be an innocuous reference to what happened on those days that he either forgot to record in the diary or recorded elsewhere. Or it might mean something less savoury. One widely respected critic has urged that this 'M' refers to masturbation, others that it indicates sexual intercourse, and still others that it alludes to defecation. In the 1760s he used this 'M' more plausibly to chronicle his defecation because he was very ill then, suffering from insomnia and wishing to keep track of his bowel movements during the night. In 1729 the first two meanings may be more likely as it is certainly possible that, especially during periods of boredom in his room, he indulged in sexual fantasies. To keep a record of instances of masturbation by way of trying to control the practice, this same critic observes, is not uncommon, and it would have been a way of dealing with his guilt over it.[24]

Apart from what, how much, and how regularly he studied, Johnson made an impression at Pembroke as an intellectual prodigy, which it pleased him to perpetuate. A number of stories circulated by Boswell,

Mrs Thrale, Hawkins and other early biographers, some embellished, no doubt, and some perhaps spurious, celebrate him as a kind of academic wonderboy there. He told Mrs Thrale, for example, who liked stories of the unconventional Johnson, that 'when he made his first declamation, he wrote over but one copy, and that coarsely; and having given it into the hand of the tutor [Jorden] who stood to receive it as he passed, was obliged to begin by chance and continue on how he could, for he had got but little of it by heart; so fairly trusting to his present powers for immediate supply, he finished by adding astonishment to the applause of all who knew how little was owing to study.' Someone else who heard him say this exclaimed that he must have been taking a huge risk, to which Johnson replied, 'Not at all, no man I suppose leaps at once into deep water who does not know how to swim.' In Oxford, a few months before he died, he was in the full flow of boasting about this undergraduate intellectual bravado in the company of Dr Adams, his daughter and other guests when Miss Adams flattered him by supposing his exercises so brilliant that he could not have made them better. 'Yes, Madam, to be sure,' he replied, 'I could make them better. Thought is better than no thought.' The point is he chose not to make them better and unquestionably in this and other ways constructed a notoriety about himself inside and perhaps also outside Pembroke.[25]

For Johnson's first 5 November celebrations or 'gaudy' at the college Jorden asked his students to compose prose Latin exercises relating to the Gunpowder Plot. Johnson failed to produce his. Instead, he composed some Latin verses for Jorden entitled '*Somnium*', a tongue-in-cheek literary prank relating a dream he said he had: 'that the Muse had come to him in his sleep, and whispered, that it did not become him to write on such subjects as politics; he should confine himself to humbler themes'. What those humbler themes may have been we do not know because the poem is lost, but Boswell saw it and judged its versification 'truly Virgilian'.[26]

Jorden's response to these unauthorised 'Virgilian' verses is unknown, but that he did not disapprove too strongly was borne out later by his asking Johnson to translate into Latin Pope's poem, the biblical-Virgilian pastoral *The Messiah* (1712), a poem imitating Virgil and drawn from the Messianic visions of the prophet Isaiah. Johnson had the leisure to write it since he stayed at the emptied college right through the Christmas vacation with a handful of other students. Hector informed Boswell, '[Johnson] told me, that afternoon at the first [attempt] he finished more than one half and in the morning concluded the remainder of Pope's Messiah'. In later life Johnson claimed combatively that the poem gave him the chance 'to show the tutors what I could do, [not] what I was willing should be done. It convinced those who were well enough inclined to punish me, that I could wield a scholar's weapon as often as I was menaced with arbitrary inflictions. Before the frequency of personal satire had weakened its effect, the petty tyrants of colleges stood in awe of a pointed remark, or a vindictive epigram.' The poem's subject suited him because of its central meditative idea that Truth speaks inwardly without the clatter of words. It gave him a chance to reflect quietly on his feelings about religion and nature, both actual and Virgilian, as well as on the pomposity of the world (and of Oxford) that the light of Christ made look so dim. The result was an unqualified success. 'He performed it with uncommon rapidity,' Boswell reports, 'and in so masterly a manner, that he obtained great applause from it, which ever after kept him high in the estimation of his College, and, indeed, of all the university.' Hawkins and Boswell circulated the story that the poem was brought to the notice of Pope who, very impressed with it, was said to have remarked, 'The writer of this poem will leave it a question for posterity, whether his or mine be the original.' High praise indeed if the story were true. For Johnson the poem was the most memorable piece he wrote as an undergraduate. 'Here I translated Pope's Messiah,' he said reverentially as he and Warton paused at the gates of the College in 1754.[27]

[7]

'Where is religion to be learned but at an university,' Johnson once said, but at Oxford he was not doing very well in that vein in spite of Hawkins's assertion that his moral character was greatly 'fixed' by 'early calls to prayer, the frequent instruction from the pulpit, [and] with all the other means of religious and moral improvement'. He took his 'lax' talking against religion with him to university, though he had to rein it in because 'it would not be *suffered* there'. He was inclined to laugh at writers on religion, and it is unknown whether he attended chapel regularly. Oxford was not then an especially congenial environment for the growth of religiousness. George Whitefield, the Methodist, when he first received the sacraments at St Mary's in Oxford was immediately 'set up as a mark for all the polite students that knew me to shoot at'. Everyone was supposed to be present at the sacraments in church at the beginning of every term, he wrote, 'yet so dreadfully has that once faithful city played the harlot, that very few masters, and no undergraduates but the Methodists, attended upon it'. Whitefield complained that fellow students threw dirt at him for attending these services; others withheld payment to him for his services as a servitor.[28]

Deep religious feeling, though still submerged, still resonated in Johnson. He was not systematically reading religious works, searching for spiritual truth, but he rediscovered religion through a book he happened to pick up, William Law's *A Serious Call to a Devout and Holy Life* (1728), a treatise on practical morality. In his words this is what happened:

> When at Oxford, I took up Law's *Serious Call to a Holy Life*, expecting to find it a dull book (as such books generally are), and perhaps to laugh at it. But I found Law quite an overmatch for me; and this was the first occasion of my thinking in earnest of religion, after I became capable of rational enquiry.

While he confided in Hector in 1778, 'my health has been, from my twentieth year, such as has seldom afforded me a single day of ease', at least help now was at hand: 'It [religion] had dropped out of my mind. It was at an early part of my life. Sickness brought it back, and I hope I have never lost it since.' The effects of *A Serious Call* upon him were life-changing. He 'studied it hard' and its influence on his moral essays was fundamental. He also turned to it in his *Dictionary* for over two hundred citations.[29]

A Serious Call appealed to him profoundly because it addressed 'every part of our common life', everyday existence, not abstract religious dogma – he called it 'the finest piece of hortatory theology in any language'. Law's insistence, for example, that one should rise early so as to wrest control of one's life spoke powerfully and immediately to him. The book called the reader to private rather than public prayer, making religion a personal and individual affair between him and God. There was hope in that but it was also a double-edged sword. 'Every man knows something worse of himself than he is sure of in others' – in Johnson's words this was one of Law's recurring themes that deeply penetrated his psyche. The battle would be fought in his mind, not in church. Law was not 'a reasoner', Johnson once said. His strength instead was an ability to rouse the reader not with expostulations to stop sinning but with entertaining character portraits, many of them satiric, illustrating the human condition in its many aspects and providing individual cautionary tales. In the unhappiness of his closing months at Oxford, Law's book provided light with which to illuminate the gathering darkness.

[8]

As it turned out, Johnson's days at Oxford were numbered. Perhaps his depression, 'the flying vapours of incipient madness', brought matters to a head and sent him packing. The prospect of again remaining at college for the Christmas holidays with a handful of other students in the 'sullen solitude' of the lifeless and empty buildings, without his parents and missing Lichfield and the old haunts, was a bleak prospect. It may have been around this time that he heard his mother's voice calling him. He told Boswell 'that one day at Oxford, as he was turning the key of his chamber, he heard his mother distinctly call *Sam*. She was then at Lichfield; but nothing ensued.'[30]

On top of all this, the money was just not there. As Christmas 1729 approached the inescapable fact was that his finances would not allow him to remain even for the vacation. He had been at Pembroke about thirteen months and no further gift or loan had come his way. Nor did the college, so far as we know, offer him a scholarship – of which there were two. He would have been eligible for one of them, but as it was worth only £10 per year, however, it would not alone have enabled him to stay. He packed his very few personal belongings and left Oxford around 12 December. 'Johnson being miserably poor set out for Lichfield early in the morning having hid his toes in a pair of large boots,' said Taylor, who accompanied him as far as Banbury and returned at night. Johnson left his small library behind in the not so conscientious care of his old friend – Johnson's remark on Taylor's having 'never relished a book in his earlier days' might allude to his having neglected it. Since his name was left on the College books for almost two more years, it is possible someone decided he might return. Surely he must have left desperately hoping for the same thing. The fact that for years he did not request his books to be sent to him suggests as much.[31]

The anger, intellectual arrogance, depression and cramped finances that characterised his time at Pembroke, terminated ingloriously by his lonely departure, would appear to be overwhelming grounds for assuming that for the rest of his life he would nourish resentment towards Oxford University. Quite the contrary, however, was the case. Boswell quoted Adams saying that 'he contracted a love and regard for Pembroke College, which he retained to the last'. He frequently boasted about Pembroke's alumni, and he visited Oxford more than any other place in England, even more than Lichfield, at least twenty-seven times from 1754 until his death. Many of those visits were for several weeks at a time, mostly at New Inn Hall and University College, not Pembroke. Part of his affection for the place understandably resulted from the huge (though not universal) respect for him there once he became the famous moralist and scholar. He became almost an Oxford institution, toasted and bowed to by dons in one common room or another and entertained by his growing group of friends. On his visit in 1754 he was delighted still to find at Pembroke college servants he knew, especially 'a very old butler, and expressed great satisfaction at being recognised by them, and conversed with them familiarly', even if the Master of the College John Radcliffe conspicuously snubbed him.[32]

Close to the end of his life he took pleasure in showing Pembroke to his friend Hannah More, the evangelical moral reformer, author and eminent member of the Bluestockings circle. 'You cannot imagine with what delight he showed me every part of his own College,' she wrote. 'He would let no one show it me but himself – "this was my room; this Shenstone's". Then after pointing out all the rooms of the poets who had been of his college, "In short," said he, "we were a nest of singing birds".' Through the prism of succeeding years he increasingly viewed his thirteen months at Pembroke with gratification, but as he left in December 1729 mostly he felt the jarring pressures of failure, injured pride and wrecked nerves.[33]

CHAPTER 6

Horrible Imaginings

[1]

When Johnson arrived home shortly before Christmas, the inner gloom with which he had co-existed for months suddenly deepened and solidified. He was entering the bleakest, unhappiest period in his life as he fell into the tight grip of depression. Whether or not it was unremitting we do not know because for the next two years there are no diary entries, no letters, and only a little testimony from others about his existence. It is as if he went into hiding. The 'morbid melancholy' he inherited, aggravated by numerous experiences at different times during his short life, had finally triumphed at Oxford, and instead of returning to Lichfield like something of the conquering hero he rode into town and fell into a deep, dark emotional hole. He was at home again in the midst of his bickering parents, the understandable complaints of his 'noisy' brother Nathaniel – who appears to have inherited his father's melancholia and could not have been thrilled about having to share home space again with his brother – and the dullness of the bookseller's world in a provincial town which must have seemed like the end of the earth after Oxford. If his parents hoped he would now pull his weight in the bookshop, they were bound to be disappointed. There was also a disconcerting new feature of his behaviour which must have worried everyone. As a result of his physical illness he began to show signs of the 'tics and gesticulations' that stayed with him for the rest of his life.[1]

Boswell described Johnson's desperation:

The 'morbid melancholy', which was lurking in his constitution, and to which we may ascribe those particularities, and that aversion to regular life, which, at a very early period, marked his character, gathered such strength in his twentieth year, as to afflict him in a dreadful manner . . . he felt himself overwhelmed with an horrible hypochondria, with perpetual irritation, fretfulness, and impatience; and with a dejection, gloom, and despair, which made existence misery. From this dismal malady he never afterwards was perfectly relieved; and all his labours, and all his enjoyments, were but temporary interruptions of its baleful influence.

Thinking possibly of this period, Johnson once told his friend John Paradise that he 'sometimes was so languid and inefficient, that he could not distinguish the hour upon the town-clock'. He admitted, 'I did not then know how to manage it.' Hector even feared he might commit suicide. He tried to exorcise these devils by describing them on paper. Whatever form it took, it is a huge loss that this piece of searching self-analysis has been lost. The only person to whom he showed it was his godfather, Dr Swynfen, who was so struck by 'the extraordinary acuteness, research and eloquence' in it that he circulated it among friends. Johnson was furious when he found out, 'so much offended that he [was] never afterwards fully reconciled to him'.[2]

Over the following months Johnson 'strove' to exorcise the black dog by other means, with 'forcible exertions' such as repeatedly walking in one day the thirty-two mile return trek between Lichfield and Birmingham. One can picture him shuffling his tall, ungainly form along swiftly, jaw set firm and fists clenched, his vacant eyes focused inward in a struggle to disentangle the turmoil inside. In a remark that Boswell chose to omit from his *Life*, Johnson said, 'I once walked a good deal. I left it off at two and twenty when I grew melancholy.' He must have meant specifically the intense, almost obsessive walking between Lichfield and Birmingham because movement of his body, either by walking, or riding in carriages, or sailing through stormy Hebridean seas with Boswell, for the rest of his life would remain a vital means of defeating stagnation and raising his spirits. 'Frequent and violent agitation of the body,' he would write later, was a recipe for subduing depression. In Birmingham Hector helped him as much as he could, such as getting his mind off his trouble by asking him to write a love poem for a friend. 'I applied to Johnson,' Hector wrote to Boswell, 'who was with me, and in about half an hour [he] dictated the verses which I sent to my friend.' Forty years later Johnson recalled that in fact he wrote the lines in five minutes when 'dear Mund' (his nickname for Hector) pressed him for 'the nonsense' people now 'keep such a stir about'.[3]

[2]

Either at Oxford (as is commonly thought) or in this following dark period, Johnson wrote his strongly autobiographical short poem, 'The Young Author'. The earlier date obviously connects with Oxford because the poem deals with the ambitions of a young writer and scholar who has vain dreams of published glory. There are reasons to think, however, that he may have written it after he had removed himself from the socially intense environment of Pembroke and could, on reflection and with bleak detachment, view his own vanity as an aspiring author with more poignant irony. From Lichfield, Oxford seemed like an oasis. While he was there he could still imagine himself blossoming into authorship. 'The great advantage of a university,' he once told the politician William Windham, 'is that a person lives in a place where his reputation depends upon his learning.' There were people around him who encouraged such hopes. After he left, he was on his own. Glancing back forty-five years later he wrote simply and powerfully to Taylor, 'The transition from the protection of others to our own conduct is a very awful point of human existence'. This was the typically oppressive mental state of the melancholic – that he not only was unlikely to succeed at anything but also could not even imagine succeeding.[4]

In 'The Young Author' he rationalised his defeat at the hands of circumstances and his own mind by depicting the saga of disappointments awaiting any youth who falls prey to delusion and casts his bread upon the precarious waters of literary fame. For such a victim of vanity and 'disorders of the intellect', as he was to put it in his moral fable and short psychological tale *Rasselas* (1759), 'fictions begin to operate as realities ... and life passes in dreams of rapture or of anguish'. The lot of the aspiring poet is delusory, 'panting for a name,/ And fir'd with pleasing hope of endless fame', because he trusts his fate to 'human kind,/more false, more cruel than seas and wind'. He sells his soul to the phantom of 'praise from nations yet unborn', scorning such 'transitory blessings' as wealth and title. What are the rewards for the self-deluding joys of his imagination? There are none except the 'hisses' of attacking pamphlets, from which the wounded young author flies, his vanity in tatters. There hidden in some refuge he is content to lick his wounds, merely 'Glad to be hid, and proud to be forgot'.[5]

Once he escaped from this particular dark night of mental illness, as he told Hector, he never really gained full control over the black dog. Neither did he ever outgrow his distrust of the imagination and how it can cheat with false hope, at every age and level. In *Rasselas* with a sombre eye turned inward, however, he has the philosopher Imlac say to young Rasselas:

> Disorders of intellect happen much more often than superficial observers will easily believe. Perhaps, if we speak with rigorous exactness, no human mind is in its right state. There is no man whose imagination does not sometimes predominate over this reason, who can regulate his attention wholly by his will, and whose ideas will come and go at his command. No man will be found in whose mind airy notions do not sometimes tyrannise, and force him to hope or fear beyond the limits of sober probability. All power of fancy over reason is a degree of insanity; but while this power is such as we can control and repress, it is not visible to others, nor considered as any depravation of the mental faculties: it is not pronounced madness but when it comes ungovernable, and apparently influences speech or action.[6]

When fantasy prevails over reality there is a 'dangerous prevalence of imagination' – that is, a condition in which imagination overcomes rational balance, judgement and perspective. It ushers in depression and, as Macbeth put it, 'horrible imaginings' that are not just monsters of darkness but thrive as happily in full daylight. It could lead to 'insanity', an 'ungovernable' madness. That was the condition in which Johnson now found himself.

There is no surviving clue as to how much Johnson's family noticed his sickness. His moodiness and sullen loneliness would have been all too apparent within the walls of their house, and perhaps his father, who was a melancholic himself, picked up on certain signs that his son was going through something close to a breakdown. His brother Nathaniel had his own problems, as we shall see, and probably little patience with yet another of his brother's displays of antisocial behaviour. Perhaps Johnson spoke to his mother about his discovery of Law's *A Serious Call*. Religion was a type of bond between them. But this was not a close family in which the members freely shared with each other their worries and fears. Happy moments there must have been, but not lasting ones. Outside the family, Johnson could confide in Swynfen, though he was now in Birmingham. Hector, too, was in Birmingham. Cousin Cornelius was in London. In the way of patrons and mentors, that left Gilbert Walmesley. He was still in Lichfield, just around the corner, ready to welcome his protégé back to the

Bishop's Palace and the society that had done so much good for him more than a year before.

[3]

Even if Johnson had been sufficiently in his right mind in 1730–31 and able to rouse himself enough to do something constructive, few obvious career options were open to him. The bookselling business was out. He had no appetite for it and his father was not a good advertisement for the kind of life one could lead as a bookseller. He was twenty and had no degree, no teaching credentials, no money, and no acumen for conducting a business. As Hawkins put it, 'His fortunes and circumstances had determined him to no particular course of study, and were such as seemed to exclude him from every one of the learned professions.'[7]

The months passed and then tragedy struck in the summer of 1731. On 22 August Cornelius died in London in Hummums, his favourite hotel in Covent Garden Piazza which served as a type of bagnio for its patrons. Virtually a resident of London by then, Cornelius had become known to Pope and a clutch of other poets and fashionable wits at various taverns and coffee houses. With lots of money to spend, he had surrendered completely to his taste for extravagance and fast living. He ran through his money, mortgaged his properties, and borrowed heavily, and only a few months before his death he landed in prison for debt. He died soon after his release. Had he lived, Cornelius could have made a monumental difference to Johnson's early literary career, though not necessarily an entirely positive one. His wayward literary life ended in prison and hastened on to impoverishment and an early death – an anticipation of the poet Richard Savage in whom Johnson took a consuming interest in his early London life.

The silence of these months in Lichfield suddenly came to an end on 30 October 1731, just over two months after Cornelius's death, when Johnson wrote his first surviving letter. Written to Cornelius's half-brother, Gregory Hickman, one of Stourbridge's prominent citizens, it reveals that the preceding summer with Hickman's help he had been making efforts to get a teaching job at the Stourbridge Grammar School.[8] Hickman's daughter Dorothy, in fact, had caught his eye when he was a pupil at the school. She was only twelve then. Now she was seventeen or eighteen and a rather more promising focus of amorousness – so much so that sometime during his summer visit to his relatives Johnson found himself falling in love and addressing an affectionate poem to her, 'To Miss Hickman Playing On the Spinet'. Disappointingly, the verses do not yield much auto-biographically. In another love poem written about this time, 'To a Young Lady on Her Birthday', possibly also addressed to Miss Hickman, he dwells somewhat more personally on the conquering spell of the girl's beauty, imploring her to be fair and just and not squander her arts and powers on coquettishness. There is also an oblique allusion in this poem to feelings of inadequacy in courtship, an awareness of his physical uncouthness and roughness, not to mention the disfigurements of disease and birth defects: 'With his own form acquaint the forward fool,/Shewn in the faithful glass of ridicule'. A third poem, 'An Ode on a Lady Leaving Her Place of Abode; Almost Impromptu', written in the late autumn or early winter of 1731, laments his love's sudden departure, for London perhaps, depriving him of her 'wit, love and mirth', as well as her warming eyes. He pleads for her return north soon to bless him with 'continu'd day'. All this was a good sign. Love poetry and the pursuit of gainful employment, as well as breaking free of Lichfield and enjoying the company of a warm, healthy and loving family, gave him a momentary new lease on life.[9]

But winter was approaching and he had to return to the greyness of his own home and unhappy family, one temporarily even more crowded now that Cornelius's two maiden sisters began boarding there for about two months. Added to that was the bad news in September that he had failed to gain the teaching appointment, which went to a graduate of Trinity College, Oxford instead. As it turned out, Hick-man's influence could not compensate for his lack of a degree. Oddly, on the heels of this disappointment – or was it his lack of success in Stourbridge with Gregory Hickman's seventeen-year-old daughter? – Hickman asked him to write a poem about his failure. The request angered him: 'Be pleased to consider that versifying against one's inclination is the most disagreeable thing in the world, and that one's own disappointment is no inviting subject.' The subject was so 'barren', he added, that it would be like trying 'to build without materials'. He concluded simply with, 'As I am yet unemploy'd, I hope you will if anything should offer, remember and recommend [me].'[10]

There was another even more personal shock to come. In early December, after an autumn of quickly deteriorating health owing to some respiratory ailment, Michael Johnson finally gave up the fight. He died from an 'inflammatory fever' at the age of seventy-five and was buried at St Michael's in Lichfield on 7 December. The family's much-loved servant 'Kitty' Chambers arranged the funeral, a sign of how intimately she had become involved in the life and affairs of the family. For the last two years the Johnsons had fallen on their hardest times yet, so Michael Johnson died thinking himself a defeated man without having provided adequately for his wife and sons. To his son he was a dispiriting example of how an able and strong man with such energy, well regarded in the community – the burial register describes him as 'a Magistrate of the City' – could fail as a result of com-prehensive business incompetence. All that was left to Sarah was a few pounds, the home, and the shop with its ample stock of books, although without her eldest son's knowledge of books to help her she and her relatively uninterested second son Nathaniel were at a loss of how to acquire further good stock. The shop kept ticking over for many years, chiefly with Kitty's help, but it was never the same again, becoming merely the equivalent of a second-hand bookshop today instead of a well known source in the region for antiquarian volumes and fine editions.

In his *Annales*, a separate diary he wrote in 1734 for the years 1725–34, Johnson mingles his sorrow over his father's death with a palpable fear. For the day of his father's death he merely scribbled the brief Latin phrase, '*Patre orbatus est*', but he also recorded that eight months later in Lichfield he collected what was due him from his father's effects, adding (as translated by Hawkins) a resolution never to let happen to him what happened to his father: 'June 15, I laid by eleven guineas; on which day I received all of my father's effects which I can hope for till the death of my mother (which I pray may be late), that is to say, nineteen pounds; so that I have my fortune to make, and care must be taken, that in the mean time, the powers of my mind may not grow languid through poverty, nor want drive me into wickedness.'[11]

Johnson collected his legacy – which today would be in the region of £2,000 – on his return to Lichfield in mid-June 1732 from Market Bosworth, Leicestershire, where he had been teaching. Back in March it suddenly looked as if his luck had turned when his application for the post of usher at the grammar school there, perhaps with Walmesley's intervention, was successful. The appointment was highly unusual because the school's statutes specified that the appointee had to have a Bachelor of Art's degree.[12] On 9 March he made his way by foot to the pleasant town, about twenty-five miles east of Lichfield, to take up his post, hoping that this opportunity could prove to be the beginning of a successful teaching career.

The salary was meagre but the appointment also provided that Johnson would reside at Bosworth Hall, the late sixteenth-century country house of the local squire, Sir Wolstan Dixie, fourth baronet, whose ancestors founded the school and who tyrannically controlled its administration. In addition to teaching, his role was to officiate 'as a kind of domestic chaplain', as Boswell called it, to this boorish 'brutal rascal' of a squire, saying grace at meals and probably treated like something of a slave. Johnson's pride promptly revolted and he took to quarrelling with the baronet. Sir Wolstan merely responded with 'intolerable harshness'. That this went on for months suggests Johnson's desperation to have and keep the job. Sir Wolstan was bad enough, but even the teaching was 'painful drudgery', as he described it to Hector in complaining letters which Hector sadly seems either to have lost or kept from Boswell to prevent him from broadcasting the full extent of Johnson's fury at the time. 'He wrote me word [that] his business was to teach Lily's grammar to a few boys,' Hector told Boswell, but it 'was hard to say whose difficulty was greatest: he to explain nonsense, or they to understand it'. A poet had caught the essence of his wretchedness at the school, Johnson added, with the phrase '"*Vitam continet una dies*" [one day contains the whole of my life]; that it was unvaried as the note of the cuckow'. He stuck it out until the end of the term in July and then bid Sir Wolstan and his school good riddance, for the rest of his life preserving 'the strongest aversion, and even a degree of horrour' for both. His lifelong detestation of bullies and domestic tyrants, especially adults who take unfair advantage of young people, was born of experiences like this.[13]

He walked disconsolately and angrily back to Lichfield. Perhaps it was time to do something entirely different from teaching. He did not have much time to cool his heels at home thinking about career choices, however, because a few days after his return he received a letter from John Corbet, his schoolfriend Andrew's younger brother, telling him of a vacancy as usher at the grammar school in Ashbourne which had suddenly become vacant. Johnson was on John Corbet's mind because they had recently seen each other on 17 July at Sir Wolstan's home. 'On being called to dinner at ... Dixie's,' Johnson wrote in his diary, 'I saw J. Corbet, a youth once very delightful to me, and not because if I am right, he then loved me very much.'

Because a replacement was needed right away, the school might also be willing to hire someone without a degree. Best of all, Ashbourne was where Taylor lived, to whom he wrote off immediately, asking him to exert any influence he could. 'If there be any reason for my coming to Ashbourne, I shall readily do it,' he added; 'Mr Corbet has, I suppose, given you an account of my leaving Sir Wolstan. It was really *e Carcere exire* [leaving prison].' Taylor was not a school governor, however, and by the 1st of August the job had gone to another applicant who failed to take up the post but was quickly succeeded by a third candidate. It was especially galling to Johnson that these two men were preferred to him and yet, like him, neither had a degree. If he did walk the thirty miles to Ashbourne for an interview, it is perfectly possible his unusual appearance and involuntary movements, quite pronounced by then, put the governors off. 'To his dying day,' wrote William Shaw, 'he never thought, recollected, or studied, whether in his closet, or in the street, alone, or in company, without putting his huge unwieldy body in the same rolling, awkward posture.' Or his reputation for prickly independence and assertiveness may have preceded him.[14]

It may have been that autumn that he wrote 'An Epitaph on Claudy Phillips, a Musician', his first known of the many epitaphs he wrote in his life. Phillips was an accomplished Welsh touring violinist who died in poverty in 1732. It seems he played in Lichfield and was heard by both Johnson and Garrick. One day when the two of them were sitting together, perhaps in the Bishop's Palace, Garrick roused Johnson by quoting an epitaph on Phillips he had recently come across. As Boswell retells the anecdote told to him by Garrick, 'Johnson shook his head at these common-place funereal lines, and said to Garrick, "I think, Davy, I can make a better." Then, stirring about his tea for a little while, in a state of meditation, he almost extempore produced the following verses.' What is interesting about Johnson's improvement in the following lines was his strong empathy for Phillips's poverty, an emotionalism that was easily aroused by the spectacle of a talented individual going to his grave unrewarded, unappreciated, and destitute:

> Phillips! whose touch harmonious could remove
> The pangs of guilty pow'r, and hapless love,
> Rest here, distrest by poverty no more,
> Find here that calm thou gav'st so oft before;
> Sleep undisturb'd within this peaceful shrine,
> Till angels wake thee with a note like thine.

From his own slough of disappointment, melancholia and indolence he could nonetheless animate himself and enter poetically and beautifully into another's distress. This was one of Johnson's most self-defining impulses in his early years and for the rest of his life, an identification with the poor and distressed that sprang from his own experience and began to trace a deeper, more meaningful Christianity within him than what his well-meaning mother had been able to impart to him.[15]

CHAPTER 7

Stirrings in Birmingham

[1]

Concerned over the vacuum and lack of direction in Johnson's life, towards the end of 1732, Hector invited him to Birmingham to live with him for an undetermined period in the apartment he was renting at the house of Thomas Warren, a bookseller across from the Swan tavern in the High Street. Johnson knew the area well. His unpleasant uncle John Harrison lived nearby, and his uncle Andrew who died three years earlier had kept a bookshop just down the road, where his aunt was still living.[1]

Hector's invitation was well-timed, and Birmingham was the perfect place for the idle melancholic to which to escape for a lengthy period. Change and excitement were in the air. Industrial forces then beginning to shape the emergent nation were all at work there as the city began its climb to keep up with Liverpool and Manchester in overtaking older cities like Bristol and Norwich as provincial centres. When Johnson joined Hector the city already possessed an intoxicating energy. Some thirty-five years later, Erasmus Darwin in a letter to Matthew Boulton, the great engineer and inventor of the steam engine, summed up where Birmingham was headed when he moaned he had to miss a meeting of the Lunar Society that Boulton had founded: 'Lord! what inventions, what wit, what rhetoric, meta-physical, mechanical, pyrotechnical, will be on the wing, bandied like a shuttlecock from one to another of your troupe of philosophers.' Johnson's remark in 1776 that Lichfield was a city of 'philosophers: we work with our heads, and make the boobies of Birmingham work for us with their hands', was merely a proud boast. He knew by then that the 'boobies' of Birmingham were at the head, not the tail, of England's future and that the Enlightenment had found its model in such groups as the Lunar Society. And on the arts side, thinking of Birmingham and Lichfield, he wrote in 1776: 'Staffordshire is the nursery of the arts, where they grow up till they are transplanted to London.'[2]

Johnson's companionship at first must have been heavy going for Hector, though from observation over preceding months Hector knew what to expect. He told Boswell he 'was afraid of Dr Johnson's head' during this period and that when, many years later, Johnson, who 'had been afraid to ask Hector for fear of an answer in the affirmative', asked him 'if he had observed in him a tendency to be disordered in his mind, Hector said he had'. In his *Life*, Boswell was sceptical of what Hector told him about Johnson's near 'madness' during these months, partly because tendencies towards insanity did not fit conveniently into the persona of his friend as the age's greatest rational moralist that he wished to perpetuate. Boswell thought Johnson 'fancied himself seized' by insanity, that 'his own diseased imagination' deceived him. It was stranger still, he added, 'that some of his friends should have given credit to his groundless opinion, when they had such undoubted proofs that it was totally fallacious'.[3]

Hector continued to do what he could to help Johnson through this prolonged depression. He tried to rescue him from his morbidity and his total lack of occupation in Lichfield by bringing him into regular contact with Warren whom he hoped would find Johnson and his knowledge of literature and bookselling useful. His generosity made a deep impression on Johnson, the memory of which he treasured more and more as the years passed. Writing to Hector in April 1755 after almost twenty years' separation and no communication, he recalled tenderly those 'evenings which we have passed together at Warren's and the Swan'. 'Gratifications and friendships of younger years operate very powerfully on the mind', he added. One month later he wrote again, grateful for the recovery of their intimate friendship in Birmingham, laced though it had been with suffering, 'Are you too come to the age in which *former days* begin to have an awful sound, and to impart an idea mixed of pain and pleasure?' Hector would have been sincerely saddened however to read this: 'From that kind of melancholy indisposition which I had when we lived together at Birmingham, I have never been free, but have always had it operating against my health and my life with more or less violence'.[4]

As it turned out, Warren proved to be very civil to him and welcomed him to his house and table with Hector, not least because he discovered Johnson could be useful to him in developing his new newspaper, *The Birmingham Journal*, by providing the occasional essay. In the after-glow of the publication of his majestic *Dictionary*, Johnson

gratefully thought back to those difficult weeks and months of desperation and uncertainty, asking Hector, 'What comes of poor
Warren? I have not lost all my kindness for him, for when I remember
you I naturally remember all our connections, which are more pleasing
to me for your sake.' We have only Hector's word for it that Johnson
earned 'a little money' writing for Warren. All issues but one of the
paper have been lost. Boswell looked high and low for copies and
came up empty-handed: 'In what manner he employed his pen at this
period, or whether he derived from it any pecuniary advantage, I have
not been able to ascertain.'[5]

[2]

While he was living in Warren's house, Johnson mentioned having
read at Pembroke College a French translation of Father Jerónimo
Lobo's *Voyage to Abyssinia* and suggested that 'an abridgement and
translation of it from the French into English might be a useful
and profitable publication'.[6] Warren liked and encouraged the idea
immediately. Travel literature was already popular on booksellers'
publishing lists. During Johnson's life 'Britons conquered Canada and
half of India, lost control of North America but won dominion over
the Pacific, sent embassies into China and adventurers into Africa,
colonised Australia and traded everywhere else, and bequeathed to
Victorians one of the most extensive empires ever known to man.'[7]

The translation describes a seventeenth-century Jesuit missionary
from Lisbon, Father Lobo, who embarked in the 1620s (at the age of
twenty-six) on a succession of hazardous journeys to the East Indies,
first to Goa and then across the Arabian Sea to the ancient Coptic
Christian country of Abyssinia where he finally arrived at the Jesuit
house in Fremona, inland from the Red Sea. He laboured in that area
of the world for many years, teaching and perilously attempting the
conversion of the locals to the Church of Rome, eventually winding
up in prison for several years before escaping from what had become
a politically complex and dangerous missionary environment. In his
sixties he returned to Lisbon and wrote up his remarkable adventures.
His manuscripts in Portuguese remained unpublished for the most
part until he showed some of them, chiefly his *Itinerário*, recounting
his hair-raising voyages and cross-country expeditions, to the British
Ambassador to Portugal, Robert Southwell, who asked him to write
a series of short scientific essays on the Nile, the palm tree and the Red

Sea, among others, which the Royal Society published anonymously in English in 1669. These proved to have an enormous appeal as many translations bearing Lobo's name followed in the next few years. Then came along a Frenchman, Joachim Le Grand, who found Lobo's manuscript of the *Itinerário* gathering dust in a library in Portugal and published a translation in French in 1728, the edition Johnson saw at Pembroke.[8]

Johnson suddenly had a substantial literary project with a clear line to publication. For what would amount to a substantial piece of translation Warren was to pay him a measly five pounds – although that was a quarter of his paltry annual salary teaching at Market Bosworth – but the project was a light breaking in on his gloom. It was his first delicious taste of writing for money. Le Grand's *Lobo* was nowhere to be had in Birmingham, so he quickly had a copy sent to him by someone at Pembroke. With that in hand in early 1733 he set to work translating selected portions of it. Warren's printer, a man named Osborn, was notified to expect copy flowing in and Johnson began giving it to him almost at once. It should have been easy sailing on a project well within his literary abilities and knowledge of French. He had learned the language unsystematically on his own along the way with the help of dictionaries – Boswell said he could understand it perfectly but could not speak it 'readily'. But he had to overcome two old adversaries: persistent melancholia and indolence.

On 1 June, after having lived with Hector in Warren's house for no fewer than six months, he deposited himself in the home of an F. Jervis when Hector moved to his own lodgings on New Street. His work then stalled. He was 'very idle, lounged about with Hector, and had a few acquaintances'. Warren became impatient, Hector worried since he was familiar with his friend's dilatory ways, and Osborn was desperate because he badly needed the income from the work. What happened next was an early display of Johnson's instinctive sympathy for the needy. Hector knew his friend could not bear the thought of being the reason that 'the poor man and his family were suffering' and put it to him that if he did not apply himself Osborn could earn nothing. Alert to the recurring theme of a 'motive for humanity' in Johnson's life, Boswell embellished the story as Hector told it to him:

> Johnson upon this exerted the powers of his mind, though his body was relaxed. He lay in bed with the book, which was a quarto, before him, and dictated while Hector wrote. Mr Hector carried the sheets to the press, and

corrected almost all the proof sheets, very few of which were even seen by Johnson. In this manner, with the aid of Mr Hector's active friendship, the book was completed.

As one critic has pointed out, there are people who do write in bed, but it would have taken no fewer than forty hours in bed to complete this 416-page translation. Nonetheless, with his back to the wall, Johnson was able even in his youth to turn near defeat into a sudden dramatic victory. What turned out to be an act of charity succeeded in getting the book done. In due course, with unaccountable delay, the book was published in 1735.[9]

Voyage to Abyssinia was his first effort in a long career of thinking and writing about travel. Exploration in the Western hemisphere was double-edged for him: it both fascinated and revolted him because of colonial atrocities committed there. Columbus 'gave a new world to European curiosity and European cruelty', he would write later. He had a similar distaste for European, especially Portuguese, imperialism along the African coastline, a subject about which he had read extensively and which would inspire his philosophical tale *Rasselas*, his play *Irene*, oriental tales in several moral essays, and general reflections on travel writing. A vogue for literary orientalism evident early in the eighteenth century in such works as Antoine Galland's *Arabian Nights* somewhat accounts for this fascination, but when he accepted the commission to translate Lobo he did so with an unusually deep knowledge of that exotic part of the world and with strongly negative views about how it was colonised.[10]

As for travel literature itself, the trick was to be the right kind of traveller. 'It may, I think, be justly observed, that few books disappoint their readers more than the narrations of travellers,' he wrote in 1760. Too frequently they are 'without incidents, without reflection' and 'tell nothing because nothing is to be told'.[11] The great object of any book of travel written for the entertainment of others should be to say something useful and revealing about 'human life' and examine the customs and laws of foreign nations. The genre was therefore extremely useful, he thought, to the health of the individual and a nation. Lobo was the type of traveller who brought back home something 'by which his country may be benefited; who procures some supply of want or mitigation of evil, which may enable his readers to compare their condition with that of others, to improve it whenever it is worse, and whenever it is better to enjoy it'. Johnson wrote in the

Preface to the *Voyage* that Lobo did not indulge in 'romantic absurdities or incredible fictions' with trite and worn-out phrases as if he were writing a romance tale. Lobo's arduous journeys and long years of first-hand observation in India and Abyssinia qualified him as a realistic observer of human nature. Apart from its theme, the Preface is remarkable for its ring of authority. It points unmistakably to the argumentative persona he had been projecting as early as his pre-Oxford days.[12]

Johnson took aim at the social and political authority and abuse that Father Lobo had brought to his attention. There is fury in the following passage, aimed here at the Jesuits:

> Let us suppose an inhabitant of some remote and superior region, yet unskilled in the ways of men, having read and considered the precepts of the Gospel, and the example of our Saviour, to come down in search of the *True Church*: if he would not enquire after it among the cruel, the insolent, and the oppressive; among those who are continually grasping at dominion over souls as well as bodies; among those who are employed in procuring to themselves impunity for the most enormous villainies, and studying methods of destroying their fellow-creatures, not for their crimes but their errors; if he would not expect to meet benevolence engaged in massacres, or to find mercy in a court of inquisition, he would not look for the *True Church* in the Church of Rome.

In spite of his definition of 'schismatick' in his *Dictionary* that suggests that the notion of the 'True Church' did exist for him, this barrage against the Jesuits, which underplays much that is positive in their mission, points to his fundamental hostility, even as a young man, towards any individual or religious group claiming to have a unique or exclusive pipeline to God, or claiming special miracles and insight denied to others. The Preface also anticipates Johnson's developing abhorrence of national and religious egotism on the part of power-hungry, imperialist, commercially predatory countries who think they know what is best for remote, less advanced nations.[13]

[3]

Johnson made only a few good acquaintances either at Warren's or Jervis's house, but among those whom he had it in mind to impress were Harry Porter, a dealer in textile fabrics and fine cloth who had a shop and house nearby on the High Street, and John Taylor, not his dear schoolmate but the clever Quaker inventor of the gild button and japanning of metals who amassed a fortune and, in 1765, with Sampson Lloyd III founded the first Birmingham banking-house that became known as Lloyds Bank. Lloyd, incidentally, was the nephew of Olivia Lloyd, the young Quaker in Stourbridge with whom Johnson had been 'much enamoured' and to whom he wrote love verses. Such people from the world of commerce and manufacturing seem to have been the extent of his contacts. Except for Warren we know of no literary friendships on his horizon, nor is anything known with any certainty of whom else he met or what he did or did not do for the next seven months while living in the Jervis house.[14]

He may have had a sexual interest, though. Hector told Boswell he did not believe certain anecdotes he had heard about Johnson's sexuality, but he did mention to him having heard from Peter Garrick, David's older brother, that on visits to Birmingham Johnson was one of three 'gallants' of the 'dissolute' wife of Lewis Paul, an inventor who later set up a cotton mill in Birmingham with the backing of several friends of Johnson's and whom Johnson also tried to help financially. One of the other gallants was 'fever powder' Robert James, his school friend six years older than he who also made appearances at Walmesley's table and whom Johnson regarded as one of the chief sources of information about his youth. The third member of this triumvirate and original source of the anecdotes was Benjamin Victor, eventually Poet Laureate of Ireland and theatre historian. Johnson met him in 1762 and described him as 'honest, indolent, conversable' with 'a great many anecdotes'. In this particular anecdote Victor told Garrick that 'the lady told him Johnson was the most seducing man she had ever known'. Boswell did not allow the anecdote into his biography, perhaps partly because it involved sexual flirtation with another man's wife and partly because he preferred to believe Hector when he said Johnson 'never was given to women' – in other words, that he was chaste and never partook of adultery: 'His juvenile attachments to the fair sex were ... very transient; and it is certain, that he formed no criminal [i.e. carnal] connection whatsoever. Mr Hector, who lived with him in his younger days in the utmost intimacy and social freedom, has assured me, that even at that ardent season his conduct was strictly virtuous in that respect.'[15]

Hector also admitted that Johnson was not always an ideal companion. 'He drank freely, particularly Bishop with a roasted orange in it' – a kind of sangria containing wine, oranges and sugar, to which Johnson was especially partial. He might well have been drunk from time to time, though Boswell informed Hector that Johnson assured him 'there was no man alive who had seen him drunk'. To this Hector replied, 'Then he had forgot me', and proceeded to tell what happened one memorable night when one of Johnson's Ford relatives from Stourbridge, not Cornelius who had died the year before but probably one of his uncles, visited him in Birmingham. In Boswell's words:

> He [Ford] was it seems a hard drinker and he engaged Johnson and Hector to spend the evening with him at the Swan Inn. Johnson said to Hector, 'This fellow will make us both drunk. Let us take him by turns, and get rid of him.' It was settled that Hector should go first. He and Ford had drunk three bottles of port before Johnson came. When Johnson arrived, Hector found he had been drinking at Mr Porter's instead of saving himself. Hector went to bed at the Swan leaving Johnson to drink on with Ford. Next morning he perceived that Johnson who had been his bedfellow had been very drunk and he damned him. Johnson tried to deny the charge. *Literally* speaking Hector had not *seen* him drunk, though he was *sure* of the fact.

It is the sort of story that easily gets stretched into the realm of fiction in the telling and retelling. Boswell also left this anecdote out of his *Life*, but not necessarily because he did not believe it. It smacks of the truth, given Johnson's situation, companions and state of mind; moreover, Boswell himself acknowledged elsewhere that even in later life, although Johnson could be 'rigidly *abstemious*', he was not 'a *temperate* man either in eating or drinking'. He could keep himself from drinking, but once he started it was hard for him to control it. Such roughness in Birmingham included and probably aggravated a bad humour in his relations with others, a tendency that Hector identified during this period in Birmingham: he would often be 'absent' – withdrawn, heedless, or neglectful – 'and talk to himself and take peevish fits and abuse Hector who would then keep aloof, upon which Johnson would come and coax him' into a reconciliation. Rough treatment like this of friends and acquaintances when he was impatient or suddenly cross was not uncharacteristic of a harshness of personality later on. The coaxing part also rings true. When Boswell describes an instance of it in his *Life*, he is quick to add that Johnson was essentially too good-natured not to attempt a reconciliation when he was aware of having gone too far insulting or humiliating someone. With Hector it would have been more a matter of jollying him along rather than coaxing.[16]

[4]

Johnson wrote in his *Annales* that in February 1734 he finally returned to Lichfield, having stretched his visit in Birmingham to just over one year. Warren either had no more work for him or he had lost interest in writing for him. In the autumn, he had received a small legacy of five pounds from his deceased godfather Richard Wakefield, but he was running out of money and had to retreat to his home where his mother, Nathaniel and Kitty Chambers awaited him. There he spent the next few months languishing without anything to do, though he could have done a bit of tutoring or teaching at his old school or helped a little in the bookshop, of which his brother was now in charge.[17]

The main effect of Birmingham was that now he wanted to earn money by writing. He was more certain than ever that he did not want to sell books. He wanted to produce them. In the spring he asked an old Pembroke College member, the Revd Robert Boyse, then living near Birmingham, to check out an edition of the fifteenth-century Italian Renaissance scholar Angelus Politian's Latin poems from the college library on his next visit there. He remembered the book was there. Boyse checked the book out on 15 June, noting it was for 'the use of Mr Johnson'. With it in hand Johnson issued in August proposals for a subscription edition of the poems. More than just an edition of the poems, this was to include a history of Latin poetry from Petrarch to Politian as well as a life of Politian. This is the first sign of his lifelong interest in writing biography – the 'biographical part of literature,' he would say later, was 'what I love most', especially the lives of 'great and learned persons'. It was the branch of literature that 'comes near to ourselves, what we can turn to use'. People were supposed to send in their subscriptions with a payment of half the price to either him or his brother at the bookshop, 'N. Johnson, bookseller of Lichfield', the rest to be paid on delivery. Subscriptions did not arrive in any number, though, and he had to give up the project. The only thing Johnson had to show for the project was the Pembroke copy of Politian, which he seems never to have returned.[18]

This stillborn project prolonged his dejection. There was no teaching job within his sights and he had little sense of moving forward. A major solace, as before, was Walmesley at the Bishop's Palace, where he again saw Garrick and met the better sort of people of Lichfield, as well as an expanding group of ladies, including the Aston girls who began to play a part in his life the following year. The odd thing is that Johnson may now have felt less at ease there. Older and more self-conscious about wearing his continuing poverty among such people, he entered in Latin a passage in his freshly revived diary about a poor man who has to devise a way of disguising his tattered and torn clothes, as he did at Oxford, when he moves among well-heeled company: 'For a poor man going among strangers, I have found useful things to be silk thread and pins of the same colour as one's clothes (silk thread, that is, of the kind used for knitting stockings)'. At home now, his mother would have been of some use here, though one of his friends in his later years spoke of his pride in being able to do things for himself: 'He knew how to mend his own stockings, to darn his linen or to sew on a button on his clothes. I am not (he would often say) a helpless man.' His confidence was boosted some time in the first three months of 1735 when his *Voyage to Abyssinia* was finally published by two London booksellers after the printed sheets had gathered dust in Warren's shop for several months. It sold very poorly but at least now he had a book to his name.[19]

Given Johnson's lethargy, it may have been Walmesley who prodded him in November 1735 to act on the bold idea of writing to the editor, printer and publisher Edward Cave (1691–1754) in London, who in 1731 had the brilliant idea of founding *The Gentleman's Magazine*. As Cave had strong links with Birmingham, someone like Thomas Warren in the publishing business there could have suggested to Johnson that writing for Cave and his new monthly magazine might prove profitable. By 1734 the magazine was a going concern. Edited by Cave under the pseudonym Sylvanus Urban, it was the first ever significant London magazine of miscellaneous interest and history and became the most famous periodical in the eighteenth century. Cave read the market perfectly. He published monthly digests of news and articles from other papers and provided general information about the London entertainment world and public and private life, much of it gossipy or in the 'Talk of the Town' *New Yorker* mode. Cave also offered a section titled 'Poetical Essays' containing reprinted and original poetry. It was a convenient and pleasurable way for Londoners to keep up with what was going on across the spectrum of city life. Cave also hit on the clever and novel idea of circulating his magazine in the provinces so that they could easily keep abreast of what was happening in the capital and internationally.

From remote Lichfield Johnson sent a letter off to Cave with characteristic audacity, for some reason concealing his identity by cautiously giving his name as S. Smith. Not over modestly, he offered to overhaul the magazine's poetry section. Cave must surely be aware, he wrote, no less than his readers, of 'the defects of your poetical article'. He offered to put the section right 'on reasonable terms' by occasionally filling a column for him. The public would thank Cave, he urged, 'if beside the current wit of the month' the magazine added 'not only poems, inscriptions, etc. never printed before' which he would take it upon himself to supply, but also 'short literary dissertations in Latin or English, critical remarks on authors ancient or modern, forgotten poems that deserve revival, or loose pieces … worth preserving'. This would make the poetry section worth the time of an intelligent reader much more than the present diet of 'low jests, awkward buffoonery, or the dull scurrilities of either [political] party'. If Cave agrees, he would like to know how much he would pay. If the publisher's offer in last month's issue of £50 for the best Latin or English poem on 'Life, Death, Judgement, Heaven and Hell' is any indication, he expects he will be 'generous'. While he was at it, he added he was willing to contribute to any other literary project of Cave's provided his ideas would not be stolen by others. Although Cave responded one week later – whether positively or negatively is unknown – nothing came of the effort. When Johnson wrote to him again in 1738 it was in his own name and as if for the first time.[20]

CHAPTER 8

Taking a Wife

[1]

In September 1734 something had happened that was to change the course of Johnson's life for ever and lift him for a time from his persisting melancholia. Harry Porter, the Birmingham dealer in textiles to whom he had been introduced by Hector, died insolvent at his shop on the High Street on 3 September at the young age of forty-three and after twenty years of marriage, leaving his widow Elizabeth and two sons and a daughter, Lucy, between the ages of ten and eighteen to survive him. Johnson had of course met Elizabeth Porter through Hector's circle of friends. Hector used to buy his clothes from Porter's shop. Anna Seward, whom several people, most vigorously Hector and Boswell, denounced for her gossipy and malicious tales about Johnson and the Porters, claimed that while Porter was ill Johnson actually 'passed all his leisure hours' at his house, 'attending his sick-bed', and that it was at this time that he secretly conceived a passion for his wife.

Elizabeth Porter was twenty years older than he. She was raised in a respectable propertied Leicestershire and Warwickshire family named Jervis, and although her father died when she was six she was accustomed to a more genteel existence than the one her husband gave her. She brought to him a dowry of at least £600, in spite of which he did not prosper. Anna Seward said that her mother 'perfectly remembered' Mrs Porter and that her beauty existed only in Johnson's imagination: 'She had a very red face, and very indifferent features.' There is a surviving portrait of her believed to have been painted in her forties, however, showing her as quite a beauty. The picture may be the same one her daughter Lucy once showed to Mrs Thrale long after her mother had died, in which Mrs Thrale thought she looked 'pretty'. 'Her hair was eminently beautiful,' Johnson told her, 'quite blond like that of a baby.'[1]

Soon after Porter's death Johnson began to court her. Her daughter Lucy saw it all begin to happen and was able as the eldest daughter to respond to this astonishing development with more equanimity than her brother Jervis. At eighteen he was old enough to see the overtures of this strange-looking interloper only seven years older than he as a humiliation and grotesque absurdity. His ten-year-old brother was too young to feel such outrage. Probably all three of the children wondered why their mother could possibly want to enter into a relationship with a young man who was poor and had no prospects, was blotched with scrofula scars, had bad eyesight (though this may not have been immediately evident), and made disconcertingly odd movements with his head and upper body.

We tend to think of Johnson as he was when Boswell knew him, overweight and famous, when flesh had concealed the massive angularity of his large bone structure. He cut a different figure in 1734, as Lucy told Boswell in the only account anyone, even Hector and Taylor, has left of his youthful physique:

> Miss Porter told me, that when he was first introduced to her mother, his appearance was very forbidding: he was then lean and lank, so that his immense structure of bones was hideously striking to the eye, and the scars of the scrofula were deeply visible. He also wore his hair, which was straight and stiff, and separated behind; and he often had, seemingly, convulsive starts and odd gesticulations, which tended to excite at once surprise and ridicule.

This was disturbing enough, but after he died Mrs Thrale in her *Anecdotes* added detail about his eyes that would have characterised him in his youth as well: 'His eyes, though of a light grey colour were so wild, so piercing, and at times so fierce, that fear was I believe the first emotion in the hearts of all his beholders.' How, then, could Mrs Porter have been attracted to him? Part of the answer to that doubtless lies in his strength, height and robustness, also highlighted by Mrs Thrale:

> His stature was remarkably high [five feet eleven inches in his stockings], and his limbs exceedingly large: his strength was more than common, I believe, and his activity had been greater I have heard than such a form gave one reason to expect: his features were strongly marked, and his countenance particularly rugged; though the original complexion had certainly been fair, a circumstance somewhat unusual.

Sir Joshua Reynolds once was supposed to have been told that he should not paint Johnson in a full-length portrait because of the 'uncouth formation' of his limbs. On the contrary, Reynolds replied, far from thinking Johnson's limbs unsightly, he thought them well-formed.[2]

That was only the body that housed the soul, as Mrs Thrale put it, and for Mrs Porter it was by far the less important part of the picture. Lucy remembered that her mother seemed not to notice his body: 'Mrs Porter was so much engaged by his conversation that she overlooked all these external disadvantages [and advantages], and said to her daughter, "This is the most sensible man that I ever saw in my life."' That his conversation and mind, his down-to-earth common sense and insight, were enough for her to be able to see beneath the surface of his distorted physique and ignore his virtual poverty says a great deal about her own perspicacity. Except for him she was looking at a life of loneliness and deterioration. Her children would eventually be going their own way, so any hostility towards Johnson on their part counted for less than they thought. Lucy was not as upset with their mother as Jervis was. One of the early biographers claimed that her brother 'offered to settle a very handsome annuity on her [their mother] for life, provided she would break her engagements'. Her quick readiness to swim against such currents in this relationship and follow her own feelings with such abandon argues not only that she fell deeply in love with him but also that she had resources and emotions inside her that had not yet been tapped. Mrs Thrale judged that as a widow with children 'she must have been in most respects a woman quite like her neighbours', with nothing to distinguish her, but 'her second choice made her a person to enquire about'.[3]

What was there to appeal to him in a woman of her years, apart from her physical attractiveness? Although her husband had died insolvent, she had about £800 (about £80,000 today) to bring to the marriage. One wonders at what point he knew about the money. Did he think his chances of marrying someone else were very limited, that women were never likely to be attracted to him romantically? If we are to believe Hector and Boswell, his religious upbringing up to this point had kept him sexually innocent. Mrs Porter's interest in him, which she must have had to make quite plain to overcome his sexual shyness and inexperience, must therefore have seemed to him like an exciting, warm and luminous breeze of unfamiliar affection. She unlocked something in him: 'In a man whom religious education has

Michael Johnson, Samuel's father. Johnson wrote impatiently of his parents that 'neither of them ever tried to calculate the profits of trade, or the expenses of living.'

Edial Hall, Lichfield, Johnson's failed school.

Elizabeth Porter, Johnson's wife and twenty years older than him, whom he called 'Tetty'. Thought to have been painted not long before they married on 9 July 1735.

First page of the only surviving letter from Samuel Johnson to his wife Tetty, 31 January 1740. He writes with a sense of guilt for having been away from her for so long, especially while she had injured herself: 'You have already suffered more than I can bear to reflect upon, and I hope more than either of us shall suffer again.'

Tea service of Chinese design belonging to Samuel Johnson.
Johnson often drank copiously, more than ten cups of tea at a sitting.
Note the small teacups without handles.

Molly Aston, Johnson's great love, who lived in Lichfield.

St John's Gate, Edward Cave's *Gentleman's Magazine* offices, where he also resided. The doorway to the right of the arch led to Cave's office, a large room above the arch, where Johnson spent much time in the late 1730s and 1740s.

An imaginary scene, painted in the mid-nineteenth century, showing Johnson working intensely in Cave's offices at St John's Gate. The girl has brought him food.

Elizabeth Carter, poet, classicist, translator and early favourite
of Johnson's in London.

Samuel Johnson by Joshua Reynolds, *c.*1755, which was
included in the first edition of the *Dictionary*.

Self-portrait by Joshua Reynolds, 1753–4. Reynolds returned
to England from his Grand Tour in 1752 and soon became
immensely rich from his painting. After Johnson's death he
referred to 'thirty years' of intimacy with him.

secured from licentious indulgences, the passion of love, when once it has seized him, is exceedingly strong; being unimpaired by dissipation, and totally concentrated in one object.' That is the way Boswell read her initial effect upon him. Beyond that, he was impressed by her family background and could read in it something of 'the born gentlewoman'. And as he later said, he was taken with her ironic, satirical sense and slight signs of literary judgement – that she 'could read comedy better than anybody he had ever heard', though 'in tragedy she mouthed too much'.[4]

Their courtship continued for about nine months somewhere in Birmingham. It was not at her house on the High Street because since she was forced to give up the shop that was connected to the house, she had no choice but to vacate the house as well. Wherever she resided in Birmingham, probably without her disgusted eldest son who could not bear the sight of Johnson's wooing, it still meant that Johnson had to make frequent visits to the city to see her. Before long, they decided to marry and it was time for Johnson to explain his decision to his mother and, if possible, obtain her approval. Johnson hoped his mother would give them her blessing, but it would not deter him if she did not. He surely told her about Elizabeth's money and that if he were to be married, Mrs Porter's sons stood to be supported very well by their rich uncle, Joseph Porter. Sadly alienated, the eldest boy Jervis vowed never to see his mother again, as a result of which neither son ever saw his mother again after her re-marriage. Only Lucy would remain with her mother.

It was not only Mrs Porter's family who disliked Johnson and the idea of his marriage to her. Lucy Porter insisted to Boswell that 'The Birmingham people could not bear Mr Johnson. She did not say why. I suppose from envy of his parts; though I do not see how traders could envy such qualities.' Envy, gossip, hostility: these undoubtedly were the reasons the couple decided to marry not in Birmingham but out of the way at St Werburgh's Church in Derby on 9 July 1735. Adding another layer of eccentricity to the whole courtship, for some reason they decided to get there on horseback, not in a carriage, and a strange enough journey it was. 'His account of the wedding we used to think ludicrous enough,' Mrs Thrale wrote: 'I was riding to church (says Johnson), and she following on another single horse: she hung back however, and I turned about to see whether she could get her steed along, or what was the matter. I had however soon occasion to see it was only coquetry, and *that I despised*, so quickening my pace a little, she mended hers; but I believe there was a tear or two – pretty dear creature!' For Boswell he added that her coquettish behaviour of riding too slow and then too fast, trying to keep him off balance, came from reading too many frivolous 'old romances', which put into her head 'the fantastical notion that a woman of spirit should use her lover like a dog'. He was not about to become, he said, 'the slave of caprice', so he rode on out of her sight. Boswell judged that his behaviour showed 'manly firmness'.[5]

An objective witness may be more disposed to think it insensitive. A woman married for twenty years in dire need of companionship is not likely to have wanted to treat her new husband like a 'dog'. This little test of wills, coming early in a married life that turned out to have quite a few quarrels, was for her mingled with a good portion of grief. Within the space of less than a year she had lost her husband, married a highly eccentric man half her years disliked by her children and other relatives, and seen her family break up in ill will. And here was Johnson riding on ahead of her in her hour of need when he should have been next to her. That in later years he liked to tell his friends about this ride to Derby in a comical vein suggests he never grasped the full meaning of her tears. He married his 'Tetty' – his nickname for her, which Boswell called a provincial contraction for 'Elisabeth' and judged to be ridiculous enough 'when applied to a woman of her age and appearance' – feeling it was 'a love-marriage upon both sides'. His wife is supposed to have worn a portrait of him in miniature in a bracelet for the rest of her life. Boswell concluded that 'his regard and fondness for her never ceased, even after her death', a fact amply borne out by his searching prayers for her year after year. Still, there were quarrels and great pressures in their marriage. She brought him some money, which helped launch them as a married couple, but they were two very different people and soon enough they began to drift apart.[6]

[2]

Tetty's faith in him was such that with her money they decided boldly in the spring or summer to start a school, for which he took steps in May to recover the more than one hundred books and private papers he had left at Oxford with Taylor. In June and July they also placed advertisements in *The Gentleman's Magazine* in London for the school, where 'young gentlemen are boarded and taught the Latin and Greek languages, by SAMUEL JOHNSON'. 'I am now going to furnish a house in the country,' he wrote to his old Lichfield chum Richard Congreve, 'and keep a private boarding-school for young gentlemen whom I shall endeavour to instruct in a method somewhat more rational than those commonly practised, which you know there is no great vanity in presuming to attempt.' He wrote this from nearby Great Haywood, Staffordshire, where in May he had accepted a job for a few weeks preparing the nineteen-year-old son of Thomas Whitby for university. Whitby was former High Sheriff of Stafford-shire, to whom Johnson had been recommended by the Revd John Addenbrooke, then the Vicar of St Chad's and eventually Dean of Lichfield – a 'kindness' Johnson recalled forty years later that included negotiating a salary.[7]

The prospect of being in charge of a school particularly excited him. No longer would he be enslaved by the whims and tyrannies of superiors who knew less about their subjects than he did, or stymied by curricula he did not think were in pupils' best interests. He was even restless to draw up a 'plan of education' for the school. He needed details of the 'different ways of teaching in use at the most celebrated schools' and asked Congreve to send him what he knew about West-minster and the methods at his own school Charterhouse – just 'under each class their exercises and authors'. He also had strong ideas of his own about teaching. Around about this time he advised his first cousin Samuel Ford about how best to prepare for university. 'Apply yourself wholly to the languages, till you go to the university' by focusing on Greek authors such as Xenophon, Homer, Theocritus and Euripides so as to be 'skilled in all the dialects'. As for Latin authors, 'it is proper not to read the later authors, till you are well versed in those of the purest ages', the likes of Terence, Tully, Caesar, Sallust, Virgil and Horace. But his main advice was rationalist and pragmatic, the earliest complete statement we have of what, above all else, as a boy and young man he had determined to master through relentless practice, and for which the world has come to know him: 'The greatest and most necessary task still remains, to attain a habit of expression, without which knowledge is of little use. This is necessary in Latin, and more necessary in English; and can only be acquired by a daily imitation of the best and correctest authors.'[8]

After only a few weeks at Great Haywood he was back in Lichfield and Birmingham, renting a farmhouse called Edial Hall for the school about two and a half miles west of Lichfield in a tiny rural crossroads in the middle of nowhere. Today it looks just as lonely as it must have seemed then. It was available and recommended by Walmesley. They moved into the house with his books and Tetty's daughter Lucy sometime late in the year or early in 1736. In the tiny group of three boarders he (with Walmesley's help) managed to net were Davy Garrick, who was then eighteen, and his younger brother George. Someone said that putting the Garricks in the school resembled the trick of country housewives of 'placing one egg in the nest of a hen to induce her to lay more'. Davy had interrupted his schooling at Lichfield Grammar School to be with his wine-merchant uncle in Lisbon, and on his return needed to be brought up to scratch in Latin before going on to university. While his father was in Granada as a captain in military service and his elder brother was away at sea, he more or less had become head of his debt-ridden family (mother and four other siblings) in Lichfield. By the time he entered the school, he had already shifted his attention from university towards a military career for himself, so his application to his studies was less earnest than it might have been. On top of which his distracting relish for theatre instead of the Romans and Greeks had already shown itself. When Johnson 'expected from him some exercise or composition upon a theme, he showed him several scenes of a new comedy, which had engrossed his time'. Forty years later Johnson was still complaining about lack of academic prowess: 'He has not Latin enough. He finds out the Latin by the meaning, rather than the meaning by the Latin.'[9]

Johnson's insurmountable problem with this school, apart from his lack of credentials, was that his frightening appearance and the same odd manner and assortment of tics and gesticulations that had put off potential employers also scared off potential parents and students. When he tried one last time in August perhaps under pressure from Tetty to secure a teaching post before going ahead with his own school, this time nothing less than as Master of Solihull Grammar School, he was rejected for this reason and because he was arrogant. One of the trustees or governors of the school wrote to Walmesley, who had spoken for him, explaining bluntly that everyone thought he was an excellent scholar but also disliked him for his insolence: 'he has the character of being a very haughty, ill-natured gentleman, and he has such a way of distorting his face (which though he cannot help) the gentlemen think it may affect some young lads'. They were looking instead for 'a soft tongue, a smooth face, or ceremonious carriage'. There was also the logistical problem at Edial Hall that with Lichfield

Grammar School so close by there was no particularly good reason for parents to send their boys to Johnson. On this fragile basis of a little band of three students at their school, then, he and his wife began their married life, hoping that when word got out about his excellent teaching the students would flock to the school. They did not flock, however, even after he ran further advertisements in *The Gentleman's Magazine*. He trawled in a few from here and there but never had more than eight, several of whom were day boys. The enterprise was looking financially disastrous. [10]

Lack of interest in the school was only one strain on the marriage. Living in a remote spot like Edial was a huge change for Tetty from living on the high street in Birmingham. She would have had to fight boredom much of the time as Johnson got on with his teaching. There was also Lucy, confused and unhappy, muddying the waters. More seriously, Tetty soon discovered that her new husband's personal habits were a trial for her. A few of Mrs Thrale's allusions in 1777 to their quarrels, long after Tetty had died, could apply just as plausibly to this period as later: 'I asked him once whether he ever disputed with his wife (I knew he adored her). Oh yes, perpetually my dear says he; she was extremely neat in her disposition, and always fretful that I made the house so dirty – a clean floor is *so* comfortable she would say by way of twitting; till at last I told her, I thought we had had talk enough about the floor, we would now have a touch at the *ceiling*.' They had their disagreements about meals, too. The Johnson Mrs Thrale knew 'loved his dinner extremely', so one day she asked 'if he ever huffed his wife about his meat? Yes, Yes replied he, but then she huffed me worse; for she said one day as I was going to say grace – Nay hold says she, and do not make a farce of thanking God for a dinner which you will presently protest not eatable.'[11]

There was a larger problem. Her conversation may have struck him as too narrow to compensate for her querulousness. Could he have been thinking of his own marriage when he said, again after her death, 'a man of sense and education should meet a suitable companion in a wife. It was a miserable thing when the conversation could only be such as, whether the mutton should be boiled or roasted, and probably a dispute about that.' With his remarks Johnson in retrospect and inadvertently sends the message that he was not an easy man to live with, whatever her housewifery was like. Very telling in a more comprehensive way was Mrs Thrale's observation that in arguments between spouses that they both witnessed, he would always take the side of the husband:

> Women (says Dr Johnson) give great offence by a contemptuous spirit of non-compliance on petty occasions. The man calls his wife to walk with him in the shade, and she feels a strange desire just at that moment to sit in the sun: he offers to read her a play, or sing her a song, and she calls the children in to disturb them, or advises him to seize that opportunity of settling the family accounts. Twenty such tricks will the faithfulest wife in the world not refuse to play, and then look astonished when the fellow fetches in a mistress. And are the hours of pleasure so frequent in life, that when a man gets a couple of quiet ones to spend in familiar chat with his wife, they must be poisoned by petty mortifications?

Such tricks as Tetty played at are behind such sour views on marriage, but a man who thought the husband always right cannot have been easy to live with.[12]

Decades later Garrick loved to tell an anecdote about Tetty and Johnson's sex life at Edial, which with his unmatchable talent for mimicry and ridicule he caricatured to devastating effect. The anecdote highlights the additional stress on their married life of having Davy and the other boys at such close quarters in the house with them. Davy, moreover, unimpressed with Johnson as a teacher, was lively and mischievous enough to perplex them even more, and he probably was the ringleader in this nocturnal episode as told inimitably by Boswell:

> From Mr Garrick's account he did not appear to have been profoundly reverenced by his pupils. His oddities of manner, and uncouth gesticulations, could not but be the subject of merriment to them; and, in particular, the young rogues used to listen at the door of his bed-chamber, and peep through the keyhole, that they might turn into ridicule his tumultuous and awkward fondness for Mrs Johnson.

Garrick, especially in his cups and in exclusively male company, when Johnson was nowhere to be seen, liked to amuse his friends by working up routines of what to him and doubtless the other boys was the easily burlesqued relationship between their highly sexed master and his older, decaying wife. Boswell reconstructs one of these from a conversation he and a friend had with the gossipy Mrs Desmoulins who was living in Johnson's house the year before Johnson died:

BOSWELL: 'Do you know, Ma'am, that there really was a connection between him and his wife? You understand me.' MRS DESMOULINS: 'Yes, yes, Sir. Nay, Garrick knew it was consummated, for he peeped through the keyhole, and behaved like a rascal, for he made the Doctor ridiculous all over the country by describing him running round the bed after she had lain down, and crying, "I'm coming, my Tetsie, I'm coming, my Tetsie! Ph! Ph!" (blowing in his manner).'

In another version Johnson is so preoccupied working on a play in his bedroom that he is fairly oblivious to Tetty's calls to him to come to bed. When he absently mistakes the bedclothes for his shirt-tails and begins to stuff them hurriedly into his breeches, she finds herself suddenly exposed on the bed. Garrick did not entirely conjure up the pictures out of thin air, but he did invest them with images of Johnson and Tetty as they were ten or more years later in London. At Edial Hall she may already have begun to feel a pressure to look and act young in deference to her younger husband, taking to excessive cosmetics to create the desired effect. He resolutely objected to her dyeing her hair black.[13]

Whatever the causes, Johnson's eyes did turn elsewhere. 'Forty years ago, Sir,' he confessed to Boswell in 1776 on their visit to Lichfield, 'I was in love with an actress here, Mrs Emmet', though Garrick mistakenly did not think he was a careful observer of the female form. But if there really was a woman with whom he fell in love during that year after his marriage and remained in love for the rest of her life, it was Molly Aston. Three years older than Johnson, she was one of eight daughters of Sir Thomas Aston of Cheshire, four of whom came to live in Lichfield. He had met her at the Bishop's Palace several years earlier when Walmesley began to cultivate the Aston girls – he married one of them, Magdalen, in 1736. When the Aston girls came on to the scene, the palace, which was always an enticing escape for him, sparkled as it never had before, and he shined as never before. Boswell described how Johnson could rise to the occasion in the company of women in Lichfield:

In such families he passed much time in his early years. In most of them, he was in the company of ladies, particularly at Mr Walmesley's, whose wife and sisters-in-law, of the name of Aston, and daughters of a baronet, were remarkable for good breeding; so that the notion which has been industriously circulated and believed, that he never was in good company till late in life, and, consequently, had been confirmed in coarse and ferocious manners by long habits, is wholly without foundation. Some of the ladies have assured me, they recollected him well and when a young man, as distinguished for his complaisance.[14]

During the increasingly exasperating and grinding year at Edial Hall, this new feminine company at the palace would have had a magnetic effect upon him. He once described Molly as 'a beauty and a scholar, and a wit and a Whig'. She was bright and daunting to other women – Anna Seward described her as 'handsome but haughty'. That she was a Whig disturbed him no more than that Walmesley was one. What really must have turned his head was her beauty and intelligence, and her breeding, all of which is attested to in a ravishing portrait of her dating from this period showing her elegant face and figure, and an abundance of auburn hair. Eager to slip into her *Anecdotes* some titillating details from Johnson's past, Mrs Thrale wrote that when her first husband asked him what had been the happiest period or moment in his life, he did not hesitate to reply: 'It was that year in which [I] spent one whole evening with M—y As—n; but thoughts of it sweetened the whole year.' 'That indeed (said he) was not happiness, it was rapture.' In her journal Mrs Thrale stated plainly that they spent the evening tête-à-tête. 'She talked all in praise of liberty', he went on, so gallantly 'I made this [Latin] epigram upon her'. It was about her beauty, '*Pulchra Maria*', to which he had become a slave – 'She was the loveliest creature I ever saw!!!!' Mrs Thrale translated the epigram immediately into, 'Persuasions to freedom fall oddly from you:/If freedom we seek – fair Maria, adieu!' Johnson added, 'The ladies never loved Molly Aston', alluding to her forthright intelligence. Mrs Thrale then pressed home by questioning him what his wife thought of this 'attachment'. His reply, which is an amazing and revealing piece of confidence to give to her, touched a nerve in his marriage:

> She was jealous to be sure (said he), and teased me sometimes when I would let her; and one day, as a fortune-telling gipsy passed us when we were walking out in company with two or three friends in the country, she made the wench look at my hand, but soon repented her curiosity; for (says the gipsy) your heart is divided, Sir, between a Betty and a Molly: Betty loves you best, but you take most delight in Molly's company: when I turned about to laugh, I saw my wife was crying.

He added quickly, 'Pretty charmer! she had no reason!'[15]
There are grounds for thinking she did have reason to cry and that

in this disclaimer to Mrs Thrale he was shielding himself from the imputation that he was in love with someone else when he married. To begin with, Molly's letters to him over the next thirty years went missing so that none of his early biographers ever saw them, though he remarked that 'they should be the last papers he would destroy'. This may mean he finally burned them in his infamous bonfire.[16]

At about the same time as Johnson first met Molly, he became very friendly with the dashing Henry ('Harry') Hervey, captain in the 1st Dragoon Guards who was posted to Lichfield around 1730 and soon became Molly's brother-in-law. As he had for others, Johnson wrote several love poems for Hervey, some included in the 'Stella' group that Hervey transcribed during their most intimate time in London between 1737 and 1743 and which Johnson published in *The Gentleman's Magazine* in 1747. Hervey undoubtedly wanted them for Molly's sister, his future wife Catherine, but it is not unlikely that Johnson got his inspiration for them from Molly herself. Two 'Stella poems', 'To Miss— on Her Playing Upon the Harpsicord in a Room Hung With Some Flower-Pieces of Her Own Painting' and 'To Miss— On Her Giving the Author a Gold and Silk Net-Work Purse of Her Own Weaving', flatter and please with pleasant though trite imagery and commonplace sentiments. 'The Winter's Walk', set in the Staffordshire countryside during the wicked winter of 1739–40, resonates more deeply, deploying winter as an emblem of life's miseries that, as it did then in Johnson's life, alternated with sunshine and joy: 'Tir'd with vain joys, and false alarms,/With mental and corporeal strife,/Snatch me, my Stella, to thy arms,/And screen me from the ills of life.' The poem is full of longing and frustration, a fantasy that with his Stella he could some day find himself in a protecting, encouraging, intellectually satisfying love. That he never, so far as we know, satisfied his passion for Molly has to be regarded as one of his greatest personal sadnesses.[17]

[3]

As the months wore on, Johnson began to realise that his school was failing, that he was not cut out to be a teacher, and that the whole enterprise was wearing him out, deepening his frustration, and initiating what was to become a relentless process of romantic disenchantment between him and Tetty. The thought and accompanying guilt weighed on him, too, that he had got her to agree to spend much of her surviving fortune on this school. On 27 August he wrote in his diary, 'This day I have trifled away, except that I have attended the school in the morning.' It must have been a feeling he had many times a week. He was wasting his talents. He began to make resolutions and 'rules' for himself to do better and do more. On 7 September, his twenty-eighth birthday, as would become his habit on his birthday, he composed a little prayer asking God for help to make use of the year in a way that would bring him comfort 'in the hour of death, and in the day of judgement'. Then he added another resolution for good measure, 'I intend tomorrow to review the rules I have at any time laid down, in order to practise them.' If such 'rules' were anything like the many he made for himself for the rest of his life, they included going to bed and getting up at reasonable hours and not giving in to laziness, with all of which he was failing too often. Perhaps Robert Burton's *Anatomy of Melancholy* helped him, which he said 'was the only book that ever took him out of bed two hours sooner than he wished to rise'. It was hard to get up in the morning and face another day of systematic, patient teaching when his whole being and intellect ached to move swiftly, if unsystematically, 'by fits and starts, by violent eruptions into the regions of knowledge'. Having to force his 'gloomy and impetuous' mind into the harness of a schoolmaster made him irritable, and that only increased his guilt. He had the highest respect for a good teacher and knew that a good temper was a requisite for the job, but he also knew he lacked one.[18]

It was therefore strange that in 1736, probably late in the year, he applied for the assistant mastership of Brewood Grammar School in Staffordshire. It is likely Tetty put him up to it. As with most of his other teaching applications, this one came to nothing, which in this instance was especially regrettable because the Revd William Budworth, the headmaster of the school, was widely esteemed as a talented and benign instructor of youth. In the years to come, Budworth lamented more than once having to reject his application 'from an apprehension that the paralytic affliction' from which he suffered 'might become the object of imitation or of ridicule among his pupils'.[19]

There was nothing for it, then, but to hope that the school might suddenly catch the fancy of local parents. In the meantime, he needed to do something else as well, something literary that would help him preserve his sanity and self-respect and, who knows, perhaps earn him some money. He decided to write a poetic drama. He would call it *Irene* and base it on a piece of Turkish history. The story takes place between the fall of Constantinople in 1453 and the death of Irene in

1456. Constantinople was an appealing subject for him, for in his reading he had worked up a deep appreciation for it and the Moham-medan world generally. 'Sir, there are two objects of curiosity', he said to Boswell, 'the Christian world, and the Mahometan world. All the rest may be considered as barbarous.' For his source he used Richard Knolles's *A Generall Historie of the Turkes* (1603), which he much admired and used in his study of the Mohammedan Empire that had already borne fruit in the *Voyage to Abyssinia*.[20]

The plot is taken from an episode in the wars between the Greeks and Turks. It concerns the fate of Irene, a ravishingly beautiful Greek slave who after the fall of Constantinople is handed over to the Sultan Mahomet II and becomes his mistress. Her beauty holds too much of a sexual power over him, though she has abandoned her Christianity for him, and he is warned by his advisers to remove her from his life and court before his people turn against him. Her Greek friend Aspasia provides the Christian theme by striving to convince her to recover her moral sense. Irene, and to a lesser extent the unworldly Aspasia, provide the moral focus. Irene's weaknesses and tormentingly ambivalent values are the source of her own destruction – 'what Anguish racks the guilty Breast' – not politics or the Sultan's cruelty, and the play concludes with him lopping off her head when he suspects her of treachery. Since the whole play is poetry, it must have seemed to Johnson as he wrote page after page of verse in that isolated farmhouse-school outside Lichfield that here at last was the vehicle for the creative fulfilment of his poetic powers and a justification for all the reading he had done about the oriental world. The play looked to him like his ticket out of Lichfield, his first step to fame and fortune.

He began to write rather chaotically in a 'fragmentary eruption' of ideas, composing speeches without being sure who would actually speak them. The original manuscript, which tradition has it someone saved from the bonfire and someone else (much later) presented to the King, looks like the work of an inexperienced dramatist who was relying on his prodigious memory, propelled first by the impulse to get the speeches down on paper that in many instances he had already composed in his head. One critic has called the first draft more of a commonplace-book than a dramatic sketch, a sign of the 'radically untheatrical quality' of his imagination – a reason why the play, even after extensive revisions, 'lacked that dynamic of interlocking, opposing personalities and ideas in vivid and sinewy conflict that thrill us in the best drama'. One finds its characters remain wooden and its didactic morality laboured and cloying, unconnected to real human experience.[21]

Johnson turned Irene's dilemma into one between worldly or materialistic glory and Christianity, but her speeches trace the more rebellious theme of independence and individuality against the oppressiveness of society. At one point he has her defend herself from male arrogance and its autocratic suppression and disregard of women:

> Do not we share the comprehensive thought,
> Th' enlivening wit, the penetrating reason?
> Beats not the female breast with gen'rous passions,
> The thirst of empire, and the love of glory?

And there are other convincing speeches on female slavery and other types of suppression. Irene is in torment because of her socially and morally divided self. The fact that she is killed at the end expresses Johnson's indignation that social order is tyrannical, cutting down those who presume to violate it. Were Molly Aston's sentiments on liberty ringing in his ears? There is, to be sure, ambivalence in his attitudes towards Irene and Aspasia. Aspasia represents conventionality, Irene independence. It is better to act now and claim today before 'interposing death destroys the prospect!'; docility and deference always perpetrate a 'gen'ral fraud from day to day' and fill the world 'with wretches undetected'. Irene may be impure in her martyrdom for the Greek cause, but she is the tragic heroine and Johnson's sympathies were overwhelmingly with her.[22]

After writing three or more acts of the play, he took it to Walmesley at the palace for a mature judgement. Walmesley was so disturbed by the pathos of the heroine's emotional and moral plight that he asked Johnson, 'How can you possibly contrive to plunge her into deeper calamity?' Johnson's comeback was, 'Sir, I can put her into the Spiritual Court!' Pleased with 'this proof of Johnson's abilities as a dramatic writer', he advised him strongly to finish the tragedy and get it on the stage. What stage would that be? Where else but in London? It was time to leave Lichfield.[23]

PART III

Slow Rises Worth

Edward Cave, founder of
The Gentleman's Magazine

CHAPTER 9

Stranger in London

[1]

The idea was timely and caught hold. He and Tetty, partly under Walmesley's influence, decided to close the school so he could travel to London to acquire literary work. He left most of their money with Tetty, who presumably continued to live with Lucy in Edial Hall, now empty of boys. Notwithstanding the awkwardness over the marriage, they could benefit from being close to his mother and could even have helped her in the bookshop. Once he established himself in London, he would send for them – a dangerously open-ended scheme. On the face of it, he was eager to get away from both of them.

The plan was to travel to London with Davy, finish *Irene* there, try to get it acted and published, and generally find his way in the professional world of letters. Davy was to lodge as a paying guest with an old friend of Walmesley's in Kent, the Revd John Colson, to be tutored by him on mathematics, philosophy and 'humane learning' with a view to his entering the Temple and being educated to the Bar. Just after Johnson and his former pupil disappeared down the road out of Lichfield on 2 March 1737, Walmesley dutifully sat down to compose for Davy a letter of introduction to Colson, also mentioning that he would be in the company of a Samuel Johnson:

> He, and another neighbour of mine, one Mr Samuel Johnson, set out this morning for London together. Davy Garrick is to be with you early the next week, and Mr Johnson to try his fate with a tragedy, and to see to get himself employed in some translation, either from the Latin or the French. Johnson is a very good scholar and poet, and I have great hopes will turn out a fine tragedy-writer.[1]

Walmesley may have hoped that Colson would take Johnson in for a few days, assist him in getting other lodgings in town, and generally help him on his way, but Colson surely would have had little idea of how to help him, short of setting him up somewhere in town closer to the hothouse atmosphere of writers and publishers.

Johnson now apparently had little money to spare for this experiment in London, and Davy may have had even less because his father was back from Spain and ill. They decided to ride to London but as the famous story goes had money enough only for one horse. Garrick used to say they adopted the proverbial 'ride and tie' method by which one of them would ride off on the horse, stopping and tethering it at some point and then walking on; when the other reached the horse he would mount it, trot past his companion, and in his turn tether it – and so on into London. The method was not conducive to sociability and one wonders whether the sudden change of their circumstances created some awkwardness between them, especially as Davy had shown little taste for learning at the school. Johnson would never have a high regard for his companion's learning. They left their master-pupil relationship behind them, however, and both knew that in a few days they would part company.[2]

The main coaching route from Lichfield to London had been remarkably consistent for centuries, with eighteenth-century horsemen and coaches following much the same route as Roman soldiers marching along Watling Street. Just as Johnson the toddler had bumped along this route with his mother in 1712 on their way to be 'touched' by the Queen, he and Garrick now passed through Coleshill, Coventry, Dunchurch, Daventry, Towcester, Stony Stratford, Dunstable, St Albans, High Barnet, and on into London. Perhaps painful sensations coursed through him at Coventry where in October 1728 he and his father had turned their horses on to the Banbury Road heading towards what they hoped would be a bright future at Oxford. The journey took Johnson and Garrick less than a week.

[2]

Whatever else happened in these first days, both suffered severe blows soon after arriving in London. Garrick heard the tragic news that his father had died while they were on the road. Grieving, he went on to Rochester, spent a few months there bored by mathematics, decided against his new plan of studying law at Lincoln's Inn, and then retreated back to Lichfield. He returned to London a few weeks or months later to set up the London end of a wine business he and his elder brother Peter had decided to go into together.

Johnson's blow was less expected: his brother Nathaniel had died at the age of twenty-five, apparently also when they were travelling to London. Nathaniel had fallen on hard times and seemed to have taken to drinking. He had plans to open a bookshop in Stourbridge, but there is a hint that while working in the family business at home he had committed some 'crime' that brought much trouble to his mother and prompted him to leave to work in some sort of extension of the business in Burton-on-Trent. It was from there perhaps that he wrote a most unhappy, dejected letter to his mother, lamenting his 'crime' but bitterly reproving her for not telling him he could have the use of certain (perhaps book-binding) tools that could have made a difference in his life. The melancholia that plagued his father and brother seemed also to have him in its grips. He lashed out particularly at his brother: 'As to my brother's assisting me I had but little reason to expect it when he would scarce ever use me with common civility and to whose advice was owing that unwillingness you showed to my going to Stourbridge ... If my brother did design doing anything for me, I am much obliged to him and thank him. Give my service to him and my sister. I wish them both well.' By his sister he meant Tetty. He planned in a couple of weeks to make a complete break by emigrating to General Oglethorpe's new North American colony of Georgia. He never got there. The letter, in fact, sounds suicidal. When asked once if he thought people who committed suicide were 'mad', Johnson's reply could well have been gloomily tinged with a stabbing memory of his own brother's fate: 'Sir, they are often not universally disordered in their intellects, but one passion presses so upon them, that they yield to it, and commit suicide, as a passionate man will stab another ... I have often thought, that after a man has taken the resolution to kill himself, it is not courage in him to do any thing, however desperate, because he has nothing to fear.'

It seems Johnson believed his brother felt things too deeply, that perhaps this had been at the root of the problem between them. In his copy of John Norris's *A Collection of Miscellanies* (1699), he wrote 'my brother' next to this passage: 'It is supposed by the Ancient Fathers, that the sufferings which our Blessed Saviour underwent in his body were more afflictive to him than the same would have been to another man, upon the account of his excellency and quickness of his sense of feeling.' Johnson almost never spoke about his brother afterwards. He did not return home for the funeral, nor noted anything about him in his diary except for 'a dream of my brother' he had many years later. He stayed in London, leaving his mother alone at home with Kitty Chambers to deal with her grief and bury Nathaniel next to his father in St Michael's Church in Lichfield.[3]

[3]

In dire need of money and on Garrick's suggestion, they both applied for it to a bookseller named J(ohn?) Wilcox, whom Garrick knew slightly. Johnson informed Wilcox that he intended to earn his living as an author, which was not a good opening. Wilcox took in Johnson's 'robust frame' and suggested instead that 'he had better buy a porter's knot'. He took pity on them, however, and lent them £5 (about £500 today). Wilcox, incidentally, kept a well-stocked bookshop in Little Britain. In an interesting coincidence, Benjamin Franklin had lodged next to this same Wilcox in 1725 and borrowed many of his books 'on reasonable terms'.[4]

Johnson's first lodging was an upstairs room or garret in the house of the staymaker Richard Norris in Exeter Street, a cul-de-sac just off the north side of the Strand, costing much less than the two shillings per week that an average poor family would have to expect to pay for a small furnished room in the house of a prosperous tradesman. He came to London hoping he could make it with the measly funds he had. He devised a system whereby he could make his coins go further and yet enjoy the society of a tavern or coffee house by day or night: 'I dined ... very well for eight-pence, with very good company, at the Pine Apple in New-street just by ... It used to cost the rest a shilling, for they drank wine; but I had a cut of meat for six-pence, and bread for a penny, and gave the waiter a penny; so that I was quite well served, nay, better than the rest, for they gave the waiter nothing.'[5]

From the beginning of his London career, it was more with tavern than coffee house life that Johnson was associated. The 'tavern chair' was for him 'the throne of human felicity'. Coffee houses were commonly the haunts of 'authors by profession' but they were more like debating societies, identified frequently by political affiliations and business interests. The coffee house has been described as the 'eighteenth-century business Internet', as well as a social centre. Taverns differed according to their clientele, but normally they were quieter and more intimate, more given to controlled and private conversation than to club-like banter or raucous contests of wit. This was the sort of environment in which Johnson luxuriated and where, whether drinking and eating or not, the solace of conversation could mitigate against the loneliness of his life in his lodgings. As for drinking, Boswell wrote, 'He at this time, I believe, abstained entirely from fermented liquors: a practice to which he rigidly conformed for many years together, at different periods of his life.' But Johnson once remarked, 'Early in life I drank wine: for many years I drank none. I then for some years drank a great deal.' 'I used to slink home, when I had drunk too much,' he admitted, but whether this early drinking refers to a period before he first came to London, this first period in London, or a year or two later when he was there with his wife, is unclear.[6]

It was a revelation to him to meet daily with these locals who rarely bothered to discover each others' names, whose practical and intellectual offerings had nothing to do with who they were or where they came from. At the Pine Apple he found a rich and varied microcosm of London, patronised by a mix of high and low life, by men who were experts in a variety of fields, men who were failures and downtrodden on the edges of society, and the luckier ones who bathed in the sunshine of success and esteem. He was beginning a lasting love affair with London. 'A man is always *so near his burrow*' in London, he exulted. The city was his 'element', his 'heaven upon earth'. One of his most famous remarks was about London: 'When a man is tired of London, he is tired of life; for there is in London all that life can afford'.[7] And on a more personal note, he freely admitted that 'the spirits which I have in London make me do everything with more readiness and vigour. I can talk twice as much in London as anywhere else.' That was where, even in a garret, 'a man's own house is truly his *castle*, in which he can be in perfect safety from intrusion whenever he pleases'. He had embarked on the period of his first genuine independence, without obligations, without family and relatives, without old friends, and (dare he think it) without his wife.[8]

By choosing this area of London, Johnson landed himself in the centre of an urban vortex renowned throughout Europe. Exeter Street was in the middle of immense activity and liveliness, where he was bound to hear all the breaking news in the city and be up to date with the political ferment in which the Prime Minister Sir Robert Walpole featured so alarmingly to Tories like him, royal gossip, new publications and the latest reports about plays in the theatres. A riot in

Drury Lane Theatre, in fact, on the very day he arrived in London would have been the sensational talking point of the moment. London was a violent city whose inhabitants were regarded by foreigners as dangerously and congenitally barbarous. Things had not improved by 1762 when, on his first visit to London, Boswell could not believe the dangers and enticements of violence all around him: 'The rudeness of the English vulgar is terrible,' he wrote in his journal. 'This is indeed the liberty which they have: the liberty of bullying and being abusive with their blackguard tongues.' To make matters worse, there was no professional police force in the city, and there would be none until Sir Robert Peel established one in 1829. Lawlessness was rife. Churches stood beside houses of pimps. Sports were violent, too: cock-fights, bear and bull-baiting, and dog fights were quite common entertainments for those who wanted a different sort of dramatic entertainment to what was offered in the theatres.[9]

London's violence and brutality existed in close proximity to unexpected tranquility and breathtaking architectural and garden beauties; where the ghastly misery of poverty watered by cheap gin often coexisted obscenely with unimaginable wealth just down a street or around a corner. It was a city of coffee houses, taverns and chocolate houses, clubs and societies, of beautiful Wren churches and innumerable chapels of nonconformist religions. In his classic study *England in the Eighteenth Century*, J. H. Plumb described this melting pot comprehensively as 'rough, coarse, brutal; a world for the muscular and the aggressive and the cunning. The thin veneer of elegance and classic form obscured but never hid either the crime and dissipation or the drab middle-class virtue and thrift.'[10]

After the Great Fire in 1666 the engines of wealth and power began to generate the renovation of London in a rebuilding and extension to the west, clearing away much of the old to make place for the commercially and fashionably new. The fire was in a way a blessing because its ancient centre had burned down, allowing the laying out of wider streets and more public spaces, the envy of cities like Paris. But it was not until around the mid-eighteenth century that the pace of growth really picked up. In 1757 the houses on London Bridge were demolished and foul Fleet Ditch was filled up. A few years later the City was opened up through the removal of its ancient gates, creating more fluid movement of trade and people. The city would not have lighting and paving throughout until the first Westminster Paving Act of 1762, the year Boswell first visited: gutters and underground drains, paving-stone replacing pebbles in the main streets, and a central system of street repair and cleaning making walking in London even safer and more pleasant. In the newer areas of London to the west lovely squares were created that became the addresses of the aristocracy and rich. As a modern historian of London has put it, 'From Covent Garden through St James's to Mayfair, the West End was wide and handsome, built to please those with money to burn and time to kill.' Indeed, Georgian London took shape as a 'well-mapped topography of pleasure', but Johnson's area, Fleet Street and the Strand connecting Westminster and the City, was the place to be to watch life pass by in all its variety. 'Fleet Street has a very animated appearance', Johnson wrote in later years, and he thought that at Charing Cross could be seen 'the full tide of human existence'.[II]

Most of all, London was the genuine city of the Enlightenment, the scene of ideas-in-action, pragmatic liberty and dashing, dazzling spirit. Eighteenth-century London was truly revolutionary long before the French Revolution, 'a revolution in mood, a blaze of slogans, delivering the shock of the new'. The French *philosophes* cast their eyes across the channel to England as the cradle of the modern, and anglophiles on the Continent 'celebrated Britain's constitutional monarchy and freedom under the law, its open society, its prosperity and religious toleration'. At just the time Johnson came to London, the city was embracing a print culture that proved to be the envy of the world, with periodicals and magazines of specialised and general interest – *The Gentleman's Magazine* was the most successful of the latter kind – cropping up out of nowhere, as well as novels, prints, and even pornography, all devoured by a hungry reading public. As Johnson put it, this was an 'age of authors' – of both sexes. There seemingly were no limits or boundaries. Travellers, 'knowledge-mongers', writers, musicians, artists, and scientists, they came in great numbers from distant regions and countries to see what it was all about, and many like Handel, Haydn, Benjamin Franklin, and Pasquale Paoli, the exiled Corsican patriot, lingered or stayed to create because their geniuses found the spirit of modernity and freedom congenial. Knowledge 'generally diffused' was the icon of the age – 'society is held together by communication and information', Johnson said. What intoxicatingly flooded into Johnson's life in those first heady days in London was uniquely English: 'England's modernisers had no stomach for indigestible scholastic husks; they were not ivory-towered academics but men (and women) of letters who made their

pitch in the metropolitan market place.' Johnson very quickly came
to subscribe to the notion of the uncloistered writer playing with social
and market forces in order to get his message out to the public.[12]

[4]

He did not have Cornelius Ford to relieve what Boswell called 'the
cold obscurity' of his first months in London by introducing him to
the world of wits and letters, but Walmesley's patronage extended all
the way to London. Henry Aston Hervey, husband to Walmesley's
new sister-in-law Catherine Aston for whom Johnson had written
poems, stepped in to help him. The younger son of the first Earl of
Bristol, he kept a house in London to which he invited Johnson to
meet some polite society. Hervey was a gambler and spendthrift, but
he did not lack wit and Johnson took to him. Johnson had an 'avowed
and scarcely limited partiality for all who bore the name or boasted
the alliance of an Aston or a Hervey,' wrote Mrs Thrale. No less
incongruously than when the worldly 'Parson' Cornelius Ford became
ordained, the high-living Hervey left the army in 1742 and joined the
Church soon after. On the principle that it was better to deliver good
sermons than bad ones, Johnson wrote several of his. Late in life he
told Boswell, 'He was a vicious man, but very kind to me. If you call
a dog HERVEY, I shall love him.' The most interesting story about
Hervey's charity towards his young Lichfield friend concerns an
alleged act of gross ingratitude on Johnson's part with which Boswell
confronted him. Boswell mentioned he had heard that at one point
Hervey had 'shown him much kindness, and even relieved him from
a spunging-house' – a place kept by a bailiff where debtors were taken
before being committed to prison – but that one day at dinner with
Johnson, after he had fallen on hard times, he was arrested for debt
and taken off to prison. As this story went, when Johnson failed to
spring to his friend's defence and just kept on eating and drinking,
Hervey's sister rebuked him for ingratitude. Boswell asked Johnson if
this were true. Absolutely not, came the answer: 'Sir, I was very
intimate with that gentleman, and was once relieved by him from an
arrest; but I never was present when he was arrested, never knew that
he was arrested, and I believe he never was in difficulties after the
time when he relieved me. I loved him much ... Sir, I would have
gone to the world's end to relieve him.' That Johnson in these earliest
London years found himself in a 'spunging-house' is a measure of

how uncertain, despite Hervey's help, his future was in London.[13]

A few disconnected reminiscences of this period in his diary for 1743, like glints of light passing through almost an opaque glass, touch on what his first 'home' in London was like. There was a cat with which his landlord's wife 'fair Esther' liked to play, as well as children. On one occasion a palm reader seems to have been called in to amuse the children with an 'inspection of the hand'. For some reason he remembered a disgruntled customer on another day returning some stays. He also recalled having to pay one guinea in advance before being allowed by Norris, his landlord, or his fair wife to climb the stairs to his room. A guinea was about three months' rent. Norris's lodgings soon proved unsatisfactory, or the neighbourhood did, probably because of noise and interruption, and in a few months Johnson fled Fleet Street for Greenwich, next to the Golden Hart tavern in Church Street, where he hoped to have more peace and quiet and finish *Irene*. At Greenwich the tranquility pleased and bored him at the same time, especially the park where he was fond of walking while composing. He stayed there no more than a couple of months but carried away fond impressions of the place.[14]

In July, before leaving Greenwich with *Irene* still unfinished, he wrote again to Edward Cave. Describing himself now 'a stranger in London' and without mentioning his earlier letter from Lichfield, he proposed a specific project this time, a translation from the Italian of the seventeenth-century Catholic priest Paulo Sarpi's *History of the Council of Trent* (1619). Like the *Voyage to Abyssinia*, the project appealed to his fascination with history, in this case the convening of the Council of Trent by Pope Paul III in 1545 to decide if papal powers should be allowed to be curbed and Church doctrine liberalised by secular states. As it turned out, Church reformers and interested Protestants were disappointed and outraged as papal authority had its own way of resisting reform. Johnson was well-equipped as a historian and linguist to take on the project and as we have seen instinctively was drawn to a translation of a book in which authority in the Church and tyranny of any kind was depicted as regressive and an obstacle to the free expression of ideas in man's relationship to God. Never mind that Sarpi's book had already been translated into English back in 1619 – that did not deter him in the least. 'You cannot read three pages of the English History without discovering that the style is capable of great improvements,' he told Cave, adding that if he wanted to see a specimen demonstrating he could do it better, he should let him know. Johnson asked for a 'speedy answer' either way. But Cave, who at the time had another hefty translation project under contract that had not yet earned him any income, rejected the proposal.[15]

In spite of Johnson's economies, it was difficult to live in London with as little money as he had in his pockets. Moreover, he had made little progress with his *Irene*, which was beginning to seem like sowing seeds in arid ground, and it had been half a year since he had seen Tetty. It was time to return to her and talk about their next steps, reunite with his mother who by now had somewhat recovered from the loss of Nathaniel, and rejoin the Walmesley set with its feminine circle of Astons, especially Molly, the object of his secret longing. So at the end of the summer 1737 he made his way home for another homecoming tinged with failure. He had little to show for the last six months, though his love affair with London had been born.

CHAPTER 10

Sons of Misery:
Finding Richard Savage

[1]

Johnson stayed in Lichfield only three months. The homecoming was hardly triumphant. Returning was an appalling anticlimax to someone geared up for literary fame who for six months had tuned himself to the tempo of sprawling, disorderly London, discovering favourite haunts where he whiled away the hours talking with all manner of 'good fellows' and generally contracting an obsession with the atmosphere of taverns in late hours.

He finally completed the last two acts of *Irene* on this visit. Otherwise nothing is known of his Lichfield homecoming except for one exchange between him and his mother that had a little edge to it. When his mother lived briefly in London 'in the last age', he told Boswell thirty-six years later, there were two sets of people, 'those who gave the wall [were deferential], and those who took it; the peaceable and the quarrelsome'. When he was at home with his mother one day after his return, she somewhat contentiously, perhaps, or at least probingly, asked him whether he was 'one of those who gave the wall, or those who took it'. Whatever she was trying to stir up, he sidestepped it: '*Now*, it is fixed that every man keeps to the right; or, if one is taking the wall, another yields it, and it is never a dispute' – as if to say, 'Now, mother, let us not quarrel.'[1]

He was reminded soon enough, as in all his homecomings, that nothing was going to happen in Lichfield to launch him into a career. One thing he was not going to do was take up the reins in the bookshop. It was decided that he and Tetty would return to London together – he could not very well leave her again – but what of Lucy? Boswell wrote vaguely that she 'was left with her relations in the country', but the warmer and more logical decision would have been to have her move in with his mother and Kitty Chambers and help them run the business.[2] If this did not happen immediately, the advanced age of Sarah Johnson soon made it not only convenient but imperative. Lucy's eventual residence in the house was a great relief to Johnson and a great boost to their growing intimacy. He mischievously told Mrs Thrale that he had 'the wit' to get Lucy 'on my side' before disputing with her mother.[3] She slipped naturally into life at the house on Market Square, helping Kitty with the running of the household, supporting his ageing mother, keeping the accounts, and generally taking charge. If Johnson and Tetty had not done so before, they gave up Edial Hall, which, if it involved the sale of household effects and furniture, would have provided additional funds. So, towards the end of 1737, off they went, this time not on horseback, for what Johnson hoped would be a happier marriage in a more stimulating and successful world than Lichfield.

The nervous couple had to find lodgings, which they did first in Woodstock Street near Hanover Square and then by April 1738 at a Mrs Crow's, No. 6 Castle Street, very near desirable Cavendish Square.[4] The address was not as good as it would become in the 1760s with the elegant development of the square and adjacent areas by the aristocracy, but it was good enough. Perhaps a mantle of peace and contentment would settle on them now and replace their quarrelling, but the Cavendish Square neighbourhood was not sustainable and over the next few years they would drift closer to the 'dungeons of the Strand' and Grub Street where his work would take him.

With *Irene* finished and burning a hole in his pocket, Johnson's first priority was to get it acted on stage. He had been dragging the tragedy around in its various stages of incompleteness for well over a year and was now sure it was fit for the stage and certain of its success. The play was ostensibly the reason he came to London in the first place, and on it rode his and Tetty's hopes for the future. There was more money in having it acted than in trying to get it published; moreover, the latter would follow easily if the play were a success on stage.

Davy was not in the picture during these early days of Johnson's Grub Street life. Ambitiously, Davy had chosen instead to cultivate the influential and affluent people he thought could help him get on stage instead of applying himself to his and his brother Peter's wine business. Peter therefore had to come to London to take over from his brother, and it was he, not Davy, who helped Johnson with *Irene*. One day they walked into the Fountain tavern and read it to each other, and with Peter's encouragement he made a move. He looked up Charles Fleetwood, a Staffordshire man who since 1734 had been the major patentee of Drury Lane Theatre, to persuade him to stage it there. Fleetwood looked at it – that is about all he did – and rejected it. In a few moments Johnson's fondest hopes for a year, a major reason for coming to London, seemed dashed. Peter thought Fleetwood rejected it 'probably because it was not patronised by some man of high rank'. Even this early, Johnson's prideful, stubborn and often arrogant insistence on getting ahead by his own merits ruled out his looking for a patron. Hawkins read this streak in Johnson well: 'Bred to no profession, without relations, friends, or interest, Johnson was an adventurer in the wide world, and had his fortunes to make: the arts of insinuation and address were, in his opinion, too slow in their operation to answer his purpose; and, he rather chose to display his parts to all the world, at the risk of being thought arrogant, than to wait for the assistance of such friends as he could make, or the patronage of some individual that had power or influence, and who might have the kindness to take him by the hand, and lift him into notice.' In an essay years later Johnson wrote on how he had learned that proud independence and aggressive intellectual self-assertion do not often win friends: 'I question whether some abatement of character is not necessary to general acceptance ... the scholar whose knowledge allows no man to fancy that he instructs him, the critic who suffers no fallacy to pass undetected ... are generally praised and feared, reverenced and avoided. He that would please must rarely aim at such excellence as depresses his hearers in their own opinion ...'[5]

For the moment he had no choice but to shelve the play. There were pressing needs for income and he could not afford to waste any more time dallying with self-deluding dreams. Writing for Cave's monthly magazine still appealed to him. He told Boswell that when he first saw St John's Gate in Clerkenwell, where Cave ran his magazine, he 'beheld it with reverence'. For seven years Cave had continued to thrive with his magazine, going from strength to strength from a combination of his natural instinct for what would appeal to the public and a keen vigilance about keeping standards and sales high. Gathering himself up, Johnson took aim again at him in late winter, sending him his flattering twenty-four line Latin ode, 'Ad Urbanum', addressed to him in the pseudonym 'Sylvanus Urban' which he used in his magazine and which hinted at his targeting both urban and rural readership. Johnson referred to his speedily written Latin offering as a 'trifle' but it was a study in tact, if a little crudely sycophantic and definitely opportunistic, defending Cave against the 'rude treatment' he had suffered at the hands of rival magazines and journals such as the *London Magazine* and *Common Sense* and celebrating him, 'indefatigable man', as too great to take notice of such 'senseless sneerings of a haughty tongue'. This biographical theme would be repeated in the *Life of Cave* he wrote just after Cave died, in which he praised him for being a self-made man, one who had overcome social and economic disadvantages and 'risen to eminence' through diligence and ability. It was a quality he valued over almost all others in his biographical heroes. The poem was the work of an hour or two. Flattering as it was, how could it miss? Cave needed to raise the quality of his poetry section and this Latin poem – there was little Latin poetry in any of the magazines at that time – seemed a good way to start doing it, so he published it in March 1738 under 'S. J.' It was Johnson's first appearance in print as a London author. A parody of it appearing in the April issue of the *London Magazine* alludes to him as writing from 'Grubstreet garrets', bribed with 'ale and gin' but unable to rescue the 'mang'ling' *Gentleman's Magazine* – an allusion to Cave's successful method of taking essays from other periodicals and republishing them in digest form, severely abridged and edited.[6]

Encouraged by this success, a few days later Johnson was emboldened to write to Cave again, 'a pleasure I shall always think it to converse in any manner with an ingenious and candid man', enclosing another poem and appealing to Cave's generosity by passing it off as the work of some other needy soul in dire need of an advance: 'I do not doubt but you will look over this poem with another eye, and reward it in a different manner, from a mercenary bookseller, who counts the lines he is to purchase, and considers nothing but the bulk.' Desperate for some money, in his letter Johnson appealed to Cave's charity: as the author 'lies at present under very disadvantageous circumstances of fortune', a reply the next day is urgent, so that 'I may know what you can afford to allow him, that he may either part with it to you, or find out (which I do not expect) some other way more to his satisfaction'. By accepting this poem Cave would 'encourage learning, and relieve distress'.[7]

The offering was *London: A Poem*, an imitation of the third satire of the second-century Roman poet Juvenal. With such translations of (chiefly) Latin poetry he clearly felt his strengths as a poet, and these translations would comprise the most important and successful body of his lifelong poetic output. Recognising the energy and powerful animus in the poem, as well as its originality and currency in the present political situation, Cave immediately spotted it as a winner. Within a day or two Johnson received a small advance from him – a 'present' he called it – his first income as a London author, apparently with the seductive suggestion that the poem should be published separately by the bookseller Robert Dodsley (1703–64), who ran his business from Tully's Head, Pall Mall. It was a thrilling proposal. As a separate item, of course, the poem could command far more attention than if it were relatively hidden in the pages of *The Gentleman's Magazine*. Moreover, Dodsley was the young innovative bookseller-publisher of the hour, having set up his business by 1735 and boldly moved into the publishing world with a swift confidence, sponsoring poetry, publishing old plays, and writing plays himself. He has been described as a 'tough, neat, humorous, and determined soul'.[8]

Johnson asked Cave to send him back the poem promptly with a note for Dodsley so he could take it to him, 'read the lines to him', and see if he would consent 'to put his name in the title page'. He kept up the pretence that the poem was someone else's and that he was merely an interested intermediary and friend: 'As to the printing, if it can be set immediately about, I will be so much the author's friend as not to content myself with mere solicitations in his favour.' It is unlikely that Cave often dealt with any author, especially one totally unknown, who proposed with such exactness that five hundred copies of the poem be printed and that, in light of Cave's offer of letting all profits be kept by the author, he would repay any of the printer's costs. He even offered to repay the advance if the author reaped profits. The poem could be printed in five sheets, he added a day or two later, which would include at the bottom of each page the corresponding lines from Juvenal's poem, 'part of the beauty of the performance (if any beauty be allow'd it) consisting in adapting Juvenal's sentiments to modern facts and persons'. Johnson did take the poem to Dodsley, who paid him ten guineas outright for the copyright and published it in folio on 13 May 1738 for one shilling, just before the rising of Parliament in mid-May, without Johnson's name on the title page. Considering the poem's attacks on the Walpole ministry, Johnson may have felt it wise not to own himself the author at this point. Or if Dodsley had discovered Johnson was the author, perhaps it was he, against Johnson's wishes, who decided that anonymity might endow the poem with some mystery and curiosity and work more to his benefit than if it appeared as the work of an unknown Samuel Johnson. It was not long before a small group of people knew this man Samuel

Johnson was the author, however. Regarding the ten guineas, Johnson told Boswell he 'might, perhaps, have accepted of less' except that another (inferior) poet recently had been paid that amount and he 'would not take less' than he. Within a week the poem sold out. Dodsley wasted no time getting a second edition out a week later, and when that sold out a third edition appeared in a couple of months. Cave was not about to be left out. By agreement with Dodsley he himself published sixty-six lines of the poem in the May issue of his magazine, so the success of the poem was like a dream come true for the young author. It was a promising step on the way out of obscurity.[9]

When Alexander Pope read the poem he declared it the work of a new, serious voice and took steps immediately to find out who the poet was. His response to the information that it was a young man called Johnson was, 'He will soon be *déterré*.' So far as we know, they never met although, for seven years, they were in London at the same time – it was one of the greatest literary events that never happened: 'No, Sir, I never *saw* Pope,' Johnson once stated emphatically.[10]

He had written the poem rapidly, in three or four days. One of the sheets of the manuscript of the poem that was found in the 1920s among Boswell's manuscripts at Malahide Castle in Ireland, reveals that he composed much of the 263-line translation in his head rapidly before writing it down in a left-hand column, with revisions appearing in a column to the right. The manuscript shows all the signs of swift work: quick deletions and additions, tentative readings, discarded lines, and so on. As we shall see, his ability to compose verse on a still larger scale was a wonder even to himself – one he loved to boast about.

The urgency behind his furious speed of composition is only partly explained by the need for money. It was also the result of his anger and frustration over what he saw around him on the streets of London, in the political climate, and in his own personal, economic and professional predicament. Garrick once said the reason the poem was so successful, so 'lively and easy', was that Johnson wrote it when he was seeing much of the Herveys and 'saw a good deal of what was passing in life'. Hervey's orbit exposed him to the high life, where he could tune into the corruption, social and political, in the metropolis in a 'lively and easy' manner. But the power of the poem is far more personal and deep than that, far more internalised. It is an eruption: a crescendo of outrage, boosted perhaps by the facile, complacent conversation he heard in the Hervey circle but rooted mostly in dark thoughts that he had carried around with him and nourished from Lichfield boyhood and adolescence to Oxford, to various teaching disappointments, to Birmingham, to marriage, and now to London.

[2]

Before looking at *London* and what it tells us about Johnson's literary progress in the city, we need to get a further reading of his mental state and introduce a powerful new personality in his life who plays a major role in the poem.

On his twenty-ninth birthday in September 1738, not long after his poem came out, he composed a prayer – 'the first solemn prayer of which I have a copy,' he wrote; 'whether I composed any before this, I question.' In writing it he concocted a sort of hybrid consisting of a formal prayer following the wording of the *Book of Common Prayer* and a journal entry that satisfied his desire for communion with God and at the same time took him into private meditation and reflection on his own personal affairs and depressed mental state. 'In the days of childhood and youth, in the midst of weakness, blindness, and danger, thou hast protected me,' it begins, 'amidst afflictions of mind, body, and estate thou has supported me; and amidst vanity and wickedness thou hast spared me.' The next sentence raises themes present in virtually all his prayers for the rest of his life – guilt over squandering his talents (and thus dishonouring God) and what he calls unkindness towards others: 'enable me by thy Grace to use all diligence in redeeming the time which I have spent in sloth, vanity, and wickedness'. He prays 'to make use of thy gifts to the honour of thy Name; to lead a new life in thy Faith, Fear, and Love'. Whether the wickedness he twice mentions alludes to anything other than unkindness to others, such as sexual temptation, is open to question.[11]

A fresh boost to his disaffection and alienation, his sensations as an outsider, was also provided by someone he met in these early months in London. His name was Richard Savage. And thereby hangs a tale. Savage (1697–1743) was one of Cave's poetry contributors, one of the few poets of ability whom he began to pay for verse in 1736 as part of his gradual move to obtain original contributions for his magazine. Johnson may have met him through their work for the magazine, at St John's Gate or perhaps at a tavern for supper with Cave. Or they may have met through the influential Thomas Birch, the biographer, historian, and adviser to *The Gentleman's Magazine*, through whom

Savage made his work known to Cave. In his manuscript diary (now in the British Library) Birch never mentioned dining with both Savage and Johnson together, or even with Cave, but he did dine with them separately many times, the first time with Johnson on 22 August 1738 after the latter's emergence from the shadows with his *London*, which he knew Johnson wrote.[12]

Since Birch dined occasionally with Savage and perhaps Cave, and more often with the rising twenty-year-old poetess and classicist Elizabeth Carter (1717–1806), whose poems Cave published in his magazine and who had become a friend of Johnson's early in 1738, it is not unlikely that by early that year Johnson was also known to Savage. Savage deeply impressed him. In April Johnson seemed fascinated enough with Savage's poetry and notoriety, though it is unlikely he had yet met him, to supply Cave with an effusive Latin epigram on him as an appendage to a poem of his appearing in that month's issue of *The Gentleman's Magazine*. Translated, it reads:

> To Richard Savage, Esquire, Lover of Mankind.
> Devotion to your Fellow Man burns brightly in your Breast;
> O! that Fellow Man may cherish and protect Thee in return.

They probably got acquainted soon after Savage read this.[13]

Savage suffered from several overwhelming problems that both turned him into a national celebrity and ruined his life: continuing controversy about his birth, a persecution complex, an uncanny ability to bite the hand that fed him, reckless dissipation, and a murder in a coffee-house brawl in 1727 for which he was arrested and tried. Pope, his benefactor at the end of his life, called him 'a wrongheaded fool'.[14] He also possessed considerable charm and literary ability.

According to Savage, his bad luck began soon after his birth. He claimed he was the rejected illegitimate son of Anne, Countess of Macclesfield (wife of the second Earl of Macclesfield) through her liaison with the dissolute fourth Earl Rivers, although the evidence on balance seems to argue that he was an impostor. To his dying day he maintained he had been denied the rights of a rightful heir. The controversy was aired in the papers of the 1720s and Londoners were divided as to whether Savage was, as he claimed, the bastard repeatedly rejected and even persecuted by his mother or a bounder and brilliant impostor. Without hope of any legacy from his mother, he turned to literature. He wrote two plays, various odes and satires, and a poem titled *The Wanderer* (1729), inspired by his own wandering in endless searching and rejection, and dedicated to his patron Viscount Tyr-connel, Lady Macclesfield's nephew who half-heartedly supported his claim as her son. Two more notable poems followed in the 1730s, the scandalous *The Progress of a Divine* and *Of Public Spirit*, a scathing political satire. Johnson was especially pleased and roused by Savage's attack on the government's greedy exploitation of colonised countries in the name of progress: 'Savage has not forgotten ... to expose the enormous wickedness of making war upon barbarous nations because they cannot resist, and of invading countries because they are fruitful; of extending navigation only to propagate vice, and of visiting distant lands only to lay them waste.' Although he did not feel that *Of Public Spirit* was well-written, these two poems, in fact, attracted him to Savage as a Grub Street companion, fellow struggling poet and kindred rebel.[15]

Savage's disarming charm and wit won him many friends and patrons along the way, including the Queen, Pope, the famous actress Anne Oldfield (who, unsolicited, gave him a generous allowance without any strings attached), the poets Aaron Hill, James Thomson and David Mallet, and Lord Tyrconnel. There seemed to be no end to his supporters, although his rebelliousness and querulousness made many of them wring their hands in exasperation. But in his sensational trial for murder presided over by a notoriously harsh judge, in which he undertook his own defence, he was convicted and sentenced to hang. Through the vigorous intervention of friends, he was pardoned in March 1728. Capitalising on the huge public interest in him and his relative success as an author, and presumably out of gratitude to his supporters and the general public, a couple of years later Savage thought well enough of himself to allow Lord Tyrconnel to propose him unsuccessfully for the poet laureateship that had recently become vacant. Angry when he failed, he cheekily started writing annual birthday poems of his own to Queen Caroline in 1732 under the sobriquet, 'Volunteer Laureate'. He kept up this audacity for five years and, quite extraordinarily, the Queen rewarded him for them with five annual allowances of fifty pounds (about £5,000 today). They stopped when she died, and at about that time a quarrel with Tyrconnel also brought an end to his patronage as well. Savage got back at him for not honouring a bill of his in a letter beginning with 'Right Honourable Brute, and Booby', that conveys the flavour of his ingratitude and forms part of a minor literary genre of the eighteenth century, the Letter to a Noble Lord, only in a different key from Johnson's famous snub and rejection of the Earl of Chesterfield over the *Dictionary* in 1756.[16]

Reduced to virtual pennilessness when Johnson knew him, Savage faced the sober reality that nobody would lend him any more money if he stayed in expensive London. Pope agreed to raise money for him and give him ten pounds himself every three months provided he left for Wales immediately. He agreed and left by stagecoach for Swansea in the summer of 1739, parting from Johnson 'with tears in his eyes'. But not long after getting there he began to complain of conspiracies against him and to criticise the 'inhumanity' of his benefactors, whom he took to calling his 'persecutors and oppressors'. In a letter to him in April 1742, Pope threatened to wash his hands of him, which he and other benefactors did soon after: 'It is with concern I find so much misconstruction joined with so much resentment, in your nature. You still injure some, whom you had known many years as friends . . . but I have no weight with you.' 'While he was thus spending the day in contriving a scheme for the morrow,' Johnson wrote, 'distress stole upon him by imperceptible degrees.' Bristol friends who had courted him began to desert him. Lodging 'in the garrett of an obscure inn', the White Lion, his money completely ran out. Pope expected him to return to London at this point, as probably did Johnson, who may have received the occasional letter from him, but he had no money for the journey. Finally, early in 1743, he was arrested with three pence halfpenny in his pocket and imprisoned in Newgate prison in Bristol for a debt of eight pounds. He died there after a sudden illness at the end of July.[17]

What particularly attracted Johnson to Savage, apart from his reputation as a poet, was his rebelliousness and readiness to challenge authority, as well as his poverty and hostility towards a society that he felt had deprived him of wealth and fame and condemned him first to eke out an existence in Grub Street cranking out hack work for Cave and others, and then, finally, to end his days in Wales. Savage was for him a damaged and spent genius. Hawkins saw him as Johnson's evil genius, equipped with 'the charms that wrought on Johnson, and hid from his view those baser qualities of Savage'. They were with each other in London less than two years before Savage was exiled to Wales.[18]

Hawkins seems not to have known Savage, but as he met Johnson in the 1740s when he himself was writing for *The Gentleman's Magazine* – Johnson gave him some help with a pamphlet titled 'Six Cantatas'

(1742) – he must have known several people who did, and who had seen the two men together. Nonetheless, one must be wary of his censoriousness. In later years Hawkins became disaffected with most of Johnson's good friends and tended to censure, underplay, and misrepresent the importance of several of them, including Savage, in his biography.[19]

'They had both felt the pangs of poverty and the want of patronage,' Hawkins wrote: 'Savage had let loose his resentment against the possessors of wealth, in a collection of poems printed about the year 1727, and Johnson was ripe for an avowal of the same sentiments ... In speculations of this kind, and a mutual condolence of their fortunes, they passed many a melancholy hour.' He and Savage took to walking out at night together as night wanderers, prowling about on the fringes of society, not just in their own Grub Street territory but also in the West End where the panorama of wealth and privilege around every corner provoked their anger even more. Finding solace in each other's bitterness, once they began declaiming it was hard for them to stop: 'Johnson has told me', Hawkins wrote, that 'whole nights have been spent by him and Savage in conversations of this kind, not under the hospitable roof of a tavern, where warmth might have invigorated their spirits, and wine dispelled their care; but in a perambulation round the squares of Westminster, St James's in particular, when all the money they could both raise was less than sufficient to purchase for them the shelter and sordid comforts of a night cellar.'[20]

But Johnson himself was no pauper at this time, receiving regular pay from Cave and having his own lodgings with Tetty in Castle Street. Savage was profligate and expected others to pay for his expenses, but he too had free accommodation if he wished to take the trouble and risk the danger of walking several miles for it in the dark. As Thomas Kaminski has put it, 'Since there was no place of retirement open to both, and since Johnson was not likely to abandon his companion, the public squares had to furnish what comfort they could. Johnson and Savage wandered the streets not because they lacked the means to procure a room, but because they cherished one another's company more than sleep.' Johnson was enjoying himself, as he did all his life when he was in conversation in the deep of night. For him Savage was an intoxicating symbol of 'an exiled poetic conscience of the age'. He *wants* to go out into the cold night air with him: 'They both with the same eye saw, or believed they saw, that the then minister [Sir Robert Walpole] meditated the ruin of this country;

that excise laws, standing armies, and penal statutes were the means by which he meant to effect it; and, at the risk of their liberty, they were bent to oppose his measures.' Johnson was thrilled with the excitement of discovery, which the night framed and dramatised into hours of heightened intellectual exchange.[21]

[3]

Johnson's *London*[22] was written in the middle of this prolonged 'night dream' with Savage, just before Savage's exile to Wales. The poem is set on the banks of the Thames at Greenwich, which Johnson knew well for its pleasant walks from a year earlier, where the poet and Thales – very likely his name for Savage in the poem although many contend that Johnson completed *London* before he knew Savage – wait with 'a sense of woe' for a wherry that will sail off for 'Cambria's solitary shore' with the 'injur'd Thales' and the meagre remains of his 'dissipated wealth'. Thales raises his contemptuous eyes towards the metropolis and launches into a dramatic monologue for the rest of the poem against all those forces he and the poet had radically and disruptively attacked on their nightly prowls in Westminster, St James's Square, Grosvenor Square, and even as far as Hyde Park, 'reforming the world, dethroning princes, establishing new forms of government, and giving laws to the several states of Europe, till, fatigued at length with their legislative office, they began to feel the want of refreshment, but could not muster up more than fourpence halfpenny'. The poem could be considered as Johnson's first version of Savage's biography. It is harsh in the manner of Juvenal, but (except that it is set in the city) also reminiscent of the eighteenth-century 'night school' of poetry in its nocturnal, reverie-like, meditative, psychologically complicated overtones. Johnson is portraying them both as frustrated, disillusioned poets, 'unacknowledged legislators' of society, buried by the night and their own personal distress. Thales's monologue can be seen also as Johnson's. His success was in adapting Juvenal's catalogue of urban evils in Rome to London, without allowing the poem to become too artificial, drawing on his own anger for the individual 'fire' of the poem.[23]

Thales depicts himself for the most part as an innocent victim, but in the lines, 'what, my friend, what hope remains for me,/Who start at theft, and blush at perjury', Johnson was thinking of himself, a newcomer, with plenty to learn and plenty more to suffer after the months of hardship he already had gone through. He had eyes and could see what reigned out there, from a generalised political evil to personal venality and aristocratic foppery. He laments the 'arts of insinuation', hypocrisy, effeminacy, pretentiousness, obsequiousness, that emaciate British manliness in a culture now that has taken to acting, playing 'a borrow'd part', that 'sap[s] the principles' of 'ancient British lineaments'.

The poem also reflects his compassion for the poor and persecuted members of society. In this he proved to be nobly different from Savage who lamented losing a fortune and feared for himself more than for the victims of wickedness and folly. All Johnson's life poverty and oppression remained a highly sensitive subject for him and roused his charity. The poem speaks ironically of 'starving merit' as if one had to be poor to be virtuous. 'When I was running about this town a very poor fellow,' he wrote many years later, 'I was a great arguer for the advantages of poverty; but I was, at the same time, very sorry to be poor. Sir, all the arguments which are brought to represent poverty as no evil, show it to be evidently a great evil. You never find people labouring to convince you that you may live very happily upon a plentiful fortune.' In the city, where vice was too often rewarded, not punished, 'All crimes are safe, but hated poverty./This, only this, the rigid law pursues,/This, only this, provokes the snarling muse'. He could have been much rougher with Mrs Thrale than he was when once she 'pertly' joked at the expense of the poor in a place in London called Porridge Island. 'Come, come (says he gravely), let's have no sneering at what is serious to so many: hundreds of your fellow-creatures, dear Lady, turn another way, that they may not be tempted by the luxuries of Porridge-Island to wish for gratifications they are not able to obtain.' Mrs Thrale wrote that when he was financially able he was not content with relieving poverty but 'wished to add also indulgence. He loved the poor as I never yet saw any one else do, with an earnest desire to make them happy.' He rounded on her severely once when she lamented the dusty roads during one summer drought and wished for rain to 'lay the dust': 'I cannot bear (replied he, with much asperity and an altered look), when I know how many poor families will perish next winter for want of that bread which the present drought will deny them, to hear ladies sighing for rain, only that their complexions may not suffer from the heat, or their clothes be incommoded by the dust; – for shame! leave off such foppish lamentations, and study to relieve those whose distresses are real.'[24]

In his opinion English poetry was fairly bankrupt of emotional representation of the poor: 'Whoever studies either the poets or philosophers, will find such an account of the condition expressed by that term as his experience or observation will not easily discover to be true ... he will read of content, innocence, and cheerfulness, of health, and safety, tranquility, and freedom; of pleasures not known but to men unencumbered with possessions; and of sleep that sheds his balsamic anodynes only on the cottage.' Pope wrote about the charity of relieving the poor, he complained, but 'never saw the miseries' which he imagined 'easy to be borne'. It is not surprising, therefore, that he reserved for poverty several of the most emotional and sardonic lines in *London*, charged with autobiographical bitterness: 'Quick let us rise, the happy seats explore,/And bear oppression's insolence no more./SLOW RISES WORTH, BY POVERTY DEPRESS'D' (175–7). This is the only line in the poem completely capitalised. The poet and Thales, or Johnson and Savage, are caught in a whirlpool of neglect and poverty, struggling to avoid being sucked through the drain to ignominy and oblivion.[25]

These are private distresses, however. There are far more sinister public dangers lurking everywhere with which the poem dismally concludes:

> Prepare for death, if here at night you roam,
> And sign your will before you sup from home.
> Some fiery fop, with new commission vain,
> Who sleeps on brambles till he kills his man;
> Some frolick drunkard, reeling from a feast,
> Provokes a broil, and stabs you for a jest. (224–9)

These 'Lords of the street, and terrors of the way/ ... Their prudent insults to the poor confine', but there is no mistaking the pervasive malaise and moral sickness infecting the whole of society. At the end, without any redeeming vision of future hope, Johnson projects his own personal future as a satirist – 'In angry numbers warn'st succeeding times; ... Thy satire point ...'

It was as a moralist, not satirist, he would eventually decide to dedicate himself as a writer, but at the centre of his own work would remain this streak of anger and impatience, the rebel and radical, to which he would add the rigorousness of an ironic commentator on vanities.

[4]

Although five years elapsed between *London* and Johnson's next literary use of Savage, the logic of the connection dictates that we pass straight to it. When Savage died, Cave possessed many of his papers, including recent correspondence from Wales and Bristol, and of course copies of all his hack work for the magazine. Public interest in Savage's controversial life had subsided somewhat, but his death in a debtors' prison revived it. Johnson saw his opening and thought he had the inside track. Savage died on 1 August and in that month's issue of the *Gentleman's Magazine* appeared Johnson's letter to 'Mr Urban' (Cave) staking his claim to and advertising a project he and Cave had already plotted: a new biography of 'the unfortunate and ingenious Mr *Savage*' to be written by a person – Johnson himself – 'who was favoured with his [Savage's] confidence and received from himself an account of most of the transactions which he proposes to mention to the time of his retirement to Swansea in Wales'. 'Others may have the same design', he informed the public, but 'as it is not credible that they can obtain the same materials, it must be expected they will supply from invention the want of intelligence, and that under the title of the *Life of Savage* they will publish only a novel filled with romantic adventures and imaginary amours'.[26]

There is a note of urgency in his next letter to Cave. He had been ill but now was ready to start writing: '*The Life of Savage* I am ready to go upon and ... reckon on sending in half a sheet a day.' But he was out of money and needed candles and good pens – Cave's messenger boy had found him 'writing this, almost in the dark, when I could not quite easily read yours': 'If you could spare me another guinea ... I should take it very kindly tonight'. Once he began, he wrote briskly, staying up one entire night to write forty-eight pages 'at a sitting' and then settling down to half a sheet per day. He appears to have completed the first draft near the end of the year, when on 14 December Cave paid him fifteen guineas for the copyright of the work. On 11 February 1744, three months before the death of Pope, Savage's last patron, and two months after he was paid for finishing the job, the book came out with the title, *An Account of the Life of Mr Richard Savage, Son of the Earl Rivers*. It was well received but sold only moderately well and did not appear in a second edition until 1748.[27]

The book turned out to be one of the earliest psychological

biographies in Western literature. Instead of trying to uncover the complexity of behaviour that made up a person, biographical writing had largely been content with external historical events and well-known personal episodes, or opted for panegyric, hagiographic celebrations in order to illustrate moral lessons. Telling the truth about human nature, its shifting complex of good and evil, remained a treacherous and neglected area because it necessarily meant that the biographer had to include the good and the bad, the public and the private.

In his biography, however, Johnson at times was too ready to defend Savage. He was too inclined to accept Savage's story about parental rejection, have a high opinion of his poetry, and take his side against society. Take, for example, this misinformed and biased description of Lady Macclesfield:

> This mother is still alive, and may perhaps even yet, though her malice was so often defeated, enjoy the pleasure of reflecting that the life, which she often endeavoured to destroy, was at least shortened by maternal offices; that though she could not transport her son to the plantations, bury him in the shop of a mechanic, or hasten the hand of the public executioner, she has yet had the satisfaction of embittering all his hours, and forcing him into exigencies that hurried on his death.

The biography takes on its own life as a defiant protest. It did not matter to him that he had not properly researched Savage's claims, nor talked to enough people who had known him. It was enough that, as in *London*, he was ready to strike at the amorphous, quashing, nullifying spectre of authority. In the process, he made the work also into a kind of autobiography. He pictured himself a troubled, struggling, angry soul on the ragged edge of society, looking up with Savage at the well-lit windows of the powerful and great in the squares of Westminster and St James's from the cold streets below. If he portrayed Savage as 'the Poet as Outcast', some of that colouring spilled on him, too.[28]

Among the most interesting passages are those that tell us about Savage and himself at the same time. Although he only once drew attention to or mentioned himself as a character in the drama, he is there as the silent witness playing the part of a companion of the night. Much of the detail is so particular that he could not have learned of it except by actually being present. In the following famous passage, for example, read 'we' for 'he':

He lodged as much by accident as he dined, and passed the night sometimes in mean houses, which are set open at night to any casual wanderers, sometimes in cellars, among the riot and filth of the meanest and most profligate of the rabble; and sometimes, when he had not money to support even the expenses of these receptacles, walked about the street till he was weary, and lay down in the summer upon a bulk, or in the winter, with his associates in poverty, among the ashes of a glass-house.

They must have spent enough nights like this for Johnson conceivably to project it as, at times, a pattern of existence for them both: glass-houses were small factories where glass of all kinds was melted and reprocessed in ovens, leaving large amounts of warm grey ash in which tramps bedded down for the night. Bulks were wooden stalls at the front of shops where food could be laid during the day and on which by night tramps could find relief from lying on cold stone. 'Mean houses' and cellars rounded off the bedding accommodation for the two night prowlers: the former were vile-smelling places of public lodging with wooden bunks for one penny per night, the latter small basement doss-houses filled with filthy sacks and people. In later years Johnson liked to tell people about these wild and raw nights, as exhilarated by the memory as he had been by the actual experience. 'Elevated speculations, useful studies, or pleasing conversation', Johnson wrote in the *Life*, were on the menu every night.[29]

Johnson gradually grew more critical of Savage as the biography progressed, and though remaining sympathetic moved away from his earlier emotional identification with him by exposing his tragically flawed response to the brutal realities of poverty in Grub Street and later in Wales.[30] This exposure also resonates with autobiographical echoes, such as in his mention of Savage's ungrateful pride in the face of charity: 'he never submitted to be treated otherwise than as an equal' and became harshly indignant if he was not. There is a passage, in fact, based on first-hand information, that brings to mind the humiliating Pembroke College shoes episode:

His clothes were worn out, and he received notice that at a coffee-house some clothes and linen were left for him – the person who sent them did not, I believe, inform him to whom he was obliged, that he might spare the perplexity of acknowledging the benefit – but though the offer was so far generous it was made with some neglect of ceremonies, which Mr Savage so much resented that he refused the present, and declined to enter the house till the clothes that had been designed for him were taken away.

Johnson read in Savage's final months and years a cautionary moral tale, a Grub Street tragedy of poverty that sounded alarm bells for him in this early period of his own career.[31]

Johnson saw Savage's lack of realism as grotesque, epitomised by his flights of fancy that Wales would become his rural paradise. This sort of pastoral nonsense, 'flattering the imagination with Arcadian scenes', was already for Johnson – the country boy who understood the realities of rural life – a species of wanton wastefulness, allowing life to slide away without self-examination. The Welsh idyll that seduced Savage destroyed him, but so did insensitive and clumsy efforts to alleviate his poverty. Johnson was enraged by society's obtuse, clumsy, ill-conceived philanthropy that organised Savage's 'miseries of dependence' and coerced him to go west. Nobody comes off very well in this biography.[32]

At the end of the book Johnson returned once again to a personal theme that by 1743 had become his own permanent cross to bear – the fear of loneliness and melancholia:

> He was generally censured for not knowing when to retire, but that was not the defect of his judgement, but of his fortune; when he left his company he was frequently to spend the remaining part of the night in the street, or at least was abandoned to gloomy reflections, which it is not strange that he delayed as long as he could; and sometimes forgot that he gave others pain to avoid it himself.

'Those are not proper judges of his conduct', he added, 'who have slumbered away their time on the down of plenty, nor will any wise man presume to say, "Had I been in Savage's condition, I should have lived or written better than Savage."' One can either succumb, however, as Savage ultimately did, or fight on. Johnson himself was a fighter and he felt he had earned the right also to declare from his heart, without yet having tasted the success for which he was battling in Grub Street, that prudence, patience and courage were resources available to all in times of affliction: 'This relation will not be wholly without its use if those who languish under any part of his sufferings shall be enabled to fortify their patience by reflecting that they feel only those afflictions from which the abilities of Savage did not exempt him ... Negligence and irregularity long continued will make knowledge useless, wit ridiculous, and genius contemptible.'[33]

CHAPTER II

'Slow Rises Worth by Poverty Depress'd'

[1]

After the artistic success of *London* and as he pushed Cave to agree to publish his translation of Sarpi's *History of the Council of Trent*, Johnson was certain he had the genius, courage and resilience to succeed in the uphill journey of establishing his literary reputation in London and earning a good income through it. At this point in Johnson's career, Cave was exactly what he needed in the way of a publisher. An honest if slow and methodical man, he was totally reliable and never kept his authors in doubt about what he thought of their writing. He also imposed strict deadlines and paid promptly. Hawkins, who began to write for the magazine in 1739, did not like him or his taciturn manner and claimed that Johnson 'saw very clearly those offensive particulars that made a part of Cave's character'. This might have been so, but Johnson also appreciated them. From his first meaningful contacts with Cave he had the highest regard for his practical literary instincts in sniffing out a good piece of prose and shaping it for his magazine. It was no accident that in eight years his magazine had become one of the most widely read in London. After Cave's death in 1754 Johnson wrote a memoir of him for *The Gentleman's Magazine* in which he admiringly remembered how Cave's taciturnity brought results: 'The same chillness of mind was observable in his conversation; he was watching the minutest accent of those whom he disgusted by seeming inattention; and his visitant was surprised when he came a second time, by preparations to execute the scheme which he [was] supposed never to have heard.' Although Johnson on his death-bed recalled Cave was a 'penurious paymaster', in these early years he was under no illusions about the going rates for hack-writing. Cave paid not significantly worse or better than other magazine editors.[1]

Until the late seventeenth century, the English press was not very free. Licensing acts enforced controls that protected the government from criticism and the Stationers' Company enjoyed a control of commercial publishing that effectively enabled it to monopolise the book trade. Near the end of the century there were only twenty master printers in London and fewer than two hundred people employed in the printing trade. It was a lucrative enough profession for those few but it was exclusive. In 1695 the Licensing Act lapsed, which removed censorship before publication, and although censorship of one kind or another persisted and taxes continued to cramp printers and publishers it was not long before this freedom bred a new and numerous generation of people in the trade. Presses sprang up in London and all over the country, making the English press the freest and most energetic in the world. By 1750 Samuel Richardson, the internationally successful author of *Pamela* and *Clarissa* and by profession a master printer, ran nine presses in his premises at Salisbury Court clattering away with about forty journeymen busy at work. Unlike Johnson, who in his youth had had enough of the bookseller's life and assiduously avoided anything to do with manufacturing and retailing books, he died rich.[2]

The new print culture into which Johnson launched himself without reservation in 1738 required some hard-headed realism. Print culture freed the author from the uncertain pursuit of patronage, but it also created its own uncertainties and pressures. For one thing, as we have already seen, it was chaotic, vulnerable to the constantly moveable feast of shifting commercial forces instead of the whims of a patron. For another, everyone seemed to be getting into the act, from all sorts of social classes and with uneven literary results. One historian of English print culture explains that print technology not only made 'simple fools into hack writers', but also turned 'honest mechanics into greedy printers and simple tradesmen into booksellers without scruples, taste, or morality, willing to steal and publish anything that will sell'. The worry was that England's literary culture would be corrupted by the growing and cheapening mass commercialism of print, contaminating the moral fabric of society, from politics to philosophy: 'A flood of printer's ink was a darkness that spread across the land, staining, as in [Pope's] memorable image of Fleet ditch running into the silver Thames, the white page, darkening the minds of the people and their rulers, obliterating polite letters.'[3]

Johnson himself wrote satirically of 'the itch of literary praise' in what had become 'the epidemical conspiracy for the destruction of paper': 'If we consider chiefly the state of our own country, [it] may be styled with great propriety The Age of Authors ... The province of writing was formerly left to those, who by study, or appearance of study, were supposed to have gained knowledge unattainable by the busy part of mankind; but in these enlightened days, every man is qualified to instruct every other man.' At the same time, he understood that print culture was now a way of life and that if he was to succeed as an author he had to plug into his age's version of 'on-line'.[4]

At the centre of this print whirlwind in London were the booksellers. A new Licensing Act in 1709 in theory threatened more explicitly than ever before their claim to own copyright, but in practice it was fairly ignored. When the bookseller commissioned or bought a work from an author, existing common law provided that he also bought the copyright and owned it in perpetuity – this in spite of the new Licensing Act granting him ownership of it for only twenty-one years in the case of existing works and fourteen for new works. It was not until 1774 that the House of Lords – in a legal case in which Boswell played a significant part – passed legislation outlawing perpetual copyright once and for always, which, in fact, had always been illegal. Booksellers were so powerful in the eighteenth-century publishing world that they had possession of copyright pretty much their own way in the intervening years.

Authors, printers, couriers – they were all dependent on the bookseller. He hired the printer and invested his money in producing the book. If he succeeded, he kept all the profits; if he failed, he absorbed all the losses. Once the author sold the book and got paid, he was out of the picture completely, earning no royalties whatever. Moreover, the bookseller commanded virtually all the resources of distribution. It was not a level playing field for the other players. Those in the printing business who decided to go out on a limb to buy copyrights from authors and publish books themselves had to scramble to round up anything like a decent distribution. There were entrepreneurial trade publishers who would occasionally try to beat the system which booksellers tyrannised by publishing works, the copyrights of which were owned by others, under their own imprint, but such efforts were minimal. If a bookseller decided to challenge such a publication with bad publicity, he could usually succeed. Johnson's estimation of booksellers was that they looked on any author as 'criminal' who tried 'to enjoy more advantage from his own works than they are disposed to allow him', such as by getting a printer to print his work directly, leaving out the bookseller, and tasting some royalties.[5]

So as Johnson plunged into the universe of London publishing he had two broad choices. He could try cultivating booksellers and sell them his original work or take the more common, safer, anonymous route for aspiring authors via the periodical press. To put it another way, he was already writing literature in its broad eighteenth-century meaning – at times grumbling about his role as a translator for book-sellers – and trying to be a poet. Thus far he had been unsuccessful with *Irene* but had managed to establish a promising relationship with Robert Dodsley by selling *London: A Poem* to him for ten guineas with Cave's help. This was the sort of writing he wished to do, but it was the more difficult route because he could not produce such works regularly enough to earn an income on which he and Tetty could live. As an unknown writer he would be paid little for such writing. Fifteen guineas for the 180 octavo pages of the *Life of Savage* was not much of an improvement on the ten guineas for *London*. He had no choice but to pursue the second alternative.

As the most successful entrepreneurial magazine publisher and editor in London, Cave was the obvious man with whom to link up, but Johnson understood the depressing dangers of becoming a Grub Street hack, which he articulated autobiographically years later in the *Rambler* with a retrospective shiver. These 'manufacturers of lit-erature', he wrote, 'have set up for authors, either with or without regular initiation, and, like other artificers, have no other care than to deliver their tale of wares at the stated time':

> They have seldom any claim to the trade of writing but that they have tried some other without success. They perceive no particular summons to composition except the sound of the clock. They have no other rule than the law or the fashion of admitting their thoughts or rejecting them. And about the opinion of posterity they have little solicitude, for their productions are seldom intended to remain in the world for longer than a week.

He also had another potential problem, procrastination and idleness. 'I had books of every kind round me,' he recalled a decade later, 'among which I divided my time as caprice or accident directed. I often spent the first hours of the day, in considering to what study I should devote the rest; and at last snatched up any author that lay upon the table, or perhaps, fled to a coffee house for deliverance from the anxiety of irresolution, and the gloominess of solitude.' Like the poor soul who was driven out of his 'literary slumber' by a creditor, he had not proved to be one of those 'heroes of negligence' who could easily turn 'the dignity of imprudence' to his advantage.[6]

Nonetheless, he could always begin with Cave in a tentative sort of way as an interim measure. The variety of ways he could contribute to the magazine – criticism, poetry, essays, histories, translations, reviews, biographies, journalistic reporting, editorial work – might prove to be enlivening and a means of broadening his grasp of British and foreign contemporary affairs and literature. As a matter of fact, like many editors of the mushrooming magazines in the city Cave was in dire need of someone who could write distinguished prose and poetry, who knew Latin, Greek, French and Italian, who was widely read, and who possessed a journalist-editor's instinct for revision and public appeal. He needed Johnson, just as Johnson needed him.

[2]

Johnson had already shown Cave his poetic prowess and epigrammatic talents and was eager to show him more. Latin and Greek poetry such as he could write easily on demand, the work of a minute, was highly unusual in a periodical magazine and had already given Cave's poetry section a sudden leg up on the *London Magazine* and other competitors. 'I have composed a Greek epigram to Eliza and think she ought to be celebrated in as many different languages as Lewis le Grand,' he wrote to Cave in April 1738 about the young authoress Elizabeth Carter. It delighted everyone, especially Carter, when Cave published it that month. In July appeared another Latin poem of his in praise of Eliza, followed by his translation of it in August, 'To Eliza Plucking Laurel in Mr Pope's Garden'. He signed it 'Urbanus', a way of indicating that the piece was from the office of Sylvanus Urban, Cave's *nom de plume*. The poem alludes to Pope's geniality and generosity in allowing Eliza to pluck her laurel from a branch as a tribute to her recognition as a poet. To reach the garden, incidentally, he would have needed first to pass through Pope's equally famous grotto, an inspiration, perhaps, for his later translation into Latin of Pope's verses on the grotto, published in *The Gentleman's Magazine* five years later.[7]

In the next few months Cave published others of his short poems. He took these pieces eagerly, together with excerpts from *London: A Poem* that he published in May. He was delighted, ranking *London:*

A Poem that month as number one in his register of books while Pope's poem *One Thousand Seven Hundred and Thirty-Eight* came in at only number twenty-two. Here was a new poet better than Pope. All the signs were that Johnson would follow up *London: A Poem* with more verse satire, modelled again on Juvenal or Horace. Nothing would have been more natural or expected.

But occasional verses, least of all epigrams, were not going to pay the bills. He needed more substantial, regular links to the magazine. In short, he needed to write prose for it – more words meant more printer's sheets filled, and more sheets meant more money. He said on his deathbed that Cave contracted 'for lines by the hundred'. Pressing him again regarding the translation of Paulo Sarpi's *Council of Trent*, he caught his interest this time and in July began working on it, receiving regular payments. These first payments made such an impression on him that he carefully recorded them on a slip of paper entitled, 'Account between Mr Edward Cave and Sam. Johnson, in relation to a version of Father Paul, &c. begun August the 2d, 1738'. Such a translation suited Cave. He badly wanted to rise in the publishing trade, like the fabulously successful Samuel Richardson, from printer and magazine publisher to the more lucrative and prestigious realm of book publishing. Authors were not about to offer him their manuscripts, however, unless he had achieved some reputation as a publisher of larger works. It was slow work but he was getting there and Johnson came along just at the right time.[8]

In less than three months after returning to London, Johnson had managed to win Cave's confidence by several means. One was personal testimony. Cave's office was a quiet, businesslike sort of place where only a few workers spent their time and where contributors were not often seen. Alehouses, coffee houses, and private dinners at homes were more likely meeting places. Birch and Savage, and also Moses Browne and Samuel Boyse, were among those few contributors with whom Cave seems to have developed personal relationships, although the snobbish Birch thought himself superior to Cave and his Grub Street world. All of them could be counted on to speak well to Cave of this young, energetic literary dynamo, his extensive reading, ideas, poetic sophistication, useful potential as a translator, and fascination with foreign (especially exotic) lands. Also impressive was his curiosity about the 'general principles of every science' which since boyhood he had dedicated himself to possess – to 'grasp the trunk' of knowledge and 'shake all the branches', as he once put it. He described his early years as so much 'running about the world with my wits ready to observe, and my tongue ready to talk'. It is revealing that with the exception of Pope and Dodsley, Johnson's earliest literary 'patronage' in London was from word-mongers and peddlers of sentences in the print factories, not from established writers and people of note and influence.

The darling of this group, the one whose testimony may have penetrated Cave's taciturnity more than the others, was Elizabeth Carter. Carter's was the most impressive female intellect he would ever encounter. The daughter of the Revd Nicholas Carter in Kent, who was an accomplished classical scholar, she was taught by her father and worked assiduously throughout her Kentish youth in Deal to attain a command of Greek and modern languages, becoming at a young age one of the most distinguished female poets and scholars in Johnson's lifetime. She had been writing poetry for Cave's magazine since 1734. It was through Cave that she first met Johnson in April 1738 – 'Poor dear Cave,' he wrote to her years later after Cave's death, 'I owed him much, for to him I owe that I have known you.' Johnson loved her at once for her blend of modesty, confident piety, intellectual brilliance and poetical talents. He once said of her, 'My old friend Carter ... could make a pudding as well as translate Epictetus from the Greek, and work a handkerchief as well as compose a poem'. He also admired her clear-headed moral understanding and independent spirit in believing that 'women had not their proper station in society, and that their mental powers were not rated sufficiently high'. Cave and his wife were very attentive to her, Birch seems to have fallen in love with her, and Johnson (eight years older) took her under his wing, becoming in a way her mentor. Occasionally, she wrote to her father back in Kent about him, apparently revelling in his attentions. Her father replied sceptically, 'You mention Johnson; but that is a name with which I am utterly unacquainted. Neither his scholastic, critical, or poetical character ever reached my ears. I a little suspect his judgement, if he is very fond of Martial.'[9]

One innovation of Cave's for the magazine especially caught Johnson's imagination. He hired William Guthrie to attend the House of Commons and Lords and report the debates there himself for the magazine instead of simply taking and digesting reports from rival periodicals, which he had been doing since 1732, much to the annoyance of his rivals. Guthrie had begun these in February 1738, but he wrote merely competently and Cave needed someone to turn them

into brisker and more imaginative prose. Johnson took them in hand
in June and in the process slid gently into the role of Cave's fellow-
editor and soon enough even his right-hand man.

Cave deployed a way of circumventing fresh parliamentary restrictions on the reporting of the debates in 1738. The Commons at that
time did not want any reporting published in the papers even during
the recess; nor did it want speakers identified by name. Either he or
Johnson hit on the clever device, adapted from the *London Magazine*,
of framing the debates as 'Debates in the Senate of Magna Lilliputia',
taking advantage of the resonating irony of Swift's consummate satire
in *Gulliver's Travels* a decade earlier. In June Cave duly published an
introduction to the Lilliputian scheme, 'State of Affairs in Lilliput',
that bears signs of Johnson's style, especially in the satiric attacks on
the government.[10]

The elaborate artifice begins with Gulliver's grandson sailing to
Lilliput to set the record straight about his grandfather. Lilliput,
Blefescu, and other kingdoms in the region, he finds, exactly resemble
Europe, and several institutions in Lilliput, mainly its parliament,
correspond perfectly to England's. Parliamentarians in Lilliput are
coyly given names resembling (but strategically not the same as) the
main players in Britain's parliament, so nobody could be in any doubt
about who was meant. This ironic camouflage created the freedom to
report and embellish the debates without fear of prosecution. While
Johnson was asked to look over Guthrie's prose, he also did a good bit
of the writing of the debates himself. It was a brilliant idea that
brought vigour and fresh esteem to the magazine, especially at a time
when Sir Robert Walpole was in the final tumultuous phase of his
rule and particularly vulnerable to such satire under the pretence of
objective reporting.

There was also a flurry of harsh pieces which Cave gave Johnson
the opportunity to write, including his first original paragraphs for
the magazine, a 'letter' from 'Eubulus' on the arrogance of British
colonialism in China. He also wrote current affairs articles on the
moral question of condolences raised by the ill-timed and ill-conceived
parliamentary panegyrics on the late Queen – his comments were also
bitterly anti-Hanoverian – and on epitaph-writing. The latter two
especially roused his anger over effusive, facile and self-regarding
expressions of sympathy which only make a sufferer feel more grief
and show frivolous insensitivity to fearful death.[11]

A couple of months after Johnson began revising Guthrie, he

became bored of sifting through his collaborator's prose. Cave apparently had a few stiff words with him about his letting too much of Guthrie's writing go unrevised, for in an August letter Johnson was defending himself:

> You seem to insinuate that I had promised more than I am ready to perform. If I have raised your expectations by any thing that may have escaped my memory I am sorry, and if you remind me of it shall thank you for the favour. If I made fewer alterations than usual in the debates it was only because there appeared, and still appears to me to be less need of alteration.

He was also unhappy about some new work for the poetry section. Cave asked him to judge poetry submitted on 'the Divine attributes' for one of the magazine's poetry prizes of £40 – a competition announced two years earlier and, given the subject, not eliciting much response from the readership. It meant a little more money so Johnson agreed, but he was constitutionally opposed to judging other people's verse in such an artificial exercise and tried to beg off, admitting 'a backwardness to determine degrees of merit, [which] is nothing peculiar to me'. He would do it if he had to, but 'I shall engage with little spirit in an affair, which I shall *hardly* end to my own satisfaction, and *certainly* not to the satisfaction of the parties concerned.' The competition eventually petered out the following year. The same ennui or depression, or perhaps problems with Tetty – all these could have been connected – struck at his translating of Sarpi: 'As to Father Paul, I have not yet been just to my proposal,' he informed Cave in August, 'but have met with impediments which I hope are now at an end, and if you find the progress hereafter not such as you have a right to expect, you can easily stimulate a negligent translator.' Cave probably did 'stimulate' him in some way – probably with a little money – because the work resumed and in October no fewer than six thousand copies of Johnson's proposal for the translation were published, with his name appearing attached to it.[12]

[3]

His first biographical offering, a 'Life of Sarpi', appeared in the November issue of *The Gentleman's Magazine* signed 'S. J.' and identifying him clearly as the translator of Sarpi. It was the magazine's means of advertising the translation Johnson had been at work on for almost half a year. Publicity was suddenly needed because soon after the proposals were published a rival translator reared his head who threatened to scuttle the whole Sarpi enterprise. Instead of backing off from the competition, Johnson and Cave decided to fight back by providing a sample biography, showing how well the translator could write and how fortunate the subscribers were to have him on the job. What it really illustrated was Johnson's powers not as a biographer but as a translator, since it is merely a severely abridged translation of an existing biography with a few of his own perspectives on Sarpi thrown in – at least to the extent that his single source could inspire any.

Cave then asked him to write a biographical piece on the famed Hermann Boerhaave, the celebrated Dutch physician and Professor of Physick at Leiden who had just died on 23 September. Johnson was naturally interested in Boerhaave because his work was responsible for 'the most widespread assumptions of medical thought' just at the time he himself was studying medicine, especially 'the study of physic'. Again, he simply took a Latin eulogium on the physician published in Leiden and wrote another translation and abridgement. Unusually lengthy for the magazine, the 'Life of Boerhaave' was published anonymously over four issues beginning in January 1739. A measure of its importance in eighteenth-century medical thought at the time is that it was included slightly revised in Robert James's *Medicinal Dictionary* in 1742 and then again in the *Universal Magazine* for 1743. James depended upon its systematised presentation of Boerhaave's and other medical knowledge in several of his later writings, including his *Modern Practice of Physic* (1746).[13]

In both these lives of Sarpi and Boerhaave he was using a single source from which to translate, and although his tactical abridgement of each shows his brilliance in taking a longer work and casting it into rhythmical and balanced English prose, he did not see himself as what we think of as a fully fledged biographer. Nor was he interested in doing any biographical research. He focused more on reflections on human nature than on researched facts. Boerhaave possessed two qualities which in Johnson's mind were among the most important in his idea of a hero: usefulness to society and, above all, self-confidence. The latter is a theme in all his biographies, a quality he extolled for the rest of his life. Without it, no human excellence and achievement was possible. It was a quality he himself clearly possessed, and knew he possessed, even if he was not sure at this point where it was leading him and what good he would be able to do society with it.[14]

Another idea for a translation that Cave and Johnson may have come up with together was that of the Swiss theologian Jean-Pierre de Crousaz's controversial attack on Pope's poem *An Essay on Man* (1733) in 1735–6. Crousaz had not liked Pope's deism in the poem, its fashionable secular moralising about man and the universe and what he thought were its logical contradictions. He condemned it in the name of both morality and religion. Cave thought Crousaz's *Commentary*, if translated, could pick up on the buzz Crousaz had caused in London. Perhaps Pope, who was taken aback by the furore, would also appreciate it. Johnson did not much like Pope's determinism either, but unlike Crousaz he was in a position to defend the brilliance of Pope's verse. The project almost collapsed when the disreputable bookseller Edmund Curll beat Cave and Johnson to it with his own translation of Crousaz. Although Cave was in no doubt that Johnson could produce a far superior translation, he thought they should consider abandoning ship, with which Johnson, stymied and disappointed, agreed: 'I am pretty much of your opinion, that the Commentary cannot be prosecuted with any appearance of success, for as the names of the authors concerned are of more weight in the performance than its own intrinsic merit, the public will be soon satisfied with it.' However, Cave then decided to push on since Curll had brought out only part of Crousaz's work and Cave thought that the whole of it might be marketable. Johnson took it up and wrote it at a furious pace, Boswell recording in his journal that he wrote six sheets of forty-eight quarto pages in one superhuman day. Cave had most of the 300-page book printed but did not publish it until November 1741, under his own imprint and without Johnson's name. It included notes by Johnson that are of particular interest because they are among his first published criticism. Cave was still sitting on unsold copies a couple of years later. Not for the first time, this publication was an unhappy literary exercise for Johnson, characterised by disappointments of money, time and lack of recognition.[15]

[4]

By April 1739, he had completed about fifty sheets of *Sarpi*, some four hundred quarto pages, a staggering amount in such a short time – four times as long as the *Crousaz*. Hence the shock when, only a quarter of the way through, Cave terminated his work. Formidable competition from a rival translator, however, turned out to be too much for them in spite of Johnson's having staked his claim with his 'Life of Sarpi'. It was too risky for Cave. Johnson's huge scholarly investment was suddenly all for nothing. Worse yet, his manuscript disappeared into the recesses of St John's Gate and was never seen again. At this point his publishing scorecard did not inspire confidence. *Irene* remained neglected, *Sarpi* had come to nothing, and *Crousaz* did little for his public reputation. He had done much to redefine and invigorate *The Gentleman's Magazine*, but hack work was hack work and he remained buried by it. He felt cheated. In his writing he had sublimated much of his anger and rebelliousness in nuanced moral reflections on a variety of subjects, but there was no mistaking the underlying acerbic tone of his thinking. Cave knew he had an angry genius on his hands who, among other things, was radicalising his magazine, prepared to lash out at many targets. The one element in Johnson's work, in fact, that sustained his morale was his satiric impulse, serving as a type of pressure valve, an original and creative release to vary the drudgery of editorial work. This was especially evident in the satirical muscles he flexed during a London periodical warfare fought for several months early in 1739, with Johnson leading the charge on behalf of the magazine and articulating various arguments against biased political writing in the public press. Cave put a stop to it in the spring fearing that his 'oracle', as someone called Johnson, was putting at risk his magazine's reputation for fairness and reliability.[16]

What were Johnson's mature views on Tories and Whigs? They certainly are not understandable in terms of neat modern oppositions between conservative and liberal, the right and left. 'A wise Tory and a wise Whig, I believe, will agree,' he insisted. 'Their principles are the same, though their modes of thinking are different.' The traditional myth of Tory Johnson that is part of the popular conception of him, and has been ever since the end of the eighteenth century, makes him into a stiff and backward-looking conservative, an unreserved defender of aristocratic hierarchy, sceptical of change, and intolerant of new ideas, especially if they threaten the established order.

A number of Johnson's Tory positions, however, were in fact strongly liberal. To be sure, he never equivocated his defence of the Church of England and its role in the lives of Englishmen. But notwithstanding his Tory-like isolationism, he was always hugely concerned, as we have seen, for the welfare of native peoples in distant and exotic lands threatened by the imperialistic policies of powerful nations; and he was always fascinated with, and frequently wrote about, their customs and manners. He was an economic isolationist, a Little Englander, stridently opposed to foreign military ventures on behalf of global British commercial interests. But in this he was, as has often been pointed out, in line with Walpole who strongly opposed such expensive and exploitative foreign policy and was frequently attacked for it by the country's powerful trading interests in the East India and South Sea companies. Johnson later despised the Whig William Pitt for ambitious foreign policies that took Britain into war – in America, for example – in greedy pursuit of economic expansionism. As Donald Greene has pointed out, this did not mean that Johnson was opposed to trade and industry, for (not surprisingly, given his own bourgeois family background) he championed the middle classes and economic policy that would ameliorate the suffering and wants of the needy in his country – and in this, he supported Pitt against the growing wealth of the Whig aristocracy. Politically, he was horrified by the threat of civil conflict from any quarter, and the accompanying spectre of anarchy, but at the same time he was very critical of the abuses of monarchs. He also felt that if Britain had to fight a war to protect itself and its reasonable interests, it should do so mightily. He did not wish America to be exploited commercially by Britain, but his anti-Americanism and vigorous desire to win the War of Independence sprang from what he regarded as the colonies' fraudulent arguments for independence and propagandistic and populist distortion of the history of their relationship to Britain.[17]

Johnson's political attitudes sprang from his embracing humanitarian heart, his distrust and scepticism where oppressive power raised its ugly head, his rooting for the underdog and all kinds of minority groups, his unwavering anti-slavery stance – all of this without creating dangers of anarchy, which he feared and hated. His charitable acts were legendary. He was highly sceptical of grandiose political plans and ingenious theories for social improvement. For his most social and political attitudes he drew simply on his own career as an ordinary citizen and human being, on 'the heart of man', not on the vagaries of political affiliations. That was where his power rested as a moralist, social and literary critic, and political satirist.

Little that he wrote was more venomous than a fifty-page pamphlet attacking Walpole in May which he titled *Marmor Norfolciense*. In this clever tour de force by a 'true Briton', as Boswell wrote rather simplistically, 'he, in a feigned inscription, supposed to have been found in Norfolk, the county of Sir Robert Walpole, then the obnoxious prime minister of this country, inveighs against the Brunswick succession, and the measures of government consequent upon it.'[18]

The Brunswick succession needs some explaining as it was another complication in Johnson's political thinking. George I had been the Duke of Brunswick-Luneburg, a historical state within the Holy Roman Empire, when the English parliament passed the Act of Settlement in 1701 placing his mother Sophia, the electress of Hanover and granddaughter of James I, first in the line of succession to the Crown. When Queen Anne died in 1714, George I became the first Hanoverian king and the Whigs returned to power in force. After the succession, however, there lingered increasingly marginal and wistful Jacobite (from the Latin *Jacobus* or 'James') sympathies in Britain for the banished James II and his return to the throne. To what extent Johnson harboured such sympathies has been hotly debated, especially in the past twenty years or so, but it is probably fair to say his was only a lukewarm attachment to Jacobitism blended with a strong dislike of Georges I and II. He was never active in support of the cause and it is certain he never wished for another constitutional crisis connected with the monarchy.

In *Marmor Norfolciense*, with 'warm anti-Hanoverian zeal', Johnson lacerated Walpole's ministry and its venal hangers-on as well as George II and kings in general. His pamphlet, as Hawkins wrote in his painful prose, consists of 'an invective against a standing army, a ridicule of the balance of power, complaints of the inactivity [i.e. cowardice] of the British lion, and that the Hanover horse was suffered to suck his blood'. Johnson enjoyed writing the pamphlet as a way of releasing his political frustrations – Pope read it and thought it was 'very humorous' – but he was harsh and deadly serious, brimming with righteous indignation. It is also recklessly angry. He spitefully attacked not only foreign policy, especially as regards the overly pacific attitude towards Spain, but also the King's morals, frivolity and intelligence, adding the brazenly Jacobite line, 'Kings change their laws, and kingdoms change their kings'. With this kind of personal innuendo against the monarch, several pages long, Johnson stood apart from most Opposition writers. It was nearly treasonous. One story Hawkins told, suspicious because the authorities would have had no trouble finding him, is that the ministry identified him as the author and initiated proceedings, forcing him and Tetty both to go into hiding in a hide-away in Lambeth Marsh until the matter blew over.[19]

One of his targets in *Marmor Norfolciense* is censorship of anti-government publications, another subject that raised his temperature so much that in less than three weeks he wrote another biting pamphlet, *A Compleat Vindication of the Licensers of the Stage*, against the abuse of liberty as well as many of the corruptions of the Walpole government he had denounced in the earlier pamphlet. Adopting Swiftian satire again, he ironically portrayed Walpole's vindicator defending all that he hated about the secrecy and obscurantism of his government. Johnson's disgust here dated back to the Government's passing of a new Licensing Act in 1737 granting and publicising new measures for the examination and suppression of plays that attacked the Walpole government. Such powers had long existed but this Act's blatant and public declaration of them especially angered Johnson and many others. His revulsion over the obscene arrogance and arrogation of power at the expense of the individual in a flawed social system plays into this pamphlet.

The autobiographical content of these pamphlets is not found in whether Johnson was now, and later, a Whig in Tory clothing, or a Whiggish Tory, or a Toryish Whig, or just a Tory. As we have seen, he hated the excesses of party politics. Hawkins and Boswell both went so far as to maintain that he had 'a high opinion' of Walpole: 'He said of him, that he was a fine fellow, and that his very enemies deemed him so before his death: he honoured his memory for having kept this country in peace many years, as also for the goodness and placability of his temper.' Rather, the pamphlets speak volumes about his social and private persona. The Government's system of forcing people into 'subordination and dependence', and of keeping the public ignorant, that his vindicator in *Compleat Vindication* extols was ever anathema to him and a sure bet to provoke his fury.[20]

[5]

None of this government-bashing in *The Gentleman's Magazine* and pamphlets took him closer to his original literary goals. It earned him a little money, though barely enough to live on. Otherwise, it was largely a self-indulgent waste of time if his object was to make his name as a man of letters. Literary London seemed increasingly a wasteland for him where his efforts to succeed were shrivelling on

Cave's vine. Moreover, London was not Tetty's favourite place, and later evidence suggests that out of boredom and neglect she may already have begun to resort to the pretence of happiness through drink and excessive make-up, with the danger of collapsing into an unattractive caricature of herself. So it is no surprise that when there was a vacancy for the headmastership in Appleby, Leicestershire, only twelve miles east of Lichfield, he decided to apply.[21] With not a little sense of failure or even despair, and leaving Tetty behind in their lodgings with the hope that she would join him soon when he got the job, he left London in August 1739. Whatever the reasons for her staying behind, it cannot have been good for her to remain in London alone.

There was a preferred candidate for the position but a division among the school's governors and trustees created a small breach that was Johnson's opportunity. The Bishop of Lincoln was to make the appointment in December, so there was time for jockeying of position and influence peddling. Johnson's lack of a degree was still his greatest handicap. His application therefore seemed pointless because the school's statutes specified that the headmaster had to have a degree from either Oxford or Cambridge. Friends came forward to support him, however, suggesting how he could get a degree.

His strong card was *London: A Poem*. First, William Adams at Pembroke was asked whether on the strength of the poem Oxford could be prevailed on to grant him a degree, but Oxford would not cooperate. Adams wrote to Boswell after Johnson's death: 'I was applied to by a common friend to know whether a Master of Arts degree could be granted him as a favour from the university, to qualify him for a school master's place which was then offered him. But this, tho' his character in the literary world began to rise [it] was thought too much to be asked.'[22]

Contacted possibly by Savage, Pope was also brought in to help. Lord Gower, Pope was told, had a friend who was an intimate of Swift, the Dean of St Patrick's Cathedral in Dublin. Could Swift be reached through this friend with a view to using his influence at Trinity College, Dublin to obtain for Johnson a Master of Arts from that university? It was very much a long shot since the school statute specified a degree from an English university. Still, would Pope write to Gower about this? Pope did and the letter that Gower duly sent from Trentham, Staffordshire on 1 August contains some interesting facts. He identified Johnson as the author of *London: A Poem* and 'some other poetical pieces', a native of Staffordshire, and much respected in the region for his probity and learning. The headmastership, worth an annual salary of £60 (about £6,000 today) that 'would make him happy for life', is not likely to come his way unless Swift can persuade the university 'to send a diploma to me, constituting this poor man Master of Arts'. Johnson was willing, Gower added, to travel all the way to Dublin to submit to the 'strictest examination', 'choosing rather to die upon the road, *than be starved to death in translating for booksellers*, which has been his only subsistence for some time past'. Gower, however, was going through the motions only because Pope had asked him to on behalf of this 'poor man'. Gower thought the exercise was bound to be fruitless: 'If you see this matter in the same light that it appears to me, I hope you will burn this, and pardon me for giving you so much trouble about an impracticable thing.'[23]

If Swift ever did do anything for Johnson, we know nothing of it. Johnson did not receive his degree, but he decided to travel up to Lichfield and Appleby anyway to be interviewed by the governors, leaving London just a month after Savage fled to Wales. Presumably he was interviewed in August but no vote was taken and he had to wait until mid-December for the bishop's decision – based, of course, on the governors' recommendation. Without a degree and plagued by his 'infirmity of a convulsive kind', he failed to secure the position. Stourbridge, Market Bosworth, Ashbourne, Solihull, Edial, Brewood, and now Appleby – seven failed applications by the age of thirty. Neither Pope, nor Lord Gower, nor his network of friends in the area, nor several of the trustees who favoured his application, nor his extraordinary talents could overcome his physically grotesque and uncouth mannerisms and lack of credentials. If this, surely last, failure to secure a teaching position did anything it was to sharpen his bitterness and add to the sense of desolation with which he left London, the deepening feeling that, like Savage, he was an outsider, on the fringe, and unable to gain acceptance except in Grub Street.

CHAPTER 12

Wandering in the Midlands

[1]

Johnson could have returned to Tetty and London promptly in August or early September, after being reunited at home with his mother, Lucy and Kitty Chambers for a decent interval. But he did not. He waited until early spring 1740, seven or eight months later. The inevitable conclusion to be drawn from this neglect of Tetty is that he preferred to be with his family and even Lucy instead of with her, at least for the time being. Reluctant also to return to the harshly competitive literary fray in London, he found richly reassuring companionship in his native corner of England which he did not want to leave.

When he left for Appleby his parting from Tetty could not have been painful. For him the trip was partly an escape, and by then she was used to being on her own and was withdrawing into herself anyway. Hawkins thought Savage was at the root of the problems between them:

> We are to remember that Johnson was, at this time, a husband: can it therefore be supposed that the society of such a man as Savage had any tendency to improve him in the exercise of the domestic virtues? Nay rather we must doubt it, and ascribe to an indifference in the discharge of them, arising from their nocturnal excursions, the incident of a temporary separation of Johnson from his wife, which soon took place, and that, while he was in a lodging in Fleet Street, she was harboured by a friend near the Tower. It is true that this separation continued but a short time, and that if indeed his affection, at that instant, was alienated from her, it soon returned.

Hawkins, however, did not take into account quarrels even before Johnson came to London and met Savage. That finances were one severe pressure on their marriage, worsening in London and continuing to be a source of friction, was highlighted by Shaw, though the following remark could apply to any period between 1739 and her death: 'She disliked the profusion, with which he constantly gave away all the money about him; and he found with astonishment and concern, that whatever he provided or laid up for family exigence, was always gone before he expected.' Another pressure may well have been Johnson's sexual fantasies. 'With all possible respect and delicacy', from what he had heard Boswell judged:

> his conduct, after he came to London, and had associated with Savage and others, was not so strictly virtuous, in one respect, as when he was a younger man ... He owned to many of his friends, that he used to take women of the town to taverns, and hear them relate their history ... Johnson was not free from propensities which were ever warring against the law of his mind ... and that in his combats with them, he was sometimes overcome.[1]

In January, after more than five months in Lichfield without apparently writing to her except presumably immediately after he failed at Appleby, Johnson sent a letter to Tetty in Castle Street tinged with a sense of guilt. It is the best surviving letter he wrote to her. She was in a sorry state, having damaged a tendon in her leg to add to her loneliness and other woes. Whether it was she or someone else who wrote to him about this is unknown, but the injury may have resulted from a fall on ice. That winter everyone was talking about the big freeze, which would long be remembered as one of the most severe in memory – 'the dreadful winter of Forty', Johnson recalled years later. The Thames froze over completely and an ice-fair was held on it; in north Staffordshire, people 'could gaze upon the result of a rivulet dripping down a rock at Ipstones, in the shape of a column of ice "10 yards 3 qrs. High, and 12 about"'. 'After hearing that you are in so much danger,' he began urgently, 'as I apprehended from a hurt on a tendon, I shall be very uneasy till I know that you are recovered, and beg that you will omit nothing that can contribute to it, nor deny yourself anything that may make confinement less melancholy ... I beg therefore that you will not more regard my happiness, than to expose yourself to any hazards.' He urged her to get the best medical help from, among others, a couple of royal physicians who were said to be 'the best' for a guinea. Never mind the expense, he added, because he and his mother had just mortgaged the family home on Market Square to Theophilus Levett, the Lichfield town clerk who befriended Johnson and his family. He was keeping twenty pounds and would soon be sending her the rest. It felt good to have some fresh cash in his pocket, and he had promising news: 'David [Garrick] wrote to me this day on the affair of *Irene*, who is at last become a kind of favourite among the players; Mr Fleetwood promises to give a promise in writing that it shall be the first next season, if it cannot be introduced now.' Not only that, the Drury Lane prompter and stage historian William Rufus Chetwood 'is desirous of bargaining for the copy, and offers fifty guineas for the right of printing after it shall be played ... I hope it will at length reward me for my perplexities.'[2]

It is possible to read the letter as an acknowledgement that all the suffering to which he said he subjected her is owing to his inability to earn enough money to take care of her properly. Her injury had awakened his remorse and made him curse his own failures: 'You have already suffered more than I can bear to reflect upon, and I hope more than either of us shall suffer again. One part at least I have often flattered myself we shall avoid[;] for the future our troubles will surely never separate us more.' His 'esteem and affection' for her 'has only contributed to increase my unhappiness when I reflected that the most amiable woman in the world was exposed by my means to miseries which I could not relieve'.

But there is more going on here than mere remorse over his failure as the breadwinner. Phrases in it like 'most amiable woman in the world', and others like 'dear girl', and 'my charming love' all may be read as efforts to placate her for his prolonged absences, past and present, yet the letter does not acknowledge he was doing anything wrong in having already been away from her for more than five months. There is a deeper sense of self-blame at work in these sentences: 'I still promise myself many happy years from your tenderness and affection, which I sometimes hope our misfortunes have not yet deprived me of ... Be assured, my dear girl, that I have seen nobody in these rambles upon which I have been forced, that has not contributed to confirm my esteem and affection for thee.' He added, 'Of the time which I have spent from thee, and of my dear Lucy and other affairs, my heart will be at ease on Monday to give a particular account, especially if a letter should inform me that thy leg is better, for I hope you do not think so unkindly of me as to imagine that I can be at rest while I believe my dear Tetty in pain.' In other words, he would feel less guilty telling her about these enjoyable visits and rambles over the past few months if he knew she was no longer in pain. Her injury had brought him back down to earth somewhat, but not enough to make him hasten back to her.

Johnson indeed appears to have enjoyed himself greatly during his absence, which is probably what lies behind his nervous assertion that he has not met anyone in his rambles who has made him forget her. If Mrs Thrale was right, he had had to reassure her like this before at Edial Hall after he met Molly Aston. The truth was he had discovered an entertaining new social world much to his liking, even more pleasing to him at the age of thirty than at the Bishop's Palace in his uncertain youth. He found most of these new delights of good society in Ashbourne and the countryside around it. His school chum John Taylor, who had recently given up law to become a clergyman, was at the top of his list of people to visit. It was about this time that Taylor took up residence in the comfortable manor of Ashbourne and began his existence as a type of eighteenth-century 'squarson', a parson who also played at being a farmer and squire, not budging too much from rural pursuits at home to see to his clerical duties in Market Bosworth. From this point on Taylor went from strength to strength. Over the years he became a local patron of Ashbourne, almost like a resident lord, and in the last fifteen years of his life Johnson made a habit of visiting Ashbourne almost annually, although his friends were mystified by what he found appealing enough in his boring and stuffy friend to detain him there that much. 'Sir, I love him,' he said to Boswell, 'but I do not love him more; my regard for him does not increase ... His talk is of bullocks.' What he found there in 1739–40 was a comfortable and quiet self-enclosed world, a dramatic change of pace from London.[3]

Taylor was the centre but not boundary of Johnson's new Ashbourne social horizon. Three miles down the road he found more animated society at Bradley, the seat of the country squire Littleton Poyntz Meynell, as insular an Englishman as could be imagined who, forty years later, Johnson remembered as having said, 'For any thing I see, foreigners are fools.' His son Hugo became famous as the so-called 'father of fox hunting'.

It was the women at Bradley who impressed Johnson the most. One of them later wrote her impressions of him at Bradley. These found their way into Boswell's hands, and he quoted as follows from them: 'During his stay at Ashbourne, he made frequent visits to Mr Meynell, at Bradley, where his company was much desired by the ladies of the family, who were, perhaps, in point of elegance and accomplishments, inferior to few of those with whom he was after-wards acquainted'. Meynell's daughter, Mary Fitzherbert, was a par-ticular delight – 'Of her, Dr Johnson said ... that she had the best understanding he ever met with in any human being'. Mrs Thrale who thought Johnson's veneration for Mary was so highly pitched that it was 'very difficult to deserve', recorded his remark that she 'loved her husband as we hope and desire to be loved by our guardian angel ... her first care was to preserve her husband's soul from cor-ruption; her second to keep his estate entire for their children: and I owed my good reception in the family to the idea she had entertained, that I was fit company for Fitzherbert whom I loved extremely.' Was Mary attractive? Mrs Thrale asked him: 'She would have been handsome for a queen (replied the panegyrist); her beauty had more in it of majesty than of attraction, more of the dignity of virtue than the vivacity of wit.'⁴

Another feminine presence who sparkled for Johnson at Bradley and the Fitzherbert's seat at Tissington Hall was young Hill Boothby, daughter of Sir Brooke Boothby of Ashbourne Hall, a frequent guest and herself of an old Derbyshire family. After Mary Fitzherbert died in childbirth in 1753, 'in the flower of her age, distinguished for her piety and fine accomplishments', her six children were raised by Miss Boothby. Johnson's affection for her persisted and grew to the point that after Tetty died he may have entertained the idea of marrying her, if she would have him.

Before Johnson could marry Miss Boothby, however – if indeed that was ever likely to happen – she died in January 1756 from an illness during which Johnson wrote to her deeply affectionate letters. In a fascinating one written at midnight on 30 December 1755, he implored her, 'Continue, my dearest, your prayers for me, that no good resolution may be vain. You think, I believe, better of me than I deserve. I hope to be in time what I wish to be, and what I have hitherto satisfied myself too readily with only wishing ... You know Descartes' argument, "I think therefore I am." ... I might give another, "I am alive therefore I love Miss Boothby", but that I hope our friendship may be of far longer duration than life.' In his next letter he addresses her, 'My Sweet Angel'. Mrs Thrale, however, poured cold water on the relationship: 'he told me she pushed her piety to bigotry, her devotion to enthusiasm; that she somewhat disqualified herself for the duties of *this* life, by her perpetual aspirations after the *next*: such was however the purity of her mind, he said, and such the graces of her manner, that Lord Lyttelton [at nearby Hagley] and he used to strive for her preference with an emulation that occasioned hourly disgust, and ended in lasting animosity.' Mrs Thrale even went so far as to make the wild claim that a negative biography Johnson wrote of Lord Lyttelton forty years later was inspired by his jealousy of Lyttelton over Miss Boothby: 'She *would* delight in that fellow Lyttelton's company', she reported him saying, in spite of 'all that I could do; and I cannot forgive even his memory the preference [for] a mind like hers'. 'You may see', he allegedly said, 'that dear Boothby is at my heart still.'[5]

Such complications were not even imagined in the autumn, winter and spring of 1739–40, however, when the Derbyshire landscape was for him one of green innocence and delight in the company of these graces. These were scenes complete with a cast of characters worthy of Jane Austen, supplied even with the colourful and eccentric rector of Bradley, Dr John Kennedy, author of *A Complete System of Astronomical Chronology* and *A New Method of Scripture Chronology*, for which Johnson wrote a Dedication and Preface respectively, who also grew into a friend.[6] One can scarcely blame Johnson for not tearing himself away from all this and rushing back to Tetty. He discovered, really for the first time at the age of thirty, without a dragging sense of inferiority or weight of melancholia, that he could hold his own in a genteel setting with fine ladies and gentlemen, appreciated for his intelligence, wit, and honesty. His Grub Street existence seemed a lifetime away.

He had to get back to Tetty, though, and in late spring 1740, he finally forced himself away, leaving his mother, Lucy, friends, and any more thoughts of a schoolmaster's life, behind him. He would not return to Lichfield and Ashbourne for twenty-two long years.

PART IV

Triumph:
The Dictionary Years

Johnson's house

CHAPTER 13

London Revived:
A Lion in Harness

B ack in Grub Street in the spring of 1740, Johnson promptly repaid Garrick's kindness for using his influence at Drury Lane on behalf of *Irene* by writing a prologue for his friend's new play *Lethe*.[1] Although in that poem he alludes to the recklessness and vanity of the dramatist like himself who 'dares to venture on the dangerous stage,/And weakly hopes to 'scape the critick's rage' even as he ducks 'the poignant orange' and tries to ignore the 'catcall's direful cry', he still had hopes that Fleetwood was serious about staging *Irene*. In the meantime, he slipped quickly again into the drudgery of revising Guthrie's debates, beginning in the May 1740 issue of *The Gentleman's Magazine*, and into some more hack work whipping into shape for the bookseller J(ohn?) Wilcox an abridged translation of an anonymous writer's *The History of Tahmas Kuli Khan, Shah, or Sophi of Persia*, a sensational French account of Nadir Shah of Persia's murderous military campaigns against Afghanistan and India. Wilcox, we recall, had lent Johnson and Garrick £5 soon after they arrived in London three years earlier. This is the only publishing venture in which Johnson and Wilcox were ever connected, notwithstanding Johnson's calling the bookseller 'one of my best friends.'[2]

While Johnson was away the political landscape had altered. Britain had declared war on Spain and suddenly buzzed with nationalistic fervour. He returned to a city hungry for patriotic writing that would remind everyone of the country's (chiefly naval) greatness. Cave was only too happy to oblige and eager to call on Johnson to provide some of this with his rousing prose. The genre the two of them chose to capitalise on this market was biography – specifically, naval biography – which suited Johnson well. Biographies for the magazine encouraged him to think he was contributing something original. In fact, he did no research for them except for consulting earlier lives and reading some correspondence that had come Cave's way.

The first was the *Life of Admiral Blake*. As his source he simply used Thomas Birch's rather dry account of this colourful hero in the *General Dictionary, Historical and Critical*, condensing and restructuring it into seven pages in the magazine – a sizeable and successful contribution that Cave then reprinted in a fifteen-page pamphlet. In this biographical sketch Johnson often crudely and with the most obvious kind of patriotic cant exploited the public's impatience for the Government to fight the Spanish with force and dignity as Englishmen did in the past, not tentatively and anaemically as it was doing now. He wrote that, faced with a refusal to let his men draw water for his troops, Blake indignantly 'curled his whiskers, as was his custom when he was angry' and summarily captured Tunis.

Johnson followed this with more patriotic chest-beating in his next biographical assignment, the *Life of Drake*, details for which again he took mainly from four pamphlets comprising *Sir Francis Drake Revived*, an exciting tale of adventure and travel in South America and the Indies offering great opportunities for observations on human nature and customs in primitive lands. Drake's life in his hands became a national symbol of heroic adventure, a tribute to the dash and bravery of British explorers of the past, but it also turned out to be an excuse for Johnson to write about his greater and more lasting interest in the history of exploration and colonisation. He took a swipe especially at the nonsense of the noble savage archetype, that 'savages' like the Patagonians were more innocent and loving than an Englishman or any other European. Human nature was uniform throughout the globe, he contended, so to construct moral and social philosophies on the fanciful utopian idea that people untouched by 'civilisation' were superior to Europeans was idiocy. His old theme about the evils of colonial exploitation also appears strongly as he scourges the slaughter of the Patagonians by the cruel Spanish 'intruders'.

Another biography he wrote quickly was about the young German intellectual prodigy, Johann Philip Baratier, who in November 1740 had died at the age of nineteen. There was much about him in the press at the time. For this one Johnson did what he knew he did best, which had nothing to do with a chronological series of actions: on the basis of a few letters Cave let him see from the boy's father, he composed a moralist's biography, stressing the lonely self of a prodigy and how it coped in the world. It was the type of life-writing he liked most of all to do.[3]

[2]

This flurry of biographical activity creates the misleading impression that Johnson was as busy as ever working for Cave in 1740. In fact, the opposite was true: he was working much less for him than the year before. Even after Guthrie got fed up and stopped writing the debates in November, Johnson did not do the obvious and start writing them himself. He was deliberately resisting getting swallowed up by the magazine, holding out for alternatives that matched his notions of the kind of writer he wanted to be. *Irene*, however, continued to be a disappointment. By September 1741, when Cave wrote to Birch for ideas about helping with the play, Fleetwood had sneaked out of his promise to Garrick to stage it that season. Even if Fleetwood had been as good as his word, the income from the play would have been a one-off affair, and what Johnson sorely needed was steady income. Nothing else materialised, however, to save him from being sucked up by Cave's journalistic whirlpool, and from December onwards he increasingly was absorbed by the magazine – chiefly in writing the weekly essays – until in July 1741 he was completely in its grip. Notwithstanding a few acerbic lines he wrote about Cave in his biography of him, towards the end of his life Johnson had only grateful words for his employer and friend. Cave's road simply meant another road not taken, at least not for several years.

In the first six months of 1741, Cave called on his services more than ever before. Filling more than six pages per issue – eighteen in January – Johnson wrote for the magazine two short parliamentary debates that spared Cave the need to raid the *London Magazine* for its material; revised and 'abridged' into virtually an original work an old 112-page pamphlet (*Monarchy Asserted*, 1660) containing the famous debate between Cromwell and Parliament in 1657 concerning the petition to have him assume the title of King; translated and condensed a 350-page French history of the Amazons into his 'Dissertation on the Amazons'; and composed one of the magazine's so-called critical weekly essays entitled 'An Essay on Epitaphs' on the proper form and function of funerary epitaphs as an art.[4] That last essay expresses his growing conviction that the best biography is about the common man from whose life one can learn far more than from society's great heroes. He wrote all this with the gnawing awareness that it was relentlessly ephemeral prose, not adding up to anything very coherent or substantial. What he needed was a firm heart and steady resolution, a patient faith in his own abilities. Surely it was only a matter of time before his great break would come.[5]

Something did come up. Johnson had done wonders with Guthrie's parliamentary reporting but had mostly performed as a copy editor, shaping them into readable and interesting prose. In the summer, Cave offered him exclusive authorship of the debates. His task was to air issues and ideas that were being debated in Parliament in connection with particular legislation. Nobody reads his debates today because they are not easily accessible in modern editions, and they are rooted in mid-eighteenth-century issues and personalities, but they are far from dead in spirit and theme. Although their rhetoric makes a show of representing the politicians with dignity – given the magazine's political neutrality he had to do this – Johnson wrote his observations on the ambiguities and vanities of human nature in any sphere of activity, especially politics, through the lens of both the moralist and satirist.

It is surprising that in the last year of his life Johnson felt penitent about his debates; he felt that they were 'the mere coinage of his own imagination' and that they 'imposed' on the public because nobody in them really said exactly what he said they did, or in the way he had them say it. Fictionalised parliamentary speeches were commonplace at the time and had been part of the historical and biographical tradition of ancient Greek and Roman writers. Compelled to write them without attending Parliament or working from rough notes surreptitiously scribbled by someone who had, did not give him much of a choice in any case. Nonetheless, he regretted he became 'an author of fictions' in writing them.[6]

Still, this uneasiness did not preclude his vanity and pride over having pulled the deception off in the first place. His friend and biographer, Arthur Murphy, told of a dinner conversation one night at the home of the actor Samuel Foote during which a classical scholar present remarked that a speech by Pitt he recalled reading in the debates was better than anything Demosthenes had ever written. Johnson was there and allowed the conversation to proceed for a while without saying anything. Then he is supposed to have dropped his bombshell, 'That speech I wrote in a garret in Exeter street' – he must have meant Castle Street (if Murphy was not misremembering) since he had not lived in Exeter Street since 1737. There was general astonishment and when the scholar asked what he could possibly mean Johnson replied:

Sir, I wrote it in Exeter Street. I never had been in the gallery of the House of Commons but once. Cave had interest with the door-keepers. He, and the persons employed under him, gained admittance: they brought away the subject of discussion, the names of the speakers, the side they took, and the order in which they rose, together with notes of the arguments advanced in the course of the debate. The whole was afterwards communicated to me, and I composed the speeches in the form which they now have in the Parliamentary debates.

Amazement turned to praise, especially for his alleged political impartiality, whereupon Johnson is supposed to have replied with this now iconic remark, 'That is not quite true. I saved appearances tolerably well; but I took care that the WHIG DOGS should not have the best of it.' On another occasion he stated that 'he always took care to put Sir Robert Walpole in the wrong, and to say every thing he could against the electorate of Hanover'. He would also have been proud (if a bit uncomfortable) had he heard that the debates had deceived Voltaire, who declared that 'the eloquence of ancient Greece and Rome was revived in the British senate'.[7]

Once the notes smuggled out of Parliament were put into his hands, he wrote at an astonishing speed. 'He never wrote any part of his works with equal velocity,' Boswell wrote; 'three columns of the magazine, in an hour, was no uncommon effort, which was faster than most persons could have transcribed that quantity.' Hawkins described how he did it: 'They were written at those seasons when he was able to raise his imagination to such a pitch of fervour as bordered upon enthusiasm, which, that he might the better do, his practice was to shut himself up in a room assigned him at St John's Gate to which he would not suffer any one to approach, except the compositor or Cave's boy for matter, which, as fast as he composed it, he tumbled out at the door.' Writing the debates as fast as he did, it is true he did not distinguish the speakers from each other by style and manner, identifying them chiefly by their positions on issues and their fictitious names. They all speak, whether vulgar or noble, pretty much in the same sustained oratorical style and without any regional accent or dialect. The dramatic give and take of debate, with sputterings, innuendo, and colloquialism, is not there. Johnson would have replied indignantly that he was interested in argument and reasoning, not characterisation.[8]

He has also been censured for deliberately putting speeches in the mouths of people who did not make them, or introducing arguments that were never uttered at all in the debates. As one of Johnson's commentators has urged, 'such a practice, abhorrent to the modern historian or journalist, was easily justifiable under the large demands of Johnson's rhetorical art. We must not forget that to value a speaker's real words, in all their paltriness, over a rhetorically perfected distillation of his meaning is a modern prejudice. It is to value the shell of a nut so greatly that it can never be cracked to get at the meat. It is to disdain the truth of art and to glorify the truth of "fact".'[9] Nonetheless, members of Parliament must surely have had some good gossip in their corridors of power about not having made the speeches with the oratorical brilliance that *The Gentleman's Magazine* published them.

As for his claim that he shaded the speeches to prevent the 'Whig dogs' from getting the best of it, a little political clarification is needed. To begin with, there were prominent Whigs in Opposition who were vicious in their clamour against Walpole, so which Whigs did he have in mind? Moreover, his constructions of Walpole's speeches are objective and characterised by his admiration of the man's expediency and pragmatic leadership. He endowed him with an understanding of the ambiguities and flaws of government and political power, and of human institutions generally, which he thought was no bad quality for a prime minister or any other leading political figure. He made Walpole sound convincing in denouncing the airy, insubstantial ranting of politicians who were not, like he is, held accountable for their fine speeches, and in defending himself with a wry, effortless loftiness. Less pleasing to Walpole would have been to read the speeches Johnson wrote for his enemies, including ones by Opposition Whigs, full of rancour and bitter reflections on his immorality and abuse of power. They have an energy and bite leaving no doubt that Johnson fundamentally thought he was a corruptive force in British life. All in all, however, it is the ambiguity of government, society and life in general that comes through. Life and human nature are complicated. Practice is more important than theory, and theory is easy to come by.[10]

In a positive and more universal vein, the debates have a life today in the libertarian vision they present. Many of the speeches are driven by Johnson's own, not the speaker's, passions regarding the individual's sanctity and freedom in the face of flawed, corrupt, and self-perpetuating institutions and government policy. Debates on Walpole's insistence on having a standing army, for example, produce arguments on whether compulsory military service is consistent with a free society. Is secrecy in government, even on behalf of national security, consistent with the individual's right to freedom of information? How much power should be vested in a leader like Walpole, who gets fat on it and uses it to tyrannise? Should the Government autocratically presume to define and legislate morality for the people – especially when it is itself corrupt? Slavery, taxation (called 'universal slavery') that especially punishes the poor, alliances and connivances that subvert freedom (not excluding those of the Hanoverian monarchy), war-mongering against Spain, and bribery and back-handing: these are all issues to which Johnson's imbedded hostility towards authority lends a fire and urgency, not unlike the virulence in *Marmor Norfolciense*. But a parallel theme is to what extent can the people be trusted? Facile, simplistic, idealistic, selfish, uninformed public resentment was useless. His scorn for impractical idealism was at times no less ferocious than his indictment of the abuses of power.

[3]

Johnson kept writing these debates until early 1744. In addition to them, he had his hand in the magazine in so many different editorial ways that, on average, he was pulling in a salary of about £100 per year (about £10,000 today). During this period he was cranking out copy at a rate of about twenty pages per issue, a significant increase over the previous year.[11]

His instincts to draw out the moral implications in issues and new publications during these months were never dormant, even in the rush to supply copy and earn his salary. It was biographies he turned to mostly to achieve this, urging its supreme importance, as distinct from history, in dwelling on common, personal details of subjects, 'in their private apartments, in their careless hours'. One such 'biography' that reflected his growing and lifelong interest in medicine was of the seventeenth-century English physician Dr Thomas Sydenham. It is the most autobiographical of his early lives. Cave wanted it because he needed the publicity for an edition of Sydenham's works he was publishing and knew that with his keen interest in medicine Johnson was the one to write it. In effect, he made something out of nothing because there was almost no factual material to go on and he made no effort to find any. Instead of writing a biography, Johnson turned the piece into a scornful denunciation of those who accused Sydenham of practising medicine purely on the basis of clinical experimentation. On top of this, Sydenham illustrates his common biographical theme, even this early, that it is not so much a man's abilities and skills in rising to eminence but his Christian virtue which principally recommends him, especially his charity and compassion.[12]

It was all anonymous work, however, and left Johnson hungrier than ever for reputation. One may wonder why he did not write new poetry for the magazine's poetry section during these months and years? After the excellent reception of *London: A Poem*, he had every reason to be confident of further success as a poet, especially with Cave and Dodsley's support. Why not another imitation of Juvenal or perhaps Horace? Writing new verse could have helped alleviate the tediousness of this maze of editorial work in which he had become entangled. Cave asked him for some, but all he came up with, except for a new translation into Latin of Pope's verses on his famous grotto, was a handful of old unpublished poems he either pulled out of a drawer or dictated from memory. Published in the July 1743 issue, they included 'Friendship: An Ode' and 'The Young Author'. Perhaps new poetry involved too great a shift of gears for him; or he may simply have felt he had no time for it. Or it may have been a matter of indolence.[13]

One critic has remarked that Johnson 'found the magazine amateur and left it professional', well on its way to a circulation of ten thousand and a readership much larger than that.[14] Instead of being run almost exclusively by Cave and occasional contributors of considerably varying abilities, by 1743 the magazine was staffed by talented professional writers like Johnson, Boyse, and an able newcomer, John Hawkesworth (1720–1773), a protégé of Johnson's who would also become a friend and his closest literary collaborator. Neither Boswell nor Hawkins acknowledged Hawkesworth's importance in his life and work, Hawkins patronisingly calling him 'a man of fine parts, but no learning'; but Johnson once said that for details of his life 'after my coming to London to drive the world about a little, you must all go to Jack Hawkesworth for anecdotes'.[15] After Johnson weaned himself from deep involvement in the magazine by 1744, it was Hawkesworth who took over the debates and others of his functions and eventually became its literary editor. The magazine was Hawkesworth's making as a man of letters, which reminds us that Johnson's indefatigable work for Cave, while it delayed his full emergence as a bright literary star, also provided a great push towards fame. It established him in the world of printers and booksellers with a wide range of contacts.

[4]

Johnson's personal life during this long vigil at the magazine is sketchy. His reasonably good income from 1741–3 undoubtedly brought some peace of mind for Tetty, but otherwise things were not improving for her. Whether she had yet begun to lapse into alcoholism or not is unknown. It was generally understood she was headed in that direction, for as Shaw noted, 'It has been said that Mrs Johnson ... had, especially in the latter part of her life, addicted herself to drinking'. In the autumn of 1742, she was ill in bed for several months. As Johnson told Taylor in the new year, 'Mrs Johnson was seized with such an illness, having not been well for some time before as will easily make you excuse my neglect at answering you. I believe it is now the twelfth week since she was taken with it, and last Thursday she walked about [her] chamber for the first time. I never saw any body do so much that did or did not recover.' She had become a 'difficult hypochondriac'. He added that otherwise 'nothing very ill has happened to me, which I know you will be pleased to hear'.[16]

In the spring of 1741 it seems he had taken lodgings again on his own 'at the Black Boy over against Durham Yard, the Strand', where Garrick had kept his wine stock during the brief time he was a wine merchant. Over the next five years it is difficult to keep track of where Tetty and he, or he on his own, lived – 'if I change my lodgings', he told Taylor, he would be sure to tell him – but almost forty years later he remembered his addresses during this period pretty much in this order: Boswell Court (Carey Street), the Strand again, Bow Street, Holborn, Fetter Lane, and Holborn again. Perhaps they were compelled to seek out less expensive lodgings, but the more serious possibility is that life was not working out between them, that Tetty was sliding steadily into the grotesque caricature Johnson's friends circulated years later and he had little sense of a home where he could work.[17]

He spent much of his time with Robert James, his old schoolfellow. Medicine kept them in touch. 'My knowledge of physic, I learned from Dr James,' Johnson told Boswell with overstatement. Musing at Mrs Thrale's house one day in 1777, on who would be his biographer, he remarked that except for Adams and Hector 'Doctor James can give a better account of my early days than most folks'. Receiving his B.A. in 1726 at Oxford and M.D. in 1728 at Cambridge and then practising in the Midlands for several years, James made his way to

London where he traded in medicine, writing about it and realising
he could make money by concocting marketable powders and potions.
Two million doses of his fever powders, which acted as a diaphoretic
and cathartic as well as emetic, were sold within twenty years of being
patented in 1746. In spite of rumours about their violent after-effects,
many testified to their positive results, including a number of Johnson's
friends. In spite of any reservations he may have had about James's
medical abilities, in the early 1740s, Johnson decided to help his old
friend, this 'lewd fellow' whom he said 'for twenty years was not
sober'.[18]

Part quack and part learned professional, James was an understandable medical phenomenon in the eighteenth century, as was
Robert Levet, later a member of Johnson's household for many years,
for medicine was something of a lottery in the mid-eighteenth century.
There were no medical journals, for example, and no forum in which
physicians could formally exchange information with each other.
Neither was there any testing of cures, the compounds of many
of which were guarded as money-making secrets: 'Testimonies and
publicity, fashion and fruitless rivalry took the place of impartial
assessment and made the advance of knowledge uncertain.' Johnson
himself acknowledged this in his *Life of Akenside* thirty-five years later,
'A physician in a great city seems to be the mere play-thing of fortune;
his degree of reputation is, for the most part, totally casual; they that
employ him know not his excellence; they that reject him know not
his deficience.'

In February 1742 James published the first part of his successful
Medicinal Dictionary, a compilation of information from previous
medical works with the purpose of distinguishing the useful from
gossipy hand-me-down remedies. It appeared each fortnight and then
was published in three volumes from 1743–5. Boswell said Johnson in
1743 'had written, or assisted in writing, the Proposals ... and being
very fond of the study of physic, in which James was his master,
he furnished some of the articles'. There is a passage in them that
encapsulates Johnson's no-nonsense denigration of inferior scholarship and points tantalisingly to the dawning of his ideas about
writing a dictionary himself. There are other medical dictionaries, he
wrote, 'by those to whom an impartial critic would have allowed
neither the wages of labour, nor the laurels of science, who have
transcribed truth and error without distinction, have been too ignorant
to lop off the superfluities of their predecessors, and too lazy to supply

their defects ... the knowledge of words must necessarily precede the study of science'.[19]

After the emergence of James's powders in 1746, Johnson distanced himself from James and his medicine. He wrote to his friend, and a leading London physician, Dr Richard Brocklesby in the last year of his life, 'I never thought well of Dr James's compounded medicines. His ingredients appeared to me sometimes inefficacious and trifling, and sometimes heterogeneous, and destructive of each other.'[20]

[5]

In June 1742 Johnson's mind ran again along the lines of a huge project as the pathway to reputation. That month Edward Harley, the second Earl of Oxford died. Harley, friend of Pope and son of Robert Harley the Tory Lord Treasurer in the reign of Queen Anne, was owner of the great estate of Wimpole Hall in Cambridgeshire. He owned a vast collection of books, manuscripts and tracts that he housed at Wimpole Hall, his house in Dover Street, and his magnificent mansion in Cavendish Square. The size of the collection included, some fifty thousand books and seven thousand volumes of manuscripts, not to mention coins, engravings, Greek and Roman antiquities, and more than five hundred paintings. His need to build elegant places to house them eventually brought on severe financial worries that may have hastened his death.

Keeping the manuscripts, which were eventually sold to the British Museum in 1753, his widow decided to sell the books as a whole instead of preserving them, as her husband had wished, as a public library. Three months after his death they were purchased (surprisingly) by the tasteless and ill-mannered bookseller Thomas Osborne for the huge sum of £13,000 but which was supposed to have been far less than what Harley had paid (£18,000) just for the bindings. Osborne is one of those eighteenth-century characters who attained a kind of immortality from the verbal and physical attacks he received from men of genius. Pope introduced him as one of the contenders for the prize of dullness among booksellers in the 1743 *Dunciad* as revenge for his outrageous violation of copyright in fraudulently selling copies of Pope's *Iliad* at half price. Building on his unsavoury reputation, biographers have used Osborne to add to the image of Johnson as the scourge of villainous bullies, a type of literary Hercules. Johnson is supposed to have knocked him down with a folio in his bookshop and then 'put his foot upon his neck'. 'Sir, he was impertinent to me,' he told Boswell, 'and I beat him. But it was not in his shop: it was in my own chamber.' 'Osborne was a man entirely destitute of shame, without sense of any disgrace but that of poverty,' Johnson later wrote in his *Life of Pope*. According to this anecdote, Osborne made a mistake not many others, given Johnson's size and strength, were foolhardy enough to make.[21]

Osborne beat the competition to buy the collection because of its sheer size and the difficulties of housing it. The Bodleian Library could not afford it and the Government was not yet into buying large libraries. He bought it in order to sell it piecemeal but it became a biblio-albatross and selling it turned out to be far from simple. He needed a convincing sales device and hit on the idea of drawing up a scrupulous, annotated catalogue of the entire collection that would appeal to scholars and men of learning, whose good will he needed if he was going to succeed. As he had met Johnson earlier through his involvement in publishing James's *Medicinal Dictionary*, and as Johnson came highly recommended in the trade, he offered him the job of compiling the catalogue. Johnson eagerly accepted. A few days later he sent Johnson's proposal, 'An Account of the Harleian Library', to Thomas Birch for his advice and with the request that he promote it among his fellow members of the Royal Society. On 9 October Johnson had dinner with Birch and two other Society members among the books in the Cavendish Square house. Osborne got more than just a money-spinning outline from Johnson's 'Account'. It amounts to a moral argument on the importance of literary culture to a nation: 'every man who considers learning as ornamental and advantageous to the community', he urged, must celebrate men like Harley as 'public benefactors who have introduced amongst us authors not hitherto well known, and added to the literary treasures of their native country'.[22]

Johnson's scheme was that 'the books shall be distributed into their distinct classes, and every class ranged with some regard to the age of the writers; that every book shall be accurately described; that the peculiarities of editions shall be remarked, and observations from the authors of literary history occasionally interspersed'. To sit down and do this for fifty thousand volumes was a thoroughly daunting task. So to help Johnson, Osborne also hired William Oldys, the able and indefatigable antiquarian and bibliographer and Harley's learned librarian who was later thrown into Fleet prison for debt and grew so fond of it that after he was released he liked to return to spend his evenings there. There is no record at all, unfortunately, of how they got on together week after week as they dived into the stacks. They set to work in Cavendish Square, but Osborne's impossible deadline of February 1743 for publication of the first two volumes covering more than fifteen thousand volumes meant many annoying compromises and shortcuts, and although the volumes with their Latin, French and English annotations turned out to be far more scholarly than the average book sales catalogue, the result fell far short of what Johnson's scheme outlined. Hawkins surmised that 'engaged in so servile an employment' Johnson 'resembled a lion in harness'. Osborne continued to frustrate Johnson's scheme and when the next two volumes duly appeared in January 1744 they were again a mediocre shadow of the original model. A fifth volume with which neither Johnson nor Oldys had anything to do came out more than a year later and consisted of not much more than routine transcriptions of titles. Osborne's sale of these books dragged on for at least twenty years.[23]

After the third and fourth volumes were published, Osborne handed over to Oldys the job of editing the *Harleian Miscellany*, a reprinting of pamphlets in the collection, and asked Johnson again to write proposals and an 'Introduction' to this venture. His 'Introduction' celebrates the 'boundless liberty' of the British Enlightenment, in which (as he wrote) the freedom to write and read pamphlets was unique, perpetuating 'new sentiments to the public without danger of suffering either ridicule or censure': 'It is observed that among the natives of England is to be found a greater variety of humour than in any other country ... where every man has a full liberty to propagate his conceptions, variety of humour must produce variety of writers.' This short 'Introduction' can be taken as one of Johnson's earliest assertions that nowhere else in Europe was the Enlightenment so robust and practical.[24]

Not from any of these Harleian publications, unfortunately, did Johnson reap any reputation with the public, much less a good income. He needed money more urgently than ever. One day in December 1743 he had to take a break in Osborne's bookshop to write urgently to Theophilus Levett, Lichfield attorney and Town Clerk, about his failure to make a £12 mortgage payment on the Market Square house because of 'a great perplexity of affairs'. He would pay the interest owed in two months, he assured Theophilus Levett. Would he allow him this grace period? As it happened, he had to turn to Aston to make the payment. And he further pleaded with Levett: 'I look upon this and the future interest of that mortgage as my own debt, and beg that you will be pleased to give me directions how to pay it, and not mention it to my dear mother.' His relief was immense when Levett replied with 'humanity and generosity'. His and Tetty's poverty had reached such a pitch by then that they even tried to claim some £35 owed to them from her late husband's estate. He asked Levett to help him get it but appears not to have succeeded. That autumn he had to beg Cave to spare him a guinea as an advance on a new project, a history of the British parliament, 'but if you do not [I] shall not think it an injury'. He worked on the new history for several months, several sheets of which were printed off, but it came to a screeching halt when Parliament unexpectedly restricted access to its manuscripts. Another scheme, another defeat. He was already intensely at work on the *Life of Savage*, but he would not be paid the fifteen guineas for that until mid-December, and it would bring only temporary relief. An embarrassing hint of the discomfort of his poverty during these months was suggested by a possibly spurious anecdote that Boswell told: 'Soon after Savage's Life was published, Mr [Walter] Harte [the writer and tutor to Lord Chesterfield's son] dined with Edward Cave, and occasionally praised it. Soon after, meeting him, Cave said, "You made a man very happy t'other day." – "How could that be," says Harte; "nobody was there but ourselves." Cave answered, by reminding him that a plate of victuals was sent behind a screen, which was to Johnson, dressed so shabbily, that he did not choose to appear; but on hearing the conversation, was highly delighted with the encomiums on his book.'[25]

[6]

Johnson's life between the publication of the *Life of Savage* early in 1744 and the summer of 1746 is largely a blank. Money troubles, defeated hopes, a disintegrating marriage, little idea of how to gain fame and reputation beyond *London* and the *Life of Savage*, and a peripatetic life between London lodgings were calls to the black dog to dance into his imagination and spirit. His first known prayer to 'almighty and everlasting God' for New Year's day 1745, is a cry for help and repentance: 'Grant, O merciful Lord, that thy call may not be vain, that my life may not be continued to increase my guilt, and that thy gracious forbearance may not harden my heart in wickedness.

Let me remember, O my God that as days and years pass over me, I approach nearer to the grave where there is no repentance...' Whether it was the paralysing effect of depression or some physical illness that lay at the root of his inactivity and despair, he wrote virtually nothing for most of 1744. It was Shakespeare who came to the rescue towards the end of the year.[26]

In the February 1745 issue of *The Gentleman's Magazine*, Cave announced that Johnson's pamphlet, *Miscellaneous Observations on the Tragedy of Macbeth* was 'speedily' to be published. It came out in April, and appended to it were 'Proposals for Printing a New Edition of the Plays of William Shakespeare, with Notes Critical and Explanatory'. Both items were anonymous, doubtless because Cave at this juncture did not want the prospects for the project diminished by a name that would not resonate at all with the public. Continuing his search for a project that would establish his reputation, Johnson had agreed with Cave that the best way to do this and at the same time provide Cave with a slice of the Shakespeare market was nothing less than a complete edition of the Bard in ten small volumes, selling at the knockdown price of one pound five shillings. It was a bold and, in theory, an inspired decision. Thomas Hanmer's edition, lavishly presented and short on critical insight, provided an easy target for Johnson's critical artillery. Moreover, more than ever before Shakespeare was fast becoming a patriotic winner in the literary marketplace. There was no better way for a critic to make a name for himself as a critic than by producing a complete edition, even though five editions had already preceded him in the eighteenth century. Johnson fell to the task probably in the summer or autumn of 1744 with characteristic intensity and energy, shutting everything else out, going through most of the plays and amassing a wealth of data and notes on Shakespeare's language and ideas in the individual plays.

Miscellaneous Observations is neither an edition of *Macbeth* nor a systematic critical analysis, but a display of the kind of commentary he could produce on selected passages. William Warburton, the friend of Pope, churchman and editor of Shakespeare, praised it as written by 'a man of parts and genius' – an endorsement Johnson remembered with gratitude for the rest of his life: 'He praised me at a time when praise was of value to me.' Much of the appeal in embarking on a Shakespeare edition was iconoclastically to rubbish the fanciful and pedantic nonsense that previous editors and commentators on the Bard had dished out to the public in edition after edition. In

Miscellaneous Observations his caustic criticism of Hanmer previewed what he hoped to do in his own edition: attack the encrusted Shakespeare establishment not only by exposing errors of judgement and textual editing but also by revealing how consistently critics have wasted their efforts by not measuring Shakespeare against what they know about life from their own experiences. People like Hanmer, whose 'harmless industry may, surely, be forgiven, if it cannot be praised', should avoid the whole subject: 'No man should attempt to teach others what he has never learned himself.' Critics should 'disdain to labour in trifles'. The whole enterprise pointed to his determination to storm the exclusive club of Shakespeare scholarship through the breach that Hanmer's incompetence had opened up.[27]

It was good and promising while it lasted, but this magnificent project was doomed to the same fate that had killed earlier projects. Jacob Tonson, the publisher of an edition of Shakespeare in 1725 by Pope – who would die only two or three months after Johnson began working on his own edition without ever meeting the young poet he so much admired – claimed the copyright of Shakespeare's plays and within a week of the announcement of the edition threatened an injunction against Cave if he went ahead with it. Had Cave decided to fight back, he might well have won because Tonson's claim was a bluff. Booksellers illegitimately claimed copyright of all sorts of titles and authors as part of their unofficial membership in the inner circle of the publishing world. They were difficult and expensive to oppose, even by the most successful magazine editor of the day. Perhaps Tonson also offered Cave a sweetener to drop the project. As Warburton's own edition would appear in 1747, Cave must also have been frightened off by him. The upshot was that he capitulated and Johnson again was left high and dry, though several months of work on Shakespeare ultimately would not go to waste. He continued to sift through the plays, as if his massive collection of notes on Shakespeare's language had developed a life of its own, regardless of how it might be used. One critic has judged that his collection on index slips of thousands of passages illustrating Shakespeare's vocabulary turned him in a matter of months into the 'greatest living authority on Shakespeare's diction'. It was linguistic ammunition waiting to be deployed in as yet an undetermined way.[28]

The gap or silence that ensued in the last half of 1745 suggests that depression at some level must have set in again, compounded by his worsening finances. He was so disillusioned over not having been able to break into the money as an author that around this time he even asked Adams at Pembroke College to discover whether he could practise as an advocate in the Doctors' Commons 'without a doctor's degree in Civil Law'. It is extraordinary that he thought he might be able to. The answer, of course, was 'no'. Nor did he have any money to study law, telling Boswell twenty-five years later that if he had had the money he might as easily (and happily) have studied law as tragic poetry. It was also at about this time that in distress Tetty was forced to sell the silver cup the generous woman in the stagecoach had bought for him when his mother took him to London to be touched by the Queen: 'The cup was one of the last pieces of plate which dear Tetty sold in our distress.' In his *Annals* he poignantly remarked that he still clung to the silver spoon the woman also bought for him at the same time. According to Boswell, Aston saved him from being arrested for debt, which if true would have happened before Aston died in 1748 and before Johnson finally emerged from obscurity in 1746 with a boldness and courage greater than he had ever shown before.[29]

CHAPTER 14

A Lifeline: the *Dictionary*

[1]

After the wretched disappointment of the Shakespeare edition, through to the end of 1745 and into the spring of 1746, Johnson at the age of thirty-seven looked at his life and saw a wife who was deteriorating and unhappy and whose welfare he blamed himself for neglecting; a mother in Lichfield who thanks to his failures had been forced to mortgage the family house; a lifestyle in Grub Street still rewarding him very little for huge amounts of work; poverty; and a career almost mysterious with false starts and cruel disappointments yielding him almost no public notice. The Shakespeare fiasco seemed like the last straw. Even Gilbert Walmesley seemed dejected about his protégé in a letter to Garrick in November 1746: 'When you see Mr Johnson pray [give] my compliments, and tell him I esteem him as a great genius – quite lost to both himself and the world.'[1]

Johnson published virtually nothing in 1746 although Dr Adams told Boswell he was playing with the idea of a life of King Alfred, a potential patriotic bestseller if ever there was one: on which, given the 'warmth with which he spoke about it, he would, I believe, had he been master of his own will, have engaged himself, rather than on any other subject'.[2] We hear no more of it. Suddenly that spring his world and existence changed, however, and light poured into his darkening consciousness in the shape of a book proposal by his friend the successful bookseller Robert Dodsley, whom he called 'Doddy'. The book was nothing less than a dictionary of the English language, a monumental project that great authors such as Pope and Joseph Addison had contemplated and given up almost before they really got going and lesser men had trembled to think of compiling even as they grumbled and protested about the dire need Britain had for a dictionary.

Through his friendship with Cave and others in the trade, Dodsley had kept track of Johnson's mostly anonymous work. He was struck by the way Johnson raised Grub Street writing to unprecedented levels, able to take the writing of other contributors to *The Gentleman's Magazine* and transform it into witty, learned, colourful and rhythmically pleasing prose. He also knew that with his 'encyclopedic' cast of mind Johnson had shown himself ready to take on large projects requiring a good deal of stamina, organisation, and classification. Johnson's high writing standards by now were well known to others in the book trade as well. Dodsley's brother James, who joined him in the business several years later, told Boswell what happened. In Boswell's words: 'When Johnson was one day sitting in his [James's] brother Robert's shop, he heard his brother suggest to him, that a Dictionary of the English Language would be a work that would be well received by the public.' Having planted the seed, he stood back and waited as Johnson mulled over the idea: 'Johnson seemed at first to catch at the proposition, but, after a pause, said, in his abrupt decisive manner, "I believe I shall not undertake it."' Thirty years later Johnson confided to Boswell, 'Dodsley first mentioned to me the scheme of an English Dictionary; but I had long thought of it.'[3]

This was a brave, even reckless idea of Dodsley's. Johnson was still unknown with no clout to his name, and this dictionary would be a far larger project than Dodsley or almost any other publisher had ever undertaken. A dictionary was financially too risky for him or any other bookseller to take on alone, so he arranged for an impressive syndicate of them to become partners in the project. In addition to Dodsley, they were at the front of the profession and all knew the quality of Johnson's writing: the brothers John and Paul Knapton, Andrew Millar, Charles Hitch and Thomas Longman. Though not a bookseller, Cave might well have been included in the enterprise if he had been willing to put up some money for it. Together these men asked Johnson to come up with a proposal, which he did briskly with his nineteen-page 'Short Scheme for compiling a new Dictionary of the English Language'. It impressed them as the work of a man who had already thought long about what such a dictionary should achieve, as well as about the massive problems lying in wait for any brave soul embarking on such a journey. He made it clear that his dictionary would be innovative, especially with his extensive use of quotations drawn from the best English literary sources in order to illustrate the meanings of words. Realising they were on to a good thing, the proprietors gave him the green light. On 18 June 1746 he met with several of them at the Golden Anchor near Holborn Bar and over breakfast signed the fateful contract, promising to finish the job in the incredibly short period of three years. They agreed to pay him 1,500 guineas (£1,575) in installments, the equivalent today of close to £150,000. It was his first substantial payment for literary labour of any kind, a large contract for any author, especially for one who was virtually unknown to the general public.[4]

The contract instantly launched him into another orbit in his professional career and must have been the source of some jubilation at home for the longsuffering Tetty. Immediately, they were able to move to new lodgings at 17 Gough Square, just north of Fleet Street, which today still stands as a memorial to Johnson in the form of a museum of Johnson's domestic life – one of the very few museums of eighteenth-century literary figures in England. Seriously damaged during the Blitz but restored faithfully, it is one of the few houses of that period to survive in the City of London. It has three main storeys in addition to a basement, garret and five bays positioned amid a tangle of narrow lanes and dark alleys in a quiet square that when Johnson moved in was not as respectable as it had been when it was created at the end of the seventeenth century. The Fleet Street neighbourhoods, the Strand, Covent Garden and Charing Cross, had been invaded by coffee houses, taverns, chop houses, and a general culture of hedonism: wig-makers, condom shops, glovers, mercers, specialists in lace, snuff dealers, and gin shops. Prostitutes walked the streets everywhere. Fleet Prison lay close by, reminding one of the dismal consequences of excess and debt. Hygiene and sanitation were deplorable. Completing the scene were foul smells from open drainage, small local industries polluting the air and an atmosphere clogged with smoke from coal transported in collier ships from Newcastle. For the Johnsons, however, the house was perfect, with even a tiny garden described by Thomas Carlyle when he saw it in the 1830s as 'somewhat larger than a bed-quilt'[5] but large enough at least for Tetty to enjoy some private space outside. Most critical of all, the top floor of the house consisted of a large attic room ideal as a workshop for the small lexicographical industry that he needed to set in motion without delay if he was to have any chance of completing this massive book in three years. The house was close to the throbbing pulse of the book trade and, most importantly, the office of the highly successful printer William Strahan at 10 Little New Street whom the booksellers had chosen to print the enormous work and who would become one of Johnson's steadfast and most useful friends.

Even with one floor devoted exclusively to the *Dictionary*, it is surprising that Johnson decided to lease such a large house for just the two of them. Perhaps signs of Tetty's decline made him realise they needed a servant or two to live in the house; or he may also have been anticipating a need in the future for more companionship to live in the house with him. The house brought a change in lifestyle. 'I am always at home,' he wrote soon after moving there. Among his visitors was almost certainly the uncouth, sullen, 'obscure practiser in physic amongst the lower people' Robert Levet, an unlicensed doctor whom he met at a coffee house and who in 1762 came to live with him permanently. Around this time he also met Richard Bathurst, a Jamaican-born physician, educated at Peterhouse, Cambridge, for whom he developed a deep affection – after his death he 'hardly ever spoke' of him 'without tears in his eyes'. In 1750 Bathurst's father brought a slave boy to England from Jamaica who would play a major part in the rest of Johnson's life. Johnson saw in Bathurst a kindred spirit: 'Dear Bathurst ... was a man to my very heart's content: he hated a fool, and he hated a rogue, and he hated a *whig*; he was a very good *hater*.'[6] Another probable visitor to Gough Square was George Psalmanazar, also a coffee-house friend, a reformed and penitent French literary impostor in his mid-sixties for whom Johnson conceived an exaggerated respect because of his later piety and penitence. He once said Psalmanazar was one of only three people he knew who lived a 'regular' or 'uniform' life 'planned by choice', able to keep resolutions.[7]

[2]

Contrary to myths that have attached themselves to Johnson's *Dictionary*, his was by no means the first English dictionary. Dozens had already appeared in the 150 years before Johnson became a lexicographer. The *Short Title Catalogue* in the British Library lists 663 dictionaries of one kind or another before Johnson's, though most of these were variations on encyclopedias, reference works on particular professions and trades, word lists for certain disciplines, and the like. Nor would his be the newest or most trendy, the most comprehensive, or the most accurate. The first English dictionaries, going back centuries, were bilingual, mostly Latin-English and English-Latin, but they had very little to do with daily life. By 1582 when the famous headmaster of Merchant Taylors' school, Richard Mulcaster, drew up a list of some eight thousand commonly used words and called for a monolingual dictionary of English, it had already become a national scandal that there was not one for Englishmen to turn to conveniently in their daily lives. The seventeenth century did not improve notably on Mulcaster, however, for the dictionaries that did appear were devoted to foreign and specialised 'hard words' and inkhorn terms, ignoring the general plea for works defining common English words. It was more useful to read Shakespeare's plays where dramatic contexts involving very real people doing real things communicated what most words meant.[8]

It was not until 1721 that a dictionary recognisable as such today was published in England by Nathan Bailey, *An Universal Etymological Dictionary*, which he followed up with his folio *Dictionarium Britannicum* in 1730 containing 48,000 head words (expanded to 60,000 in a second edition). His *Etymological Dictionary* became the most useful English dictionary in Britain before Johnson's and at a good price was even more commercially successful than his, appearing in twenty-eight editions over the rest of the century and still going strong in the next. Its etymologies were good but its definitions were often paltry – a strawberry was 'a well known fruit', for example, and 'to wash' meant 'to cleanse by washing' – so that while it made life easier for a lot of people it did not define the language in a manner consistent with the greatness of the nation and its literary, cultural and scientific history. Then finally in 1748, while Johnson was hard at work on his dictionary, came Benjamin Martin's *Lingua Britannica Formata*. This one gave Johnson many sleepless nights, not least because Martin was the first lexicographer ever to give the multiple meanings of words. Although these dictionaries were competitive in the lexicographical market, by the mid-eighteenth century Britain still lagged behind both France and Italy in lacking a full dictionary of its language that with careful and multiple definitions, etymology, orthography and illustrative quotations could reflect the pride the British had in their tongue.[9]

Both the Italians and French could boast of dictionaries that honoured their national tongues, but both had been created by national academies, not by one struggling individual. In France, for example, Cardinal Richelieu founded the Académie Française in Paris in 1635, which assembled leading linguistic scholars to establish fixed rules for the French language and produce a dictionary that dictatorially would 'fix' it – that is, prevent or at least retard its changing. Some forty or so academicians began work in 1639 and no fewer than fifty-five years later the Académie published the *Dictionnaire de l'Académie* (1694). As one historian has put it, the *Dictionnaire* set the language in stone.[10]

The English had no Academy to produce a dictionary. The closest they came to one was the Royal Society of London for the Improvement of Natural Knowledge, founded in 1662. Its brief was science, not language, however, and although the Society set up a committee in 1664 to look into organising a grammar, normalising spelling and compiling a list of words, it met only four times and then disbanded. Over the next half century a succession of great writers called vigorously for a national dictionary: John Evelyn, John Dryden, Daniel Defoe, Addison, Pope and Swift. Swift complained bitterly that the language was a mess, a riot of chaos, inconsistency, foreign imports, abuses, and absurdities. More than anything else, he and others wanted a dictionary that, like the French and Italian, would put a stop to mindless, corrupting 'innovations', the province of dunces. His was like a voice crying in the wilderness. The English temper did not, it seems, travel well in the mode of committees and academies. Johnson himself was against creating an Academy. If ever an academy were to be formed, he later wrote, 'English liberty will hinder or destroy' it. His entrance into the dictionary arena, alone and well-armed from a lifetime of reading, was a patriotic, courageous, quintessentially English entrepreneurial publishing venture.

[3]

Dodsley and the other proprietors read the national mood well. Britain's extremity was their opportunity. They gambled that there was a marvellous publishing opportunity awaiting them. Boswell wrote that Johnson knew exactly what he was getting into and 'had a noble consciousness of his own abilities, which enabled him to go on with undaunted spirit'. One day the inquisitive Dr Adams, with whom he continued to stay in touch, dropped in at Gough Square to visit him in the early stages of the work. Seeing books, slips of paper, notebooks, and boxes strewn all over the attic room, and a handful of assistants scurrying about, Adams exclaimed, 'But, Sir, how can you do this in three years?' Johnson replied, 'Sir, I have no doubt that I can do it in three years.' But 'The French Academy, which consists of forty members, took forty years to compile their Dictionary,' Adams persisted. 'Sir, thus it is,' Johnson answered playfully; 'this is the proportion. Let me see; forty times forty is sixteen hundred. As three to sixteen hundred, so is the proportion of an Englishman to a Frenchman.' It remained to be seen whether such bravado held up.[11]

It took him more than a year to come up with a comprehensive statement of what kind of dictionary he was going to write and how he was going to go about it. *The Plan of a Dictionary of the English Language*,[12] a thirty-four page pamphlet recasting his 'Scheme' and published in August 1747 under his own name, was both a declaration of intent and a publicity move to present himself and stake out his territory. It immediately made him a focus of public attention and scepticism such as he had never experienced before. To begin with, he and the proprietors decided they had to aim very high and dedicate it to Philip Dormer Stanhope, the fourth Earl of Chesterfield, generally thought of as 'the Maecenas of the age', one of the most respected arbiters of taste and high culture, and a highly regarded diplomat-politician and Member of Parliament who had just been appointed Secretary of State. He was also a prominent literary patron. Johnson explained to Boswell in 1777 how the Dedication came about: 'I had neglected to write it by the time appointed. Dodsley suggested a desire to have it addressed to Lord Chesterfield. I laid hold of this as a pretext for delay, that it might be better done, and let Dodsley have his desire. I said to my friend, Dr Bathurst, "Now if any good comes of my addressing to Lord Chesterfield, it will be ascribed to deep policy, when, in fact, it was only a casual excuse for laziness."'[13]

Encouraging the view that he was something of an authority on language, Chesterfield declared an interest in becoming the project's aristocratic champion. At about this time he and Johnson even appear to have met and talked about language: 'in the conversation which I had with him,' Johnson remarked, 'I had the best right to superiority, for it was upon philology and literature.' Whatever Johnson thought privately about Chesterfield's grasp of the subject, Dodsley and the others were desperate to have his Lordship's name attached to their enterprise. Thus Chesterfield became Johnson's patron. He gave him £10 as a token of the arrangement. It was all he would ever give. In the *Plan* Johnson insinuated Chesterfield's linguistic credentials and made it seem as if he was his spokesman: 'I may hope, my Lord, that since you, whose authority in our language is so generally acknowledged, have commissioned me to declare my own opinion, I shall be considered as exercising a kind of vicarious jurisdiction, and that the power which might have been denied to my own claim, will be readily allowed me as the delegate of your Lordship.' It looked like a good move. Who could argue with Chesterfield's 'delegate'?[14]

Chesterfield's umbrella of patronage therefore enabled Johnson to deflect criticism and shield himself from the general astonishment that one man, an unknown man at that, had the presumption to write the dictionary. Another method of deflecting criticism was self-deprecation: 'I knew, that the work in which I engaged is generally considered as drudgery for the blind, as the proper toil of artless industry,' he wrote, 'a task that requires neither the light of learning, nor the activity of genius, but may be successfully performed without any higher quality than that of bearing burdens with dull patience, and beating the track of the alphabet with sluggish resolution.' 'The unhappy lexicographer holds the lowest place', so he has 'enter'd with the pleasing hope, that as it was low, it likewise would be safe'. Then at the conclusion he gave this show of diffidence a patriotic spin. He would be the new benign, trembling invader of Britain's sacred shores: he was 'frighted' at the extent of his own ambition as stated in the *Plan*, but 'like the soldiers of Cæsar' he looked on Britain's language as a 'new world, which it is almost madness to invade'. If he could not hope to 'complete the conquest' at least he could 'discover the coast, civilise part of the inhabitants, and make it easy for some other adventurer to proceed farther, to reduce them wholly to subjection, and settle them under laws'. He could not be faulted for trying should his achievement prove to be 'below the excellence of other dictionaries', for at least he will have fought the good fight and 'retired without a triumph from a contest with united academies and long successions of learned compilers'. It was a clever exercise in artful humility, for the benefit of both patron and public.[15]

Sandwiched in between this opening and concluding dissimulation, Johnson laid out his scheme and method with striking authority. He went so far as to claim that 'were he still alive, solicitous as he was for the success of this work', Pope 'would not be displeased that I have undertaken it'. He rolled up his sleeves and sent out this ringing challenge to the 'arrogant stupidity' of some would-be critics: 'I shall not be solicitous what is thought of my work, by such as know not the difficulty or importance of philological studies, nor shall think those that have done nothing qualified to condemn me for doing little.'[16]

[4]

As he began to plow through the lexicographical terrain in the *Plan*, he discovered a minefield of issues that threatened to blow up in his face if he did not tackle them head-on. The crucial thing was to sound confident about his tactics. He sounded so confident, in fact, that some commentators have judged the *Plan* to have even an overt moral cast about it, that he aspired to tame the language's licentiousness, dress up as a social and linguistic reformer, a champion of stability. The argument is that like many others in the past he wanted to 'fix' or freeze the language in a backward-looking, conservative sort of way, keeping it pure from several aggressive modes of corruption.[17] What comes across, however, in such sentences as the following in which he castigated the profligate spawning of words is the voice of the satirist at least as much as of the moralist: 'By tracing ... every word to its original, and not admitting, but with great caution, any of which no original can be found, we shall secure our language from being over-run with *cant*, from being crowded with low terms, the spawn or folly or affectation, which arise from no just principles of speech, and of which therefore no legitimate derivation can be shown.'[18]

   He recognised that the imposition of embalming strictures of usage on language flew in the face of what language is all about although in the course of writing the *Dictionary* his ideas about the nature of language changed and remain complex. In the *Plan* such glimpses as there are of a desire to fix the language, which to a large extent are utterances meant to accommodate and please Chesterfield and reassure his readership, are countered by his care and statements about linguistic realities: 'Language is the work of man, of a being from whom permanence and stability cannot be derived.' Like humans, words do not remain in a time warp, a linguistic limbo: 'Like their author, when they are not gaining strength, they are generally losing it. Though art may sometimes prolong their duration, it will rarely give them perpetuity.' The 'decrees of custom' are not those of the most recent, sloppy instances of the 'licentious' but of broadly determined precedents by the 'correctest writers', and he saw it as his job to examine the evidence 'on both sides'. He honoured popular language as robustly as any lexicographer had ever done: 'words of general use; words employed chiefly in poetry; words obsolete; words which are admitted only by particular writers, yet not in themselves improper; words used only in burlesque writing; and words impure and barbarous'. Certainly not backward, that forcefully progressive position may well have made Chesterfield more than just a little uncomfortable. One wonders, in fact, if his feeble £10 gift and subsequent lack of interest in the project may be traced to it. One influential Johnson critic has written, 'The habit of talking about Johnson's lexicography as "normative" or "dictatorial" or "authoritarian" is completely wrong'; his rationalism 'is prior to his traditionalism; and if a recognition of the priority of rationality is to be taken (as some insist) as the distinguishing mark of the liberal or radical political temperament, then Johnson must be classed as such a liberal or radical.' In the published Preface to the *Dictionary* Johnson stated his position unreservedly, in spite of (with an eye on Chesterfield) having 'flattered' himself momentarily in the tradition of prescriptiveness:

> When we see men grow old and die at a certain time one after another, from century to century, we laugh at the elixir that promises to prolong life to a thousand years; and with equal justice may the lexicographer be derided, who being able to produce no example of a nation that has preserved their words and phrases from mutability, shall imagine that his dictionary can embalm his language, and secure it from corruption and decay, that it is in his power to change sublunary nature, and clear the world at once from folly, vanity, and affectation.

The shifting meanings of words can no more be frozen 'than a grove, in the agitation of a storm, can be accurately delineated from its picture in the water'.[19]

Johnson's practical and liberal lexicography was evident from the start as he considered which words to include: 'The value of a work must be estimated by its use'; 'It is to little purpose, that an engine amuses the philosopher by the subtlety of its mechanism, if it requires so much knowledge in its application as to be of no advantage to the common workman.' However, if they have been sufficiently 'naturalised' by usage and familiarity, certain foreign words and terminology of science, the arts, common law, 'controversial divinity', medicine, professions, and war and navigation (for readers of travel books and history) would be included.[20]

His liberal view extended also to orthography and etymology. His 'chief rule' here would be compliance with 'general custom' and 'to make no innovation'. An imposition of rules, technically logical though they may appear as laid down by experts and etymologists, would inflict the language with yet another layer of chaos: 'The present usage of spelling, where the present usage can be distinguished, will therefore in this work be generally followed.' As for etymology, his strategy might often seem 'capricious' in its empiricism, he warned, but that is the nature of the beast: 'Our language is well known not to be primitive or self-originated, but to have adopted words of every generation, and either for the supply of its necessities, or the increase of its copiousness, to have received additions from very distant regions.' Neither can syntax be reduced to rules. It can be learned only by examples from the best writers.[21]

Finally, he acknowledged that the most challenging task, as others before him had discovered, was to define the words. The most common words were the most difficult because there is often only one word for one idea, and certain words like 'bright' and 'sweet' are often explainable in another language more easily, or because like certain verbs they have dozens of meanings. But he would not be content until he exhausted the following nuances and senses: the 'natural' or 'primitive' meaning, the metaphorical, the consequential or accidental, the poetical, the familiar, the burlesque, and the 'peculiar' as found in individual authors. And the definitions will be crowned by quotations that he intended as one of the glories of the *Dictionary*, quotations that he had already spent a year or more laboriously collecting from thousands of books, 'preferring writers of the first reputation to those of an inferior rank; of noting the quotations with accuracy; and of selecting, when it can be conveniently done, such sentences, as, besides their immediate use, may give pleasure or instruction by conveying some elegance of language, or some precept of prudence, or piety'.[22]

The *Plan* was well received. While Thomas Birch grudgingly approved, 'it is an ingenious performance, but the style too flatulent', Pope's learned friend John Boyle, the Earl of Orrery, was less equivocal, 'I think the specimen is one of the best that I have ever read ... the language of Mr Johnson's is good, and the arguments are properly and modestly expressed ... I have great expectations from the performance.' Notices in the press were also very positive, the upshot of which was that the *Plan* suddenly made Johnson known and encouraged the public to imagine he was smoothly and well into the book and would complete it promptly.[23]

[5]

In the attic room at the top of his house – frequently compared to Sir James Murray's famous Scriptorium at Oxford, for decades the engine room of the *Oxford English Dictionary* in the late nineteenth century – Johnson assembled the materials and people he needed, turning it into something resembling a 'counting house'. Hundreds of books (many of them large folios) had to be brought in to supplement his own collection, shelves were constructed, tables had to be set up to accommodate the various stages of research and the physical process of transcribing and cutting and pasting slips, boxes for filing had to be organised, and the odd chair and stool brought in for him and his assistants. Joshua Reynolds mentioned 'his books, all covered with dust' and 'a crazy deal table, and a still worse and older elbow chair, having only three legs'. That three-legged stool became legendary in his lifetime, following him from this study to others he would have in London.

As for books, he treated them, then and later, with a roughness for which modern librarians would have regarded him as a public nuisance. The problem, as Hawkins wrote, was that Johnson did not care about the external condition of books, 'tearing the heart' (as the poet Mary Knowles said) out of them and as likely as not leaving them on a table or on the floor after he was done with them. Hawkins described Johnson's library as 'a copious but miserably ragged one'. Nor were the books he borrowed for the *Dictionary* exempt from abuse. He treated them as tools, not as precious items in collections. He marked them up with black lead pencils and although he maintained that all the marks could be removed with breadcrumbs, they could not; nor did he try very hard to remove them, if at all. So notorious did he become for this treatment of books that people eventually were reluctant to lend him what he needed. Hawkins wrote that he often returned them 'so defaced as to be scarce worth owning, and yet, some of his friends were glad to receive and entertain them as curiosities'.[24]

By any reckoning, to finish the *Dictionary* in three years – even in six, or nine for that matter – would require herculean efforts and demand more of him by far than had any other previous task, especially since much of this was on the face of it dull work. '*To make dictionaries is dull work,*' he would write in his entry for 'dull', in the same self-deprecatory vein as his definition of 'grubstreet' as a place 'inhabited by writers of small histories, dictionaries, and temporary poems, whence any mean production is called 'Grubstreet', and of 'lexi-cographer' as 'a writer of dictionaries; a harmless drudge, that busies himself in tracing the original, and detailing the signification of words'. But he had a heroic sense of mission about the job. A recent writer on the *Dictionary* has summed up what the task required: 'It called for all the skills of the writer, but also for those of the editor, the explicator, the anthologist and the hod-carrier, the book-muncher, the page-maker and the cultural steeplejack, and was as many as a dozen labours rolled into one.'[25] If he were ever to finish at all, never mind on time, he needed steady help.

Oddly, considering his legendary sniping at Scotland, of which there will be more later, he chose five Scots to help him – six amanu-enses in all, five of whom had poverty in common. Boswell could not resist the comment, 'Let it be remembered by the natives of North-Britain, to whom he is supposed to have been so hostile, that five of them were of that country.' Never would all six work at one time in the attic – generally only four or fewer according to the stage of the work and whether there was anything at the time useful for them to do.[26]

Francis Stewart was the first to come on board. Johnson paid him, like the others, out of the advance from the booksellers, in spite of their poor salaries an expense that turned out to be a significant drain on his resources and made the advance quickly look much smaller than at first. Stewart's task was chiefly to copy illustrative quotations from hundreds of books that Johnson had already marked up in the early spring. He also helped Johnson define 'low cant phrases; all words relating to gambling and card-playing'. The others were hired in the weeks and months to follow and seem to have been paid equally poorly. Two of them, the brothers Alexander and William Macbean, entered the fray around 1748 and stayed until about 1754. They brought with them some practical experience with reference works. The eldest, Alexander, 'a very learned Highlander', appears to have provided Johnson with some sort of moral or even spiritual encouragement, perhaps having something to do with his melancholia. Not long before he died, Johnson remembered fondly that Alexander 'was one of those who, as Swift says, *stood as a screen between me and death* ... He was very pious. He was very innocent ... He was very highly esteemed in the house.' He was more than a copyist for Johnson, actually writing a few of the definitions for him and mischievously slipping into the text both his own name and a little of his own poetry. Robert Shiels was a fourth, a hack writer and sometimes biographer. He died of consumption two years before the *Dictionary* was published, lamented by Johnson as 'a man of very acute understanding, though with little scholastic education'. The fifth Scot was a 'Mr Maitland', about whom we know nothing, and the sixth an Englishman, V. J. Peyton, a linguist who later published a French grammar and was described by Johnson's friend Giuseppe Baretti, probably incorrectly given Baretti's strong prejudices, as 'a fool and a drunkard'. Peyton and Alexander Macbean were the ones still working for Johnson when the *Dictionary* was published. Johnson later would not be entirely pleased with the work of either of them.[27]

These 'laborious brethren' were among his first set of household guests in what would be forty years of having odd collections of indigent or otherwise needy souls living with him for varying periods of time. He not only gave them work but also allowed them occasionally to sleep at Gough Square or visit him during unsocial hours. Long after the *Dictionary* was published, he continued to help them. 'Peyton and Macbean are both starving, and I cannot keep them,' he wrote in 1775, but he did, raising money for them, finding them lodgings, and paying for Peyton's funeral expenses. He wrote poignantly to Mrs Thrale about Peyton's death in 1776, how for many years 'he sat starving by the bed of a wife not only useless, but almost motionless, condemned by poverty to personal attendance, and by the necessity of such attendance chained down to poverty.' Stewart died before the *Dictionary* was published, but as late as 1780 Johnson was imploring Boswell not to forget his sister in Edinburgh, for 'the memory of her brother is yet fresh in my mind'.[28]

[6]

From the very beginning, the progress on the *Dictionary* was difficult. He was beset with doubts, plagued with persistent melancholia, and not entirely certain how to proceed. He was working in a vacuum, without a useful model. Nobody had done before what he wanted to do, not at any rate the way he wanted to do it. His work with the Harleian Library had familiarised him with specimens of dictionaries in the past, but mostly they provided lessons on what to avoid. His courage cannot be overstated. In the *Rambler* (essay number 122, written on 18 May 1751 when he was still a long way from reaching the summit of the lexicographical mountain he was trying to scale), he reflected with some agony on the chronic human dilemma of biting off more than one may be able to chew: 'Nothing is more subject to mistake and disappointment than anticipated judgement concerning the easiness or difficulty of any undertaking, whether we form our opinion from the performances of others, or from abstracted contemplation of the thing to be attempted.'[29]

He started by making a word list, then looked for the quotations to illustrate definitions. Obviously he had never tried to find quotations for less common words, otherwise he would have realised quickly enough that he would not have been able to complete his work in thirty years, much less three.[30] Instead, he built his word list of some 43,000 words from the quotations he took from what he considered the best authors, augmenting it by raiding earlier dictionaries, chiefly Bailey's. His governing principle was that the books of great writers determine the language. The method he used was to plunge into a volume, underline a word he decided to include, write it in the margin, and mark with vertical lines the beginning and end of the passage that contained it. He decided to choose his English authors from the period between Sir Philip Sidney and the Restoration, which Edmund Spenser described as 'the wells of English undefiled' – before the language was heavily influenced by French and after the 'rudeness' of earlier eras – though in practice he ended up going further back for a few, such as to Chaucer and Sir Thomas More. The quotations turned out to be a map of his intellect and astonishingly vast range of reading. His favourite authors included Sidney, Spenser, Bacon, Milton, Thomas Browne, Richard Hooker and Dryden. He also drew on John Locke, Isaac Watts, Addison, Pope, Swift and William Law, among other post-Restoration writers, as well as on several 'living authors' such as his friend Samuel Richardson, in spite of having declared that he would ignore them lest he 'be misled by partiality, and that none of my contemporaries might have reason to complain'. Indeed, he even included himself and friends, several women among them including Charlotte Lennox, 'when my heart, in the tenderness of friendship, solicited admission for a favourite name'. After the *Dictionary* came out, Garrick told him people were grumbling that he had lowered the dignity of his work by including living authors. He replied famously, 'Nay, I have done worse than that: I have cited *thee*, David [under 'giggler'].'[31]

He amassed many more than the 116,000 quotations he included in the *Dictionary*, finding that because of the incredible bulk to which the volumes would swell and 'fright away the student' he was reduced to 'the vexation of expunging' thousands of them, or reducing them to 'clusters of words', or even rewriting them. Many he could not bear to purge or 'mutilate' because they 'intersperse with verdure and flowers the dusty deserts of barren philology'. As it was, the formidable fatness of the published volumes would be due chiefly to the quotations, which embrace encyclopedically virtually all knowledge in literature, religion, philosophy, science, law, manufacturing technology, crafts, and so on, making it 'part dictionary, part encyclopedia, part textbook'.[32]

Mitigating against the reputation of the *Dictionary*, however, as a universal and progressive display of knowledge, has been the controversial contention that Johnson's quotations reveal a moral, religious, philosophical and political bias. This is partly because he admitted he wanted quotations to do more than just illustrate a word: 'I therefore extracted from philosophers principles of science; from historians remarkable facts; from chemists complete processes; from divines striking exhortations; and from poets beautiful descriptions.' But which philosophers, divines and poets? There is no doubt that he chose or rejected many authors for their beliefs. It is clear at least that neither the quotations nor the definitions reflect a 'primary commitment' to these biases. Johnson is primarily illustrating words, not principles, but as a human being with strong feelings and ideas his choices do frequently reflect his attitudes and points of view. As Robert Folkenflik notes, 'dictionaries are ideological. They cannot be otherwise.' Johnson's *Dictionary* 'has a mind of its own. We can safely say what the *Dictionary* thinks; it is more difficult to make the claim about what Johnson thinks on the basis of *Dictionary* illustrations or even definitions. Controversial terms do not always call for a tendentious response.' Johnson's decisions 'come out of a head, not out of a hat'. As religion was central to Johnson's life and thought, for example, Christian writers such as Law, Richard Hooker, Robert South and John Tillotson are extremely well represented, as is the Bible (4,617 quotations) and the *Book of Common Prayer*. Other religious writers he omitted on account of their theological views. His exclusion of Thomas Hobbes and Bernard Mandeville and other 'wicked' writers – although he thought highly of Mandeville in other respects – was impelled by his intense dislike of both their 'principles' or unorthodox religions and social views and the damage he feared they could do to impressionable readers. 'I scorned, sir, to quote him at all', Johnson said of Hobbes.[33]

Readers have also censured the way Johnson allowed his personality to intrude: that he used the work to promote his own views, standing in the way of progress by misrepresenting the contemporary intellectual milieu. He has also been accused of reinforcing the contemporary status quo, religious, political, and cultural. He was involved in suppressing insubordination and dissent, some of the argument goes. Given Johnson's vast range and catholicity of sources, these judgements sound extreme, for any points of view introduced by his illustrative quotations keep company with thousands of others that undercut them. It is unreasonable to claim that the *Dictionary* embodies any coherent political, social or personal orientation. Another way of looking at this issue is that the *Dictionary* was 'public', as Robert DeMaria has pointed out, and that for some of the same reasons accounting for his tact in the *Plan* he was wary of alienating potential purchasers, aiming at 'a broad but economically stable, politically conservative stratum of British society'.[34]

[7]

The booksellers were eager to see manuscript copy and have the printing begin, and Johnson himself, whose hunting through books for quotations was done in a void, needed to see how his method of collecting them first and then adding definitions, etymologies and other lexicographical material later would work. He therefore began to compose the text very early in the project. In order to contain the manuscript he and his assistants created as many as eighty notebooks by folding and cutting paper into quarto format and creating with it gatherings or sections of pages, slipped within each other. If, as Boswell said, each notebook contained two quires of paper, or about twenty-four quarto sheets, and each sheet eight pages, then each of these cumbersome notebooks numbered close to four hundred pages. Each page was divided into two columns. Johnson and his amanuenses then wrote the words to be defined in the columns; he had them copy the quotes from transcribed slips or (to save work) directly from the books into the spaces allotted for the particular word being defined. He judged the space he needed between words on the basis of how many quotations for a word he had already collected, how many senses of the word he had come up with, and what other lexicographical information he knew or anticipated he would include. Obviously he would have to add leaves and gatherings as he introduced new words, so he tied the notebooks loosely rather than stitched them together.[35]

Everyone had something to do and they made rapid progress in the first two or three years. As this was noticed, there was a buzz in the air that the *Dictionary* would soon be finished. But all was not well in the garret, and it is hard not to believe that Johnson had not for some time realised the huge problem that was rearing its nightmarish head.

If he had had a word processor, his sleepless nights would have been less troubled. With all the additions, expansions and revisions that inevitably continued, he constantly ran out of space under the entries and the text often became a confusing jumble. To begin with, he attempted to insert quotations before he had collected all of them. Many (with some difficulty) could continue to be slipped or written in wherever possible, though many could not. If the order in which he wished them to appear had to be changed, he was often out of luck. There was no room to do that. The fragile and chaotic state of the manuscript resulting from this alone would have been horrendous for the printer. Glued slips could fall out, as the manuscript notebooks were moved around the printing house. A bigger problem was the definitions. He continually underestimated the number of senses and variety of usage of words. His quotations were revealing by the hour how richly diverse and infinitely alive the language was in meaning, throwing up all kinds of meaning from usage that his earlier etymological scheme or straitjacket of tracing words down from their primitive meanings could not accommodate.[36] Extended definitions drawing on his reading had to be squeezed in where possible and the text rearranged. There were other problems. The amanuenses often entered the wrong headword, or entered it in the wrong place, if they reasoned incorrectly as to how to read a phrase Johnson had marked. His amanuenses gave him vital help and companionship, but inadvertently they interfered with his authorial control. Also, since quotations had been written into the manuscript from early in the process, Johnson's hands were tied if he wished to alter their wording, as he often did.[37]

The whole thing became a mess. The deeply depressing day finally arrived in 1749 or early 1750 when his worst dreams came true and he had to abandon both his method and manuscript, realising that instead of using confining notebooks he would have to adopt a more flexible method of using loose sheets that could be added as needed. This catastrophic decision brought a crisis both of mind and career. He understood the new method he had to use, and this gave him some hope, but, although he had not exactly wasted three years, the book-sellers who hoped to publish at the end of that time thought he had and were not at all happy. He had used up all the advance and Tetty was in a more parlous state than ever, making more demands on the little money they now had left. Was he back where he had started three years earlier? Was this just another failure? For a time his work appears to have come to a screeching halt.

CHAPTER 15

Poetic Interludes

S oon after arriving in London with Johnson in 1737, Garrick had given up the wine business and begun to prosper on the stage. With his innovative emotional, naturalistic acting style, by 1747 he had made himself one of the leading actors in the country, in both comedy and tragedy. He would soon be swept up by Garrick fever in a theatrical world already ornamented with stars such as James Quin, Peg Woffington, Kitty Clive, Charles Macklin, Samuel Foote, Hannah Pritchard, and Susannah Cibber. His drawing power at the box office became enormous, mainly at the Theatre Royal in Drury Lane, which he had made his theatrical home since debuting there in 1742. In the spring of 1747 he decided to purchase a half-interest in Drury Lane for £12,000 as one its two patentees, thereby catapulting himself into the world of theatrical management to augment his powers on the stage. After a summer of structural improvements at the theatre and working out the repertory for the coming season and new contracts for his battalion of more than fifty actors, he opened his first season as manager on 15 September with a performance of *The Merchant of Venice*. What he did there for more than thirty years transformed the British stage and became legendary.

That opening night was the occasion of a minor collaboration between Garrick and Johnson. They had not seen much of each other for years while Garrick was rising to stardom, in the course of which their relationship became complex. While publicly acknowledging Garrick's acting genius, Johnson clearly envied his meteoric success and was repelled by his vanity, chronic name-dropping and artful social climbing. 'His being outstripped by his pupil in the race of immediate fame,' wrote Boswell, 'as well as of fortune, probably made him feel some indignation, as thinking that whatever might be Garrick's merits in his art, the reward was too great when compared with what the most successful efforts of literary labour could attain.' Neither did Johnson like what he regarded as Garrick's and others' 'artificial tone and measured cadence in the declamation of the theatre', especially in the acting of Shakespeare. One night in a tavern, after seeing Garrick act, Johnson remarked, 'the players ... have got a kind of rant, with which they run on, without any regard either to accent or emphasis'. Arthur Murphy told of 'being in conversation with Dr Johnson near the side of the scenes during the tragedy of *King Lear*, when Garrick came off the stage, he said, "You two talk so loud you destroy all my feelings". "Prithee", replied Johnson, "do not talk of feelings, Punch has no feelings." Admirable as Garrick's imitation of nature always was, Johnson thought it no better than mere mimicry.'[1]

Indeed, Johnson seems to have been irritated especially by Garrick's role in transforming the nation's consciousness about Shakespeare, in turning him into a national icon, the Bard, a patriotic literary champion of Englishness. And yet, 'Dr Johnson considered Garrick his property,' said Reynolds, and 'would never suffer any one to praise or abuse him but himself'. 'It is certain', wrote Murphy, 'that he esteemed and loved Garrick; that he dwelt with pleasure on his praise; and used to declare, that he deserved his great success, because on all applications for charity he gave more than was asked. After Garrick's death he never talked of him without a tear in his eyes.'[2]

From isolated remarks by his contemporaries, the prevailing (and overstated) opinion seems to have been that Johnson did not have much use for the theatre. Boswell thought he was lukewarm about the theatre because he could not see or hear well enough and felt bitter about his failure to get *Irene* acted, as well as because of his envy of Garrick. Johnson's friend the Shakespearean critic George Steevens said he had it from Johnson himself that his eyesight was his great handicap at the theatre: 'To speak the truth, there is small encouragement there for a man whose sight and hearing are become so imperfect as mine'. There was perhaps a more fundamental reason for his ambiguities about the stage – the face rather than the page, as the saying goes: he was not about to 'chase the new-blown bubbles of the day' which the 'wild vicissitudes of taste' on stage every day held up as a mirror to the 'publick voice', a mockery of the great national theatrical tradition.[3]

Nonetheless, he did attend plays at Drury Lane, Covent Garden and elsewhere and, as we shall see, for a time even enjoyed lingering backstage at Drury Lane. And he was pleased to accept Garrick's

invitation to write a prologue for that opening night of his management at Drury Lane. Writing the sixty-two lines of the prologue
for the big night gave him a chance, with Garrick's encouragement
and perhaps even at his request, to describe the moral degeneration
of contemporary English drama, which he thought was a national
disgrace, a plague threatening to infect the other arts – 'the licentiousness and dissolute manners on stage', as Boswell put it. It was a
timely message: the new era Garrick was launching at Drury Lane
promised change and the prologue provided a manifesto for it. He
claimed that after composing the entire poem in his head, 'I did not
afterwards change more than a word in it, and that was done at the
remonstrance of Garrick. I did not think his criticism just, but it was
necessary he should be satisfied with what he was to utter.'[4]

The poem begins with an appropriate celebration of the former
glories of the stage in which Shakespeare's 'flame' and Ben Jonson's
'art' thrived. The trouble began in the Restoration, when thespian
'wits' opted for 'easier ways to fame'. Johnson's harsh language leaves
no doubt as to where he stood on the moral vacuum that had ensued:
'Intrigue was plot, obscenity was wit./Vice always found a sym-
pathetick friend;/They pleas'd their age, and did not aim to mend'
(lines 20–22). The theatre became nothing less than a 'pimp' for future
generations. On top of that, its art declined, 'crush'd by rules' and
'refin'd' into effeminate weakness. Tragedy declined through 'frigid
caution' and 'declamation roar'd, while passion slept'. Virtue and
'Nature' fled, leaving the stage open for productions of vapid panto-
mime and song. But the audience that night was lucky and privileged:
Garrick's new reign at Drury Lane was about to rescue the London
stage. 'The pomp of show' was about to be chased off the stage by
'useful mirth and salutary woe', the moral radiance of truth and virtue.[5]

How much Johnson believed all this is open to question, but he
was paid for the poem and surely it had already occurred to him that
one favour deserved another and that Garrick now was in a position
to help him with *Irene*. He was right. Garrick encouraged him to put
some finishing touches to the play and promised to stage it at Drury
Lane. To Johnson it must have seemed like a dream come true, a
fulfilment or closure of those struggling years before and after moving
to London. The play's resurrection also meant some badly needed
income since it was customary for the playwright to receive the profits
from every third performance.

First, there was work to be done on the play. More than a decade had elapsed since he wrote most of it, and the pseudo-classical pomposity of many of its lines struck Garrick as virtually unactable, even by the great actors and actresses he had in his stable under contract. Even after revisions, Hawkins judged, 'The diction of the piece was cold and philosophical; it came from the head of the writer, and reached not the hearts of the hearers.' One might have expected Johnson to respond gratefully to Garrick's recommendations based on years of acting and knowledge of the mechanics of the theatre, especially since he knew the play was an example of his writing when he was only in his twenties. But not so. He seems to have resisted Garrick's suggestions at every turn and was still resentful of what he saw as his friend's pushiness many years later. Enlisting Taylor to intervene after a 'violent dispute' between them, Garrick got an earful for his efforts: 'Sir, the fellow wants me to make Mahomet run mad, that he may have an opportunity of tossing his hands and kicking his heels.' (Garrick did not play Mahomet, perhaps as a result of their disagreements.) Nonetheless, Garrick had his way on many passages and on 29 November 1748 this note appeared in the *General Advertiser*: 'We hear a new tragedy called *Mahomet and Irene* will be acted at the Theatre Royal in Drury Lane after Christmas.'[6]

The play opened seven weeks later on 6 February. On the opening night Johnson paced anxiously up and down the theatre dressed totally out of character in what he thought was appropriate for a playwright, a scarlet waistcoat braided with gold and a gold-laced hat. Recognising quickly the absurdity of the figure he was cutting backstage in the Green Room as well as out in the side boxes, 'I soon laid aside my gold-laced hat, lest it should make me proud.' 'At that period all the wenches knew me', he remarked, 'and dropped me a curtsey as they passed on to the stage.' According to one unreliable story Boswell tells in his journal (and in an early draft of the *Life* that he later somewhat bowdlerised to make less racy), Garrick informed David Hume that Johnson, during these performances or later, 'out of considerations of rigid virtue', decided that he had to put an end to his backstage visits: 'No, David said he[,] I will never come back. For the white bubbies and the silk stockings of your actresses excite my genitals.' For publication, Boswell replaced 'genitals' with 'amorous propensities'. Johnson's nervousness on the opening night was not helped by the hissing and catcalls that issued from the audience before the play began. Once Johnson's combative Prologue began to be spoken, though, the audience grew silent, surprised by its strident note of defiance and indifference towards criticism. He was not about to get on his knees to the audience: 'Ye fops be silent, and ye wits be just!'[7]

In spite of a wonderful set and lavish costumes, and the best actors, Garrick's efforts proved insufficient. The play in several respects was beyond repair for the stage, though one of Garrick's revisions created its own problems. Against Johnson's wishes, he insisted that Irene (acted by the popular Mrs Pritchard) was to be strangled onstage in the fifth act, not out of view as Johnson wrote it, speaking her last two lines 'with a bow-string round her neck'. The melodrama proved too much for the audience, which cried '*Murder! Murder!*', and from that moment the scene crumbled in a chaos of jeers and taunts: Mrs Pritchard 'several times attempted to speak; but in vain. At last she was obliged to go off the stage alive.' The next night Irene expired safely offstage, but the hissing lingered on in subsequent performances. The play was not a flop, but its reception was only lukewarm. Garrick kept it going for nine nights, a good run for the eighteenth century, so that his friend could reap almost £200 in profits from a benefit every third performance, but he never liked it. He told Murphy decades later, 'When Johnson writes *tragedy, declamation roars, and passion sleeps*: when Shakespeare wrote, he dipped his pen in his own heart.' When asked how he had felt about the lukewarm reception of his play, Johnson replied, 'Like the Monument', unmoved and stoic. The income softened the blow, but he was far from unmoved. He stewed somewhat with mixed feelings about the actresses. Alluding to a typical attitude of actors in the eighteenth century, he complained of the superb Mrs Pritchard, whom Mrs Thrale said he blamed for the failure of the play and whom once he described as a 'vulgar idiot' in common life: 'She no more thought of the play out of which her part was taken, than a shoemaker thinks of the skin, out of which the piece of leather, of which he is making a pair of shoes, is cut.' As for Susannah Cibber in the role of Aspasia, he said he would rather 'sit up to the chin in water for an hour than be obliged to listen to the whining, daggle tailed Cibber'. The pain of not having a smash hit on his hands was eased by his selling the copyright to Robert Dodsley for £100, who published it on 16 February. In just over a week he made more money than previously in any entire year.[8]

Poetry and fable were safer. Several months earlier he had published a piece of visionary prose fiction on the theme of the futility of human happiness, *The Vision of Theodore: The Hermit of Teneriffe*, which

Dodsley published in his *Preceptor: Containing a General Course of Education*. He also wrote the Preface for the *Preceptor*, which gave him a chance to draw on his strong feelings about his own education and the social imbalances in the education system.[9] *The Vision*, which he wrote in one night, fit nicely into Dodsley's publication because it is an allegory about how to acquire wisdom and morally constructive 'habits, sentiments, and passions'. Like other allegories of his, it turned out to be one of his more popular pieces with the reading public. A 'preceptor' or teacher, in a manner anticipating Johnson's great work *Rasselas* a decade later, instructs his 'dear pupil' in morality and tells him of a fable he heard related by a friend in the form of a 'a vision' illustrating how moral choices determine the happiness and fate of the individual. Theodore, a hermit, begins the ascent of a high peak in Teneriffe, the largest of the Canary Islands, but on the way up he has a dream in which a 'protector' appears to him and directs him to look down upon multitudes struggling up the mountain slopes. Some are making it up to a 'Temple of Happiness', others beset by 'a troop of pygmies' (human habits) are being waylaid by vices such as indolence, ambition, despair, intemperance and avarice. The whole allegory is draped in the archetypal tradition of a mountain gloom, mountain glory journey of discovery so popular in sixteenth and seventeenth-century English literature, the most famous example of which was *A Pilgrim's Progress*.[10]

What is disturbingly evident in this 'dream' is Johnson's pre-occupation with the temptations of his own bad habits and how they continually threatened his own happiness. 'Remember, Theodore,' concludes the preceptor, 'and be wise, and let not Habit prevail against thee.' Also at the core of unhappiness is the failure to check Admiration or Wonder, Fear, Pride, Anger and Love with 'prudent Sentiments and Opinions'. In his New Year's Day prayer in 1748, he had struck just that theme, as he would in prayer after prayer, year after year: 'Almighty and most merciful Father ... grant that I may so remember my past Life, as to repent of the days and years which I have spent in forgetfulness of thy mercy and neglect of my own Salvation, and so use the time which thou shalt yet allow me, as that I may become every day more diligent in the duties which in the Providence shall be assigned me.' Diligence is a rational faculty, and, as in this petition to God, he recognised that prayer or obedience in his own life must be expressed through a capacity to be disciplined. Theodore himself is told by a sweet nymph who calls herself 'Reason' that his only protection is obedience, and that 'Reason' is the way to Religion. This was a weighty moral problem for Johnson, knowing as he did that his own obedience had always been a huge struggle, and explained the emotional force behind his dread of entangling, seducing vices – 'inchained by Habits, and ingulfed by Despair'. Indolence, especially when it teamed up with melancholia, terrified him:

> The captives of Indolence had neither superiority nor merriment. Discontent lowered in their looks, and Sadness hovered round their shades; yet they crawled on reluctant and gloomy, till they arrived at the depth of the recess, varied only with poppies and nightshade, where the dominion of Indolence terminates, and the hopeless wanderer is delivered up to Melancholy: the chains of Habit are riveted for ever, and Melancholy having tortured her prisoner for a time, consigns him at last to the cruelty of Despair.[11]

All of this was very close to the bone and may have impelled him to tell Percy it was 'the best thing he ever wrote' – 'best' in the sense of being morally self-defining.

Just before *Irene* was staged, he took up the theme of human happiness again in a new poem in heroic couplets, *The Vanity of Human Wishes*, an imitation of the tenth satire of Juvenal. It was his greatest achievement in poetry and the first time his name ever appeared on the title page of one of his works, but as he was still unknown to the public as a poet, Dodsley paid him only fifteen guineas for it. He wrote *Vanity* probably in the early autumn 1748, very rapidly for some quick money, as he stated in a characteristic boast: 'I wrote the first seventy lines ... in the course of one morning, in that small house beyond the church at Hampstead. The whole number was composed before I committed a single couplet to writing.' He told Boswell the same thing when describing his customary and eccentrically precocious way of composing verses: 'The great difficulty is to know when you have made good ones. I have generally had them in my mind, perhaps fifty at a time, walking up and down in my room; and then I have written them down, and often, from laziness, have written only half-lines. I remember I wrote a hundred lines of *The Vanity of Human Wishes* in a day.'[12]

The poem is, as the title suggests, essentially a Christian sermon rooted deeply in human nature. Its great Christian theme is that it is idle and dangerous for humans to seek to hold on 'permanently to human happiness, or even to try to find it, for that matter, for life is slippery and on the whole unhappy, mainly a preparation for the afterlife. The great sin or human folly is to imagine that through either self-deception or prideful ego one can escape that profound fact.'

Johnson's deteriorating progress with the *Dictionary* and the gloom that stole over him as a result possibly prompted him to write the *Vision of Theodore* and *Vanity of Human Wishes*,[13] both of which are about the inability to make the right choices frequently enough and therefore the vanity of aspiring to lasting happiness. Emulating Juvenal, the Stoic, and adapting his satire to modern conditions, *Vanity* savagely chronicles how misguided hopes cruelly, ridiculously and pridefully have disappointed generation after generation. 'All times their scenes of pompous woes afford,' he writes. In a cavalcade of historical characters he drives the point home, from English political figures like Cardinal Wolsey who 'lost the pride of aweful state', the first duke of Buckingham who was murdered in 1628, and Robert Harley who suddenly fell from power when Queen Anne died in 1714, to continental legends like Charles XII of Sweden, Xerxes and the Holy Roman Emperor Charles VII.

In this poem he is still the angry young man who now is almost forty. The poem opens with a general, bleak assessment of mankind's parlous state in a dark and dangerous world:

> How hope and fear, desire and hate,
> O'erspread with snares the clouded maze of fate,
> Where wav'ring man, betray'd by vent'rous pride,
> To tread the dreary paths without a guide,
> ... Shuns fancied ills, or chases airy good.

Everywhere 'Fate wings with ev'ry wish th'afflictive dart', and there is no end in sight of those who are betrayed by their restless ambition:

> Unnumber'd suppliants croud Preferment's gate,
> A thirst for wealth, and burning to be great;
> Delusive Fortune hears th'incessant call,
> They mount, they shine, evaporate, and fall.

Inviting the laughing philosopher Democritus to mock the folly and ghastly farce of human existence, he tells the reader he is going to 'Survey mankind, from China to Peru' – the great and powerful as well as the weak, foolish and vulnerable, like mothers and scholars – to determine how justified the mockery is. He finds that nobody is spared, but (unlike Juvenal) he pities mankind, as in his sketch of Cardinal Wolsey's fall from royal grace, 'With age, with cares, with maladies oppress'd' while 'Grief aids disease' as he hastens towards death.[14]

One of the most moving sections is on old age, the keynote to which Johnson sums up in the line, 'That life protracted is protracted woe.' Time has shut up 'all the passages of joy' and rendered 'the dotard' who has prayed for long life incapable of any sensuous enjoyment. All that is left to him is senile bullying and demands, 'perversely grave, or positively wrong'. He becomes a target of gathering sneers by bored, avaricious would-be heirs. His end is far more bleak than Jacque's portrait of old age in Shakespeare's *As You Like It*: 'Unnumber'd maladies his joints invade' as his avarice still flourishes and he turns his 'anxious heart and crippled hands' to his gold, which he counts up to the minute of his death. This appalling picture Johnson counters with a portrait of an ageing but wise and gracious woman who Mrs Thrale maintained was modelled after his own mother, 'The gen'ral fav'rite as the gen'ral friend.' But even she is afflicted with sorrows in old age. She decays until her 'with'ring life' is at last released by 'pitying Nature'.

There is also another sketch of a girl whose parents vainly pray that she will grow up to be pretty. The passage sympathetically concentrates on the vanity that inevitably germinates within such a girl and the moral pressures that women in general have to suffer in a society that stridently and cruelly programs them into conventional private and domestic roles:

> Ye nymphs of rosy lips and radiant eyes,
> Whom Pleasure keeps too busy to be wise,
> Whom Joys with soft varieties invite,
> By day the frolick, and the dance by night,
> Who frown with vanity, who smile with art,
> And ask the latest fashion of the heart,
> What care, what rules your heedless charms shall save,
> Each nymph your rival, and each youth your slave?

The poor girl does not realise in the fullness of blooming youth and beauty that she is already on a slippery slope to rivalry, age, neglect and obscurity: 'Now beauty falls betray'd, despis'd, distress'd,/And hissing Infamy proclaims the rest.'

Where then, Johnson asks, 'shall Hope and Fear their objects find?

Must helpless man in ignorance sedate, 'Roll darkling down the torrent of his fate?' God is a very present help in trouble, he urges, to whom we must leave 'the measure and the choice,/Safe in his pow'r, whose eyes discern afar/The secret ambush of a specious pray'r'. Love, patience, and faith are the 'goods' for which we should all aspire, ordained by heaven. This is a spiritual happiness which has nothing to do with vain human wishes and provides the ultimate mockery of vanity. It may strike the reader that this conclusion is too easy and abrupt in terms of the profound complexity and tragedy of human sorrow that the poem has richly and emotively portrayed. But there is no alternative except terrible oblivion, Johnson thought, and oblivion is not the fate of those who call honestly upon God.

The poem was received tepidly, and no other separate edition of it appeared in his lifetime. Many thought it was too bleak in the abstract, though Garrick paradoxically judged that Johnson wrote the poem after 'he became more retired' – more comfortable and settled at Gough Square – than when his poverty and sense of alienation pro-duced the more realistic pictures of 'common life' in *London*. It is 'as hard as Greek', Garrick complained: 'Had he gone on to imitate another satire, it would have been as hard as Hebrew.' The Romantics disagreed. Lord Byron found it a 'grand poem' of great truth: 'The lapse of ages *changes* all things – time – language – the earth – the bounds of the sea – the stars of the sky, and every thing . . . *except man himself* . . . The infinite variety of lives conduct but to death, and the infinity of wishes lead but to disappointment.' And Sir Walter Scott remarked that he had more pleasure in reading *London* and *The Vanity of Human Wishes*, than 'any other poetical composition he could mention'. In the mid-twentieth century, T. S. Eliot declared that Johnson's claim as a major poet rested chiefly with *Vanity*; and in our own time, the poem has been judged as the first in a series of writings that has established him as a moral genius, or almost secular prophet, in modern thought.[15]

CHAPTER 16

Tetty and 'Amorous Propensities'

[1]

Hawkins knew Johnson fairly well during the late 1740s and had a bleak view of his mental state at the end of 1748. He stated flatly that his indolence and melancholia were chronic and mostly unrelated to his professional work and domestic life. This misconception undoubtedly was due to Johnson's scrupulousness in not speaking of himself and his anxieties. Even if he did not stress the isolating pressures of the *Dictionary* and demoralising effects of his life with Tetty, however, Hawkins did judge that Johnson's loneliness impelled him to found the Ivy Lane Club in the winter of 1748–9. Chance meetings in coffee houses were not enough; left largely to himself by Tetty at Gough Square, he needed to meet regularly for lively debates with people he enjoyed being with. As one of the founding members, Hawkins confirmed it was:

> a great relief to Johnson after the fatigue of study, and he generally came to it with both a corporal and mental appetite; for our conversation seldom began till after a supper, so very solid and substantial, as led us to think, that with him it was a dinner. By the help of this reflection, and no other incentive to hilarity than lemonade, Johnson was, in a short time after our assembling, transformed into a new creature: his habitual melancholy and lassitude of spirit gave way; his countenance brightened; his mind was made to expand, and his wit to sparkle: he told excellent stories; and in his didactic style of conversation, both instructed and delighted us.[1]

The birth of the Ivy Lane Club marked the emergence of Johnson as the 'great Cham' or monarch of literature, an expression first used by the novelist Tobias Smollett in 1759 to describe him; or (in Hawkins's words) as a 'symposiarch, to preside in all conversations'. The club met every Tuesday evening at the King's Head, a beefsteak house in Ivy Lane between Newgate and St Paul's Cathedral. Every Tuesday

Johnson would make his way to the King's Head with a spring in his step and 'a disposition to please and be pleased', for a few hours losing himself in humour and vigorous debate, forgetting 'painful reflections'. The club's members, in addition to Hawkins, included John Hawkesworth, his friend and associate at *The Gentleman's Magazine* since 1740; Dr Richard Bathurst, whom Johnson kept mentioning in his prayers for many years afterwards, the only person outside his family to be singled out in this way; and Samuel Dyer, the highly regarded dissenting scholar and linguist who thought Hawkins 'a man of the most mischievous, uncharitable, and malignant disposition' and, in later years, with too much money on his hands, became something of a 'sober sensualist', a tendency that Johnson tried to counter by attempting unsuccessfully to persuade him to write a life of Erasmus. Johnson occupied his tavern throne of human felicity, as he thought of it, during club sessions, from which he sometimes vexed other members by dominating the conversation intellectually. Hawkins noted he was able to 'reason and discuss, dictate and control' by his exactness of expression and also deploying his rich fund of humour, 'in which there hardly ever was his equal'.[2]

[2]

By 1748, Johnson was living mostly on his own at Gough Square in 'my recluse kind of life', oppressed by melancholic loneliness to a degree he had not felt since before his marriage. That year the deterioration of Tetty and their estrangement at last became well known when she moved out of the house and took simple lodgings in Hampstead.[3]

Whether or not Peter Garrick's remark to Boswell that Johnson once seduced 'a very fine woman' is true is something we may never know, but there is no doubt about his amorous propensities (in Boswell's phrase) and his drive to be gallant to women such as Hill Boothby. Neither are we ever likely to know if Johnson on occasion visited a prostitute. It is unlikely he did while Tetty was alive, but who knows what has remained secret in a pocket-book diary he began the year after she died – he was desperately worried when it went missing while he was on his deathbed. Hawkins had taken it to keep others (so he said) from reading it and never revealed what was in it, although at Johnson's house in 1776 Boswell secretly made a copy and used parts of it in his *Life*. The diary was destroyed shortly before Johnson's death. The fact that Johnson made a point of noting in this diary that during Tetty's funeral he was 'never once distracted by any thoughts of any other woman' suggests perhaps that before she died he frequently had been. Boswell did not use such passages in the *Life*, most likely because he did not wish to diminish Johnson's devotion to Tetty.[4]

After the contract for the *Dictionary*, Johnson was at home almost all the time, but up in the garret and totally preoccupied with the extraordinary demands the project placed on him – demands which worried him and themselves aggravated the tension between him and Tetty. She lost sexual interest in him and one day decided to deny him any more sexual favours for the rest of their married life, which for someone with such strong sexual appetites as his must have been a dismal development. Finally, she persuaded him (we may presume) to let her have her own lodgings in Hampstead, surely another source of strife and an expense they could ill afford but a place where at least she could enjoy healthier rural air in the higher ground of the village. Johnson's account of this move was that she was advised to sleep out of town and that she 'complained the staircase was in very bad condition, for the plaster was beaten off the walls in many places'. Not to worry, said the owner, 'that's nothing but by the knocks against it of the coffins of the poor souls that have died in the lodgings!'. If this remark was actually made, very likely it felt ominous to them both. Johnson visited this 'small house beyond the church' regularly while Tetty was in residence, composing the first seventy lines of *The Vanity of Human Wishes* there.[5]

It is pertinent at this point to bring in a conversation Boswell started with Johnson in October 1779 in London on the subject of conjugal infidelity. Johnson's personal revelations in the exchange strike the modern reader as outlandishly chauvinistic, even in Johnson's society of double standards regarding secular morality where female chastity was central to the marriage market of a hierarchical and propertied society, as well as to the need for absolute clarity regarding the inheritance of property and title. The 'friend' in the following passage is almost certainly Boswell himself:

I mentioned to him a dispute between a friend of mine and his lady concerning conjugal infidelity, which my friend maintained was by no means so bad in the husband as in the wife. JOHNSON: 'Your friend is right, Sir. Between a man and his Maker it is a different question; but between a man and his wife a husband's infidelity is nothing. They are connected by children, by fortune, by serious considerations of community. Wise married women don't mind it. They detest a mistress but don't mind a whore.'

Then came the bombshell:

> 'My wife told me I might lie with as many women as I pleased provided I loved her alone.' BOSWELL: 'She was not in earnest.' JOHNSON: 'But she was. Consider, Sir, how gross it is in a wife to complain of her husband's going to other women. It is that she has not enough of—'

This dash at the end suggests that even in his journal Boswell could not bring himself to include what Johnson, perhaps crudely, said Tetty lacked, if indeed she said it. He later scribbled 'tail' above the dash, though in his final version he wrote, 'what she would be ashamed to avow'. He persisted:

> BOSWELL: 'And was Mrs Johnson then so liberal? To be sure, there is a great difference between the offence of infidelity in a man and his wife.' JOHNSON: 'The difference is boundless.' BOSWELL: 'Yes, boundless as property and honours.' JOHNSON: 'The man imposes no bastards upon his wife.' BOSWELL: 'But Sir, my friend's lady argued that a wife might take care that her infidelity should not be worse than that of her husband, which, said she, it would not be if she never went astray but when she was with child by her husband.' JOHNSON: 'Sir, from what you tell me of this lady, I think she is very fit for a bawdy-house.' BOSWELL: 'Suppose a woman to be of such a constitution that she does not like it. She has no right to complain that her husband goes elsewhere'. JOHNSON: 'If she refuses it, she has no right to complain.' BOSWELL: 'Then as oft as a man's wife refuses, he may mark it down in his pocket-book and do as he pleases with a safe conscience.'

Boswell had gone too far, however, and Johnson reined him in, 'Nay, Sir, you must consider: to whore is wrong in a single man, and one cannot have more liberty by being married.' Nonetheless, as far as Boswell was concerned, he had elicited Johnson's real sentiments about Tetty, though when he came to write the *Life* he could not bring himself to publish all of this conversation. The last passage cited above was actually printed for the first edition in a revised state but he withdrew even that at the last moment. As he wrote in 1791, he could not believe he had almost 'admitted this to the public eye'. At least one friend, the MP William Windham whom Johnson 'highly valued', was struck by the 'indelicacy' of it. It is however mighty good stuff,' Boswell added, but in spite of this he did not want to run the risk in the *Life* of either tainting Johnson's moral authority or of having the indelicacy of the passage 'hurt the book'.[6]

According to what he heard from Mrs Desmoulins, who, before she was married, lived with Tetty at Hampstead – probably at Johnson's request – Tetty mistreated Johnson: 'She indulged herself in country air and nice living, at an unsuitable expence, while her husband was drudging in the smoke of London, and that she by no means treated him with that complacency which is the most engaging quality in a wife.' Why did Johnson tolerate this? Putting the best spin on it he could, Boswell had an answer: 'This is perfectly compatible with his fondness for her, especially when it is remembered that he had a high opinion of her understanding, and that the impression which her beauty, real or imaginary, had originally made upon his fancy, being continued by habit, had not been effaced, though she herself was doubtless much altered for the worse.'[7]

Johnson's strong sexual appetite appeared to cause him mildly to sublimate his frustrated feelings by petting Mrs Desmoulins when he visited her in Hampstead. Or so at least Mrs Desmoulins herself told Boswell in an exchange that Boswell again decided to keep out of the *Life*.[8] It fills five pages of his journal under the heading of 'Tacenda' and begins when he and the painter Mauritius Lowe cornered Mrs Desmoulins one day at Johnson's house in April 1783, while he was taking a nap, to extract as much as they could from her about Johnson's sex life. Making allowances for Mrs Desmoulins's vanity and gossipy disposition, the account nonetheless rings true. Lowe first primed the pump: 'Now, Ma'am, let us be free. We are all married people. Pray tell us, do you really think Dr Johnson ever offended in point of chastity? For my own part I do not believe he ever did. I believe he was chaste even with his wife, and that it was quite a Platonic connection.' Mrs Desmoulins would have none of it: 'Ah, Sir, you are much mistaken. There never was a man who had stronger amorous inclinations than Dr Johnson. But he conquered them.' Baiting her, Boswell interjected, 'I have heard people … talk of Dr Johnson's seraglio [in his household], which included you as well as her, Madam. But nobody had a serious belief of anything for a moment.' And Lowe chimed in, 'I do still think the Doctor never has had any inclination for women.' 'But he has,' she replied. Lowe demurred, 'I do not believe his marriage was consummated.' She insisted that it was most certainly consummated back at Edial Hall, according to Garrick, at least, but adds:

They did not sleep together for many years. But that was her fault. She drank shockingly and said she was not well and could not bear a bedfellow. And I remember once when at Hampstead a young woman came on a visit. I lay in the room with Mrs Johnson in a small bed. She said, 'It will not hold you both. So if you promise not to tell Mr Johnson, you shall sleep with me. But if he should know this, he'd say, "If you can bear a bedfellow, why not me as well as another?"' LOWE (waggishly): 'He has been so bad a bedfellow she could not bear him, and this has made her take drinking. He has had no passion.' MRS DESMOULINS: 'Nay, Sir, I tell you no man had stronger, and nobody had an opportunity to know more about that than I had.'

At this both Boswell and Lowe bolted upright in their chairs, craving more revelations. 'You'll forgive me, Madam', Boswell continued, 'but from what you have said, I beg leave to ask you if the Doctor ever made any attempt upon you?' 'No, Sir, I have told you he commanded his passion. But when I was a young woman and lived with Mrs Johnson at Hampstead, he used to come out two or three days in a week ... The maid went to bed, as she could not be kept up, and I used to sit up for him; and I have warmed his bed with a pan of coals and sat with him in his room many an hour in the night and had my head upon his pillow.' Amazed, Boswell could not leave it alone, 'What, when he was in bed, Madam?' 'Yes, Sir,' she replied, 'He'd desire me to go out of the room, and he'd go to bed; but to come back in a little while and talk to him – and I have come and sat on his bedside and laid my head on his pillow.' Then Boswell tried to bring these revelations to a climax:

BOSWELL: 'And he showed strong signs of that passion?' MRS DESMOU-LINS: 'Yes, Sir. But I always respected him as a father.' BOSWELL: 'What would he do? Come now, would he fondle you? Would he kiss you?' MRS DESMOULINS: 'Yes, Sir.' BOSWELL: 'And it was something different from a father's kiss?' MRS DESMOULINS: 'Yes, indeed.' LOWE (approaching his hand to her bosom): 'But would he, eh?' MRS DESMOULINS: 'Sir, he never did anything that was beyond the limits of decency.' LOWE: 'And could you say, Madam, upon your oath, that you were certain he was capable?' MRS DESMOULINS: 'Y-yes, Sir.' BOSWELL: 'But he conquered his violent inclin-ation?' MRS DESMOULINS: 'Yes, Sir. He'd push me from him and cry, "Get you gone." Oh, one can see.'

The upshot of the interview was that as an unhappily married man of forty Johnson had strong urges which, according to Mrs

Desmoulins, he was able to control. Edmund Burke, to whom Boswell confidentially related this conversation, thought it was 'just common human nature' for Johnson to act this way, but Boswell got Mrs Desmoulins to admit that if the lexicographer had indeed 'proceeded to extremities', 'such was my high respect for him, that I could not have had resolution to have resisted him', even though she had never been sexually attracted to him. When Boswell remarked that he could not imagine any woman being attracted to him this way, as 'his figure [was] so terribly disgusting', she offered the considered view that there was nonetheless something sexually appealing enough about him at the age of forty to attract a woman – 'his mind is such'. She was convinced that if a woman like the beautiful and engaging Duchess of Devonshire tried to seduce him, he might succumb if he momentarily allowed himself 'to deliberate'. Otherwise, he would 'spurn' her with ease in 'contempt and indignation'.

While Boswell packaged his portrait of Johnson's marriage with delicacy and restraint, others did not. Mrs Thrale, for example, was happy to transmit Garrick's brutal remark that Tetty was 'a little painted puppet [or 'poppet'], of no value at all, and quite disguised with affectation, full of odd airs of rural elegance'. Garrick, in fact, was especially unkind about her, perhaps still disgusted with rec-ollections of the absurd incongruity of the figure she and Johnson cut together at their Edial school. Boswell did allow into the *Life* Garrick's harsh depiction of her looks: 'very fat, with a bosom of more than ordinary protuberance, with swelled cheeks, of a florid red, produced by thick painting, and increased by the liberal use of cordials; flaring and fantastic in her dress, and affected both in her speech and her general behaviour'.[9]

William Shaw maintained that although Johnson had no children to interfere with his work on the *Dictionary*, he did have his wife whose addiction to drinking and opium may have driven him to other women. He also reminded his readers, however, that Johnson's peevishness induced by study and disease did not make him easy to live with at home. Robert Levet, one of Johnson's long-term house-hold guests, rounded it off by recalling that 'she was always drunk and reading romances in her bed'. Hawkins thought that Johnson's widely proclaimed love for her was embarrassing and did not ring true, and that her indifference to his personal appearance and habits in the 1740s bespoke a comprehensive indifference to him: his 'negligence of dress seemed never to have received the least correction from her, and who, in the sordidness of his apparel, and the complexion of his linen, even shamed her. For these reasons I have often been inclined to think, that if this fondness of Johnson for his wife was not dissembled, it was a lesson that he had learned by rote, and that, when he practised it, he knew not where to stop till he became ridiculous.' It was almost as if they were acting out an absurd, grotesque charade: 'As, during her lifetime, he invited but few of his friends to his house, I never saw her, but I have been told by Mr Garrick, Dr Hawkesworth, and others, that there was somewhat crazy in the behaviour of them both; profound respect on his part, and the airs of an antiquated beauty on hers.'[10]

[3]

Tetty was on a rapid downward curve even in the more salubrious air of Hampstead or with visits to hotels in Covent Garden known as 'hummums' where there were hot water and vapour baths – 'my wife went to the Hummums,' Johnson once recalled, 'it is a place where people get themselves cupped' – i.e. bled with a little 'glass-bell ... upon the skin'. She was very ill when she was back again at Gough Square for a few days in July 1749. 'Your poor Mamma is come home but very weak,' he informed Tetty's daughter Lucy in Lichfield, 'yet I hope she will grow better', otherwise she would have to return to Hampstead. 'She is now upstairs and knows not of my writing.'[11]

He was nervous also about his own mother's health and, as he thought, imminent death. Death was on his mind: 'I was afraid your letter had brought me ill news of my mother, whose death is one of the few calamities on which I think with horrour. I long to know how she does and, how you all do.' He appeared to be preparing himself to deal with grief. When the mother of his friend James Elphinston, the Scottish schoolmaster and Strahan's brother-in-law, died in September 1750, he wrote to him a remarkable letter of consolation worth quoting in full for its capacious understanding:

> I hope you will not think me incapable of partaking of your grief. I have a mother now eighty-two years of age, whom therefore I must soon lose, unless it please God that she rather should mourn for me. I read the letters in which you relate your mother's death to Mrs Strahan and think I do myself honour when I tell you that I read them with tears but tears are neither to me nor to you of any further use, when once the tribute of nature

has been paid. The business of life summons us away from useless grief, and calls us to the exercise of those virtues of which we are lamenting our deprivation. The greatest benefit which one friend can confer upon another, is to guard, and excite and elevate his virtues. This your mother will still perform, if you diligently preserve the memory of her life.

The best way to increase his wife's happiness, he added, was to be true to her values and virtue: 'Surely there is something pleasing in the belief, that our separation from those whom we love is merely corporeal; and it may be a great incitement to virtuous friendship, if it can be made probable that union which has received the divine approbation shall continue to eternity.' It felt to him as if the death of either Tetty or his mother might soon reveal to what extent the melancholic torment of grief would turn on him and how effectively he could fight it.[12]

CHAPTER 17

The Triumph of the Moralist

[1]

In spite of all he had done by 1750, Johnson still was relatively unknown to the public. *The Vanity of Human Wishes* put his name before the public for the first time with a published work, as distinct from the advertised and distant promise of the *Dictionary*, but it brought neither financial rewards nor wide recognition as a promising new literary personality. All that changed with his *Rambler* essays, which once they began to be published made people begin to talk and write about him and seek him out. He quickly became known as 'the Rambler'.

His distresses as a struggling author, scholar, and melancholic, his loneliness and anger over an oppressive society, and the shock of temporary defeat at the hands of the *Dictionary* shaped his philosophic and moral 'voice' for the *Rambler*. The 208 essays, which he began publishing on 20 March 1750 and which endowed him with a public identity, were crucial to his own mental health as well as to thousands of readers who were looking for essays with a hard moral realism blended with Christian benediction. As a modern editor of the *Rambler* has put it, with these essays Johnson established himself as 'one of the great moralists of modern times – as one of a handful of men, during the last three centuries, whose writing on human life and destiny has become a permanent part of the conscience of mankind'. As a distillation of his experience of life, they comprise his most representative single body of writing. And yet, for one of the great works of English literature, it is not often read today.[1]

With the *Dictionary* stalling, one might not think it was a propitious time for him to embark on a major new writing and publishing venture. But he needed the two guineas (about £200 today) per essay that Edward Cave and two other publishers were ready to pay him. Also, he had not written much prose for several years except for *Dictionary* entries and was hungry to express himself again fully and roundly in some literary way. The following remark in his penultimate essay (207) on 10 March 1752, on the complex psychology of writing for publication, is plainly autobiographical if we imagine Johnson at the end of the *Rambler* road reflecting on why he started writing these essays in the first place: 'if by the necessity of solitary application he is secluded from the world', an author 'listens with beating heart to distant noises, longs to mingle with living beings, and resolves to take hereafter his fill of diversions, or display his abilities on the universal theatre, and enjoy the pleasure of distinction and applause'. The *Rambler* satisfied this longing, providing him with a platform from which to interact with the reading public, not as a scholar but as a fully engaged guide to the human mind. It enabled him to escape from his study for immediate and regular discourse with the public, although it meant relentless deadlines twice per week for two years. In the last issue on 14 March 1752, he confessed to the pressures this had placed on him: 'He that condemns himself to compose on a stated day, will often bring to his task an attention dissipated, a memory embarrassed, an imagination overwhelmed, a mind distracted with anxieties, a body languishing with disease: he will labour on a barren topic, till it is too late to change it; or in the ardour of invention, diffuse his thoughts into wild exuberance, which the pressing hour of publication cannot suffer judgement to examine or reduce.'[2]

As a literary periodical, the *Rambler* was not modelled slavishly on the tradition of the periodical essay established by Addison and Richard Steele. It is not as topical and rooted in the eighteenth century as is the *Spectator*, for example, to which it has always been compared, though it does take up current talking points such as education, marriage, wealth, the pride of Londoners, the legal profession and criminality, the arts and theatre, fops, drinking and gambling, prostitution and poverty. In his last essay, in fact, Johnson made a point of distancing the *Rambler* from the topical periodical essay: 'I have never complied with temporary curiosity, nor enabled my readers to discuss the topic of the day.'[3] Indeed, the essays were often criticised for being too sombre. He rejected criticism with relish, feeling he was on a superior trajectory. Nevertheless, only half of Johnson's *Rambler* essays are strictly speaking what we can call 'moral essays'. And there are obvious resemblances in style and form to the contemporary popular periodical with a 'letters to the editor' format, literary criticism (including a few essays on Milton's versification), and most of all contributions written to a deadline with a roughly consistent average of 1,500 words.

If the individual issues were going to sell in any number approaching the *Spectator*'s circulation of 10,000, they had to have some 'hot off the press' immediacy of appeal for the general reader and look like a pamphlet or magazine that could be plucked casually off bookshop counters by people passing by. This feel to the essays was achieved partly by their pages being joined by a pin instead of being sewn together. (Complete sets of the original issues are extremely rare today.) For posting to readers in the provinces, they were folded lengthways. Even the name of the periodical conveys the idea of a casual, wandering sort of table talk. Johnson remarked he had been going around in circles deciding what to call it until one night 'I sat down at night upon my bedside, and resolved that I would not go to sleep till I had fixed its title. *The Rambler* seemed the best that occurred, and I took it.' Boswell did not think the name 'suited to a series of grave and moral discourses', noting in 1773 that the Italians had translated the periodical under the name '*Il Vagabondo*'. It was true that 'ramble' to Johnson's contemporaries had a somewhat racy connotation, he himself defining 'ramble' in his *Dictionary* as 'to rove loosely in lust'. Otherwise, it has a sense of casualness and impermanence, even idleness, about it. But in *Rambler* 106, on the vanity of authors who hope for the 'bubbles' of fame, he made it clear that he was hoping for the largest possible audience by comparing his essays to those of the great Bacon, who first popularised the English essay, whose essays 'come home to men's business and bosoms'. So he was in a sense trying to have it both ways: appeal to casual readers wanting entertainment and also write what he hoped would amount to a lasting compendium of his breadth and depth as a practical moralist.[4]

He composed these essays 'hastily', often because he procrastinated until almost the last moment and then found himself 'every moment more irresolute' while his ideas 'wandered from the first intention, and I rather wished to think, than thought, upon any settled subject'. Mrs Thrale told of how people spoke of his composing number 134 on procrastination, of all subjects, at Reynolds's while a messenger boy from the press waited 'to carry it to press'. 'There was however some pleasure in reflecting', he noted, 'that I, who had only trifled till diligence was necessary, might still congratulate myself upon my superiority to multitudes, who have trifled till diligence is vain.'[5]

Hastily written or not, he took the essays very seriously, composing a short 'Prayer on the Rambler' just before the first number appeared, petitioning God 'that in this my undertaking thy Holy Spirit may not be withheld from me, but that I may promote thy glory, and the Salvation both of myself and others'. The *Rambler* became the most personal and psychologically sensitive body of prose he ever wrote. He never kept a private journal with the scope and consistency of a Pepys or Boswell, but the essays, with their reflections on the human predicament, go some way towards supplying us a commentary on his own life. He was immensely proud of them, once describing his other writings as 'wine and water' whereas 'my Rambler is pure wine', and in his last essay summing up his sense of triumph over what he had achieved in them: 'I ... look back on this part of my work with pleasure which no blame or praise of man shall diminish or augment. I shall never envy the honours which wit and learning obtain in any other cause, if I can be numbered among the writers who have given ardour to virtue, and confidence to truth.'[6]

Precisely because they were so personal, initially he published these essays anonymously, not wishing to have himself measured against his own intricate moral reasoning and the sharp satire which characterise many of the essays. He was proposing to dive deep into human egotism and the complex texture of morality where he thought any man (especially he) was bound to feel naked and be found wanting. As he wrote in the autobiographically charged number 14, 'a man writes much better than he lives ... We are, therefore, not to wonder that most fail, amidst tumult, and snares, and danger, in the observance of those precepts, which they laid down in solitude, safety, and tranquillity, with a mind unbiased, and with liberty unobstructed.' His rich sympathy with the fallibility of human nature made him angry at those who with knee-jerk, accusative stuffiness 'charge with hypocrisy him that expresses zeal for those virtues, which he neglects to practise'.[7] For the time being, it was best to remain relatively anonymous. A more mundane reason for anonymity may also have been that he did not want to be censured for playing truant from the *Dictionary*.

Very soon after the early numbers appeared, Garrick and others 'who knew the author's powers and style from the first' – the sonorous rhythms and elegant, balanced syntax transmitting an air of authority and dignity[8] – 'unadvisedly asserting their suspicions, overturned the

scheme of secrecy'. It was not long before his name was on everyone's
lips. After reading the first thirteen, Samuel Richardson told Cave he
was 'inexpressibly pleased' with them, unable to remember anything
in the *Spectator* 'that half so much struck me'. He added sincerely, 'for
its own sake, I hope the world tastes them! There is but one man, I
think, that could write them; I desire not to know his name, but I
should rejoice to hear that they succeed, for I would not, for any
consideration, [hear] that they should be laid down through discouragement.' 'I am vexed that I have not taken larger draughts of
them before,' he added, 'that my zeal for their merit might have been
as glowing as now I find it.' Cave replied, admitting that 'Mr Johnson
is the *Great Rambler*, being, as you observe, the only man who can
furnish two such papers in a week, besides his other great business.'[9]

The *Rambler* provided Johnson with a large canvas on which to
protest aggressively against the Establishment and power-elites – the
egotism, venality, selfishness, stupidity, discrimination, alienation and
cruelty in society. He expressed his indignation in the last number: 'I
have never been much of a favourite of the public, nor can boast that,
in the progress of my undertaking, I have been animated by the
rewards of the liberal, the caresses of the great, or the praises of the
eminent ... If I have not been distinguished by the distributors of
literary honours, I have seldom descended to the arts by which favour
is obtained. I have seen the meteors of fashion rise and fall, without
any attempt to add a moment to their duration ... I did not feel much
dejection from the want of popularity.' There were festering wounds
not far beneath the surface of these disclaimers.[10]

As for the essays themselves, they are brimming with reductive,
ironic, biting wit; with character sketches of ludicrous people who dig
deeper and deeper holes for themselves in the pursuit of their pitiful
illusions and self-delusions; and with disdainful accounts of certain
social institutions, customs and attitudes. Take, for example, the portrait of Gelidus in number 24, a prototype of cold and absurd 'men of
learning', 'uninterrupted by their passions', who care not a fig for the
welfare of mankind, nor even for their own families, so long as nobody
disturbs them and they are left alone 'to study anything rather than
themselves'. In this essay he vented his hostility towards the imposition
of such people and the sometimes irreparable harm they do. It is one
of the reasons he reprehended pedants in teachers' clothing who had
no business meddling with young minds and hearts.[11]

Another signpost of Johnson's stridency is the abundance of 'tart, fidgety'[12] phrases, such as in this passage in number 183 on envy: 'The cold malignity of envy may be exerted in a torpid and quiescent state, amidst the gloom of stupidity, in the coverts of cowardice.' Or in number 144: 'Those that cannot make a thrust at life are content to keep themselves in play with petty malevolence, to tease with feeble blows and impotent disturbance.' He reserved special venom in number 136 for patrons, one of his favourite targets, who expect 'indecent and promiscuous dedication' and thus degrade literature: 'For what credit can he expect who professes himself the hireling of vanity, however profligate, and without shame or scruple celebrates the worthless, dignifies the mean, and gives to the corrupt, licentious, and oppressive, the ornament which ought only to add grace to truth, and loveliness to innocence?' Elsewhere he described patrons as proper company for 'cheats, and robbers, and public nuisances'.[13]

But he did not embrace the persona of a railing Juvenalian or Swiftian satirist.[14] 'Though no man perhaps made such rough replies as Dr Johnson,' wrote Mrs Thrale, 'yet nobody had a more just aversion to general satire ... and for the most part professed himself to feel directly contrary to Dr Swift.' He was more interested in moral direction and Christian devotion. The *Rambler* essays configure moral landscapes of reconciliation and community, in which humans need to participate in each other's lives and try to understand each other. Commitment to community is all. Johnson does not cast himself as the detached preacher or teacher holding forth from a lofty perch. He is one of us, saying that we all have the same temptations and weaknesses, the same hopes and fears; he describes pitfalls all of us may fall into. Readers have always found it reassuring to have him analyse relentlessly this shared humanity from so many points of view and in such detail.[15]

[2]

Even in her distress, Tetty was touched by his having launched himself into this new orbit of literary vitality. 'Johnson told me, with an amiable fondness', Boswell noted, 'a little pleasing circumstance relative to this work. Mrs Johnson, in whose judgement and taste he had great confidence, said to him, after a few numbers of the *Rambler* had come out, "I thought very well of you before; but I did not imagine you could have written any thing equal to this."' That Johnson thirty-four years later still remembered this remark so vividly as to be able to quote it suggests that it was far more than just 'a little pleasing circumstance' for him.[16]

Tetty was not alone among women readers in praising the *Rambler*, but there were problems with the public response in general, and with women's response in particular. Keeping to his publishing track record thus far, in terms of sales Johnson did not succeed with the *Rambler*. Fewer than five hundred copies of any one number were sold. The essays proved to be insufficiently light or topical to crack the mass market of literate London. To achieve this it was felt by many that he needed to have come across as less 'solemn' and 'dictatorial' and more sprightly. Ironically, one of a handful not written by him, Samuel Richardson's *Rambler* 97 on courtship advice to unmarried ladies, was the bestseller. Richardson was particularly disappointed, in fact, that Johnson's papers were not selling: 'The encouragement, as to sale, is not in proportion to the high character given to the work by the judicious, not to say the raptures expressed by the few that do read it.' As Murphy noted, although Johnson had his four guineas per week for them, the bookseller lost money from the enterprise.[17]

Richardson provided clues, in his letters as well as in his essay, as to why the essays did not sell well. Much had to do with women. His essay consists of a letter from a correspondent urging the Rambler to write more for women, about the manners of women, 'the better half of the human species', and the foibles thereof. Women are plagued today, he moaned, with 'modern time-killers' and need instruction: 'Set, dear Sir, before the youthful, the gay, the inconsiderate, the contempt as well as the danger to which they are exposed. At one time or other, women, not utterly thoughtless, will be convinced of the justice of your censure, and the charity of your instruction', especially as they negotiate their way through the marriage market. Johnson recognised Richardson's sensitive understanding of women and referred approvingly to his famous novels *Pamela* and *Clarissa* as 'lectures of conduct and introductions to life'. On the other hand, he also felt that Richardson was too precious in his sensibilities and limited in his society: 'His love of continual superiority was such, that he took care to be always surrounded by women, who listened to him implicitly, and did not venture to controvert his opinions.' Richardson was stifled by an unquenchable thirst for applause: 'He could not be content to sail gently down the stream of fame unless the foam was continually dashing in his face, that he might taste it at every stroke of the oar ... that fellow died merely for want of change among his flatterers: he perished for want of *more*, like a man obliged to breathe the same air till it is exhausted.' Richardson, however, was unapologetic, 'My acquaintance lies chiefly among the ladies; I care not who knows it.' The eminent editor and children's author, Anna Letitia Barbauld (1743–1824), put her finger on why Richardson's single essay in the *Rambler* had sold well and Johnson's essays had not, fastening on what she saw as Johnson's obtuseness, his assumption that everyone had to be as 'grave' as he was in his *Rambler* or as serious as in the *Dictionary:* 'The ladies he [Richardson] associated with were well able to appreciate his works. They were both his critics and his models, and from their sprightly conversation, and the disquisitions on love and sentiment, which took place, he gathered what was more to his purpose than graver topics would have produced. He was not writing a dictionary, like Johnson, or a history like Gibbon. He was a novel writer; his business was not only with the human heart, but [also] with the female heart.'[18]

Elizabeth Carter and her friend Catherine Talbot, both of whom contributed essays to the *Rambler*, were two other women who were certain they knew what Johnson needed to do in the *Rambler* to sell more copies. Their chatty letters are especially interesting because they highlight a unique mode of critical idolatry Johnson suddenly found was focused on him by intelligent women after his essays began to appear. One moment he was a 'harmless drudge' secreted in his garret at work on his *Dictionary*, the next a celebrated moralist and essayist who could nonetheless do with a bit of female advice. Talbot felt he needed to include more letters from correspondents and be more deferential towards them, use fewer 'hard' words (a common complaint) such as 'equiponderant' and 'adscititious' (number 20), and attempt 'papers of humour' for which London provided an endless swarm of 'amusing' material: 'odd clubs, advertisements, societies, meetings, and devices of various kinds, which this age produces'. In effect, she wanted the *Rambler* to be more like the *Spectator*. 'Any hint that is known to come from you', she urged Carter, 'will have great weight with the Rambler, if I guess him right, particularly given in that delicate manner you so well understand.'[19]

Perhaps because Elizabeth Carter spoke to him, Mrs Talbot became hopeful that Johnson might surprise them all by introducing 'humorous descriptions of, and reflections on, the London follies and diversions', and reign in his exaggerations: 'Mr Johnson would, I fear, be mortified to hear that people know a paper of his own by the sure mark

of somewhat a little excessive, a little exaggerated in the expression.' A
case in point was number 59 on Suspirus the 'human screech-owl', a
perpetually complaining cynic and malcontent – 'so *many* merchants
discouraged, so *many* ladies killed, matches broke, poets dismayed!
The numbers are too large, five or six is enough.' If only Elizabeth
Carter could have a word with him again: 'I have set my whole heart
upon the success of the Rambler (what a noble paper his last [no. 78]
upon death)'. She wrote on 17 December 1750, 'You could talk more
persuasively to the author than anybody.' He must write more on 'the
living manners of the times'. 'I say all this with fear and trembling,'
she admitted, for 'humour and manners of the world are not his fort.'
What he does excel in are 'the serious papers, that seem to flow from
his heart, and from a heart amiable and delicate to a great degree'.
When the *Rambler* ended, all was regret and exasperation that the
periodical had not matched the *Spectator*'s commercial success. Carter
was appalled, 'a good deal out of humour with the world, and more
particularly with the great and powerful part of it'.[20]

In spite of poor initial sales, the *Rambler* had a considerably wider
exposure from the common practice of hundreds of pirated issues of
the periodical published in a multitude of journals, magazines and
London and provincial newspapers. There were over three hundred
reprintings in magazines and over three hundred in provincial newspapers. Editors thought that individual issues made good feature
articles. This was not all. Even before Johnson finished writing the
essays, the publishers Bouquet and Payne – and Cave also got into
the act, for Johnson assigned the copyright over to him in April 1751
and he printed the volumes – began to put together a collected 'correct
and beautiful edition' of them in four volumes at twelve shillings, for
which Johnson heavily revised the essays. Johnson said he stopped
writing them because this edition had mushroomed to six volumes.
He revised them for other editors as well in the next four years.
Boswell was incredulous when, years later, Johnson told him he still
could improve the *Ramblers*, 'But I will, Sir, if I choose. I shall make
the best of them you shall pick out, better.' Most readers became
familiar with the *Rambler* through these printed editions. Ten in all
appeared in Johnson's lifetime, more than twenty by 1800, helping to
establish his reputation as the greatest essayist of the age. By the end
of the century and throughout the nineteenth century the *Rambler*
was more popular even than the *Spectator*.[21]

[3]

Obviously it is not possible to represent accurately enough the wide range of the *Rambler*'s moral subjects and themes in a few paragraphs. One needs to read all the essays to obtain a sense of their uncanny coherence. A good way to appreciate their weight, moreover, is to connect them to certain stages, conditions and themes in his life, when often what he says is found to be forcefully autobiographical.

In addition to those already mentioned, his subjects and methods include allegory and fictional narratives; literary criticism including essays on the new rage for fiction and a revolutionary one on biography (number 60) which is constantly anthologised; and social reform concerning prisons, orphanages, prostitution, slavery and capital punishment. Among the many moral topics, often constituting thematic clusters, are family tyranny, private and public abuse of authority, women and marriage, envy, happiness, endless incarnations of tormenting self-delusion, tragic waste of time, absurd preoccupation with the future, idleness and procrastination, vanity, grief, melancholia, biography, death, authorship, and the proper responsibilities of the worlds of learning and authorship. An overarching principle embracing Johnson's complex morality in all these essays is that it is no good trying to be virtuous in the abstract, or judging others from 'speculative reason': 'It is not but by experience, that we are taught the possibility of retaining some virtues, and rejecting others, or of being good or bad to a particular degree' (number 7). Complicated human behaviour cannot be reduced to easy choices. Nobody can attain perfection, so to judge others is a dangerous and misguided business.[22]

There is a restless, persistent probing in the typical *Rambler* moral essay, as he took up an idea, explored it from various angles, qualified and amplified it. Very little of the argumentative process is sustained with reference to Christianity. He kept pushing for human connections and revelations, telling readers about themselves, insisting on honesty (his own and ours), realism, and truth to experience. Just when the reader thinks Johnson has dealt with some aspect of an idea and is about to drop it, he is on his way again, casting yet more light on the dark corners of the mind, appealing to the uncompromising demands of common sense. He was a rebel-moralist, overturning and reconstructing. It was all given an inimitable strength by his balanced elegance of style, which is inseparable from the force and energy of his argument – 'truth is recommended by elegance, and elegance sustained by the truth'. And in spite of frequent complaints about his 'hard' words, it is all kept down to earth by the insistent concreteness of his imagery that matches his practical morality. It is a humane journey of scepticism and reassuring, if sometimes painful, moral clarity.

CHAPTER 18

Darkness Falls

[1]

Johnson wrote about 170 of the 208 *Rambler* essays while he did nothing on the *Dictionary*. He knew the proprietors were waiting impatiently for him to finish it, but in his anxiety over the huge amount left to be done and what appears to have been a taste of writer's block, he did not return to it until late November 1751, by which time the *Rambler* had only three and a half months left to run. Several of the *Rambler* essays contain clues to his fear, timidity, and deepening angst, to what felt like idleness and was exposing him to melancholia again. In number 134 (29 June 1751), he wrote bleakly: 'Life is languished away in the gloom of anxiety, and consumed in collecting resolution which the next morning dissipates; in forming purposes which we scarcely hope to keep, and reconciling ourselves to our own cowardice by excuses, which, while we admit them, we know to be absurd . . . every submission to our fear enlarges its dominion.' Indecision about how to proceed was paralysing him. If he was going to return to the work, not 'freeze in idleness', clearly it would take a huge display of self-discipline and courage.[1]

A stiff word or two from Strahan on behalf of the other disgruntled proprietors, threatening to cut off money and supplies if he did not get back to work and start sending copy again to the printer, jolted him. After five years of work only 'A', 'B' and a little of 'C' had been printed, and they had been completed several months back. They demanded to meet with him for the purpose of exerting more pressure. Not surprisingly, he did not like their complaints and took his anger out on Strahan in November 1751 with a stinging reply. He would not write if he did not want to – 'I shall *not* write' – nor would he meet with any of them until it suited him: 'my resolution has long been, and is *not* now altered, and is now *less* likely to be altered, that I shall *not* see the Gentlemen Partners till the first volume is in the press', which they may support or not as they liked. And he issued this threat: 'Be pleased to lay this my determination before them this morning, for I shall think of taking my measures accordingly tomorrow morning, only this that I mean no harm, but that my citadel shall not be taken by storm while I can defend it, and that if a blockade is intended, the country is under the command of my batteries.'[2]

[2]

In the meantime, a new woman came into his life, the novelist and dramatist Charlotte Lennox (1729–1804), who became another in his string of female protégées. Lennox was something of an enigma, definitely an outsider. Though well known for her novels, not much is known of her life. Born probably in Gibraltar, she moved to New York in 1739. Her father was a lieutenant in the British army. When he died in 1743, she emigrated to London where she briefly came under the patronage of Lady Isabella Finch. She had no money there and was in the process of preparing herself for a position at court when, at the age of eighteen, she unwisely married the impoverished and useless Scot Alexander Lennox who worked for Johnson's printer Strahan. He provided no relief from her relative poverty, so she was reduced to trying to make her way as a writer and actress. In 1747 she published *Poems on Several Occasions* which won her some literary attention – Horace Walpole described her as 'a poetess and deplorable actress'; and then in 1750 she came out with her first novel *The Life of Harriot Stuart*, among other things an indictment of the system of patronage.

Johnson had liked her when they met through her husband's connection with Strahan, but when her novel came out he was so taken with it he decided to organise a big dinner party in her honour, 'a whole night spent in festivity', at a meeting of the Ivy Lane Club at the Devil Tavern near Temple Bar. At eight o'clock Lennox, her shiftless husband, and eighteen others assembled. Hawkins, who was there but did not want to be, described the event: 'Our supper was elegant, and Johnson had directed that a magnificent hot apple pie should make a part of it, and this he would have stuck with bay leaves, because, forsooth, Mrs Lennox was an authoress, and had written verses; and further, he had prepared for her a crown of laurel, with which, but not till he had invoked the muses by some ceremonies of his own invention, he encircled her brows.' The night passed in 'pleasant conversation' and 'harmless mirth'. At five in the morning Johnson was in full stride, his face shining 'with meridian splendour, though his drink had been only lemonade; but the far greater part of us had deserted the colours of Bacchus, and were with difficulty rallied to partake of a second refreshment of coffee, which was scarcely ended when the day began to dawn'. The waiters were all asleep, so nobody could get the reckoning for hours and it was eight before 'the creaking of the street door gave the signal for our departure'. The only sour note was provided by Hawkins himself who wrote that as he walked out the door a 'sensation of shame' overwhelmed him because of the evening's resemblance to 'a debauch'. Hawkins thought Johnson depended on nights like this to drive away melancholia, 'which the public now too well knows was the disease of his mind'. The longer he stayed up, the longer he could delay stepping back into his loneliness at home. Hawkins even maintained that he may have had to stop writing the *Rambler* because its intensity threatened 'the relaxation of his mind'.[3]

Bright young spirits like Charlotte Lennox were good medicine for Johnson. Boswell recorded his comment a few months before his death that of all the young female authors he had known well, she was the one whom he thought was the ablest: 'I dined yesterday at Mrs Garrick's, with Mrs Carter, Miss Hannah More, and Miss Fanny Burney. Three such women are not to be found: I know not where I could find a fourth except Mrs Lennox, who is superior to them all.' It was not, however, a sentiment shared by his other female friends. She was quarrelsome, quick-tempered, and tempestuous, acquiring a reputation for ingratitude. Mrs Thrale once remarked that although Lennox's books were read, 'nobody likes her'. Regardless, Johnson admired her satirical audacity and energy, her independence and status as an outsider. He warmed to *Harriot Stuart* because it was a spoof on the exaggerated romantic expectations of women in heroic romance novels of the day, agreeing with her about the pernicious effects upon young, sensitive minds of such novels featuring heroines who expect 'nothing less than vows, alters, and sacrifices'. He took a detailed interest in her next ironical novel, *The Female Quixote* (1752), a highly successful imitation of Cervantes, spoofing again the young girl who gluts herself on romances and then sets out herself to live in a world of fantasy. He may have written all or part of the penultimate chapter for her, as well as the dedication, and helped her convince Richardson to publish it – 'our Charlotte's book', he called it. When she later bravely faulted Shakespeare in her three-volume *Shakespear Illustrated* (1753–4), a study of Shakespeare's sources, for which he wrote the dedication to the Earl of Orrery, Johnson and Garrick both joked that the book would have been more aptly titled *Shakespeare Exposed*. Johnson wrote to her wryly, with a Miltonic allusion, 'When Shakespeare is demolished your wings will be *full summed* and I will fly you at Milton; for you are a bird of prey, but the bird of Jupiter' – the god of tempests and thunderbolts. At times, however, even he became exasperated when she sprang at him for some imagined offence or insult: 'I wish you would for once resolve to use any method of transacting with your friends but that of letters. You will, in whatever part of the world you may be placed, find mankind extremely impatient of such letters as you are inclined to favour them with . . . I have no inclination to continue quarrels.'[4]

Johnson was the most important person in Lennox's literary life – unlike Elizabeth Carter who once remarked, 'I may make my fortune very prettily as Mrs [Elizabeth] Montagu's owl.' She remained part of, and very familiar with, his professional life for the rest of his days, although her publishing declined after the 1750s and she neither moved in his circles nor had anything to do with the Bluestocking circle of Mrs Montagu within which she might well have prospered. After he died she languished in distress for years with family problems, seeking charity and publishing a final novel in a desperate effort to earn income. She died in 1804. Very regrettably, she never kept a diary or wrote memoirs. If she had, we would surely have a valuable increment to our knowledge of Johnson as a friend and professional man of letters, especially in the 1750s.

[3]

The combined pressure of renewed penury, his remorse at not working on the *Dictionary* for about two years, together with the complaints of the proprietors, had swollen to such a pitch that by late 1751 Johnson finally had summoned up courage and forced himself to turn his attention to it again. In the next three or four months he appeared to make progress, completing and copying out for the printer words between *Carry* and *Dame* (some fifty sheets), and adding to material for *Dame* to *Kyd*. But it was difficult for him to concentrate and lead a normal life because Tetty's health was rapidly deteriorating. 'Poor Tetty Johnson's illness will not suffer me to think of going any whither, out of her call,' he wrote worriedly to Lennox on 12 March 1752. 'She is very ill, and I am very much dejected'. Then during the night of 17/18 March, only three days after the last *Rambler* and four days after he had presented her with the tender gift of his just-published four-volume edition of the essays, he received the news at Gough Square that her largely unhappy and lonely life since she married him had come to an end at her scruffy, rented lodging in Hampstead in which she had chosen to live the last months of her life.[5]

The effect Tetty's death had on him was profound. It was in many ways a pivotal moment in his life. Perhaps one has to experience the premature death of a spouse or extremely close loved one to appreciate properly the inconsolable grief that overwhelmed him. Immediately, the oppressiveness of loneliness was unbearable. In the anguish of the night he scribbled out a note to Taylor at his house in the Cloisters, Westminster, to come at once. At three in the morning Taylor flew over to Gough Square and found him weeping uncontrollably. The next morning Johnson implored him to come again, 'Let me have your company and your instruction. Do not live away from me. My distress is great.'[6]

Tetty was buried at Bromley in Kent, where John Hawkesworth lived and was able to organise her funeral, but he could not bring himself to attend it, and composed a sermon to be spoken by Taylor which was never delivered. According to Hawkins, who, unlike Boswell, did not hesitate to describe their marriage as largely a failure, he was dissuaded from 'so ostentatious a display of the virtues of a woman, who, though she was his wife, was but little known'. He could not summon up the courage to visit the grave for more than a year. When he got there on Easter Day 1753 he wrapped himself in a tissue of frantic prayers: 'I repeated mentally the commendation of her with utmost fervour . . . before the reception of each element at the altar. I repeated it again in the pew, in the garden before dinner, in the garden before departure, at home at night.' He did not get around to placing a memorial stone of black marble by her grave until shortly before he died, most likely because he could never bring himself to see or even think about the grave. His friend John Ryland, Hawkesworth's brother-in-law, saw to the stone for him. 'Shall I ever be able to bear the sight of this stone?' he asked him. He preferred to reflect on Tetty's continuing blessings on him and whether or not he was worthy of them. In Latin he wrote on the stone, here translated: 'Beautiful, polite, ingenious, pious . . . much loved and long lamented'.[7]

Four prayers crying for God's mercy that he composed between 24 April and 6 May go some way towards conveying his fear of grief and sense of desolation, combined as they were with remorse for not being a better, more patient husband and an abounding guilt over not having used his time better – time he felt should have made Tetty's life happier and more comfortable. He prayed repeatedly to be spared 'fruitless grief' and the pernicious onslaught of 'tumultous imagination' or wayward thoughts. 'Speak peace to my troubled soul,' he pleaded, that his thought might dwell on what made her life 'acceptable' and through the forgiveness of his sins enable him 'to begin and perfect that reformation which I promised her, and to preserve in that resolution, which she implored Thee to continue, in the purposes which I recorded in thy sight, when she lay dead before me'. He wrote these resolutions down and consulted them repeatedly over the next few years in an attempt to live more purely and consistently: 'to rise early', 'to lose no time', and 'to keep a journal'. He even asked God's approval for Tetty's spirit 'to have care of me . . . that I may enjoy the good effects of her attention and ministration, whether exercised by appearance, impulses, dreams'. This was no idle, sentimental prayer, for he did believe in the appearance of spirits, although he was concerned about the potential impiety of doing so.[8]

In his prayer for 6 May, in addition to a futile resolution to leave off grieving and 'return to the duties of my present state', he put his finger on a central problem of his mental health, calling upon 'our heavenly Father' to protect him from the idleness and perpetual 'negligence' that would 'lay me open to vain imaginations'. He became almost obsessive in his prayers against idleness. His verse paraphrase of *Proverbs* 6:6 just a few days after Tetty's death, entitled 'The Ant', pointed to another crisis of paralysis and a fresh chill of horror about lost time:

> How long shall sloth usurp thy useless hours,
> Year chases year, with unremitted flight,
> Till want, now following fraudulent and slow,
> Shall spring to seize thee like an ambush'd foe.

Very soon after Tetty's death he was also surprised to find himself indulging in sexual fantasies. He never referred to them in prayers before her death. These were insistent and would last for years. Lacking a woman in his house and life, even Tetty who had been unavailable to him sexually in the last few years, he prayed relentlessly to be spared these fantasies and the ensuing anguish over sensuality and sin. 'Habitual wickedness and idleness': he tended to lump them together in asking for protection against 'unchastity, idleness, and neglect of public worship', 'vain longings of affection', 'lust', 'sensuality in thought', 'pollutions', 'sinful habits', 'wickedness', 'thoughts clouded with sensuality'. There was, however, no way of beating down these devils. Tetty's death had opened up a sluice-gate for a stream, sometimes torrent, of private guilt and morbidity.[9]

His thoughts also ran to remarriage, which brought with them their unique baggage of guilt. On Easter Day thirteen months following her death, after having attended the service in Bromley, he wrote: 'As I purpose to try on Monday to seek a new wife without any derogation from dear Tetty's memory, I purpose at sacrament in the morning to take my leave of Tetty in a solemn commendation of her soul to God.' On Easter Monday he was relieved to be able to add, 'During the whole service I was never once distracted by any thoughts of any other woman or with my design of a new wife which freedom of mind I remembered with gladness in the garden.'[10]

His grief seemed to his friends all out of proportion with the nature of the marriage. Hawkins said everyone was mystified that he was 'incapable of consolation' and 'could derive no comfort' from religion, especially as 'their marriage was not one of those which ... young people call love-matches'. 'The melancholy, which seized Johnson,' he added, 'was not, in degree, such as usually follows the deprivation of near relations and friends: it was of the blackest and deepest kind.' The quarrelsome Italian Giuseppe Baretti (1719–89), who knew and became friends with Johnson perhaps as early as 1751, the year he came to live in England, told Mrs Thrale that when this lady died, Dr Johnson was almost distracted with his grief; and ... the friends about him had much ado to calm the violence of his emotion'. By the time he met Mrs Thrale in the 1760s, Johnson had escaped the gnawing pain over his loss, but she remarked nonetheless that 'he never rightly recovered the loss of his wife'. In 1778 he said to the cheerful Oliver Edwards, his old contemporary at Pembroke whom, as he was walking down a London street with Boswell, he encountered for the first time in fifty years, 'Sir, I have known what it was to have a wife, and (in a solemn tender faltering tone) I have known what it was to *lose a wife*. It had almost broke my heart.' Shaw's description of the effects of Tetty's death on him was the most compelling: 'Johnson often said he never knew how dear she was to him, till he lost her. Her death affected him so deeply, that he grew almost insensible to the common concerns of life. He then stayed little within, where her image was always recalled by whatever he heard or saw. Study disgusted him, and the books of all kinds were equally insipid. He carefully avoided his friends, and associated most with such company as he never saw before.' He took to walking the streets at night, often with Baretti: 'This for many a lonesome night was his constant substitute for sleep.' For the rest of his life he kept the wedding ring he had given her in a little round wooden box, which after his death his servant Francis Barber offered to Lucy Porter. She declined it.[11]

CHAPTER 19

Once More unto the Breach:
Back to the *Dictionary*

[1]

Although Tetty had spent little time at Gough Square in the last months of her life, Johnson now felt the house unbearably empty. Within two weeks of her death he took into his household as servant a Jamaican boy, formerly a slave (called 'Quashey' back home) brought to England by Colonel Richard Bathurst in 1750 and renamed Francis Barber, or 'Frank', as Johnson and everyone else called him. It was through the colonel's son, Johnson's dear friend Richard, that Frank (c.1742–1801) came into Johnson's life. It appears to have occurred to Richard Bathurst that the boy was perfect for Johnson's hour of need.

Johnson quickly developed an affection for the boy, who was about ten, and in years to come 'whenever disputes arose in his household among the many odd inhabitants of which it consisted, he always sided with Francis against the others'. Mrs Thrale, who with Hawkins and other friends disapproved of Frank's volatility after Johnson died, felt that he 'was scarcely as much the object of Mr Johnson's personal kindness, as the representative of Dr Bathurst, for whose sake he would have loved any body, or any thing'. But Johnson's affection for Frank was beyond doubt, as was the strong bond that was forged between them for the rest of his life, not least on the basis of Johnson's hatred of slavery and his strong support for its abolition. Even more incredible was Mrs Thrale's contention that 'When he spoke of Negroes, he always appeared to think them of a race naturally inferior, and made few exceptions in favour of his own'. On the contrary, it delighted him that Richard Bathurst had inherited no slaves from the colonel and that in his will in April 1754 his father gave Frank his freedom and twelve pounds. This was highly unusual. In 1772 the black British population was about 15,000, most of whom were slaves. Moreover, there was from early in the century a deeply entrenched racism in British culture and politics. Johnson had no truck with this.

On one occasion in Oxford in 1777 he expressed his fierce disapproval of slavery by proposing a toast in the company of 'some very grave men' to 'the next insurrection of the Negroes in the West Indies'. As Boswell put it, 'he had always been very zealous against slavery in every form.' 'No man is by nature the property of another,' Johnson wrote. As we shall see, in later years he directed his scorn on this subject at the hypocrisy of the Americans who kept slaves and yet issued the 'loudest yelps for liberty'.[1]

At home in Gough Square in 1752, this boy was a godsend. Frank told Boswell that when he came into Johnson's service he found his master in 'great affliction' from his wife's death. Aware of his desolation, the *Dictionary*'s proprietors left him alone for a while. Though there is no doubt that he was completely thrown off his work by Tetty's death, in later years he tended to dismiss the notion that grief such as his could paralyse a writer, thinking it an affectation. George Steevens remembered that when Johnson once was informed of a certain critic's public announcement that he could not bring himself to attack Steevens's work any more because he had suddenly lost his wife, Johnson observed coldly, 'I believe that the loss of teeth may deprive the voice of a singer, and that lameness will impede the motions of a dancing master, but I have not yet been taught to regard the death of a wife as the grave of literary exertions. When my dear Mrs Johnson expired I sought relief in my studies, and strove to lose the recollection of her in the toils of literature'. This was, however, after months of mourning, and according to Steevens it was then only in his garret that he could do anything: 'After her death, though he had a whole house at command, he would study nowhere but in a garret. Being asked the reason why he chose a situation so incommodious, he answered, "because in that room only I never saw Mrs Johnson".'[2]

[2]

In November the wheels began to turn again. It may have been John Hawkesworth who got him moving by establishing a new twice-weekly periodical, *The Adventurer*, in November 1752. Johnson did not begin to contribute essays to it until the following March, but he helped Hawkesworth think through the scheme and agreed to contribute a Latin motto (with translation) for each of the numbers. Boswell stressed that Hawkesworth helped Johnson take his mind off

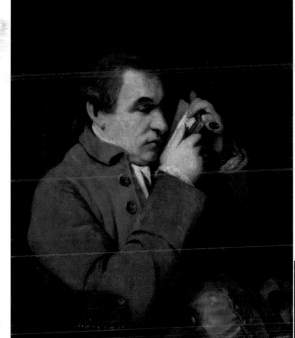

Giuseppe Baretti, after Joshua Reynolds. The temperamental Baretti, although he was a close friend of Johnson's and several Club members, never had much chance of being elected to the Club.

James Boswell at twenty-five, painted by George Willison in Italy while he was on his Grand Tour in 1765, during which he occasionally corresponded with his famous friend Johnson.

Mrs Hester Lynch Thrale and her daughter Queeney, by Joshua Reynolds *c*.1779.
With Mrs Thrale Johnson enjoyed a deeper if unsettled intimacy than with anyone else.

Streatham Place, the Thrales' home in Southwark which for almost twenty years
served Johnson as a second home. It sometimes irritated Johnson's friends that they
could not find him because he was at Streatham.

Samuel Johnson in the late 1760s, by Joshua Reynolds. He appears to be gesticulating awkwardly with his hands, in deep thought and in a manner described by Frances Reynolds 'as if he had been seized with cramp'.

Anna Williams, Johnson's blind and quarrelsome housekeeper and member of his household on and off for more than thirty years, by Frances Reynolds. When she died, Johnson was devastated.

ABOVE: Charlotte Lennox, author and poet, whom Johnson once described as 'superior to them all'.

Detail from *Mr & Mrs Garrick Taking Tea Upon the Lawn of Their Villa at Hampton*
by Zoffany, 1762. Johnson is said to have remarked, 'It is the leaving of such places that makes
a death-bed terrible'.

FACING PAGE: *The Nine Living Muses of Great Britain* by Richard Samuel, 1778.
The figures include Elizabeth Carter, Anna Laetitia Barbauld, Catherine Macaulay,
Elizabeth Montagu and Hannah More.

The so-called 'Streatham' portrait of Johnson, by Reynolds, *c*.1773.

his grief in this way as well as relieve the drudgery of the *Dictionary* once he started working on it again in earnest. Hawkesworth's idea was for a periodical containing essays about grave moral issues but also, in Johnson's words, lighter 'pieces of imagination, pictures of life', appealing to a wider readership. At first Hawkesworth and another anonymous contributor carried it, but his helper faltered and by the spring he needed Johnson to come to his rescue. Johnson agreed to contribute essays regularly. The paper paid two guineas per essay.³

The arrangement was that Hawkesworth would write forty-six, and Johnson and Joseph Warton (Thomas's elder brother) twenty-three each, though Johnson ended up writing twenty-nine and may have been tempted to write more except that the *Dictionary* beckoned and he was loath again to 'condemn himself to compose on a stated day'. The intervals between his essays vary between one and seven days, five being the most common. He also wanted Richardson and perhaps Elizabeth Carter to pitch in, but neither of them 'found the leisure' to contribute anything. The edition continued for 140 numbers and concluded in March 1754, with Johnson's last essay (number 138) appearing on 2 March.⁴

His friendship with the Wartons was not one of undiluted mutual admiration. Joseph Warton said that he and Johnson had 'contracted close friendship' in the autumn of 1752 and that he was 'quite intimate' with him. Johnson did at first reciprocate fully, 'I enter my name among those that love [you]', he wrote to him in March 1754. Warton was a clergyman and schoolmaster and would become Headmaster of Winchester College in 1766 for a long run of almost thirty years. Thomas became Oxford Professor of Poetry in 1757 and Poet Laureate in 1785. His greatest achievement was his *History of English Poetry* (1774–81), the first comprehensive assessment or 'ordering' of the subject ever written. Visited by Johnson often in Oxford over the years, he was a closer and more sympathetic friend to Johnson than his brother the headmaster, and was more of a kindred spirit. Johnson found neither of them communicative enough, however. 'A little, thick, squat, red-faced man', Thomas seemed to him cold: 'Johnson has been known to declare in terms of severity ... that Tom Warton was the only man of genius, whom he knew, without a heart'. 'Your brother ... is a better correspondent than you,' Johnson rebuked him. 'You might write to me now and then, if you were good for any thing. But ... professors forget their friends'. As for Joseph, when he published the first volume of his important *Essay on the Writings and*

Genius of Pope in April 1756, Johnson was put out that he had not mentioned anything of it to him in advance: 'When you and your brother were in town you did not think my humble habitation worth a visit ... That way of publishing without acquainting your friends is a wicked trick.' He is once supposed to have said, 'I wonder that Joe Warton, a scholar by profession, should be such a fool.'[5]

Johnson needed the two guineas for each *Adventurer* paper but may have kept little or none of the money for himself. His friend Bathurst had fallen on hard times as a physician and apparently needed money even more than he did. Boswell recorded that, according to the blind poet Anna Williams who in 1754 appears to have taken up residence at Gough Square, Johnson dictated his essays to his friend who then could say he had written them and be paid for the effort: 'As he had *given* those essays to Dr Bathurst, who sold them at two guineas each, he never would own them; nay, he used to say he did not *write* them: but the fact was, that he *dictated* them, while Bathurst wrote.' Boswell said that when he read to Johnson what she had said, 'he smiled, and said nothing'. 'As his purse was ever open to almsgiving,' wrote Mrs Thrale, 'so was his heart tender to those who wanted relief. He gave away all he had, and all he had ever gotten, except the two thousand pounds he left behind.' And Murphy noted, 'It has been truly said that the lame, the blind, and the sorrowful, found in his house a sure retreat.' Bathurst lingered on in London, failing as a doctor, until January 1757 when he moved to Barbados. He died of a fever in Havana while serving as physician on the British naval expedition against Cuba during the Seven Years' War. For years Johnson continued to remember Bathurst in his prayers.[6]

Johnson initially did not reveal he was the author of any of these essays, identifying them merely with a 'T'. Warton, Hawkesworth and other contributors used other letters to conceal their authorship as well. Almost everyone was fooled, although Richardson was among several who noticed a resemblance of style between those written by 'T' and the *Rambler* essays. Catherine Talbot was on the right track in a letter to Elizabeth Carter in January 1753, 'I discern Mr Johnson through all the pages that are not marked A, as evidently as if I saw him through the keyhole with the pen in his hand.' When Hill Boothby, perceiving Johnson's hand in them, asked him outright about them, at first he was silent. After she persisted, he finally admitted writing them, to which she replied, 'I wonder not at your hesitating to impart a secret to a woman; but am the more obliged to you for communicating it as a secret, after so hesitating. Such a mark of your deliberate confidence shall be strictly regarded; and I shall seek for letter T, that I may read with *redoubled* pleasure.'[7]

[3]

The *Adventurer* with its multiple authorship proved to be a greater commercial success than the *Rambler*, partly because the *Rambler* had prepared the way for it and partly because its essays were lighter and more diverse. 'I like the *Adventurers*,' Talbot informed Carter, 'we all like them exceedingly; and I fancy they will soon become very fashionable ... They do not abound in hard words, they are varied with a thousand amusing stories, they touch with humour on the daily follies and peculiarities of the times.' Realising after the *Rambler* that if he were ever to be involved in another periodical he would have to write essays easier to read, Johnson wrote this new batch with larger brush strokes for more casual readers. But he was no less indignant in exposing human flaws and vices. If anything, his language is even more strident. Several of them are also quite bleak.

His essays cover a few of the subjects and themes he had already written about in the *Rambler*, several of them under the general moral theme of vanity and its dangers: flattery, lying, learning, retirement, egocentricity, complacency, the 'contagion of desire', happiness, and the pride of 'singularity' or thinking of yourself as the exception to the rules that bind the rest of mankind. Writing with an autobiographical edge, he urged that life is a warfare and one must fight the good fight, although there is no assurance of victory either for the mind or soul: 'To strive with difficulties, and to conquer them, is the highest human felicity; the next, is to strive and deserve to conquer.'

Predictably, he devoted *Rambler* 39 to sleep and how life without enough of it is unendurable: 'A perpetual vigil [at night] will appear to be a state of wretchedness ... Sleep is necessary to the happy, to prevent satiety and to endear life by a short absence; and to the miserable, to relieve them by intervals of quiet.' He often complained of nights of fitful sleep, when his imagination would run rampant and like a mole burrow away at him, unearthing hidden fears. As a result he would sleep late. 'I do not remember that since I left Oxford I ever rose early by mere choice, but once or twice at Edial, and two or three times for the *Rambler*,' he entered in his diary in 1753.[8]

Authorship is a subject to which he turned with the scars of his own struggles on Grub Street. Is a life of writing of any real use and does it bring happiness to an author? The last two of his essays are about this (numbers 137 and 138), the first of which he launched with a motto from Pythagoras, 'What have I been doing?' How worthwhile can the *Adventurer*, or any other kind of writing for that matter, really be? 'Much of my time has sunk into nothing, and left no trace by which it can be distinguished, and of this I now only know, that it was once in my power and might once have been improved.' As for the *Adventurer*, he has had good intentions but wonders 'what has been the consequence of my labours', and whether the hours spent on them have been to 'good and laudatory purpose' or 'suffered to fume away in useless evaporations'. 'That the world has grown apparently better, since the publication of the *Adventurer*, I have not observed,' he concluded, but perhaps some readers have caught some benefits from 'single sentiments'.[9]

His last essay on authors describes the personal suffering, isolation, self-deprivation and loneliness in a life of writing: 'Composition is, for the most part, an effort of slow diligence and steady perseverance, to which the mind is dragged by necessity or resolution, and from which the attention is every moment starting to more delightful amusements.' Moreover, just because a writer has worthwhile ideas does not mean he is going to find the words for them. Every writer at times finds himself 'deficient in the power of expression . . . obliged to ransack his memory for terms adequate to his conceptions, and at last unable to impress upon his reader the image existing in his own mind'.[10] The writer's lot is 'study and vexation', a private hell of incarceration within the four walls of his study or garret.

[4]

In November 1752 he knew he had to get back to the grind of the *Dictionary*. The proprietors could not tolerate any more delays. By then he had been working on it for six years and reached only as far as the word *dame*. The gravity of the moment was reflected in a prayer he composed at the start of the month titled, 'Before Any New Study', asking God to help him 'shun sloth and negligence' and keep him from lavishing away his time on 'useless trifles' and wasting his talents on 'searches after things which thou hast hidden from me'.[11]

By 3 April 1753 he had completed the first volume, leaving space in it for the preface and history of English grammar which he had not yet begun, and was moving into the second volume. At this point he began to work incredibly fast. Within the next eighteen months he completed the rest of the text, an astonishing eighty per cent of the whole book, with only Peyton and Alexander Macbean to assist him. Completing the text by late spring 1754, he was now able to devote himself almost entirely to proofreading and therefore dramatically increase the rate of printing the work.[12]

Such rapid progress was made possible by his new method. To begin with, he needed to decide what to do with the manuscript notebooks he had abandoned for letters A, B and the first part of C. Since the chaos of these manuscripts made them useless as printer's copy, he began by marking them up with revisions to be transcribed by Peyton and Macbean, shaping it in the way he wished it to appear in the book. In loose sheets, not in disastrously confining notebooks such as he had first used, they wrote down the entry-words, etymologies, definitions, illustrations, and anything else he had written in the old notebooks, leaving spaces for him to introduce additional information later. In the process Johnson also trimmed many of the illustrative quotations. He made these deletions on the manuscript itself, after which the amanuenses copied the cropped quotations directly on to the sheets. It all became more compact and clear. Many of the original entries, however, especially under A, tended to remain encyclopedic in content because he had too little time to keep working on them, or to tailor the quotations further.[13]

His progress became steady and more efficient with entries beginning with C, which were shorter, but the real retrenchment began with D. He abridged the illustrative quotations chosen for inclusion and shaped them to fit smoothly in entries after being transcribed from source texts. He continued to gather new ones to fill in gaps, but just about all of them for volume II had already been marked in books and transcribed by March 1753. This was crucial for rapid progress because he could now focus on preparing text and proofing copy. Similarly, Peyton and Macbean could now prepare copy for the printer more quickly because they no longer had to divide their time between that and transcribing quotes on to slips. He himself was humming along and, to the delight of Strahan and the proprietors, was for a change actually composing copy faster than it was being printed. He was also producing printer's copy that was manageable and easier to read, in spite of the sloppy copying that Peyton and Macbean often produced in an effort, as Johnson put it, 'to get to the end of a day's work'. 'One cannot always be on the watch,' he defended himself to Strahan. As for writing the text of the entries, he neared the end of that process by late spring 1754, when he was also revising the *Adventurer* and *Rambler* essays for new editions. He had been composing at the rapid rate of fifty-four to seventy pages per week. Probably by agreement with Strahan, he completed the whole of the manuscript for volume II before handing it over in May 1754. Typesetting and proofing then began and printing was completed in March 1755.[14]

Once he had handed over all the copy, Johnson was free (except for proofing) to prepare the collected edition of the *Rambler* in June and travel to Oxford in July to do extensive research in the Bodleian for his Preface, 'History of the English Language', and 'Grammar of the English Tongue'. His work 'now draws towards its end', he informed Thomas Warton on 16 July 1754, but he could not finish it 'without visiting the libraries of Oxford' in a couple of weeks: 'I know not how long I shall stay or where I shall lodge, but shall be sure to look for you at my arrival.' For his long five weeks there he lodged at Kettel Hall, near Trinity. The visit was more of an escape than a research trip, more social pleasure than drudgery. Warton told Boswell, 'he collected nothing in the libraries for his *Dictionary*'.[15]

He spent much of the time with Warton at Trinity and paying visits to other colleges. Their visit to Pembroke was a disappointment. Warton recalled that 'the master did not choose to talk on the subject [of the *Dictionary*], never asked Johnson to dine, nor even to visit him, while he stayed at Oxford. After we had left the lodgings, Johnson said to me, "*There* lives a man, who lives by the revenues of literature, and will not move a finger to support it. If I come to live at Oxford, I shall take up my abode at Trinity."' One day they walked out to the village of Elsfield, three miles out of town, to visit the Revd Francis Wise, the Radclivian librarian and Keeper of the Archives at Oxford, whose superb library of Northern literature, a 'nest of British and Saxon Antiquities', Johnson perhaps intended to, but appears not to, have used in researching the preliminary material for the *Dictionary*. In a different key, there was the pleasure of meeting Mary Jones, an 'ingenious poetess and ... a most sensible, agreeable, and amiable woman' who 'was often of our parties'. Johnson took to calling her the 'Chantress' because she was the sister of the Chantor of Christ Church Cathedral at Oxford. A new world of friendships had opened up for him at Oxford, and he was loath to return to London to pick up the hard work of proofing copy.[16]

But return he did. Strahan's presses kept churning out the proofs rapidly and he had some catching up to do. More than just checking for printing errors, he was also altering quotations and definitions and rearranging text on a large scale. It was now he who was cracking the whip, and Strahan was not slow to respond. Everyone involved in the project was now bearing down hard. He composed most if not all of his Preface, 'History' and 'Grammar' in the autumn. The latter two he wrote carelessly and perfunctorily, impatient with them as hurdles over which he still needed to jump to conclude this massive work.[17]

The Preface was a different matter and revealed a great deal about him personally. What makes it such a powerful statement is that he invoked his own emotions and experience in explaining to the reader what he, as a mere mortal, has had to go through to produce this work.[18]

His strategy in the Preface was conventional in that it is an *apologia* for what he has done, a way of anticipating and deflecting criticism. But it is also a remarkably honest and moving personal revelation, although prefaces to dictionaries were often personal, even lugu-brious – a tradition reaching back to the Renaissance. His own life, he confessed, especially in the nine years since he launched himself into treacherous lexicographical waters, had been an allegory of triumph and despair, hope and defeat in 'this gloom of solitude'. Art is long and life is short. He had discovered that lexicographers are 'unhappy mortals' who rather than 'aspire to praise' can 'only hope to escape reproach': 'When first I engaged in this work, I resolved to leave neither words nor things unexamined, and pleased myself with a prospect of the hours which I should revel away in feasts of literature ... and the triumph with which I should display my acquisitions to mankind ... But these were the dreams of a poet doomed at last to wake a lexicographer ... I saw ... that to pursue perfection, was, like the first inhabitants of Arcadia, to chase the sun, which, when they had reached the hill where he seemed to rest, was still beheld at the same distance from them ... much of my life has been lost under the pressure of disease; much has been trifled away ... a whole life cannot be spent upon syntax and etymology.' He had been on his own, 'with little assistance of the learned, and without any patronage of the great; not in the soft obscurities of retirement, or under the shelter of academic bowers, but amidst inconvenience and distraction, in sickness and in sorrow'. And it had taken so long that much of the pleasure from publication had perished with several of those dear to him: 'I have protracted my work till most of those whom I wished to please, have sunk into the grave, and success and miscarriage are empty sounds: I therefore dismiss it with frigid tranquillity, having little to fear from censure or from praise.' That last sentence was putting a brave face on it. He had much to fear.[19]

It was an enormous boost to his confidence that just before publication he was awarded what he had long coveted. He had no academic credentials, yet his credibility as the author of what he and the publishers hoped would be Britain's most celebrated *Dictionary*, as well as the book's saleability, must surely suffer without them. He very likely hinted something of this to Warton and Wise in Oxford, who talked about it and decided there was still time for a degree to be conferred on him before publication, 'that he may be able to write himself A. M. in the title page'. By 21 December the deal was virtually done. 'I will keep back the title page for such an insertion as you seem to promise me,' he informed Warton. 'I have mentioned it to none of my friends,' he wisely added, 'for fear of being laughed at for my disappointment.' There were frustrating and anxious delays but on 25 February 1755, he opened his front door at Gough Square and received Dr William King, Principal of St Mary Hall, who came bearing the gift of the diploma itself. In recommending the degree to the university, the Chancellor, the Earl of Arran, had praised him in terms that healed Oxford wounds long open: he had 'very eminently distinguished himself by the publication of a series of essays [*The Rambler*], excellently calculated to form the manners of the people, and in which the cause of religion and morality is every where maintained by the strongest powers of argument and language; and ... shortly intends to publish a Dictionary of the English Tongue, formed on a new plan, and executed with the greatest labour and judgement'. The public would now begin to know him as 'The Rambler' and 'Dictionary Johnson'. A few days after the news, the title page was run off with the letters 'A. M.' after his name.[20]

[5]

This was heady stuff, though it was soured by the unhappy news that Dodsley, his literary confidante, had suddenly lost his own wife. He felt his friend's pain far more than most, confiding in Warton, 'I hope he will not suffer so much as I yet suffer for the loss of mine', and adding a passage that revealed the depths of his own continuing grief, as if he were looking in at his own life through a window from the cold outside: 'I have ever since seemed to myself broken off from mankind a kind of solitary wanderer in the wild of life, without any certain direction, or fixed point of view. A gloomy gazer on a world to which I have little relation.'[21]

On the threshold of unimaginable fame, his heart also went out to two melancholic poets. William Collins (1721–59), whose lyrically intense poetry in the 1740s helped redefine English poetry in the second half of the century, had attended Winchester College where he met and shared poems with Joseph Warton, and then proceeded to Oxford where as a precocious student at Johnson's own college, Pembroke, he published his *Persian Eclogues*. Johnson met him in 1744 when Collins was trying to scrape together an existence in London; after that, he kept track of him through the Wartons. In around 1750, Collins began to suffer from depressive melancholia, a 'dreadful malady' for which he was shut up in a madhouse in Chelsea. 'I knew him a few years ago,' Johnson told Joseph Warton, 'full of hopes and full of projects, versed in many languages, high in fancy, and strong in retention.' Now his 'busy and forcible mind' had fallen into an abyss which, for much of his own adult life, Johnson feared might be his own fate. By 1754 'poor dear Collins' was living with his sister in Chichester. 'Would a letter give him any pleasure', Johnson asked Thomas Warton, 'I have a mind to write.' He did write but the letter has not survived; if it were found, it would surely provide further fascinating insight into the terrors of melancholia. Collins never replied, so far as we know, and Johnson was left to reflect on the vulnerability of the human mind in a letter to Joseph Warton: 'The moralists all talk of the uncertainty of fortune, and the transitoriness of beauty; but it is yet more dreadful to consider that the powers of the mind are equally liable to change, that understanding may make its appearance and depart, that it may blaze and expire'. 'Madmen are all sensual in the lower stages of the distemper,' he said to Boswell. 'They are eager for gratifications to sooth their minds'. 'I have often been near his state, and therefore have it in great commiseration.'[22]

After Collins died in 1759 at thirty-eight, Johnson sketched out a 'character' of his life for a collection of his verse in 1763, which he used later as the nucleus for his 'Life of William Collins'. He could be writing about himself as he touched on Collins's rough London days,

'A man, doubtful of his dinner, or trembling at a creditor, is not much disposed to abstracted meditation or remote enquiries ... About this time I fell into his company ... By degrees I gained his confidence; and one day was admitted to him when he was immured by a bailiff that was prowling in the street.' It was probably Johnson who helped Collins on that occasion escape prison by promptly persuading a publisher to pay him an advance for a promised literary work, much as he would do for his friend Oliver Goldsmith. But 'man is not born for happiness,' he wrote, and there was little more he could do. 'His disorder was not alienation of mind, but general laxity and feebleness, a deficiency rather of his vital than intellectual powers.' Boswell thought Johnson's account of 'the melancholy depression with which Collins was severely afflicted, and which brought him to his grave' was 'one of the most tender and interesting passages in the whole series of his writings'.[23]

The other mentally troubled poet was Christopher Smart (1722–71) who had recently hatched a plan to publish a periodical journal, *The Universal Visiter*, in collaboration with the miscellaneous writer Richard Rolt. Johnson met him through Arthur Murphy and had earlier written the 'Life of Cheyne' (1751), a Presbyterian who was President of St John's College, Oxford, for Smart's magazine, *The Student*. Smart's dilemma was that he was going mad at the time with a religious mania showing itself in an obsessive need for constant prayer. It was an affliction with which Johnson instinctively identified. When Smart for a short time was incarcerated in St Luke's Hospital, out of 'compassionate regard' Johnson stepped in to write at least three essays in the short lifespan (twelve issues) of Smart's new journal: 'I wrote for some months in "The Universal Visiter", for poor Smart, while he was mad,' he stated, 'not then knowing the terms on which he was engaged to write, and thinking I was doing him good. I hoped his wits would soon return to him. Mine returned to me, and I wrote in "The Universal Visiter" no longer.' Boswell tells of an exchange he heard between Burney and Johnson about Smart's insanity a few years later, by which time the poet had been locked up in a private madhouse in Bethnal Green for four years. When Burney asked for the latest about Smart, Johnson replied, 'It seems as if his mind had ceased to struggle with the disease; for he grows fat upon it ... I did not think he ought to be shut up. His infirmities were not noxious to society. He insisted on people praying with him; and I'd as lief pray with Kit Smart as any one else.' He added as an afterthought, 'Another charge was, that he did not love clean linen; and I have no passion for it.' Smart was committed for debt to the King's Bench prison in 1770 and died there a year later, for the most part forgotten until the twentieth century in spite of having composed superb religious poetry like *A Song to David* while he was in the madhouse.[24]

[6]

Johnson was nervous as he awaited publication of the *Dictionary*. 'I now begin to see land, after having wandered ... in this vast sea of words. What reception I shall meet with upon the shore I know not, whether the sound of bells and acclamations of the people ... or a general murmur of dislike'. He was ready for criticism, though, and if it came at him like Polyphemus he would 'have at his eyes', he said, ignoring for the sake of the proverbial phrase the fact that Cyclops had only one eye. He knew himself and his combative spirit: 'I am a little afraid of myself, and would not willingly feel so much ill will in my bosom as literary quarrels are apt to excite'. This apprehensiveness was well founded. When his supposed 'patron' Lord Chesterfield, on hearing that the *Dictionary* was soon to be published, rushed into print with two puffs for it in the periodical *The World* (nos. 100 and 101), condescendingly praising Johnson, parading his own superficial and trivial knowledge of the language, and generally revealing a lack of understanding of Johnson's work, he struck at him with a frontal attack much as he promised he would fly at Polyphemus, in one of the most celebrated letters in English literary history. Chesterfield was too late and his casual return to the role of Johnson's patron was insufferable. Chesterfield had ignored both him and the project for nine years. Now on the eve of publication he was trying to move on to centre stage with Johnson. Johnson was furious. 'I have sailed a long and painful voyage round the world of the English language,' he said to Garrick, 'and does he now send out two cock-boats to tow me into harbour?' It was additionally galling that Dodsley, who was interested in sales, had plans to promote this intolerable fiction. He had to act immediately.[25]

Boswell went to considerable trouble to recover the letter from Johnson himself, who dictated it from memory in 1781 with 'an animated glow in his countenance' as he recalled his 'high-minded indignation'. In it he unloaded decades of bitter frustration and anger over his neglected genius and poured out his grudge that when Chesterfield had a chance to help him after Tetty died he did not. It is a letter professors love to introduce to their students as one of history's greatest and most public snubs:

> I have been lately informed by the proprietor of *The World* that two papers in which my Dictionary is recommended to the public were written by your lordship. To be so distinguished is an honour which, being very little accustomed to favours from the Great, I know not well how to receive, or in what terms to acknowledge.
>
> When upon some slight encouragement I first visited your lordship I was overpowered like the rest of mankind by the enchantment of your address, and could not forbear to wish that I might boast myself Le Vainqueur du Vainqueur de la Terre, that I might obtain that regard for which I saw the world contending, but I found my attendance so little encouraged, that neither pride nor modesty would suffer me to continue it. When I had once addressed your lordship in public, I had exhausted all the art of pleasing which a retired and uncourtly scholar can possess. I had done all that I could, and no man is well pleased to have his all neglected, be it ever so little.
>
> Seven years, my lord[,] have now past since I waited in your outward rooms or was repulsed from your door, during which time I have been pushing on my work through difficulties of which it is useless to complain, and have brought it at last to the verge of publication without one act of assistance, one word of encouragement, or one smile of favour. Such treatment I did not expect, for I never had a patron before.
>
> ... Is not a patron, my lord, one who looks with unconcern on a man struggling for life in the water and when he has reached ground encumbers him with help. The notice which you have been pleased to take of my labours, had it been early, had been kind; but it has been delayed till I am indifferent and cannot enjoy it, till I am solitary and cannot impart it, till I am known and do not want it.
>
> I hope it is no very cynical asperity not to confess obligation where no benefit has been received, or to be unwilling that the public should consider me as owing that to a patron, which Providence has enabled me to do for myself.[26]

The letter was more than a mere personal rebuff. It has been said that when Boswell first published it the year before the *Life of Johnson* (in which it also appeared), it tolled the death of literary patronage in England. One critic has described it as 'the Magna Carta of the modern author, the public announcement that the days of courtly letters were at last ended'. It was an important skirmish in 'a dramatic power struggle for control of the language': the old polite world of letters pitted against 'living speech' of writers who wished chiefly to communicate and explore. In the almost ten years of work on the *Dictionary* Johnson had left well behind him both Chesterfield and the accepted notion that linguistic authority was invested in a privileged social class. He had none of the patience left that he mustered when, at Dodsley's request, he submitted to Chesterfield at the start. Other writers, too, were demonstrating in the hothouse of professional letters and the print revolution that the Chesterfields and their class were become irrelevant to language and letters: 'There is no absolute language, no ideal meanings for words, no set of eternal rules governing form and development of languages.' The 'King's English' had been democratised into the 'Authors' English'. Johnson's *Dictionary* was nothing if not revolutionary in this respect; his lexicographical vision was almost prophetic, neither conservative nor traditionalist. He and other good writers, not Chesterfield, were authorising the language. Who was Chesterfield anyway? As Johnson openly announced, he was not 'a Lord among wits; but only a wit among Lords'. His definition of 'patron' revealed the extent of his personal animus: 'Commonly a wretch who supports with insolence, and is paid with flattery'. In a revision of *The Vanity of Human Wishes* in 1755, he also changed the word 'garret' to 'patron' as one of the pernicious evils along with toil, envy, want and jail set to ambush the young scholar or writer.[27]

On a personal level, Johnson was indeed now known and did not need Chesterfield, but on 1 March in a pre-publication effort to promote sales, and now fully aware of Johnson's anger over Chesterfield's attempt to win credit as a good patron where no credit was due, Dodsley distributed free of charge 1,500 copies of Johnson's *Plan* with the address to Chesterfield now almost ten years old. That was what the general public saw. Chesterfield knew, though, that more privately a number of influential people were aware of, or actually had read, Johnson's stinging letter to him. So he may have tried to make the best of the situation and perhaps save face. The story got around, in fact, true or not, that he himself was so proud of being the target of such a consummate snub that he left a copy of the letter lying around in his house for visitors to read. His literary hauteur may not have let him acknowledge defeat. It is just as conceivable, of course, that Johnson, greatly incensed, saw to it that various people read his letter.

Johnson's boat finally made it safely to the shore when he sent his messenger to Andrew Millar with the last proofed sheet in April. Millar was not reticent in expressing himself when he received it: 'Thank God, I have done with him.' When the messenger later told Johnson what he said, he replied with a smile, 'I am glad that he thanks God for any thing.' The *Dictionary* was published on 15 April 1755, available in two folio volumes running to more than 2,500 pages in two columns at a price of £4. 10s. Strahan printed 2,000 copies. The volumes weighed twenty pounds, unwieldy for just about everyone, 'proud in its prodigious bulk', as he boasted to Thomas Warton. According to Hawkins, Johnson had received a total of at least £1,575, more than his contract stipulated, in fact, and although he may have hoped that the publishers would give him some more as some sort of bonus out of gratitude, he was disappointed when he learned that because of the work having stretched to nine years their own expenses had well exceeded their expectations and they were not about to give him any more.[28]

The reviews on the whole were extremely good. The *Public Advertiser* on 10 October even published a remark by the President of the Accademia della Crusca, the Marquis Nicolini, who had been presented with a copy by the Earl of Orrery, that the work would be 'a perpetual monument of fame to the author, an honour to his country in particular, and a general benefit to the republic of letters throughout all Europe'. Adam Smith recommended it in the *Edinburgh Review* (June 1755) as the best to be had, though he thought the definitions were somewhat chaotic and that there should be more from the author prescribing usage. Many reviews patriotically bore witness to the huge scale of Johnson's achievement for the glory of Britain. The poet Christopher Smart wrote nine months after publication that he looked on the *Dictionary* as he did St Paul's Cathedral: 'each the work of *one* man, each the work of an *Englishman*'. And Garrick composed a patriotically back-thumping poem on the occasion of the work's completion in which the last two lines read, 'And Johnson, well-arm'd like a hero of yore,/Has beat forty French, and will beat forty more'. The patriotic theme, repeated for decades in an increasingly jingoistic manner, was one that Johnson himself struck in his Preface: 'I have devoted this book, the labour of years, to the honour of my country, that we may no longer yield the palm of philology to the nations of the continent. The chief glory of every people arises from its authors.'[29]

He happily announced to Thomas Warton in June that the work

'sells well', but because of its price and unwieldy size it did not. Efforts to promote sales through publishing schemes did little better until a considerably condensed abridgement in a cheaper two-volume octavo third edition was published in January 1756 at ten shillings, one-ninth of the original price. All five thousand copies of that sold in the next four years; and other editions in 1760, 1766 and 1770 each sold a further five thousand. In 1773, Johnson came out with his extensively revised fourth edition in folio, for which he was handsomely paid £300 (about £30,000 today).

[7]

Much attention has been given to several of Johnson's humorous, idiosyncratic, overly wordy, personally charged, biased, self-deprecating definitions which have given the *Dictionary* a sensational and bizarre reputation and made it useful fodder for after-dinner talks and lively conversation. Many of them have gained currency in our language because they trip off the tongue easily and are perfectly shaped for one-liners and quick, witty effects. Johnson remarked that the definitions are 'that part of my work on which I expect malignity most frequently to fasten', partly because of mistakes, such as his definition of *pastern* as the 'knee of an horse' when it is in fact part of the foot. People seemed to make a sport of finding errors, though he was unflappable in the face of them. When a woman asked him how he came to get *pastern* wrong, Johnson (according to Boswell's embellishment) simply shrugged, 'Ignorance, Madam, pure ignorance.' He also expected criticism from 'critics of the coffee house', because many of the definitions are strongly opinionated, facetious, or malicious, such as: *Tory* ('one who adheres to the ancient constitution of the state, and the apostolical hierarchy of the church of England'), *Whig* ('the name of a faction'), *party* ('a faction'), *pension* ('in England it is generally understood to mean pay given to a state hireling for treason to his country'), *freethinker* ('a libertine'), *oats* ('a grain, which in England is generally given to horses, but in Scotland supports the people'), *enthusiasm* ('a vain belief of private revelation; a vain confidence of divine favour or communication'), *poetaster* ('a vile petty poet'), *stockjobber* (or stockbroker, 'a low wretch who gets money by buying and selling shares in the funds'), *foxhunter* ('a man whose chief ambition is to show his bravery in hunting foxes'), *excise* ('a hateful tax levied upon commodities, and adjudged not by the common judges of property, but wretches hired by those to whom excise is paid'), and *dedication* ('a servile address to a patron'). There is enough in that short list to have angered quite a cross-section of British society. But, of course, they are an infinitesimal few among thousands.

He suspected that his tendency to wordy definitions, sometimes leaving the reader not much the wiser, would also subject him to ridicule. A famous example is *network*: 'any thing reticulated, or decussated, at equal distances, with interstices between the intersections'. Was a recent journalist inspired by this definition when explaining that the tennis professional Guillermo Vilas bore a thirty-year-old grudge against fellow-competitor Ilie Nastase for defeating him with 'a spaghetti string racket that imparted all manner of odd spins with its pattern of non-intersecting strings on independent planes'? Another is *cough*: 'a convulsion of the lungs, vellicated by some sharp serosity'.

He also knew he would be mocked for his huge selection of 'hard' or out-of-the-way foreign and obsolete words. One waggish commentator once remarked that Johnson wrote the *Rambler* to make the *Dictionary* necessary and the *Dictionary* to explain the *Rambler*. A few examples from the *Dictionary*: *dealbation, digladiation, dodecatemorion, enneatical, slubberdegullion, immarcessible, impennous, repullulate, sciomachy, captation, tentiginous, conterraneous, dapatical, fabaceous, furacious*, and *gemelliparous*. Johnson loved them. A popular pastime was to look up words to see if Johnson included them, and if not, to roll one's head in disbelief. Catherine Talbot wrote smugly to Elizabeth Carter, 'We have looked in Johnson for *athlete*, no such word there, nor any thing of the kind by *athletic*, with explanations everybody knows'. The *Dictionary* was fair game for all manner of scrutiny: it was national property.[30]

An enriching dimension to the *Dictionary* is its function as an encyclopedia. Johnson was candid about it in the Preface when he stated his intention 'to pierce deep into every science, to enquire the nature of every substance': 'When first I engaged in this work, I resolved to leave neither words nor things unexamined'. Even without the quotations the *Dictionary* would be more encyclopedic than any of its predecessors. One critic has divided the encyclopedic entries into three groups: complicated artefacts (*airpump, geneva, grenade, orrery*); natural objects and phenomena such as *vine* (which included a survey of no fewer than thirty-four species), *seahorse, crocodile, light, diamond*, and *epilepsy*; and human institutions and fields of learning (*jury*, *justice*, *architecture*, *astronomy*, *chemistry*, *logarithm*). Johnson borrowed most of these definitions from specialised reference works but reworked them carefully with his own readers in mind. These sources alone illustrate the breadth of his reading.[31]

The *Dictionary* was a supreme embodiment of eighteenth-century culture and ideas about language, an astonishing achievement. It made a huge impression on the nation, becoming a standard work against which past and future dictionaries were measured. It made Johnson famous overnight.

PART V

Depression, Shakespeare, Travel and Anger

Thomas Davies's house

CHAPTER 20

Stalled

[1]

S uddenly Johnson was celebrated but his letters suggest he was not happy. It is as if many of the problems, physical as well as mental, that he suppressed while he lost himself in the mighty concentration of the last three years rushed forward once his 'shackles' were broken. Writing at midnight on 30 December 1755 to Hill Boothby, whom he was now possibly hoping to marry, his mood was as dark as in the 'waste hour of darkness and vacuity': 'If I turn my thoughts upon myself what do I perceive but a poor helpless being reduced by a blast of wind to weakness and misery ... Of the fallaciousness of hope, and the uncertainty of schemes every day gives some new proof ... something rather felt than seen.' Publication of the *Dictionary* had brought him fame but no financial security. His confidence was 'depressed': 'No man can know how little his performance will conform to his promises, and designs are nothing in human eyes till they are realised by execution.' Each year after this he resolved to read the Bible through, until 1772 when he felt he had 'attained to know, even thus hastily, confusedly, and imperfectly what my Bible contains'. Except for the Bible, however, his resolutions evaporated.[1]

It deeply depressed him that he had squandered vast amounts of time on the *Dictionary* through blunders in the first years, blunders that had cost him the pleasure of presenting the finished work to Tetty before she died. He had not even had the pleasure of witnessing Cave's response to it as his former employer ('poor dear Cave, I owed him much') died on 10 January 1754. Arthur Murphy noted that 'it was a mortification to the author of that noble addition to our language, that his old friend did not live to see the triumph of his labours'. One of Cave's last acts was 'to press the hand that is now writing this little narrative,' Johnson wrote in a short life in *The Gentleman's Magazine*.[2]

It was his own knowledge of the *Dictionary*'s imperfections that weighed on him most. While he had now released the book to the public, it had not released him. He knew he had made lots of mistakes and felt he had not prevailed satisfyingly over the inexact science of lexicography. He also fretted that sooner or later he would have to return to the grind of revisions. About fifteen years later, when the Thrales put him in mind of 'four or five faults' and encouraged him to publish a revised edition, Johnson moaned, 'Alas ... there are four or five hundred faults instead of four, but it would take me up [to] three months labour, and when the time was out, the work would not be done'. Young Charles Burney (1726–1814), then the organist of St Margaret's Church in King's Lynn in Norfolk who had taken a distant interest in the project ever since reading the *Plan* in 1747, wrote to him a few days before publication asking when he would be able to get a copy. Johnson replied, 'If you find faults, I shall endeavour to mend them; if you find none, I shall think you blinded by kind partiality.' Burney, incidentally, like Langton, had long ago become a disciple of the *Rambler* and was deeply frustrated he was stuck in Norfolk teaching music and unable to meet Johnson. He determined at least to forge a relationship by post: 'It is the fate of men of eminence to be persecuted by insignificant friends as well as enemies; and the simple cur who barks through fondness and affection, is no less troublesome than if stimulated by anger and aversion'. Johnson's heart was warmed, 'I have too much pleasure in pleasing men like you, not to feel very sensibly the distinction which you have bestowed upon me.' He hoped to receive 'another letter; and another yet, when you have looked into my Dictionary'. Burney's further praise two and a half years later – they still had not met – elicited a startling admission from Johnson, 'Your praise was welcome ... because praise has been very scarce ... among all my acquaintance there were only two who upon the publication of my book did not endeavour to depress me with threats of censure from the public, or with objections learned from those who had learned them from my own preface. Yours is the only letter of good will that I have yet received.'[3]

He was also sick from bronchitis for several weeks at the end of 1755, 'seized with a hoarseness which still continues'. From the 'convulsions' of a violent cough he once even fainted. His imagination was playing tricks on him and he feared the worst for his lungs. 'My physician bled me yesterday and the day before, first almost against his will, but the next day without any contest. I had been bled once before, so that I have lost in all 54 ounces.' It was the third time he was bled that winter. Like many of his contemporaries, he was already well into phlebotomy, the surgical opening or puncture of a vein to draw out blood, a lifelong madness that he inflicted on his ailing body with more assiduity than most. Rather than wait on a physician, he often impatiently bled himself with grisly deliberateness for all manner of ailments: coughs and colds, flatulence, an 'inflamed' eye, and especially breathing difficulties and shortness of breath. Fifty-four ounces is a great quantity of blood, though to the end of his life he believed that the practice was effective only if it were done in copious amounts. It was a horrible manifestation of his self-belief as an amateur medical practitioner. He wrote to his 'sweet angel' Hill Boothby, for example, who was alarmingly ill in December, 'Give me leave, who have thought much on medicine, to propose to you an easy and I think a very probable remedy for indigestion and lubricity of the bowels.' His remedy featured not phlebotomy but the use of dried orange peel, which he became known for scraping, cutting into pieces, and carrying in his pocket. He remained secretive about his use of the peel when Boswell questioned him closely about it in 1775, but in this instance he recommended that Hill Boothby either grind it into powder and drink it in a glass of port, or eat it first and then wash it down with heated port: 'This is a medicine not disgusting, not costly, easily tried, and if not found useful easily left off.' 'I love you and honour you, and am very unwilling to lose you,' he added.[4]

In his illness he also depended on Dr Thomas Lawrence (1711–83) whom he had met a couple of years earlier and who later was president of the Royal College of Physicians. Johnson would describe him as 'one of the best men whom I have known'. Lawrence recommended oil and sugar for his bronchitis, but he drank some Rhenish wine and water instead and promptly recovered his voice.[5]

These gloomy contours of body and mind deepened suddenly when Hill Boothby, 'his dear little miss', his 'dearest dear', died in January 1756, leaving him lonelier and emptier than ever. It was all his friends could do to 'calm the violence of his emotion'. He sought comfort in composing another prayer, 'Hill Boothby's Death', thanking God for her 'good example' and praying that he might learn from 'the knowledge of her life, and by the sense of her death'. In his prayer on the anniversary of Tetty's death on 28 March, he mentioned his life 'bereft of worldly comforts', an allusion not only to what now was his double grief over her and Hill Boothby but also to his dire finances. He was arrested on 16 March for a debt £5 18s. While the bailiff waited impatiently, he shot off a letter to Richardson who rescued him from the sponging-house by promptly sending him six guineas. It was a near escape that induced him the following year to write two essays on the evils of imprisonment for debt. It was also a wake-up call that in his post-*Dictionary* doldrums he could not afford the luxury of feeling sorry for himself. He needed money and he needed it quickly. He had to think up new projects.[6]

[2]

Johnson did soon get down to earning some money. One of his sources of income was writing prefaces, introductions and dedications at the request of booksellers, friends and acquaintances. Although he did not generally like to be asked for them by friends who may sometimes have thought he would write them for nothing, he churned out more than thirty over the next dozen years. Moreover, he became an easy but unwilling target for people who simply wanted him to look over their manuscripts, especially friends like Lennox, Burney, Baretti and Reynolds. As for payment, he told Mrs Thrale he 'hated to give away literary performances, or even to sell them too cheaply: the next generation shall not accuse me of beating down the price of literature: one hates, besides, ever to give that which one has been accustomed to sell.' Boswell heard more or less the same thing: 'I am very unwilling to read the manuscripts of authors, and give them my opinion. If the authors who apply to me have money, I bid them boldly print without a name; if they have written in order to get money, I tell them to go to the booksellers, and make the best bargain they can.' If he agreed to write something on behalf of a work, often he would merely 'peep' into it before doing so. In February 1756, for example, he wrote a preface to Richard Rolt's *Dictionary of Trade and Commerce*: 'I never saw the man, and never read the book ... I knew very well what such a Dictionary should be, and I wrote a Preface accordingly.' In November, he had produced a dedication to Lennox's edition of Sully's *Memoirs*, and in January he produced a dedication to William Payne's *The Game of Draughts*. And so it went. He could easily have eaten up most of his time writing these.[7]

He also got heavily into writing reviews of books on a wide range of subjects. His diary entry mentioning the 'infelicity'[8] of existing London review journals suggests he thought they were in a wretched state, especially ones that could review scholarly books and have an international focus. In *Rambler* 3 he had scolded overly critical reviewers who with 'elation of malignity' in that 'virulent generation' of mushrooming journalism 'either imagine it their duty, or make it their amusement, to hinder the reception of every work of learning or genius, who stand as sentinels in the avenues of fame, and value themselves upon giving ignorance and envy the first notice of a prey'. And in many reviews he did indeed act, as one critic has put it, as the author's defence attorney and client, pleading the case for the book and then leaving it to the readers to make up their own minds.[9]

To supply the need, he decided to edit a commercially promising new monthly review magazine for the 'general perusal' of a middlebrow readership entitled *The Literary Magazine*. He threw himself into it beginning with the first issue in May 1756 – in which, among other things, he again excoriated the slave trade by describing Jamaica as a 'dungeon of slaves'. This began a sustained period of intense creativity, his most important effort in the field of journalism. The magazine lasted for two years but his connection with it was only for about a year, in the course of which he wrote several editorial pieces and no fewer than forty reviews of books. In his prefatory essay, 'To the Public', for the first issue he wrote there was so much literary rubbish in the book trade that only a few books and pamphlets 'will deserve the distinction of criticism, and a few only will obtain it'.

He was an ideal reviewer because he could express informed judgements on a breathtaking variety of subjects, among them manufacturing processes, sciences (chemistry, zoology, biology, electricity, Newton's optics), medicine, geography, natural history, cartography, politics, international relations, public affairs, military science and what Boswell called 'the useful arts of life': beekeeping, tanning, bleaching, dairy products, china, meat, brewing, coinage, peat digging, kelp gathering, and many others. There was nothing highbrow about any of that. 'The meanest artisan or manufacturer', he wrote, 'contributes more to the accommodation of life, than the profound scholar and argumentative theorist ... the public would suffer less present inconvenience from the banishment of philosophers than from the extinction of any common trade.'[10] He also reviewed books on moral philosophy, drama, poetry, travel, classical literature and journalism.

Having represented a good reviewer as one who kept himself pure from the 'elation of malignity', in his own reviews for *The Literary*

Magazine he could turn quite hostile if he judged authors ignorantly egocentric and complacent or if certain political issues and topics inflamed him sufficiently. These hostile reviews are now more interesting for what they say about Johnson's personality and individuating, simmering anger than for his opinions of the books themselves. One book he attacked with the club of Hercules was Thomas Blackwell's *Memoirs of the Court of Augustus*. His review abounds with scornful words and phrases: he is 'disgusted' with Blackwell's 'vanity' and hubris; the author 'ought not to boast himself as a great benefactor to the studious world'; his language is loaded with 'gaudy or hyperbolic' epithets; he 'heated his imagination' and is 'bold in fighting shadows'.[11]

In a different key, Soame Jenyns's amateurish *A Free Inquiry into the Nature and Origin of Evil* provoked him to write a vitriolic, sardonic and sparkling review in three instalments from May to July 1757. Jenyns was a dilettantish poet, long-time member of Parliament and essayist. Some have claimed that this long review is the single most important statement of Johnson's philosophy. He was offended by Jenyns's incompetence as a philosopher – 'swelled in sound, and diffused in bulk' – as well as by his shallow optimism. No less repelling in his eyes was Jenyns's presumption that he had all the answers to perplexing moral and religious dilemmas. This violated his deep sympathy for suffering humanity in a complex world. The world he knew did not match Jenyns's rosy view: 'He decides too upon questions out of the reach of human determination, with too little consideration of mortal weakness, and with too much vivacity for the necessary caution.' The final straw was when Jenyns argued that there may be superior beings in the universe who treat us for diversion much in the way we treat animals. Johnson bristled with irony: 'Many a merry bout have these frolic beings at the vicissitudes of an ague, and good sport it is to see a man tumble with an epilepsy'. The one question he wished to put to Jenyns is, 'why he that has nothing to write, should desire to be a writer'.[12]

Inflammatory wording and political indignation in other reviews and editorial contributions were fired by the outbreak of the convulsive Seven Years' War in May 1756, which he opposed fiercely as warmongering and economic madness. The first issue of *The Literary Magazine* coincided with the declaration of war on France by Britain, so it was bound to focus on current affairs. The war was truly a global conflict, a clash with France (chiefly) for control of parts of Europe, the Mediterranean and Africa, the West Indies, North America and India. By the end of it, in 1763, Britain had succeeded beyond her wildest dreams, the Peace of Paris that year carving out the largest single accretion of the Empire in British history.

The early months of the war, however, with French gains on all fronts, were discouraging for Britain, bringing a sharp decline of national morale and confirming Johnson in his conviction that British foreign policy was benighted. It did not seem to him in this time of national gloom that much of anything was going right in the nation's politics, conduct of the war, foreign entanglements and exploitations or naval policy. He disliked William Pitt, the Elder (1708–78), Secretary of State in the new coalition government with the Duke of Newcastle, for his imperialist policies on the development of a standing army; nor did he think much of his speeches in the House of Commons, which he thought more histrionic than brilliant. He unloaded his frustration about the war and Pitt's determination to expand overseas in several extremely strident political essays in 1756–8 about military glory and imperial aggrandisement, notably in three editorial pieces of 'literary vituperation' for *The Literary Magazine* in 1756: *Remarks on the Militia Bill* (1756), *An Introduction to the Political State of Britain* (1756) and *Observations on the State of Affairs in 1756* – as well as in four other short 'Observations' in a new weekly paper in 1758, *The Universal Chronicle*. They amount to a self-portrait of a highly independent thinker stripping away the 'ideological clothing' with which Pitt had justified the war and exposing the plunder of other nations that he believed lay behind the war effort. They also point up Johnson's courage and combativeness in waging his own war against the reigning political establishment and its current cant and jingoism, for his views during this time of fevered 'patriotism' were highly unpopular.

His *Introduction to the Political State of Great Britain*, which began prominently on the first page of the first issue of the magazine, is a long historical survey of British foreign policy since Queen Elizabeth by way of a background to how Britain got into this sorry war to begin with. Its theme is the immorality of foreign exploitation. He concluded by remarking that British conduct towards the native Americans in the American colonies had been scandalous: 'Our factors and traders having no other purpose in view than immediate profit, use all the arts of an European counting-house, to defraud the simple hunter of his furs ... we continue every day to show by new proofs, that no people can be great who have ceased to be virtuous.' In his *Observations on the Present State of Affairs*, which Boswell described as glowing 'with as animated a spirit of constitutional liberty as can be found anywhere', he was even more indignant towards the fraud and injustice of Britain's war with France over the boundaries of settlements in America which 'neither can occupy but by usurpation and the dispossession of the natural lords and original inhabitants'. He described the British Government as little more than 'a gang of bandits' trafficking in 'new modes of usurpation' and 'new instances of cruelty and treachery'.[13]

The proprietors of *The Literary Magazine*, however, were not pleased with the stridency of his tone and may even have forced him out since his extreme views on the evils of the Seven Years' War differed dramatically from theirs and had hurt sales of the magazine from the beginning. The magazine never did recover and it expired in July 1758. Even after the war had taken Britain to the threshold of glorious victory, Johnson's anger over government policy and its accompanying cant was undiminished – and at the time highly unusual. Indeed, the four sardonic anti-government 'Observations' that he wrote for the *Universal Chronicle*, in the spring of that year proved to be so upsetting to 'patriotic' readers that the publishers of that paper also slammed the door in his face, refusing to publish anything more from him on this theme.[14]

[3]

Johnson's household and personal life was in a state of flux. He had the boy Frank Barber living with him as a servant, but otherwise he was still lonely and rattling around in a large house. What he needed was immediate companionship and more people in his home; there were now plenty of bedrooms, especially now that after completing the *Dictionary* he had moved his library up to the garret. There was less natural light up there but the rest of the house had too many memories.

When little Frank, slight and delicate, first moved into Gough Square in 1752, Johnson did not really need him as a servant. From the start, he took pains to provide the boy with a good education. But Frank was volatile and in the autumn of 1756 'upon some difference', possibly having to do with schooling, he ran away to an apothecary in Cheapside and worked for him for two years as his assistant, 'during which he called sometimes on his Master and was well received' with the understanding that he would return to him. In December 1758, aged sixteen and restless, he ran away to sea. Somewhat stunned, Johnson later explained, 'Being disgusted in the house he ran away to sea, and was in the summer on board the ship stationed at Yarmouth to protect the fishery.' After two long years, 'in great distress' because Frank was 'of a delicate frame' and suffered from 'a malady in his throat', Johnson set in motion plans to recover him. He had a very low opinion of life at sea and could not imagine Frank was happy with it: 'No man', he once said, 'will be a sailor who has contrivance enough to get himself into a jail; for being in a ship is being in a jail, with the chance of being drowned.' He disliked the novelist Tobias Smollett but wrote to him anyway to see if, with his contacts in the navy, he could intervene to have Frank discharged. Smollett in turn called on John Wilkes, a political firebrand to whom Johnson would refer as 'a new retailer of sedition and obscenity' – Wilkes had mocked aspects of the *Dictionary* – to ask if he would write to the Admiralty on behalf of Johnson's 'lackey', in the process giving Johnson a tag by which he has been known ever since Smollett's letter became public in Wilkes's *Miscellanies* in the nineteenth century: 'I am again your petitioner, on behalf of that great CHAM of literature, Samuel Johnson. You know what manner of animosity the said Johnson has against you; and I dare say you desire no other opportunity of resenting it than that of laying him under an obligation. He was humble enough to desire my assistance on this occasion, though he and I were never cater-cousins.' Doubtless bemused, Wilkes wrote to Sir George Hay, one of the Lords of the Admiralty, and after a long delay Frank was discharged against his will in August 1760 and returned to Johnson who by then had moved out of Gough Square and was living less expensively in chambers at No. 1 Inner Temple Lane.[15]

The story of another boarder in Gough Square, Anna Williams (1706–83), is an unhappy one. Johnson's relationship to her was the result of a need for companionship, a desire to assist her and her father in their poverty, a mild respect for her poetry and other literary skills, and a curiosity regarding her interest in science. She developed a taste for science through her father Zachariah, who thought of himself as an inventor and whose great obsession was to win the £20,000 prize offered by the Government to anyone who could come up with a reliable method of measuring longitude at sea. In 1729, he became a pensioner of the Charterhouse, 'that asylum of age and poverty' founded in 1611 as a hospital for pensioners in buildings near Smithfield which had once housed a Carthusian monastery. His daughter, who had except for one brief period been blind since 1740, was unhappily prevented from living there with him, and in 1748 he himself was unceremoniously removed and reduced to living in poverty with her in unknown lodgings until he died seven years later.

Johnson took her in at Gough Square at intervals out of charity, originally while Tetty was still alive, for a brief spell around 1754, and finally more or less constantly shortly after her father died when she was penniless and alone. But he did more than this. To generate money and publicity for the indomitable but indigent Zachariah, who had not given up on the Longitude prize, he boned up on his invention and wrote a pamphlet under the inventor's name published as *An Account of an Attempt to Ascertain the Longitude at Sea* (1755). It failed to promote Williams's chances for the prize, and in any case Williams died that year. As for Anna, in 1752 he organised (with Hawkins's help) and paid for a painful cataract operation at Gough Square to restore her sight. It was unsuccessful and she remained blind for the rest of her life. To foster her literary ambitions, he also introduced her to Samuel Richardson by showing him a poem she had written in praise of the high moral tone of his recent novel *Sir Charles Grandison*. Later, when in desperate poverty, she tried to capitalise on Richardson's favour and influence by compiling a dictionary of scientific terms that he might promote, Johnson pressed him to help her: 'If you think her dictionary likely to shift for itself in this age of dictionaries, you will be pleased to encourage her.' Nothing came of the idea. Finally, one of her literary efforts did pay off because Johnson brought in Garrick who agreed to stage her play, *Merope*, in January 1756 for one benefit night. Johnson saw to the tickets being printed just the right way and talked up the play among his friends, with the result that she received £260, which for her was a fortune. By then she was running Johnson's home, even in blindness.[16]

It was a feature of Johnson's household that once he began to take in non-paying lodgers, 'whole nests of people', as Mrs Thrale put it, there was a good deal of quarrelling in it. What he gained in companionship, he lost in tranquility. 'Easily provoked to anger', Anna (known as Mrs Williams), was at the centre of his household's jarring lack of harmony and jealousy. For a start, she took a dislike to Frank. Hawkins praised her prudence and 'enlightened understanding', maintaining that she blessed Johnson with much good practical advice while he instructed her on 'religious and moral improvement', and Boswell especially enjoyed late-night cups of tea with her in the kitchen, but everyone agreed she was cranky. According to Hawkins, she was full of complaints about Frank's 'inattention to the interests of his master'. She would fly at Johnson about Frank, 'This is your scholar! Your philosopher! Upon whom you have spent so many hundred pounds!' Frank allegedly resented her 'for the authority she assumed over him, and [which she] exercised with an unwarrantable severity'.The churchman and anti-quarian Thomas Percy remarked: 'So far from being a constant source of disquiet and vexation' to Johnson, 'although she was totally blind for the last thirty years of her life, her mind was so well cultivated, and her conversation so agreeable, that she very much enlivened and diverted his solitary hours'.[17]

Robert Levet, another argumentative and permanent addition to the household, was also presently lodging with Johnson intermit-tently. Mrs Thrale colourfully described him in 1777 as 'a super-annuated surgeon' who had care of the whole *ship's company* in the house. He was never licensed as a physician but had gained good practical knowledge of the subject in France and Italy from experts in anatomy and pharmacy and was now prescribing medicines among the poor in London for 'whatever provisions his patients could afford him'. Sullen and something of a heavy drinker, he won Johnson's admiration for his good heart. 'Levet, Madam,' Johnson said to Mrs Thrale, 'is a brutal [awkward] fellow, but I have a good regard for him, for his brutality is in his manners, not his mind.' He was not a pretty sight in his mid-fifties when he moved into Gough Square, standing at five-feet five-inches tall, extremely thin, grey, and scarred by smallpox. Many of Johnson's friends found him grotesque, and his quarrels with Mrs Williams frequently descended to the vicious. He rarely spoke when company was present. Nevertheless, it was enough for Johnson that he was poor and miserable.[18]

One hanger-on, who did not join the 'nest' of lodgers, was the Frenchman and forger George Psalmanazar who further illustrated Johnson's charitable and instinctive attraction to the indigent, eccen-tric and even fraudulent fringes of society. 'I used to go and sit with him at an alehouse in the city,' Johnson remarked. Old Psalmanazar lived in Ironmonger Row off Old Street, where Johnson used to visit him, and it was at a 'club' or alehouse on Old Street that they used to pass the hours. Psalmanazar was a fraud and literary impostor, passing himself off in London during the early part of the century as a native of Formosa and concocting a new name and elaborate Formosan language and mythology to support his totally fraudulent book, *Historical and Geographical Description of Formosa* (1704). He enacted this pretence successfully until a religious conversion in the 1720s propelled him on a journey of penitence eventually bearing fruit in his *Memoirs* (1764), a published confession. From the 1720s until his death in 1763, he lived a religiously blameless life of poverty. In his novel *Humphry Clinker*, Tobias Smollett pauses to describe him as one 'who, after having drudged half a century in the literary mill, in all the simplicity and abstinence of an Asiatic, subsists upon the charity of a few booksellers, just sufficient to keep him from the parish'. Even children who passed him on the street would show 'the usual signs of respect'. Asked once whether he ever contradicted Psalmanazar, Johnson replied, 'I should as soon have thought of contradicting a bishop'. 'George Psalmanazar's piety, penitence, and virtue exceeded almost what we read as wonderful even in the lives of saints', he told Mrs Thrale with not a little exaggeration; he was the 'best' man he had ever known.[19]

Speaking of Grub Street and the 'regular' education Johnson nostalgically believed was to be had in that school of hard knocks, there was another man, a tailor, with whom he and Psalmanazar would retreat into the shadows of that club in Old Street and whom they dubbed the 'metaphysical tailor' because of the sage advice he dispensed. When the year before he died Johnson discovered to his surprise that his good friend John Hoole was this obscure tailor's nephew in Grub Street, that they had been 'brother authors' there in 'the mansions of our progenitors', he shouted, 'Let you and I, Sir, go together, and eat a beef-steak in Grub-street.'[20]

[4]

There were other, more socially respectable, friends. The mercurial and exceptionally able Giuseppe Baretti was one, introduced to him by Charlotte Lennox. Baretti was too hot-tempered and opinionated to be friends with everyone, but Johnson and his circle were steady in their loyalty towards him and once teamed up to get him acquitted at a murder trial. Johnson had the highest regard for 'my Baretti', as he called him. Philosophical about his erratic behaviour, he admonished Mrs Thrale: 'Poor Baretti! Do not quarrel with him, to neglect him a little will be sufficient. He means only to be frank, and manly, and independent, and perhaps, as you say, a little wise. To be frank he thinks is to be cynical, and to be independent, is to be rude ... his misbehaviour, I am afraid, he learned part of me.'[21] Johnson wrote prefaces to Baretti's *Introduction to the Italian Language* (1755) and *A Grammar of the Italian Language* (1760), among others, helped with his *Italian Library* (1757), and actually planned several of Baretti's other works for him.

A more tender friendship was with young Bennet Langton (1737–1801), who entered Trinity College, Oxford, in 1757 and studied under Thomas Warton. Tall and gangly at six feet six inches – Johnson nicknamed him 'Lanky', a 'very tall, meagre, long-visaged man, much resembling a stork standing on one leg' – Langton was quite thrown off balance by Johnson, whom he reverenced, when 'down from his bed-chamber, about noon, came, as newly risen, a huge uncouth figure, with a little dark wig which scarcely covered his head, and his clothes hanging loose about him.' But he was quickly seduced by his hero's conversation, and for his part Johnson, undoubtedly equally taken aback by Langton's prodigious height, took to the young man for his youthful zest, piety and 'exalted character', as well as for his old Lincolnshire family.[22]

While at Oxford, Langton met a young rake and fellow student, Topham Beauclerk (1739–80), the great-grandson of Charles II and Nell Gwyn and grandson of the 1st Duke of St Albans, who may be mentioned now although Langton did not introduce him to Johnson until the latter's next visit to Oxford in June and July 1759. Langton and Beauclerk cemented an affectionate friendship with each other at Oxford that never wavered. Apparently Johnson also took to Beauclerk immediately, whom he called 'Beau', although his friendship with this 'gay, dissipated' young man raised a few eyebrows. 'What a coalition!' said Garrick when he heard of it, with Falstaff in mind, 'I shall have my old friend to bail out of the Round-house.' 'Thy body is all vice, and thy mind all virtue,' Johnson once said to Beauclerk, who could take more liberties with his older friend, and get away with them, than anyone else. With Langton and Beauclerk Johnson had more sheer fun, often in youthful 'frisks', than with anyone else except, in different ways, later with Boswell. 'What, is it you, you dogs! I'll have a frisk with you', he announced to them 'with his little black wig on the top of his head, instead of a nightcap'. They had rapped at his door in Inner Temple Lane at three one morning in the early 1760s to commandeer him on a ramble into Covent Garden, 'where the green-grocers and fruiterers were beginning to arrange their hampers, just come in from the country'. After a few hours in a tavern drinking 'Bishop', a favourite drink of Johnson's made of a mixture of wine, oranges, and sugar, they boarded a boat and rowed down the Thames to Billingsgate. They were going to keep this up throughout the day but Langton abandoned them for breakfast with what Johnson teasingly described as 'a set of *un-idea'd* girls'. When Garrick caught wind of this escapade, he had to say, 'I heard of your frolic t'other night. You'll be in the Chronicle.'[23]

There is no doubt that his warmest and closest male friend was Joshua Reynolds (1723–92) who, since returning from Italy in 1752, had been on the fast track to becoming Britain's greatest and wealthiest portrait painter. To Cordelia Knight, a young woman growing up in London in the 1760s and 1770s, 'his features were coarse, and his outward appearance slovenly', and 'his pronunciation was tinctured with the Devonshire accent' that was a pleasant complement to John-son's own Staffordshire accent. Nobody knew Johnson like Reynolds. 'If I should lose you, I should lose almost the only man whom I call a friend,' Johnson once said to him. He was his 'oldest and kindest friend'. He simply regarded Reynolds as a 'great man'. Reynolds maintained that Johnson 'formed my mind' and 'brushed off from it a deal of rubbish'. They appear to have met in 1756–7, the rough date given to their meeting by Reynolds's sister Frances, who had moved in with her brother in 1753 to keep house for him. In one of his memo-like pocket-books that listed such things as the sitters for portraits and sales he attended, he mentioned Johnson for the first time in January 1757 as sitting for a portrait, so it is likely they met not long before then.[24]

Frances Reynolds ('Renny', as Johnson called her), whose family thought she could have married Johnson if she had wanted to, remem-bered those early days fondly in her diary, especially 'the impression I felt in his favour, on his saying that as he returned to his lodgings about one or two o'clock in the morning, he often saw poor children asleep on thresholds and stalls, and that he used to put pennies into their hands to buy them a breakfast'. Even his 'best dress was, at that time, so very mean', she added, that at times he was mistaken for hired help and not introduced properly, which made him growl. A painter herself, she was somewhat highly strung. Charles Burney's daughter Fanny described her as 'in a habitual perplexity of mind and irresolution of conduct'.[25]

Renny is of particular interest because she painted a portrait of Johnson and also showed herself fascinated by his eccentric physical movements and appearance, especially the compulsive tics and gesticulations, the conspicuous movements and sounds. These included ritualised 'extraordinary gestures or antics with his hands and feet, particularly when passing over the threshold of a door, or rather before he would venture to pass through *any* doorway'. Boswell also commented on his counting his steps before passing through a doorway or carefully touching posts as he walked along a street. As for his foot movements, Renny added, they were 'scarcely credible': 'Sometimes he would make the back part of his heels to touch, sometimes the extremity of his toes, as if endeavouring to form a triangle, or some geometrical figure, and as for his gestures with his hands, they were equally as strange; sometimes he would hold them up ... sometimes at his breast in motion like those of a jockey on full speed; and often would he lift them up as high as he could stretch over his head, for some minutes.' One day while walking in Twickenham meadows with him, she was distressed to see him suddenly launching into 'antics both with his feet and hands, with the latter as if he was holding the reins of a horse like a jockey on full speed'. This was so extraordinary that 'men, women, and children gathered round him, laughing. At last we sat down on some logs of wood by the river side, and they nearly dispersed.' The movement that she said astonished the most 'was his stretching out his arm with a full cup of tea in his hand, in every direction, often to the great annoyance of the person who sat next him, indeed to the imminent danger of their clothes ...; sometimes he would twist himself round with his face close to the back of his chair, and finish his cup of tea, breathing very hard, as if making a laborious effort to accomplish it.' It is now widely suspected that these movement disorders were symptoms of what has become known as the neurological disease that some now call Tourette's Syndrome, except without the extremes of profanity that often characterise it.[26]

By the time Boswell had met Johnson, it is possible that these jerks, gesticulations and other movement disorders had become even more severe and astonishing to onlookers. His description of them is even more complete and remarkable than Renny's:

while talking or even musing as he sat in his chair, he commonly held his head to one side towards his right shoulder, and shook it in a tremulous manner, moving his body backwards and forwards, and rubbing his left knee in the same direction, with the palm of his hand. In the intervals of articulating he made various sounds with his mouth, sometimes as if ruminating, or what is called chewing the cud, sometimes giving a half whistle, sometimes making his tongue play backwards from the roof of his mouth, as if clucking like a hen, and sometimes protruding it against his upper gums in front, as if pronouncing quickly under his breath, *too, too, too*: all this accompanied sometimes with a thoughtful look, but more frequently with a smile. Generally when he had concluded a period, in the course of a dispute, by which time he was a good deal exhausted by violence and vociferation, he used to blow out his breath like a whale ...

In a character sketch of Johnson after he died, Joshua Reynolds disagreed with Boswell's assertion that Johnson lapsed into these movements both when actively engaged with persons around him and when he was alone or musing, lost in thought. He maintained that the movements were not wildly involuntary and were noticeable only when Johnson withdrew into himself: 'His mind appeared to be preying on itself; he fell into a reverie accompanied with strange antic gesticulations. But this was when his mind was absent or deep in thought; he never did when his mind was engaged by the conversation.' Reynolds's opinion was that the movements 'proceeded from a habit which he had indulged himself in, of accompanying his thoughts with certain untoward actions'. Mrs Thrale never saw him move like this in church, and Renny plausibly maintained that without the ability to control his body he could hardly have sat for portraits that her brother and she painted of him. In any case, retrospective medicine is a risky business, and whether or not Johnson's well-publicised eccentric physical movements were due to Tourette's Syndrome exclusively remains a complicated matter.[27]

[5]

What Johnson looked like the year after the publication of the *Dictionary* brings us to the portrait of him by Reynolds in 1756–7. Reynolds's annual income by the early 1760s was about £6000, in the region of £600,000 today, but it is unlikely that Johnson had anything in his pocketbook at all to spare for this first portrait of himself. That so soon after meeting him Reynolds should paint a full portrait of such an eccentric-looking writer – a huge departure from his usual lucrative aristocratic subjects – is a measure of his fascination with the appearance of the now famous lexicographer and his desire to record an image from his post-*Dictionary* fame. Indeed, the portrait is commonly referred to as 'Dictionary Johnson' and now hangs in the National Portrait Gallery in London, attacked recently by a deranged knife-wielder. It shows Johnson sitting uncomfortably in a simple chequered-covered chair without arms, at a table covered with a plain green cloth. His face is open, clean, and relatively youthful with a smooth brow. There are no deep furrows and signs of worry. There is a coarseness about the face, though, with its fleshiness, large jaw, large nose and thick lips. He looks much as one may have expected Reynolds to represent a literary figure – without any social pretentiousness and looking, in his simple coat, like someone who may not have had too many other clothes to choose from in which to be painted.

Boswell said that when he first met Johnson he felt he was not looking at him for the first time because of this portrait: 'I found that I had a very perfect idea of Johnson's figure, from the portrait of him painted by Sir Joshua Reynolds soon after he had published his *Dictionary*, in the attitude of sitting in his easy chair in deep meditation which was the first picture his friend did for him, which Sir Joshua very kindly presented to me.' Boswell did not meet Reynolds until 1769, and since in his journal he never says he had seen the painting, he must be saying this for effect. As there is no look of 'deep meditation' in the original portrait, when Boswell set about having the painting engraved by James Heath, engraver for the Royal Academy, for the Frontispiece of his *Life* thirty-five years later, Reynolds (who had kept the portrait until he gave it to Boswell in 1789) thought the image 'was too young and not thoughtful enough' and advised Heath to make him look more like the now famous moralist and lexicographer, with another quill pen and inkpot and a copy of the *Dictionary* on the table, a face slimmed and frowning with more prominent eyebrows, his wig roughed up, and his clothes more respectable. It was a case of Johnson's reputation reaching back to the original portrait and altering it.[28]

Johnson would be painted by twelve painters during the rest of his life, and by Reynolds three or four more times. Only Pope was painted more often in the eighteenth century, but Pope was rich and had many aristocratic friends. Johnson was quite taken with the honour of Reynolds's portrait and the depth of understanding of his character, the 'colouring' of the mind, that he felt the painter had caught in it.

Three years later he dearly hoped Reynolds would not squander his talents by painting 'historical pictures': 'I should grieve to see Reynolds transfer to heroes and to goddesses, to empty splendour and to airy fiction, that art which is now employed in diffusing friendship, in reviving tenderness, in quickening the affections of the absent, and continuing the presence of the dead.'[29]

CHAPTER 21

'Suffering Chimeras'

[1]

If Johnson were not to remain stalled and poor, wasting hours in taverns, writing ephemera for magazines, and providing prefaces and dedications for friends and booksellers which did him personally little material good, he had to throw himself decisively into another major project. Hawkins wrote that in this hour of need it was again a consortium of booksellers led by Jacob Tonson who came to his rescue: they 'had their eyes upon Johnson' and were alarmed at the 'misapplication of his talents'. Tonson, we recall, claimed perpetual copyright in Shakespeare and defeated Cave's effort a decade earlier to have Johnson produce an edition of the Bard. Now on the strength of Garrick's stupendous popularisation of Shakespeare on the stage, Tonson himself decided there was an ideal market for a new complete edition of Shakespeare and that it was better to have Johnson, whom he realised was the ideal man to produce it, on his side. He and the others concluded correctly that Johnson's deep study of Shakespeare's language for the *Dictionary* and collection of thousands of quotations from the plays placed him in the best possible position to take on the edition.[1]

The contract dated 2 June 1756 specified that profits from a subscription to the first edition would be his, and the booksellers would keep the copyright. The edition would be 'elegantly printed' in eight volumes in octavo size. He would be supplied with 250 sets free of charge to sell to subscribers for two guineas each in loose sheets – the purchaser would have to see to his own binding. After that he would have to pay one guinea for subscriber sets. So Johnson would stand to make five hundred guineas if he could get that many subscribers. To round up as many as possible he turned to friends. He told Hector in October he was even bringing his aged mother into service: 'I have undertaken a new edition of Shakespeare, and that the profits of it are to arise from a subscription. I therefore solicit the interest of all my friends, and believe myself sure of yours without solicitation. The proposals and receipts may be had from my mother to whom I beg you send for as many as you can dispose of, and to remit to her money which you or your acquaintance shall collect.' Concerned for his mother's well-being, he added a month later, 'As you receive three or four guineas send them to my mother. She may want them.'[2]

On 8 June he published his *Proposals* for the edition, deploring the imperfections of early editions and the mangled state of the text in Shakespeare's lifetime and since, claiming a crucial need for yet more notes to shed the needed light: 'to correct what is corrupt, and to explain what is obscure'. He was hard on previous editors: Nicholas Rowe and Pope were 'very ignorant of English literature', William Warburton was 'detained by more important studies', and Lewis Theobald was content only with as much analysis as enabled him 'to embellish his page with the expected decorations'. None of them possessed the 'critical sagacity' which he would display in his own edition. Compounding the textual problems, he added, were obscurities of language and sources veiled by the mists of time: 'the figures vanish when the canvas has decayed'. 'With regard to obsolete or peculiar diction,' he declared, 'the editor may perhaps claim some degree of confidence, having had more motives to consider the whole extent of our language than any other man from its first formation'. He also needed to examine the literary context of each play and perform 'a careful collation of the oldest copies' for variant readings of the text, for which he made a desultory effort to round up books from public libraries and friends like Birch, Thomas Warton and Garrick.[3]

Potential lenders would have done well to think twice before lending him any, however, given his treatment of the books he borrowed for the *Dictionary*. As Boswell observed, 'considering the slovenly and careless manner in which books were treated by Johnson, it could not be expected that scarce and valuable editions should have been lent to him'. Garrick, however, did lend him volumes from his fine collection of old plays and Shakespeare quarto editions, one of the finest in the country, leaving a key to it with his servant and instructions to light a fire in the library so that Johnson could use it in comfort any time he wished. He was upset when he read this passage in the Preface to the edition, 'I collated such copies as I could procure, and wished for more, but have not found the collectors of these rarities very communicative.'

Johnson's pride would not let him acknowledge the favour, especially since he regarded Shakespeare's text his own province, not Garrick's, and resented his crossing the line from stage to page through the power of his collection. When Boswell asked him why he did not mention Garrick in his Preface to the edition, he mocked his old pupil's alleged influence of the public's perception of Shakespeare: 'I would not disgrace my page with a player. Garrick has been liberally paid for mouthing Shakespeare. If I should praise him, I should much more praise the nation who paid him. He has not made Shakespeare better known. He cannot illustrate Shakespeare. He does not understand him'. Moreover, he denied that Frank Barber ever received any of Garrick's books. In his journal Boswell put this tempest in a teapot down to Johnson's jealousy, 'that *Davy* Garrick, who was his pupil and who came up to London at the same time with him ... should be so very general a favourite and should have fourscore thousand pounds, an immense sum, when he had so little'. In an exasperated letter to Johnson in May 1765, Garrick said he could scarcely believe it when his brother asked him if he had subscribed to the edition: 'I told him yes, that I was one of the first, and as soon as I had heard of your intention; and that I gave you, at the same time, some other names, among which were the Duke of Devonshire.' Nonetheless, Johnson complained later that 'Garrick got me no subscriptions.'[4]

Johnson confidently agreed in the contract to finish by Christmas 1757. He knew his powers, but in retrospect eighteen months seemed to him and others totally unrealistic. Among other things, he underestimated the work involved in sifting through and dealing with previous editors on whose commentary and textual decisions he had to provide notes. Personal problems also lurked ahead to confound him. Still, he threw himself into the work and, remarkably, in December 1757, felt sanguine enough to be able to write to Burney, who had rounded up six subscribers among Johnson's Norfolk admirers, 'I shall publish about March.' He was hard at it but March came and still there was no edition. 'I am ashamed to tell you', he wrote to Burney that month, 'that my Shakespeare will not be out so soon as I promised my subscribers ... It will however be published before summer ... I have printed many of the plays and have hitherto left very few passages unexplained.' When he could not explain them, he added, he was confessing his ignorance, 'which is seldom done by commentators'. But if any subscribers needed reassurance that the edition would be out by then, he instructed Burney to let them read Arthur Murphy's 'splendid encomium' the previous April on his editorship: 'one of the best critics of this age ... who has approved himself, in various branches of writing, an English classic of the first magnitude ... possessed of a genius to which we may apply what was said of Caesar, "The Alps and the Pyreneans sink before him."'[5]

Burney still had not met him but in the winter of 1758 finally dropped in at Gough Square where 'he dined and drank tea with him, and was introduced to the acquaintance of Mrs Williams'. Johnson even took him up to his garret, where Burney could see for himself the sacred space where the *Dictionary* was created but which now was littered with Shakespeareana. There Johnson showed him the plays already printed as evidence that he was indeed getting on with the project. They spoke of literature and it was then that Johnson first conceived his respect for Burney's mind and enthusiasm, even if in his ambivalence about music he was less than enthusiastic that Burney was a musician. 'Music excites in my mind no ideas, and hinders me from contemplating my own,' he once remarked. The meeting was enough to push Burney's hero-worship of Johnson into the regions of idolatry. When he finally moved to London in 1760 with his wife and six children, he cultivated Johnson's company assiduously. He even perpetuated the reverence of his friend and fellow Norfolkian William Bewley by surreptitiously cutting off 'a few bristles of his hearth-broom' and posting them to Bewley as a type of relic. Learning of this, Johnson later called Bewley 'the Broom Gentleman'.[6]

By this time Johnson had attained the reputation as a superman among scholars. Shenstone wrote to Thomas Percy in January 1758, 'Do you hear that Mr Johnson's Shakespeare will be published this winter? I have a prejudice ... in favour of all he undertakes; and wish the world may recompense him for a degree of industry very seldom connected with so much real genius.' Percy had met Johnson in the summer of 1756 at Gough Square and immediately promised to help collect subscriptions from his Northamptonshire and Shropshire friends, but he had his doubts when Johnson told him confidently he hoped to publish before Easter 1758. Indeed, Johnson's predictions of a publication date soon dried up. In spite of books lent him and notes which Warton, Percy and others sent his way, he encountered what Boswell called 'severe and remittent' obstacles, emotional and practical. Hawkins's overstated opinion was that the edition was not a labour of love and that this prevented him from really getting down to it. Johnson told him, 'I look upon this as I did upon the *Dictionary*:

it is all work, and my inducement to it is not love or desire of fame, but the want of money, which is the only motive to writing that I know of.' Hawkins also claimed that Johnson not only failed to apply himself to systematic reading but also much of the time drifted about doing almost nothing: 'It was provoking to all his friends to see him waste his days, his weeks, and his months so long, that they feared a mental lethargy had seized him, out of which he would never recover.' Much to the confusion of subscribers and the general public, the edition did not appear in 1758 or the next year, or the year after that.[7]

One of the reasons for the delay may well have been complications arising from his methods.[8] He had already overshot his deadline by close to a year, and inasmuch as he had virtually finished what for him was the easiest part of the process, explication of themes and language in the plays, and was about to embark on the more troublesome textual work, it is likely he lost his drive to publish anywhere near his advertised deadline. The problem was that in the *Proposals* he had boasted he would undertake 'a careful collation' of 'all the copies that can be found'. It did not surprise him that when it came down to it he had no taste for combing the bibliographical landscape for early printed copies of the plays and exhaustively collating them.

Johnson had more accessible public libraries at his disposal than did preceding editors, so there was no excuse for his negligence in acquiring books he needed. The British Museum had been established in 1753 and formally opened its doors in January 1759 at the seventeenth-century mansion Montagu House in Bloomsbury, and even as he was working on his edition part of the Royal Library was transferred to it by George II in 1757. But rather than delight him, the dramatic increase in the availability of books made him sceptical. He saw darker meanings in the vast accumulations of printed volumes. While in *Adventurer* 85 he had derided those who believed libraries were filled only with 'useless lumber' from which 'men of parts' needed 'no assistance', he also was suspicious of them as 'bubbles of artificial fame' that could swallow up lives 'in vain endeavours'. For him a vast library, 'crowded on every side by mighty volumes', embodied 'the vanity of human hopes'. His approach instead was to balance research with the imaginative and pragmatic, to discover in literature not facts but a mirror to nature, the truth about human existence, 'appealing wholly to observation and experience'. A scholar who buries himself in manuscripts and wears out his days in 'perpetual research and solitary meditation', risks 'losing in his elocution what he adds to his wisdom'; he is in danger of approaching writing 'overloaded with his own notions, like a man armed with weapons which he cannot wield'. Squandering hours in the imaginatively deadening precincts of a library was the last thing he wanted to do. 'A ready man is made by conversation.'[9]

The real monster he feared was the textual work. He knew there were better Shakespeare editors out there who would censure him for slipshod work, and such a prospect troubled and somewhat paralysed him. It was not lost on him that critics had vigorously attacked Warburton's edition. So, in the Preface, he decided it might help to attack potential critics first by portraying them as maliciously irrelevant: 'The one stings like a fly, sucks a little blood, takes a gay flutter, and returns for more; the other bites like a viper, and would be glad to leave inflammations and gangrene behind him.' What he knew he really needed, though, was a textual collaborator who could have dealt with this meddlesome part of the labor – someone like George Steevens, one of the great Shakespeareans of the late eighteenth century who became his friend only in the later stages of the project, when it was too late. It was easy to write in the Preface that he wished for more early editions to collate, but he was loath to chase after them.[10]

As for notes from friends, even though he planned an appendix as a catch-all for any he received after the relevant plays were already printed, he found himself sticking in notes to the plays 'by means of asterisks and obelisks ... interspersing them between the notes numbered numerically'. This practice was just not sustainable, for after a while it would involve drastic and expensive reconstituting of entire pages. It was all becoming a jumble, and the confusion postponed publication.[11]

[2]

The weight of anxiety about how the edition was going set in motion mutually reinforcing aggravations and worries. It was nourishing soil for the ever-lurking black dog and made him feel he *was* idle. 'Much of my time past has been lost in sloth,' he moaned in his Easter Day prayer on 26 March 1758, and then in his birthday prayer in September he implored God to 'enable me to improve the time which is yet before me', repenting 'days misspent in idleness and folly, that I may henceforward diligently attend to the business of my station in this world'.[12]

He was also worried about his mother, now just short of ninety and seriously ill in Lichfield. 'I will, if it be possible, come down to you,' he wrote in some panic on 20 January 1759 to Lucy, who was still living with her at home. 'God grant I may yet see my dear mother breathing and sensible. Do not tell, lest I disappoint her.' He did not go. Instead, her illness elicited from him a rare series of short letters to her, efforts partly to palliate or 'efface' his guilt over not having seen her for twenty years. 'The account which Miss gives me of your health, pierces my heart,' he wrote on 13 January. He suggested both spiritual and temporal remedies. Lucy could read to her from 'the Passion of our Saviour' and she should take 'a strong infusion of the bark'. 'Do, dear Mother, try it.' Then poignantly he added, 'forgive all that I have done amiss to you'. 'I know not how to bear the thought of losing you,' he wrote to his mother on 16 January. 'You have been the best mother, and I believe the best woman in the world. I thank you for your indulgence to me, and beg forgiveness of all that I have done ill.'[13]

He did not have money enough for an emergency flight to Lichfield, which he hoped to make before she died. Nor did he believe he could afford her funeral expenses when the sad event occurred. So he sat down and began to write a short philosophical tale or moral fable, to be titled *The Choice of Life or The History of—— Prince of Abissinia*, eventually better known as *Rasselas*. He used the printer Strahan as his literary agent to settle on terms with Dodsley and another prominent bookseller William Johnston: £100 for the first edition and £25 for the second. Baretti thought he had sold it too cheaply: 'Any other person with the degree of reputation he then possessed would have got £400 for that work, but he never understood the art of making the most of his productions.'[14]

On the same day Johnson wrote to Strahan about this, Lucy wrote to say his mother had died. 'If she were to live again', he wrote to Lucy on the 23rd, 'surely I should behave better to her.' That was the day of her funeral. 'It is not of any use for me now to come down,' he wrote to her two days later, 'nor can I bear the place.' That same day he composed a prayer, asking forgiveness for unkindness towards her and committing to God 'the soul of my departed Mother'. Four days later he dashed out an essay on losing a loved one, with this telling passage: 'Every calamity comes suddenly upon us, and not only presses us as a burden, but crushes as a blow ... The life which made my own life pleasant is at an end, and the gates of death are shut upon my prospects.' All that was left was a 'state of dreary desolation in which the mind looks abroad impatient of itself, and finds nothing but emptiness and horror'.[15]

Johnson felt a new kind of loneliness, which, with a dark look at himself, he expressed in *Rasselas* almost immediately: 'I have neither mother to be delighted with the reputation of her son, nor wife to partake the honours of her husband.' He reached out to Lucy like a drowning man: she was 'the only person now left in the world with whom I think myself connected ... I have nobody but you ... If you and Kitty will keep the house, I think I shall like it best'. Just the thought of them in it helped: 'Kitty may carry on the trade for herself, keeping her own stock apart, and laying aside any money that she receives for any of the goods which her dear good Mistress has left behind her ... My mother's debts, dear mother! I suppose I may pay with little difficulty ... I fancy Kitty can do nothing better, and I shall not want to put her out of a house where she has lived so long and with so much virtue ... You must have what part of the house you please while you are inclined to stay in it, but I flatter myself with hopes that you and I shall sometime pass our days together.' All he asked was that she write to him once a week, 'for I am now very desolate, and am loath to be universally forgotten'. Perhaps taking in lodgers, she continued to live there until 1763.[16]

He was especially vulnerable to these new sensations of loneliness and dislocation because the previous September he had been forced to give up the lease on Gough Square, no longer able to afford it. 'I have left off housekeeping,' he informed Langton, with under-statement that belied the upheaval he must have felt. It meant of course that his household of non-paying guests would have to disperse. Mrs Williams and Dr Levet suddenly had to move out and find other places. She was fortunate to be able to move to a boarding school in Bolt Court off Fleet Street, not far from Gough Square, where she continued to live for many years until she rejoined Johnson in a house large enough to take her and others in. He saw her every day, dropping in after midnight for his customary tea before going to bed.[17]

[3]

It would have been extraordinary if the awkwardness of having to move out of Gough Square had not interrupted his Shakespearean work. *Rasselas*, however, his 'little story book', he appears to have written almost on the run. He told Reynolds that in the urgency of raising money for his mother he 'composed it in the evenings of one week, sent it to the press in portions as it was written, and had never since read it over'. The book exploded from him. As Shaw wrote, it was 'an early conception, on which ideas were matured long before the completion of the work'. It was published anonymously – it was not long before he was discovered as the author – in two volumes on 20 April 1759 for five shillings, a bestseller if ever there was one in his life, translated several times over the next few years into Italian, French, German and Dutch, and eventually published in America in 1768. It reached fifty editions before the century was out.[18]

Johnson's most popular work, *Rasselas* was his only attempt at a lengthy piece of prose fiction. It is an extended moral parable in the style of the oriental or eastern tales he wrote for several of the *Rambler* essays. In it he expressed again his strong views about self-delusion and benighted efforts to find human happiness, about how mortal existence overflows with 'vanity and vexation of spirit'. 'Human life is everywhere a state in which much is to be endured, and little to be enjoyed,' says the philosopher and poet Imlac. The tale tells of a young and hopeful prince, Rasselas, and his sister Nekayah, who, although they have all their desires satisfied, feel bored, imprisoned and shut off from life's variety in 'the happy valley' surrounded by mountains that was the ancient residence of Abyssinian royalty. 'I have already enjoyed too much,' says the prince, 'give me something to desire ... I shall long to see the miseries of the world since the sight of them is necessary to happiness.' He spends much of his time bemoaning his fate. Under the tutelage of Imlac, he and his sister finally escape from the valley through the mountains to find the 'choice of life' that will bring them happiness. They make their way to Cairo where they encounter spectacles, some of them ludicrous and pitiful, of misguided efforts to find happiness and fulfilment.[19]

The very first sentence of the book is strongly cautionary and leaves no doubt about the overarching theme to follow: 'Ye who listen with credulity to the whispers of fancy, and pursue with eagerness the phantoms of hope; who expect that age will perform the promises of youth, and that the deficiencies of the present day will be supplied by the morrow; attend to the history of Rasselas prince of Abissinia.' If Johnson needed any confirmation of this theme in his own life, he needed only to reflect on the failure of the *Dictionary* to bring him the

happiness and comforts for which he longed, and on the confusion
rocking him all over again with his Shakespeare edition. He voiced
his own despondency with his description of the prince's: 'His imagination was now at a stand; he had no prospect of entering into the
world; and, notwithstanding all his endeavours to support himself,
discontent by degrees preyed upon him, and he began again to lose
his thoughts in sadness.' Dominating all the major early biographies
of Johnson by Boswell, Piozzi, Hawkins and Murphy was the theme
that Johnson's despondency and melancholia were responsible for the
bleakness of the tale.[20]

The tale consists mostly of moral reflections and philosophical
scepticism through dialogue, with virtually no action to relieve it. After
their long and sobering journey the travellers return to Abyssinia, wiser
in the understanding that no single place or philosophy can shield
men and women completely from the pain, suffering, disease, grief,
disappointment and sadness of life. Throw away 'the encumbrance of
precepts', Imlac demands. 'Be not too hasty to trust, or to admire, the
teachers of morality: they discourse like angels, but they live like
men.'[21]

One day in Cairo, Rasselas tells Imlac that he intends henceforth
to devote all his days to 'literary solitude'. Imlac, who often may be
taken as Johnson's own voice and has already warned Rasselas that
there is nobody who does not dread 'the moment when solitude should
deliver him to the tyranny of reflection', warns him immediately and
firmly that before making this choice he 'ought to examine its hazards,
and converse with some of those who are grown old in the company
of themselves'. For Imlac too much isolated study in the vain hope of
impressing the world leads to selfishness and the precincts of insanity.
An astronomer they meet, who says he has always suspected himself
of madness, chimes in bitterly with the same warning: 'I can only tell
that I have chosen wrong . . . I have missed the endearing elegance of
female friendship, and the happy commerce of domestic tenderness'.
Whatever he has gained from retirement and isolated study has been
costly in terms of 'fear, disquiet, and scrupulosity'; and with a crescendo of dismal finality he announces, 'I now see how fatally I betrayed
my quiet, by suffering chimeras to prey upon me in secret; but melancholy shrinks from communication.'[22]

Imlac then launches into what we may read as one of Johnson's
fullest analyses of insanity. A few passages will convey his sense of
urgency and fear on the subject. 'All power of fancy over reason is a

degree of insanity,' says Imlac; 'it is not pronounced madness but when it comes ungovernable, and apparently influences speech or action. To indulge the power of fiction, and send imagination out upon the wing is often the sport of those who delight too much in silent speculation. When we are alone we are not always busy ... the mind dances from scene to scene ... Then fictions begin to operate as realities.' Religious 'scruples' about 'futurity', vain speculations on the afterlife, also conspire against reason. And grief, too, can foster fear and propel one towards melancholia. It is a devilish congregation of mental scorpions. The astronomer later says to Imlac, 'I am like a man habitually afraid of spectres, who is set at ease by a lamp, and wonders at the dread which harassed him in the dark, yet, if his lamp is extinguished, feels again the terrors which he knows that when it is light he shall feel no more'. Imlac responds with the last word on this disease:

> No disease of the imagination is so difficult to cure as that which is complicated with the dread of guilt: fancy and conscience then act interchangeably upon us, and so often shift their places, that the illusions of one are not distinguished from the dictates of the other. If fancy presents images not moral or religious, the mind drives them away when they give it pain, but when melancholic notions take the form of duty, they lay hold on the faculties without opposition, because we are afraid to exclude or banish them. For this reason the superstitious are often melancholy, and the melancholy almost always superstitious.[23]

But as in the *Rambler* essays, the picture is far from totally bleak. Courage plays a great part. Johnson portrays the main characters with piety and compassion, hope and at times humour. Rasselas and Nekayah, in spite of their experiences and Imlac's counsel, return home with sustaining hope, but realising at the same time that they are not likely ever to obtain their desires. The final chapter is titled, 'The conclusion, in which nothing is concluded'. The important thing is to keep moving and aspiring. As Nekayah realises at the end, it is not the 'choice of life' but the 'choice of eternity' that is crucial to understand.

The critical reception of *Rasselas* was mixed. Shenstone thought the tale 'below Mr J'. The poet and essayist Hester Mulso (later Chapone), an intimate member of Richardson's literary coterie – his 'little spitfire' – and friend of Elizabeth Carter, was 'grievously disappointed' in 'the giant Johnson' because she thought the tale was too bleak, uninstructive (even harmful) therefore for young people, unnatural in its characterisation, ill-contrived, and inconclusive. 'I think the only maxim one can deduce from this story,' Mulso wrote to Carter in a gossipy vein, 'is that human life is a scene of unmixed wretchedness and that all states and conditions of it are equally miserable'. She admitted her anger that with his 'poisonous' inferences 'poor Mr Johnson ... had considered the worst side of the character of human nature, and seems to be but little acquainted with the best and happiest of its affections'. The general complaints were also that *Rasselas* uses too many 'hard' (especially polysyllabic) words, its characters are indiscriminate cardboard figures who are merely mouthpieces for Johnson's ideas – the women come across as 'Johnson in petticoats' – and speak in an unrelieved high style, its narrative lacks emotional force, its tone is dictatorial, and its plot is anaemic. On the positive side it was praised for its sublimity, purity of diction, elegance and eloquence and moral insights on human affairs. It was also praised for its fine Eastern fable.[24]

[4]

After months in residential limbo, Johnson described his move on 23 March 1759 to Staples Inn as 'a change of outward things' which he hoped would be answered by 'a reformation of my thoughts, words, and practices'. Staples Inn is a well-preserved late sixteenth-century clutch of buildings around a courtyard with a half-timbered front that takes one by surprise today on a walk along noisy High Holborn. Then in an unattractive neighbourhood, the building was a lodging house for law students as well as others who came recommended. That summer he escaped to Oxford again for no fewer than seven weeks, staying at All Souls and Trinity colleges as a guest of Warton and Robert Vansittart, Regius Professor of Civil Law from 1767–89, whom he 'much esteemed'. He let himself go on this Oxford visit with boyish abandon, relieved to escape for a couple of months the gloom and impermanency of his life in London. He took to wearing his academic gown 'almost ostentatiously', which was 'at my first coming quite new and handsome'. 'I have swum thrice, which I had disused for many years. I have proposed to Vansittart climbing over the wall, but he has refused me.' And he joined in a procession in his gown to hear a lecture at the Sheldonian Theatre on the occasion of the installation of the seventh Earl of Westmorland as Chancellor of Oxford – 'I clapped my hands till they are sore', he wrote, after listening to the speech by Dr William King, Principal of St Mary Hall, who had personally brought Johnson's MA diploma to him in London in February 1755. Soon after he returned to London, he left Staples Inn for Gray's Inn until August 1760, when he moved yet again to chambers one flight of stairs up at 1 Inner Temple Lane. There he fixed himself until 1765.[25]

[5]

While he was working, or not working, on Shakespeare at the end of the decade, he felt the need again to get involved in writing he could do regularly without much effort and which would be read by the public immediately. In 1759, at the invitation of John Newbery, he wrote an Introduction to *The World Displayed*, a collection of short travel narratives published by Newbery between 1759 and 1761, in which he returned stridently to the theme of colonial and missionary exploitation of Africa, America and Asia by Europeans, chiefly the Spanish, Portuguese and Belgians, but also the British ('English barbarians'). His Introduction is loaded with outspoken anti-imperialism. It also attacks the start of the slave trade. Newbery also had him help choose the travel books for the collection and serve as one of its editors. In December that year he also wrote three letters to the *Daily Gazeteer* on behalf of the architect John Gwynn's entry in the competition for the erection of the new Blackfriars Bridge, in which he revealed a familiarity with engineering issues relating both to the bridge and architecture in general.[26]

Running steadily along every Saturday between 15 April 1758 and 5 April 1760 were Johnson's anonymous *Idler* essays, the third of his protracted periodical series. Newbery once more seems to have encouraged him to write them. Having decided to start his weekly eight-page newspaper, the *Universal Chronicle*, Newbery needed something original with which to launch the paper and lure readers.[27] Since the paper took almost all its copy from other periodicals, it was no surprise that readers turned to it mainly for the *Idler* essays published each week on the first page. Again, it did not take people long to discover Johnson was their author. Contending that Johnson accepted the commission to write them because of an 'aversion to a labour he had undertaken' – i.e. the Shakespeare edition – Hawkins maintained that the essays 'were extemporaneous compositions, and hardly ever underwent a revision before they were sent to the press'.

'Sir, you shall not do more than I have done myself,' he said when Langton asked to read one he was about to rush into the post. He wrote all but twelve of the 103 *Idler* essays.[28]

In order to attract more readers, he wrote them with 'less body and more spirit ... more variety of real life'. As a result, readers turning to them for the accustomed depth of the *Rambler* often were, and still are, disappointed. Shorter and with briefer sentences and an easier style, many of their subjects are less consequential and more topical. Tired of writing periodical essays and impatient with weekly deadlines, Johnson did not appear to have his heart in them. Nonetheless, the essays were widely read and pirated by other journals and papers. The piracy grew so extensive, in fact, that he was driven in the 5 January 1759 issue of the *Universal Chronicle* to threaten retaliation by raiding other periodicals – he would 'degrade them ... contract them into a narrow space, and sell them at a humble price'. The piracies so depressed the market that Newbery's first collected edition of them in 1761 sold only 1,500 copies over four years. With two-thirds of the profits, Johnson earned only about £85.[29]

There are a number of serious essays in the series, however. These include eighteen critical literary essays, as well as ones on history, slavery, the wisdom of self-denial, the frustrated expectations of pleasure, the frustrated expectations of achievement, the vanity of authorship, the oppression of native Americans by white invaders, the vacuity of much travelling and travel writing, weather as a psychological barometer, and the uncertainty of friendship. But of the greatest value to the biographer are essays for which Johnson once more turned the searchlight upon his own mental and physical state. At least sixteen essays are emotionally loaded biographically and autobiographically.

Returning to the subject of biography that he had eloquently considered in *Rambler* 60, he wrote urgently in *Idler* 84 about what he thought might be the most important moral imperative for any author: to write honestly about his private self. He never made a distinction between biography and autobiography – indeed, the word 'autobiography' did not then exist. Because biography is 'most easily applied to the purposes of life', the great issues of good and evil and vice and folly, in 'honest and impartial biography' we may be told 'not how any man became great, but how he was made happy; not how he lost the favour of his prince, but how he became discontented with himself'. The kind of biography that is most valuable, then, is that in which the writer includes 'his own story'. He has 'at least the qualification of an historian, the knowledge of the truth'. The problem, as always, was that although he admonished a number of people to write regularly about themselves in journals, he himself on the whole was failing to do so. And he recognised this, as he made clear in the penultimate essay (102) of the *Idler* series: 'the author, however conspicuous, or however important, either in the public eye or in his own', unfortunately all too often 'leaves his life to be related by his successors, for he cannot gratify his vanity but by sacrificing his ease'. And yet, scholars and authors, the 'sons of literature', capable of eloquent introspection and victims of the same distresses as everyone else, have more to impart than most. The lives of writers are perpetual purgatory – and here he is writing under the burden of the Shakespeare edition he had yet to finish: 'They are entangled by contracts which they know not how to fulfil ... Every publication is a new period of time from which some increase or declension of fame is to be reckoned. The gradations of a hero's life are from battle to battle, and of an author's from book to book.'[30]

Johnson saw in his own humanity a type of epitome of mankind. The most famous example of this is *Idler* 31 on idleness, about Sober, a fictitious figure Mrs Thrale insisted was a self-portrait. Sober is the portrait of an idle man who deceives himself. Idleness is pernicious and subtle because it is 'a silent and peaceful quality, that neither raises envy by ostentation, nor hatred by opposition'. It is often disguised by 'turbulence and hurry' and is the bedfellow of procrastination, the connoisseur of 'petty business'. Sober takes obsessive pleasure in conversation: 'there is no end of his talk or his attention; to speak or to hear is equally pleasing ... and [he] is free for the time from his own reproaches'. He is fearful of solitude: 'there is a time when he must go home, that his friends may sleep' – 'these are the moments of which poor Sober trembles at the thought'. Sober has devised hobbies to suppress the misery of this fearful loneliness, momentarily at least, one of which is chemistry: 'He has a small furnace, which he employs in distillation, and which has long been the solace of his life. He draws oils and waters, and essences and spirits, which he knows to be of no use; sits and counts the drops as they come from his retort, and forgets that, while a drop is falling, a moment flies away'.[31]

Johnson repeats these themes in several other *Idler* essays. As in the last chapter of *Rasselas*, the only certain conclusion is that 'nothing is concluded'. The only real solution is to turn to God, of which the coincidence of the 1760 Easter season with the last *Idler* was an apt reminder. Easter is a time for 'the examination of conscience': 'the review of life, the extinction of earthly desires and the renovation of holy purposes'. This is when 'the imagination of the heart shall be brought to judgement, and an everlasting futurity shall be determined by the past'. In his birthday prayer that year, he resolved 'to reclaim imagination', to keep it from being overrun by chimeras.[32]

CHAPTER 22

'Vain and Corrupt Imaginations'

[1]

The crisis of Johnson's mental history beginning in the early 1760s was severe. It would last for most of the decade. Arthur Murphy, who was well tuned to Johnson's life at this time, composed a profile of his lassitude, debilitating self-doubt and fear of insanity in describing his worst sustained attack since immediately after quitting his studies at Oxford:

> Indolence was the time of danger: it was then that his spirits, not employed abroad, turned with inward hostility against himself. His reflections on his own life and conduct were always severe; and, wishing to be immaculate, he destroyed his own peace by unnecessary scruples. He tells us, that when he surveyed his past life, he discovered nothing but a barren waste of time, very near to madness. His life, he says, from his earliest years, was wasted in a morning bed; and his reigning sin was a general sluggishness, to which he was always inclined, and, in part of his life, almost compelled, by a morbid melancholy, and weariness of mind ... An apprehension of the worst calamity that can befall human nature hung over him all the rest of his life, like the sword of the tyrant suspended over his guest. In his sixtieth year he had a mind to write the history of his melancholy; but he desisted, not knowing whether it would not too much disturb him.

Several times he referred to his 'depression', but whether it was acute enough to have been regarded as madness by his own era's definitions – as he suspected it was – was something he would not discuss with anyone. He feared that if he spoke of it, what he hoped might be fictions of the imagination might 'begin to operate as realities, [and] false opinions fasten upon the mind'.[1]

His lodgings in Inner Temple Lane, where he lived in mild poverty between August 1760 to July 1765, did not do much to raise his spirits. The painter Ozias Humphry visited him there and remarked that the lodgings consisted of four filthy, dingy and worn-out rooms, one of which was like 'an old counting house' where the great man sat 'waving over his breakfast like a lunatic'. The furniture included 'a very large deal writing-desk, an old walnut-tree table, and five ragged chairs of four different sets'. According to Hawkins, Johnson also used the garret above his rooms as a chemistry laboratory where he carried on simple experiments to distil 'peppermint, and the dregs of strong beer, from the latter whereof he was able to extract a strong but very nauseous spirit, which all might smell, but few chose to taste'. Indeed, Humphry could not help thinking he was looking upon a madman: 'He is a very large man, and was dressed in a dirty brown coat and waistcoat, with breeches that were brown also (though they had been crimson), and an old black wig: his shirt collar and sleeves were unbuttoned; his stockings were down about his feet, which had on them, by way of slippers, an old pair of shoes.' It was one o'clock in the afternoon and Johnson had just got up from bed: 'He seldom goes to bed till near two in the morning; and Mr Reynolds tells me he generally drinks tea about an hour after he has supped.' Johnson's conversation was overbearing: 'every thing he says is as *correct* as a *second edition*: 'tis almost impossible to argue with him, he is so sententious and so knowing'. On another day, a Cambridge student and his friend who called on him there were amazed at what they saw. The student wrote that the wainscoted and dark entrance room led to the study, 'into which, a little before noon, came rolling, as if just roused from his cabin, the truly uncouth figure of our literary Colossus, in a strange black wig, too little for him by half, but which, before our next interview, was exchanged for that very respectable brown one in which his friend Sir Joshua so faithfully depicted him'. Thus he held court to those who could find him and were emboldened to look him up – which were many, according to the neighbour on the corner who told Hawkins that 'during the time he dwelt there, more inquiries were made at his shop for Mr Johnson, than for all the inhabitants put together of both the Inner and Middle Temple'.[2]

Visitors to Inner Temple Lane did not always come to see him. Hawkins reminisced that when he knocked on the door and Frank answered, 'a group of his African countrymen were sitting round a fire in the gloomy ante-room.' This is the first mention of Frank's use of Johnson's house as a meeting place for blacks, another sign of his master's sympathy for their plight as slaves in London.[3] Except for the mistake of thinking Frank an 'African', the image sounds credible enough, a glimpse of the informal, bohemian existence Johnson was leading. Frank's duties included waiting on the table when there were guests, running errands and answering the door. He and his master continued to live together until in the late 1760s Johnson sent him to a school in Hertfordshire for some serious schooling.

[2]

In 1760 he wrote little apart from drawing the *Idler* to a conclusion. In January he wrote in Baretti's name the Dedication to his *Dictionary of the English and Italian Languages*, an immensely successful book frequently reprinted for a century afterwards. In August he contributed the Introduction to the *Proceedings of the Committee for Cloathing French Prisoners*, a reminder of his generous commitment to humanitarian causes. Thomas Hollis, the political writer and republican friend of Benjamin Franklin, and benefactor of Harvard College whom Johnson described as a 'strenuous Whig' and defended as 'a dull poor creature as ever lived', asked him to write it for five guineas in an effort to ameliorate the condition of French prisoners during the Seven Years' War. In December at a meeting of the Society for Promoting Arts and Commerce, Hollis also suggested that the Society tempt Johnson with another five pounds to write a piece on the 'polite and liberal arts'. Johnson remembered in 1781 that Hollis 'pointed me out as the man who could do it best. This, you will observe, was kindness to me.' Kindness or not, he 'slipped away, and escaped it' with the spurious reason that he was 'not sufficiently informed' to do it.[4]

On 25 October 1760, between seven and eight in the morning, King George II died of a stroke in his water-closet at Kensington Palace and his grandson acceded to the throne as George III. At noon the next day he was proclaimed King outside Savile House in Leicester Fields. The bells of churches rang out and that night bonfires lit the night sky. Johnson had a low opinion of the first two Georges, but this one was different. 'We were so weary of our old King', he wrote in June 1761 to Baretti in Italy, 'that we are much pleased with his successor; of whom we are so much inclined to hope great things, that most of us begin already to believe them. The young man is hitherto blameless.' Horace Walpole immediately thought well of the new King when he kissed the King's hand three days later, remarking that there was none of that German insularity about him and that he enjoyed walking about and actually talking to people in good English. 'Farmer George', as he was called, was determined to please the people and, perhaps most important for Johnson, supported the arts, artists and writers. Anticipating the Coronation he 'lent his friendly assistance' to John Gwynn by writing the first four paragraphs of his *Thoughts on the Coronation* the preceding summer, urging in his best democratic spirit that the procession needed to be re-routed so that it could be seen by the public: 'Magnificence in obscurity is equally vain with *a Sun-dial in the Grave*.'[5]

Reynolds, for one, was sanguine about the prospect of royal patronage, though he appears to have offended the King right at the start by agreeing to do a sketch in oil of the Coronation procession to the Abbey a year later in September but for no less than one thousand pounds. The King, who doubtless thought he had honoured Reynolds sufficiently by asking him to do it in the first place, would have none of it and thereafter maintained a coldness towards him, disappointing his hopes of being appointed Painter to the King. When Johnson was asked if Reynolds minded being passed over, he replied that 'it has ever been more profitable to be popular among the people than favoured by the King: it is no reflection on Mr Reynolds not to be employed by them; but it will be a reflection on the Court not to have employed him'.[6]

Johnson was more discreet than Reynolds in dealing with the new monarch. In January 1761, he wrote an 'Address' to him on behalf of the 'Painters, Sculptors, and Architects' of the Society of Artists, patriotically championing British artists and praising the King's apparent appreciation and patronage of the arts: 'It is our happiness to live in the age, when our arts may hope for new advances towards perfection, assisted by the favour of a British King, of a monarch no less judicious to distinguish, than powerful to reward: who knows the usefulness and value of that skill, which delights the eye with beauty, but not corrupts the manners by unlawful passions.' This enthusiastic glorification of the arts seems to come from nowhere to many who believe Johnson had little interest in and appreciation of the arts. After all, had not Mrs Thrale (who met Johnson a few years later) stated plainly: 'Dr Johnson's utter scorn of painting was such, that I have heard him say, that he should sit very quietly in a room hung round with the works of the greatest masters, and never feel the slightest disposition to turn them if their backs were outermost, unless it might be for the sake of telling Sir Joshua that he *had* turned them.' He was 'too blind to discern the perfections of an art', she insisted, nor could he understand why Reynolds brushed his genius on such a perishable material as canvas. It was better to use copper. Sculpture came off even worse. Boswell heard him say, 'a fellow will hack half a year at a block of marble to make something in stone that hardly resembles a man. The value of statuary is owing to its difficulty. You would not value the finest head cut upon a carrot'.[7]

Johnson's activities, however, suggested he was far from indifferent to artists and their affairs. To begin with, he was the intimate friend of Reynolds, the most popular painter of his day, from whom he absorbed a belief in the importance of painting. And it was largely through him that he became involved in the encouragement of painters and sculptors. In December 1756 he was elected to the Society of Arts, founded in 1754 as the Society of the Encouragement of Arts, Manufactures and Commerce to promote a partnership between the fine and practical arts. It was the first organisation ever set up in Britain to benefit both the arts and sciences. His name appeared on the first membership list along with other members of the famous Turk's Head Club, generally known simply as The Club: Reynolds, Burney, Goldsmith, Garrick and Gibbon. They were in good company, for the list also included a galaxy of the age's greatest painters, sculptors, writers, architects and musicians. In *Idler* 45, he urged that while 'genius is chiefly exerted in historical pictures' there was room in the nation for patronage of 'painting through all its diversities'. The next year he took the part of painters in the Society of Artists, a distinct group, by writing a letter for them to the Society of Arts asking for the use of its new Great Hall at Beaufort Buildings in the Strand to stage what would be the first ever public exhibition of art in England. In a 'Plan' he drafted to accompany the letter he justified the exhibition by declaring the need to prevent artists of ability from languishing in obscurity. The exhibition of 130 paintings by 69 artists, which took place in Sir William Chambers's innovative double-cube room eighty feet long and forty wide, was spectacularly successful, at least from the Society of Arts' point of view, with over twenty thousand people attending.[8]

But the exhibition turned into a mad scramble, almost a riot, which dramatised the differences in the approach to art between the artists and the Society. A portrait of Garrick as Richard III, for example, was so popular that the mob broke windows crowding in to see it. When a few months later the artists asked Johnson to draft a second letter to the Society of Arts for another exhibition, he obliged by urging the Society this time to charge an entrance fee of a shilling in order to deter multitudes of ignorant viewers, 'no proper judges of statuary or painting', from attending and turning the event into something of another commercial circus. As a result of its refusal, a philosophical and organisational schism between the two groups occurred and eminent artists like Reynolds, Hogarth and Gainsborough staged their own independent exhibition in Cock's auction rooms in Covent Garden. Eventually that schism led to the founding of the Royal Academy in 1769. An indication of his high profile as literary apologist for the art world at this time was the publication of a caricature, 'The Combat', featuring him as 'Toastmaster General' of the Society of Arts and author of what might be termed the Society of Artists manifestos.[9]

[3]

In the winter of 1761–2, for the first time in twenty years, Johnson travelled up to Lichfield. Both the town and Lucy were a disappointment to him. 'My daughter-in-law [stepdaughter], from whom I expected most,' he wrote to Baretti, 'and whom I met with sincere benevolence, has lost the beauty and gaiety of youth, without having gained much of the wisdom of age.' As for the town itself, the streets seemed shorter and narrower 'inhabited by a new race of people to whom I was very little known'. His old 'play-fellows' were now old and he felt himself 'no longer young'. He 'wandered about' for five days and then hurried back to London where 'if there is not much happiness, there is at least such a diversity of good and evil, that slight vexations do not fix upon the heart.'[10]

[4]

After 19 July 1762, Johnson had much more about which to write to his friends than merely the account of an uneventful 'journey of a wit to his own town' or local gossip. On that day, Alexander Wedderburn (Boswell's boyhood friend and later Lord Chancellor) informed him that the First Lord of the Treasury, Lord Bute, had approved and the King granted him an annual pension of £300 (about £30,000 today). More than anything else, it was a long-delayed expression of gratitude from a nation that thus far had deplorably neglected its lexicographical hero and great moralist. One moment he was desperate for money, moving dangerously close again to the fringes of Grub Street, the next he was lifted out of poverty and reflecting on the unfamiliar sensations of financial security. At first he hesitated to accept the award. People might think, in light of his past virulent attacks on government and especially his definition of *pension* as 'pay given to a state hireling for treason', that this was a payoff by the Government to keep him quiet in the future. But he canvassed his friends, especially Reynolds, for their opinions, and everyone agreed it was not a government bribe. When Johnson went to see him, Lord Bute told him, 'It is not given you for anything you are to do, but for what you have done.' Bute repeated this twice, to make sure Johnson understood. So he decided to accept it, though inevitably critics would continue to claim that he had been bribed, which made him wish the pension had been twice as much so that his critics might make 'twice as much noise'. To Bute he later wrote, 'You have conferred your favours on a man who has neither alliance nor interest, who has not merited them by services, nor courted them by officiousness; you have spared him the shame of solicitation, and the anxiety of suspense.' The money was slow in coming, however, and there was one little moment of awkwardness in November when he had to write to Bute to ask him to facilitate the payments.[11]

There was another financial windfall, less than a year later, but it only indirectly affected him. In the spring of 1763 Lucy's brother Jervis died, leaving her £10,000 (about £1,000,000 today). This changed Johnson's relationship with her significantly. She was no longer dependent on him and no longer needed to live in the family home with Kitty.

Johnson's friends now expected him to move out of Inner Temple Lane and begin to live in a manner more fitting the literary celebrity he had become. He did no such thing. His clothing remained shabby and he stayed in his 'decrepit' lodgings for three more years. 'Now that I have this pension,' he said to Boswell, 'I am the same man in every respect that I have ever been; I retain the same principles.' He could not help adding tongue-in-cheek, 'It is true, that I cannot now curse (smiling) the House of Hanover; nor would it be decent for me to drink King James's health in the wine that King George gives me money to pay for. But, Sir, I think that the pleasure of cursing the House of Hanover, and drinking King James's health, are amply overbalanced by three hundred pounds a year.' Neither did the money have any perceptibly positive effect in lifting him out of his melancholic inertia, which may have been the reason he just stayed where he was.[12]

In August 1762 Reynolds decided that a trip with Johnson to Devon might just be the medicine he needed. Now a rich man earning approximately £5,000 a year (about half a million today), Reynolds had not been back to his native county for ten years. It turned out to be a great adventure, from which Johnson thought he had taken 'a great accession of new ideas'. He kept no known record of it, but Reynolds did.[13]

After spending two nights with Joseph Warton at Winchester College, they proceeded to Salisbury and visited the Earl of Pembroke's Wilton House about ten miles to the west of the cathedral town. Then it was on to Dorchester and nearby Corfe Castle. At Kingston Lacy there was a moment of embarrassment when Johnson became bored by the owner's explanations of the paintings in the house and (according to Frances Reynolds who heard of it from her brother) 'began to exhibit his antics, stretching out his legs alternately as far as he could possibly stretch; at the same time pressing his foot on the floor as heavily as he could possibly press, as if endeavouring to smooth the carpet, or rather perhaps to rumple it, and every now and then collecting all his force, apparently to effect a concussion of the floor'. 'Dr Johnson, I believe the floor is very firm,' the guide remarked, which made him stop. From Dorset they made their way to Exeter and Plymouth, stopping first at Torrington to see Reynolds's two other sisters Elizabeth and Mary – Renny was also there – where Johnson nonplussed everyone by swallowing no fewer than thirteen pancakes at a single sitting. They stayed three weeks in Plymouth at the home of Reynolds's boyhood friend the celebrated surgeon John Mudge, whose son William became Johnson's godson a few months later. He is supposed to have amazed his hostess there, too – who was counting assiduously – by drinking seventeen cups of tea in one sitting. When he asked for one more, she cried out, 'What! Another, Dr Johnson?', to which he replied, 'Madam, you are rude.'[14]

The splendour of the navy in Plymouth harbour and the industrial bustle of shipbuilding there fascinated him. When he was not prowling around the docks and sailing, he and Reynolds were entertained at a number of noble estates in the area, including Mount Edgcumbe with its glorious gardens. Perhaps it was on his birthday on 18 September that at one of these seats he exhibited the athleticism he had displayed as a youth. All someone needed to do to set him off was to mention having climbed this or that tree or wall in youth, or make an idle physical boast of athleticism. It was likely to be answered with Johnson's challenge to run a race, roll down a hill, leap over a wall, or jump into a pond for a swim. An anonymous writer in the *European Magazine* in 1798 remembered such feats as 'childish playfulness': 'It was no uncommon thing to see him hop, step, and jump.' Renny described a race at some country house near Plymouth where this time his competition was female: 'A young lady present boasted that she could outrun any person; on which Dr Johnson rose up and said, "Madam, you cannot outrun me"; and, going out on the lawn, they started. The lady at first had the advantage; but Dr Johnson, happening to have slippers on much too small for his feet, kicked them off up into the air, and ran a great length without them, leaving the lady far behind him, and having won the victory, he returned, leading her by the hand, with looks of high exultation and delight.' Bennet Langton had another example, recalling a rolling incident from the top of a hill at Langton, his Lincolnshire home. Looking down the hill, Johnson announced he had a mind 'to take a roll down'. Langton and others present attempted to stop him, but he persisted that 'he had not had a roll for a long time'. Emptying his pockets, he laid down 'parallel with the edge of the hill' and 'descended, turning himself over and over till he came to the bottom'. Stories abounded about his physical strength, including separating large fighting dogs, subduing thieves in London streets, threatening the actor Samuel Foote with an oak stick if he ever deployed his talent for mimicry in ridiculing him on stage, and throwing someone into the pit in a theatre, chair and all, who had taken his seat.[15]

[5]

They were back in London in late September, having been away for almost six weeks. The fresh air, exercise and change of scene had been a tonic for Johnson. In October, however, he received a sobering jolt from the poet Charles Churchill who mocked him in his poem *The Ghost* for delaying the Shakespeare edition. A very witty and effective satirist, not easy to ignore but ignore him Johnson did, Churchill took him to task in *The Ghost* for deceiving his subscribers: 'He for subscribers baits his hook,/And takes their cash – but where's the book?' (3:801–2). In December, Johnson took a second break by visiting

Oxford again, this time staying at University College as the guest of young Robert Chambers. The main reason he gave for the visit was to get rid of a 'violent' cough by escaping London air, but the visit had the look of still another flight from Shakespeare. Little is known of this visit.[16]

His friendship with Chambers (1737–1803) was one of several with young scholarly men that were blossoming around this time. There was a strong element of mentorship in several of them. Chambers had been consulting with Johnson about an academic legal career ever since 1758 when the Vinerian chair of law was established at Oxford and the distinguished jurist Sir William Blackstone was elected to it, thus inaugurating the academic study of law in Britain. They first met in the summer of 1754 at Gough Square when seventeen-year-old Chambers began studying law at the Middle Temple. And when he began his study that autumn at Lincoln College, Oxford, Johnson began supervising his studies and counselling him in general. 'Johnson, whose kind attractive Call/Led me at Learning's Shrine to bend,' Chambers wrote in a poem of gratitude in 1766. Their friendship would expand into a three-year clandestine legal collaboration after Chambers succeeded Sir William Blackstone as the second Vinerian professor of English law. Chambers turned to Johnson somewhat desperately for help with many of the sixty public legal lectures he was required to give, a series amounting to a comprehensive review of English law patterned after Blackstone's own lectures that were the nucleus of his famous *Commentaries on the Laws of England* (1765–9). They reveal an extensive knowledge of English law that Johnson picked up over the years through reading and many friendships with lawyers like Walmesley, Taylor, Hawkins, Murphy, Burke and two later members of the Club, Sir William Jones and William Scott, first Baron Stowell, a famous jurist who once remarked that if Johnson had followed law instead of literature he 'might have been Lord Chancellor of Great Britain, and attained to the dignity of a peerage'.[17]

Beauclerk and especially Langton were two other young men with whom he was continuing to develop even closer ties. One piece of entertainment Beauclerk provided Johnson in 1763 was a visit to his shabby lodgings by the sparkling, beautiful and famous Madame de Boufflers, the mistress of the Prince of Conti, advisor to Louis XV. At her home in Paris she was well known as hostess to prominent writers, musicians, scientists, politicians and notables such as Mozart, Rousseau, David Hume and Jean D'Alembert. In London that summer she told Beauclerk she would like the novelty of meeting Johnson. Beauclerk sprang to it and took her around to see his famous friend. Years later he told Boswell that after 'she was entertained with his conversation for some time' they had just emerged from the house on to the street 'when all at once I heard a noise like thunder. This was occasioned by Johnson, who it seems upon a little recollection, had taken it into his head that he ought to have done the honours of his literary residence to a foreign lady of quality, and eager to show himself a man of gallantry, was hurrying down the staircase in violent agitation. He overtook us ... and brushing in between me and Madame de Boufflers, seized her hand, and conducted her to her coach. His dress was a rusty brown morning suit, a pair of old shoes by way of slippers, a little shrivelled wig sticking on the top of his head, and the sleeves of his shirt and the knees of his breeches hanging loose. A crowd quickly gathered to watch all this and 'were not a little struck by this singular appearance.'[18]

Langton, who had recently returned from doing the Grand Tour in Italy with Beauclerk from March to August 1763, lugged home a copy of the French Academy's *Dictionnaire*, which he presented to Johnson as a present from the members of the Academy in token of their admiration for his *Dictionary*. After that he and Jonhson became good friends. It never seemed to matter to him that Langton did not fulfil his literary promise and scarcely ever published anything. 'The earth does not bear a worthier man than Bennet Langton,' he once announced. 'I know not who will go to heaven if Langton does not' – an allusion to what he called Langton's 'evangelical virtue'. But there was something of the ridiculous about him. Apart from mismanaging his affairs, living expensively in London, and lacking focus and a sense of direction, he was thought to be absurd as well as very odd-looking. Mrs Thrale was confused by him: 'Mr Langton seems to stand in a very odd light among us ... he is acknowledged learned, pious, and elegant of manners – yet he is always a person unrespected and commonly ridiculous.' And yet he corresponded frequently with several members of the Club, among them Reynolds, Garrick and Burke, who liked and respected him. He married the Countess of Rothes in 1770 and had no fewer than ten children whom he indulged and who, on visits to the family, Johnson tended to find exceedingly wearing. He was more circumspect and equable than Beauclerk in his conversation with Johnson, more gentle and discreet. Even so, there was one courageous moment when Langton surprised Johnson by telling him that the one quality above all he should overcome in himself was his habit of being rough in conversation; and he occasionally urged Boswell not to encourage that in him by playing the fool.[19]

There was one other young admirer in the wings in 1763, a young Scot who in the last twenty years of Johnson's life would commit a large part of his life and soul to the 'Rambler' and, in the process, shape enormously the world's knowledge of him. For Johnson, who in this case was sought out and his friendship zealously cultivated by the young worshipper, the relationship was one of two new intimate friendships in the next two or three years that would help him through a deepening mental crisis.

CHAPTER 23

Boswell and Mrs Thrale

[1]

By 1763, Robert Levet had gone into hiding in Inner Temple Lane with Johnson and Frank. He joined them there after the prostitute he had disastrously married was arrested for street theft. From then on he lived with Johnson permanently until he died in 1782. There was no room for Anna Williams there but soon after receiving his pension Johnson began to give her an allowance. In addition to dropping in on her regularly at her lodgings, he made her life more interesting by occasionally taking her along with him on Sundays to dine with friends. She did not usually make a good impression: 'from her manner of eating, in consequence of her blindness, she could not but offend the delicacy of persons of nice sensations'.[1]

After taking Levet in, Johnson very likely discussed with him the complications and dangers of passion and marriage. He had strong views on the subject, which he had expressed frequently in his moral essays. On learning that in Italy Baretti had fallen hopelessly for the daughter of a friend in Milan, he was quick to point out dangers: 'There is indeed nothing that so much seduces reason from her vigilance, as the thought of passing life with an amiable woman; and if all would happen that a lover fancies, I know not what other terrestrial happiness would deserve pursuit. But love and marriage are different states.' John Taylor was also on the receiving end of his marital advice when his wife left him alleging he had had an affair with their household servant, which Taylor denied. For a clergyman and prominent owner of the manor of Ashbourne, the accusation was dynamite, true or not. 'Do not let this vexation take possession of your thoughts,' Johnson cautioned, 'or sink too deeply into your heart ... The happiness of conjugal life cannot be ascertained or secured either by sense or by virtue, and therefore its miseries may be numbered among those evils which we cannot prevent and must only labour to endure with patience, and palliate with judgement.' His wife would return, Johnson reassured him, and 'mend her behaviour' when she ran out of money. 'Nature has given women so much power that the law has very wisely given them little.' Above all, Taylor must protect himself 'from melancholy and depression of mind, which is a greater evil than a disobedient wife. Do not give way to grief, nor nurse vexation in solitude'.[2]

Johnson had reached the stage in his life when he was ready and very willing to administer counsel. It veritably issued from him in a stream of moral and practical wisdom, especially for young people, whose company he particularly sought. 'I love the acquaintance of young people because, in the first place, I don't like to think myself growing old. In the next place, young acquaintances must last longest, if they do last; and then ... young men have more virtue than old men ... I love the young dogs of this age: they have more wit and humour and knowledge of life than we had' – though they were not such good scholars, he added. It was propitious, therefore, that when Johnson walked into Thomas Davies's bookshop near Covent Garden on 16 May 1763, and met a young Scot aged twenty-two who was taking tea with the bookseller, he discovered a person needing his mentorship and sage counsel, eager to drink it in more greedily than any other person he had ever met or would meet. Their meeting turned out to be one of the most important encounters in English literary history. From it and the friendship that ensued would come a great biography and a huge amount of what we know today about Johnson's life and thoughts. The Scotsman was, of course, James Boswell (1740–95).[3]

Boswell was in London to get away from Scotland and his dour and relentlessly pragmatic father, one of the fifteen judges on the High Court of the Judiciary of Scotland. His father was already convinced he was a fool, whose literary interests and fascination with English culture frivolously and irresponsibly distracted him from the central business of practising law in Edinburgh and preparing for the day he would take over as laird of Auchinleck, the family seat in Ayrshire. He was in love with the Edinburgh theatre to the immense annoyance of his father and had taken to keeping a journal. He had already shown signs of melancholia, experiencing at the age of seventeen a nervous breakdown. He also nourished a disgust for the provinciality of Scottish life and told his incredulous father he was little inclined to practise law. All this was a recipe for disaster for the father-son relationship, which, as the years passed, became more hostile on the father's side until he even contemplated disinheriting his son. The visit to London was the result of a temporary truce and agreement: James agreed to study law in Utrecht for one year, which seemed to him one of the dullest prospects on earth, in exchange for being allowed to spend a few months in London and (after the year in Utrecht) tour the loose federation of independent German principalities for several weeks. He promised his father that after this time abroad, which was not supposed to last much more than a year, he would finish his legal studies and knuckle down at home to the life of an advocate with a rich wife who could replenish the coffers of the depleted Boswell estates. To his father it seemed a tidy programme and a good bargain that would enable him to have his way in the end.

When Boswell met Johnson, he had already been in London six months, ecstatic over his new freedom and bridled only by the limited allowance his father sent him. He lived the life of a rake, doing his best to hobnob with aristocracy and meet famous political and literary personalities whom, back in Scotland, he could only dream of knowing. He was frequently at the theatre and gaming parties and in the beds of prostitutes. We know all of this in enormous detail from his now famous journal. His greatest ambition in London was to meet Johnson, for whom he confessed 'a kind of mysterious veneration' based chiefly on the *Rambler*. As Johnson frequently popped in to see Davies, Boswell repeatedly did the same, hoping he would appear one day while he was there. He finally did, Boswell wrote: 'a man of most dreadful appearance. He is a very big man, is troubled with sore eyes, the palsy [convulsive tics], and the king's evil. He is very slovenly in his dress and speaks with a most uncouth voice ... He has great humour and is a worthy man. But his dogmatical roughness of manners is disagreeable.'

Boswell's account of the event is one of hundreds of beautifully crafted scenes in his journals and the *Life*:

> Mr Davies mentioned my name, and respectfully introduced me to him. I was much agitated; and recollecting his prejudice against the Scotch, of which I had heard much, I said to Davies, 'Don't tell where I come from.' – 'From Scotland,' cried Davies, roguishly. 'Mr Johnson, (said I) I do indeed come from Scotland, but I cannot help it.' ... 'That, Sir, I find, is what a very great many of your countrymen cannot help.'[4]

Stunned and struggling to recover, Boswell then foolishly strayed into dangerous waters by ignorantly offering an opinion on Garrick.

Johnson pounced on him: 'Sir, (said he, with a stern look), I have known David Garrick longer than you have done: and I know no right you have to talk to me on the subject.' Poor Boswell was down but not out: 'I now felt myself much mortified, and began to think that the hope which I had long indulged of obtaining his acquaintance was blasted.' But he 'remained upon the field' and heard some good conversation. Davies then left them alone for a while, just long enough for Boswell to discover 'there was no ill-nature in his disposition'. As Boswell walked out of the shop, he whispered to Davies he was afraid he had botched the meeting, but Davies reassured him, 'Don't be uneasy. I can see he likes you very well.' Johnson would take it as a compliment, he said, if he visited him at his chambers.[5]

Boswell spent the next few days madly doing the social rounds: meeting John Wilkes the political firebrand who had just founded his anti-government journal the *North Briton* and was anathema to Johnson; finding another future adversary of Johnson's, James Macpherson, whom he dubbed the 'Sublime Savage' and who read to him a few of the controversial Highland poems by the legendary Ossian he claimed to have discovered; and foolishly glutting himself on several prostitutes without 'armour [condoms]'. Surfacing for air 'from this chorus, which was rather too outrageous and profane', he finally decided to look in on his hero. He arrived at his 'slovenly' chambers to find there were people already there. When they got up to leave, he did, too: 'No, don't go away,' Johnson cried. 'Sir, I am afraid that I intrude upon you,' Boswell blurted out; 'It is benevolent to allow me to sit and hear you.' Johnson replied he was obliged to any man who visited him. They sat down to talk. Boswell, whose melancholia was fed partly by religious scepticism, was comforted by Johnson's argument in favour of Christian Revelation and resolved to read a few of the books he was then reading on the subject, including Zachary Pearce's *The Miracles of Jesus Defended* (1729). He got up to leave but Johnson still would not let him go and unexpectedly found himself confiding in this raw youth: 'He said he went out at four in the afternoon and did not come home, for most part, till two in the morning.' Boswell's reply illustrated the audacity for which he would become well known, 'I asked him if he did not think it wrong to live so and not make use of his talent.' Johnson could only nod, 'He said it was a bad habit.' Three weeks later he pleased Johnson by calling on him again: 'He shook me by the hand at parting, and asked me why I did not call oftener. I said I was afraid of being troublesome.

He said I was not; and he was very glad to see me. Can I help being vain of this?'[6]

Two weeks later they had a meal together at the Mitre Tavern, a popular haunt to dine and meet in Fleet Street. 'I was quite proud to think on whom I was with,' Boswell purred, though Johnson's ravenous way of eating amazed him: 'When at table, he was totally absorbed in the business of the moment; his looks seemed riveted to his plate; nor would he, unless when in very high company, say one word, or even pay the least attention to what was said by others, till he had satisfied his appetite, which was so fierce, and indulged with such intenseness, that while in the act of eating, the veins of his forehead swelled, and generally a strong perspiration was visible.' He had been longing to confide in Johnson about his life and fortunes, to lean on him as a substitute father-figure. On mentioning he was a strict Christian but had strayed into 'infidelity' and finally recovered his faith, Johnson declared, 'Give me your hand, I have taken a liking to you.' Encouraged, Boswell told him of troubles with his father. 'A father and a son should part at a certain time of life,' Johnson consoled him. 'I never believed what my father said. I always thought that he spoke *ex officio*, as a priest does.' He then offered to put the young man on a reading programme to increase his general knowledge. Boswell could scarcely believe his luck: 'I put out my hand. "Will you really take a charge of me?" ... "Sir, I am glad we have met. I hope we shall pass many evenings and mornings too together."' They stayed at the Mitre talking until the early hours of the morning, finishing off a couple of bottles of port before Johnson pulled himself away reluctantly to return to his solitude at home.[7]

In the ensuing days, their conversation eventually got around to the Irishman Oliver Goldsmith (*c.*1728–74) whom Johnson described as 'one of the first men we now have as an author, and he is a very worthy man too'. It is his earliest known reference to Goldsmith, though they had already met through Percy about four years earlier. A proof-reader for Richardson and hack writer, Goldsmith was not yet well known but would soon become 'one of the brightest ornaments of the Johnsonian school'. Johnson recognised him as an extraordinarily versatile literary genius and loved his good nature and generosity. As Boswell's *Life* frequently illustrates, however, Johnson made a habit of poking fun at him. Aware that others called him an 'idiot inspired', he regarded him as a jealous and at times ridiculous man, as well as affected and a bit of a fool in conversation. Garrick threw up a couplet once by way of an epitaph on him: 'Here lies Nolly Goldsmith, for shortness call'd Noll,/Who wrote like an Angel, but talked like poor Poll'. When it came to defending and helping him, however, Johnson was unhesitating, as in the case of Goldsmith's novel *The Vicar of Wakefield*. According to Boswell's account,[8] on the verge of being thrown out of his lodging in October 1762 by an irate landlady demanding he pay his overdue rent, in a panic Goldsmith scribbled a message to Johnson imploring him to come quickly. Sending off a pound ahead of him, Johnson hurried over to discover that the landlady had Goldsmith under arrest and was about to have him removed. Spotting the manuscript of Goldsmith's incomplete novel on a table, he glanced over it and decided instantly to sell it to a publisher to obtain the rent money. As he was stepping out of the room with it he told the landlady firmly he would return promptly. He found the bookseller John Newbery, sold the manuscript to him for sixty guineas, and then flew back with the money to pay the landlady. The novel was published to popular acclaim.[9]

Now totally at ease as Johnson's companion, Boswell knew he had been truly allowed into the inner sanctum of Johnson's confidence when Levet took him up secretly to see his chaotic library located in the two garrets above his chambers. Manuscripts in Johnson's handwriting lay scattered everywhere and he half expected to see those of *Rasselas* and the *Rambler* lying about like gold dust. His departure for Utrecht was approaching and at the Turk's Head tavern in Gerrard Street, Soho, one day the talk turned to travel. Johnson recalled that when he was a boy his father had put into his hands a copy of Martin Martin's *Description of the Western Islands of Scotland* (1703), which made a deep impression. 'He said he would go to the Hebrides with me, when I returned from my travels, unless some very good companion should offer when I was absent, which he did not think probable; adding, "There are few people to whom I take so much to as you … my dear Boswell, I should be very unhappy at parting, did I think we were not to meet again."' Whether or not Johnson was serious about the 'romantic fantasy' of a Hebridean expedition, the idea stuck in Boswell's mind.[10]

Three days later, again at the Turk's Head, Boswell asked for his advice on a method of study at Utrecht, upon which Johnson shouted out, 'Come, let us make a day of it. Let us go down to Greenwich and dine, and talk of it there.' Arm-in-arm they walked down the Strand back to Inner Temple Lane. The following Saturday they hired a sculler at nearby Temple Stairs and off they sailed down the Thames. They disembarked above London Bridge and, to avoid the rapid water, walked to Billingsgate where they 'took oars and moved smoothly along the silver Thames' on a lovely day. Walking in Greenwich Park, Boswell surprised Johnson by plucking out of his pocket a copy of *London: A Poem* and reading aloud the lines on the village. 'Is not this very fine?', Johnson asked. 'Yes, Sir; but not equal to Fleet-street.' 'You are right, Sir.' They ended the day back at the Turk's Head where Boswell regaled Johnson with accounts of his seat at Auchinleck. 'I must be there, Sir,' Johnson exclaimed, indulging in another fantasy, 'and we will live in the old castle; and if there is not a room in it remaining, we will build one.' That also stuck in Boswell's mind.[11]

Suddenly, these magical weeks with Johnson were at an end and Boswell had to move on to Utrecht. Reluctant to part, Johnson decided to go with him to Harwich, his port of embarkation: 'I must see thee out of England.' Johnson's humour, to which Boswell responded as fully than anyone who ever knew him, broke out en route as he entertained a woman at an inn about his travelling companion: 'that gentleman there (pointing to me) has been idle. He was idle at Edinburgh. His father sent him to Glasgow, where he continued to be idle. He then came to London, where he has been very idle; and now he is going to Utrecht, where he will be as idle as ever.' In the church at Harwich, Johnson made Boswell kneel: 'Now that you are going to leave your native country, recommend yourself to the protection of your CREATOR and REDEEMER.' Then they walked down to the beach together and embraced. As Boswell stood on deck watching the receding shore, he kept his eyes focused on Johnson's lonely figure: 'As the vessel put out to sea, I kept my eyes upon him for a considerable time, while he remained rolling his majestic frame in his usual manner: and at last I perceived him walk back into the town, and he disappeared.'[12]

[2]

Johnson advised Taylor to dissipate his 'vexation' of mind with short journeys and a 'variety of scenes', but he does not appear to have taken his own advice except for a few days in January 1764 with Langton and his parents at their family home in Lincolnshire. In February his depression set in. He had little desire to see anyone – 'the most fatal symptom of that malady', especially for him who (as Reynolds put it) thought 'any company ... better than none'. Dr Adams, his Oxford tutor, came to visit and as an old friend was 'admitted'. He found him 'in a deplorable state, sighing, groaning, talking to himself, and restlessly walking from room to room'. At one point Johnson cried out, 'I would consent to have a limb amputated to recover my spirits.'[13]

Alert to his despondency and loneliness, in February 1764 Reynolds proposed to him they form a new club of like-minded individuals with strong literary interests and good backgrounds in the classics. Johnson was at first reluctant but came around to the idea. It would be an intellectual and social dining club meeting at the Turk's Head one evening per week at seven, until late at night if anyone wished. It would be called the Turk's Head Club, or simply the Club. Politics and religion would be forbidden topics, and a minimal requirement of all members was 'clubbability'. The nine founding members were Johnson, Reynolds, Goldsmith, Langton, Beauclerk, Hawkins, Burke, Christopher Nugent (Burke's father-in-law) and Anthony Chamier (a politician with links to Burke). It became the most famous club in the eighteenth century, a period generally famous for its London clubs.[14]

After Johnson, Burke (1729–97) was the Club's most imposing member. They had met on Christmas Day in 1758 but curiously there is little evidence of their friendship until the Club was formed. Beyond sharing a high regard for trust, honesty and consideration for others, and personal charity towards the unfortunate, they had the highest admiration for each other's intellects. Burke had one of the greatest minds in the eighteenth century and was widely celebrated for his conversation and parliamentary speeches. Just a few months before he died, Johnson said of Burke, 'if a man were to go by chance at the same time with Burke under a shed, to shun a shower, he would say, "this is an extraordinary man"'. There was a magnetism and force about him that became almost legendary in his lifetime, even if many disagreed strongly with his views. By 1764 he was an intimate friend of Reynolds's as well, which is one of the reasons he was included as a founding member of the Club. Fanny Burney summed up Burke and Johnson by calling Burke 'the second man in this Kingdom' and Johnson 'the first of *every* kingdom'.[15]

One founding member who became distinctly unpopular was Hawkins, especially after rudely attacking Burke one night. Johnson called him 'a most unclubbable man'. He was more or less pushed out, though he put it about that he 'seceded' because the meetings were interfering with his family life. It is surprising that Hawkins was included in the original nine and not Garrick. Soon after the Club was formed Reynolds mentioned it to Garrick who piped up, 'I like it much, I think I shall be of you.' Reynolds reported this to Johnson whose classic comment was, '*He'll be of us*, how does he know we will *permit* him? The first Duke in England has no right to hold such language.' Perhaps Johnson was afraid that Garrick's 'buffoonery', as he put it, would devalue the conversation. Mrs Thrale reported Johnson as saying, 'If Garrick *does* apply, I'll black-ball him. Surely, one ought to sit in a society like ours, "unelbow'd by a gamester, pimp, or player"', although Boswell accused her of misrepresenting Johnson with the remark. All it took was one black ball to doom an application. Garrick was not admitted until 1773. Johnson was against the rapid growth of the Club in any case: 'He said it was intended the Club should consist of such men, as that if only two of them chanced to meet, they should be able to entertain each other, without wanting the addition of more company to pass the evening agreeably.' In 1768 the number was expanded to twelve, and by 1776 Johnson felt the Club 'was now quite spoiled by the introduction of too many members, and that without attention to their being agreeable to all the rest'. He seldom attended in the final years of his life. When he died there were thirty-five members, none of whom ever was a woman because the Club was conceived as a gentlemen's private club for dining and drinking.[16]

Even with the Club to sustain him, Johnson fought an uphill battle against his advancing despair. Physical ailments did not help. He was going to bed at two or three in the morning, often rising at two in the afternoon, sleeping badly, experiencing flatulence, defecating with difficulty – he used the symbol 'M' to keep track of his bowel movements[17] – and experiencing unfamiliar physical pains in his face while he tried to sleep. 'My memory grows confused, and I know not how the days pass over me,' he complained. When he was out in society, he was also struggling to give up wine – he 'resolved or hoped to combat sin and to reform life, but at night drank wine,' he wrote on 17 January. Late-night tea vigils with Mrs Williams were a comfort, but sometimes he would not return home from her until four in the morning.[18]

There was a pressing need for him to be able to work because he had wound himself up again to make a final push on his Shakespeare edition. The only way to write was to sit down and write, he once said, but in late June 1764 he succumbed instead to another diversion. To raise his spirits with more 'variety of scenes' he took time off to travel to the village of Easton Maudit in Northamptonshire with Frank and Mrs Williams for a long-delayed visit to Percy and his wife Anne. Percy had been dreaming of this visit for five years and later remarked he had never found Johnson more 'cheerful or conversible' than during those weeks. There were rural pursuits that helped take him out of himself, among other things helping Anne Percy feed her ducks, making excursions in the district, and reading proof sheets of *Othello* which arrived regularly for his corrections. Back in London in mid-August, he soon became restless again and had to spend a few days in October with Chambers in University College. While he was there he received a bizarre invitation from Renny to accompany her and others on a cruise to the Mediterranean courtesy of a Captain George Collier. 'I cannot go now. I must finish my book [his edition of Shakespeare]', Johnson replied, adding that he did not think 'the grossness of a ship' suitable for a lady.[19]

[3]

There was another woman who, in January 1765, threw him a lifeline. On the 9th he scribbled into his diary cryptically, 'At Mr Trails'. This was Henry Thrale, husband to Hester Thrale (1741–1821). In her *Thraliana* for September 1777, she remembered this was the first time she ever laid eyes on Johnson: 'Murphy[,] whose intimacy with Mr Thrale had been of many years standing, was one day dining with us at our house in Southwark; and was zealous that we should be acquainted with Johnson, of whose moral and literary character he spoke in the most exalted terms; and so whetted our desire of seeing him soon, that we were only disputing *how* he should be invited, *when* he should be invited, and what should be the pretence.' Aware of Johnson's compassion and empathy for the poor, they and Murphy came up with a plan of inviting to dinner a shoemaker-poet called [James] Woodhouse, who was then being talked about as something of a literary oddity, and using him as 'a temptation to Mr Johnson to meet him'. Johnson came. Woodhouse knew what was going on and thought Johnson regarded him as some kind of 'wild beast from the country', but he played along. The truth was that Johnson scoffed at the supposed novelty of a poet-cobbler and was not at all curious

about Woodhouse: 'They had better furnish the man with good imple-
ments for his trade, than raise subscriptions for his poems. He may
make an excellent shoemaker, but can never make a good poet.'
Murphy had given the Thrales fair warning of Johnson's figure, dress
or behaviour, including his mannerisms and noises. They hit it off so
well with him that they met again the following week, this time
without the shoemaker. After that he dined with them 'every Thursday
through the winter', Mrs Thrale wrote, and 'has remained till this day,
our constant acquaintance, visitor, companion and friend'.[20]

Mrs Thrale was the daughter of a wealthy Welsh landowner.
Against her will she found herself in 1765 at twenty-four in a loveless
marriage to a dull, prosperous, gentleman-like London brewer in
Southwark with little hope of ever feeling any passion for him. Nor
did he have much of a taste for culture. She once reminded Johnson
that in the first six years of her marriage 'I never set my foot in any
theatre or palace of entertainment at all.'[21] It did not help that he kept
a mistress. Nevertheless, she successfully promoted his efforts (with
Johnson's help) to become a member of Parliament for Southwark
from 1765 to 1780. Her greatest joy and solace were her children –
there were twelve births over a period of fifteen years, only four of
whom (all girls) survived into adulthood. She also had considerable
literary interests and was a highly successful hostess at her 'charming
villa' in Streatham, ten miles south of central London. A small woman,
she was not a beauty, but her lively intelligence, wit and wide reading
pleased Johnson. From that first meeting, the Thrales (especially
Hester) held centre stage in his life, so much so that his closest London
friends from time to time complained they could not find him at home
because of the frequency and length of his visits to Southwark and
Streatham.

Boswell, who still was not back from his travels, later became jealous
of Johnson's dependence on her and was of the opinion that she took
him in chiefly because he was a literary ornament to her social life, a
prize she liked to show off. But this was unfair, even if it was true that
once Johnson became a regular feature at her Streatham dinners her
social standing as a hostess of poets and artists soared. He soon fell
into a regular pattern of sleeping several nights a week there which
continued for almost the rest of his life. Indeed, he came to think of
the place as a second home. In the autumn, he 'followed' the Thrales
to the small fishing village then called Brighthelmstone (Brighton):
'When business is done what remains but pleasure? And where should

pleasure be sought but under Mrs Thrale's influence?' The village had recently become known as a good place for sea-bathing. The Thrales were among the first to make holidaying there fashionable and shortly after meeting Johnson bought a house on West Street, about fifty metres from the sea. Johnson never liked Brighton but would spend several holidays there with them. The first one did not get off to a good start, however. Arriving on their doorstep, he was annoyed to discover they had left because of Mrs Thrale's advanced pregnancy. So he went swimming on his own. The man whose job it was to dip people into the sea was impressed: 'Why Sir (says the dipper), you must have been a stout-hearted gentleman forty years ago.' There were painfully poignant moments for him there as well. In a meditation fifteen years later, he recalled gazing out at the sea on this visit, overcome with renewed grief for Tetty: 'When I recollect the time in which we lived together, my grief for her departure is not abated, and I have less pleasure in any good that befalls me, because she does not partake it. On many occasions I think what she would have said or done. When I saw the sea at Brighthelmstone I wished for her to have seen it with me.' At least now he could tell himself he had in Mrs Thrale a new friendship that promised him comfort and healing.[22]

Free now from the onerous drudgery of heavy Shakespearean editing, on his return from Brighton he threw himself into some electioneering in Henry Thrale's campaign for a parliamentary seat. It was good therapy, a rough-and-tumble change of pace. Thrale had lost two previous elections elsewhere, but this time the signs were good because of his family's reputation in Southwark. Johnson wrote at least one 'advertisement' for him to the electors, though his main value seems to have been in interacting with the populace, at which Mrs Thrale wrote he excelled because of his empathy for 'the lower ranks of humanity' dating from those earlier days when 'he and they shared pain and pleasure in common'. The election illustrated 'his toleration of boisterous mirth, and his content in the company of people whom one would have thought at first sight little calculated for his society'. He could throw his hat 'up in the air and huzza' with the best of them when Thrale won.[23]

With his pension, a new confidante in Mrs Thrale, the unfamiliar comforts of Streatham at his disposal, and his edition about to be published, it seemed that at last everything had begun to come right for him in his external life. Topping it off, in July he was awarded the 'spontaneous compliment' of an LL.D. (*Legum Doctor*) by Trinity

College, Dublin, making an Irish university the first to create the title 'Dr Johnson' by which he became known in his lifetime and to posterity. It was another sweet reward for decades of labour in his now vanished wilderness of literary and social neglect. In March he had also managed his first triumphant visit to Cambridge with Beauclerk where he was a star attraction. One of the fellows, Dr John Sharp, recalled the visit in a letter published in 1785: 'He drank his large potations of tea with me, interrupted by many an indignant contradiction, and many a noble sentiment. He had on a better wig than usual. Several persons got into his company the last evening at Trinity, where [at] about twelve, he began to be very great; [metaphorically] stripped poor Mrs [Catherine] Macaulay to the very skin' – she was the historian whose republican views impelled him to make crude jokes about her – 'then gave her for his toast, and drank her in two bumpers'. Sharp referred to him as 'Caliban' who 'was not roused from his lair' before noon on Sunday, the day after he arrived in town, surmising that 'his breakfast probably kept him till night'. Nobody saw anything of him until Monday afternoon. He also dropped in at Emmanuel College to look in on Richard Farmer who the following year would publish his own celebrated piece of Shakespeareana, *An Essay on the Learning of Shakespeare*. Farmer promised him 'an habitation in Emmanuel College' whenever he chose to come again. The judgement of another Fellow was less happy, 'I don't believe Dr Johnson belongs to us; I only wish he did. But we do not deserve him.'[24]

In August he finally roused himself to move from the shabby lodgings in Inner Temple Lane to a spacious and more comfortable house where he lived for the next twelve years. Number 7 Johnson's Court, off Fleet Street, was named after a tailor who had lived in the square for many years. And perhaps that same summer the 'Mr Johnson' Reynolds entered in his Sitters Books was him, posing for a portrait then and several times more in 1766–7 that undoubtedly became the one dated 1769 in which Reynolds said his mind was 'preying on itself in a reverie, accompanied with strange antic gesticulation'.[25]

CHAPTER 24

Shakespeare and the Living World

[1]

After years of delay and intermittent work, Johnson completed the final two volumes of his Shakespeare edition, completed the notes in the Appendix, and wrote the Preface in the summer of 1765. At last, he breathed the deepest sigh of relief when *The Plays of William Shakespeare* appeared in eight volumes on 10 October. Now after all those years, as with the *Dictionary*, he felt anticlimax. 'To tell the truth,' he confided in Joseph Warton the day before, 'I felt no solicitude about this work, I receive no great comfort from its conclusion; but yet am well enough pleased that the public has no farther claim upon me.' More than twenty years of literary drudgery were behind him, and with his pension he no longer needed to play hostage to the public in an unceasing effort to make a living by his pen. Moreover, he wanted nothing to do with distributing the edition to friends who had gathered subscriptions for him. Selling briskly, the first impression of one thousand copies was gone in one month.[1]

The edition was maligned in the nineteenth century for slovenliness and careless scholarship and had to wait until the twentieth century for a recovery of its reputation, but when it appeared it was well received as a noble critical effort that urged on readers the emotional truth of their national poet. Among its best qualities is that it is enjoyable to read. This is because of the illuminating common sense Johnson applied to explaining passages in the plays, for which he was linguistically more qualified than any previous critic. More intensely than ever before, he insisted that if literature was to be worth reading it had 'to enable the reader better to enjoy life, or better to endure it'. 'The end of writing is to instruct; the end of poetry is to instruct by pleasing.' What we are struck with in his edition is his imaginative and moral identification with Shakespeare. His power as a critic was forged not in academe but in the labyrinths of his own human career.

He was above all an experiential critic, subjective, impatient with abstract critical principles. He understood the poet's greatness as located in what Harold Bloom has called 'a diversity of persons':

> For Johnson, the essence of poetry was *invention*, and only Homer could be Shakespeare's rival in originality. Invention, in Johnson's sense as in ours, is a process of finding, or of finding out. We owe Shakespeare everything, Johnson says, and means that Shakespeare has taught us to understand human nature ... One way of defining Johnson's vitality as a critic is to note the consistent power of his inferences: he is always sufficiently *inside* Shakespeare's plays to judge them as he judges human life, without ever forgetting that Shakespeare's function is to bring life to mind, to make us aware of what we could not find without Shakespeare.

To paraphrase Pope, Johnson found that nature and Shakespeare were the same.[2]

There is little pedantry in his edition, little accumulation of commentary and textual notes merely to display his learning and superiority to previous editions, or with which to prop himself up, although he felt bound to include many of the notes of previous editors and friends: 'I do not always concur with my friends in their opinion, but their abilities are such as make me less confident when I find myself differing from them, and the public might justly complain if I suppressed their sentiments either by pride or timidity.' This modesty was a protection against being thought an authoritative critic arrogantly donning the mantle of a legislator or literary dictator, for the proper role of criticism was not, in his view, a matter of dictatorial and fashionable pronouncements. In this sense he was a disinterested critic, against what in *Rambler* 93 he called the critic's 'interest and passion' that disturb the innocency of a reader's response: 'Critics, like all the rest of mankind, are very frequently misled by interest ... kindness or malevolence, veneration or contempt'. In his *Proposals*, he had written, 'The editor, though he may less delight his own vanity, will probably please his reader more, by supposing him equally able with himself to judge of beauties and faults.' Furthermore, he was not going to indulge in 'cruelty to crush an insect who had provoked me only by buzzing in my ear'. It was from the poetry, not the joint authority of critics cited in the notes of a Shakespeare edition, that he would draw whatever authority he could claim.[3]

Still, 'he that writes may be considered as a kind of general challenger, whom every one has right to attack ... To commence author is to claim praise, and no man can justly aspire to honour, but at the hazard of disgrace.' His own glosses on about two thousand words and phrases number among the most insightful and helpful ever provided. The components of his edition equipped it also with all that it needed for him and the booksellers to claim that this was now the complete up-to-date Shakespeare, the defining edition beyond which the public need not look any further. He included a variety of elements or critical 'apparatus' that turned the edition into what is generally called a variorum edition. Shakespeare had become such a commodity and so many were getting into the act as commentators, jostling for advantage, that this kind of institutional authority was deemed crucial as well.[4]

As for collating and textual work, he did a good amount but nowhere near so much as a few of his predecessors and many of his immediate successors. He adopted William Warburton's 1747 edition as a copy-text, augmented by Lewis Theobald's text when a new edition of his work came out. To a great extent it could be said Johnson was stuck with these. He was far from systematic in gathering variant readings from earlier editions. The troublemaking, spiteful critic Joseph Ritson may have had a greater portion of character defects than most Shakespeareans, but he was a superb textual editor and he called it as he saw it, declaring that Johnson 'never collated any of the folios' – not entirely true – and left the text in the 'same state of corruption as was in the time of Rome'. Thomas Babington Macaulay continued this line of attack a few decades later by sneering that 'it would be difficult to name a more slovenly, a more worthless edition of any great classic'.[5]

Johnson's edition was soon superseded by others, but the Preface remained a triumph in his lifetime, acclaimed as another example of his sturdy common sense and brilliant humanly anchored moral insight. It was too progressive for Voltaire, who criticised Johnson for his defence of Shakespeare's violation of the classical unities of time, place and action. Johnson retaliated by comparing Voltaire's brand of remarks to the 'petty cavils of petty minds'. The Romantics, who thought the edition was too institutionalised, not sufficiently imaginative, manhandled it in the next century – Samuel Taylor Coleridge, for instance, accusing Johnson of not understanding the character of Hamlet. They particularly disliked Johnson as a Shakespeare critic because they concluded he was defending classical literary 'rules' in enumerating the poet's literary shortcomings. They tended to dump him indiscriminately into the outmoded neoclassical bucket without valuing sufficiently what he was writing throughout the Preface about Shakespeare's sublime imagination and his judgement of the poet's genius in representing the infinitely 'mingled drama' of life on earth – what Johnson called 'the real state of sublunary nature'. The Romantics therefore accused him of defending neo-classicism while Voltaire and other neo-classical critics accused him of violating it.

The eminent Shakespearean critic David Nichol Smith wrote at the start of the twentieth century that by then those nineteenth-century critical opinions had not changed: 'Johnson's *Preface* in particular was remembered only to be despised. It is not rash to say that at the present time the majority of those who chance to speak of it pronounce it a discreditable performance ... [it] has received scant justice'. He added, 'Not only was Johnson's edition the best which had yet appeared; it is still one of the few editions which are indispensable'. By 1910, Walter Raleigh in his *Six Essays on Shakespeare*, a landmark in the turn towards Johnson's work, felt that 'the Romantic attitude begins to be fatiguing'. Johnson was able 'to go straight to Shakespeare's meaning, while the philological and antiquarian commentators kill one another in the dark'. By 1928, Smith was writing of the Preface that 'by common consent nowadays it is one of the greatest essays on Shakespeare that has ever been written'.[6]

Johnson's Preface is his earliest detailed analysis of any writer. It speaks of his gratitude to Shakespeare's genius for striking a chord with his own inner moral convictions and psyche, for projecting the realities of human nature with 'common conversation and common occurrences'. His characters 'are the genuine progeny of common humanity, such as the world will always supply, and observation will always find. His persons act and speak by the influence of those general passions and principles by which all minds are agitated, and the whole system of life is continued in motion.' While he wrote that Shakespeare's 'first defect' was not going far enough in projecting what mankind should be, and thus not rising to 'a writer's duty to make the world better', he nonetheless believed that Shakespeare's portrait of a vast panorama of human behaviour and thought conveyed (without being didactic) what mankind ought to be like. 'This therefore is the praise of Shakespeare,' he wrote, 'that his drama is the mirror of life; that he who has mazed his imagination, in following the phantoms which other writers raise up before him, may here be cured of his delirious extasies, by reading human sentiments in human language, by scenes from which a hermit may estimate the transactions of the world, and a confessor predict the progress of the passions.'[7]

As for the classical unities, he observed that 'a play read, affects the mind like a play acted. It is therefore evident, that the action is not supposed to be real, and ... that no more account of space or duration is to be taken by the auditor of a drama, than by the reader of a narrative, before whom may pass in an hour the life of a hero, or the revolutions of an empire.' In invoking the authority of Shakespeare to demolish the critical tyranny of the unities, he knew he was in dangerous territory: 'I am almost frighted by my own temerity; and when I estimate the fame and the strength of those that maintain the contrary opinion, am ready to sink down in reverential silence.' To sink into silence was not something he was about to do, however.[8]

Although he called explanatory and textual notes 'necessary evils' by which the text is 'refrigerated', his own are, next to the Preface, where the chief value of his edition lies. They amount to a sustained commentary on the individual plays and rank as the finest literary criticism he ever wrote. Several of them like the sketch of Polonius in *Hamlet* or Falstaff in *Henry IV* are among the best ever written about these characters, impregnated with a humane largeness of mind and a refusal to descend to myopic, sanctimonious, moral censure. They are like character sketches in his moral essays. The redeeming quality he singles out in Falstaff, for instance, 'thy compound of sense and vice; of sense which may be admired but not esteemed, of vice which may be despised, but hardly detested', is one he especially valued when he encountered it in his own life: 'the most pleasing of all qualities, perpetual gaiety ... an unfailing power of exciting laughter ... easy escapes and sallies of levity, which make sport but raise no envy'.[9]

His 'General Observations' at the end of each play often contain an assortment of short, critical comments on, among other subjects, the sources of the play, Elizabethan versus modern taste, the propriety or not of the language, and the believability or not of character and action. Many of them are highly personal and to a degree as unpredictable as his critical judgements could be in his conversation. About *As You Like It*, he remarks, 'I know not how the ladies will approve the facility with which both Rosalind and Celia give away their hearts. To Celia much may be forgiven for the heroism of her friendship.' He properly castigates Bertram in *All's Well That Ends Well*: 'I cannot reconcile my heart to Bertram; a man noble without generosity, and young without truth; who marries Helen as a coward, and leaves her as a profligate: when she is dead by his unkindness, sneaks home to a second marriage, is accused by a woman whom he has wronged, defends himself by falsehood, and is dismissed to happiness.' Of Edmund's evil art in *King Lear* he takes note of the 'important moral, that villainy is never at a stop, that crimes lead to crimes, and at last terminate in ruin'. But he is unhappy with Cordelia's tragic death because of the moral failure of the play in allowing the wicked to prosper: 'Since all reasonable beings naturally love justice, I cannot easily be persuaded, that the observation of justice makes a play worse; or, that if other excellencies are equal, the audience will not always rise better pleased from the final triumph of persecuted virtue.' He actually preferred the happy ending of Nahum Tate's 1681 adaptation in which Cordelia survives. He was emotionally shocked by Shakespeare's conclusion, just as he was terrified as a boy by Hamlet's ghost: 'if my sensations could add any thing to the general suffrage, I might relate, that I was many years ago so shocked by Cordelia's death, that I know not whether I ever endured to read again the last scenes of the play till I undertook to revise them as an editor.' Equally, of Desdemona's murder in *Othello* he confesses, 'I am glad that I have ended my revisal of this dreadful scene. It is not to be endured.' He is in no doubt that the fall of Macbeth is correct emotionally, ethically, and morally: 'The passions are directed to their true end. Lady Macbeth is merely detested; and though the courage of Macbeth preserves some esteem, yet every reader rejoices at his fall.'[10]

Johnson believed that the best way to learn about a Shakespeare play was to read it as a type of ethical poem, not to see it on the stage. He appears even to have felt that seeing one of the plays on stage could be an impediment to a proper understanding of it. He was once supposed to have said, 'It would afford him more entertainment to sit up to the chin in water for an hour than be obliged to listen to the whining, daggle-tailed [Mrs] Cibber, during the tedious representation of a fulsome tragedy without the possibility of receiving from it either pleasure or instruction.' Goldsmith confronted him over his alleged indifference to the theatre in February 1766: 'I think, Mr Johnson, you don't go near the theatres now. You give yourself no more concern about a new play, than if you had never had any thing to do with the stage.' According to Boswell, Johnson agreed at that moment, 'our tastes greatly alter. The lad does not care for the child's rattle, and the old man does not care for the young man's whore'. Whores and rattles aside, years after seeing Goldsmith's *She Stoops to*

Conquer in 1773, he 'could scarce recollect having seen the inside of a playhouse ... To speak the truth, there is small encouragement there for a man whose sight and hearing are become so imperfect as mine.'[11]

Nonetheless, he continued to attend the theatre over the years, especially to see Shakespeare, and the year before he died he delighted in a visit from Sarah Siddons, the great tragic actress of the day and some said a rival of Garrick's in tragedy. She came with her brother, the popular actor John Philip Kemble. When she told him that her favourite tragic role was Catherine in *Henry VIII*, he replied that if she were ever to act the part again he would 'once more hobble out to the theatre' to see her. She then promised she would 'do herself the honour of acting his favourite part for him'. He then demonstrated a close knowledge of the contemporary stage by running through what he thought were the strengths of the leading actors and actresses in his lifetime, especially Garrick whose praises he sang for both comedy and tragedy. He had seen him in probably all his Shakespearean roles, particularly in Richard III, Hamlet, King Lear and Macbeth as well as in his comic hit as Benedick in *Much Ado About Nothing*. 'Garrick, Madam, was no declaimer,' he told Mrs Siddons, 'a true conception of character, and natural expression of it, were his distinguishing excellencies.'[12]

[2]

The Thrales were now a regular and comforting feature of his existence, but he wanted Boswell back, who was in Paris on his way home when he wrote to him there in January 1766. Johnson's esteem for him had steadily increased as the young man coursed through Germany, Switzerland, Italy, and finally Corsica, cultivating relationships with Rousseau, Voltaire, Paoli, and a multitude of other eminent persons: 'I long to see you and to hear from you, and hope that we shall not be so long separated again. Come home and expect such a welcome as is due to him whom a wise and noble curiosity has led where perhaps no native of this country ever was before.' He was referring to Boswell's hazardous journey across Corsica by foot to find Paoli.[13]

Boswell arrived in London on 12 February 1766 and the next day dropped in on Johnson at his new 'good house' in Johnson's Court. He found Mrs Williams was occupying an apartment on the ground floor and Levet had taken over a room in the garret. Their separation by two floors was calculated to reduce strife in the house. This was the beginning of the long final period of Johnson's life when he had these two, and several years later also Elizabeth Desmoulins and Poll Carmichael, living with him constantly, not to mention others who would come and go for short periods.

Boswell walked in, fell on his knees before Johnson, and immediately asked for his blessing. Johnson hugged him 'like a sack' and grumbled, 'I hope we shall pass many years of regard.' Later they dined alone at the Mitre and talked of Boswell's travels and their mutual friends. For Boswell, their reunion climaxed when Johnson enthusiastically endorsed his idea of writing an account of Corsica – 'Give us as many anecdotes as you can,' he urged him – although by late summer, months after Boswell had returned to Scotland, he had changed his tune: 'You have, somehow or other, warmed your imagination. I wish there were some cure, like the lover's leap, for all heads of which some single idea has obtained an unreasonable and irregular possession. Mind your own affairs, and leave the Corsicans to theirs.' A couple of days later they were together again at the Mitre, talking of Boswell's having struck up friendships with Rousseau and Wilkes, not exactly two of Johnson's favourite characters. Johnson was incensed. Rousseau had recently retreated from Switzerland to England to escape the abuse he was receiving there for his progressive and scandalous writings on society and education. Johnson glared at Boswell: 'If you mean to be serious, I think him one of the worst of men; a rascal, who ought to be hunted out of society as he has been. Three or four nations have expelled him.' Boswell simply thought to himself that Johnson misread Rousseau's 'heart', but the resentment ran deeper than that, for Johnson regarded Rousseau a seductive threat to society as he knew it, an enemy of the Judeo-Christian tradition of learning and rational philosophy.[14]

The following day they spoke of another infidel, David Hume, whose religious scepticism Johnson deplored, and of hierarchy and subordination within society. Even this early, with the somewhat affected habits he had picked up on the Continent of pressing people in conversation, Boswell began to irritate Johnson. 'My dear Bozzy,' Johnson broke in when he thought Boswell was going to oppose him again, 'let us have no more of this. It is extremely disagreeable to me. You are making nothing of this argument. I had rather you'd whistle me a Scotch tune.' When Boswell persisted with pesky questions, Johnson had had enough: 'This now is just such stuff as I used to talk to my mother when I first began to think myself a clever fellow, and she ought to have whipped me for it.' Boswell, however, was resilient – 'You ought then to whip me' – but he was surprised by Johnson's 'roughness', that he 'tossed and gored' people in conversation, which seemed 'more striking to me now, from my having been accustomed to the studied smooth complying habits of the Continent'. Goldsmith had noticed Johnson's greater impatience and irritation, too. 'Don't you think that head's failed?' he asked Boswell ten days later. 'No, Sir, I think he is rather more impatient of contradiction than he was'. Goldsmith agreed. 'No man is proof against continual adulation.'[15]

The impulse came upon him in the spring to write a short fairy tale, *The Fountains*, to be included in a volume of Mrs Williams's poems, *Miscellanies in Prose & Verse*, for which as far back as 1750 he had written proposals but had done nothing since to promote. The obstacle to publication still was that Mrs Williams had not written enough pieces to fill a volume, so he asked Mrs Thrale and a few others if they had written or could write anything they would be willing to have appear in the volume and charitably pass off as Mrs Williams's. Mrs Thrale promptly came up with something, upon which Johnson himself (in her words) rose to the occasion: 'He said come Mistress, now *I'll* write a tale and your character shall be in it; so he composed The Fountains in the same book.' He wrote it swiftly, either in Southwark or Streatham, basing the main character of a clever and witty young woman Floretta on Mrs Thrale and setting the story appropriately at the renowned and magical Mount Plinlimmon in Wales, her homeland. The story is framed by the so-called 'choice of life' theme central to both *The Vision of Theodore* and *Rasselas*. The point is that Floretta, like Mrs Thrale, unwisely made choices based on earthly happiness. In addition to this fairy tale, Johnson wrote or revised seven of his own poems for the *Miscellanies*, including 'The Ant', 'The Happy Life', and 'An Ode on Friendship'. Percy, Mrs Thrale and Renny (who painted Mrs Williams's portrait for the volume) contributed poems as well. The volume was published by Thomas Davies in April and enjoyed modest praise. Catherine Talbot thought *The Fountains* was 'enchantingly beautiful' but too depressing and melancholy in having Floretta ultimately sink under the weight of human folly.[16]

All these were good signs, but a mental crisis was fast approaching. He was already in its early stages.

[3]

For several months, perhaps as long as a year, Johnson had been physically ill, and early in 1766 his condition worsened. He scarcely ever attended the Club. On the day before Easter, worries haunted him about his religious frame of mind, 'I do not feel myself today so much impressed with awe of the approaching Mystery.' He prayed that he might be neither 'harassed with vain terrors' nor 'linger in perplexity, nor waste in idleness that life which thou hast given and preserved'.[17]

Then all of a sudden he succumbed to a severe mental breakdown. While Boswell wrote nothing of this, Mrs Thrale highlighted it in her *Anecdotes*. She and her husband had been keeping a close eye on him and feared that something like this was coming. She wrote that for weeks 'he could not stir out of his room in the court he inhabited'. He 'often lamented to us the horrible condition of his mind, which he said was nearly distracted'. One day near the end of June they found him imploring a guest to pray for him 'in the most pathetic terms'. Shocked, Thrale 'involuntarily lifted up one hand to shut his mouth'. Then and there, Mrs Thrale decided to take over, removing him from his 'close habitation in the court' and whisking him off to Streatham Park where for three months she nursed him until his physical (if not mental) health returned.[18]

Those three months were a turning point in his life. For the next sixteen years he spent much of his time with Mrs Thrale and her husband at Streatham and Southwark, virtually as a member of the family. His relationship with her became, apart from his marriage to Tetty, the most important one in his life. She became his 'Mistress' and Thrale his 'Master'. The 'Master' did his part, prevailing on him 'to change his shirt, his coat, or his plate, almost before it became indispensably necessary to the comfortable feelings of his friends'. After the death of their infant daughter (they already had one daughter, Queeney) the previous October, Johnson was another focus for Mrs Thrale's maternal instincts. In him she now also had an intellectual companion for lively talk and banter, as well as someone with whom to compose poetry and discuss literature. An invitation to her house often meant a chance to meet and talk with the famous Samuel Johnson. He drew there the likes of Reynolds, Goldsmith, Burke, the Burneys and other geniuses. The one irritant for her was her aged mother, Mrs Salusbury, who lived with her much of the time and disliked Johnson, a feeling he reciprocated because of her constant gabble about what she read in the papers. They disliked each other also because each thought the other had too much influence over Mrs Thrale. He could not really complain, however, for he had never known anything like the domestic pleasures in his elegant new 'home' that now dropped plentifully into his lap: the finest and most nutritious food, a lovely garden, wonderful country walks, and the constant stream of distinguished visitors from the literary, artistic, religious, political and highest social ranks of English society. They also set him up with an apartment 'over the counting house [of the brewery in Southwark] two pairs of stairs high – and called it the *Round Tower*'.[19]

Johnson and Mrs Thrale quickly fell into the habit of sharing secrets. He believed she was little more than a kept mistress, 'shut from the world, its pleasures, or its cares'. She complained frequently to him about her life, complaints to which her husband turned a deaf ear, although she was ever loyal to him, a talented and shrewd support in his political and business affairs as a successful brewer, and a dutiful and worried mother. On the other hand, she wrote that having Johnson as a frequent and prolonged guest soon enough became a cross she had to bear. When after his death she wrote her *Anecdotes* about him, based on her journal and commonplace book, *Thraliana*, many people – especially those in his circle – called her ungrateful, 'a little artful impudent malignant devil'. They felt that when she described her long relationship to him as 'a *bondage*, which she had endured *to please Mr Thrale*, but when he was dead … became insupportable', she revealed her true colours.[20]

What were her complaints? For one thing, he wanted her to exercise her intellect and not be such a slave to her family, but he never challenged Thrale's authority in the house and in squabbles between man and wife almost always defended him. 'I know no man', Johnson once said, 'who is more master of his wife and family than Thrale. If he but holds up a finger he is obeyed.' His conversation was brilliant but also trying if people had places to go, such as retiring to bed. After he had lectured the assembled company at length one day and was about to embark on a new subject, Thrale interrupted, 'There, there, now we have had enough for one lecture … we will not be upon education any more till after dinner, if you please.' Mrs Thrale wrote that his social habits were so sprawling that he upset family routines. His insomnia and fears of loneliness often forced her to stay up with him into the early morning hours. 'Mr Johnson loved late hours extremely, or more properly hated early ones. Nothing was more terrifying to him than the idea of retiring to bed, which he never would call going to rest, or suffer another to call so. "I lie down (said he) that my acquaintance may sleep; but I lie down to endure oppressive misery, and soon rise again to pass the night in anxiety and pain."' As a result, she claimed, 'I hurt my own health not a little by sitting up with him when I was myself far from well'; she was 'forced' by 'his vehement lamentations and piercing reproofs, not to quit the room, but to sit quietly and make tea for him, as I often did in London till four o'clock in the morning'. At Streatham she said she fared better because often there was some guest there who could take her place sitting with him late into the night.[21]

Her recitation of his personal habits was so stinging that one suspects it is exaggerated and overcharged, the result of accumulated vexations: he 'would not rise in the morning till twelve o'clock perhaps, and oblige me to make breakfast for him till the bell rung for dinner, though much displeased if the toilet was neglected, and though much of the time we passed together was spent in blaming or deriding, very justly, my neglect of economy, and waste of that money which might make many families happy'. She maintained he was frequently 'on the verge of a quarrel'. 'Have a care,' she said she heard him saying to a guest one day just as she walked into the drawing room, 'the Old Lion will not bear to be tickled.' She protested that helpful as he was with Queeney and later the other children, he was insufferably opinionated in advising her how to bring them up. She also disliked what she felt were his overbearing opinions of women's clothes he did not like, which at times caused distress to the women concerned. At first, she felt it was all worth it because she and her husband saw themselves as saving him; later, she chafed under a 'perpetual confinement' that was 'terrifying in the first years of our friendship, and irksome in the last'. She insisted that after her husband's death in 1782, she could scarcely bear his capriciousness and roughness in the house. She felt the world owed her a debt of gratitude because 'the shelter our house afforded to his uneasy fancies' and 'the pains we took to sooth or repress them' enabled him to continue to write.[22]

There was something even more disturbing in his relationship with Mrs Thrale, a darkness that went deeper than her irritation with him, reached to his melancholia and terrifying fear of madness, and placed her in compromising, even unsavoury situations.

In May 1779 she entered a passage in her *Thraliana* that is as mysterious as it is intriguing. She noted that in 1767 or 1768 'our stern philosopher Johnson trusted me ... with a secret far dearer to him than his life', one that placed him 'in her power' as his nurse or warden. This passage, hotly contested by critics and biographers, has remained an enigma. Some have supposed the secret was his past enslavement to another woman. Indeed, Mrs Thrale recorded his comment once that 'a woman has *such* power between the ages of twenty five and forty five, that she may tie a man to a post and whip him if she will'. 'How many times', wrote Mrs Thrale, 'has this great, this formidable Doctor Johnson kissed my hand, ay & my foot too upon his knees!' She acknowledged that she herself would not have such 'power' over him were she not a woman, for he never would have trusted any man with 'such secrets' 'entrusted to me'. But more psychologically complex explanations than mere sexual passion have been offered for the meaning of this 'secret'.[23]

The editor of Mrs Thrale's journal long ago made a connection between the secret and another reference of hers to 'the fetters & padlocks [probably just one] [that] will tell posterity the truth'. The padlock and mysterious fetters undoubtedly were the same ones that turned up among her effects sold at auction in 1823, which she identified as 'Johnson's padlock, committed to my care in the year 1768'. What were the fetters and padlock for? The likelihood is that he asked her to chain him with them, fearing perhaps sleepwalking and the insanity that he thought was a present possibility and could do him physical harm. In 1767–8 his desperate thoughts ran to such extremes. And there is evidence that his self-delusory thoughts of insanity continued, perhaps not so violently, throughout the next few years. On 24 March 1771, for example, he wrote in his pocket-diary (in Latin), 'Insane thoughts on fetters and hand-cuffs'. Perhaps he even enjoyed the idea of being confined in this way by his nurse and warden, the feeling of being secure in her control.[24]

Katherine Balderston's suggestion that Johnson may have taken a perverse sexual pleasure in such confinement has been discredited. It is based on a letter he wrote in French to Mrs Thale in early June 1773 while he was in the house staying with her. Balderston called it a 'pathological document' exhibiting 'erotic maladjustment' and 'masochistic fantasies'. Johnson was there in the house at an awkward time for her because her mother was dying and he was left largely on his own, in 'profound solitude', while she attended to her. In this letter he was either merely sulking at being left alone so much or genuinely worried that given his mental state he could not vouch for his behaviour during such unrelieved solitude. The letter pleads for help, 'Tell me whether you wish me to wander abandoned or to confine myself within certain prescribed limits.' If this was merely about staying out of the way at a time when Mrs Thrale was preoccupied with nursing her dying mother, a plea for order in a disordered house where children were also sick and builders were being disruptive, not about strict confinement, one wonders what the padlocks and chain were for. He added, 'if it seems best to you that I should remain in a certain place, I beg of you to spare me the necessity of constraining myself by taking away from me the power to leave the place where you want me to be. Which will not cost you more than the trouble to turn the key in the door twice a day ... your judgement and vigilance may come to the rescue of my weakness ... I desire, my patroness, that your authority should always be palpable to me, and that you should hold me in the slavery that you are well able to render happy'.[25]

Mrs Thrale's in-house letter to him, apparently in immediate response to his, has been read by some as simply a recognition that his letter was a plea for loving attention. But there was more going on here than that, even if we do not accept the wild theory that Johnson was a flagellant demanding to be scourged and manacled. The leading medical historian among Johnson scholars has reasoned that in the late 1760s the Thrales had turned Streatham into a retreat, a centre for therapy, with her as the therapist. Johnson was in the grips of a severe mental crisis of melancholy, when the black dog was 'upon his back' – a phrase in current use at Streatham to describe both Johnson and Henry Thrale's melancholia. They would use the phrase, wrote Mrs Thrale, as 'a sort of *byword* or *hack joke* here at Streatham, and in the letters I published between Dr Johnson & myself, it is almost perpetually recurring'. He desperately needed and wanted some loving confinement, whether enforced by a padlock or his own self-discipline. Her letter alludes to this need in kindly urging him, after six or seven years, to use self-discipline instead of making her resort to an 'irksome and dangerous idea' – namely, having recourse to strict confinement. She was gentle and tactful but did not want anything more to do with 'fetters to the body': 'If it be possible shake off these uneasy weights, heavier to the mind by far than fetters to the body. Let not your fancy dwell thus upon confinement and severity. I am sorry you are obliged to be so much alone.' She had become 'an unwilling performer in Johnson's psychopathological drama'. She also recognised that Boswell could teach him a thing or two about how to sweep his mind clean of melancholic rubbish.[26]

Apparently an agreement was reached that determined the pattern of his life with the Thrales for almost the rest of his days: he would normally have the run of the house, interacting fully with the family, but when his melancholia was severe and he felt the need to confine himself, he would shut himself up in his room for lengthy periods. There he would be without distractions and provocations, could occupy himself with complicated mathematical computations that he commonly used to combat the phantoms of madness, and read. Mrs Thrale thus patiently combined confinement with kindness as a recipe to 'sooth' Johnson and attempt to shake off the black dog. It is cruelly ironic that soon after his death she registered in her diary her fear that the phalanx of biographers lining up to write his life 'will leave *nothing untold* that I laboured so long to keep secret; & I was so very delicate in trying to conceal his fancied insanity, that I retained no proofs of it – or hardly any.' It was she of all the eventual biographers who wrote most of his phobia about madness and whom Boswell chiefly had in mind when he mentioned disdainfully those who wishing 'to depreciate him, should, since his death, have laid hold of this circumstance, and insisted upon it with very unfair aggravation'.[27]

[4]

By December, Robert Chambers, the new Vinerian Professor of Law, still had not come up with any of the lectures expected of him. It was time for concerted action, Johnson wrote: 'Come up to town, and lock yourself up from all but me, and I doubt not but lectures will be produced. You must not miss another term ... Come up and work, and I will try to help you.' Chambers came and they began a secret collaboration which lasted three years. In January 1767, Johnson was urging Chambers to come again 'to sit very close, and then there will be no danger, and needs to be no fear'. A week after returning home from three months in Streatham, he departed hurriedly to Oxford for a month. University College again gave him a room. Chambers would draw him to Oxford no fewer than eight or nine times during the next three years for work on the lectures.[28]

Chambers's *Course of Lectures on the English Law* was the fruit of the largest intellectual collaboration in Johnson's life. Because the lectures were not published until 1985, his work on them has not until recently been studied and appreciated. They posed problems for Chambers because after Blackstone's *Commentaries on the Laws of England* he ran the risk of treading over the same ground. His and Johnson's solution was to simplify Blackstone's lengthy legal explanations by stressing the need for law and order. Such a theme reflected Johnson's characteristic humanitarian insistence that the British Constitution must respond to human institutions and needs in order to be properly used and understood. He supervised the writing and Chambers may have used paragraphs and entire lectures written by Johnson, but their collaboration was balanced, a joint authorship.[29]

[5]

In February 1767, Lucy urged Johnson to pay a visit to Lichfield, but he saw no point in it except to see Kitty who was seriously ill and dying. Lucy herself seemed to be cold towards him these days. It was a good thing he did not go. That month he was distinguished with 'one of the most remarkable incidents' of his life, an interview with the King that raised his spirits considerably. He jotted down the conversation (the so-called 'Caldwell Minute') immediately afterwards for a friend, Sir James Caldwell, from whom Boswell obtained it. Reynolds, Goldsmith, and a few others afterwards heard him talk with undisguised pride and earnestness about it. The scene of the interview was the King's Library in the royal residence known as the Queen's House, formerly Buckingham House, on the site where Buckingham Palace now sits. This great library was built from 1762–6 by Sir William Chambers to accommodate the great collection of books and manuscripts George III had amassed. The royal encounter came about because when the King was informed that Johnson, the most distinguished man of letters in England, occasionally came to the royal library to study, he made it known that he would like to meet him on his next visit. Seeing Johnson enter and settle down with a book by the fire in the library, the King's godson and future Librarian, Sir Frederick Barnard, promptly informed the King and led him briskly by candlelight along some dark passages and through a private door into the library. When Barnard whispered into his ear, 'Here is the King', Johnson 'started up' and stood motionless facing the sovereign. The King walked over to him and they began to talk.[30]

This encounter has been represented, particularly as rendered by Boswell, as a cordial confrontation between the old courtly, aristocratic world of letters and patronage and the new professional, Johnsonian world of print culture where the market did the bidding, not kings. Boswell dramatised his source, the 'Caldwell Minute', making Johnson and the relatively new print culture the heroes of his beautifully orchestrated scene. The King is cast as the supreme patron pressing the Aeneas of British literature and culture to perform again for the good of the country. Perhaps he wondered whether the pension he had granted him had in fact been good for him if it had silenced his pen. He questioned him about his writing four separate times. First the King asked if he 'was then writing anything', to which Johnson replied, 'he was not, for he had pretty well told the world what he knew' and had to do more reading. A few minutes later, the King tried again, urging him 'to continue his labours'. This time Johnson told him what in exasperation, bordering on anger, he had told others who prodded him to write more, that he thought he 'had already done his part as a writer'. Cordially, the King remarked he would agree with him if he had not written so well. At this Johnson remained silent, struck deeply by the compliment. Finally, with one more effort the King recommended he write 'a literary biography of this country', for nobody else could do it. This time Johnson gave way and 'signified his readiness to comply with his Majesty's wishes'.[31]

Boswell wrote that throughout this interview Johnson conducted himself in the 'firm manly manner' befitting a respectable professional man of letters, not in the obsequious mode of a suppliant. When later at Sir Joshua's house Johnson regaled his host, Goldsmith, and others with an account of the exchange, they all hung on his words as a kind of returning hero who for a few minutes before the sovereign – 'the finest gentleman I have ever seen' – had enacted the new era of independence of artists and writers in the public face of patronage. Often jealous of Johnson's ability to dominate and take command of conversations, Goldsmith at first sulked on a sofa, but he finally came forward with a telling compliment to the man of the hour: 'Well, you acquitted yourself in this conversation better than I should have done; for I should have bowed and stammered through the whole of it.'[32]

CHAPTER 25

Coliseum of Beasts

[1]

In the summer of 1767, shortness of breath, especially in bed, made Johnson's mind race with fears of worse things. He also began to experience spasms in his stomach, throat and neck. Flatulence (possibly caused by a gall stone) and rheumatic pains, which had been a problem for years, rounded out the dreary procession of ailments. All his would go on for years. In April 1770 he complained in his diary of 'lumbago, or rheumatism in the loins, which often passes to the muscles of the belly, where it causes equal, if not greater, pain'. He wrapped himself up in flannel at night with 'a very great fire near my bed', but lying down only increased his pain and he could stay in bed only for a couple of hours at a time. He was also resorting to blisters on his back and opium.[1]

His inability to breathe properly increasingly made him feel incapable of rising to occasions, to settle to work and get on with life. His references to uneasiness, disturbed and unsettled nights and 'freedom of mind' were coded references to depression. While he was in Oxford in early 1768 helping Chambers again with his lectures, he suffered another severe attack of physical illness and melancholia, which forced him to extend his stay in New Inn Hall to two entire months. He remembered this attack vividly fifteen years later in a letter to Chambers, who was then in Calcutta: 'That dreadful illness which seized me at New Inn Hall left consequences which have I think always hung upon me. I have never since cared much to walk. My mental abilities I do not perceive it impaired.' Over the years since, he added:

> my constitutional maladies pursued me. My thoughts were disturbed, my nights were insufferably restless, and by spasms in the breast I was condemned to the torture of sleepiness without the power to sleep. Those spasms after enduring them more than twenty years I eased by three powerful remedies, abstinence, opium, and mercury, but after a short time

they were succeeded by a strange oppression of another kind which when I lay down disturbed me with a sensation like flatulence or intumescence which I cannot describe.

'I have been really very bad', he wrote in April to Mrs Thrale who had recently given birth to another daughter, 'and am glad that I was not at Streatham, where I should have been troublesome to you' ; and again later that month, 'I am better, having scarce eaten for seven days.' These were 'disorders of the body, and disturbances of the mind very near to madness' which now made up so much of his life that he could not bear to think of them. 'I have now begun the sixtieth year of my life,' he wrote in his birthday prayer: 'How the last year has past I am unwilling to terrify myself with thinking. This day has been passed in great perturbation.'[2]

Instead of returning to London from Oxford in May, he rushed to Lichfield because Kitty Chambers was on her deathbed. It was a measure of his deep affection for his family's servant of over more than forty years. After seeing how very ill she was, he wrote desperately to his physician Thomas Lawrence in London with detailed accounts of her symptoms to determine if she could be cured. The letters are extraordinarily clinical, anticipating his letters about his own sicknesses in following years. 'Kitty is, I think, going to heaven,' he wrote. She hung on for two more months, forcing him to stay in town depressingly longer than he had anticipated. Waiting for her to die became a kind of enforced idleness. 'My old melancholy has laid hold upon me to a degree sometimes not easily supportable,' he wrote to Robert Chambers in Oxford. He pined for the comforts of Streatham Park, complaining to Mrs Thrale about 'the shackles of destiny' he felt in Lichfield − 'there has not been one day of pleasure, and yet I cannot get away'. 'I hope soon to return from exile.' Finally, unable to wait any longer, he took his leave of 58-year-old Kitty in mid-October, recording the moments of parting in a touching passage: 'I desired all to withdraw, then told her that we were to part for ever, that as Christians we should part with prayer, and that I would, if she was willing, say a short prayer beside her. She expressed great desire to hear me, and held up her poor hands, as she lay in bed, with great fervour, while I prayed, kneeling by her ... I then kissed her. She told me that to part was the greatest pain that she had ever felt, and that she hoped we would meet again in a better place. I expressed with swelled eyes and great emotion of tenderness the same hopes. We kissed and parted.' The person he was most sorry to leave, apart from Kitty, was Elizabeth Aston, for whose sister Molly he had nourished such a strong, even amorous, affection. Elizabeth had never married and lived alone up at Stowe Hill, the house she had built just outside Lichfield. She would be his most intimate friend in Lichfield on future visits, a warm and vital compensation for the otherwise dreary and barren months he would spend there.

He rushed back to Oxford, regretting he could not bring himself to stop for a few hours with Hector in Birmingham: 'A few serious and a few jocund hours would have brought back a little of our former lives. Surely we shall meet some time again.' With his health and spirits as they were, it may have occurred to him this would never happen.[3]

[2]

There was not much to occupy him in London in the next several months. He did a little reading of Pascal's *Pensées*, continued helping Robert Chambers, and wrote the Dedication for William Payne's *Introduction to Geometry*. He thought of geometry as 'the primary and fundamental art of life', extending throughout all 'operations of human skill'. Mrs Thrale was particularly struck by the psychological use to which he could put his delight in mathematical computations, even to the point of timing how long it would take a fingernail to grow. She wrote that he had 'a singular power of withdrawing his attention from the prattle he heard round him, and would often sit amusing himself with calculating sums while there was a noise in the room enough to perplex any common mortal. He used indeed to be always tormenting one with showing how much time might be lost by squandering two hours a day, how much money might be saved by laying up five shillings a day, how many lines might be written by putting down only ten every day with a hundred such like propositions.' Once he got over an attack of stomach spasms by calculating the national debt, which he said if converted to silver would 'make a meridian of that metal' around the circumference of the earth, which could be called 'the *Meridian* of *London*'.[4]

When Parliament was dissolved early in 1768, Johnson assisted Thrale again in another campaign for re-election. This national election turned out to be especially violent because the hard-hitting John Wilkes was back in London stirring up public discontent. He had fled to France four years earlier when both houses of Parliament sought to prosecute him for seditious libel in attacking the King and his Ministers in his periodical *The North Briton* (no. 45), and for his pornographic *Essay on Woman*. He was now campaigning to re-enter Parliament as Member for Middlesex, flying in the face of the political establishment, the King and the Prime Minister by whipping up a frenzy of public support for his radical reforms in favour of popular rule, including enfranchisement for the poor. A rallying point for the 'patriot' Opposition, he was suddenly the people's hero and cries of 'Wilkes and Liberty!' echoed in the streets as rioting broke out. Benjamin Franklin, then living in London, described how the mob required 'gentlemen and ladies of all ranks, as they passed in their carriages, to shout for Wilkes and liberty, marking the same words on all their coaches with chalk, and No. 45 on every door'. On the road to Oxford from London, Boswell was fascinated by people 'roaring with "Wilkes and Liberty", which, with "No. 45", was chalked on every coach and chaise'. Although Wilkes was a magnetic and likeable personality, he was suspected of being less interested in the people's rights than in restoring his own personal fortunes because a Member of Parliament could not be arrested for debt. He won the March election but the following month was arrested on the old charges, fined £1,000, and promptly thrown in jail for twenty-two months. That the new MP for Middlesex should be stewing in prison only incited further mob violence. Then he was unwisely deprived of his office, an act that raised constitutional issues later taken up by Johnson in his political pamphlet, *The Patriot*, in 1770. As for Thrale, who opposed Wilkes strongly, he narrowly won his seat for Southwark in March thanks in no small part to his wife's untiring campaigning efforts while carrying another baby due in April.[5]

In the spring of 1768 Boswell, who (so far as we know) had not had a letter from Johnson since August 1766, re-entered his life. He had been busy in Edinburgh earning his living as a new advocate and looking for a rich wife, but he expended most of his creative impulses in authorship. Drawing on his colourful journal record of his intrepid visit to Corsica, in February 1768 he published his *Account of Corsica*. The book sold so well that for a time he became famous as 'Corsica Boswell'. With the delicious glow of fame lighting his way, he was eager to get to London on his new footing of literary success, although he was also nervous about seeing Johnson because without his per- mission he had included in his book a passage from one of his letters to him in Paris in January 1766. Someone had told him Johnson was 'offended'. 'In short, I was quite in the dark concerning him,' Boswell scribbled in his journal. It was just as well he had left Edinburgh before reading Johnson's letter: 'I could now tell why I should not write, for who would write to men who publish the letters to their friends without their leave?' He added that while he would be glad to see him, 'I wish you would empty your head of Corsica, which I think has filled it rather too long.' When he got around to reading *Corsica*, Johnson liked the personal part of the book because it was full of images 'which operated strongly upon yourself', but as for the history of the island he thought it was borrowed and dull.[6]

Finding Johnson was in Oxford, Boswell followed him there. He checked in at the Angel and quickly made his way to New Inn Hall, where Chambers received him graciously and gave him tea. A little while later Johnson came in and promptly quieted all his anxieties: 'He took me all in his arms and kissed me on both sides of the head, and was as cordial as ever I saw him.' He was flattered his young friend had come all the way to Oxford just to see him and delighted to hear he was now earning £200 per year as an advocate: 'What, Bozzy? Two hundred pounds! A great deal.' Immediately, Boswell took in the Johnsonian ether and began to record their conversations. They spoke also of the legal profession and literature, especially of Goldsmith, and Johnson renewed his promise to visit the Hebrides with him. Chambers invited Boswell to spend the night with them and the next evening they supped together at the Angel.[7]

The conversation flowed at the Angel, running in and out of subjects with ease and jollity. At one point, Johnson's sense of humour got the better of Boswell's bizarre ideas about reincarnation. 'Why not allow a dog to be immortal', Boswell blurted out. When he remarked that whenever he saw a very intelligent dog he did not know what to make of him, Johnson 'growling with joy', replied, 'No, Sir, and when we see a very foolish fellow, we don't know what to make of him.' He then suddenly rose from his chair, 'bounced along, and stood by the fire, laughing and exulting over me'. Boswell was struck again by Johnson's determination to talk for victory: 'When Mr Chambers was getting the better of him in an argument, he said to him as to a boy, "My dear Chambers, take it to you, take it to you, since you will have it so", as if he made a concession to please him, when in reality he did not know how to answer him.' They spoke of how they felt a woman's adultery is so much more to blame than a man's because her 'crime' breaks the peace of families and introduces the 'confusion of progeny' whereas the man's, though 'criminal in the sight of God', injures only her. As for chastity, Boswell asked Johnson whether it was fair that a woman's 'deviation' from it should absolutely ruin her. Johnson replied: 'The great principle which every woman is taught is to keep her legs together. When she has given up that principle, she has given up every notion of female honour and virtue, which are all included in chastity.' Completely out of touch with Johnson's mental and physical ordeals in Oxford, Boswell noted only his energy, laughter and cheerfulness: 'His mixing more in society had dissipated much of that gloom which hung upon his mind when he lived much alone, when he brooded in the Temple.'[8]

Johnson returned to London at the end of April to find that Boswell, feeling 'really the *Great Man* now', was still there though recovering in his room in Half-Moon street from one of the seventeen attacks of gonorrhoea he endured during his lifetime. He called to see him one morning. Already thinking of cashing in on his friendship with Johnson, Boswell asked him if he would object to his publishing his letters after his death. 'Nay, Sir,' Johnson answered, 'when I am dead, you may do as you will'.[9]

Johnson continued to take an interest in the development of the Royal Library, writing in May 1768 an uncharacteristically long letter to the King's Librarian, Frederick Barnard, containing detailed advice on what rare books to buy by 'ransacking other countries': 'every country has literature of its own which may be best gathered on its native soil ... you must catch up single volumes where you can find them. Try every place, things often occur where they are least expected.' Reflecting his own interest in geography, topography and the history of printing, he strongly recommended acquiring maps and first editions of early printed works as 'great ornaments' for the library.[10]

On 7 June Boswell arranged a dinner for Johnson at the Crown and Anchor in the Strand which included Percy, Langton and Davies, as well as two distinguished members of the Edinburgh literati who wished to see him, Dr William Robertson the historian who became principal of Edinburgh University in 1762, and Dr Hugh Blair the divine and critic who since 1762 had been Regius Professor of rhetoric and belles-lettres at the university. Blair, who once criticised Johnson's style in the *Rambler* for being 'too pompous', had met him in 1763 and remembered the rough treatment he received then from 'the Giant in his den'. Defending the authenticity of the Ossianic poems, he now came in for a bit more. He asked Johnson if he still thought 'any man of a modern age could have written such poems?' Johnson turned on him, 'Yes, Sir, many men, many women, and many children.' After that the dinner proved disappointing for Johnson because, according to Boswell, Robertson and Blair were so cowed by him that 'they hardly opened their lips, and that only to say something which they were certain would not expose them to the sword of Goliath; such was their anxiety for their fame when in the presence of Johnson.' And on that night it was a good thing they did not confront him. Davies took some direct hits, as did Percy who characteristically got up and left in a huff. In the morning, before leaving for home, Boswell found Johnson pleased with his 'colloquial prowess'. 'Yes, Sir,' Boswell observed, 'you tossed and gored several persons.'[11]

By then Johnson's reputation for conversational roughness, even rudeness, was widely known. Horace Walpole, who went out of his way to avoid meeting Johnson and therefore remained largely dependent on rumour, did not mince his words, describing him in 1775 as 'an odious and mean character' whose 'gross brutality' made him want 'to fling a glass of wine in his face'. 'I have no patience', he added, 'with an unfortunate monster trusting to his helpless deformity for indemnity for any impertinence that his arrogance suggests, and who thinks that what he has read is an excuse for everything he says.' The epithet circulating was that he was a 'bear'. Baretti thought that with more polish he might have been 'a dancing bear'. Boswell heard Goldsmith say in his defence, 'Johnson, to be sure, has a roughness in his manner; but no man alive has a more tender heart. *He has nothing of the bear but his skin.*'[12]

Sometime in 1768, or perhaps earlier, Johnson sent Frank off to Bishop's Stortford Grammar School in Hertfordshire to be educated properly. Hawkins disapprovingly remarked that Frank stayed at the school for five years and (according to Mrs Williams) cost Johnson no less than £300 (some £30,000 today) over that period. He thought it was money down the drain. But Johnson never wavered in his determination to raise the boy with the advantages of a good education, writing more than two years later, 'I am very well satisfied with your progress ... Let me know what English books you read for your entertainment. You can never be wise unless you love reading.' He was even ordering clothes for him and promised he would never forget or forsake him.[13]

He visited Oxford three times in 1769 to see his friends and continue helping Chambers, including six weeks in the spring and summer soaking up the attention and comforts he received there. In September the Thrales took him on a short excursion into Kent, hoping that a change of scene would benefit his health, and there were plans that autumn also for some time in Brighton with them which did not materialize. When their baby girl Lucy Elizabeth was born on 22 June, he was 'honoured' to be asked to be her godfather. He 'insisted' on her being called Elizabeth in memory of Tetty. 'I always wished it might be a Miss,' he wrote. 'Surely I shall be very fond of her. In a year and half she will run and talk.' Ominously, he slipped in the comment, 'how much ill may happen in a year and a half'. It took longer than that, but his goddaughter, Mrs Thrale's favourite, died four years later.[14]

His prayer on his sixtieth birthday in September recorded his horror once again that he was not achieving anything and that his physical recovery was slow: 'My days are easier, but the perturbation of my nights is very distressful. I think to try a lower diet. I have grown fat too fast. My lungs seem encumbered, and my breath fails me, if my strength [is] in any unusual degree exerted, or my motion accelerated.' Such worries bred fears of an unprepared death that cropped up frequently in his letters: 'though I feel all these decays of body, I have made no preparation for the grave. What shall I do to be saved?' Boswell's compelling passage on 26 October describing Johnson's mind in combat with itself, elicited by Garrick's remark that he believed Johnson 'to be harassed with doubts', is the most vividly terrifying ever written by someone who had the chance to study him closely:

> His mind resembled the vast amphitheatre, the Coliseum at Rome. In the centre stood his judgement, which, like a mighty gladiator, combated those apprehensions that, like the wild beasts of the *Arena*, were all around in cells, ready to be let out upon him. After a conflict, he drove them back into their dens; but not killing them, they were still assailing him. To my question, whether we might not fortify our minds for the approach of death, he answered, in a passion, 'No, Sir, let it alone. It matters not how a man dies, but how he lives ... It will do him no good to whine.'

Brave but desperate words. Boswell was in forbidden territory but foolishly persisted talking about death: 'He was so provoked, that he said, "Give us no more of this"; and was thrown into such a state of agitation, that he expressed himself in a way that alarmed and distressed me; showed an impatience that I should leave him, and when I was going away, called to me, sternly, "Don't let us meet to-morrow." Licking his wounds, the next day Boswell bravely called to apologise and managed to soften his 'ferocity' so successfully that as he was leaving Johnson stopped him 'and smiling said, "Get you gone – *in*"; a curious mode of inviting me to stay, which I accordingly did for some time longer'.[15]

[4]

'My friends at Lichfield must not think that I forget them', he had told Lucy in June 1768, 'neither Mrs Cobb, nor Mrs Adey, nor Miss Adey, nor Miss [Anna] Seward, nor Miss Vise'. Elizabeth Aston also was waiting for him up at Stowe Hill. With the prospect of a warmer Lucy, 'my dear darling', there to welcome him, in August 1769 he ventured another Lichfield visit. Lucy's well-being had been especially on his mind and there was a string of other women he wished to see. He set out on 10 August with Frank, who was spending the holidays at home. Lucy received them warmly – she saved 'her best gooseberries upon the tree for me', he exulted, though they were no match for the pineapples and strawberries and cream which he identified with the plentitude of Streatham Park. 'Not yet well', he 'rambled' out into the countryside, pleased (in Horace's words) with 'the familiar streams and sacred springs' and courting the 'cooling shades'. On the other hand, the town council's (those 'wicked men' and 'audacious aldermen') had 'violated' 'ill-fated' George Lane in town by denuding it of its lovely trees. This time there was less chance to get bored with the town, as he also squeezed in a visit to Taylor at Ashbourne.[16]

He fretted he might not be able to get back to London in time to accompany the Thrales to Brighton. As it happened, he had to make his way there on his own in mid-August, where the days passed pleasingly enough. Not with enormous pleasure, one imagines, he hunted on the Downs with Thrale; more pleasurably, he swam in the sea with Mrs Thrale and little Queeney. While he was there he received a letter from Boswell who had arrived in London at the beginning of September and, dressed flourishingly as a Corsican patriot, was on his way to Stratford to participate in Garrick's famous extravaganza known as the 'Shakespeare Jubilee' – a few days of festivities in honour of the Bard which were washed out in torrential rains. Boswell thought it was shameful that Johnson, the great modern editor of Shakespeare, was in Brighton and not in Stratford, getting wet with the rest of them: 'almost every man of eminence in the literary world was happy to partake in this festival of genius, [and] the absence of Johnson could not but be wondered at and regretted'.[17]

When he returned to London in late September, Boswell could not devote himself to him as completely as on previous visits. The reason was that Paoli, who had failed in his valiant struggle for Corsican independence from the French, had fled the island in the summer and was forced into exile in London. Boswell saw it as his 'duty, as well as my pleasure, to attend much upon him', which included the thrill of introducing the famous Corsican and the greatest literary personality of the age to each other: 'They met with a manly ease, mutually conscious of their own abilities and of the abilities one of each other.' Immediately, Johnson conceived a lasting respect for the noble ideals and dignity of the Corsican patriot, telling Boswell later at his lodgings in Old Bond Street, while they drank tea late into the night, that Paoli 'had the loftiest port' he had ever met in a man. Even so, Johnson was still fed up with all of Boswell's chatter about Corsica. At Streatham, to which at Johnson's request Boswell was invited for dinner one October evening, Johnson was in a mocking, hilarious mood at the expense of both Scotland and Corsica. This was not the first or last time that in the company of Mrs Thrale he felt the impulse to be especially hard on Boswell, in this instance shocking him with his violent declamation against Corsican failure to take one single fortified town from the Genovese in twenty years: 'They might have battered down the walls and reduced them to powder in twenty years. They might have pulled the walls in pieces, and cracked the stones with their teeth in twenty years.' There was no opposing him that night. As Goldsmith once remarked about Johnson's 'talking for victory', adopting the words of a character in one of Colley Cibber's plays, 'There is no arguing with Johnson, for "when his pistol misses fire, he knocks you down with the butt end of it."'[18]

The last intimate moment with Johnson that Boswell recorded on this London visit was of his returning to Johnson's Court with Johnson on 26 October to have tea with Anna Williams. The scene provides a snapshot of her in Johnson's home and Johnson's silent forbearance of her. She made the tea with 'sufficient dexterity notwithstanding her blindness, though her manner of satisfying herself that the cups were full enough was a little awkward. She put her finger down a certain way till she felt the tea touch it'. They quietly sipped and talked.

Boswell could have hugged himself with the 'elation at being allowed the privilege of attending Dr Johnson at his late visits to this lady': 'I willingly drank cup after cup, as it had been the Heliconian spring."[19]

[5]

After Boswell left London on 10 November, the 'tedious and painful rheumatism' that flared up in the spring of the new year brought Johnson another layer of considerable suffering. Drawing to a close his collaboration with Chambers, who by the end of the academic year in July had given all his required Vinerian lectures and been paid for them, he was in Oxford for four days in January and then again a week in April, but during the latter visit he was in great pain. He tried blistering and took opium when he got back to London, only imagining he felt some relief from the former. After briefly taking refuge again at Streatham, he returned home on Good Friday because of his rheumatic discomfort, to treat himself and fast 'unobserved'. 'I came home late, and was unwilling to carry my rheumatism to the cold church in the morning, unless that were rather an excuse made to myself.' He tried to be philosophical: 'The pain harasses me much, yet many have the disease perhaps in a much higher degree with want of food, fire, and covering, which I find thus grievous with all the succours that riches and kindness can buy and give.' On Saturday he sat up to compose a lengthy Easter prayer, and 'having ordered the maid to make the fire in my chamber at eight went to rest, and had a tolerable night'. He resolved again to read the Scriptures every Sunday, which he was failing to do: six hundred verses in the Old Testament 'in any language' and two hundred in the New Testament in Greek every week, from which sometimes he would read a little 'with a solemn hum, and sometimes talk to himself, either as meditating or as praying'. To help him adhere to this plan he even kept tables of how much of the Bible he was reading.[20]

He greeted the new decade with shame and guilt that the black dog was still his regular companion and he could rouse himself neither to work nor take command of his thoughts and days. 'For the last year I have been slowly recovering both from the violence of my last illness, and, I think, from the general disease of my life.'[21]

CHAPTER 26

Back to Shakespeare and the *Dictionary*

Johnson sat down one night in January 1770 at the Thrales's South-wark house and began writing his first political pamphlet, *The False Alarm*, since being granted a pension in 1762. He thus embarked on a period of political writing in the early 1770s in which he produced four pamphlets in the persona of an *enfant terrible*, a role he relished. They brought him widespread criticism partly because he was thought by many to have accepted his pension on condition he would not stray again into politics. There were accusations of ingratitude. It took him about a day to write the twenty-five pages. Mrs Thrale wrote she would never forget the pleasure it gave him to write it. Just the sensation of letting his pen flow again freely must have been exhil-arating. Strahan rushed the pamphlet into print, publishing five hundred copies on 16 January, followed by three more impressions of five hundred copies each in February and March. It was published anonymously but as usual in a very short time everyone knew he was the author.[1]

Johnson saw the pamphlet as a way to get back at Wilkes (that 'abusive scoundrel') for ridiculing in *The North Briton* (nos. 11 and 12) several of his definitions in the *Dictionary* when it first came out. But there were more important reasons for writing it. One was a letter to the *Public Advertiser* by Junius, whose identity remains unclear even today, defending Wilkes's right to take his seat in the House. Junius had also taken delight in repeatedly attacking the King, for whom at this point Johnson had a very high regard, so this was his small way of evening the score on behalf of the monarch, too. Of Wilkes, he said he wished to say little except that 'lampoon itself would disdain to speak ill of him of whom no man speaks well. It is sufficient that he is expelled from the House of Commons, and confined in jail as being legally convicted of sedition and impiety ... We are now disputing . . . whether Middlesex shall be represented or not by a criminal from a jail'. Beyond this, there was a constitutional issue raised by Wilkes having been denied his seat by the Commons. Johnson's main argument was that this so-called 'alarming crisis' (a favourite expression of the Wilkites) was a manufactured spin, a false alarm, and that the Commons was perfectly within its constitutional right to allow another man, who obtained far fewer votes, to take up the seat instead. His position is another complicating factor in the misdirected effort to fix on him the label of either Tory or Whig.[2]

As a monarchist and defender of the established Church, as one who had a revulsion for republicanism and dissenting attitudes towards religion, Johnson was understood to be a Tory by his contemporaries. Both monarchy and the Church of England, in his view, protected the nation from constitutional, religious and moral instability. But when it got down to social and economic realities, to the individual welfare and condition of human beings, he appeared much more like the 'liberal' of today. It has also been argued that because Johnson defended Parliament's right to control its own membership, in spite of what the electors decided, he was behaving like a strong Tory. Another view, however, is that the latter was in fact a 'Whig' position, that Johnson – even as he encouraged political awareness and concern by the average citizen – regarded inflammatory politicking by fire-brands like Wilkes, the chaotic cant of mobs that could rouse the populace to rioting, and vague talk about 'rights' without an under-standing of political realities, as dangerous to the fabric of effective government, harmony of society and happiness of the individual. 'The perpetual subject of political disquisition is not absolute, but comparative good.' Anarchy was itself a kind of tyranny.[3]

His language grows angry and abusive in the pamphlet over what he saw as irresponsible electoral agitators who have whipped up 'this tempest of outrage'. Boswell described it as 'extreme coarseness of contemptuous abuse' from one accustomed to wielding such language against the establishment but now aiming it against the 'declaimers or the plotters of a city-tavern'. His fury was stoked by the spectacle of the ignorant, uneducated masses, even mobs, presuming to dictate to Parliament how to govern. The 'weeping patriots' were 'puny con-trovertists': 'If infatuation be, as the proverb tells us, the forerunner of destruction, how near must be the ruin of a nation that can be incited against its governors, by sophistry like this.' His temperature rose as he sarcastically exposed the bathos of 'fever of epidemic patriotism'.

Every moment brings a new crisis, 'quiet and security are now at an end', 'we hear the thunder while the sky is clear': 'the tailor slips his thimble, the drapier drops his yard, and the blacksmith lays down his hammer; they meet at an honest alehouse, consider the state of the nation, read or hear the last petition, lament the miseries of the time, are alarmed at the dreadful crisis, and subscribe to the support of the Bill of Rights.' The entire conduct of this 'despicable faction' could be summed up as 'plebeian grossness, and savage indecency', fired by 'the insolence of invective'. These 'low-born railers' have insulted the King with rudeness when they should rather have been grateful that he is the first monarch in a century who has desired and tried to deserve their affections and be 'the common father of all his people'. The Tories, moreover, have been shameful with their 'frigid neutrality' towards the 'fomenters of sedition, and confederates of the rabble', their chronic suspiciousness of whatever administration was in power in Westminster.[4]

As a historical postscript to this pamphlet, Wilkes was elected for Middlesex again in the general election of 1774 and allowed this time to retain his seat. With the financial assistance of powerful backers from both politics and trade who enabled him to recover financially, he later became Mayor of London. Two years after his election he would meet Johnson, with unexpected results.

[2]

Johnson may or may not have attributed to his fervent prayers for a return of literary activity an intense period of revision of both the Shakespeare edition and the *Dictionary* in the early 1770s. By January 1770 he had begun revising his edition, for which he called on the scholarly help of Steevens, whom one critic has called the nastiest person in Johnson's circle. This was because of his sly and treacherous relish for tricking people into arguments with each other. He was fond of writing embarrassing pieces for the newspapers and attributing them to others, inventing information to decoy and trap rival scholars, and attacking his friends in anonymous articles for newspapers. When once at Langton's house for dinner in 1778, Johnson remarked he would 'be sorry if any of our Club were hanged', though 'I will not say but some of them deserve it', Beauclerk piped in, 'You, Sir, have a friend [Steevens] who deserves to be hanged; for he speaks behind their backs against those with whom he lives on the best terms, and

attacks them in the newspapers. *He* certainly ought to be *kicked* ...
He is very malignant'. Johnson did not entirely agree, 'No, Sir; he is
not malignant. He is mischievous, if you will. He would do no man
an essential injury; he may, indeed, love to make sport of people by
vexing their vanity.' 'If he is a man of principles,' Beauclerk insisted,
'he does not wear them out in practice.' As a Shakespearean and
Renaissance scholar, however, Steevens definitely knew his way
around and was extremely well read in Elizabethan literature. He
appears to have been among those with whom Johnson supped in the
Temple on the night before publication of the 1765 edition, and who
kept him up until after five in the morning. According to Steevens,
when Johnson looked at his watch, he exclaimed, 'This is sport to
you, gentlemen; but you do not consider there are at most only four
hours between me and criticism.'[5]

Without Steevens, he could not have completed the Shakespeare
revision, which became known as the Johnson-Steevens edition, published in 1773. The edition contained eighty-four new notes signed
by Johnson to which possibly Steevens added without telling him.
Steevens also was the chief contributor of supplementary notes for
the three appendices that conclude the tenth and final volume. And
he took the textual editing far beyond anything Johnson attempted
for the original edition, although the crotchety critic and giant-killer
Joseph Ritson complained that in this, and the next edition in 1778,
Steevens and Johnson had 'never collated any of the folios'. Even
Johnson's friend, the scholarly Irishman Edmond Malone, who will
soon come into his life (although they had met briefly in 1765 when
Johnson was living in Inner Temple Lane), had a low regard for the
textual editing and felt that Shakespeare's text after the Johnson-
Steevens edition was in such a sorry state that he needed to do a whole
new edition of his own, which was eventually published in 1790.

[3]

Johnson spent a couple of weeks in July 1770 with Lucy in Lichfield,
where it was wet and miserable, he ached with rheumatism, and failed
to see his favourite Miss Aston because she was away. He then dallied
with rural novelties at Ashbourne for a couple more, feeding the fawns
from his hand upon the lawn, measuring Taylor's 'great bull', and
haymaking. Mrs Thrale missed him sorely, 'I hope we shall all spend
our Christmas comfortably together.' He was home in the first week

of August where he did not find much to do for five months except help Goldsmith with what became one of the most famous of eighteenth-century poems, *The Deserted Village*.[6]

In December, Spain provoked an international crisis that banished thoughts of measuring bulls and haymaking from his mind and concentrated it instead on writing another political pamphlet. With a sudden show of naval force Spain invaded the Malvinas or Falkland Islands and succeeded in removing the miniscule English garrison there. When news of the invasion got back to London, Lord North's ministry rapidly prepared a naval force to sail back and reclaim the islands. But William Pitt (the Elder) and others in opposition contrived to trip up Lord North. They urged a war against Spain that they were sure England would lose because of the enemy's probable alliance with France, talking up the ugly face of the impending war in order to induce North to lose courage and accept a humiliating defeat. This, they hoped, would force him to resign as Prime Minister, whose ministry Johnson supported.

Perhaps at Strahan's request and with information he was given by the Government, in late February or early March 1771, Johnson wrote *Thoughts on the Late Transactions Respecting Falkland's Islands*, which was out on the streets by 16 March. Although it was not as controversial as *False Alarm* and to his mind lacked its 'subtlety of disquisition', it had 'fire'. It attacked 'the howl of plebeian patriotism' broadcast by the likes of Wilkes and Junius, the exploitative greed of the trading interests of the City, and Pitt, Lord Grenville, and the Opposition in general. 'Like vultures waiting for a day of carnage', Pitt and his cohorts played the game of 'domestic sedition', Johnson wrote. Neither of these scenarios came to pass and England on the contrary humiliated Spain into backing down and getting out of the Falklands without a single shot being fired – all this in spite of what Johnson called 'the machinations of these pygmy rebels', 'the noisy faction which has too long filled the kingdom, sometimes with the roar of empty menace, and sometimes with the yell of hypocritical lamentation.'[7]

Johnson took aim at the warmongers who stood to get rich by war, and the patriotic cant of the rabble whipped up by the power brokers in order to realise their own personal ambitions. His indictment of war is an eloquent, incensed plea against the 'diseases of animal nature' that send young men to their deaths marching to slogans, doomed by political ideology: 'It is wonderful with what coolness and indifference the greater part of mankind see war commenced. Those that hear of it at a distance, or read of it in books, but have never presented its evils to their minds, consider it as little more than a splendid game; a proclamation, an army, a battle, and a triumph.' He also struck again at Junius's 'blaze of impudence' and 'thirst of blood': 'He cries *havoc* without reserve, and endeavours to let slip the dogs of foreign or of civil war, ignorant whither they are going, and careless what may be their prey.' Junius 'drew the rabble after him as a monster makes a show'. As Boswell said, we find Johnson in this pamphlet 'lashing the party in opposition with unbounded severity, and making the fullest use of what he ever reckoned a most effectual argumentative instrument – contempt'.[8]

Strahan, a Member for Parliament as well as successful printer, was so impressed by Johnson's two recent political pamphlets, by his relish for entering into the fray, that he got it into his mind that Johnson should himself become a Member of Parliament and be able to influence current affairs more directly. Presumably with Johnson's approval, he wrote to the House of Commons in March 1771 proposing he would make 'an excellent figure' there and asking that the idea be presented to Lord North. Johnson had all the necessary credentials, he urged, eloquence, sharp analytical powers, 'extraordinary sense and unimpeached virtue', an amazing capacity for work, and strong support for the ministry. Friends of the King would 'find him a lamb', his enemies 'a lion'. But Johnson now was widely regarded as too politically independent. Back in 1762, when recommendations were sought for his pension, Richard Farmer wrote to Lord Bute: 'I am told that his political principles make him incapable of being in any place of trust, by incapacitating him from qualifying himself for any such office – but a pension My Lord requires no such performances.' As for Johnson's willingness to be a Member, 'Yes, yes, he would have *approved* it,' Mrs Thrale noted regarding Strahan's idea. However, the matter raises the question whether or not Johnson would have been any good as a speaker in the House since the long, sustained speeches required there were not in his mode of 'sententious brevity'. Boswell thought he would have been a sensation; others disagreed. There is almost no knowledge of Johnson delivering speeches to large assemblies, except several times at the Society of Arts and Sciences when the reception was mixed. On one of those occasions, he himself admitted, 'all my flowers of oratory forsook me'.[9]

[4]

For a year and a half after his marriage to his cousin Margaret Montgomerie – who did not bring him the wealth he had hoped for through marriage but who turned out to be the perfect wife for him – Boswell had turned his mind away from Johnson, London, and the attractions of gambling and whoring that had patterned his existence since returning from the Continent. He broke his silence in April 1771 by inviting his friend to Scotland for the tour of the Highlands and Hebrides they had kept alive in imagination for years. 'Whether we climb the Highlands, or are tossed among the Hebrides,' Johnson replied two months later, 'I hope the time will come when we may try our powers both with cliffs and water.' The next day he was off again with Frank on another 'furlough' (as Mrs Thrale put it) to Lichfield and Ashbourne. He wanted to be well away at the end of another of her difficult pregnancies. He could leave with the pleasing sensation of improved relations with her mother, for whose breast cancer he was constantly trying to find remedies and seek medical advice. For her part, Mrs Salusbury had decided after all that following her death Johnson would remain a good, protective influence for her daughter as friend and counsellor.[10]

As usual he found little in Lichfield 'to please me' because Elizabeth Aston was not well, another of his schoolfellows had died, and there were 'no temptations to prolong my stay'. His vanity was aroused, however, by hearing from Lucy that the portrait of him Reynolds finished in 1769, of which a copy had been painted for her, was 'much visited and much admired'. 'Every man has a lurking wish to appear considerable in his native place.' His thoughts were often on the Thrales and what by now he thought would be the new 'pretty little stranger in the cradle'. As it turned out, the baby was a month overdue, causing considerable pain and anxiety to the mother. He imagined that at this rate the baby would be 'a giant' like Richard III, not an especially pleasing thought. In late June he made his way to Ashbourne, where there was nothing new to entertain him. Trying to take his mind off the rheumatism that he again experienced in his face and mouth by looking forward to seeing the 'furnace' or chemical laboratory the Thrales were building at his urging in the kitchen garden at Streatham, he promised to bring back some iron, copper and lead ore so the children could see lead smelted in it. He also bought Queeney a cabinet in which to keep such curiosities as shells and minerals as he managed to obtain on his travels.[11]

[5]

On his return to London, there was a large task awaiting him, a revision of the *Dictionary*. As Mrs Thrale also declared, the initiative for revision came from the proprietors: 'the booksellers suggested the project' and 'paid Johnson well' – some £300, the same amount as his annual pension.[12]

Because existing common law in practice gave London booksellers (i.e. publishers) copyright ownership of a book in perpetuity, in spite of the Copyright Act of 1709 giving authors, not booksellers, proprietary ownership of their own works and the option to assign to booksellers the rights to publish for only two fourteen-year periods before a work entered the public domain, Johnson, like all authors, had to do their bidding and could not decide on his own to have any of his works republished. Having been asked by Strahan and the other publishers twice in the space of a year to revise his two major publications, Johnson found himself thinking freshly about literary property. Also, in July 1773, Boswell won a highly important 'cause' (the Scottish term for a legal case) in the Edinburgh Court of Session regarding literary property on behalf of the Edinburgh bookseller Alexander Don-aldson's fight against the London booksellers. Johnson read his notes on the cause and offered his viewpoints on them before they were published separately as a pamphlet early in 1774. On being asked by Strahan in March to state his ideas on copyright as part of the London publishers' efforts to appeal the Edinburgh ruling to the House of Lords, he clearly laid out his ideas on the subject in a balanced and impartial way that could not have entirely pleased Strahan: 'The author has a natural and peculiar right to the profits of his own work ... It is inconvenient to society that a useful book should become perpetual and exclusive property ... an author should retain during his life the sole right of printing and selling his work'. Still, authors had to live in the real world: 'the author must recede from so much of his claim, as shall be deemed injurious or inconvenient to society'; and an author's claim would indeed prove to be harmful if fifty years down the line a revision were badly needed and could not be done because the text was not in the public domain. Therefore, by his scheme a book 'may continue the property of the author or of those who claim from him about fifty years, a term sufficient to reward the writer without any loss to the public'. In effect, Johnson offered Strahan a commonsense compromise between what he saw as the author's rights as creator of an original work and the realities of the book trade and how it might protect him from piracy and earn him a profit.[13]

He went at the revision meticulously, using notes he had kept over the years of changes and additions he wanted to make if he ever got around to it; resurrecting the manuscript notebooks crammed with text and recyclable quotations that the desperate crisis in his original method had forced him to reject; eliminating many illustrative quotations and adding thousands of new ones; and correcting, deleting and adding to the definitions and notes on etymologies and usage. He also made some minor changes in the prefatory essays. He never revised any other of his other works so extensively.

Working with two of his old assistants, Peyton and Alexander Macbean, in an effective division of labour over which he maintained strict control, his efficiency was exemplary. From the outset his successful strategy was more or less simultaneously to complete large portions of the text across the alphabet so that Strahan's men could print several sections of the work at the same time. Except for one delay caused by the loss of the interleaved first edition sheets, he never delayed the printing process, varying his working methods as required and marking the changes directly on printed sheets of the first edition. In a review of 1772 – 73 in his diary he noted, 'I was able in those seasons to examine and improve my dictionary, and was seldom withheld from the work, but by my own unwillingness.' He was spared any illness until a few days after the fourth edition was published when he succumbed to a cold which grew violent for some ten weeks.[14]

Of all the changes he made in the *Dictionary*, by far his most substantial consisted of the illustrative quotations he deleted and added. There were largely three categories of additions: the Bible (drawn almost entirely from Alexander Cruden's *Concordance*), reflecting his systematic reading of the scriptures; poetry from the sixteenth, seventeenth and eighteenth centuries, mainly by Milton and Edward Young (whose death in 1765 freed Johnson to use him heavily); and religious prose by orthodox Anglican apologists and controversialists. The poetry quotations were dominated by Milton, whom he cited even more than Shakespeare. 'I think more highly of him now than I did at twenty,' he told Boswell a month after the edition was published, signifying that Milton's poetry, heavily inspired as it is by the Bible, was now a greater spiritual experience for him than ever before. What is interesting about all these additions and adjustments are the religious shifts in emphasis they introduce. His intention was to increase the religious and meditative associations of some words, making the entries sometimes feel like mini-prayers on the need for a stronger faith.[15]

There is another theme governing the illustrative quotations Johnson added that concerns Christianity in a political and doctrinal rather than inspirational way. He drew on a wide variety of writers, not always especially good ones, for hundreds of passages of theological prose to shore up his defences against aggressive pressure from many quarters for reform of Church of England doctrine. The passages, described by one critic as a 'stream of reminders', amount (in such a large work) to a necessarily diffused polemic against dissident writers and thinkers, potential parliamentary legislation affecting doctrine, and what he described as the irresponsible 'yelps' against the King and Lord North's ministry, particularly in the early 1770s. More personally, he felt that the chipping away at the Anglican liturgy, the Thirty-Nine Articles of the Church, the *Book of Common Prayer*, and the role of the clergy was endangering Christian faith in general and his own in particular. 'I think that permitting men to preach any opinion contrary to the doctrine of the Established Church tends, in a certain degree, to lessen the authority of the church,' he insisted to Langton, 'and consequently, to lessen the influence of religion.' He was hostile towards any challenge to the Church in the guise of Whig liberalisation.[16]

Reform of Church doctrine, in fact, was one of those subjects, along with death, Wilkes, America, monarchy, and a few others, that could make him erupt angrily in conversation if he were resisted. Although he was on the whole lax about attending church and taking Communion, except in the Easter period, such talk cut to his deepest fears about faith and salvation. On one occasion, when Boswell strayed into the always dangerous territory of Church doctrine, he witnessed Johnson's 'explosion of high-church zeal' – 'he had come close to my chair, and his eyes flashed with indignation'. Boswell 'bowed to the storm' and this time sensibly changed course.[17]

Johnson was finished with his *Dictionary* work in early October 1772 (except for reading of proofs) and the revised fourth edition came out in March 1773. It did not make much of a splash, receiving scarcely any critical attention in the press beyond what was written when the first edition came out almost two decades earlier. A couple of months after publication, he considered, 'Whether I shall ever revise it more, I know not.' He did not.[18]

[6]

Frank Barber, who was now living with Johnson again after five years at school, showed Boswell to the upstairs study in Johnson's Court when he arrived for his spring visit in mid-March 1772. 'Frank and I were pleased to renew our acquaintance', Boswell noted. 'I waited a little and then heard the great man coming upstairs. The sound of his feet upon the timber steps was weighty and well announced his approach. He had on an old purple cloth suit and a large whitish wig'. Delighted to have Boswell's 'noisy benevolence' with him again, Johnson embraced him, 'I am glad to see thee, I am glad to see thee. Come sit you down.' As he was leaving late at night after tea with Mrs Williams, Johnson burst out, 'I do love thee. I do love thee ... Good night, dear Sir. I am glad to see you again, very glad to see you again.' Thus began another of Boswell's annual recharges in Johnson's company.[19]

It was on this London visit, after dinner with him at General Paoli's on 31 March, that he first confided in his journal his momentous decision to write Johnson's biography: 'I have a constant plan to write the life of Mr Johnson. I have not told him of it yet, nor do I know if I should tell him. I said that if it was not troublesome and presuming too much, I would beg of him to tell me all the little circumstances of his life, what schools he attended, when he came to Oxford, when he came to London, etc., etc.. He did not disapprove of my curiosity as to these particulars, but said, "They'll come out by degrees".' Johnson had just remarked that 'nobody could furnish the life of a man but those who had eat and drank and lived in social intercourse with him', so Boswell felt pretty good about his chances. There is no evidence that Johnson had given much serious thought to who was best qualified to be his biographer, but with two intimate friends keeping journals, both of whom he encouraged to do so, the matter must occasionally have crossed his mind. At Johnson's Court late that night, he and Boswell spoke of their mutual friends and of writing biographies. 'I hope you'll write all their lives,' Johnson threw out.[20]

For the present, Mrs Thrale was too wrapped up in her family problems even to contemplate such a fanciful idea as writing the *Life* of her great friend, although she had far more opportunity throughout the year to hear him talk and observe his behaviour than Boswell did. Johnson involved himself in the welfare of the children and Mrs Salusbury ever more deeply and relished the chemical experiments he was able to conduct in the new laboratory Thrale had set up for him, 'drawing essences and colouring liquors'. Regrettably for him, his mad scientist behaviour one day spelled the abrupt end to the laboratory when, with the children and servants watching, he almost set himself on fire, or at least according to Mrs Thrale her husband thought so: 'the master of the house [was] persuaded, that his short sight would have been his destruction in a moment, by bringing him close to a fierce and violent flame. Indeed it was a perpetual miracle that he did not set himself on fire reading a-bed, as it was his constant custom, when exceedingly unable even to keep clear of mischief with our best help; and accordingly the fore-tops of all his wigs were burned by the candle down to the very net-work.' Thrale closed down the laboratory immediately. There were more serious problems at Streatham than that. Three of the little girls were ill with either rickets, scurvy, boils, hernias or ear infections. At least five-year-old Harry was 'strong and lively', and exceedingly bright, though not (in his mother's eyes) very attractive.[21]

In June calamity struck. After a run of foolish speculation and investments in his brewery business through which he hoped to out-flank the rival brewer Samuel Whitbread, Thrale found himself facing bankruptcy. Neither Mrs Thrale nor Johnson had ever taken much of an interest in the business, but now they sprang to his aid with the help of the chief clerk John Perkins, taking over the management of the brewery from the dazed Thrale. Mrs Thrale obtained several loans which, along with the pacification of the restive employees and reforms of business practices, enabled them to keep things going in the face of mounting debts. It would take nine years to pay them off. The crisis had a lasting effect on Thrale as he succumbed to the black dog, a 'horrible stupor which at last quenched entirely the spark of life'. To add to the misery, an eighth child was born in September and died ten hours later. 'One cannot grieve after her much,' Mrs Thrale wrote stoically, 'and I have just now other things to think of – this has been a sad lying in: my mother dying – & everything going wrong.'[22]

Johnson's role at this point was to steady Thrale who in his extremity and relative helplessness now resented the business being run by

Perkins so effectively, and to assist his wife by encouraging her and the children. Mrs Salusbury too, very ill, relied on him in her last days and in gratitude gave him the present of a chair that her daughter had covered in needle-point as 'a good little girl'. They all needed him, so it was a huge loss to them when he left again for Staffordshire. 'I am about to set out at nine tonight,' he wrote to Mrs Thrale on 15 October, comforting her as best he could: 'Do not be dejected, send for me, if I can do you either service or pleasure.'[23]

CHAPTER 27

The Road to the Hebrides

[1]

The only thing that seemed to occupy his attention in Lichfield was the state of affairs at Streatham. 'The brewhouse must be the scene of action,' he reminded Mrs Thrale. Unless the beer could be produced more economically, 'nothing can help us', but the problem was the fluctuating price of malt. The big news from her was that in her self-appointed role as 'skinflint' she had decided for the time being to move the family in November from Streatham to the Southwark house she hated. The role that Johnson took on in helping with the family finances appealed to his mathematical logic: 'Suppose that our former mode of life kept us on the level, we shall by the present contraction of expense, gain upon fortune a thousand a year, even though no improvements can be made in the conduct of the trade. Every two thousand pounds saves an hundred pound interest, and therefore as we gain more we pay less. We have a rational hope of success ... Let us therefore not be dejected'. 'If I make haste' to return, he asked, 'will you promise not to spoil me?' After spending November with Taylor watching the grass grow and admiring the bulls again, 'sometimes reading, and sometimes talking, not sleeping much', he was home by mid-December, bearing a gift of shells for Queeney from Miss Aston.[1]

Unfortunately, he could not resume his life with the Thrales because he suffered his first attack of gout and another onslaught of violent coughs – 'a vexatious catarrh' – that kept him housebound and feeling sorry for himself until the end of February 1773 as he waited for the revised *Dictionary* to be published. 'Here am I, sitting by myself, uncertain whether I shall dine on veal or mutton,' he grumbled to Mrs Thrale. 'I have been sometimes near fainting'. For more than ten weeks Frank and Mrs Williams allowed no one in to see him except Mrs Thrale for breakfast a few times when she came into town on

business. His house was fuller than ever because Frank had recently
married a white woman, Elizabeth Ball (Betsy) who was now also
living there. 'Frank has carried the empire of Cupid farther than many
men,' Johnson told Mrs Thrale. It was not a happy marriage.[2]

In March his health improved somewhat and by April he was
getting about town again. There was cheerful news about Goldsmith.
His new comedy, *She Stoops to Conquer*, was produced by George
Colman on 15 March at Covent Garden and was proving to be a smash
hit. Johnson had to use 'a kind of force' to get Colman to stage it.
Goldsmith's comment to Boswell was that 'stage earning is the dirtiest
money that ever a poor poet put in his pocket, and if my mind does
not very much alter, I have done with the stage'. Johnson loved the
play, 'I know of no comedy for many years that has so much exhilarated
an audience, that has answered so much the great end of comedy –
making an audience merry.' But his relationship with Goldsmith
remained a work in progress. Beauclerk told Boswell when he arrived
in town in early April for six weeks that they remained as testy as ever
with each other. The problem Johnson recognised in Goldsmith was
that 'he should not attempt [to talk] as he does, for he has not the
temper for it. He's so much hurt if he fails'. For all that, after an
evening's wrangling with Johnson, Goldsmith was seldom reluctant
to walk home with him, who was never slow to praise Goldsmith to
the skies as a literary genius – 'he stands in the first class'. Johnson
even felt that Goldsmith could be his 'best' biographer except that he
distrusted him: 'his particular malice towards me, and general disregard for truth, would make the book useless to all'.[3]

To Boswell's astonishment Johnson asked him to dine with him on
Easter Sunday – 'Sir, I generally have a pie on Sunday'. Boswell had
never heard of any of his friends ever having dined at his house 'in the
dusky recess of a court in Fleet Street'. He imagined they would be
eating the anticipated pie without the use of knives and forks, but
what he was served was a feast of soup, boiled leg of lamb and spinach,
a veal pie, rice pudding, pickled walnuts and onions, and wine. By
then Johnson knew his Scottish friend seriously intended to write his
Life, 'I hope you shall know a great deal more of me before you write
my Life', and he proceeded to shower him with details of his boyhood
in Lichfield.[4]

The climax of this London visit for Boswell was when Johnson
asked Goldsmith to propose him on his behalf for membership in the
club. He would have done it himself except he was on his way to

Oxford. Johnson later revealed to Boswell that 'several of the members wished to keep you out ... [but] knew, that if they refused you, they'd probably never have got in another. I'd have kept them all out.' When he heard he had been elected, Boswell rushed over to the Turk's Head and 'was introduced to such a society as can seldom be found. Mr Edmund Burke, whom I then saw for the first time ... Mr Garrick [elected that same spring], Dr Goldsmith ... Upon my entrance, Johnson placed himself behind a chair, on which he leaned as on a desk or pulpit, and with humorous formality gave me a *Charge*, pointing out the conduct expected from me as a good member of this Club'.[5]

[2]

Before leaving for Scotland, Boswell firmed up with Johnson their plan that in August he would travel up to Edinburgh for their tour of the Highlands and Hebrides. All the signs were now positive, though Goldsmith seemed sour about the tour and talked it down to Boswell, saying 'he would be a dead weight for me to carry, and that I should never be able to lug him along through the Highlands and Hebrides'. Only time would tell if Boswell would be able to pull it off.[6]

Throughout the summer everyone was uncertain if Johnson would actually embark on this great adventure. He suffered from fevers, a severe eye inflammation, numerous purges, and dreadful nights. 'It is not a very happy state,' he wrote to Mrs Thrale, 'when the mere preservation of life becomes its chief business.' Neither was he happy about abandoning Mrs Thrale when her family problems were increasing. Her mother was on her deathbed, his goddaughter Lucy Elizabeth was very ill, and Mr Thrale was turning his back on them all. She did not want him around and told him so, though he insisted that he live at Streatham part of the summer, adding another gloomy layer to her life just then. The Hebridean tour seemed to her what Johnson needed. She would be spared having to care for him in addition to everyone else, and for a while he would be able to get out of himself: 'Dissipation is to you a glorious medicine,' she told him, 'and I believe Mr Boswell will be at last your best physician'.[7]

The time of his departure was determined by the end of the summer term of the Court of Session in Edinburgh, which required Boswell's attendance, and also by the plans of Robert Chambers who, within the year, would leave for Bengal to take up his post there in the Supreme Court and who wished to bid farewell to his relations in Newcastle. The plan was for him to accompany Johnson this far. 'What an intellectual feast is before me!' Boswell wrote excitedly to Langton on 14 August, 'I shall never murmur though he should at times treat me with more roughness than ever.' With no small amount of encouragement and coaxing, much of it rigged by Boswell, Johnson launched himself from the metropolis on 6 August 1773.[8]

On the way up Johnson did his best to slide into the tourist mode in preparation for months of travel with Boswell. He and Chambers stopped at York, Durham and Alnwick Castle, the seat of Percy's patron the Duke of Northumberland who welcomed them for a few hours and showed them around the estate. Arriving in Newcastle, they were entertained by Chambers's mother for a night. After a night in Newcastle, where he parted company with Chambers, Johnson made the last leg to Edinburgh by 14 August. He sent word to Boswell from Boyd's Inn off the Head of Canongate that he had arrived. Boswell rushed down the High Street to meet him and arm-in-arm they marched back up it. On the way, with the evening effluvia wafting pungent all around them, Johnson leaned towards his host and said teasingly, 'I smell you in the dark!'[9]

Johnson had had no experience of travel, not having money for it until his pension and then finding himself constitutionally indisposed to do it except for short trips to Devon, Brighton and Staffordshire. If his pension had come his way twenty years earlier, he commented, he 'should have gone to Constantinople to learn Arabic', but now it was almost too late. He spoke from time to time of visiting Cairo, the Red Sea and the Great Wall of China, among other places – and the act of moving, getting somewhere, appealed to him greatly. The Hebridean journey had been initially his idea, a fulfilment of his fascination with the Hebrides ever since his father introduced him to Martin Martin's *Description of the Western Islands*. One of the (as yet) untapped resources he had in abundance as a potential traveller, as Boswell soon discovered, was his great physical strength and lack of squeamishness. Most of his friends were not up to such a journey. When Boswell mentioned to Voltaire in Ferney in 1764 that he and Johnson had spoken of such an adventure, Voltaire looked at him as if he had mentioned the North Pole: 'You do not insist on my accompanying you'?' 'No, Sir'. 'Then I am very willing you should go.' Adventure and the prospect of observing the lives, culture and manners of distant peoples in sublime and obscure regions at the edges of the

planet – wild, primitive, or savage life – were what ultimately persuaded Johnson in this instance to overcome his resistance to translating his dreams into reality. His good fortune was to have in Boswell
an ideal travelling companion – full of 'good humour and perpetual
cheerfulness'.[10]

Boswell did not anticipate the extent to which Johnson, even in the
remote Hebridean islands, would keep thinking about Mrs Thrale. Her
'enchantment over him seldom failed,' he wrote.[11] Johnson seemed constantly to be writing to her, letters he later used as the basis of his account
of the trip in *Journey to the Western Islands of Scotland* (1775). It would
have depressed Boswell to know that his companion, now in the spirit
of travel, was already planning a trip to Wales with the Thrales.

Johnson stayed with Boswell and his wife Margaret for three days
in their house in St James's Court. For most of that time the 'great,
the learned, and the elegant' filed through the house at all hours of
the day to meet him – for breakfast, dinner, teas and supper. Margaret
agreed to pour tea for him and guests anytime it was needed, and
according to her husband she insisted in giving up her own bed-
chamber to him. But all was not well with her. 'The truth is,' Boswell
wrote in the *Life*, 'his irregular hours and uncouth habits . . . could not
but be disagreeable to a lady'. As a result, Johnson incurred her
displeasure which it took him years of patient cajoling to overcome.
This was, after all, the man who was pulling her husband away from
her to London almost annually and who she thought had altogether
too much influence over him. On the very first night he and Boswell
sat up until two, long after Margaret had gone to bed. He also felt
'poorly' and probably needed some special attention from her. On top
of that, his frightening appearance threw her off balance. Boswell
described him: 'He was now in his sixty-fourth year, and was become
a little dull of hearing. His sight had always been somewhat weak . . .
His head and sometimes also his body shook with a kind of motion
like the effect of a palsy; he appeared to be frequently disturbed by
cramps or convulsive contractions, of the nature of that distemper
called St Vitus's dance.' As for Edinburgh, it did not impress him,
reminding him of 'the old part of Birmingham'. All in all, it was a
nervous beginning. With a sigh of relief, Boswell finally got him into
a post-chaise on 18 August with his servant and off they went towards
St Andrews on a journey that would last more than three months.[12]

Johnson's travels in Scotland

[3]

The first leg of Boswell's itinerary took them up the east coast via St Andrews to Aberdeen. In both places Johnson was received with wonder and plaudits from all manner of people, especially university faculty who were eager to meet him. He seemed less interested in the professors at St Andrews, however, than in an old woman who lived in the ruins of the cathedral vault with her cat and 'claimed a hereditary residence in it'. What interested him about her was what would chiefly interest him throughout the trip as a 'moral explorer' and amateur anthropologist – the way people lived their lives: 'Her habitation contained all that she had, her turf for fire was laid in one place, and her balls of coal dust in another, but her bed seemed to be clean.' Although he was given the freedom of the city in Aberdeen, Boswell became annoyed that the professors at Marischal College were afraid to speak to him.[13]

Towns were not, in any case, what Johnson had come to Scotland for. 'He always said', wrote Boswell, 'that he was not come to Scotland to see fine places, of which there were enough in England, but wild objects – mountains, waterfalls, peculiar manners'. He hoped to throw himself into the wilderness of the Highlands and Hebrides and participate in the primitive culture he found there. 'I have now the pleasure', he would write from the Isle of Skye, 'of going where nobody goes, and seeing what nobody sees.' Continuing north from Aberdeen, his spirits rose as they passed through rugged, wild, romantic beauty. His energy level soared. They came to Dunbuy Rock – 'just an island covered with seafowl' – and Bullers of Buchan, a large and dangerous basin surrounded by 'tremendous rocks' through one of which the sea boiled in furiously. They walked around this 'monstrous cauldron' on very narrow rocky edges 'so that it is somewhat horrid to move along'. Johnson warmed to the adventure and took off over the rocks with alacrity and courage. Boswell was alarmed to see him 'poking his way'. They clambered into a little boat and launched themselves into the thrashing waters, a foretaste of what lay ahead in tempestuous Hebridean waters: 'He was stout and wonderfully alert.'[14]

Travelling along the north-east coast, they then headed for Inverness, passing on the way 'the bleak and blasted heath' where Macbeth met the witches. 'I have had great romantic satisfaction in seeing Johnson upon the classical scenes of Shakespeare,' Boswell wrote to

Garrick. Johnson did admit to their imaginations being 'heated' but was not otherwise solemn, as Boswell was, on seeing the heath. Instead, he managed to spook Boswell that night with warnings that 'the witches would come and dance' at the foot of his bed. Boswell became so jittery he had to sleep with the door of his room open to Johnson's: 'This gave me security, and I soon fell asleep.'[15]

[4]

Their comfort level dropped suddenly after they turned south from Inverness. There they had to mount horses and with guides to lead the way ride along Loch Ness to Fort Augustus and then west to Glenelg, a little outpost next to the narrow channel they had to cross over to Skye. At Inverness, wrote Johnson, 'the appearance of life began to alter' as Highland manners became more evident. 'We were now to bid farewell to the luxury of travelling, and to enter a country upon which perhaps no wheel has ever rolled.' As they trekked down Loch Ness, Johnson's curiosity about the modes of life in this savage country came into full play, and even the sublime landscape somewhat stirred him: 'On the right the limpid waters of *Lough Ness* were beating their bank, and waving their surface by a gentle agitation. Beyond them were rocks sometimes covered with verdure, and sometimes towering in horrid nakedness.' Even so, it was not the wild beauty as much as the topography, geology, climate, movement of water and animal life that he found absorbing. Sitting down on a bank, 'such as a writer of Romance might have delighted to feign', with trees whispering over his head and 'a clear rivulet' streaming at his feet, he felt the calm soft air and that 'all was rudeness, silence, and solitude'. 'Whether I spent the hour well I know not,' he noted, referring mock-modestly to the fact that it was there he got the idea for his *Journey to the Western Islands of Scotland*.[16]

When they spotted a Highland hut on the banks of the loch – Boswell called it a 'wretched little hovel' – on an impulse they turned their horses towards it since 'our business was with life and manners'. In his *Journey* Johnson describes carefully how the hut was built and how the old woman they found within lived. The only light inside came through the front door and a hole in the thatch and, on entering, they could just make out the woman boiling goat's flesh in a kettle. Johnson questioned her about her family (five children and an eighty-year-old husband), their diet and 'whole system of economy', and religion. It is amazing he was able to understand her. Outside she had some poultry, a potato garden, goats, and some barley: 'She has all this from the labour of their own hands, and for what is necessary to be bought, her kids and her chickens are sent to market.' He was struck that such primitiveness could still exist in modern, industrial Britain: 'Such is the general structure of the houses in which one of the nations of this opulent and powerful island has been hitherto content to live.' The woman 'with true hospitality' then asked them 'to sit down and drink whisky', asking if they had any snuff to spare. The visit turned out to be richly comic when she said she was afraid they wanted to go to bed with her. Later they made merry over it, Boswell insisting it was Johnson 'who alarmed the poor woman's virtue. "No, sir," said he. "She'll say, there came a wicked young fellow, a wild young dog, who I believe would have ravished me had there not been with him a grave old gentleman who repressed him. But when he gets out of the sight of his tutor, I'll warrant you he'll spare no woman he meets, young or old." "No," said I. "She'll say, there was a terrible ruffian who would have forced me, had it not been for a gentle, mild-looking youth, who, I take it, was an angel!"'.[7]

Boswell spotted further comedy and incongruity in the spectacle of Johnson on a horse. A few days earlier, the tediousness of travel beginning to get to him, Johnson had complained about the prospect at some point of having to mount one. 'If we must *ride* much, we shall not go and there's an end on't'. 'You're a delicate Londoner,' Boswell teased him, 'you can't ride!' Johnson would have none of it, 'Sir, I shall ride better than you. I was only afraid I should not find a horse able to carry me.' Boswell had been spellbound by the sight of Johnson on a horse as they rode out of Inverness, 'As I saw him now for the first time ride along ... I thought of *London, A Poem*, or the *Rambler*, or *The False Alarm;* and I cannot express the ideas which went across my imagination.' He later found other words to describe him on a horse as they approached Glenelg down a steep hill when both Johnson and the horse, which 'staggered' under his weight, were fatigued after having climbed in 'the dreariness of solitude' over one thousand feet in three miles. The scene blends rich humour with an outbreak of Johnson's anger: 'As Mr Johnson was a great weight ... it did not go well, and he grumbled'. Boswell was entertained by the sight of the guides trying to distract him from the dangers by whistling at the goats and then saying to him, 'See such pretty goats', as they ran off: 'Here was now, a common ignorant horse-hirer imagining that he could divert, as one does a child, *Mr Samuel Johnson!* ... I laughed immoderately, and must laugh as often as I recollect it'. Johnson did not see anything funny in it, 'the only moment of my journey, in which I thought myself endangered'. As darkness came, Johnson became furious when Boswell suddenly rode off ahead to enquire about the inn at Glenelg: 'Mr Johnson called me back with a tremendous shout, and was really in a passion with me for leaving him.' They quarrelled and later Johnson told him, 'had you gone on, I was thinking that I should have returned with you to Edinburgh and then parted, and never spoke to you more.' Later at the inn Johnson admitted he had spoken in a 'passion' and that storming back to Edinburgh would have been ten times worse than Boswell's 'incivility'.[18]

On top of their fatigue and hunger, it was a bleak arrival at the watery threshold of the Hebrides because, as Johnson explained to Mrs Thrale, they found that the innkeepers were ill-prepared, with 'neither wine, bread, eggs, nor anything that we could eat or drink. When we were taken upstairs, a dirty fellow – "black as a Cyclops from the forge" – bounced out of the bed in which one of us was to lie.' The landlord produced some chops they could not eat and killed a couple of hens, 'of which Boswell made his servant broil a limb, with what effect I know not. We had a lemon, and a piece of bread, which supplied me with my supper'. 'Mr Johnson was calm,' Boswell wrote; 'I said he was so from vanity. "No," said he, "'tis from philosophy."' They then bedded down for the night on hay. Margaret Boswell had slipped sheets into their baggage, lest they 'catch' something along the way, but Johnson had his doubts: 'I thought sheets a slender defence, against the confederacy with which we were threatened, and by this time our Highlanders had found a place where they could get some hay; I ordered hay to be laid thick upon the bed, and slept upon it in my great coat. Boswell laid sheets upon his hay and reposed in linen like a gentleman.'[19]

They rose in the morning 'rustling from the hay' and crossed over to Skye, making their way to Armadale, the home of Sir Alexander Macdonald and his wife. There they found miserly and boorish hospitality, Boswell's portrayal of which in the *Tour* more than a decade later infuriated Macdonald so much that he challenged Boswell to a duel. There was some compensation for them in Johnson's mimicry of the beautiful Lady Macdonald, whose apparent stupidity was beyond belief to them. 'This woman would sink a ninety-gun ship,' Johnson complained. 'She is so dull – so heavy.' He kept mimicking her throughout the trip, adding later, 'the difference between that woman when alive, and when she shall be dead, is only this. When alive she calls for beer. When dead she'll call for beer no longer.' And Skye did not at first impress Johnson: 'A walk upon ploughed ground in England is a dance upon carpets, compared to the toilsome drudgery, of wandering in Skye.' Neither did he find, 'as zoologist', anything besides a huge otter to interest him. He reminded Mrs Thrale that he was not journeying through paradise: 'The use of travelling is to regulate imagination by reality, and instead of thinking how things may be, to see them as they are.' Everything at this point looked wildly bleak to him and the landscape bored him, 'a naked desert' with scarcely a village to be found. Philosophers like Rousseau who try to argue that life in such a place is happy, he wrote to Mrs Thrale, are deluding themselves.[20]

Matters improved when they were rowed in an open boat out of Broadford Bay ten miles out to the lovely island of Raasay for a few days at the invitation of the Macleod clan. Johnson sat 'high on the stern like a magnificent Triton', the wind whipping up the seas all around them. Boswell began to get sick but Johnson exulted, 'This now is the Atlantic. If I should tell at a tea-table in London that I have crossed the Atlantic in an open boat, how they'd shudder and what a fool they'd think me.' At Raasay they found hospitality, charm, grace, excellent food, dancing and intelligent conversation, 'all the marks of improved life'. It seemed as if people were coming out of the woodwork to see them.[21]

[5]

Returning to Skye they mounted horses again for Kingsburgh, where they met the famous Flora Macdonald who had helped the Young Pretender Prince Charles Edward, more popularly known as Bonnie Prince Charlie, escape after the Battle of Culloden, smuggling him dressed as her maid from Lewis to Portree, from where the Macleods took him to Raasay. Johnson slept 'in the bed in which the Prince reposed in his distresses', remarking facetiously, 'I have had no ambitious thoughts in it.' He told Boswell he would have given anything not to have slept in the bed, but at least he was not sleeping in the Prince's sacred sheets, 'which were never put to any meaner offices, but were wrapped up by the lady of the house, and at last, according to her desire, were laid round her in her grave'. It is not certain whether any Jacobite sentiment stirred in him as he lay there, but Boswell summed up his feelings about the Stuarts: 'Mr Johnson is not properly a *Jacobite*. He does not hold the *jus divinum* of kings ... He said to me once that he did not know but it was become necessary to remove the King at the time of the Revolution; and after the present family have had so long a possession, it appears to him that their right becomes the same that the Stuarts had ... I have heard him say he was so dubious that if holding up his right hand would have gained the victory to the Highland army in 1745, he does not know if he would have done it.'[22]

On the way to Flora Macdonald's beautiful home, Dunvegan Castle, built upon a rock overlooking the sea, Johnson fell off his horse, the only time this happened on the entire journey. It was so comfortable at Dunvegan that the foul weather making them extend their stay did not disturb him unduly. The gentle and soft-featured mistress of the house charmed him. But there was a sad awareness that financial plight would soon force her and her husband to emigrate temporarily to North Carolina, which they did the following year.[23]

After eight days the storms eased and they moved on to other Macleod homes at Ullinish and Talisker. The latter, like Raasay, turned out to be a model of grace and hospitality: 'You find that all the islanders even in these recesses of life are not barbarians'. A visitor while they were there, Donald Maclean or 'young Coll', who pleased Johnson with schemes of improving the family estates 'without hurting the people or losing the ancient Highland fashions', offered to take them on a tour of the smaller islands of Eigg, Muck, Coll and Tyree on the way to Mull, but there was unnerving news while they were there of shipwrecks along the coast in wild weather. Added to this, Johnson was becoming impatient with the weather and restless to return to Edinburgh: 'we grow afraid of deviating from our way home lest we should be shut up for months upon some little protuberance of earth, that just appears above the sea, and perhaps is scarcely marked upon a map.' He had had enough of the primitive.[24]

'I cannot but laugh to think of myself roving among the Hebrides at sixty,' Johnson observed while they waited to launch themselves on the next watery stage of their trip, 'I wonder where I shall rove at fourscore.' Upon the sea at last on 3 October in a twelve-ton vessel that had a little 'den' in the forecastle with two beds and a fire in it, this time it was Johnson who began to turn green. 'I exulted in being a stout seaman,' Boswell wrote, 'while Mr Johnson was quite in a state of annihilation', but soon he also became 'woefully sick'. They made for Iona, known also as Icolmkill. It was a furious and dangerous voyage and in an emergency, with night falling, they had to change course for the harbour at Coll with no guarantee that even if they could get there the waves would allow them to enter it. A man with one eye steered. After hours of dramatic plunging into the sea, well after midnight, they made it. Kept in some ignorance below, Johnson 'had all this time been quiet and unconcerned. He had lain down on one of the beds, and having got free of sickness, was quite satisfied ... He was lying in philosophic tranquility, with a greyhound of Coll's at his back keeping him warm'. They spent the night in the boat cold and wet.[25]

The greater trial for Johnson was the tedium of being marooned for ten days on Coll, a 'barren island' where there was almost nothing to do while the storm blew and it rained incessantly. Coll had an unused elegant house there in which they waited. Johnson grew peevish. 'I want to be on the mainland, and go on with my existence,' he protested. 'My eye is ... not fully recovered, my ears are not mended, my nerves seem to grow weaker, and I have been otherwise not as well as I sometimes am ... This climate is perhaps not within my degrees of healthy latitude.' They were reduced to arguing over whose bed had the best linen and bed posts. 'If you have the best posts,' Johnson declared, 'we'll have you tied to 'em and whipped.' Finally, they found a sloop carrying kelp and convinced its master to take them to Tobermory in Mull from where Johnson hoped they could easily return to the mainland, perhaps without seeing Iona.[26]

When Boswell bragged that Mull was now the fourth Hebridean island they had set foot on, Johnson was not impressed: 'Nay, we cannot boast of the number we have seen. We thought we should see many more. We thought of sailing about easily from island to island; and so we should, had we come at a better season.' Still, he admitted they had seen enough for a good idea of 'the system of insular life'. Boswell was determined that they would not miss Iona, so after a couple of days of confining rain, they mounted little Mull horses for a seriously rugged, exhausting ride 'over rocks naked and valleys untracked' towards the western side of the island where they could cross to the beautiful tiny island of Inchkenneth, leased by Sir Allan Maclean. At one point they had to plunge into deep water to cross a rivulet. Johnson was cranky and totally disinclined to hear the history of the Maclean clan. 'I'd rather hear the history of the Thrales,' he muttered. Arriving at the western coast of Mull in the dark 'weary and dejected', without any place to sleep, they were rescued luckily by an Irish boat on which they crossed to Ulva, a small island just off the coast, where they spent the night. The following day they crossed to Inchkenneth, an island a mile long and half a mile wide to stay with the Macleans in their humble cottage. They were the only family on the island. [27]

Leaving Inchkenneth behind as they rowed off with Maclean towards Iona some forty miles down the coast, Johnson showed his mettle again when by candlelight they penetrated five hundred feet into Mackinnon's Cave, accessible only in low tide. Emerging well before the tide could trap them, they continued down the coast while the rowers sang Erse songs, took a quick meal on some black rocks, and found themselves again in the dark at sea as they approached Iona. To their right they had been able to make out the island of Staffa, described by Sir Joseph Banks the previous year as one of the world's greatest natural curiosities, but it was late and the sea was too rough to contemplate landing on it in order to see the famed Fingal's Cave, immortalised in 1830 by Mendelssohn in his *Hebrides Overture*. 'This is roving among the Hebrides, or nothing is,' Johnson shouted out. They ploughed through rough water by moonlight. The lights of the little village on Iona then came into view and soon they were safely ashore at 'the venerable seat of ancient sanctity, where secret piety reposed.' Boswell and Maclean were carried ashore by the rowers, but Johnson 'sprang into the sea and waded vigorously out'. They slept that night in a barn 'well stocked with hay'. [28]

Taking in all the religious sites the next morning, which Johnson described at length in his *Journey*, they returned to Mull the same day and, taking leave of Maclean, were back on the mainland on 22 October. 'The difficulties of peregrination' (as Johnson put it) now at an end, they immediately struck out by horseback for the Duke of Argyll's seat at Inveraray where Boswell had an invitation for them to stay for two days, awkward ones for him as it turned out, since the duchess disliked him. From there they made their way down through 'a black and dreary region', the hills 'streaming with waterfalls' filled with almost constant rain, to the banks of Loch Lomond, then to Glasgow, and finally further south to meet up with Boswell's father at the family estate at Auchinleck just east of Ayr. Johnson did not mention it in his letters to Mrs Thrale, but in spite of Boswell's warning he fell into a violent argument with Lord Auchinleck in the upstairs library over Whiggism, Presbyteriansim, Toryism and Episcopacy. Boswell was desperately unhappy over the anger that ignited between these two 'intellectual gladiators', and was helplessly caught between them. On 9 November the two travellers returned to Edinburgh, eighty-three days after leaving it. Again people streamed into Boswell's house to see the famous scholar and moralist fresh from his remarkable expedition, and again Margaret found herself devoting 'the greater part of the morning to the endless task of pouring out tea for my friend and his visitors'.[29]

None too soon for her, on 19 November, Johnson left the city in a post-chaise and, stopping at various places on the way, arrived home on the 26th. 'I know Mrs Boswell wished me well to go; her wishes have not been disappointed,' he wrote to Boswell the day after. 'She is a sweet lady,' he added the following March, 'only she was so glad to see me go, that I have almost a mind to come again, that she may again have the same pleasure.' Now there were other things to think about. The epic Hebridean odyssey had whet his appetite for another lengthy expedition and he was already setting his sights on one to Wales with the Thrales. She had written to him in October: 'When you sigh for an island of your own remember that Rasselas could never settle the limits of his imaginary dominion, but a sight of Wales in the meantime may not be amiss. 'Tis long since I saw my own country, but there are untrodden paths in it which may perhaps be as curious as any in Scotland; barefooted girls too in plenty as I remember.' 'I am grown very superior to wind and rain,' he wrote from Auchinleck, 'and am too well acquainted both with mire and with rocks, to be afraid of a Welsh journey.' For three months Boswell had him all to himself. Now it was the Thrales's turn.[30]

CHAPTER 28

Politics and Travel

[1]

He set to work immediately gathering materials for his *Journey to the Western Islands of Scotland*, through the winter and into the spring badgering Boswell to provide him with what he needed. In addition to what Boswell and a few others sent him, he had a few notes of his own to draw on – more like a haphazard notebook than a journal – which have, unfortunately, been lost, and his letters to Mrs Thrale which as always she was careful to keep. Boswell's journal was a goldmine of information but he did not bring it with him to London until his next visit in March 1775, too late to be of any help.[1]

Once he got down to composing his *Journey* in the spring, he wrote it rapidly. He delivered almost the entire manuscript to Strahan on 20 June. By mid-October 240 pages had been printed and he anticipated that the book would be out in a month or so, 'a pretty book, I hope, it will be.' The printing, however, was not finished until about mid-December and two thousand copies of the book not published until 18 January 1775 at a price of five shillings. Strahan thought the book would sell well, so while it was printing he decided on another two thousand copies for a second edition. Johnson received 200 guineas for the book.[2]

It was favourably reviewed in London and sold briskly, and in Dublin three pirated reprints appeared within a few months. It was the talk of the town. He sent a copy in December to the King who 'fell to reading the book as soon as he got it, [and] when anything struck him, he read aloud to the Queen'; the Queen, however, 'would not stay to get the King's book' and borrowed her own copy. When Boswell came to London in the spring, Lord Mansfield greeted him with, 'We have all been reading your travels, Mr Boswell.' Concerned that Johnson would say things in the book that would embarrass him at home, Boswell had asked him if he could read the book in manuscript. Johnson reassured him it was all right because he was dealing 'more in notions than facts'. He also ignored his fellow traveller's offer to correct errors in the first edition. What was more difficult to ignore was the hue and cry raised by many in Scotland.[3]

Just before publication Strahan showed James Macpherson some passages ridiculing his claim that he used authentic Gaelic manuscripts for his *Ossian*. In the book Johnson called Macpherson a fraud and demanded the only proof that would satisfy him: the manuscripts. Macpherson was by then accustomed to his fame as the man who had brought Ossian to the attention of European writers, artists and composers. Proud and incensed at Johnson's challenge, he wrote to him rudely, demanding a retraction. We do not have this letter, but we have Johnson's celebrated response on 20 January 1775, which is about as famous as his snub of Lord Chesterfield: 'I received your foolish and impudent note. Whatever insult is offered me I will do my best to repel, and what I cannot do for myself the law will do for me. I will not desist from detecting what I think a cheat, from any fear of the menaces of a ruffian ... I thought your book an imposture from the beginning ... You may print this if you will.' Macpherson 'little knew the character of Dr Johnson,' Boswell wrote, 'if he supposed that he could be easily intimidated.' The controversy continued for years, however, and Johnson even became cross with Boswell for his mild prevarication on the matter: 'You then are going wild about Ossian? ... If there are manuscripts, let them be shown, with some proof that they are not forged for the occasion.' Beyond Macpherson, as Johnson told Hector, 'the Scotch are angry'. His prejudice against the Scots and alleged Jacobitism were revived in Scottish reviews as he was comprehensively accused of rudeness and downright obtuseness by insisting, for example, that Scotland had virtually no trees. Boswell felt this was grossly unjust: 'Johnson treated Scotland no worse than he did even his best friends, whose characters he used to give as they appeared to him, both in light and shade.'[4]

Far less personal and autobiographical than Boswell's *Tour to the Hebrides* (1785), the *Journey* is a sweeping and far deeper assessment of life in the Highlands and Hebrides, including the clan system, the nature of an oral society, mountain isolation, Gaelic culture, the unexpected appearance of civilised culture in the middle of the primitive, Catholicism unaffected by the Protestant Reformation, and the poverty and customs of crofting life that made him reflect on the benefits of civilisation and culture. One important effect of the book was an increased awareness of the economic plight of the Highlanders and what was driving them to emigrate to America. It also accelerated interest in travel to the Highlands and more generally the north of Britain, which became popular tourist destinations in the late eighteenth century, the subject of popular travel accounts in the nineteenth century, and the setting for musical compositions, novels and poetry.[5]

[2]

Chambers's departure for Calcutta, newly married, in the spring of 1774 genuinely saddened Johnson. They would never see each other again although Johnson's imagination travelled with him. His deep affection for the young judge never dimmed and he continued to write to him, maintaining his considerable interest in the culture and traditions of India. His oriental tales in the *Rambler* were all set in the country. In a letter to his acquaintance Warren Hastings, Governor-General of India, which Chambers personally delivered, he declared his desire for information about India and the 'traditions and histories of the East' and urged Hastings to explore the 'remains of its ancient edifices, and trace the vestiges of ruined cities' so that on his return to England 'we shall know the arts and opinions of a race of men from whom very little has been hitherto derived'. He himself had cherished dreams of emigrating to India ever since the early 1750s when he almost accompanied his friend Joseph Fowke who was returning there to make a fortune with the East India Company. 'Had I thought then, as I do now,' he remarked in 1776, 'I should have gone.'[6]

He suffered the greatest shock, however, in early April 1774. 'Chambers . . . is gone far,' he wrote to Langton, 'and poor Goldsmith is gone much further.' Goldsmith had suddenly and tragically died of a fever, just a few months following the stage triumph of his *She Stoops to Conquer*. It was widely suspected that his death was hastened by the use of Dr Robert James's fever powder. He was forty-four. The members of the club took this 'catastrophe' badly, although none attended his burial on 9 April 1774 in the Temple Church burial ground. Boswell wrote to Garrick, 'I have not been so much affected with any event that has happened of a long time.' Johnson was quiet in his letters about the tragedy except for this qualified eulogy to Langton: 'He died of a fever exasperated, as I believe, by the fear of distress. He had raised money and squandered it, by every artifice of acquisition and folly of expense. But let not his frailties be remembered. He was a very great man.' Reynolds later organised a monument for him in Westminster Abbey, paid for by the Club, for which Johnson wrote a Latin inscription; and in 1776 Johnson took over from Percy the task of writing his biography, which he never accomplished. There would now be no more quarrels with 'Goldie' at the Club.[7]

Happier days were ahead. The Thrales were planning a tour through Italy with Baretti as their guide. Now in the travelling mode, Johnson had his heart set on it far more than he had on the Hebridean tour. For a long time he had been thrilled with the expectation of a visit to the 'classic ground' of Italy as a fulfilment of his studies as a classical scholar. But Mrs Thrale was preoccupied with her inheritance on her mother's death of some Salusbury family property at Bach-y-Graig in Flintshire of which she was eager to take possession. So after much indecision the Italian tour was shelved and replaced by the less promising scheme of a trip to Wales to see to the family home, visit friends along the way, and have a look at the northern part of the country. Leaving Baretti behind in charge of Streatham, on 5 July 1774 the Thrales, Queeney and Johnson, rather grandly in Thrale's coach with four post-horses, left for Wales via Lichfield and Ashbourne. They did not plan on the trip consuming as many as ten weeks.

The Thrale expedition made its way first to Lichfield where they stayed three days. Johnson kept the Thrales busy there, taking them to Richard Greene's museum, his home which filled Mrs Thrale 'with emotion', and the cathedral. They also visited Erasmus Darwin – never one of Johnson's favourites – at his house in the Close, Lucy at her large house who showed them Reynolds's portrait of Johnson and one of her mother, and Elizabeth Aston at Stowe Hill, whom Mrs Thrale described as something of an 'oddity' but 'a high-bred woman, quite the remains of an old beauty'. At Ashbourne, Mrs Thrale was astonished by the 'magnificence' of Taylor's seat – no wonder, she must have thought, Johnson came to visit him so often. From there they made an excursion to Chatsworth which did not please her in any way, and Kedleston Hall which did not please Johnson – 'more cost than judgement'. They stayed ten days with Taylor, 'one of the happiest of the human race', as Mrs Thrale oddly described him.[8]

So much for the part of the journey Johnson planned. The rest was up to the Thrales as they passed into northern Wales at the end of

July, keeping close to the north coast. When they reached Bach-y-Graig they were all disappointed. The house was small, the woods were sparse, and there was no garden, though Mrs Thrale felt the place had potential. Johnson's diary reveals he was not slow to belittle what struck him as the ordinariness of certain Welsh scenes like the River Clwyd, which he called 'a brook'. 'Let us', he proposed to Mrs Thrale, 'jump over it directly, and show them how an *Englishman* should treat a *Welch* river.' He appeared to be little interested in buildings, especially ruins, although Boswell noted he agreed that Wales abounded with magnificent castles: 'One of the castles in Wales could contain all of the castles he had seen in Scotland'. What aroused his enthusiasm most were signs of modern industry. At Holywell, it was not the history and beauty of St Winifred's Well, one of the so-called Seven Wonders of Wales, that spurred him to write in his diary at length but the brass, copper and iron works nearby where the river turned nineteen mills in the space of two miles. 'I have enlarged my notions', he wrote. The busy spectacle of such 'multiplied operations' of manufacturing processes lifted his spirits and temporarily made him forget his ailments.[9]

After reaching as far as Carnarvon and the foot of Mt Snowdon, they began their faster return journey. Crossing into England, they rode south in a downpour into the landscape of Johnson's youth, very near Stourbridge and Pedmore and full of memories for him of Cornelius Ford and his old grammar school. Hagley Park was next, the seat of the Lytteltons, where 'respect and kindness' were wanting, reviving for Johnson not entirely pleasant memories of his visit there as a boy with Cornelius. 'We made haste from a place where all were offended,' he wrote.[10]

They spent a night with Hector and his sister in Birmingham and saw more manufacturing wonders, including the factory of Matthew Boulton, who in partnership with James Watt, invented the steam engine. The factory turned out Sheffield plate, buttons, spoons and other items. It frustrated him that his eyesight did not allow him to see the 'enginery' distinctly. The next stop was Blenheim, which made little impression on Johnson, and after that Oxford, which greatly impressed Mrs Thrale. They spent the next few days there, visiting the Bodleian and several colleges and dining splendidly with their host John Coulson in the Hall at University College and with Johnson's good friend the melancholic Robert Vansittart, Regius Professor of Civil Law, who cornered Johnson to talk to him about melancholia.[11]

The last stop before returning to London was Burke's seat Gregories near Beaconsfield in Buckinghamshire, where they spent the night. They were received with 'open arms', though Burke had to be away the next day and returned late, said Mrs Thrale, 'much flustered with liquor'. They awoke to the news that Parliament had been dissolved and there was to be a new general election, distressing news for Mrs Thrale who realised immediately they would now have to return to dreary Southwark to campaign for her husband's seat instead of easing into the bucolic peace of Streatham with the family after almost three months on the road.[12]

While Johnson found the country 'beautiful and rich', he assured Boswell in October that Wales 'is so little different from England, that it offers nothing to the speculation of the traveller'. 'I am glad that I have seen it,' he told Taylor, 'though I have seen nothing, because I now know that there is nothing to be seen.' When Boswell became restless in the autumn of 1777 for another journey with Johnson and spoke of travelling to Wales, Johnson was nonplussed: 'Except the woods of Bachycraigh,' he wrote to him, 'what is there in Wales? What that can fill the hunger of ignorance, or quench the thirst of curiosity?' 'Shall we go to Ireland,' Boswell suggested, 'of which I have seen but little?' Johnson's mind was turning on something much more exotic and adventurous, a trek to the Baltic and perhaps some 'more northern regions' that Boswell had half seriously suggested when they were on Skye but now was 'shrinking' from.[13]

The trip to Wales had not been a huge success. Queeney had been ill much of the time, Thrale uncommunicative, and Johnson on the whole unimpressed and unimpressive, at least to Mrs Thrale. Indeed, she wrote in her journal, 'Travelling with Mr Johnson I cannot bear'.[14] She, too, was ill for much of the second half of the journey. She hated the rough roads, and was, moreover, pregnant again. She knew Johnson would never produce a book about their travels to match the one he was about to publish about the Hebrides. He knew it, too.

[3]

It was timely that Johnson should hear of the new election while staying at Gregories since Burke would play such a large part in it. His admiration for Burke's intellect was greater than ever, but there was a persistent political tension between them. When he first met Burke at Garrick's house in 1758, and Burke firmly disagreed with him on the subject of Bengal and the Government's efforts to control the East India Company's activities there, Johnson suddenly conceived a liking for the man. He said to Arthur Murphy later, 'If this be the kind of man he is, would that he were ours' – that is, he would be better politically employed in what in some respects might have passed for Tory circles. In 1765, when the Whig Marquess of Rockingham became prime minister, Burke became his private secretary, and after he was elected member for Parliament in 1766 joined the so-called Rockingham Whigs. 'Burke is a great man by Nature, and is expected soon to attain civil greatness,' Johnson said – but his controversial views and fiery obsessiveness kept him down. He is 'unequal', Johnson said, 'he is a lion, who lashes himself into a fury with his own tail'. He tended to divide the world into friends and enemies, which Johnson thought was his worst enemy.[15]

They also differed in that Burke was idealistic and Johnson sceptical and rational. Burke was drawn to abstract ideals whereas Johnson tended to reason from the more complicated 'moral' standpoint of individual human beings. The two men did not discuss politics seriously in the presence of each other, but what Johnson objected to was Burke's narrow party adherence, 'right or wrong', in the belief that in order to rise to power his best option was to stick with the Rockingham Opposition. This smacked of dishonesty to Johnson: 'I do not say that he is *not* honest; but we have no reason to conclude from his political conduct that he *is* honest.' For his part, Burke's judgement of Johnson's politics was equally harsh, asserting, even after Johnson's death, that in his pamphlet on the Falklands he knew he was wrong in charging that the Opposition were 'endeavouring to involve the nation in a war on account of the Falkand Islands'. Boswell thought Burke was even abusive on the subject.[16]

Johnson's part in what Mrs Thrale called 'this filthy election' was to help her husband by writing three brief political addresses to the electors of Southwark. 'We lead a wild life', Mrs Thrale wrote to him on 4 October 1774 at Johnson's Court, but it would be all over in a week. She felt Thrale would win but not by much. 'The patriots have the mob of course,' she added. It was at these 'patriots' of the opposition Johnson took aim in his third major political pamphlet of the 1770s, *The Patriot*, published anonymously on 12 October. Boswell worried when he heard about his pamphlet that it had taken time away from his work on the *Journey*, but Johnson reassured him he wrote it in one day and had 'heard little of it' since.[17]

The pamphlet was an excuse to take another swipe at Wilkes by attacking the popular cant about 'patriotism'. It was obviously not that Johnson failed to support liberal ideas of personal, social and religious freedom central to the Enlightenment. Far from it. Since the 1730s he had argued for them in all sorts of ways. Rather, his anger was over the appropriation of these ideas by the loud malcontents who indiscriminately slung around the term 'patriot' on behalf of political expediency, to rouse up the masses for selfish personal ends, especially in opposition to the King and even to the point of rejoicing in the successes of Britain's foreign enemies: 'A man may have the external appearance of a Patriot, without the constituent qualities; as false coins have often lustre, tho' they want weight.' These are fraudulent patriots 'who rave and rail' yet do not care for the public, hoping 'to force their way to riches by virulence and invective, and are vehement and clamorous, only that they may be sooner hired to be silent'. And looking across the Atlantic to the growling turbulence in America, he anticipated his next explosive pamphlet: 'That man therefore is no Patriot, who justifies the ridiculous claims of American usurpation; who endeavours to deprive the nation of its natural and lawful authority over its own colonies: those colonies, which were settled under English protection; were constituted by an English charter; and have been defended by English arms'.[18]

The pamphlet had no influence on the election because it was published after it was over. Thrale won anyway with a reduced majority over candidates who were Wilkes supporters and had provoked a good deal of rioting in the borough. 'Mr Thrale has had a very violent and formidable opposition which he has very triumphantly overcome,' Johnson announced to Taylor on 20 October 1774. While Mrs Thrale, her family and Johnson rejoiced that the 'cruel fatigues' of the election were behind them, Johnson was primed to write something else about 'patriots', the American problem and the political state of Britain in general.[19]

After obliging Charlotte Lennox first thing in January by writing 'Proposals' for her *Works*, he was ready to turn his attention to America. 'I am going to write about the Americans,' he informed Boswell on 21 January 1775 – 'But mum, it is a secret'. The reason it was secret was that Lord North's ministry had asked him to write a reply to a so-called 'Bill of Rights' that the American Continental Congress – which Johnson in the third edition of the pamphlet in 1775 called 'a

seditious meeting punishable by law' – had drawn up during its
first ever session held between 5 September and 26 October. That
document insisted on colonial autonomy regarding fiscal legislation
and rehearsed the grievances and justification of the Colonies in the
face of what it described as British oppression. By the end of February,
Johnson had completed his *Taxation No Tyranny* and Strahan had
printed it.[20]

The Americans were complaining that British taxation of them was
unconstitutional because as subjects of a sovereign state they could be
taxed only by their consent through representation in Parliament, and
such representation did not exist. They protested they were too far
away to be directly represented. Johnson devoted the first part of his
pamphlet to disproving both these contentions. 'In sovereignty there
are no gradations', and Americans could not expect any special treatment among the many British colonies. 'A colony is to the mother-
country as a member to the body ... the body may subsist, though
less commodiously, without a limb, but the limb must perish if it be
parted from the body'. Perhaps, he continued, 'Our colonies ...
however distant, have been hitherto treated as constituent parts of the
British Empire', and as such they have their privileges and obligations.
The American colonies 'as subordinate communities are liable to
taxation, because they all share the benefits of government'. It is
incumbent on them to prove 'that the Parliament ever ceded to them
a dispensation from that obedience, which they owe as natural-born
subjects'. By seditiously raising armies and forming alliances with rival
countries, they run the risk of forfeiting their colonial charters and
having to be subdued by 'stricter laws and stronger obligations'. In the
second part, Johnson accuses them of ingratitude and being hood-
winked by 'patriots' and self-seeking anarchists. In response to the
efforts of American 'croakers of calamity' and 'dictators of sedition'
to spread terror in British hearts by suggesting that if the British
Government could make slaves of them in North America, it could
just as easily make slaves of its subjects at home, his anger swelled: 'I
should gladly see America return half of what England has expended
in her defence ... But probably in America, as in other places, the
chiefs are incendiaries, that hope to rob in the tumults of a conflagration, and toss brands among a rabble passively combustible'.
Agitators like the 'master of mischief' Benjamin Franklin, he protested, are in the business of putting 'in motion the engine of political
electricity' – an allusion to Franklin's electrical experiments that, in

Samuel Johnson. Generally accepted as the 1775 'blinking Sam' portrait by
Reynolds. It shows Johnson poring over a book, obviously near-sighted
and struggling to make out the words.

Unfinished portrait of Johnson by James Barry, *c*.1777–80.

A Young Black by Reynolds, *c.*1770. It is now generally accepted that this is Francis Barber, Johnson's servant, who at the age of ten in 1752 was placed in his care.

blessing of God, is to contend with
them, and, if I can, to conquer them.

 My Resolutions are
To conquer Scruples. Dij.
To read the Bible this year.
To try to rise more early.
To Study Divinity.
To live methodically.
To oppose Idleness.
To frequent Divine Worship.

 Almighty and most mer-
ciful Father, before whom I now appear ~~gone~~ loaden with the sins of
another year, Suffer me ~~once more~~ yet again
to call upon Thee for pardon and
peace. O God, grant me repentance,

A page from his diary in which Johnson lists resolutions 'to conquer scruples.
To read the Bible this year. To try to rise more early. To Study Divinity.
To live methodically. To oppose idleness. To frequent Divine Worship.'

Frances ('Fanny') Burney, author of the bestseller *Evelina* (1778). She was a personal favourite of Johnson's, a young friend and admirer.

Hannah More, philanthropist and religious writer, by Frances Reynolds, c.1780. She was befriended by Johnson and was a great success in his and Elizabeth Montagu's circles.

Frances Reynolds, painter and sister of Joshua Reynolds. Members of her family thought she might have married Johnson if she had wished to.

Edmund Burke in the 1780s. Burke was a member of the Club and one of Johnson's closest and most respected friends.

A plaster cast of the 1784 bust of Johnson by William Cumberland
Cruikshank and James Hoskins, incorporating the death-mask.

fact, he much admired. It is all absurd cant, just as it is in Britain in the mouths of Whigs like Wilkes. 'If slavery be . . . fatally contagious,' he asks, 'how is it that we hear the loudest yelps for liberty among the drivers of Negroes?' The hypocrisy of the American position, he gasped, was breathtaking.[21]

There is more than just a hint of Johnson's repulsion over the American thirst for independence in the diary of the Revd Thomas Campbell, an Irish clergyman who came to London in the spring of 1775 specifically to meet Johnson and a few other luminaries. Befriended by the Thrales, he was invited by them several times to dinner where he met Johnson, Boswell, Langton, Murphy, Baretti and Dr Nathan Wetherell, the new Master of University College, Oxford. Johnson called him 'a fine showy talking man'. The diary provides a rare glimpse – apart from Boswell – of the Johnsonians relaxing with each other over good food and unguarded conversation. He recorded Johnson saying that one of the measures he advocated to humble the Americans, which 'the Ministry expunged', was 'to quarter the army in the cities, and if any refused free quarters, he would pull down that person's house, if it was joined to other houses, but would burn it if it stood alone'. When Campbell 'coolly' suggested that the Government had not 'succeeded so well in burning the cities, and roasting the inhabitants of America', Johnson agreed that Britain had erred on the side of too much diplomacy: 'had we treated the Americans as we ought, and as they deserved, we should have at once razed all their towns – and let them enjoy their forests'. This was no exaggeration of his violent attitudes regarding the Americans. Three years later at Charles Dilly's house one evening in the company of the Quaker Mrs Mary Knowles, he was still fuming over them: 'I am willing to love all mankind, *except an American*.' Boswell was surprised by the ferocity of his remarks, that he 'breathed out threatenings and slaughter', called the Americans 'rascals – robbers – pirates', and exclaimed that he would 'burn and destroy them'. When checked by someone, he 'roared out another tremendous volley, which one might fancy could be heard across the Atlantic'.[22]

The pamphlet went into four editions in 1775, and was reprinted with the other three political tracts of the 1770s in *Political Tracts* the following year under his name. It was greeted with a howl of criticism in a stream of hostile pamphlets, newspapers, and reviews. 'The patriots pelt me with answers,' he noted. Fretting somewhat that the pamphlet had not sold enough, he said to Boswell, 'I think I have not been attacked enough for it. Attack is the re-action; I never think I have hit hard, unless it rebounds'. The response in America was of course predictably hostile. When someone said his works would no longer be admired there, Boswell piped up, 'No, we shall soon hear of his being hung in effigy'. 'I should be glad of that,' Johnson replied, 'that would be a new source of fame'. Nonetheless, the Government was grateful and three weeks later he received an honorary D.C.L. from Oxford. 'They have sent me a degree of Doctor of Laws', he wrote to Mrs Thrale from Oxford on 1 April, 'with such praises in the diploma, as, perhaps ought to make me ashamed; they are very like your praises. I wonder whether I shall ever show them to you.' With the approval of Lord North, the degree had been organised by his new friend Nathan Wetherell of University College, who anticipated and met with some opposition to awarding the degree. When he and Johnson visited Oxford together the following March, Boswell got the impression from Wetherell that 'there were at Oxford some who did not admire and reverence Mr Johnson as some of us do'.[23]

[4]

Johnson's political pamphlets, especially *Taxation No Tyranny*, landed him in political skirmishes within a highly vexed political environment. These fed the adrenalin in his naturally combative temper, but they brought him notoriety more than literary praise as England's most esteemed author. Some were even saying they could no longer read his moral essays with undiluted satisfaction knowing now that he had 'prostituted' his talents 'under the character of a political writer'.[24] When it came down to it, he himself felt he had written them only for the moment and that they had left him with an empty feeling. He did after all tell Boswell, 'politics are now nothing more than means of success in life', devoid of principles, although the subject continued to fascinate him.[25]

On his spring visit in 1775, Boswell noticed that Johnson seemed to have become more extreme than ever in many of his opinions, something of a caricature of himself. His views on America were especially exaggerated. 'Such extravagance is really ludicrous,' Boswell noted. Dr Campbell was not at all pleased when he first met Johnson at this time: 'he has the aspect of an idiot, without the faintest ray of sense gleaming from any one feature – with the most awkward garb, and unpowdered grey wig, on one side only of his head – he is forever dancing the devil's jig, and sometimes he makes the most drivelling effort to whistle some thought in his absent paroxysms.' He 'flew in[to] a passion' rather too much. His remarks on people were inordinately critical. About Thomas Gray, whose poetry he did not on the whole admire, he was contemptuous: 'he was dull in company, dull in his closet, dull everywhere. He was dull in a new way; and this made many people think him great.' 'You are not a lukewarm man,' Campbell had the temerity to say to him. At Oglethorpe's for dinner, Johnson could not bear Boswell's questioning any longer and simply got up and abruptly left. On the way home in Langton's coach, he complained, 'Boswell's conversation consists entirely in asking questions, and it is extremely offensive.'[26]

None of this alienated Boswell, who was as bold as ever asking frank questions. He understood that 'Johnson's roughness was only external, and had no participation with his heart,' and also that he often seemed unaware of the bludgeoning he often gave people. On a coach ride to Twickenham to dine with the minor poet Owen Cambridge at his beautiful seat on the Thames, Johnson stretched himself out and amazed Boswell with, 'I look upon *myself* as a good-humoured fellow.' Boswell came back at him, 'No, no, Sir; that will *not* do. You are good-natured, but not good-humoured. You are irascible. You have not patience with folly and absurdity.'[27]

Boswell saw Johnson everywhere, at the Thrale's's, Reynolds's, Strahan's, Dilly's, Davies's, Beauclerk's, the Club, and the Mitre, but it was their private meetings he valued the most. He sought his advice about moving to London permanently. 'If you come to settle here,' Johnson answered, 'we will have one day in the week on which we will meet by ourselves. That is the happiest conversation where there is no competition, no vanity, but a calm quiet interchange of sentiments.' They took their ritual teas with Mrs Williams deep into the night. On Good Friday, as Boswell tells it, 'after we had drank tea with Mrs Williams, he asked me to go upstairs with him, and we sat a long time in a sort of languid, grave state, like men watching a corpse; or nearly like that'. They spoke only when Johnson started a subject. Boswell was thrilled when Johnson offered him a room, 'where I might sleep occasionally, when I happened to sit with him, to a late hour. I took possession of it this night'. Attended by Frank, he was surprised to find everything 'in excellent order'. Breakfast in the morning was quite an affair: 'His tea and rolls and butter, and whole breakfast apparatus were all in such decorum, and his behaviour was so courteous' that another guest present was 'quite surprised ... having heard so much said of Johnson's slovenliness and roughness'. The last impression Boswell leaves us as he departs in late May 1775 is of Johnson's laughter: 'I never knew a man laugh more heartily ... Johnson's laugh was as remarkable as any circumstance in his manner. It was a kind of good humoured growl. Tom Davies described it drolly enough: "He laughs like a rhinoceros."'[28]

[5]

Johnson had delayed his next Staffordshire visit to accommodate Boswell: 'I had no great reason for haste, and therefore might as well gratify a friend ... Boswell would have thought my absence a loss, and I knew not who else would have considered my presence as profit'. He was also delayed by Thrale's insistence that a suit of his 'be made like other peoples, and they are gone to the tailor'. After ten days in Oxford, he and Frank 'thundered' away on 8 June for Lichfield, where he stayed until the end of the month in the lap of all his lady friends, Elizabeth Aston and her sister Jane Gastrell at Stowe Hill, who gave him 'good words, and cherries, and strawberries', and Mary Cobb and Mary Adey to whom he behaved 'with a kindness and easy pleasantry, such as we see between old and intimate acquaintance'. Restless afterwards at Ashbourne watching Taylor garden, he dreamed of seeing 'other forms of existence' by going to Cairo 'and down the Red Sea to Bengal' and taking 'a ramble in India', which would give more 'variety to the eye, and amplitude to the mind' than building and planting. While he was there he heard from Mrs Thrale that little Ralph Thrale, sick for some time, had died from brain damage. He was home by mid-August.[29]

[6]

The Thrales again delayed plans for an Italian excursion, but there was now a window of opportunity for a shorter trip to France since Mrs Thrale was not, for a change, pregnant. The trip would be a trial run for Italy the following year and Baretti, whose published guides for the European traveller made him an ideal guide and who would be expected to continue giving Queeney her Italian lessons, would come, too. Mrs Thrale would keep a journal again, and this time Johnson promised he would keep one, too. Unfortunately, only one of three journal notebooks he kept during the tour has survived. 'Shall we have *A Journey to Paris* from you in the winter?' Boswell asked him. This would be his first visit to the Continent. They left Streatham on 15 September and met Baretti at Dover for the smooth crossing on a sloop to Calais.[30]

If Johnson thought this two-month journey would enrich him with a new assortment of imagery and an excitement about unfamiliar manners and modes of existence, stimulating him to write another travel book, he would soon be disillusioned. The way Baretti, mostly, and Mrs Thrale organised the route to Paris, comfort and convenience were absolute requirements. Johnson wrote to Boswell from Calais on his birthday that their 'regular recommendations' along the way would keep them from being mistaken for 'vagabonds'. With Mrs Thrale and eleven-year-old Queeney in the group, they could hardly have travelled any other way – the hardships they had encountered in Wales had been occasions for much moaning, though not by Johnson. If they had travelled in France more as vagabonds, more as he and Boswell did through the Highlands and Hebrides, Johnson surely would have been more animated and less detached. As it was, they made a 'prodigious fine journey' of it, taking in the main tourist sites, travelling in two coaches, staying in good accommodation, and spending a huge amount of money. The fifty-nine days cost Thrale more than £800 (some £80,000 today), which he could not really afford.[31]

From Paris, he wrote to Boswell, 'Paris is, indeed, a place very different from the Hebrides, but it is to a hasty traveller not so fertile of novelty, nor affords so many opportunities of remark.' 'I have seen nothing that much delighted or surprised me,' he told Hector when he got home. Paris 'in general makes a very mean appearance'. He could not really say, as he had after the Hebrides, that he had seen 'a new region'. Most important, he confided in Taylor that the trip had not made any impression on his feelings about himself and sense of direction: 'Is not mine a kind of life turned upside down. Fixed to a spot when I was young, and roving the world when others are contriving to sit still, I am wholly unsettled. I am a kind of ship with a wide sail, and without an anchor.' The main benefit of the trip was that 'the French have a clear air and a fruitful soil' that improved his health. At Versailles he felt so good that 'I ran a race in the rain this day, and beat Baretti.'[32]

Mrs Thrale's journal is conspicuous for seldom mentioning John-

son's conversation and actions. When she did mention him, it was
often with impatience and irritation or to find fault with him. One
reason for this is simply that he did not command the attention on
the journey that normally he was accustomed to in a gathering at
Southwark or Streatham. There were other things to think about, and
his interaction with the French was limited by his reluctance to speak
French, which he could not do as well as read or write it. She allowed
a few glimpses of him, however, such as when a Parisian wig he had
acquired almost proved to be too much for some Frenchman who
'refrained from laughing out with the greatest difficulty'; or when one
evening in Paris she sat at home with him while others went out: 'we
criticised & talked & were happy in one another – he in hugging
me, & I in being hugged'; or when an Irishman living cheaply in Paris
'found the way to Dr Johnson's heart by abusing the French'. Such
French bashing extremely annoyed Baretti who was extolling French
virtues right and left throughout the trip, but it had long been typical
of English tourists. Johnson certainly indulged in his share of stereo-
typing the French with an assortment of stock prejudices against them:
'Their meals are gross', 'the French have no laws for the maintenance of
their poor', 'in France there is no middle rank', and 'nobody but mean
people walk in Paris'. He remained firm in these views of Paris, for at
Reynolds's house for dinner three years later he declared, 'I question
if at Paris such a company as is round this table could be got together
in less than half a year.' Boswell heard Johnson say that the meat
markets in Paris were 'such as would be sent to a gaol in England'.[33]

Johnson's own journal – what we have of it – is on the whole
predictably impersonal, though he made an effort to be descriptive of
some of the palaces, libraries and churches he saw. Libraries appealed
to him most, especially the King's Library, where he had the thrill of
handling the Gutenberg Bible, and the libraries at the Sorbonne and
St Germain des Prés. He was 'well used' by the English Benedictine
monks, and while Mrs Thrale went off yet again to see the pictures at
the Palais Royale he spent the last day in Paris entirely with them,
speaking Latin and exploring their library: 'I lived at the Benedictines,
meagre day. Soup meagre, herrings, eels, both with sauce. Fried fish.
Lentils, tasteless in themselves ... I parted very tenderly from the
Prior.' The Prior, Father Cowley, who offered him the use of a cell
anytime he wished it, would remain a friend and visit him in London
in 1777. 'I dined in their refectory, and studied in their library, and had
the favour of their company to other places, as curiosity led me.' He

was not as pleased with the lives of the English Austin nuns at Nôtre Dame de Sion where he came to fetch Mrs Thrale one afternoon at tea time. He disapproved of the religious austerity there and said to the Lady Abbess, 'Madam, you are here, not for the love of virtue, but the fear of vice.' She replied she 'would remember this as long as she lived'. His lengthiest description was of an entirely different realm of French life, the process of manufacturing at a mirror factory in Paris, having the day before seen the mirrors in the great gallery at Versailles.[34]

The trip was a pleasure and success for the Thrales but not for Johnson. He was virtually ignored by the eminent French authors, philosophers and scientists, who either seemed unaware that he was there or were uninterested in seeing him. Like the Welsh trip, this excursion to Paris was for the Thrales mostly about sightseeing. He met fewer scholars than even Boswell did when he was there in his early twenties. What Johnson did take back with him above all else was a distaste for the wastefulness and 'luxuriousness' of the French aristocracy, ripe for destruction in the French Revolution, as well as with the corrupt social system and dismal poverty it created. 'The French are a gross, ill-bred, untaught people,' he said a few years later. 'What I gained by being in France was, learning to be better satisfied with my own country.'[35]

PART VI

Biography and 'The Race with Death'

Token with Johnson's head

CHAPTER 29

'A Very Poor Creeper upon the Earth'

Even before returning home in mid-November 1775, they all began making plans for an expedition to Italy in the spring. Queeney would be included and Baretti was to be in charge again of making all the arrangements and acting as their courier. He had in mind no short excursion this time but a Grand Tour over a whole year, the chief part to be spent in Tuscany for the winter. Johnson was amenable to a year, as was Thrale, but Mrs Thrale insisted on only six months from April to October because she wished to be back when young Harry entered Westminster School.

The expensive plan was to leave on 8 or 9 April in three post-chaises with a maid and two manservants, hiring additional servants in cities where they would be staying for some time. 'With money one can do everything,' wrote Mrs Thrale tentatively. They would head for Lyons via Paris, cross the Alps to Turin, proceed to Genoa and Milan, and then turn south to Rome. Baretti was all for making short stops in small towns so that his relatives could meet Johnson, whom he described to an Italian friend as 'my British sack of learning, my Samuel Johnson'. Wishing to prepare a relative for meeting this remarkable and unusual man, Baretti also cautioned that he was 'a nasty old man, a giant both in body and mind, always absent-minded, fierce, touchy, dirty, full of unpleasant habits, always shifting his body when he is seated, and always moving his jaw like an ox chewing the cud; but as he is rightly believed to possess more learning than any other man in this kingdom, he is feared and respected by all, perhaps more than he is loved.' Baretti proposed an excursion even to Sicily before returning north to winter in Tuscany, but Johnson was concerned that with such an itinerary they might not properly see the major cities: 'We must, to be sure, see Rome, Naples, Florence, and Venice, and as much more as we can.' He insisted on changes. Baretti could not actually take them to Venice because if he did so he risked being arrested there for some politically daring writings. Johnson began brushing up on his Italian and wondered if he might write a book about his travels there. 'I do not see that I could make a book upon Italy,' he remarked to Boswell, 'yet I should be glad to get two hundred pounds, or five hundred pounds, by such a work.' Thinking this 'a proof that he supposed he *might* compose a valuable journal', Boswell and others were thrilled at the prospect that some day Johnson might well be offering the public his insights on Italy 'through his noble intellectual glass'.[1]

In the spring Boswell was preparing for his annual dose of the Johnsonian ether, but Johnson was concerned that he was coming chiefly to cling to him in the hope of shaking off months of melancholia that were ruining his life: 'I am very sorry that your melancholy should return and should be sorry likewise if it could have no relief but from my company . . . if you will come to me, you must come very quickly' before they left for Italy. If he hurried, they might even be able to squeeze in a trip to Oxford, Lichfield and Ashbourne.[2]

Johnson had his own problems. There was the alarming example of Charles Congreve, a classmate of Taylor, Hector and his whom he had recently discovered languishing in a stupor in a London room ten-foot square, 'willing, I am afraid, to forget the world, and content to be forgiven by it, to repose in that sullen sensuality, into which men naturally sink, who think a disease a justification of indulgence.' Johnson feared that very sullenness and despondency in himself. He could see Congreve had allowed himself to descend into a form of madness. His Easter Day diary entry sounds as worried as any he ever wrote: 'My reigning sin, to which perhaps many others are appendant, is waste of time, and general sluggishness, to which I was always inclined and in part of my life have been almost compelled by morbid melancholy and disturbance of mind. Melancholy has had in me its paroxisms and remissions, but I have not improved the intervals, nor sufficiently resisted my natural inclination, or sickly habits.' If only he could rise at eight and feel more regularly the 'radiations of comfort' obtainable by turning to the 'Holy Spirit', the rest of the day might properly fall into place.[3]

One method of getting out of himself was to help others. In January he had tea with the gentle moral reformer and educator Hannah More (1745–1833) and read her freshly published poem *Sir Eldred*. 'We fell upon *Sir Eldred*,' she wrote, for which he suggested 'some little alterations' and composed a new stanza. She had recently arrived in London from Bristol, where she kept a boarding school with her sisters. When they first met at Reynolds's house in June 1774, she was astonished to discover he knew something of her writings. He met her 'with good humour in his countenance, and continued in the same pleasant humour the whole of the evening'. They took to each other immediately, although it may have been this same evening that he not so mildly rebuked her, as he often did Mrs Thrale, for constantly flattering him: 'Dearest lady, consider with yourself what your flattery is worth, before you bestow it so freely.' They next met a few days later when Renny took it upon herself to take her and her sister to 'Dr Johnson's *very own house*'. On the way, with their hearts palpitating, the three ladies broke into raptures over him, 'Abyssinia's Johnson! Dictionary Johnson! Rambler's, Idler's and Irene's Johnson!' When they got there Hannah seated herself in Johnson's great chair in the parlour, 'hoping to catch a little ray of his genius'. He laughed when he heard of it, but informed her he never sat in that chair. Renny told Johnson of their 'rapturous exclamations' on the way, on which he looked at Hannah and said, 'She was a *silly thing*'. 'Why should she flatter *me*?' he asked. 'I can do nothing for her. Let her carry her praise to a better market'.[4]

Hannah became a great favourite of his. For tea at Reynolds's house one day the following year, she 'was placed next him, and they had the entire conversation to themselves . . . The old genius was extremely jocular, and the young one very pleasant'. At Elizabeth Montagu's splendid house in Portman Square, the 'Queen of the Blues' and 'female Maecenas' (as she was called) about whose writings and friendships with Horace Walpole and Thomas Gray Johnson had mixed feelings, she sorted her way through 'half the wits of the age' assembled there and finally sat down next to him for the rest of the evening. She then accompanied him home, 'although Mrs Montagu publicly declared she did not think it prudent to trust us together, with such a declared affection on both sides'. He invited himself to tea with her and her sister the following day 'that we may read Sir Eldred together . . . He repeats all the best stanzas by heart, with the energy, though not the grace of a Garrick'. This great Dr Johnson had found his way into her heart: 'To enjoy Dr Johnson perfectly, one must have him to oneself, as he seldom cares to speak in mixed parties.' For her part, in addition to her exemplary and modest moral nature, she provided him the uncluttered female grace and wit he craved to keep up his spirits.

Hannah's sister even joked a wedding might be in the offing between the 'mother of Sir Eldred, and the father of my much-loved Irene'. Mrs Montagu chimed in that this was not that improbable since Johnson could be overheard calling her 'child', 'little fool', 'love', and 'dearest' through the din of conversation. She once playfully called him her 'beau' and 'gay libertine'. 'I love you both,' he declared to her and her sister – 'inamorato', as Hannah related it. He promised to visit her and her school in Bristol, which he did with Boswell in the spring.[5]

Garrick also frequented these parties – laughing boisterously with Johnson about their Lichfield youth, as did Dr Burney. Johnson wrote the Dedication to the Queen for Burney's monumental four-volume *General History of Music*, the first volume of which was published in January; he also added to it his translation of a passage from Euripides on 'the joys of music' and read proofs. Such involvement could be taken as evidence that he was more appreciative and understanding of music than most of his friends believed. He remarked about Burney's book that it 'evidently proved that the author of it understood the philosophy of music better than any man who had ever written on that subject', a comment prompting Renny to write, 'it must be supposed that he had felt its power, and that he had a taste for music'. On the other hand, his writings and other sources are sprinkled with his comments that he took little pleasure from music, and not entirely because he was hard of hearing. He could be quite scornful and dismissive of both music and musicians: 'no man of talent, or whose mind was capable of better things, ever would or could devote his time and attention to so idle and frivolous a pursuit'. On being asked at Burney's house a question about Bach, he replied mischievously, 'And pray, Sir, *who is Bach*? Is he a piper?' 'Music excites in my mind no ideas, and hinders me from contemplating my own,' he is supposed to have said – at least according to the biased Hawkins whose own *History of Music*, also published in 1776, was mocked by Johnson and club friends. Although with such comments Johnson was knowingly acting out the popular notion that he had little use for music, Dr Burney himself is our most reliable witness when he asserted that he was 'wholly deaf & insensible to it'.[6]

Boswell arrived in London in mid-March, eager to have at least two or three weeks with him before he left for Italy. He discovered on his arrival at Johnson's doorstep that he had recently moved to a house in a narrow alley at No. 8, Bolt Court, very close to his previous residences just off Fleet Street – a 'much better one' with 'good rooms and a pretty little spot of background'. Johnson was at the Thrales's so Boswell 'sailed to Southwark' from Blackfriars Bridge where he found his hero in 'the full glow of conversation'. Johnson confirmed that before leaving for Italy he would indeed take a 'jaunt' to Oxford, Birmingham and Lichfield. 'I shall go in a few days,' he announced, 'and you, Boswell, shall go with me'. This would be Boswell's first opportunity to walk in the footsteps of his hero's early years and interview Hector and others about them. Three days later they were on their way.[7]

They were well into their stay at Lichfield when a letter from Mrs Thrale brought an end to it. Reading it during breakfast at Lucy's, Johnson solemnly announced, 'One of the most dreadful things that has happened in my time … Mr Thrale has lost his only son'. This meant they had to cut short their time in Lichfield and after a short stay at Ashbourne rush back to London so Johnson could comfort the Thrales. For the time being, in any case, he had run out of patience with Boswell's biographical mission and endless questions and note-taking. Boswell complained that the 'rattling' of the wheels of the chaise as they thundered their way south drowned out Johnson's answers to questions, whereupon Johnson shouted at him, 'Then you may go hang yourself.' A few days and many questions later, he was equally forceful, 'You have but two topics, yourself and me, and I'm sick of both.'[8]

Mrs Thrale, Baretti and Queeney were just leaving for Bath when Johnson arrived at Streatham. He declined to go with them, preferring to stay and comfort Henry Thrale in his grief. Inconsolable, Thrale sent him away. That same day Johnson sat down and wrote a perceptive letter to Mrs Thrale on grieving: 'I know that such a loss is a laceration of the mind. I know that a whole system of hopes, and designs, and expectations is swept away at once, and nothing [is] left but bottomless vacuity. What you feel, I have felt.' He wrote to her almost every other day until in mid-April he joined her in Bath. By then he had met with a huge disappointment. The Thrales yet again had cancelled the Italian tour. Only he and Baretti still had any heart for it. He pretended to Mrs Thrale he was not that disappointed. She wrote to him, 'Baretti said you would be very angry … but I knew you better … Mr Thrale says he shall not die in peace without seeing Rome, and I am sure he will go nowhere that he can help without you.' That was small consolation. Without seeing Italy, he felt incomplete, as he told

Boswell at Paoli's house before hearing the bad news: 'A man who has not been in Italy is always conscious of an inferiority ... the grand object of travelling is to see the shores of the Mediterranean. On these shores were the four great empires of the world: the Assyrian, the Persian, the Grecian, and the Roman. All our religion, almost all our law, almost all our arts, almost all that sets us above savages, has come to us from the shores of the Mediterranean.'[9]

From Bath he summoned Boswell, 'Come ... as soon as you can'. In a matter of a few days Boswell was there. The most memorable event in their time there together was an excursion to Bristol to look into the authenticity of manuscript poems at St Mary Redcliffe Church allegedly written by Thomas Rowley, a fifteenth-century priest. Just as Johnson had demanded of Macpherson proof of the authenticity of Ossian's poetry in the form of authentic Gaelic manuscripts, he now wanted to satisfy himself regarding another controversial forgery of the day. Thomas Chatterton, 'the marvellous boy', as he was called for his poetic genius, had published these manuscript poems which he claimed he found in the church archives. The fact was he had written the beautiful verses himself, and soon after publishing them had moved to London where in 1770, in a lonely garret, without any money, he appears to have poisoned himself at the age of eighteen – an act memorialised magnificently by Henry Wallis's painting, *Chatterton*, one of the minor masterpieces of the Pre-Raphaelite movement. But for years the controversy about their authenticity continued, with names of believers and disbelievers published occasionally in the newspapers. Johnson pronounced the alleged 'originals' impostures the moment he saw them. Indeed, he found 'this wild adherence to Chatterton more unaccountable than the obstinate defence of Ossian' even as he and many others wondered at Chatterton's poetic skills: 'This is the most extraordinary young man that has encountered my knowledge. It is wonderful how the whelp has written such things.'[10]

On his return to London, he was greeted with the just-published octavo edition of his *Political Tracts* containing *Taxation No Tyranny* and the three other pamphlets; somewhat ironically, in light of the signing of the American *Declaration of Independence* in July and General George Washington's major success in driving the British from Boston and New York that year. More satisfactory to him politically than what was happening in America was Parliament's rejection of Wilkes's Bill for Parliamentary reform. The timing could not have been better, therefore, for one of Boswell's greatest coups on 15 May when he brought together Johnson and Wilkes for dinner at Charles Dilly's home in the Poultry, where Johnson said he always found a good dinner. It was the prospect of such a dinner that Boswell, who was staying in the room set aside for him in Johnson's house, used as a lure to get him to Dilly's house that night. Johnson of course knew nothing of the plan, which Boswell hatched with Dilly's collusion, to have Wilkes there as well. Boswell was playing with fire. It was just the sort of awkward situation he longed to put Johnson into in order to see how he would behave. When he suggested a meeting between him and Mrs Macaulay, for instance, Johnson scolded him, 'No, Sir, you would not see us quarrel, to make you sport.' When the evening at Dilly's arrived the plan nearly unravelled because Johnson had forgotten about the dinner and ordered a quiet meal instead at home with Mrs Williams and Boswell. Mrs Williams came to the rescue, however, after some persuasion from Boswell, and in a few minutes Johnson was calling out, 'Frank, a clean shirt'. Soon they were in a hackney coach on their way to the Poultry.[11]

When they got to Dilly's, almost immediately Johnson wanted to know who a man in lace across the room was. 'Mr Wilkes, Sir,' was the simple answer, whereupon he grabbed a book sulkily and sat down to compose himself. Dinner was then called. Wilkes, who had little problem with Johnson being there even though, alluding to his pension, he regarded him 'a slave of the state', sat down boldly next to him and was so attentive and cordial, seeing to it that Johnson was served with all that he wished, that Johnson gradually began to melt. '"Sir, Sir, I am obliged to you, Sir"', Johnson grumbled, 'bowing, and turning his head to him with a look for some time of "surly virtue".' Before long he had relaxed and was enjoying sparkling conversation with the man whom he had described as 'a criminal from a gaol'. Boswell sat back hugging himself, not minding at all their ganging up on him as Johnson began 'breaking jokes with Jack Wilkes upon the Scots'. At Bolt Court later, Johnson was all praise for his arch-enemy and the evening. Burke learned of this encounter later – 'there was nothing to equal it in the whole history of the *Corps Diplomatique*,' he told Boswell. With the glow from his triumphant stage-managing warming him, Boswell left London the next day. 'Pray take care of him, and tame him,' Johnson wrote to his wife. 'The only thing in which I have the honour to agree with you is, in loving him; and while we are so much of a mind in a matter of so much importance, our other quarrels will, I hope, produce no great bitterness.'[12]

That summer Johnson suffered a strong attack of gout: 'I enjoy all the dignity of lameness ... I am a very poor creeper upon the earth, catching at anything with my hands to spare my feet.' 'It is of my own acquisition, as neither my father had it nor my mother.' For mental and physical relief he trudged off to Brighton again with the Thrales in the last week of September and stayed until the end of October. He even tried swimming, 'though I know not that it does me any good'. He still disliked the town, he wrote to Boswell: 'The place was very dull, and I was not well; the expedition to the Hebrides was the most pleasant journey that I ever made. Such an effort annually would give the world a little diversification. Every year, however, we cannot wander.' Mrs Williams was seriously ill, too, in November, 'in a feeble and languishing state, with little hope of growing better', though Dr Levet remained 'sound, wind and limb'. There was also trouble at Streatham when (in Johnson's words) after one too many quarrels with Mrs Thrale 'in some whimsical fit of disgust, or ill-nature' Baretti put down his teacup at breakfast one morning in July and walked out of the house without saying a word, resolving never to see her again. The timing of this was not wonderful since she was pregnant again.[13]

His health continued poor into the spring. Desperate to sleep one night, he took ten ounces of his own blood so inexpertly that Frank and Levet had to help him 'stop the stream'. Thrale was furious when he heard he had put his life in danger like this. Lawrence bled him again later, making it thirty-six ounces in two or three days. He spent much of every night sitting up in bed. Good sleep was hard to come by. Also common was the claustrophobic feeling of helplessness: 'Days and months pass in a dream, and I am afraid that my memory grows less tenacious, and my observation less attentive. If I am decaying it is time to make haste. My nights are restless and tedious, and my days drowsy. The flatulence which torments me, has sometimes so obstructed my breath, that the act of respiration became not only voluntary but laborious in a decumbent posture.' Neither was he attending church, having missed almost every Sunday of the year thus far. He looked to Reynolds, Burney and Mrs Thrale for moral support and comfort, as well as to Boswell from afar – 'your kindness is one of the pleasures of my life' – and he was cheered that his 'old enemy' Margaret Boswell had shown him some affection by sending him a jar of her marmalade – 'she is after all a dear, dear lady'. 'We must all help one another,' he wrote to her.[14]

One of the new and brightest lights on his horizon that spring was Dr Burney's twenty-five-year-old daughter Fanny, whom he met for the first time at a morning party at the Burney house. In a few months she would secretly publish her classic bestseller, *Evelina*, keeping her authorship unknown for months, even from her publisher, because of her shyness and the terror of the stigma of female authorship. She was an undiluted joy for Johnson, young, shy, charming and intelligent, and she reciprocated his regard with a deep affection for him for the rest of his life. Her journal was all that Mrs Thrale's, with her family troubles and constraints, could never be: full and rich with the novelist's wit and vibrantly recorded scenes that make it, along with Pepys's and Boswell's, among the most engaging in British literary history.

Fanny Burney was taken aback when she first saw Johnson: 'He is, indeed, very ill-favoured; is tall and stout; but stoops terribly; he is almost bent double. His mouth is almost continually opening and shutting, as if he was chewing. He has a strange method of frequently twirling his fingers, and twisting his hands. His body is in continual agitation, *see-sawing* up and down; his feet are never a moment quiet; and, in short, his whole person is in *perpetual motion*.' As for his dress, it was 'as much out of the common road as his figure' with 'large wig, snuff-colour coat, and gold buttons, but no ruffles to his shirt ... and black worsted stockings'. She said his near-sightedness was so bad that not until someone held out a hand to him did he know who it was. Inspecting the library shelves, which he did within five minutes of being announced, he almost touched the backs of the books with his eyelashes. He plucked a book off the shelf and fell solitarily to reading it, much to the dismay of others in the room who longed to hear him talk. Fanny quickly caught on that if Johnson was to talk he first had to be 'drawn out'. She was a fine acquisition for him, another young female admirer of delicacy and taste, with a fine satiric impulse, who had little patience with affectation, buffoonery, and hypocrisy – one on whom he doted extravagantly, at times somewhat to her embarrassment, as when in front of a roomful of people he drew her 'very unexpectedly towards him, and he actually kissed me!'.[15]

[2]

Two major events occurred in the early months of 1777, one criminal, the other literary. The literary development was that on 29 March he was approached by a consortium of no fewer than forty-two book-sellers and six printers to write brief biographical vignettes or *Prefaces* for each of the poets in their projected collection of British poetry. 'I am engaged to write little Lives, and little Prefaces, to a little edition of the English poets,' he announced lightly to Boswell four days later. His old friends Davies, Strahan and Thomas Cadell came to him to propose the project on behalf of the other booksellers. The idea was their immediate retaliation to an offensive by the Scottish bookseller John Bell, who announced he would publish over one hundred volumes of English poets that threatened commercially to bury once and for all any claim London booksellers still had to English authors as their exclusive literary property. 'Johnson' was the name they wanted at the head of the publishing venture in order to endow it with the merchandising clout and literary prestige it needed.[16]

Johnson almost certainly had advance notice of the project, perhaps from Steevens who appears to have recommended him for it. He was pleased and accepted 'very politely'. Their project had a patriotic twist to it since he felt 'the chief glory of every people arises from its authors' and England, facing the revolution in the American colonies, the financial and political pressures it created, and threats of French and Spanish invasion, needed to be reminded of its greatness. He profoundly believed that no other country on the Continent could come close to rivalling it as 'the capital of literature'. The downside of the commission was that at an advanced age, and amid growing health worries, it saddled him with a literary project requiring several years of hard work, painful self-sacrifice and confinement to his study. Left to decide how much he would be paid, he modestly (and foolishly) agreed to do the Prefaces for 200 guineas, later revised to £300, feeling this was a respectable sum given the original agreement that he would provide only 'a concise account' for each poet. He felt he could supply the booksellers easily and quickly with what they wanted – and they wanted it quickly in order to compete with Bell's edition. Later, he defended the contract price: 'The fact is, not that they have paid me too little, but that I have written too much.' He ended up writing over fifty lives, several of them very long. It would be his greatest biographical effort.[17]

The criminal event had a more immediate personal and emotional effect on him.[18] The Revd William Dodd, 'the macaroni parson', as he was called because of his recklessly extravagant social climbing, was a high-spending clergyman and somewhat successful author who through luck and industry had managed to gain some prominence in high society. He was chaplain to the King and Bishop of St David's and (ironically as it turned out) tutor to Philip Stanhope, godson of Johnson's would-be patron for the *Dictionary*, the fourth Earl of Chesterfield. By the time of the crime the godson had succeeded to the earldom. A hopeless spendthrift, Dodd was so desperate for money that he forged the signature of the fifth Earl to a bond valued at £4,200. In less than a week he was exposed and arrested, charged for the capital offence of forgery. He came to trial at the Old Bailey on 22 February, at which he made a melodramatic speech defending himself. It did no good. He was found guilty and on 16 May sentenced to hang, by which time the press had reported the trial so sensationally that the public wept to hear the man's fate. After fainting, Dodd was carted off to Newgate to await execution.

In his extremity he apparently recollected Johnson's *Rambler* essays (especially no. 114) on modern justice and the legal system and asked for his help through the Countess of Harrington and his friend, the printer Edmund Allen, Johnson's landlord and neighbour in Bolt Court. Johnson read Lady Harrington's letter to him 'walking up and down his chamber ... much agitated, after which he said, "I will do what I can."' 'Poor Dodd was sentenced last week,' Johnson informed Taylor on 19 May. 'It is a thing almost without example for a clergyman of his rank to stand at the bar for a capital breach of morality. I am afraid he will suffer ... How little he thought six months ago of being what he now is'. He kept up the fight over the next four months. He wrote 'The Convict's Address to his unhappy Brethren', a sermon that Dodd delivered to fellow prisoners at Newgate on 6 June, two letters to the Lord Chancellor, one to Lord Mansfield, the Lord Chief Justice of the King's Bench, 'A Petition from Dr Dodd to the King', 'A Petition from Mrs Dodd to the Queen', several pieces for the newspapers, and 'Dr Dodd's last solemn Declaration'. He implored Dodd not to let it be known that he wrote the letter to the King: 'I hope I need not tell you, that I wish it success. But do not indulge hope. Tell Nobody.' Dodd and he exchanged several letters, carried back and forth by Allen, who was a friend of the Keeper of Newgate, but Johnson never visited him in Newgate, feeling 'it would have done *him* more harm, than good'.[19]

Johnson's plea to the Under-Secretary of State came back with a 'dreadful answer'. He knew the die was cast and wrote immediately to Allen on 17 June, urging him to tell Dodd to write 'the history of his own depravation' for the moral benefit of the public. And he was definite on one particular point: 'Let him ... shut his doors against all hope, all trifles, and all sensuality' and turn to God for mercy and salvation. But still he did not give up, imploring Lady Harrington on 25 June to make a direct appeal to the King and pressing Allen to send the Newgate sermon to anyone who might be able to help, even to the King and the highest ministers in the land. There was an element of panic in his last efforts. To Dodd, finally, he wrote on the 26th, telling him to prepare for death: 'Be comforted: your crime, morally or religiously considered, has no very deep dye of turpitude. It corrupted no man's principles; it attacked no man's life'. Hawkins, who chaired the Grand Jury that brought Dodd to trial, differed from Boswell in maintaining that Johnson privately did not think Dodd worthy of his efforts to save him, judging that the effort was another example of Johnson's misplaced 'indiscriminate humanity'. Dodd was finally executed on 27 June. 'Poor Dodd was put to death yesterday,' Johnson told Boswell angrily, 'in opposition to the recommendation of the jury – the petition of the city of London – and a subsequent petition signed by three-and-twenty thousand hands. Surely the voice of the public, when it calls so loudly, and calls only for mercy, ought to be heard ... He applied to me often. He was, I am afraid, long flattered with hopes of life; but I had no part in the dreadful delusion.'[20]

[3]

The sermon Johnson wrote for Dodd was one of more than forty he wrote in his lifetime. Their bulk comprises one of his most impressive literary and spiritual achievements – especially impressive, in personal terms, because he wrote them secretly for 'sundry beneficed clergymen' at their request – twenty-five were for Taylor alone – with the demand that they must never reveal his authorship. That it was not an uncommon practice for clergymen to have sermons written for them, and that he charged two guineas each for them and felt, therefore, he had no further right to be identified as their author, does not diminish the selflessness and charity of the act in a lifetime of writing anonymously for others in a multitude of ways. When someone told him he doubted Dodd wrote the sermon to the Newgate convicts because he lacked 'the force of mind' needed, he coyly kept up the deception: 'Depend upon it, Sir, when a man knows he is to be hanged in a fortnight, it concentrates his mind wonderfully.' Hawkins was one of the few who suspected he wrote many of Taylor's sermons. He claimed later that he recognised Johnson's 'sentiments, style, and method' in them when he heard Taylor ineffectively deliver several at the Church of St Margaret in Westminster.[21]

He wrote the sermons rapidly. 'The composition of sermons is not very difficult,' he wrote in 1780 to Thomas Lawrence's son who had recently been ordained deacon. 'Invent first and then embellish ... Set down diligently your thoughts as they rise in the first words that occur'. 'I have begun a sermon after dinner, and sent it off by the post that night'. On 20 April 1778, he noted in his diary that he had written a 'little' of the *Lives* and composed more sermons 'as readily as formerly' in spite of 'a vacillation and vagrancy of mind' owing to his 'unsettled' life, the feeling that for the last year his life had been 'very melancholy and [a] shameful blank', and 'painful and fatiguing' nights affected by breathing difficulties so severe that 'asthma was suspected'. Modern medicine has tended to agree it was emphysema more than asthma. The concentration on deeply religious thought in his sermons during the late 1770s occurred to him as not unrelated to a sudden remission of these terrifying 'convulsions' in his breast and breathing difficulties on 18 June 1779. A year later he was so grateful still to be free from them that he composed a prayer of 'Thanksgiving' for 'that recovery and continuance of health which thou hast granted me'.[22]

'Manly sense, deep penetration, and ardent love of virtue': such words have often been used to describe Johnson's sermons. Steeped in the English homiletic tradition of the sixteenth and seventeenth centuries, especially the sermons of Richard Hooker, John Tillotson and Jeremy Taylor, the sermons are much more than standard variations on Anglican theological themes of communion, vanity, repentance and charity, among others. With their strong moral reflections, they make one think immediately of the *Rambler* essays and their insight into the recesses of the human mind. They are all about making one's way as best as one can in this mortal existence with realism, dignity and spiritual sensitivity and devoutness. The themes Johnson wrote about include marriage, the vanity of human wishes and self-deception, arrogance and intellectual pride, envy, war, death, law and morals, capital punishment, idleness, charity and the 'compassionate heart', friendship and God. It has been well understood that Taylor's hot-tempered character, ambition and avarice – he was called 'Midas' by his Ashbourne neighbours – all made him an unlikely deliverer of these sermons, quite apart from his intellectual inability to write them and his apparently poor performance in the pulpit. But we can forgive all this because if he had not asked Johnson to write them on visits to Ashbourne, they simply would not exist.[23]

[4]

In 1777 Johnson took on another lodger, Tetty's old friend Mrs Desmoulins, who for many years had been living in Chelsea in poverty. Although he did not much like her, he felt a lingering obligation to her not only on account of Tetty but also because she was the daughter of his godfather, after whom he had been named and who had helped him get to Oxford with some small financial assistance. He gave her an allowance of half a guinea per week and allowed her (with her daughter) to move into the same room with a 'Scotch wench', Poll Carmichael, whom Johnson may have taken in as early as 1773, if she was one and the same as the prostitute he found nearly lifeless in the street one day and carried home on his back. He took care of Poll tenderly for years and had long been assisting her to recover a small patrimony she said she had been unjustly denied. She did not work out in the house as well as he had hoped: 'we could spare her very well from us; Poll is a stupid slut', he remarked to Mrs Thrale in 1778.[24]

Desmoulins and her daughter brought to seven the total number of dependants living at Bolt Court in the summer of 1777. She completed the recipe for domestic chaos in the house, for she and Mrs Williams despised each other and the normal bickering in the house increased exponentially. Mrs Thrale was both amused and horrified that Johnson's house was 'overrun with *all* sort of strange creatures, whom he admits for mere charity', 'but as they can both be occasionally of service to each other, and as neither of them have any other place to go to, their animosity does not force them to separate'. None of the inhabitants, in fact, liked Mrs Desmoulins. 'Mr Levet who thinks his ancient rights invaded, stands at bay, *fierce as ten* furies', Johnson grumbled to Mrs Thrale; 'Mrs Williams growls and scolds, but Poll does not much flinch.' After a year with all of them, Johnson summed up the turmoil in the house: 'We have tolerable concord at home, but no love. Williams hates everybody. Levet hates Desmoulins and does not love Williams. Desmoulins hates them both. Poll loves none of them.' Mrs Williams was so ill during the summer that in July, Johnson sent her out into the countryside for her recovery, but he feared the worst. Levet, in spite of feeling besieged by all those women, and Frank were the only stable ones among them. The seventy-two-year-old Levet was good company for Johnson, breakfasting with him and costing little because of his medical attentions to the poor and indigent living in the neighbourhoods of Marylebone for which they were able to pay him one way or another. Johnson's deep affection for Levet and his charitable work never wavered. However, lengthy visits to Staffordshire became more than ever a way to escape the cacophony of argument at home. This pattern of existence would last to the end of his life.[25]

CHAPTER 30

Biographical Straitjacket

Instead of seeing Boswell in London in the spring of 1777, Johnson proposed they meet up at Taylor's in September: 'If you live awhile with me at his house, we shall have much time to ourselves, and our stay will be no expense to us or to him ... Our ramble in the islands hangs upon my imagination, I can hardly help imagining that we shall go again ... When we travel again let us look better about us'. He stopped in Oxford for a week on the way north in late July and this time stayed with his friend William Scott, Professor of Ancient History, during which he made a cursory inspection of biographical materials for the *Lives* – 'and a little I have got'. In Lichfield he lived with Lucy for a month, 'barren of entertainment', looking in occasionally on Elizabeth Aston who was recuperating from a stroke and 'in great danger'. Stowe Hill was 'a collection of misery' with everyone there ill in some way. His own health was uncertain: 'When I came hither, I could hardly walk, but I have got better breath and more agility ... But I have miserable, distressful, tedious nights'. 'I could not walk but with great difficulty from Stowhill to Greenhill.' By the end of August he was in Ashbourne where the tedium did not surprise him much: 'if you were to lay a pebble' on Taylor's mantel-piece, 'you would find it there next year'. There was little to do but get on with the lives of Cowley and Denham, write to Mrs Thrale, and wait for Boswell's delayed arrival. Shocked by his efforts to medicate himself there, Mrs Thrale implored him not 'to torture that iron constitution of yours quite to ruin, because you have nothing else to do. It were better to bind books again as you did one year in our thatch'd summer house,' she wrote, than inflict on himself 'doses of Mercury and Opium which are not wanted, and then complain that you are *hermetically seal'd* ... Oh dear Sir, do pray try to govern your own [health], and do not take physic for fun.' 'Mr Boswell will make

Ashbourne alive better than three hautboys and the harpsichord', she hoped.[1]

Johnson was not eager to talk to Boswell about the *Lives of the Poets*, which he now worried was a very large project for a man his age, but one evening they spoke of death: 'He lied,' Johnson exclaimed, when Boswell told him that David Hume, who had died several months earlier, had been 'easy at the thought of annihilation … Dr Dodd would have given both his hands and legs to have lived'. Impatient of the morbid subject, he preferred to think of other things: 'If I had no duties and no reference to futurity [life after death], I would spend my life driving briskly in a post-chaise with a pretty woman, one who could understand me, and would add something to the conversation'.[2]

One evening after supper Johnson dictated an argument to help him plead a cause in the Court of Session in Edinburgh on behalf of Joseph Knight, an African slave brought to Scotland who was petitioning for liberty. Johnson's argument was totally consistent with his lifelong hostility towards slavery. Only the previous July, he had written to Boswell in support of the decision in 1772 by Lord Chief Justice William Murray, the first Earl of Mansfield, that a slave by law was free the moment he set foot on British soil; and in *Taxation No Tyranny* he endorsed a proposal to set free all the slaves in America, for which an enraged Benjamin Franklin denounced him for inciting slaves to rise up against whites. The argument he dictated to Boswell was a strong anti-slavery statement, especially castigating racism and violence as its basis: 'His colour is considered as a sufficient testimony against him. It is to be lamented that moral right should ever give way to political convenience.' Boswell used the argument successfully in obtaining Knight's freedom, but in the *Life* he asserted that Johnson's zeal was 'owing to prejudice, and imperfect or false information'. The abolition of slavery, he argued, would be 'wild and dangerous' and would interfere with commercial interests.[3]

The most unpleasant moment occurred when they fell into a furious quarrel about the Americans, the only subject, Johnson maintained, of 'great importance' that Parliament had ever debated in his lifetime. Sympathetic to the American revolutionary cause, Boswell refused to submit, making Johnson explode in anger: 'the violent agitation into which he was thrown, while answering, or rather reprimanding me, alarmed me so, that I heartily repented of my having unthinkingly introduced the subject'. They both returned to their rooms, Johnson steaming and Boswell badly bruised. True to form, the next morning Johnson had cooled off and was in a conciliatory mood as Boswell sat on his bed and they talked. Boswell left the next morning, content with having 'derived a considerable accession to my Johnsonian store'.[4]

[2]

Johnson lingered at Ashbourne, 'awkward at departing', on 6 November finally rejoining his feuding household in Bolt Court after a three-month ramble of 'very little pleasure'. At Ashbourne he had acknowledged one of the reasons for dallying there: 'You know, I have some work to do. I did not set to it very soon, and if I should go up to London with nothing done, what would be said, but that I was – who can tell what? I therefore stay till I can bring up something to stop their mouths.' Six months had disappeared since he agreed to write the *Prefaces*. 'Little lives and little criticism may serve,' he tried to tell himself unconvincingly. Soon after his return, he began to write the *Life of Edmund Waller*, receiving proofs of it by mid-April, but by then he still did not have the momentum he and the booksellers expected, although by December the *Life of Cowley* was being printed, complete with his long, innovative, critical discussion of what he called the 'metaphysical' poets of the seventeenth century. He indulged in another small procrastination in January when he accompanied Burney and his son to Winchester College to make sure, through his friendship with Joseph Warton, that the boy was 'well received'. On Easter Monday in 1778, he looked back over the year with the stark realisation, 'so little has been done that days and months are without any trace'. It was imperative that he pick up the pace. If only he could keep at bay 'the hand of time, or of disease . . . very heavy upon me'.[5]

After Easter he shot ahead on a new trajectory, no longer comforting himself with notions of 'little' Prefaces that never seemed to ignite his enthusiasm and resolving to write long, substantial ones, solid with literary criticism and reflections on literature. *The Life of Dryden*, which he began in the spring, was a dramatic turning point. It turned out to be one of the longest and most complex. 'You have now all *Cowley*,' he wrote in late July to John Nichols (1745–1826), the printer, editor and author. 'I have been drawn to a great length, but *Cowley* or *Waller* never had any critical examination before. I am very far advanced in *Dryden*, who will be long too. The next great life I purpose to be *Milton's*.' Familiar with the publishing world inside out and later editor of *The Gentleman's Magazine*, Nichols now moved to centre-stage in helping Johnson get his Prefaces edited, revised and printed. He was only thirty-three, but with his voracious appetite for literature and tracking down anecdotes and fugitive poems which he knew Johnson would never find without him, he was a goldmine of biographical and other kinds of literary information. Years later, Nichols wrote of Johnson: 'In the progress of his "Lives of the Poets", I had the good fortune to conciliate his esteem, by several small services; though, at the same time, I was perpetually goading him to furnish the press with copy'. 'You now have the life of Dryden, and you see it is very long,' he wrote again to Nichols in mid-August. These 'big' lives at last satisfied the booksellers that he was sailing.[6]

A distinctive feature of his labours on the Prefaces was that they were to some extent the result of teamwork. Nichols (especially), Steevens, Isaac Reed (another great Shakespearean), Thomas and Joseph Warton, Percy and other scholars and librarians sent him facts and books in response to his requests. He even asked Boswell in Scotland to gather up what he could on the Scottish poet James Thomson. When a biography was freshly printed, he would take the proof sheets to Streatham and let Mrs Thrale, Fanny Burney and others read them aloud over breakfast or tea. 'Dr Johnson was very communicative concerning his present work of the Lives of the Poets,' Fanny observed. She recounted the playfulness with which he floated the biographies among them: 'I was then looking over the Life of Cowley, which he had himself given me to read, at the same time that he gave to Mrs Thrale that of Waller. They are now printed, though they will not be published for some time. But he bid me put it away ... "Do,["] cried he, ["]put away that now, & prattle with us ... I can't make this little Burney prattle ... and I am sure she prattles well[."]' 'I could not help remarking how very like Dr Johnson is to his writing,' she added, 'and how much the same thing it was to hear, or to read him ... but that nobody could tell that, without coming to Streatham, for his language was generally imagined to be laboured & studied, instead of the nice common flow of his thoughts.'[7]

[3]

Boswell was in London in the spring of 1778, recording more than 150 pages of Johnson's conversation. One of the most famous scenes in the *Life* he captured on this visit was Johnson's ill-tempered quarrel with the priggish Percy over the literary merits of Thomas Pennant's *Tour in Scotland* (1771). Johnson praised the book but Percy 'opposed Johnson eagerly' because Pennant did not like his precious patron the Duke of Northumberland's estate at Alnwick. To Johnson this was nonsense and self-interest. They fell to arguing about whether or not Pennant was correct in describing Northumberland's gardens as excessively 'trim', a criticism that could sting anyone who wished to be thought of as at the forefront of the new natural style of landscaping. Percy was so fired with indignation he foolishly said to Johnson he was in no position to judge anyway because he was short-sighted. Johnson retaliated by accusing Percy of 'the resentment of a narrow mind'. The temperature rose when Percy blurted out, 'Sir, you may be as rude as you please'. Johnson shouted back, 'Hold, Sir! Don't talk of rudeness; remember, Sir, you told me (puffing hard with passion struggling for a vent) I was short-sighted. We have done with civility. We are to be as rude as we please'. A few minutes later Percy, realising his horrible blunder, rushed across the room to apologise and they were immediately reconciled. 'I am willing you shall hang Pennant,' Johnson then announced. 'Hang him up, hang him up.' As he confessed to Mrs Thrale, 'I am always sorry when I make bitter speeches, & I never do it, but when I am insufferably vexed.' 'But you do suffer things to vex you, that nobody else would vex at. I am sure I have had my share of scolding from you!'[8]

Another memorable exchange was at Dilly's between Johnson and the 'ingenious Quaker lady' Mary Knowles. Except for their belief in an 'inward light' that ruled out any need for the clergy, Johnson maintained a respect for the piety of Quakers: 'I have always loved the simplicity of manners, and the spiritual-mindedness of the Quakers ... the essential part of religion [is] piety ... and many a man [is] a Quaker without knowing it'. But he bolted at the progressive Quaker position on the social roles of women. When she complained that men had much more liberty than women, his reply was intensely conservative, 'Madam, women have all the liberty they should wish to have'; he argued that men have all the dangers and that all they do is for women: 'If we require more perfection from women than from ourselves, 'tis doing them honour. And women have not the same temptations we have. They may always live in good company. Men must mix indiscriminately.' She resisted, ending with, 'Well, I hope that in another world the sexes will be equal.' He had the last word: 'You are too ambitious. We may as well desire to be angels.' Such views of his on women were only part of the picture. In coaxing Boswell to abandon his unreasonable plan to entail his estate so as to exclude the female line, he took a position he had long argued: 'Women have natural and equitable claims as well as men, and these claims are not to be capriciously or lightly superseded or infringed.' On the subject of death, Mrs Knowles's remark that it was the 'gate of life' had a different effect on him, drawing a curtain momentarily on his cheerfulness as he stood 'with his face to the chimney and [with] a serious, solemn and somewhat gloomy air, said that no rational man would die without apprehension'.[9]

There was no time for his annual summer-autumn visit to Stafford-shire in 1778. Instead, he paid Langton a five-day visit in September at Warley Camp in Essex. In spite of an injured knee and other ailments, Langton recalled, 'he sat, with a patient degree of attention, to observe the proceedings of a regimental court martial', did the rounds of the camp at eleven one night, and entered with informed interest into conversation on military subjects, especially gunpowder. It was damp and cold, and he worried over his own and Langton's health.[10]

In London there was plenty of elegant socialising to keep him busy, especially at Streatham and with the Burneys and the grand Elizabeth Montagu. When he had to miss one dinner with Mrs Montagu because of a cold and cough, he had to reassure her he was not making up excuses. He himself felt slighted when she neglected to give him a print of herself after a portrait by Reynolds: 'I shall think myself ill rewarded for my love and admiration if she does not give me one ... But I never could get anything from her but by pushing a face'. When she heard of his disappointment, she quickly sent him one.[11]

[4]

During these years and to the end of his life Johnson was especially amenable to having his likeness cut in stone or painted, and artists were clamouring to be allowed to 'perpetuate his image'. In 1777 his friend the prominent sculptor Joseph Nollekens, who had sculpted a monument for Goldsmith in Westminster Abbey which Johnson supplied with an epitaph, carved his bust and exhibited it at the Royal Academy. Johnson was not unaware of the honour done him by this, sending a cast of it to Lucy in Lichfield who, along with Mrs Thrale, Renny, Sir Joshua and Garrick's wife, did not like it. 'I think my friend Joe Nollekens can chop out a head with any of them,' he once remarked, but the head did not much please him because he thought it deprived him of his individuality by showing him with too much hair – 'the flowing locks of a sturdy Irish beggar' – and making him look like just another ancient poet in an art gallery. He seemed to be covering his embarrassment by dismissing the bust as not his idea: 'These things [like paintings of him] have never cost me anything, so that I do not much know the price.' The bust was made for the exhibition at the Royal Academy in 1777, he added, 'and shown for the honour of the artist, who is a man of reputation above any of the other sculptors'. He sat for this third portrait by Reynolds in 1774 or 1775 and in October 1778 sat for him twice for his fourth.[12]

The third, possibly the one commonly called the 'Blinking Sam' portrait, shows Johnson poring over a book, obviously near-sighted and struggling to make out the words. He was unhappy with it, too, according to Mrs Thrale, remarking that he 'would not be known by posterity for his defects only, let Sir Joshua do his worst'. Reynolds apparently had no such vanity since his self-portrait then hanging in the Library at Streatham, said Mrs Thrale, depicts his difficulty in hearing. Johnson was unimpressed. 'He may paint himself as deaf if he chooses', Johnson insisted, 'but I will not be blinking Sam.' There are problems in connecting with any certainty the account by Mrs Thrale to this painting, but the portrait itself is a penetrating study of Johnson at the age of sixty-six, not long after the Hebridean tour, as if in the act of reading some political pamphlet which he was about to attack with relish. The 1778 portrait pleased him and others more. Known as the Streatham portrait (now at Tate Britain) because it was painted as one of a series of eminent friends of the Thrales to hang in the new library there, it shows him in a white wig with something of a pained look on his face, as if struggling for breath. Hawkins had a different take on it: 'There is in it that appearance of a labouring, working mind, of an indolent reposing body, which he had to a very great degree.' Johnson was concerned most with how it would please Mrs Thrale: 'Sir Joshua has finished my picture, and it seems to please everybody, but I shall want to see how it pleases you.'[13]

[5]

By October 1778, the booksellers had finished printing almost all the the *English Poets*. Publication waited only on Johnson. Cadell tried to push him. 'I am exceedingly sorry for the delay,' Johnson explained, 'but you see I have taken a course very different from what I originally thought on. I thought to have given four or five pages to an author ... There are however but eight upon whom I can think of dilating, and of those when Dryden is finished, four are done.' The booksellers had little option but to go ahead and publish all fifty-six volumes of the *English Poets* in the autumn and at the same time publish a separate volume of the Prefaces he had finished, including 'Milton' and several short ones which he could churn out quickly. The Prefaces would be available only to purchasers of the complete set, a strategy that backfired somewhat when people took to borrowing the volumes of Prefaces instead of acquiring them by buying the *English Poets*. Feeling the booksellers breathing down his neck, he completed 'Milton' by January and then went to work immediately on the short ones, several of which were relatively insubstantial and based almost entirely on *Biographia Britannica*. The following February he told Renny he had 'about a week's work to do'. By 1 March he had turned in twenty-two biographies of a total of fifty-two poets, making up four volumes that appeared that month as *Prefaces, Biographical and Critical, to the Works of the English Poets*. Fifteen hundred copies were printed, one of which he sent to the King, thus fulfilling a promise in that memorable interview in 1767 that he would someday publish 'a literary biography of this country'. 'If the King is a Whig, he will not like them,' he wrote to Mrs Thrale, 'but is any King a Whig?'[14]

Whigs, in fact, did not like the Prefaces, though most people admired Johnson's critical energy and insight in them. Edmond Malone gently pointed out that unfortunately his 'political principles break out' in them, especially in 'Waller' and 'Milton'; others were less gentle in lamenting his 'Tory' political prejudices. 'The hounds of Whiggism have opened in full cry', Boswell wrote. Malone also mentioned that while the 'critical parts' were 'amusing and instructive', the biographical sections were flawed by 'want of industry': 'He hates much trouble. A man of infinitely inferior parts (Horace Walpole, for instance) would have collected a great many anecdotes, and made a more entertaining work.' Johnson wrote in 'Dryden' that he did not know of any description of the poet's appearance, but Malone coolly observed, 'There are few English poets of whose external appearance more particulars have been recorded.' What did deeply impress Malone was the humanity and wisdom in the Prefaces that could never be matched by a mere accumulation of facts. Many reviewers and readers regretted Johnson had failed to turn up much new biographical information. Others were astounded that a man of seventy could write 'with so much fire'.[15]

[6]

The pleasure of publication was dampened considerably by the sudden death of Garrick on 20 January 1779. Swallowed up by his work, Johnson had been less alert to Garrick's illness than he would otherwise have been – 'a death, I believe, totally unexpected'. In his *Life of Smith*, he concluded with this famous comment on Garrick's death: 'What are the hopes of man! I am disappointed by that stroke of death, which has eclipsed the gaiety of nations, and impoverished the public stock of harmless pleasure.' Just over a year later, Beauclerk, too, would die suddenly on 11 March 1780 at the age of forty. 'Another will not often be found among mankind,' Johnson felt, although there was in his last days a dark side to Beauclerk's love for him. 'At his age he should be thinking of better things than to abuse people,' Beauclerk had grumbled. And Burke described a bitter quarrel between them at the Club as 'between Fury and Malevolence'. As usual, all was soon forgiven. In April 1781, as Johnson and Boswell were leaving Eva Garrick's house in the Adelphi Terrace after a happy and nostalgic evening with David's widow and friends including Hannah More, Elizabeth Carter, Reynolds and Burney, they paused by the rails and looked out over the Thames. Boswell reminded Johnson that they had recently lost two dear friends who lived in the Adelphi. 'Ay, Sir,' Johnson answered tenderly, 'and two such friends as cannot be supplied.'[16]

Johnson awoke on Good Friday, 1779, after a bad night and a 'disorder in my breast', went through the motions of fasting, and ended the day weighed down with post-publication melancholia. All he felt he had to show for the year was 'dismal vacuity', broken health, and the biographies, as well as a 'little charity' – which actually was quite a lot on behalf of Levet, Mrs Desmoulins, Mrs Williams, Tom Davies, Phoebe Herne, and a number of others including a few young people and pensioners. On Easter eve, his review of his life was 'comfortless': 'Little done ... my mind has neither been improved nor enlarged. I have read little, almost nothing, and I am not conscious that I have gained any good, or quitted any evil habit.' He was under no illusions about the Prefaces, expecting to be attacked. 'The worst thing you can do to a man is to be silent. An assault of a town is a bad thing, but starving it is still worse,' he wrote, and 'It is very rarely that an author is hurt by his critics.'[17]

Fanny Burney failed to notice his melancholy. 'Dr Johnson has more fun, & comical humour, & laughable & ... nonsense about him, than almost anybody I ever saw,' she wrote. 'I mean, though, when with those he likes; for otherwise, he can be as severe & bitter as report relates of him.' She herself thought twice before writing to him, as she said to him in a letter in November: 'How could I live so much at Streatham, & not perceive your cruelty to letter scribblers? Have I not again & again seen irony gathering in your eyes, & laughter trembling upon your lips as you have glanced over their unfortunate productions?' 'What pity that he will not curb the vehemence of his love of victory and superiority!', she observed a year later after he had savaged someone on the matter of Pope's wit, behaving, as usual, in a manner that made him 'dreaded by all, and by many abhorred'. According to Fanny, he was now 'constantly omitted' in invitations, 'either from too much respect or too much fear'. Mrs Thrale complained, too, which elicited this remarkable admission from him about his temperamental 'genius': 'have you not observed in all our conversations that my *genius* is always in extremes ... I am very noisy, or very silent; very gloomy, or very merry; very sour or very kind? And would you have me cross my *genius* when it leads me sometimes to voracity and sometimes to abstinence? You know that the oracle said follow your *Genius*'.[18]

After a month away in Lichfield and Ashbourne in late spring 1779, where he said he had eaten more fruit than since he was twenty, his good spirits returned again. 'I grow light and airy,' he scribbled to Mrs Thrale in Brighton. 'A man that does not begin to grow light and airy at seventy, is certainly losing time, if he intends ever to be light and airy.' That autumn, however, the nation was feeling far from 'light and airy'. There was a good deal of political restlessness and concern: the American war was dragging on and there was economic recession from diminished trade and harsh taxation. There was also a lingering fear of invasion by the French and Spanish, who in June with a combined fleet of sixty-six ships and twelve frigates – sometimes referred to as 'the other Armada' – had sailed to within sight of Plymouth on their way to landing on the Isle of Wight and at Portsmouth. There were forty thousand troops at Le Havre and St Malo waiting to follow them. Confusion, perhaps an easterly wind, and illness among the French and Spanish sailors prevailed and the fleet was forced to sail back to Brest without having fired a cannon ball. The threat persisted, however. 'I suppose you are all frighted at Lichfield and indeed the terror has been very general,' Johnson wrote to Lucy on 24 August. 'Our ships are said to have greater guns, and to be better manned,' he tried to reassure her, adding that the battle promised to be 'of greater consequence than any battle in our time'. If they spilled ashore at Portsmouth, 'we ... must fight for ourselves upon our own ground ... If we are invaded the King is said to have resolved that he will head his own army'. It was also expected that Lord North's ministry would fall, but when Parliament reconvened in November, North saw off the challenge from the Opposition. 'Those are happiest who are out of the noise and tumult,' Johnson said on reflection.[19]

[7]

As winter drew on, he felt hemmed in by the large amount of work still to be done with the *Lives*. Boswell had tried to help him in May 1778. One day he stopped by the home of the Earl of Marchmont, once an intimate friend of Pope's who had much to tell about the poet. Marchmont modestly asked Boswell to tell Johnson he was willing to help him any way he could and that he would even call on him. Boswell agreed to arrange a meeting for the following day. Excited by the valuable and easy source of anecdotes he had secured for Johnson, that evening at Streatham he proudly announced the good news. 'I shall not be in town tomorrow. I don't care to know about Pope,' Johnson answered. Everyone was nonplussed except for Mrs Thrale, 'I suppose, Sir, Mr Boswell thought, that as you are to write Pope's Life, you would wish to know about him'. Johnson would have none of it: 'Wish! Why yes. If it rained knowledge I'd hold out my hand; but I would not give myself the trouble to go in quest of it.' It was a matter of pride, a protest against being drawn into 'a state of obligation' by Boswell's forward meddling. Still, he allowed that sometime or other he might draw on Marchmont. The meeting did not occur until an entire year later, when, after drinking chocolate at Paoli's, and dressed 'in his best suit and Parisian wig', he and Boswell called on the old statesman. Walking home after two hours, Johnson admitted, 'I would rather have given twenty pounds than not have come.' 'Pope' would be his last life and he would not earnestly begin work on it until six months later.[20]

Just when he needed it most a literary hoard fell in his lap, a fair copy of the manuscript of Joseph Spence's collection of anecdotes and observations on literature (chiefly Pope), later published as *Anecdotes* in 1820. Spence was a friend of Pope's in his later years and the important notes he kept of the poet's remarks and observations were a hugely valuable source that Johnson was the first ever to use extensively. He was given the chance to read Spence's notes by Sir Lucas Pepys, the Thrales's physician as well as his own in the last two years of his life, who arranged the loan with the owner of the manuscript, the Duke of Newcastle. Johnson disappointed a number of people by not properly acknowledging Newcastle as his benefactor in this instance. He did not use the manuscript much right away, but the possession of it spurred him on. By April 1780 he was not exactly in a gallop, rather more in a fast jog. He thought he would 'bolt upon' Mrs Thrale in Bath if he could finish 'Addison', 'Prior' and 'Rowe' before she returned to London, but he fell behind and she did not have a spare room for him anyway. He had about nineteen remaining, a total of 250 pages in the modern edition, of which those on Edward Young, Swift and (especially) Pope were going to be lengthy.[21]

Longing to be out of his biographical straitjacket, he envied Mrs Thrale who was among the living conquering hearts in 'places of high resort', while he was 'seeking for something to say about men of whom I know nothing but their verses, and sometimes very little of them'. He still had not finished 'Rowe' nine days later because of a stream of visitors. Neither did it help that he was dining out almost every night, 'I have had I am afraid, too many dinners of late', though for several months he had controlled his diet and brought his weight down considerably, and had made himself feel better than he had for twenty years. Colds and coughs continued to disturb his nights, for which he was being bled. 'My Lives creep on,' he declared, not knowing when he would 'smell hay, or suck clover flowers' again at Ashbourne. There was a brief, enjoyable change of pace at the Royal Academy exhibition in the newly opened Somerset House (designed by Sir William Chambers) on 1 May, where he was struck by the contrast of the 'contour' and 'grace' of the paintings to the dull monochrome of his existence. In June he began sitting for a portrait by Renny, which delighted him since it gave him the chance to relax with her. The summer of dejection wore on with no great results: 'I have sat at home in Bolt Court, all the summer, thinking to write the Lives, and a great part of the time only thinking . . . I still think to do the rest.' 'Pope', however, loomed on the horizon like Everest: 'I wish the work was over, and I was at liberty' – to do what, he was not sure in a life full of plans 'never brought into practice'. He pined to travel to Europe, Asia and Africa with Boswell. Particularly enticing was Henry Thrale's impulsive revival of an Italian tour, planned by Baretti, even if, like Mrs Thrale, he felt it was a foolish idea in light of the brewer's mental and physical health. Nevertheless, if the trip did happen he was determined not to be left behind'.[22]

[8]

In addition to the six remaining volumes of Prefaces that were published on 15 May 1779, the booksellers decided in March to print three thousand copies of a separate edition of all of them in four volumes, scheduled for publication also in May but delayed until June. The title for the first time identified the biographies as *The Lives of the Most Eminent English Poets; With Critical Observations on Their Works*. A purchaser of this set would get all the Prefaces and make it unnecessary for anyone to buy the complete set of the *English Poets* to acquire them. This decision was less a charitable act towards people who had not purchased the set in 1779 than a ploy to pre-empt Dublin booksellers trying to get in on the act. In August and September 1782 Johnson revised the *Lives* – chiefly with additions that Nichols, Boswell, Steevens and others had turned up, although he was fairly indifferent about the process – and in February 1783, three thousand copies of a new edition, 'considerably altered', was published, for which he was paid £100. Thus ended six long years of labour on the project.[23]

Johnson's achievement in the *Lives of the Poets* was uneven. While 'Milton', 'Dryden', 'Swift' and 'Pope' were book-length, and 'Cowley', 'Waller', 'Prior', 'Addison' and 'Young' were also lengthy, many were very short, perfunctory, ill-researched, borrowed, and merely adapted from existing biographies. The lengths were at times oddly disproportionate. Edmund Smith, Sir Richard Blackmore, Ambrose Philips and Nicholas Rowe, for example, not exactly giants in the English literary canon, commanded more pages than William Collins and Thomas Gray, whose poetry he disliked but who were among the most loved and influential poets of the late eighteenth century. Gray's odes are 'forced plants, raised in a hotbed', Johnson announced, 'and they are poor plants; they are but cucumbers after all', fit for hogs. 'I said to the Doctor he might have been kinder to Gray,' Boswell wrote in his journal. 'He very justly said he could not be kind ... He was to tell what he thought; and if people differed from him, they were to tell him so.' Several poets were chosen simply because the booksellers decided to include them in their collection, not because Johnson saw them as promising or worthy subjects. Modern readers scratch their heads over the inclusion of poets like Broome, Duke, Halifax, Pitt, Smith, Somervile, Stepney and West most of whom are not even included in the *Oxford Companion to English Literature*, and are mystified that he left out of the *Lives* the following major poets: Richard Crashaw, Richard Lovelace, Robert Herrick, Andrew Marvell and Goldsmith. The omission of Goldsmith was not his fault but due to a bookseller who owned the copyright of one of his works and refused to allow him to be included.[24]

He divided the longer and middle-sized lives into three sections: the biographic, a character sketch, and literary criticism. As already mentioned, he was not resourceful in gathering biographical material, which he acknowledged somewhat disingenuously in his 'Advertisement': 'the succession of facts is not easily discovered ... I must be supposed to have engaged in it with less provision of materials than might have been accumulated by longer premeditation. Of the later writers at least I might, by attention and enquiry, have gleaned many particulars, which would have diversified and enlivened my biography.' The character study was crucial because it mediated between literature and life, thus enabling him to demonstrate how a poet's life and works interacted with one another.[25]

What especially engaged his critical imagination and genius was the critical section. As in his Preface to his Shakespeare edition, in these biographies he took the reader into a more complex and discriminating critical study of literature than had ever before been attempted. This was not the work of an industrious commentator or editor but the fruit of a penetrating, enquiring, iconoclastic critic. It is putting it mildly to say that his readers did not always agree with his critical judgement, but he forced them to reason and to think about literature in ways that very few people were accustomed to doing with the existing English literary canon. In short, again, instead of literary fashion his endlessly flexible but pragmatic compass guided him to consider whether poetry conforms to 'truth' and the centrality of life. If he felt it did not, typically he was brisk and uncompromising in telling the reader forcibly why not, often exaggerating (as in conversation) to make his point. That led him to make many unconventional literary judgements which landed him in deep water. This drive to establish his critical principles and then apply them quickly to the experiences of life constituted his powerful voice and stability as a critic. 'To circumscribe poetry by a definition', he wrote in 'Pope', 'will only show the narrowness of the definer.' Literature was not for him a rarefied aspect of human expression but part of ordinary and endlessly complicated life itself; it was another of life's pleasures.[26]

His political bias, evident strongly in 'Milton', 'Waller' and 'Lyttelton', also outraged many. He called Milton 'an acrimonious and surly Republican'; and his contemptuous (and largely inexplicable) dismissal of the Staffordshire Whig George, Baron Lyttelton incurred the disapproval and even wrath of much of London polite society, friends as well as enemies, and notably Elizabeth Montagu and the bluestockings who struck him off their list. He told Mrs Thrale he had already begun 'to tremble for my admission' in Mrs Montagu's new house. 'I doubt I shall never see the inside of it.' Mrs Montagu's anticipated rejection prompted his priceless remark to Boswell: 'Now, Sir, there are people whom one should like very well to drop but would not wish to be dropped by.' His strong religious views also affected his critical judgement, openly in 'Milton', for example, and implicitly in the biographies of 'profane' authors like the Restoration dramatists Thomas Otway and William Congreve. His general view was that 'The ideas of Christian theology are too simple for eloquence, too sacred for fiction, and too majestic for ornament; to recommend them by tropes and figures is to magnify by a concave mirror the sidereal hemisphere.' He censured Milton's wonderful pastoral-Christian poem Lycidas for this reason.[27]

Above all, he did not get himself personally out of the way in many of the Prefaces, either critically, politically, socially or morally. As one commentator has put it, 'The individual, standing in the full shaft of light, is identical with the moving spirit of the whole vast impersonal enterprise.' One of his dominant autobiographical themes is the economic and social distress an author frequently endures. Money and indigence are often themes, as are the slipperiness of reputation and the monster of despair that spectrally haunts the imagination with the realisation that life is ebbing away. Writer's block and the notion that one can write only in a particular place or at a particular time are particular nonsense, he argues in 'Milton': 'The author that thinks himself weather-bound will find ... that he is only idle or exhausted; but while this notion has possession of the head, it produces the inability which it supposes. Our powers owe much of their energy to our hopes ... When success seems attainable, diligence is enforced; but when it is admitted that the faculties are suppressed by a cross wind, or a cloudy sky, the day is given up without resistance.'[28]

There were other hazards of authorship he understood intimately. Explaining why Pope took five years to translate the *Iliad*, he wrote feelingly about the rival claims of art and life and the folly of self-deluding deadlines to projects agreed to in the sunshine of early hope. He drew on his painful recollections of a career full of delays:

> It is natural to suppose, that as much as has been done today may be done tomorrow; but on the morrow some difficulty emerges, or some external impediment obstructs. Indolence, interruption, business, and pleasure, all take their turns of retardation; and every long work is lengthened by a thousand causes that can, and ten thousand that cannot, be recounted ... He that runs against time, has an antagonist not subject to casualties.

Pope was equal to such challenges. Addison sometimes was not and turned to the bottle. Johnson, who dedicated much of his life to avoiding wine and talking of its dangers, as well as to the use of conversation to resist loneliness and melancholia, wrote about Addison: 'From the coffee-house he went again to a tavern, where he often sat late, and drank too much wine. In the bottle, discontent seeks for comfort, cowardice for courage, and bashfulness for confidence ... He that feels oppression from the presence of those to whom he knows himself superior, will desire to set loose his powers of conversation; and who, that ever asked succour from Bacchus, was able to preserve himself from being enslaved by his auxiliary?' Nor could Addison, any more than anyone else, control the vicissitudes of reputation: 'Time quickly puts an end to artificial and accidental fame ... Every name which kindness or interest once raised too high is in danger lest the next age should by the vengeance of criticism sink it in the same proportion.' This turned out to be one of the major themes of the *Lives* – it was the old, persistent theme of the vanity of human wishes.[29]

[9]

The years 1778 to 1780 were difficult for the Thrales. Even as he continued to rely on them for support and comfort and threw himself into the *Lives of the Poets*, Johnson entered completely into their troubles. In spite of the help of friends and able assistants and managers, Thrale had been mismanaging his brewery business largely by brewing too much beer. He had also eaten up capital in 1777 on lavish improvements to Streatham instead of investing it in the business. Inevitably, in April 1778 there was a financial crisis. 'Here is a new agony,' Mrs Thrale bitterly complained to Johnson, 'my master dispirited and almost in despair about pecuniary matters ... looks like death ... and is likely to die himself instead of me'. She and others had to scramble to round up some money quickly to stave off bankruptcy. Thrale's melancholic moods were also vexing his wife as much as ever, making her feel ignored and unwanted. 'All sorrow that lasts longer than its cause is morbid, and should be shaken off as an attack of melancholy, as the forerunner of a greater evil than poverty or pain,' Johnson warned them. Not until November was Thrale better. This time the black dog had 'gnawed him to the bone', Johnson gloomily observed. The next time the dog was likely 'to pick my master's heart out'. The following June Thrale suffered not an attack by the dog but a severe stroke from which he recovered quickly but without ever regaining his strength completely. Johnson's advice to Mrs Thrale was to keep her husband 'cheerful' and herself 'airy' – 'be a funny little thing'. For months afterwards Johnson offered advice to Thrale on exercise, diet and mood to prevent another attack. Another cruel blow to Mrs Thrale was a miscarriage on 10 August 1779, 'in the utmost agony before they could get me into bed, after fainting five times'. Then the roof more or less fell in at the general election of September 1780, in the wake of a severe economic recession in 1779, when Thrale lost his Southwark seat in Parliament. 'Mr Thrale's loss of health has lost him the election,' Johnson reported to Boswell. From that moment, Thrale deteriorated rapidly.[30]

Then in June 1780, six days of violent civil unrest known as the Gordon riots did not help anyone's frame of mind, least of all the Thrales'. The Catholic Relief Act of 1778, freeing Catholics from restrictions on land ownership and inheritance, lay behind it. Lord George Gordon led a procession of fifty thousand people from Southwark to Westminster to call for a repeal, but inevitably the crowd turned hostile, attacking and burning the homes of prominent politicians and judges thought to be responsible for the Act, most sensationally Lord Mansfield's, even burning his possessions in the street. The mob targeted Catholic residences and businesses and opened all the major prisons and released prisoners, a chilling anticipation of the storming of the Bastille in Paris nine years later. They also set fire to the prisons, the flames of Newgate rising high into the sky. London had not seen fires like this since the Great Fire of 1666, as Johnson reported to the Thrales in Bath: 'At night they set fire to the Fleet [prison], and to the King's Bench [in Southwark], and I know not how many other places; you might see the glare of conflagration fill the sky from many parts. Some people were threatened, Mr Strahan moved what he could, and advised me to take care of myself. Such a time of terror you have been happy in not seeing.' The Thrales were terrified by his account and what they heard from their own sources because their brewery was in immediate danger. Had it not been for the courage of their manager John Perkins, who spoke to the rioters and offered them free beer, they probably would have burned it down as well. The episode marked a low point in the Thrales' roller coaster fortunes of recent years.[31]

Whatever elation Johnson may have felt on completing his *Prefaces* at the end of 1780 was checked suddenly in April 1781 by Henry Thrale's death at the age of fifty-two. Johnson was with him in his last hours: 'I felt almost the last flutter of his pulse, and looked for the last time upon the face that for fifteen years had never been turned upon me but with respect or benignity. Farewell.' Johnson urged Mrs Thrale to hold on to the brewery and manage it herself for a salary of a maximum of about £2,000 per year (about £200,000 today) – and he would help her. This did not seem like much to her. Before her husband's death, she had written on 29 January 1781, 'Mr Thrale *may* die, and not leave me sufficient to keep Streatham open as it has been kept, and I shall hate to live in it with more thought about expenses than I have done.' It was likely, she guessed, she would have to say 'farewell [to] pretty Streatham, where I have spent many a merry hour, and many a sad one'. On the strong advice of her husband's executors, however, within two months she had sold the brewery to Perkins and the Barclay family for £135,000 (about thirteen million today). Instead of income from the brewery, therefore, she would live on the interest from £30,000 (her portion of the sale proceeds), somewhat more than the projected brewery income; she also had both the Streatham and Southwark houses, and all the furniture in each. The rest of the sale proceeds would be held in trust for the children. Under Perkins, to whom she generously and out of gratitude gave the Southwark house and all the furniture in it, the brewery prospered, but in light of the manner in which she was accustomed to living her own finances were now cramped and she would have to take in her sails. Life now at Streatham would never be the same for Johnson.[32]

CHAPTER 31

Losing Ground

[1]

Thrale's death was a severe blow to Johnson. He told Mrs Thrale that no death since Tetty's 'has ever oppressed me like this ... I am afraid of thinking what I have lost'. 'I never had such a friend.' The loss signalled a changed world for him. 'With him were buried many of my hopes and pleasures,' he entered into his diary for Good Friday, 1781. 'I enjoyed his favour for almost a fourth part of my life.' The changes in store for him as a result of Thrale's death were far greater and less pleasing than he anticipated.[1]

Boswell's London visit that spring did not yield as large a crop of Johnson's conversations as did earlier visits, but it was notable for a bawdy *jeu d'esprit* he composed at Reynolds's house, *Ode by Dr Samuel Johnson to Mrs Thrale Upon Their Supposed Approaching Nuptials*. That he wrote it eight days after Thrale's death and only one after his funeral seems a supreme instance of bad taste. Since the song had Johnson saying to his 'dearest darling' that he was her 'slave', that Tetty 'no longer shall be prais'd', and that now Thrale was in his grave he was rescued from 'lonely gloom' in the 'Blissful Bower' by an 'aphrodisian spasm' with 'our limbs entwin'd/And lip in rapture glued to lip', it is not surprising that for months he was terrified lest either should learn of it. While Johnson never did, Mrs Thrale read it for the first time in the *Life*, never suspecting Boswell wrote it. For the sake of a bawdy song, Boswell was registering what he feared and enabling himself to laugh about it. Hawkins's daughter Letitia summed it up: 'On the death of Mr Thrale it was concluded by some that he would marry the widow; by others that he would entirely take up his residence in her house, which resembling the situation of many other learned men, would have been nothing extraordinary or censurable.' But on Hawkins's wife asking him if he was going to join Mrs Thrale at Bath, Johnson 'roared out', '*I* know nothing of Mrs

Thrale', and stormed out of their house. In Johnson's own house and well out of his hearing, his good friend William Scott (one of his executors) and Boswell 'agreed that it was possible Mrs Thrale might marry Dr Johnson, and we ... wished it much' – a notion that anyone familiar enough with Mrs Thrale's heart and mind would have found ludicrous.[2]

[2]

After Thrale's death, the family at first picked up the pieces well enough to restore life at Streatham through the summer of 1781 with a pleasing routine and some semblance of happiness, with Johnson there almost constantly now that he had completed the *Lives*. He urged Mrs Thrale to put grief behind her, 'the world is all before us ... I hope we shall never lose the kindness which has grown up between us'. He continued to instruct Queeney and occasionally Fanny (who spent most of the summer at Streatham) in Latin, and the children kept at their harpsichord lessons with Dr Burney. There was a relatively new figure present – another Italian besides Baretti – the singer and composer Gabriel Piozzi who taught the girls singing and encouraged them to translate Italian poetry. Liked by everyone including Johnson, Piozzi was a fixture there until early July when he left for a visit to Italy. Little did Johnson then suspect how Piozzi's presence ultimately would torment him and disrupt others' lives. Piozzi's cheerfulness and helpfulness enveloped Mrs Thrale with a feeling of warmth, consideration and affection that threw Johnson's demanding and critical presence into greater negative relief for her than ever before. She needed uncritical support. Suffering from nervousness, a rash that lasted for the month of September, and depression, she was losing weight and told Johnson, 'I fear I shall never be happy again in this world.' She did not let on to anyone, perhaps not even to herself, but the reason for her unhappiness was Piozzi's absence until late November. It is telling that Boswell's few visits to Streatham in the spring were enough to alert him to the especially warm relationship between her and Piozzi because in his *Ode* he joked that Johnson once saw Piozzi as a rival: 'Piozzi once alarm'd my fears/ ... Indignant thought to English pride!/That any eye should ever see/Johnson one moment set aside/For Tweedledum and Tweedledee' – that is, for a musical performer.[3]

Having missed Lichfield the previous year, Johnson was determined to go in October 1781. He found Lucy deafer than ever and 'very inarticulate': 'I can scarcely make her understand me, and she can hardly make me understand her. So there are merry doings.' Her health was 'broken' and she ate and exercised little. He was relieved to find, for a change, that Elizabeth Aston's health had not deteriorated and that Mrs Gastrell was 'brisk and lively'. From his tired perspective, time seemed to stand oppressively still in Lichfield: 'All here is gloomy, a faint struggle with the tediousness of time, a doleful confession of present misery, and the approach seen and felt of what is most dreaded and most shunned.' He looked to Boswell and Mrs Thrale for rejuvenation. 'What enjoyment has a sick man visiting the sick?' he asked Boswell. 'Shall we ever have another frolic like our journey to the Hebrides?' And longing for Streatham, he sought to encourage Mrs Thrale with the thought that when he and Piozzi returned 'you will have two about you that love you'.[4]

'Dear Dr Johnson is at last returned,' Mrs Thrale entered in her journal on 17 December, but his appearance shocked her: 'My fear is lest he should grow paralytic, there are really some symptoms already discoverable I think, about the mouth particularly; he will drive the gout away . . . when it comes, and it must go *somewhere*.' More serious, immediately on his return the chronic bronchial infection from which he had suffered intermittently for twenty years became acute and developed into emphysema. Very concerned, over the next five months he wrote a series of letters to Dr Lawrence in Latin – Lawrence always insisted on discussing medical questions in Latin – reciting the symptoms and informing him what he had done and wished to do to alleviate his discomfort. With Lawrence's help, he began bleeding himself at an alarming rate, over fifty ounces in the next ten weeks, sometimes fairly certain it was doing him good, at other times not. His breathing was so difficult he often had to sleep, or try to sleep, sitting up in a chair. The opium he took only subjected him to the 'tyranny of vain imaginations'. It did not help that on 17 January Levet suddenly died at the age of seventy-seven. His 'faithful adherent for thirty years', Levet had been the healthiest person at Bolt Court and now he was gone.[5]

In March and April 1782 he composed an elegy, 'On the Death of Dr Robert Levet', which has been called 'one of the noblest short elegies in the language'.[6] It was published in the August 1783 issue of *The Gentleman's Magazine*. With its moving biographical realism it illustrates Johnson's habitual resistance to vague and

conventional eulogy. Levet is no literary paragon of virtue but
'Officious, innocent, sincere/ ... Obscurely wise, and coarsely kind;/
... His virtues walk'd their narrow round'/ ... Unfelt, uncounted'.
The poem celebrates Levet's particular and eccentric mode of charity
amid real poverty, the 'power of art without the show', in the faceless
London streets where 'hopeless anguish pour'd his groan,/And lonely
want retir'd to die'. It is a feeling, soulful tribute to a sincere
Christian who aspired to no material rewards. Death 'free'd his soul
the nearest way' and his eternal destiny was in no doubt, even if
'letter'd arrogance' may have been inclined to scoff at his 'single
talent well employ'd'.[7]

Levet's death did not interrupt Williams and Desmoulins's continued quarrelling, even when they were both ill. 'This little habitation
is now but a melancholy place, clouded with the gloom of disease and
death,' he moaned in early February. He helped Burney with the
conclusion of his *General History of Music*, raved about Fanny Burney's
new novel *Cecilia* in the summer, and wrote and edited for Shaw and
Lawrence parts of works on which they were engaged; but otherwise
there was little in the literary vein to occupy him. He prayed with and
instructed Frank in religion and read the Bible regularly, scarcely
stirring from home for months except to Mrs Thrale's where, as he
recklessly told Malone (who had recently been elected to the Club),
'I can use all the freedom that sickness requires'.[8]

Even the political situation wearied him. The American war had
been lost, and when Lord North resigned in March 1782, he prayed
in gratitude with Frank. Lord Rockingham's succession elicited only
his scorn: 'The men are got in whom I have endeavoured to keep out,
but I hope they will do better than their predecessors; it will not be
easy to do worse.' Then when Rockingham died in July and Lord
Shelburne and Pitt took over, only to be thrown out in February 1783
by a Charles James Fox-Lord North coalition, he threw up his hands
in disgust: 'We have now neither power nor peace, neither influence
in other nations nor quiet amongst ourselves.' The state of the nation
was deplorable: 'I cannot but suffer some pain when I compare the
state of this kingdom with that in which we triumphed twenty years
ago. I have at least endeavoured to preserve order and support monarchy.' The weakness of George III, however, and the 'tumultous'
succession of weak and divided governments appalled him. He longed
for the powerful prime ministers of the past. 'I'd as soon have a man
break my bones as talk to me of public affairs, internal or external. I

have lived to see things all as bad as they can be,' he complained bitterly to Boswell.[9]

Mrs Thrale felt stranded at Streatham as winter came on and decided at the start of the new year to take a house in Harley Street for three months even though she knew it would raise suspicion she was hunting for a husband. At least she was closer to Johnson there and could keep an eye on him. Back in Streatham by mid-April 1782, she had to rescue him from Bolt Court on 11 May, 'so very ill that I thought I should never get him home alive – such spasms on his breath; sure enough one would have believed on Thursday that he could not have lived till now: & old Lawrence his physician worse than he, dead [paralysed] on one side'. Johnson decided to try Oxford for a week or so in June for a 'change of air', but while there his thoughts were mostly on her: 'When I come back to retirement, it will be a great charity in you to let me come back to something else.'[10]

Something else other than what? He had felt her drifting away. Piozzi was to blame. She was restless and looking to the future. He represented the past while Piozzi could take her and her girls away from claustrophobic, gossiping London. She knew she and her family could not continue to live at Streatham on her smaller income, so in August she decided to act. She would remove the family to Italy, with Piozzi as their courier, where she could live more cheaply and expose the girls to that wonderful culture. Piozzi was behaving 'like an angel' and would follow her anywhere and take care of her. By this time the girls and several friends knew she had fallen completely in love with him, and he with her, though she did not tell Queeney and Fanny Burney plainly until November. She did not tell Johnson even then. She would let Streatham for three years and rent a house in London for the winter. The tricky thing was how 'my monitor, my friend, my inmate, my dear Mr Johnson' would respond. She knew that at seventy-four and in his precarious health he could not come with them.[11]

He had been feeling somewhat better after a few days in Oxford, so one sunny August day at Streatham she decided to tell him about Piozzi, Italy – everything. He had seen this coming but the news was profoundly disturbing for him, especially since it meant he would once again be denied the sight of Italy. He put a brave face on it, however, so brave that she was thrown off balance and imagined herself slighted: 'See the importance of a person to himself! I fancied Mr Johnson could not have existed without me forsooth, as we have now lived together above 18 years, & I have so fondled and waited on him in sickness & in health. Not a bit on't! he feels nothing in parting with me, nothing in the least; but thinks it a prudent scheme, & goes to his book as usual.' It was only her husband he had loved, she thought.[12]

In September 1782, she let Streatham to no less a personage than Lord Shelburne, the Prime Minister, and by early October she was packing. Suffering from a cold and an injury to his leg incurred as he was stepping down from a coach, Johnson attended church at Streatham and bade it goodbye 'with a kiss'. Afterwards, they all met for a final supper in the dining room: 'I took my place in no joyful mood ... When shall I see Streatham again?' On the evening of 6 October, he sat for the last time in the library, haunted by voices from the past, where portraits of 'Johnsonians' looked down on him. Alone in his room later, he prayed that he 'may with humble and sincere thankfulness remember the comforts and conveniences which I have enjoyed at this place and that I may resign them with holy submission, equally trusting in thy protection when Thou givest and when Thou takest away. Have mercy upon me, O Lord, have mercy upon me'. The next morning they set off early together for a stay in Brighton until 20 November, joined by Fanny Burney a few weeks later. It was a fairly disastrous six weeks. Johnson fell prey to a cold and he was cranky and wounded by Mrs Thrale's lack of attention. Fanny found him embarrassing when they went out – 'I dread him before strangers.' He was so noisy and rude, in fact, that people seldom included him in their invitations. 'I am sorry for it,' Fanny wrote, 'as he hates being alone'. This behaviour of his had been a problem for some time now, and although he was invited to large parties with Mrs Thrale and Fanny, his behaviour and the sting of his tongue, if he was displeased by something like a meal or a remark he disliked, could be offensive. A three-day excursion from Brighton on 8–10 November with Philip Metcalfe, a member of the Club, to Arundel (where 'my breath would not carry me to the old castle'), Chichester (whose cathedral charmed him with 'the final transition from the massive Norman to the lighter Gothic style') and Cowdray House in Midhurst, and then back via Petworth House ('furniture magnificent but chapel ... gloomy'), Storrington, Steyning and Bramber in West Sussex, restored his spirits somewhat in early November.[13]

Johnson's 'sickly and melancholy year' of 1782 seeped into 1783. Short of breath and in pain from gout in his foot, Johnson began to sleep downstairs in January. By April he was feeling the delicious reprieve of 'a lucid interval': 'The cough goes and comes, but is not violent, I breathe with tolerable freedom, and the pain in my foot is gone. I may perhaps, with a little caution, have an easy summer'. Until she left for Bath, Mrs Thrale rented a house in Argyll Street that served him as a temporary sanctuary. For months London society and the newspapers had buzzed with gossip and indecent squibs about her scandalous love affair with Piozzi, a foreigner far beneath her socially. It was widely suspected that he was after her money. Fanny implored her to reconsider and Queeney (now age nineteen) was cruelly cold and calculating, threatening to set up house for herself and her sisters. The pressure on her was enormous, and finally before leaving for Bath where she could escape the furore, she surrendered, telling poor Piozzi in late January she could not marry him. 'Adieu to all that's dear, to all that's lovely. I am parted from my life, my soul! My Piozzi!' she cried into her journal. Suffering and undemanding, he continued to teach singing to her daughters for two months and finally parted from her 'courageously' on 6 April when the family, except for the two youngest girls (who remained behind to attend a boarding school in Streatham and one of whom died in a few days), left for Bath. The day before this, she also parted from Johnson who was full of compassion. 'I took leave of Mrs Thrale,' he entered into his diary on 5 April 1783, probably with a trembling hand; 'I was much moved. I had some expostulations with her. She said that she was likewise affected.' They never saw each other again.[14]

It was a crushing development aggravated in May when he began to 'languish' again in health, feeling forlorn and lonely. With Levet in his grave and two sick women in the house, he now had nobody to talk to in hours of solitude. When the two women did talk they quarrelled – at least until Mrs Desmoulins surrendered and in May left the house for a year, after which he had only Mrs Williams 'to fight or play with'. The death in June of Lawrence from a stroke, another old friend gone, only added to his loneliness.[15]

With an increased 'steadiness' from having become Laird of Auchinleck on his father's recent death, Boswell again came to his rescue for a couple of months in the spring – 'He is all that he was, and more,' Johnson wrote. Looking pale and breathing with perceptible difficulty, Johnson welcomed him with open arms, 'I am glad you are come. I am very ill . . . You must be as much with me as you can. You have done me good. You cannot think how much better I am since you came in.' They spent Good Friday and Easter Sunday together as usual. The day before leaving London at the end of May, Boswell invited him to make a return visit to Auchinleck, now that he was Laird. 'I cannot come this year,' Johnson answered. 'But when I grow better, as I hope I shall, I should gladly come. I should like to totter about your place, and live mostly on milk, and be taken care of by Mrs Boswell. We are good friends now, are we not?' Then came the supreme compliment that had never been possible while Mrs Thrale was in the ascendancy: 'If I were in distress, there is no man I would come to so soon as you. I should come to you and have a cottage in your park.' But Boswell was also nervous when they parted: 'I got up from him. He took me in his arms, and said with solemn fervour, "God bless you for Jesus Christ's sake" ... I walked away ... with agitation and a kind of fearful apprehension of what might happen before I returned'. He had a word with Mrs Williams before he left, who said Johnson had not yet made a will. Less than four months after Boswell's departure it was she who was to die.[16]

Johnson sat for a painting in June, perhaps an ongoing one by Renny which he thought made him look like 'a grimly ghost'. Now at Haverford College in Pennsylvania, it was assumed to be the fifth of him by her brother, finished perhaps in early 1783. It is an intimate portrait of a suffering, ill, asthmatic old man, looking tiredly at the painter, almost as if he is struggling not to fall out of his chair and with his open, pouting lips struggling for breath. It could have been painted only by someone he knew very well – someone for whom he had sat many times before and in his extremity was willing to sit for again. It may have been that the June sitting was for John Opie, a bold and exciting new Cornish genius who became Professor of Painting at the Royal Academy in 1805 and briefly carried on a courtship with Mary Wollstonecraft. He was certainly sitting on 3 September for Opie, whose known portrait shows him solemn and thoughtful but also haggard or ill, in a very bushy powdered wig, slightly stooping, looking out with eyes dim with age, and with lower lip rather pouting. Perhaps because it showed him so weary Johnson remarked it was 'not much admired'.[17]

[3]

Ever since April 1783 his legs and feet had begun to swell from an excess of watery fluid, an ailment known then as 'the dropsy' and today as oedema, which made it painful for him to walk. The night after sitting for this last portrait, at about three in the morning, he awakened suddenly with 'a confusion and indistinctness in my head which lasted, I suppose, about half a minute'. To test whether or not it was a stroke and had affected his mind, he immediately composed a prayer to God in Latin, discovering to his infinite relief that 'the lines were not very good, but I knew them not to be very good'. However, he also discovered he could not speak. Calmly, he drank 'two drams' of wine 'to rouse the vocal organs' and 'put myself into violent motion', but his speech would not come. He could say 'no' but not 'yes'. He then fell asleep. Thomas Davies felt great pity for him, writing to Mrs Thrale on 18 June: 'Yesterday morning early Dr Johnson was afflicted with a paralytic stroke ... He is really much to be pitied. He has no female friend in his house that can do him any service on this occasion. Mrs Du Moulin [Desmoulins] has left the house for what cause, I do not know, and I would not ask.' But Johnson did not keep the crisis from Mrs Thrale in a letter that contains many writing errors and corrections, indicating a disorder known as 'dysgraphia' in which a person has difficulty expressing himself coherently in writing. He admitted to her, 'My hand, I knew not why, made wrong letters.' 'Dreadful event!' she wrote in her diary in Bath when she heard of the stroke, 'and I at a distance – poor fellow!'. A few days later he could repeat the Lord's Prayer, confident also that he had not lost any of his memory. Despite his doctors's hideous prescription of putting blisters on his back and throat (to draw noxious humours away), his voice improved steadily in the following weeks, though it was weaker and easily worn out with too much exertion. In July he was able to ride out to Hampstead and attend the Club. It was a narrow and remarkable escape, for which he wrote prayers of thanks.[18]

His diseases were becoming so complicated he decided to begin a regular, informal medical diary for Mrs Thrale, sending her close reports, diagnoses, and accounts of remedies. It makes for morbid reading, as he acknowledged to her, 'You will forgive the gross images which disease must necessarily present ... The journal now like other journals grows very *dry*, as it is not diversified either by operations or events. Less and less is done ... The first talk of the sick is commonly of themselves, but if they talk of nothing else, they cannot complain if they are soon left without an audience.' He thought of these letters as medical 'treatises', a sort of trial run for a more serious medical diary or 'Sick-Man's Journal' he was to keep in Latin later.[19]

Another effect of disease and its consequent solitariness was the intensification of his melancholia: 'The black dog I hope always to resist, and in time to drive [out] though I am deprived of almost all those that used to help me ... When I rise my breakfast is solitary, the black dog waits to share it, from breakfast to dinner he continues barking ... After dinner what remains but to count the clock, and hope for that sleep which I can scarce expect.' In the morning the whole cycle repeated itself. 'What shall exclude the black dog from a habitation like this? If I were a little richer I would perhaps take some cheerful female into the house.' It was not that he did not receive many callers, but that he could not frequently or easily get out of the house. If he could just feel well enough, he would try to 'change the air frequently this summer'.[20]

He got just that chance in mid-July, taking a two-week excursion to stay with Langton and his family in Rochester. Living with eight spoiled children in a small house does not seem like the perfect prescription for a sick and irritable man, but it turned out to be the best possible cure. The house was airy and full of light, overlooking the Medway and blessed with gentle sea breezes. After the fortnight there he felt better than he had for years. His good health continued through an extreme drought and heat wave and into September, when he accepted an invitation from William Bowles, a new friend from Wiltshire, to visit his estate, Heale House, not far from Salisbury, where Charles II had hidden in disguise for a week in October 1651. The gardens there impressed him perhaps more than any he had ever seen, like the scene of a romance, and he saw Stonehenge for the first time, immediately conceiving theories about its ancient history and function. Like everyone else's at the time, of course, they were incorrect. Salisbury Cathedral also thrilled him and he described the two places as 'the first essay and the last perfection in architecture'. Trying to keep Johnson diverted from his creeping melancholia, Bowles proposed that they take a short journey to Weymouth to see Mrs Thrale, who had gone there for the summer from Bath, but he discovered that Johnson 'had no great mind to see Mrs Thrale,' undoubtedly because Piozzi had complicated their relationship.[21]

Before he had left for Wiltshire, Mrs Williams's condition had turned critical, and while he was at Heale House she died on 6 September 1783. He received the news by messenger on the same day. This was the final increment to his loneliness: 'when I come home I shall return to a desolate habitation,' he moaned, for Frank and his wife had recently moved out of Bolt Court. He arrived home on 18 September, 'not well enough to go much out' and reduced 'to sit, and eat or fast alone' on his birthday. On 15 August he had composed a prayer for her preservation, 'Permit, O Lord, thy unworthy creature to offer up this prayer for Anna Williams, now languishing upon her bed, and about to recommend herself to thy infinite mercy.' Now he wrote another of gratitude for her friendship over more than thirty years, 'make me to remember, with due thankfulness, the comforts which I have received from my friendship with Anna Williams.' His immobility at that point was due to yet another acute physical problem. For some time he had experienced minor discomfort from testicular swelling, which had grown worse after Rochester and extremely painful at Heale House. A well-known Plymouth surgeon to whom he wrote about it in detail recommended an immediate operation, but he waited until he was home to consult with Dr William Heberden, a distinguished London physician who had made a particular name for himself by identifying the difference between chickenpox and smallpox, and two other surgeons, William Cruikshank and Percival Pott, both of whom prevaricated about 'the fire and sword' of surgery. It turned out to be a 'sarocele' or tumour. The only solution seemed to be surgery, which at his age, without an anaesthetic, was dangerous. A flare-up of his gout delayed the operation, so in the meantime Cruikshank pierced the testicle to drain it, and gradually it did drain with the result that its size and pain subsided and it healed naturally. Johnson thus escaped yet another dangerous medical crisis. 'What a man am I!', he said to Hawkins, 'who have got the better of three diseases, the palsy, the gout, and the asthma.' He was ready to fight these illnesses wherever the cures may take him.[22]

Temporary relief in October 1783 enabled him to entertain theatrical celebrities Sarah Siddons and John Philip Kemble for tea, and to engage in a few minor distractions lifting him above the demoralising monotony of his sickness and immobility. One was a hot-air balloon craze that had begun in France in the summer and swept London in the autumn. Horace Walpole was amazed: 'All our views are directed to the air. Balloons occupy senators, philosophers, ladies, everybody.' With his quick scientific curiosity, Johnson considered the chemistry and physics of the invention, but most of all he was interested in its uses: 'If a case could be found at once light and strong a man might mount with his ball, and go whither the winds would carry him ... The cases which have hitherto been used are apparently defective, for the balls come to the ground.' In spite of having written in *Rasselas* about the dark possibilities of flight, the idea of flying appealed to him psychologically, anchored heavily as he was to earth by his diseased body and destined to grope about with gout. It remained to be seen how soon someone would become airborne in a balloon and sustain a flight for some distance.[23]

Another more substantial diversion he took steps to provide for himself was clubbing. At first he and his old friend John Ryland, both original members of the Ivy Lane Club back in 1749, 'warmed ourselves into a wish' for a reunion and revival of the surviving members of that club. The old meeting-place had shut down and the neighbourhood was now unsavoury, so with Hawkins and the bookseller John Payne, the only other surviving members they could track down, they dined elsewhere in late November. 'One of us thought the other grown very old,' he commented ruefully, and their meeting was 'somewhat tender'. As Hawkins described the evening, 'when we were collected, the thought that we were so few, occasioned some melancholy reflections ... We dined, and in the evening regaled with coffee'. They broke up early, however, at ten, 'much to the regret of Johnson, who proposed staying; but finding us inclined to separate, he left us with a sigh that seemed to come from his heart, lamenting that he was retiring to solitude and cheerless meditation'. Their idea was to meet once a month, but Johnson's health did not allow more than one further meeting in mid-April when they were 'as cheerful as in former times' except that he 'could not make quite so much noise' because of his weak voice.[24]

In any case, it was better to start a new club with a good membership, so with Brocklesby in December 1783 he founded the Essex Head Club as an alternative to the large, heterogeneous, commercially and professionally based Club with which he was now disaffected. This would be 'a little evening club' meeting three days a week in the Essex Head tavern kept by an old servant of Thrale's in Essex Street, close to home just off the Strand. Johnson specified rules that would ensure the orderly election and more or less regular attendance of its twenty-four members, including an obligatory payment of sixpence per person at each meeting and a fine of twopence for every meeting missed. Anyone who failed to attend for three months would be dropped. Among the members were Brocklesby, Nichols, Murphy, John Hoole, who wrote the most complete account there exists of Johnson's last three weeks and who was one of his most loyal friends in the last few years, the Virginian landowner John Paradise, and the athletic and eminent Whig politician William Windham who since 1778 had also been a member of the Turk's Head Club. Johnson invited Reynolds to join, but as his rival James Barry, who was Professor at the Royal Academy and also painted Johnson (c.1778–80), was also to be a member, he declined. The club was a good idea because Johnson could attend its meetings conveniently in his neighbourhood to escape 'the solitude of the long evenings' at home. The first one was on 8 December, but sadly after that he was 'hindered from attending ... by want of breath'.[25]

Indeed, want of breath shut him down for four months. 'I am severely crushed by my old spasms,' he moaned near the end of December, which prevented him from getting any sleep at all at night. 'Spiritless, infirm, sleepless, and solitary, looking back with sorrow and forward with terror', he began to take opium copiously. Contrary to Hawkins's assertion that he had begun to take opium 'in large quantities' as early as 1764, he had taken his first opium in 1770 at Oxford for 'rheumatism in the loins'. But always wary of the drug and its dangers of addiction, he never took it heavily until his last months, as he explained to his friend John Ryland: 'When I first began to take opium, my usual dose was three grains, which I found was in the opinion of physicians a great quantity. I know not however that it ever did me harm, for I did not take it often; yet that the demands of my constitution might not increase, I tried to satisfy it with less, and the event is, that I have sometimes attained my purpose of appeasing spasms or abating chilness by half a grain ... it is by frequent intermissions that so small a dose can preserve its efficacy.' The dropsy came on furiously in January. 'My legs and thighs are very much swollen with water, [with] which I should be content if I could keep there, but I am afraid that it will soon be higher ... I am extremely afraid of dying.' He longed for a warmer climate like Italy, but with 'a diseased body', no companion, and even with his pension insufficient money for a long trip there was no chance of experiencing this.[26]

What was now beginning was a mighty battle, a warfare against accepting what sometimes seemed like the inevitable. Heberden told him he was all right, and that when the warm weather came he would perspire more and thus the 'watery disease' would at least drain partly away. But he knew Heberden was wrong: 'The sun has looked for five thousand years upon the world to little purpose, if he does not know that a sick man is almost as impatient as a lover.' He took matters into his own hands.[27]

Phrases like 'my physicians endeavour to make me believe' and 'the physicians pertinaciously told me that I was not very near death' indicate he had lost a good deal of faith in them. They tried to convince him, he told Boswell, that 'vernal breezes and summer suns' would help drain his 'half drowned body'. He wanted to believe in them, as he had in the past, but now the stakes were higher and he felt he knew as much or more about his condition than they did, and also how to treat it. On 13 February, for example, he asked Cruikshank to send him 'a large adhesive plaster' fourteen inches long as a 'defensative' (bandage) for his breast and specifying 'Pix Burgundica' (Burgundy pitch) as a healing ointment. On the 17th he commanded him to cut into his thigh 'to drain away the water'. There was something else he did, against the advice of his doctors, that was both dangerous and a potentially powerful remedy. On the 16th or thereabouts he took a very large dose of squill powder – he always believed in large doses of medicine, drastic bleedings, and extreme incisions in his body – a diuretic medicine that was used to regulate the heart and get rid of excessive fluids. After five days of misery when he thought he was going to die, the alarming result of the large unattenuated dosage, he rejoiced that he had 'emitted in about twenty hours, full twenty pints of urine, and the tumor of my body is very much lessened'. This was followed in a day or two by a remarkable recovery. Brocklesby wrote disapprovingly of Johnson's disobedience but also rejoiced in a letter to another doctor that 'every night and morning ever since his [dosage] excretions have surprisingly exceeded his liquids taken in and he is by this time entirely evacuated of all preternatural fluids in his legs and thighs as well as from his chest'.[28]

The dropsy had been vanquished, it seems. It was a divinely bestowed miracle, Johnson thought, following a day's intense prayer and preparation for death. Against Heberden's advice, he also dramatically reduced taking opiates, which were making him delirious. Not having left his house since 13 December, on Easter Day 1784 he took the Sacrament at home. His prayer that day thanked God for his intervention in 'my late deliverance from imminent death'.[29]

Finally on 21 April, after 129 days of being house-bound, he walked over to St Clement's Church to give thanks for his recovery; and on the 24th he showed himself to the public again at the annual exhibition of the Royal Academy where he 'admired nothing but myself' – his ability to walk up all the stairs 'without stopping to rest or to breathe'. He moved briskly with easier 'respiration' than he had known for two years. Brocklesby would not, however, go so far as to allow him to venture out into the chill night air to attend an Essex Head Club meeting. By May he had 'broken loose' into a number of friends' homes for dinners: 'I do not now drive the world about; the world drives or draws me.'[30]

[4]

Mrs Thrale's health in Bath had been wretched through the winter as a result of her heartbreak over Piozzi. In January the girls had been so concerned over her that they agreed – Queeney especially reluctantly – to call Piozzi back from Italy. Released as from a spring in a box, she wrote to him frequently during the next few months, promising to marry him and agreeing to live in Italy although she knew it would mean a separation from her children. He agreed to return and marry her. Her health improved overnight and she waited impatiently for him. Johnson simply admonished her on 26 April, 'Settle your thoughts, and control your imagination, and think no more of Hesperian felicity' – a reference to her former desire to live in Italy which he thought had permanently been put to rest. It was he who was not controlling his imagination, however. He knew Piozzi would soon arrive in England but did not assume she would then necessarily marry him. She had been convinced to reject him once and could always send him away again.[31]

In town again in May, Boswell found him 'greatly recovered' and helped take his mind off her. They attended a meeting of the Essex Head Club in which Johnson was in 'fine spirits', and a few days later he was even willing to engage Boswell on whether or not he was rough in conversation. 'And who is the worse for that,' he objected. 'It hurts people of weak nerves,' Boswell replied. 'I know no such weak-nerved people,' Johnson shot back. Hearing Boswell describe this exchange later, Burke could only shake his head, 'It is well if when a man comes to die he has nothing heavier upon his conscience than having been a little rough in conversation.'[32]

Not having been in Oxford for two years, Johnson decided he must go in the first few days of June since he had in Boswell, 'my old fellow traveller', the perfect companion. It would prove to be an inspired decision because in the few days they were there Boswell was able to glean from Adams, with whom they stayed at Pembroke, many recollections of Johnson's early years. There were two particularly emotional discussions he recorded that speak volumes about Johnson's gloomy anxiety about dying soon. One arose when he mentioned his idea of compiling a book of prayers from other sources, adding his own, and prefixing the volume with a discourse on prayer. But he protested vigorously when Adams and Boswell pressed him to do it, 'Do not talk thus of what is so awful. I know not what time GOD will allow me in this world. There are many things which I wish to do.' When Adams persisted, Johnson shouted, 'Let me alone! Let me alone! I am overpowered!' He covered his face with his hands and lowered his head to the table. On another occasion he shocked the company 'with a look of horror, that he was much oppressed by the fear of death', adding dismally that he was convinced he was 'one of those who shall be damned'. Asked what he meant by damned, he replied, 'Sent to Hell, Sir, and punished everlastingly.' Boswell felt this was another instance of Johnson's melancholia surfacing in conversation. When the others present contradicted him, in 'gloomy agitation' he shouted them down, 'I'll have no more on't.' He maintained that life was definitely more miserable than happy: 'I would not lead my life over again though an archangel should request it'.[33]

At Oxford he began again to take squills and sleep poorly, once or twice in a chair because he was too hot and sleepless in bed. Back in London on 16 June, his breathing became difficult and his sleep fitful. The dropsy also was 'watching an opportunity to return'. Boswell proposed to him they travel north together as far as Ashbourne, and Johnson liked the idea – 'I love to travel with him,' he remarked – but Taylor was doing repairs to his house and could not have him. Hearing him more than once express a fear of the coming winter and wistfully express a wish to go to Italy to avoid it, unknown to him Boswell and a few others at Paoli's a few days later hatched a plan to try to get him there. They decided the ideal companion for him would be his Italian friend Francesco Sastres, the teacher and writer, who had settled in London in 1777 and was a member of the Essex Head Club. For such a trip, Johnson would need an increase in his pension, about which, after consulting Reynolds and just before leaving for Scotland on 2 July, Boswell wrote to Edward Thurlow the Lord Chancellor. On the strength of Thurlow's encouraging reply and promise to take the matter up with the King, Reynolds thought Boswell should now tell Johnson about the plan. Johnson's eyes filled with tears as he heard

Boswell describe the scheme. 'God bless you all,' he exclaimed. Boswell, too, shed tears. After a few minutes of silence during which neither was able to speak, Johnson quickly left the room to recover his composure, returning a few minutes later. They agreed to dine quietly with Reynolds the next day and then Boswell promptly left Bolt Court, not knowing it was for the last time ever – 'I never was again under that roof which I had so long reverenced.'[34]

At their 'friendly confidential dinner' the next day, Johnson allowed himself to indulge in thoughts of additional money, either a doubling of his pension or a single payment that would enable him to live in 'splendour' before he died. Reynolds and Boswell tempted his imagination with scenes of happy and sunny Italy. 'Nay,' he said, 'I must not expect that. Were I going to Italy to see fine pictures, like Sir Joshua, or to run after women, like Boswell, I might to be sure have pleasure in Italy. But when a man goes to Italy merely to feel how he breathes the air, he can enjoy very little.' Afterwards, Reynolds's coach took him and Boswell to Bolt Court for what would prove to be their final parting. Boswell described the scene vividly in his journal: 'When we came to the entry of Bolt Court, he asked me if I would not go in with him. I declined it from an apprehension that my spirits would sink. We bade adieu to each other affectionately in the carriage. When he had got down upon the foot-pavement, he called out, "Fare you well!" and without looking back sprung away with a kind of pathetic briskness ... which seemed to indicate a struggle to conceal uneasiness, and was to me a foreboding of our long, long separation.'[35]

Cruelly, Italy again was not to be. In September Johnson heard the King had decided against an increase of his pension. Thurlow instead offered a mortgage on the pension, but in a letter to him Johnson declined, adding somewhat bitterly that he had not expected to hear a refusal but that since he had not had time to 'brood hope' nor 'rioted in imaginary opulence, this cold reception has been scarce a disappointment'. It was, of course, a huge disappointment, the final nail in the coffin of a lifetime of Italian dreams.[36]

On 6 July 1784 he began his 'Sick-Man's Journal', which for four months recorded the return of his ailments. But a couple of days before Boswell left he suffered a more devastating blow to his peace of mind than anything asthma, dropsy and a multitude of other diseases could inflict on him. On 30 June Mrs Thrale had sent him and the children's other guardians an announcement that she was about to marry Piozzi, who was just then arriving in Bath to claim her. Queeney confirmed the news from Brighton, to which she and her sisters had fled before Piozzi arrived. The Thrale family had in effect disintegrated. Before her marriage she wrote Johnson a note asking for 'pardon for concealing from you a connection which you must have heard of by many, but I suppose never believed', and declaring that all was 'irrevocably settled'. His reply was brutally stern, 'If I interpret your letter right you are ignominiously married, if it is yet undone, let us once talk together. If you have abandoned your children and your religion, God forgive your wickedness; if you have forfeited your fame, and your country, may your folly do no further mischief.' Regretting his harshness, six days later he 'breathe[d] out one sigh more of tenderness perhaps useless, but at least sincerely'. He was ready to contribute to her happiness in repayment 'for that kindness which soothed twenty years of a life radically wretched'. Thinking of the children, he implored her to persuade Piozzi to settle down with her in England, where she could live a more dignified and secure life: 'only some phantoms of imagination seduce you to Italy'. What she wanted almost as much as Piozzi himself, however, was to leave England. 'My heart rejoiced when I saw the shores of England receding from my view,' she wrote after they left the country in early September.[37]

There was bitter irony for him in the knowledge that she was departing for Italy's 'softer climate' with Piozzi while at least twice he had been denied the thrill of visiting the country with her and Thrale – an irony that deepened when the King closed the Italian door for him in September. 'The tears stand in my eyes,' he concluded, barely able to write more. London society did not shed tears; it was horrified by the marriage. Apart from the widespread hostile coverage of the marriage in the papers, Fanny Burney was numbed and Elizabeth Montagu said what many were thinking: 'I am, myself convinced that the poor woman is mad . . . I bring in my verdict [of] lunacy in this affair.' As for Johnson himself, he was done with her: 'If I meet with one of her letters, I burn it instantly. I have burnt all I can find. I never speak of her, and I desire never to hear of her more.' That was not entirely true, for he spared many of her letters from his bonfire.[38]

After seeing to it that his inscription would at long last be carved on Tetty's stone in Bromley, Johnson left for Staffordshire on 13 July 'in hope of air from the country' but mostly in pursuit of the comfort and peace to be gained from feeling secure at home with Lucy and friends in his native countryside. He was away over four months. From distant London he heard of the first successful balloon ascent in England by Vincenzo Lunardi which travelled twenty-four miles, and that Reynolds had been appointed Painter to the King, having against his inclination asked for the position. He also wrote the Dedication for Burney's *Commemoration of Handel*. The single, meagre recreation he enjoyed was a visit to Chatsworth again, this time meeting the beautiful, charming Georgiana, the Duchess of Devonshire, who told her mother 'he look'd ill, but, they say, is wonderfully recover'd. He was in great good humour and vastly entertaining tho' his first début was dry ... the Duke took him under the lime trees'. Other than that, he was a sick man contriving desperately to do anything he could to get better, writing to numerous correspondents about little else than the progress of his health and his self-administered medication – among these were a series of nineteen dreary, morbid and dramatic letters to Brocklesby crammed with medical details. All of this was in addition to the medical journal he was keeping in Latin, recording minutely each day his sleep, bowel movements, urine discharge, and the fluids and drugs he gave himself. It was an obsessive warfare against his asthma and dropsy, what he knew might well be his final battle. He even used military metaphors to describe his medical arsenal: bottles of squill vinegar were among his 'weapons' and squill pills were his 'perfect bullets'. How 'perfect' remained to be seen.[39]

At first his breathing remained difficult and made motion painful, making him feel 'feeble, and very dejected' in spite of opiates, and under the influence of the squills his dropsy ebbed and flowed. 'I struggle hard for life ... but who can run the race with death?' he told Burney. Then on 13 August he awoke to a wonderful remission of his asthma after giving himself a violent purge and a huge dose of squill, enabling him to move 'with more ease than I have enjoyed for many weeks'. As for the dropsy, it 'rises, though it does not rise very fast'. The remission lasted for weeks during which he seemed convinced that he was making progress, or at least that things were not getting worse. The dropsy completely disappeared. Then suddenly in October he began to complain of losing ground again, moaning to Brocklesby that for the past three weeks he had 'gone backwards'. Wretched nights followed. His dejection was now once more a mighty enemy. He fell prolifically to purges and taking drams of diacodium, numerous grains of opium and an abundance of squills. His breath was short and the water was beginning 'to threaten' again. He spent several nights sleeping in a chair. His strength evaporated – 'God have mercy,' he wrote desperately in the middle of the increasingly ghastly, farcical drama of drugs to which he was subjecting himself. He took so many opiates at one point that he described himself as 'comatose'. Just before leaving Lichfield, he informed Hawkins, 'I am relapsing into the dropsy very fast.' On 8 November 1784 he stopped writing his medical journal.[40]

On his way home he stopped for a last visit with Hector and his sister, and a few days with Adams in Oxford, feeling he was now 'in a right frame of mind' for writing his book on prayers.[41] While he was there his condition worsened dramatically, the dropsy rising aggressively and an increasing sense of helplessness beginning to overwhelm him.

CHAPTER 32

The Last Days

That winter was very cold and severely snowy, just the sort of weather Johnson dreaded and had hoped to avoid by going to Italy. In the next weeks at home, full of pain, he was courageously busy. He carefully adjusted his will at Hawkins's insistence, beginning the enumeration of his legacies with what was for him the most important of all: 'I bequeath to GOD, a soul polluted with many sins, but I hope purified by JESUS CHRIST'. He tried to provide for his relations but was disappointed in being unable to discover enough about how and where they were. He left most money – a greater amount than he was generally thought to have – to Frank, some £1,500, including an annuity of £70 to be paid to him by Langton, which he frittered away in the next few years before moving to Lichfield with his wife where he opened a school in 1797. He died in 1810. Hawkins was irritated about this large bequest to Frank, grumbling something about 'a caveat against ostentatious bounty and favour to negroes'. Johnson also left to Langton £750, to the brewers Barclay and Perkins £300, and to Percy £150 – though nothing to Lucy, who was offended at being left out. He specified that the proceeds from the sale of the Lichfield house should be dispersed among people scarcely known to him, such as his godchildren and the children of the painter Mauritius Lowe. He also left £100 to his 'lunatic' cousin, Elizabeth Herne, for her maintenance at the madhouse in Bethnal Green where he had placed her. His large library was dispersed among his friends. He wrote an epitaph for his father, mother and brother which he asked Richard Greene to see to being engraved on a 'deep, massy and hard' stone to cover their graves. And he had Cadell send a package of his major publications to Adams for the Pembroke library. He gave George Strahan the manuscripts of his prayers for publication.[1]

As we know, in late November or early December, he did the almost unthinkable and burned a mass of his papers, having stated several times that the contemplation of his past filled him with misery, whereas there was hope in the future.

If Johnson's preparations and his seemingly endless talk about the progress of his illness and rapid deterioration comprised early scenes in the drama of his death, his final two weeks in his house and on his deathbed could be seen as a production in which he orchestrated the climactic final act. There was a steady stream of friends coming to Bolt Court to speak to him, including John Hoole, Langton, Reynolds, Burke, Taylor, Fanny and Charles Burney, Steevens, Malone, Sastres, Hawkins, Nichols, George Strahan (to whom he dictated his will on 8-9 December), Windham, John Ryland and John Perkins. To most of these he had memorable things to say, including advice on how to live the rest of their lives. He spoke much of his own life, fears and hopes. The doctors who were chiefly in attendance were Heberden, Brocklesby, Cruikshank and Richard Warren as supporting actors. Among those who saw him regularly as he was dying, Hoole and Hawkins wrote the most extensive accounts. Fanny also entered into her own diary what she saw and heard, as did Windham whose servant was in attendance much of the time and added firsthand observations. Boswell's account at the end of his *Life* is the most dramatic, well-rounded narrative, drawing not only on Hawkins and Hoole but also on a number of people like Sastres and Reynolds whom he asked for reports. The newspapers also carried daily reports of his progress. 'It may be said,' wrote Arthur Murphy, 'the death of Dr Johnson kept the public mind in agitation beyond all former example. No literary character ever excited so much attention; and, when the press has teemed with anecdotes, apothegms, essays, and publications of every kind, what occasion now for a new tract on the same threadbare subject?'

On Sunday, 28 November, Hawkins, who is a reliable witness of what happened in the closing days, wrote:

> I saw him about noon; he was dozing; but waking, he found himself in a circle of his friends. Upon opening his eyes, he said, that the prospect of his dissolution was very terrible to him, and addressed himself to us all, in nearly these words: 'You see the state in which I am; conflicting with bodily pain and mental distraction: while you are in health and strength, labour to do good, and avoid evil, if ever you hope to escape the distress that now oppresses me.' — A little while after, — 'I had, very early in my life, the

seeds of goodness in me: I had a love of virtue, and a reverence for religion; and these, I trust, have brought forth in me fruits meet for repentance; and, if I have repented as I ought, I am forgiven. I have, at times, entertained a loathing of sin and of myself, particularly at the beginning of this year, when I had the prospect of death before me; and this has not abated when my fears of death have been less; and, at these times, I have had such rays of hope shot into my soul, as have almost persuaded me, that I am in a state of reconciliation with God.'

The following Sunday was even more dramatic as Johnson felt even more severely the inexorable end. Hawkins again tells what happened: 'I communicated with him and Mr Langton, and other of his friends, as many as nearly filled the room. Mr Strahan, who was constant in his attendance on him throughout his illness, performed the office. Previous to reading the exhortation, Johnson knelt, and with a degree of fervour that I had never been witness to before, uttered [a] most eloquent and energetic prayer.'

He was now suddenly grown so weak, unable even to kneel in prayer, Hawkins recalled, 'it was thought necessary that a man should watch with him all night; and one was found in the neighbourhood, who, for half a crown a night, undertook to sit up with, and assist him.' Nonetheless, he was not beyond thinking of where and how his stone would be placed: 'When the man had left the room, he, in the presence and hearing of Mr Strahan and Mr Langton, asked me, where I meant to bury him. I answered, doubtless, in Westminster Abbey: "If", said he, "my executors think it proper to mark the spot of my interment by a stone, let it be so placed as to protect my body from injury." I assured him it would be done. Before my departure, he desired Mr Langton to put into my hands, money to the amount of upwards £100, with a direction to keep it till called for.'

What several of the written accounts of these last days reveal is that the two dominant, opposing keynotes of his mental state during the last weeks of his life were desperation and calm acceptance of God's mercy. His desperation to try anything to survive gradually evolved into some measure of peace about what he realised was his imminent death, but it appears also that his desperation did not cease until very shortly before he died, and that a last frantic clutching at the possibility of life may indeed have hastened his end. He was not about to go gentle into that good night.

Most everyone in the room on that occasion understood that

Johnson was repenting that it had taken him so long fully to accept God's grace and trust to his salvation. To do so was to be part of an inherited 'holy dying' tradition in which an eminent person's death could provide a religious example to others. Several witnesses, and in turn Boswell who cited a few of them, contended that several days before his death he had come to terms spiritually with the idea of dying and had resigned himself completely to the peaceful end of his mortal existence. Strahan, for example, from whom Johnson took communion a few days before his death in front of a number of people including Frank, said unequivocally that 'some time' before his death 'all his fears were calmed and absorbed by the prevalence of his faith'; and Boswell's brother David whom Boswell asked to interview Frank Barber, reported Frank's observation that Johnson appeared 'perfectly resigned' and 'seldom or never fretful or out of temper' once he knew his death was near. Boswell added that after Johnson asked Brocklesby to tell him plainly whether he thought he could recover and was told not without a miracle, he announced, 'Then ... I will take no more physic, not even my opiates; for I have prayed that I may render up my soul to God unclouded.' It was also consistent with this view of his own death that in the middle of all the suffering he could still counsel Hoole regarding religion, repeatedly call his guests to his room for prayers by his bedside, bless a number of them, and admonish others regarding their future behaviour to remember 'that life is short, and that eternity never ends'. There is little reason to doubt that when the end finally came he was at peace, although the holy tradition these witnesses all hoped Johnson's manner of dying would illustrate may have prejudiced their comments somewhat.[2]

But it is unclear how soon before Johnson died he came to such a strong faith or 'conversion' that the afterlife would not, as he had feared all his life, hold any terrors for him. Whenever that was, it is at least clear that he defiantly and frantically, even violently, fought the battle against death. To begin with, he burned his papers, not the act of a man at peace with himself. Brocklesby reported that eight or ten days before he died, 'low and desponding', he cried out to him part of Macbeth's speech that begins with, 'Canst thou not minister to a mind diseas'd?' And when five days before his death John Ryland attempted to comfort him that there was great hope for everyone in the afterlife, Johnson replied quickly, 'Yes, we have hopes given us; but they are conditional, and I know not how far I have fulfilled those conditions.'[3]

What he most definitely did not want to hear were compliments on what a virtuous life he had led. Furthermore, the story Boswell told about his signing off medicine once Brocklesby told him only a miracle would save him, clearly misrepresents what happened since he took plenty of medicine afterwards and resorted to other physical means to recover. Nichols told Boswell that less than a week before his death Johnson had such little fear of the pain of a needed surgical puncture of the revived sarcocele that when Brocklesby began to take his pulse he grabbed his wrist and 'gave him a look of great contempt, and ridiculed the judging of his disorder by the pulse'. Instead, he asked 'if a puncture would not relieve him', and when Brocklesby advised that Cruikshank was the best judge, Johnson shouted, 'How many men in a year die through the timidity of those whom they consult for health! I want length of life, and you fear giving me pain, which I care not for.' Johnson tried to bully Cruikshank, too, when he appeared later, but the surgeon refused to pierce the sarcocele. Then he commanded him to make incisions in his legs to release the pressure of the hateful dropsy. The surgeon was again afraid a 'mortification' might set in from any deep penetration of the knife and was in the process of merely lancing the surface of the legs when Johnson cried out again, 'Deeper, deeper; I will abide the consequence: you are afraid of your reputation but that is nothing to me.' 'I would give one of these legs for a year more of life, I mean of comfortable life, not such as that which I now suffer,' he is supposed to have said.[4]

His truly terrifying and courageous act came on the morning of the last day of his life. From his servant's report, Windham recounted what happened:

> He had compelled Frank to give him a lancet, and had besides concealed in the bed a pair of scissors, and with one or the other of these had scarified himself in three places, two in the left leg, etc. On Mrs Desmoulins making a difficulty of giving him the lancet, he said, 'Don't you, if you have any scruples; but I will compel Frank ...' He then made the three incisions above mentioned, of which one in the leg [was] not unskilfully made; but the other in the leg was a deep and ugly wound from which, with the others, they suppose him to have lost nearly eight ounces of blood.

Frank told Hawkins that he and the servant seized Johnson's hand when he tried to slip the lancet under the covers and implored him not to do anything rash. He said he would not but he had the lancet and seconds later they saw his arm move under the covers. They immediately pulled the covers off and saw 'a great effusion of blood, which soon stopped'. Soon after that, Johnson took scissors and 'plunged them deep in the calf of each leg'. He was so convinced dropsy was the root of most of his illness that he was determined to do anything in his power to get rid of it. 'He looked upon himself as a bloated carcass; and, to attain the power of easy respiration, would have undergone any degree of temporary pain,' Hawkins wrote. 'He dreaded neither punctures nor incisions.' If that butchering of his own body did not hasten his death, the experimental drug, digitalis, which he was given that last day in a major overdose, did.[5]

Boswell chose not to say anything about this self-mutilation, perhaps again because he did not trust Hawkins as a source or because he did not wish to conclude his biography on the note of Johnson's mental and physical turmoil at the end. Hawkins had no reservations: 'Many persons have appeared possessed of more serenity of mind in this awful scene ... it may be deemed a discouragement from the severe practice of religion, that Dr Johnson, whose whole life was a preparation for his death, and a conflict with natural infirmity, was disturbed with terror at the prospect of the grave.'[6]

The final high drama of the death scene occurred on 13 December. Johnson slept for most of the day, taking some milk which he complained had not been given to him properly, and blessing a Miss Morris who had come in off the street totally unexpected to receive his benediction, but otherwise speaking to nobody. Nobody spoke to him because he seemed in a type of doze, breathing in short, regular breaths. Shortly after seven in the evening he took his last breath, awakening from his doze (according to Hawkins) just seconds before to say to Sastres, 'iam moriturus' ('now I am about to die').[7]

Hamilton said of Johnson what all the Johnsonians felt when it sank in that they no longer had with them the literary colossus who had touched and altered English life and the literary landscape so considerably in the last half of the century as well as their own lives in deeply personal ways: 'He has made a chasm, which not only nothing can fill up, but which nothing has a tendency to fill up. – Johnson is dead. – Let us go to the next best: – there is nobody; – no man can be said to put you in mind of Johnson.' Up in Scotland, Boswell heard of his death on the 17th and in his numbness could bring himself to write only the following in his journal: 'I was stunned and in a kind of amaze ... I did not shed tears. I was not tenderly affected. My feeling was just one large expanse of stupour.' 'His death

made a kind of era in literature,' remarked Hannah More. It was hard
to believe that such a life had finally ended. John Hoole wrote of 'the
most awful sight of Dr Johnson laid out on his bed, without life!'[8]

A sermon on his death was preached in St Mary's, Oxford, and
there were numerous obituaries, the longest by Langton. Malone and
Reynolds saw to it that a monument was raised in his honour beneath
the dome of St Paul's Cathedral – unveiled in 1796. The critics had
their innings, which made one observer remark, 'Ay, now that the old
lion is dead, every ass thinks he may kick at him.' In 1786 Mrs Thrale
published her *Anecdotes* that infuriated the Johnsonians, especially
Boswell and Malone, and in 1788 she came out with an edition of
her correspondence with Johnson. In 1787 the industrious Hawkins
produced the first complete edition of Johnson's works, in which he
included his *Life*, also the first complete biography to appear. Boswell
was hard at work on his but would not be rushed. His *Tour to the
Hebrides* appeared in 1785 and his monumental *Life* not until 1791,
the year that Thomas Paine published *The Rights of Man*, William
Wordsworth began his travels in revolutionary France, and William
Wilberforce succeeded in having his motion for the abolition of the
slave trade passed in the House of Commons. A new age was dawning
as Boswell published his coda on one that was ending.

As for Johnson's funeral in Westminster Abbey on 20 December, it
was a huge disappointment, even a scandal. As one of Johnson's
executors, Hawkins saw to arranging it with the Abbey and chose the
cheaper service without music because, as he put it, Johnson had little
sensitivity to music anyway. The entire service proceeded without the
sound of the organ or voices of the choristers. Moreover, the service
was conducted by Taylor, a prebendary of Westminster, who delivered
the sermon in a conspicuously lacklustre way, much as he had delivered
the sermons Johnson had written for him, offending just about all of
Johnson's friends. As Dr Burney wrote the day after the funeral, 'The
executor, Sir John Hawkins, did not manage things well, for there was
no anthem, or choir service performed – no lesson – but merely what
is read over every old woman that is buried by the parish ... Dr Taylor
read the service – but so-so.' All the members of the Club who were
in town attended, from whose ranks the pallbearers were drawn:
Joseph Banks, Burke, Charles Bunbury, George Colman, Langton
and Windham. They deposited the lead coffin in Poet's Corner, not
far from Goldsmith's memorial slab and Garrick's grave at the foot of
the famous Shakespeare monument. In his biographical memoir of

Johnson published soon after his death, his friend Thomas Tyers wrote, 'Who should have thought that Garrick and Johnson would have their last sleep together.' An inscription was placed over the grave stating simply his name, degree, death date and age. When he was told days before his death that he was going to be buried in the Abbey, he replied simply, 'place a stone over my grave that my remains may not be disturbed'.[9]

NOTES

Abbreviations

WRITINGS OF JOHNSON

(1) Yale Works:

The Yale Edition of the Works of Samuel Johnson, 15 vols, 1958 onwards (not consecutive volumes because not all have been published)

Diaries: Diaries, Prayers, and Annals, ed. E.L. McAdam, Jr, with Donald and Mary Hyde, vol. I (1958)

Adventurer and *Idler: The Idler and The Adventurer* (ed. W.J. Bate, John M. Bullitt and L.F. Powell), in *Works*, vol. II (1963)

Rambler: The Rambler (ed. W.J. Bate and Albrecht B. Strauss), vols III-V (1969)

Poems: Poems, ed. E.L. McAdam, Jr, with George Milne, vol. VI (1964)

Johnson on Shakespeare: Johnson on Shakespeare, ed. Arthur Sherbo (with an introduction by Bertrand H. Bronson) vols VII and VIII (1968)

Journey: A Journey to the Western Islands of Scotland, ed. Mary Lascelles, vol. IX (1971)

Political Writings: Political Writings, ed. Donald Greene, vol. X (1977)

Sermons: Sermons, ed. Jean Hagstrum and James Gray, vol. XIV (1978)

Voyage to Abyssinia: A Voyage to Abyssinia, ed. Joel J. Gold, vol. XV (1985)

Rasselas and Other Tales: Rasselas and Other Tales, ed. Gwin J. Kolb, vol. XVI (1990)

Commentary on Pope: A Commentary on Mr Pope's Principles of Morality, Or Essay on Man (A Translation from the French), ed. O.M. Brack, vol. XVII (2005)

Johnson on the English Language: Johnson on the English Language, ed. Gwin J. Kolb and Robert DeMaria, Jr, vol. XVIII (1990)

(2) Other Johnson editions:

Early Biographical Writings: David Fleeman, *The Early Biographical Writings of Samuel Johnson* (1973)

Journey: Samuel Johnson, *A Journey to the Western Islands of Scotland*, ed. J.D. Fleeman (1985)

Letters: The Letters of Samuel Johnson, ed. Bruce Redford (5 vols, 1994)

Lives of the Poets: The Lives of the Most Eminent English Poets, ed. Roger Lonsdale (4 vols, 2006)

EDITIONS, BIOGRAPHIES AND CRITICAL WRITINGS

AJ: The Age of Johnson: A Scholarly Annual, edited by Paul Korshin and Jack Lynch, 18 vols (1989–)

Boswell's Journals:
Applause: Boswell: The Applause of the Jury 1782–1785, ed. Irma S. Lustig and Frederick A. Pottle (1981)
Defense: Boswell For the Defence 1769–1774, ed. William K. Wimsatt, Jr, and Frederick A. Pottle (New York 1959, London 1960)
Extremes: Boswell in Extremes 1776–1778, ed. Charles McC. Weis and Frederick A. Pottle (1970)
Hebrides: Boswell's Journal of a Tour to the Hebrides with Samuel Johnson, LL.D., 1773, ed. Frederick A. Pottle and Charles H. Bennett (1963)
Laird: Boswell: Laird of Auchinleck 1778–1782, ed. Joseph W. Reed and Frederick A. Pottle (1977; rpt. Edinburgh University Press, 1993)
London Journal: Boswell's London Journal 1762–1763, ed. Frederick A. Pottle (New York, 1950; London 1951)
Ominous: The Ominous Years 1774–1776, ed. Charles Ryskamp and Frederick A. Pottle (1963)
Wife: Boswell In Search of a Wife 1766–1769, ed. Frank Brady and Frederick A. Pottle (1957)

Boswell's Notebook: R.B. Adam, *Facsimile of Boswell's Notebook* (1919)
BP: Boswell Papers, Beinecke Rare Book and Manuscript Library, Yale University
Burney's Diary: The Early Diary of Frances Burney, 1768–1778, ed. Annie Raine Ellis (2 vols, 1913)
Burney Early Journals and Letters: The Early Journals and Letters of Fanny Burney (1788–94) vol. III, ed. Lars E. Troide and Stewart J. Cooke (1994); vol. IV, ed. Betty Rizzo (2003)
CCSJ: The Cambridge Companion to Samuel Johnson, ed. Greg Clingham (1997)
Dictionary: David Crystal (ed.), *Dr Johnson's Dictionary* (2005)
Early Biographies: The Early Biographies of Samuel Johnson, ed. O.M. Brack, Jr, and Robert E. Kelley (1974)
Fifer: The Correspondence of James Boswell with Certain Members of the Club, ed. Charles N. Fifer (1976), Yale Research Editions: Correspondence, vol. III
Fleeman Bibliography: David Fleeman, *A Bibliography of the Works of Samuel Johnson* (2 vols, 2000)
Gleanings: Aleyn Lyell Reade, *Johnsonian Gleanings* (11 vols, 1909–52; reprinted 1968)
Greene Politics: Donald Greene, *The Politics of Samuel Johnson* (1960, 2nd edn 1990)
Hawkins's Life: Sir John Hawkins, *Life of Samuel Johnson, LL.D.* (1787), ed. Bertram H. Davis (1961)
JE: Pat Rogers, *The Samuel Johnson Encyclopedia* (1996)
JM: Johnsonian Miscellanies, ed. George Birkbeck Hill (2 vols, 1897)
JRL: Thrale letters, John Rylands Library, University of Manchester
Life: Boswell's Life of Johnson, ed. George Birkbeck Hill and L.F. Powell (5 vols, 1934; reprinted 1979)

Murphy's Essay: Arthur Murphy, *Essay on Johnson's Life and Genius* (in *JM*, vol. I)

New Light on Boswell: New Light on Boswell: Critical and Historical Essays on the Occasion of the Bicentenary of The Life of Johnson, ed. Greg Clingham (1991)

Nichols Literary Anecdotes: John Nichols, *Literary Anecdotes of the Eighteenth Century*, ed. Colin Chair (1967)

Piozzi Anecdotes: Hester Lynch Piozzi, *Anecdotes of the Late Samuel Johnson, LL.D. during the Last Twenty Years of His Life* (1786), ed. Arthur Sherbo (1974)

Reddick: Allen Reddick, *The Making of Johnson's Dictionary 1746–1773* (1996)

Redford Life: James Boswell's Life of Johnson: An Edition of the Original Manuscript, ed. Bruce Redford (Boswell Yale Editions: Life of Johnson, vol. II, 1999)

Shaw's Memoirs: William Shaw, *Memoirs of the Life and Writings of the Late Dr Samuel Johnson* (1785), ed. Arthur Sherbo (1974)

Thraliana: Thraliana:The Diary of Mrs Hester Lynch Thrale (Later Mrs Piozzi), 1776–1809 (2 vols, 1951)

Waingrow: Marshall Waingrow, *The Correspondence and Other Papers of James Boswell Relating to the Making of the Life of Johnson* (Boswell Yale Editions: Correspondence, vol. 2)

Waingrow Life: James Boswell's Life of Johnson: An Edition of the Original Manuscript, ed. Marshall Waingrow (Boswell Yale Editions: Life of Johnson, vol. 1 (1994), vol. II (1998)

Works: The Works of Samuel Johnson, ed. Arthur Murphy (1801), 12 vols

PREFACE

1. Bloom, *Shakespeare: The Invention of the Human*, p. 227.
2. Frances Reynolds, 'Recollections of Dr Johnson', *JM*, II: 274.
3. Ruskin, *Praeterita and Dilecta* (Everyman, 2005), pp. 198–200.
4. *Life*, IV: 275.

CHAPTER I: Anecdotes of Beggary

1. *Letters*, I: 206; BP (C9801), box 20, f. 451.
2. Howard Clayton, *Coaching City: a Glimpse of Georgian Lichfield*, Chapter 1.
3. *Letters*, III: 49, 51, 166; I: 327; IV: 424; *Life*, I: 465; *Letters*, I: 345–6.
4. *Dictionary*, p. 300.
5. See Percy M. Lathwaite, *A History of St Chad's Church* (1938); Revd Thomas Harwood, *History and Antiquities of the Church of Lichfield* (1806); Mary Alden Hopkins, *Dr Johnson's Lichfield* (1952). The earliest history of Lichfield on which later historians have drawn is John Jackson, *History of the City and County of Lichfield* (1795).
6. *Boswell's Journal: Ominous Years*, p. 293; Defoe, *A Tour Thro' the Whole Island of Great Britain* (1724–26), as quoted in the edition by Pat Rogers (1992), p. 144.
7. *Thraliana*, I: 125.
8. *Diaries*, pp. 7, 10; *Piozzi Anecdotes*, p. 148.
9. *Piozzi Anecdotes*, p. 163; *Diaries*, p. 66.
10. *Diaries*, p. 20; *Life*, I: 38, 35; *Diaries*, p. 6; *Piozzi Anecdotes*, p. 154.
11. *Gleanings*, X: 12–17. I have drawn on this monumental series, published painstakingly

and lovingly across a span of more than forty years, for much of the detail about Johnson's early life, relatives, and early friendships in Lichfield, Birmingham and the nearby countryside.

12. *Diaries*, pp.19–20; *Life*, V: 59–60.
13. *Piozzi Anecdotes*, p. 148; *Life*, I: 35, 37. Reade argues factually against this story in *Gleanings*, III: 14–17, although he documents certain family and other links between Michael Johnson and Elizabeth Blaney. The story first appeared in *The Gentleman's Magazine* (Feb. 1785, p. 100) and then in *Hawkins's Life*, p. 3, from which Boswell got it.
14. *Life*, II: 261; *Gleanings*, X: 2–3.
15. For an approximate idea of the value of contemporary currency, one needs to multiply it by one hundred.
16. *Diaries*, pp. 7–8.
17. The Ford family made the settlement more complicated through the provision of a Trust to be spent on property and any children's education, to which Michael himself was supposed to, but did not, contribute £100 within a year (*Gleanings*, X: 15–16).
18. *Gleanings*, X: 15–20.
19. Frances Reynolds, 'Recollections of Dr Johnson', *JM*, II: 257; *Life*, I: 35; *Piozzi Anecdotes*, p. 148.

CHAPTER 2: Stepping on the Duckling

1. *Diaries*, p. 3.
2. *Diaries*, pp. 4–5 and notes; *Life*, IV: 210; Piozzi *Anecdotes*, p. 63.
3. *Diaries*, pp. 5–6 and notes. See also *Gleanings*, X: 22. Much has been written about Johnson's poor health, but the reader will benefit from a recent short summary by Graham Nicholls, '"The general disease of my life": Samuel Johnson and his Health,' in *The Tyranny of Treatment: Samuel Johnson, His Friends and Georgian Medicine*, ed. Natasha McEnroe and Robin Simon (2003). For a more lengthy analysis, see John Wiltshire, *Samuel Johnson in the Medical World* (1991), which deals also with Johnson's developed interest in medicine.
4. *Diaries*, pp. 6–7; *Gleanings*, X: 68–9.
5. *Diaries*, pp. 9–10. I and J were treated as the same letter in the eighteenth century.
6. *Nichols Literary Anecdotes*, p. 524; *Diaries*, pp. 8–9; Marc Bloch, *The Royal Touch: Sacred Monarchy and Scrofula in England and France* (1973).
7. *Diaries*, pp. 8–9; *Piozzi Anecdotes*, p. 63; Clayton, *Coaching City*, p. 19; *Life*, I: 43.
8. *Life*, I: 39. One problem with the story is that Sacheverell's only known visit was when Johnson was one year old. Also, he stopped preaching 1710–13.
9. *Diaries*, p. 10; *Piozzi Anecdotes*, p. 69.
10. *Diaries*, p. 10; F.A. Pottle, *James Boswell: The Earlier Years*, p. 2; *Life*, I: 67.
11. *Life*, I: 40; Charles E. Pierce, Jr., *The Religious Life of Samuel Johnson*, pp. 65–6.
12. *Piozzi Anecdotes*, pp. 63–4.
13. *Piozzi Anecdotes*, pp. 64–5; *Life*, I: 40; *Yale Works: Poems*, p. 54. Boswell's citation of the poem is his *Notebooks* version.
14. *Piozzi Anecdotes*, pp. 62–3; *Rasselas* (line 302), *Yale Works: Poems*, p. 105. Many pages of his *Annals* are missing, however, beginning about the time his brother was born.
15. *Piozzi Anecdotes*, pp. 65, 63; *Life*, IV: 8, n.3, I: 71n.1, II: 408; Johnson's *Observations on Macbeth* (1745), note xx; *Life*, I: 70.
16. *Piozzi Anecdotes*, pp. 66–7.

CHAPTER 3: Leaping Over the Rail

1. *Lives of the Poets*, III: 1.
2. *Life*, I: 43, 39; *Boswell's Notebook*.
3. *The Weekly Journal or British Gazeteer*, 14 April 1716; *Life*, I: 43; *Gleanings*, III: 79–80; Thomas Harwood, *Lichfield*, p. 460; *Life*, I: 67–8.
4. *Life*, IV: 215; *Piozzi Anecdotes*, p. 66. See Pierce, *The Religious Life of Samuel Johnson*, pp. 25–7.
5. For a history of the school, see P. Laithwaite, *A Short History of Lichfield Grammar School* (1925).
6. *Diaries*, pp. 11–17.
7. Ibid.
8. *Diaries*, pp. 19–20.
9. *Life*, I: 44–5.
10. *Diaries*, pp. 17–19.
11. *Diaries*, pp. 22–3.
12. Davies, *Memoirs of the Life of David Garrick, Esq.* (4th edn, 1808), I: 4; *Life*, I: 44.
13. *Life*, II: 146, I: 451, 46.
14. *Life*, I:47; *Letters*, II: 163, 301–2, I:9, 115.
15. John Campbell, *The Lives of the Chief Justices of England. From the Norman Conquest till the Death of Lord Mansfield* (1849), II: 279; *BP*, Box 71, f. 1454 (C1524); *Life*, IV: 135; *Diaries*, p. 225; *Life*, I: 48.
16. *Hawkins's Life*, p. 4.
17. *Piozzi Anecdotes*, p. 70; *Letters*, II: 297, IV: 372; *Life*, I: 159.
18. *Life*, I: 48; 'On the stream flowing away from the Stowe Mill at Lichfield', trans. John Wain (*Johnson on Johnson*, 1975, p. 21).
19. *JM*, II: 395–6.
20. *Piozzi Anecdotes*, p. 119; *Letters*, IV: 182; *Life*, II: 339; *BP*, Box 24, f. 567 (C1523).
21. *Yale Works: Poems*, Introduction, pp. xi–xxiv, 3–4.
22. *Piozzi Anecdotes*, pp. 67, 68.

CHAPTER 4: Two Benefactors

1. *Piozzi Anecdotes*, p. 65.
2. *Letters*, II: 308; *Hawkins's Life*, pp. 268–9. In his Will, Johnson left £200 to 'the representatives of the late William Innys, bookseller'.
3. 'Life of Fenton', *Lives of the Poets*, III: 89; *Life*, III: 348.
4. *Thraliana,I:171*; *Piozzi Anecdotes*, p. 65.
5. *Letters*, I: 369; *JM*, II: 208–9.
6. *Life*, I: 50.
7. *Poems*, pp. 4–27. Johnson told Mrs. Thrale that when he was sixteen he had made a start at translating Anacreon's verses on a dove, the first Greek verses that struck him when he was a boy. He completed the poem when he was sixty-eight (*Piozzi Anecdotes*, pp. 75–6).
8. *BP*, box 24, f. 567 (C1524); *Letters*, I: 146.
9. *Hawkins's Life*, p. 5.
10. *Life*, IV: 372–3; *JM*, II: 426–7.
11. *Life*, I: 56–8, 445; *Shaw's Memoirs*, p. 8.

12. *Life*, I: 445. The best analysis of Johnson's reading is by Robert DeMaria, *Samuel Johnson and the Life of Reading* (1997).
13. *Lives of the Poets*, II: 178–9.
14. Ibid.
15. *Greene Politics*, p. 43.
16. *Greene Politics*, pp. 43, 65–6.
17. Cited in M. Ashmun, *The Singing Swan: An Account of Anna Seward and Her Acquaintance with Dr Johnson, Boswell and Others of their Time* (1931).
18. *Life*, I: 82; *JM*, II: 326, 252.

CHAPTER 5: Oxford: Wielding a Scholar's Weapon

1. *Life*, I: 43.
2. *Correspondence of Alexander Pope*, ed. George Sherburn (1956), I: 430.
3. *Life*, I: 59, 57.
4. *Life*, I: 59–60.
5. *Life*, I: 59–60, 272; *Piozzi Anecdotes*, p. 70; *Waingrow*, p. 162. On 12 July 1786 Adams denied Piozzi's assertion that Johnson ignored most of Jorden's lectures (*Waingrow*, p. 162).
6. See *Gleanings*, V: 33–6.
7. *Life*, I: 79, 61; *Piozzi Anecdotes*, p. 72; *Life*, I: 272.
8. Lawrence Stone, 'The Size and Composition of the Oxford Student Body, 1580–1910', in *The University in Society* (1975), p. 37; *Boswell's Journals: Ominous*, p. 281; *The Correspondence of Gray, Walpole, West & Ashton* (1915), I: 51. For background on Oxford, I have relied on Graham Midgley's *University Life in Eighteenth-Century Oxford* (1996).
9. Richard Graves, *Recollections of some particulars in the Life of the late William Shenstone Esq.* (1788), p. 30 (as quoted in Midgley, p. 66).
10. *Letters*, I: 245. See Lionel Salt, 'Samuel Johnson and His Pembroke College Contemporaries' (unpublished), Pembroke College 2005.
11. *A Plea Against an Order to Inhibit Wine-Cellars* (1734), Bodleian Library, G.A. Oxon. 4 6 (11); *Life*, III: 302–4.
12. Midgley, p. 91; *Life*, I: 273.
13. *Hawkins's Life*, p. 4.
14. *Life*, I: 73–4. See James L. Clifford, *Young Samuel Johnson*, p. 121 and 337 n.26; and *Waingrow*, p. 57, n.10.
15. *Life*, I: 73.
16. *Hawkins's Life*, p. 11; *Life*, II: 153; Goldsmith, *The Present State of Polite Learning*, chapter 13.
17. *Life*, II: 444, 529, and III: 23; *Gleanings*, V: 14–15, 129–35.
18. *Hawkins's Life*, pp. 6–7.
19. *Life*, I: 76–7. Boswell received most of his information about the shoe episode, Taylor's matriculation and the Bateman lectures from Taylor himself, recording them in 'Communications concerning Dr Johnson from the Revd Dr Taylor,' *BP*, box 32, f. 825 (C2641).
20. *Hawkins's Life*, p. 8; *Life*, I: 446.
21. *Life*, I: 446, 70, 57.
22. *Hawkins's Life*, p. 7; *Life*, I: 446, 272, 274 (Warton's testimony).

23. *Diaries*, p. 26; *BP*, box 24, f. 567 (C1524); *Life*, I: 74, 72.

24. See these articles: Donald Greene, 'A Secret Far Dearer to Him than His Life': Johnson's "Vile Melancholy" Reconsidered', *AJ*, 4 (1991): 1–40; Barry Baldwin, 'The Mysterious Letter "M" in Johnson's Diaries', *AJ*, 6 (1994): 131–45; J.D. Fleeman, 'Johnson's Secret', *AJ*, 6 (1994): 147–9; and Aaron Stavisky, 'Johnson's "Vile Melancholy" Reconsidered Once More', *AJ*, 10 (1998): 1–24.

25. *Life*, I: 71; *Piozzi Anecdotes*, p. 70; *Life*, IV, 399.

26. *Life*, I: 60–62.

27. *BP*, box 24, f. 567 (C1524); George Steevens, *Anecdotes*, *JM*, II: 312–13. Two prose exercises and two poems of Johnson's, both in Latin, survive in the Pembroke College library.

28. *Life*, II: 187; *Hawkins's Life*, p. 1; Revd Luke Tyerman, *Life of Whitefield* (1876), I:19.

29. *Life*, I: 68, IV: 147–8, 215; *Thraliana*, I: 421.

30. *Life*, IV: 94.

31. *BP*, box 32, f. 825 (C2641); Waingrow, p. 185. Under December 1729 in his *Annales* Johnson wrote 'S.J. Oxonio rediit'. See *Gleanings*, V, chapter 4.

32. *Piozzi Anecdotes*, p. 72; *Life*, I: 74; *Letters*, I: 8.

33. *Memoirs of Hannah More*, ed. William Roberts (1834), I: 261–2.

CHAPTER 6: Horrible Imaginings

1. See Lawrence C. McHenry, Jr, 'Samuel Johnson's tics and gesticulations', *Journal of the History of Medicine and Allied Sciences*, 22 (1967), pp. 152–68.

2. *Life*, I: 63–4, 66; *Life*, I: 64; *Hawkins's Life*, p. 273. Donald Greene expressed considerable doubt about the idea of a severely melancholic Johnson who in this period almost lapsed into insanity ('"A Secret Far Dearer to Him Than His Life": Johnson's "Vile Melancholy",' *The Age of Johnson*, IV [1991]: 28–34). Boswell, incidentally, confounded the date of Johnson's abandonment of Oxford, thinking that he returned to the University after the 1729 Christmas holidays and continued there until 1731.

3. MS. *Life*, *BP*; *Poems*, pp. 79–80. See *Life*, I: 92–9 and n. 2; *Waingrow*, pp. 80–81, 439 and no. 2, 575–6. The poem was published in Robert Dodsley's *A Collection of Poems* in 1747, and later in the *Gentleman's Magazine* (1768), p. 439.

4. *The Diary of the Right Hon. William Windham* (1866); *Letters*, II: 199.

5. *Poems*, pp. 72–3. The poem was first printed in *The Gentleman's Magazine*, July 1743, p. 378.

6. *Yale Works: Rasselas and Other Tales*, XVI: 150–51.

7. *Hawkins's Life*, p. 9.

8. *Letters*, I: 3.

9. *Yale Works: Poems*, pp. 36, 38–40.

10. *Letters*, I: 3.

11. *Diaries*, pp. 28–30.

12. *Gleanings*, X: 91.

13. Hector to Boswell, 15 July 1786, *BP*, box 4, f. 117 (L637); *Life*, I: 84–5.

14. *Shaw's Memoirs*, p. 10; *Diaries*, p. 30 (translated from Latin); *Shaw's Memoirs*, p. 8.

15. *Life*, I: 148–9; *Yale Works: Poems*, pp. 68–9.

CHAPTER 7: Stirrings in Birmingham

1. Hector to Boswell, 28 March 1785, *Waingrow*, pp. 85–7 (*BP*, box 71, f. 1454 [C1524]).
2. Darwin cited from *The Age of Johnson*, ed. A.S. Turberville (1965), II: 245; *Boswell's Journal: The Ominous Years*, p. 292; *Life*, II: 464.
3. *Waingrow*, pp. 90–91; *Life*, I: 66.
4. *Letters, I:* 104–6, 107–8 (13 May 1755), 143 (7 October 1756). Roy Porter examined attitudes towards madness at this time in *Mind-Forg'd Manacles: A History of Madness in England from the Restoration to the Regency* (1987).
5. *Life*, I: 87.
6. *Waingrow*, pp. 87–8.
7. Thomas M. Curley, *Samuel Johnson and the Age of Travel* (1976), p. 1.
8. *Life*, I: 85–9. For a background introduction to Lobo and his travel accounts see *Yale Works: Abyssinia*, pp. xxxii-xxxix; *Life*, I: 86.
9. *Waingrow*, p. 88; *Life*, I: 87. See Paul Korshin, 'The Mythology of Johnson's Dictionary', *Anniversary Essays on Johnson's Dictionary*, ed. Jack Lynch and Anne McDermott (2005), pp. 10–23.
10. This background is much indebted to Thomas Curley's first chapter, 'Johnson's Lifetime 1709–1784: The Age of Travel', in *Samuel Johnson and the Age of Travel*, pp. 7–46.
11. *Idler*, no. 97 (23 February 1760), *Yale Works: Adventurer and Idler*, p. 298.
12. *Yale Works: Adventurer and Idler*, pp. 298–300; *Yale Works: Abyssinia*, pp. 3–4.
13. *Yale Works: Abyssinia*, pp. 4–5. See Curley, *Samuel Johnson and the Age of Travel*, p. 24.
14. *Waingrow*, p. 88; *Letters*, II: 310.
15. *Waingrow*, pp. 88–9; *Life*, I: 93–4. Waingrow says he found no evidence that either Johnson or James did not know Mrs Paul (*Waingrow*, p. 89 n.28); nor did he find evidence they did. See *Gleanings*, III: 124n, 164, 177 ff.
16. *Waingrow*, pp. 90–91; *Life*, I: 468.
17. *Diaries*, p. 32.
18. *Life*, I: 90 and n. 2, 425; *JM*, II: 8.
19. *Diaries*, p. 33 (including the translation); *Waingrow*, p. 250. See H. W. Liebert, 'Dr Johnson's First Book', *Yale University Library Gazette*, XXV (1950), p. 28.
20. *Letters*, I: 6–7.

CHAPTER 8: Taking a Wife

1. *Waingrow*, p. 80; *Thraliana*, I: 178.
2. *Life*, I: 94–5 and note 4; *Piozzi Anecdotes*, pp. 157–8.
3. *Life*, I: 95; *Shaw's Memoirs*, p. 11; *Thraliana*, I: 178. I have benefited from Graham Nicholls's thoughts on Johnson and Mrs Porter's relationship as presented in his unpublished lecture about her and Sarah Johnson on 6 October 2004 to the Samuel Johnson Society of Lichfield.
4. *Life*, IV: 395–6; I: 94. See *Gleanings*, X: 108–13.
5. *Gleanings*, X: 111; *Boswell's Notebook*, p. 10.
6. *Life*, I: 98–9, 96. The artist and present whereabouts of the miniature are unknown. The earliest attention drawn to it was in the *Gentleman's Magazine*, LXXXVIII (March 1818), p. 194.
7. *Life*, I: 97; *Gleanings*, X: 104–5; *Letters*, I: 7–8, 10.

8. *Letters*, I: 11–12 and II: 156–7. A more complete version of the educational scheme he sent his cousin is in the *Life*, I: 99–100.

9. *Hawkins's Life*, p. 20; Ian McIntyre, *Garrick* (1999), pp. 22 ff.; Thomas Davies, *Memoirs of the Life of David Garrick, Esq.* (1780, 1808), I: 8; *Life*, II: 377.

10. *Hawkins's Life*, pp. 19–20; *Life*, I: 96, 531 (Appendix G); *Shaw's Memoirs*, p. 11. The letter to Walmesley is in the Pembroke College manuscripts.

11. *Thraliana*, I: 177–8.

12. *Piozzi Anecdotes*, pp. 110–11.

13. *Life*, I: 98–9; *Boswell's Journals: Applause*, p. 111; *Thraliana*, I: 178. See also *Life*, I: 531 and *Piozzi Anecdotes*, pp. 110–11. Edmond Malone thought Garrick's entertainment at Johnson's expense was mostly 'invention' (*Life*, I: 531).

14. *Life*, II: 464–5, I: 82.

15. *Piozzi Anecdotes*, p. 112–13; Anna Seward, *Correspondence*, p. 116; *Thraliana*, I: 538; *Piozzi Anecdotes*, p. 113; *Poems*, p. 43.

16. *Piozzi Anecdotes*, p. 113.

17. *Yale Works: Poems*, pp. 77–8, 82–4.

18. *Diaries*, p. 35; *Life*, II: 121, I: 97–8.

19. *Life*, IV: 407–8 and n. 4; *GM* (3 January 1785), LV, i.

20. *Life*, IV: 199, I: 100; *Rambler*, no. 122 (18 May 1751), *Yale Works: Rambler*, pp. 290–91.

21. The MS of the first draft is in the King's Library (British Library). See Bertrand H. Bronson, *Johnson Agonistes and Other Essays* (1965), pp. 100–55. See also Marshall Waingrow, 'The Mighty Moral of *Irene*', *From Sensibility to Romanticism* (1965), ed. F.W. Hilles and Harold Bloom, pp. 79–82.

22. Act II, sc. vii, 55–8 (*Yale Works: Poems*, pp. 147, 148–9, 155).

23. *Life*, I: 101.

CHAPTER 9: Stranger in London

1. *Life*, I: 102.

2. *Life*, I: 101, n.1; *BP*, box 31, f. 807 (C2543).

3. *Gleanings*, I: 1; *Life*, I: 229.

4. *Life*, I: 102 n.2.

5. *Life*, I: 105, 103.

6. Liza Picard, *Dr Johnson's London: Life in London 1740–1770* (2000), p. 199; *Johnson's England*, I: 180–81; *Life*, III: 305, 389, 381. *Life*, I: 103, n.3 reviews Johnson's drinking and on slender evidence maintains that Johnson never drank between 1736 to at least as late as 1757.

7. This famous remark about London has sometimes been denied Johnson on the grounds that it is not in Boswell's journal. Although in the *Life* Boswell quoted it for the year 1777, he often did draw on sources he knew from later in Johnson's life (and are therefore not in the daily journals) to illustrate earlier attitudes.

8. *Life*, III: 378–79, IV: 358, III: 178, 246.

9. Peter Ackroyd, *London: A Biography* (2000), 'Violent London' (chapter 52), pp. 477, 482; Boswell, *London Journal*, pp. 74 (11 December 1762), 86–7 (15 December 1762).

10. J.H. Plumb, *England in the Eighteenth Century* (1959), p. 33.

11. Ackroyd, *London: A Biography*, pp. 308–9; Roy Porter, *London: A Social History* (1994), pp. 125, 168ff.

12. Porter, *Enlightenment: Britain and the Creation of the Modern World* (2000), pp. 3, 6,

xxiv, 11. See Pat Rogers, *Grub Street* (1972); also Roy Porter's *London: A Social History* (1994), chapters 5, 6, and 7 (pp. 93–184).

13. *Piozzi Anecdotes*, p. 112; *Life*, I: 106, V: 483–84, III: 194–6. On Johnson's sermon on Charity for Hervey-Aston, no. 27, see *Yale Works: Rasselas and Other Tales*, pp. 287–99.

14. *Diaries*, p. 39; *Life*, I: 460–61.

15. *Letters*, I: 12–13.

CHAPTER 10: Sons of Misery: Finding Richard Savage

1. *Life*, V: 230.

2. There is no firm evidence that Lucy moved in with Sarah Johnson then, but Seward (*Letters*, I: 116) says she 'boarded' with her and several letters in following years argue in favour of that (see *Life*, I: 110, n.3).

3. *Piozzi Anecdotes*, p. 110.

4. Castle Street is now called Eastcastle Street and his house stood partly on the site of what is now the Hotel York.

5. *Life*, I: 111; *Hawkins's Life*, pp. 27–8; letter to Thomas Birch, Birch MSS, BL Add. Ms. 4302; and *BP*, box 57, f. 1206; *Rambler*, no. 188, *Yale Works: Rambler*, p. 221.

6. *Life*, I: 112, III: 322; *Yale Boswell: Poems*, pp. 40–43. See Robert Folkenflik, *Samuel Johnson: Biographer* (1978), pp. 61–3.

7. *Letters*, I: 14–15.

8. *Letters*, I: 15; Jenny Uglow, *Dr Johnson, His Club, and Other Friends*, p. 24.

9. *Letters*, I: 15–16, 16–17; *Life*, I: 124. On this matter of the poem's anonymity, see *Early Career*, p. 20.

10. *Life*, I: 129; *Correspondence of Alexander Pope*, ed. George Sherburn (1956), IV: 194; *Life*, I: 534.

11. *Life*, I: 194; *Diaries*, pp. 37–8.

12. Letter to Birch, Birch MSS., BL Add. Ms. 4302; *BP*, box 57, f. 1206.

13. *Life*, V: 255, I: 159. The most readable source for Savage and his connection to Johnson, although it is not without its factual errors, is Richard Holmes' *Dr Johnson and Mr Savage* (1993), from which the translation of Johnson's epigram on Savage is cited (p. 177). See also *Early Career*, pp. 186–9; and Clarence Tracy, *The Artificial Bastard: A Biography of Richard Savage* (1953).

14. *Correspondence of Alexander Pope*, IV: 431.

15. *Lives of the Poets: Life of Savage*, III: 163. I cite here and below from Johnson's revised version in the *Lives of the Poets*.

16. *Life*, I: 161 n.3. I am indebted for this idea of 'Letter to a Noble Lord' genre to Robert Folkenflik.

17. *Lives of the Poets: Life of Savage*, III: 175, 177, 178; *Correspondence of Alexander Pope*, IV: 392.

18. *Hawkins's Life*, p. 29.

19. See Bertram A. Davis, *A Proof of Eminence: The Life of Sir John Hawkins* (1973) and Holmes, *Dr Johnson and Mr Savage*, chapter 3 ('Night'). The following account of *London* and *The Life of Richard Savage* is (with a few caveats) partly indebted to Holmes' reading of Johnson's anti-authority, satirical, psychologically intense, rebellious persona.

20. *Hawkins's Life*, pp. 29–30.

21. Kaminski, *Early Career*, p. 89.
22. *Yale Works: Poems*, pp. 47–61.
23. *Murphy's Essay*, p. 371. Thomas Kaminski argued against the identification of Thales and Savage in 'Was Savage "Thales"', *Bulletin of Research in the Humanities*, 85 (1982), pp. 322–35; for other views see *Waingrow*, p. 233 and n.6.
24. *Life*, I: 441; *Piozzi Anecdotes*, pp. 88–9, 95.
25. *Rambler*, no. 202, *Yale Works: Rambler*, pp. 287–8.
26. *Letters*, I: 32–3, 35–6.
27. *Letters*, I: 35–6; *Life*, V: 66–7. See J.D. Fleeman, 'The Making of Johnson's *Life of Savage*, 1744', *The Library* 22 (1967).
28. Holmes, *Dr Johnson and Mr Savage*, pp. 353, 351.
29. *Lives of the Poets: Life of Savage*, III: 165.
30. See Folkenflik, *Samuel Johnson: Biographer*, pp. 195–213.
31. *Lives of the Poets: Life of Savage*, III: 172.
32. *Lives of the Poets: Life of Savage*, III: 174.
33. *Lives of the Poets: Life of Savage*, III: 186, 188.

CHAPTER 11: 'Slow Rises Worth by Poverty Depress'd'

1. *Hawkins's Life*, pp. 26–7; 'Life of Cave', *GM* (1754), pp. 55–58. There is no complete modern biography of Cave.
2. See John Brewer on eighteenth-century authors, publishers and literary culture in *The Pleasures of the Imagination: English Culture in the Eighteenth Century* (1997), especially section II, chapters 3–4.
3. Alvin Kernan, *Printing Technology, Letters & Samuel Johnson* (1987), pp. 13, 7–8, 16–18.
4. *Adventurer*, No. 115 (11 December 1753), *Yale Works: Adventurer and Idler*, p. 457.
5. Kaminski, *Early Career*, pp. 65–7.
6. *Yale Works: Rambler*, IV: 336.
7. *Letters*, I: 17; Kaminski, *Early Career*, p. 21–2.
8. *Life*, I: 135.
9. *Letters*, I: 126; Pennington, *Memoir*, I: 447; *Life*, I: 139; Pennington, *Memoir*, p. 26; Kaminski, *Early Career*, pp. 34–40; *Life*, II: 319. See Norma Clarke, *Dr Johnson's Women* (2000), chapter 2.
10. Kaminski, *Early Career*, pp. 42–3.
11. John Nichols, *GM* (1785), p. 6; *Political Writings*, pp. 11, 16; Kaminski, *Early Career*, pp. 46–49.
12. *Letters*, I: 18–19.
13. William Cullen, *First Lines in the Practice of Physic* (1772), pp. xxxiii; John Wiltshire, *Samuel Johnson in the Medical World*, pp. 75–9; 'Life of Boerhaave', *GM*, 1739, pp. 37–8, 72–3, 114–16, 172–6.
14. Kaminski, *Early Career*, p. 54; *Life*, IV: 430. See Robert Folkenflik, *Samuel Johnson: Biographer*, pp. 58–62 (and his chapter, 'Johnson's Heroes').
15. *Letters*, I: 20; *A Commentary on Mr Pope's Principles of Morality, or Essay on Man* (1742), p. 123. See Kaminski, *Early Career*, pp. 77–8.
16. Kaminski, *Early Career*, pp. 54–9.
17. *Greene Politics*, pp. 236–42.
18. *Life*, I: 141.
19. *Correspondence of Alexander Pope*, IV: 194; *Hawkins's Life*, p. 41. See Greene, *Political*

Writings, pp. 19–51; Kaminski, *Early Career*, pp. 100–1.
20. *Hawkins's Life*, p. 227; *Political Writings*, pp. 63, 72.
21. *Gleanings*, VI, chapter ix.
22. *Waingrow*, p. 58; *Life*, I: 133–4, 373.
23. *Gleanings*, X: 148; Kaminski, *Early Career*, pp. 73–6.

CHAPTER 12: Wandering in the Midlands

1. *Hawkins's Life*, p. 49; *Shaw's Memoirs*, p. 34; *Life*, IV: 395–6.
2. *Gleanings*, VI: 120; *Letters, I: 22–4.
3. *Life*, III: 180–81.
4. *Gleanings*, VI: 125; *Life*, I: 82–3, III: 149; *Piozzi Anecdotes*, pp. 113–14.
5. *Letters*, I: 117–18; *Piozzi Anecdotes*, p. 114.
6. *Life*, I: 366, 547. See *Letters*, III: 169 and n.5, 371.

CHAPTER 13: London Revived: A Lion in Harness

1. *Yale Works: Poems*, p. 67.
2. *Life*, I: 102, n.2. See F.V. Bernard, 'The History of Nadir Shah: A New Attribution to Johnson', *British Museum Quarterly*, 34 (1970), pp. 92–104.
3. On the lives of Drake, Blake and Baratier, see Folkenflik, *Samuel Johnson: Biographer*, p. 99; Curley, *Samuel Johnson and the Age of Travel*, pp. 31–2, 61–4; Robert DeMaria, Jr, *The Life of Samuel Johnson* (1993), pp. 74–6; and Kaminski, *Early Career*, pp. 110–13.
4. Kaminski, *Early Career*, pp. 116–22.
5. 'Essay on Epitaphs', in *Samuel Johnson*, ed. Donald Greene (Oxford Authors, 1984), p. 101.
6. *Gentleman's Magazine*, XXIII (March 1753): 148; *Life*, IV: 408–9, I: 152.
7. *Murphy's Essay*, pp. 378–80.
8. *Life*, I: 314; *Hawkins's Life*, p. 56. For eloquent analyses of Johnson's method and achievement in the debates, see *Greene Politics*, pp. 112–40, and Kaminski, *Early Career*, chapter vii, on both of which I draw for my discussion.
9. Kaminski, *Early Career*, p. 131.
10. On the debates, see *Greene Politics*, pp. 122–9.
11. Kaminski, *Early Career*, pp. 166–70, 240 n.23, 148–53.
12. *Samuel Johnson*, ed. Greene, pp. 113–14; *GM* (1742), p. 634; Folkenflik, *Samuel Johnson: Biographer*, p. 64; Wiltshire, *Samuel Johnson in the Medical World*, pp. 101–2, 80; Kaminski, *Early Career*, pp. 158–61.
13. *GM* (1743), p. 550.
14. Kaminski, *Early Career*, p. 171.
15. *Piozzi Anecdotes*, p. 70.
16. *Letters*, I: 31.
17. *Life*, III: 405; *Letters*, I: 32.
18. *Thraliana*, I: 173; *Life*, I: 159.
19. *Early Biographical Writings*, p. 89; Wiltshire, *Samuel Johnson in the Medical World*, pp. 94, 99–100; *Lives of the Poets*, III: 415; *Life*, III: 355.
20. *Letters*, IV: 372; 'General Account of the Work' [James's *Medicinal Dictionary*] as cited by Wiltshire, *Samuel Johnson in the Medical World*, p. 74.

21. *Life*, I: 154; Kaminski, *Early Career*, pp. 174–84.
22. Osborne to Birch, BL Add. Ms. 4316, f. 98; 'Account of the Harleian Library', in *Samuel Johnson*, ed. Greene, pp. 117–19.
23. 'Account', pp. 117–19; *Hawkins's Life*, pp. 60–61, 63.
24. 'Introduction to the *Harleian Miscellany*', in *Samuel Johnson*, ed. Greene, pp. 123–4. The 'Introduction' is otherwise known as his 'Essay on the Origin and Importance of Small Tracts and Fugitive Pieces'.
25. *Letters*, I: 36, 37–9; *Life*, I: 163n.
26. *Diaries*, pp. 40–41. See *Early Career*, pp. 193–4.
27. *Johnson on Shakespeare*, p. 45.
28. *Johnson on Boswell*, p. xiv.
29. *Life*, I: 318, 134; *Hebrides*, p. 20; *Diaries*, pp. 9–10; *Life*, III: 195. Aleyn Reade contends that Adams's request dates very likely from this period, not in 1738 as Boswell claimed (*Gleanings*, VI: 116).

CHAPTER 14: A Lifeline: the *Dictionary*

1. *The Letters of David Garrick*, ed. D.M. Little and G.M. Kahrl, I.
2. *Life*, I: 177.
3. *Life*, I: 182–3; III: 405; *Letters*, I: 40–41.
4. The best comprehensive account of Johnson's work on the *Dictionary* is by Allen Reddick, *The Making of Johnson's Dictionary 1746–1773* (revised edn, 1996), to which I am heavily indebted. More recently, see Henry Hitchings's erudite and entertaining *Dr Johnson's Dictionary: The Extraordinary Story of the Book that Defined the World* (2005).
5. Thomas Carlyle, *Samuel Johnson* (1832, 1853), p. 75. 'It is a stout, old-fashioned, oak-balustrated house', wrote Carlyle.
6. *Piozzi Anecdotes*, p. 88.
7. *Diaries*, p. 134.
8. Jack Lynch has published an edition of selections from the *Dictionary*, with a useful Introduction: *Samuel Johnson's* Dictionary: *Selections from the 1755 Work that Defined the English Language* (2002, 2004). Because it is more widely available I cite from David Crystal's edition, *Dr Johnson's Dictionary* (2005).
9. *Reddick*, pp. 13–17; Lynch, *Samuel Johnson's Dictionary*, pp. 2–3; Hitchings, *Dr Johnson's Dictionary*, pp. 56–9.
10. Jonathon Green, *Chasing the Sun: Dictionary Makers and the Dictionaries They Made* (1996), p.211.
11. *Life*, I: 186.
12. On the text of the *Plan*, see Gwin J. Kolb, 'Establishing the Text of Dr Johnson's Dictionary of the English Language', *Eighteenth-Century Studies in Honor of Donald F. Hyde*, ed. W.H. Bond (1970), pp. 81–7.
13. *Life*, I: 183. See *Reddick*, pp. 19–23; Paul Korshin, 'The Johnson–Chesterfield Relationship: A New Hypothesis', *Publications of the Modern Language Association*, 85 (March 1970); and Howard Weinbrot, 'Samuel Johnson's *Plan* and Preface to the *Dictionary*: The Growth of a Lexicographer's Mind', in *New Aspects of Lexicography*, pp. 73–94.
14. *Life*, I: 332–3.
15. *Dictionary*, pp. 1, 17–18.

16. *Dictionary*, pp. 16, 18.

17. For example, Hitchings, *Dr Johnson's Dictionary*, pp. 67–8. See also Green, *Chasing the Sun*, pp. 22–3, 234.

18. *Dictionary*, pp. 11, 16, 10.

19. Hitchings, *Dr Johnson's Dictionary*, p. 68; *Dictionary*, pp. 11, 15, 16; *Greene Politics*, p. 34; *Dictionary*, pp. 37–8, 29. Lynch agrees that Johnson 'was usually adamant that usage should be determined by consensus, not by fiat' *(Samuel Johnson's Dictionary*, p. 8); see also Robert DeMaria, *The Life of Samuel Johnson*, p. 115. See also Robert Folkenflik's recent essay, 'The Politics of Johnson's *Dictionary* Revisited', *Age of Johnson*, 18 (2007), pp. 1–17, for a considered view of the controversy.

20. *Dictionary*, pp. 5–7, 16.

21. *Dictionary*, pp. 7–11.

22. *Dictionary*, pp. 12–18.

23. *The Orrery Papers*, ed. the Countess of Cork and Orrery, 2 vols. (1773), II: 43 (August 1747).

24. *Hawkins's Life*, p. 77. See also *Life*, I: 435–6, 328.

25. Hitchings, *Dr Johnson's Dictionary*, p. 60.

26. *Life*, I: 187, 536.

27. *Letters*, IV: 336. See J.D. Fleeman, *A Preliminary Handlist of Documents and Manuscripts of Samuel Johnson* (1967), p. 6, no. 35.

28. *Life*, I: 187, II: 379; *Letters*, II: 207–8; *Life*, III: 421; *Letters*, II: 315.

29. *Yale Works: Rambler*, IV: 286–7.

30. Hitchings, pp. 70–71.

31. *Dictionary*, pp. 32–3; *Life*, IV: 4.

32. Lynch, *Samuel Johnson's Dictionary*, p. 13. See also DeMaria, *Johnson's Dictionary and the Language of Learning* (1986), p. 37.

33. *Dictionary*, p. 32; *Thraliana*, I: 34; Thomas Tyers, *A Biographical Sketch of Dr Samuel Johnson* (1785), in *The Early Biographies of Samuel Johnson*, ed. O.M. Brack, Jr and Robert E. Kelley (1974), p. 82. See Robert Folkenflik, 'The Politics of Johnson's *Dictionary* Revisited', *Age of Johnson*, 18 (2007), pp. 1–17.

34. Green, *Chasing the Sun*, pp. 222–23; Rod Mengham, *The Descent of Language: Writing in Praise of Babel* (London, 1993), p. 113; Hitchings, *Dr Johnson's Dictionary*, p. 103; DeMaria, *The Life of Samuel Johnson*, pp. 122–27.

35. *Reddick*, pp. 37–41. See Folkenflik, 'The Politics of Johnson's *Dictionary* Revisited', *Age of Johnson*, 18 (2007), pp. 1–17.

36. *Reddick*, p. 54.

37. *Reddick*, pp. 42–51. Recently, the results of Reddick's careful reasoning were modified by Anne McDermott's own minutely researched conjectures presented in a lecture, 'How Johnson's *Dictionary* Was Made', at the Pembroke College, Oxford, conference on the *Dictionary* in August 2005. See also her essay, 'Johnson the Prescriptivist? The Case for the Defense', *Anniversary Essays on Johnson's* Dictionary, ed. Jack Lynch and Anne McDermott (2005), pp. 92–112.

CHAPTER 15: Poetic Interludes

1. *Life*, I: 167, 168.

2. *Murphy's Essay*, p. 457.

3. *JM*, II: 318.

4. *JM*, II: 318, 314.

5. 'Prologue Spoken at the Opening of the Theatre in Drury Lane, 1747', *Yale Works: Poems*, pp. 87–90.

6. *Hawkins's Life*, p. 85; *Life*, I: 196.

7. *Life*, I: 200, 201, 196; *Waingrow*, pp. 146–7, 427; *JM*, II: 318.. A racier version of Garrick's anecdote (omitted by Boswell) has Johnson referring to 'the white bubbies & the silk stockings' of the actresses that 'excite my genitals' (*Life*, I: 538–39).

8. *Life*, I: 197–8; *Murphy's Essay, JM*, I: 387; *Life*, I: 199 and n.2, II: 348–9. See *Waingrow*, pp. 106 and n. 45, 22.

9. *Works*, ed. Murphy (1801), II: 236–8.

10. *Yale Works: Rasselas and other Tales*, pp. 195–212.

11. *Diaries*, p. 41; *Yale Works*, XVI: 202–3, 212.

12. For Johnson's boast, see *Works* (1787), XI: 212; *Life*, II: 15.

13. *Yale Works: Poems*, pp. 90–109.

14. See Howard Weinbrot's insightful essay, 'Johnson's Poetry', in *CCSJ*, pp. 34–50.

15. *Life*, I: 193; Pat Rogers, *The Samuel Johnson Encyclopedia*, p. 410; *Life*, I: 194; Byron, *Works* (1835), V: 66; James Lockhart, *The Life of Sir Walter Scott* (1837–8), II: 307; Bate, *Samuel Johnson*, p. 278. *The Vanity of Human Wishes* appeared in a revised text in Robert Dodsley's *Collection of Poems* in 1755. The complete manuscript of the entire poem in an earlier version is in the Hyde collection at Harvard.

CHAPTER 16: Tetty and 'Amorous Propensities'

1. *Hawkins's Life*, pp. 105–6.

2. *Hawkins's Life*, pp. 110–11; *Life*, I: 28, n.1 .

3. *Letters*, I: 42.

4. *Diaries*, p. 53; *Life*, IV: 395–6. See Donald and Mary Hyde, 'Dr Johnson's Second Wife', in *New Light on Dr Johnson*, ed. F.W. Hilles (1959), pp. 133–51.

5. *Life*, I: 192 and n.4, 238.

6. *Boswell's Journals: Laird*, pp. 142–3; *Life*, IV: 200; letter from Boswell to Edmond Malone, 10 February 1791, *Waingrow*, p. 384.

7. *Life*, I: 238.

8. *Boswell's Journals: Applause*, pp. 110–13.

9. *Piozzi Anecdotes*, p. 110; *Life*, I: 99.

10. *Shaw's Memoirs*, p. 33; *Thraliana*, I: 178; *Hawkins's Life*, pp. 129–30.

11. *Life*, I: 349; *Dictionary*, p. 167; *Letters*, I: 43–4.

12. *Letters*, I: 43, 45–6.

CHAPTER 17: The Triumph of the Moralist

1. *Yale Works: Rambler*, III: xxi, xxiii. See Lawrence Lipking, 'Johnson and the Meaning of Life', in *Johnson and His Age*, ed. James Engell (1984), p. 20.

2. *Yale Works: Rambler*, V: 312 (no. 207), 318 (no. 208).

3. *Yale Works: Rambler*, V: 316.

4. *Life*, I: 202; *Yale Works: Rambler*, IV: 204. On the publication and distribution of the essays, see Paul Tankard, 'A Petty Writer: Johnson and the *Rambler* pamphlets', *Age of Johnson*, X (1999), pp. 67–87. See also Introduction, *Yale Works: Rambler*, III: xxvi-xxvii.

5. *Yale Works: Rambler*, IV: 345–46; *Piozzi Anecdotes*, p. 76. Johnson was not as unprepared as he made out. Boswell tells that he had in his possession a commonplace book in which he wrote 'a variety of hints for essays on different subjects' (*Life*, I: 204–7).

6. *Diaries*, p. 43; *Yale Works: Rambler*, V: 320.

7. *Yale Works: Rambler*, III: 76.

8. On Johnson's style, see W.K. Wimsatt, Jr, *The Prose Style of Samuel Johnson* (1941) and *Philosophic Words: A Study of Style and Meaning in the* Rambler *and* Dictionary (1968); and Mark E. Wildermuth, 'Johnson's Prose Style: Blending Energy and Elegance in *The Rambler*', *The Age of Johnson*, VI (1994): 205–35.

9. *Correspondence of Samuel Richardson*, ed. Anna Letitia Barbauld (1804), I: 169, 164–5 – hereafter cited as *Richardson Correspondence; Yale Works: Rambler*, V: 317.

10. *Yale Works: Rambler*, V: 316.

11. *Yale Works: Rambler*, III: 132–3.

12. *Yale Works: Rambler*, III: xxviii.

13. *Yale Works: Rambler*, V: 198, 4; IV: 356, 197.

14. See W. Jackson Bate, 'Johnson and Satire Manqué', in *Eighteenth-Century Studies in Honor of Donald F. Hyde* (1970), pp. 145–60.

15. *Piozzi Anecdotes*, pp. 97, 150.

16. *Life*, I: 210.

17. *Life*, I: 213; *Richardson Correspondence*, I: 168; *Murphy's Essay*, p. 393.

18. *Yale Works: Rambler*, IV: 157, 159; *Richardson Correspondence*, V: 281–2; Norma Clarke, *Dr Johnson's Women*, p. 79; *Hebrides*, p. 386; *Thraliana*, I: 173; *Richardson Correspondence*, IV: 317; *Life*, V: 396, n.1; *Richardson Correspondence*, I: 164–6.

19. *A Series of Letters between Mrs Elizabeth Carter and Miss Catherine Talbot, from the year 1741 to 1770*, ed. Revd Montagu Pennington, I: 229–30.

20. Pennington, *A Series of Letters*, I: 235, 244, 295.

21. *Yale Works: Rambler*, III: 315; *Letters*, I: 57.

22. *Yale Works: Rambler*, IV: 5–6. Paul J. Korshin succinctly reviewed a few of the recurring moral themes in 'Johnson, the Essay, and the *Rambler*', *CCSJ*, pp. 51–66.

CHAPTER 18: Darkness Falls

1. *Yale Works: Rambler*, IV: 346–7.

2. *Letters*, I: 50–51. I am indebted for several details regarding the chronology of Johnson's work on the *Dictionary* to Anne McDermott's lecture, 'How Johnson's *Dictionary* was Made', at the Pembroke College conference on the *Dictionary* in August 2005.

3. *Hawkins's Life*, pp. 121–2, 123.

4. *Life*, IV: 275; Chauncey Tinker, *Dr Johnson and Fanny Burney* (1911), p. 205; *Letters*, I: 71, 56; V: 10–11. See Norma Clarke, *Dr Johnson's Women* (2000), pp. 221–5. On whether or not Johnson wrote the penultimate chapter of Lennox's novel, see Margaret Dalziel's edition (Oxford, 1970), pp. 414–15, and the Appendix to the edition by Duncan Isles, 'Johnson, Richardson, and *The Female Quixote*', pp. 418–27.

5. *Letters*, I: 59.

6. *Letters*, I: 61.

7. *Hawkins's Life*, p. 130; *Diaries*, pp. 52–3; *Letters*, IV: 430, 435. The poem was printed in Anna Williams's *Miscellanies in Prose and Verse* (1766), p. 1. He wrote 'The Ant' on a leaf dated 14 April 1752.

8. *Diaries*, pp. 44–7, 50.

9. *Yale Works: Poems*, p. 263; *Diaries*, p. 47 and *passim*.

10. *Diaries*, pp. 52–3. Johnson once almost asked his wife to promise that she would not marry again if he died before she did (*Life*, II: 77). Boswell did not like that, commenting that her marriage to him was a second marriage and that he overlooked that her first husband had a prior claim.

11. *Hawkins's Life*, pp. 130–31; *Piozzi Anecdotes*, p. 114; *Life*, III: 305; *Diaries*, p. 50; *Shaw's Memoirs*, p. 34.

CHAPTER 19: Once More unto the Breach: Back to the *Dictionary*

1. *Piozzi Anecdotes*, pp. 130–31; *Life, III: 200*; *Taxation No Tyranny*, in *Yale Works: Political Writings*, p. 454. James G. Basker delivered an overview of Johnson's strong abolitionist stance on slavery at the Johnson Society of London in July 2006, but it has not yet been published: 'Johnson, Boswell, and the Abolition of Slavery'. Aleyn Reade tells Francis Barber's complete story in *Gleanings*, II: 1–115.

2. *Life*, I: 241; *JM*, II: 316–17.

3. *Letters*, I: 63–4 (9 July 1752); *Yale Works: Adventurer and Idler*, II: 323–36; *Letters*, I: 67. See David Fairer, 'Authorship Problems in *The Adventurer*', *Review of English Studies*, 25 (1974), pp. 144, 148–9.

4. *Life*, I: 252.

5. *Life*, IV: 33, 300; *Letters*, I: 78; *Probationary Odes for the Laureateship* (1785), p. 116; *Letters*, I: 97, 133–4; *Life*, III: 84 n. 2.

6. *Life*, I: 242 and n.1; *Diaries*, p. 79.

7. *Life*, I: 254; *Piozzi Anecdotes*, pp. 159, 95, 99; *Letters Between Mrs. Elizabeth Carter and Miss Catherine Talbot*, I: 320; *An Account of the Life of Dr Samuel Johnson, Written by Himself*, ed. Richard Wright (1805), pp. 47–8 – this edition is the first time Hill Boothby's letters to Johnson were printed; *Life* (3rd edn), I: 219n.

8. *Yale Works: Adventurer and Idler*, II: 346–7; *Diaries*, pp. 54, 55.

9. *Yale Works: Adventurer and Idler*, II: pp. 487–92.

10. *Yale Works: Adventurer and Idler*, II: 494–5.

11. *Diaries*, p. 48.

12. *Diaries*, p. 50.

13. *Reddick*, pp. 56–9, 70.

14. *Reddick*, pp. 70–71; *Letters*, I: 73. I am indebted to Anne McDermott's lecture at Pembroke College in 2005 for this probable schedule. See also *Reddick*, pp. 72–4.

15. *Letters*, I: 81–2; *Life*, I: 271; *Letters*, I: 94.

16. *Life*, I: 270 n.5; *Letters*, I: 88; *BP*, Box 35, f. 893 (C3075); *Life*, I: 271–2.

17. *Reddick*, pp. 75–7; *Letters*, I: 253. See Robert DeMaria, Jr, 'Johnson's Extempore History and Grammar of the English Language', *Anniversary Essays on Johnson's Dictionary*, pp. 77–92, based as he says on his and Gwin J. Kolb's edition, *Yale Works: Johnson on the English Language*, vol. XVIII.

18. *Dictionary*, p. 24.

19. *Dictionary*, pp. 21, 35, 40, 41. On the tradition of biographers' lugubrious characterizations of their tasks and lives, see *Yale Works: Johnson on the English Language*, Introduction, pp. xxii-xxv.

20. John Wooll, *Memoirs of Warton* (1806), p. 228; *Letters*, I: 88, 89–90, 98; *Life*, I: 280.

21. *Letters*, I: 90.

22. *Letters*, I: 77–8, 88, 89, 91; *Life*, III: 176.

23. *Lives of the Poets*, III: 335–40; *Life*, I: 383.
24. *Life*, II: 345, 397. Three essays for the *Universal Visiter* that it is known Johnson wrote were: 'Some Further Thoughts On Agriculture', 'An Essay on Epitaphs' (featuring Pope), and 'Reflections on the Present State of Literature' on self-deluded authors.
25. *Letters*, I: 92, 101; *Murphy's Essay*, p. 405.
26. *Life*, I: 260, IV: 128; *Dr Johnson's Dictionary*, p. 101; *Letters*, I: 94–7.
27. Alvin Kernan, *Printing Technology, Letters and Samuel Johnson*, pp. 199–203.
28. *Life*, I: 287, 304; Hitchings, *Dr Johnson's Dictionary*, pp. 192–3; *Letters*, I: 100, 105.
29. *Reddick*, pp. 83–8; *Life*, IV: 4; *The Universal Visiter*, January 1756, p. 4; *Dictionary*, p. 40. For a discussion of the encyclopedic nature of the *Dictionary*, see Jack Lynch, 'Johnson's Encyclopedia', *Anniversary Essays on Johnson's* Dictionary, pp. 129–46.
30. Woodman, *A Preface to Samuel Johnson*, p. 136; Hitchings, *Dr Johnson's Dictionary*, p. 134; *Letters Between Mrs Elizabeth Carter and Miss Catherine Talbot*, I: 390.
31. *Dictionary*, p. 35; Lynch, *Johnson's Encyclopedia*, in *Anniversary Essays on Johnson's Dictionary*, pp. 129–46.

CHAPTER 20: Stalled

1. *Letters*, I: 117; *Diaries*, pp. 56–8.
2. *Murphy's Essay*, pp. 403–4; *The Gentleman's Magazine*, February 1754.
3. *Thraliana*, I: 165; *Letters*, I: 103; Madame d'Arblay, *Memoirs of Dr Burney* (1832), I: 119–20; *Letters*, I: 157. See Roger Lonsdale, *Dr Charles Burney* (1965), pp. 45ff.
4. *Letters*, I: 116; Wiltshire, *Samuel Johnson in the Medical World*, p. 66; *Letters, I:* 120–21. For Johnson's evasiveness regarding orange peels, see *Life*, II: 330–31.
5. *Life*, IV: 143; *Letters*, I: 122.
6. *Piozzi Anecdotes*, p. 114; *Diaries*, pp. 59–60, 61; *Idler* nos. 22 and 38 (*Yale Works: Adventurer and Idler*, II: 69–71, 117–21).
7. *Piozzi Anecdotes*, p. 152; *Life*, II: 195, I: 359.
8. *Diaries*, p. 56.
9. *Yale Works: Rambler*, III: 15.
10. *Yale Works: Rambler*, V: 8.
11. *Literary Magazine*, II: 167, I: 239.
12. *Literary Magazine*, II: 299, 171; *Life*, I: 315.
13. *Yale Works: Political Writings*, pp. 147, 150, 186–8; *Life*, I: 310.
14. *Yale Works: Political Writings*, pp. 268–9.
15. *Waingrow*, pp. 164–9; *Reddick*, pp. 66–7; *Yale Works: Political Writings*, p. 333; *Letters*, I: 145, 188; *Life*, I: 348; *Gleanings*, II: 12. 'Cham' was 'the title of the Sovereign of Tartary . . . well applied to Johnson, the Monarch of Literature' (*Life*, I: 349 n.5). See Lyle Larsen, *Dr Johnson's Household*, chapter 3.
16. *Letters*, I: 79, 124, 126, 127.
17. *Thraliana*, I: 184.
18. *Thraliana*, I: 185; *Life*, I: 243.
19. *Life*, III: 314; *Hawkins's Life*, pp. 245–6; *Life*, III: 443–9 (Appendix A); *Piozzi Anecdotes*, p. 119.
20. *Life*, I: 296 n.2, IV: 187.
21. *Letters*, II: 248 (15 July 1775).
22. *Life*, I: 247.
23. *Life*, I: 249, 250–51.

24. Knight, *Autobiography*, ed. J.W. Kaye (1861), I: 9; *Letters*, I: 244 (August 1764); Reynolds, *Portraits*, p. 66; *JM*, II: 294; F.W. Hilles, *The Literary Career of Sir Joshua Reynolds* (1936; rep. 1967), p. 12 n.2; James Northcote, *The Life of Sir Joshua Reynolds* (2nd edn 1818), I: 79.

25. *JM*, II: 251, 259, 261; Frances D'Arblay, *Memoirs of Dr Burney*, I: 332.

26. *JM*, II: 273, 274, 297. See *Life*, I: 484. On Tourette's Syndrome, see Lawrence C. McHenry, Jr, 'Samuel Johnson's tics and gesticulations', *Journal of the History of Medicine and Allied Sciences*, 22 (1967), pp. 152–68, Wiltshire, *Samuel Johnson in the Medical World*, pp. 24–34, and T.J. Murray, 'Doctor Samuel Johnson's Movement Disorders', *British Medical Journal*, I (1979), pp. 1, 610–14.

27. *Life*, I: 485–6; Reynolds, *Portraits*, p. 70; *Life*, IV: 183 n.2, I: 144. See Wiltshire, *Samuel Johnson in the Medical World*, p. 29.

28. *Life*, I: 392; *The R.B. Adam Library* (1929), vol. II. Several of the alterations in Heath's engraving (which went through several stages) may well have been based on alterations Reynolds himself supervised over the years, as was his general practice, long before he gave Boswell the portrait in 1789. For a full history of this painting see Irma S. Lustig, 'Facts and Deductions: The Curious History of Reynolds's First Portrait of Johnson, 1756', *The Age of Johnson*, pp. 161–80; also Kai Kin Yung, *Samuel Johnson 1709–84* (1984), pp. 79–81.

29. *Yale Works: Idler*, II: 140.

CHAPTER 21: 'Suffering Chimeras'

1. *Hawkins's Life*, pp. 150–52.

2. *Life*, I: 545; *Letters* I: 142, 147, 153, III: 19 n.3.

3. *Johnson on Shakespeare*, VII: 51–6; *Letters*, I: 135.

4. *Boswell Journals: Defence*, pp. 123–4; *Life*, II: 192; *Letters of David Garrick*, ed. D.M. Little and G.M. Kahrl (1963), II: 460; *Hebrides*, p. 207.

5. *Letters*, I: 158, 159; *London Chronicle* (12–14 April 1757), pp. 358–9.

6. *Life*, II: 103, IV: 134. See Lonsdale, 'Johnson and Dr Burney', *Johnson, Boswell and Their Circle*, pp. 25–26.

7. *The Correspondence of Thomas Percy & William Shenstone*, ed. Cleanth Brooks, in *The Percy Letters* (1977), VII: 6; *Hawkins's Life*, pp. 151–2.

8. The bibliographical morass Johnson got himself into by working and printing too fast off the starting blocks is outlined by Arthur Sherbo in *Johnson on Shakespeare*, VII: xvi–xxvi.

9. *Rambler*, IV: 200; Preface, *Johnson on Shakespeare*, VII: 59; *Yale Works: Adventurer and Idler*, II: 412–14. See Alvin Kernan, *Printing Technology, Letters, and Samuel Johnson*, pp. 243–5, 249.

10. *Johnson on Shakespeare*, VII: 100, 94.

11. *Letters*, I: 162.

12. *Diaries*, pp. 64–5.

13. *Letters*, I: 177, 174, 176.

14. James Prior, *Life of Edmond Malone* (1860), pp. 160–61.

15. *Letters*, I: 179, 180; *Diaries*, p. 67; *Idler* no. 41, *Yale Works: Adventurer and Idler*, II: 129, 131.

16. *Letters*, I: 182, 184.

17. *Waingrow*, p. 90; James Clifford, *Dictionary Johnson*, p. 201; *Letters*, I: 173. See Larsen, *Dr Johnson's Household*, pp. 38–9.
18. *Shaw's Memoirs*, p. 39.
19. *Yale Works: Rasselas and Other Tales*, XVI: 16, 18, 19.
20. *Yale Works: Rasselas and Other Tales*, XVI: 7; *Life*, I: 341–4.
21. *Yale Works: Rasselas and Other Tales*, XVI: 87, 74.
22. *Yale Works: Rasselas and Other Tales*, XVI: 66, 142.
23. *Yale Works: Rasselas and Other Tales*, XVI: 146–53, 162.
24. *Posthumous Works of Mrs Chapone* (1807), I: 108–10 (28 April 1759), I: 111–13 (15 July 1759), 118 (n.d.).
25. *Diaries*, p. 69; *Life*, I: 348; *Letters*, I: 186, 187.
26. Curley, *Samuel Johnson and the Age of Travel*, pp. 61–2; *Daily Advertiser*, 1, 8, and 15 December 1759; *Letters*, III: 46; *Hawkins's Life*, pp. 157–8; *Life*, I: 352. See Morris Brownell, *Samuel Johnson's Attitude to the Arts*, pp. 107–26 and (on Gwynn) 126–36.
27. Johnson wrote the two introductory essays to the journal that appeared in the first number on 8 April.
28. *Yale Works: Adventurer and Idler*, II: xv–xix; *Hawkins's Life*, p.152; *Life*, I: 331.
29. *Life*, I: 330–31, 345 n.1; *Yale Works: Adventurer and Idler*, II: xx–xxiii.
30. *Yale Works: Adventurer and Idler*, II: 262–3, 312, 313–14. See Robert Folkenflik, *Samuel Johnson: Biographer* (1978), p. 27.
31. *Piozzi Anecdotes*, p. 76; *Yale Works: Adventurer and Idler*, II: 96, 97, 98.
32. *Yale Works: Adventurer and Idler*, II: 315, 316.

CHAPTER 22: 'Vain and Corrupt Imaginations'

1. *JM*, I: 409; *Diaries*, p. 264 (Easter Day 1777); *Yale Works: Rasselas and Other Tales*, p. 152; Jackson, *Melancholia and Depression*, pp. 142–6.
2. *JM*, II: 400–1; *Hawkins's Life*, p. 178; John Nichols, *Literary Illustrations* (1817–1831), VI: 147–8; *Hawkins's Life*, p. 161.
3. John Nichols, *Literary Illustrations*, VI: 148.
4. *Life*, IV: 97–8, 197, 97; *Johnson's Prefaces and Dissertations*, ed. Allen T. Hazen, p. 193.
5. *Letters*, I: 198; Hazen, *Johnson's Prefaces and Dedications*, p. 42. See Ian McIntyre, *Joshua Reynolds* (2003), pp. 129–30.
6. *JM*, II: 401–2.
7. The 'Address' is cited by Morris Brownell, *Samuel Johnson's Attitude to the Arts*, p. 50; *Piozzi's Anecdotes*, p. 93; *Life*, II: 439. Robert DeMaria pointed out that in the *Dictionary* Johnson only sketchily covered the fine arts, the nomenclature of which he either omitted or poorly defined (*Johnson's Dictionary and the Language of Learning*, pp. 217–18).
8. *Yale Works: Adventurer and Idler*, II: 140.
9. Brownell, *Samuel Johnson's Attitude to the Arts*, pp. 46–55; Ronald Paulson, *Hogarth: His Life, Art and Times* (2 vols, 1971), II: 313–14; Hazen, *Johnson's Prefaces and Dedications*, pp. 204–5. See J.L. Abbott and D.G.C. Allen (eds.), *The Virtuoso Tribe of Arts and Sciences* (1992).
10. *Letters*, I: 206.
11. *Letters*, I: 207; *Life*, I: 374–5; *Letters*, I: 212.
12. *Life*, I: 429; *Letters*, I: 206.
13. Reynolds's engagement book is in the Royal Academy. See James Clifford, 'Johnson's

Trip to Devon in 1762', *Eighteenth-Century Studies in Honor of D.F. Hyde* (1970), pp. 3–28.

14. *JM*, II: 275; *Life*, I: 145, 379.

15. *Life*, I: 377–79; *JM*, II: 278, 396; *Life*, II: 299, V: 329; *Life*, I: 477 n.1.

16. *Letters*, I: 216.

17. 'An Epistle from R.C. to Doctor Samuel Johnson on the Choice of Life, written about the Year 1766', ed. Herman W. Liebert, printed for the Annual Dinner of the Johnsonians, 19 September 1969; *Life*, III: 309–10. See Thomas M. Curley, 'Johnson, Chambers, and the Law', *Johnson After Two Hundred Years*, ed. Paul Korshin (1986), pp. 187–209; and Pat Rogers's convenient summary, *JE*, pp. 225–8.

18. *Life*, II: 405–6.

19. *Life*, III: 161, IV: 280; *Thraliana*, I: 106; *Life*, I: 249. See *Correspondence of James Boswell with Certain Members of the Club*, ed. C.N. Fifer (1976), pp. lii–lxxv.

CHAPTER 23: Boswell and Mrs Thrale

1. *Life*, III: 26.

2. *Letters*, I: 214, 225–7, 234, 228–9. See James G. Basker, 'Dancing Dogs, Women Preachers and the Myth of Johnson's Misogyny', *The Age of Johnson*, III (1990), pp. 63–90.

3. *Life*, I: 445. There are several modern biographies of Boswell: F.A Pottle, *James Boswell: The Earlier Years 1740–1769* (1966), Frank Brady, *James Boswell: The Later Years 1769–1795* (1984) and Peter Martin, *A Life of James Boswell* (1999).

4. *Life*, I: 383–4; *Boswell's Journals: London Journal*, p. 260; *Life*, I: 392.

5. *Life*, I: 392–5.

6. *Boswell's Journals: London Journal*, pp. 261–8, 279.

7. *Boswell's Journals: London Journal*, pp. 282–5; *Life*, I: 468.

8. Boswell said he had this story from Johnson's 'exact narration', but there is no record of it in his journals or *Life* papers (*Waingrow Life*, I: 287 n.7).

9. *Life*, I: 408, 417; *Boswell's Journals: London Journal*, p. 105; *Lives of the Poets*, II: 49; *Portraits by Sir Joshua Reynolds* (The Yale editions of the Private Papers of James Boswell, 1952), p. 41; *Life*, I: 416.

10. *Life*, I: 417, 421, 422, 425, 427, 433, 435–6, 445, 450.

11. *Life*, I: 457–62.

12. *Life*, I: 462, 465, 471, 472.

13. *Life*, I: 483; *Portraits by Sir Joshua Reynolds*, p. 68.

14. *BP*, 25, f. 606 (C1690); *Life*, I: 477–81. After Johnson's death the Club became better known as The Literary Club.

15. *Life*, IV: 275, II: 16–17.

16. *Life*, I: 479–81; Percy to Boswell, 29 Feb. 1788, *BP*, box 29, f. 733 (C2234) (*Waingrow*, p. 269); *Boswell's Journals: Ominous*, p. 200.

17. Donald Greene thought the 'M' could refer to masturbation, but this has not generally been accepted: see Greene, '"A Secret Far Dearer to Him than His Life": Johnson's "Vile Melancholy" Reconsidered', *The Age of Johnson*, 4 (1991), pp. 8–11; and Barry Baldwin, 'The Mysterious Letter "M" in Johnson's Diaries', *The Age of Johnson*, 6 (1994), pp. 131–45.

18. *Diaries*, pp. 84, 92, 89.

19. Robert Anderson, *The Life of Samuel Johnson, LL.D.* (1815), 3rd edn, p. 300n.; *Letters*,

I: 247. See Bertram H. Davis, *Thomas Percy: A Scholar-Cleric in the Age of Johnson* (1989), pp. 120–25.

20. *Thraliana*, I: 158–9; *Life*, II: 127; *Piozzi Anecdotes*, pp. 101–2. For biographies of Mrs Thrale, see James L. Clifford, *Hester Lynch Piozzi (Mrs Thrale)* (rev. edn 1987); and W. McCarthy, *Hester Thrale Piozzi: Portrait of a Literary Woman* (1985).

21. 24 June 1775, JRL, Eng. Mss. 538, letter 12.

22. *Letters*, I: 250; *Piozzi Anecdotes*, pp. 98, 147; *Diaries*, p. 127.

23. *Piozzi Anecdotes*, pp. 131–2. On Johnson's electioneering, see David Fleeman, 'Dr Johnson and Henry Thrale, M.P.', in *Johnson, Boswell, and Their Circle*, p. 175.

24. *Life*, I: 487, 517.

25. *Diaries*, p. 103; *Portraits by Sir Joshua Reynolds*, p. 70. See Brownell, *Samuel Johnson's Attitude to the Arts*, pp. 87–8, and K.K. Yung, *Samuel Johnson*, p. 103. This is the so-called Type II Reynolds portrait. It was first displayed to the public in 1770.

CHAPTER 24: Shakespeare and the Living World

1. *Letters*, I: 255–6.

2. *Yale Works: Johnson on Shakespeare*, VII: 67; Harold Bloom, *Shakespeare: The Invention of the Human* (1998), pp. 1–2.

3. *Yale Works: Johnson on Shakespeare*, VIII (Appendix): 1049; *Yale Works: Rambler*, IV: 131–3; *Proposals* in *Yale Works: Johnson on Shakespeare*, VII: 57. I am indebted to Robert Folkenflik's paper, 'Samuel Johnson and the Authority of Shakespeare', delivered in June 2007 at the Pembroke College, Oxford, conference on Johnson and the theatre.

4. *Yale Works: Rambler*, IV: 133–4.

5. Ritson, *Remarks, Critical and Illustrative, on the Text and Notes of the Last Edition of Shakespeare* (1783). See Edward Tomarken, *A History of the Commentary on Selected Writings of Samuel Johnson* (1994), pp. 92–103.

6. *Yale Works: Johnson on Shakespeare*, VII: 71–4; Smith, *Eighteenth-Century Essays on Shakespeare* (1903), p. xxxi; Raleigh, 'Johnson on Shakespeare', *Six Essays on Johnson* (1910), pp. xviii, 84; Smith, *Shakespeare in the Eighteenth Century*, p. 68. See Steven Lynn, 'Johnson's Critical Reception', *CCSJ*, p. 245.

7. *Yale Works: Johnson on Shakespeare*, VII: 61–3, 65.

8. *Yale Works: Johnson on Shakespeare*, VII: 78–9, 80–81.

9. *Yale Works: Johnson on Shakespeare*, VII: 92–111, 523.

10. *Yale Works: Johnson on Shakespeare*, VII: 264, 404; VIII: 704, 1045, 795. Philip Small-wood writes of Johnson's sometimes dread of Shakespeare's force, in 'Shakespeare: Johnson's Poet of Nature', *CCSJ*, pp. 143–60.

11. The Cibber comment was recorded by Daniel Astle, a clergyman who met Johnson in a tavern in 1765 and was struck by his argumentative, satiric turn of mind (BP, Box 9, f. 258, C43); *Life*, II: 14; *JM*, II: 318.

12. *Life*, IV: 242–42; *Johnson on Shakespeare*, VII: xxxv-xxxvi. See James Gray, "'I'll come no more behind your scenes, David": A Fresh Look at Dr Johnson as Theatre-goer', *English Studies in Canada*, II (1976), pp. 27–60.

13. *Letters*, I: 261–2.

14. *Life*, II: 5–7; Macaulay, *Essays*, I: 390; *Life*, II: 7–8; *Letters*, I: 273.

15. *Boswell's Journals: GT* (ii), pp. 302–3, 312–13; *Life*, II: 66, 14–15.

16. Clifford, *Piozzi*, pp. 61–3; *Yale Works: Rasselas and Other Tales*, XVI: 215–29, 248; Allen Hazen, *Johnson's Prefaces and Dedications*, pp. 213–16; Pennington (ed.), *Letters between*

Mrs Elizabeth Carter and Miss Catherine Talbot, III: 136.

17. *Diaries*, pp. 106–7.

18. *Piozzi Anecdotes*, p. 102.

19. *Piozzi Anecdotes*, p. 106; Clifford, *Piozzi*, pp. 66ff.

20. Edmond Malone, who has been called the midwife to Boswell's *Life*, a great champion of Johnson and determined to see Boswell's biography accepted as the only truly authoritative one, made most of these accusations. Peter S. Baker et al. (eds), *The Correspondence of James Boswell with David Garrick, Edmund Burke and Edmond Malone* (1986), in the *Yale Editions of the Private Papers of James Boswell: Correspondence*, IV: 314–17. See Peter Martin, *Edmond Malone* (1995), pp. 145–7.

21. *Piozzi Anecdotes*, pp. 155, 101, 156.

22. *Piozzi Anecdotes*, pp. 156, 155, 158, 154–5, 156, 158.

23. *Thraliana*, I: 384–5, 386, 415.

24. *Thraliana*, I: 415 and n. 4.

25. *Letters*, I: 39 (cited in translation from Wiltshire, *Samuel Johnson in the Medical World*, pp. 44–5). Balderston elaborated on this idea in a psychological and sexual direction in her controversial essay, 'Johnson's Vile Melancholy', in *The Age of Johnson*, ed. F.W. Hilles and W.S. Lewis (1949), pp. 3–14. Her theory was attacked by James Gray, '*Arras! Hellas!*, A Fresh Look at Samuel Johnson's French', in *Johnson After Two Hundred Years*, ed. Paul Korshin (1986).

26. Wiltshire, *Samuel Johnson in the Medical World*, pp. 47–9; *Thraliana*, II: 785; JRL, Eng. Let. 539, letter 30.

27. *Thraliana*, II. 625.

28. *Letters*, I: 276–8. For the text of these Vinerian lectures and the help Johnson gave Chambers with them, see Thomas Curley (ed.), *A Course of Lectures on the English Law* (1986).

29. Curley, 'Johnson, Chambers and the Law', *Johnson After Two Hundred Years* (ed. Korshin), p. 195.

30. *Letters*, I: 274–5; *Life*, II: 34–42; *Letters*, II: 307–14.

31. Alvin Kernan has discussed this interview as such a confrontation in *Printing Technology, Letters and Samuel Johnson*, pp. 24–47.

32. *Life*, II: 42.

CHAPTER 25: Coliseum of Beasts

1. *Diaries*, p. 115.

2. *Diaries*, pp. 127–8; Wiltshire, *Samuel Johnson in the Medical World*, pp. 40–43; *Letters*, IV: 125, I: 302, 305; *Diaries*, p. 119.

3. *Letters*, I: 282–3, 284, 287, 286, 289; *Diaries*, pp. 116–17; *Letters*, I: 291.

4. Hazen, *Prefaces and Dedications*, p. 152; *Thraliana*, I: 190–91.

5. *Letters*, I: 294, 296; Franklin, *Writings*, V: 122 (16 April 1768); *Boswell's Journals: Wife*, p. 156; *Letters*, I: 296. On the Wilkes affair, see *Yale Works: Political Writings*, pp. 314–15.

6. *Boswell's Journals: Wife*, pp. 155–6; *Letters*, I: 298.

7. *Boswell's Journals: Wife*, pp. 156–8.

8. *Boswell's Journals: Wife*, pp. 164, 166–7.

9. *Life*, II: 60–61.

10. *Letters*, I: 307–14.

11. *Life*, I: 396, III: 172, 173, II: 62–6.

12. Walpole, *Letters*, IX: 313.

13. *Hawkins's Life*, pp. 138–9; *Letters*, I: 315, 350, 353.

14. *Letters*, I: 325, 326.

15. *Diaries*, p. 123; *Life*, II: 106–7.

16. *Letters*, I: 301, 317, 327 and n.3.

17. *Life*, II: 69; *Letters*, I: 329.

18. *Boswell's Journals: Wife*, pp. 333–4, 336; *Life*, II: 71; *Boswell's Journals: Wife*, p. 26.

19. *Boswell's Journals: Wife*, p. 347. In his recasting of this scene for the second edition of the *Life*, Boswell has Mrs Williams only touch the surface of the tea, not sink her finger into it (*Life*, II: 99; *Waingrow Life*, II: 51 n.7).

20. *Boswell's Journal: Defence*, p. 131; *Diaries*, pp. 128–9.

21. *Diaries*, p. 143.

CHAPTER 26: Back to Shakespeare and the *Dictionary*

1. *Piozzi Anecdotes*, p. 73; *Fleeman Bibliography*, II: 1172–4. The pamphlet was reprinted in Johnson's *Political Tracts* in 1776, slightly revised.

2. *Life*, I: 394; *Yale Works: Political Writing*, pp. 319, 343. The Wilkes controversy behind *The False Alarm* is discussed by Donald Greene in *Political Writings*, pp. 313–17 and *Greene Politics*, pp. 205–11. The 'Junius' letters were published in the *Public Advertiser* between January 1769 and January 1772.

3. *Life*, I: 394; *Yale Works: Political Writings*, pp. 318, 319, 327.

4. *Life*, II: 112; *Yale Works: Political Writings*, pp. 330, 335, 341, 342, 344.

5. *Life*, III: 281–2; *JM*, II: 320; *Letters*, I: 254.

6. *Letters*, I: 343, 344, 349; JRL, Eng. Let. 539, letter 6; *Life*, II: 77.

7. *Boswell Journals: Defence*. p. 43; *Yale Works: Political Writings*, pp. 361, 363, 379.

8. *Life*, II: 134; *Yale Works: Political Writings*, pp. 370, 376–7; *Life*, II: 134.

9. *Life*, II: 137–9 and n.1.

10. *The Correspondence of James Boswell with David Garrick, Edmund Burke and Edmond Malone*, IV: 42; *Life*, II: 139–40; *Letters*, I: 362–3.

11. *Letters*, I: 364 *passim*.

12. *Piozzi Anecdotes*, p. 78.

13. *Life*, I: 438; *Life*, II: 259; *Letters*, II: 130–31. On copyright, see Alvin Kernan, *Printing Technology, Letters and Samuel Johnson*, pp. 97–102.

14. *Diaries*, p. 154.

15. *Life*, II: 239. See Reddick, *The Making of Johnson's Dictionary*, chapters 6 and 7, especially pp. 122–30.

16. *Life*, II: 254; Robert DeMaria, *Johnson's Dictionary and the Language of Learning* (1986), p. 244. See Reddick, *The Making of Johnson's Dictionary*, chapter 7.

17. *Life*, II: 458, I: 464.

18. *Letters*, II: 30.

19. *Boswell Journals: Defence*, pp. 41, 54.

20. *Boswell Journals: Defence*, pp. 86–7.

21. *Piozzi Anecdotes*, p. 139.

22. *Thraliana*, II: 805; Hyde, *The Thrales of Streatham Park*, pp. 54–5.

23. *Chapman Letters*, I: 283; *Letters*, I: 396, 399, 398.

CHAPTER 27: The Road to the Hebrides

1. *Letters*, I: 401, 404, 406, 404, 409.
2. *Letters*, II: 10; JRL, Eng. Let. 539, letter 19.
3. *Letters*, II: 26; *Boswell's Journals: Defence*, p. 160; *Life*, II: 233; *Boswell's Journals: Defence*, p. 191; *Piozzi Anecdotes*, p. 70.
4. *Boswell's Journals: Defence*, pp. 180, 183; *Life*, II: 215–16; *Diaries*, p. 156.
5. *Life*, II: 240 and n.1.
6. *Life*, II: 260; *Boswell's Journals: Defence*, pp. 45–6.
7. *Letters*, II: 40; JRL, Eng. Let. 539, letter 30.
8. JRL, Eng. Let. 539, letter 30; *Members*, p. 33.
9. *Letters*, II: 46–51.
10. *Hebrides*, pp. 3–4; *Letters*, II: 115.
11. *Hebrides*, p. 4.
12. *Life*, II: 269 n.1; *Hebrides*, p. 8; *Letters*, II: 51.
13. *Letters*, II: 55–6.
14. *Hebrides*, p. 81; Peter Levi (ed.), *Samuel Johnson and James Boswell* (1984), p. 12; *Letters*, II: 62; *Hebrides*, pp. 71–72.
15. *Yale Works: Journey*, pp. 18–19; *Hebrides*, p. 84.
16. *Yale Works: Journey*, pp. 21–24, 30–31.
17. *Yale Works: Journey*, p. 25; *Hebrides*, p. 100.
18. *Hebrides*, p. 58, 109–10, 112; *Journey*, p. 38.
19. *Letters*, II: 76–7; *Hebrides*, p. 112.
20. *Hebrides*, p. 304; *Letters*, II: 77–9; *Hebrides*, p. 117; *Letters*, II: 88.
21. *Hebrides*, pp. 127–8, 133, 152.
22. *Letters*, II: 90; *Hebrides*, p. 160.
23. *Hebrides*, p. 165; *Letters*, II: 92.
24. *Letters*, II: 93; *Hebrides*, pp. 212–13.
25. *Hebrides*, pp. 244, 247–51; *Yale Works: Journey*, p. 99.
26. *Hebrides*, pp. 271–2, 265; *Letters*, II: 98.
27. *Hebrides*, pp. 302–3.
28. *Yale Works: Journey*, p. 122; *Hebrides*, p. 328; *Letters*, II: 107.
29. *Yale Works: Journey*, p. 132; *Hebrides*, pp. 375–6, 386.
30. *Letters*, II: 120, 128; JRL, Eng. Mss. 538, letter 9; *Letters*, II: 114.

CHAPTER 28: Politics and Travel

1. *Letters*, II: 133.
2. *Letters*, II: 151.
3. *Letters*, II: 166; *Life*, II: 290 n.2; *Boswell's Journals: Ominous*, p. 98; *Letters*, II: 145. See Mary Lascelles, 'Notions and Facts: Johnson and Boswell on Their Travels', *Johnson, Boswell and Their Circle*, pp. 215–29.
4. *Letters*, II: 168–9, 174, 180; *Life*, II: 298, 306. See Fleeman's edition, pp. xxviii-xxxviii, for an account of the book's reception.
5. *JE*, pp. 214–15.
6. *Letters*, II: 136; *Life*, III: 20. See Thomas M. Curley, 'Samuel Johnson and India', *Re-Viewing Samuel Johnson*, ed. N. Jain (1991).
7. *Letters*, II: 147; *Correspondence of James Boswell with Garrick, Burke and Malone*, IV:

60. See *Life*, III: 81–5.

8. *Letters*, II: 149, 151; A.M. Broadley, *Dr Johnson and Mrs Thrale* (1910), pp. 160–75; *Diaries*, pp. 168, 170, 175.

9. *Life*, V: 441 n.4; *Life*, II: 285; *Diaries*, pp. 186–7.

10. *Diaries*, p. 211; Broadley, p. 206; *Letters*, III: 68; Broadley, p. 209; *Diaries*, pp. 217–18; Broadley, pp. 213–14.

11. *Diaries*, p. 220; *Boswell's Journals: Ominous*, p. 284.

12. Broadley, pp. 217, 219.

13. *Letters*, II: 149, 151 and III: 65–6; *Life*, III: 134. See Curley, *Samuel Johnson and the Age of Travel*, pp. 79–112.

14. *Thraliana*, I: 525 n.2.

15. *Life*, II: 450, IV: 19–20; *Boswelliana*, p. 299; *Life*, II: 138–9; *Murphy's Essay*, p. 421; *Life*, V: 575. On Johnson's friendship with Burke, see Elizabeth R. Lambert, 'Johnson on Friendship: The Example of Burke', *Johnson After Two Hundred Years* (ed. Korshin), pp. 111–23.

16. *Life*, II: 223, 348; 'Johnson on Friendship', p. 120. See *Greene Politics*, pp. 252–3.

17. JRL, Eng. Mss., vol. 539, Letter 33; *Life*, II: 288 n.2; *Letters*, II: 155.

18. *Greene Politics*, pp. 211–12 and *Yale Works: Political Writings*, pp. 387–9, 390–91.

19. *Letters*, II: 151.

20. *Letters*, II: 170, 173; *Yale Works: Political Writings*, pp. 401–2.

21. *Yale Works: Political Writings*, pp. 423, 425, 429, 442, 454.

22. Campbell, 'Anecdotes', *JM*, II: 53, 55, 56; *Life*, III: 290.

23. *Letters*, II: 198; *Life*, II: 335; Campbell, 'Anecdotes', *JM*, II: 51; *Letters*, II: 193–4; *Boswell's Journals: Ominous*, p. 144.

24. *Life*, II: 316.

25. *Boswell's Journals: Ominous*, p. 152.

26. *Boswell's Journals: Ominous*, pp. 87, 100; Campbell, 'Anecdotes', *JM*, II: 41, 48; *Boswell's Journals: Ominous*, pp. 126, 105.

27. *Boswell's Journals: Ominous*, p. 150.

28. *Life*, II: 359; *Diaries*, pp. 224–6; *Boswell's Journals: Ominous*, p. 145; *Life*, II: 375–6, 378; *Boswell's Journals: Ominous*, p. 274.

29. *Letters*, II: 205, 211, 217, 230, 235; JRL, Eng. Mss. 538, letter 13; *Letters*, II: 243.

30. *Letters*, II: 260.

31. *Letters*, II: 271; Moses Tyson and Henry Guppy (eds), *The French Journals of Mrs Thrale and Doctor Johnson* (1932), p. 143.

32. *Letters*, II: 274, 273, 276, 277, 274; *Diaries*, p. 249; *Letters*, II: 273.

33. *Letters*, II: 271; *French Journals*, pp. 163–4, 88–9, 143, 141, 142; *Diaries*, pp. 229, 231, 238, 239 and note; *Boswell's Journals: Extremes*, p. 254; *Life*, II: 402. See Curley, *Samuel Johnson and the Age of Travel*, pp. 108–12.

34. *Diaries*, pp. 233, 253; *Letters*, II: 338; *Life*, II: 435.

35. *Life*, III: 352.

CHAPTER 29: 'A Very Poor Creeper Upon the Earth'

1. *Life*, III: 19; Baretti cited in E.S. De Beer, 'Johnson's Italian Tour', *Johnson, Boswell and Their Circle*, pp. 159–62; *Boswell's Journals: Ominous*, p. 317; *The Correspondence of James Boswell and William Johnson Temple*, ed. Thomas Crawford (1997), I: 412.

2. *Letters*, II: 299.

3. *Letters*, II: 301; *Diaries*, p. 257.

4. W. Roberts, *Memoirs of Hannah More* (1834), I: 64; *JM*, II: 179; *Life*, IV: 341; *JM*, II: 180; *Life*, III: 293.

5. *JM*, II: 182–5, 187.

6. *Letters*, III: 196, 205; *JM*, II: 404, 286; *Dr Johnson and Fanny Burney*, ed. Tinker, p. 4; *Hawkins's Life*, p. 133. See Roger Lonsdale, *Dr Charles Burney* (1965), p. 252; and Brownell, *Samuel Johnson's Attitude to the Arts*, chapter 1.

7. *Boswell's Journals: Ominous*, pp. 255–6, 258; *Life*, II: 428.

8. *Boswell's Journals: Ominous*, pp. 295, 351.

9. *Letters*, II: 313; JRL, Eng. Mss. 538, letter 15; *Boswell's Journals: Ominous*, p. 329.

10. *Life*, III: 50–51; *Letters*, IV: 14.

11. *Life*, III: 185, 64–79.

12. *Life*, III: 77; *Letters*, II: 332; *Life*, III: 183, 330.

13. *Diaries*, p. 258; *Letters*, II: 339, 341, 347, 358, 360–61, 365.

14. *Letters*, III: 4, 11, 21, 9, 43; *Diaries*, p. 267.

15. Burney's *Early Journals and Letters*, III: 110.

16. *Letters*, III: 20.

17. *Life*, III: 110–11; John Nichols, *Literary Anecdotes*, VIII: 416–17 n.

18. See *JE*, pp. 121–3.

19. *Life*, III: 139–48; *Letters*, III: 25.

20. *Letters*, III: 27–8, 32–33; *Hawkins's Life*, p. 231; *Letters*, III: 33–4.

21. *Life*, III: 167; *Hawkins's Life*, pp. 167, 295. See *Yale Works: Sermons*, pp. xxi–xxix. The sermons for Taylor were first published in two volumes in 1788–9 by Revd Samuel Hayes. They were identified as 'left for publication by John Taylor, LL.D', but immediately many people were convinced that Johnson had written all of them.

22. *Life*, V: 67; *Letters*, III: 311–12; *Diaries*, pp. 276, 277, 279, 292, 300. See Wiltshire, *Samuel Johnson in the Medical World*, pp. 37–40.

23. *Monthly Review*, LXXIX (Dec. 1788), p. 529; *Yale Works: Sermons*, p. xxxi–xxxii.

24. Burney's *Early Journal and Letters*, III: 148, 146–7.

25. *Letters*, III: 140.

CHAPTER 30: Biographical Straitjacket

1. *Letters*, III: 41, 45, 51, 55; *Diaries*, p. 292; *Letters*, III: 81; *Boswell's Journals: Extremes*, p. 184; *Letters*, III: 61, 67–8, 81; JRL, Eng. Mss. 538, letter 16, Eng. Mss. 540, letter 71.

2. *Boswell's Journals: Extremes*, pp. 155, 162; *Letters*, III: 68, 83.

3. *Life*, III: 200–4.

4. *Life*, III: 206, 208.

5. *Life*, III: 189; *Letters*, III: 83; *Diaries*, pp. 291–2; Lonsdale, *Dr Charles Burney*, p. 242; *Letters*, III: 100. See *Lives of the Poets*, I: 1–103.

6. *Letters*, III: 122, 124; Nichols, *Literary Anecdotes*, II: 550 n; *GM*, 1785, p. 9.

7. *Lives of the Poets*, I: 28–9; *Burney Early Journals and Letters*, III: 105, 150, 153–4.

8. *Life*, III: 271–8; *Letters*, III: 113–14; *Burney's Early Journals and Letters*, III: 32.

9. *Life*, II: 457, III: 287; *Boswell's Journals: Extremes*, pp. 284–5, 290; *Life*, II: 416–23, III: 294.

10. *Fifer*, p. 316.

11. *Letters*, III: 110, 127.

12. *Letters*, III: 108–9.

13. *Piozzi Anecdotes*, p. 142; *Works of Samuel Johnson*, ed. Hawkins (1787), XI: 204; *Letters*, III: 134. See H.W. Liebert, 'Portraits of the Author: Lifetime Likenesses of Samuel Johnson', *English Portraits of the Seventeenth and Eighteenth Centuries* (1974), pp. 45–88; and *Life*, IV: 447–64.

14. *Lives of the Poets*, I: 30–31 (letter cited courtesy of the Hyde Collection, Harvard); *Waingrow*, p. 13; *Letters*, III: 151, 156.

15. *Reports of Historical Manuscripts Commission*, XII, 10: 344–5; *Life*, IV: 40, 206; *Boswell's Journals: Laird*, p. 80; Malone, *Prose Works of John Dryden* (1800), I: 430–37.

16. *Letters*, III: 152; *Lives of the Poets*, II: 179; *Boswell's Journals: Auchinleck*, pp. 83, 92; *Life*, IV: 99.

17. *Diaries*, p. 293–5; *Boswell's Journals: Laird*, p. 58.

18. *Burney's Early Journals and Letters*, III: 255–6, 436; *Dr Johnson and Fanny Burney*, ed. Chauncey Brewster Tinker (1911), pp. 151–2; *Letters*, III: 284.

19. *Letters*, III: 193, 202, 180–81, 197.

20. *Life*, III: 344–5, 392.

21. *Thraliana*, I: 424; *Letters*, III: 228, 233.

22. *Letters*, III: 237, 238, 248, 254, 264, 250, 273, 278, 303, 285.

23. *Lives of the Poets*, I: 47–52 (on Johnson's 'assistants' see pp. 52–80).

24. *Life*, IV: 13; *Boswell's Journals: Laird*, p. 295.

25. *Lives of the Poets*, I: 189.

26. *Lives of the Poets*, I: 189. See Clingham, 'Life and Literature', p. 164.

27. *Burney's Early Journals and Letters*, III: 151–2; *Life*, IV: 73; *Lives of the Poets*, II: 53–4.

28. John Wain, *Johnson on Johnson* (1976), p. xv; *Lives of the Poets*, I: 266–7.

29. *Lives of the Poets*, IV: 16, III: 21, 23.

30. Hyde, *Thrales of Streatham Park*, p. 201; *Letters*, III: 128, 139–40, 176 and n.6; *Thraliana*, I: 401; *Letters*, III: 318.

31. *Letters*, III: 268–9.

32. *Diaries*, p. 304; Hyde, *Thrales of Streatham*, pp. 227–32; *Thraliana*, I: 482, 491.

CHAPTER 31: Losing Ground

1. *Letters*, III: 330, 332, 334; *Diaries*, p. 304–5.

2. *Boswell's Journals: Laird*, pp. 319–21; *JM*, II: 140; *Boswell's Journals: Laird*, p. 324.

3. *Letters*, III: 342; JRL, Eng. Mss. 583, letter 24.

4. *Letters*, IV: 23; *Diaries*, p. 310; *Letters*, III: 361–79, IV: 4.

5. *Thraliana*, I: 521; Wiltshire, *Samuel Johnson in the Medical World*, pp. 39–40; *Letters*, IV: 9; *Diaries*, p. 312.

6. *JE*, p. 231.

7. *Yale Works: Poems*, pp. 314–15.

8. *Letters*, IV: 14.

9. *Letters*, IV: 29, 124; *Boswell's Journals: Applause*, p. 82.

10. *Thraliana*, I: 535; *Letters*, IV: 55–6.

11. *Thraliana*, I: 525.

12. *Thraliana*, I: 540–41.

13. *Diaries*, p. 338, 339, 346.

14. *Letters*, IV: 101, 133; *Thraliana*, I: 557; *Diaries*, pp. 358–9.

15. *Letters*, IV: 139.

16. *Letters*, IV: 126; *Boswell's Journals: Applause*, pp. 74, 152, 154.

17. *Boswell's Journals: Ominous*, p. 149; *Letters*, IV: 151, 193 and n.1.

18. *Letters*, IV: 151–3, 164; *JM*, II: 311.

19. *Letters*, IV: 154ff, 272. See Wiltshire, *Samuel Johnson in the Medical World*, pp. 51–3.

20. *Letters*, IV: 160.

21. *Letters*, IV: 168, 173–4, 222, 192; *Life*, IV: 523.

22. *Letters*, IV: 195, 199; Wiltshire, *Samuel Johnson in the Medical World*, pp. 53–4.

23. *Horace Walpole's Correspondence*, ed. Lewis et al. (1937–83), XXV: 449; *Letters*, IV: 204, 235, 272–3, 279, 281.

24. *Letters*, IV: 246–7, 259, 316; *Hawkins's Life*, p. 256.

25. *Letters*, IV: 256–7; *Hawkins's Life*, p. 259; *Life*, IV: 254 n.5; *Letters*, IV: 264.

26. *Letters*, IV: 260, 266, 285, 388–9. See Wiltshire, *Samuel Johnson in the Medical World*, pp. 67–8.

27. *Letters*, IV: 275.

28. *Letters*, IV: 300, 286 9; *BP*: C579. See Wiltshire, *Samuel Johnson in the Medical World*, pp. 54–60; and W.W. Fee, 'Samuel Johnson's "Wonderful Remission" of Dropsy,' *Harvard Library Bulletin*, 23 (1975), pp. 271–88.

29. *Letters*, IV: 297; *Diaries*, p. 368.

30. *Letters*, IV: 319, 321, 325.

31. *Letters*, IV: 321–2; *Boswell's Journals: Applause*, p. 213.

32. *Boswell's Journals: Applause*, p. 216.

33. *Boswell's Journals: Applause*, pp. 231, 234–5, 238; *Life*, IV: 299.

34. *Letters*, IV: 334, 335–6; *Life*, IV: 326–7, 337.

35. *Boswell's Journals: Applause*, pp. 254–5.

36. *Letters*, IV: 400.

37. *Letters*, IV: 338 and n.1; JRL, Eng. let. 583, letter 32; *Letters*, IV: 343–4.

38. *Letters*, IV: 344; Hyde, *The Thrales of Streatham Park*, p. 242 n.14, 241; *Diary and Letters of Madame D'Arblay*, ed. Austin Dobson (1904), II: 271.

39. Letters, IV: 398 n. 5; Wiltshire, *Samuel Johnson in the Medical World*, p. 58. See *Diaries*, pp. 371–418.

40. *Letters*, IV: 353, 354, 368, 370, 422; *Diaries*, p. 403; *Letters*, IV: 436.

41. *Life*, IV: 376.

CHAPTER 32: The Last Days

1. The accounts of Johnson's final days are compared by Paul J. Korshin, 'Johnson's Last Days: Some Facts and Problems', *Johnson After Two Hundred Years*, pp. 55–76. For Johnson's will, see *Life*, IV: 405, n.2.

2. *Life*, IV: 416–18, 415. I an indebted to Graham Nicholl's '"The Race with Death": Samuel Johnson and Holy Dying', *The New Rambler* (2005–6), pp. 11–21.

3. *Life*, IV: 400; *JM*, II: 156.

4. *Life*, IV: 409.

5. *Life*, IV: 400; *Hawkins's Life*, pp. 272–73; *Life*, IV: 409; *JM*, II: 386; *Hawkins's Life*, p. 275; Wiltshire, *Samuel Johnson in the Medical World*, pp. 61–63.

6. *Hawkins's Life*, p. 275.

7. *JM*, II: 159.

8. *Life*, IV: 420–23.

9. *Life*, IV: 420–23; Johnstone, *Parr*, I: 533; *JM*, II: 378; *Boswell's Journals: Applause*, p. 271; *JM*, II: 378.

BIBLIOGRAPHY

Primary Sources

JOHNSON'S WORKS

The Yale Edition of the Works of Samuel Johnson, presently 15 vols, not consecutive (New Haven: Yale University Press, 1958 onwards):

Diaries, Prayers, and Annals, ed. E.L. McAdam, Jr, with Donald and Mary Hyde, vol. I (1958)

The Idler and The Adventurer (ed. W.J. Bate, John M. Bullitt and L.F. Powell), in *Works*, vol. II (1963)

The Rambler, ed. W.J. Bate and Albrecht B. Strauss, vols III–V (1969)

Poems, ed. E.L. McAdam, Jr, with George Milne, vol. VI (1964)

Johnson on Shakespeare, ed. Arthur Sherbo (with an introduction by Bertrand H. Bronson), vols VII and VIII (1968)

A Journey to the Western Islands of Scotland, ed. Mary Lascelles, vol. IX (1971)

Political Writings, ed. Donald Greene, vol. X. (1977)

Sermons, ed. Jean Hagstrum and James Gray, vol. XIV (1978)

Voyage to Abyssinia, ed. Joel J. Gold, vol. XV (1985)

Rasselas and Other Tales, ed. Gwin J. Kolb, vol. XVI (1990)

Johnson on the English Language, ed. Gwin J. Kolb and Robert DeMaria, Jr, vol. XVIII (1990)

A Commentary on Mr Pope's Principles of Morality, or Essay on Man (a Translation from the French), ed. O.M. Brack, vol. XVII (2005)

The Works of Samuel Johnson, LL.D. (with life), ed. John Hawkins, (15 vols, 1787–89)

The Dictionary of the English Language (1st edn 1755)

The Dictionary of the English Language (4th edn 1773)

Lynch, Jack (ed.), *Samuel Johnson's Dictionary* (2002)

Crystal, David (ed.), *Dr Johnson's Dictionary* (2005)

Hazen, A.T. (ed.), *Samuel Johnson's Prefaces and Dedications* (1937)

Fleeman, J.D. (ed.), *The Complete English Poems* (1971)

Fleeman, J.D., (ed.), *Journey to the Western Islands of Scotland* (1985)

Chapman, R.W. (ed.), *The Letters of Samuel Johnson* (3 vols, 1952)

Redford, Bruce (ed.), *The Letters of Samuel Johnson* (5 vols, 1992–94)

Biographies, Editions and Critical Works

This is a selective list of editions and writings that have most influenced this biography.

Abbott, J.L., *John Hawkesworth* (1982).

Adam, E.L., and L.F. Powell, *Dr Johnson and the English Law* (6 vols. 1934–50; vols. V and VI, 2d ed., 1964)

Adam, R. B., *Facsimile of Boswell's Notebook* (1919)

Baker, Peter et al. (eds), *The Correspondence of James Boswell with David Garrick, Edmund Burke, and Edmond Malone* (1986)

Balderston, K.C. (ed.), *Thraliana: The Diary of Mrs Hester Lynch Thrale* (2 vols, 1942)

Balderston, Katherine, 'Johnson's Vile Melancholy', in *The Age of Johnson*, ed. F.W. Hilles and W.S. Lewis (1949), pp. 3–14

Barbauld, Anna Laetitia (ed.) *Correspondence of Samuel Richardson* (6 vols, 1804).

Bate, Walter Jackson, *Samuel Johnson* (1977)

—— *The Achievement of, Samuel Johnson* (1955)

Bloch, Marc, *The Royal Touch: Sacred Monarchy and Scrofula in England and France* (1973)

Bloom, E.A. and L.D. Bloom (eds), *Piozzi Letters* (2 vols, 1989)

Bloom, E.A., *Samuel Johnson in Grub Street* (1957)

Bloom, Edward A. and Lillian D. Bloom (eds), *The Journals and Letters of Fanny Burney* (Madame D'Arblay) (12 vols, 1978)

Bloom, Harold, *Shakespeare: The Invention of the Human* (1998)

Bond, William H., *Eighteenth-Century Studies in Honor of Donald F. Hyde* (1970)

Boswell, James, *Journals: The Yale Editions of the Private Papers of James Boswell* (listed chronologically):

Boswell's London Journal 1762–1765, ed. Frederick A. Pottle (1951)

Boswell in Search of a Wife 1766–1769, ed. Frank Brady and Frederick A. Pottle (1956)

Boswell for the Defence 1769–1774, ed. William K. Wimsatt, Jr. and Frederick A. Pottle (1960)

Boswell's Journal of a Tour to the Hebrides with Samuel Johnson, LL.D., 1773, ed. Frederick A. Pottle and Charles H. Bennett (1961)

Boswell: The Ominous Years 1774–1776, ed. Charles Ryskamp and Frederick A. Pottle (1963)

Boswell in Extremes 1776–1778, ed. Charles McC. Weis and Frederick A. Pottle (1970)

Boswell: Laird of Auchinleck 1778–1782, ed. Joseph W. Reed and Frederick A. Pottle (1977; rpt Edinburgh, 1993)

Boswell: The Applause of the Jury 1782–1785, ed. Irma S. Lustig and Frederick A. Pottle (1981)

——*Notebook*, ed. R.B. Adam (1919)

Boswell Papers, Beinecke Rare Book and Manuscript Library, Yale University

Boswell's Life of Johnson, Together with Boswell's Journal of a Tour to the Hebrides and Johnson's Diary of a Journey into North Wales, ed. G.B. Hill, revd and enlarged by L.F. Powell (6 vols, 1934; rpt 1979)

Boulton, James T., *Johnson: The Critical Heritage* (1971)

Brack, O.M. and R.E. Kelley, *The Early Biographies of Samuel Johnson* (1974)

—— (eds), *The Shorter Prose Writings of Samuel Johnson* (1987)

Brady, Frank, *James Boswell: The Later Years 1769–1795* (1984)

Broadley, A.M., *Doctor Johnson and Mrs Thrale* (1910)

Bronson, Bertrand H., *Johnson Agonistes and Other Essays* (1965)

Brooke, John, 'The Library of King George III', *Yale University Library Gazette* 52 (1977)

Brooks, Cleanth (ed.), *Correspondence of Thomas Percy and William Shenstone.* (1977)

Brownell, Morris, *Samuel Johnson's Attitude to the Arts* (1989)

Burney, Fanny, *The Early Diary of Fanny Burney*, ed. A.R. Ellis. (1889)

Burney, Frances, *The Early Journals and Letters of Fanny Burney* (vol III: part I, 1778–1770', ed. Lars E. Troide and Stewart J. Cooke (1994)

—— *The Early Journals and Letters of Fanny Burney* (vol. IV: part II, 1780–81), ed. Betty Rizzo Rizzo (2003)

Chambers, Robert, *A Course of Lectures on the English Law*, ed. Thomas M. Curley, (1986)

Chapin, C.F., *The Religious Thought of Samuel Johnson* (1968)

Chapman, R.W. (ed.), *The Letters of Samuel Johnson* (3 vols, 1952)

Clark, J.C.D., *Samuel Johnson: Literature, Religion and English Cultural Politics from the Restoration to Romanticism* (1994)

Clifford, James L., (ed.), *Dr [Thomas] Campbell's Diary* (1947)

—— 'Johnson's Trip to Devon in 1762', in *Eighteenth-Century Studies in Honor of Donald F. Hyde* (1970)

—— *Dictionary Johnson* (1979)

—— *Hester Lynch Piozzi* (1941, 1952)

—— *Young Sam Johnson* (1955)

Clingham, Greg (ed.), *The Cambridge Companion to Samuel Johnson* (1997)

Cochrane, J.A., *Dr Johnson's Printer: The Life of William Strahan* (1964)

Copeland, T.W. et al. (eds.), *The Correspondence of Edmund Burke* (1958–70)

Crystal, David, (ed.), *Dr Johnson's Dictionary* (2005)

Curley, Thomas M., *Samuel Johnson and the Age of Travel* (1976)

—— *Sir Robert Chambers: Law, Literature and Empire in the Age of Johnson*

—— (ed.), *A Course of Lectures on the English Law* (1986)

D'Arblay, Madame Frances, *Diary and Letters of Madame d'Arblay* (edited by her niece, 1842)

Davies, Thomas, *Memoirs of the Life of David Garrick* (1808)

—— *Miscellaneous and Fugitive Pieces* (1773)

Davis, Bertram H., 'Johnson's Visit to Percy', in *Johnson After Two Hundred Years*, ed. P.J. Korshin (1986)

—— *The Life of Samuel Johnson, LL.D. by Sir John Hawkins* (1961)

—— *Thomas Percy: A Scholar-Cleric in the Age of Johnson* (1989)

DeMaria, Robert, Jr, *The Life of Samuel Johnson* (1993)

—— *Samuel Johnson and the Life of Reading* (1997)

—— *Johnson's Dictionary and the Language of Learning* (1986)

Dobson, Austin, *The Diary and Letters of Madame D'Arblay* (1904)

Eaves, T.C.D., 'Dr Johnson's Letters to Richardson', *PMLA*, 75 (1960)

Eaves, T.C.D. and B.D. Kimpel, *Samuel Richardson* (1971)

Fairer, David, 'Oxford and the Literary World' in *The History of the University of Oxford*, vol. 5 (*The Eighteenth Century*), ed. L.S. Sutherland and L.G. Mitchell (1986)

—— 'Authorship Problems in *The Adventurer*', *Review of English Studies*, 25 (1974)

Fifer, C.N. (ed.), *The Correspondence of James Boswell with Certain Members of The Club* (1976)

Fleeman, J.D., *A Bibliography of the Works of Samuel Johnson* (2000)

—— *A Preliminary Handlist of Documents and Manuscripts of Samuel Johnson* (1967)

—— 'Some Notes on Johnson's Prayers and Meditations,' *Review of English Studies*, n.s. 29 (May 1968), 172–9. [Corrections of Yale ed., vol. I]

—— (ed.), *Samuel Johnson: A Journey to the Western Islands of Scotland* (1985)

—— (ed.), *Early Biographical Writings of Samuel Johnson* (1973)

—— (ed.), *Samuel Johnson: The Complete English Poems* (1971)

Folkenflik, Robert, *Samuel Johnson: Biographer* (1978)

—— 'The Politics of Johnson's *Dictionary* Revisited', *Age of Johnson*, vol. 18 (2007), pp. 1–17

—— 'Johnson's Politics', in *The Cambridge Campanion to Samuel Johnson* (1977), pp. 102–13

Forbes, Margaret, *James Beattie and His Friends* (1904)

The Gentleman's Magazine (1731–1907)

Gray, James, 'Arras! Hellas!, A Fresh Look at Samuel Johnson's French', in *Johnson After Two Hundred Years*, ed. Paul Korshin (1986), pp. 85–6

Greene, Donald, *Samuel Johnson's Library* (1975)

—— 'Dr Johnson's "Late conversion": A Reconsideration', *Johnsonian Studies*, ed. Magdi Wahba (1962)

—— *The Politics of Samuel Johnson* (1960, 2nd edn 1990)

Grundy, Isobel, *Samuel Johnson and the Scale of Greatness* (1986)

Guppy, H. and M. Tyson (eds), *The French Journals of Mrs Thrale and Doctor Johnson* (1932)

Hagstrum, Jean, *Samuel Johnson's Literary Criticism* (rev. edn 1967)

Hanley, Brian, *Samuel Johnson as Book Reviewer* (2001)

Harwood, Thomas, *History and Antiquities of Lichfield* (1806)

Hawkins, Sir John, *The Life of Samuel Johnson, LL.D.* (2nd edn 1787)

Hazen, Allen T., *Samuel Johnson's Prefaces and Dedications* (1937)

Hemlow, Joyce, *The History of Fanny Burney* (1958)

Hill, G. Birkbeck (ed.), *Johnsonian Miscellanies* (2 vols, 1897)

—— and L.F. Powell (eds), *Boswell's Life of Johnson* (5 vols, 1934; reprinted 1979)

Hilles, Frederick W. (ed.), *New Light on Dr Johnson* (1959)

Hitchings, Henry, *Dr Johnson's Dictionary: The Extraordinary Story of the Book That Defined the World* (2005)

Holmes, Richard, *Dr Johnson and Mr Savage* (1993)

Hopkins, M.A., *Dr Johnson's Lichfield* (1952)

Hyde, Mary, *The Impossible Friendship: Boswell and Mrs Thrale* (1972)

—— *The Thrales of Streatham Park* (1977)

—— 'The Library Portraits at Streatham Park,' *The New Rambler*, (1979), pp. 10–24

Isles, Duncan, 'The Lennox Collection', *Harvard Library Bulletin* 19 (1971).

Jackson, John, *History of the City and Cathedral of Lichfield* (1805)

Jackson, Stanley W., *Melancholia and Depression: From Hippocratic Times to Modern Times* (1986)

Johnson, Boswell and Their Circle: 1965. *Essays Presented to L. F. Powell* (1965) by Mary M. Lascelles, James L. Clifford, J. D. Fleeman and John P. Hardy

Jonard, Norbert, *Giuseppe Baretti* (1963)

Kaminski, Thomas, *The Early Career of Samuel Johnson* (1987)

Kernan, Alvin, *Samuel Johnson and the Impact of Print* (1989)

Knight, Ellis Cordelia, *The Autobiography of Miss Knight*, ed. Roger Fulford (1960)

Kolb, G.J., 'Johnson's "Little Pompadour": A Textual Crux and a Hypothesis', in *Restoration and Eighteenth-Century Literature*, ed. Carroll Camden (1963)

Korshin, Paul J., 'Johnson and the Earl of Orrery', *Eighteenth-Century Studies in Honor of Donald F. Hyde* (1970).

—— (ed.), *Johnson After Two Hundred Years* (1986)

Larsen, Lyle, *Dr Johnson's Household* (1985)

Leslie, C.R. and Tom Taylor, *Life and Times of Sir Joshua Reynolds* (1865)

Lewis, W.S., *The Yale Edition of Horace Walpole's Correspondence*, ed. W.S. Lewis et al. (1937–83)

Liebert, H.W., 'Portraits of the Author: Lifetime Likenesses of Samuel Johnson', in *English Portraits of the Seventeenth and Eighteenth Centuries* (1974)

Lillywhite, Bryant, *London Coffee Houses* (1963)

Lipking, Lawrence, *Samuel Johnson: The Life of an Author* (1998)

Little, D.M. and G.M. Kahrl (eds), *The Letters of David Garrick* (3 vols, 1963)

Lonsdale, Roger (ed.), *Samuel Johnson: The Lives of the Poets* (4 vols, 2006)

—— *Dr Charles Burney* (1965)

Lustig, Irma S., 'The Myth of Johnson's Misogyny in the *Life of Johnson:* Another View,' in *Boswell in Scotland and Beyond*, ed. Thomas Crawford (1997), pp. 71–88

—— '"My Dear Enemy": Margaret Montgomerie Boswell in the *Life of Johnson*,' in *Boswell: Citizen of the World, Man of Letters*, ed. Irma S. Lustig (1995)

Lynch, Jack and Anne McDermott (eds), *Anniversary Essays on Johnson's Dictionary* (2005)

Lynch, Jack (ed.), *Samuel Johnson's Dictionary* (2002)

Lynn, Steven, 'Locke's Eye, Adam's Tongue and Johnson's Word: Language, Marriage and the Choice of Life', *Age of Johnson*, 3 (1990), 35–61

Martin, Peter, *A Life of James Boswell* (London, 1999; Yale, 2000)

—— *Edmond Malone, Shakespeare Scholar: A Literary Biography* (1995)

Mathias, Peter, *The Brewing Industry in England, 1700–1830* (1959)

Maxted, Ian, *The London Book Trades, 1775–1800* (1977)

McGuffie, H.L., *Samuel Johnson in the British Press, 1749–1784* (1971)

McHenry, Lawrence, 'Samuel Johnson's Tics and Gesticulations,' *Journal of the History of Medicine and Allied Sciences*, 22 (1967), pp. 152–68

McIntyre, Ian, *Garrick* (1999)

Menninger, Roy W., "Johnson's Psychic Turmoil and the Women in His Life," *The Age of Johnson*, 5 (1992), pp. 179–200

Midgley, Graham, *University Life in Eighteenth-Century Oxford* (1996)

Morgan, Lee, *Dr Johnson's 'Own Dear Master': The Life of Henry Thrale* (1998)

Murphy, Arthur, *An Essay on the Life and Genius of Samuel Johnson* (1792) in *Johnsonian Miscellanies*, vol. I

Namier, Sir Lewis and John Brooke, *The House of Commons, 1754–1790* (3 vols, 1964)

Nicholls, Graham, '"The Race with Death": Samuel Johnson and Holy Dying', *The New Rambler* (2005–6), pp. 11–21

Nichols, John, *Literary Anecdotes of the Eighteenth Century* (9 vols, 1812–1815).

Northcote, James, *Life of Sir Joshua Reynolds* (1818)

Pennington, Revd Montagu (ed.), *A Series of Letters between Mrs Elizabeth Carter and Miss Catherine Talbot 1741–1770* (2 vols, 1809)

Percy, Thomas, 'Diary', BL Add. MS. 32, 332–6, 337 (begins 17 June 1753)

Piozzi, Hester Lynch, *Anecdotes of the Late Samuel Johnson, During the Last Twenty Years of his Life* (1786)

—— *Letters To and From the Late Samuel Johnson, LL.D.* (2 vols, 1788)

Porter, Roy, *Enlightenment: Britain and the Creation of the Modern World* (2000)

—— *London: A Social History* (1994)

—— *Mind-Forg'd Manacles: A History of Madness in England from the Restoration to the Regency* (1987)

Pottle, Frederick A., *James Boswell: The Earlier Years, 1740–1769* (1966)

—— *The Literary Career of James Boswell, Esq.* (1929)

Reade, A.L., *Johnsonian Gleanings* (11 vols, 1909–52; reprinted 1968)

Reddick, Allen, *The Making of Johnson's Dictionary, 1746–1773* (1990, 1996)

Redford, Bruce (ed.), *The Letters of Samuel Johnson.* (5 vols, 1992)

—— *James Boswell's Life of Johnson*, The Yale Editions of the Private Papers of James Boswell: Research Edition, vol. 2: 1766–1776 (1998)

Roberts, William (ed.), *Memoirs of the Life and Correspondence of Mrs Hannah More* (2 vols, 1834)

Rogers, Pat, *The Samuel Johnson Encyclopedia* (1996)

Rudé, George, *Wilkes and Liberty* (1962)

Sachs, Arieh, *Passionate Intelligence: Imagination and Reason in the Work of Samuel Johnson.* (1967)

Schwartz, R.B, *Samuel Johnson and the New Science* (1971)

Seward, Anna, *The Swan of Lichfield: Correspondence of Anna Seward*, ed. Hesketh Pearson (1936)

Shaw, William, *Memoirs of the Life and Writings of the Late Dr Samuel Johnson* (1785)

Sherbo, Arthur (ed.), *Hester Lynch Piozzi: Anecdotes of the late Samuel Johnson, LL.D. during the Last Twenty Years of His Life* (1974)

—— (ed.), William Shaw, *Memoirs of the Life and Writings of the Late Dr Samuel Johnson* (1785, 1974)

—— *Samuel Johnson, Editor of Shakespeare* (1956)

Sledd, J.H. and G.J. Kolb, *Dr Johnson's Dictionary* (1955)

Small, M.R., *Charlotte Ramsay Lennox* (1935)

Smallwood, P.J., *Johnson's Preface to Shakespeare* (1985)

Thrale, Hester Lynch, *Thraliana: the Diary of Mrs Hester Lynch Thrale, 1776–1809*, ed. Katharine C. Balderston (2 vols, 2nd edn 1951)

Tomarken, Edward, *A History of the Commentary on Selected Writings of Samuel Johnson* (1994)

Tracy, Clarence, *The Artificial Bastard: A Biography of Richard Savage* (1953)

Twining, the Revd Thomas, *Recreations and Studies of a Country Clergyman of the Eighteenth Century* (1882)

Tyson, Moses and Henry Guppy, (eds), *The French Journals of Mrs Thrale and Doctor Johnson* (1932)

Vance, John A., *Samuel Johnson and the Sense of History* (1984)

Wain, John, *Johnson on Johnson* (1976)

—— *Samuel Johnson: A Biography* (1974)

Waingrow, Marshall (ed.), *The Correspondence and Other Papers of James Boswell Relating to the Making of the 'Life of Johnson'* (1969), The Yale Edition of the Private Papers of James Boswell: Research Edition, Boswell's Correspondence, vol. 2

—— (ed.), *James Boswell's Life of Johnson*, The Yale Editions of the Private Papers of James Boswell: Research Edition, vol. 1: 1709–1765 (1994)

—— (ed.), *James Boswell's Life of Johnson*, The Yale Editions of the Private Papers of James Boswell: Research Edition, vol. 2: 1766–1776 (1998)

Weinbrot, Howard D., 'Johnson, Jacobitism and the Historiography of Nostalgia,' in *The Age of Johnson*, vol. 7 (1996), pp. 163 ff.

—— 'Johnson and Jacobitism Redux: Evidence, Interpretation and Intellectual History,' in *The Age of Johnson*, vol. 8 (1997), pp. 89–125

—— 'Meeting the Monarch: Johnson, Boswell and the Anatomy of a Genre,' in *The Age of Johnson*, vol. 18 (2007), pp. 131–50

Wendorf, Richard and Charles Ryskamp, 'A Bluestocking Friendship: The Letters of Elizabeth Montagu and Frances Reynolds in the Princeton Collection', *Princeton University Chronicle*, 41 (1979–1980), pp. 173–207

Wendorf, Richard, *Sir Joshua Reynolds: The Painter in Society* (1996)

—— *The Elements of Life: Biography and Portrait-Painting in Stuart and Georgian England* (1990)

Wheatley, Henry B., *London Past and Present: Its History, Associations, and Tradition* (3 vols, 1891)

Wiltshire, John, *Samuel Johnson in the Medical World* (1991)

Wimsatt, William K., *The Prose Style of Samuel Johnson* (1941)

Windham, William, *The Diary of the Right Hon. William Windham 1784–1810*, ed. Mrs Henry Baring (1866)

Wooll, John, *Biographical Memoir of the Late Rev. Joseph Warton* (1806)

Woolman, Thomas, *A Preface to Samuel Johnson* (1993)

Wright, J.D., 'Unpublished Letters of Dr Johnson', *Bulletin of the John Rylands Library* 16 (1932)

Yung, K.K., *Samuel Johnson, 1709–1784: A Bicentenary Exhibition* (1984)

ACKNOWLEDGEMENTS

I am grateful to the staffs of the following libraries for allowing and helping me to use their books and manuscripts, and permitting me to quote from their collections: the Beinecke Rare Book and Manuscript Library at Yale University; the Bodleian Library, Oxford University; the Cambridge University library; the Hyde Collection in Houghton Library, Harvard University; the British Library; Princeton University Library; the John Rylands Library, University of Manchester; the Lewis Walpole Library in Farmington, Connecticut; and the Pierpont Morgan Library in New York. For permission to quote from published material I am especially indebted to the Yale Edition of the Works of Samuel Johnson, the Yale Editions of the Private Papers of James Boswell (and their director Gordon Turnbull), Edinburgh University Press and Oxford University Press. For permission to publish illustrations I would like to thank the National Portrait Gallery; the British Museum; the Hyde Collection, Houghton Library, Harvard University; the Huntington Library in San Marino, California; Dr Johnson's House, Gough Square, London; the Johnson Birthplace Museum, Lichfield, Staffordshire; Lord Rees-Mogg; Tate Britain; the Beaverbrook Art Gallery, New Brunswick; the Scottish National Portrait Gallery; Museum of the Order of St John, St John's Gate, London; Dover City Museum; the Menil Collection, Houston, Texas; the Bridgeman Art Library; Pembroke College, Oxford University.

Note on quotations: For the sake of clarity, I have modernised spelling and capitalisation except in poetry and when the spelling reveals some idiosyncrasy of Johnson's.

INDEX

THIERS
1797–1877

THIERS
1797–1877
A POLITICAL LIFE

J. P. T. Bury and R. P. Tombs
University of Cambridge

London
ALLEN & UNWIN
Boston   Sydney

Allen & Unwin (Publishers) Ltd,
40 Museum Street, London WC1A 1LU, UK

Allen & Unwin (Publishers) Ltd,
Park Lane, Hemel Hempstead, Herts HP2 4TE, UK

Allen & Unwin, Inc.,
8 Winchester Place, Winchester, Mass. 01890, USA

Allen & Unwin (Australia) Ltd,
8 Napier Street, North Sydney, NSW 2060, Australia

First published in 1986

British Library Cataloguing in Publication Data
Bury, J. P. T.
   Thiers, 1797–1877 : a political life.
1. Thiers, Louis-Adolphe 2. France—
Presidents—Biography
I. Title II. Tombs, R. P.
 944.081'2'0924 DC280.T5
ISBN 0–04–944013–6

Library of Congress Cataloging-in-Publication Data

Bury, J. P. T. (John Patrick Tuer)
   Thiers, 1797–1877.
Bibliography: p.
Includes index.
1. Thiers, Adolphe, 1797–1877. 2. France—Politics
and government—19th century. 3. France—Presidents—
—Biography. 4. Historians—France—Biography.
I. Tombs, Robert. II. Title.
DC280.5.T5B87 1986 944.06'092'4 [B] 85–22969
ISBN 0–04–944013–6 (alk. paper)

Set in 10 on 12 point Sabon by
Mathematical Composition Setters Ltd, Salisbury
and printed in Great Britain by
Mackays of Chatham

Contents

For M. E. B. and I. S. L. T.

Foreword

There are few works on French political and social history in the nineteenth century in which the name of Thiers does not occur. As a young political journalist in the 1820s he was a vigorous opponent of the reactionary policies of Charles X. After the Revolution of 1830, in which he played an important part, he was prominent in government or opposition under three successive regimes, and in 1871 became the first President of the Third Republic. Yet the present book is, so far as we know, the first 'scholarly' political biography of him in any language. Of previous works, the fullest is Henri Malo's *Thiers 1797–1877*, published as long ago as 1932. Despite its merits, this deals superficially with Thiers's political career, presupposes much background knowledge and lacks all documentary and bibliographical references; it is, moreover, difficult to obtain. Similar drawbacks are shared in varying degrees by other French biographies, while the two latest in English, one, John M. S. Allison's *Monsieur Thiers*, was published more than fifty years ago, and the other, René Albrecht-Carrié's *Adolphe Thiers or the Triumph of the Bourgeoisie* (1977), though excellent for its purpose, was intended to provide only a brief summary.

Such neglect is presumably a reflection of the deep disfavour with which Thiers has been regarded by recent generations of French historians and their public. We hope that as foreigners we have been able to consider him dispassionately, providing a straightforward, up-to-date and relatively concise account and assessment of the different facets of his exceptional career. Since Thiers, even in his roles of journalist, historian and would-be philosopher, was particularly concerned with politics, this is essentially a political biography. We trust that it will be of use to many inside and outside France who take an interest in the history of France during the nineteenth century, when parliamentary government and Liberal values, now threatened in many parts of the world, were fought for and ultimately secured.

Acknowledgements

We are glad to acknowledge the kindness of many friends and colleagues who provided information or suggestions, including Monsieur Pierre Laroque, Professor Lee Johnson, Dr Rainer Hudemann, Dr Paul Smith, Mr Lawrence Jacobs, Dr Tim Blanning, the late Professor J.-B. Barrère, Dr Iain Hamilton, Professor David Landes, Professor Derek Beales, Ms Sharon Cather, Dr Hugh Gough and Professor Daniel L. Rader. Monsieur and Madame Denis Bussy kindly checked documents in Paris. Dr John Keiger made most valuable comments on the text, as did our wives, who also helped in other ways, including typing. We are also grateful for the assistance of Madame Benoît and Monsieur Fossier, of the Bibliothèque Thiers; the staff of the manuscripts section of the Bibliothèque Nationale; Madame Meyer and Monsieur Alcouffe of the department of *objets d'art* of the Louvre; Monsieur Ronsin, director of the Bibliothèque Municipale de Saint-Dié; and Madame Desmed-Thielemans, of the Archives Générales du Royaume, Brussels. The British Academy and the Masters and Fellows of St John's and Corpus Christi Colleges, Cambridge, provided generous financial assistance. All responsibility for errors committed and opinions expressed is, of course, ours alone.

List of Illustrations

[1]

Early Years

Marie-Joseph-Louis-Adolphe Thiers was born out of wedlock in Marseilles on 15 April 1797. His father, Louis Thiers, was the ne'er-do-well son of a not unprosperous lawyer from Aix-en-Provence, who for twenty years (1770–90) had been Keeper of the Archives of the city of Marseilles. Louis, a spendthrift adventurer, had already espoused and neglected one wife, Claudine Fougasse, but happily for his illegitimate son, the subject of this biography, she died shortly before he was born. Seemingly smitten by rare pangs of conscience, Louis married the girl he had seduced, the baby's mother, Marie-Madeleine Amic, nine weeks after Claudine's death. The wedding took place on 13 May. Four months later he vanished. For over a quarter of a century he virtually ceased to exist so far as his wife and son were concerned. Louis-Adolphe, or Adolphe, since his mother understandably preferred not to use his father's name, was brought up in a one-parent family. Yet he would often refer to his 'two mothers', for his maternal grandmother lived with her daughter. The two devoted themselves to caring for him and for much of his life he depended on older women for the stable background his father had so signally failed to provide.

The Amic family were all-important for Adolphe's early upbringing. Unfortunately we know little about them, except that Claude Amic, his grandfather, was a merchant in Marseilles with a small trade in cloth in the Levant[1], and that the grandmother who helped to look after him was a Greek, née Marie Santi-Lhomaca, whom Claude had married at Constantinople. Her sister was wife to Louis de Chénier, the father of the two poets André and Marie-Joseph Chénier. It is interesting to note that, of the two statesmen who, some seventy years later, played a principal part in establishing the Third French Republic, both were southerners and that one, Adolphe Thiers, had a half-Greek mother, and the other, Léon Gambetta, an Italian father.

The young Adolphe's early years were spent in straitened circumstances. There was little money to spare in his 'two mothers'' household at 15 Rue des Petits-Pères in Marseilles. Not only had the resources of his grandfather, the archivist, been drained by Louis's extravagance, but in 1793, two years before the archivist's death, they had been further reduced because, when he went to live with one of his daughters at Menton, then on Sardinian

1

territory, he had been placed on the émigrés' list and had his property con-fiscated. The revolutionary wars had likewise ruined the Amics' fortunes. So two other women, Louis's sister, Victoire, who had married a man of some substance at Menton, and Adolphe's godmother, Madame Paul, helped to defray the cost of the boy's education. He was sent first to a private day-school and then in 1809 to the Lycée of Marseilles to which he won a part scholarship and where he spent six years. We know little of the private school or of the lessons he received at home, but the six years in one of the barrack-like Lycées of the First Empire were a tough experience, men-tally and physically. Later he referred to it as a military school from which the senior boys were drafted each year into Napoleon's armies. But the experience, for all its harsh discipline, was rewarding. The education he received was broader than in many schools of the time, for the curriculum of the Napoleonic Lycée included mathematics and science as well as history, classics and philosophy. Mentally he demonstrated his immense capacity for hard work: he took innumerable notes–a habit continued throughout his life–won many prizes and left with glowing testimonials. Physically he attributed his iron constitution to the development of a capacity to overcome the rigours of life at the Lycée.

Here, however, heredity no doubt also played a part. Both Louis Thiers and his father lived to be over 80. In three other ways also young Adolphe took after his picaresque parent. He inherited his diminutive stature–when full grown he was no more than 5 ft 2in–his facility of speech (both were ceaseless, persuasive and omniscient talkers); and his adventurous ambition. But whereas the father, mendacious, charming, dishonest, and improvi-dent, indulged in wild schemes and compromising liaisons and frequently got into trouble, the son, despite a mischievous streak, kept his caprices, for the most part, under control and combined shrewdness with self-discipline. Much later his mother is said to have remarked that anyone who let her son mount behind their carriage might be sure that he would very soon be occu-pying their place inside.[2] Adolphe would indeed have a sharp eye for the main chance. Unlike his father, he learnt both how to earn money and how to keep it.

But for Leipzig and Waterloo he might well have been swept into the armies of the emperor whose admiring historian he later became. As this prospect was ruled out, however, he was urged to go to the bar like so many bright French lads who later took to politics. The nearest law school was at Aix, his grandfather Thiers's old home town north of Marseilles, and there he was enrolled as a student in November 1815. After a spell in modest lodgings he was joined in 1818 by his mother and grandmother who moved from Marseilles to make a new home for him. It was in Aix that he spent the best part of another six years, first as a law student and then as a needy young barrister.

These were stimulating years. For all his studiousness, Adolphe Thiers was no recluse. Adoring talk and argument with fellow-students, he led an active social life, joined in undergraduate pranks, made friends, dreamt dreams, planned great works, and harboured vast ambitions. Of his friendships, much the most important was that with a tall, fair, good-looking young man a year his senior, named François Mignet. They soon became inseparable. For Adolphe, the fatherless only child, the calm Mignet, who had only sisters, was like an elder brother. Later, some historians said that M. Thiers was incapable of friendship. This was not true. The friendship formed at Aix endured for sixty years and ended only with Adolphe's death in 1877. As for the great works, he composed thirteen sections of a hoped-for masterpiece 'towards the age of twenty'.[3] Only one man, wrote the young author, had hitherto conceived the kind of plan he had in mind, namely Rousseau in the *Savoyard Vicar's Profession of Faith*. 'The order of ideas is as follows, man, the universe and God, and my book would have no other title were this title not too high-flown.' The work was to be 'a complete corpus of rational philosophy'. Needless to say, like the 19-year-old Napoleon's Dissertation on Royal Authority or the history of civilization from the barbarians to Dante later dreamt of by the young Catholic writer Frédéric Ozanam, it was one of the innumerable 'great works' projected by clever young men that never saw the light of day. Yet, as will be seen, the idea of writing some such book was intermittently a hobby horse of Adolphe's throughout his life.

Although Adolphe's embryo 'great work' dealt with abstract concepts, its author, completing his studies in the difficult years following Napoleon's fall could hardly fail to be interested in politics. Louis Thiers had, if anything, been a supporter of the Revolution who later developed Bonapartist leanings, but as the Revolution had ruined the family fortunes it is not surprising that the sympathies of his wife and mother-in-law seem to have been with the Bourbons. So were those of most Provençals. In the later 1790s Marseilles and the surrounding countryside had suffered from constant insecurity and brigandage. During the First Empire the city's prosperity had been damaged by the British blockade and Napoleon's Continental System. In consequence, during the Hundred Days the majority of Marseillais were hostile to Napoleon, and after Waterloo Provence generally was a propitious terrain for Royalist reaction. Aix, Adolphe's new home, conformed to this pattern and its municipal authorities ceremoniously celebrated every royal occasion.[4]

Against such a family and regional background it might seem surprising that Adolphe emerged as a Liberal and a devotee of the leading critics of the Restoration regime. Yet the probable reasons are not far to seek. First of all, we know that in all ages some clever young men delight in showing independence by taking the opposite line to their parents and persons in authority. Secondly, there were no doubt particular circumstances which determined Thiers's evolution. The young rationalist did not like political extremism and part of his life at Aix coincided with the ascendancy of the Ultra-Royalists—one of his friends, Emile Teulon, a Protestant from Nîmes, had his family home sacked during the White Terror; it also coincided with extreme manifestations of religious fervour by Catholic clergy eager to seal and maintain an alliance of throne and altar. It is easy to suppose that these were distasteful to a young man whose family Catholicism appears to have been superficial,[5] who at 19 or 20 wrote that he had been in turn materialist, atheist, dogmatist and believer,[6] and who had a sceptical cast of mind. Thirdly, Aix was not devoid of Liberals among its notables, especially the magistrates, and some of these Adolphe and François Mignet may well have met at the house of Dr Arnaud, a prominent personality who sought to bring men of different views together. But the most compelling reason which drove the two friends into the Liberal ranks was probably a very practical one, the lack of opportunities for employment. The collapse of Napoleon's European empire meant that too many able young Frenchmen were pursuing too few jobs; whereas, earlier, the principle of 'la carrière ouverte aux talents' had frequently operated, the government now sought to fill posts with its own Royalist supporters who expected to be rewarded for their loyalty.

Thiers and Mignet were enrolled as members of the bar at Aix in November 1818, but Aix, a town of only 24,000 inhabitants, was in economic decline, outstripped by the far larger Marseilles and also by Avignon.[7] With Royalists in the ascendant and economic prospects poor, the young men were too often briefless barristers. Adolphe, who hated inactivity, filled in his time with literary projects. He planned a tragedy on Tiberius Gracchus which his friend Teulon was to put into verse; he wrote a comedy and short stories as well as a eulogy of the Polish hero Kosciuszko. But, above all, it was the prizes offered by regional academies which came to Adolphe's and François's relief. Such academies were largely late seventeenth- or early eighteenth-century foundations, but their prizes and commendations were still coveted and in 1818 Adolphe was awarded a prize of 300 francs by the Academy of Aix for an *Histoire de l'éloquence judiciaire* and in 1821 one for an *Eloge de Charles VII dit le Victorieux et le Restaurateur de la France*.

Most prize essays are soon forgotten, but the *Eloge de Vauvenargues* (1820) is remarkable for the way in which it too won a prize and for what France's most notable nineteenth-century literary critic later said about it. When the competition was first held one particular entry was praised with undue enthusiasm by the Marquis d'Arlatan-Lauris, a member of the jury and one of Adolphe's admirers. The competitors wrote under mottos rather than their names, but suspecting that the young Liberal might be the author, d'Arlatan's more conservative colleagues voted to make no award and hold the competition again the following year. Adolphe thereupon said that he would rewrite his essay and compete anew. But, fearing a repetition of what

had happened the year before, he also wrote a second version and arranged
for it to be sent in from Paris under a different motto. This was the essay
to which the judges awarded the prize and one can imagine their dismay
when they opened the envelope containing the author's name and
discovered that it was that of the young man they thought they had turned
down.[8] The episode vividly illustrates Adolphe's pertinacity, his facility
with his pen and his readiness to indulge in a practical joke. Sainte-Beuve,
however, was concerned with the content of the essay. He was impressed
by the delicacy and justness of the young author's appreciation of
Vauvenargues. He noted the absence of rhetoric in his style which later
would become 'a fanatical desire for simplicity', and he was struck by
Adolphe's predilection for action. In one passage, for instance, Adolphe
showed that it seemed to Vauvenargues that 'since man is here below in
order to be active, the more active he is the more he fulfils his purpose'.
Sainte-Beuve commented that while this early work might have exaggerated
Vauvenargues's need for action it already revealed much about its author,
M. Thiers.[9]

The trouble was that Aix offered all too few prospects for purposeful action and a useful career. In July 1819 Adolphe told Teulon that he had
pleaded two or three times at the Assizes, but had neither the stature nor
the voice (his voice was thin and high-pitched) to make a good impression.
He was sometimes very hard up. In the same letter he said that he would
like to visit Teulon at Nîmes, 'but my mother gives me money for food not
travel'. In November 1820 he confessed to being restless, ambitious,
unhappy, poor and discontented with his profession. He could not afford
to pay for a practice and become a solicitor like Teulon, and while he would
like to become a deputy to a public prosecutor he did not see how he could
enter the closed world of the magistrature. The only way to earn money was
perhaps to write books and get them published in Paris.[10]

Curiously enough, the first book which he eventually had published in
Paris, a collection of articles relating to a journey to the Pyrenees, contained
a lyrical description of the magnificent view of his native city, Marseilles,
as travellers suddenly beheld it when they went south from Aix. He expressed
his admiration for its inhabitants as 'a seafaring, trading people ready to
take risks, as speculators always are' and called it 'the most democratic of
all French towns'. Why did he not return to the city of his birth and
schooling? Its prosperity was slowly beginning to return, his maternal
grandfather had been a merchant, and he himself had an excellent head for
figures, an insatiable curiosity about how things worked, and a remarkable
capacity for mastering detail. He might well have become a more affluent
merchant or financier than any of his forebears. Did he ever contemplate
such a prospect? Apparently in 1814, when finishing his studies at the
Lycée, he had thought of doing so in order to help his family, but one of
his masters had strongly urged him not to hide his talents under the bushel

of trade and his mother had not tried to press him into a commercial career.[11] Success in law or literature carried more social prestige and it is evident that Adolphe's spare-time intellectual preoccupations at Aix were predominantly literary or philosophical. So were those of François Mignet and other close friends such as Etienne Rouchon-Guigues and Teulon, both of whom were poets and versifiers as well as lawyers. The great literary prizes were to be won in Paris, not Marseilles, and it was a fresh literary success of François's that helped to ensure that Adolphe should go north, not south.

A prize he won at Nîmes encouraged François Mignet to enter for the much more prestigious competition sponsored annually by the Académie des Inscriptions et Belles-Lettres. The subject set was one in French mediaeval history and in July 1821 he learnt that he was one of the two successful candidates and should go to Paris to receive his share of the award. The chance to visit the capital and try to earn a living there was too good to be missed. He went, decided to stay, and quickly urged Adolphe to follow.

Adolphe had been shattered by the sudden separation from his 'brother'. It quickened the resolve he had formed eight or nine months earlier 'to mount a portfolio and take my wares to the big market, namely Paris'.[12] But were the wares saleable and would they procure him a job? By a happy chance a philanthropic nobleman, the Duc de La Rochefoucauld-Liancourt, was at this time looking for a bright young man to act as his secretary. Somehow he had heard of Adolphe, perhaps through Jean-Joachim Pellenc, who had once been deputy for Aix to the States General in 1789 and at one time secretary to Mirabeau. Pellenc, however, reported that he did not think Adolphe was the kind of young man the duke needed. 'M. Thiers', he said, 'is very small in stature and the sound of his voice is not very agreeable. He has a strong accent, he reads badly and although his head is full of Aristotle and Plato in almost equal doses you might well find him... too much of an ideologue... I think he was born and brought up especially to be eloquent and that his principal talent is a literary talent.' In Pellenc's opinion there was much room for stylistic improvement in the unfinished literary works he had seen so far. Yet he discerned 'prodigious talent' in an essay on the superiority of classical to romantic literature and, in a new 'brochure', 'statesmanlike qualities in two or three chapters, sophisms in several others and rhetoric everywhere'.[13] The duke was intrigued by what he had heard and read—he, too, had read the 'brochure'; he ignored Pellenc's advice and made the appointment.

Adolphe's family had so little money to spare that he had to borrow 400 francs from Teulon and 180 from the Rouchon-Guigues, father and son, to defray the costs of the journey to Paris[14] and presumably of clothing fit for service in a ducal household. 'I leave tomorrow,' he wrote to a friend on 17 September. 'I am overcome with tears; my two mothers break my heart with their grief... I am ill; I am feverish; my breast burns; I breathe with difficulty... The future is awful but the present is unendurable... I must go, no matter what it costs.'[15] So after a tearful parting, he set off by coach to Avignon. Thence a boat took him to Lyons where he boarded another coach for Paris. He left behind not only his 'mothers' and young men friends but a girl named Emilie Bonnefoux who regarded herself as his fiancée.

For a young man of 24 who had seldom left home and probably never set foot outside Provence the long journey must have been alarming. In Paris it was a great consolation to find François again, but his bare and dismal room in a seedy lodging house near the Palais Royal did not make for cheerfulness. Moreover, they met only to part, since Adolphe's duties required him to work in the duke's château at Liancourt in the Oise. It was no wonder that he was very homesick and that he did not hold his secretarial post for long. Pellenc had doubted whether he was the right man for the job and François was eager for Adolphe's company. The two young men wished to be together in the capital, to do similar work and once more share their experiences. They soon contrived to do so. In November François was taken on as a contributor to an advanced Liberal paper, the *Courrier Français*, and soon afterwards Adolphe was offered the opportunity of working for another Liberal journal, the *Constitutionnel*. He took it, despite having told Teulon in August that he had decided to go to Paris but not to become a journalist there,[16] and he speedily joined François in his lodging house. A few months later, in February 1822, he obtained a contract from the publishers Lecointe and Duret to write a history of the French Revolution, and in May François signed one with another firm for a work on the same subject. These were remarkably shrewd moves. Now that nearly a quarter of a century had passed since the *coup d'état* of Brumaire, which in effect put an end to the Revolution and brought Napoleon to power, men were eager to read about the events of 1789 and after which had so dramatically changed the course of French and European history. Hitherto, apart from Madame de Staël's important *Considérations sur les principaux événemens de la Révolution Française*, published posthumously in 1818, they had had to be content with the numerous memoirs of survivors. It was time, said the prospectus of Adolphe's work, 'for writers of the present generation who hold to the revolution only by the common interest of justice and liberty, to become the historians of this memorable epoch and retrace for us its useful and instructive "*souvenir*"'.

Adolphe frankly admitted that he had undertaken a difficult task, for after the distractions of war and conquest the passions aroused by the Revolution were reviving under the Restoration. 'No doubt, we, the sons and heirs of the men who had taken part in it', he wrote, in the preface, 'will be unable to free ourselves entirely from their passions, and posterity will perhaps dispute that we have the disposition necessary to write their history. However, whilst supporting the same cause we do not have to defend their conduct and we can separate liberty from those who have served it well or ill.' For him and François 'the cause' was the cause of Liberalism.

Sometime in the same year their fortunes had so far improved that they were able to move to better lodgings in a house in the Rue Choiseul occupied by a German bookseller and publisher, Alexander Schubart. They had found their feet and were in Paris to stay. 'Our life is here', François told Rouchon in August 1822. 'At Aix there are relations and friends but there is no bread.'[17] Within less than a decade the two friends who had had no vocation for the law were to be widely known as journalists and historians.

Neither had money to spare when he first arrived in Paris but each had letters of introduction to leading Liberals, including Jacques Manuel, a former Aix lawyer who now represented the Vendée in the Chamber of Deputies and was one of the Bourbons' most determined opponents. They reached Paris at a time when the Liberals were hard pressed: they had been weakened by the death of one of their leaders, Camille Jordan; the Carbonari conspiracies in which some of them had rashly become involved were being uncovered; and a new wave of Ultra-Royalist reaction was threatening. Manuel and his friends were therefore delighted by the possibility of enlisting young and able recruits for the Liberal newspapers. The recruits were fortunate in beginning their careers at a time when the political press in parliamentary countries was exceptionally powerful. It was not long since Napoleon had declared that three hostile newspapers were more to be feared than a thousand bayonets, and across the Channel in 1828 Macaulay would call the reporters in the gallery of the House of Commons 'a fourth estate'. 'Opinion', wrote Balzac in 1840, 'is made in Paris; it is manufactured with ink and paper.' Governments knew this only too well and were anxious to control the manufacture if they could.

Most provincials who embarked on Parisian journalism began by writing for periodicals or specialized journals, so Adolphe was particularly fortunate in being taken on by a political journal and that one of the most prosperous of the day. After numerous vicissitudes and changes of name during the early years of the Restoration, it had re-emerged as the *Constitutionnel* in 1819 and, thanks to an able staff which eventually included Antoine Jay, Evariste Dumoulin, Pierre François Tissot, Léon Thiessé, Cauchois-Lemaire and Charles Etienne, the man who had offered Adolphe his job, its circulation and the value of its shares increased. It was stoutly Liberal and often malevolently anti-clerical, but dexterously managed to avoid head-on collisions with the authorities. In consequence by 1826 its circulation of approximately 20–21,000 copies accounted for about two-fifths of that of all the Parisian papers. 'What café, what reading room is there in Paris and the whole of France...', wrote the author of a report drawn up for the chief minister, Villèle, 'that does not have one (or several) copies of the *Constitutionnel*?'[18]

'We write articles', François had told a friend at Aix, Séverin Benoît, in December 1821, 'I think we shall never lack for this kind of work and that we shall even have more of it than we need.'[19] Neither he nor Thiers was confined to the paper which first took him on, but whereas, before 1830, François wrote laboriously and limited himself mainly to literary or historical reviews or articles on foreign policy which reflected his deterministic view of history in general and of the French Revolution in particular, Adolphe was far more versatile and productive. As his friend said, he 'can do anything quickly and well because of his astonishing faculty of assimilating everything in a moment and of always being ready'.[20] So, in addition to writing on a variety of subjects for the *Constitutionnel*, he contributed to a few other French papers and, from the end of 1823, became a regular correspondent of the German *Allgemeine Zeitung*, or *Gazette d'Augsbourg*, as it was widely known.

His versatility was shown from the outset. Within the first year of his journalistic career his articles included a powerful refutation of the views expressed by the eccentric Comte de Montlosier in a pamphlet entitled *De la Monarchie française au 1er mars 1822*, a series of articles on the art exhibition or Salon of 1822, and those already mentioned on the Pyrenees and the South of France in November and December 1822. The refutation of Montlosier was later called by Sainte-Beuve 'un article-ministre';[21] the articles on the Salon were thought good enough to be collected and published as a brochure soon after their appearance in the *Constitutionnel*; and those on the Pyrenees, although not all printed in the paper, were not only similarly collected and published in 1823 but brought him sudden fame.

All these writings are significant when we consider Adolphe's career as a whole. The reply to Montlosier was one of the earliest expositions of his views on the French Revolution and a few sentences are worth quoting to indicate their tenor:

> No, before '89 we did not have all that we have had since; for it would have been senseless to rebel without any motive and a whole nation does not go mad in a moment ...
>
> Remember that before '89 we had no annual representation, no freedom of the press, no individual liberty, no voting of taxes, no equality before the law, no eligibility for offices. You claim that all these things were in people's minds, but it needed the Revolution to make them legal realities; you claim that they were written down in the *cahiers*, but it needed the Revolution to send out the *cahiers*.

The articles on the Salon were among the first indications of a lifelong interest in art, in the pursuit of which he became both a patron and a zealous collector. They reflect, too, the remarkable speed with which he had widened the circle of his acquaintance. He had obtained an introduction to the artist Gérard and watched him paint a portrait of the Duchesse de Broglie as 'Corinna at Cape Misenum';[22] he had visited the studios of Girodet and Horace Vernet. Now, in his articles he warmly praised Gérard's 'Corinna', gave advice to Vernet who was eight years his senior, and discerned the genius of a young man two years his junior, Eugène Delacroix.[23] Adolphe was barely 24 but, as one historian has remarked: 'one would have said he was a redoubtable elderly critic whose opinion makes or destroys a reputation'.[24] Curiously, his future political rival François Guizot had also tried his hand at art criticism; when he was 23 he had written a pamphlet on the fine arts and the Salon of 1810. But Guizot's approach was more philosophic than aesthetic. For all the doubtfulness of his taste, particularly later in life, the young Adolphe had flashes of artistic insight which were denied to his rival and, without positive evidence to support the allegation, it is unfair to him to believe that he praised Delacroix only because he was rumoured to be the son of Talleyrand.

The *choses vues* in his three articles printed in January 1823 in the *Constitutionnel* (which soon afterwards formed part of a brochure entitled *Les Pyrénées et le Midi de la France*) were wholly different. After a year's intensive work in or near Paris, 'the centre of all activity and all knowledge', Adolphe told Etienne that he intended to take a holiday, but that, as he would see many things, he would write some articles. He would go home by way of Switzerland, but he said nothing of his intention to go on to the Pyrenees, 'the last bastion of European liberty'.[25] The result was one of the most original examples of early newspaper reporting. The reporter's aim was threefold; to puff his native city and the south of France 'so little known and so misjudged'; to collect material for his history of the French Revolution; and to throw light on the situation on the border with Spain. Incidentally, of course, he contrived to see his 'mothers' – his grandmother was now ailing – and several friends at Aix and Marseilles. His reports showed the variety of his talents: amusing irony in narrating encounters with police officials; a sense of history in analysing the relations of Aix and Marseilles; a command of facts in recounting the vicissitudes of Marseilles's commerce and manufactures; and a remarkable power of grasping the geographical elements of a landscape and describing them with a poetic feeling which charmed his readers. More than twenty years later this moved Sainte-Beuve so much that he called Adolphe's almost Romantic picture of the valley of Argelès, seen from the priory of Saint-Savin, 'perfection itself'.[26]

But politically minded Frenchmen were concerned not with the beauties of Pyrenean scenery, but with the Spanish question and its implications for France. In 1820 conservative governments had been dismayed by a military coup in Madrid which had obliged the Bourbon king to accept once more the Liberal constitution of 1812 which he had jettisoned in 1814. Various Royalist factions hoped that the French Bourbons would come to the rescue, for without funds and arms they could not hope to defeat the regular army unaided. By the autumn of 1822 the French had done no more than mobilize an observation corps on the frontier, but one so-called 'pure' Royalist group of 'Soldiers of the Faith', led by the Marquès de Mataflorida, had raised the standard of revolt, thereby starting what has been called the first Spanish Civil War, and set up a regency in Seo de Urgel, south of Andorra. But by the end of November, when Adolphe Thiers, his mule, and his guide made their way through the snow from Prades in Roussillon up mountain gorges to the Col de la Perche and across the frontier to Puycerda, the Army of the Faith was in flight, and he passed 'King' Mataflorida and his suite on their melancholy route to refuge in France. Adolphe had little commendation for the Soldiers of the Faith or the monks who had fled in front of them, but he was impressed by the 'constitutional' troops who had taken Puycerda unopposed, for 'despite their dirtiness and the kind of neglect that pervaded their ranks' he saw in them 'perhaps the most veteran troops in Europe today'; here were the *bandes* that had for so long measured themselves against the Grand Army of Napoleon.

This Pyrenean journey which ended at Bayonne did not make Adolphe's fortune but it made his reputation. No other reporter had had the initiative or physical stamina to see for himself what things were like on the Spanish frontier. Moreover, his articles were eminently readable and relevant to one of the burning topics of the day. Would there or would there not be war? Should the French army of observation be ordered to intervene in Spain and free the Spanish king? The French Liberals, some of whom appear to have sponsored Adolphe's Pyrenean journey, were for the most part bitterly opposed to intervention and argued that the Spaniards would resist it as they had resisted Napoleon[27]. Several sentences in Adolphe's pamphlet supported their arguments. The Spaniards, he said, would always give the foreigner a hostile reception. They had not changed and so 'the rashness which would lead our young fellow-citizens into a country in which the bravery of our veteran troops could not succeed' was to be deplored. Men like the 'constitutional' troops he saw at Puycerda 'pouvaient rendre bon compte de nos braves'. Furthermore, civil war in Spain and the presence of the French *cordon sanitaire* along the frontier had temporarily damaged or threatened the trade of places such as Tarbes and Bayonne. But Adolphe had also perceived that the rank and file of the new army of the Restoration were indifferent to politics and ideology, and not long afterwards he revised his opinion and declared that Spain was 'an extinct Vendée'. When in April 1823 the French troops, the standard of whose food and clothing he had praised, did march in they proved him right. Their intervention was a walk-over and the war was 'a political triumph for the dynasty, the government and the party that had made it'.[28] Most French Liberals were confounded and their discomfiture was increased by the losses they suffered in the elections of 1824.[29] The position of the Ultra-Royalists and the able chief minister, Villèle, was for the time greatly strengthened.

Some Liberal newspapers were victims of the reaction that followed.

Among them was the *Tablettes Universelles*, bought in 1822 by Jacques Coste, a businessman who, with Guizot's encouragement, sought to make of it a forum for reconciling all aspects of liberalism. Coste had enrolled several young men to write for it. They included François Mignet, Adolphe Thiers, and Adolphe's exact contemporary Charles de Rémusat, who later became his lifelong associate and friend. Among those who inspired some of Adolphe's trenchant political articles was no less a person than the Prince de Talleyrand, who expressed the wish to meet him early in 1823. Despite its small circulation, the government regarded the *Tablettes* as dangerous, and in January 1824, when Coste was in financial difficulties, they succeeded in buying it; the editorial staff refused to carry on and the last number appeared in March.[30] 'The young Guard is beaten' said Adolphe to Rémusat when next they met.

But a defeat did not mean surrender, least of all for Adolphe Thiers. Ever since his arrival in Paris he had continued to work with extraordinary energy as well as with his accustomed facility. 'Paris', he once said, 'belongs to the man who gets up early.' He normally rose at 5 a.m. and worked until noon. He then lunched with Mignet and other friends and spent the afternoon at the office of the *Constitutionnel* and the evening in 'society'. His reputation as a journalist now established, his reputation as an historian was made by the appearance of his *Histoire de la Révolution* between 1823 and 1827. This was not because all ten volumes were good history – he himself recognized the defects of the first two – but because, like the Pyrenees articles, they were readable and, as has been said, one of the first narrative accounts of a subject in which most educated Frenchmen were passionately interested.[31] Already at the end of November 1823 he had begun the correspondence which paved the way for his contributions to the influential *Gazette d'Augsbourg*. In 1824 he wrote for a while for a new paper, the *Globe*, which was in some sort the successor of the *Tablettes Universelles*,[32] and projected acquiring one of his own along with François Mignet and another Provençal, Alphonse Rabbe. Before the end of the year two more volumes of the *Histoire de la Révolution* had followed and their young author had refused an overture inspired by Villèle inviting him to write articles in defence of the government's plan for converting government stock. It was significant that such overtures could be made; Adolphe had added finance to his many interests, made the acquaintance of leaders of the financial world such as Delessert, Ternaux, Baron Louis, and Laffitte, and become known for the lucidity with which he could expound financial problems. It was fortunate for his reputation that he could afford to turn the overture down and that, despite his respect for Villèle's financial expertise, and his approval of his second conversion bill, he was shrewd enough to do so.

Adolphe's first nine years in Paris throw interesting light on certain aspects of French society and journalism. 'Some of us', wrote Charles de

Rémusat in an article of 1844 referring to the Liberals of Restoration days, 'at first obscure, unknown, and come from afar, owed everything to our own efforts. No family tradition, no conspicuous position had predestined them to active opposition ... Brought up far from Paris they quickly acclimatized themselves in this new world, whilst retaining some of the energy that derived from a harsh education, free from softness and distractions.'[33] Thus from Nîmes and Geneva Guizot at the age of 18 had come to Paris without money and virtually friendless. For such young men, it was a time to make influential friends, to frequent the salons in which people of consequence might be met, and to be ready, if need be, to render service. So in the evenings, as we have seen, Adolphe and François were constantly in society. One of their most generous hosts was the wealthy Liberal banker Jacques Laffitte, to whose house Manuel and the song-writer Béranger were regular visitors. It was there that Adolphe had been introduced to Talleyrand, and in Laffitte's country home, the Château de Maisons west of Paris, Adolphe is said to have written much of his *Histoire de la Révolution*.[34] He and François shone as the most brilliant talkers in the salon of the d'Aubernons, who regularly entertained the staff of the *Courrier Français* as well as its occasional contributors such as Stendhal, Victor Cousin, Duvergier de Hauranne and the painter Ary Scheffer. They also frequented the homes of foreign hostesses in Paris, of Mrs Clarke and her daughter, Mary, who entertained historians and philosophers such as Augustin Thierry, Benjamin Constant, Guizot and Quinet, and, in 1828 and after, of Lady Blessington in whose salon they met Lord John Russell.

In such places it was important to see and be seen; in these salons Adolphe the historian could make contacts with useful survivors of the Revolution and collect items of news useful also to Adolphe the journalist. His articles, as was generally the custom of the day, were anonymous. But the author of a particular type or series of articles might have some distinguishing mark: thus Adolphe's contributions to the *bulletin politique* of the *Tablettes Universelles* were signed with three asterisks and for a time people supposed them to be written by Etienne of the *Constitutionnel*. It was, of course, an advantage to a talented journalist for his identity to become known to influential people. Journalism was not regarded as a regular profession until much later and it was not a particularly well-paid pursuit. One historian thinks Adolphe was arbitrarily exploited by Etienne because of the meagre payment he received for his articles on his trip to the Pyrenees,[35] and the editor of his letters to the *Gazette d'Augsbourg* points out that during the six and a half years in which he wrote for that paper he was paid 200 francs a month without any increase, despite the exceptional quality of his contributions.[36] What made the needy young barrister of 1821 a relatively prosperous man-about-town by 1828 was not his income as a journalist, but the handsome sums he derived from the original

13

edition of the *Histoire de la Révolution Française* (14,000 francs), and from the revision of the first two volumes (15,000 francs), as well as from becoming a nominal shareholder in the *Constitutionnel*. It was one thing to write for one of the two most flourishing papers in France, quite another to be one of its shareholders and sit on its board of management.

The advantages of being a shareholder appear to have been drawn to the attention of a wealthy German, proprietor of the *Gazette d'Augsbourg* and other papers, Baron Johann-Friedrich Cotta, by Adolphe's and François's landlord, Schubart, who was agent for some of Cotta's Parisian business. But to become a shareholder was not easy. There were only fifteen *Constitutionnel* shares compared with the *Courrier Français's* forty, and there could be a legal obstacle in the way of foreign ownership of one of them. The way round this obstacle was to appoint a Frenchman as the nominal holder and Schubart suggested that Adolphe would admirably play this part. When, however, in 1824 a shareholder emerged who was ready to sell one of his shares for 100,000 francs, another purchaser appeared on the scene, the journalist Cauchois-Lemaire, backed by a rich deputy, Gévaudan. The immediate upshot was that half the share went to Cotta and the other to Cauchois-Lemaire, while Thiers became its nominal owner. After further complicated transactions Cotta eventually became real owner of the whole, but Adolphe for his services received the surplus income from half a share after certain fixed payments had been deducted. Since the value of the shares had been rising appreciably, his net dividends amounted to 6,250 francs both in 1826–7 and 1828–9, and 8,000 in 1827–8. As the historian of his relations with Cotta remarks: 'It was a good income for a man who had not contributed one franc's worth of capital apart from a refund of 5,000 fr. given to Schubart to console him for having been deprived of any part of the business.'[37]

It was on Schubart's recommendation that Cotta enrolled Adolphe as one of the French correspondents of the *Gazette d'Augsbourg*. This may have been the journalistic task that Adolphe most enjoyed. In his political articles for the *Tablettes Universelles* or the *Constitutionnel* he had constantly to take care not to bring his paper into gratuitous conflict with the authorities, but for the *Gazette d'Augsbourg* he could write as he pleased, since the responsibility for eluding censorship lay with the editor of the paper and the men he employed to translate foreign correspondents' letters into German. It was for them to soften Adolphe's style or strike out risky passages. Thus many scornful references to Charles X disappeared, as did derogatory remarks about his ministers such as one in a letter of 21 January 1829: 'M. Portalis est un lourd personnage, bien gros, bien médiocre, bien dévot.'[38] Cotta also sought to preserve the anonymity of correspondents of another nationality. This was naturally very important and the precautions taken by both sides were so strict that Adolphe's identity was unknown even to some of Cotta's closest collaborators. This secrecy enabled him to continue his contributions for six and a half years until the French revolution of July 1830.

These contributions further illuminate both his methods of working and his views. They were full of grammatical slips and spelling mistakes and bore every sign of being written in haste, but their style was clear and incisive and they were frequently enlivened by touches of humour and irony. They were well informed and, as with his articles on the Salon, their author wrote with an air of authority despite his youth. Such qualities made them very readable, like his Pyrenees articles, and Charles de Rémusat's son Paul later claimed that it was Adolphe who had invented *la Presse légère*; he revealed, he wrote, 'what was new in those days, the details which made up the life of governments, the gossip about the secret side of public affairs, all the workings of movements inside the Council of Ministers and diplomatic conferences'.[39] These revelations also revealed some of Adolphe's own prejudices. He had no respect for Louis XVIII or Charles X or indeed for any of the Bourbons except for a while for the Duc d'Angoulême whom he once referred to as 'this excellent prince'.[40] He was contemptuous of almost all aristocrats except for his first employer, the Duc de La Rochefoucauld-Liancourt, and the Duc de Broglie, both Liberals, and he was firmly anti-clerical, not because he detested the clergy as such but because he could not tolerate their interference in politics.

During this period Adolphe certainly endeavoured to be a good son. Now that he was prospering materially he sent money to his mother instead of receiving it, and after his grandmother died in 1824 he brought his mother to live with him and moved from his lodgings in the Rue Choiseul to the Rue du Faubourg Montmartre.[41] But Madame Thiers, now over 50, and seemingly a difficult woman, was lost in the big city in which she had never lived and had no friends. In April 1826 she returned to Provence. Her son accompanied her as far as Fontainebleau and spent some time at Aix when she was ill there in December 1827. But when she went back to Paris after Adolphe's marriage some years later his in-law family kept her at arm's length. Meanwhile he had arranged that in the event of his dying before her she should receive for her lifetime the income from the *Constitutionnel* which would have come to him.

He also in these years had two unpleasant reminders of the past. His letters to Emilie Bonnefoux, the girl he had left behind him at Aix in 1821, had become less frequent and then ceased as he became increasingly absorbed by Parisian life. In 1824 in Paris he was suddenly confronted by Emilie's irate father, a former officer in Napoleon's army, who challenged him to a duel with pistols. He could not avoid the encounter and Manuel and François Mignet acted as seconds. Fortunately neither antagonist was hurt and honour was satisfied. Some years later Adolphe, admitting that he had been in the wrong, secretly procured for the man who might have been his father-in-law a post in the departmental administration of the Bouches-du-Rhône. The second reminder was in 1825. Realizing that his abandoned son had now become well known and presumably well-to-do, Louis Thiers re-emerged and wrote him the first of a series of begging letters that continued almost until Louis's death in Provence in 1843 at the age of 84. After initially refusing help to a man 'whose name I bear, whose son I am, but who was never my father and whom I shall never regard as such,[42] Adolphe eventually sent him 100 francs a month and found money and jobs for the five half-brothers and sisters, only one of them legitimate, who soon followed their father in making themselves known and holding out their hands. As one historian has remarked 'Thiers must often have envied Guizot. His father, at least, died on the scaffold of the Revolution.'[43]

With increasing prosperity, Adolphe, unlike François Mignet, sought to cut a dash as a young man-about-town, wearing extravagant clothes, learning to ride and becoming the owner of fine horses. To some these extravagances, perhaps another attempt to compensate for his small stature, might seem ridiculous, but, as could be expected, he tackled his new equestrian accomplishment with zest; someone later expressed surprise that his eagerness to be a horseman had not led him on to become a jockey. Social extravagances and family upsets, combined with an ever strenuous life, naturally took it out of him from time to time. In July and August 1825 he 'suffered horribly' from an attack of nerves. In August 1828 he was again unwell and in September his doctor ordered him to take the waters for a fortnight: accordingly he went first to Aix-les-Bains and then to Zurich. In a letter to Cotta in October he referred to his impaired health and, when he discovered grey hairs, he prophesied that his hair would be white by the time he was 40. But in general his health was good and in 1829 the restlessness that he had known at Aix and that had perhaps impelled him to the Pyrenees in 1822 beset him once more. Having finished his *Histoire de la Révolution*, the last two volumes of which appeared in November 1827, and added to his reputation by his study of John Law and his financial system, published in 1826, he needed new worlds to conquer. Under the moderate Martignac ministry, formed after the fall of Villèle in January 1828, French politics appeared more stable and less exciting. Disinclined as yet to embark upon the history of the Consulate and Empire for which Schubart had bought the publication rights in 1826, his mind reverted to a vaster project, not the History of Philosophy dreamt of in his adolescent years, but a General History in which the course of human development would be explained by reference to the earth's geography. For this, he thought, he needed to travel widely.

It so happened that at this time an expedition was being prepared which appeared to offer just the opportunity he wanted. Periodically the Ministry of Marine was wont to despatch a warship to show the French flag in different parts of the globe. In 1829 plans were being made for the corvette *Favorite* to go round the world for this purpose and also undertake survey work. Adolphe got in touch with its commander, Captain Laplace. The

Minister of Marine, Hyde de Neuville, was approached, saw the aspiring passenger and gave his consent. (This is said to be the only time that Adolphe, in little more than three years' time a minister himself, had any formal dealings with a minister of the Restoration period.) But on 6 August 1829, the Martignac ministry fell and was succeeded by a reactionary one headed by the king's close friend, Prince Jules de Polignac, an Ultra-Royalist of the deepest dye. Sooner or later a major confrontation between such a ministry and the forces of Liberalism looked inevitable. Adolphe's friends persuaded him that he would be needed and could not possibly leave France at such a time.

So on 30 December the *Favorite* left Toulon for the Canaries, the Cape of Good Hope and the Ile de Bourbon off Madagascar without him. It visited Pondichéry in India, went on to the Philippines and called at ports in Australia and New Zealand. Then it crossed the Pacific to Valparaiso, rounded Cape Horn and put in at Rio de Janeiro before returning to France in 1832. The voyage had taken the best part of three years and Laplace published an account of it in five volumes.[44] We may be sure that, had Adolphe acted as its chronicler, as Hyde de Neuville had suggested, the account would have been more sparkling; but whether the voyage would have given him the data he needed for his general history no one can say. In 1831 another young man, an Englishman, embarked on a voyage round the world in a naval vessel called *The Beagle*. For all his vast curiosity and interest in the history of mankind it is unlikely that Adolphe Thiers's observations would have led him to anticipate Charles Darwin's theory of the origin of species.

[2]

The Liberals, the *National,* and the Revolution of 1830

As we have seen, at Aix Thiers was regarded as a Liberal and when he went to Paris it was to prominent Liberals such as Manuel that he had introductions, with Liberals that he chiefly consorted, and on the staff of a Liberal paper, the *Constitutionnel*, that he was employed.

Like many political labels, 'liberal' was a loose term applied to a whole range of people whose views and personalities often conflicted, but who were held to share the same general outlook.[1] Broadly speaking the outlook of the Liberals of Restoration France derived from the Encyclopaedists of the eighteenth century and their followers or spiritual descendants, commonly known as the Ideologues. From them they drew their basic notions such as faith in reason and belief in the rights of man, as well as their religious scepticism. When Pellenc told the Duc de la Rochefoucauld-Liancourt that he might find the young Thiers 'too much of an ideologue', he meant that his conversation and writings reflected the influence of such men. Politically the Liberals were people who detested the *ancien régime* and, however much they differed about some of its phases, exalted the main principles of the Revolution of 1789, as did Thiers in his historical writing. Many also distrusted the Restoration regime because they suspected the Ultra-Royalists of seeking to scrap some of the cherished gains of the Revolution. Like Thiers and Mignet they were mostly middle-class men who resented the return of émigré aristocrats to place and power, Voltairian anti-clericals, temperamentally as well as rationally opposed to clerical influence in matters of state. Several had served the First Republic or Napoleon and some were still Republicans or Bonapartists at heart. Some had been implicated in conspiracy and attempted insurrection, others eschewed violence. But for all their differences, as the name of their most popular paper, the *Constitutionnel*, implied, the majority shared a common belief in or paid lip service to the virtues of constitutional government based on the Charter of 1814. Such a government was, as Mignet later described it, '*ce beau régime* in which right is respected, laws are by consent, speech

18

is free and public opinion consulted'.[2] Although by constant repetition of its virtues those who admired such a *beau régime* succeeded in making 'Vive la Charte!' a truly popular cry, they did not necessarily admire democracy or dream of pushing public consultation as far as universal suffrage.

The Restoration was no great age of political thought and Thiers was no great political thinker – few journalists or historians are. He was a man of action (whose incessant writing was a form of action), more interested in fact than theory. His ideas were borrowed: his talent was to express them simply and reiterate them with clarity and force. His brand of Liberalism, already voiced anonymously in the *Constitutionnel* and the *Gazette d'Augsbourg*, emerges with stark simplicity in his own paper, the *National*, in 1830. He was not a crypto-Bonapartist, despite his interest in the army and his admiration for Napoleon as a military leader. He was not a Republican, although he sometimes sailed near the Republican wind and, like Manuel earlier, recognized that 'some men with lively and generous minds' favoured a Republic. Indeed, a celebrated article in the *National* on 19 February 1830 vigorously denied that France's wish to govern herself reflected a Republican spirit. It reflected her belief that she was competent to operate the system of representative government within the framework of constitutional monarchy based upon and confined within the constitutional Charter. If the monarch ignored or broke through the confines, then, as had happened in England in 1688, he should be changed. Like many Frenchmen, not least his future rival, Guizot, Thiers believed in a strong executive power, but he did not think that France was ripe for an American type of republicanism – that, moreover, was a model of doubtful value since the political climate of the New World was so different from that of the Old. It would take years of disillusionment with constitutional monarchy and its supporters before he was convinced that a Republic was preferable for France because it was the form of government that divided Frenchmen least.

'Still young and full of enthusiasm', wrote Rémusat of the journalists who contributed to the *Globe* and the *National* in 1830, '. . . we had one thought in common, that of bringing the French Revolution to an end by making representative government a reality.'[3] It is essential to remember that the idea and practice of representative government were still relatively new in continental Europe. What West Europeans have so long taken for granted was in Restoration days the subject of a continuing debate. A section in Madame de Staël's *Considérations sur les principaux événemens de la Révolution Française* was headed 'Des circonstances qui rendent le gouvernement représentatif plus nécessaire maintenant en France que partout ailleurs'. Guizot wrote pamphlets about it and it was a theme treated by Chateaubriand and Benjamin Constant. Indeed the Duc de Broglie once remarked that Constant was the man who really taught representative government to the new France while Chateaubriand taught it to the émigrés and country gentlemen.[4] Public opinion, it has been said, was the basis of *La Monarchie selon la Charte* as Chateaubriand expounded it: 'the Chamber expressed it and, through it, the ministry . . . All this went to make of the King a purely decorative personage.'[5] So thought Thiers when, *à propos* of an incident in February 1825, he wrote in a letter for the *Gazette d'Augsbourg* that the new King, Charles X, had forgotten that he or his name should never appear or exert influence in a representative government.[6] Later, in the *National*, he would express this view more memorably: 'Le Roi règne et ne gouverne pas.'

As they were not France's first teachers of representative government so Thiers and Mignet did not originate the idea of a French 1688. Many writers had been fascinated by the English Restoration period and looked for parallels in their own day. As early as 1818–19 in his *Lettres Normandes*, one of the *Constitutionnel's* journalists, Léon Thiessé, had suggested the possibility of a 1688 in France, and in March 1826, in an article for the *Gazette d'Augsbourg*, Thiers made his first public allusion to the fall of the Stuarts 'who had perished not from anger but from disgust'.[7] Nearly a year later he more outspokenly referred to the theme on which the *National* was to harp in 1830: 'It was not a popular rising which drove out the Stuarts, it was the aristocracy itself which deserted them. No doubt we should not think ourselves near to such an outcome but the isolation of the existing family has never been so apparent.'[8]

Although the Polignac ministry was formed in August 1829, the Chambers were not summoned to meet again until 2 March 1830. In the interval the press furnished the main political battlefield and the Liberals, aware of the unpopularity of the new government and fearful that it would seek to narrow the electorate and stifle free expression, sought to make it more unpopular. They were already in a strong position because their papers were widely read in working-class circles. Now they seized the chance to strengthen their arsenal and take the offensive. In October 1829 a new Liberal paper, the *Temps*, whose avowed purpose was to defend the liberties guaranteed by the Charter, was founded by Coste. In January 1830 it was followed by the *National*, and in February the weekly *Globe* became a daily paper and overtly political in character. At the same time two previously short-lived opposition journals, the *Journal de Paris* and the pungent *Tribune des Départements*, were revived.

It was not the first time that Thiers had thought of founding a paper. The previous attempt had failed, but now the climate was more propitious, though the precise circumstances leading to the creation of the *National* remain obscure. We do not know whether the initiative came from Thiers or his backers or even who all these were. In mid-February 1830 Thiers wrote that he had been 'dragged into this extraordinary enterprise by a series of bizarre circumstances'.[9] What they were he tantalizingly failed to reveal, but the word 'dragged' suggests that the initiative proceeded from others, probably including the ultimate backers. There is a strong probability, too, that the most influential of these were Laffitte and Talleyrand. Thiers and Mignet – for the two friends naturally collaborated in the new venture – had long been on friendly, even intimate, terms with Laffitte; they had also been intermittently entertained by Talleyrand and were generally believed to have reflected his views in some of their articles. They and Armand Carrel, who was to direct the new paper with them, are known to have visited the Prince in Touraine late in 1829. When in a letter to Cotta on 21 April 1830 Thiers boasted of the new paper's success, he singled out Laffitte and Talleyrand, along with Royer-Collard and Sébastiani, as men of judgement who thought it had become France's leading journal.[10]

The likelihood is that, in the critical situation resulting from the advent of the Polignac ministry, Laffitte and Talleyrand were anxious for their own views to be forcefully expressed and believed that Thiers and Mignet were just the men to do this for them since their political outlooks coincided. At one moment Thiers appears to have doubted whether there was room for three new papers and proposed that the *Globe* and the *National* should join forces, but negotiations came to nothing; the *Globe* preferred to intensify its activities independently.[11] Whether Thiers's and Mignet's association with Carrel was one of some standing or whether it was pressed upon them is another uncertainty, but the choice was appropriate. This handsome ex-army officer had in 1827 produced an *Histoire de la contre-révolution en Angleterre*, a book which one French historian has described as 'a long and menacing parallel between the Stuart and Bourbon restorations'.[12] Its publisher was Sautelet, the young man who three years later published the *National*. The three directors agreed to assume the executive responsibilities in rotation, Thiers taking the first year's turn.

To give moral support is one thing; to supply financial backing quite another. Laffitte doubtless furnished both,[13] but the less affluent Talleyrand perhaps contented himself with bestowing his blessing and advice. That at least was Chateaubriand's view, but then he could not abide the former Bishop of Autun. 'M. le prince de Talleyrand', he wrote in his famous *Mémoires d'outre-tombe*, 'did not contribute a sou; he simply sullied the tone of the paper by pouring into the common fund his measure of corruption and treachery.'[14] If we exclude Talleyrand, the others who put money into the venture, apart from Laffitte, seem to have been Thiers and Mignet themselves, Auguste Chambolle, formerly a colleague of Mignet on the staff of the *Courrier Français*, Albert Stapfer, whose Swiss father was a well-known literary figure and who had himself translated Goethe into French, and some young publisher friends of Auguste Sautelet and Victor Paulin, the men who were to produce the paper.[15]

The *National* was, in fact, a young men's production which often voiced the scornful aggressiveness of relative youth. Thiers and Mignet were still in their early 30s, Carrel was 29, Chambolle 28 and Sautelet and Paulin belonged to the same generation. It was Sautelet's name that appeared at the bottom of the last page as *propriétaire-gérant*; as such he was given three of seven free half-shares in the venture.

The paper's office was established in the Place des Italiens, 10 Rue Neuve-Saint-Marc, a busy area not far from the opulent new Bourse, but until mid-March, because of difficulties made by the government, it was printed elsewhere. It was not heralded by any advance prospectus and we do not know who gave it its name. Perhaps it was Talleyrand, remembering that in 1814 he had suggested to the Marquise de Coigny that, if Napoleon fell, it might be possible to erect 'un trône national avec M. le duc d'Orléans'.[16] This at least is an agreeable fancy.

The first issue appeared on 3 January 1830. The début of any new venture is a tense moment for its prime movers – at the end of the month Thiers could still refer to the 'horrible burden' he and his colleagues had undertaken – and when he sent a copy of the first issue to Chateaubriand his covering note betrayed his concern. He said that all his collaborators joined him in hoping that the great man would be willing to consider himself not as a subscriber but as a reader of good will: 'If in this first article, which is a source of great anxiety to me, I have succeeded in expressing opinions that you approve, I shall be reassured and certain of finding myself on the right path.'[17]

The paper Chateaubriand received was, like most daily journals for many years to come, limited to four pages. In the upper half of the first two foreign news had precedence – Thiers had asked Cotta to help him find correspondents in Munich, Berlin and London and on 9 February told him that he had received two good letters from Lindner in Munich[18] – and at the bottom there was often a *feuilleton* devoted to some cultural subject such as the proceedings of the Academy of Science, a course of lectures by Cuvier, or the most recent plays. Among the paper's literary critics were J.-J. Ampère and the young Prosper Mérimée whose reviews of a French translation of Byron's Memoirs and of a new edition of those Memoirs appeared on 7 March and 3 June. The last page, as was usual with daily papers of the time, was partly given over to items such as stock exchange news, lists of theatre performances and miscellaneous advertisements. The day when newspapers could be bought singly from a street vendor or at a shop or kiosk had not yet dawned, though it was not far off; a police report in April might refer to its free distribution in the Seine department but regular readers of the *National* had to subscribe for it, paying what was then the average price of 20 francs for three months, 40 for six, and 80 for a year.[19]

Whether or not Chateaubriand deigned to reply, Thiers continued as he had begun. His 'first article' was of course a political one, the first of some 160–200 that Thiers wrote for the *National* between 3 January and 27 July,[20] and it expounded the theory of representative government which he

Plate 1 Thiers aged thirty-three

so frequently reiterated during those seven months. Such government, it explained, was composed of three main parts, a hereditary and inviolable monarch who was obliged to entrust the exercise of governance to responsible ministers, a hereditary and reasonably endowed peerage, sensitive to public opinion, yet conservative by tradition and outlook and so able to 'resist the general impetuosity of human minds', and, lastly, an elective assembly of men distinguished in various walks of life whose task was to represent the country, proclaim the nation's mind and indicate who should be chosen as ministers. This, Thiers declared, was the most stable, free, balanced, and vigorous form of government, the one most desirable for France. He was, he told a contributor, a 'passionate disciple of the English school'.[21]

This exposition of the virtues of representative government was combined with constant attacks on the Polignac ministry. As early as 5 January 1830 Thiers stated the ministry's dilemma. It was unacceptable to the Chamber, and therefore faced the choice of resigning or dissolving Parliament. It might well choose dissolution and then, to prevent the return of a Chamber still more hostile, 'violently' change the electoral law. Men said, he wrote insidiously, that the idea of dissolution by means of a *coup d'état* had been advised. On 26 February, four days before Parliament was due to reassemble, he asserted that the 'faction opposed to the Charter' wished to attack the freedom of the press as well as the electoral system. Two days later he made a forecast: the Chamber would be prorogued if the reply to the address to the throne led the government to fear that the deputies would refuse to vote the budget; meanwhile there would be an attempt to do something dazzling at Algiers and preparations would be made for new elections. If the new Chamber was no better than the old 'on montera à cheval' – a vivid contemporary phrase for a *coup de force*.

Thiers was well informed. When Parliament met on 2 March the speech from the throne contained a scarcely veiled threat that 'unforeseen obstacles' would be overcome by force.[22] The deputies replied with a vote of no confidence in the ministry. It had been drafted by Thiers's former colleague on the staff of the *Constitutionnel*, Etienne, together with Guizot, and 221 deputies voted for it. The King's response was to prorogue Parliament until 1 September and then, after considerable hesitation over dates, to dissolve it in May and order fresh elections to be held on 23 June and 2 July. In the meantime 'something dazzling' was under way at Algiers.

An incident in August 1829, following upon years of friction between France and the Dey of Algiers, induced the Polignac government to intervene directly to destroy a nest of pirates who had preyed on Mediterranean trade for more than three centuries. French troops landed on Algerian soil between 14 and 18 June 1830 and by 5 July Algiers itself was theirs. Their commander, Bourmont, in a rightly proud proclamation, told them that twenty days had sufficed 'to destroy a state whose existence had wearied

Europe for three centuries'. French casualties were few and the treasure found in the Dey's coffers more than covered the cost of the expedition. The government had every reason to rejoice over a brilliant success.

Like the Spanish war earlier, the Algerian enterprise placed France's Liberals in something of a dilemma, as the sixteen articles Thiers devoted to it in the *National* clearly show. At first Liberals clearly condemned it because it was mounted by the detested Polignac Cabinet which could do nothing right in their eyes and because some of them genuinely feared that it would land France in a confrontation with England. Yet the Spanish expedition had been successful. What if the Algerian succeeded likewise? At first Thiers's tone was wholly condemnatory. Just as Talleyrand in May called it *une étourderie* so Thiers had already denounced 'the mad expenditure of men and money'. Before the expedition set out he enlarged upon the difficulties and dangers; he ridiculed going to such lengths just to punish 'un imperceptible barbare, un écumeur de mer'; and he accused the government of shirking an explanation of the expenditure on an expedition not authorized by the Chambers.[23] Yet in April he wrote eight articles describing its historical background. Then gradually his tone changed. On 6 and 13 June, when the fleet was on its way, he hoped for and expected success, thanks to the admiral's caution, 'the devotion of our brave sailors and the valour of our soldiers', but of course expressed reservations. On 12 July, when success had been achieved, he voiced the *National's* lively satisfaction but added that there was no reason for the ministry to exult as though it was their work.

Two days later the nationalist born in Marseilles came fully into the open. He had already been glimpsed on 6 February when he wrote that, if something really lasting was required, France should found a colony in Algeria with the approval of all Europe. He had dreamt expansionist dreams in the last historical articles when he said that Algiers was ill placed for commerce, but Tunis and Tripoli were a different matter: 'if we could push our conquest as far as that we should make a huge acquisition; we should have one of the shores of the Mediterranean . . . valuable colonies capable of growing all the crops suited to the New World . . . we should open trade with the interior of Africa the extent of whose wealth cannot yet be evaluated'. Here was a pointer towards the illusory visions of the interior later seen by men such as Soleillet in *L'Avenir de la France en Afrique* (1876). But such dreams in 1830 were wild and Thiers himself threw cold water on them by adding that England would not permit their realization. In July, however, he was unblushingly defiant and annexationist. The city must be France's 'for keeps'. Never were there more sacred rights of conquest. France must stand up to England; the expedition now had an objective, namely to occupy Algiers, bring it civilization, exploit its resources, and form a settlement there which would provide an opening for middle-class Frenchmen. All nations had an interest in Algiers being occupied and civilized by a Christian nation, especially by France.[24] Thiers's personal interest continued for many years.

The thorny problem of the future of Algiers was left for another French regime to try and resolve. It would in any event probably have been impossible to dazzle by success in Africa men of a generation which, it has been said, could conceive of war and glory only 'as something in Europe across the Rhine and across the Alps'.[25] As it was, Charles X and Polignac had mismanaged their timetable. Had they really hoped by military success and clever propaganda to influence the electors, they should have deferred the polling dates to give their forces time to be sure of victory. When the first poll took place the troops were still in the difficult early phase of engagements on land and, at the time of the second, victory, though well in sight, was still incomplete.

The election dates had been fixed in May 1830, a month in which Charles and his chief minister had again shown their blindness and incorrigibility. As Thiers had foreseen, the Cabinet understandably had to consider what to do should the electors return another hostile majority. When they did so Polignac refused to rule out recourse to Article 14 of the Charter and restriction by ordinance of both the freedom of the press and the size of the electorate. In consequence two ministers resigned. The resignations offered Charles and Polignac the chance to reinforce the Cabinet and bring back the ablest or most prestigious of the dynasty's supporters. It was hardly strengthened by the inclusion, in place of the men who had resigned, of one of the most unpopular members of Villèle's ministry and of a man known chiefly as an election manipulator. 'People don't understand', Thiers told the readers of the *Gazette d'Augsbourg*, 'what party interest can have induced the King on the eve of the elections to take men who are sure to lose him ten thousand voters.' This 'inconceivable folly' showed that the new ministry was formed with a view to the morrow of the elections 'when it will be necessary to resort to *coups d'Etat*'. 'In that case we should at once enter upon this great counter-revolution that we are all expecting and which will bring all this to an end.'[26] It was indeed a tense summer. When the Duc d' Orléans gave a ball at the Palais Royal on 30 May for the King of Naples and his family, many of the deputies present betrayed their anxiety; one wryly remarked that it was a truly Neapolitan fête – they were dancing on a volcano.[27]

Soon afterwards the *National* inserted an extra page in its issue of 13 June. Called a prospectus, it was devoted to a summary of the paper's political stance and a justification of the first five months of its existence. These had often been difficult. Like other outspoken opposition papers, it was vulnerable to prosecution. The issue of 20 February had been seized by the police. On 10 March Sautelet, as *propriétaire-gérant*, had appeared before a police tribunal, and on 3 April the *National* and the *Globe* (also seized in February) were both condemned, their managers having to undergo a period of imprisonment and pay a fine. This, a further prosecution early in May, and an unhappy love affair placed Sautelet under excessive strain and on 13 May he committed suicide.[28] His successor was another young man, Prosper Gauja, born in 1801, who later became a prefect in the Second Republic.

Despite these difficulties, the directors of the *National* expressed satisfaction with its progress. But the prospectus may well have been an attempt to boost circulation. The restrictive press laws rendered precarious the financial viability of many papers and in April the *National* was said to have printed only 1,590 copies daily. By the end of July it had probably increased this figure to 2,320.[29]

Notwithstanding intense official pressure, the results of the elections were a catastrophe for the government.[30] Thiers in the *National* of 25 May had urged the electorate to vote for the 221 deputies who opposed the government if they thought that rule according to the Charter was the only good and firm type of government, if they believed that the elector *à cent écus*[31] should continue to be invested with the right to participate in this government by choosing deputies, and if they wished the press to inform them every morning of what it was in their interest to know. They had responded in large numbers to this appeal and to those of other opposition journals and politicians. Only 143 of the government's supporters were returned. The ranks of the opposition had increased from 221 to 274. Direct confrontation between the Cabinet and its opponents seemed imminent. On 18 July in the *National* Thiers described the government's situation as an insuperable nightmare, in which there were but two fearful 'idées fixes: VIOLER LES LOIS OU SE RETIRER'. On the 21st and 22nd he reported sinister rumours that there would be a *coup d'état* before the end of the month and declared that if the press were threatened it would use every means to protest against violation of the law.

The rumours were only too true. On Monday the 26th four ordinances were printed in the official government paper, the *Moniteur*. As Thiers had foretold, the government had invoked Article 14 of the Charter; 'the great counter-revolution' had begun. The ordinances suspended the liberty of the press, dissolved the newly elected Chamber, radically reduced the size of the electorate and ordered fresh elections to be held in September. The *coup d'état*, so long talked of, had taken place. Those most immediately affected were the newly elected deputies, many of whom risked losing their seats, and the journalists and other writers whose freedom of expression was drastically curtailed. No newspaper, periodical or semi-periodical, was henceforth to appear without an authorization that had to be renewed every three months. Papers and periodicals which contravened this regulation were to be seized immediately and the presses and type used in printing them were either to be placed in a public depository under seal or put out of commission.

Since the Parliament elected in June and July was not expected to meet until 3 August many deputies and peers were away from Paris, but the city was of course still full of journalists. No sooner had the content of the ordinances been digested than some of them, together with such deputies as could be found and a handful of lawyers, met to consider their legal implications. Thiers, as we have seen, had already stigmatized them as a violation of the law. This view was confirmed by the lawyer and deputy, André Dupin, in whose house the first meeting was held and who asserted that the journalists had the right, even the duty, to disobey the ordinances. After a second meeting at the Paris home of another prominent opposition deputy, Casimir Perier, some of those present adjourned to the offices of the *National*. Mostly journalists, they understandably went there because the offices were conveniently central and spacious and also because of the sustained and forceful role the paper had played in opposing the Polignac government.

Little time was lost in agreeing on the need for a protest. Thiers took a lead in determining its form. He argued successfully in favour of a collective protest and was asked to draft one, along with Cauchois-Lemaire of the *Constitutionnel* and Chatelain of the *Courrier Français*. They left the task to him and his draft was accepted virtually without amendment. But who should sign it? Should there be a collective signature or should as many journalists as could be induced to do so sign it individually? Thiers, Carrel, Mignet, and Rémusat of the *Globe* urged individual signatures and again prevailed. Forty-four journalists from eleven papers appended their names. Their protest was categorically defiant. It ended with the words: 'Today the government has lost the legal character by which it commands obedience. As far as concerns our own rights we will resist to the utmost. As for France, let her decide how far she should carry resistance against tyranny.' In a letter to a friend in June, Talleyrand had written that the year 1830 was morally and physically *aux orages*. The big storm had now broken. The moral conflict was clear, but would it have physical consequences? Were the journalists' references to resistance a deliberate call to arms?

It was one thing to draft a protest and obtain the signature of a number of opposition journalists; it was quite another to secure its general publication. On the morning of 27 July 1830 only three opposition papers, apart from the *National*, dared to publish such an inflammatory document in defiance of the ordinances. But Thiers and his colleagues had foreseen the difficulties. They had run off copies on handbills and had them circulating on the streets and in cafés in the afternoon and evening of the 26th. Moreover, on that same day the *National* had brought out a special supplement containing its own protest and appeal to disobedience. The Chamber and electorate, it said, had already done their duty by returning a majority opposed to reactionary government; it was now up to the taxpayers to 'save the cause of law' and refuse to pay taxes. Later, on the 31st when all was over, it printed a special number which reproduced all its issues during the revolutionary period, beginning with the supplement of the 26th. These issues were only single sheets and nothing appeared on the 29th. Nevertheless, the paper claimed that seven or eight thousand copies had been distributed gratis each day. If this was so, Thiers and his colleagues had triumphantly overcome the problems of publicity and distribution in a crisis that rapidly became revolutionary.

The idea of refusing to pay taxes was not new. During the Hundred Days, Lainé, one of Napoleon's most prominent critics, had recommended withholding payment of taxes.[32] After the advent of the Polignac ministry the *Journal de Commerce* had revived the idea, and in September 1829 a body called the Breton Association had been founded to implement it if need be. Other local bodies had discussed it and in the summer it had been debated by a meeting of lawyers and deputies at the Duc de Broglie's house. The *National*, too, had given it publicity – indeed on 8 May it wrote that the idea was in everyone's head. Now its appeal to taxpayers to 'save the cause of law' was a logical sequel to its earlier attitude and shows that Thiers and his colleagues, like many other professional people, were preoccupied by legality. It shows also that they were sure that many serious-minded citizens, who abhorred the *coup d'état* but eschewed violence, would be ready to organize or take part in such a form of passive resistance. The *National's* own protest was certainly not a call to arms.

Two other forms of protest on the 26th deserve mention: at two meetings, one at the Hôtel de Ville and another at a café, some businessmen were said to have resolved to close their shops and workshops the following day,[33] and that evening there were gatherings near the Bourse and the Palais Royal of printers' journeymen whom the ordinance threatened with unemployment. Windows at the Ministry of Finance were stoned.

The weather was fine and hot and on 27 July the effervescence and agitation on the streets intensified. Signs bearing the royal arms were torn down and gunshops pillaged. Belatedly scenting trouble, Charles X sent for the reluctant (and, unfortunately, unpopular) Marshal Marmont and appointed him commander of the Paris garrison with instructions to deal with disorders. By 5 p.m. his men had occupied the main strategic positions in the city without serious difficulty. Nevertheless they had encountered some resistance, a couple of barricades had been erected and, ominously, the first blood had been shed.

It was incumbent on the authorities to deal with defiance of the ordinances as well as disorder. Accordingly, on learning of the journalists' protest, the Prefect of Police sent men to seize or dismantle the presses of the papers which had dared to publish it. When they came to the offices of the *National* Thiers and his colleagues refused to admit them to the machine room and so they eventually broke down the door and dismantled the presses.[34] Nevertheless, as we have seen, Thiers suceeded in having a single-page *numéro de fortune* printed on each of the following days except the 29th.

Meanwhile, on the 27th the paper's offices were the venue of 'an almost continuous meeting'.[35] Thiers was certainly there for part of the time and it seems clear both that he sought to attend two other meetings that day and that in general he tried to restrain young hotheads and promote non-violent resistance.

Once the journalists had shot their bolt it was the opposition deputies' turn to give a lead. Indeed the journalists' protest had included an appeal to them to resist the violation of the laws to the best of their ability. At the *National* meeting some militants urged that it was time to take up arms, but when it was known that deputies were to meet that afternoon at Casimir Perier's house Thiers urged restraint and the need to keep in touch with the country's elected representatives. In consequence he was asked to lead a small deputation to spur the deputies into action.[36] One account says they were to be told of the existence of a plan for a decisive armed revolt, another that they were to be urged to encourage the use of the electoral committees of Paris to co-ordinate opposition such as refusal to pay taxes. When Thiers and his companions reached their destination, however, they found that most of the deputies had already dispersed, having merely asked Guizot and two others to draft a protest and arranged to meet and consider it the following day. Casimir Perier received the unexpected visitors and, in reply to one who said that the people of Paris were beginning to stir (it was about 3 p.m. that the first insurgent was killed), besought them to keep within the law and refrain from inciting to rebellion. When the disappointed party walked away and talked among themselves Chevalier is said to have scorned Perier's caution and declared his belief that an insurrection might succeed. Thiers was less sure, but suggested that even an unsuccessful rising could help to estrange the people from the Bourbon dynasty. The remark, if made, reflected his sometimes Machiavellian realism. It was also consistent with the campaign he had waged in the *National*; if the dynasty remained incorrigible its position should be made untenable.

The second meeting, mainly of deputies and journalists, was in the evening at the house of Cadet-Gassicourt, an elector of the 4th Paris *arrondissement*. Thiers again, apparently, insisted that resistance should continue to take legal form; pursuing a line advocated earlier in the offices of the *National*, he urged the mobilization of electoral committees and suggested ways in which they might act as centres of resistance. In this he was warmly supported by Cauchois-Lemaire and Boulay de la Meurthe, a National Guard officer, who reported that the committees of the 11th and 12th *arrondissements* had already been organized. It was significant that Cadet-Gassicourt was a member of the executive committee of the society called 'Aide-toi, le ciel t'aidera' which had helped to drum up support for opposition candidates in the recent parliamentary elections. Many other members of the committee had been at a gathering in the *National's* offices on the previous evening;[37] in its later brief summary of the events of the 29th the paper said that its offices had become a directing centre from which issued a constant stream of notices, proclamations and orders, emanating above all from the gallant committee which had popularized in France the slogan *aide-toi, le ciel t'aidera.*[38]

But by the time of the meeting at Cadet-Gassicourt's, fighting had already begun. The decisive confrontation for Marmont and the government was not with recalcitrant taxpayers but with citizens in arms who were not content to wait for slow-moving and legalistic deputies to give a lead.

If Thiers slept at home after that meeting on the evening of 27 July it was not for long. In an unpublished memoir Boulay de la Meurthe expressed his admiration for the journalists who had had the courage to sign the protest against the ordinances, for he thought they risked imprisonment. The Republican Louis Blanc went further and wrote that it was 'but just to say, that most of those who signed, believed that they did so at the risk of their lives'.[39] On the evening of the 27th the government ordered their arrest and between 8 and 9 p.m. warrants were handed to the Prefect of Police for execution next day. Had the order been given earlier and acted on before nightfall Thiers, Mignet, and many others would almost certainly have been clapped in gaol;[40] had the government won the day, Thiers, as one of the ringleaders of resistance, would no doubt have been harshly dealt with. As it was, he, Mignet and others got wind of their danger and wisely went into hiding. Sometimes before or soon after midnight the two friends slipped away to the suburb of Bessancourt where Madame de Courchamp, sister of one of the *National's* contributors, gave them asylum.[41] Their friend Rémusat took refuge with the Duc de Broglie who lodged him in a servant's attic room in his porter's lodge.

During the absence of Thiers and Mignet the insurrection gained momentum. As early as 8 a.m. on the 28th Marmont reported to the king: 'It is no longer a rising, it's a revolution.' The effects of a severe economic depression which began in 1825 were still being felt in France and they had been aggravated by bad harvests and, in 1829–30, an exceptionally severe winter. On 13 February, in almost the only article on economic problems published in the *National* during his editorship, Thiers had written that from one end of the world to the other people were complaining of unexampled distress: 'their agriculture suffers; their manufactures are full of products they cannot sell; their workers are dying of hunger. Where people beg, the streets are full of beggars; where they steal, the roads are no longer safe... traders complain of shortage of funds.'

By the summer things had improved, but Paris was now a great overcrowded city of about 800,000 people and there were still many artisans and others who were unemployed or whose livelihood was precarious – men who, as in various demonstrations in the 1820s, would gladly vent their feelings against the government. Many older men had fought in the armies of the Revolution or Empire and had military experience which could be useful to insurgents, while the younger, not least the students of the Polytechnic and other great schools, had every reason to oppose a government whose illiberal measures reduced their prospects. There was thus plenty of spontaneously combustible human material and, once a few bold spirits had erected barricades, or returned fire, or put on National Guards' uniform, or hoisted the tricolour on Nôtre Dame and elsewhere, they were sure of widespread support, especially among the skilled workers who suffered many casualties. By the evening of 28 July Marmont had lost 2,500 men and been obliged to withdraw his forces from advanced positions and concentrate them near the Louvre and the Tuileries.

Thiers and Mignet were no doubt informed of this turn of events, for they returned to the capital early on the 29th. By then they were in no danger of arrest. That morning at dawn the Prefect of Police had burnt his compromising papers and fled.

The 29th, the last of what became known as *les trois glorieuses*, was the decisive day. By the afternoon virtually the whole city was in the hands of the insurgents and Marmont's troops were falling back on Saint-Cloud. The *National*, as we have seen, did not apppear. Two days later it explained: 'Our printers, without concealing the importance of their task, could not but think that they would perform one that was still more useful by defending France and liberty with their guns. Most of the staff themselves were carried away into following the impetus given by the heroic people of Paris whom they had called to arms.' The last phrase was interesting. As we have seen, the journalists' protest was ambiguous; it might or might not have been regarded as a call to arms, but increasingly, ordinary people had interpreted it and other denunciations of the government as though they were. Now that victory had been achieved by force and not by withholding taxes the *National* rejected ambiguity and claimed its share in the summons to real battle.

By the 29th many deputies had returned to Paris. Among them were two of the best known opposition leaders, Lafayette, the Republican 'hero of two worlds', and Laffitte, whose house at once became the headquarters of the 'non-combatant opposition'. On the 28th they had endorsed Guizot's draft protest and sent a deputation asking Marmont to persuade the King to revoke the ordinances and change his ministers. But the King had not yet admitted defeat and there was no news of concessions. As the insurgents, 'the people', forced the troops to retire, deputies like Casimir Perier shifted their position and openly said they must now back the people. It was sometime on that day that Talleyrand, looking out of his window and seeing regular troops retreating in disarray, is said to have consulted his watch and remarked: 'A few more minutes and Charles X will have ceased to be King of France.'[42]

If this were so, who should take his place? On the 29th Charles was still

King but there was a growing power vacuum in the capital. This gave Thiers and Mignet, who joined the throng in Laffitte's house, the chance to press the solution more than once broadly hinted at in the *National*. One such hint in an article of 12 February had explained that in order to complete a revolution of principle brought about in 1640, English society had effected a simple change of persons in 1688 and placed on the throne a family 'imbued with the new faith. England was then so far from being revolutionary... that she chose the family most nearly related to the fallen prince.' Another article soon after asserted that, although France loved genius, she did not want another Napoleon. What she required were simple virtues, modest and solid, that could always be ensured by a good education and that could not be spoiled by a limited power. In the France of 1830 'the family most nearly related' to Charles X was that of Orléans which, despite its royal lineage and vast wealth, was believed to exhibit just those homely virtues that the *National* extolled.

The idea of placing Louis-Philippe, Duc d' Orléans, on the French throne was not new. On the eve of Napoleon's overthrow in 1814 it had been considered by the Tsar and toyed with by Talleyrand. After Waterloo it had again been mooted. In one of his letters to the *Gazette d'Augsbourg* in 1824 Thiers himself had let slip the name 'Philippe VII' and in 1825 he had referred to the possibility of the throne passing to the Duc d'Angoulême, then thought to be a Liberal, and 'perhaps to the Duc d' Orléans'.[43] In December 1827 Cauchois-Lemaire had caused a stir by publishing a *Lettre au duc d'Orléans* in which he appealed to the Duke to emerge from his retreat, show a little courage and take within the monarchy the place that Lafayette would occupy in a Republic, namely that of France's first citizen.[44] It was not surprising that, by the summer of 1830, some of the government's critics were openly saying that its policies were playing into the hands of the Orléans family.[45] For Thiers and Mignet, who were obsessed by the history of the Stuarts and had no wish for a Republic, the Duke must necessarily be France's William III. But the great question was whether historical analogies made practical politics. Could the deputies be induced to see as Thiers and Mignet did; could Orléans, whom they had never met, be persuaded to play the part for which they had cast him and would 'the people' accept him in that role?

On the way to Laffitte's house Thiers and Mignet had observed that, while shopkeepers had dismantled signs bearing the royal arms they had left undisturbed those bearing the Orléans escutcheon. This was an encouraging straw in the wind. At Laffitte's they insisted that only the Duke could avert the Republic for which many insurgents were clamouring. After most of his other visitors had gone, Laffitte, a willing listener, agreed and recognized the need for urgent action if the Orleanist solution was to have any chance of prevailing. With his approval the two friends promptly drafted the famous unsigned proclamation that publicized the Orleanist cause and was posted all over Paris next day. The first three sentences made its purpose crystal clear:

> Charles X can never again enter Paris: he caused the blood of the people to be shed.
> The Republic would expose us to frightful divisions: it would embroil us with Europe.
> The Duc d' Orléans is a prince devoted to the cause of the revolution.

The three following sentences extolled the duke. In them the two historians of the great Revolution astutely recalled it:

> The Duc d' Orléans was at Jemappes.
> The Duc d' Orléans is a Citizen King.
> The Duc d' Orléans has carried the tricolour under the enemy's fire.

The last two boldly asserted:

> The Duc d' Orléans has declared himself: he accepts the Charter as we have always wanted it. It is from the French people that he will hold his crown.

So eager was Thiers to succeed by giving the impression of a *fait accompli* that he is said to have suggested that this and other pro-Orleanist posters should bear the words: 'de l'imprimerie du gouvernement'.

But there was no *fait accompli*. The young journalists had gone too far and in a later printing of the proclamation the wording of the penultimate sentence was changed to something closer to the truth. It now read: 'The Duc d' Orléans does not commit himself. He awaits the expression of our wishes.'

In fact the Duke's views were unknown. Residing on his estate at Neuilly, as was usual during much of the summer, he had no wish to go on his travels a third time because of revolution. Neither did he wish to be placed under preventive arrest by Charles X or to become the cat's paw of the insurgents, although his family's sympathies were with them. On hearing the news of the ordinances and the ensuing disturbances he wisely kept a low profile. At Laffitte's he was thought to be at Neuilly but no one knew for certain. It was essential that contact should be made with him as soon as possible. Young, active, and a fervent advocate of the Orléans candidature, Thiers volunteered to be the envoy.

Armed with an introduction from General Sébastiani and a brief note from Laffitte asking the Duke to listen to what the bearer had to say 'en toute confiance', he set out on horseback on the morning of the 30th. The day was intensely hot and the roads were dusty. He was accompanied by Ary Scheffer, a well-known artist who was also drawing-master to the Orléans princesses, and, to ease their passage if need be, by an officer of the National Guard. When the three men reached Neuilly they learnt to their dismay that the Duke had retired to another of his estates, Le Raincy on the north-eastern side of Paris. Thiers had to explain his mission to two ladies, the duchess and her more forceful companion, the duke's sister, Madame Adélaïde.[46]

Soon after his return Thiers wrote an account of their conversation.[47] It has never been contradicted and there is no reason to doubt the accuracy of its main tenor. After the Duchess had reproached Scheffer for coming on a mission to persuade the Orléans to be disloyal to Charles X and after Madame Adélaïde had expressed her fear that Europe would think the Duke had intrigued to overthrow him, Thiers developed his arguments. His first two sentences might have come from the *National*: 'We want a representative monarchy... We need a new dynasty which owes the crown to us and which, because it owes it to us, is ready to accept the role assigned to it by the representative system.' Everyone would know that the Orléans family had not been seeking the crown, 'for today it is certainly too fraught with danger to be an object of ambition'. But, he warned, the field was still wide open. Some people would still put up with Henri V (the Duc de Bordeaux, Charles X's grandson); others, faithful to the memory of Napoleon, were thinking of the Duc de Reichstadt (Napoleon's only son, in exile in Vienna). Still others would go straight for a Republic. Speed was essential: 'Today those who act most promptly will be the most adroit: thrones belong to those who first take possession.' He added what he called a last decisive argument: 'Thrones are gained at the cost of victories and dangers.' The Duke should come at once to the centre of Paris and declare his support for the July Revolution. There were indeed great risks: Charles X was still at Saint-Cloud with resources at his command, 'But risks are necessary.' If his candidate showed physical courage and braved the risks, Thiers reckoned that his chances would surely be improved.

Madame Adélaïde was impressed. She rose and replied that if Thiers thought the revolution would benefit from her family's support then they would give it. She was ready herself to go to Paris, provided that Laffitte and Sébastiani would themselves come and fetch her. Thiers answered that so long as one member of the family was committed it did not matter which it was. Her promise was sufficient. He had gained what he wanted and, in his delight, told her: 'Aujourd'hui vous placez la couronne dans votre maison.'

They agreed that a letter should be written at once to Orléans explaining why he should act as suggested. Then Thiers, having accomplished his mission, returned post-haste to Paris. There he learnt that some sixty deputies were meeting at the Palais Bourbon under the chairmanship of Laffitte. It was to them that he reported the result of his interview. Laffitte and Sébastiani agreed that Princess Adélaïde had indeed committed the whole Orléans family and that the most important thing now was, as Thiers put it, to be able 'to go boldly forward and say that the Duc d' Orléans could be persuaded to accept the crown'. Many deputies, however, as well as peers like Broglie, preferred to hurry slowly. After a long discussion it was agreed to begin by inviting the Duke to become Lieutenant-General of the Kingdom. Now back at Neuilly, but still undecided whether to follow the course advocated by Thiers, he is said to have sent a messenger to elicit Talleyrand's advice. The answer was short and to the point: 'He should accept!' Before midnight the Duke was in Paris as Thiers had wished.

Meanwhile, to restore law and order, a new centre of local authority had emerged the day before. On the 29th at 4 p.m. a single-sheet number of the *Globe* had announced the formation of what it called a constitutional committee – the proper name was *commission municipale* – and informed its readers that Lafayette had accepted the post of commander-in-chief of the Parisian National Guard. These arrangements had been made by the deputies meeting at Laffitte's house that morning. Both the commission and Lafayette and his staff had installed themselves in the Hôtel de Ville. It was there in the evening that an envoy from the King met the commission and told them that Charles was ready to revoke the ordinances, but the commission was unmoved, for the envoy had no formal document of revocation with him. It was not until early next morning that Charles signed the revocation ordinances, and when the Duc de Mortemart, whom he had appointed to succeed Polignac, brought them to Paris he could find no one to print them. The commission, of which Laffitte was a member, jeered when they were read and soon afterwards issued a proclamation declaring that Charles X had ceased to reign. But did this pave the way for a Republic or for an Orleanist monarchy?

The Republicans believed that they had won the day now that Lafayette was in a commanding position. They offered him the presidency and, convinced that he would accept and give the regime they wanted the necessary prestige, planned to proclaim the Republic at midday on the 31st.

They were disappointed. Lafayette refused. He was the same age as Charles X and hesitated to assume so onerous and perhaps dangerous a position at 73. He accepted the Orleanist solution in principle and, once Orléans had formally accepted the deputies' offer of the Lieutenant-Generalcy, was prepared to welcome him, thereby averting the risk of civil war. When the two men publicly embraced on the balcony of the Hôtel de Ville the Orleanist or July Monarchy was as good as made. But the Duke was not formally acclaimed as King of the French until 9 August and an interesting article in the *National* of the 4th shows that Thiers was still anxious. He described the partisans of 'the Republican utopia' as still formidable and expressed his impatience with the timorous people who wanted to take into account the rights of the young Duc de Bordeaux in whose favour Charles X had now abdicated. He need not have worried. The Lieutenant-General himself soon swept them aside, thereby creating an irreparable breach between the Houses of Bourbon and Orléans and, in the long run, weakening the monarchy itself.

Thiers was not a peer or deputy or even an officer of the National Guard.

After his visit to Neuilly his main role, apart from that of championing the Orleanist cause in the *National*, was over. But one curious incident deserves mention, both because it arose out of his first meeting with Orléans and because of the divergent interpretations put upon it. After being presented at the Palais Royal to the man he had tried to meet at Neuilly, Thiers asked him if he would receive some of his friends who were dissatisfied and wished to 'discuss their political difficulties with him'.[48] The Duke agreed and before long Thiers returned with six young men, five of whom had taken part in the assault on the Tuileries two days earlier. Their sympathies were Republican and if, as has been suggested, Thiers hoped that such a conversation would convert them to Orleanism, he must indeed have been disappointed. One, Godefroy Cavaignac, was to be one of the Republicans' most dynamic leaders during the next few years, and another, Jules Bastide, would be a sincerely Republican minister in 1848.

But one French historian put a different construction on Thiers's action. He suggested that Thiers induced his friends to go to the Palais Royal in order to avert any possibility of trouble and that by agreeing to go the young Republicans were 'accepting the *fait accompli*'.[49] Whatever Thier's motives, the Republicans were realistic enough to understand that, once Lafayette had failed them, it was useless to attempt a fresh rising to overturn the work of the deputies. As Godefroy Cavaignac later told Duvergier de Hauranne: 'It was too hard to make the people, who had fought shouting *Vive la Charte*!, understand that their first act after victory should be to take up arms to destroy it.'[50]

'The people': who were the people? This is not the place to discuss a problem which has caused recent historians to spill so much ink. But it is worth noting that the question arose very soon after the July Revolution and that the *National* was at pains to assert that they were not simply the working class, but also 'the writers who were the first to resist arbitrary action, the young people who read out their protests mounted on benches, the foremen, manufacturers and printers who closed their workshops, the Polytechnicians and the students of the schools of law and medicine, the National Guards, the deputies who had given moral support, and the troops of the line who refused to massacre Frenchmen'. Whatever the means they used to resist, 'the Blouse and the Frock Coat', as one historian has called them,[51] had fought together in defence of 'liberty'.

By the time this article appeared on 18 August Thiers had written his last leader for the *National*, while his last contribution to the *Gazette d'Augsbourg* had appeared on 25 July. On 29 August the *National* printed the following announcement: 'Since MM. Thiers and Mignet have assumed public duties they have ceased to take part in editing the *National*. From today M. Carrel, who has returned to Paris from a mission in the departments, continues as sole editor.' Within a year or so Carrel would turn it into a Republican paper.

The year 1830 was crucial for Thiers as well as for France. The events just described throw light on his character, they mark the climax and termination of his career as a journalist, and they demonstrate the power of journalists and historians to exercise political influence. They reveal that the little man who, ten years earlier, had summarized Vauvenargues's view of man in the words 'The more he acts, the more he fulfils his goal', was himself more than ever a man of action, not lacking in courage, physically tireless and mentally determined and quick, living up to his own maxim 'the nimblest will be the cleverest'.

Later, loving a Napoleonic comparison, he called his campaign in the *National* his 'siege of Toulon' and every history of the fall of the Restoration regime records the role of the *National* and its executive editor. Yet it must be remembered that it was only one of a number of vehement opposition papers, and that in an article of nearly fifty pages on 'The Public Journals' in Paris, published later in the year, the author, Sir Charles Morgan, mentioned it only briefly and Thiers not at all.[52] It was at first sight indeed remarkable that a new paper with a circulation not exceeding 1,500–2,320 subscribers should have exercised so much influence and gained such celebrity. It is less remarkable when we recall that leading Republican papers like the *Tribune des Départements* and *La Révolution* printed only 500 or even fewer than 200 copies of each issue, and when we remember who were the *National's* probable backers, and the way in which day after day the paper relentlessly pursued its aim of confining the Bourbons within the Charter. In addition the paper's celebrity was greatly enhanced by the use made of its offices and by the lead given by its staff, headed by Thiers, in launching the journalists' protest at the beginning of the July Days.

Moreover, the *National's* opposition had a particular historical dimension which must be of interest to historians. As Thiers's and Mignet's histories of the great Revolution were intended to demonstrate that it was a logical sequence of cause and effect, not an arbitrary series of events, so it was with their 'siege of Toulon'. Their friend Rémusat later said that they pictured the revolution in France as a curve on which all the points had been fixed in advance by the course of the English revolution,[53] and Mignet's biographer, assessing his relatively modest role in 1830, has written: 'His real revolutionary responsibility is wholly contained in the *National* articles in which his historical determinism shows the necessity of the change of dynasty. In this sense the July Revolution is indeed the triumph of the historians.'[54]

Thiers's responsibility was much greater than Mignet's. Of all the revolutions in which he was caught up, 1830 was *par excellence* 'his', the one in which he was most actively concerned to effect a change. But it had cost more than 2,000 casualties. In the *National* Thiers had pointed out that there was now no Bastille to take or night of 4 August to accomplish.[55] He had hoped that the very relentlessness of Liberal opposition would cause the government to change course. Yet in 1829, soon after Martignac's fall, he is said to have remarked that trials and condemnations, bloodshed and shooting would provoke national revulsion before Charles X departed in the same way as had James II.[56] The historian of the French Revolution was no sentimentalist. If the dynasty was driven *monter à cheval*, for all his preference for refusing to pay taxes and other sorts of passive resistance, he can hardly have supposed that there would be no physical clashes or that no one would interpret as a call to armed opposition the journalists' protest that he himself had drafted. There is no knowing how far the casualties affected him, but in April 1831 he made his apologia: 'If the Revolution has to cost blood or gold the fault belongs not to us but to those who forced us to make a revolution.'[57]

Thiers did not merely wish to be rid of the Bourbons. To ensure the success of representative government as he envisaged it, he wished for a specific kind of change. The sequence of events led some to suspect that he was privy to a deep-laid Orleanist conspiracy. But, although he had Orleanist sympathizers among the backers of the *National*, this has never been proved and Thiers always strenuously denied it.[58] The Orléans family were in the wings, not wholly unready should a call come in conditions they were prepared to accept, but not engaged in the dangerous business of plotting. What the *National* did was accustom men to the notion that the need for such a call could arise, and when in Thiers's view it did, he again showed himself adept at drafting the kind of proclamation that would appeal to the multitude. It was in this sense that one French historian could call him the inventor of the Orleanist idea.[59] Rémusat, philosophically inclined, expressed this view in the context of historical determinism, later writing that Thiers and Mignet actually wanted what they thought necessary, a change of dynasty: 'Thence sprang a rational, not absolute, Orleanism, not in any way connected with the House of Orléans.'[60]

A few months after the July Revolution, in his brochure *La Monarchie de 1830* Thiers subscribed to the idea of inevitability by declaring that King Louis-Philippe, as Orléans had become, was 'the King indicated by all intelligent people'. But crowds are swayed by sentiment as much as reason, and at the end of the July fighting the Orleanist outcome was hardly 'inevitable'. Late twentieth-century political philosophers are said to argue over the proposition that 'only that which is uttered is an event: history is people doing things with words'.[61] If this is so, Thiers did a vast amount, but he also had to mount his horse and use his legs if his words were to influence the right people at the right time. The little historian gave 'inevitability' a push or two to ensure the 'necessary' result, and being, as well as an egoist like most of us, an historian and journalist used to daily recording, he fortunately recorded for us the push he had given at Neuilly. Together with the 'siege of Toulon', the journalists' protest, and the proclamation in favour of the Duc d' Orléans, it was a shining example of an historian shaping history in a country in which, he had once written, 'all is achieved by enthusiasm (*entraînement*)'.[62]

[3]

The King's Minister,
1830–1839

The regime installed by her Liberal politicians and consolidated during the year following the July Revolution was designed to make France safe for representative government. The way had been indicated by Thiers and Mignet's celebrated proclamation of 29 July: 'The Duc d'Orléans. . . awaits the expression of our wishes. Let us proclaim those wishes and he will accept the Charter as we have always wanted it. It is from the French people that he will hold his crown.' A few days later the *National* declared that the nation had found its William III: 'it will dictate the Bill of Rights'. In effect that 'Bill' was a revised version of the Charter, hastily drafted by a commission appointed by the Chamber of Deputies which had reassembled on 3 August. After approval by the Chamber on the 7th it was formally presented to the Duke two days later in the presence of both Houses of Parliament. It did away with the preamble which stated that the King had freely granted his people rights, since these were now regarded as essentially theirs. The Duke was invited to accept and swear to observe this revised Charter and then to assume the title of King of the French. Once he had done so the contract was sealed which, as Thiers later put it, bound the new monarch to the nation, and from which his legitimacy was derived.

Many of the revisions to the old Charter were important. The France in which Thiers, at the age of 33, now began a new career was one in which the blue, white, and red of the tricolour, 'the beautiful colours of regenerated France' as he later called them, had replaced the white flag of the Bourbons, and in which – a change of vital moment for him – the age limits for becoming a deputy or elector had been respectively lowered from 40 to 30 and from 30 to 25. The National Guard was formally re-established and allowed to choose its officers. Laws were promised and before long passed which provided for elective municipal and departmental councils. This humble expression of representative government, for which the *National* had campaigned before the Revolution, was very important, for it gradually accustomed men even in the remotest areas to the idea and practice of choosing those responsible for the welfare of their local communities. Another law was also significant: by lowering the tax qualification it increased the parliamentary electorate from about 90,000 to about 166,000. This was less than one-third of those enabled to vote as a result of the Reform Bill of 1832 in England[1], but many people on the Left in France hoped that it was a first stage in a steady progress towards universal suffrage. Thiers expressed his satisfaction. In a brochure published at the end of 1831 he claimed that concessions had been made 'in one go' which would otherwise have taken years to obtain: above all a larger portion of the population had been called on to take a part in governing itself.[2]

One criticism of the new rulers was that they had acted in undue haste, rushing through a revised Charter instead of consulting the country anew about its wishes and arranging for a Constituent Assembly to draw up a new constitution. In their defence Thiers rightly and understandably emphasized the need there had been for acting quickly to put an end to uncertainty and disorder, but he made no mention of the fact that only 252 deputies out of 430 had been present when the vote was taken and that only 219 had actually voted for the revision.[3] This was grist to the mill of those who disliked the Orleanist solution. They could say that Thiers and his friends had conjured away the Republic, they could deride the new King's 'quasi-legitimacy' and they could argue with amused disdain whether he was King because of or in spite of his Bourbon blood. But the Orleanists themselves would soon be divided. While Thiers continued to believe that the King should reign but not rule, Guizot and others, following authors such as Benjamin Constant and Lanjuinais, held that he might properly exercise a moderating influence. As Guizot later put it, the throne was not an empty chair.

Amid such divergent interpretations, the new regime, in one French historian's view, instead of closing an era of revolutions opened one of equivocations.[4] Evidently Louis-Philippe, 'this grave, simple, enlightened, witty and eloquent prince', as Thiers called him in *La Monarchie de 1830*, would have a difficult row to hoe. Much would depend on his character and intelligence and on his own interpretation of the constraints of representative government.

The celerity of constitutional change in 1830 was matched by the rapidity with which changes were effected in ministerial and administrative personnel. The Revolution of July 1830 has been called the revolution of the job seekers,[5] and through his courageous and enterprising part in it Thiers was one of many excellent candidates for public office. On 9 August, the day on which Louis-Philippe took his oath, Thiers was appointed to a commission to study reform of the electoral law (in which he supported, with success, a reduction in the *cens*, the tax qualification for electors, from 300 to 200 francs). Two days later he was appointed to a senior post at the Ministry of Finance. On 20 August he was appointed to the Conseil d'Etat, one of the most coveted legal appointments at the heart of central government, and assigned as personal assistant to the new Minister of Finance, the veteran of the Empire, Baron Louis, Thiers's sometime tutor in financial lore. These appointments compared favourably with the rewards obtained by contemporaries and former colleagues: Armand Carrel, to his chagrin, was merely offered a remote prefecture.

It could not be foreseen that Thiers was one of a handful of men who, emerging to prominence in 1830, were to dominate the political history of the July Monarchy.[6] During the next ten years he was to hold office in six governments, and emerge as one of the brightest of a new generation of young men who were to make politics their profession. With the ending of the dominance of the nobility in 1830, they were to give leadership to the political nation of landowners, professional men and businessmen. The ascendency of the new political leaders was founded not on birth or wealth, but on parliamentary powers of oratory and manoeuvre vital in a Chamber barely disciplined by parties, on journalistic talent, and on intellectual ability: the July Monarchy was governed to a large extent by its intellectual elite, several of them historians. Of these, Guizot and Thiers were the most outstanding.

Thiers faced an important barrier to high office. He was not rich enough to be eligible for the Chamber of Deputies, or even to be an elector. Here the Dosne family, whose salon Thiers and Mignet frequented, for the first time played an important role in his career. The financier Alexis-André Dosne, co-owner of a property company, sold Thiers one of its houses, at 3 Rue Neuve Saint-Georges, in the smart new bourgeois quarter of Notre Dame de Lorette. The terms were somewhat special: 100,000 francs (ten years' salary for a Conseiller d'Etat) to be paid only after two years. The 'down payment' seems to have been the simultaneous appointment of Dosne as Receiver-General of Taxes for Brest.[7] Without wealth of his own, Thiers had thus become a man of property, and a payer of sufficient tax on the house to be eligible for parliament. Three days after the house became legally his, on 21 October 1830, he was elected deputy for Aix-en-Provence in a by-election by 177 votes out of 220 cast, having persuaded a potential rival to stand down.[8]

Having entered the Chamber, he was immediately appointed Parliamentary Under-Secretary at the Ministry of Finance in the first elected government of the July Monarchy, presided over by Laffitte who was also Minister of Finance. The outlook for the government and the country was grim. Political agitation had not been ended by the change of regime. War with the European powers seemed likely, and the economy and state finances were gravely affected. The immensity of the problems and the likelihood of failure no doubt explain why Thiers, still a minor figure, was at first offered the ministry itself; he was clever, hard-working and expendable. He refused: 'I could be minister tomorrow and sacked the day after.' But he could not refuse the King's and Laffitte's insistent requests that he should take over the technical side of the ministry, while Laffitte held the portfolio: 'I accepted with repugnance and the desire to get out as early as possible.' As Parliamentary Under-Secretary he did the hard work of the ministry – 'I get up at 4 o'clock in the morning and only go to bed at midnight.'[9] He spoke only twice in the Chamber, on technical financial matters. His journalistic talents too were used by Laffitte in preparing major speeches and also served the new regime, as has been seen, through his pamphlet *La Monarchie de 1830*. This was distributed throughout the country, and in his own territory of Bouches du-Rhône by the prefect, Thomas, who was acting as Thiers's electoral agent.

Thiers was dissatisfied with his position in the Laffitte government, and unwilling to commit himself to it as mere political factotum, for its fortunes were sinking as ministers disagreed, opposition on Right and Left mounted, and economic, political and external problems grew. But he was unsure of the best way forward for himself and the country. Foreign relations, he believed, would decide internal politics, as in the 1790s. 'If peace prevails, the moderate system may prevail. . . If war prevails, we shall go over to the extreme Left.'[10] His belief, during the winter of 1830–1, was that war would come.

There were weighty reasons for this belief, which was widely shared in Europe. The Belgian Revolution, which was breaking up the Kingdom of the Netherlands, one of the buffer states placed on France's border by the 1815 treaties, brought into the open French ambitions and the suspicions of the former allies of Waterloo about the recurring tide of French nationalism. Also dangerous were revolts in Poland late in 1830 and in Italy early in 1831, the former the satellite and ally of the Napoleonic period to which the French public retained a strong sentimental attachment, the latter a traditional French sphere of influence closed to her in 1815. While Louis-Philippe and his ministers were desperately trying to preserve peace without outraging nationalist opinion too dangerously, the Left – a mixture of Liberals, Republicans and nostalgic Bonapartists – was campaigning in Parliament and the press for war, which, it argued, was inevitable anyway, and which would be victorious, for the oppressed peoples of Europe would rise to welcome the French as liberators. For the Left, the 1830 Revolution was above all a national revolution, revenge for Waterloo. Revolutionary war was its inevitable culmination, necessary to strengthen it inside France by rallying the people and keeping counter-revolution at bay, and outside France by destroying its enemies in the old monarchies. In the press, the campaign was led by Thiers's old paper, the *National*, and his former colleague and friend, now rapidly becoming an enemy, Armand Carrel, who was impatient to hear ' the cannon of national victories', and to 'settle the quarrel between the old and the new Europe'.[11]

Thiers was watching and waiting, not simply from opportunism, but also because the dilemma in which France was placed existed in his own mind. Like so many of his generation, he felt himself the heir of the Revolution and of the Napoleonic Empire, seen as its glorious culmination. He was one of the creators and beneficiaries of the Revolution of 1830, which seemed, in those first months, not a pale imitation of 1789 but its full-blooded reincarnation. The most enthusiastic supporters of 1830 could see it as a return to the fearsome glories of the 1790s, when France could turn the world upside down and young heroes perform unimaginable feats. Yet Thiers was also a practical man, priding himself on his grasp of reality; he was a man of order and government, excited, as his *History of the Revolution* showed, less by upheaval than by the restoration of order and the creation of a new state upon the ruins of the old: this he had seen as the great achievement of both the Convention and Napoleon. To this intellectual leaning was added the insight of a newly fledged under-secretary at the Ministry of Finance of a state close to bankruptcy, and the prudence of one who was no longer a footloose young journalist but a man with office and property at stake: 'I fear... the results of war for private and public wealth. I am a Councillor of State and a deputy. The King honours me with his favour. I wait, I watch events, quite ready to do my duty if needed. I hate disorder as much as I love liberty. I hope that they do not force us, by humiliating us, into military lunacy.'[12]

Thiers's ambiguous position, and his view that in certain circumstances revolutionary fervour, well directed, might be of value to the regime both internally and externally, was shown in his reaction to the serious rioting of February 1831. This was provoked by a commemoration service held at the church of St Germain l'Auxerrois for the Duc de Berry, assassinated in 1820. The service was interpreted as a demonstration of support for the hated Bourbons. A crowd disrupted the ceremony and sacked the church. The Prefects of the Seine and of Police, both prominent Liberals, made no attempt to control them, and the local mayor – a leading actor in the 1830 Revolution – himself ordered the cross to be pulled down from the church. Other churches were also attacked, and the following day the crowd looted the archbishop's palace. The authorities did not intervene, and pro-government voices in Parliament and the press blamed the trouble on Legitimist provocation. Thiers, having gone to the scene of the rioting, actually ordered a battalion of National Guards not to intervene – an act for which he was later criticized. He had been greatly impressed by the power of the mob and, according to Rémusat, to whom he recounted the incident later that day, he had immediately thought that such power could be used, as Mirabeau, Danton and Napoleon had used it, especially if war came. He also believed that the King should appoint some able and determined Left-wing ministers whom power would make more moderate yet who would have greater dynamism than the Laffitte government could generate. But Louis-Philippe, although he did not wish to break with the Left, had no intention of venturing any further in that direction than Laffitte, as above all he feared war with Europe.[13]

The February riots and the authorities' uncertainty, bad for confidence and for business (government funds had plummeted), led to increasing attacks on the ministry. Laffitte was considering a Cabinet reshuffle that would bring in a greater Left-wing element, and a dissolution of Parliament. This was too much for the King, who had kept Laffitte in office so as not to break with the Left and because he was an easy-going minister who let the King run foreign policy himself. Louis-Philippe resembled Thiers in being clever, talkative and self-opinionated. Confident in his own wide experience, he proved unwilling to yield to any minister in matters vital to the security of his throne. In foreign affairs especially he intended to have the last word.

By March, as street demonstrators clamoured for war with Russia to liberate Poland, Louis-Philippe had decided that Laffitte should go. Thiers, eager to escape his thankless task at the Ministry of Finance, had offered his resignation a month earlier, but it had been refused. Now he agreed to deliver the King's message to Laffitte asking for his resignation – an act many considered ungraceful on the part of protégé to patron.[14]

To replace Laffitte, the King reluctantly summoned Casimir Perier, another banker but one of hard conservative stamp, who declared that 1830 was not a revolution but merely a change in the person of the head of state. Be that as it may, Perier was as determined to reduce the King to a limited constitutional role as he was to clear the streets of revolutionary demonstrators. Although a man with a taste for power, Perier had hesitated to accept office, so serious was the situation: war seemed close as the Poles fought on against Russia, Austrian troops marched against Italian rebels, and negotiations over Belgium were near to breakdown. Internally, the government was seriously challenged by a workers' uprising in Lyons – the first of several. As conditions of his accepting office, Perier imposed control over the King, the other ministers, and the civil service. He also set out to discipline Parliament by calling repeatedly for votes of confidence. This was the first but not the last attempt under the July Monarchy to split the changeable and unattached deputies into stable and identifiable government and opposition groups.

There was much to attract Thiers, with his taste for order and authority and belief in parliamentary government, to this 'policy of Resistance', as it was called. But it did not resolve the conflict within him, for neither politically nor emotionally had he broken with the 'party of Movement'. Believing that war or peace would determine who would rule France, and with war still threatening, he remained watchful and uncommitted during the spring and summer of 1831. Like Thiers, Perier realized that war would mean further revolution, but he was also aware that to survive the regime must show that it could defend French interests, so he risked sending an army to resist the Dutch invasion of Belgium.

Thiers, although he did not hide his uncertainty from his friends, was coming to think that Perier would succeed in maintaining both peace and internal order. During the late summer of 1831, he began to appear in the Chamber as an ally of the government. In August, he supported it in the debate on the King's Speech. In September, he was one of a small group that defended the retention of a hereditary element in the Chamber of Peers. This demonstrated his new conservatism, but it was in fact an idea he had expressed in 1830 in the *National*, and it was a familiar element in the thinking of Liberals who believed that Britain was the historic political model.

His support for Perier's policy of Resistance drew vituperative attacks from the Left. At the end of April 1832, he made a rare visit to his consti-tuency of Aix and his home town of Marseilles. Although the sober electors of Aix offered him a banquet, the rowdier elements organized a *charivari* at his door. In this traditional manifestation of disapproval and mockery, horns were blown, pots and pans rattled and empty barrels banged amid whistling and a torrent of invective – 'Down with the renegade patriot! Down with the traitor to Poland and Italy!' In Marseilles, things took a nastier turn. A demonstration against him was broken up by troops, and the following day he escaped a booing crowd by hastily embarking in a small boat. Rémusat thought that these experiences opened Thiers's eyes to the dangerous character of the party of Movement, causing him to ally himself with the party of Resistance. As has been seen, however, this evolu-tion had been in progress for several months, and if the *charivari* had any importance it was to show publicly his change of position, and help him to gain acceptance by the conservatives and the King.[15]

Already by the spring of 1832, Thiers was a leading member of a group of young deputies who called themselves the 'brigade', among them, Rémusat, Duvergier de Hauranne, Jaubert and Duchâtel. Several of them were to be ministerial colleagues of Thiers's; Duvergier, like Rémusat, was to become a lifelong friend. Although still outside the government, the 'brigade' set themselves to defend its policy. All former opposition jour-nalists under the Restoration, they wished to show that they were capable of more than mere criticism and were able and willing to take responsibility for the state that they had helped to create: 'We felt that the state was our thing', recalled Rémusat, who admitted that in their zeal to defend the new regime, they had 'defended more than one abuse'.[16] In the 'brigade' Thiers began to find his parliamentary feet, taking particular interest in budgetary matters, of which he believed his studies of John Law and of the French Revolution had given him a firm grasp.

His parliamentary debut, as Under-Secretary in the Laffitte government, had not been successful. His small stature, high-pitched nasal voice and Marseilles accent did not lend themselves to the declamatory style of the day: and those who were jealous of his rapid ascent were eager to mock. At first discouraged, he soon began to modify his speaking style (with

Talleyrand's advice, it was said), abandoning great effects in favour of informality. He was an overwhelming and at his best dazzling conversationalist, and he began to talk to the Chamber as he liked to talk in a salon. Thus began one of the great parliamentary careers of that age of oratory, and the effect was rapid, as opponents grudgingly testified. Within a few months Thiers had become one of the government's major parliamentary allies. His airs of self-appointed minister without portfolio were said to annoy Perier; nevertheless the government had his speeches printed and distributed along with those of Perier himself.[17]

The consolidation of the government was interrupted less by riots in Grenoble and a Legitimist rising in the Vendée than by the cholera epidemic that struck Paris during the summer of 1832. Among its victims were Perier and a bellicose orator of the nationalist Left, General Lamarque. The funeral of the latter on 5 June, attended by huge crowds, was exploited by extremist secret societies – Bonapartist, Republican and Legitimist – who, by provoking acts of violence, succeeded in igniting an insurrection in several parts of Paris. Thiers – heedless of cholera – was dining at the famous Rocher de Cancale, close to the principal scene of the fighting. His reaction, very different from that at the time of the anti-clerical riots in 1831, was to help organize the pro-government forces at National Guard headquarters, and advise the King to proclaim martial law.[18] Most of the National Guard, solid citizens tired of disorder, rallied to the government, and crushed the remnants of the rebellion the following day.

Perier had to be replaced in a situation full of danger. Though the Left had been beaten and the Legitimist rising had been a fiasco, neither party had given up its efforts. The dashing Duchesse de Berry, mother of the Legitimist pretender, was at large in the Vendée, hoping that a war over Belgium might afford her another chance to raise revolt. War was indeed possible, for the Dutch refused to evacuate Antwerp, awarded to the new Kingdom of Belgium by an international conference in London. Moreover, Perier's death encouraged the Austrians to take a stronger line in Italy, while in the Middle East France was left a mere spectator as Russia increased her influence over an Ottoman Empire enfeebled by war with its nominal subject, the Pasha of Egypt. In spite of these multiple problems, Louis-Philippe, glad to 'drive his own cab' now that Perier had gone, was acting as his own chief minister and prolonging the interregnum. Guizot and Thiers, as two major parliamentary allies of the Perier government, were brought into the negotiations over the formation of a new ministry. Guizot was unpopular because of his previous association with the Bourbons and his conservative theories of constitutional monarchy; he had therefore to be content with the secondary post of Minister of Public Instruction. Thiers, however, was still too much of a lightweight to arouse much opposition and his talents were useful. So, in his first full ministerial office, he received the important portfolio of the Interior.[19]

He was, however, a Minister of the Interior with a single mission.[20] Local government was removed from his control and, to his annoyance, given to the Minister of Public Works. He had responsibility for internal security only, with a free hand to find the Duchesse de Berry. Although the dangers of a successful Legitimist revolt were small, the Duchess's clandestine presence in France was an irritant, an incentive to plotters, and damaging to the regime's prestige abroad. Moreover, the new government, unpopular with moderates and the Left, wanted to prove that it could deal with the Legitimists. That such responsibility was given to Thiers shows that his colleagues were aware of his ability and determination (for he had special reason to show that in spite of his new conservatism he was still a man of 1830 who would have no truck with Legitimism). But there was probably a less flattering reason that Thiers could only have partly suspected. Catching the Duchess would bring little glory; the Cabinet did not even wish to know how it was done. Thiers, young, still in the second rank politically, with a reputation already tarnished by slander, a man of the lower classes, could be a useful tool for a task to which more distinguished men would not stoop.

Thiers bought the services of a former agent of the Duchess and was quickly put on her track. He realized the embarrassment of using all the might of the state against a young and courageous princess, and leaked warnings to Legitimist sympathizers in the hope of scaring her out of the country. She refused to budge, however, and her arrest became unavoidable. Thiers, characteristically thinking of Napoleon's blunder with the Duc d'Enghien,[21] gave orders that there should be no violence and no accident. On 7 November 1832, she was found in a chimney in a house near Nantes. Wisely, the government decided not to put her on trial, as the Legitimists and the Left wanted, but not daring simply to send her back to Holyrood, as they would have preferred, they interned her at the fortress of Blaye. This was of doubtful legality, but Thiers stoutly defended his action in the Chamber on the grounds of public necessity, and dissuaded the deputies from voting for a trial. The government's embarrassment was alleviated when the widowed Duchess proved to be mysteriously pregnant. This was enough to disillusion her sympathizers, and in June 1833, after the child's birth, she was allowed to leave the country. If not very gloriously, Thiers had strengthened the government, which meanwhile had achieved a more substantial success by sending an expedition to seize Antwerp from the Dutch.

Thiers himself was the butt of bitter attacks from Legitimists, who had the sympathy of many who preferred aristocratic ladies in distress to jumped-up little politicians, and the activities of Thiers's disreputable and importuning family also gave plenty of material for malicious gossip. Unwilling to become the policeman of the regime, he resigned from the Interior and obtained on 1 January 1833 what was to be a congenial field for his non-political interests, the Ministry of Commerce and Public Works. Himself an art critic and enthusiastic collector, he thus became the leading official patron of the arts in France, and he took advantage of it. His major project was to finish the great uncompleted Parisian monuments, including the Arc de Triomphe, the Place de la Concorde, the Pantheon and the Madeleine. Awaiting restoration were several important buildings, such as the basilica of St Denis, the Collège de France, the Palais Bourbon and the Bibliothèque Royale. A Bill for these projects and for provincial roadworks, canals and preparatory work for railways was presented in April 1833. It was a costly programme for the time – 100 million francs over five years – yet Thiers, who combined a liking for spending public money with a devotion to financial orthodoxy, managed to finance it without raising a loan.

He supervised the Parisian buildings with relish, choosing the sculptures for the Arc de Triomphe and commissioning from his friend and protégé Delacroix important murals for the Palais Bourbon.[22] But this great programme was not art for art's sake. Public works created employment. Moreover, he was glad to provide the opportunity for the regime to enjoy some of Napoleon's reflected glory by finishing his buildings and replacing his statue on the Vendôme column. This was done with great ceremony in July, the anniversary of the 1830 revolution, when Thiers, in uniform and on horseback, accompanied the King in saluting the Emperor.

At the same time, the government implemented an important legislative programme – concerning primary education, divorce, and local government – and Thiers, as ever, was eager to speak in the Chamber on a variety of subjects. Meanwhile, in his own department, he had created the first government statistical service. When Parliament was in recess, he bustled off to inspect the industries of the north of France and of England in his first trip across the Channel, where he visited Stourbridge and Sheffield as well as the salons of London. As usual he saw everything, took copious notes, talked to everyone and gave opinions about everything.[23] In June he was elected to the French Academy – a simple process for a distinguished historian who was also a minister. In November 1833 he found time to get married.

This was done in as brisk and businesslike a fashion as anything in his career: he proposed to his bride-to-be the day after her 15th birthday when she came of age; that evening, the civil wedding was performed; next day, the church ceremony; the morning after that, he left on an official tour of the port of Le Havre. This was no sudden passion, but a well-organized alliance, less between Thiers and his bride, Elise Dosne, than between him and the Dosne family. The first step had come with the sale to Thiers in 1830 of the house which made him eligible for the Chamber. The 100,000 francs were due in October 1832. The money was not paid, though no doubt Thiers could have raised it; perhaps it was never really intended to be. Instead it was decided that Thiers should marry the Dosnes' elder daughter. Alexis-André Dosne was delighted when, in October 1833, Thiers wrote asking for her hand: he at once replied giving his blessing – after complaining to Thiers that the income from his Receivership at Brest was poor, and asking for leave of absence with pay. His wife Sophie, by now Thiers's confidante and counsellor, was no doubt even more delighted, for the marriage cemented a relationship that was in some ways to become the most important in both their lives. Mignet tried to dissuade Thiers from the marriage, both because of his 'flightiness' and because of the scandal that might be caused by his friendship with Madame Dosne.[24] Thiers too was worried, and with reason: his enemies, and not a few of his friends, were ready to believe that he had married the daughter of his mistress. It was the scarcely veiled theme of a satirical play, *L'Ecole des journalistes*, and was echoed in the marriage of Balzac's ambitious and unscrupulous character Rastignac who, like Thiers, had come from the provinces to conquer Paris.

No one would have claimed that he married for love, though he seems to have been 'in love' once the marriage was decided: 'I am as nervous as is proper, and I love my young wife more than is proper for a man of my age', he confessed to the Duchesse de Dino, who thought him 'very much in love, very jealous', and found Elise quite pretty but graceless, dull, sulky and seemingly indifferent to her husband.[25] Thiers's infatuation was apparently short lived, and for some years, until she found consolation in celebrity and political influence, she appears to have fitted the stereotype of the victim of an arranged marriage, unhappy, petulant, capricious and in delicate health. They never had children. Yet in many ways the marriage was successful, and by the standards of the time eminently so. To the Dosne family it gave spectacular social ascent, and even though their petty-bourgeois origins were never forgotten (nor was the gossip surrounding the marriage), the Dosne ladies were placed on friendly terms with queens and princesses. To Alexis-André it gave the immensely profitable Tax Receivership of Lille. To Thiers it gave financial security, for although he was careful to keep out of debt (except, of course, to the Dosnes), he was not financially independent, and needed his ministerial salary. The dowry, rumoured to be two million francs, was a more modest though still substantial 300,000. Beyond this, Thiers became for the rest of his life the centre of the Dosne household, with his needs met from the Dosne fortune. As important as financial security was the emotional security that the Dosne women – Sophie, Elise and her younger sister Félicie – gave him. In them, says Pomaret caustically, he had 'l'Administration, la Poupée, l'Admiration' – all he really wanted from women was an audience, a secretariat and a commissariat.[26] It was unquestionably in many ways a lopsided relationship, but there can be no doubt of the loyalty and devotion of Thiers and 'the ladies', whose letters display affection, good humour and mutual concern. The closest bond was that between Thiers and Madame Dosne,

MADAME DOSNE.

Plate 2 Madame Dosne in later years

who became like a mother (his third!) to him, as well as confidential political secretary.[27] She appears to have provided constant support and encouragement rather than political guidance: an *alter ego* rather than an *éminence grise*.

In March 1834 Thiers moved back to the Ministry of the Interior. This followed the resignation of the Liberal pro-British Duc de Broglie from Foreign Affairs, which produced the usual Cabinet crisis as Louis-Philippe tried to obtain a more pliable ministry than that dominated by Guizot, Broglie and Thiers, whom he found uncomfortably like a three-man Casimir Perier. Finally, a government was formed under the titular presidency of Marshal Soult, in which Thiers and Guizot were the real leaders.

Thiers resumed the Interior (this time with local government and economic responsibilities as well as police) in the midst of a crisis. Since their defeats in 1830 and 1832, the extreme Left, from the radical wing of the parliamentary opposition to the semi-clandestine jacobin, socialist and Bonapartist groups, had worked to cover France with newspapers and societies. A potential mass following came from workers whose economic existence was threatened by increased competition, changing work practices and mechanization: 1834 was a year of exceptional strike activity, especially in the skilled trades centred in Paris and Lyons. The government's response was to try to limit the attempts by Left-wing politicians to 'exploit' unrest by legal attacks on their newspapers and associations. In January and February 1834, before Thiers took over the Interior though of course with his support, it introduced Bills extending press restrictions to all publications, forbidding vendors to distribute them without permission, and plugging the loophole by which associations had been able to escape legal restrictions by dividing themselves into sections. These laws provoked an outcry, ostentatious defiance and consequent arrests and riots.[28]

Thiers's appointment was taken as a sign that the government intended to deal toughly with the crisis. Yet at once he proposed public works projects to try to calm workers' unrest: this was one of the few remedies available to nineteenth-century Liberal governments, but it was irrelevant to the plight of skilled workers determined to protect their crafts. Thiers also told the Prefect of Lyons not to 'precipitate a confrontation', while in Paris he refused the Prefect of Police permission to make preventive arrests of the leaders of the revolutionary Société des Droits de l'Homme. However, if the Left went on to the offensive, he gave orders to 'suppress the attempted insurrection with the last ounce of energy you have'.[29] It was to this outcome, despite Thiers's relative caution, that the logic of the situation led.

On 9 April the trial of Lyons workers for belonging to a trade union – such societies being forbidden by the 1791 Le Chapelier law – caused mass demonstrations which turned into armed insurrection. When the news reached Paris by semaphore telegraph, Thiers's first thought was that he and the young Duc d'Orléans, the heir to the throne, should go to the city to direct the battle. However, a false report that the troubles were over changed his mind, and the interruption of telegraphic communications meant that for two days the government was unaware of events in Lyons. Only on 12 April did they learn that the troubles were still serious. News also came of disturbances in Strasbourg and political unrest in the army. It must have been this seeming proof of widespread conspiracy that persuaded Thiers and the Cabinet to make pre-emptive arrests in Paris, for which the new law on associations now gave powers. There were 150 arrests made, and a few barricades were demolished by troops. Leaders of the Société des Droits de l'Homme still at liberty called their men to arms, declaring that Lyons was in rebel hands, and that a provisional Republican government had been proclaimed. During the afternoon of 13 April, barricades were built on both sides of the Seine, and at about 7 p.m. the first shots were fired. Thiers assured the Cabinet that he could control the situation: there were 40,000 troops in Paris under Marshal Bugeaud. The rebels were concentrated in the crowded old central area north-west of the Hôtel de Ville, already the centre of revolt in 1830 and 1832. During the night of the 13th, it was invaded by two columns of troops. Thiers insisted on leading one of the columns, at Bugeaud's side. They came under occasional fire, and one of Thiers's civilian aides was killed. At daybreak, a general attack cleared the remaining barricades. A company of infantry from the other column, searching for a suspected sniper, killed several people in a house in the Rue Transnonain. The 'Massacre in the Rue Transnonain', immortalized in a Daumier lithograph, was a reproach against Thiers for the rest of his life. The next day, 14 April, he was at the Chamber reassuring agitated deputies, calm himself, but, according to Rémusat, making no attempt to calm their anger. He was congratulated on his stern handling of the revolt but refused the offer of a monetary recompense, saying that any money should be distributed to victims.[30]

On 15 April, news came from Lyons that the fighting was finally over. Thiers was determined to take advantage of these military victories to put an end to the Left-wing political societies. He signed an order that insurgents should be tried by the Chamber of Peers. He sent a reassuring dispatch to the Prefect of Bas-Rhin, saying that the law on associations would deal a final blow to the 'factions', and, on learning that the sections of the Droits de l'Homme in still-restive Strasbourg were meeting in permanent session, he ordered all 2,000 men to be arrested. Arrests were also carried out in Paris and Lyons. Thiers intended to prove what conservatives had always asserted: that the unrest was the outcome of conspiracy by political extremists both Republican and (if it could be shown) Legitimist. The trial before the Peers was to demonstrate this, and he ordered the Prefects to find the evidence. The Prefect at Lyons was told to proceed 'as though there were a war' in making searches and harrying all political and workers' societies. As in the hunt for the Duchesse de Berry, Thiers was not afraid to accept responsibility for acting outside the law if necessary. He promised to cover the Prefect's acts, and told him 'to communicate directly to me. I will write to you myself because I do not want any official correspondence in these matters of great moment.' Finally, he conducted an investigation of the Rue Transnonain killings, doing his best to arrange a cover-up.[31]

Public opinion, alarmed by the disorders, was running in favour of the government, and in the June 1834 general elections the government won successes; Thiers himself was elected in three constituencies. The Left was wiped out. However, independents and supporters of the 'Tiers Parti' (a centrist group placing itself between the 'Resistance' majority and the Left) also gained – a sign that some electors felt that revolution had now been defeated and some thaw was possible. A month later, Thiers and Guizot united to eliminate the nominal head of the government, Marshal Soult, who was a political liability and personally disagreeable (he was known to refer to Thiers as *le foutriquet* – 'the runt'). There followed the now habitual struggle between the king and the leading politicans. Thiers and Guizot tried to force him to accept Broglie as head of a new government. He refused, and the manoeuvring began: the Tiers Parti tried to form a government and failed. The King then tried to win Thiers over from his colleagues and form a government with him. Thiers, however, was still committed to his partnership with the Doctrinaires[32] – he knew that he and Guizot made a strong partnership and balanced each other's strengths and weaknesses. He was even ready for a period out of office, for he was once again being heavily criticized, and was vulnerable to attack due to the discreditable doings of his paternal relatives and to a Rabelaisian, harmless but undignified 'orgy' (as the press called it) at the Château of Grandvaux, in which he was said to have been a prominent participant. There followed several months of uncertainty until March 1835, when the King was forced to accept Broglie, with whose policy of *entente* with Britain and coldness towards the continental powers he disagreed. Thiers by now was somewhat unhappy at the Doctrinaires' strength within the government, but Broglie and Guizot were conciliatory, offering a diplomatic mission to Mignet (which that retiring scholar refused) and being assiduously polite to Madame Dosne.[33]

So Thiers remained at the Interior. In April 1835, the trial of the insurgents began and was to last two years, giving them a platform for their attacks on the regime. July was the anniversary of the 1830 Revolution. The King, accompanied by a numerous staff of ministers, officers and officials (among them Thiers, on horseback and in uniform complete with cocked hat), was reviewing the National Guard in the Boulevard du Temple when a volley of musketry rang out from an upstairs window. It came from an 'infernal machine' of musket barrels fastened to a frame and fired simultaneously.

The King was barely scratched. Thiers's white trousers were splashed with blood but he was untouched. Fourteen people were killed and twenty-two wounded. The would-be assassin was at once arrested. He was Joseph Fieschi, a former Bonapartist connected with the Société des Droits de l'Homme.[34] Strong public reaction against yet another assassination attempt, and the realization among the political class that even after the defeat of the Lyons and Paris insurrections the regime was not safe, gave the government support for new repressive measures, the 'September Laws', which were principally Thiers's work. The most important were aimed at the Republican and Legitimist press: new offences were defined (insulting the King, adhering to the Republic), penalties increased, and legal procedures altered to facilitate conviction. The revolutionary Left, with their societies outlawed and their press now broken, were reduced to impotence. Besides, with the propertied classes tired of upheaval, the rural population largely indifferent, the artisans of Lyons and Paris beaten, and unemployment alleviated by a period of economic growth, the times did not favour them. Thiers's last months at the Interior were quiet. He had done what was expected of him, actively suppressing disorder, and setting up public works to create employment. He had shown no particular imagination or flexibility, though there was little room for them. For the regime and its enemies had no common ground, nor did they seek any. Whenever political or social crisis loomed, the political imagination was filled not with projects of reform but with memories of the wars and upheavals of the 1790s, to which one side looked back with horror, the other with nostalgia. Such a political and ideological context left little place for gradual reform and compromise, much for revolt and repression. However, with the threat from the extreme Left now apparently defeated, Thiers himself soon became the instrument by which the embattled Resistance majority was broken up and a movement of conciliation made towards the moderate Left, the party of Movement.

On 5 February 1836, the Broglie government resigned after defeat on a technical financial matter. Their fall had been engineered by the Tiers Parti, the centrist group led by Dupin, which wanted to see an end to Doctrinaire dominance, new men in office, and less intransigence in domestic policy. Louis-Philippe too was glad to see the break up of the trio Broglie, Guizot and Thiers, and Broglie's elimination. The usual round of negotiations to form a new government took place, but probably the King was aiming throughout at a Thiers ministry. This would give an appearance of a new departure in domestic policy, Thiers being one of the leading men of 1830, but with no risk of weakness from a man who had crushed revolt and passed the September Laws. On foreign policy, Thiers's views had moved towards those of the King, largely under the influence of Talleyrand, who was disillusioned with the *entente* with Britain and urged *rapprochement* with Austria. Talleyrand had worked to persuade Thiers and others that Thiers could bring this about and reconcile Europe with the July Monarchy; to the

King he presented Thiers as a usable mouthpiece for royal policy.[35] He was still regarded as a useful man, but not as a weighty political figure in his own right. At first Thiers refused to consider forming a government, hesitating to break with his former colleagues and perhaps doubtful of success. However, great efforts of persuasion were made by the King, Talleyrand, Thiers's political friends and members of the Left opposition – enough to change 'a firmer, more austere and more faithful heart'[36] than that of such an ambitious young politician whose personal relations with the haughty and high-minded Doctrinaires were cool. He asked Broglie to consent to his taking office. Broglie answered that he was quite free to do so; but he is said to have warned Louis-Philippe of the dangers of making Thiers prime minister, fearing that if ever such a clever and ambitious man had to be dismissed, he would become a dangerous opponent.

Thiers took office on 22 February 1836. From the beginning his position was delicate. The proclaimed defender of parliamentary government, he owed his rise in part to royal favour, and two of his ministers were staunch allies of the King. Three others came from the Tiers Parti (about 120 men) and from the vague 'Centres', many of whom were supporters of any government that enjoyed the King's favour. This, however, did not give a majority: he also needed support from some of the hundred or so Doctrinaires – but he had excluded them from office for the first time in five years – or from the seventy men of the Dynastic Left. At first there was no problem: the King's followers and the Tiers Parti were dependable; the Doctrinaires were not hostile; and the Dynastic Left were delighted to see a government without the Doctrinaires. But it was a majority liable to break up if controversy arose. Consequently, Thiers's strategy was to steer a middle course, avoid controversy and attempt by word and deed to please the various groups by what was nicknamed a *politique de bascule* (seesaw policy).[37] Thiers hoped to be able to persuade at least part of the Right that no dangerous changes were being made and that order would be maintained, while satisfying at least part of the Left that a watershed had been reached, and that, however gradually, the government was ready to relax the policies of Resistance and make concessions. Thiers's mouthpiece, the *Constitutionnel* declared that 'the new government... must help to heal the nation's wounds and calm its hatreds', supported by those deputies who had 'broken with the harsh policy of recent governments'.[38] At the same time, Thiers pursued a busy programme of practical legislation (a vitally important Bill on local roads, and measures on railways and tariffs) which kept the Chamber occupied with non-partisan matters important to the material interests of deputies and their constituents.[39] They were questions on which Thiers loved to show his expertise.

More than this was needed to consolidate an unstable majority. Thiers needed success in foreign policy. He had for some time been tempted to take a more active part in diplomacy. His ambition to master the workings of high politics and his parvenu's taste for treating with princes over the great affairs of Europe were certainly stimulated. But there was more here than short-term parliamentary tactics or individual ambition. The inter-relation of foreign and domestic policy was a vital question. Thiers believed that no government, and no regime, could long survive in France unless it could play a world role able to stand comparison with the glories of a past uncomfortably recent and alive. Such patriotic gestures as completing the Arc de Triomphe or replacing Napoleon's statue on the Vendôme Column could try to establish the July Monarchy as the inheritor of the glories of the Revolution and Empire, but only a successful foreign policy could consolidate it. This belief was widely shared. As has been seen, the extreme Left was vehemently nationalistic. Men of the moderate Left such as Barrot and Tocqueville saw diplomatic success as a necessary buttress of the sort of regime they advocated, which would otherwise sooner or later be swept away by revolution.[40] Many conservatives agreed. Casimir Perier had ordered intervention in Belgium and Italy; while the Restoration had sent expeditions to Spain, Greece and Algiers. Among the leading statesmen, Louis-Philippe was least tempted by foreign adventures, believing that if war came it would be disastrous and inevitably revolutionary, as in 1792. In this he could be sure of the support of politicians who thought more of the immediate interests of the stock market and trade than of winning laurels for the July Monarchy. His heir the Duc d'Orléans, however, favoured assertiveness, more impressed perhaps by the rise of Napoleon than by the fall of Louis XVI.

When Thiers came to power in February 1836, however, he and the King were in agreement: their priority was to find a bride for the Duc d'Orléans, if possible a Habsburg princess. Marriage would consolidate the dynasty, for its continuation, once grandchildren came, would depend less and less on Louis-Philippe's life, so often the target of assassins. Marriage would also break the unity of the conservative monarchies against the upstart of 1830, help to reintegrate France into the European system, and make war less likely. While Thiers shared these aims, he also calculated that a *rapprochement* with Austria would increase France's freedom of action. No longer dependent on the *entente* with Britain to keep her from diplomatic isolation, she would be an equal partner in the diplomatic game, able to assert her own interests in Spain rather than being the instrument of British interests, and – if circumstances were favourable – able to bargain with Britain and Russia when each sought her support against the other. Then the prize might be a glittering one indeed: the end of the 1815 straitjacket, with the gain perhaps of the 'natural frontiers' in the Alps and on the Rhine.

The royal family and Thiers decided to pursue the Habsburg marriage without delay, and the Duc d'Orléans and his brother left in May to show themselves to advantage in Berlin and Vienna. This was the second approach in just over a year, the first having failed in March 1835 (when

Thiers was still at the Interior) after Metternich politely indicated that the time was not ripe. Now, however, the King and the Duc d'Orléans were determined to break through Metternich's evasiveness, and in case of refusal conclude a 'little marriage' with a less august House. Thiers hoped to bring off the Habsburg marriage by adroit diplomacy; Talleyrand and other oracles were convinced that a *rapprochement* with France was in Austria's interest, for it would help her to defend her Near Eastern position against Russia.[41]

Thiers was willing to be conciliatory to the continental powers: he warned Switzerland to expel Left-wing refugees; protested weakly when independent Cracow was occupied by Austrian, Prussian and Russian troops; and took no action to support the Constitutionalist government in Spain against Carlist rebels. These were concessions more of form than of substance: the hard words to Switzerland had no concrete effect; Poland was beyond aid (as Thiers had always said); and in Spain, where he had been a consistent advocate of French intervention (both to assert French influence and to defend a friendly Liberal regime), his intention was merely to defer action until the *rapprochement* with Austria was sealed by matrimony and France was in a stronger position to carry out her own policy.[42]

The situation suddenly changed in August when the Austrians finally refused the marriage on the pretext that yet another attempt on the King's life had shown that Paris was too dangerous for a Habsburg princess. Thiers and the King had been prepared for the refusal, which confirmed them in their growing contempt for the Austrians. Sour grapes apart, they had misjudged Austrian policy, which aimed to weaken the French *entente* with Britain, but not to create a French *entente* with themselves. French statesmen never grasped the suspicion of French ambitions shared by all the other Powers. Thiers set out to make a virtue of necessity. He still needed a diplomatic success, for he had no wish to appear before the country as the author of a policy of *rapprochement* with the 'Holy Alliance' which would displease the Left and had anyway failed. He could see the advantage that could be drawn from a 'little marriage' with a non-Habsburg, presented as a sign that the July Monarchy had not renounced its revolutionary origins. Most important, he could return to a more active policy of aid to the Liberal government in Spain. He had consistently – even before 1830 – argued that the assertion of influence in the Peninsula was a historic French interest. It was now a way of repaying the Austrian snub, winning the support the government needed at home – 'I'll recuperate in Spain' – and strengthening ties with Britain by suggesting joint action.[43] If the King refused to accept this policy, Thiers could leave office as a patriotic statesman thwarted by royal intransigence.

In May 1836, a pro-French government came to power in Madrid, but was soon under attack from both Carlist reactionaries and radicals. Thiers pressed for intervention against the latter, enlisting the support of the Duc d'Orléans, the King of the Belgians and the British government to try to overcome Louis-Philippe's reluctance.[44] Neither the King nor Thiers wished to precipitate another Cabinet crisis, and as a compromise they agreed that while there should be no direct intervention, the Foreign Legion, already lent to Spain, should be reinforced and that French volunteers could serve with the Spanish forces. Thiers, in direct contact with the officer commanding, tried secretly to increase the size of the Foreign Legion beyond the figure agreed by the King – 'I take that on myself.'[45] On 16 August, after the King refused to appoint Marshal Bugeaud to command the force, Thiers offered his resignation in a long, emotional and outspoken letter: 'There is no place in the world for a system of weakness... To wish to avoid perils at any price is not prudence but self-deception... One conquers security with courage. The King is personally very brave; may I, must I, tell him that he is less so in mind than in body.' France would lose Spain and the British alliance, he argued, and the reaction of the Chambers and the electorate to foreign policy failures in Austria and Spain would be bad. While protesting his affection for the King, he ended by saying that he wished 'to reserve myself to serve him when we are completely in agreement. I do not know when I shall be his minister again; perhaps never.'[46] But the resignation was withdrawn when a Left-wing army mutiny in Spain brought a government to power on whose behalf neither Thiers nor the King was ready to intervene. Thiers, however, continued to build up forces on French soil, and it was the King's insistence at the end of August that these should be disbanded – which Thiers regarded as 'the beginning of the total abandonment of Spain' – that finally brought his resignation on 26 August.[47]

Thiers's defeat meant a rapid loss of French influence in Spain, and problems for the future when Guizot tried to restore it in the 1840s. From this point of view, Thiers's policy had been correct: intervention was necessary if France was to maintain a voice in Madrid, and a friendly Liberal government on her borders. Such a policy would not have been resisted by the continental powers and could have strengthened the *entente* with Britain. A problem that Thiers never faced, however, was the practicality of military intervention: while the King and many others were alarmed by the precedent of the 'Spanish ulcer' in the 1800s, he was content to assert that military intervention would be easily effective, as in 1823. His assertion was never tested, for no government was strong enough to carry out such a risky and potentially unpopular policy. Cabinets would be divided on the issue, the Chamber of Deputies – strongly aware of the costs and risks of war to the property-owning class – would be unlikely to support it, and so the King could make his view prevail. Thiers's supporters, strong in the Parisian press and the progressive urban middle class, carried little weight on such an issue in Parliament.[48]

The major consequences of Thiers's first government were, however, in domestic politics. His acceptance of office split the 'Resistance' coalition, and the circumstances of his fall widened the split. He now became leader of an enlarged Left-Centre in Parliament, made up of Tiers Parti men and some followers attracted from both Right and Left. The group was characterized by youth and ambition, and had relaxation of Resistance and a bolder foreign policy as its programme. For Thiers personally, in Rémusat's opinion, the attainment of supreme office at the age of 38 was to prove a liability, which he later regretted. He had now either to lead a government or remain out of office: for most of the next 35 years, it was the latter.[49]

The dissolution of the Resistance coalition began a period of parliamentary impotence and growing royal authority. After Thiers's resignation, the King appointed a government of whom the leading members were Molé and Guizot. This lasted from September 1836 to March 1837, when Guizot's resignation led to the usual ministerial crisis. After the customary negotiations the King reappointed Molé, a peer without any personal following in the Chamber of Deputies, who was able to remain in power for nearly two years because he was the King's man. His parliamentary support came from conservatives who wanted stability at home and peace abroad – Louis-Philippe's natural allies – and included a sizeable contingent of civil servants, businessmen and bankers, especially from the southern half of the country and from the northern and eastern industrial fringes. This gave Molé nearly half the Chamber, and, with the opposition parties divided and the government confining its legislation mainly to technical matters, he was able to govern. During the summer recess of 1838, some Doctrinaires, led by Duvergier de Hauranne, began a press campaign urging a united attack by all the opposition parties on the government. Neither Thiers, who was in Italy, nor any of the other party leaders were involved until the opening of the next session, when they took over the movement organized by their followers. For the first time, all the opposition groups from Legitimists to crypto-Republicans were prepared to join in the attack, though the big battalions of the 'Coalition', as it was called, were Thiers's Left-Centre (now sixty-two men), Barrot's Dynastic Left (sixty-five) and – the new and vital reinforcement – Guizot and thirty Doctrinaires. The Coalition was criticized as a cynical attack of 'outs' against 'ins', and ambition certainly played a part. But it was also an attack by parliamentary politicians against the royal prerogative (nine of the eleven former ministers in the Chamber joined the Coalition) and by all the parties identifiable by some ideological label against the amorphous 'ministerial Centre'.[50]

The attack reached its climax in the debate on the Address, the reply to the King's Speech, the greatest political set-piece of the parliamentary calendar and on this occasion one of the great parliamentary battles of the July Monarchy.[51] The Coalition had its leaders – including Thiers, Guizot, Passy and Duvergier de Hauranne – elected to the commission which drafted the Address, which was in consequence unambiguously critical of foreign policy and the royal prerogative, calling for a 'prudent and firm' policy 'making the dignity of your Throne respected abroad', and a government founded on powers 'contained within their constitutional limits' with the Crown covered by the 'responsibility' of ministers. The debate lasted twelve days (7–19 January 1839), the attack being led by Guizot (who spoke twelve times), Thiers (thirteen times), Duvergier and Barrot. The burden of defence was borne by Molé (who spoke seventeen times) powerfully aided by an unexpected ally, Lamartine. Thiers, as usual, was combative and witty; Guizot was unusually violent, provoking an outraged reaction from government supporters. The Coalition accused the government of weakness abroad. Thiers blamed their failure to maintain the alliance with England: 'from this stems your weakness in Belgium, your timidity in Italy'. This was an implied attack on Louis-Philippe, who was known to exercise a veto in foreign policy and to aim at closer links with the European powers (a policy which Thiers had briefly tried to carry out with the Austrian marriage project). The passage of the Address concerning constitutional limits was an open attack on what one of Thiers's journalist allies called 'the most stubbornly self-confident and least constitutional prince in the world'. At the end of the debate, Molé scraped a majority of 221 to 208, but regarding this as inadequate, he resigned.

After an approach to Soult that was merely a matter of form, the King dissolved the Chamber, and in the ensuing March 1839 elections Molé's supporters lost their slim majority. This was a defeat for Louis-Philippe. The Coalition, however, which was united only in its opposition to Molé and the Crown prerogative, proved unable after long negotiation to agree on a government. Thiers, who would only accept office on terms unacceptable to Guizot or the King, was a major obstacle; and although the Left-wing press blamed Louis-Philippe for the long ministerial crisis, many of the Centre-Left blamed Thiers and broke with him. No viable government had been formed when, on 12 May, the clandestine Left-wing Société des Saisons, encouraged by the political crisis, staged an armed rising in Paris. This enabled the King to form an emergency government under Soult, with the participation of the anti-Thiers faction of the Centre-Left. Thus the King regained the political authority and initiative that the parliamentary and electoral success of the Coalition had threatened to deny him, but at the cost of openly entering the political fray. His clashes with Thiers brought the role of the monarch into the forefront of national politics, with dangerous consequences for the regime. Thiers's motives in raising obstacles to the formation of a Coalition government are obscure, but they had culminated in his political defeat. The new government was, Duvergier said, a Centre-Left government made against Thiers. He also failed to be elected to the Presidency of the Chamber, thanks to the opposition of the 'ministerial Centre', the Doctrinaires, and the dissident Left-Centre.[52]

Thiers was impatient to continue the fight, but although most of the press was hostile to the government, he could find little enthusiasm in the Chamber for more instability. Moreover Guizot was now prepared to defend the government. So, with little chance of a speedy return to power, Thiers began a major project, the *History of the Consulate and Empire*, a fruit of his devotion to the progressive nationalist cause, and the means by which he would draw for the French nation the political lessons of the Empire. It also provided useful cash, now that a ministerial salary seemed remote.

In January 1840, however, historical research was dropped as an unexpected political opportunity presented itself. The government proposed a financial endowment for one of the King's sons, the Duc de Nemours. This aroused a wave of opposition inside and outside Parliament, a combination of resentment against the Crown born of the political struggles of the past few years and simple parsimony among government supporters. Thiers, while despising the latter feeling, seized his opportunity. On 20 February 1840, in a secret vote and without debate, the opposition, organized secretly by Thiers, and reinforced by forty defectors from the government side, defeated the Bill by six votes, administering a resounding slap in the face to the Crown. 'It is like Constantinople', complained a defeated minister. 'We have been strangled by mutes.' 'That', he was told, 'is often the fate of eunuchs.'[53] The King had no choice but to call on Thiers.

[4]

The Syrian Gamble, 1840

Thiers's return to power on 1 March 1840 marked, in Molé's opinion, 'a new era' in which government would move to the Left.[1] It was a resumption of the policy of 1836, by which Thiers intended to replace the permanent conservative majority in the Chamber with one of the centre, drawing on the support of the moderate Left. This time, however, Thiers had come to power not with royal favour, but after the defeat in the Chamber of a government supported by the King who had been snubbed personally and seen his use of the royal prerogative forthrightly criticized. Moreover, the Dynastic Left was eager to play its part in Thiers's new majority. In these circumstances, certain prominent conservatives refused to join the new Cabinet. This suited Thiers, who was thus free to form a Cabinet of new men of which he, as president and foreign minister, was the undoubted master. His colleagues came from that part of the Left-Centre that had remained with him in spite of his refusal of office after the Coalition of 1839, and from the progressive wing of the Doctrinaires, most notably Rémusat as Minister of the Interior. Their presence helped to reassure potential supporters on the Right and to persuade Guizot, the newly appointed ambassador in London, to stay at his post, where he was no political danger.

Since the mid-1830s respectable arguments had been made out for the creation of such a centrist government: that the social and political dangers that had followed 1830 had now passed; that a policy of Resistance was no longer needed; that the time was ripe to heal the wounds of the political nation. This, in the jargon of the day, was called 'transaction'. As Rémusat put it in a circular to the prefects, 'the government... has clearly announced that its policy would be one of transaction... You could not possibly approve any language [in the government-subsidized press] which was not that of conciliation and the bringing together of the parties.'[2]

There was, of course, a less idealistic side to this policy. If the 'transaction' succeeded, Thiers and his allies would have smashed the old parliamentary balance and made themselves masters of the Chamber. Moreover, there was in it an element of duplicity: while announcing its benevolence to the Left, the government was quietly reassuring the Right. Rémusat wrote to Guizot that 'it is clear that it will seem. . . especially for the first month, to be moving to the Left. These will be the appearances. . . but I answer for the reality on the essential points' – which were to refuse electoral reform and the dissolution of Parliament. Thiers was willing to tell the Right that he regarded his new government as a reincarnation of the old Resistance coalition 'astride the Channel', including his old ally Guizot in London, and at the same time tell the Left that what he was really doing was neutralizing Guizot and the Doctrinaires.[3] As in 1836, Thiers planned to rally his majority by a 'national' foreign policy. He was later to say that this had been understood as part of the bargain: 'I accept your honorable support. . . in giving you a common theme that you can all openly accept.'[4]

The first parliamentary test of confidence was the debate on the secret service funds. Thiers's opponents planned an attack, hoping to rally Molé's supporters, many Doctrinaires and dissidents of the Left-Centre. In his defence Thiers firmly upheld the principle of the new government, welcoming the support of the Dynastic Left as a worthy party of government: 'I have no prejudice against any party. . . I do not believe that there is here one party exclusively devoted to order and another devoted to disorder. . . There must be no exclusions', for that had been the fatal error of the Restoration. The Left was eager to grasp this outstretched hand, and, in spite of bitter attacks from Lamartine on the Right and Garnier-Pagès on the extreme Left, who implied that the Dynastic Left was letting itself be both corrupted and duped, its leader Odilon Barrot promised his support for the government in the name of patriotism and good sense. When the vote came, the government won a suprisingly large majority: 246 to 160. 'It is inconceivable', said Louis-Philippe to Thiers. 'Where did you find them?' 'Where no one had ever been to look for them', he replied – in other words, on the Left.[5] But apart from Barrot's supporters, Thiers had also won the grudging votes of the dissident Left-Centre and about sixty conservatives, who preferred to keep the new government in office rather than face a period of renewed political uncertainty. In this they reflected the view of business circles, which were becoming reconciled to Thiers's experiment: a fortnight after his arrival in office, share prices and the *rente*, which had fallen when the Soult government resigned, recovered. The hostile 160 were made up of about 140 resolute Molé conservatives and Doctrinaires, and about 20 Legitimists and Radicals.[6]

In spite of his parliamentary victory, Thiers could by no means relax. The expectations of his disparate supporters had somehow to be satisfied, or Lamartine's prediction that his 'false equilibrium' could not last would be fulfilled.[7] In part this could be done by a careful choice of words both in parliamentary debate and in private, when Thiers buttonholed deputies in order to make 'individual conquests' for the government by means of flattery, persuasion and patronage. The Left, starved of these delights, was gratified with a 'veritable administrative purge' in its favour, with the removal of unfriendly prefects and the appointment to administrative and judicial office of Left-wing notables and their clients.[8] The 'balancing act' also featured more resounding political gestures: extension of an existing amnesty for political offences (to please the Left); expressions of support for the French protégé Mehemet Ali, the Pasha of Egypt (to please the nationalist Left) coupled with criticism of Great Britain (to please the Right); the project to bring Napoleon's remains from St Helena to Paris (to please nationalists, especially on the Left); and Thiers's emphatic rejection (to please the Right) of a selection of electoral reforms presented with a petition to Parliament in May.[9]

Part of Thiers's strategy was, as in 1836, 'to occupy the Chamber for the rest of the session with... measures of material interest'.[10] An impressive number of Bills was introduced, several of great importance, which could be expected to attract support across party lines. They also accorded with Thiers's liking for spending public money, especially at a time of economic slump. Measures voted included improvement of inland waterways so important to the French economy, harbour building at Saint-Nazaire, the establishment of a steamship service to North America, the renewal of the status of the Bank of France, and the first state guarantee of interest on railway bonds. Modernizing and favourable to business, these measures appealed to the Left. Thiers threw himself into the debates with his usual energy and mastery of business, speaking thirty-two times (without counting the budget debates) during the remaining three months of the session: 'never have I taken such pains', he wrote in June, relieved that 'in one week I shall be free of the Chambers'.[11] Thus the government reached the haven of the parliamentary recess without accident, though there were many critics who doubted that such piloting could be repeated.

Thiers's policy of 'transaction' has been frequently criticized, either on the grounds that there was a fundamental political cleavage between Right and Left and to attempt to bridge it was unprincipled and dangerous (a conservative criticism of the time and for some decades afterwards), or more generally that it was cynical and motivated by the crudest self-seeking. The first criticism is difficult to maintain: there was much common ground between moderate conservatives and the Dynastic Left, and to exclude the latter would add dangerously to the tensions of the following decade. The second criticism is partly accurate but largely irrelevant. In the French system, although it was in some ways less openly corrupt than the British, no politician who held office (and few who did not) had entirely clean hands. The centralized state placed vast powers of patronage in the hands of ministers, who all used them to influence a small electorate for whom local and personal interests weighed heavily. Thiers was not exceptional in these matters. His motives, however, were judged harshly. Certainly, he enjoyed intrigue and manipulation; he had a frank appetite for power, as had many leading politicians brought to prominence in 1830; and he was openly indifferent to much of the political ideology of his contemporaries, which he dismissed as mere prejudice, irrelevant to the real business of running the country. In all this he displayed a careless effrontery which made him vulnerable. He encountered too that mixture of snobbery and calumny which had already done him harm. He fitted one of the stereotypes of that period of economic growth and political and social change: the man from nowhere who succeeds too quickly, the type of Balzac's character Rastignac, or even the stock villain of popular melodrama Robert Macaire. Thus his motives were inevitably interpreted unfavourably: he was described as 'a man who arrived from the South poor, with immense ambition', a man 'utterly without convictions, but full of pride, of ambitious desires and of thirst for gold'.[12] Thiers was not the only politician who was the butt of such attacks; indeed, following the 1839 Coalition politicians in general tended to be tarred with the same brush, and even the high-minded Guizot was accused, with equal injustice, of corrupting Parliament. But Thiers's personal reputation was particularly bad, and in 1836 and 1840 he simply did not have the political or moral stature to be taken at face value when trying to reconstruct the pattern of politics, as he was to do in very different circumstances in the 1870s.

The new government was not to have an easy passage. The country was suffering the effects of an international economic depression – a combination of a new type of financial crash, which had spread from the United States and Britain, and the old type of general slump caused by bad weather and harvests. Latent discontent was to break out in strikes and demonstrations during the summer of 1840. It was foreign problems, however, which brought the government to grief. In 1839 there had been a resurgence of the Eastern Question caused by an outbreak of fighting in the Ottoman Empire between the Sultan and his over-mighty subject Mehemet Ali, the Pasha of Egypt, who had gained control of much of Arabia, the whole of the Levant to the borders of Asia Minor, and Crete. When an Egyptian army routed the Sultan's forces in April 1839, the Great Powers decided, partly at French instigation, to act together to save the Turkish Empire from collapse.[13] Soult's government – in which Louis-Philippe was known to have a strong voice in foreign policy – had associated France with this action, signing a collective Note to the Ottoman Porte on 27 July 1839 announcing their intention to impose a settlement, which meant in practice that the Great Powers collectively would protect the Sultan against Mehemet Ali. The French government, however, in fact favoured Mehemet Ali, and their true intention had been to delay action by the Great Powers, while encouraging a direct settlement between the Sultan and Mehemet Ali which would favour the latter.

During the summer and autumn of 1839, negotiations between the Great Powers were pursued in London, and the British Foreign Secretary, Lord

Palmerston, repeatedly urged the Soult government to join in collective action. The French refused, in spite of concessions profferred to Mehemet Ali by Palmerston. Privately, the French foreign ministry thought that at the very least they could hold up any action by the Powers and extract further concessions for Mehemet Ali. It was the orthodox view in France that the other four Powers – and especially the arch-rivals Britain and Russia – would not succeed in coming to a workable agreement in the face of French opposition.[14]

While France had large and well-established commercial interests in Egypt and the Levant, they alone were not enough to explain the pro-Egyptian line taken by successive French governments with the support of a public opinion as vocal as in the Belgian crisis of 1831. Part of the explanation was the desire not to permit France to be treated as of no account by the other Powers. In addition, Mehemet Ali enjoyed a special source of popularity. He was seen in France as a late-developing disciple of the French Revolution, the seeds of which had been taken to Egypt by Napoleon in his much romanticized expedition. Mehemet, inspired by French 'imported civilization', his defenders asserted, had transformed Egypt into a modern state, and was capable of rejuvenating the whole Turkish Empire; moreover, he would remain the protégé and friend of France, a valuable counterweight to Britain and Russia. 'The question of Egypt', the Legitimist Berryer told the Chamber, 'is a question of life and death... for France.'[15]

The Left-wing parties in particular were eager to encourage support for Mehemet Ali. Since the July Revolution they had been pressing for a 'national' foreign policy to strengthen France's external security, to unite the French people at home and to prevent the July Monarchy from declining into a materialistic, degenerate and despised regime. The monarchy could not endure, said Tocqueville in 1839, 'if the idea is allowed to grow that we, once a strong and great nation... now intervene nowhere... and allow everything to go on without us... such an idea would be more fatal to us than the loss of twenty battles, and... [would] lead to the burial of the monarchy itself beneath the ruins of our national honour'.[16]

Thiers had special reason to take an interest in Egypt. With its traces of an ancient civilization and its links with Napoleon, in whose footsteps he could once more try to follow, it was bound to appeal to his imagination. As a strong advocate of French expansion in North Africa, and as the leading 'national' statesman setting out to establish a new popular government, he thought it was the moment to sound the patriotic theme. He had done so in January 1840, before coming to power, in an important speech in the Chamber. In this he tried to reconcile his position as a supporter of the alliance with Britain with the widespread patriotic wish to aid Mehemet Ali, by asserting (erroneously, as events would show) that fundamental French and British interests in the Middle East coincided, and that frank

and friendly discussion between the two governments could resolve difficulties complicated by the blunder of the Soult government in involving the
other Great Powers. He ended with a patriotic flourish which, in the context,
was an appeal to the Left for support in a future government:

> Give me back, M. Barrot has said, the enthusiasm of 1830. I promise my
> country to give back to it that enthusiasm of 1830... just as great, just as
> fine, just as unanimous; but on one condition: have a great patriotic interest,
> a great motive of national honour, and you will see... that fine enthusiasm
> of the first days of our revolution reappear.[17]

Yet although Thiers and his close allies such as Duvergier de Hauranne, his
supporters, who included Barrot and Tocqueville, and the Left-wing press
– the *Constitutionnel* and the *Siècle* in the lead – were eager to find a
patriotic cause, it was not they who manufactured the Eastern Crisis of
1840 or the popular support for Egypt. As has been pointed out, they
inherited the essentials of the problem from Soult, and soon found that
Egypt was not merely a party slogan, but a universal concern of the whole
political nation. 'There is no government, indeed no dynasty,' wrote
Tocqueville to Thiers, 'that would not be exposing itself to destruction if
it wished to persuade this country to stand idly by while Russia and England
put an end by force to the quarrel of the Pasha and the Sultan, and brought
about the ruin of the former.'[18] Thiers's government did no more than
follow the general tide of opinion, and continue the policy they had
inherited: 'I defy him to invent anything new', wrote one diplomat.[19]

On taking office, Thiers made brief overtures to the British government,
on the lines of his January speech, hoping that his known support of close
relations with Britain might win concessions. The distance between the two
governments, however, was too wide to be so easily bridged. The problem
was Syria.[20] Palmerston believed that the Sultan's power could only be
preserved if Mehemet Ali gave up Syria, in return for the hereditary possession of Egypt; the French believed that he was strong enough to hold Syria,
and that the Sultan and the Powers could be brought to acquiesce. Like his
predecessors, Thiers turned down Palmerston's suggested compromises in
the expectation that further concessions would follow. His argument to
other governments had become a familiar one on French lips: the impossibility of forcing Mehemet Ali into excessive concessions lest he march on
Constantinople and 'set the East and the West on fire'.[21] Louis-Philippe too
was eager to expatiate before foreign diplomats on the formidable military
strength of 'the new Alexander', Mehemet Ali. But it was largely bluff: 'I say
that the Pasha is invincible', Thiers told his consul-general in Alexandria.
'I speak very loudly at the tribune of the support France intends to give him;
but all that is said for Europe.' In reality, Thiers knew that Mehemet Ali
was not invulnerable, especially against four Great Powers if they finally
acted against him; he feared that Syria might be induced to rebel against the

Egyptians; and he feared the more distant possibility of Russian troops invading Syria overland through Armenia and Mesopotania. Moreover, he did not intend to give Mehemet Ali military support, and made sure that he knew it. His intention was to 'secure him a few months respite', and to do this he was prepared to risk France's being diplomatically isolated. But these few months must be used by Mehemet Ali to come to terms with the Sultan, whom the French believed was ready to compromise, and thus forestall the action of the Great Powers. Mehemet Ali must be pressed to show 'wisdom and moderation'; he must offer the Sultan territorial concessions; 'we shall not risk our alliance with England by supporting inflated pretensions'.[22]

Thiers continued this policy from March to July, during which time the Eastern Question was out of the French headlines, and the government concentrated on its energetic display of domestic activity. By the beginning of July, Thiers believed the game nearly won. 'We have prevented everything by our inertia alone'; the other governments, aware of the danger of breaking with France and the difficulties of taking military action in the Middle East, were, he believed, ready to acquiesce in Mehemet Ali's being given by the Sultan hereditary possession of Egypt and life possession of Syria. 'This plan has not yet been proposed to us, but we know that it will be, and we also know that it is the final concession we can hope for.' Thiers believed this to be a sufficient victory both for France and for Mehemet Ali.[23]

Thiers's optimism was soon shattered. On 15 July, Britain, Russia, Austria, Prussia and Turkey signed a Convention in London which amounted to an ultimatum to Mehemet Ali: unless he accepted the Sultan's offer of hereditary possession of only the southern part of Syria, the Powers would use force against him. This was far less than Thiers had expected as a final offer – the whole of Syria for life. Moreover, it ended his hope of forestalling the Powers by arranging a direct agreement between Mehemet Ali and the Sultan – indeed, news from Constantinople of this attempt by the French had helped to provoke the ultimatum. 'The mine, in short, by which M. Thiers meant to blow up Lord Palmerston was met by a counter-mine which blew up M. Thiers.'[24] Thiers could not have been too surprised: he had for several months been aware that the other Powers might act without France, and if necessary had been willing to accept that. On 17 July, just before the news of the Convention reached the French government, he had warned Alexandria that 'some undesirable resolution, harmful to the peace of Europe... is being prepared in London'. Both he and Guizot, however, had thought that they still had time in hand, and, more important, expected merely to receive a Note from the Powers once more asking France to adhere to collective action.[25] Instead, they were informed that a Convention had been signed without them – testimony to the annoyance of the other Powers that Thiers had tried to outwit them. Thiers's and Guizot's misjudgement of the situation was probably due to their reliance on the good will of pro-French elements on the Left of the Whig party and within the British Cabinet, and on the moderating influence of Austria and Prussia.

The signature of the Convention, interpreted as a studied insult and a return to the anti-French alliance of 1814, caused an immense public outcry in France. The Prefect of Police reported 'lively indignation, even among usually calm and peaceful people', and the press – including the conservative and business newspapers – was full of warlike talk.[26] The conservative *Journal des Débats* (29 July) wrote: 'The treaty is a piece of insolence that France will not endure. . . It is necessary for her to prepare for war.' The Left-wing papers – the *Siècle*, the *Temps*, the *National* – were as bellicose as ever. Heinrich Heine felt around him in Paris 'a joyful warlike enthusiasm. . . Except for the Legitimists, all Frenchmen have rallied round the tricolour, and their unanimous cry is: War on perfidious Albion!'[27] The 'enthusiasm of 1830' that Thiers had promised in his January speech had come with a vengeance. 'Never since 1830 have I seen such pronounced and sustained enthusiasm'. wrote a French politician to one of the leading pro-French Whigs. 'It is the national spirit showing itself without bravado. . . You may be certain that if the government did not respond to the Treaty of London with an energetic attitude, it would be overthrown by a revolution.'[28]

Thiers made no attempt to calm this public anger, but rather sought to use it to alarm the other Powers. His basic policy, however, was unchanged: to continue to do all he could to discourage action by the Powers while trying to arrange a compromise between Mehemet Ali and the Sultan which would leave the Powers without a leg to stand on. This assumed that Mehemet Ali was strong enough militarily to resist for a long time any attempt by the Powers, by blockade, bombardment or amphibious landing, to bring him to heel. French military and naval experts, diplomats, politicians and the King all considered this to be certain.[29] Thiers was not entirely convinced, but nevertheless considered the Egyptians strong enough to resist seaborne landings. He realized that the Lebanon, where the Christians were in revolt against the Egyptians, was the weak point. He repeatedly urged Mehemet Ali to pacify the province, by force and by concessions, and sent a French Lazarist missionary to act as an intermediary. He also dispatched military advisers to Egypt, and offered surreptitious money and arms. He was confident that, with prudence, Mehemet Ali was militarily secure for the time being.[30]

If so, he assumed that the London Convention would become a dead letter, and that the resolve of the allies would weaken. He would encourage this by a calculated policy of sabre rattling, into which the King and the pro-government press threw themselves with brio. On 29 July, Thiers announced the first measures of rearmament. At the same time he inspired, or perhaps drafted, an anonymous article in the *Revue des Deux Mondes* (1 August) which threatened, 'If certain limits are exceeded, it is war, total war... whichever the government.' He sent out a similar message through his ambassadors, warning the Russians that if war came it would be revolutionary war, and that Poland would rise; hinting to the Prussians and Austrians that war would spread to the Rhine and Italy; and warning the British, through Guizot, that 'the pasha is capable if threatened... of setting light to the powder... [He] crosses the Taurus and blows up Europe with him.' He was simultaneously warning Mehemet Ali, however, that if he did any such thing he would inevitably be destroyed.[31] Louis-Philippe, who was genuinely angered by the London Convention, and resentful that the other governments should cause him such dangerous embarrassment at home, sabre-rattled as loudly as Thiers: 'They owe the peace of Europe and the security of their thrones to me, and this is their gratitude!' There were noisy scenes at the palace, with the King shouting at ambassadors, 'this time, do not believe that I shall go against my government and my country; you want war, you shall have it, and if necessary I shall unleash the tiger' – revolution.[32] The alliance of Thiers and the King was not based on entire trust. Louis-Philippe, concerned for his popularity, was not prepared to give Thiers a pretext for resignation and himself take the responsibility for a diplomatic disaster: 'I shouted louder than he, and left him grappling with the problems.' Thiers, with public opinion behind him, felt that if the King weakened, he would be 'carried along by the tide of opinion, that no dam could hold'.[33]

A further link between King and Minister was that both were glad of the opportunity to increase the size of the army, run down by cost-cutting Parliaments, and begin a huge programme of fortifications for Paris. There had been angry debate about forts round the capital ever since 1830, with critics of the regime accusing Louis-Philippe of thinking more of internal repression than foreign invasion. Whether this had been in Thiers's thoughts is not clear, but he certainly wished to close a gap in French defences that he believed had been fatal to Napoleon in 1814. Moreover, ostentatious military preparations would lend substance to the French sabre rattling.[34]

The essence of bluff is, of course, that it should be believed. That of Thiers and Louis-Philippe was believed 'at Windsor', and by some of the British government – Russell, Clarendon, Holland – who made Palmerston's life in Cabinet difficult, pressing for concessions, threatening resignations and even passing on confidential information to Guizot. But Palmerston, who counted most, did not believe it.[35] The diplomatic world of 1840 was remarkably transparent. Both Thiers and Palmerston received confidential information about each other; Thiers, however, had more to hide. Moreover, if Palmerston had to reckon with Cabinet opposition and pressure from Windsor, Thiers had worse stumbling-blocks placed in his way by Louis-Philippe, members of his own government, and Guizot. The King, who had never meant his threats seriously, soon made it clear to his ministers and ambassadors that he would never go to the point of war. Worse, he let foreign goverments know too.[36] In consequence, Thiers had the mortifying experience in mid-September, when he attempted to give a solemn warning of the danger of war to the British chargé d'affaires, Bulwer, of being shown by the latter his draft dispatch calmly telling Palmerston, 'you need not have the slightest apprehension as to the King's acceptance of M. Thiers' programme... the King will accept [his resignation] without a moment's hesitation'. Thiers protested that 'the King is far more bellicose than I', but failed to convince Bulwer or Palmerston, who had never believed that the French would fight. Palmerston replied to Bulwer that if Thiers ever tried threats again, 'convey to him in the most friendly and inoffensive manner possible, that if France... begins a war, she will to a certainty lose her ships, colonies and commerce... that her army of Algiers will cease to give her anxiety, and that Mehemet Ali will just be chucked into the Nile'. Palmerston also told Bulwer that 'Guizot is getting conveyed to me... that if we would but make the most trifling concession... the French government would jump at our proposals.'[37]

With his threats discounted by those who mattered most, Thiers's only hope of salvaging his policy depended on Mehemet Ali's ability to conduct a successful defence against the limited military means that the Powers had immediately available: this Broglie called 'our best card'.[38] If they were denied an easy success, Thiers still hoped that they would have second thoughts, especially as in a few months French rearmament would be well under way – he planned to have over 600,000 men by the spring of 1841. But in September Thiers began to receive information that caused him a 'secret fear' that Mehemet Ali was 'weakening', and therefore the whole basis of French policy was crumbling.[39] He realized that Mehemet Ali was inclined to surrender completely to the Powers, and would already have done so but for French support. To avoid utter humiliation, Thiers now had to encourage Mehemet Ali to hold out, and not to accept the terms of the 15 July Convention. He tried to keep all this secret, but Palmerston soon heard about it through the gossip of Thiers's opponents, conveyed through the Rothschilds. This merely accorded with what Palmerston had always believed: that Mehemet Ali was a man of straw, who 'would not dare move his little finger in hostility to England'.[40]

Though the news had not reached Paris, the Pasha's weakness had already been demonstrated. On 11 September, a mainly British naval squadron landed a force of Turkish soldiers and Austrian and British marines a few miles from Beirut. The French government had been assured by its naval commander on the spot that this was impossible because of the winds and currents; but the British had steamships.[41] Faced with the allied force, which joined hands with the Lebanese rebels, the Egyptian troops at once began to withdraw, and Beirut fell. On 2 October, the news reached Paris. Thiers's 'best card' had been trumped. 'Pray try to persuade the King and Thiers that they have lost the game, and that it would be unwise now to make a brawl about it', wrote Palmerston.[42]

This was not how things appeared in Paris. The news of the allied landing, and that the Sultan had decreed Mehemet Ali's deposition, caused 'an agitation here beyond all imagining'. The press, which had begun to waver, was again nearly unanimous, and the pro-government Left-wing papers urged Thiers to act: 'The government has our fleets and armies at its disposal', wrote the *Siècle* (3 October). 'Let it choose the place and the time... [France] will respond on the Continent, if need be, as in the Mediterranean.'[43] The situation had never been anywhere near as grave, Thiers wrote to Guizot. 'It is impossible to say what will happen, or what the government's resolutions will be.'[44] He, the King and the Cabinet now had to consider seriously the possibility of war or retreat. The King's view was well known. The Cabinet was divided ('still more divided than others we know of', joked Palmerston).[45] Thiers's own view shows how little, when faced with the decision, he could ever have intended war:

> the violent party wants war for the sake of war; Beirut has given them a marvellous theme; the wise and patriotic people desire peace, have little hope of it and yet prefer war to dishonour... in fact, we are not ready. We shall soon have 489,000 men; thanks to determined efforts we shall have 639,000 by next April or May... Our navy is excellent but not sufficiently numerous; it would win the first battle and lose the last... we must not make war except for an absolutely obligatory reason.[46]

Although Thiers's policy of frightening other governments was not working, he had succeeded only too well in frightening public opinion, in France and abroad. Throughout Germany, threatened with war on the Rhine, there had been an extraordinary outburst of patriotic and anti-French feeling among all classes. The emotion was expressed in patriotic songs that won lasting popularity, including 'Deutschland über alles' and 'Die Wacht am Rhein'. A lasting stimulus was given to German nationalism.[47] In France, stock-market prices were unstable throughout the summer, and businesses, especially those involved in foreign trade, were hit by destocking and uncertainty. This came on top of the poor economic situation left by the slump of the late 1830s. Unemployment was serious in Paris, and during the summer several strikes broke out. The nationalist and revolutionary rhetoric in the Left-wing press had alarming consequences. Louis-Napoleon Bonaparte was encouraged to land at Boulogne on 6 August, to try to raise a military revolt. The campaign for electoral reform was renewed, and several reform banquets were held, including a militantly radical one on 31 August at Châtillon. Conservatives were greatly disturbed, especially as the government was unwilling in the circumstances to repress public disorders. Memories of 1831, when political radicalism and jingoism had also been closely linked, were frequently evoked. When belief that war was imminent began to ebb in well-informed circles, the government was even more strongly criticized for having inflamed agitation unnecessarily. The conservative press repeatedly demanded the recall of Parliament, seen by early autumn as a means of safeguarding peace rather than, as during the summer, a possible stimulus to rash resolutions.[48]

On 15 October, soon after the news of the attack on Beirut arrived, there was an attempt on the King's life by a worker named Darmès, who, when questioned, muttered something about Beirut, and it was soon discovered that he had attended the notorious Châtillon banquet in August.[49] Clearly, the attack had been made because of Louis-Philippe's ill concealed opposition to war. Madame Dosne was unsympathetic: what else could be expected 'if . . . one has the intention of loading cannons and rifles without using them, especially if one is imprudent enough to let that intention show'.[50] The victims of Darmès' bullet were Thiers and the government, for it was now dramatically evident that the excitement caused by the foreign crisis was putting the hard-won stability of the previous few years in danger. The conservative party raised its head, Guizot wrote to Broglie to say that he was more worried by the internal situation than the external, and the King himself now seemed more ready to stand up to the government.[51]

Faced with foreign intransigence and domestic opposition, the government was in some confusion.[52] Soon after the news of Beirut, they voted at Thiers's insistence – though by only five votes to four – to send a Note of protest to the Powers, recall Parliament to ask for further credits, and send the fleet to Alexandria to protect Mehemet Ali. The King would not agree.[53] Thiers, having consulted his parliamentary and press allies, was determined to persist, believing that public opinion demanded 'a reparation or a demonstration', and denying that it would endanger the regime. He offered his resignation.[54] Many observers believed that he was seeking a pretext to resign as the patriotic victim of royal cowardice, and thus evade his responsibilities: 'M. Thiers will be the national minister', said Louis-Philippe, 'while I shall be the foreigners' king.' Under pressure from the bellicose Duc d'Orléans and from some conservative politicians concerned for the monarchy's popularity, Louis-Philippe procrastinated.[55] Eventually, on 7 October, King and government agreed on a compromise suggested by Broglie. A Note was to be dispatched, Parliament recalled and (the major compromise) the fleet withdrawn to Toulon.[56] The King's agreement was grudging: 'if I can find a chance to get out of this peacefully, I shall take it'. The government, its reason for resignation gone, was somewhat surprised to find itself still in office. 'He gave in, and forced me to stay', wrote Thiers.[57]

The Note that Thiers was to draft would show the government apparently taking a firm stand, by loudly proclaiming that France would go to war if the Powers tried to deprive Mehemet Ali of Egypt. The Pasha had officially been deposed by the Sultan – for the fourth time in his eventful career –

but immediately after the capture of Beirut, both Palmerston and Metternich had hastened to assure the French government that his deposition would not be implemented. It was therefore safe, as all the governments realized, for Thiers to deliver his Note on 8 October.[58] As the British chargé d'affaires was later to put it, Thiers, 'in order to appear to do something without doing anything... said that if the Powers did what they said they would not do... France would oppose such an act'.[59] This Note made it clear to those with eyes to read that there was not going to be a war, for the French *casus belli* would not occur; it was, critics pointed out, in reality a *casus pacis*. Thiers had tacitly accepted what he had previously refused to accept – that Mehemet Ali might now lose the whole of Syria, more than he would have lost under the July Convention.[60]

Nevertheless, Thiers had not given up the struggle. 'Now [Mehemet Ali] must fight to the last in Syria', he wrote to Alexandria on 9 October, 'above all let him prolong the war there. If he can do that all can be saved; if he holds on until winter, our armaments being completed, we shall negotiate at the head of our forces, and we shall perhaps have an advantageous peace.' Thiers was banking on bad autumn weather interrupting the allies' sea communications. Then nothing more would happen until spring, when, with France prepared for war, 'Europe would not have sacrificed its peace and quiet for some slice of Syria'.[61] Some slice of Syria was what Thiers was quite ready to settle for as he sought desperately for a face-saving concession to salvage his policy. On 15 October he promised the British ambassador that if the Powers would only begin negotiations he would adjourn the Chambers without asking for further spending on armaments, and later suggested that Mehemet Ali might now accept the offer made under the July Convention, 'trusting to the generosity of the Sultan to bestow an additional pashalik [governorship] on one of his sons'.[62]

For Louis-Philippe, however, enough was enough. The prudent course for him would have been, as some of his advisers urged, to wait for Parliament to meet and leave to it the responsibility of bringing Thiers down. Acute observers – including the British chargé d'affaires and stock-market speculators – believed that the Chamber would decide for a policy of peace. The King, however, did not wait. It is possible that he was unsure of the dispositions of Parliament, though in that case to dismiss Thiers beforehand and risk his being brought back by a chauvinistic Parliament was more dangerous than to do nothing. Perhaps, on the contrary, sure of conservative approval, he was glad to take the initiative himself, in order to show the country how necessary he was to prevent its parliamentary politicians from running amuck and thus take a belated revenge on Thiers and his allies for their campaign over the previous two years against the royal prerogative. He had already approached Molé and Guizot, and the latter was ready to form a new government under the presidency of Marshal Soult.[63]

While domestic political considerations predisposed the King to break with Thiers, the final pressure came from abroad. Encouraged by their sympathizers in England, Louis-Philippe and Guizot had become openly convinced that the other Powers were ready to respond to a conciliatory attitude on their part with concessions that they had refused to make to Thiers's threats. [64] But if French threats continued, they would soon provoke military counter measures. The Austrian and Prussian governments, pressed by excited nationalist opinion, were beginnning reluctantly to consider common defence, while in London the peace party had shot its bolt and Lord Melbourne was on the point of recalling Parliament to ask for naval credits. On 16 October, Queen Victoria wrote to Leopold of the Belgians that England was ready to be conciliatory, and urged him to pass to Louis-Philippe the message that 'if France... were to *cease arming*, I think all would do;... if France goes on arming, we shall hardly be justified in not doing the same, and that would be very bad'. [65] On 17 October, Louis-Philippe showed himself very reluctant to support further rearmament when he met Thiers and his colleagues at Saint-Cloud. 'When I armed, I hoped to frighten England; but today I see that my armaments have not produced that effect on Lord Palmerston', who, he thought, really was prepared to go to war. That would destroy them all, he told Thiers; 'you, me, my sons, my family, my wife, your wife' and– in a vain attempt to touch Thiers's heart – 'your mother-in-law'. Armaments, said the King, should wait, and the Speech from the Throne contain only 'vague things'. Thiers took the opposite view: 'if the King would let me act, I would prepare him an honourable peace', but 'if, when I speak firmly to the ambassadors... the King talks peace, promising everyone that we shall have it... he makes all favourable negotiation impossible'. [66]

The government seems to have concluded that it must show Europe that Thiers had prevailed over the King, and that consequently war was still a possibility unless France was offered concessions. Or if – as seemed likely – Louis-Philippe refused, at least they could resign with their nationalist reputation intact. Rémusat therefore drafted a Speech from the Throne which brought the matter to a head: it spoke of 'new measures' of armament and of France's being ready to act 'the day she believes the European balance seriously menaced' (a reference to the Note of 8 October guaranteeing Egypt). It ended with a flourish: 'No sacrifice would be too great to keep [France] her position in the world... she will not buy [peace] at a price unworthy of her, and your King... wishes to leave intact to his son that sacred heritage of independence and national honour which the French Revolution has placed in his hands.' On 21 October, having read through the draft, Louis-Philippe refused it, and almost without discussion the government offered its resignation. Neither side was surprised; both, indeed, seem to have been somewhat relieved. [67] On 22 October, Thiers wrote a graceful letter to Guizot promising to cause him no difficulties. [68]

It was rumoured in Paris that Thiers no longer thought of returning to power under Louis-Philippe, but was waiting for the Duc d'Orléans to succeed him.[69]

When the Chambers met, Thiers was violently criticized by members of the new conservative and centre majority. His policy, as one critic put it, had amounted to 'throwing themselves without fixed plan into the chances of a war that they themselves did not want'; and having shrunk from war they had brought about what Lamartine called 'the Waterloo of French diplomacy'.[70] Undeniably, Thiers had exacerbated the diplomatic difficulties he inherited. He had refused to compromise during the long negotiation in the spring of 1840, wanting nothing less than complete success. However, given the mood of the country and the practically universal belief in the strength of the French and Egyptian position, it would have needed a remarkably timid and pessimistic politician, and one quite insensitive to public opinion, to follow any other course. Thiers was certainly not such a man; at that moment neither were Louis-Philippe or Guizot. Once the initial failures began, Thiers, belying his reputation for changeableness, persisted with remarkable stubborness in the same policy of temporizing, bluffing and placing ever higher stakes on the 'Syrian card'. This was a perfect example of one of Thiers's strong characteristics: determination to follow a certain logically conceived course of action, having persuaded himself and others that it must be right, even if events were proving it wrong. Thence the conviction that the Anglo-French alliance must be fundamentally sound (even though the English were ready to abandon it); that a genuine Anglo-Russian *rapprochement* was impossible (in spite of the willingness of the English and the Russians to bring it about); that the Four Powers must split; that Mehemet Ali, the progressive emulator of the Revolution and Napoleon, must be strong and determined; that the Four Powers must give way to French threats. This determined wrong-headedness made defeat, when it came, all the worse – defeat inflicted by a pragmatic, and much better informed, Palmerston. Thiers, was, as Rémusat noted in another connection, bad at understanding what he had not actually seen and resistant to ideas that did not fit his logical scheme of things. An excellent debater, he was a bad negotiator.

Yet his policy, the errors of which are so evident in retrospect, frequently seemed at the time very near to success: Mehemet Ali did come close to making peace with the Sultan; the Egyptian possessions did seem impregnable until the Syrian revolt provided a loophole for the allies; Palmerston was dangerously isolated in the Cabinet and vulnerable to any military reverse in Syria; and Austria and Prussia were bullied into offering concessions. That Thiers held an apparently strong hand encouraged him to raise the stakes. It is impossible to be sure whether he would have gone to war. His policy was based on avoiding war, but appearing to be ready for it. Yet many of his closest associates were convinced that he would eventually have fought if necessary.[71] The uncertainty about his real intentions meant that conservatives would not trust his 'brinkmanship'.

In the debate on the reply to the Speech from the Throne in December – which became a battle between Thiers and the leader of the new government, Guizot, and their respective policies – Thiers and the Left mustered only 161 votes, against 247 for the government.[72] Most of the political nation had been badly frightened by the possibility of war and the surge of internal agitation, and they were angry at Thiers's vast military expenditure.[73] There was to be no more experimentation with Left-Centre governments, and a conservative political course was fixed until 1848. Attacks on Thiers in the Chambers, the press and political society were extraordinarily bitter, and pushed him near to despair. Rémusat thought that 'for thirty or forty years. . . no such ordeal had been inflicted on anyone'. It might well have been the end of his career: 'I hope that people will understand', wrote one critic, 'that war, revolution and he are synonymous.' But far from being finished, Thiers and his remaining allies were prepared to fight on: 'a long. . . determined battle for the emancipation of the country is about to begin', wrote one of them.'I want. . . the greatness of France before liberty and progress. . . We shall first bring down the enemy within; and then we shall deal with the enemies without.' On the other side of the fence Guizot, Louis-Philippe's willing instrument in the maintenance of peace and order, had a similar view. It was 'the beginning of a long and hard campaign'; he hoped that a new conservative majority would coalesce: 'It has begun. The Chamber is cut in two.'[74] Although the July Monarchy was to enjoy eight years of unprecedented political stability, this gulf would never be bridged.

Thiers, from 1836 to 1840, came to be a distruptive force in the politics of the constitutional monarchy he had done much to invent. He was a man entirely committed to the revolutions of 1789 and 1830. Yet he was equally committed to upholding the authority of the state, and had no sympathy for further substantial political and social reform. His solution was to reconcile the moderate Left to a policy of domestic conservatism by minor political concessions – 'transaction' – backed up by a foreign policy worthy of a nationalist revolutionary state. This proved impossible in 1836 and in 1840 because of opposition from the King and most of the political nation of *notables* – men of established wealth and position – whose alarm at the dangers of foreign conflict and single-minded preoccupation with material interest Thiers and his supporters despised. Paradoxically, only a widening of the franchise might have enabled them to overcome the conservative resistance, but a widening of the franchise was something their political strategy was designed to avoid. Consequently, their anger was directed against the royal prerogative, and Louis-Philippe became the scapegoat for their failure.

It was not only domestic conditions that caused the failure of Thiers's foreign policies, however. In the case of the Austrian marriage project in

1836 and in that of the Eastern Crisis of 1840, French policy was fundamentally misconceived. Some of the errors were worsened by Thiers's mistakes, but they were never his mistakes alone. Some were caused by the over-eagerness for success of governments that needed it politically. Some were compounded by the professional failing of a highly politicized diplomatic corps. But many stemmed from the world view of the Liberal intelligentsia and its understanding of recent historical development. Two fallacious beliefs that led to disaster in 1840 were that a relationship based on shared liberalism must necessarily exist between France and Britain, and that fundamental antagonism must exist between Britain and Russia. Conservatives (who in this case included Louis-Philippe and Guizot) were equally mistaken in believing that other governments would make concessions to them in return for their curbing revolution. French policy, said a Russian diplomat, could be summed up as 'evading' under Soult, 'threatening' under Thiers, and 'begging' under Guizot.[75] They all failed.

It was difficult for French statesmen of all parties to recognize that any reappearance of French expansionism would unite the other Powers against them. Thus the French dilemma, as Thiers and his allies pointed out, was whether to accept a secondary position in world affairs or to brave a coalition of the other Great Powers. In 1840 Thiers gambled that in such a contest France could prevail by bluff. Quite reasonably, the majority of the political nation was not prepared to risk it. For all these reasons, the July Monarchy was unable to draw strength from success abroad, except in Algeria which (as for the Restoration) was not enough. Only when both the international and the domestic situation had been transformed in the wake of 1848 was Louis-Napoleon able, for a time, to reap the benefits of policies such as his predecessors had not been able, or had not dared, to pursue.

[5]

Opposition and Revolution, 1840–1848

'Disraeli', wrote one of his biographers, 'was to spend a longer time in opposition than almost any statesman of comparable stature in our history.'[1] Thiers's biographers might well make the same remark about him. After his fall from power in October 1840 he was out of office and generally in opposition, sometimes muted, sometimes active, for over thirty years. At the end of 1840, despite his temporary discredit and the hostilities he aroused, no one could have predicted that he would be so long absent from government, least of all Thiers himself; had he not, in a curious letter written even before his fall, confidently declared 'Thrown aside, I shall return'? Those who thought that French politics in the 1840s would continue in the pattern of the previous decade might well suppose that in two or three years' time he would be back in power.

This was not to be. The King had had a scare. He regarded his fallen minister as too adventurous, too independent, and too anxious to curtail royal prerogative. Thiers's return to office under the July Monarchy could henceforth be possible only if the King was willing or forced to call upon his services. Louis-Philippe was not willing and when, in February 1848, he was forced to do so, it was too late. Thiers, as we shall see, was unable to control a situation that had become revolutionary, and the situation had in part become revolutionary because with advancing years Louis-Philippe, like Charles X, was increasingly inflexible and unwilling to make concessions while there was still time.

Many of Thiers's critics, among them one of the most eloquent, the poet Lamartine, assumed that his dominant passion was greed for office and that he would do anything to get back into power.[2] They misjudged him. Some years earlier they might have been right, but now he was eager for it only if he could hold it on his own terms. His attitude to power had become more independent, partly because he did not need it for financial reasons. Besides, he had an alternative employment and ambition, his *chères études* and the enhancement of his reputation as an historian. As early as 1827 he had signed contracts to write separate histories of the Consulate and of the Empire, but, apart from gathering some material, he had not got far with this new work before the July Revolution. Then, for the best part of the ensuing decade, politics absorbed his energies. In June 1839, however, he signed a new contract for a single history of the same subjects. This was a very important commission financially as well as historically. It enabled him for the first time to become a man of substantial property – a *grand notable*, because he was paid the enormous sum of 500,000 francs for the first ten volumes – the equivalent of Macaulay's receipts for his great *History of England*.

He appears to have set to work in earnest soon after October 1840. Michelet was later to criticize him for not having done research in archives, but he could not accuse him of neglecting the terrain of many of Napoleon's greatest military exploits. In 1841 he travelled to Holland, Germany and Austria in pursuit of his 'historic hero and his gigantic adventures'.[3] He spent a day exploring the battlefield of Austerlitz, and in 1843 in Switzerland he examined the terrain of the battle of Zurich. In the autumn of 1844 the leader of the Dynastic Left, Odilon Barrot, found him at Lille busy correcting proofs, and in 1845 he was doing the same at Vichy. In that year the first three of the twenty volumes that, very literally, constituted his *magnum opus* appeared in print. Before it was over another two had been published. Volumes 6 and 7 followed in 1847 and Volumes 8 and 9 in 1849.[4] Meanwhile, in August 1845, Thiers had taken his younger friend, Walewski, whom he was encouraging to become a diplomat, to Spain to see the sights and tour the battlefields of the Peninsular War.[5] His mother-in-law, Madame Dosne, was nervous about what she called his 'mania' for travelling by train on Sundays,[6] but Spanish railways, still in their infancy, gave him little opportunity for such self-indulgence. In a countryside of bad roads and brigands he was almost as active and tireless as he had been in the Pyrenees in 1822. It was the former dandy and dilettante Walewski who was exhausted.

Return to the *métier* of historian was one of Thiers's consolations for loss of office. Another was his election, on 26 December 1840, to the Académie des Sciences Morales et Politiques. This distinguished body, originally created by the Convention in 1795, had been revived in 1832 by Guizot, and among its earlier members who reappeared in the 1830s were two well-known and venerable Ideologues, Destutt de Tracy and Merlin de Douai. It was appropriate that Thiers, thought by Pellenc twenty years earlier to be too much of an Ideologue for the Duc de La Rochefoucauld-Liancourt's taste, should now become a member. Eight years later one of his best-known brochures was published under the Academy's auspices.

So much literary activity did not mean that Thiers had no time for politics. The 1840s were the period of his great political rivalry with Guizot whose temperament and personality were as antipathetic to him as were Gladstone's to Disraeli. He was a leader of the opposition to the Soult–Guizot ministry which remained in office for more than seven years, but his opposition was fitful, unpredictable, and opportunist. It depended partly upon the extent to which he was engrossed by his historical labours, partly upon the degree to which he suffered disillusionment and, like Lord Stanley in contemporary England, had spells of aversion from politics, and partly on the opportunities for effective attack. His role as an opposition leader thus falls into two phases, the first from October 1840 to his speech on the question of a regency in August 1842 and the second from January 1844 until, in February 1848, he was abruptly summoned to form a new government. In between there is a period of sixteen months when he was almost wholly absorbed by his *chères études* and spoke only once, very briefly, in the Chamber.

Apart from his unsuccessful attempt to defend his Eastern policy, Thiers's first preoccupations after leaving office were less with opposition than with two proposals arising from his own policies. The first was Napoleonic, the second military.

It had been on Thiers's initiative that the King and Cabinet had asked for the return of Napoleon's ashes from Saint Helena to re-inter them ceremonially in the church of the Invalides in Paris. He was no longer Prime Minister when the ceremony took place in December 1840 but he could be gratified by its success. Despite bitter cold the crowds were vast and, however mixed the reactions of educated people, there was no mistaking the enthusiasm of ordinary Parisians. Humble poetasters celebrated Thiers's role and Victor Hugo hailed 'the magnificent poem in action' for which he had been responsible. For Thiers, no doubt, the political motive was to win Bonapartist support for the July Monarchy. Perhaps, too, he believed that by giving a boost to the Napoleonic legend he would strengthen the allegedly weakening national fibre. His former colleague on the *Constitutionnel*, Cauchois-Lemaire, was, however, more perceptive; he remarked that it was a good day for the prisoner of Ham. The prisoner was the Bonapartist pretender, Louis-Napoleon, whose attempt at raising the Bonapartist standard at Boulogne in August had ended in fiasco. He had been captured by the French authorities, tried, and sentenced to perpetual imprisonment in the fortress of Ham. But he had pertinently asked how long perpetuity lasted in France and, in a new foreword to his little book, *Des Idées Napoléoniennes*, first published in 1839, he had observed that it was not only the ashes of the Emperor but also his ideas which must be brought back to France. There is no evidence that Thiers, whose paper, the *Constitutionnel*, had dismissed the Boulogne episode as ridiculous[7], had any inkling of the long-term dangers of the kind of fervour aroused by his 'poem in action' in 1840.

The second unresolved problem was the long-debated question of fortifying Paris. Some people were in favour of a continuous line of defence, others of detached forts; many objected to the whole idea. As we have seen, the question had come to a head with the danger of war in 1840, and on

4 September, encouraged by the Duc d' Orléans, Thiers had persuaded the King and Cabinet to agree to a plan which included detached forts as well as a continuous rampart. When the proposal came before Parliament, Thiers was no longer in office, but he acted as *rapporteur* on the Bill which was backed by the government. The debate in January 1841 was notable not only for the eloquence with which Thiers discoursed on the problems which had confronted Vauban and Napoleon, but also for some of those exchanges between protagonists of the offensive and defensive which so often recurred in French history. One of the former was Lamartine, who characteristically preferred an *offensive redoutable* to a timid defensive 'repugnant to an enthusiastic people such as we are'. Despite the poet's opposition the government carried the day with a majority of seventy-five. Before long Paris was surrounded by a defensive wall some twenty-four miles in length with ninety-four projecting bastions. Further out and commanding all approaches to the capital, seventeen detached forts were constructed. Thiers was delighted with the new defences and in 1846 spent the greater part of a day exhibiting them to his old British antagonist, Palmerston. Earlier, when he heard that they were to go ahead, another British Foreign Secretary, Lord Aberdeen, had divined in them 'a measure of incalculable importance which, if completed,' would 'exercise some great influence' (what, he could not tell) on the future destiny of France.[8] Happily, it would be many years before the efficacy of Thiers's fortifications was put to the test and before it could be seen whether Aberdeen's prediction had any substance.

Immediately, however, the effect of their construction was disadvantageous to Thiers. Although they provided temporary employment for thousands of provincials they cost a very large sum of money, over 140 million francs, and in October 1841 the government was obliged to raise a loan to make ends meet. This expenditure, on top of the outlay necessitated by Thiers's war preparations in 1840, was most unpalatable to many thrifty French electors.[9] For them Thiers was not only a warmonger but also a spendthrift; this view was doubtless reflected in the election results of 1842 and 1846, both of which returned Guizot to power with a comfortable majority.

Between these two dates Thiers had to some extent shifted his political stance. At first, still denounced on account of his alleged adventurism and lack of principle, he emphasized his moderation, the relative insignificance of the differences between him and Guizot, and the need for the majority in the Chamber to be anchored in the centre. The ministry, he argued, had been trying to build its majority *en arrière*, and he thought it should be *en avant*. What Thiers elusively urged in the Chamber[10] was spelt out by his friend and political ally, Duvergier de Hauranne, in the *Revue des Deux Mondes*: the one way to obtain a stable majority, he urged, was by means of another 'transaction', an alliance of the moderate Right with the moderate Left.[11] In effect Thiers and his friends hoped that such a 'transaction' – a key word in March 1840 when he was seeking to consolidate his own majority[12] – would come about whenever Guizot's position weakened. The new grouping would sponsor a few moderate reforms and be led, of course, by Thiers.

In February 1842 it looked as though such hopes would be realized. One of the reforms envisaged by Duvergier de Hauranne had long been mooted. On 7 March 1830 the *National* had pointed out that since Villèle's ministry (1821–8) many people had asked whether government officials should not be ineligible 'for electoral and legislative functions'. Such exclusion, it argued, would not, as some had said, be unjust but it would be against the interest of the state for its legislators to be deprived of administrative experience or its administrators to be without direct knowledge of the legislative processes. Since then Thiers had changed his mind. The inducements to and pressures upon deputies who were also government officials to be lackeys of the government in power were only too obvious. When, in February 1842, a member of his group, the Left-Centre, tabled a motion to exclude most government employees from Parliament its consideration was rejected by only eight votes. Guizot's position looked precarious, but in the summer, on a vote of confidence, his majority increased to forty-one and he astutely decided to dissolve Parliament and hold new elections on 9 July.

At first it looked as though he had miscalculated. Not for the first or indeed the last time Paris showed its recalcitrance; ten out of twelve of its new deputies supported the opposition. But the results from the provinces were very different and in the end the government had an overall majority of about forty. The new Chamber contained nearly as many civil servants (263) as the old (272) and two-thirds of them supported the government.[13] At Aix the Legitimists, who had taken no part in elections there since 1832, had re-entered the fray and put up a candidate to oppose Thiers. They had waged such a violent compaign against him in the local *Mémorial* that, mindful perhaps of the *charivari* of 1832, he was said to have been afraid to go there before polling day.[14] But his friend Aude, mayor of the town since 1835, had in 1841 founded a rival paper, the *Echo de Provence*, to support him and he was returned by 247 to 110 votes. He immediately went to Aix to thank his constituents, but in view of the Legitimists' strength, Mignet, who often advised him on local affairs, urged him to press for regional benefits. Opposition deputies might denounce Guizot's government as the rule of interests, but they were well aware of the importance of the interests of their own voters. In 1843 Mignet congratulated his friend on the forthcoming installation at Aix of an Ecole des Arts et Métiers: 'Everyone here knows that but for you they would not have got it.'[15]

There was one development of great significance to Provençals which affected but also transcended local interests. The railway age had arrived and as early as 1836 Thiers, at first characteristically cautious when confronted by a novelty, had declared that railways were destined for a huge development.[16] One of the first main lines planned was from Paris to Marseilles and it was proposed that the southernmost section should pass through Arles. Thiers backed a counter-proposal to route this stretch through Aix, but in May 1837 he had to bow to the superior technical arguments that favoured Arles.[17] The defeat confirmed the stagnation of Aix, but had not prevented Thiers's re-election.

While plans abounded, France's actual construction of railways lagged far behind that of Belgium, the United Kingdom and the USA, partly as a result of government reluctance to finance new lines. At the beginning of 1842 there were still only some 350 miles of track and, pressed to take action, the government introduced a Bill to speed the development of lines radiating from Paris. Thiers repeated what he had said in 1840, that he had never shared the popular enthusiasm for railways but had always believed in their future. Now in view of foreign competition, he recognized that they were of sufficient national interest to warrant a special effort; but, in order not to disperse resources, he urged, as he had in 1838, concentrating on the one most useful line from the Mediterranean to the English Channel and the Rhine. He emphasized the importance of trade between Paris and Belgium, for whose railways and steam navigation he again expressed admiration, and stressed the military value of a link from Lille to Marseilles by way of Paris and Lyons. Once this line had been built the others could be dealt with in succession.[18]

The amendment he supported was lost by seventy votes. The line he favoured so eloquently was advantageous to Marseilles if not to Aix and he was of course right in urging its military importance now that France was in the process of conquering Algeria. Whether in stressing its commercial value he was aware of the growing economic imbalance between the prospering north of France and the relatively static south is much less certain.

Soon afterwards, when Thiers was at Vichy with his ladies, news came that the popular heir to the throne, the Duc d' Orléans, had been killed in a carriage accident in Paris. At once the future of the regime seemed less secure. Louis-Philippe was now 69 and the new heir, the Duc d' Orléans's son, the Comte de Paris, was only 4. It looked as though sooner or later a Regency would be inevitable, and most sensible men, including the King himself, recognized that it was essential to legislate for such an eventuality. But who should be Regent? Many politicians of the Left and Centre favoured the Duke's widow, since she was more popular and supposedly more liberal than the King's second son, the Duc de Nemours, who was regarded as shy and stiff. But the Duchess was a German Princess and Louis-Philippe was emphatic that, whatever her virtues, the Regency should not be entrusted to a foreigner. He was anxious that it should go as of right to the prince next in succession, namely Nemours. Thiers, who had hurried to

Neuilly to condole with the grief-stricken royal family, agreed. According to Madame Dosne, he had already, before seeing the King, made up his mind that this was the right course and in the debate on the Regency Bill in August he vigorously supported it.[19] He declared that he was 'profoundly monarchist' and that he would never reproach himself for having voted for a hereditary peerage. His stance is understandable: it was important to affirm the hereditary principle in a new dynasty, and he may well have remembered that if the last feminine regency in France, that of Marie Louise in 1813–14, was no great success, the recent one (1835–40) of Maria Cristina in Spain had been far from edifying.

The Duc d' Orléans's death profoundly affected Thiers as well as the future of the regime. Although Thiers denied that they had been friends the two men had esteemed one another and it was commonly said that when Orléans ascended the throne he would gladly countenance more Liberal and forceful policies and that Thiers would be his chief minister. Now that prospect had vanished. Thiers might hope that his statesmanlike attitude over the Regency question would induce the King to change his views and after all to regard him as an acceptable alternative to Guizot. But Guizot's parliamentary position had, as we have seen, been strengthened by the recent elections, whereas Thiers's had weakened because of a breach with Odilon Barrot, the leader of the Dynastic Left, and his supporters who had failed to back him on the regency issue. Unless Guizot committed some inexcusable blunder there seemed no reason why Louis-Philippe should change his ministers for months to come.

Temporarily then Thiers's political fortunes went into decline like those of the newspaper, the *Constitutionnel*, with which he was still associated and to which he still gave directives. Its circulation had been steadily falling; from 20,000 in 1830 it would sink to 3,600 in 1844. The paper had failed to keep up with the times: its rivals regarded its subscribers as typically stupid and naive members of the bourgeoisie and satirized its sleepiness by depicting it as a cotton nightcap shaped like an extinguisher. It was now eclipsed by a journal launched in 1836 by the other great parvenu of the time, Emile de Girardin, and this, the *Presse*, was hostile to Thiers. It owed its success to the revenue it derived from the advertisements on its last page, to Girardin's boldness in halving the normal subscription price from 80 to 40 francs per annum, and, last but not least, to the serial stories for which it started a vogue. It was not until 1845–6, after its purchase, in 1844, at Thiers's suggestion, by one of its shareholders, the enterprising Dr Véron, that the *Constitutionnel* followed suit and its circulation again reached 20,000. Little is known about Thiers's precise relations with it during this period, but it looks as though his attitude to newspapers was similar to his attitude to railways. It was one of 'wait and see'; let others experiment and take risks with new machines and techniques; he was no visionary and needed time to be convinced that they were worth adopting. Meanwhile he might derive comfort from the fact that the hostility of the *Presse* was to some extent countered by the friendliness of the *Siècle*, also founded in 1836. Regarded as the organ of the Dynastic Left, its political editor was his friend Chambolle, and it had a circulation of 30–40,000. It too had taken to printing serial stories, notably Dumas's *Three Musketeers*.

For many months after the regency debate Thiers was very much an absentee from politics. It was not until January 1844 that he re-entered the fray. Then, in a speech critical of the government in the customary debate on the address at the beginning of a new session, he said that he had come to believe that the art of government consisted in making timely concessions and that, despite his distrust of progress – 'everyone talks of living in an age of progress' – he was now convinced that there were useful reforms which needed to be made.[20] Somewhat surprisingly, in his next major speech he reported favourably on a government Bill put forward to try and settle the vexed and highly important question of freedom of education. Just as in England it was not yet established doctrine that the duty of an opposition was to oppose, so there was no need for a French politician, whose party was out of office, and certainly not for a politician as independent as Thiers, invariably to attack the men in power. Legislation to provide for freedom of education had been promised in the revised Charter of 1830 and any law at last agreed upon by Parliament could well be regarded as a useful reform. But Catholics who had been fighting for the right for their secondary schools to be free from the control of the secular and, for many, 'godless' University, as the state teaching corps was called, were bitterly disappointed. The Bill devised by the Minister of Education, Villemain, retained this control at certain key points and Thiers firmly supported him. His report, a devoted servant of the House of Orléans told one of the King's sons, had dealt with questions of public education in masterly fashion: the July Revolution had been the triumph of all the principles which the report had enunciated in such a lively and often eloquent manner.[21] Those principles were secular and no one acquainted with Thiers's earlier views could be surprised that he had come out as a defender of *l'esprit laïque*.

Thiers's education report enhanced his parliamentary reputation and temporarily embarrassed Guizot who had not wished for such an ally, but it had no practical consequences, for Guizot, who wished to conciliate the Catholics, soon found an excuse to drop Villemain's Bill. The issue of freedom of Catholic secondary education remained unresolved as long as the July Monarchy lasted and Thiers continued to express secularist views. In May 1845, not for the first time, he joined in the popular sport of hunting the Jesuits. In recent years several religious orders had returned to France without authorization. Conspicuous among them were the Jesuits, always the object of deep suspicion among anti-clericals, and Thiers, too, denounced them and demanded that the government should enforce the laws relating to the orders. A year later he declared that he was not an enemy to religion but was convinced that 'to entrust the education of youth to the hands of ecclesiastics was not to bring it closer to religion'; what he wanted was a 'great national system of education entrusted to laymen'. [22]

Thiers's treaty of alliance with Barrot was no doubt concluded partly to strengthen the Left-Centre and Dynastic Left before the next general election. But it was unavailing. In deciding to go to the polls in August 1846 Guizot again showed a good sense of timing. In the preceding four years France had enjoyed renewed prosperity as well as peace. The electors, preoccupied as Mignet lamented with material interests, [23] were satisfied with Guizot. All Thiers's eloquence, his criticisms of foreign policy, his reiteration of his devotion to constitutional monarchy, and the wry humour with which he indicated that he would be ready to take office provided he could pursue his own policies were insufficient to make them wish for a change of government. [24] Indeed, Catholics preferred Guizot, who had reasserted his belief in freedom of education, and many were probably alarmed by Thiers's move to the Left, just as many civil servants who hoped to be re-elected must have been dismayed by his support in March for another move for parliamentary reform, this time a proposal by Barrot to render certain classes of official ineligible. He himself singled out for disqualification the members of the royal household and his language was forthright. After repeating his principle that the King should reign but not rule, he concluded 'instead of sacrificing royalty what are we asking for? . . . that the men attached to its service should be sacrificed . . . in a word that it is better to sacrifice the King's *aides de camp* than the King himself.' [25] Louis-Philippe was not amused.

The elections were a victory for the civil servants as well as Guizot. The government gained eighteen seats; the number of officials returned rose by 24 from 263 to 287, 200 of whom were reckoned to be government supporters. [26] Despite his own triumphant re-election at Aix by 222 out of 238 votes Thiers and his friends were naturally dejected. Guizot's position looked impregnable. Mignet spoke of the Opposition's increasing impotence and urged Thiers, without neglecting his duties as Opposition leader, to concentrate on finishing his history. Thiers himself in October talked of quitting politics. He did not of course do so, but he did concentrate on the Consulate and Empire and was almost as silent in the Chamber in 1847 as he had been in 1843.

But there were consolations apart from the numerous congratulations on his history. One was the purchase of a share in the famous Anzin coal-mining company near Valenciennes of which he became a director in 1849 and president in 1869. [27] The share and the directorship, which he held for over twenty-five years, provided him with a regular income of about 10,000 francs rising to about 20,000 during the boom years of the Second Empire. Another consolation was a visit to Aix in December 1846 which was said to have been 'an apotheosis'. [28] A third must have been an invitation from electors in Marseilles in 1847 to be a candidate in his native city at the next election. The invitation was probably a recognition not only of his efforts on behalf of the Paris–Marseilles railway but also of his championship of the conquest and colonization of Algeria. He had advocated such a policy in the 1830s, he had emphasized the importance of the port of Algiers in 1842, and in January 1845 he had said that what France must now do was 'to people our colony, and enable it to feed itself and supply recruits for our cadres lest in time of war it should be cut off from the mother country'.[29] In these years, too, he maintained a regular correspondence with Algeria's governor, Marshal Bugeaud. Thiers, wrote Louis Blanc, was 'the only prominent personage to show strength of will regarding Africa. Imperialism being the basis of his ideas, Algeria pleased him as a nursery of soldiers.' This was undoubtedly true, but Thiers himself also recorded that his interest in Algeria was due to his passion for geography and to reports which revealed the wealth and resources of this conquered territory.[30] Whatever his motives there could be little doubt that the development of commerce and military traffic with Algeria would benefit Marseilles. But Thiers tactfully declined the Marseilles electors' invitation. He revisited his native city and his old school there in August 1847 and gave 300 francs to found a half scholarship at the Ecole Normale, but he could hardly desert the Aixois who had so recently given him such support.

When Thiers and Barrot signed their treaty of alliance in December 1845 they had agreed that on forming a ministry they would introduce parliamentary and electoral as well as other reforms. But after the elections of 1846 it looked as though they would have no prospect of office unless reform came first. So in 1847 parliamentary and, still more important, electoral reform became the rallying cries of the Opposition. As we have seen, Thiers had latterly supported attempts to obtain parliamentary reform. His attitude to electoral reform was however, less clear and in 1840, while admitting that no one had ever said that it should never take place, he had declared that the time for it was not yet ripe.[31] But by 1846 the electorate had increased only to some 240,000 on the basis of a taxpaying qualification of 200 francs, and there was nothing sacrosanct about this figure. Although they argued about what exact degree of reform Thiers had said he could accept,[32] there is no reason to believe that Thiers disapproved of the very modest plan tabled by Duvergier in the Chamber in March 1847; it proposed increasing the number of electors by 200,000 and of deputies from 459 to 538.[33] It was rejected by ninety-eight votes, but in the following month a proposal for parliamentary reform put forward by Rémusat was turned down by only forty-eight. Guizot had staved it off by saying that the subject would be debated before the end of the legislature.

The drop in his majority was encouraging for reformers but there seemed little hope of legislation unless outside pressures were brought to bear. Accordingly some Opposition leaders, including Duvergier, influenced by the success of the Anti-Corn-Law agitation in the United Kingdom, decided to continue their campaign outside Parliament. Since the laws allowed no rights of public meeting or demonstration, the reformers had recourse to subscription banquets at which toasts were given and speeches made to advertise their cause. Such a 'banquet campaign' accompanied by a number of articles and brochures, had rather turbulently but ineffectually been organized in 1840.[34] The 1847 campaign was intended to be a more efficient affair and its prospects looked better because of the numerous difficulties now besetting the government.

In 1846 Guizot had benefited at the polls from the fat years of the early 1840s, but once the elections were over the lean years began with dramatic swiftness. The corn and potato harvests of 1846 were catastrophic and a credit crisis – the nemesis of over-speculation in the railway boom – and a general recession soon followed. Discontent and distress were widespread. As always men blamed the government for many of their ills and the enemies of the regime, particularly the Republicans, sought to exploit the situation. Guizot's standing in the country as a whole declined; it could be hoped that soon he would be vulnerable even in Parliament.

These hopes were only partly fulfilled. Some seventy banquets, involving about 17,000 guests, were held up and down the country between 9 July and the end of December 1847, but despite the publicity they attracted they do not seem to have made a great impression in the provinces. Moreover, this sort of appeal to the country over the heads of the Chambers was still enough of an innovation to divide the Opposition and Rémusat, Dufaure, and Thiers were unwilling to take part.[35] Barrot thought the reason for Thiers's abstention was that he was doubtful of his popularity or believed he was 'trop rapproché du pouvoir'.[36] In fact he seems to have disliked speaking to audiences of any size outside Parliament, no doubt because of the weakness of his voice. In addition, when he realized that many of the banquets were being organized by Republicans for their own ends and that some speakers attacked Louis-Philippe himself, he must have preferred not to be involved. He feared, he wrote later, that the agitation aroused might not be peaceable and he had no wish to have to listen to speeches of which he did not approve.[37]

Meanwhile, whatever the influence of the banquet campaign, the general situation had further deteriorated. Scandals involving former ministers and persons in high society gave additional currency to the idea that the ruling circles were corrupt: on 29 January 1848 the *Constitutionnel* could assert that 'whether one was talking of laws or roads or railways, pensions, scholarships or decorations, compensation for hail, flood or fire, everything was distributed with a view to electoral or parliamentary votes'.[38] Well before then there was widespread anxiety. In a letter to Monckton-Milnes Guizot had once said that it was his *métier* to see a little clearly into the future,[39] but in September 1847 Thiers might well deplore 'the blindness of our governors'. He was afraid that before long circumstances would deteriorate for everyone.[40] One correspondent wrote to him that things were profoundly wrong and he did not know whether there was still time to put them right: 'the lower classes are organizing and making ready for a fight. They have only contempt for those who govern them and nothing is more dangerous.'[41]

In such a situation it looked as though the next session of Parliament would be critical. The Opposition hoped that Guizot would at last see the need to make concessions or that by their attacks they could force him onto the defensive and ultimately oblige him to resign. When the session opened on 28 December 1847 it was soon clear that concessions were not on Guizot's agenda. His most perceptive biographer has claimed that he had 'no fundamental objection to slight changes in the electoral or parliamentary systems',[42] but the King, now 74, was, as his sons themselves perceived,[43] increasingly authoritarian and tragically inflexible in his old age. He had come to dread change, to rely on Guizot, and to have something of an *idée fixe* that reform would mean new elections which would sooner or later oblige him to accept Thiers as chief minister and that Thiers would mean war.[44] Accordingly the tone of the address from the throne was as tactless and intransigent as that of the address delivered by Charles X in March 1830. It castigated the reformers as men moved by 'blind and hostile passions' and so stirred the troubled waters instead of calming them.

Provoked and put on his mettle by the address, and spoiling for a fight with his old enemy Guizot, Thiers went on to the attack, speaking no fewer than six times in eighteen days, criticizing Guizot's financial policy and, above all, his handling of foreign affairs. This he had done many times before and his speeches had been interesting for their indication that 1840 had taught him a lesson – France should never again allow herself to be isolated and alone in a European crisis – and for the repeated emphasis he put on the importance of the 'English alliance'. Since he himself had shattered it in 1840, his criticisms of Guizot for jeopardizing it in 1842–4, when there was Anglo-French friction on account of France's annexation of Tahiti and other Pacific islands, and for shattering it in 1846 as a result of the quarrel over marriages into the royal house of Spain, were less telling than they might have been. But in the course of a visit to England in 1845 he had made it up with Palmerston and since then, like Molé, he had become intimate with the new British Ambassador to Paris, Lord Normanby. By 1848 he was on stronger ground, for Guizot, likewise anxious since the rift with England that France should not be isolated, had effected a *rapprochement* with the conservative Powers of Europe. Unfortunately for him he had done so at a time when the constitutional and nationalist movements with which French Liberals and nationalists generally sympathized were threatening the stability of the countries ruled by his new friends. Louis-

Philippe, enthroned by a revolution, was proud of having become a pillar of European order against revolution, but his doing so at such a juncture added to his now widespread unpopularity.

Once again, as so often later in the twentieth century, Europe was sharply divided. In these new speeches on foreign policy Thiers made no bones about it. Having recognized that it was necessary to maintain a balance between states under absolute and under free governments, he roundly declared that whenever an absolute government disappeared and a free one arose, France lost an enemy and gained a friend. This did not mean that by force or propaganda she should introduce liberty to countries which did not possess it, but she should protect it where it had developed freely. Of the 1815 treaties he said that they must be observed but detested, and, after a trenchant attack on the government for meddling in Swiss affairs, he asserted that he was not a radical but that at home and abroad he was 'of the party of the Revolution'; he would like this to be in moderate hands, but if it fell into more ardent ones he would still be of that party.[45] His fiercest assault was on 10 February when he denounced government policy as counter-revolutionary and anti-national: 'You may say that I am mad and wish to ruin my country, that I am a weak man dragged along by a party. I reply that you are the instruments of a government that is blind and leading the country to its destruction.'[46] In Sainte-Beuve's opinion he had made three 'great and magnificent speeches'.[47]

Before sitting down Thiers referred to 'this tumult which has been alarming all citizens for the past four days'. It was not speeches inside Parliament, however eloquent, but the complications and eventual bloodshed arising from 'this tumult' outside it which would force a change of government far sooner than anyone expected – in a fortnight's time. Unfortunately for France and for Thiers they were to topple the regime itself, not only the government.

The 'tumult' concerned a reform banquet. Since the banquets had so far achieved little or nothing, some National Guard officers suggested that another should be held in the poorest and most radical district of Paris, the 12th *arrondissement*, but the Prefect of Police, understandably fearing disorders, had forbidden it. What were the reformers to do? Chambolle, a deputy as well as an eminent journalist, proposed that he and the others who were deputies should resign *en masse* in the hope of forcing a dissolution of parliament. Thiers supported the proposal as the lesser of two evils, but most of the organizers preferred to go ahead with the banquet, changing the time and place and devising a face-saving transaction. This, however, was not what the Republicans wanted and one of them, Marrast, took it upon himself to publish in the *National* of 21 February a programme making the affair into an elaborate public ceremony involving the National Guard, whose interests the government had for many years foolishly neglected. Thereupon the authorities renewed their ban, reminding the reformers that the National Guard could not be paraded by an unofficial group. At another agonized meeting of opposition deputies Thiers was insistent that the banquet should be called off. The majority agreed but decided, as a gesture to mollify their disappointed supporters, on drawing up a Bill of impeachment against the ministry. Thiers, believing that, like the banquet, this would simply stir up public excitement, preferred a petition to the King asking for a change of government.[48] But he was overruled.

After the meeting he walked a short distance with two Legitimists, one of whom, Falloux, expressed his fear that they were on the eve of a revolution. Thiers, Falloux alleged, pooh-poohed the idea and said that the government had ample forces to deal with any *émeute*. The National Guard would give Guizot a good lesson and the King 'having a sharp ear, will see reason and yield in time'.[49] Thiers might have been whistling in the dark and refusing to admit to Legitimists that revolution, in which they might have an interest, was a possibility. On the other hand his success in restoring order as Minister of the Interior in 1834–5 might well have made him over-confident that violence could be dealt with with equal ease in 1848. If so he was sadly mistaken. The meeting of Opposition deputies on the 21st had adjourned further discussion of an act of impeachment until the 24th. Before that day was over revolution had occurred.

As in 1830 trouble began in the streets. On the 22nd large crowds gathered near the Madeleine and in the Champs-Elysées, not knowing that the banquet had been cancelled. As Thiers saw for himself on a walk across the Champs-Elysées, some barricades had gone up, and when he was recognized he was greeted by mingled cries of 'Vive Thiers! A bas Guizot!' and – much less agreeable to hear – 'A bas les bastilles! A bas les lois de Septembre!'; stones were thrown in his direction.[50] Before the day ended there had been fatal casualties. The situation was serious and, as a French historian has written, the 23rd might well have been a *journée* or day of insurrection.[51]

At a meeting ten days earlier Thiers was recorded to have remarked sarcastically: 'If we are ready for a revolution, give your banquet.'[52] The moderate reformers by no means wanted a revolution but this could not be said of all Republicans and certainly not of the Republican secret societies who were at their strongest in Paris. On the 23rd there was fighting at several places and many National Guards, called out to help restore order, showed that their sympathies were with the opposition. This was not surprising when the reformers were likely to give them the vote so far refused by Guizot and his colleagues. Dismayed at his government's inability to master the situation, Louis-Philippe was persuaded to accept Guizot's resignation and send for Molé to form a new Cabinet. Thus it was the National Guards and the people in the street, not the Opposition leaders in Parliament who were forcing a change of government.

Thiers had for some time expected that if Louis-Philippe was ever obliged to part with Guizot he would first call on Molé and have recourse to Thiers himself only in 'a dangerous extremity'.[53] So it was now. Reluctantly Molé began the ritual consultations. They included a visit to Thiers who refused to take office under him but promised unconditional support. Some time before Molé's arrival Thiers had had other visitors. A crowd had gathered outside his house. He and his family had talked to them and allowed them into the courtyard. They went away delighted when Madame Dosne, like many other Parisians, had arranged for lighted candles to be set in all the windows to demonstrate her household's pleasure in the change of government and the prospect of reform. Two had then come back, saying they were hungry – one was an unemployed hairdresser – and the ladies had seen that they were fed and Thiers had given them 20 or 25 francs apiece.[54] All had gone well and, with luck, the news of Guizot's resignation and the likelihood of reforms (although Molé was no ardent reformer, he was an experienced enough politician to know that reforms would have to be made) would suffice to restore calm. Unlike Charles X, who had clung too long to Polignac, it could be hoped that Louis-Philippe had got rid of Guizot in time.

But there was no luck. Thiers's two young visitors had not long departed when a man came to his *concierge* and bade him tell his master to have the lights put out; there was no longer any reason to rejoice.[55] Fighting in various parts of the city continued and now the situation had worsened dramatically. Soldiers posted in front of the Ministry of Foreign Affairs, scared by a procession of demonstrators led by disaffected National Guards, had fired on them, killing twenty and wounding over fifty.[56] All too many people jumped to the conclusion that the incident was a deliberate act of treachery on the part of the King and his advisers. The elderly aristocrat, Molé, was not the man for such a situation. He renounced his mission and towards 1 a.m. on the 24th Louis-Philippe sent for Thiers. Nine precious hours had been lost.

So the time for Thiers to fulfil his pact with Barrot had come at last, but the 'extremity' was even more dangerous than he could have imagined. Moreover, before he reached the Tuileries towards 3 a.m., Louis-Philippe, without waiting to consult him, had given command of the troops and National Guards to Marshal Bugeaud. Bugeaud was a good friend of Thiers and the King's move was understandable since Bugeaud had successfully quelled the Paris rising of 1834. But it was of doubtful wisdom since Bugeaud was wrongly regarded as having been responsible for the 'massacre' of the Rue Transnonain[57] and was accordingly very unpopular with Parisians. People could easily believe that his nomination heralded another bloody repression, for which indeed he was initially diposed.

At the Tuileries the King, reluctantly agreeing to a Thiers–Barrot ministry, urged Thiers to get a Cabinet together with the utmost speed but refused to hear of a dissolution of Parliament. Thiers began his consultations at once; before daybreak he had discussed the military situation briefly with Bugeaud, whose impressions were not encouraging, and agreed with Barrot both on a Cabinet and on the reform policies already envisaged at the end of 1845. Inevitably these would mean dissolution and fresh elections. Meanwhile many friends and colleagues had impressed upon him the unwisdom of Bugeaud's appointment. Sometime between 7.00 and 8.30 a.m. Thiers returned to the Tuileries along with Barrot and others and eventually induced Louis-Philippe to agree both to a dissolution and to the transfer of command of the National Guard to the more popular General Lamoricière under Bugeaud's general direction. Conciliation, not repression, was to be the new government's policy. Towards 10 a.m. the following proclamation was drafted:

> Citizens of Paris, the order has been given to cease fire everywhere. We have been commissioned by the King to form a new ministry.
> The Chamber will be dissolved. There will be an appeal to the country.
> General Lamoricière has been appointed Commander-in-Chief of the National Guard.
> MM. Odilon Barrot, Thiers, Lamoricière, Duvergier de Hauranne are appointed ministers.
> Liberty, order, reform.
>   Odilon Barrot and A. Thiers

But there were great difficulties in getting the proclamation printed and circulated and meanwhile the military situation had sharply deteriorated. In 1830 the defection of two regiments of the line had turned the tide against Charles X. On the morning of 24 February 1848 the demoralization of General Bedeau's men, who started to fraternize with insurgents and threw down their arms when Bugeaud ordered them to withdraw to the Place de la Concorde, had a similar effect. By 9 a.m. the north of the city between the Hôtel de Ville and the Place de la Concorde was for the most part in the hands of the National Guard and the insurgents. Thiers is said to have urged that, if things got worse, the King should withdraw to Saint-Cloud and thence call up sufficient troops to take the offensive, but the King ignored this advice, if indeed it was given, and eventually contented himself with a half-hearted attempt to rally the National Guard on duty near the palace.[58] Meanwhile Thiers's own situation had deteriorated. Some of the many people who now found their way into the Tuileries declared that his name was also too unpopular to influence the insurgents and that Barrot should head the new ministry. He agreed to step down, but at the King's request stayed at the palace to give advice.

So Thiers's third Cabinet was still-born. His unpopularity had disarmed him and it was left to Barrot to try and quell the insurrection and save the regime. Yet he, too, proved powerless to do so. The Republicans, done out of their victory in 1830, were bent on revenge. Much better organized and

Citoyens
DE PARIS

L'ordre est donné partout de suspendre le feu.

Nous venons d'être chargés par le Roi de former un nouveau ministère.

La chambre va être dissoute. Un appel est fait au pays.

Le général Lamoricière est nommé commandant en chef de la garde nationale de Paris.

MM. ODILLON BARROT, THIERS, LAMORICIÈRE DUVERGIER DE HAURANNE sont nommés ministres.

Liberté, Ordre, Réforme.

ODILLON BARROT et A. THIERS.

Im primerie Lange Levy et comp., rue du Croissant.

Plate 3   Thiers' abortive ministry. Proclamation of 24 February, 1848 far more numerous than before, they had successfully suggested that only Louis-Philippe's abdication would satisfy the people. Then, after the king had complied and abdicated in favour of his 10-year-old grandson, the Comte de Paris, and it was up to the deputies to arrange for a regency, the Republicans promoted the invasion of the Chamber. A Republic, the second of its name, was proclaimed at the Hôtel de Ville.

The events of 23 and 24 February 1848 were a shattering experience for many well-to-do Parisians who feared that the Republic would mean social anarchy, and for none more than Thiers. After the abdication he appears to have felt that all was over so far as he was concerned. He made his way to the Chamber but stayed for only a brief time, sitting in a state of dazed gloom and mechanically repeating to those who asked him questions: 'The tide is rising. The tide is rising.' A robust colleague, Talabot, took him home by a circuitous route, first on foot as far as the Bois de Boulogne and then in a cabriolet by way of the outer boulevards. He alleged that during the journey Thiers had gesticulated and sobbed and talked incoherently. The rumour spread that he had gone mad. It even reached England whence, about a month later, Henry Reeve wrote to Léon Faucher asking if Thiers had lost his reason.[59] He had not, but he had been up all night trying to form a Cabinet, trying to cope with an old and difficult ruler, trying to size up an ever worsening military situation, at the same time listening to hordes of people giving contradictory advice and, when he went from the Tuileries to Bugeaud's headquarters and, later, to the Chamber, perhaps risking his life at the hands of a hostile crowd.[60] It was understandable if, after such physical and emotional strain, ending with the collapse of all his hopes, he had suffered a profound nervous reaction.

It is said that, when it was suggested that the King should abdicate, Thiers was asked for his advice but refused to say anything, and that when Louis-Philippe made up his mind and was in the act of signing the abdication act the Queen, in an emotional outburst, accused Thiers of being the ruin of the regime. Some contemporaries agreed with her, for instance Dr Véron, who, it is true, had broken with Thiers by the time he wrote his well-known *Mémoires d'un bourgeois de Paris*, and so have some of his French biographers. Thus one of the most hostile, Lucas-Dubreton, accused Thiers of giving the monarchy the final blow by advising a cease-fire and thus disarming Bugeaud; Pomaret wrote that involuntarily Thiers had been one of the most *sûrs artisans* of the unexpected revolution; and the Duc de Castries has declared that he was one of the persistent 'artisans' of the fall of the regime,[61] deliberately bringing about the abdication of a King who had not esteemed him at what he thought his proper worth.[62] Another writer, speaking of divisions in the Opposition, said that some of its members, 'like Thiers', were simply intriguers motivated by personal ambition and seeking to overthrow Guizot in order to take his place.[63]

To consider whether there is any justification for such charges we need to put them in the context of representative government as Thiers saw it and as it was then practised in England which he and so many other Frenchmen regarded as a model. The last charge is the most easily dealt with. When parties are not organized in the twentieth-century sense and politicians adhere to different and often shifting groups, there is bound to be frequent manoeuvring. Thus it has been said that for the two main parties in England at this time, 'politics or the struggle for power was largely a matter of bargaining with the other groups in Parliament'.[64] The floating vote was in the House of Commons itself. The position in the Chamber of Deputies was not dissimilar. Largely by his use of patronage Guizot succeeded in building an unusually homogeneous majority, but the Opposition was much divided, for there were in it Legitimists and Republicans who opposed the regime itself as well as Orleanists of different shades. Any credible Opposition leader was bound to bargain – his opponents would naturally say 'intrigue' – for sufficient support to make his opposition effective, and it is to Thiers's credit that when the crisis came in 1848 he stood by his bargain with Barrot and the Dynastic Left and made it clear to the King that he must share power with them. As for personal ambition, politics being by definition the struggle for power, every opposition leader has the ambition to overthrow the prime minister in office and at the right juncture take his place. This does not mean that he must be denied a sincere belief that he could serve his country better than the present incumbent or that Thiers was not sincerely convinced of the mistakenness of Guizot's policies and the advisability, in the country's interests, of the change of course which he and Barrot had thought out more than two years earlier.

What of the other charges? As one of the architects of the July Monarchy Thiers could hardly be expected to wish to destroy it deliberately, and there is no evidence that disillusionment induced any such desire. On the contrary he held firmly to the view of representative government that he had enunciated from the outset, namely that the King should reign but not rule, while his political activities as a representative were for the most part scrupulously confined to the parliamentary arena and, like those of other politicians, to exercising influence through the press.[65]

Yet it can be argued that Thiers, and ultimately the regime, were victims of his rashness and belligerency on the one hand and of his caution and wish to adhere to parliamentary procedures on the other. As two French historians have maintained, his belligerent attitude in 1840 convinced the ruling classes in France of the need for a more stable and oligarchical government.[66] Hence representative government remained too narrowly based. Moreover, the King shared this conviction and, as we have seen, did not subscribe to Thiers's view of the monarch's role. After 1840 attacks on foreign policy over which, everyone knew, the King sought a directing influence, inevitably reflected on both Louis-Philippe and Guizot. Some of

Thiers's speeches early in 1848 were no fiercer than Disraeli's celebrated onslaught on Peel a year before, and it is difficult to know how much influence they had outside Parliament. However, it could be argued that they were unnecessarily inflammatory when tensions in Europe were rising and when the banquet question was stirring emotions in Paris, the capital of a country in which there was no general consensus of allegiance to the Crown. In England the miniscule Republican movement did not reach its zenith until about 1870; but in France the Legitimists were irreconcilable and the Republicans outside Parliament a growing force.

At the same time Thiers can be taxed with excessive caution and calculation. Had he come out sooner and more boldly in favour of reform and fearlessly espoused the banquet campaign, the argument would run, he would have regained popularity and many Parisians, above all the National Guard, would have rallied and enabled him to save the situation on the crucial morning of 24 February. Lack of courage was the implied charge in a curious anonymous letter of 20 February in which the writer told Thiers that his inactivity during the last two or three years had discredited him and discouraged his friends. His recent speeches had done good, 'but we always remember the prediction: "You will have as many speeches as you want from M. Thiers, but never an act."'[67] This was a remarkable comment on the erstwhile admirer of Vauvenargues who had once seemed to be a human dynamo. So, too, various critics implied that the Revolution would have been halted and suppressed had Thiers had the courage to leave Bugeaud in command with a free hand to continue hostilities. All these 'ifs' are big ones. For one thing, there is evidence to suggest that already, before Thiers's return to the Tuileries, Bugeaud had decided to renounce the use of force in favour of persuasion.[68] For another, given his unpreparedness, it is by no means certain that Bugeaud could have done any better than Marmont in 1830 or achieved in February 1848 what, at great cost, Cavaignac accomplished in June. Nor can we be sure that the regime could politically have survived the inevitable slaughter.

Whatever Thiers's errors of omission or commission, the fall of the regime was the last thing he intended. Nor is there any clear evidence that he actively schemed to bring about the King's abdication. There was certainly no love lost between the two men after 1840 and each said rude things about the other,[69] but Louis-Philippe was an old man and Thiers, as he once laughingly told Guizot, could afford to wait. As for the final crisis on the morning of 24 February the evidence is contradictory: Beaumont asserted that Duvergier and Thiers recommended abdication, Rémusat denied it.[70] Other accounts say that Thiers remained silent when asked for his opinion and that silence was naturally regarded as meaning assent.[71] There may well be truth in the assertion that he was angry that the King had put him in what he thought was an impossible situation.[72] He might well sadly have felt that the sovereign who had lost so much time by at first refusing him permission to dissolve Parliament and had then rejected his advice to withdraw to safety (Saint-Cloud?) was beyond saving and that, if he did not abdicate, his unpopularity might even cost him his life.

This said, one grave charge remains which is difficult to rebut. Once Louis-Philippe had abdicated, there is no indication that Thiers, who had taken such pains over the Regency Bill in 1842 and who on 31 May 1846 had told a friend that the monarchy was indispensable,[73] did anything to ensure that monarchy's continuance by proclaiming or defending a regency on 24 February 1848. In a revolutionary situation there was indeed little hope of support for Thiers's formerly preferred candidate, the relatively unknown and unpopular Nemours, but whatever Thiers's views about a woman regent, the Duchesse d'Orléans had popularity and courage as she showed when she herself went to the Chamber with her son after the King's abdication. She was then the monarchy's last hope. As one of Thiers's most hostile critics said, he too should have had courage, the courage to remain in the Chamber to stem the mounting tide; he should have defended the Regency 'in one of those speeches he was so good at improvising'.[74] To his credit this was what Odilon Barrot did, although in vain, whereas Thiers, now wholly incapable of happy improvisation, had broken down and gone home. The breakdown can be explained; it is less easily excused in an *homme de gouvernement* who had once displayed clear qualities of leadership.

[6]

Problems in a Republic, 1848–1849

On 28 July 1830 Thiers and Mignet had prudently spent a night away from home in order to avoid arrest. Now, on 24 February 1848, exhausted after the ordeals of another revolution, Thiers was again advised not to sleep at home owing to the risks of fighting nearby or even an attack on his house in the Place Saint-Georges. This time he took refuge in the suburban villa of a young Italian friend, Countess Taverna-Martini. It was there that he learnt that the Orleanist monarchy had been swept away and a Republic proclaimed. At about the same time Guizot, much more likely to be an object of popular violence, was hiding in the house of his old friend, Madame de Mirbel, before joining Louis-Philippe in exile in England.

Thiers, a leader of the parliamentary opposition under the fallen regime and advocate of moderate reform, had no need to quit France. He was a resilient man; he soon returned home, recorded his account of the revolution he had just passed through[1] and resumed work on his history of the Empire. On 26 March Madame Dosne reported that her son-in-law was wonderfully well and writing twenty pages every morning.[2] But he was a political animal as well as an historian and soon had to decide how far and in what ways he should adjust himself to the new political situation.

This was far more radical than could have been envisaged a few months earlier. As in 1830, the revolution was in part a triumph for the opposition press. But the *Constitutionnel* and the *Siècle*, papers associated with Thiers and Barrot, had counted for nothing. The organs with which most of the members of the new Provisional Government were connected were the Republican *National* and, still further to the Left, champion of social as well as political changes, the *Réforme*. And with men such as Carnot, Ledru-Rollin, and Louis Blanc, who were now in power, that most eloquent of poets, Lamartine, who admired Thiers's writing but detested his politics, had thrown in his lot. The change in governing personnel was radical, the change in governing outlook was radical, and, as in 1830, revolution was followed by unbridled freedom of the press and of meeting, frequent demonstrations and continuing disorder.

But France's new governors were caretakers whose care was to provide for a properly constituted and, they hoped, permanent Republican regime. On 5 March they issued the most crucial decree of their brave new era. They ordained that elections should be held in April for a national Assembly which would draft a Republican constitution. The elections were to be held by universal male suffrage. At a stroke of the pen the electorate was increased from some 240,000 to some 9,000,000. This great leap forward was also a leap into the dark.

On the day before the decree was promulgated Thiers told a friend that a moderate Republic was now the regime most to be desired.[3] This was basically his position throughout the next few years. He and his friends recognized that for the time being a restoration of monarchy was out of the question. In a celebrated speech six months later he said that they had neither made nor desired the Republic but that they accepted it: 'We have always wanted the kind of liberty which shields the country's affairs from the dual pressure of courts and streets. We have wanted good financial administration, prestige for the country, and a policy in accord with national interests. We shall pursue all this in the future as in the past.'[4] The question was how they should do so. For Thiers, of course, Parliament was the principal arena in which to exercise influence, and when it was known that elections were to be held it was natural that he should receive invitations to be a candidate. He accepted one to stand again in his native department of Bouches-du-Rhône, but did so in a very half-hearted way, unsure, it seems, whether it might not be too soon to re-enter political life. He would not go to Aix, he told one of his friends there, or publish an election letter: 'My past life should answer for my life to come.'[5] Yet he hoped to be returned unopposed and when he learnt that there were to be rival candidates he hastily wrote an election address. It was a very honest document but fatalistic and lacked his normal confident pungency. He did not disavow his past or want a Republic. But Providence had decided otherwise, and, though he was ready to resist any tyranny, he would never resist 'la force des choses'. He thought that his political experience might be of use and so it was out of a sense of duty that he had accepted a candidature. But he begged his friends not to compromise themselves by making efforts on his behalf. If he were unsuccessful he would happily return to retirement and study.[6] To Rémusat he was more explicit; he dreamt of a little house in Rome and of working there on the history of the world which had been his dream since childhood.[7]

The elections of 23 April were held by *scrutin de liste*, which meant that each elector was entitled to cast as many votes as there were to be deputies representing his department. In the Bouches-du-Rhône there were twenty-two candidates for ten seats, and Thiers came eighteenth, securing only 22,042 votes compared with the 72,084 polled by the Republican Barthélemy. His defeat was not surprising. His candidature had been strenuously opposed by the regime, as well as by Catholics and Legitimists, and voters were unlikely to flock to support a candidate so lacking in enthusiasm. In his address Thiers had said that he would not be disconcerted if he failed, but when the news came he privately admitted to bitterness at having been beaten by 'bankrupts, briefless barristers and charlatans', while his mother-in-law seethed with indignation that Aix had repudiated 'sa plus belle gloire moderne'. The defeat rankled all the more since 'M. Thiers has the honour of being almost the only opposition deputy to be rejected'. The Bouches-du-Rhône had put itself beyond the pale. 'Henceforward', Madame Dosne declared, 'we renounce this department. Whatever happens... M. Thiers would never agree to represent it, it is a divorce during his life and after his death.'[8] Yet in the by-elections of June his name again went forward there, only to be once more rejected. Thereafter it would be fifteen years before Thiers consented to be a candidate in the Bouches-du-Rhône and then, too, in 1863, he was defeated. Yet he tried again in 1869. Successful in winning the support of an electorate of some 400, he had found it difficult to conquer one of more than 30,000.

The setback in April 1848 was only temporary. In opposition earlier in the 1840s Thiers had seldom made a speech without telling his audience that he was an old hand in politics; in his recent electoral address he had reminded his former constituents of his experience. It was indeed by now considerable. He had sat continuously in Parliament for more than seventeen years, he had twice been prime minister and for seven years one of the main leaders of the opposition; moreover he was renowned not only as an orator but also for his ability to master technical subjects. The newly elected National Assembly, which met for the first time early in May, was a vast gathering of 900 'representatives', of whom only 165 had sat in previous parliaments. Dismayed by his rejection in April, many men of moderate views believed that Thiers would have much to contribute to such an inexperienced chamber and should enter it as soon as possible. He did not have long to wait since several by-elections were to take place on 4 June. In mid-May Thiers told a supporter that he had had invitations from electoral committees in ten or twelve departments. Now, both sought after and clear in his own mind that he wished to be elected, he was returned in four departments and chose to sit for Seine-Inférieure.[9] Thus in this year 1848, which saw so many dramatic changes in fortune and reputation, Thiers was again a rising star. But his rise was far less dramatic than that of a newcomer elected at the same time. This newcomer preferred not to take his seat for the time being and resigned. When, however, he was elected in five departments in September and some weeks later intimated willingness to become President of the Republic, no one could ignore him. The newcomer's name was Louis-Napoleon Bonaparte.

The National Assembly had been sitting for a month when Thiers joined it. Called by one historian an assembly of rural Girondins,[10] many of its members, like Thiers himself, were reasonably well-to-do and few were very youthful. A majority were moderate men or monarchists who had not been obliged to take an oath of allegiance to the new regime but who, at any rate for the time being, favoured a moderate Republic. What they did not want at any price was the kind of democratic Socialist Republic championed by some of their extreme colleagues on the Left and by many Parisian workers' clubs that had sprung to life since the revolution. They wanted it still less after their session on 15 May was interrupted by a mob, one of whose leaders pronounced the Assembly's dissolution and the formation of a new provisional government at the Hôtel de Ville. The coup failed, but it naturally alarmed the representatives, impaired their confidence in the Executive Commission they had just appointed to replace the Provisional Government, increased their distrust of Parisian extremists, and drove them to greater conservatism.

With such men Thiers could sympathize. As early as 4 March he had expressed his fear that France was threatened 'not by an agrarian law, which is too difficult to apply, but by the communism of the workers which will, if it is not restrained, make industry and trade impossible and ruin the country from top to bottom'.[11] Industry and trade were indeed flagging. Continuing disorders and political uncertainty caused a run on the banks and increased unemployment which became a grave problem. To relieve the situation the Provisional Government had set up National Workshops, which were soon full not only of the genuinely unemployed but also of men who refused to return to work in the poor conditions which had prevailed before the revolution. Some of these had been among the invaders of the Assembly on 15 May, and after that traumatic event the majority of representatives sought to end what some saw as a permanent organized strike. After the end of the month, when the numbers in the Workshops had swollen to 103,000, they were all the more eager to do so, since the presence of so many men occupied by largely useless labour appeared to pose a continuing threat to orderly government. On 21 June the Minister of Public Works began what was intended to be the process of dispersal by decreeing that workers between the ages of 18 and 25 should join the army or leave for the provinces. The measure was harsh. It was no real remedy for what was a grave social problem and it provoked a violent confrontation, the rising of the June Days, which required three days of bitter fighting to put down. Order and relative confidence were restored by Cavaignac, a Republican general of unimpeachable integrity, to whom the Assembly gave dictatorial powers in the emergency. The Executive Commission was superseded and, when the fighting was over and Cavaignac laid down his office, the Assembly in gratitude entrusted him with executive power and the title of President of the Council of Ministers. More than twenty-two years later Thiers himself would hold a similar position in not dissimilar circumstances.

Such was the most dramatic part of the background to Thiers's first month as a representative in the National Assembly. He was living in dangerous times and when the June Days trouble began, mindful no doubt of the events of 15 May, he was said to have suggested that the Assembly should make contingency plans to leave for some provincial town such as Bourges; on hearing this, Cavaignac is alleged to have commented that if M. Thiers repeated such a suggestion, he would have him shot.[12] Thiers was not shot, but during the rising a mob threatened to pillage and burn down his house, and on 5 August a bullet, presumably meant for him, pierced Mignet's hat as he was about to visit his old friend. After such incidents it is not surprising that Thiers kept pistols in his pocket for at least a year. They came in handy in 1849 for a different reason: first, he nearly fought a duel with one of his Republican colleagues, Trélat; then, when another colleague, Bixio, attributed to him derogatory remarks about Louis-Napoleon which he regretted having spoken, he denied them and promptly called him out to the Bois de Boulogne. It was only later in the day that he told the ladies of his household that he had fought a duel.[13] Fortunately, as happened in most of these political 'affairs of honour' which continued in France throughout the nineteenth century, both combatants came through unscathed.

Meanwhile, in the National Assembly his expertise was much in demand. In an undated letter, probably written soon after the June rising, he described his day. At 8 a.m. he went to the Finance Committee and at 11 to his bureau; from 2 to 7 he attended the general session of the Assembly and then, after allowing an hour for dinner, made his way to a meeting in the Rue de Poitiers. He never, he said, got home before 11 p.m.; it was 'a frightful life', but he thought he had never been more useful: 'I perorate constantly in the Bureaux and Committees whilst waiting for the moment for speaking from the tribune to come.'[14]

Such moments came at the end of July, the beginning of August, and the middle of September. On 26 July he scathingly denounced as an attack on property a complicated Bill proposed by the Socialist, Proudhon, for the relief of debtors through a great expansion of cheap credit and a reduction in state salaries and pensions. The Assembly was indeed with him – it rejected the Bill by 691 votes to 2, condemning it as 'an odious attack on the principles of public morality' and as a measure 'that appealed to the worst passions'.[15] On 2 August the majority of his hearers again approved when he voiced the Finance Committee's recommendation that a tax on mortgage loans, introduced by the Provisional Government in April (it fell, he said, on the poorest class of investors who sought security), should be removed, but when he had the apparent temerity to assert that the new tax which deserved to be most seriously considered and even perhaps tried was an income tax there were cries and movements of dissent. In view of the dire financial plight of France in 1848, he appeared to support such a tax, quoting the precedent of England, where the tax had been 'the object of a kind of reprobation' at first, but 'good sense . . . recognizing its necessity, had ended by accepting it'.[16] It seems, however, that his apparent support was a scarecrow and that, as with Gladstone, an income tax was the last thing he really wanted. In later years he strenuously opposed it.[17]

His third speech from the tribune, on 13 September, concerned an amendment to the preamble of the draft constitution. In May, soon after it first met, the National Assembly, mindful that it was a constituent assembly, had appointed a constitutional committee. Had Thiers been elected in April he might well have been one if its members. The fact that he was not was perhaps the sole serious disadvantage which he suffered from his rebuff in the Bouches-du-Rhône. Too late to join the committee as a member, he could meet it only as one of the delegates of the fifteen bureaux who were invited to proffer their views.[18] Thus he had no direct influence on the structure of the new constitution; indeed his strong plea that the future Parliament should consist of two chambers, not one, was rejected both by the committee and the Assembly. Whether the existence of two chambers would have made any difference to the subsequent fortunes of the new Republic, once it had been decided that its President should be elected by universal suffrage instead of by the National Assembly, is a moot point.

On two controversial issues Thiers's interventions certainly represented the views of many well-to-do people regardless of party. The first was whether the Assembly should accept an amendment to Article VIII of the preamble whereby the Republic would categorically recognize the right of all citizens to work, one of the great slogans of 1848. Thiers vigorously opposed such recognition. He knew that the people were indeed suffering, but asserted that in general the workers' lot had much improved in the last half century. Property, liberty and competition were the bases of society. The basis of property was work. What did the Assembly wish to substitute for the principle of hard work – such words as commonalty, association, reciprocity, and fraternity? Association spelt industrial anarchy. The right to work, he declared, meant 'a salary for idle workers congregated in large towns'. The evil his hearers wished to remedy was unemployment. Aid to relieve it should not be made a right, but, according to circumstances, the state should provide public work for the unemployed to whom private work was not available.[19] Thiers was of course right in saying, as he had in his bureau, that if industry came to a standstill because of successive crises it would be impossible for the state to provide work for from 1,500,000 to 2,000,000 workers.[20] People living in the latter part of the twentieth century are only too aware of the impossibility of guaranteeing the right to work. In 1848, however, the tone of the debate, in which such eminent representatives as Tocqueville and Lamartine also opposed the amendment was only too evidently and understandably coloured by memories of the National Workshops and the June Days. The amendment was rejected by 596 to 187.

Napoleon once said that a constitution should be short and obscure. The Republican constitution of 1848 was the reverse. It was very long and its authors sought to spell everything out. Thus, whereas the Charters of 1814 and 1830 had left the details of manning the armed forces to a subsequent law on recruitment, the authors of the draft constitution of 1848 specifically did away with the right of a conscript to provide a substitute saying: 'Substitution is forbidden.' In doing so, they had the approval of two generals, Cavaignac and the Minister of War, Lamoricière. In the Assembly in October a great debate ensued, in which, it has been said, there was 'a confrontation not only between the democratic and the bourgeois concepts of the army but also between the technical notions of a professional army (*armée de métier*) and a nation in arms'.[21] Thiers spoke passionately, as he would throughout his life, in favour of the long-service professional army. The abolition of substitution, he said, would necessitate shortening the term of service and be the ruin of the army. The system of substitutes meant that the army obtained a good soldier instead of a bad one. The army gave the peasant a better life; he was better fed and clothed and after seven years he returned home 'plus fort, plus moral et mieux instruit'. With a shorter term of service it would be necessary to adopt the system which Prussia had developed because of her small population and her wish to play the role of a Great Power. But *l'esprit militaire* could not be acquired in six months.[22]

Twenty-two years later the superiority of the Prussian system was dramatically demonstrated to the detriment of France, but Thiers's views were not changed. Meanwhile he and those who thought like him had as good as won a victory. The clause prohibiting substitution was reworded to say that the facility for each citizen to free himself from personal military service would be regulated by the recruitment law. There is no reason to doubt the sincerity of Thiers's belief in the superiority of the *armée de métier*, but he also earned the gratitude of many upper- and middle-class parents who could afford to pay for substitutes and did not wish their sons to serve; substitution had long been a part of France's social pattern and Cavaignac himself had admitted that its abolition would be a shock to existing habits.[23]

Some of these grateful parents he no doubt encountered at the meetings in the *salle des séances* of the Académie de Médecine in the Rue de Poitiers, to which he had referred in the letter relating his day's activities. These meetings had been started at the end of May by a number of representatives, mostly from the provinces, who had never sat in a parliament before and wished to exchange views. After a while they opened their doors to men who had previously been deputies. These were mostly conservative in outlook and it was not surprising that before long old hands such as Molé, Berryer, and Thiers came to exercise a dominating influence in their deliberations and that, as the numbers attending the meetings were often between 300 and 400, the Réunion de la Rue de Poitiers came to function as an effective pressure group. This was largely due to Cavaignac's difficult political position. A Republican of the moderate *National* school, he was detested by the more extreme Republicans for his suppression of the June rising, and, not having a large enough following of his own, he was obliged from time to time to sacrifice men and measures to the pressures of Thiers and his friends.[24] Such pressures did not make for good relations between Thiers and the head of the government. Thiers described Cavaignac as 'a sorry pilot'; Cavaignac, no doubt, regarded Thiers as a reactionary intriguer.[25] Their mutual antipathy was of particular importance when it came to electing a President of the Republic.

But before that election campaign Thiers had won fresh acclaim from conservatives, this time as an author. In 1849 his old antagonist, Guizot, was to publish a pamphlet entitled *De la démocratie en France* which was speedily translated into English and hailed by the Tory John Wilson Croker as the finest defence of property since Burke.[26] But Thiers had anticipated him. Sometime in the late summer in the quiet of Franconville, a demesne near Luzarches in Seine-et-Oise belonging to the Massa family, who were connected by marriage with the Dosnes, he had written a tract for the times. It was at first serialized in the *Constitutionnel* and then, in November, published as one of a series of 'little treatises' sponsored by the Académie des Sciences Morales et Politiques. The title was *Du droit de propriété*. The series was intended to deal with questions relating to social order and to educate the new electorate. Thiers's speeches during the summer and early autumn had clearly revealed his preoccupation with property as a basis of social order and it was appropriate that he should also defend it with his pen. He had not written a booklet since *La Monarchie de 1830* in 1831, but his hand had not lost its cunning. What he wrote was very readable and just what property-owners wanted to read. Congratulations poured in and, in at least one instance, the little work was literally used to educate the people. A landowner in the Loire wrote that he had read extracts aloud to his peasants one Sunday and that they had enjoyed what they heard so much that they wished to bring their wives and children on the following Sunday.[27]

Du droit de propriété, which Thiers had in mind as early as 1845, was no original contribution to political thinking, but it is of interest on two counts, apart from developing the fairly commonplace thoughts on property and social order scattered in his speeches. First of all, with its references to God, the unity of divine laws, and the planets, it is the published work most nearly akin to a fragment of the great historico-philosophical work that he dreamt of but never wrote. Secondly, there are two passages which characteristically display the independent attitude he wished to adopt towards the world or which hint at a private problem. The independence was voiced in a sentence in which he said that he had already arrived at 'a mature age, which in a few years would become old age' (he was 50), and that he had witnessed several revolutions and expected and desired nothing from any power on earth. The problem is suggested by a moving description of a rich man who was childless and therefore adopted a nephew or niece or, if he had no nephew, went to 'a poor woman of the field to borrow from her an object of love'. Thiers was relatively rich, although he, like many others, was said to have suffered financially from the commotions of 1848, and he was childless. Was this passage merely conventional sentimentality or did it reflect a personal pang? Would he have liked to adopt a child but been opposed by his three ladies? Without further evidence it is impossible to say.

The constitution of the Second French Republic – 'the very worst', thought Normanby, 'that ever reached that finishing stage of manufacture'[28] – was approved by the Assembly on 4 November. It was agreed that the first task was to choose the President, who had been invested with considerable executive powers and, like the single-chamber Parliament, the Legislative Assembly, was to be elected by universal suffrage.[29] He was to be responsible for the government's acts and could choose and dismiss his ministers who need not necessarily be members of parliament. Designed to produce strong government and facilitate the continued restoration of order after the anarchy of the earlier months of 1848, the new system, ironically, was in some ways the antithesis of the kind of representative government for which Thiers and his friends had striven in 1830. As a check upon any quasi-monarchical ambitions that the holder of such powers might possibly entertain, the Assembly had, however, prescribed one important restraint: he was not to be immediately re-eligible for office. Moreover, although Presidents would normally hold office for four years, the first President's term was to expire in May 1852. Both the powers and the limitations were of immense importance; they resulted from a series of compromises by well-meaning but largely inexperienced legislators and were to pave the way to dictatorship.

Had the choice of President been left to the Assembly, as some had wished, the most likely candidates would have been Cavaignac, already in the saddle, Marrast, the President of the Assembly, and Thiers, the veteran parliamentarian.[30] But election by universal suffrage and the emergence of Louis-Napoleon as a candidate put quite a different complexion on the contest. After his re-election to the Assembly in September, the Bonapartist pretender had decided to take his seat and had subsequently intimated his readiness to stand for President. He might make a poor showing in Parliament, but there was no gainsaying the magic of his name for the uneducated masses.

By the beginning of November there were two firm candidates, Cavaignac and Louis-Napoleon. Both courted Thiers,[31] who for a time was much perplexed as to whether he, too, should stand, whether the Réunion de la Rue de Poitiers should put up a candidate, and, if not, whom they and he should support. Wisely he decided not to stand and risk the sort of defeat he had experienced in April. He also dissuaded his friends from putting forward a man of their own, arguing that this would only split the moderate vote with the result that no candidate would obtain a clear majority and that then the choice would revert to the Assembly which would be sure to elect Cavaignac.[32] But they could not, as a body, agree which of the two existing candidates to support and, with some reluctance, Thiers himself plumped for Louis-Napoleon as the lesser evil.

His motives seem to have been a mixture of fear, self-interest, and fatalism – fear that Cavaignac, once in power for more than three years, might carry the Republic too far to the Left,[33] self-interest in that he, like Mignet and many of his other friends, believed that the Prince was an inexperienced fool whom they could easily manipulate, and fatalism because he thought that the Prince was bound to win and saw no point in swimming against the tide. Whether his choice was in any way affected by the curious fact that, in a proclamation at the time of his abortive coup at Boulogne in 1840, Louis-Napoleon had designated him as his prime minister there is no means of knowing.

Thiers did not meet the man whose good or ill fortune meant so much for his own career during the next twenty-one years until 17 November. He then formed the opinion that the Prince's character was gentle and good and his mind cultivated but a little chimerical. He was soon to have glimpses both of his obstinacy and his deviousness. Having climbed on the Prince's bandwagon Thiers and some of his friends attempted to write the Prince's election manifesto for him. Drafts went to and fro but the Prince quietly stuck to his own version and incorporated only a few of the phrases proposed by his new advisers. The deviousness appeared not long after when it seemed that he was privy to an abortive attempt to filch the *Constitutionnel* from Thiers's control.[34] A few months later, however, Thiers's long connection with the paper was finally severed. Dr Véron, the proprietor, succumbed to the blandishments of Louis-Napoleon's associates, became to all intents and purposes a Bonapartist, and repaid Thiers and his friends the 100,000 francs they had invested in the journal. Thus for the first time in many years Thiers was a politician without a Parisian paper at his command.

For the time being, however, Thiers and Louis-Napoleon needed one another and civilities, once begun, continued. At the end of the first polling day, an auspiciously sunny 10 December, Louis-Napoleon and two of his cousins, Prince Napoleon and Princess Mathilde, dined with the Thiers and some of their friends. On the following night when the results so far known suggested that victory was his, he returned their hospitality. In February, when as President of the Republic he gave his first ball at the Elysée, it was a proud Madame Dosne whom he led into supper.[35]

Louis-Napoleon's electoral triumph was greater even than many of his most ardent supporters had dared to hope. It is likely that he would have won outright even had the moderates of the Rue de Poitiers fielded a candidate. Indeed Rémusat later wrote that all the efforts made by Thiers and his friends on his behalf – among other things they enlisted the *Constitutionnel* and a number of moderate provincial papers in his cause – probably contributed no more than 50,000 of his 5,534,520 votes.[36] Above all it was what Marx called 'the peasant revolution' that swept him to victory.

The Prince-President, as he was soon generally known, invited Thiers to preside over his first Cabinet. Perhaps he thought that the ambitious historian of the Consulate and Empire who had such admiration for his uncle would be a ready and willing tool, and hoped that he could form a ministry of all the talents which would give lustre to the new era over which he was about to preside. To his credit Thiers was not to be caught. He still had a certain loyalty to the House of Orléans and that he, a founder of the July Monarchy should be foremost in taking office under a Bonaparte would indeed have been discreditable. No doubt he agreed, too, with King Leopold of the Belgians who urged him not to assume power when so many great problems, especially economic ones, seemed insoluble, but to keep himself in reserve and, like Peel in England, exercise influence from outside the government.[37] He held to this line at the end of May 1849 when the Prince-President again wished to form a strong government to cope with the new Legislative Assembly. By pursuing it consistently might he not even have a chance of being Louis-Napoleon's successor in 1852?

Meanwhile he was, as ever, free with his advice and readily counselled the President on how he should conduct his household and government, and, since he had campaigned as a man of order, pointed out how important it was for him to lean on the support of *le grand parti modéré*.

For a while the President heeded Thiers's advice in many things. At his suggestion he took Odilon Barrot as head of his first ministry and under Thiers's influence a number of men who had lost their places as a result of the February Revolution gained some sort of position under the new dispensation.[38] But privately, and not always privately enough, each chafed and certainly each worried about the future. Louis-Napoleon was vexed that neither Thiers nor Molé had consented to take office and that he had to take for his first ministers a set of 'understudies',[39] and, although he listened patiently to Thiers's exhortations, he did not necessarily relish them. For their part Thiers and his friends had grossly miscalculated in supposing that the President could be treated as a puppet. They had never before had to deal with an inscrutable half-foreigner who had the backing of five million French voters and regarded himself as a Man of Destiny. Thiers quickly had misgivings. As early as 19 December he had told his mother-in-law that the Prince was a trickster (*un fourbe*) and he feared that they were only at a 'port of call and not the final haven'.[40] For nearly eight months he did his best to keep him 'on the right path' but in the summer the prince asserted his independence and not long afterwards there was a rift. It was soon clear that the harbour towards which the President sought to steer was not that of true parliamentary government. Before the end of 1849 it was an open secret that he wished to restore the Empire.

For Thiers these eight to ten months were characterized by revealing bouts of depression – at Easter he wrote of being without hope: 'Aged 50 I have nothing more but a long wait for the end, and I do not know what is the purpose of the ten or twenty years of life that remain.'[41] During the spring and summer there was also a different cause for depression, a serious recrudescence of cholera. Cholera was no respecter of persons. 'We are dying like flies' wrote Thiers in June.[42] Among those it carried off were Thiers's father-in-law, M. Dosne, and Marshal Bugeaud, whom Louis-Philippe had summoned to restore order in February 1848. Bugeaud was an ambitious soldier who might still have played an important part in French affairs. Both losses affected Thiers personally, for in recent years Bugeaud had become a friend and frequent correspondent. Thiers wrote, too, a charming letter of condolence to his old friend J. -J. Ampère on the death of another cholera victim, the celebrated Madame Récamier, who, he knew, had been to Ampère 'toute une famille'.[43]

Thiers's last speech in the Constituent Assembly had been in an important debate on foreign affairs at the end of March 1849. Even before then he and his colleagues of the Rue de Poitiers had begun preparing for the forthcoming elections to the Legislative Assembly and he, with Molé and Berryer, had acted as a triumvirate to direct a committee of seventy-two appointed for the purpose of co-ordinating the activities of local conservative election committees. They had done their work well. The trend begun in April 1848 had continued, and their so-called Party of Order were the chief gainers, winning approximately 450 of the 750 seats. The moderate Republicans, however, had been far outdistanced by those further to the Left, the Democratic Socialists or Montagnards, as they were beginning to be called, who polled more than 2.5 million votes and obtained 210 seats. Had the positions been reversed there might have been a chance of real parliamentary government, with the alternation of power between the two main parties which generally characterized political life across the Channel. But the polarization towards the extremes which resulted from the elections made this impossible and played into the hands of Louis-Napoleon who claimed to be above parties.

The year 1849 was less tragically revolutionary in France than 1848 yet there were still disturbances enough both there and in Europe as a whole. One of Gladstone's biographers has written that for most members of the House of Commons in the 1860s 'order and strong government were regarded as the essential foundation of liberty, justice, and every other good'.[44] Great Britain in the 1860s was an oasis of calm compared with

France in 1849, and when it is remembered that Thiers more than once had reason to fear for the safety of his family and they for his it is easier to understand why at that time he regarded order and strong government as the prime requisites. At the end of January there was a danger that Left-wing Republicans, angered by a moderate proposal that the Constituent Assembly should end its labours in May, would stage another *journée*, and Madame Dosne, warned of a possible attack on Thiers's house, sent her daughters to sleep elsewhere.[45] On 28 May when the Legislative Assembly met for the first time, Thiers, as he came away, risked being assaulted by young Republicans for refusing to cry 'Vive la République démocratique et sociale',[46] and on 13 June there was another *journée*, the last for many years to come, but no one could be sure of that at the time. The alarm it caused naturally affected the tone of the press Bill introduced by the government at the end of the month and debated in the Legislative Assembly at the end of July. Thiers's intervention is noteworthy on two counts. It clearly stated the limitations of French Liberalism while reaffirming his orthodox Liberal belief that much recent revolutionary unrest was due to mischievous writing which raised false hopes. He could tolerate freedom to discuss the government's acts, but not freedom to dispute its existence or 'give a call to arms and provoke a class war'. So what he wished to veto was 'not a discussion of systems – far from it', but writings 'full of bile and violence in which the people are told that there is a supreme good which can in a moment put an end to everyone's sufferings, that it needs only a single effort of will by the majority to obtain it, but that we do not wish to make it because we are the wicked rich interested in perpetuating the present situation'. No one could bring about the happiness of nations in the twinkling of an eye.[47]

It was foreign policy which provoked this last *journée* and an eventual rift between Louis-Napoleon and Thiers.

When France became a Republic in 1848 many, including Thiers, had feared that one consequence might be a war for which she was unprepared. However, thanks to the prudence of her foreign ministers and the preoccupation of the other Great Powers with their own domestic troubles, war had been averted. Thiers himself had learnt his lesson in 1840. Although in 1850 he would be quite ready to contemplate armed negotiation on behalf of French interests in Uruguay, since this would merely be one of those wars 'which maritime nations should know how to wage when they wish to be respected in the world',[48] he never failed to insist that France must not risk a war in which she would be one against many. Such influence as he was able to exert in 1848 had been wholly on the side of peace. Thus, for example, he had done all he could to impress on the Foreign Minister, Bastide, the risks that France would run on the Rhine if she sent an army into Italy.[49] He was already concerned by the danger to France of a unified Germany.

Italy was the critical area, and, whereas in 1848 France skilfully avoided

113

armed intervention in the peninsula, in 1849 it proved impossible for her to do so. France and Austria had long been rivals there and in January 1848 when the stirrings of Liberal nationalism were gathering momentum Thiers had declared that France wished Italy to be independent, free, and happy, which meant free from the rule and influence of the Austrians whom he called his country's 'inveterate enemies'.[50] He had friends among Italian exiles both in France and in England, and his interest in the history of Florence, which he intended to write, had brought him into contact with many Tuscans, while Mignet had had a liaison and then an enduring if stormy friendship with another celebrated exile, Princess Belgiojoso. Sentimentally everything predisposed Thiers to favour the Italian cause, and in March 1848, when most events at home and abroad were reason for deep anxiety, he had told Rémusat that his one consolation was that the Austrians had been driven from Milan.[51]

A year later the situation was very different. Despite the advice of Thiers and King Leopold of the Belgians, Charles Albert of Sardinia-Piedmont had again gone to war with Austria and, as Thiers had foreseen, been swiftly crushed. What was France to do? In a debate on 31 March he made a powerful speech supporting the government's proposal to negotiate on the basis of the integrity of Piedmontese territory and opposing the Left's demand for military intervention. Such intervention, he said, would mean war with the continent for which France's resources were insufficient. He defied his adversaries to maintain that 'she should embark on a general war for a question of influence'.[52] The motion giving the government a free hand was passed by 444 to 320. King Leopold congratulated Thiers on his speech, but the Venetian patriot Tommaseo rightly found it harsh and protested that Thiers's assertion that Italy was now 'in the hands of feeble and ridiculous agitators' was undeserved by Venice.[53]

When Thiers uttered those contemptuous words he was undoubtedly thinking of the men who in November 1848 had risen against Pope Pius IX, assassinated his distinguished Liberal minister, Rossi, and, having caused him to take refuge in Gaeta, deprived him of his temporal power, set up a Roman Republic, and declared war against Austria. After defeating Piedmont in March 1849, Austria prepared to move further south and deal with Mazzini's radical regime in Rome. Whatever their views about the Pope and the Temporal Power – and those of Thiers were highly debatable[54] – Frenchmen were virtually unanimous in wishing to prevent Austria from dominating most of Italy. An expedition was therefore dispatched in April with the twofold object of forestalling the Austrians by a peaceful occupation of Rome and of reconciling the Pope with his rebellious subjects. It was a programme 'easier to conceive than to fulfil'.[55] Everything went wrong from the start. It was hoped that as the French troops were to protect them from the Austrians, the leaders of the Roman Republic would welcome them as friends; instead they repulsed them as enemies and it was not until 3 July that they entered Rome by force. It was hoped, too, that when papal government was restored the Pope would resume the liberal reforms upon which he had originally embarked in 1846, but by the beginning of August this hope looked illusory.

Thiers, who received confidential reports from Italy, was twice publicly involved in the events arising from this Roman imbroglio. On 12 June when, egged on by the Roman Republicans, Ledru-Rollin and the Montagnards tabled a motion impeaching the President and his ministers for violating the constitution by sending armed forces against Rome, Thiers defended the government's action, saying that they had been sent not against true liberty, but against demagogy.[56] Defeated in the Assembly, Ledru-Rollin and his friends had organized a large demonstration on the following day, intended no doubt to intimidate the government into changing its Italian course. It was dispersed fairly easily by Changarnier, the commander of the Paris garrison, relatively few workers answering the extremists' call to arms. The last of the *journées* was another setback for the Mountain and Ledru-Rollin fled to exile in England.

Once French troops had occupied Rome the government had to ask for credits to maintain them there. This occasioned Thiers's second involvement, for he was appointed *rapporteur* on the Bill presented for this purpose. It was also the occasion of a rift with the President, in whose eyes Thiers's report committed a grave sin of omission. Annoyed by the reactionary attitude of the commission of Cardinals whom the Pope had sent to administer the Papal States until he himself returned to Rome, Louis-Napoleon had on 18 August, without prior consultation with his ministers, written and subsequently made public a letter to Edgard Ney, one of his aides-de-camp in Rome; in it he succinctly stated that France had not dispatched an army to stifle freedom there: 'I summarize the re-establishment of the Pope's temporal power as follows: general amnesty, secularization of the ministry, Napoleonic Code, and liberal government.' But the Pope had no intention of going so far. In his indirect riposte, a *Motu Proprio* issued in September, he promised the minimum of reforms.[57] He knew that he could count on the support of the French Catholics who were an important and, in Thiers's view, indispensable component of the Party of Order on whose support the French Cabinet relied. Louis-Napoleon's letter, another indication that the President regarded himself as above party and had no intention of always falling into line with the men of the Rue de Poitiers, was therefore for Thiers most untimely and vexing. He showed his disapproval by making no reference to it in his report. Louis-Napoleon was furious and soon after, convinced that his ministers, too, had given insufficient support to the policy advocated in the letter, he replaced them. The outgoing ministry, the second to he headed by Barrot, had been laboriously constructed with the help of Thiers at the end of May. The new, little-known men appointed on 31 October were the President's own nominees.

Tocqueville, one of the outgoing ministers, thought the crisis had been due partly to Louis-Napoleon's conviction that he and his friends would not help him in the final *coup d'état* and partly to his wish to govern and be seen to govern. He believed that the breach between Louis-Napoleon and Thiers was irreparable: 'the latter has realized that he has no role to play with this man who is as ungovernable as he is incapable of governing'.[58]

Whether Tocqueville was right would remain to be seen. Meanwhile, it is worth noting that at the end of his report Thiers declared that it was in France's interest to make her occupation of Rome as brief as possible. In fact troops remained there intermittently for the best part of twenty-one years. But that was Louis-Napoleon's headache, not Thiers's.

[7]

The Liberals' Waterloo,
1850–1851

Thiers's growing personal mistrust and dislike of the Prince-President did not as yet cause him to withdraw his public support. But he no longer had any illusions that he could influence him through advice given privately. For some months Madame Dosne and other friends had urged him to keep himself in reserve, 'retiring to his tent' and avoiding involvement in the stopgap and rather disreputable governments of Louis-Napoleon or the factional squabbles of the Party of Order. Duvergier and Mignet were glad that he was absorbed in historical labours – Volumes 10 and 11 of the *Consulate and Empire*. Rémusat considered that he had practically relinquished leadership of the Liberals, and later wrote, mistakenly, that Thiers had remained silent in the Legislative Assembly for nearly eighteen months.[1] In fact, Thiers was giving much time to parliamentary affairs. In the Assembly he could be sure of the cheers of a comfortable conservative majority, while his oratorical verve was stimulated by the noisy minority on the Left. He was also involved in the work of commissions studying legislation on public assistance, which came before the Assembly in January 1850; on education, debated in February; and on the suffrage, debated in May.

The Commission on Public Assistance was the Assembly's response to the 'social question' – all the new problems created by industrialization and urbanization – first posed in the 1820s. These problems had largely contributed to the unrest of the 1830s, most notably the Lyons silk workers' revolts during Thiers's tenure of the Ministry of the Interior, and had swelled popular opposition to the July Monarchy during the Guizot years. During the 1840s remedies for the social question and denunciations of governmental indifference had multiplied: from Romantic conservatives such as Lamartine and Romantics *tout court* such as Hugo; from philanthropic Catholics such as Lamennais and his more paternalistic co-religionist Armand de Melun; from visionary technocrats, the Saint-Simonians, and their disciple Louis-Napoleon Bonaparte, who wrote *The Extinction of Pauperism* in 1844 in his prison at Ham; and from the various 'utopian Socialists'. So strong had Socialist ideas become among the Left-wing politicians and workers of Paris that, when the July Monarchy unexpectedly fell in February 1848, they had at once obtained the establishment of the Luxembourg Commission, under the Socialist Louis Blanc, to study remedies for the social question, the recognition of 'the right to work', and the institution of National Workshops to provide employment. As has been seen, the abolition of these precipitated the insurrection of June 1848. The political climate, therefore, demanded some action and reform. In June 1849, Armand de Melun urged the Assembly to set up a commission to study means of improving the moral and material conditions of the people: it agreed to do so unanimously, spurred on by the need to dish the Socialists. Thiers was elected to the commission, and charged with drafting its report to the Assembly, which he presented on 26 January 1850.

Thiers's main qualification for this prominent role in major social legislation was, of course, that he was a leader of the Party of Order. He was also a long-recognized authority on public finance who had, since June 1848, been in the lists as champion of economic rationality against socialist utopianism. His verbal battle with the Left, in print, in Parliament and in the commission, was a dialogue of the deaf. This was partly temperament, as Thiers, one of the few self-made men in politics, without feelings of religious or social guilt, stressed the virtues rather than the vices of the society that had permitted his success, and proclaimed that hard work and social mobility were the remedies for its ills. Poverty and inequality were part of the nature of things: they would in time be alleviated by economic growth, and might in the short term be somewhat relieved by private or public charity, but could not be abolished. Thiers's quarrel with the Left was intellectual as well as temperamental: it was the conflict of the realist and the visionary, with Thiers and his supporters arguing in terms of present economic and social reality, against a Left wishing to transcend that reality. Thiers challenged them to propose, not the 'transformation of humanity', but 'an immediately practicable proposal, a precise, drafted Bill . . . for us to examine . . . for the Assembly does not discuss science, it is not an academy but a legislative assembly'.[2] But the Left were not willing to discuss 'practicable' minor reforms, the details of pension funds, poor relief or public works projects. They insisted on their great and simple schemes for social transformation, and their voices were being increasingly heard in the country.

Thiers fought back before the Commission on Public Assistance, repeating many of the arguments he had been propounding since 1848 and had published in *Du droit de propriété*. Socialist nostrums were hollow and if tried would lead to disaster. The 'right to work' was a meaningless and impossible obligation, amounting in practice to unrestricted right to the dole, which society could not and should not confer. 'Universal credit' would simply mean vast inflation and speculation. 'Association' – the reorganization of industry in workers' co-operatives – would mean inefficiency, the squandering of public money, and monopoly. Yet he was elected to draft the commission's report in preference to the leading reformer, Armand de Melun, who supported Thiers – though with misgivings – as being an experienced politician whose voice would be listened to. For Thiers did not oppose all reform in public assistance. Many conservatives were eager to improve charitable provision, and show that they too were sensitive to the sufferings of the poor. The Church was eager to take the lead in organized charity as one way of winning back the urban masses to Christianity. Thiers, in his report, was determined to moderate the commission's impetuosity without giving the blank refusal of action advocated by the *laissez-faire* 'ultra-economists'. Consequently, he reported that there was 'little to invent, much to improve' in public assistance. Limiting central control and leaving a large place for religious and private charities, the report produced piecemeal proposals concerning child welfare, apprenticeships, poor relief, state aid to housing, sanitary regulations, state encouragement of friendly societies (which implied supervision of potentially subversive organizations), aid to voluntary pensions schemes and planned job creation in state industries – this last, seemingly, a pet scheme of Thiers's, quite in accordance with his moderately interventionist leanings. The report also urged consideration of colonies as a remedy for unemployment, especially in North Africa, 'the French India', development of which he had elsewhere described as the great national task, 'the only great deed accomplished in thirty years'.[3]

These measures were, of course, inadequate – indeed, no measures in the political and economic circumstances of the time could have been adequate.[4] Moreover, not all the proposals reached the statute book – Thiers's project for co-ordinated job creation did not – as the Assembly turned its attention to what it considered more urgent political matters. In fact, Thiers's report was never debated as a whole. The Assembly was no doubt eager to play down such dangerously controversial matters. 'If full of useful information and precise data, the inventory of the ideas of the Orleanist bourgeoisie', notes one historian, 'theory and practice was to draw from it neither general doctrine nor efficacious solution.'[5] But Thiers appeared content with his sole foray into social reform, having done his best to 'diminish the fatal and dangerous mass of benefit promised but unfortunately impracticable'.[6]

Further measures for reducing dangerous expectations were press control (which Thiers had advocated for precisely this reason in the previous July) and the reform of state education. Education was one of the great political battlefields of the nineteenth century, for all political groups assumed that this mighty instrument of social engineering and indoctrination held the key to the future. Nowhere was this more true than in France under the Second Republic. Thiers asserted that the army and education were his chief preoccupations, and he played a leading part in the struggle to control the schools in the cause of conservatism.

119

An extra-parliamentary commission had been set up in January 1849 by the Minister of Education, the Catholic Comte de Falloux, to devise a system providing 'liberty of education' – especially for the Church. It included representatives of the Church, notably the Abbé Dupanloup, a leading intellectual, and a layman, Comte de Montalembert, in politics a Liberal; of the University, notably Thiers's old friend the liberal philosopher Victor Cousin; of the Protestant churches and of the private schools. Falloux had only accepted office on condition that Thiers, as leader of the non-Catholic element of the Party of Order, pledged support for his plans, and Dupanloup too wanted Thiers in the commission.[7] For in spite of his having attacked clerical encroachment into education in 1844 and 1845, he had announced publicly that, in the turmoil following February 1848, such disputes had lost significance and that the real danger was disorder and subversion. The Catholics had welcomed him like a lost sheep – one cardinal hailing him as the 'saviour of religion'[8] – and he was appointed chairman of the extra-parliamentary commission and then of the parliamentary commission that drafted the Education Bill, which he defended vigorously before the Assembly in February and March 1850. Although known as the Loi Falloux, it could well have been called the Loi Thiers.

In the discussions of the extra-parliamentary commission, Thiers, in spite of his Left-Centre background, took a harder line than most of his colleagues, and in the confidentiality of the commission (whose minutes he insisted should be kept secret) he was even less inclined than usual to mince words. He repeatedly stressed his suspicion of the very principle of 'inordinately extending' elementary[9] education: 'I do not wish to indulge in obscurantism', but 'the child who has been to school too often does not want afterwards to follow the plough'; 'reading, writing, counting, that is what must be taught, the rest is superfluous'; 'education is. . . a beginning of affluence and affluence is not reserved for all'; it was a consequence not a cause of increased wealth, 'a luxury', where 'inequality is the law of God'. This statement provoked 'numerous exclamations', and from the deist Victor Cousin of all people the protest 'Are you forgetting, Monsieur Thiers, that we are Christians?', causing Thiers to 'withdraw the expression, as it shocks certain people'. But Thiers did not change his views: 'I consider things as they are: I cannot consent to light a fire under an empty pot.'[10]

While fearful of the long-term dangers of education in a society he conceived of as static and essentially agrarian, Thiers was even more fearful of the immediate danger that the school system was becoming an instrument of Left-wing political propaganda. His attention, like that of other conservatives, had probably been drawn to this threat in 1848, when the Republican Minister of Education, Carnot, had introduced a Bill to provide free and compulsory education in order to destroy social inequality and 'make the whole of France as republican in heart and mind as it is today in its institutions'. Furthermore, Carnot had attempted to use the *instituteurs* – the elementary school teachers – as electoral agents in the April 1848 elections, sending them 'manuals of civic instruction' – hastily written Republican catechisms – to distribute and expound.[11] Thiers, with the dogmatic extremism characteristic of him at that time, had decided that the *instituteurs* as a whole were rotten with Socialism, the consequence of their own 'pride' and 'devouring ambition' when they were taken out of their class (nearly all were sons of peasants or artisans) and over-educated, yet had no prospects beyond a village school and a slender salary. It was not simply as teachers that Thiers feared them, but as agitators outside the schoolroom, 'thirty-seven thousand socialists and communists', each one 'reading aloud in a café... the nasty little newspaper to which he subscribes', and 'on Sundays, after Mass... dispensing [to discontented peasants] teaching that certainly no inspector will ever find [him] professing to the children in school'. They were the only rival of the Church – 'veritable anti-priests' – in reaching the peasant masses.[12]

Thiers advocated a simple and sweeping solution. As far as possible they should be got rid of. He realized, however, that this was not immediately practicable: 43,000 lay teachers could not simply be sacked, and the Church had not the resources to take over the whole elementary system. In the meantime, he urged 'draconian legislation' to bring the *instituteurs* under the authority of the prefects, for 'feeling the weight of the iron hand of the administration [they] will be humble and submissive'. As for the training colleges (*écoles normales*), 'the most abundant fountain of the evil', where subversive doctrines were learnt and a dissident *esprit de corps* developed, they should be abolished: 'one does not need them to learn a, e, i, o, u'.[13]

His long-term desire was to give exclusive influence in elementary education to the clergy, because it was 'aimed at the masses, the masses need imposed truths, the faith must be their only philosophy' – 'that good philosophy that teaches man that he is here to suffer'. He hoped that eventually clerics would predominate in elementary school teaching, and that any lay teachers would be trained and employed by them. The Catholic representatives assured Thiers that the Church would willingly undertake that task.[14]

He expressed a different opinion concerning secondary education, for it was 'aimed at the middle classes of society, whose spirit, which desires as a right free philosophical discussion, would revolt against imposed doctrines'. The middle classes, of course, were not a cause of political disquiet, nor were their teachers. Religion, believed Thiers, was neither a necessary nor a possible foundation for middle-class morality, given 'the lack of religious faith... in our present societies', concerning which 'we can do nothing by force'. Indeed, religious secondary schools, he argued, tended to turn their pupils against religion and in consequence experienced a lower standard of morality in their pupils than state schools. While Thiers was concerned to maintain the classical curriculum as the foundation of a secular morality –

here he expressed the pure orthodoxy of the University – and to reject vocational and technical education as materialistic and barbarous, producing 'little Americans', he was content to reach a compromise. The Church should be allowed to have its own secondary schools without restriction, and present their pupils for the all-important *baccalauréat*; but the state must have the right to supervise all secondary education, to 'strike youth in its own effigy', to prevent 'young Frenchmen [from being taught] to hate the government of their country', whether by Jesuits or Socialists. To make this acceptable to the clergy, they would be allowed to participate in that supervision, as would local notables, as a solid conservative safeguard. [15]

After a long and bitter debate, the law was voted on 15 March 1850. It gave Thiers much of what he had fought for: the elementary school curriculum was limited largely to religious instruction and the three Rs, and although *écoles normales* were not abolished, they were no longer to be an obligatory charge on the departments, and their curriculum was reduced. One administrator summed up the new spirit to his *instituteurs*: 'Society, so deeply disturbed in our day, demands of you more than literary or scientific knowledge. It orders you to soak your teaching in the changeless waters of Catholicism.' Several thousand *instituteurs* were disciplined, some by dismissal. [16] The Law permitted a steady growth in Catholic education over the next generation. Yet the state gained overall supervision: there was not to be complete liberty of education. The Church was permitted to extend its activities in so far as this was believed to serve the Party of Order. In other words, the Church was cast as the propagandist of conservatism, intensifying the struggle between Left and Right over Catholic education that marked the rest of the century and beyond. This long ideological dispute overshadowed the social inequality of French education, divided into two separate systems, elementary and secondary, which survived well into the twentieth century. Moreover, the cut-back in the primary school curriculum must have been a disadvantage in preparing farmers and workers for economic growth and modernization.

Thiers was right in thinking that the bishops, prompted by the Pope, would accept this new 'concordat'. His alliance with his old opponents was sealed, and he received flattering letters from clergy and laity. He also began a lifelong friendship with Dupanloup, soon Bishop of Orléans, who quoted Thiers on the nation's need for faith in the preface to his famous *Catéchisme chrétien*. Not all Catholics were equally pleased. Some intransigents, angry that the law recognized the ultimate authority of the state over all education, looked to Louis-Napoleon for a more favourable bargain. One commented sourly that all Thiers was interested in was to have 'a corps of gendarmes in cassocks'. The idealistic young Catholic Frédéric Ozanam commented, in a shaft that must have been aimed at Thiers, that 'there is today no Voltairian afflicted with some thousand pounds of income who does not want to send everyone to Mass, on condition of not having to set foot there himself.[17] If Thiers's attitude was utilitarian, and even cynical, it was not – as critics frequently said – inconsistent. In the 1840s he had defended the authority of the state in education for the elite, and he continued to do so in 1850, though with concessions to the Church for the sake of conservative unity. But he had always believed in the necessity of religious indoctrination for the masses, as had Napoleon, whose original Concordat he so admired. He had written of it in 1844:

> Religious belief and worship are necessary in any human society... The double motive of re-establishing order in the state and the family, and satisfying the moral needs of souls, had inspired in Napoleon the firm resolution to replace the Catholic religion on its old footing, except for the political attributions that he regarded as incompatible with the present state of French society. Is it necessary... to inquire whether he acted by the inspiration of religious faith, or rather by policy and ambition? He acted wisely... that is enough. The rest is a mystery... which matters little.[18]

During his speech on the Loi Falloux, Thiers used a phrase that became famous: 'the Republic... is of all governments that which divides us least'.[19] This was not a new thought. Many years before he had spoken of a Republic as a possibility for France if constitutional monarchy, which he openly preferred, proved a failure. Since 1848, he had frequently declared his acceptance of the Republic as the *de facto* government, preferring it to the dangers of further upheaval. Now, however, in one of those pithy formulas for which he had a journalist's knack, he was implying positive support. This was heartily endorsed by Duvergier, who tended to be slightly further to the Left, and by Madame Dosne, who detested the Legitimists and despised the Bonapartists: 'if the Republic lasts', she assured him, 'one day you will lead it'.[20] That day was probably far off; yet Thiers had taken a step towards acceptance of the Republic that he never entirely reversed. It was, however, a particular kind of Republic – one that divided not just Frenchmen least, but above all the ruling classes least, for it would enable them to put aside their dynastic loyalties and form a regime capable of maintaining order. For Thiers wanted a Republic controlled not by those who had always fought for it, but by those who, having unsuccessfully resisted it, were ready to accept it for their own purposes. A few days later, he taunted the Left with this very point: if the Republic survived, it would be because its former enemies had taken control of it from its partisans who were ruining it: 'If it lasts, you will not govern it, and it will only last because of that', a phrase that had Lamartine gritting his teeth and muttering 'little scoundrel'.[21] His support for the Republic, therefore, was hardly a peace offering to the Left, who, after his ruthless wrecking of their plans for social reform and education, were in a bitter mood.

They showed it in by-elections in March and April 1850 called to replace thirty Left-wing deputies expelled from the Assembly after the insurrection

123

of June 1849. Although the Union Libérale (as the Party of Order was officially known) won ten seats, this success was overshadowed by the three results in Paris, in which the moderate Left joined with the 'Montagnards' to win a victory that horrified conservatives. For the three successful candidates were de Flotte, an insurgent in June 1848, Carnot, former Minister of Education whose policies had been brusquely reversed by the Loi Falloux, and Vidal, a close associate of Louis Blanc in the Luxembourg Commission and thus a symbol of those aspirations to social change that Thiers's Report on Public Assistance had declared utopian. Finally, on 28 April, the popular novelist Eugène Sue, literary defender of the downtrodden and hammer of the Jesuits, was also elected in Paris.

The first thought of the conservative leaders, Thiers, Molé, Broglie and Berryer, was to draw closer to Louis-Napoleon and take office themselves. Mutual suspicions brought this to nothing. There was talk of a *coup d'état*. But Thiers preferred the idea of changing the electoral law: 'I don't want the Empire. I am for keeping the Republic', but 'we must tear up. . . the dirty placard of the gentlemen of the *National*', that is, the 1848 constitution. In return for his aid, Thiers was willing to offer Louis-Napoleon an extension of his term of office (not the first time this possibility had been discussed) but the Legitimist leader Berryer demurred. The government agreed, however, that a new electoral law should be prepared by a commission of seventeen conservative leaders, including Thiers.[22]

Their hastily drafted Bill had two aims: to reduce the working-class electorate without too blatantly contravening the constitutional provision of universal male suffrage; and in particular to disfranchise the so-called 'dangerous classes', that conservative nightmare of a vagrant, semi-criminal sub-proletariat which, cut off from local roots, family restraints and the influence of social superiors, was assumed to vote for the extreme Left. Consequently, the main provisions of the Bill were to disfranchise the indigent and men convicted of a variety of offences (not only criminal or political, but also commercial and moral such as bankruptcy and adultery); and to increase the residence requirement from six months to three years, proof being provided by tax registers. Some Liberals felt that the law was dishonest, harsh and perhaps impolitic; some Legitimists, with loyal peasant electors, objected that many poor conservative voters would be disfranchised.[23] But most Liberals, always afraid of universal suffrage, believed that at last they might have a potent weapon against the 'Reds'. Among them was Thiers.

The Bill was debated during the last week of May 1850. Molé had urged Thiers to speak in order to 'raise the level of the discussion':[24] he did so perhaps more than he intended, and one phrase in his speech became the most notorious of his career. Attacking the Left for misleading the electorate and respecting the constitution and universal suffrage only when it suited them, he told them that they ought to support the disfranchisement

IDYLLES PARLEMENTAIRES.

LE SECRET CONFIÉ AU DIEU FAUNE

Je feins d'aimer la jeune République | Mais je prétends, loin d'être platonique,
D'une discrète et tendre passion: | Violer un jour sa Constitution!

Plate 4 Thiers and Molé conspiring (by Daumier, February 1851) of 'the dangerous part' of the population: 'real Republicans fear the mob, the vile mob (*la vile multitude*) that has. . . delivered over to every tyrant the liberty of every Republic'. So notorious did this phrase become that Thiers later explained it away as a parliamentary trick, decided in advance, to provoke the Montagnards to rage and frighten the wavering moderates into voting with the Right.[25] Another possibility was that Thiers, like other conservatives, was convinced that the Reds were planning revolution and hoped that the Bill might lure them into a premature rising that would be crushed.[26] His language – like that of some conservative newspapers – might have been a deliberate provocation, and was at best irresponsible in that tense atmosphere. But had he been trying to stampede the moderates or enrage the Mountain, to obtain maximum effect he would perhaps have spoken just before the vote. As it was, the vote (in which the Bill obtained a large majority) came a week later, when the passions he had aroused might be expected to have cooled; yet he did not speak again to rekindle them. On the contrary, he at once tried to moderate the effect of his words by saying that he was not attacking 'the people', but 'the mob', which was quite different. The simplest explanation of the incident would be that he lost his temper during an angry debate when Left-wing deputies tried repeatedly to drown his voice. Whatever the explanation, Thiers certainly believed what he had said, as did the many who applauded him, for the notion of the 'dangerous classes' was a commonplace of liberal and conservative thinking – other representatives spoke of 'the dangerous people', 'the immoral', 'the army of evil'.[27] In his speech Thiers placed this belief, as was his custom, in historical context, referring to ancient Rome, seventeenth-century Holland, revolutionary France and renaissance Florence (which he was studying as a paradigm of the problems of democracy). He was to repeat the same idea of mob rule leading to despotism in 1873, but then the Republicans applauded.[28]

The Bill was voted on 31 May by 433 votes to 341. Its effect was to reduce the electorate from 9,680,000 to 6,800,000, but no elections under its regulations were ever to be held. Laws restricting political clubs and the press followed within days. The Left did not attempt to resist by force. Thiers and his allies thought that they had won. But their legislative victories had undesired consequences.

The politicians of the Party of Order – the 'party of fear', Hugo called them – soon found that their repressive laws had cut them off from moderate Republicans who shared their fundamental principles, as well as from the electorate. They had actually increased the popularity of the Montagnards, who organized vocal campaigns against the electoral law, and had given a political weapon to the Bonapartists. Thiers, supposedly the wiliest of tacticians, had greatly contributed to his party's predicament. He had underlined the negative aspects of the Public Assistance proposals; he had stressed the repressive and reactionary character of the Loi Falloux and he had called the three million disfranchised electors 'a vile mob'. Hugo mocked the Right:

> Go on! Take away three million electors, take away four, take away nine. . .
> What you will not take away are your own mistakes, all the contradictions
> of your policy of repression, your fatal incapacity, your ignorance of the
> country today, the antipathy that you feel for it and that it feels for you.[29]

Thiers and the Liberals were, in Tocqueville's phrase, 'like river oarsmen. . . called upon to navigate their boat in mid-ocean'.[30] They were of all political parties the least capable of riding the swell of universal suffrage. Having always regarded the masses as apolitical or passive, they were unable to think of winning votes except by the moral and social pressure of clergy and notables, and their instinctive reaction if that failed was repression.

The Liberals' fears are understandable in the context of recent history, which Thiers brought to mind in the discussions of the education commission: 'May not the scaffold soon be raised again in our squares, for our fathers, and even the oldest among us, have already seen that terrible guillotine; and the masses are so easy to deceive.' Yet the spectre of Jacobin terror seems to have alarmed Thiers less in 1850 than his apprehension that 'modern society might fall to nothing' – become 'a vast Tipperary', as one contemporary put it – through chasing an impossible utopia, a danger of which Benjamin Constant had warned years earlier. 'Governments know very well that they have only a wooden sword to defend us against that collapse,' said Thiers, 'less bloody perhaps than that of the past, but assuredly more ignominious; it would be utter and irreversible annihilation.'[31] Some of his fears and criticisms were prescient, but his imagination gave him too lurid an impression of danger. He feared not only the worst, but the worst overnight, seeing French society as 'a wooden house, menaced on all sides'.[32] Hence his fear of the power of words and ideas – the 'right to work', the right to education, social equality, progressive taxation – which he believed would, in a democracy, force governments under the pressure of 'the mob' into ever more desperate extremes. He seems to have had no conception of the management of democracy, of necessary concessions (for which, however, he praised the English aristocracy), or of slogans as substitutes for action rather than as calls to action. These things both the Left and Louis-Napoleon well understood.

The Montagnards, despite official harassment, continued their activities in the provinces. Their targets now were the dual elections of 1852, when both President and Assembly would go to the country almost simultaneously, and when the 'vile mob' of the disfranchised intended to exercise their vote by force if necessary. Both Left and Right were becoming convinced that 1852 would mark the beginning of social revolution through the ballot box. More than ever conservatives turned to Louis-Napoleon as the saviour.

Ironically, Thiers and his little band, who had expressed Liberal fears so stridently, seem to have grown more confident that the menace from the Left had been staved off once the electoral law had been passed. But their relative optimism was shared by few.

After the passage of the law of 31 May 1850, Thiers left Paris before the Assembly adjourned, missing debates on the press and on political clubs, in order to visit the dying Louis-Philippe at St Leonard's-on-Sea. He liked to think that he and the King had been fond of each other – 'I shall weep when he dies', he used to tell Rémusat – but he was still bitter that Louis-Philippe had rejected his policy in 1840 and thus, he was convinced, doomed the regime. He had no ties with the rest of the Orléans family; indeed, he often commented on the ingratitude and unreliability of princes. He had seemingly discounted a restoration, writing in July: 'the monarchy ruined itself wilfully by being unable to make a minor sacrifice in time. But in France, kings cannot make concessions and the people cannot be patient' – an opinion he had already expressed in his *History of the French Revolution*. 'Consequently, the regime that suits England so well appears in France only to demonstrate its impossibility.'[33] When in Brussels in August (to see Metternich concerning his *Consulate and Empire*, on which he was working busily) he discussed the Orléans family's future with his friend and their relative King Leopold, but without reaching any conclusion. They mentioned the possibility that Louis-Philippe's grandson the Comte de Paris might succeed Louis-Napoleon when he came of age, but that meant four years' wait and so implied a second term of office for the Prince-President. In October Thiers assured the Orléans family that for the time being there was nothing for them to do.[34]

This was very soon to change when Thiers finally – though not yet openly – decided to resist Louis-Napoleon, and to use the Orléans family as a weapon. The decision may have been taken after he returned to Paris that autumn and was informed of the President's activities during the recess.[35] Louis-Napoleon had made a much publicized quasi-royal progress through France, and in successive speeches had hinted clearly that he intended to remain in office for a second term, which the constitution forbade. This his supporters were mounting a powerful campaign to have altered. The Bonapartist press heaped scorn on the Party of Order as well as on the Montagnards. 'If you think that the country is with you, you are wrong', wrote the *Moniteur du Soir* on 26 July. 'What would the electorate reply if they were told tomorrow: between the Assembly and the President, choose!' Most alarmingly, Louis-Napoleon had blatantly tried to win personal support from the army. In August he gave banquets at the Elysée for officers and NCOs, and in September and October held manoeuvres followed by handsome *déjeuners sur l'herbe* for the troops, including wine and cigars, with his compliments. When marching past, regiments were encouraged to shout 'Vive l'Empereur!' This displeased many senior officers and one of them, General Neumayer, ordered the troops to keep silence, as regulations prescribed. He was swiftly transferred to another post.[36]

This had extra significance because Neumayer was second-in-command to General Changarnier, on whose instructions he was thought to have acted, and Changarnier, Commander of the Army of Paris and a member of the Assembly, was self-appointed defender of parliamentary liberty against the President's dictatorial ambitions. The conservatives in the Assembly had come to rely on his protection against both the mob and the Elysée, and Louis-Napoleon was not yet prepared to face the political storm that removing Changarnier himself would arouse. In January 1851, however, he found a pretext to sack him, and dismissed those ministers who demurred. Rémusat, encouraged by Thiers, interpellated the government and forced a debate.[37] This clash between Assembly and President marked Thiers's final and open break with Louis-Napoleon.

In his speech on 17 January, he solemnly recounted the history of his and the conservatives' support for Louis-Napoleon. He recalled the disquieting events of the past few months and appealed to all parties to make peace and to accept the Republic, for 'perhaps. . . the destinies of modern nations lead them to the American system', 'the government of everyone, of all parties', which humiliated no one. Yet the government, he asserted, far from seeking political peace, had issued an intolerable challenge to the Assembly in sacking Changarnier and leaving it defenceless. Thiers's peroration caused a sensation. If the Assembly surrendered, 'its weakness is so obvious to all that it is finished'. There would no longer be two powers in the state, but only one. 'And when there is only one, the form of government is altered; it matters little when the word and title come. . . the Empire is made.' Thiers's call to resist helped to rally the Assembly, which voted no confidence in the government by 417 votes to 278.[38] It was a hollow victory: the government resigned, but Louis-Napoleon replaced it with a non-political Cabinet of his own creatures.

Thiers was now determined to fight the President to the finish. His resources were slender. The Left, still angry with the reactionary laws of 1850, had declared that while they mistrusted Louis-Napoleon, they mistrusted Thiers and Changarnier even more. The die-hard Legitimists were unwilling to support any other cause than that of Henri V. Worst of all, many Orleanists and Legitimists, led by Broglie and Montalembert, had decided that there was no alternative to Louis-Napoleon but chaos and revolution, and that he must be appeased. They reflected conservative opinion in the country: at every victory of the President, the stock exchange rose. Moreover, the economy was at last moving out of depression in France, as all over Europe, and the government received much of the credit. Agricultural prices remained seriously depressed, but that helped the Montagnards. Thiers found his forces reduced to a handful of uncompromising Liberal deputies: the irrepressible Duvergier, Rémusat, the faithful Chambolle, and about two dozen others. He also had the Orléans family: 'I know of only one way to prevent the Empire, more or less dissimulated, that is the candidature of the Prince de Joinville in the presidential election of 1852.'[39] It was not absolutely necessary for Joinville, one of Louis-Philippe's sons, to win: if he obtained enough votes to prevent Louis-Napoleon from gaining an absolute majority, it would be for the assembly to elect a President. Or at least Joinville might win enough votes to deny Louis-Napoleon a majority so overwhelming that his re-election could not be contested, whatever the constitution said.

Thiers's instinctive strategy was once more to try to create an alliance of moderate Right and moderate Left. He believed that moderate Republicans could be induced to rally to Joinville to avert Bonapartist dictatorship. This meant resisting 'fusion', the union of Orleanists and Legitimists through recognition by the Orléans princes of the prior claim to the throne of the Comte de Chambord as Henri V. Fusion was advocated by Guizot, and the struggle within the Orleanist ranks was in an odd way a continuation of the struggle of the 1840s. Thiers was aware of this, and wrote to the Orléans family that ever since 1830 there had been a fatal division among the Orleanists between those attached to the Revolution (led by himself), and those who wished as far as possible to return to the old monarchy (led by Guizot). The family should remember that they 'represent the Revolution, the good French Revolution'.[40] The Orléans family were willing to follow Thiers's lead, and to adopt retrospectively his view of the 1840s: he had been right, and Guizot and Louis-Philippe had been wrong. After all, Thiers was offering them a role and a hope, however slender, whereas Guizot and Broglie could only urge them to accept defeat gracefully, and yield their ambitions and their principles to either Bourbon or Bonaparte. When a Legitimist delegation went to the Orléans' new home in Surrey to pave the way for fusion it was coldly received. Joinville wrote to Thiers describing the encounter in 'burlesque terms', and Thiers and Duvergier gleefully showed his letter round on the benches of the Assembly, and made sure that the Legitimists knew. Yet to follow the Thiers line that they represented the Revolution of 1789 might oblige the Orléans family to accept something almost as distasteful as fusion – the Republic.[41]

Thiers put his arguments in a forceful (and highly secret) letter to the family on 2 March 1851. If Joinville were to be elected, 'he must be President in good faith, for the sake of his honour and ours, and having the advantage of being in power, if by the course of events, always stronger than men, the Republic were to fall'. But the Republic might not fall, in which case Joinville would have to leave office gracefully, when his term expired, with the satisfaction that 'the House of Orléans would have added to the eighteen years of a good monarchy, four years of a good Republic'. To reasons of principle Thiers added reasons of practicality: a majority of the Assembly was needed to repeal the 1848 law exiling the Orléans family.

The support of the Legitimists, won by fusion, might bring 120–130 votes; but it would lose 150–180 on the Left. The effect in the country would be 'much worse' and would strengthen the Bonapartists. The only hope was to rally support on the Left, at an opportune moment, when the threat of a Bonapartist dictatorship seemed imminent. To this end, they should put themselves absolutely in Thiers's hands.[42]

The family balked, replying that they had decided on 'absolute abstention' from politics. They found an alliance with the Left repugnant. Moreover, Joinville feared that he would be beaten and become 'a figure of fun'. So they refused to make any public declaration. Yet they soon indicated that they would not prevent Thiers from going ahead with his project, and were prepared to obey if the country summoned them to duty. This was enough for Thiers and his little band, who began their campaign. But he intended that the Orléans family should commit themselves at least privately, and asked them for 600,000 francs for campaign expenses. Both sides tacitly understood that this was a pledge of good faith – Thiers did not trust princes. They paid: he had convinced them that his was the only way. It was, wrote Joinville, 'a new phase in our relations with *le petit*'. The Duchesse d'Orléans was enthusiastic, for she believed that if Joinville could serve four years as President, her son the Comte de Paris, by then of age, could succeed him, with the road to the throne open.[43]

These manoeuvres had not caused Thiers to cease his efforts to influence policy through Parliament. On 3 May 1851 he made a technical speech on the strategic and economic effects of alternative railway projects in western France (which, now that he sat for Seine-Inférieure, were also constituency matters).[44] On 27 June he made one of his greatest speeches, a long, devastating attack on free trade and *laissez-faire* economics, a classic statement on the subject. He had made various note-taking forays, including one to the Great Exhibition in London, and amassed much ammunition from English and French businessmen. Economic liberalism, he asserted, bore no relation to political liberalism. The system that gave advantages to Britain would 'smash [French prosperity] like a glass'. Free trade in food, which great English landlords had consented to for political reasons, would ruin the vast class of small French peasants, and 'when you ruin the land, you ruin everyone'. Free trade in industrial products, which the British needed to find markets for their vast production of a small range of cheap, mass-produced goods, and which they could afford to pay for by the sacrifice of less important industries, would give no benefit to France, whose industry was diversified, whose exports were mainly higher-quality articles little affected by tariffs, and whose cheaper products supplied a home market that would be wrecked by British dumping. The advocates of free trade argued that France might not be able to compete in iron or cotton, but instead could make more silks and wine: 'Would you grow mulberry trees in Lille and Rouen? Would you make wine in Lille and Rouen?' It had been tried

131

Plate 5   Thiers tempting Joinville (by Daumier September 1851)

before, 'and there was a wretched population in the streets of Rouen, starving, rioting, and cursing the authors of the 1786 treaty'. Finally, there was the argument of Thiers the strategist. The two great countries of the future, Russia and America, rightly rejected free trade. England now depended for one-third of her food on imports, which she had the greatest navy in the world to protect: France could not possibly take such a risk. And even England: 'suppose a change in the world balance, suppose a change in the relative force of navies, what would happen to that nation. . . ?'[45]

He was delighted by the reception the speech received: 'Complete success', he wrote to Madame Dosne. 'I spoke for three hours, and I saw attention, enthusiasm, even tears. . . The general feeling is that I surpassed myself.' She, of course, basked in his success and was only mildly annoyed by a note of criticism in 'that goose the *Constitutionnel*', which dared to 'lecture M. Thiers'. Amid the celebrations, Thiers and Elise went for a few days to Anzin, where he was a director of the famous Mining Company. His fellow-directors must have been loud in their praises of his defence of protectionism. Madame Dosne's affectionate and good-humoured solicitude accompanied him: 'No *gigot à l'ail*, none of that excellent salad that M. Perier does so well, nor those fine crayfish. . . When I consider all that your head can produce. . ., and your kindness too. . . when the cut and thrust does not carry you away, [I think] you only lack the looks of Adonis to be perfect.'[46]

Just over two months later, in the calm of the summer recess, Chambolle's new paper *L'Ordre* – the only reliable organ of Thiers's little group – flew the first kite in the Joinville campaign. It suggested that illegal re-election of Louis-Napoleon could mean civil war, and so another candidate must be found – the Prince de Joinville. The response was disappointing: the Republican press was hostile; the Legitimists were contemptuous; and there was little support even from supposedly Orleanist papers in Paris or the provinces.[47] Moreover, there was a growing divergence between Thiers's group and the Orléans family: Thiers, regardless of their views, was presenting Joinville as a republican candidate and courting Republican support.

This divergence, and the little progress the campaign was making, led both Joinville and Thiers to call a halt. Duvergier, who had been extremely active, was annoyed, and wrote twice to Thiers on 6 October hoping that 'they', having compromised us, will not 'let us down': 'In politics one must never count too much on princes.' If necessary the fight must continue with another candidate such as Changarnier, even though his chances would be less.[48] The press reported that Thiers's group were ready to support Changarnier, and perhaps for this reason the Orléans family had another change of heart, and again fell in with Thiers's plans: he is 'in the country', wrote Joinville, 'we must let him act as he sees fit'.[49]

Just then, however, these decorous, old-fashioned and utterly unsuccessful salon politics were overshadowed by portents of a *coup d'état*. In July the Assembly had debated revising the constitution to permit Louis-Napoleon to stand for a second term. Thiers did not speak, but he and his group joined the Republicans in voting against, and their combined 270 votes were enough to deny the necesssary three-quarters majority. This provoked rumours of a coup. The situation worsened in November, when Louis-Napoleon demanded repeal of the 1850 electoral law so as to restore universal male suffrage. Now the political imprudence of the law became clear. It gave the President both motive and pretext for a *coup d'état*: motive, because the reduction in the size of the electorate made it more difficult for him to win the absolute majority plus two million votes required by the constitution for direct election (and conversely made a spoiling candidature such as Joinville's a more credible threat); and pretext, the defence of democracy. It enabled him to discredit the Assembly as reactionary and restart the quarrel between Left and Right which the law had caused and which Thiers wanted forgotten. After an angry debate, the Assembly refused repeal, with Thiers's group and the Republicans voting on opposite sides.

The government had resigned, and on 27 October Louis-Napoleon installed a Cabinet of trustworthy supporters, including the unscrupulous General de Saint-Arnaud as Minister of War. Like travellers who see a band of robbers approaching, wrote Tocqueville, the Assembly looked for its pistols.[50] On 6 November, its quaestors Le Flô and Baze (the officers responsible for its administrative arrangements and security) tabled a motion asserting the right of the President of the Assembly to requisition troops for its protection. This was the Assembly's last feeble show of self-defence. The 'Elyséens' thought it unwise. The Bonapartists opposed it, asserting that it was a plot by Thiers and Changarnier for an Orleanist coup. This the Republicans, angry at the refusal to repeal the electoral law, were willing to believe, and they shouted Thiers down when he spoke in support of the motion on 17 November. It was defeated by a majority of 108 votes, including nearly all the Republicans, the 'Elyséens', and many other conservatives. Even had it been carried, it might well have precipitated, rather than prevented, the coup.[51] The diehard Orleanists had been routed. Some, including Thiers and Changarnier, consoled themselves with the thought that Louis-Napoleon had won so completely that there was now no reason for an immediate coup, and that they had a short respite. In England, the Orléans princes began planning to re-enter France and rally resistance to the expected coup. Vague soundings were made in Amiens, believed to be a friendly town and a suitable base. Thiers was probably informed but not directly involved. He and his friends were still planning parliamentary action, by means of Bills making incitement to violate the constitution high treason and defining the circumstances for impeachment. But it was not clear when these might be debated, let alone voted.[52]

Thiers was still not expecting an immediate coup. On the evening of 1

December he told the company at dinner at the Duchesse de Galliéra's that having just lost a by-election the Bonapartists would hesitate; moreover, they would not act before the Christmas and New Year festivities were over, for it was an important season for Parisian commerce. Perhaps he was whistling in the dark, for one guest thought that 'Thiers seemed fearful, and spoke quietly to Molé and Mignet'.[53] That same evening, the Prince-President was holding his usual Monday reception at the Elysée. All seemed normal; but during the reception and immediately after it, he quietly gave his last orders for 'Operation Rubicon'.

During the early hours of 2 December, the police rounded up those whom the conspirators considered their most dangerous opponents. In the Assembly these were seven Montagnards, the six Orleanist or Republican army officers, including Changarnier, Cavaignac and the quaestor Le Flô, and the diehard Orleanists, Thiers, Roger and the quaestor Baze. Louis-Napoleon and his advisers seem to have taken the Orleanist 'plot' – the quaestors' motion for requisitioning troops, the Joinville candidature, and the vague plans for countering a coup (documents concerning which they may have intercepted) – seriously.[54] Thiers, like the others, was asleep when a Commissaire of Police arrived at the Place Saint-Georges to arrest him, and like them was rushed to Mazas Prison. From there he dashed off a note reassuring 'the ladies' that he was safe. Madame Dosne burnt compromising papers, including her own notes for 1851.[55]

Bonapartist accounts portrayed Thiers as terrified, convinced that he was about to be shot, and pleading with bribes and promises to be left in peace. Similar discrediting stories were told about the other men arrested. All were rejected contemptuously as smears by early historians of the coup. It is an interesting example of Thiers's posthumous unpopularity that most later historians have readily accepted the Bonapartist story.[56]

Throughout Paris, the well-planned coup unfolded: the Assembly was occupied and the Imprimerie Nationale guarded, newspapers were closed, proclamations posted, militants arrested and troops mustered. There were several meetings of shocked parliamentarians. Thiers's friends, perhaps by prearrangement, gathered at Barrot's house, where Madame Thiers joined them.[57] Most soon went on to the *mairie* of the 10th *arrondissement*, where about 300 mainly conservative deputies had met to proclaim the President's deposition and offer symbolic resistance. When they refused to disperse they were marched off to a nearby barracks but released as harmless after an insultingly brief detention. There was a flurry of resistance in some working-class districts, in which a Montagnard deputy was killed, while panicky shooting on the boulevards killed a number of elegant by-standers. But observers were invariably struck by the indifference of Parisians of all classes to the fate of the Assembly.[58]

Over the next few days as the news of the coup reached the provinces, a surge of minor uprisings broke out in hundreds of towns and villages in the regions where the Montagnards were entrenched. The army suppressed them without great difficulty and tens of thousands were arrested. This rebellion, the largest of the century, terrified conservatives and reconciled the great majority to the *coup d'état*. For it appeared that Louis-Napoleon had not merely taken action against his mainly conservative parliamentary opponents, but had nipped a vast socialist conspiracy in the bud. The conservative newspapers were full of hair-raising fantasies of Red atrocities. Even previously firm opponents were convinced that Louis-Napoleon had saved society and that to oppose him would be folly. The Orléans princes dropped their vague plans of resistance. A plebiscite approved the coup by 7,439,216 votes to 640,737.[59]

So hollow had the Orleanist threat shown itself to be that the 'conspirators' were quickly released. The Duc de Morny, Minister of the Interior, wrote to Madame Dosne on 6 December that he was 'most happy to be able to inform you that the President has just given the order to release M. Thiers. I hope that this sad and damp sojourn has not affected his health.'[60] The no doubt emotional reunion of Thiers and his ladies was brief, however, for he was escorted to the frontier and then, by a decree of 9 January 1852, 'temporarily removed' from France. On leaving he drafted a formal protest.[61] Seventeen other deputies were similarly exiled, among them Duvergier – 'most honoured' at the distinction 'but not at all grateful'[62] – Chambolle, Rémusat, Changarnier and various Liberals and Republicans. Five Left-wing deputies were transported, and sixty-six banished, among them Hugo. During the next few months, some 10,000 real or suspected disturbers of public order were condemned to various forms of exile, including transportation to Algeria or Cayenne.[63]

The policies followed by Thiers and his allies during the Second Republic are striking in their inadequacy to meet the great political challenges of those years. Their efforts to influence and then to resist Louis-Napoleon were shaken off. Their measures to defeat the Left were ineffective. They succeeded only in isolating themselves politically, and when the *coup d'état* came they were powerless, finding that the country was polarized, with no place for a liberal *juste milieu*.

Thiers's determination to resist Louis-Napoleon at all costs and promote Joinville's candidature, however slim the chances of success, was characteristic. In 1840 he had shown the same tenacity in following a chosen course to the end, regardless of risk. This was unlike the common conception of Thiers as an unprincipled opportunist. Contemporaries puzzled over his motives. Typically, some assumed a deep-laid plot to seize power: Broglie's son later concluded that Thiers had calculated that when the Joinville candidature failed, he himself would be the Liberals' choice.[64] There is no evidence for such a belief, which demonstrates the suspicion with which he was habitually regarded rather than his real intentions. He was sufficiently aware of his own unpopularity in both the Assembly and the country to realize that Changarnier, not he, would be the alternative to Joinville. He was aware too that even Joinville, with the advantage of a great name, had only 'a chance, not a certainty' of success, while 'any other would fail utterly'.[65] Ironically, Joinville's popularity stemmed from his part in Thiers's ill-starred brainchild, the return of Napoleon's remains from Saint Helena in 1840; but, as an unkind Republican put it, where the reflected glory of the Emperor was concerned, 'the nephew beats the undertaker'. Yet the chance that Joinville might win enough votes to be an embarrassment contributed to Louis-Napoleon's decision to strike first.[66] Thiers's opposition to Bonapartism was certainly in part personal; moreover, the continuation of his own political influence demanded the defeat of the would-be Emperor. But there is no reason to doubt the sincerity of his conviction that a Bonapartist dictatorship would be 'an immense danger and a lamentable degradation',[67] and that a parliamentary system was the only foundation for orderly and rational government in France.

[8]

'Les Chères Études'

The *coup d'état* and his arrest and exile left Thiers without illusions as to the completeness of the Liberals' defeat. He did not share Mignet's short-lived confidence that the new regime could not last, writing to Cousin on 1 January 1852 that he saw no alternative to 'resignation'; as for the Orléans family, 'it can do even less than we... I have thought enough and acted enough to know what the share of man is in human events, and to wish never to be the gadfly of providence.' Soon he and Mignet were entirely agreed that, in 1852 as always, history could not be changed by individuals: 'one does not change the course, one must let it exhaust itself'. Mignet wrote approvingly of Thiers's 'judicious thoughts and wise dispositions... the very natural impatience of exile in no way clouds your mind'.[1]

Emotionally he was less serene. While eager to reassure his ladies as to his safety, he admitted that 'my morale is not as good as my physical condition. It breaks my heart to have left you all three, and I cannot write without tears in my eyes.' He had always been subject to loneliness and homesickness, and his friends and fellow exiles Duvergier and Chambolle were no substitute for his family and for Mignet, from whom he had never been so long separated in thirty-seven years. After a short stay in Brussels, he left for London, unwilling to embarrass King Leopold with a presence that could neither be safely acknowledged nor decently ignored. In April the ladies came to see him, braving the Channel (which usually made Madame Dosne seasick) and surviving a railway accident on the way to London. As yet, there was no question of their remaining with Thiers permanently, for his movements and even the duration of his banishment were uncertain. Hope of a speedy return alternated with a gloomy conviction that banishment would be long, perhaps permanent.[2]

Thiers had his usual distractions in times of tribulation, travel and work. The two were invariably linked, for he was not a man for aimless sight-seeing, but busily gathered information for his literary projects. In England early in 1852 he visited cathedrals, notably Winchester and Peterborough. Passing through Belgium in April, en route for Italy, he stopped at Liége to inspect the churches, and gave an impromptu lecture to the clergy on their own architecture. They rewarded him with wine of an ancient vintage – 'I took a glass from politeness', he assured his wife – and an armful of drawings. In Florence he bought a dozen volumes of historical documents and made his usual pilgrimage to the Uffizi. In Rome he took notes on the monuments as well as calling on politicians and the Pope.[3]

In the late summer, he travelled to Vevey in Switzerland for a true holiday, surrounded by his ladies and friends, including Mignet, Duvergier, Chambolle and Roger and family. Thiers was in the best of spirits, sprinkling Mignet with a watering can from an upstairs window, an exploit reminiscent of pranks of earlier years, of which he was as proud 'as if he had won a great victory at the tribune'. He seemed reconciled to a life of exiled retirement, and the family planned to settle abroad. He would have preferred Italy, his great love, or England. But the ladies, Elise in particular, did not wish to cut all ties with Paris, and so they chose Switzerland, with winters to be spent at Nice, then Piedmontese territory.[4]

From the first, Thiers had refused to accept special treatment from the new regime in France: 'I can neither negotiate nor have others negotiate for me.' He turned down an approach in March 1852, refusing to make any gesture of recognition of the new regime, or even to return without conditions unless as part of a general measure covering other political exiles – 'I am thinking only of my dignity.' He made no secret, however, of his intention to abstain from political activity if allowed to return. No doubt he wished to reassure the government that he would not cause trouble, but his assertion that political activity for the time being was not only useless but absurd accorded with his belief in the inevitability of great historical events.

> I do not believe that the present government will fall soon, but would even believe in its longevity if it would adopt the role that the two branches of the house of Bourbon let slip. But it is carried away by imitation of the Empire, and it will meet either a terrible war without, or invincible resistance within, not from such and such a party but from the human mind. To add oneself to all that, as an extra difficulty awaiting it, would be ridiculous.[5]

Nevertheless he refused to contemplate returning to France 'like a repentant sinner, head bowed, mouth shut', and felt a pardonable pride in his own fortitude. In the early days he had asked Mignet to send him Cicero's Letters as the only possible consolation in his woe, but was soon reporting jauntily to Madame Dosne that he was enduring his exile better than the great orator, whose sadness he found 'excessive'.[6]

Such stoicism was not unbroken. Watching the State Opening of the British Parliament provoked melancholy reflections on the failure of constitutional monarchy in France. During these months his mind was full of forebodings of revolutions and great European wars. In 1852 he made a new will redolent of depression and despair:

> I ask my family and Mignet to love me always without lamenting me. I had nothing more to do here below, not having been able to give constitutional

government to my ungrateful country [crossed out] inconstant country. I leave to them the care of my memory, so unworthily treated by cowardly and implacable enemies. I affirm that if the pain of my family were not before my eyes when I think of death, I should look upon it without sorrow. I love my country and truth, and have not for a single day had the reward of my devotion.[7]

The self-pity and self-righteousness were perhaps a balm for his feelings. He had an urge to justify himself, as if to admit having been wrong would destroy his last reserves of strength: 'I myself must not abandon myself, and allow injustice to be added to persecution.'[8] Perhaps Thiers, whose claim to authority was that he understood the necessities of history and politics, could not admit to error without feeling disqualified from public life.

As consolation he had, as in 1836 and 1840, his *chères études*, 'after all... a truer vocation'.[9] So thought many other Liberal politicians in these bitter years, and the result was a remarkable efflorescence of scholarship: during the 1850s and 1860s, Broglie worked on philosophy and his *Vues sur le gouvernement de la France*; Guizot produced five books on religion and morality, as well as his memoirs; Rémusat turned to political thought, philosophy and British history; Duvergier wrote his important ten-volume *Histoire du gouvernement parlementaire en France*; and Tocqueville began his celebrated *L' Ancien Régime et la Révolution*. Thiers finished his *Histoire du Consulat et de l'Empire*, and planned a history of renaissance Florence, a project cherished since the early 1830s. But his first idea after the *coup d'état* was to write a work of 'pure philosophy', far removed from the 'sad present'. No doubt he was inspired by reading Cicero, who had also philosophized in exile; moreover, such a work did not require the documentary impedimenta of a major work of history. But it was shelved. First he wrote that he could not work, and needed to travel for a couple of months. Then the philosophical work and the history of Florence were postponed in favour of the *Consulate and Empire*. Finishing this absorbed his attention for the next ten years.[10]

With Mignet's help and the co-operation of the Archives Nationales he was able to work in exile. His secretary Goschler laboured full time summarizing and copying documents, aided when necessary by two assistants.[11] In August 1852, however, the decree exiling the Liberal deputies was rescinded, and Thiers felt that he could honourably return to France; he felt no solidarity with the Montagnard deputies or the December insurgents who were still in exile or confinement.

It would be wrong to see Thiers's writing of history as merely a hobby or a consolation for loss of office. An activity that absorbed immense time and effort over more than half a century, produced thirty volumes of political history, and accumulated much material for works of even vaster scope, was more than dilettantism. From his youth, Thiers had high intellectual ambitions. During his political career, he frequently declared his reluctance to take office and leave his *chères études*, or his relief in returning to them. Contemporaries and historians have often regarded these protestations as hypocritical or self-deluding. His friends, however, did not regard them as such, and as Thiers, once youthful ambitions had been fulfilled, was not greedy for office for its own sake, there was probably some truth in his declarations. Duvergier assured him in 1855 that his glory as a historian 'is well worth political glory', and quoted Macaulay on being pressed to re-enter Parliament: 'Can you tell me who was prime minister when Gibbon published his history?'[12]

Thiers was typical of his time in making history the rock on which his political thinking rested: the early decades of the nineteenth century witnessed an unprecedented fascination with the past and its meaning. Thiers always viewed contemporary events from a historical perspective. For example, as mentioned earlier, the 1830 revolution was seen as part of a pattern that the 'glorious Revolution' of 1688 and the American Revolution had already illustrated. Guizot, a rival in history as well as politics, was contemptuous: 'At one time he imitates Louis XIV, at another the Jacobins; today the Directory and tomorrow Napoleon. It seems as though . . . he has no other way of helping himself out of a difficulty than by asking himself "How would the Monarchy, how would the Republic, how would the Empire have acted under these circumstances?"'[13] This was not true. Thiers's mind was fertile enough not to need ready-made policies plucked from historical analogies. Yet he did not try, by rigorous analysis of the past, to deepen his own or his readers' understanding of the profound nature of the changes of the previous century. Although similar in many of his ideas to Tocqueville (whom he admired) and Guizot, he did not seek as they did to test or explore those ideas, but rather to illustrate conclusions he regarded as self-evident: historic trends were inevitable; liberty balanced by order was desirable; despotism was ultimately destructive.

Thiers also received from the past an emotional and imaginative stimulus when he conceived of the struggles of his time as the unfolding of great historic processes. He frequently impressed contemporaries by placing everyday political questions in an historical context, and had no doubt of his qualifications to speak for history. On one occasion, when criticizing a policy of Metternich's, he wrote that history would not excuse it – 'I am an historian, and I can answer for that.'[14] Moreover, he felt himself worthy to be an historic figure. This was his deepest ambition, stemming from what Princess Lieven called his 'pride of Satan'. It can be seen in his care to preserve his papers, keep copies of important lettters, and confide his 'memory' to Mignet and his ladies, who fully shared his concern for the judgement of history. Such reflections and precautions are doubtless common among public figures, but Thiers's preoccupation seems unusually strong. He spoke frequently, especially later in life, about his place in history, and concern about it affected his actions. His seeming carelessness for office, which puzzled contemporaries, was ascribed to impenetrable deviousness or even frivolousness. Rather it seems that Thiers, encouraged by his family and friends, was consciously holding back from humdrum politics and lost causes and reserving himself for great deeds if the opportunity for them arose. If not, he would concentrate on history and philosophy. He seems to have decided that his mission would be to bring stable government to France, convinced that no one was as well fitted as himself, a 'child of the Revolution', a realist and man of experience, and an historical thinker, to understand the necessities of the new age, avoiding the anachronism of the Right and the utopianism of the Left. Failure brought him near to despair, particularly in 1852, when he felt he had 'nothing more to do here below'. But by 1873 he was convinced that he had judged rightly and made his mark on history: 'I do not refuse the judgement of history, and I deserve to appear before it.'[15]

It was not only as a statesman that Thiers wished to appear before history. His epitaph, laid down in the fresh will be wrote in 1870, was *Patriam dilexit Veritatem coluit.*[16] It was as a seeker after truth, a philosopher and thinker, that he also wished to be remembered. Perhaps his principal intellectual ambition was to write a great work of philosophy. It was an ambition of his youth, returned to in exile in 1852, taken up again in the 1860s, and cherished until his death. While he doubtless drew inspiration from the great philosopher-statesmen Cicero and Machiavelli (whose bust adorned his study) he had distinguished models among his acquaintances too – Royer-Collard, Cousin, Humboldt, Guizot, Broglie – in an age when politics were no disqualification from high thinking. The great philosophical work was never written, indeed hardly begun, interrupted not only by political activity but also by his historical writings. These, his great intellectual achievement, almost monopolized his output. The histories took far longer than intended – most of the time between 1822 and 1862 that was not devoted to politics. The historical subjects that he chose – the Revolution, the Consulate, and Empire, and renaissance Florence (worked on over a period of eight years but never written) – were derived from his political preoccupations, and in part from the needs of political debate.

His first major work, the *Histoire de la Révolution française*, was written as part of the struggle between Liberals and Ultra-Royalists in the 1820s, in which arguments for and against the Revolution were of central importance. 'We want to set [the Revolution] against its enemies' wrote Mignet, and he and Thiers were 'its first historians properly so called',[17] the first to attack that burning subject head on in comprehensive histories for a wide readership. Thiers's publishers noted that 'the moment is difficult, perhaps even dangerous for writers' – an over-dramatization, but probably the reason why the original project was for a short book, one of a series of fairly elementary textbooks, which would not make too great a stir. But the scale of the work grew (Thiers's histories invariably did) once he burrowed more deeply into the politics, warfare and administration of the revolutionary state. Originally planned as two small volumes, then three, it eventually filled ten.[18] The first, and for a generation the only, book on such a scale, it was a great success and became the standard work, going through twenty editions by 1848.

The book is a narrative – simple, detached and highly readable – of the politics of the Revolution. Unlike other Liberal writers such as Benjamin Constant, Madame de Staël or Mignet, Thiers saw the Revolution as essentially a political phenomenon, the breakdown – 'sooner or later inevitable'[19] – of an anachronistic political system, and its replacement by another. This emphasis on politics caused him to neglect the problem of underlying causes, and his first paragraph takes the reader from the ancient Greeks to Louis XVI, ignoring the Frankish invasion, the rise of the middle class, the English revolutions, intellectual developments – subjects that other Liberals maintained were of the utmost importance to the understanding of the French Revolution. An important implication of Thiers's approach was heavily underlined by Mignet's *Histoire de la Révolution française*, which contemporaries regarded as the theoretical companion to Thiers's longer narrative.[20] Mignet stated clearly the doctrine of what was called *le fatalisme historique*, 'historical inevitability': that certain political developments were logically determined by changes in social and economic structures. 'When a reform has become necessary, and the moment to accomplish it has arrived, nothing prevents it and everything aids it'; the various phases of the Revolution 'were almost obligatory, so irresistible was the force of the events that produced them!'[21] Similar ideas had been developed eighty years earlier in Montesquieu's influential *De l'esprit des lois*. Furthermore, Rémusat thought that Mignet and Thiers had been influenced, through Victor Cousin, by German philosophers, presumably Hegel and Schelling.

Whatever the precise influences, they could hardly have remained untouched by some idea of determinism at a time when, in an intellectual development of immense importance, the idea of history as a relentless and purposeful process had appeared as the explanation of political and social change. Thiers held to *le fatalisme historique*, but never fully worked the idea out in his writings. It is not clear what he considered the historically determining factor to be. For Constant and de Staël it was the progress of ideas, and for Mignet socio-economic development. Thiers appears simply to have taken determinism for granted and, although the idea was already present in his *French Revolution*, later in life he stressed its providential nature as the unfolding of some unspecified design. He described political action as being contained within this overall development. 'I see a man in a boat descending a river; he can follow the current, or else he must row, go upstream, cut across, in short, come to terms with the current. That is what man can do when he grapples with *la force des choses*.'[22] But

143

he always believed that *la force des choses* would ultimately prevail. In the 1820s, the significance of his and Mignet's assertion of *le fatalisme historique* was that it constituted a vindication of the French Revolution, for, said Mignet, 'to explain it is to justify it, as with all necessary things'.[23] Thiers's narrative, as contemporaries realized, was intended to show not an arbitrary and accidental series of events, but a necessary succession of cause and effect, emerging 'with such lucidity, plausibility and logic, that one finishes, or very nearly, by judging [it] inevitable. To go on from there to excusing, absolving, even sometimes admiring the men who took part... is only a short step, and the historian, if one is not careful, leads one to take it.'[24]

Thiers's narrative approach, retained throughout his historical works, fitted his temperament, for he was a dazzling if loquacious talker, and an indefatigable explainer and describer. Moreover, he was, in that heyday of romanticism, an enthusiastic admirer of the visual arts and wanted his history to be artistic and colourful, 'to unite poetry and philosophy... things as they are, alive and yet linked, both detailed and general'.[25] Yet while Thiers's narrative can be dramatic, it is striking not for any emotional tone, but rather for its cool detachment which, in the circumstances of the time, amounted to a kind of effrontery that shocked many contemporaries. For he was describing as mere incidents in a political process what the enemies of the Revolution regarded as atrocious crimes. The trial and death of Louis XVI as told by Thiers are not great drama or sacrilege, but acts of policy: the King is not a hero or a martyr but a political pawn, significant only because his execution was a declaration of war by the Revolution against the old order. 'The person of the King almost disappeared in this immense question ... Only the result was seen, and the victim on whom the blow was to fall was lost from sight.'[26]

Conservative and some Liberal critics reacted sharply. The *Journal des Débats* spoke for many when it attacked Thiers for putting 'politics in the place of pity, and necessity in the place of morality'. He and Mignet were evading the historian's duty to make a moral judgement on the Revolution and the Terror, which 'must encounter today all the severity of history'. Many Liberals preferred to applaud 'the great results of 89', while condemning 'the bloody aftermath'. Thus Guizot, for example had earlier asserted that it was wrong to 'take the past *en bloc*'. Now Thiers and Mignet appeared to be telling their large readership to do precisely that: the Revolution had been 'sublime and atrocious at the same time'. Moreover they seemed not greatly moved by the fate of the eggs broken in making the omelet. Benjamin Constant vehemently disapproved such a view. 'To justify the reign of 93, to picture its crimes and frenzies as a necessity that weighs heavily on peoples when they seek freedom, is to harm a sacred cause, to do it more damage than its avowed enemies.'[27]

Thiers did not merely excuse the excesses of the Revolution on the grounds of historical necessity. For the first time he described its positive achievements in constructing a new state upon the ruins of the *ancien régime*, and defending France against reactionary forces. In his third volume he turned to the Convention, until then habitually described in the blackest terms. Thiers, even when criticizing individuals, was willing to admit their qualities (for example, Robespierre's incorruptibility) and to see merit in their policies. He described the men of the Convention

> rousing the nation ..., putting 1,800,000 men under arms, taming the heroism of the Vendée, thwarting the policy of Pitt and breaking the coalition of Europe; at the same time creating a new social organization, a new civil military administration, a new economic and financial system; inventing new measures of time, weight and distance, and adding to the boldness of their concepts an inexorable vigour of execution; ... using successively the language of the market place and that of the most sublime eloquence; issuing 44 million of paper money and dining on fourpence a day; treating with Europe and going to the Tuileries on foot and in everyday clothes; sometimes combining unprecedented political cruelty with the greatest personal kindness.[28]

Here too conservative critics raged. Thiers had dared to bring to life 'blood-thirsty' men, 'their filthy language, their gross behaviour, their cynical and atrocious ferocity ... It is perhaps necessary to analyse their crimes, but to analyse them in order to brand them with the mark of infamy.'[29]

Thiers's aim was not solely polemical. Believing that the Revolution had begun the creation of the modern French state he wished to understand its workings. He conceived his history as training in statecraft both for himself and for the political class of the country. He consulted documents and leading experts of his day – particularly Baron Louis, a former Minister of Finance – in order to understand and explain to his readers the hard facts that made statesmen behave as they did. 'I have not feared to enter into the details of loans, taxes, paper money ... bread, soap and candles ... I believed that it was an attempt to be made, that of complete truth in history.'[30] His notion of what constituted complete truth was, however, a limited one. His technical explanations fully covered finances, in which he was passionately interested, but neglected broader economic and social developments and popular movements. Much attention too is paid to military matters. He had learnt, and would never forget, Baron Louis's lesson: finances and the army were the sinews of power. He treated constitutional texts negligently, and dismissed the Declaration of the Rights of Man as serving no other purpose than 'gratifying ... philosophical minds'. This accorded with contemporary Liberal thought and especially that of Constant, for whom only underlying political principles were vital, whereas constitutional forms had a strictly relative and secondary importance.[31] Thiers the politician would practice what he preached.

The book was not based on archival research, but on monographs, memoirs and printed documents, supplemented by conversations with survivors. Partly, no doubt, this was dictated by the need to produce quickly a work that was to become 'a war machine against the absolutism of Charles X'. [32] Besides, it was not a 'scholarly' work, but a book for the general public. While well documented by the standards of its time, it lacked footnotes, documentary citations, and often even dates. Its readers were to be wearied with only enough technical detail to permit them to follow the author's argument. 'Thiers', noted Lord Acton, 'relieves you of the trouble of thinking.' [33]

The public response was not immediate. But from Volume 3 (1824), dealing with the Convention, interest grew. Royalists attacked the book, influential Liberals praised it, and the Liberal public bought it. The last volume appeared in 1827; by 1833, 150,000 volumes had been sold, and by 1845, 80,000 complete sets – equivalent to one third of the electorate. In later years Thiers could boast that it was a book that 'my century has read'. It was one of the major channels by which the Liberal view of the Revolution became established: it was a cardinal event in history; it was a necessary and inevitable result of social change; its excesses were caused by internal resistance and foreign interference; the phase of violence and terror was ended by the necessary and desirable restoration of order by the Directory and Consulate, when the Revolution began its culminating phase of creating a modern state. His presentation of the last years of the Republic had a clear political message: that finally the Revolution had raised France to heights which the Restoration could not equal:

> When was our country ever finer or greater? . . . It was only for a moment; but there are only moments in the lives of peoples, as in those of individuals. We were about to regain affluence with calm; as for liberty and glory, we had them already! . . . Frenchmen, we who have seen since then our liberty stifled, our country invaded, our heroes shot or betraying their own glory, let us never forget those immortal days of liberty, greatness and hope! [34]

The trend of the argument in the last volumes seemed to call for a sequel covering the years of Napoleon's domination, which in the last lines of Volume 10 Thiers defined as the next phase of the Revolution, during which it was spread and defended by military force. But it was more than ten years before he began the *Histoire du Consulat et de l'Empire*, his greatest work. His intention had been to begin at once, but his journalistic activity of the late 1820s and his rise to political prominence in the 1830s forced him to postpone these plans. [35] Thiers still wielded his pen as a political weapon, however, witness *La Monarchie de 1830*, which justified the new regime as resulting 'from necessity alone' – a restatement of the argument in his *French Revolution*. Of almost equal political relevance was his projected 'general history of government', first thought of in the late 1820s, and for which he seems to have begun reading very widely at about this time. It was intended to cover the ancient world, mediaeval and modern Europe and the United States. He was also interested, as shown in lists of books he intended to read and buy (his library eventually contained over 5,000 works), in South America and Asia. He was concerned with the fashionable question of how socio-political systems were affected by differences of climate, geography and culture. [36] This typically vast enterprise appears never to have gone beyond the note-taking stage, and Thiers turned to a more clearly defined subject, renaissance Florence, still virgin territory for the historian.

Thiers, like many of his countrymen, loved Italy. He knew some Italian, and was an enthusiast for Italian art. All of this must have whetted his interest, but mere enjoyment was never a sufficient motive for Thiers, who, in all his historical works, sought insight into the political problems of his own day. He was forming the view – similar to that of Tocqueville – that one of these was a trend towards democracy which tended to degenerate, as the Revolution seemed to show, into anarchy followed by despotism. Whereas Tocqueville sought elucidation in America, Thiers looked back to Florence, which he believed to have had the most democratic system of government in history, but which had ended under the despotic rule of the Medicis. He was also interested in the social foundations of its great cultural achievement, for Florentine art was a particular hobby, and nursed the idea that his great philosophical work would include a philosophy of art or possibly a universal history of the arts.

He began background reading in the early 1830s, and in 1838 engaged a young Italian scholar, Giuseppe Canestrini, to work as a researcher in Florence, directing him towards three main areas: the history of the guilds, the economy of the city and the guilds, and architecture. At the same time Thiers was doing research in Paris. In 1843 he wrote to Canestrini that he was much occupied with architectural history; his notes on the work of the fifteenth-century Florentine architect Alberti still remain. No doubt he also read all he could find on the political history. The knowledge acquired added to his stock of political ideas, or at least provided ammunition to defend some he already held, such as the desirability of a mediating aristocracy, the danger of despotism emerging from democracy, and the creative function of wealth. He was to express these ideas forcefully after the 1848 revolution. He must also have been struck by Machiavelli's view, so similar to his own and Mignet's *fatalisme*, that wise statesmanship must obey the dictates of necessity.

Great though his enthusiasm was, the book was never begun. Political affairs delayed a serious start until after his resignation in 1836, but then, despite having engaged Canestrini, he decided that the Consulate and Empire came first. Characteristically, he underestimated the magnitude of the task. In the late 1830s and early 1840s he repeatedly assured Canestrini that he would have it finished in a few months. By 1845, he had realized what he had taken on, and wrote disconsolately, 'I am 47 years old, I have been at work for thirty years and when I have finished the history of the Empire God knows if I shall have the courage for anything else. However, if I can still hold a pen it will be to write the history of that fine Florentine republic.' But it took another seventeen years to finish the Consulate and Empire, and by then other works had been published on Florence, including one by Canestrini himself. Thiers did not care to be one scholar among many, and so, in his mid-60s, he again turned his attention to his youthful ambition, a work of philosophy.[37]

It was, therefore, the *Histoire du Consulat et de l'Empire* (twenty volumes, 1845–62), even more than politics, that absorbed his time and energy during his years of maturity. He had excellent reasons to take on the subject. The success of his *French Revolution*, which called logically for a sequel, and his political prominence, meant that public and publishers were eager: 50,000 subscribers are said to have been waiting for the first history of what to many Frenchmen was the apogee of their national existence.[38]

Thiers, who had completed and inaugurated the Arc de Triomphe, replaced Napoleon's statue on the Vendôme column and had his remains brought back from Saint Helena, had the chance of creating another national monument. Furthermore, he would add to his credentials as the leading patriotic statesman who had twice fallen from office because of his determination to pursue a more assertive foreign policy. The book was intended to rekindle a patriotic flame that many Liberals felt had burnt out. Moreover, he sincerely admired Napoleon, whom he regarded as 'the greatest human being since Caesar and Charlemagne'.[39] Even when criticizing him politically, he presented him as a great and noble character, accepting on the whole Napoleon's own account of his actions and motives and passing over or excusing the less attractive episodes. In short, 'the dominant motive is admiration, and more than admiration – affection, love'.[40] Acton wrote of 'a joy, an intellectual prize, such as was seldom or never given to any writer — the prodigious intellectual sympathy of so gifted a man with one still more richly gifted than himself'.[41]

As well as being a leading patriotic politician, Thiers was of course a leading Liberal, an advocate since the beginning of his journalistic career of parliamentary government and limited monarchy, and a victim of Louis-Philippe's use of the royal prerogative. He had every reason, therefore, to pursue his attacks on 'despotism' in his historical writings. Moreover, having been less than successful in high office, he could not have been unaware of the advantages for his reputation of adopting the role of elder statesman educating his country in the ways of liberty: he was, wrote a British commentator, posing as professor of politics to his compatriots. The friendly *Siècle* thought him admirably qualified: 'Are there many men in Europe who have received such an historical training? Is it not at least the equal of that of the universities of Cambridge and Oxford?'[42]

There was, then, an ambiguity – more of feeling than of logic – in a work that was simultaneously a critique of despotism and a celebration of national glory. Furthermore, Thiers's message seemed to be affected by the circumstances in which the book appeared: the first seven volumes during the Guizot years, the rest during the Second Republic, the rise of Louis-Napoleon Bonaparte, and the first decade of the Second Empire. Even if it were true, as Thiers insisted, that these events did not affect what he wrote, they could not but alter what the public thought it read. During the 1840s, it was the 'national' message that Liberals looked for. Reviewing the first three volumes in 1845 the *Siècle* exclaimed, 'What a contrast between this conduct of the First Consul and the *bonne politique* of our day ... giving in to everything and finding ... everyone against it.' Saint-Aulaire, Thiers's old ally as ambassador in Vienna, wrote to him that France should be grateful for his 'forcing [his] readers to feel enthusiasm and emotion for something other than material interest or the price of railway shares'.[43] Thiers's friends in the press denied that he was stirring up trouble for the government or drawing facile parallels with the present day, but they certainly shared his dim view of what he privately called 'a dull and spiritless generation'. Mignet urged him to finish 'this fine monument ... to the glory of a great man who did great wrong, and to a great nation that now only wishes to be a prosperous nation. Be severe on the passions and excesses that have made us sick of greatness and have wearied us to the point of exhaustion.' Mignet hoped that the phase of timid materialism, though inevitable, would pass once the dynasty was established and the bourgeoisie 'satisfied'.[44] Thiers's history was a means of setting the country back on the patriotic path.

In the 1850s and 1860s, with the Empire in power, the book was interpreted very differently, even in the same circles. Duvergier urged Thiers to use history as a political weapon against the regime: 'we must choose subjects that permit us to defend, by another means, the principles we have always defended. In your last volumes on the Empire, when you are on the slope that leads to the Isle of Elba, you will not lack opportunity, and you can show quite naturally where ... despotism leads.' He was delighted with the results. Volume 12, appearing in 1855, showed Napoleon 'in his illusions and mad dreams ... In the last pages especially you judge Napoleon severely. And yet your narrative is far more severe than your judgement ... If you want to believe that the man was basically good and that despotism corrupted him, so be it; but corrupt or corrupted, he is an abominable scoundrel.' Volume 14 was even better: 'whether it is your intention or not ... [it] is crushing for Napoleon' – especially when written by 'a sincere admirer who regrets his hero's faults'.[45] Other Liberals devoured the book with similar relish: Roger, Montalembert, Prévost-Paradol ('one day, thanks to you, only those who cannot read can be admirers of military despotism'), and the Duchesse d' Orléans, who looked forward to reading about 'the fall of the Empire'. The Legitimist Berryer too was eager for the concluding volume and its lessons.[46] Thiers drew the moral in his closing words, which seem to reflect not only the bitter experience of Waterloo, but the more recent blows of the 1848 revolution and the 1851 *coup d'état*:

> the country must never be handed over to one man, no matter who the man, no matter what the circumstances. In finishing this long history of our triumphs and our defeats, this is the last cry that comes from my heart, a sincere cry that I would wish to carry to the hearts of all Frenchmen, in order to persuade them all that liberty must never be given away, and, so as not to risk its being lost, must never be abused.[47]

Thiers, however, had not changed as much as many of his readers. He had all along intended both to attack despotism and to celebrate national glory, and the 1851 *coup d'état* did not change that. 'I am not and shall never be Bonapartist', he wrote in 1857, 'but one must tell the truth, and beware of wounding national feeling.'[48] In his preface to Volume 8 written in 1855, he went so far as to praise the 'victors of Sebastopol' and end with a compliment to the government: 'The greatest compensation for being nothing in one's country is to see the country being all that it should be in the world.' His admiration for Napoleon the Romantic hero and his taste for military history – which forms the largest element in the book and which Mignet and Duvergier urged him to cut down – do much to offset the effect of his political criticisms. Consequently, while Liberals applauded the criticisms, he also received applause from the great Empire families – Ney, Davoût, Cambacérès, Walewski – for his celebration of the glories of their ancestors.[49] Above all, he enjoyed the approval of the Bonapartes themselves. King Jerome, Napoleon I's brother, for years called on Thiers for advice, even concerning his daughter's future. Napoleon III spoke flatteringly of Thiers in private, and in public referred to him as 'our national historian'.[50]

The qualities that won approval for the *Consulate and Empire* from conservatives drew fire from the Left: it was too much a military saga and neglected internal politics and the growth of opposition to Napoleon. Moreover, critics asserted, extravagant praise of the emperor's genius made meaningless criticism of the faults of 'despotism' leading to Waterloo.[51] Thiers, on the contrary, thought that the praise reinforced the lesson of the criticism, for 'if ever a country had excuses for giving itself to one man, it was France when in 1800 she took Napoleon as her master ... [but] absolute power carried within itself incurable madness, the temptation to do everything when one can do everything, even evil after good'. Consequently, 'however great, however wise, however vast the genius of a man, never must the destinies of a country be delivered completely to him'.[52] There was therefore no logical reason why Thiers should not emphasize the greatness of the man and the glories of his epoch, and indulge his own taste, and that of his readership, for a prolonged military epic.

But was the consistency of Thiers's logic enough? He indignantly rejected the reproach that he had contributed to the 1851 *coup d'état* by encouraging the Napoleonic myth. Yet in spite of the clear and repeated warnings of disasters even in the early volumes, and the strong criticisms of Napoleon in the later volumes, the overall effect is ambivalent. Napoleon, in spite of everything, is not for Thiers the 'abominable scoundrel' he was for Duvergier, and the disasters he brought do not blot out the benefits. Thiers describes himself as 'an historian ardently admiring Napoleon', 'deploring' his faults, but 'immensely grateful to him for having left us . . . glory, which is moral greatness and with time restores material greatness'.[53] The effect on opinion of a work of history – even one that went through dozens of French and foreign editions – is impossible to gauge. Thiers, however, in one of the major books of the century shared, reflected and gave substance to a view of the recent past in which military glory played a central part, and this first under the July Monarchy, that was bitterly criticized for its supine foreign policy, and then under the Second Empire, that tied its prestige, with fatal consequences, to continuing the glories of the First.

Thiers had other lessons to teach: 'the secrets of administration, finance, war, diplomacy . . . this purely technical part of history [deserved] as much attention from serious minds as the dramatic part'.[54] Here he had no reproaches to make, regarding Napoleon as the inspired creator of the modern state, as well as the greatest soldier of modern times. Especially praiseworthy was his restoration of Catholicism not as the state religion, but as the religion of the French people. Royer-Collard told Thiers that he had written the history of the Concordat as if he would like to have made it, and indeed, in Thiers's account, Napoleon's views of religion and the state – deist, sceptical, utilitarian – seem identical with his own: religion was necessary for the masses in a civilized state, and in France that religion was Catholicism, 'consecrated by time'.[55] As in his *French Revolution*, Thiers intended to further the political education of the nation by showing the hard realities on which political decisions were based: 'He considered that he was addressing a society which had advanced further than any other in public affairs . . . [which] makes its own laws, governs itself.' He must have been gratified by the response of one of his female readers: 'Since reading M. Thiers, I have become financier, administrator and general, and no novel has ever interested me as much as his history.'[56]

Guizot too found reading Thiers like reading a novel, but he did not mean it as a compliment.[57] Thiers, as with his *French Revolution*, was not writing for scholars, but for the whole reading public, and he succeeded in reaching it. Even a hostile critic admitted that 'all who read, inside and outside France, have read this book'. They included Metternich, Napoleon III, Wellington almost at the end of his life, Cavour on his deathbed, and

Gladstone, who avoided visitors when reading the latest volumes. The style, like that of the *French Revolution*, was suited to a wide readership who were not to be wearied with a scholarly apparatus of footnotes, archival reference and textual citations. This was partly the style of the time, but also, perhaps, because Thiers was not presenting evidence in support of an academic hypothesis, but instructing his readers as an authority; he was inviting not discussion, but assent. He was presenting, he believed and asserted, not an opinion but the facts. Like many contemporary historians – foremost among them Ranke – Thiers was a militant realist, believing that the task of the historian was to ascertain and understand objective reality, and present it in simple language. He went to great lengths to verify certain details: as we have seen, he delighted to visit battlefields, notebook in hand, so that topographical descriptions should be exact, and he read and annotated 30,000 of Napoleon's letters. His appetite for facts explained the unanticipated and apparently uncontrollable growth in the size of his books and the time spent on them. 'I have thus sometimes taken a year to prepare a volume which two months was enough for me to write.'[58]

He was also a fanatic for simplicity, a characteristic of his earliest writings, and one which he declared to be as difficult to achieve as 'the finest verse'.[59] Although he shared some of the characteristics of Romanticism, he detested what he considered its excesses, in literature and history. Victor Hugo, his *bête noire*, was equally contemptuous about Thiers's lack of poetry: 'M. Thiers is writing the history of Napoleon. O Monsieur Scribe, translate Homer!'[60] Thiers shared, of course, the orthodox admiration for the Latin and Greek classics and those of seventeenth-century France but he considered that the time for writing like a Bossuet or a Pascal had passed. Modern writers, he declared, should aim at 'a simple, true, thought-out style, a scientific, polished style'.[61] Here (as in much else) his model was Napoleon, whom he called the greatest writer of the age. His own style is generally simple, relaxed and readable, and it has aged well. Hugo's sarcasm was not generally echoed at the time (though it has been since); indeed, as the later volumes appeared, Thiers's prose was extravagantly praised: it was 'rich and precise, energetic and supple, colourful and almost as naked as a wrestler of antiquity'; 'no one has written like this since the masters of classical antiquity'; its last twenty pages would 'always count among the masterpieces of the French language'.[62]

But his prose no longer figures in anthologies, and though his century read the *Consulate and Empire*, ours does not. This, no doubt, is partly due to the decline in his reputation that began soon after his death. Furthermore, *juste milieu* Liberals, with the exception of Tocqueville, have until recently inspired little sympathy or interest. Thiers's books are also very long, even by the standards of the time. Length, admittedly, does not prevent new editions of Michelet, but Thiers, unlike Michelet, wrote a history that no longer catches the imagination: it is the history of states and statesmen, not of societies and peoples, and even his military history concerns the moves of the chessboard rather than the excitement of combat. He is not even a quarry for professional historians, for (except perhaps in his beloved maps) he does not provide fundamental material that might still be useful. Above all, although he liked to think he was addressing future ages, his preoccupations were entirely those of his own day, and what brought him contemporary success condemns him to subsequent neglect: he was the first to tell an epic story that is now familiar, while if the dangers of despotism require further demonstration, there are more recent and terrible examples.

When the *Consulate and Empire* was finished, Thiers found that after all he still had the courage to hold a pen. Although the chance of being the first modern historian of Florence had passed, he retained his interest in the history of art, now apparently to be part of his old and most ambitious project, a great universal philosophy, which was also to include the philosophy of science and of ethics (reminiscent of the influential Eclecticism of Victor Cousin, the leading academic philosopher and Thiers's old friend, which argued that the three 'faculties' of man were reason, sensibility, and will to pursue *le Vrai*, *le Beau* and *le Bien*. Thiers was already enthusiastic and quite knowlegeable about the arts (*le Beau*) and during the 1860s and 1870s set out with equal enthusiasm to further his knowledge of one aspect of *le Vrai*: science.

During the 1820s, as has been seen, he had embraced art criticism as a normal part of the journalistic task, and had praised early controversial works by Delacroix at the Salons of 1822 (in particular the *Barque of Dante*) and 1824, great events in the history of Romantic painting.[63] It is noteworthy, in view of Thiers's 'fatalistic' philosophy of history, and his 'amoral' treatment of the violence of the French Revolution, that one of these paintings, *The Massacres of Chios*, was a 'dispassionate treatment of horrific suffering', a portrayal of submission to fate, which Delacroix was to call 'that eternal necessity'.[64] During the 1830s, as Minister of Commerce and Public Works and then Minister of the Interior, Thiers was the official patron of the arts, able to commission works for public buildings and monuments. His most courageous and important decision was to invite Delacroix to paint the murals of the Salon du Roi in the Palais Bourbon, the room in which the King performed the state opening of Parliament, although Delacroix was a controversial figure outside the artistic establishment, who had never handled such a large scheme. He followed this successful initiative by securing major commissions for the libraries of the Palais Bourbon and the Palais du Luxembourg for Delacroix, who later said that Thiers was the only public figure who had ever helped his career. Thiers also commissioned the masterpiece of the greatest sculptor of the Romantic period, Rude – the famous 'Marseillaise' of the Arc de Triomphe. More prosaically, he was keen to expand the teaching collection of copies

153

of great works possessed by the Ecole des Beaux Arts. His delight in being patron and protector of the arts put him on cordial terms with several artists, even the prickly Ingres (who was, however irritated by Thiers's opinionated views on painting). He collected his own materials on the arts, both the notes on painting, sculpture and architecture that he indefatigably took on all his visits, and his 'little museum' at the Place Saint-Georges, much of which he bought when travelling in Italy 'like a renaissance prince', in Chateaubriand's phrase. At his death it consisted of 1,470 pieces of all kinds, including Egyptian antiquities, Venetian glass, renaissance sculpture (notably two important pieces by Verrocchio), oriental art, reproductions of Old Masters, and Madame Thiers's collection of porcelain (which contained some of the rarest pieces of all). This collection has been mocked for its eclecticism (in Thiers's youth a fashionable characteristic) and alleged lack of refinement. The reproductions were a particular object of scorn, the assumption being that for Thiers, the archetypal vulgar bourgeois, a reproduction was as good as an original. This was not so. Many artists, including Delacroix, made and collected copies as part of their studies, and Thiers – a youthful painter of watercolours – no doubt considered himself and his copies in the same light, for his collection had a practical purpose. It was planned with expert advice as 'documentation' for the projected book, and therefore required examples of every aspect of world art that contemporary taste considered significant. Hence Thiers was willing to sell most of his collection of prints in order to buy pieces that filled gaps. Hence too his copies of great works and his collection of oriental art, in which he took an early interest and concerning which, needless to say, he theorized. The collection was, then, a reflection of the orthodox view of art history, centred on renaissance Italy, and with China and Japan the only significant non-European elements.[65] Contemporary works were practically absent – a striking omission considering Thiers's distinguished artistic friends. Thiers was relatively unimpressed by their achievements, however: 'Today ... artists ... are only imitators undecided which models to prefer.' Even Delacroix was 'defeated', going 'endlessly from one system to another, leaving everywhere the traces of a fine talent, but never able to settle'.[66]

Science, a fashionable pursuit, was Thiers's other intellectual passion during the 1860s and 1870s. He hoped to use it to demonstrate the existence of order throughout the universe, combatting materialism by proving the existence of God, author of that order, and deducing the laws of human behaviour. His interest led him in the 1860s to attend lectures on chemistry and to make contact with some of the greatest scientists of the day, including Pasteur, the astronomer Le Verrier, and the naturalist Agassiz. Whether scientists liked it or not, their work was widely considered to have clear implications for politics: the invention of 'Social Darwinism' and stress on the 'scientific' nature of Marxist dialectical materialism are the most famous but not the only examples. Thiers, and all who thought like him,

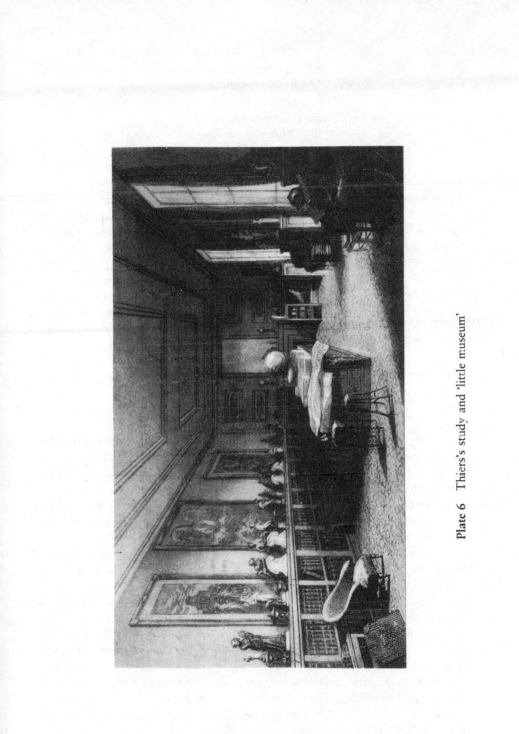

Plate 6 Thiers's study and 'little museum'

felt that in combating materialist scientists whose ideas, notes one historian, became by the 1850s practically synonymous with a radical, anti-religious *Weltanschauung*,[67] they were defending the intellectual foundations of morality and the social order, so shaken in 1848.

Thiers wrote in 1871 that 'three questions have agitated the scientific world in the last quarter of a century: the pretended transformation of species, so-called spontaneous generation, and the composition of heavenly bodies'.[68] Darwin's *Origin of Species* was published in 1859, the same year as the equally controversial *L'Hétérogénie*, written by the distinguished French biologist Pouchet (which claimed to show experimentally that microbes were generated spontaneously from inanimate organic matter). Despite the protestations of their authors, the two works were taken as providing a materialistic explanation of the origins of life: Pouchet showed that simple life forms arose spontaneously from inorganic matter; Darwin showed how they developed into higher forms. Belief in an ordered, intelligent universe was undermined. As Pasteur put it in a lecture at the Sorbonne in 1864 attended by 'all Paris' – surely Thiers would have been there – 'Great problems are in question today ... the unity or multiplicity of human races; the creation of man several thousand years or several thousand centuries ago; the fixity of species or the slow and progressive transformation of one species into another; the eternity of matter ...; the idea of a God unneeded.'[69] Pasteur and Agassiz, followed and encouraged by Thiers, were eager to enter the lists.

Agassiz, Swiss by birth and a professor at Harvard, discoverer of the Ice Age and pioneer in the classification of fossil species, was a leading scientific opponent of Darwin's. He argued, from his work with glaciers and fossils, that life had been created in successive stages, and had not evolved from a single source. In short, he staunchly defended the idea of a universe designed by an intelligent 'creative power'. Thiers congratulated him on work that had been 'the most conclusive against the materialist scientists of Germany and England'.[70] Pasteur's intervention in the controversy over spontaneous generation during the early 1860s was inspired by motives similar to those of Agassiz. He saw it as part of a battle between 'materialism' and 'spiritualism': 'What a victory for materialism if it could be affirmed that it rests on the established fact that matter ... takes on life itself.'[71] The scientific duel between Pasteur and Pouchet and their supporters attracted much public interest. Pouchet was seconded by anti-clericals and the Left, Pasteur by the scientific, political and religious establishment. The Academy of Sciences was eager to endorse Pasteur's claim to have disproved Pouchet's theories. His experiments were brilliant, but not entirely conclusive: he and his backers stifled any doubts on religious and political grounds. Thiers visited Pasteur's laboratory at the Ecole Normale to have the experiments explained to him, and, with typical self-assurance, gave public lectures on the question in 1867.

Less satisfactory was his next foray into scientific controversy, when in 1868 he placed his influence and reputation behind a set of recently unearthed manuscripts which purported to prove that Pascal had discovered the laws of gravity years before Newton ('a timid mind', pronounced Thiers), to whom Pascal had communicated the discovery. Thiers had ingeniously worked out to his own satisfaction that Pascal, having discovered the existence of the vacuum, 'must have drawn the conclusions' leading to the discovery of gravity. Alas for Thiers – who had ignored the opinion of his friend Le Verrier – it soon became clear that the manuscripts were rather crude forgeries. He looked worse than foolish. Sainte-Beuve, once an admirer, wrote of him as 'this presumptuous man' who 'wishes now to make us believe that he understands higher geometry ... What cleverness, but what conceit and what impertinence!' Renan judged that Thiers's error came from 'national pride, as misplaced as could be, that makes him see in the puerile inventions of a forger titles of glory for France'.[72]

Thiers was willing to help his friends and further the common anti-materialist cause. In 1867 he used his influence to induce the parliamentary Left to overlook Pasteur's mishandling of a student political demonstration at the Ecole Normale, which might otherwise have led to his leaving the school. In 1871, when in power, Thiers encouraged the building of new laboratories at the Jardin des Plantes, and also considered dismissing or demoting scientists who had followed the materialist English and German schools and been promoted by the Empire, which 'liked to flatter false doctrines in order to please the democracy which it idolized in order to dominate'. In 1874 he supported Pasteur's successful request for a state pension.[73]

Of all the sciences, astronomy was Thiers's favourite, for, like his hero Napoleon, he enjoyed star gazing, a spectacle that confirmed his spiritualist conviction that the universe was the creation of a mighty intelligence. Le Verrier, who jokingly addressed him as 'Monsieur l'Astronome', gave him observations and calculations to carry out, and they became friends, in spite of Thiers's disapproval of his political tendencies.[74] For Le Verrier's work in completing the mathematical analysis of the movement of heavenly bodies, in which he had achieved 'a near perfect agreement of theory and observation', could not fail to fascinate Thiers, concerned to show the orderly nature of the universe.[75] Thiers was also aware of important advances in spectroscopy during the 1860s in discovering the material composition of planets and stars; he knew of the pioneering work of the Frenchman Janssen, the discoverer of helium. Such discoveries were seized upon by philosophers as shedding light on the evolution or separate creation of the various parts of the universe – the questions that Pasteur and Agassiz were working on from the other end of the scale. Thus Thiers obtained the material for his lectures on the 'philosophy of nature', showing how, by studying the 'infinitely great and the infinitely small, one can hope to see the

157

first glimmers of divine thought'.[76] Ironically, Le Verrier had met a problem with which Thiers must have been acquainted: the movement of the planets showed a slight irregularity.[77] It was not until Einstein's General Theory of Relativity that the problem was solved, and Newtonian physics, upon which Le Verrier had based his work and Thiers sought to base a general philosophy of order, was found not to apply.

When head of government in 1871 Thiers wrote in typically lofty vein to Guizot that one day he would leave the sordid business of politics and again be 'what I am most in fact, a real philosopher, liking in human affairs only the spectacle of the universe conducted by God . . . a spectacle that I often permit myself at the Observatory, and which is the only one worthy of elevated and mature minds'.[78] After his resignation in 1873 he was able to give ample time to such pleasures, and remained a regular visitor to Le Verrier. He helped to organize a large and elaborate observation of the passage of Venus across the sun in 1874, and for his work and support was awarded a medal by the Academy of Sciences. His pleasure is easy to imagine. Pasteur too remained in contact, and in 1874 urged him to return to the struggle against materialism, by giving 'one of those luminous expositions of which you have the secret or one of those philosophical declarations to undermine the presumptuousness of atheism'.[79] This was indeed Thiers's desire, the end to which his scientific studies had been directed. At last he set out to write his great philosophical work, entitled *L'Harmonie universelle: certitude, concordance et succession.*

Only a short outline of under 4,000 words was ever written, and Thiers admitted that 'I do not know whether I shall have the time or the strength to finish the work I propose to begin today.'[80] We might suspect that the outline was a manifesto of beliefs and aspirations rather than the realistic synopsis of a book. It is enormous in its scope and ambitions: proof of the existence of God, demonstration of order in the universe, deduction of moral laws governing human societies, and philosophies of art and history. Reminiscent of the works of Thiers's old friend Cousin in its eclecticism and clear political overtones – providing 'incontestable truths' to combat 'malcontents' and furnish 'solid foundations for all necessary beliefs' – the outline does not give the impression that the book could ever have been written, except perhaps as a superficial tract on the lines of *Du droit de propriété.* Its main interest is to show how Thiers, often considered as an unprincipled opportunist, tried to base his political ideas on a philosophical foundation which, near the end of his life, had scarcely altered from the liberal philosophy of his youth.

Since childhood, declared Thiers, he had 'found good that which is not fortuitous but permanent'.[81] A concept of determinism lay at the heart of his historical and political beliefs. It was the most noticed feature of his and Mignet's histories of the Revolution, and drew favourable comment from Engels and Lenin for prefiguring the ideas of 'scientific socialism'. But

Thiers's determinism was never developed into a philosophy of history comparable with those of Hegel or Marx, claiming to explain the whole of human history and even to predict future development. It was an attitude of mind rather than a worked-out theory: a conviction that the universe was hard and unyielding, full of obstacles that might be negotiated but not swept aside. A shock came in 1848, when disorientated Liberals feared that after all history might not be on their side. Even Thiers was tempted to rebel, arguing that the duty of an honest man was 'to fight to the end and ... make a tottering regime last another twenty years'.[82] This diehard conservatism did not last long,[83] and the *coup d'état* of 1851 seemed to prove its futility. Thiers returned to that attitude summed up in a phrase from Virgil that he and Mignet often quoted: *Fata viam invenient* (let the fates find a way). Wisdom lay in accepting what was inevitable, and steering down the river rather than vainly battling against the current.

Thiers often spoke, even in his younger days, of providence, and he always proclaimed his spiritualism, but such language seemed little more than conventional. Towards the end of his life, however, in his philosophical outline, such thoughts are more prominent. He seemed to need to reconcile his deeply rooted deterministic and relativistic views of history and society on one hand with his repugnance for materialism and his desire for religious belief (both for personal consolation and as a social cement) on the other. 'Necessity' is thus consecrated as 'a beautiful and moral design', an 'evident moral intention in the composition and direction of the universe'.[84] Yet his religious belief was never orthodox: 'when the end comes', he wrote to a friend, 'God will put us elsewhere, I don't know where, but in any case a place that will I think be very different from what my priest says and yours'.[85]

Thiers's *chères études* were motivated by high ambitions. He regarded them as a worthy alternative to political activity, and he seems at times to have believed them more important. Yet these high ambitions were not entirely fulfilled in spite of his brilliant intellectual gifts and his remarkable contemporary success, for his crowning philosophical work was never written, and posterity does not mourn its loss. It is impossible to say whether Thiers's intelligence might have produced historical, philosophical or scientific works of lasting value, but an obvious condition would have been that politics should play a less prominent part in his life, not only because of the time they took, but more importantly because political pre-occupations channelled his thoughts in certain preconceived directions, and led him to desire to reach and influence a large contemporary audience. His success in doing so encouraged his frequently mocked pretentions to omniscience, as he attempted to be a great historian, a great philosopher and a great statesman all at once. Even his exceptional cleverness and appetite for work could not suffice for a task which brought out his worst intellectual vices: over-confidence, prejudice and jumping to conclusions (which he saw as 'intuition, that divinatory inspiration').[86] All was buttressed by his dazzling gifts of exposition and argument, with which he not only convinced others, but also convinced himself.

While he often became bored with run-of-the-mill politics and turned with pleasure to study, it is impossible to imagine Thiers abandoning wider political preoccupations for an ivory tower of scholarship, and in the 1860s, he duly returned to Parliament. In his early and highly revealing work, the *Eloge de Vauvenargues*, he makes clear the attraction of a life of action over one of contemplation. In other writings, and in many sayings attributed to him, the same urge to action is manifest: 'never is life more endurable [to man] than when he acts forcefully; when he forgets himself and ceases to use his mind to doubt [and] blaspheme'.[87] The urge to self-forgetfulness and the rejection of doubt may not be the best frame of mind for philosophical exploration. Moreover, he was faced by no nagging intellectual problem affecting him personally, unlike Tocqueville, an aristocrat in an age of democratization, or Guizot, a Christian in an age of scepticism. Thiers had no difficulty in accepting prevailing beliefs, and this rendered his political ideas commonplace to sophisticated minds in search of originality, while for millions of ordinary citizens maxims such as 'the king reigns but does not rule' or 'the Republic is the government that divides us least' took on the force of proverbs. His mind was like a brilliant mirror held up to his age, and it reflected the fundamental elements of political liberalism to the nation at large. Never was this more so than in the 1860s.

The Old Hand:
In Parliament Once More,
1862–1870

The twentieth and last volume of *The History of the Consulate and Empire* appeared in 1862. Apart from the philosophic book of his dreams, which has just been described, Thiers now had no literary commitments.[1] He was a free man just when political life, stifled since December 1851, began to stir anew. After a decade of popularity and success characterized by economic expansion and military victories in the Crimea and in Italy the authoritarian regime of Louis-Napoleon, transformed into the Second Empire in 1852, had begun to lose impetus. The economic horizon darkened and foreign complications developed. Republicans in the large cities maintained their opposition while criticism of the regime affected even its supporters. These were among the factors which had induced Napoleon III to change course. On 24 November 1860 Napoleon III had issued the first of a series of decrees which initiated the authoritarian Empire's hesitant progress towards liberalism. The Chambers were permitted to vote an address in reply to the annual speech from the throne, their powers of discussion were to be widened, the government's measures were to be presented not, as Thiers sarcastically put it, by a 'poor little councillor of state', but by ministers without portfolio, and their debates could be printed and published in entirety.

When asked by the Duc d'Aumale, Louis-Philippe's youngest son, what he thought of the decree, Thiers replied that 'the liberal monarchist party' certainly ought to take part in discussing state business since it was invited to do so. It should discuss business for business's sake, as in the first year of the revolution of 1848 when it had been able to do good service. As for individuals, young newcomers could have no objection to being active at once, but, lacking authority and experience, they might not suffice for their task unless they were well directed. This created a problem for people like Thiers since the matter of their 'dignity' was immense. For his part he had maintained his 'dignity' since he quitted the political struggle. If a crisis as grave as that of 1848 threatened the country he might feel impelled to re-enter it. 'Otherwise I shall advise my party to be active while I myself maintain 'la dignité du repos'.[2]

It was easy enough to preserve this 'dignity' when two volumes of the *Consulate and Empire* had yet to be written, but when that was done and 1863 was a general election year things looked different. Moreover, Thiers had already been courted by both sides. He might, as the Emperor well knew, be a difficult ally, but he could be a still more dangerous foe. The speech in which, as early as 1857, Napoleon had hailed him as an illustrious national historian might have been interpreted as a gesture toward reconciliation. Soundings were subsequently made on Napoleon's behalf both by Walewski and the well-known writer Mérimée, but in vain. Nor did the Prussian Minister in Paris, Count Otto von Bismarck, whose fame was yet to come, fare better. Thiers did not respond to his cheerful suggestion that he should make it up with the Emperor since sulking was not a policy.[3] In fact there was for the time being an unbridgeable gulf. Napoleon III had no intention of relinquishing his personal power, whereas return to a regime in which the monarch reigned but did not govern was now as ever Thiers's ultimate objective. If the government had the wisdom to give way, he had told Aumale, critics like himself must surrender, not in order to become ministers, but to show their approval. Until then if Thiers returned to parliament he would evidently take his place in the opposition.

At first, when approached about being a candidate in the 1863 elections he hesitated as in 1848, but this time, it seems, mainly because of the objections of his wife and mother-in-law. For them Thiers's re-entry into politics in 1848 had meant fresh fears for his safety and, eventually, a spell in exile. They thought him sure of a place in history and had no wish to experience anew the sort of anxieties they had suffered under the Second Republic. But eventually, missing the joys of exercising political influence, he responded to what other members of the opposition represented as the call of duty, helped those others to overcome their scruples about taking the oath of allegiance required of Members of Parliament, and agreed to stand for election. Despite his rebuff there in 1848 he did so again in the Bouches-du-Rhône's second constituency, as well as in the sixth constituency of the Nord, the fourth of the Côtes-du-Nord, and the second of Paris.

In the Bouches-du-Rhône his good but eccentric and deaf friend Borély was an original canvasser. From time to time he got off his horse and entered a café, striking to left and right with his riding crop to arouse the customers' attention. Then he would say to them: 'If you want a good-looking man as your deputy choose M. Bournat; if you want a statesman and superb orator, I know one who is not much to look at; he's small, he's even ugly, but he's wonderfully talented. I'm choosing my friend Thiers. Do you do the same.'[4] Unfortunately Calixte Bournat, a local man, was the official candidate, and the administration, bent on thwarting Thiers, swung votes his way by timely favours. Voting was to take place on 31 May and

Plate 7   Thiers aged sixty-five

in mid-April the government gave the go-ahead for an irrigation canal for which local people had long been pressing.

Partly as a result Thiers was defeated in the Bouches-du-Rhône; he was also unsuccessful in the Côtes-du-Nord and, despite his connection with the Anzin Mining Company, in the Nord. But in Paris he fared better. The Minister of the Interior, Persigny, overreached himself by an ill-judged attack on Thiers's past record, and Thiers defeated the official candidate, a chocolate manufacturer and influential municipal councillor named Devinck, by 11,112 to 9,845 votes. The working-class electors in the constituency were unlikely to be enthusiastic on behalf of the man who had referred to *la vile multitude*, but some railway workers were reported to have said: 'We are taking M. Thiers as an extra horse to help us get up the hill.'[5] Although Persigny hailed the elections as a government victory, the Liberal, Laboulaye, claimed that they marked a return to the principles of 1789; the opposition vote had doubled since 1857 and instead of only five Republicans there were now thirty-two deputies of various shades of opinion who counted as opponents of the still largely authoritarian regime. Thiers himself was 'worth an army'.[6]

Meanwhile it is worth noting that Thiers had just taken part in a contest that made as much stir in academic circles as did the general elections in the nation at large. In April 1863 he supported the candidature of Emile Littré, the eminent lexicographer, to replace a scientist, Biot, in the French Academy. But one fellow-Academician, the Bishop of Orléans, Dupanloup, was appalled at the prospect of the Academy's admitting an atheist, and vigorously campaigned against him, bombarding his friend Thiers with letters and visits in which he urged him to change his mind. To his credit Thiers was unmoved, even when Dupanloup quoted Napoleon in support of his arguments. His reasons showed his common sense: 'To make a dictionary and not to have M. Littré with us would be a nonsense. . . The Academy', he maintained, 'should represent the genius of France in all its diversity, freedom and independence, without claiming to represent any party, opinion, or even religion, no matter how respectable or venerable that religion might be.'[7] Dupanloup's campaign was nevertheless successful, but when Littré, who took his defeat with great dignity, tried his luck again in 1871 the climate had changed and Thiers, who once again voted for him, was vindicated. Littré was elected by a handsome majority.

After nearly twelve years' intermission Thiers now resumed his parliamentary career. He was 66 but lived as active a life as ever and seemed at least ten years younger. Like his friend Mignet he still rose at 5 a.m. Sometimes he received visitors while he dressed and shaved with infinite care after an early breakfast. Then he worked and read the papers until midday and after a light lunch probably saw more visitors until 2 p.m., sometimes walking with them in his charming garden or in the conservatory. In the afternoon he often went to museums or exhibitions and sales,

Plate 8   Thiers's house in the Place Saint-Georges

perhaps taking with him one of his lady friends such as Princess Julie Bonaparte, granddaughter of Napoleon I's brother Lucien. She remarked on his old-world politeness – he never put on his hat so long as he was in her carriage when she gave him a lift home. From 4 to 6 p.m. he usually visited his *amies*, the closest of whom was now the princess's 44-year-old cousin by marriage, Malvina, Duchesse d'Albuféra, 'an adorable creature', the daughter of a Prussian banker.[8] In their company he delighted to relax and talk of anything but politics. Then he went home for a nap before dinner at 8 at which old friends such as Mignet and Barthélemy Saint-Hilaire, whom someone called 'the house dogs',[9] and Duvergier de Hauranne were frequent guests. At about 10 many more guests would arrive to be entertained by *ces dames* and listen to the talk, as witty as it was erudite, of the master of the household. This was M. Thiers's salon, presided over by Madame Dosne.[10] Once Thiers had re-entered politics his day, when Parliament was sitting became busier (although one observer, Ludovic Halévy, thought him by no means as regular in his attendance as he should have been[11]) and at his salon there were often as many politicians and diplomats as men of letters.

Thiers's political influence was now exerted in three ways. He was an eminent member of the small but growing opposition, taking part in many of its manoeuvres and private consultations but generally preserving his independence. He had friends who could give his views publicity in the press, and, above all, he could express them in Parliament.

Eighteen opposition deputies were Republicans, but one of them, Emile Ollivier, an ambitious youngish man, before long indicated his readiness to accept and work for a Liberal Empire and in January 1870 became Napoleon III's chief minister in the Empire's final liberal phase. Thiers, while retaining his freedom of action, sympathized with him rather than the Republicans, many of whom were too radical for his liking. 'You are right', he told Ollivier in January 1866, 'we must have two oppositions, one for the fools, the other for reasonable people.'[12] Thiers prided himself on being an eminently reasonable person.

As for the press, Thiers was no longer a director or important shareholder with a newspaper at his beck and call, but sympathetic journalists were no doubt glad to report his opinions. In particular he had as a neighbour at 47 Rue Saint-Georges one of the most brilliant of the younger writers. Prévost-Paradol had also composed an essay on Vauvenargues and in 1857 Thiers had helped him to a place on the still important *Journal des Débats*, a paper with Orleanist tendencies. Paradol had a firm belief in representative government and his articles in the *Débats* and later in the relatively new *Courrier du Dimanche* often coincided with or reflected Thiers's way of thinking.[13]

People went to hear Thiers talk at home; they soon flocked to listen to him in the Palais Bourbon. In opposition during the last seven years of the

July Monarchy he had made forty-four speeches there; in the last seven years of the Second Empire he would also deliver forty-four. This was when he reached his zenith as a parliamentary orator. It took him a little time to find his feet in a Chamber where many deputies were strangers and there were few old friends and associates to cheer him on – Rémusat, Barrot, Montalembert and others had all been defeated in the elections of 1863. He had to be asked to speak up. Critics said that he was repetitive and didactic – more like a professor of the Collège de France than a statesman – seeming to believe that his every speech needed to be a *discours-Ministre*, which meant spinning out to three hours (with the help of cold coffee) what would be better said in one. Why, in a speech on foreign affairs, bring in Louis XI and Charlemagne?[14]

There was much in these criticisms, and yet for the most part Thiers's audience listened and often asked for more. It was an age when people were accustomed to long speeches and sermons – across the Channel, Gladstone, Disraeli, and many preachers could give great measure when they were in the mood. After hearing Thiers on 3 May 1866 Ludovic Halévy, then a *sécretaire-rédacteur* in the Legislative Body, forgot his adverse comments and wrote: 'What a speech! A masterpiece, a real masterpiece. And the way in which it was spoken and listened to!'[15]

It was Halévy who most vividly recorded his impression of Thiers during this later phase of his parliamentary career:

> I can still see this little man so often sketched by my friend Cham.[16] I hear a little thin, sharp voice, the driest and most disagreeable of voices issuing from his small body. On the faces of several deputies who had never heard M. Thiers one could clearly read the thought: 'What, that's M. Thiers, that's all he is. But M. Rouher will swallow him up in one go.' Two or three members of the Right cried Louder! Louder!
>
> Don't worry, M. Thiers replied, you will soon hear me better. And the fact is that suddenly one heard the little voice. It took on emphasis, volume, and authority. There was profound silence![17]

A Belgian observer who heard him in 1870–1 recalled that, 'gradually dominated by his subject', he seemed to grow in stature as he spoke while his voice 'took on the intonations of a preacher'.[18]

He was not, of course, without rivals among his fellow deputies. In the opposition ranks the moderate Republicans Jules Favre and Emile Ollivier and, later, the more radical Gambetta had a more passionate, sentimental, and physically powerful eloquence, and on the government side, the Minister of State, Rouher, soon nicknamed Vice-Emperor, was a formidable opponent, who did not let himself be intimidated by Thiers's cutting criticisms.[19] What men heard when they listened to Thiers was the still small voice of reason usually tempered by wit and, except when he was interrupted, good humour. Moreover, as its owner seldom failed to remind his audience, it was the voice of an elder statesman.

As in the 1840s Thiers again spoke on many subjects. They varied from rebates on taxes on colonial sugar (18 April 1864), the state of the merchant marine (14 and 18 April 1866) and of agriculture (10 March 1866) – 'a gothic speech', commented Ludovic Halévy: 'in political economy this liberal is the greatest reactionary imaginable'[20] – to the annual call-up (30 June 1870). But, finance apart, the subjects on which he was effective were freedom and foreign affairs. Two speeches on 11 January 1864 inaugurated what became two whole series on freedom, and one on foreign affairs. In the latter series, among other things, he eloquently upheld international law and the rights of small states.[21] Thus at the outset of this phase in his career, he urged the Empire to continue its new Liberal course and called it to account for the blunders of its foreign policy. He made clear what he stood for and reasserted his authority.

The first of the two speeches of 11 January was the most celebrated, the speech in which Thiers with great charm, skill and courtesy demanded what he called the essential freedoms (*les libertés nécessaires*). These were individual freedom or freedom from arbitrary interference with one's personal safety, freedom of the press, freedom of elections, freedom for deputies to initiate business with the government's agreement and freedom to call the ministers to account, in other words ministerial responsibility. The last three-quarters of a century had proved that freedom was something needed by rational men, 'a need which must be profoundly felt in a nation like ours which is one of the proudest and most intelligent on earth', and he was sure that the freedoms for which he asked were perfectly compatible with France's existing institutions, 'provided of course that the happy source from which the decree of 24 November emanated does not dry up'. It was simply a question of developing the institutions in the direction which they had already taken, of beginning France's political education, and not leaving her in a state of perpetual tutelage compared with other countries. The government which gave such freedoms would be frankly and sincerely accepted by all, and he himself would then be counted among the Empire's grateful citizens. He made his request, he said, with respect, but ended with a warning. The country, as yet barely awakened, might one day exact what was now so deferentially requested.[22]

No such call for freedom had been heard in any Parliament of the Second Empire. Overnight Thiers became again a national as well as a parliamentary figure and, knowing the importance of his speeches, he had this one printed as a brochure by two separate publishers under the title *Discours de Thiers sur la politique intérieure*. Most of his subsequent speeches during this period were also separately printed.

Needless to say the walls of Jericho did not collapse at the sound of his deferential trumpet. A few days later Rouher replied that the government had no intention of yielding power to the representatives of a sickly parliamentarianism, and a year later the speech from the throne derided 'the exaggerated tendencies of those who would provoke change with the sole object of undermining what it had established'. Accordingly, on 28 March 1865, in the debate on the address, Thiers returned to the attack. He reminded his hearers that the Emperor himself had in 1853 referred to freedom as 'the crowning of the edifice'. France, he concluded, possessed all the elements necessary for freedom. If, sadly, the edifice were not to be crowned it would not be the materials that were lacking but the architect who failed! 'But I reject this idea for it is incumbent on peoples to keep hoping, just as it is a duty for governments to let them do so.'[23]

A year later the architect had shown no signs of returning to the drawing-board and in a lengthy but masterly speech in February 1866 Thiers reiterated his five necessary freedoms, demonstrating that they all derived from the great principles of 1789 which the first article of the constitution of 1852 recognized, confirmed and guaranteed as 'the basis of the public law of the French'. He ended with a reflection. Having long thought about the definition of a free nation he had, he said, concluded that it was a being that reflected before taking action.[24] Was it about the same time that he privately remarked that Napoleon III was a sovereign who all his life had confused the verbs *rêver* and *réfléchir*?[25]

Like water eroding stone Thiers's campaign slowly took effect. In March 1866 an amendment to the address, moved by an Orleanist, Buffet, echoed Thiers's appeal:

> France, firmly attached to the dynasty which guarantees order, is no less attached to liberty which she believes to be necessary for the fulfilment of her destinies. The Legislative Body therefore believes that it is interpreting public opinion by bringing to the foot of the throne the wish that Your Majesty should give to the great act of 1860 the development that befits it.

Buffet's amendment won sixty votes. The opposition of 1863 had nearly doubled and the members of the non-Republican Liberal opposition, now often called by the revived name of Tiers Parti, grew in importance.

It was ten months before Napoleon responded. Then a decree of 19 January 1867 did away with the address but instead gave deputies the right, for which Thiers had vigorously pressed, to interpellate the government. Individual ministers could now be called upon to take part in debate and answer for their departments. Furthermore, the Emperor promised to recognize the right of meeting and promote a new press law. He was, he said, giving the institutions of the Empire all the development of which they were susceptible without compromising the power conferred upon him by the nation. But when men like Rouher and Baroche, who seemed to epitomize authoritarian policies, were maintained in office Thiers was mistrustful. 'It is a confidence trick', he told the Emperor's radical cousin, Prince Napoleon, 'but we shall know how to profit by it.'[26]

The Emperor never learnt the wisdom of the Latin adage *bis dat qui cito dat.*[27] The promised press law was not submitted for debate until 29 January 1868, by which time it appeared to be a grudging concession on which Thiers commented in no fewer than six speeches between 30 January and 22 February.[28] Of all his five freedoms he said it was the most necessary: 'If you deprive the nation of freedom of the press you render it deaf and blind.' Yet though he found many shortcomings in the measure he said he would vote for it because it contained two significant improvements, the abolition both of the preliminary authorization hitherto required to found a paper and of censorship, for the system whereby a paper was liable to suspension after three warnings was 'tantamount to censorship'. As Thiers no doubt foresaw, the concessions, such as they were, greatly increased the weapons in the opposition arsenal. Unfortunately, as he no doubt also foresaw when he admitted the difficulties of ensuring moderation in a free press, the press that ensued in France after the passing of the law in 1868 eventually became one of the most scurrilous and vitriolic in the world. But we may guess that for Thiers this was still a price worth paying for freedom. He had already braved press calumnies and come through, he claimed, unscathed.

One freedom, however, he did not champion: freedom of trade. A lifelong protectionist, he had been dismayed by the Anglo-French treaty of 1860 which lowered tariffs, and in 1868–70 he supported his protectionist friends, the cotton spinners of Normandy and coal owners of the north-east, in an unsuccessful drive to secure its abrogation.[29]

The Emperor's halting progress towards liberalism might have been still slower but for the weaknesses of his foreign policy. Had he died in 1860 Napoleon III would have been regarded as a conspicuously successful ruler. In 1856 France and her British ally had been victorious in the Crimean War. After the Treaty of Paris of that year she was the pre-eminent power on the European continent. In 1859 in conjunction with Sardinia-Piedmont she had defeated Austria and liberated part of Italy. But then things began to go wrong because of Napoleon's misjudgements and hesitations, and because he was outmanoeuvred by cleverer and equally unscrupulous statesmen. The failure of the Mexican expedition, which Rouher once misguidedly called the great idea of the reign, was a humiliating blow to his prestige, while the unification of Italy and subsequent aggrandizement of Prussia, as a result of her defeat of Denmark in 1864 and Austria in 1866, upset the balance of power, greatly weakened France's standing in Europe, and faced her with grave dilemmas.

In April 1862, when Nassau Senior asked Thiers whether he had approved of Napoleon III's 'Russian war', he replied: 'Yes, but not of his Italian war, or his Syrian war, or his two Chinese wars, or his Mexican war. The last four have merely wasted our money and our blood. The Italian war has given us a powerful rival...and irrevocably weakened the power most useful to the European equilibrium – Austria.'[30] A week earlier he had been particularly scornful of the Mexican war and though, had he himself been in power, the Syrian and Chinese expeditions might have fitted into the category of those small maritime wars which, he once said, a great power ought to wage,[31] he was right to have been so. To send an army and a fleet to put an Austrian archduke on the Mexican throne was, he declared, 'a madness which has no parallel since Don Quixote undertook the cause of the Princess Antonomasia'.[32] Nearly two years later the Mexican expedition was the subject of Thiers's first public onslaughts on Napoleon's foreign policy. On 26 January 1864, after a lucid exposition of the way in which the affair had grown from a simple debt-collecting venture into something far more grandiose, he launched his attack. He might, he said, have been brought up too narrowly, but for France in the existing state of the world to undertake the establishment of a great monarchy at such a distance without any clear goal, obvious usefulness or evident necessity confounded his reason. France was in a false position and he urged the government to cut its losses. Since the Archduke Maximilian had not yet sailed for Mexico, France's honour was not pledged, but 'once the Prince has left with your backing and your guarantee, you will have to support him whatever happens'.[33]

Thiers's warning went unheeded. The Archduke set sail and established a precarious empire until events elsewhere and the serious threat of war with the United States, once the American Civil War was over, forced Napoleon to withdraw his troops in the winter of 1866–7. Without French support Maximilian's cause was hopeless and within a few months he was taken prisoner and shot. Shortly after, Thiers spoke again and said that for the rest of his life he would regret not having been more persuasive in 1864: the sorry affair more than ever showed the need for ministerial responsibility.[34]

Thiers's criticisms of foreign policy applied much nearer home than Mexico. Italy had for many Frenchmen long been an abiding preoccupation. In 1849 Thiers had favoured the formation of an Italian confederation.[35] In 1852, a year in which he met Cavour and expressed admiration for Piedmont, he was still of the same mind, telling Nassau Senior that the Pope might have been Arch-Chancellor, but 'Sovereign only of Rome with the Campagna and the old patrimony of St Peter'. The advantage of a confederation was that it is 'seldom aggressive and always gives you... warning...We should have repaid ourselves [for helping to set it up] by taking Savoy...this would give us a good frontier.'[36]

Such schemes he admitted not having thought out, but they approximated closely to the aims of Napoleon III when he went to war with Austria in 1859. Nevertheless Thiers by then was opposed to war, either because France had no ally except Piedmont, or because he already feared that Austria's defeat would lead to Italian unification. He therefore sought to exert what little influence he had on behalf of peace. With the approval of Walewski, Minister for Foreign Affairs since 1855, he appealed to Metternich to support a proposal that the Central Italian states, in which Austria had a particular interest, should be placed under a European guarantee. But Metternich, old and out of office, declined to intervene.[37]

Napoleon III had promised Piedmont Lombardy-Venetia, but he did not succeed in liberating Venetia from Austrian rule because, fearing a possible Prussian attack and alarmed by French casualties, he concluded peace with Austria before that could be achieved. Piedmont had, in consequence, to be compensated with the Central Italian states which Austria was no longer able to defend, while Napoleon took Nice and Savoy, thereby acquiring for France the 'good' Alpine frontier which Thiers had coveted. But Piedmont's southward thrust, the acuteness of Cavour, and Garibaldi's unpredictable success in invading Naples led to the unification which Thiers so much opposed. This was an outcome which Napoleon, too, had originally envisaged with reluctance; it would, he had told Walewski, 'create difficulties in France because of the Roman question' and because 'France would not see with pleasure the rise on her flank of a great nation which might diminish her preponderance'.[38]

A united Italy wanted Rome for its capital but French troops were still garrisoning the city and French Catholics, whose support Napoleon needed, regarded the preservation of the Pope's temporal power as essential for the maintenance of his spiritual sovereignty. This was the dilemma presented by 'the Roman question' in its new phase. In September 1864 Napoleon attempted to resolve it by concluding a convention whereby the Italian government would transfer its capital from Turin to Florence and, in return for the withdrawal of French troops not later than 1866, undertake not to attack the remaining papal territories and to allow the Pope to raise his own force for their defence. Many of the Left wing of the opposition, sympathizing with the Italian nationalists and regarding the Pope as a reactionary ruler, approved of the convention, and their papers rounded on Thiers when he criticized it sharply in April 1865. For him the Italians had not renounced Rome, they had merely said they would not go there forcibly. If there was a revolution in Rome after France had withdrawn her troops, would she send them back again? If she did not, the Pope, he said, would lose his independence and the unity of the Church be shattered.[39]

As the British Minister to the Vatican pointed out in 1868, the temporal independence of the Pope had already ceased to exist,[40] but otherwise Thiers was only too clear-sighted. The French troops left in December 1866. Soon afterwards Garibaldi and his followers were in the Papal States bent on revolution. Napoleon had to dispatch his men again to protect the Pope; the Roman question, which he now hoped vainly to resolve by a conference, was back where it had been in 1864. When it was debated anew in December 1867 Thiers's attitude was unwavering. 'Once again', he told the deputies, 'I would say to Italy: I have sacrificed all my interests for you;. . . for your sake I have allowed people to doubt my word; but there is one thing I will not give up for you and that is my honour.' Honour demanded that France should not abandon the Pope.[41] She did not. Hard pressed in the debate, Rouher made his famous declaration that she would never do so. Thiers had gained another victory, one that in Montalembert's view re-established parliamentary government.[42] French troops remained in the Papal States until the Franco-Prussian war broke out in 1870.

Thiers's clear-sightedness was not confined to Rome. He rightly saw that Italian unification was a disaster for France not only because of the way in which she had been outwitted in Italy, but because, as he put it in April 1865, Italian unity was destined to be 'the mother of German unity. On the day when Prussia has forty million Germans in her hands and adds Hamburg and Bremen to Danzig. . . and the port of Kiel which she is about to create she will expose France to the greatest dangers. . .'[43] A year later, in his great speech of 3 May 1866, when Prussia and Austria were about to come to blows over the ill-gotten gains they had won by war with Denmark and there was a general war scare in Europe, he uttered a still more celebrated warning: if Prussia won the war she would annex some of the other North German states and subject the rest to a Diet under her influence. The result would be a new German empire – 'the empire of Charles V which used to have its seat in Vienna will now have it in Berlin and. . . be supported by Italy instead of Spain'. What could be done to preserve the peace which subsequent analysis has shown that French public opinion ardently desired?[44] Thiers suggested two courses of action: tell Prussia politely but firmly that France could in no way associate herself with her dangerous policies, and tell Italy that if she goes to war she must take the consequences and not look to France for support against Austria. In fact he envisaged France as remaining neutral and said it would be crazy to suggest a preventive war.[45] If Prussia ignored her warning France should maintain an ominous silence. Thus an American historian commented that his policy was 'a curious combination of "speak up" and "shut up" with no tolerance for "putting up" a show of force to back the protests'.[46]

This of course was the weakness of French policy both before and after the war which Thiers's intervention was too late to avert – his speech, it was said, was like mustard served after dinner.[47] But it was mustard that stung the emperor himself to reply three days later at Auxerre and declare his detestation of the 1815 settlement which Thiers in his speeches had approved in relation to Germany.[48]

In July, two months after this exchange, to the confounding of most military experts and other observers including Thiers, Prussia routed Austria at Sadowa. Thiers's worst fears were about to be realized and France did nothing. Eight years later Bismarck said that Prussia would have been hard put to it had France then sent troops into Germany to support Austria and her South German allies, but Napoleon's first decision to intervene seems to have been speedily reversed by the counter-arguments of those who emphasized public opinion's hostility to war. What Thiers himself would have done had he been in power we do not know, but eight months later, when France had on her Rhine frontier a nation of 40 million people, 'young, active, bold and devoured by ambition', he gave wise advice. In such a situation France needed to be well armed and have allies. She ought formally to declare that she would defend threatened interests and not herself threaten any European interest. He ended with another celebrated warning. His audience should follow this policy of good sense, for, 'I tell you, there is not a single blunder left to commit.'[49]

In fact the final blunder would be committed three years later. Meanwhile Thiers's reputation and influence had steadily grown and, despite the rebuffs inflicted in the elections of 1869 by what Madame Dosne called *le vrai bétail* of universal suffrage, they continued to do so.

The rebuffs must have been dismaying. He had been invited to stand in a dozen or more constituencies and did so in four, in the Nord, the Bouches-du-Rhône, Finistère, and Paris. Yet he succeeded in only one, and that with some difficulty. At Marseilles, outdistanced on the first round by de Lesseps and by the young and enthusiastic Gambetta, who twice visited the city during the election period whereas Thiers did not go near it, he withdrew. In the Nord, where he called himself a Liberal and defender of *travail national* he was nonetheless soundly defeated by des Rotours, the candidate favoured by the administration and the Church;[50] in Catholic Finistère, however, he did well to poll 12,681 votes to the successful candidate's 15,032. In Paris, as a result of changes decreed at the end of 1867, the boundaries of his constituency had been altered to his disadvantage,[51] and on the second round he had to face a Left-wing opponent as well as his old antagonist, Devinck. But in the end he was returned with a majority of more than 6,000 over Devinck. Between the two ballots a reporter of the *Figaro* went to interview him very early one morning. His account gives a rare glimpse of Thiers at home in the last years of the Second Empire. He was shown into Thiers's study or library with its fine well-bound books gleaming behind glass and above them 'a host of works of art, busts and pictures, statuettes, china and bronzes. At the end of the gallery', he went on,

> a small fire was glowing in the elegant fireplace. The windows were wide open and the scent of flowers came in from the garden and a multitude of sparrows was chattering in the trees. But where was M. Thiers?
>
> At last by the fire I saw a small pair of slippers followed by a pair of small legs and half hidden by the *Journal des Débats* the intelligent head of the former minister.
>
> Near by, on a minute table, a cup of black coffee was getting cold.[52]

The last entry in Madame Dosne's intermittent diary was a lively account of the suspense in the Thiers household on the following day when the votes were being counted.[53] A month later she was taken ill and at the end of August she died aged 76. Thiers was overcome with grief. Not only had he been devoted to her for more than thirty years but she had played the chief part in running his household. Her death was 'the greatest misfortune that could happen to us'; moreover it completely upset and altered his home life.[54] Meanwhile in January 1867 he had had to mourn the death of a once close friend, Victor Cousin, in September 1868 that of Walewski whom he had regarded as the most sensible of Napoleon III's ministers, and, more serious for France, in the same month as Madame Dosne, that of Marshal Niel, the Minister for War. In 1870 there followed the deaths of his old colleague Broglie and of Montalembert with whom he had been on good terms ever since they allied in defence of freedom of education in 1848–9. 'At my age', he told Princess Julie, 'life is a wood in which a terrible woodman fells trees around you. One must be philosophic and wait without worry or bitterness.'[55]

The 1869 elections had a threefold importance. They revealed the strength of a resurgent republicanism which triumphed in Paris and the big cities. They showed the extent to which Napoleon had lost prestige, and, despite the failure of many Orleanists,[56] they demonstrated the growing demand for parliamentary government. They were a success not only for the previous opposition but also for candidates who had broken loose from official control and labelled themselves 'Liberals' or 'independents'. They formed a large and varied Tiers Parti who were almost unanimous in wanting ministerial responsibility to a Parliament sprung from free elections.[57] Their natural mentor was, of course, the little veteran who had never ceased to demand the essential freedoms or to expose the blunders of the Empire's foreign policy. As the wits said, the Tiers Parti had in a very real sense become the Thiers Parti. When Thiers went to the special session of the new Legislative Body at the end of June for *la vérification des pouvoirs* he was greeted by cries of 'Vive Thiers!' and soon afterwards 116 deputies signed an interpellation asking that the country should be more effectively associated with the conduct of government.

At last the Emperor took heed. On 28 December the *Journal Officiel*, successor to the *Moniteur Universel* whose contract had expired, published a letter from Napoleon to Ollivier asking him to designate 'a homogeneous Cabinet faithfully representing the majority in the Legislative Body'. The edifice was about to be crowned.

Thiers had not been invited to form the new ministry and there is no reason to suppose that he would have agreed to any more than he had when Louis-Napoleon had invited him to do so in 1848. He was ready to approve, give Ollivier support and counsel and encourage particular individuals like Comte Daru to take office, but, as he had told Aumale in 1861, not to be a minister himself.[58] On becoming Foreign Minister Daru showed his appreciation by asking Thiers to go to Rome on a mission to expound France's attitude to the forthcoming Vatican Council. When Thiers declined he could not have dreamt that in eight months' time he would embark on a far greater tour abroad, the one vital diplomatic mission of his life.

Under the remodelled constitution of 1870 the Emperor was still responsible to the people 'to whom he always has the right of appeal'. Encouraged by Prince Napoleon and probably by Rouher, Napoleon III adroitly made use of that right without delay, arranging for a plebiscite on 8 May to approve the liberal reforms effected since 1860 and to ratify the new constitution. At the cost of two ministers, who resigned in protest, the Ollivier government went along with the Emperor's wish. Thiers in private strongly opposed this vote. There was no place in parliamentary government as he envisaged it for a plebiscite such as this, a 'Caesarian procedure' which his friend Paradol called 'a monstrosity'. But he did not wish to embarrass the new Liberal government by public opposition.[59] In sharp contrast to the 1869 elections the *Ouis* outnumbered the *Nons* by some 7,300,000 to 1,570,000. Although there were nearly 1,900,000 abstainers (including Thiers) and the *Nons* were again concentrated in the big towns, the result appeared to be a massive vote of confidence in the Liberal Empire. Had it lasted eight years instead of eight months and abandoned 'Caesarian procedures', Thiers might possibly have changed his mind about becoming a minister. But that was not to be. Two months later the ultimate blunder was committed.

[10]

Vae Victis,
1870

On 4 July 1870, it became known in Paris that Prince Leopold of Hohenzollern-Sigmaringen, distantly related to the Prussian royal family, was likely to be chosen to ascend the vacant throne of Spain. Given the dangerous rivalry between France and Prussia since 1866 this was grave news. It was assumed that the Prussian government was behind Leopold's candidature, with the intention of bringing Spain into its orbit and gaining a possible ally to divide French forces in case of a Franco-Prussian war. Emile Ollivier told the British ambassador, Lord Lyons, that no French government could permit a Prussian prince to rule Spain. He had warned Lyons a few months before that in the atmosphere of tension between France and Prussia, an insult from the latter would mean war: the new Liberal government in France 'must show firmness and spirit or we shall not be able to cope with Revolution and Socialism at home'. Lyons reported to London his fear that the French government wanted war.[1]

Of Thiers's reaction to the news from Madrid there could be no doubt. Since 1866 he had frequently warned of the danger of Prussian aggrandizement, and throughout his political life he had upheld French influence in Spain. On 5 July, with the agreement of the government, he arranged for one of his followers, Cochery, to raise the matter before the Legislative Body so that the government could officially state its policy, and the foreign minister, Gramont, duly made a strong declaration that unless the candidature were withdrawn, the government would fulfil its duty 'without hesitation and without weakness'. Bismarck's reaction was that 'this certainly looks like war'.[2]

The defence of national interests had been the rallying cry of Thiers and his followers during the July Monarchy, and it is easy to imagine Thiers in power taking a similar line to Gramont. Indeed, he privately assured Napoleon III on 10 July of his support if a conflict proved unavoidable, and the Emperor considered appointing him Minister of War.[3] Yet at the same time he was alarmed. Like many opposition politicians, he suspected the intransigent Bonapartists of welcoming war in the hope of reversing the liberalization of the last few years in case of victory. For Liberals and

177

Republicans this was the major reason for opposing war, since they, like most people, expected a French victory. Thiers, however, had other reasons for disquiet. To his message to the Emperor promising support he added a warning that France was not as ready for war as Napoleon's advisers claimed. He feared too that a war between France and Prussia would become a European war with unpredictable and devastating consequences.[4]

His fears concerning the state of the army were real, if somewhat vague and even misconceived.[5] He mistrusted the military reforms of the late 1860s; he worried because he himself was not in charge; and his recent examination of the military budget (when, at the Emperor's secret request, he had argued in Parliament on 30 June against a reduction in the size of the army) had convinced him that funds and manpower were insufficient. He had said then that Prussia's defeat of Austria at Sadowa had doubled the strength of Prussia, and it was not enough for France to have an army after Sadowa that had been adequate before it.[6] He was to write to Rémusat just after the declaration of war, 'God knows what will happen. The Minister of War says that he is ready; I fear that . . . he is extremely rash. God grant that the army's spirit may make up for the inadequacy of the preparations.'[7] Moreover, he was unwilling to contemplate war unless blatant Prussian aggression isolated her from her unwilling South German allies and secured the moral or material support of Europe for France. He was therefore immensely relieved when it was announced on 12 July that the Hohenzollern candidature had been withdrawn, giving France a great and bloodless diplomatic victory.

The satisfaction of Thiers and the government was shattered when the Bonapartist Right, in Parliament and the press, made their discontent stridently clear. They insisted that an explicit guarantee that the candidature would never be renewed must be given by the King of Prussia, and the Foreign Minister, Gramont, imprudently set out to obtain it. Thiers saw this as a dangerous and unnecessary attempt to humiliate Prussia and, urged on by equally alarmed colleagues, he set out on the afternoon of 12 July to lobby ministers and organize a pro-peace group within the Legislative Body. He could count on the support of part of the Liberal and Republican press and, he later claimed, 'at least a hundred' Centre deputies. He harangued five ministers in private on their 'great blunder' which made war 'probable', and thought he had persuaded them: 'they swore by all the gods that they would be careful'.[8] At the next Cabinet meeting on 13 July, they did indeed declare themselves satisfied with the withdrawal of the candidature and criticized Gramont for demanding more. At that same meeting, advice arrived from the British government to accept Leopold's withdrawal. Thiers kept up his pressure on any minister he could find, and during the 14th, part of the Cabinet held firm to the moderate line he urged. That evening, however, came news of the notorious Ems telegram, in which Bismarck announced the failure of the French ambassador to extract the required guarantee from King William of Prussia, who told him that he had nothing more to say on the subject. Bismarck's version deliberately implied that the ambassador had been insulted and gave the supposed insult maximum publicity. The Cabinet met in haste, and the ministers badgered by Thiers dropped their conciliatory line. A statement for Parliament was drawn up that amounted to a declaration of war, and it was decided to call up reserves. A British offer to mediate was ignored.[9]

On the morning of 15 July, there was an explosion of public anger in the streets and the press against the German 'insult'. Ollivier in the Legislative Body fanned the flames, even reporting – inaccurately – that Prussia had begun military preparations, and declaring that 'we are going to prepare to withstand the war that is offered to us'.[10] In an emotional atmosphere Thiers intervened, provoking one of the most famous parliamentary scenes and perhaps the most dramatic of his career. It was 'a difficult duty . . . to resist patriotic . . . but imprudent passions', he declared. 'More than anyone I want reparation for the events of 1866; but I find the occasion dreadfully badly chosen.' Amid violent heckling he accused the government of 'breaking off relations in a fit of pique', and insisted that they should produce the dispatches in which the alleged insult was contained.[11] This attempt to gain time, to force the government to prove its point, was clearly an attempt to rally those hundred or more deputies whom Thiers believed ready to support him. The same demand for proof was repeated later in the debate by the Republicans Favre and Gambetta, with no more success.

Thiers was answered by Ollivier. The government, he said, had never, unlike Thiers, advocated revenge against Prussia, but now war was being forced on them: Prussia had broken off relations with an unforgivable insult and was beginning military preparations. He accepted war, he said (in a phrase that was to haunt him), with 'a light heart'. Thiers returned doggedly to the fray, attacking the government amid the shouts of the Right: 'we have war because of a government blunder'; the Hohenzollern candidature had been withdrawn, Prussia had suffered a humiliation, but the government, under Bonapartist pressure, had foolishly demanded further guarantees which raised 'questions of pride between two equally sensitive nations, and war became inevitable'. The government should have given Europe time to mediate.[12]

If Thiers could have shown that the government was reading too much into Bismarck's telegram, opposition to their war policy might have rallied. But amid the violence of pro-war feeling inside and outside Parliament it was a slim chance. Thiers's language suggests that he realized this: 'The Chamber will do as it wishes; I am expecting what it will do, but as for myself I decline responsibility for a war so little justified.' He was protesting against, more than trying to prevent the decision to go to war, and when the vote came he, like Gambetta, voted for war credits; only ten deputies of the Left voted against or abstained.[13]

If Thiers had little hope of stopping the rush to war, he was determined to record his dissent for the sake of his own reputation and that of the opposition and the parliamentary system: 'history is watching us . . . As for myself, concerned for my memory . . . I do not wish it to be said' (interruptions) 'that I took responsibility for a war founded on such motives.'[14] With equal awareness of the eyes of history, he wrote long letters explaining his actions to Duvergier and Rémusat, urging the former to 'keep this letter . . . and if in future it is found it will explain to our descendants how this odious war was decided upon'.[15] Duvergier understood and approved: 'At least it will not be said that it was the Liberal or Radical party that wanted war and that M. Thiers, the most bellicose of men as the English newspapers say, pushed the lamb who reigns over France into it.'[16]

These letters recount Thiers's general view of the state of Europe as he had expressed it in the Chamber. In favourable circumstances, a victorious war might enable France to 'remake the old German Confederation, or take territorial guarantees on the Rhine', but at present Austria was 'resolutely neutral' and Britain 'angrily neutral'. Thiers recalled his efforts to organize a peace party in the Chamber and to lobby ministers, warning Ollivier that 'this war could be calamitous . . . you must not run the risk'. But French diplomatic blunders and an 'imprudence' by the King of Prussia – 'not an insult, as has been said' – had been exploited by the Bonapartist Right 'who believe they can win back power' by war. Finally, the Cabinet and Parliament, afraid of a political crisis, 'have sent the French to the slaughter'. In the debate of 15 July – 'in the forty years I have been in Parliament I have not had a struggle like it' – he was so angry, he said, that 'what they call my courage cost me nothing at all . . . I got up on an uncontrollable impulse, and then all the rage of the Bonapartists burst over me . . . This event which will take away either our liberty or our greatness has broken my heart . . . for us now there is nothing but sadness.' To Rémusat he concluded, 'Victorious we shall come under arrogant personal government, and if we are defeated we shall see France terribly treated. But far better victory, a hundred times better.'[17]

Thiers's analysis cannot be seriously contested. Ollivier later accused him of over-dramatizing his role, but he was forced to admit his fundamental criticisms. He also accused him of acting solely for party advantage, opposing war because it would strengthen the regime, but never believing or saying that the war might be lost. But there is evidence, given above, that Thiers felt and expressed his fears well before fighting began, and there is no reason to doubt the genuineness of his alarm over the dangers threatening France. He did not conceal that his opposition to the war was also political, because the Bonapartists seemed intent on using it as a means to threaten the liberalization of recent years. While Ollivier denied this, he did not deny his concern to strengthen the regime.[18] Thiers in office might have taken a similar view, as in 1840, but Thiers in opposition was unwilling to risk French liberties and French greatness to bolster the Second Empire.

When war broke out, Thiers was pilloried as a tool of Prussia. He was insulted in the streets and, not for the first time, an angry crowd demonstrated in the Place Saint-Georges. When Parliament was prorogued on 21 July, he withdrew to Trouville. The first French defeats at the beginning of August transformed the political situation, to the scarcely concealed joy of some on the Left. Parliament was recalled, and Thiers, travelling up by train, repeated to his companions that there would be 'deplorable events'; one of them thought that he felt a bitter satisfaction at the vindication of his own position and the discomfiture of his opponents.[19] The Ollivier government fell on 9 August, and was replaced by a ministry led by a soldier, the Comte de Palikao. With the Emperor at the front, ultimate authority was exercised by the Empress Eugénie as regent. The parliamentary opposition, with Thiers its leading figure, accepted the Palikao government as a stop-gap, but intended that in due course the Legislative Body itself should take power by electing a parliamentary commission to appoint and supervise ministers.

The military defeats of July and August called the survival of the regime into question and vindicated Thiers's opposition to the war. 'Little Thiers knows more in his little finger,' it was said 'than all the government and all the Legislative Body.'[20] Events were proving him right: this was the source of his growing prestige in the country at large, only matched by that of two soldiers, General Trochu and Marshal Bazaine, both summoned to be saviours of the country as much for their previous opposition to Napoleon III as for their military abilities.

By the middle of August France faced a military and political crisis. The main army, under Bazaine, had been forced to retreat to the fortress of Metz, where it had been cut off. A reserve army had been hastily assembled under Marshal de MacMahon at Châlons, between Metz and Paris. The government, largely for political reasons, wished to send MacMahon's army on the hazardous enterprise of relieving Bazaine. The other course, politically more dangerous but militarily more prudent, was to withdraw MacMahon to the huge fortress of Paris as the core of a new defensive strategy. Thiers, supported by much military opinion, advocated the latter course, and even referred to a coming battle beneath the walls of Paris in an open session of the Legislative Body on 17 August.[21]

In this crisis the Empress sent Prosper Mérimée, their mutual friend, to ask Thiers to come and see her. Probably he could have taken power had he wished, but he had no intention of involving himself in the Empire's disasters. He told Mérimée that he did not want to see the Empress, and that his advice would be unacceptable: the abdication of the Emperor, the withdrawal of available forces to Paris, and the arming of the population. Even if she agreed, he told Mérimée, 'I would refuse to lend my name to a desperate enterprise, not even knowing what resources I should have.'[22] Two days later, the Austrian ambassador came on the same errand. Thiers replied that he had insufficient information to give firm advice, and could only repeat that the best hope was to fight before Paris. He wrote this in a letter to the Empress which was 'correct and cool, and calculated not to compromise him if ever it became known'.[23]

On 22 August he refused to join the committee set up by the government to organize the defences of Paris, although he frequently visited the formidable fortifications whose building he had begun in 1840 and which were now for the first time being made ready for war. The government, however, nominated him to the committee none the less, and he asked Rémusat what he should do. They agreed that he could not refuse to serve, but should do so only if the Legislative Body voted approval, which it did at once.[24] Some thought that this was a prelude to Thiers's taking power – precisely what he did not want – but his misgivings did not stop him from entering into the committee's work with characteristic energy. He visited the fortifications daily, and made endless suggestions for siting batteries, building defences and collecting supplies to withstand a siege. The deliberations of the committee were soon dominated by the government's determination to send MacMahon's army to rescue Bazaine. Thiers rightly mistrusted the motives for this decision, and strongly criticized it, insisting that all troops not already committed should be concentrated in Paris. The arguments became heated: Thiers 'gave a rough time' to his old acquaintance Marshal Vaillant, and told Rémusat that he encountered only 'puerility, weakness, sycophancy. Nothing serious, nothing patriotic.' Vaillant for his part noted on 19 August, 'M. Thiers causes discord . . . he wastes our time'; and on 2 September, 'M. Thiers talks and talks; we bicker; we decide nothing; politics dominate all Thiers's good instincts.'[25] The bickering was ended by the news of Sedan, where MacMahon, surrounded on his way to join Bazaine, had been utterly defeated, and the whole army, and the Emperor himself, taken prisoner.

News of the disaster reached Paris on 3 September, and caused the Empress to renew her appeals: Mérimée and Metternich again entreated Thiers to take office, or at least say what should be done. He told them both that after Sedan there was nothing to be done, and that he would not know what advice to give.[26] In the Legislative Body, however, all parties were now prepared to accept the Left's demand that a parliamentary commission should take power. During the night of 3 September and the next morning various combinations were discussed. Both Left and Right were eager for Thiers to take a leading part. He refused, wishing to leave the Bonapartists – 'the repentant Legislative Body' – in charge for the time being until an armistice was signed. He advised the Opposition that it was neither their duty, nor was it in their interest, 'to take on themselves the burden of overwhelming events of which they were not the cause'. Consequently, when he moved in the Chamber that a governing commission should be set up, his motion did not proclaim the overthrow of the empire.[27] The Legislative Body accepted his view; but the vast crowd which surrounded and then invaded the Chamber put an end to parliamentary manoeuvres. The Republican deputies of Paris declared the Empire overthrown and hurried to the Hôtel de Ville to proclaim a Republic and prevent the revolutionary Left from seizing power. No one, from the Empress down, thought of resisting, and no blood was shed. Thiers regretted the revolution, which had burdened the opposition with a hopeless task, but he realized its inevitability. He had not followed his Republican colleagues to the Hôtel de Ville, and he refused to be a member of the new provisional Government of National Defence, the only Paris deputy not to serve. He did, however, prevent the Legislative Body from trying to embarrass it. On the evening of 4 September, the rump of the Chamber met for the last time. Thiers was chosen to preside. He told the deputies that to oppose the new government would be 'an unpatriotic act'. When several Bonapartists protested against the illegality of the day's events, Thiers could not resist reminding them of the 1851 *coup d'état*, and that he himself had been 'a prisoner at Mazas'. It was not the moment for protests: 'In the presence of the enemy . . . I think that there is only one thing for us to do: to retire with dignity'.[28]

Thiers set an example, going home to the Place Saint-Georges to console himself with his *chères études* on science, and nurse a chill. Behind the scenes, however, he was not inactive. On 5 September he met Orleanist leaders and urged them heatedly to keep their princes away from Paris so that they should cause no difficulties for the government. On the 6th he met Lord Lyons, to seek British help in securing an armistice.[29] He took elaborate precautions of secrecy to avoid outraging public opinion drunk with post-revolutionary fantasies of victory *à la* 1792, and also perhaps to avoid public responsibility for the catastrophe that he believed inevitable. He had firmly refused to lead the Government of National Defence, which was presided over instead by General Trochu, but feared that sooner or later he would be pressed to take charge of negotiations with a victor who, he had foreseen, would 'treat France terribly'.

> Everyone was begging him to sacrifice himself. Now at no price would he attach his name to a peace that would be nothing but a capitulation. Even though he thought it necessary . . . it was for others than he to accept it; and he said with just pride that he believed himself the man . . . who had most right to refuse to endure the last and harshest consequence of a war that he had wanted to spare the country.[30]

This, believed Rémusat, was one reason why on 9 September he accepted the invitation of the new Foreign Minister, Jules Favre, to leave for London as the envoy of the new government. He had only been Favre's second choice after Gladstone's friend Michel Chevalier, the free-trade economist and Imperial Senator, whom the rest of the government turned down. Thiers suggested widening his mission to take in St Petersburg and Vienna.[31]

He had long been in contact with Favre and their views on policy accorded. 'Jules was dying to make peace', reported the Austrian ambassador on 8 September, and Thiers encouraged him in this resolve.[32] Favre wanted to contact Bismarck secretly to ask for an armistice. He deluded himself that after the fall of Napoleon III Germany would offer easy peace terms and be satisfied with a large monetary indemnity. But 'neither a stone of our fortresses nor an inch of our territory' could be conceded, he declared on 6 September. Thiers, however, expected harsh terms: more than once he told Rémusat that 'we shall lose Alsace'. He never wavered in his view that the longer the war continued the worse the outcome would be. Consequently, his aim was to arrange a speedy armistice. He had already raised this with Lord Lyons, and his first task in London would be to facilitate contact between the new French government and Bismarck. Indulging his well-known taste for intrigue, he commissioned his friend the beautiful and notorious Comtesse de Castiglione, formerly an agent of Cavour and mistress of Napoleon III, to act as a go-between. Thiers also intended to try to obtain recognition and support from the neutral Powers, but was not sanguine. He planned to go no further than this: the final peace negotiations would be the task of someone else. He did, however, elaborate to several governments, including the Prussian, an idea previously mentioned in the press: that France might take Belgium as compensation for the loss of Alsace, and Leopold II of the Belgians (the son of Thiers's old friend) become King of the French.[33]

Thiers and 'his ladies' left for London on the evening of 12 September eight days before the Germans surrounded Paris. He arrived at 7 a.m. on the 13th to find London crowded with French refugees and was forced to 'camp' in the embassy, empty since the 4 September Revolution. At noon Lord Granville, the Foreign Secretary, called for the first talks. Thiers launched into a prepared speech: the war was the fault of the Bonapartists, not the country; the new government was honest and necessary; and Britain, from loyalty and in her own interests, should support France in seeking an honorable peace. This took some time, and Granville was somewhat disconcerted when on finishing his speech Thiers went to sleep. Having ascertained that he had not died, he tactfully aroused him and replied in what Thiers thought a friendly but evasive manner, stating firmly that Britain would remain neutral. Britain had, however, already suggested to Bismarck that he should see a French emissary.[34] The Prime Minister Gladstone came that evening, and was subjected in his turn to Thiers's eloquence. He noted that he 'seemed vague as to purpose'. Admittedly, Thiers talked a great deal, and Gladstone's French left much to be desired. Gladstone read him Bismarck's discouraging answer to the British initiative:

that he doubted whether the Paris government was in a position to negotiate, as it would probably not be obeyed by the army. Thiers repeated that the Government of National Defence was the effective government of France, which Lord Lyons's reports confirmed. It was decided that the British government would again urge Bismarck to talk to Favre, though without recognizing the Paris government officially, as Thiers had requested. On the 14th, a note was sent to Bismarck asking him to meet Favre, and he agreed: the Germans were not as unwilling as Bismarck pretended, and the Prussian ambassador in London had approved the British note before it was sent. [35] This was a less than brilliant achievement, but it was what Thiers had hoped for. As a result, on 19 September (when Thiers was already on his way to St Petersburg) Favre slipped secretly out of Paris and met Bismarck at Ferrières. He was shocked when Bismarck demanded as a condition of an armistice the surrender of several fortresses including heroically resisting Strasbourg, and peace terms which included the annexation of Alsace and part of Lorraine. Favre broke off talks at once. [36]

Thiers's first small success thus came to nothing. However, he had also set out to persuade the British to support France by formally stating their opinion of what would constitute 'an equitable and durable peace' that respected 'the European balance' – in other words, by opposing German annexations. He was delighted when at their first meeting Gladstone appeared to agree, but when Thiers returned to this point over the next two days he thought that Granville and Gladstone had gone back on the concession. [37] In fact, there was a difference of opinion between the Foreign Secretary and the Prime Minister: Granville wished to say nothing that departed from neutrality, but Gladstone was prepared to make clear his opposition to annexation. This difference emerged after Thiers had left London for St Petersburg. Gladstone, urged on not only by Thiers, but also by the press, by such Liberal luminaries as Michel Chevalier and John Bright, and not least by his own conscience, felt obliged to draft a memorandum in reply to a circular received from Bismarck on 22 September declaring his intention to annex French territory. Gladstone wished to reply that such a procedure had 'led to many wars and disturbances; is hard to reconcile with considerations of equity; and is repulsive to the sense of modern civilisation'. [38] Such strong words were just what Thiers had asked for. But it was not his arguments that had carried weight: his assertion that the balance of power was at risk through the annexation of Alsace was not taken seriously, and to his suggestion that the inaction of Gladstone's government would embarrass it in Parliament, Gladstone was tempted to answer 'teach your grandmother to suck eggs'. Gladstone's opposition to annexation was founded on self-determination. He admitted that he would have been relieved if the Alsatians had been willing to become German, but was 'much oppressed' at their being transferred 'like chattels'. This, commented Granville, was 'the sort of thing Thiers should have said but did not'.[39] But the French, whether through the voice of Thiers or during later generations, would never officially admit that their claim to Alsace and Lorraine rested on the will of the inhabitants. Rather they insisted on the principle of the integrity of national territory – an argument scorned by Gladstone when presented by a country that had so recently annexed Savoy, entertained designs on Belgium and the Rhineland, and owed its possession of Alsace and Lorraine to Louis XIV's successful aggression. But Gladstone's memorandum was never sent, for Granville persuaded the Cabinet to reject it on 30 September. Gladstone fell back on the Thiers-like device of publishing an anonymous article in the *Edinburgh Review* expressing the same sentiments – a less than effective way of stopping Bismarck.[40]

In short, Thiers's London talks contributed to two minor initiatives – the Ferrières meeting and the Gladstone memorandum – which finally came to nothing. He told Favre on 15 September that from Britain there was 'nothing to fear and not much to hope': she was set on neutrality, concerned only for the Eastern Question and Belgium; 'the European balance, of which we speak to her endlessly, is not much changed for her ... the sleepless nights that France used to cause her will now come from Prussia ... Besides, war terrifies her. She is not ready; no one is, neither Austria nor Russia, and she does not wish to speak [to Germany] to no purpose.' This accurate summary shows that if Thiers was not always a tactful diplomat, he was a shrewd analyst. He had realized that the key was Russia: 'I have great hopes in that direction.' If Russia made a declaration of support, Britain and Austria would follow, and that could tip the balance when peace was negotiated. While still talking to Granville and Gladstone he was eager to be off to St Petersburg.[41]

His trip was delayed by confusion over transport. The original plan had been to travel by sea, escorted by a powerful squadron of French ironclads lying off the Thames estuary. Bad weather forced them back to Cherbourg, and Thiers decided first to take a British merchantman from Hull, and then to travel overland by special train – still accompanied by his devoted ladies, who feared he might fall ill in some remote Polish village en route. He left London on 18 September, passed rapidly through Tours, where a delegation of ministers from the Government of National Defence in beleaguered Paris had set up a government for the provinces, and reached Vienna, via Turin and Venice, on the 23rd. He made a brief courtesy call on the Chancellor, the anti-Prussian but devious Beust, 'among all the men I have known, the one who has the least air of believing what he says'.[42]

On 27 September he arrived in St Petersburg via Warsaw. He first met an old acquaintance, the Chancellor Gorchakov, 'grown ripe ... with long years of uninterrupted and successful power', then, two days later, the Emperor. He gave them his usual speech, but convincing them that the new Republic was 'honest and necessary' was a more difficult task than with

Granville and Gladstone, owing to the Russian fear of revolution in general and disturbances in Poland (which the French Left in the past had encouraged) in particular. This was a major reason for the Emperor's preferring the victory of conservative Prussia. Nevertheless, the Russians were not without misgivings over the scale of Prussian victories and the danger these created for the balance of power and their own security. It was immediately made clear to Thiers, however, that there was no possibility of Russia abandoning her neutrality, and his request that Russia should place herself at the head of the neutrals for collective mediation was flatly refused: Prussia would anyway ignore it, objected Gorchakov.[43] Thiers had 'a very long conversation' with Gorchakov 'in which he spoke of the past, the present and the future', but 'proposed nothing of a practical character'. Given the Russian refusal to engage in mediation, there was little he could propose. Gorchakov agreed with many of Thiers's comments on 'the future' – of the dangers of Prussia's 'ever-increasing ambition' – but the problem was the present: the French needed an alliance at once, while the Russians, as Thiers realized, were thinking of an alliance at some time in the future, when they could obtain the friendship of a defeated and resentful France without risk. He had learnt from the Austrians that Russia had been prepared at the start of the war for mediation by the neutrals, but Sedan, as he guessed, had frightened them off for good.[44] Strong hints of French support in the Near East evoked no response: the Russians had already made plans in that direction. Realizing the inevitability of a Prussian victory and their own impotence to influence events, they had decided to accept the proffered support of Prussia in securing a face-saving 'consolation prize', the ending of the demilitarization of the Black Sea imposed by the 1856 Treaty of Paris. Thiers had wind of this, but had no idea that matters had progressed so far: the first overtures had been made as early as August, and the final steps were taken only three weeks after Thiers's departure.[45]

The Emperor and Gorchakov, however, were prepared to make a limited gesture of support for France. First, the Emperor agreed to advise the King of Prussia to make an 'acceptable' peace, though on a purely personal basis (the King was his uncle) and without any hint of a threat. Secondly, Gorchakov offered to ask the Germans to grant Thiers safe conduct so that he could consult the French government in Paris and then negotiate an armistice with Bismarck in Versailles. This was far less than Thiers had asked, but perhaps nearer to what he had seriously thought he might get, and he clutched at the offer. Gorchakov assured him, and he was eager to believe it, that the Germans themselves desired a speedy end to the war, and consequently that the Tsar's personal intervention might help to obtain 'a tolerable peace'.[46] Yet Russian support was flimsier than he liked to think: a few days after he left, Gorchakov turned down a tentative British suggestion that the two countries might agree on what would be 'acceptable terms of peace', which they would communicate to the combatants. Instead he urged the British to convince the French that they should make peace quickly and accept the loss of Alsace at least. But Thiers felt that a chance had offered itself, and he was impatient to return to France and seize it. Protocol imposed delays. He was obliged to spend some time in Vienna with the Emperor Francis-Joseph and his ministers, and he had also accepted an invitation to see King Victor-Emmanuel and the Italian government.[47]

He arrived in Vienna on 8 October, only to be told again by Beust and Andrássy, the Hungarian Prime Minister, that Austria-Hungary was obliged to remain neutral. He reported that the Dual Monarchy was too divided to help actively, but that there was much sympathy for the French cause in a country still smarting from defeat in 1866.[48] In reality, however, the Austrians' sympathy was mitigated and cynical. They were willing to encourage Italy to fight on the French side with the intention of earning French gratitude if they won and perhaps attacking the Italians if they lost. Once it was clear that the French were losing catastrophically the Austrians had no choice but to adapt themselves to the new Prussian power, aware that annexation of French territory would draw Prussian ambitions away from themselves and cause a lasting and useful enmity between France and Prussia.[49] Consequently, Beust was determined to remain uncommitted, and 'with undignified eagerness ... bowed Thiers out of Vienna with assurances that he would get all he wanted at Florence'. Beust promised to raise no objections to Italian military aid; he also promised to follow a British or Russian lead in collective mediation – something Thiers now knew to be unlikely.[50]

Thiers's last engagement was in Florence. This had not been his own idea. The Italians themselves seem not to have wanted to be left out, and their ambassador in St Petersburg had pressed Thiers to go there. Equally in favour were Favre, who dreamed of an alliance of Latin states, his friend Sénard, sent as envoy to Florence, and Chaudordy, Favre's representative at Tours. They had elaborated a fantastic plan for a lightning Italian military expedition up the Rhône valley to threaten Prussian communications and snatch victory from the jaws of defeat.[51] Thiers tactfully concealed his opinion of this idea (which Gladstone described as 'almost insane'); he can hardly have been optimistic, especially after being assured by the Italian ambassador in Vienna that his government would never give military aid.[52] Moreover, he only arrived in Florence on 12 October, and his brief informed him that military intervention must begin on 15 October at the latest, before the Alpine passes snowed up. Finally, when he spoke to Sénard (whose earlier optimism had ebbed when he found the Italians 'astonished' by his military suggestions), he 'was made aware that we would obtain nothing'. He saw the King, all the ministers and the army commander General Cialdini, and argued 'with as much ardour as if I were full of hope', promising a subsidy (on his own responsibility), and a military campaign that would be without risk and short, as Prussia would quickly come to terms and France was only seeking 'a modest and honorable peace'.[53] It has been said that Thiers admitted his own scepticism over military intervention.[54] This is possible, for he was certainly no poker-faced diplomat; but it can hardly have made any difference. He thought that the King was tempted by the adventure, but the ministers were unshakeable: 'here they fear the Parliament', reported Thiers, 'and the Parliament fears the country, and the country fears the Prussians'. But he advised that contact should be kept up, for something might be obtained if the war continued – 'for it might continue, even though one must hope not'.[55]

It was with the firm intention of stopping it that Thiers returned to France, avoiding, on coded instructions from Tours, the turbulent cities of Marseilles and Lyons. There his mission would not have met with the approval of the population as it did in smaller towns, where reception committees turned out to greet his train.[56] His arrival in Tours coincided with the appalling news that Bazaine and his army had surrendered. This was a catastrophe: an important bargaining counter had disappeared; the regular troops that had survived the early battles had now been made prisoner; and the German army besieging them was free to reinforce the invading forces further west. Paris now became even more important as the sole remaining stronghold, and pressure on the hastily raised armies in the provinces to relieve the capital became greater just as the odds against their success increased. The bleak military position confirmed Thiers in his determination to seek an armistice and elections to a National Assembly. This had been the original intention of the Government of National Defence, but after the shock of Ferrières and the harshness of German demands, elections had been postponed. Gambetta in particular opposed them, fearing that they would return an Assembly that was conservative and in favour of peace. Thiers advocated them partly for that very reason. He also believed that they would strengthen the French negotiating position: the British, for example, had promised to recognize the provisional government as soon as elections were held; and Bismarck would no longer be able to avoid negotiating, or threaten the French with the restoration of the Bonapartes.

Thiers met the Tours delegation, the government representatives in the provinces, on 21 October, bearing Gorchakov's offer to ask for safe conduct for him to go to Paris and Versailles. Thiers's contention that a diplomatic opportunity had presented itself and should not be missed seemed confirmed by the arrival of a British offer to propose to both belligerents in the name of the neutrals that they should conclude an armistice to permit elections (thus sparing the French the humiliation of making the first move). The Tours delegation agreed unanimously to accept Gorchakov's offer, for it was 'indispensable' that Thiers should go to Paris to consult the beleaguered government. But Léon Gambetta, Minister of War and the

Interior and the most energetic member of the delegation, opposed acceptance of the British offer, because he was against calling elections. Finally, it was agreed to submit these points to the Paris government. Gambetta was willing to accept an armistice (which implied elections) only on condition that its terms should favour France militarily: a cease-fire of at least twenty-five days (giving more time to organize new armies), and agreement to the revictualling of Paris (extending its capacity to resist should hostilities be renewed). It is difficult to accept Sorel's argument that the British offer would have led to a favourable peace settlement brought about by neutral mediation, but that Thiers, preferring his own pro-Russian diplomacy, let the chance slip. The British had never considered imposing a mediation that the Prussians consistently refused. In fact, the British and the Russians wanted the same thing: an armistice leading to a French acceptance of defeat, including if need be the loss of at least Alsace.[57]

Thiers's mission was delayed by a dispute with the Germans over his safe conduct: they wanted him to come to Versailles, and he insisted on going to Paris first. It was eventually decided that he should go to Paris via Versailles. While waiting, it is possible that he helped to dissuade General d'Aurelle de Paladines, commander of the Army of the Loire, from advancing on Orléans. Thiers did not want the negotiations upset by an offensive, and was pessimistic about the military prospects. So was d'Aurelle, who needed little persuasion.[58] The delay caused the army to miss a temporary numerical advantage before German reinforcements arrived from Metz, though the final military outcome could have been little altered. Thiers was also in contact at this time with two oddly contrasting unofficial intermediaries: his old friend Bishop Dupanloup and his newer friend the Comtesse de Castiglione, both of whom assured Thiers that the Germans wanted peace. The Countess had written to Bismarck asking him to meet Thiers, and was convinced that it was thanks to her potent influence that peace was in sight.[59]

After a difficult journey through war-damaged country, Thiers arrived in Versailles on 30 October, met Bismarck briefly, and was escorted to the German outposts at Sèvres. Amid much blowing of bugles and showing of white flags, he crossed the Seine in a small boat (the bridge had been blown up) and reached the French lines. Late that evening, he met the government at the Quai d'Orsay. He could not have arrived at a worse moment: the Paris garrison had just lost Le Bourget; he brought the news of the fall of Metz; and his very presence was taken as a presage of surrender. After a long discussion the Paris government agreed with their colleagues at Tours that they should seize the opportunity offered by the British and Russian proposals to seek an armistice to be followed by elections, but only on the strict conditions of a twenty-five day armistice, with revictualling of Paris, and freedom of elections and communications throughout France.[60]

Thiers snatched three hours' sleep before going to the Place Saint-

Georges, where several friends, including Mignet and Roger, were waiting. He found the house in perfect order, with fire buckets on every floor in case of bombardment. He discussed the political situation with 'a crowd' of visitors, including Rothschild. The rest of the morning he spent at the Ministry of Commerce calculating the precise quantities of food and fuel that Paris would need during the armistice. Then came his return to confront the Germans at Versailles. The *Manchester Guardian* commented that 'when he sues for peace . . . the vainglorious spirit of his country, which he personifies, has at last been sufficiently chastised'.[61]

He met Bismarck on 1, 2 and 3 November. At first he was convinced that he was making progress. Bismarck made only a passing mention of restoring Napoleon III; he agreed to a twenty-five day armistice, and, with this admitted in principle, Thiers suggested that they leave the details of revictualling Paris until later; and on the question of elections, where Thiers had feared that difficulty would arise over voting in Alsace, he believed that matters were 'in a fair way of settlement'. On the third day, however, the tone changed. Bismarck told Thiers that there had been a revolution in Paris, and insisted on suspending the talks until further news had arrived.[62] There had, in fact, been a serious, though fortunately bloodless, rising in Paris on the 31st, provoked by the news of Metz, Le Bourget, and Thiers's talks with Bismarck. The government had been held prisoner for several hours inside the Hôtel de Ville by an angry crowd of National Guards, but finally the dissidents had been ejected and the government had survived.

When talks resumed, Bismarck, to the consternation of Thiers, stated that the Germans would not permit Paris to be revictualled unless one of the Paris forts were surrendered. An armistice on the French terms, said Bismarck, would give a great military advantage to France: it would keep the Germans in their siege positions throughout the winter, give the defence of Paris a new lease of life, and afford the new armies in the provinces time to organize. Thiers could only say that Germany would derive a moral and political advantage to set against the military advantage given to France. Bismarck was unmoved. Thiers said that he could not agree to what amounted to the surrender of Paris, and broke off the talks. He drafted an angry memorandum intended for Bismarck saying that if this had been Germany's fixed position from the beginning, there had been no point in opening negotiations at all: either something had changed Bismarck's mind, or else he had simply made a show of negotiating so as not to offend the neutral Powers. France, 'whose greatness and glory date not from yesterday but from centuries past', would not accept injustice and dishonour 'whatever the trials sent to her by Providence . . . for she is one of those works that Providence does not destroy when once it has created them'.[63]

Thiers's suspicion that Bismarck had never intended the talks to succeed was not implausible. Bismarck had told him that the Germans, advancing victoriously, did not need an armistice. Yet it would have been embarrassing to turn down the British and Russian requests completely. Consequently, Bismarck was miserable and ill-tempered during the talks, but in much better spirits when they failed: 'Well, that rids us of any more negotiations with Thiers.' On the other hand, ever prudent, he was genuinely seeking an early peace if the terms were favourable, both for domestic and diplomatic reasons. The terms suggested by Thiers – especially the revictualling of Paris – were described by Bismarck as 'exorbitant'; possibly he let the talks continue in order to demonstrate his reasonableness to the neutrals and to 'pump' Thiers, who could not conceal his pessimism and whose detailed demands for revictualling Paris helped the Germans make a reasonable guess as to its remaining food and fuel stocks.[64] The French, Thiers included, were strangely naive if they thought that the Germans would not realize what a military advantage an armistice on their terms would give. Thiers soon convinced himself that Bismarck had refused his demands only because the insurrection in Paris and a defiant proclamation from Gambetta on 30 October made him doubt that the French really wanted peace. Consequently, 'next day after long reflection' he decided to resume negotiations with Bismarck, and did not deliver his angry note. Finally, after another day of talks, he agreed in desperation to suggest to the Paris government either that they should accept an armistice without revictualling, or that they should call elections (to which Bismarck consented) without an armistice at all.[65]

On 5 November he crossed the Seine again for consultations, which this time were held furtively in a ruined house near the front line, for fear of fresh disorders if he were seen to enter Paris. Trochu remained at headquarters and Thiers was met only by Favre and General Ducrot. Later accounts, by Favre, Ducrot and Thiers himself, show him urging acceptance of the German terms as France could no longer fight on with any hope of success. But when Ducrot reported on the meeting to the government that evening the minutes record him as saying 'that M. Thiers had been the first to consider the Prussian conditions as unacceptable', while both Jules Ferry and Trochu complained of Thiers's 'silence' on the general situation of France.[66] Perhaps Thiers was still determined to avoid taking political responsibility for the outcome of the war and to limit himself strictly to the role of diplomat, reporting to the government and pointing out possible choices, but refusing to deliver a clear opinion himself.

This was the tone he adopted in an important memorandum written on 5 November. What, asked Thiers, was to be done? The answer depended on the Army of the Loire and on Paris, which the Germans would not attack but simply starve out. Could the Army of the Loire, which would soon be outnumbered by the German troops released by the fall of Metz, hold on? Could the Paris garrison break out and raise the siege? If the answers were yes, 'then the course to take is indefinitely prolonged and all-out war'; if not, then resistance could only continue until Paris ran out of food. In that event,

What will the peace be like? That is the supreme question ... It must be admitted that every day of resistance ... will be paid for in billions and in territory. A prompt peace, if we are not counting on a miracle, could be paid for with one province and two billion; a delayed peace will be two provinces and four or five billion, plus a month or two of dreadful devastation ... That is the question – I do not answer it ... I ask it.

But, he argued, only an elected Assembly could decide such a question, and the Germans were willing to permit elections.[67] This the government would not contemplate, knowing public opinion in Paris would reject any sign of weakness while means of resistance still existed. Moreover, they knew that Gambetta was determined to fight on, and he had given them a more hopeful view of the military prospects than Thiers. They ordered Thiers to break off negotiations and return to Tours. He travelled through the war zone, and arrived sitting on a pile of coal in the cab of a locomotive – the last stage of a journey of over five thousand miles and lasting six weeks, no mean feat for a man of 73.[68]

Two stark choices were placed before the government by Thiers and Gambetta, the former speaking for an increasing body of provincial and conservative opinion, and the latter supported by the Left, especially in the cities. Gambetta believed that if France held on throughout the winter, even if Paris fell and the northern half of the country were entirely occupied, the Germans would be worn down and forced to offer a reasonable peace. Even if France surrendered at once, the Germans would still annex Alsace and Lorraine; but in no circumstances could they ever annex more. So France had nothing to lose. Thiers, however, believed that a reasonable peace could be obtained by offering it at once, before France was utterly defeated and while she could still bargain. The Germans were too strong to be worn down and, as Thiers realized, were prepared to occupy the northern half of the country indefinitely, 'drawing a line' across France, in Bismarck's words, and incorporating the eastern provinces into Germany without waiting for the end of hostilities. Thiers, like nearly all conservatives, also feared the internal consequences of prolonging the war: the intensification of Gambetta's 'dictatorship', the breakdown of central authority with revolutionary regimes in Lyons and Marseilles, and the possible collapse of the French state. In that case, Broglie wrote to him, 'the King of Prussia will be more master of France than any conqueror since Alaric has been of any country'.[69]

As we have seen, Thiers hoped that a quick peace would mean that the monetary indemnity would be smaller and would damage the state finances less, enabling postwar recovery to be faster, and that less territory would be lost. The British and Russian governments, and Bismarck in the November talks, had encouraged this conviction. Was it well founded? As early as August the Prussian government had drawn up the boundaries of the territories it was eventually to annex, and Bismarck had frequently and publicly stated that he would insist on Metz and Strasbourg.[70] Thiers himself accepted the loss of Strasbourg. He thought – with Bismarck's encouragement – that the reward for a quick peace would be Metz.[71] Metz was an immensely important strategic position, controlling one of the routes into Germany, which is why Bismarck and the army wanted it. On the other hand, unlike Alsace it was French speaking, and this caused Bismarck and others misgivings on political grounds. Even in February 1871, with France beaten to her knees, he had grave doubts as to whether Germany should annex French-speaking territory, and he spoke of demolishing the Metz fortifications and building another fortress further east, in German-speaking territory.[72] Possibly, therefore Thiers was right: had France made peace in November, with Paris still able to resist, and with armies in the field, she might have kept a demilitarized Metz – a solution that Britain certainly and Russia probably would have favoured. Bismarck would have had weighty reasons to make such an offer and persuade his King to agree.

Yet is is doubtful whether such a concession would greatly have lessened the harm done by the war to Franco-German relations in the long term. Any mutilation of France would have given rise to a festering resentment against Germany: this was the opinion of both Bismarck and Gambetta. Nor would nationalist anger against a government accepting annexations have been allayed by a modification of boundaries, however strategically important.

Thiers's active role finished on 5 November when his talks with Bismarck were broken off. From then until the end of the war he remained with the Delegation in Tours and then in Bordeaux, where it retreated on 10 December. He offered to go again to London, but there was little point: with the failure of his talks with Bismarck there was no further diplomatic initiative. By December, Lord Odo Russell, British envoy to German headquarters at Versailles, was reporting that Bismarck would now only accept unconditional surrender, and that he intended to annex Alsace and Lorraine and to occupy Champagne for several years.[73] Thiers was little more than a spectator, bitterly critical of, but powerless to prevent, Gambetta's policy of refusing elections and dissolving local councils to disarm opponents of the war.

The Government of National Defence in Paris followed the counsel neither of Thiers nor of Gambetta. Against Thiers's advice, it prolonged the resistance until the food stocks in Paris were exhausted; but then, when it signed an armistice on 28 January 1871, not only Paris was covered – which would have allowed Gambetta to fight on in the south – but the whole country.[74] Thiers encouraged the government to persist in its decision and to overrule, and if necessary arrest, Gambetta, who was defiantly seeking means to continue the struggle from Bordeaux. Gambetta, for his part, was rumoured to be considering a *coup d'état* in which Thiers would be one of those arrested. But what Thiers would have called 'la Force des choses', political and military, was overwhelming, and Gambetta and his supporters gave in. Elections for a National Assembly were to be held at once. For months Thiers's admirers had been assuring him that he would be called to power. The country believed that events had proved him right, and that he was the best man to limit the damage done by the errors he had denounced.[75]

Since July he had held firmly to the view that the war was unjustified and disastrous, and must be ended as soon as possible. When the first calamities occurred, he refused the pleas of the Empress, the Legislative Body and the Government of National Defence to lead the nation in war. His political past and his historical work seemed to destine him for that task: 'If you save France . . . you will have accomplished a near miracle', an old friend, Casimir-Perier, wrote; 'if you fail, your honour will be no less great'.[76] But he was not tempted by the prospect of a gallant but hopeless struggle, and turned to diplomacy and compromise. Only when the worst had happened, when the war had been lost by others, and when an Assembly had been elected to take 'a major part of the responsibility'[77] was he willing, indeed eager, to come forward as the saviour of the nation. An important motive was his concern for his posthumous reputation. 'I often dream of posterity', he said on a later occasion, 'I think of my future reputation. Jules Favre forgot his.'[78] Oddly for an historian, he seems to have been confident that history would judge dispassionately; but history has been kinder to Gambetta's heroic prodigality than to his own calculating realism. No doubt he lacked Gambetta's youthful boldness. Did he also lack understanding of what has been called the first modern war of nations? Indeed not: he and Gambetta were equally aware of what popular struggles entailed, for Thiers had been the historian of the revolutionary wars, the romanticized legend of which inspired the Republican nationalists in 1870. But Thiers feared a repetition of such turmoil, and warned that a Franco-German struggle might lead to a devastating 'universal war'.[79] His belief that the conflict could be limited and the damage to France minimized was not the view of another age, but the experience of the recent wars in the Crimea, Italy, Denmark and Austria. Since 1866, he had sought to strengthen France and weaken Prussia if an opportunity arose, but he tried to avert war in the 'dreadfully badly chosen' circumstances in 1870: 1840 had taught him of the need for allies. After Sedan, he wished to secure an acceptable peace and preserve French strength for the future, and for possible revenge. All these aims he shared with Gambetta. It was their assessment of costs that differed, and here – at least from the point of view of contemporaries – Thiers was clearly the better judge.

[11]

'M. Thiers's Republic'
1871–1873

In spite of the haste in which they were held, the elections to the National Assembly on 8 February 1871 gave unambiguous results. Only nine days elapsed between announcement and polling, but the elections had been expected since October, and many preparations, such as the establishment of electoral committees and the drawing up of lists of candidates for the multi-member departmental constituencies, had already been carried out.[1] Moreover, the issue at stake – war or peace – was so simple that a clear result was facilitated. The campaign for peace united Legitimists, Orleanists and moderate Republicans in the broadest political alliance of the century, reminiscent of the 'Party of Order' of 1849. Thiers was its unrivalled champion. A friend assured him in January that his election would be acclaimed: he had warned against the war, his fortifications had saved Paris, he had obtained the offer of an armistice from the neutral Powers, and he alone, with his European reputation, could soften the German peace terms. The result was a triumph for the peace party, and gave the Royalists a large majority. Only in some of the large cities – most ominously Paris – and in the eastern provinces menaced by annexation did Left-wing candidates win major successes with their campaign for continuing the war.

Thiers had won a personal triumph. His name had been placed on many lists – sometimes rival ones – in twenty-six departments, and in all twenty-six he had been elected. In other words, he had been chosen by nearly a third of the country. 'All eyes are turned towards you', wrote an old adversary, Montalivet, on 31 January; 'there is not one sensible man who does not see with confidence the government of the country in your hands, in whatever form it may be'.[2]

The Assembly met in Bordeaux on 13 February. It elected Thiers 'almost unanimously' as Chief of the Executive Power of the French Republic. Early in the war he had foreseen that responsibility for ending it might one day be his, but, as we have seen, while the fighting lasted he had held back. Now, although he lamented that he was 'the official receiver of a huge bankruptcy', his reluctance vanished. The task was still daunting: 'anyone who nurtured any illusions concerning the fate of the government that inherited the humiliations of 1871 would be blind indeed', as an Orleanist wrote to him tactlessly.[3] A few months earlier, Thiers would perhaps have agreed. But now the country was behind him in wanting peace, and an elected Assembly was there to bear the final responsibility. In these circumstances, as Duvergier assured him, to take power would be the glorious culmination of his political life.[4] He had at last found his historic mission: to shield France from German vindictiveness, rebuild the power of the state, and give the country lasting political institutions.

The most urgent task was to meet Bismarck, for the armistice had only another week to run. This overshadowed two scarcely less urgent problems: the avoidance of bankruptcy and the restoration of order in the large towns, especially Paris, where the government's writ had practically ceased to run.

There was no immediate possibility, in these circumstances, of deciding the great question of France's future regime. The Assembly agreed, after a statement from Thiers on 19 February, that the choice should be postponed until it no longer threatened 'the existence and safety of the country' – an agreement soon christened the Pact of Bordeaux. Yet Thiers had taken a significant step: he had named a government that did not reflect the Royalist predominance in the Assembly. Only one of the nine ministers was an avowed Royalist; five, like Thiers himself, were uncommitted; and three were confirmed Republicans. Moreover, the Republicans held key posts: Ernest Picard (Interior), Jules Favre (Foreign Affairs) and Jules Simon (Public Instruction and Worship).[5] One reason why Thiers made this choice and the Assembly acquiesced in it was probably their desire that Republican ministers from the Government of National Defence should share responsibility for the harsh peace: 'if the Republic did not exist one would have to invent it', wrote one Orleanist to Thiers.[6] Also, Thiers had come to know and apparently like these men, especially as, chastened by defeat and politically discredited, they were admiring and obedient subordinates. Yet there were weightier reasons too. For many years Thiers had toyed with the thought that a Republic might be inevitable in France, and now it had the merit of being the *de facto* government. A restoration had several drawbacks. The Royalists were divided over who should succeed to the throne and on what terms. Thiers had little love for the Orléans princes, who would not do as he told them, and he had long complained of their 'ingratitude'. Worse, the Legitimists, whom he had always opposed, were so strong in the Assembly that any restoration would have to be on their terms, which Thiers was bound to find unacceptable.

Consequently, although he had made no open or irrevocable decision, he believed that circumstances favoured the Republic: 'if the Republic misses its chances', he told Jules Simon, 'it will be the Republicans' fault, not mine'. To those with ears to hear in the Assembly, he said, 'if we succeed in this reorganization [of France] it will be done under the form of the Republic and to its profit ... The Republic is in your hands, it will be the prize of your good behaviour and nothing else.' Duvergier urged Thiers to stick to 'the government that divides us least' and eschew 'dynastic fantasies', recommending as a motto 'the Republic with the conservatives'. He believed that Thiers was 'entirely of this view', and he was right: it was a slightly modified version of Duvergier's slogan that Thiers would later make his own: 'the conservative Republic'.[7] The time, however, was not yet ripe: the Pact of Bordeaux remained in force as long as unity was required to tackle the problems of peace negotiations, financial solvency and public order.

Spurred on by Bismarck's threats to resume hostilities, Thiers spent from 21 to 25 February in Versailles negotiating a preliminary peace treaty. He told Bismarck that he hoped the terms would be no harsher than those discussed in their November negotiations, but Bismarck replied that now he would insist on Metz as well as Alsace, and an indemnity of 6,000 million francs. On 22 February, Thiers saw the new German Emperor and the Crown Prince to plead for generosity, but, unsurprisingly, got nothing. The Crown Prince was struck by his 'bright, sagacious eyes through big, sharply focussed spectacles, looking searchingly straight at my face. His exterior is more that of an oldish countryman living on his means than a statesman; his short, thick-set figure, for all his white, but strong, short hair, gives no indication of his seventy-four years.' He was not an ideal negotiator. He was, the Crown Prince felt, 'resigned', and while he bargained as best he could, he was convinced that terms would necessarily be harsher than those he had negotiated four months earlier, and that France had no means of resisting them. Bismarck knew this, and took advantage of the moral ascendancy it gave him, conducting himself with 'monstrous brusquerie and intentional rudeness'.[8] In reality, however, Bismarck was not sure whether he should or could obtain Metz, and was trying to muster support within German headquarters for its abandonment. Thiers was not able to take advantage of these doubts, which indeed he never suspected.

Bismarck astutely overcame his half-hearted resistance to the loss of Metz by offering to let France keep Belfort instead and making Thiers believe he had won this by stubborn negotiation. He also got him to agree to the politically dangerous concession of a triumphal entry by the German army into Paris as further payment for Belfort. Finally, he forced Thiers to agree to the huge indemnity of 5,000 million francs, which many experts, even among Bismarck's advisers, thought an impossible sum. It had apparently first been mentioned by Favre at Ferrières, when he hoped to tempt the Germans into giving up territorial claims; and the figure had stuck in Bismarck's mind as one the French could pay. He got it by the simple tactic of demanding 6,000 million and letting Thiers and Favre think they had beaten him down. The Germans were surprised at such advantageous terms: the Kaiser considered them an 'incredible result'. Thiers and the parliamentary commission that had accompanied him to Versailles agreed that they had no alternative but to sign, for Bismarck threatened to 'start shooting on Monday . . . That language you would certainly understand.'[9]

The French won one small success. It had been agreed that the Germans would occupy part of Paris until ratifications were exchanged. Thiers therefore rushed down to Bordeaux by special train, and asked the Assembly for immediate ratification. The debate on 1 March was painful: the nationalist Left opposed ratification; Thiers demanded that they should explain by what means the war could be continued. Amid general emotion, the final vote was 546 for ratification, 107 against. The ratification document was taken post-haste by special messenger to Favre, who hurried with it to Bismarck and demanded that German troops should leave Paris forthwith. In consequence, the Kaiser missed his own triumphal entry and complained that the Germans were 'as good as being chased out of Paris'. It was a meagre consolation, and did nothing to calm the anger of Parisians.[10]

Paris was now the government's principal problem. The hardships and disappointments of the war had caused remarkable political radicalization. Moderate Republicans such as Favre and Picard were discredited, and in the February general elections Paris had elected a predominantly Left-wing and pro-war deputation to the Assembly, in stark contrast to the Royalist and pro-peace majority, whom Parisians suspected of treachery and conspiracy against the Republic. The danger of insurrection was magnified because a large part of the Parisian population was armed and organized in the National Guard, many of whose 275 battalions had elected as their officers militant patriots, most of them Republicans, some revolutionary activists. While this turbulent force had been left with its rifles under the armistice terms, the regular garrison, except for a mere 12,000 men, had been disarmed. The German triumphal entry had caused a large section of the National Guard to mobilize, seize several hundred cannon from army depots, and set up a Republican Federation, outside government control, in which 215 battalions were said to be to some degree involved.

By early March, the capital was in a state of incipient insurrection. Yet the government was less alarmed than might have been expected. Those ministers who had remained in Paris, veterans of the Government of National Defence and the siege, had become hardened to popular agitation. Only Favre, the least phlegmatic of men, tended to panic, and even he calmed down after the German troops left. Thiers, scarcely sleeping, hurrying between Versailles and Bordeaux, busying himself with financial problems, diplomacy, the chaotic administration and the restive Assembly, had more than Paris to worry about: 'you reproach me with thinking of nothing but Paris', protested Favre. 'I reproach you with neglecting it.' Thiers was indeed willing to leave the problem to those on the spot: 'I approve all the measures you describe for the maintenance of order . . . I leave you to judge the opportune moment to get back the cannon' – those seized by the National Guard, which had become symbols of the independent power of the Republican people in arms. Thiers's own opinion was that 'nothing should be done hastily ... patience and ridicule have every chance of triumphing'.[11]

He did agree, under pressure from Favre, who was threatening to resign, to move with the Assembly closer to the capital. Favre and his Republican colleagues believed that this would calm feeling in Paris by demonstrating that the government and Assembly were not plotting against the Republic in some provincial fastness, and also make the authority of the government more effective. The Royalist majority, however, were determined not to return to Paris where their debates would be subject to 'the paving stones of the mob'. Thiers, who at first thought of Fontainebleau as a compromise, finally decided on Versailles, and let it be known that he would resign if the Assembly refused. But what Thiers saw as a concession, Parisians took as renewed provocation. Feelings were further heightened by tactless measures taken by the authorities. Consequently, when Thiers arrived in Paris on 15 March the agitation had not disappeared, and the 400 cannon seized by the National Guard were more than ever the symbol and rallying point of the dissidents. The government hoped to arrange their peaceful return. Negotiations had been going on for some days but they broke down soon after Thiers's arrival.[12]

On 17 March, Thiers and his colleagues decided to try to capture the cannon by surprise during the early hours of the 18th. It was one of the most disastrous decisions he ever took, and one which weighs heavily on his reputation, for it was the immediate cause of the bloodiest civil war of the century. His enemies, at the time and since, accused him of provocation aimed at crushing the 'vile mob' which he had feared and fought ever since the 1830s: March 1871 has been seen as following on from the 'massacre of the Rue Transnonain' in 1834, the September Laws of 1835 and the electoral law of May 1850. Thiers lent substance to this view by characteristically maintaining that he had foreseen everything.[13] The documentary evidence, however, suggests lack of preparation and confusion.

Until 17 March, Thiers (just as when he was Minister of the Interior in 1834) had consistently instructed his colleagues and the army to take no precipitate action: 'the rowdies will quarrel and get tired, and during that time our reinforcements will arrive [and] we shall dominate the disorder almost without opposition'.[14] The government's troops were relatively few and unreliable, and the army commanders, having made no preparations whatever, wished to postpone military action. Furthermore, any serious conflict would damage the government's diplomatic position and their chance of raising loans to meet current expenditure and the enormous German indemnity. The ambassador in London had written to Thiers on 11 March that 'a movement of insurrection in the provinces ... or in Paris can set everything ablaze', and make a loan in the London market impossible. Favre agreed and added, 'the Prussians ... this time would come right into

200

our house.' It would also damage hopes of *rapprochement* with Russia, the principal aim of French diplomacy. [15] On 16 March, however, a negotiated attempt by government troops to repossess some of the contentious cannon was thwarted by National Guards obeying the dissident Republican Federation. Thiers regarded this as an open challenge: the dissidents 'had acted so blatantly, so arrogantly, that I, who hesitated to give combat, felt there was no longer any way out'. The National Assembly was due to meet at his insistence at Versailles on 20 March, and would expect order to have been restored in Paris.

So on the evening of 17 March Thiers persuaded his colleagues and the military to take a risk, which, if it succeeded, would strengthen the government, discredit the dissidents, rally the moderates and facilitate pacification of the capital. Thiers's streak of recklessness, displayed in 1840, was again apparent. He eagerly listened to bad advice when it promised a quick victory: he and his colleagues were assured that the dissidents were almost ready to give in, and that no serious opposition need be expected if the troops moved before dawn. If the operation failed, things would continue as before. If the dissidents counter-attacked, Thiers mentioned the possibility of evacuating the city – an idea that had come to him in 1848. But there is no evidence that this was seriously considered and it formed no part of the military plan. [16]

With hindsight it is clear how dangerous the 18 March operation was. The rules of urban operations were ignored, and when the city awoke the troops were swamped by crowds of Parisians determined to defend 'their' cannon and prevent what many assumed to be a monarchist *coup d'état*. Officers and men were unwilling to precipitate civil war, and some broke ranks or handed over their rifles. They were hastily withdrawn, for the government and the generals feared that, as during previous revolutions, the army might disintegrate if left in contact with the civilian population. Thiers himself seems to have panicked as in February 1848, and left with unseemly speed for Versailles. The other ministers and the Mayor of Paris, Jules Ferry, were determined to hang on in the city, however, probably believing that the insurrection was little worse than those they had braved during the siege. Finally, it was the army commanders, fearful for the discipline of their troops, who decided to retreat to Versailles several hours after Thiers had left. This decision, which Thiers had been the first to advocate, left Paris with its fortifications, vast arsenal, wealth and 1.5 million inhabitants in the hands of the surprised and disorganized insurgents. Perhaps no revolutionaries have ever won so great a prize with such ease. [17]

Thiers, his ministers, the Paris garrison and the National Assembly gathered at Versailles. There was disagreement about what should be done. The Right-wing majority was determined to make no concessions to the rebels, and some were eager to attack the city. The government, aware of its military weakness, had no choice but to temporize. The mayors and

Republican deputies of Paris, who supported the legal government while sympathizing at least partly with the insurgents' demands, pleaded for compromise. They hoped to persuade the government, the Assembly and the insurgent Central Committee of the Republican Federation of the National Guard to authorize new elections in Paris for a municipal government which they expected to head. This body, both legal and popular, would, they hoped, be recognized by both Versailles and the rebels, and could negotiate a compromise that would satisfy Parisian opinion by guaranteeing the existence of the Republic and wide autonomy for the city.[18]

Thiers's attitude was ambiguous. He encouraged the mayors' mediation attempt, yet doubted their chances of success.[19] He had to avoid the appearance of weakness before an intransigent Assembly, yet he was aware of the dangers of open conflict. He promised through the mayors that elections in Paris would be held, yet on 21 March he spoke strongly against holding them too hastily, and when a government Bill was produced, it merely provided for municipal elections in April for the whole country, with a municipal council for Paris which would have none of the autonomy insisted on by the Left.[20] At the same time he was trying to avert an armed clash, discouraging action by loyalist National Guards inside Paris and refusing their requests for arms, equipment and men to help them resist the rebels.[21] He also kept the Assembly in near inactivity for the first few days, partly muzzling the extremists of the Right. On 24 March, the insurgent Central Committee called elections for 26 March, with the reluctant consent of the mayors. Thiers, although aware of the suspicion of the Right in the Assembly and pessimistic himself concerning the likely result of the elections, refrained from disavowing them.[22] But their results confirmed his pessimism: the new municipal government, the Commune, was dominated by the extreme Left, and the moderate minority soon resigned.

It has often been asserted that Thiers never contemplated compromise but was merely playing for time until ready to launch a military attack on Paris. Certainly he needed time, for his military forces were weak and disorganized, and revolt threatened or had broken out in Lyons, Marseilles, Narbonne and other towns. But temporization did not only favour the government: it enabled the insurgents to organize too, and establish a certain legitimacy by holding elections. Had the insurgents been willing to reach a compromise with the mayors of Paris acceptable to most of the inhabitants, it would have been difficult for Thiers to set it aside. During this 'worst time of my life' he may even have lacked the will to fight back: 'Once already I have pulled France drowning out of a revolution; I am not young enough to do it a second time.'[23] Diplomats were told that the government's first hope lay not in military intervention but in the possibility of the insurgents' quarrelling among themselves or arousing opposition in Paris; it was reported that only one minister favoured military action when the government met on 25 March. As Rémusat put it, 'First, it was necessary not to show oneself eager to use force . . . One could possibly hope that time . . . difficulties . . . and the belief that many of [the Commune's] members must have of the impossibility of success . . . could bring some readiness to . . . negotiate.'[24]

But there was no readiness among the insurgents to abandon a revolution that still seemed in the ascendant. On the contrary, reports came from Paris that they were preparing to attack Versailles. On 1 April Thiers insisted that a reconnaissance in force should be carried out to test the insurgents' intentions, and on the morning of the 2nd, government troops attacked their advanced positions west of Paris. Next day the Parisians, in retaliation, launched a large-scale but unsuccessful attack on Versailles, and the civil war began in earnest.[25]

Largely cut off from the rest of France, the Paris Commune and its mainly working-class supporters set out during April and May to improvise, from an unplanned, patriotic, anti-monarchist uprising, a model people's Republic, democratic, secular, egalitarian and mildly socialist.[26] The capital was governed in a relatively orderly and efficient manner. Yet, as fighting dragged on in the suburbs, the property-owning classes and probably the majority of the country, encouraged by the propaganda of the government and the Right, came to envisage the Commune as the reincarnation of the worst horrors of 1793 and an anti-patriotic movement putting France at the mercy of the Germans. While many Republicans still sympathized to some degree with Paris and blamed the Assembly and government for precipitating the conflict, few were prepared to join the fray, mostly confining themselves to vain appeals for reconciliation and compromise.[27]

During the fighting Thiers had three major tasks. The first was military: to organize an army and reoccupy Paris. The second, diplomatic: to resist German attempts to exploit the government's difficulties. The third, political: to keep the support of public opinion, especially in the potentially dangerous Republican cities of the south.

Into the first of these tasks Thiers threw himself with what Rémusat called 'a kind of joy . . . a pleasure related to childishness'. As has been seen, military matters had always been one of his passions, both as a politician and as a historian. Now for the only time in his life he exercised his vast accumulated knowledge. As commander-in-chief he chose Marshal de MacMahon, whom he found to be of a striking 'modesty and simplicity' – which meant, Rémusat remarked, that he had no ideas of his own and was willing to be Thiers's docile instrument.[28] He chose a group of senior generals who were both able and politically mixed – two Legitimists, two Bonapartists and even a Republican. They soon experienced one of Thiers's most irritating traits; his inability to 'chat five minutes with a potato-chip seller without teaching him the secrets of frying'.[29] He told them against which section of the formidable ramparts they should launch their assault (the south-western salient) and how they should go about it (with heavy artillery). He insisted on arranging directly with a private contractor the building of a monster gun battery on the Montretout heights, and was immensely pleased with the speed with which this was done and the effect of the fire. The generals were unimpressed. The attack on the south-western ramparts was obvious because it enabled the army to remain close to Versailles; while the guns held back for Thiers's battery at Montretout could have been better used elsewhere, according to one general. When the battery did at last open fire it bombarded positions abandoned several days earlier. Thiers also had an underhand – and in the opinion of some soldiers disreputable – method of retaking Paris. He tried to arrange the surrender at one of the Paris gates, sending agents with promises of money and safe conduct even to highly placed insurgent commanders. This exposed his own forces to the risk of ambush, and twice large forces were kept in the Bois de Boulogne under the guns of the Paris ramparts waiting in vain for a gate to be opened. He tried similarly to secure the surrender of Fort Issy, which commanded the chosen south-western approach, but without success.[30]

Thiers's administrative efforts were more successful. His energy in supervising the mustering and supply of an army which eventually reached nearly 140,000 men was generally recognized. He also concerned himself with the vital question of morale, and enjoyed visiting camps and outposts believing, no doubt, that those he visited enjoyed it too. He was apparently generous with medals, especially for the wounded, and promises of promotion, not always kept. He later declared that he had paid special attention to the troops' food and living conditions, but they still left much to be desired; there was, after all, a limit to what even so energetic a busybody as Thiers could do in a relatively short time. Probably his most important contribution to the military campaign was political: to resist pressure from the Assembly, the press and the Germans to hasten the military operations. He provided time for the army to build up its strength and organization and thus made the final outcome certain.[31]

Whether because he was aware of the generals' resistance to civilian interference, or mistrustful of their political loyalty, or simply through an ingrained preference for individual contact, Thiers sought allies and informants outside the official military chain of command – a colonel here, a general there – who were encouraged to communicate with him privately and were treated as old friends, much to the annoyance of the army hierarchy. The most important was the able and unscrupulous General de Cissey, commander of 2nd Army Corps, with whom Thiers maintained assiduous contact, and whom he was to appoint Minister of War in June 1871.[32]

Thiers's second task was to stand up to Bismarck. The preliminary peace treaty placed a limit of 40,000 on the army Thiers could deploy. The civil war demanded greater strength, for which Germans permission was required. German generals suspected that France might use the occasion to rebuild her armed forces rapidly and so strengthen her negotiating position. Bismarck appeared to share, or at least make use of, these fears, which may have had some substance. Friction ensued between the French and German military authorities over the movement and total permitted numbers of French troops before Paris. Tentative contacts between Bismarck and the Commune were made, with Bismarck considering mediation and the occupation of Paris in order to 'guarantee us against the bad faith of the French government'. Also, the German representatives at the final peace negotiations at Brussels and Frankfurt hardened their demands. On 29 April, Favre complained to Bismarck of 'decisive support given to the insurrection and an act of hostility against the legitimate government of France'.[33] Bismarck's answer was an ultimatum delivered on 7 May: unless Germany was given further 'guarantees' of the French government's good faith (principally an extended period of occupation), she would insist on the withdrawal of French troops beyond the Loire and German troops would occupy Paris. Thiers and Favre had no choice but to agree to the German terms. Their position was improved by the capture of Fort Issy on 9 May, which showed that they were winning the war. Favre offered to sign a peace treaty immediately, Bismarck gladly agreed and it was done on 10 May. Thereafter the problem was not German obstruction but encumbering offers of help. Thiers was determined not to permit German interference in the civil war, and on 21 May he 'beseeched' Bismarck, 'in the name of the cause of order, to let us carry out this repression of banditry ourselves ... To act otherwise would be a further disservice to the party of Order in France and hence in Europe.' It would discredit the government at home and also – though of course Thiers did not say so – weaken it diplomatically in its relations with Russia. Bismarck would not promise to refrain from intervening, but the entry of French troops into Paris that same day removed his pretext.[34]

Thiers's third task was to reassure Republicans. In order to lessen the danger of disturbances and prevent their giving aid and comfort to the Commune, Thiers had to convince provincial Republicans (whose strength was demonstrated in the April local elections) that his government was the Republic's best safeguard, and that the defeat of the Commune would not lead to a restoration of monarchy. In meetings with deputations of businessmen, freemasons and Republican local councillors during April and May he had considerable success. Hénon, the veteran Republican mayor of Lyons, wrote soon afterwards, 'My friends and I trust you, but we mistrust the Right ... Count on us ... as you direct us, we shall act.'[35]

Many conservatives suspected that Thiers might 'get involved in a sort of deal *in extremis*' with the Commune. Favre, the Foreign Minister, even suggested this on 7 May as a way of strengthening his diplomatic position against Bismarck.[36] But soon afterwards the military tide turned against the insurgents. Thiers refused to consider direct negotiations which would imply some recognition of the Commune. He would not release the imprisoned revolutionary activist, Blanqui, in exchange for the release of the Archbishop of Paris and others held hostage by the Commune, on the grounds that to give in would encourage further hostage taking. However, shooting of insurgent prisoners by the army, the original cause of the hostages' arrest, was quietly stopped.[37] Neither would Thiers accept any of the Commune's political demands, though he made certain offers and concessions in public statements and privately: the lives of those who laid down their arms would be safe; payments to 'needy workers' (to replace National Guard pay) would continue. Confidentially he went further: the mayor of Bordeaux and a delegation of Parisian Republicans were given the impression that a large measure of autonomy would be granted to Paris and that insurgent leaders would be allowed to escape.[38]

Conservatives were alarmed and angered when reports of these conversations leaked out. On 11 May, an old Orleanist friend of Thiers's, Mortimer-Ternaux, questioned the government in the Assembly about the reports, apparently hoping that they would be denied. But Thiers replied with a smokescreen of bad temper, complaining of the 'pestering' of the Assembly, threatening to resign, nowhere denying the reports and adding a calculated insult to the Right: 'There are imprudent men among you who are too hasty. Let them wait another week; at the end of the week there will be no more danger and the task will be proportionate to their courage and their capacity.' Thiers demanded a vote of confidence which a deflated Assembly carried by 490 to 9.[39]

The more radical Republicans were far from satisfied with Thiers's attitude, but they were in no mood to fight. By mid-May, the government was strong enough to forbid a congress of Republican local authorities called by the mayor of Bordeaux to discuss mediation.[40] Yet however few concessions he made to the demands of the delegations that besieged him, Thiers appears to have been impressed with this further evidence of the strength of Republican feeling in the country. The Republic seemed confirmed as the only foundation for strong and stable government.

During the second week in May, as the besiegers' shells did widespread damage inside Paris, Thiers suffered a reprisal against his own property. On 10 May the Commune's Committee of Public Safety ordered that his house in the Place Saint-Georges should be demolished. On the 11th the work began. 'M. Thiers has taken the assassination of his house nobly', wrote Jules Ferry; 'he has lamented his bronzes and his souvenirs, but, after all, it is not something that happens to everybody, and it is one form of glory.' Thiers had never been immune to self-pity. He threw his sufferings in the faces of his Right-wing critics during the row over Mortimer-Ternaux's interpellation, and complained pathetically to Duvergier and Sénard four days later that 'I no longer have hearth or home, and that house where I received you all [for] forty years is destroyed to the foundations. My collections dispersed! Add a few slanders and you have all that one gains from serving the country!' Much was destroyed; but shortly before, papers and choice works of art (including some of Madame Thiers's fine porcelain) had been placed in safety.[41]

On 21 May, government troops slipped through an undefended sector of the Paris ramparts. This was the beginning of *la Semaine Sanglante*, the 'Bloody Week' of 21–8 May, during which the army fought its way across Paris, engaged in hundreds of sometimes bloody skirmishes, and killed on the barricades, shot summarily or executed after drumhead court martial thousands of suspected insurgents. Like the St Bartholomew's Day massacre and the Terror, the slaughter of May 1871 left a scar on the collective memory of Frenchmen.[42] 'The ground . . . is strewn with their corpses', Thiers proclaimed. 'May this dreadful sight serve as a lesson.'[43] His ultimate responsibility, as head of the government and energetic prosecutor of the civil war, is undoubted, and it has made him one of the most detested historical figures in France.

Yet his personal role during the tragedy is less than clear. It was frequently explained later, by members and supporters of the government, and by Thiers himself, that the slaughter had been a regrettable consequence of bitter street fighting, aggravated by the arson and murder of hostages committed by the Communards. 'I gave the strictest orders in the endeavour to restrain the soldier's wrath', stated Thiers in his memoirs, 'and the Marshal, for his part, did all he could to prevent bloodshed.' 'But', declared MacMahon, 'in some places [my] instructions were forgotten.'[44]

The evidence, fragmentary though it is, does not permit responsibility to be so easily evaded. Orders were given, perhaps informally, to shoot insurgents 'taken carrying arms' – the phrase is frequently encountered in the writings of observers and in official reports and dispatches. It seems unlikely that such orders would have been given without Thiers's knowledge and consent. Indeed, certain of his declarations were phrased in a way that suggests that those taken in arms could not expect quarter: 'As for the insurgents, except for murderers, *those who lay down their arms* will have their lives spared'; 'We have repeated . . . that we will spare the lives of *those who lay down their arms*.'[45] One general later reported that National Guards 'taken carrying arms . . . were executed . . . on the very spot where they were arrested',[46] and this happened in many parts of the city.

Moreover, several drumhead courts martial were set up and sentenced large numbers of suspects to summary execution. There is no evidence to link Thiers directly with these courts. A certain Gabriel Ossude, who acted as prosecutor before one of them, stated later that he had received his commission from Thiers personally – an assertion that received some publicity. He is at best an unreliable witness, and official reports made by him while actually involved with the proceedings of the court martial appear to contradict his later assertion.[47] It seems to have been the army commanders who were responsible for the massacre.

Thiers must have been aware of much that was happening in Paris, even though he could not have known all the details or the scale of the killing, which indeed has never been precisely established. While the army was not under his or anyone's direct control in the circumstances of the street fighting, he saw reports and dispatches referring to courts martial and summary executions, including one from his protégé Cissey containing instructions to shoot on the spot prisoners taken carrying arms. Besides, much of the slaughter took place publicly and was reported in the press. It seems therefore that Thiers accepted at least tacitly that a harsh lesson was to be given to the insurgents.[48] Favre, who had asked Bismarck to intern fugitive rebels (which would have saved them from summary firing squads) and Ferry, who reported his alarm over the executions, appear to have been more concerned than Thiers to avert excesses. Thiers expressed his disapproval to Ferry on 27 May: 'We do not consent to any execution once a man is taken prisoner. During the fighting we can do nothing, and it would be useless to get ourselves mixed up in it.'[49] Yet Thiers may have taken some restraining action at that time, for on 27 or 28 May, as fighting died down, orders came 'from Versailles' to stop summary executions, and the worst massacres ceased.[50] By then much blood had already been shed. Had Thiers tried to interfere earlier, it might well have been useless, for the army had considerable autonomy on the urban battlefield and much of the Assembly and public opinion favoured harsh treatment of the rebels. However, many soldiers went much further than the shooting of insurgents 'taken in arms' and the slaughter became an embarrassment. *The Times*, whose influence Thiers appreciated, was vehemently critical on 26, 27 and 29 May. Such developments may explain the belated orders 'from Versailles'. One of the most ruthless executioners was Cissey. There is no firm evidence to show whether he acted with Thiers's encouragement or (as seems more likely) took advantage of his favoured position to pursue his own purge of those he considered 'a gang of criminals'. In any case, his relations with Thiers were unaffected, for on 31 May Thiers announced to him personally his appointment as Minister of War.[51]

Nearly 50,000 prisoners were taken. Their disposal posed a practical and political problem, and Thiers complained of those 'heartless' people 'without political sense' who were going too far in making arrests. He twice declared before the Assembly that 'expiation' would be 'complete', but that it would be 'in the name of the law and through the law': there would be no wholesale transportation and no special tribunals as in 1848 and 1852.[52] Thiers doubtless remembered his own revulsion against the *coup d'état* of 1851, and he argued that French governments should act within the law and escape from the cycle of the illegal and the arbitrary. The consequence was, however, that arrests and trials by court martial dragged on for several years.

Broglie and other conservatives were convinced that Thiers and the government were facilitating the escape of Communards to England. The oldest (and very moderate) member of the Commune, Charles Beslay, was certainly allowed to escape to Switzerland. The notorious Left-wing journalist Henri Rochefort believed that he owed his life to the intervention of Thiers, who feared that the massacres would 'stain his memory'. Such cases were exceptional, but the suspicious conservatives in the Assembly insisted that the right of clemency should be exercised not by Thiers, but by a Commission of Pardons. When the Commission ordered the execution of three men convicted of the murder of Archbishop Darboy, Thiers wrote 'I would have preferred no executions, but it was impossible.' He was glad that the Assembly was incurring part of the odium of the repression, even though its doing so was a sign of his deteriorating relations with the Right.[53]

In the dangerous circumstances of 1871, it would have been difficult to avoid grave civil conflict. Thiers, by his disastrous miscalculation of 18 March, was responsible for precipitating it. After the first attempts at conciliation failed, he prosecuted the civil war with relentless energy. He was the formidable director of a policy of repression that any government attached to the survival of the national state and the existing social order would have pursued. In the circumstances of 1871 the Paris Commune could hardly have escaped destruction. As one of those who had tried to bring the two sides to negotiate wrote despairingly, 'the improbable success of the Commune will bring back the Prussians. The hardly doubtful success of the government will be the signal for an intense reaction.'[54] By destroying the Commune, Thiers, at great cost, averted the first danger and limited the second: having made no great efforts to save the Communards from ferocious reprisals, he did much to prevent the reaction from assailing the Republic and Liberal government. Did he ever feel guilt or remorse, or even deep emotion, over the horrors of the civil war? Few have thought so. No doubt he would have said that what he had done was right and necessary, and that the true responsibility for the bloodshed and damage lay with the insurgents and their (similarly unremorseful) leaders.

The tragedies of the war and the Commune were deeply demoralizing to many Frenchmen of all political views, who feared that French society was decadent and France's greatness lost. The newspapers drew gloomy analogies with the fall of the Roman Empire and the partitions of Poland. Thiers, however, now that the country was following his lead, was less pessimistic. Finances and the army, he had always believed, were the sinews of the state: he set out to show how strong they still were. On 27 June, only a month after the defeat of the Commune, a state loan of 2,000 million francs was successfully floated, enabling the first instalments of the German indemnity to be paid. On 29 June, Thiers reviewed the army at Longchamps: 120,000 men, in uniforms stained by combat against Germans and Communards, marched past as evidence of both the victory of order and the rebirth of national strength. 'In the old imperial stand . . . [stood] M. Thiers . . . with tears in his eyes, lowering and raising his spectacles, hardly able to contain himself, stamping his feet, beating time with the march past.'[55] This was only two weeks after the German victory parade in Berlin, and Thiers had the satisfaction of receiving a protest from the Germans, alarmed at this rapidly resurgent militarism.

Three days later, on 2 July, the electors of forty-eight departments 'massively approved' Thiers's rule: in by-elections Republicans won ninety-nine (eighty of them gains) to only twelve won by Royalists and three by Bonapartists. This was the first of a long series of by-elections in which the massive Royalist majority began to melt away as the country turned increasingly towards 'M. Thiers's Republic' as a haven of peace and stability.[56] Another blow was struck at Royalist hopes on 5 July, when the Bourbon pretender, the Comte de Chambord – 'Henry V' – published a letter refusing to make concessions to facilitate his restoration, and insisting that France must renounce the revolutionary tricolour for the Bourbon white flag. The letter marked the beginning of the end of monarchist hopes, for the Orleanists would not accept an absolutist Henry V, while the Legitimists would not allow an Orléans prince to replace him. Chambord, quipped Thiers gleefully, would go down in history as the French Washington – the founder of the Republic.[57]

Thus, in the few weeks that followed the defeat of the Commune, the agenda for the next two years was clearly laid down: national recovery, especially financial and military, in order to end the German occupation and regain liberty of action and prestige at home and abroad; and the form of government, to be fought over by monarchists and Republicans who were themselves divided. National recovery took priority over constitutional disputes. Patriotism and self-interest induced all parties to postpone the trial of strength until the most urgent tasks had been accomplished: paying off the indemnity and completing negotiations with Germany. Here Thiers was still indispensable. He alone had the prestige to reassure domestic opinion, foreign governments and international finance.

As early as August 1871 came a clear sign that Thiers was prepared to steer the Assembly towards a constitutional choice. One of his supporters, Rivet, undoubtedly with his consent or indeed with his prompting, proposed that Thiers should be entitled President of the Republic – an important symbolic step – and also that he should be given a fixed term of office of three years, thus making him more independent of the Assembly. The Right, already suspicious of his intentions, refused to 'abdicate' by giving him a fixed term. He was instead appointed for as long as the Assembly lasted, but his 'responsibility' to it was reaffirmed. The law was voted by

491 to 94, the majority being drawn from the centre groups, with the Legitimists voting against, and Gambetta's radicals (who denied that the Assembly had constituent powers) opposing or abstaining. It was now clear that Thiers was set on founding a durable Republic, the only regime, he believed, that could be both conservative and popular.[58]

For the time being, however, the constitutional question was postponed, and until the spring of 1873 Thiers governed France more completely than any man since his hero Napoleon. He had no political rival. His ministers acted on his detailed instructions, and he often communicated directly with prefects, ambassadors or generals. As throughout his life, his working day began at first light. He would see ministerial colleagues 'as early as possible without too greatly disturbing your habits',[59] and brief friendly journalists while shaving, for as always he carefully cultivated his relations with the press. In April 1871, he had enlisted the support of Henri Vrignault, a professional journalist and editor of the *Bien Public*, which became Thiers's recognized mouthpiece, supported by secret subsidies. A 'quality' evening paper, it reached a substantial middle-class Parisian readership, as well as setting the tone for friendly provincial papers. Thiers was also on close terms with Hector Pessard, editor of the *Soir*, and used several lesser go-betweens – some of them rather dubious figures – to maintain contact with both Right- and Left-wing papers. The rest of the morning would be occupied with meetings and reading and answering papers, with help from his devoted assistant, the professor of literature and Republican deputy, Barthélémy Saint-Hilaire. When the Assembly was sitting, the afternoon and early evening would be taken up with parliamentary business. The rest of the evening would be spent receiving friends and colleagues at home (now the Versailles Prefecture), when Thiers, as usual, did most of the talking except when he took a nap in an armchair. He also held receptions – almost open house – at the Elysée, though he had to hurry back to Versailles by the last train, as he was not permitted by the Assembly to reside in Paris. Cabinet meetings too tended to be monologues – 'insupportable chatter', wrote Rémusat tartly, 'which, with age, tended towards dotage'. Thiers would arrive

> preoccupied by one or two matters, often not the most important, but which interested his mind, his mood or his person . . . he would launch into a panegyric of his ideas, his experience, his firmness, let fly some invective at those not of his opinion, and decorate the whole with irrelevant digressions and unreliable anecdotes. He has spent a two-hour Cabinet like this without any of us managing to get a word in . . . We are invariably obliged to take away our portfolios full without obtaining a decision or a signature . . . This man, so hard-working . . . was in at least half his task slow, negligent, indecisive . . . there was something of the spoilt child in all this, a thing has to amuse him for him to do it . . . Seen from close to, the activity of the government is beneath criticism.[60]

This rings true; and yet, seen from more than a century later, the negligence is undetectable, and what is striking is the grip exercised by Thiers over so many important areas of government: diplomacy, finance, army, internal administration, as well as the business of politics. Reading Thiers's dispatches gives quite a different impression from Rémusat's complaint: his orders were precise, reasoned and short – very different from the complicated if interesting essays he wrote to his subordinates in the 1830s. It may be that Thiers indulged his loquacity in Cabinet because he managed serious business – that which 'amused him' – on his own. As Rémusat admitted, 'his judgement is nearly always exact and sure'; 'the government has done good things, difficult things; . . . it is taken very seriously by France and Europe and perhaps will have a good place in history. And all that it will owe to one man.'[61]

Nowhere was this truer than in the matter of the war indemnity. The sum of 5,000 million francs, equal to the entire state budget for two and a half years, was in the opinion of many well-qualified men – among them Gladstone, Baring, perhaps even Bismarck – difficult or impossible to pay. The state would be financially crippled, the power of Germany in French affairs prolonged, and military reorganization starved of funds. Such a vast sum could hardly be raised at once by increased taxation, nor was it clear that it could be borrowed. No loan of such size had ever been attempted; a Russian flotation had recently failed; while recent French loans had been on very onerous terms. Fortunately, good harvests, an upsurge in foreign trade, and low international interest rates gave a chance of success. Understandably and characteristically, Thiers followed a prudent, orthodox path. The first step was a loan of 2,500 million (later reduced to 2,000) in 5 per cent *rentes* (government bonds), at an attractive rate of return, in close collaboration with the international merchant banks. Ideas for special tax levies, subscriptions or printing money were ruled out, and the French clearing banks were little consulted. To guarantee success, the great banking houses – principally Rothschilds and Barings – underwrote the second *milliard* for a sizeable commission. Thiers's Minister of Finance, Pouyer-Quertier, had fallen in fairly easily with the bankers' plans at a meeting in London, and the main lines had been agreed as early as March 1871: one of the Rothschild's agents assured Baring that 'the risk is not of course insignificant, but . . . the prospects of success are great'. The Paris insurrection interrupted these plans, but on 27 June, after much last-minute negotiation and hesitation, the government floated the loan at a rate of 82.50, giving a high real return of 6.06 per cent. There was plenty of capital looking for such an attractive investment, and the government was offered 4,897 million, more than double what it had asked for. There was criticism that Thiers had been too generous with interest and commission. But it was vital that the loan should succeed, and this, Alphonse de Rothschild later asserted, seemed 'very doubtful to the most competent men of the time. It was in fear and trembling that M. Thiers fixed the first flotation at 2,000 million francs, an enormous sum.'[62]

The success of the first loan made the second a less fearful prospect, even though 3,000 million francs was by far the largest sum ever raised. Thiers was at first doubtful that a second loan could succeed soon after the first, and considered waiting for three years and telling the Germans that they could not pay by the treaty date of 1874. Finally, however, he decided to go ahead in 1872 and end uncertainty. Clearly, he had no plan to hasten the payment of the indemnity for domestic political advantage, but was feeling his way forward as the money markets allowed. As it became clear that the second loan would be covered, interest and commissions were made less generous and spread more widely, with French clearing banks being brought in and eager German banks kept out. Alphonse de Rothschild decided to take a large slice, first as 'a patriotic duty', and second as 'an excellent investment'. For Thiers and the experts the problem was not now raising the money, but paying over the enormous sum to Germany without risking serious monetary and balance of payments problems. Consequently, with the help of the banks (who this time earned their profits here rather than on the loan itself), large quantities of negotiable commercial bills of exchange were bought in advance. The Germans agreed to accept part of the indemnity in this form.[63]

The loan was floated on 28 July 1872, again in 5 per cent *rentes*, but this time at a higher price of 84.50, giving a real return of 5.92 per cent. It was hugely over subscribed, 43,826 million francs being offered by 934,276 would-be investors. In Paris, they queued in a 'fête-like atmosphere'. More than half the offers came from abroad, many from Germany. Thanks to the government's precautions, helped by a large trading surplus and by the money subscribed from abroad, the transfer of funds to Germany caused no balance of payments difficulties, and the exchange rate of the franc was hardly disturbed. 'It was like crossing Niagara on a tightrope with a full glass of water and not spilling a drop.'[64]

This success, taken as evidence of prosperity and strength and a presage of German evacuation of French soil, caused public rejoicing all over the country. Windows were illuminated and bands played in the streets. It was a personal triumph for Thiers. Certainly he had followed expert advice and been helped by favourable circumstances, but his prestige and financial expertise, even if sometimes exaggerated – he was regarded as an expert by those who were not, a critic remarked – had encouraged confidence. As Reuters telegraphed excitedly, 'eagerness country entrust savings state proves that, under Thiers Republic, order, law, property will be respected and that France has confidence in its destiny'.[65]

Thiers's policy was successful and popular; but was it wise? It has been unfavourably compared with that of Germany in the 1920s, paying relatively lighter reparations as slowly and grudgingly as possible. Yet the price was high: military occupation of the Ruhr, financial chaos and catastrophic political instability. France, had she followed a similar policy, would have risked similar consequences. As it was (in the words of one Austrian newspaper), 'France, freed from occupation, will be completely herself again.'[66]

In other areas of national recovery, Thiers's policies commanded less support, and he repeatedly clashed with the Assembly. Unlike most politicians and intellectuals, whether of the Right or Left, he was not convinced that defeat and civil war meant that France was decadent and needed strenuous moral and institutional renewal by the pieties of Catholic royalism or the austerities of radical Republicanism. This was a remarkable change from his attitude in 1848–51, when he had been a leader and spokesman of the 'party of fear'. Now he wanted to reassure the country, to rebuild on existing foundations and follow policies that caused least disturbance and ensured greatest stability. He was convinced that this was what the country needed and wanted. In insisting on it, he stood at times practically alone in the Assembly. The first clash had come in April 1871, when both Left and Right – especially the latter – nostalgic for local freedoms, the nurturing of civic virtue and the exercise of patriarchal influence, wished to loosen central control of local government. Thiers was hostile, insisting that mayors of towns must be nominated, not elected, and that the powers of prefects must remain intact.[67]

A harder struggle occurred over financial reform. The finances of the state had to be restored, the costs of the war met, and the immense debt incurred to pay the indemnity serviced. Thiers insisted that all this could be done by tariffs supplemented by minor increases in the existing (mainly indirect) taxes created by the Revolution. Against him was a large majority in the Assembly: an all-party alliance of free-trade economists of Right and Left, representatives of export industries, trading and financial interests, and agriculture. For more than a year Thiers fought an obstinate parliamentary campaign against them, as hard as any in his career. He used every tactical ruse and exploited his personal authority to the limit, heedless of an opposition that even included many of his habitual protectionist supporters from manufacturing industry, whom he had led in the anti-free-trade campaign of the 1860s.[68]

Thiers's financial opinions were long held. The same arguments and language as in the 1830s and 1840s reappeared in 1871–2: first, protection of 'national industry' as essential for social stability and state power; second, rejection of income tax (and all progressive personal taxation) as arbitrary and oppressive, 'socialism through taxation', 'civil war by finance', unthinkable in a country as politically divided as France where taxation would be a weapon of party strife and class conflict.[69]

He had invented a way of killing these two birds with one stone: a tariff on raw materials. This, he believed, would raise enough revenue to regain financial solvency without income tax, and moreover would restore tariff protection by the side door, for the increase in costs to French manufacturers would be balanced by 'compensatory duties' on foreign goods. Thus French industry would be rescued from what he considered the disastrous effects of the free-trade policies of the 1860s.

The struggle began in June 1871 and reached an angry climax in January 1872, when Thiers, his raw-materials tariff defeated by what he called 'the effrontery of combined vested interests', resigned. Amid general consternation, the Assembly was obliged to bow the knee, voting on 20 January a unanimous motion of confidence in Thiers and appealing to his patriotism. Having thus demonstrated where political power for the moment lay, he consented to return to office. However, he did not immediately have his way. It took months of manoeuvre and debate (during which he was 'like a sparrow on a hot plate') before the raw-materials tariff was finally accepted in July as a central element of a financial strategy acceptable to him. But the Assembly, as stubborn as Thiers, would only agree to a low rate, and so far less revenue was raised than he had hoped. Moreover, his policy became enmeshed in diplomatic complications, as France's trading partners – especially Britain – proved unwilling to accept his interpretation of trade treaties. Consequently, the great battle ended in a draw: Thiers blocked income tax, but failed to engineer a return to protectionism by means of a high tariff on raw materials. After his fall from office the tariff was repealed. This turned out to matter little: what met France's pressing financial needs was a sharp expansion of trade and thus of revenue from the old-established taxes and duties.[70]

It is an example of a not uncommon historical paradox that Thiers's stubborn conservatism had the future on its side. His case for protectionism was strong, and over the next twenty years France followed the United States, Germany and Russia in raising tariffs to protect not only the old-fashioned but also the developing sectors of its economy. Income tax, having been blocked by Thiers when postwar self-abnegation was at a peak, was not to be introduced for forty-five years, amid the necessities of another war, and when greater political stability and internal cohesion made it a less daunting prospect.

Thiers's other conflict with the Assembly, during June and July 1872, concerned the army. The defeats of Sedan and Metz had been defeats of a medium-sized semi-professional army by a huge conscript army, and so most soldiers and politicians, irrespective of party, wished to rebuild the army on the basis of universal conscription. Moreover, nationalists of Right and Left seized on the notion of universal military service as a school of patriotism and national unity. While Thiers was enthusiastic for some reforms – new artillery and an improved high command – for which 1870 had shown the need, he opposed the adoption of what he liked to call 'the Prussian system'. As in 1848 and 1870, he displayed almost proprietary devotion to the methods of the great Napoleon, enshrined in his *History of the Consulate and Empire*. The only good soldiers, he argued, were old soldiers, and the defeats of 1870 were caused not by faults in the military system, but by political blunders. Moreover, selective service was cheaper and easier for the country to bear. His arguments were not unlike those he used in the taxation debates: selective service was like indirect taxation, in that the country was used to it and it caused no disturbance to the social order. Finally – though this was not an argument for public expression – foreign governments (and particularly the German, with whom he was busy negotiating) must not be alarmed by vast military expansion. France, they were assured, was not planning 'revenge' (though Thiers privately told Rémusat that his aim was precisely that), but simply resuming 'her place in the world'. The German government was mollified; it supported Thiers with hints and promises, and with threats in the press that policies other than his would be unacceptable.[71] Thiers's resistance to universal short-term conscription was unpopular in the country as well as among experts. He was unmoved, and again threatened resignation to force the Assembly to vote in 1872 for five-year service, too long a term for its universal application to be feasible.

The debate about detailed army reform then passed to the Conseil Supérieur de Guerre, a committee of senior officers and experts chaired by Thiers. Supported by Cissey, he continued to oppose Prussianization, especially the organization of the army in regional formations, which would make mobilization faster but which would create 'armies of Bretons, Provençaux, Picards', which Thiers thought far too dangerous for France. The reformers were led by MacMahon, whose unresolved disagreements with Thiers over military matters may have made him willing to replace Thiers in the Presidency. After Thiers's fall in 1873, the reformers had much of their way, and his hard-won five-year law (like his raw-materials tariff) was circumvented and soon dropped by its opponents in politics and the administration.[72]

Thiers gladly admitted that he was no innovator; Rémusat noted that his mind was 'as if closed to all that tries to knock from outside, and, as if better to defend the door, he floods the approaches with the torrent of his words . . . things that he has not himself thought have the greatest difficulty in entering'.[73] When experts disagreed, he sided with the more conservative. Considering himself, not without reason, a virtuoso in the techniques of government, he wished to see no fundamental change in the system he had admired and mastered in the 1830s. Stubbornly devoted to his own concep-tion of the good of the state, he was prepared to ignore political and vested interests. If there is a common thread – apart from personal inclination – in his conservatism in this period, it is surely his determination to return to normality and to disturb as little as possible a society seen as satisfactory in its fundamentals and above all needing political repose. It was one of his followers who coined the famous witticism, which he must certainly have appreciated, that France was a country of tranquil people and agitated legislators. His resistance to change had mixed success. Over taxation and provincial administration his victories lasted for 45 and 102 years respectively, but over tariff reform and the army, as has been seen, his victories were hollow. His determination to frustrate the reformist enthusiasm of a broad cross-section of the political class wore many tempers thin: 'M. Thiers alone', wrote a conservative newspaper in January 1872, 'will only manage to reorganize the ruin of France.'[74]

The power to force his views on a reluctant Assembly Thiers derived primarily from his indispensability in foreign affairs. It was undisputed that he was the man who could negotiate with Bismarck and 'liberate the territory'. This was the first step towards restoring France's position as a Great Power: 'when we no longer have the enemy's foot on our throats, then we shall see'. Thiers accepted that recovery would be slow, and that meanwhile French diplomacy had to be prudent and non-committal: *Friends of all the world*, that for some time yet is the conduct that serves France's interests.'[75] He was particularly non-committal with Britain. He had realized during the war that Britain could not or would not help France in Europe: for him, once the leading advocate of the Anglo-French alliance, the *entente cordiale* was no more, though he could envisage at some future time a 'union' of Britain, France and Russia. In the meantime, he was suspicious of British colonial rivalry and above all did not wish to be drawn into Anglo-Russian quarrels. He was flattered to be saluted by a British naval squadron while on holiday near Le Havre, but when British and French officers in the wardroom of *HMS Sultan* talked of 'the common enemy' – 'if it was Prussia I would not be so worried, but probably it was Russia' – he took pains to reassure Russian diplomats that it meant nothing.[76]

His principal concern with Britain was the long and difficult commercial negotiation which he closely supervised. His aim, as noted above, was protection by the side door, but this the British would not permit. Finally a new treaty was agreed in November 1872, 'not as protectionist as I would like, but acceptable for the moment'.[77] Elsewhere his policy was to defend traditional interests as far as obvious French weakness permitted: 'words are no use when we cannot act'. The Algerian revolt was bloodily suppressed by the colonists without involvement of the central government. Quiet support for the papacy as the authority for France's claim to protect Catholic interests, especially in the Levant, culminated in pressing offers to Pius IX to reside in France – even 'advanced Republicans' were in favour – should he decide to leave Rome. In Spain, another area in which France, and Thiers, had traditionally been concerned, he wanted to buttress internal stability by repressing Carlist activity on French soil, if necessary arresting prominent French Royalists involved. In the Mediterranean, he was keen to send a naval squadron to show the flag in the Levant (better than sailing up and down between Nice and Toulon, he thought), but was unwilling to get involved in the affairs of the Suez Canal Company, although he feared English designs on this important French interest: 'even for this . . . I would not like to begin a quarrel of national influence'.[78] His only real priorities were Russia and Germany: 'the most probable alliance for the future seems to be with Russia, but, uncertain of the future that awaits us we must be extremely prudent'. Neither Britain nor Germany must be alarmed. On the contrary, it was in France's interests to reassure Germany so as to end the occupation of French soil. He believed that at least a temporary understanding was in the interests of both countries, for Bismarck too wanted peace, knowing that 'if Europe quarrelled . . . it is natural that we should want to profit from the occasion'.[79]

In his desire to accelerate the end of German occupation, Thiers was obeying the heartfelt wish of the country. The occupation was a humiliation, a means of interference in French affairs, an economic burden and a source of constant friction and even violence between the often heavy-handed occupying troops and the inhabitants. As the peace treaty required, German troops had withdrawn gradually from the northern and Paris regions as the first instalments of the indemnity were paid. But they were to continue to occupy six eastern departments and Belfort as security for payment of the final 3,000 million francs due in 1874. Shortly after the success of the first loan, Thiers, as has been seen, realized that he could raise the whole 5,000 million more quickly than expected. For France to benefit fully, it was necessary to persuade the Germans to withdraw progressively from the still occupied areas as each instalment of the indemnity was paid. But the Germans asserted that the treaty gave them the right to occupy all six remaining departments and Belfort until the very last centime had been received.[80]

Thiers and Bismarck did not meet during the negotiations, which were somewhat hampered by the intrigues of the German ambassador in Paris, Count von Arnim, who disliked the consolidation of the Republic and feared that Thiers was growing dangerously strong. Fortunately the German military commander, General von Manteuffel, acted as a go-between, and he had developed respect and indeed affection for Thiers, who had ensured that his nephew, when sick and a prisoner of war, was well treated. More importantly, Bismarck had decided to encourage stability in France – at least until the indemnity was paid – by helping to keep Thiers in power, and so he was prepared to meet Thiers's wish to hasten evacuation. The principle that progressive payments would bring progressive troop withdrawals was recognized in a convention signed in June 1872. Thiers immediately floated the second loan, and in December was able to promise that final payment would be made during 1873. After much ill-tempered haggling, final agreement was reached in a convention signed in

March 1873: the remaining money was to be paid between June and September, by which time the Germans would have withdrawn all but a small garrison at Verdun.[81]

From a comfortable distance in time it has seemed to some a fairly small advantage that the occupation had been made less onerous and shortened by eight months. But it was received with joy by the country and Thiers seems to have thought that it made his political position impregnable. When the March convention was announced to the Assembly by the Foreign Minister, Rémusat, Thiers was acclaimed, and his supporters proposed the traditional motion that he had 'deserved well of the country'. Striking proof of how far his relations with the Right had soured, however, was their reluctance to vote the motion: one conservative deputy remarked acidly that 'three-quarters of an hour of apotheosis is enough'. Although Thiers's popularity in the country was immense, his very success meant that he was no longer indispensable. Jules Simon remarked to him that the time had come to say his *Nunc Dimittis*.[82]

He departed, though not in peace or willingly, in May 1873 when the Assembly voted its lack of confidence in the political course he was setting for France. He had declared repeatedly that the Republic must be maintained and be conservative. His acceptance of a Republic reflected his belief in the inevitability of historical change and his political realism. He had referred to the possibility of a Republic in France in 1830. During the July Monarchy he concluded, like Tocqueville, that modern societies displayed an inevitable tendency towards democratization, and in consequence he studied the Florentine Republic in an attempt to elucidate the process and its dangers. In 1850 he defined the Republic as 'the government that divides us least'. During the Second Empire, he stayed aloof from projects of Orleanist restoration, and after the 4 September Revolution strongly discouraged the Orléans princes' desire to return to France. On acceding to power, he repeatedly promised to take no part in attempts at restoration, and to preserve the Republic as the established form of government. During the Commune, as has been seen, it was an open secret that he had repeated this to provincial Republicans to dissuade them from supporting the Parisian insurgents. He also resisted Royalist pressure to dismiss Republican prefects.

He believed a Republic to be the only viable conservative regime for France for two reasons. First, it was in his view a 'neutral' form which the ruling classes, dangerously divided by the rivalry of three fallen dynasties, could accept: hence the phrase 'the government that divides us least'. Secondly, acceptance of the Republic would satisfy the moderate Left, respectable and socially conservative men such as Favre, Grévy, Simon, Ferry and Picard, with whom Thiers had worked in the 1860s and during the war and who had supported his government since 1871; and with them they would carry a large body of lower-middle class and peasant voters.

This would leave the extreme Right and Left isolated. Moreover, he hoped that acceptance of the Republic by the Assembly would induce Republicans in the country to accept in return a conservative constitution with a strong executive, a restraining upper chamber and a 'good' electoral law, which could control that still rare and disturbing phenomenon, universal suffrage. 'Strength and justice, these are the only resources against disorderly passions . . . That is what one must ask of liberty, and what I wish to bring out of it.'[83] Such a regime could prevent the fall into despotism that Florentine and recent French history had convinced Thiers was the nemesis of democratic excess, a despotism that brought 'certain and irremediable ruin'.[84]

To secure his conservative Republic, Thiers needed votes from all the centrist groups in the Assembly to overcome the resistance of over 100 Legitimists, who would never agree to constitute a Republic, and of some 200 Republicans who balked at its being made conservative. The Left-Centre (who most closely mirrored Thiers's own evolution from constitutional monarchism to conservative Republicanism) mustered fewer than 100 votes. Therefore, Thiers had to attract substantial support from both the moderate Republicans (*Gauche Républicaine*) and the unconverted Orleanists (Right-Centre) led by the Duc de Broglie: he would need to win about 150 votes from each group, the greater part of their membership. The parliamentary groups, especially those of the centre, overlapped; many deputies were members of more than one group, showing that minds had not been irrevocably made up. In the right circumstances, therefore, Thiers had a chance of creating a majority.[85]

But between Thiers and the Right-Centre deep misunderstanding developed. He, pragmatically indifferent to outworn forms and symbols, had no patience with their Royalist scruples; whereas they regarded his insistence on accepting the Republic permanently as selling the pass. Each mistrusted the other's motives. This misunderstanding bedevilled Thiers's attempts to create a Republic in which the ideological divisions – 'the passions of the parties' – bequeathed by the Revolution would at last be laid aside, and politics become what Thiers perhaps most enjoyed: commonsensical debate about practical policy.

Into the gap between Thiers and the Right-Centre the Radicals, led by Gambetta, drove a wedge. On 9 June 1872, four by-elections took place. Two were won by Radicals. The Right-Centre, alarmed at what they saw as a resurgence of the doctrines of the Commune, sent a deputation to Thiers to insist on his co-operation in a struggle against Radicalism by imposing press controls, purging Republican prefects, and influencing elections. Thiers (supported by the Left-Centre) replied that the only remedy was to abandon thoughts of monarchy and accept the Republic. Broglie believed that this was deliberately to confuse matters: the form of government and the struggle against Radicalism were separate questions. The logic of Thiers's argument, of course, was that they were two aspects

Ni trop de blanc, ni trop de rouge! Mélangeons....

Plate 9 Mixing the red and the white: the 1872 vintage

of the same question, for if the Republic were safe, moderate Republicans would separate from the Radicals. He coolly assured the Right-Centre that they were exaggerating the danger: 'aristocrats like you', he said sarcastically, found the Radicals 'very nasty, very vulgar . . . crude and ill mannered', but 'that's democracy and one can live with an ill-mannered government' – especially as people with Radical ideas 'do not always apply them when they are the masters'.[86] For the time being Thiers – negotiating for the evacuation of French soil – was invulnerable; but to the Right-Centre he had become the tool of the extreme Left.

There was something here of a return by Thiers to his plebeian and revolutionary origins as he paid back the 'aristocrats' for the disdain with which they had often treated him.[87] He believed that the Royalists were rendered powerless by their divisions, and that if they tried to fight him the majority of the country would support him, including the Radicals, who needed him as the most powerful defender of the Republic. Gambetta had indeed been conciliatory, asking the government's permission before undertaking the speaking tours which had contributed to the by-election successes of his party. Thiers had given permission: there was no point in quarrelling with Gambetta amid 'the beneficent calm that reigns' in the country. 'Pacification is our masterpiece', he told the Minister of the Interior, 'and we must try to complete it.'[88]

Thiers was too optimistic. He assumed that once peace and order returned, political agitation would subside, leaving the extremists of Right and Left high and dry. He underestimated both. Although for the time being conciliatory, the Radicals had little love for Thiers, who had called Gambetta a 'raving madman' for continuing the war and had crushed the Commune. While in public Gambetta was complimentary, in private he wrote of Thiers as 'the greedy old man who governs us', who was to be used and compromised: 'he will still struggle often enough in the net which envelops him . . . but at bottom he is powerless to disentangle himself and ruin us'.[89] In the autumn of 1872, sure that the country was calm, Thiers again gave Gambetta permission to go on a speaking tour. His complacency received a shock when on 26 September in Grenoble, Gambetta called for the dissolution of the Assembly, attacked feigned acceptance of the Republic by reactionaries, refused an electoral alliance between true and false Republicans, and proclaimed that 'new social strata' would provide the Republic with a new governing class 'far from inferior to its predecessors'. This outraged conservatives as an appeal to class war. Thiers was summoned from his well-earned holiday at Trouville (where he was happily experimenting on the beach with new models of cannon) to give his comments to members of the Assembly. He seemed and perhaps really was angry, for Gambetta's speech was a direct attack on Thiers's latitudinarian Republic, declaring that far from being neutral and indivisive, a Republican state would be the exclusive domain of proven Republicans.[90]

The Assembly returned in November 1872, and on the 13th Thiers delivered his opening message. No doubt he had been encouraged by five (mostly moderate) Republican victories in six by-elections on 20 October, and by another uncompromising proclamation by the Comte de Chambord which emphasized the split within royalist ranks. In the message he pressed more explicitly than ever for a conservative Republic, making stinging attacks on both Royalists and Radicals in an attempt to rally a centrist majority. In a detailed account of the state of the nation, he declared that the Republic was working satisfactorily. But, he argued, 'the Republic will be conservative or nothing'. Replying implicitly to Gambetta's Grenoble speech, he attacked the idea that by universal suffrage one could bring 'the triumph of one class over another' or 'establish a Republic which would be that of one party, it would last only a day'. In a passage very similar to his notorious 'vile mob' speech of 1850 he declared that agitation of the masses by extremists led inevitably to despotism, when they 'throw themselves into the chance arms of a master, and pay with twenty years of slavery a few days of disastrous licence'. In 1850 the Left had been outraged. This time they cheered, for Thiers's attack on radicalism was completely overshadowed by his firm rejection of a restoration of the monarchy. 'The Republic exists, it is the legal government of the country: to want anything else would be a new revolution, and the most fearsome of all.' In consequence, the Assembly should without delay vote the constitution which Thiers now portrayed not merely as a political convenience, but as the triumph of the great principles of 1789: 'true social justice . . . proclaimed and applied for the first time on earth'.[91]

This speech was felt by the Right 'like boiling oil on an open wound'. Thiers probably miscalculated the effect of his words, as what was apparently meant to be an even-handed attack on Legitimists and Radicals alike was generally interpreted as an attack on the Right alone. He made no attempt to withdraw, however, telling critics on the Right that he welcomed an examination of the message by the Assembly 'in the face of the country' – a scarcely veiled threat of dissolution.[92]

The angry Royalists retaliated by proposing to limit Thiers's right to address the Assembly and to define ministerial responsibility so as to make him a 'political puppet'. He considered resigning and trying to force the Assembly to dissolve. But the continuing negotiations with Germany prevented this *dénouement*: Thiers dearly wished to be the 'liberator' of French soil, and none of his opponents were prepared to disrupt his efforts – they would, wrote Broglie, have been stoned in the streets.[93] So Thiers stayed on.

He also lured the Right into a trap: he agreed to accept their somewhat complicated regulations governing his appearances before the Assembly – which he sarcastically called *chinoiseries* – but only on condition that the Assembly agreed to legislate on the system of government as a whole, not

UN BON PÈRE, par JOB

C'est elle!.. C'est ma fille!

Plate 10   The proud father of the conservative Republic

just his part in it. Otherwise he would regard the *chinoiseries* as an expression of no confidence, and resign. On 29 November, the Assembly duly voted, by 372 votes to 335, to set up a Commission of Thirty to prepare the necessary legislation. This majority was composed of the whole Left (including Gambetta and his followers, who had apparently forgotten their denial of the Assembly's constituent powers), reinforced by what Broglie called 'a sizeable defection of timid conservatives'. The vote was greeted with shouts of 'Vive la République!' The crestfallen Right thought that the Republic was as good as established by an alliance of Thiers and the Radicals. [94]

It soon became clear, to general astonishment, that this was not Thiers's view. Yet his thoughts are not hard to deduce. First, the majority was highly precarious, depending on two dozen Royalist defectors. Moreover, the Radicals could not be depended on to vote the kind of constitutional laws that Thiers wanted, with a strong executive and a restraining second chamber. On the contrary, their true designs were shown by their campaign to have the Assembly dissolved. This culminated in a debate on 14 December which showed the Assembly's real temper: dissolution was rejected by 483 to 196, with the majority of 29 November split down the middle. Thiers's only way of getting a conservative constitution was to seek a majority from among the 483, by winning over a substantial part of the Right-Centre.

He took the initiative over the next few weeks with concessions to the Right reminiscent of the old 'see-saw policy' of the July Monarchy: some Radical newspapers were prosecuted, several conservative prefects appointed and – most important of all – a deputy of the Right-Centre, Goulard, was made Minister of the Interior. 'I oscillate', joked Thiers, 'my ministers see-saw.' The Left was horrified, but for Thiers the important thing was to survive the next few months, finish the negotiations with Germany, and secure a majority for his constitutional laws: 'He calculates his voting figures, that is his whole policy.' [95] After that, the Assembly would dissolve and the future would necessarily lie with the Republic, especially as Thiers would preside over the general elections, lending his prestige to conservative Republican candidates and preventing prefectoral pressure from being used against them.

In his negotiations with the predominately conservative Commission of Thirty he was equally conciliatory. He accepted their *chinoiseries*, and in return Broglie and the Right-Centre agreed to a package of fundamental legislation which – a key concession – would be drafted by the government and presented to the Assembly shortly. Many deputies saw no particular significance in this agreement: but some Legitimists realized that Thiers had baited his trap. The Assembly, warned one, was on 'the slippery slope' to *faits accomplis*. If they voted the proposed measures, asserted another, they would be carrying out 'the last act of [their] constituent power', and Thiers

225

could say that in practice they had followed the advice of his November message and established the Republic; then would come dissolution. This was a prescient warning. Thiers was setting precisely that course and already planning which parliamentary candidates he would support in the general elections – a wide 'moderate' spectrum, excluding only the Legitimists and the Radicals.[96]

In February and March 1873, progress down the slippery slope seemed unstoppable. Thiers was still most careful to conciliate the Right. In an important speech on 4 March the Republican rhetoric of the November message was replaced by a more characteristic appeal to practical common sense: 'Under the Empire I demanded necessary liberties; today I demand necessary institutions.' There need be no proclamations, no miracles, no 'eternal and unalterable' decisions, but simply the minimum of institutions to provide stable government for the immediate future. These were persuasive arguments for all but the most intransigent Royalist, especially as the Comte de Chambord had just made another uncompromising statement that seemed to make a restoration impossible as long as he lived. Broglie himself found Thiers's arguments 'more or less irresistible', and another prominent Royalist, Lacombe, was convinced by the beginning of March that 'constitutional laws are the only resource'; the Right-Centre was 'pleased' and even the Legitimists 'undecided'. The Left – even Thiers's faithful Left-Centre – were worried by his *entente* with the Royalists, and there were comical scenes at Thiers's evening receptions when deputies from rival parties did all that decorum would allow to deny their opponents the President's ear. On one occasion, the Left-Centre deputy Ricard installed himself on a sofa and remained on duty until the last Royalist had left, 'like the first footman of the household'.[97]

Despite the mistrust and recrimination, Thiers's strategy seemed to be working. From 5 to 8 March, the Assembly voted on the composite law regulating the President's prerogatives and ministerial responsibility, and – most importantly – pledging that it would pass laws on the transmission of power that would follow its dissolution, on a second chamber and on electoral qualifications, for all of which the government would draft Bills. Each article was passed by a large majority, with only about 200 Legitimists and Radicals consistently opposing. It seemed not to matter that the majority was racked by doubt and equivocation. For Thiers, all that counted was the vote. He did not conceal his conviction that the only conceivable outcome was the Republic and that the Assembly's days were numbered: one newspaper reported that the constitutional Bills would be presented in May, and that the Assembly would dissolve in October.[98]

Circumstances seemed to favour Thiers. His popularity was so great as to deter his opponents from open conflict: in a general election, predicted one deputy, he could expect 'an incalculable majority'. If the Assembly were to turn down his reasonable-sounding request for 'necessary institutions', it would seem irresponsible and obstructive. With the 'liberation of the territory' in sight, there would be no further excuse to delay the passing of constitutional laws and subsequent dissolution. The Assembly was thus in a cleft stick: to pass the constitutional package meant a step towards dissolution; to refuse meant further unpopularity and the risk of a probably disastrous conflict with Thiers. The majority showed by their votes that as one deputy said, it was 'impossible to maintain the status quo any longer'.[99]

Although his goal seemed to be in sight, Thiers was, thought Broglie, 'sour' at having had to put his relations with the Left in jeopardy in order to conciliate the Right-Centre. He consoled himself that he would soon be able to 'shovel those people out'.[100] The Radicals, however, were unwilling to wait for his stratagems to bear their Republican fruit, especially as a 'conservative Republic' was for them a contradiction in terms. Their counter-attack came over the city government of Lyons, in the hands of Radicals whose doubtfully legal anti-clerical acts outraged the Catholics. Thiers was inclined to turn a blind eye, repeating, as he generally did, that left alone things would calm down. In the case of Lyons he had particular reason to be unworried: ever since the Commune he had had an understanding with the local Republicans and their leader Hénon, who regarded him as the bulwark of the Republic. During the summer of 1871, Thiers had protected Hénon, his deputy Barodet and their colleagues from the reactionary zeal of the regional military commander.[101] However, the Right-Centre Minister of the Interior, Goulard, went ahead with a Bill to abolish the Lyons municipality, which was voted on 4 April 1873. This was the kind of anti-radical measure the Right was eager to undertake, with or without Thiers. The Radicals replied by choosing the deposed mayor of Lyons, Hénon's successor Barodet, as candidate in a by-election to take place in Paris on 27 April.

Thiers, however, hoping to take advantage of his successful negotiations with Germany to win proof of popular support, had already arranged for his Foreign Minister and old friend Rémusat to stand in the same election. Rémusat could not withdraw without humiliating the government. Gambetta, ignoring the protests of the moderate Left and the doubts of many Radicals, would not permit Barodet to withdraw either. 'Your friends are mad', protested Thiers to a leading Radical. 'Don't they see that they are playing the Royalists' game . . . ? They will be responsible for my fall'. Gambetta was indeed prepared to go as far as that if Thiers persisted in trying to constitute a conservative Republic with the aid of the Right-Centre. More than a million posters were put up in the first 'American-style' campaign in France, and the turnout was high. Barodet won decisively, beating Rémusat by 45,000 votes. There was consternation in conservative and centrist circles at what appeared to be a 'revenge of the Commune'. Thiers protested with some reason that the vote was directed not against himself but against the Right. Even so, the Radicals were clearly not under the control of Thiers and his moderate allies.[102]

The Right-Centre, and even some of the Left-Centre, concluded that Thiers must go. Broglie and many of his supporters, their hopes of restoration for the time being dashed, had been willing to acquiesce in Thiers's idea of a conservative Republic. But the electoral successes of Radicalism brought out the fundamentally different interpretation that they gave to that term. Thiers, taking a long-term view, meant that a Republic was the only regime strong enough to be conservative – 'the only government ... that can speak to democracy with sufficient authority'.[103] But to Broglie and his followers it meant that in return for their recognizing a 'provisional interim' Republic 'at least momentarily', Thiers should relinquish power to a government of monarchists which would repress Radicalism while tacitly maintaining 'legal and easy access' to a monarchist restoration when Chambord changed his mind or died.[104] Thiers's objection was that 'one can crush a rising with cannon shot, but one cannot lead universal suffrage like that'.[105] Broglie was contemptuous: Thiers he wrote, had grown too old to 'begin a struggle with a power that has broken so many thrones and spilt so much blood ... M. Thiers has never passed for a hero.'[106]

With his wings crumbling and his centre giving way, Thiers fought back. 'I am making a last effort', he wrote, 'without knowing what the result will be. But it will be the last.'[107] A Cabinet reshuffle eliminated Goulard. On 19 May, the government presented its draft constitution, which provided for a strong executive President, elected by Members of Parliament and representatives of local authorities; a Senate to which only certain categories of notables would be eligible (such as generals and members of the Institut – 'very few hooligans there', commented Thiers);[108] and a Chamber elected by universal suffrage, but which the President would have the right to dissolve. This accorded with many of the ideas of the Right-Centre, but now they would not even discuss it, joining the Legitimists and the Radicals in refusing it a debate. Instead, they tabled a hostile motion aimed at bringing Thiers down. On 23 May, Broglie, opening the debate, attacked him as the 'dupe' of the Radicals, and had the satisfaction of seeing him 'start as if stung'.[109] Restricted by the *chinoiseries*, Thiers could not reply until next day, and the ministers who did speak proved feeble substitutes. It was not certain that he would be defeated and he seems to have retained a cautious optimism. Even defeat would not be the end: he doubted that the Right would manage to agree on a successor or a policy, and expected to be back in power 'in three months'.[110] Yet certain passages in his defiant speech on 24 May suggest a proud farewell: 'I do not fear for my memory, for I do not accept the judgement of the parties ... but I submit myself to the judgement of history, and I deserve to appear before it.' He made no concessions to the Right, but forcefully repeated the arguments of his November message: only a Republic was viable; it had served France well;

monarchy was impossible and so to support it was irresponsible; a Republic must be moderate, and would be but for monarchist agitation. The Right, he asserted, had no majority except with Bonapartist support, and their only recourse was to dictatorship: 'the dictatorship of great men ruined you; that of little men ruins you no less, and ... without the glory!'[111]

The *chinoiseries* required the session to be interrupted and the vote to be taken in Thiers's absence. His eloquence was to be afforded no further opportunity to sway waverers. He had 'laughed at what he called our *chinoiseries*', recalled Broglie, but 'the only day they were applied he did not laugh at all'. The defection of a sub-group of the Left-Centre and the support of the Bonapartists enabled the no-confidence motion to be carried by sixteen votes. It was a straight vote of Right against Left, with all from the Left-Centre to the Radicals voting for Thiers – the first round of a struggle that would last for the next six years, and leave traces as long as the Third Republic lasted. 'I am more conservative than any of you', wrote Thiers to a Royalist deputy. 'You thought you were safeguarding future elections, and I fear you have ruined them. It was necessary to pacify, and you have angered. That is what has been done for fifty years, and no government can become established ... You have all served the Radicals more than the conservatives.'[112]

Although his term of office lasted as long as the Assembly itself, he resigned at once: there was no advantage in compromising himself as the figurehead of a Broglie government. Marshal MacMahon, whom Thiers was convinced would refuse to succeed him, had already been won over by the Right. He was elected by 390 votes, the whole of the Left abstaining.

The reign of 'Adolphe I', as Bismarck called him, has been harshly judged. The 'judgement of history', swayed by the testimony of his political opponents, has tended to explain his acts in personal terms: 'senile ambition' (as one of them put it) led him to any expedient to retain power. Thiers was, of course, ambitious; also vain, self-opinionated and cantankerous; and he gloried in a popularity he had never before known. Broglie commented venomously that Thiers was 74 years old and childless, implying that, heedless of the future of the country, he thought only of enjoying present power and glory. But Broglie himself admits that had Thiers sided with the monarchists they would have given him power – he could have had a seven-year tenure and 'finished his days in a semi-royal position'.[113] It was surely because Thiers was 74 and childless that he *did* think of the future – of his 'memory' and his 'half a line in universal history'. His ambition was to assure the liberation and recovery of France after a crisis even worse than that of 1815 and to establish the first stable regime since 1789: 'the Republic, natural government of democracy, will be, in time, the final form of government of our country'.[114]

But it was not to be precisely Thiers's Republic; what Pomaret harshly called the Republic of reason, opportunism and egoism. The Third Republic did not escape opportunism and egoism, but it added a sectarianism that Thiers had wished to avoid. Could he have succeeded? He believed to the end that had his advice been followed a conservative Republican constitution might have been obtained from the Assembly, followed by dissolution and 'moderate' elections, and that broadly accepted ideological truce could have ensued. But he was too hurried and too high-handed; Gambetta too impatient; Broglie too short-sighted and suspicious. We should not, however, ascribe his failure solely to the personal and the incidental, for it demonstrates a recurring characteristic of French politics: a centrist position was difficult to sustain electorally. However much the moderate Left and the moderate Right might agree upon practical questions, over the great symbolic issues – Monarchy, Republic, the Church – they were forced to choose sides. Thiers, always contemptuous of what he called 'the passions of the parties' – both their ideological shibboleths and their material ambitions – thought that such questions could simply be laid aside.

A further difficulty was that the centre groups were composed of notables, and were organizationally weak. Legitimists and Radicals had their organizing committees, their activists, their enthusiastic followers. Neither the Left-Centre nor the Right-Centre did. Consequently, Thiers, in spite of his popularity and strong backing in the press, found himself without organized support in the country or a disciplined majority in the Assembly. It is striking that Thiers, the great advocate of parliamentary government, had never tried hard to create his own party in Parliament (in the old days he had relied on Duvergier to be 'chief whip') or to master the electoral side of politics (for which he had relied on his friends to act as agents). In 1873 he was popular enough to have won a plebiscite, yet he fell because his parliamentary majority did not trust him and because he could not ensure that his supporters won by-elections. He tried almost single-handedly to redraw the map of French politics and failed. It would be many generations before a regime emerged that enjoyed the consent of the whole nation, and so met Thiers's criterion by which 'the Republic is a contradiction in terms if, instead of being the government of all, it is the government of a party'.[115]

[12]

The Last Four Years

A statesman vacating high office often has to leave his official residence with what, to a private individual, seems indecent haste in order to make way for his successor. So it was with Thiers and his ladies in May 1873. Moreover, since their old house in the Place Saint-Georges was not yet rebuilt, they had no home of their own to go to. They stayed for a while with a relation of Madame Thiers and then rented a house in the Faubourg Saint-Honoré, the Hôtel Bagration. It was May 1875 before they were able to return to the Place Saint-Georges.

The new house, built with the aid of a state grant of 1,050,000 francs, closely resembled the old but was slightly more imposing. Madame Waddington, the wife of a future Prime Minister, remembered it as big and gloomy, but the German Ambassador, Prince Hohenlohe, described it as 'pretty, with a green lawn in front, and on the other sides a well-kept garden with turf and trees'. Thiers's bedroom, he noted, was also his writing-room. It looked on the garden and was 'very delightful'. The bed had a green silk damask cover with curtains to match.[1]

As of old, Thiers's home was much used for entertaining as well as study. On Sundays there was usually a gathering of old friends, joined sometimes by scientists and learned foreigners and, in the evenings, probably soon after his fall from power, he had resumed his salon. Hohenlohe gives us a glimpse of one evening in February 1875 when the family were still at the Hôtel Bagration:

> There were some elderly gentlemen with Thiers. Amongst them Emanuel Arago ... Madame Thiers slept soundly, Mademoiselle Dosne dozed from time to time. Thiers sat at the fire, and related to Princess Trubetzkoy and Arago his experiences during the revolution of February 1848 ... and how he ... was seized by the throat, and dragged about on the ground in the Place de la Concorde. 'Mais le people n'est plus méchant. Ils m'ont un peu secoué, mais je n'en ai pas eu grand mal.'[2]

But it was not just aged friends and savants and a stray princess who visited the Hôtel Bagration or the house in the Place Saint-Georges of an evening. As in the old days there were active politicians and diplomats, among the latter, besides Hohenlohe, the Russian ambassador, Prince

Orlov, and the American Minister, Washburne. One of the politicians later even claimed that the salon of the Place Saint-Georges 'was the real centre of opposition to the regime inaugurated on 24 May'.[3]

Thiers had assumed great responsibilities and worked like a Trojan since September 1870. Freed from office at the age of 76 he might have been expected to rejoice in the opportunity to rest and devote the remainder of his days to his *chères études*. But this was not so. As we have seen he did indeed renew his scientific interests and made a determined attempt to begin the grandiose philosophical work which, he told a journalist, was to be his last will and testament,[4] but he no more thought of abandoning politics than did his contemporaries Gladstone, Disraeli and the Russian Foreign Minister, Prince Gorchakov, or, for that matter, than would many twentieth-century septuagenarians for whom politics was the breath of life.

In several ways the pattern of his life in the mid-1870s resembled that of earlier periods of his career when he was out of office. Having, in Rémusat's words, been driven from the Presidency as unceremoniously as a steward dismissed by a *grand seigneur*, he might understandably be resentful and, since he still enjoyed relatively good health, periodically harbour the hope of return to power. This being so, he was inevitably looked to as a leader of opposition, someone of whose views and intentions it was important to be apprised, but, as in the 1840s, he bore the demands of leadership lightly and did so with much more justification now that he was an elder statesman. He again found time for travel, apart from journeys within France, going to French-speaking Switzerland three years running and in 1874 paying a last visit to Italy where he spent lavishly on *objets d'art* to reconstitute the collection destroyed by the Commune.

There were, however, notable differences from the 1840s. Although Thiers resumed his seat in the Assembly as a simple deputy only three days after resigning the Presidency and was loudly cheered by the Left on his reappearance there, he spoke in only one debate, in March 1874, on fortifications, on which he had so long regarded himself as an expert. Old friends like Duvergier more than once urged him to intervene on wider topics, but he did not respond.[5] Again, in the Parliament which succeeded the Assembly in 1876 he spoke only in committee as President of the Army Commission, not in public discussion. His abstinence in the Assembly was for reasons of dignity: 'if it were necessary to speak to the country perhaps I should be the speaker most likely to be heard by it; but when it is a matter of addressing the Chamber with which I had broken on 24 May, other speakers will be more welcome'.[6] Later, in 1876–7, he may well have felt too frail to embark on the long set speeches which he used wrongly to believe were required of him. Hence his opposition leadership was mainly exerted behind the scenes and his public speaking addressed to deputations of admirers. But he could still make his views more widely known in the *Bien Public* until it was bought by the chocolate manufacturer Menier in

January 1876, and thereafter he occasionally inspired articles in the *Journal des Débats*.[7] He seldom forgot the importance of the press.

During the four years that followed his fall the Republicans, with whom he had been forced to throw in his lot, had three main battles to fight. The first was to counter the danger of a Monarchist restoration, which seemed imminent in the summer and autumn of 1873; the second to secure an explicitly Republican constitution, a goal achieved in 1875; and the third to resist the Right-wing counter-offensive of 1877 after Thiers's successor, MacMahon, in what is known as the *Seize Mai* crisis, had virtually dismissed his Republican ministers and, with the aid of a new Right-wing government, secured the dissolution of the Chamber of Deputies and the holding of fresh elections. Many people feared that these events would be the prelude to a *coup d'état* should the Right fail to secure an election victory.

In each of these struggles the veteran Thiers was more or less active. He was never so popular with the growing number of Republicans as after his fall. His prestige was great and he attracted respect and sympathy not only because of the manner of his fall but because it was he who had negotiated the terms under which Germany's occupying troops were to quit French soil. In August 1873, on his way to Switzerland, he was enthusiastically greeted at Belfort and Mulhouse, and when Nancy was evacuated earlier in the month the city was placarded with inscriptions such as 'Honneur à Thiers!', 'Honneur au petit bourgeois!' Moreover, acclaim came not merely from townsfolk or the middle classes. On 15 September, the day before the last German soldier was due to leave, Jules Ferry, a native of St Dié close to the new eastern frontier, wrote a remarkable letter to one of his friends:

> Here the restoration of divine right is a lost cause. The peasant is *thiériste* for the time being . . . M. Thiers's name has taken the place of Gambetta's in the enthusiasm of the crowds . . . The 'little bourgeois" picture is in every cottage and the poor annexed people of Alsace have inserted his name in little children's prayers. The children recognize him when they turn the pages of the family album and point him out with their fingers, saying 'Uncle Thiers'.[8]

Moreover, Thiers now had a new title to be applauded: in 1874 at Ouchy in Switzerland and at Arcachon he was hailed as 'the liberator of the territory'.

Meanwhile he had been diligent in the battle against restoration. In a letter of 29 September 1873 to the Mayor of Nancy he declared that restoration would endanger 'all France's rights, her civil, political and religious liberties, her flag, her social condition and the principles of 1789'.[9] A week later an English diplomat reported that the ex-President was 'the virtual leader of all the anti-Conservative forces'.[10] But he did not have to fight this particular anti-Conservative battle much longer. The flag was the crucial issue. At home in France it appeared that the Legitimists and Orleanists had at last buried the hatchet and agreed upon the 'fusion' vainly attempted in

1849–51. Preparations were made to draft a constitutional Bill whereby the Legitimist Pretender, the Comte de Chambord, would become king with the title of Henri V, while the flag essential to the Orleanists who had restored it in 1830, the tricolour, would be maintained. But on 30 October a Legitimist paper published a letter from Chambord reaffirming his inability to sacrifice his honour or abandon the white flag of the Bourbons. The Pretender himself had dealt the death-blow to his restoration. On hearing the news, Thiers, who had had so many dealings with French Monarchists during his long career, is said to have exclaimed: 'They are incorrigible!' and added that, to show that he could make something still more stupid than democrats, God had created aristocrats and then rested, realizing that he could go no further.[11]

The Monarchists were in disarray, but they still had a majority in the Chamber and could either delay the making of a constitution or hope to establish one which would avoid overt recognition of the Republic and keep the way open for the Comte de Paris, should Chambord, who was childless, die before too long. Their first step was to extend MacMahon's term of office to seven years, their second to resist Republican efforts to secure a Republican constitution. For their part the Republicans sought to whittle away the Monarchists' majority both by winning as many by-elections as possible and by clever tactics and propaganda within the Assembly and the country as a whole.

In this second battle it was essential for the Republicans to stay united and to present the Republic in a reassuring guise. Here two men, Thiers and Gambetta, played a key part. Although as yet there seems to have been little intimacy between them – Thiers's wartime epithet, 'raging madman', still rankled with Gambetta – and although in the Assembly, despite Gambetta's efforts to achieve a fusion, the Republicans were divided into three groups, they worked to the same end. Thiers took a keen interest in the by-elections and, while Gambetta occasionally complained of his greed in trying to get Republicans of his own persuasion adopted,[12] there were no serious rifts.

As of old, Thiers had resumed his role as a leader of the Left-Centre in Parliament.[13] The Republicans of his own persuasion who were his closest political associates, although they did not all see eye to eye on protection, were mostly men of substance such as Léon Say, Jules Simon, Marcère, Casimir-Perier, son of the minister of 1831–2, Waddington, a former Cambridge rowing blue and subsequently Prime Minister, and Calmon, the friend who later edited Thiers's speeches. Through them he could hope to win over large numbers of the middle classes to the conservative Republic that continued to be his goal. The tactics of 'Major-General Thiers', as 'Royalist prints' were alleged to have called him, in lobbies and parliamentary *conciliabula* are ill-documented, but outside Parliament when he received deputations from Frenchmen at home and abroad he seldom lost the opportunity to point out that a conservative Republic was essential to avert civil war and facilitate productive labour.[14] This was his theme, too, when he was abroad; his Italian tour in the autumn of 1874 was called by one paper a kind of 'propagandist progress' on behalf of the Republic; his friend Barthélemy Saint-Hilaire wrote of its 'triumphs'.[15]

Significantly and shrewdly Gambetta in June 1874 paid a public tribute to 'the illustrious citizen' who had given 'experienced parliamentarians, great landowners, important industrialists, great merchants, considerable citizens of all kinds' an example in sacrificing his old opinions to the higher interest of France.[16] Shrewdly, too, Thiers let the Left-Centre make the running in bringing the constitutional issue to the fore. They were aided to some extent by a resurgence of Bonapartism, which followed the collapse of the Monarchists' hopes of restoration. Bonapartism was a useful bogey and it can hardly have been without Thiers's approval that Casimir-Perier moved that, in view of the Bonapartist threat, the Assembly's Constitutional Committee should organize the Republic on the basis of a Bill put forward by one of Thiers's ministers, Dufaure, a few days before his fall in 1873, or that, when this was turned down, another of Thiers's henchmen proposed that general elections should be held in September and that the Assembly should dissolve immediately afterwards. This was rejected by only twenty-nine votes. Most people then thought that, once the Assembly gathered after its long summer vacation, it would have to produce a constitution or leave the task to a new Parliament.

They were right. The battle for the constitution resumed in January and February 1875. Thiers was not a member of the Constitutional Committee and played no public part in the proceedings apart from casting his vote, but it was no doubt with his blessing that the Left-Centre again pressed for Casimir-Perier's wording. This time it was rejected by twenty-three votes, but on the following day an amendment proposed by a quiet, scholarly deputy named Wallon was carried by a majority of one. This was the historic vote that made the Third Republic, for the words 'the President of the Republic' appeared in the second clause. The first article of the organic law of 25–8 February, in which this clause was finally embedded, declared that the legislative power was to be exercised by two assemblies. Here Thiers had evidently played an important part behind the scenes in over-coming resistance from the Left rather than from the Right. As a French political scientist has observed, the strength of Republican opposition to a second chamber which might put a brake on rash policies is curious: 'it needed all Thiers's finesse and all Gambetta's presence of mind to secure the acceptance of the Senate'.[17] Otherwise, as Rémusat's son remarked, Thiers contented himself with 'voting in ironic silence for a constitution . . . that strongly resembled the one he had put forward two years earlier and which had led to his fall'.[18]

The Republicans had won their constitutional victory by the narrowest of margins; they still had to clinch it by getting a majority of their own men

235

Plate 11 The key to the situation (June 1874)

into the new Parliament. Before elections could be held, however, the mode of voting had to be decided, and on this they were not agreed. In 1873 Thiers had favoured *scrutin d'arrondissement* whereby each department was divided into constituencies according to its population and each constituency entitled to one deputy; it was a system which was supposed to favour local influences. But by September 1875 he had come to prefer the rival method of *scrutin de liste* in multi-member constituencies. His reasons were that the times were exceptional and that this was the only way to produce a homogeneous and moderate Assembly. Gambetta, too, strongly favoured *scrutin de liste*, but when the issue was put to the vote it was rejected despite his eloquence. The government was said to have preferred *scrutin d'arrondissement* because it feared that with *scrutin de liste* Thiers might be as successful as in February 1871 and thus greatly embarrass his successor.[19]

In October 1875 Thiers made an important speech at Arcachon with an eye to the forthcoming elections. He emphasized the need to ensure the success of the Republic now that it had been voted for; at the same time he admitted his own conservatism and reminded his hearers of the tasks ahead: France still had her financial system to complete, her military legislation to revise, her commercial treaties to renew, and her education to develop 'in accordance with the basis of modern society' – a phrase which he forbore from clarifying.[20] The elections themselves took place in three phases: the choice by the outgoing Assembly of the seventy-five senators who were to hold office for life, the election of the remaining 225, and, finally, the election of the deputies. Of Thiers's activities during the election period we have only occasional glimpses. When, in the hard bargaining over the choice of Life Senators Gambetta in masterly fashion exploited Monarchist divisions, Thiers warmly encouraged him to 'sweat the last sovereign from the cards', while on occasion he fought vigorously for the selection of one of his own supporters.[21] In the elections for the remaining senators in February 1876 84 of the 149 successful Republicans were members of the Left-Centre – there was little doubt that the Senate, which Thiers regarded as 'excellent', would be a conservative body after his own heart.[22] Without being a candidate he himself was elected for Belfort – a nice gesture by the still grateful citizens of the town he had saved from annexation by Germany – but he preferred to try his chance once more as a candidate for the Chamber of Deputies. Throughout his long parliamentary career he had always sat in the lower house. After toying with a candidature in the North he stood in the 9th Paris *arrondissement*, which included the Saint-Georges district, and was elected by 10,399 to his opponent's 5,923 votes.

Meanwhile it is to be noted that if, as someone remarked, Thiers when abroad had been a counterpart of Gambetta at home, a commercial traveller selling the Republic,[23] such influence as he still exercised in foreign affairs was all in favour of peace and at least a measure of reconciliation with Germany. Thus he continued to be in touch with Manteuffel and made a point of being on good terms with the new German ambassador, Hohenlohe. Furthermore, in 1875, when there was a scare that Germany was projecting a fresh attack on France, he is said to have offered his services to the government if they thought he could help dispel misunderstanding,[24] while at Arcachon that autumn he tried to pour oil on the lately troubled waters by drawing an idyllic picture of a peaceful Europe in which everyone was everyone else's ally.[25] As we have seen, his real hope was probably for an alliance with Russia, but for the time being there is little doubt that he continued in the opinion he had so firmly expressed in 1872, that it was in France's best interest to be the friend of all the world.[26]

By the time he became a deputy in the first Chamber of Deputies of the Third Republic, which met for the first time in March 1876, he was nearly 79 and inevitably beginning to show his age; yet despite two indispositions before June 1877, his health appeared to be generally good.[27] In August 1875 he had redrawn his will for the last time and, apart from certain specific bequests, had left everything first to his wife and then to his sister-in-law. Since a great part of his fortune came, he wrote, from the Dosne family, it was right that it should return to it.[28] He had outlived several old friends, colleagues, or former antagonists. Guizot and Ledru-Rollin had both died in 1874, and he had attended the funerals of Odilon Barrot in 1873 and of his good friend Rémusat in 1875. His greatest loss, however, was to come when he was 80. In May 1877 he was overwhelmed with grief at the sudden death of his 'incomparable friend' of twenty-years' standing, Malvina, Duchesse d'Albuféra. In her company, he told Princess Julie Bonaparte, he had found a calm refuge in which there was 'sweetness, exquisite good sense, incomparable kindness and, above all, a loftiness of feeling which made one feel transported with her to a height above everything that surrounded one'.[29]

By then he was engaged in the last of the three great battles, the fight against MacMahon and the Right-wing government called to power in May. In an interview in September 1875 he had said that he had no notion of resuming office, for 'that would be a sign that France has not yet settled down'.[30] But there is little doubt that he cherished hopes of being President once more. In January 1876 Hohenlohe reported that Thiers (never afflicted by false modesty) 'considered himself more and more as the only decisive personality', and in March 1877 Thiers told Marcère that he would never guess how many letters he received from people who asked if he would not return to power.[31]

When the Marshal as good as dismissed his Republican Prime Minister, Jules Simon, on 16 May, Simon's first act was to seek Thiers's advice. The two men agreed not to resist but to leave the President with the full burden of responsibility for his rash action.[32] A few days later both were among the 363 deputies who signed a protest against that action which they regarded as against the spirit if not the letter of the constitution. The fight was on and Thiers and Duvergier de Hauranne could think themselves back in 1830 in the days of the struggle of the 221 against Polignac.[33]

When, as Thiers put it in a letter at the end of June, 'maniacs, fools' were fouling the poor country on the reefs on which she had so often been wrecked,[34] it was evident that France had not settled down. He hoped, he told Hohenlohe, that the Republicans would return 400 strong and that the Marshal would in consequence resign.[35] In a speech on 31 May Gambetta had already designated him as the most suitable replacement and, despite a later profession of reluctance, there is little doubt that Thiers rejoiced at the prospect. His prestige and experience made him the 'ace in the Republican pack',[36] an ace whose value had been movingly enhanced by an unforeseen incident in a debate on 16 June. Upon the Minister of the Interior referring to the National Assembly as having liberated the territory, someone pointed to Thiers sitting in his place and cried 'There is the liberator of the territory!' Thereupon the Left and Centre rose to their feet and applauded their octogenarian colleague for several minutes. It was an emotional scene which caught the public imagination and brought Thiers more than ever into the limelight.

He enjoyed being there and in the next two and a half months was busy advising, warning and encouraging the Republican forces mustering for the election campaign which followed the Marshal's dissolution of the Chamber. But the main brunt of the Republican effort naturally fell upon younger men, especially the most eloquent and forceful of them, Gambetta. The names of Thiers and Gambetta were constantly coupled in Republican propaganda by word and image. The 'vieux de la montagne Saint-Georges'[37] and the man half his age (Gambetta was 39) were now on good terms and seemingly made tentative plans for the aftermath of a Republican victory. According to one source Thiers would ask Gambetta to form a Cabinet and take charge of foreign policy. He had already in July presented him to Hohenlohe, now he would 'present him to Europe'.[38] Gambetta, for his part, told a friend that it would be necessary to form a strong ministry and carry out an administrative purge (the government had installed many Right-wing prefects and other officials), but that they would have to be patient concerning reforms, 'for M. Thiers is always M. Thiers', by which he no doubt meant still wedded to the idea of a conservative Republic.[39]

These plans never materialized. At Saint-Germain-en-Laye towards the end of August Thiers was busy as ever, writing and revising his election manifesto – he was standing for re-election in the 9th *arrondissement* – receiving politicians, among them Waddington, Marcère and the Italian statesman Crispi, and planning to meet Gambetta in Paris on the afternoon of 3 September. On 1 September a cartoon depicted him giving a helping hand to Father Time 'who was portrayed in the last stages of decrepitude, no longer able even to carry his scythe . . . of which his companion had kindly relieved him'.[40] But the Foreign Minister, Decazes, who was of course in the opposite camp, had been told that Thiers's doctor was pessimistic, and he himself wrote contemptuously to the French ambassador in Berlin: 'Thiers no longer exists either as an intelligence or as an influence. The sad old man is nothing but an unconscious instrument of the great conspiracy which flatters and exploits him.'[41]

The end came suddenly. On 3 September he had a choking fit at lunch, asked for fresh air, was escorted on to the terrace but started shivering and went to bed. Soon afterwards he lapsed into a coma and some hours later died. In July, speaking to Hohenlohe about the Presidency, he had said that he could not avoid his duty to his country, 'though it should cost him his life'.[42] The strain and excitement of his last battle had indeed meant that that was the cost.

After hearing the news of his death Bismarck expressed sincere regret and called on his companions to drink in silence to his memory; while Thiers's near contemporary, Gorchakov, exclaimed that another light had gone out at a time when so few people could see clearly.[43] For many people Thiers's passing marked the end of an era.

The government immediately decreed a state funeral, but Madame Thiers wished herself to fix the order of the ceremony and the authorities were unable to agree that this should be regulated by a private individual. Nevertheless there was an impressive ceremony in which troops played their part and the mourners, after hearing the Agnus Dei in the church of Notre Dame de Lorette not far from the Place Saint-Georges, processed to the family resting-place in the celebrated cemetery of Père Lachaise. Many Republicans who took part were greatly moved: Jules Ferry thought it 'the most touching and imposing spectacle men had ever looked upon', and Gambetta, with characteristic southern hyperbole, called it the most magnificent ceremony of the century: 'Caesar returning from Gaul met nothing like it in Rome and Bonaparte had no such civic splendours after Austerlitz.' Above all both men were impressed by the respectful orderliness of the great crowds of spectators who stood for hours in the rain. 'What could be more surprising', wrote Gambetta, 'and at the same time more politically reassuring than this passionate crowd of the people of Paris who six years ago were bombarded, shot down and bled white by M. Thiers and now . . . have the courage to pardon the victor and number him among the gods?'[44]

Thiers had died, said one contemporary, like Moses, in sight of the Promised Land. Yet for a while the Promised Land partly receded. When the elections took place in October 1877, the 363 returned not 400 strong but a mere 326 and, although they still had a majority of 119 over the Right, MacMahon did not resign for another fifteen months. The Republicans had obviously been dismayed by Thiers's death, which the Right had done their best to exploit, and between him and Jules Grévy, the man the Republicans chose as his successor, there was, as Duvergier said,

Plate 12　Thiers's funeral procession

'a huge distance';[45] Grévy had none of Thiers's vivacity, governmental experience, or European prestige. It is impossible to know how much difference Thiers's death made to the Republican vote but it is probable that it confirmed MacMahon in his decision to stay at his post. For Thiers himself, however, Tacitus's phrase is apposite: he was 'felix opportunitate mortis'. When MacMahon did eventually resign on 30 January 1879 Thiers, had he lived, would have been only a little over two months short of his eighty-second birthday. Although Decazes's judgement was too harsh and there is no justification for thinking that 'the grand old man', as Gambetta called him after his death,[46] was a mere puppet in the hands of Gambetta and his friends, there were indications that his powers had, not surprisingly, begun to diminish. He never got to grips with the great philosophical book that was to have been his last will and testament; he had become too prone to reminisce; and while his last written work, his election manifesto of which, it is true, he had only time to revise a part, contained interesting points it was far too long. He would indeed have been 'a sad old man' if the electors in 1879 had thought him too frail to be President or if, once elected, he had become too feeble to perform the duties of the office which he had formerly filled with such energy and devotion.

[13]

Conclusion

Thiers's death marked the end of an unstable era punctuated by revolutions and overshadowed by the great Revolution of 1789 of which he had been the popular historian. He had played a part in each of France's nineteenth-century revolutions, in 1830 aged 33 opposing counter-revolution, in 1848 aged 51 appearing to have become a counter-revolutionary, and in 1870–1 helping to pick up the pieces after a great disaster, crushing another insurrection, and establishing a new regime. Born under the First Republic, he had lived under seven regimes. None of the first six had lasted more than eighteen years, but the last, the Third Republic, of which he was a prime founder, endured for seventy. Once a protégé of Talleyrand (born in 1754), and a disciple of Baron Louis (born in 1755), he had lived to be a father-figure to young Republicans such as Gambetta, Ferry, and Waldeck-Rousseau. His was a remarkable life which embraced three careers and which, despite many apparent paradoxes, was remarkably consistent.

To understand Thiers's life and how contemporaries saw it, it is important to remember some salient features of his make-up and background. First, we should recall that, like the much younger Gambetta, he was one of the few southerners to play a dominant part in French politics in the century after Napoleon's overthrow. He had a southerner's fluency and vivacity and, despite his apparent self-confidence, something of the mercurial temperament often attributed to men of the south – his private letters sometimes revealed moods of great despondency. Secondly, he was exceptionally small, and this was of fundamental importance. Small stature sometimes goes with extraordinary vitality, intelligence and capacity for hard work. So it was with Frederick the Great, with Napoleon, the man Thiers so much admired, and to a lesser degree with Thiers's contemporary, the Socialist Louis Blanc and, later, with Théophile Delcassé, the well-known Foreign Minister. To make themselves seen, heard and felt, very small boys and young men, not born in the purple, have to be particularly self-assertive. Thiers had a compulsive need to be up and doing, the intelligence to discern what he could do with greatest advantage, and the strong constitution and will to work which enabled him to do it. As a young man with a living to make he was a veritable 'workaholic'. He was also physically brave without being foolhardy.

243

Conversation spiced with wit was in an age devoid of radio or television another means of advancement. Thiers's conversation had wit as well as charm and could easily be heard – 'What wit! . . . what an unbroken torrent!' exclaimed Sainte-Beuve after an evening with him in December 1842[1] – but to make his thin, small voice audible in the Chamber and become a leading parliamentary orator, with a clarity of style that matched his historical writing and makes his speeches still readable, was a triumph of perseverance and intelligence almost equal to that of Demosthenes. There was another reason, too, why people enjoyed hearing him: he combined great width of interests with phenomenal powers of assimilation; he could, and did, talk on any subject. As with his contemporary Whewell, Master of Trinity College, Cambridge, omniscience was his foible. Omniscience lent him authority, but it could be a snare, leading him and others to suppose that he was more expert than he really was and induced him to be too sure of the rightness of opinions formed early in his career. Thus, paradoxically, it could narrow, not widen, his vision. It no doubt contributed, too, to his vanity, to which he confessed: 'I may be vain, and I may be irritable, but I do not think that I ever was jealous'; he also diagnosed vanity, envy, and ambition as 'the real passions' of the French.[2] Indeed, if he was vain and preoccupied with his reputation, so were other celebrities such as Chateaubriand, Lamartine and Victor Cousin who in the nineteenth century combined literature with politics.

Two other traits are worth recalling. Thiers possessed a lively although limited imagination and there was a mischievous streak in his make-up. Imagination, allied to a sense of history, could lead him to make striking prophecies, as when in 1847 he foretold that the two young giants, Russia and the United States, would one day dominate the world and inevitably clash. But Guizot thought he was much less good at understanding things close at hand: 'Mon cher', he once said, 'vous devinez et vous ne voyez pas.'[3] The mischievous trait was reflected by a liking for practical jokes and for shocking people he had no love for by coarseness or extravagance in his conversation. In politics it could be more serious; he liked to buttonhole his colleagues and sometimes confuse them so that critics regarded him as an intriguer and too clever by half. He was indeed clever and since, in his more pessimistic moments, he regarded men as 'naturally idle, false and timid' and dismissed them as stupid, he doubtless enjoyed exploiting their weaknesses.[4]

A man's rise to power is usually due both to talents and luck. Of Thiers's talents there is no doubt. They were immense and nurtured both by ambition, that other passion of the French – even Tocqueville confessed to being extremely ambitious – and by the indigence of his two 'mothers', whose menfolk had been ruined by the Revolution or their own fecklessness. To make a living and a name were thus imperative necessities. When there were no openings at Aix it was certain that sooner or later he would find his way to Paris, always a magnet for needy and ambitious young provincials. The luck came in having Mignet to pave the way, in having a useful introduction which speedily led to others – the importance of introductions can seldom be exaggerated – and in so soon being enlisted to work for an influential newspaper. This achieved, talents and hard work did the rest, while the political opinions he had formed at Aix ensured that his first Parisian career would be in the ranks of the Liberal Opposition.

Politics gave his three careers a unity. Although he wrote articles on varied topics, he was primarily a political journalist, just as he was a political historian; both these occupations gave him insights and means of influence which paved the way for and assisted his third career as politician and statesman.

He began almost simultaneously at the age of 24 his first two careers of active journalist and historian. The first lasted only nine years, whereas the second extended intermittently over forty, but he, again intermittently, retained connections with the press throughout his life. His experiences as an active journalist introduced him to the drudgery and hazards of the profession but also to the delights of influencing a much wider audience than fellow-students or the denizens of the law courts at Aix-en-Provence. He was fortunate in working for the newspapers at a time when the press was approaching the zenith of its political power; he used his great talents to become a doughty polemicist and, in 1830, he waged a campaign which gave him and his new paper the *National* a quite exceptional influence in the July Revolution. In that campaign he reiterated the ideas about representative government which were the enduring basis of his political creed. At the same time the success of the Revolution demonstrated how journalism could be the stepping-stone to a career in politics. Etienne of the *Constitutionnel* and Guizot were already deputies under the Restoration. After the July Revolution several of Thiers's fellow-journalists entered Parliament with or soon after him, although few, apart from him, held the highest offices.

'Only a hyphen', it has been said, 'separates the journalist and the historian in the Restoration.'[5] Just as Guizot and Augustin Thierry both wrote regularly for certain papers, so Thiers and Mignet worked on and published their histories of the great Revolution while they were fully engaged by the *Constitutionnel* and the *Courrier Français*.

Thiers's histories focused on problems that concerned his own time, and he was convinced that they gave him expertise in government, especially in diplomacy, finance and military affairs. He did not always convince experts – one of whom remarked that to read Thiers's technical explanations was to read 'a very clever man . . . writing about what he does not understand' – and yet few denied that his all-round command of business was unmatched. Even the unfriendly Bagehot conceded that although he 'may not comprehend the facts accurately . . . he can give the needful orders,

245

select the needful men, set the machine going in fact in the direction in which he wishes it to go'.[6] Along with journalism, historical study gave him his first insights into the machinery of power; it gave him too a long perspective on the events of the day, however misleading that perspective sometimes proved. In diplomacy, it convinced him of the logical necessity of an alliance with Britain, the other great liberal power, of the importance of France's historic role in Spain and Italy, the usefulness of the papacy as a political and ideological ally, the threat to Europe of Russian expansion, and the danger that a disruption of the European balance would lead to general war. In finance, his studies of John Law and of the Revolution and Empire underpinned his orthodoxy and his stubborn defence of the indirect taxes of the Revolutionary period, and they left him opposed to *laissez-faire* liberalism. In matters of internal administration, too, he willingly followed the path of Napoleon, always with the aim of increasing the solidity and power of the state. If his opinions were often contested, their authority was never denied, and his skill and self-confidence on occasion served him well, as when he raised the indemnity loans in 1871–2. His self-assurance could also lead him into difficulties. His belief in his military capacities, derived from historical study alone, led him to plan military intervention in Spain in 1836 and to risk major war in 1840, when in practice, though not in title, he became that rarest of French phenomena, a civilian Minister of War, having (thought a British Field Marshal) 'more administrative power and knowledge of what is required for an army in the field than any other man in Europe'.[7]

Thiers's belief in historical necessity had a clear effect on his political actions. In their earlier days, he and Mignet used confidently to predict what must necessarily happen in politics. They were at least as often wrong as right. Yet if *le fatalisme historique* was of little use in forming everyday policy, Thiers never abandoned it as a fundamental belief. The reproach was made more than once that this was merely the self-justification of the victors – the political victors of 1830 and the social victors of 'bourgeois' society. Yet after 1851 Thiers clung to the same belief in defeat: it was vain to resist 'the tide'. He retired from politics for twelve years, and when he returned was not an intransigent enemy of Napoleon III, for he looked like making his peace with the Liberal Empire. Similarly, in the 1870s, he accepted as inevitable a Republic that he had never regarded as ideal, and left power in 1873 rather than help the Royalists play King Canute. Like many men of his time – including his antagonists Napoleon III and Bismarck – he was ready to come to terms with change. In 1841 the former had written: 'March at the head of the ideas of your century, and those ideas will follow and support you; march behind them and they will drag you after them; march against them and they will overthrow you.' Thiers's view was characteristically more prudent: 'A government is in its true position when it has the enemy party behind it and its own supporters a little ahead of it.'[8]

246

Yet Thiers would always consider himself to be 'of the party of the Revolution', for root and branch opposition to change was worse than useless. Historic trends must be accepted, understood and controlled. 'I have always', he wrote, 'been a faithful back-bench supporter of Providence.'[9]

'To be of the party of the Revolution' – this was a keynote to the career of Thiers the politician. Despite his family's sufferings through that Revolution, there were good reasons for his throwing in his lot with the Liberals. The Revolution had proclaimed *la carrière ouverte aux talents*, and encouraged freedom of expression; its cause, as Thiers the historian explained, was the cause of liberty. But the restored Bourbon governments had their own supporters to reward, regardless of talents, and, like most governments of the time, feared freedom of expression. It was natural for Thiers, whose social origins were modest, to become a Liberal recruit like many other talented young men in life or literature. Yet, for all his 'siege of Toulon' and part in the Revolution of 1830, he was not temperamentally or in fact a revolutionary. For him being 'of the party of the Revolution' meant being opposed to the parties of the Counter-Revolution both in France and Europe, because they wished to put back the clock and threatened 'liberty' and representative government, which Thiers regarded as the chief gains of the Revolution and prime requisites of the modern state. In this context it is essential to remember that in the 1820s and 1830s opposition between the forces of revolution and Counter-Revolution was as sharp and constantly in men's minds as is the opposition between the free and Communist worlds in the second half of the twentieth century. If, as in 1830, this opposition came to a head in an armed clash, Thiers was ready to face it, but it would be unfair to the young man with a legal training not to recall his appeals for peaceful and legal methods of resistance. Again, when in 1848 he was summoned to take office and men were already fighting, his first and only proclamation ordered a cease-fire, while in 1870 after Sedan he sought a peaceful transfer of power to a government commission appointed by the Legislative Body.

Thus the politician who was 'of the party of the Revolution' and, in the 1860s, the champion of 'essential freedoms', could also be of the 'Party of Order'; he wished the freedoms of which he spoke so eloquently to be enjoyed within a strong, orderly and centralized state. The historian who expounded the Revolution to his countrymen was also the patriotic historian and admirer of the Consulate, in which Napoleon had brilliantly remoulded and stabilized French institutions after the upheavals of the revolutionary decade. True representative government as Thiers would have it, free of undue pressure from the 'court or the street', could not function smoothly without good order. Hence the seeming paradox that the Liberal was not afraid to suspend freedoms and ruthlessly repress disorder in the street if it appeared to threaten the security or unity of the state. Had he on such occasions been taxed with inconsistency and betrayal of the Liberal cause he might well have replied that his conduct was a matter of good sense: 'a man who governs', he said in 1834, 'should have good sense, that is the foremost political quality' and also 'the courage to show that he has it'. [10] Thiers was essentially a pragmatist who dealt with situations as they arose and scorned idealism and idealistic plans for social and other reforms as utopian and visionary. He is even said on occasion to have disowned the epithet 'Liberal', and the English historian Lord Acton considered that he was not a Liberal because he was 'averse to popular education and to freedom of trade, and not averse to war'. [11] There is,.however, no reason to doubt his belief in certain basic freedoms. The great problem in nineteenth-century France, one of the many awkward legacies of the great Revolution, was to secure conditions in which such freedoms could be enjoyed without striking fear into the hearts of the rulers.

Despite his influence over various newspapers Thiers for much of his career had a bad press. As a young journalist he had dealt hard blows, as a politician he received them in ample measure. Unscrupulous or envious opponents did their best to blacken his character during the first decade of the July Monarchy. They denounced him as a charlatan, an ill-mannered parvenu devoid of moral sense, a mischief-maker, a corrupt and cynical self-seeker greedy for office and its spoils. So much mud was flung that some inevitably stuck and as early as 1840 one of his friends believed that this had ruined Thiers's reputation. [12] Thus it was easy for later critics to rake over the old muck and repeat the old charges, slightly altered to suit the times; they derided his conceit, alleging that he was convinced that France's main interest was to be governed by M. Thiers, that he understood everything except moral greatness, epitomized bourgeois mediocrity and narrowness and had adroitly hidden his pettiness in the cloak of Napoleonic grandeur like a sparrow nesting in the Arc de Triomphe. [13]

There is no smoke without fire. Ambitious men are seldom at their most attractive between the ages of 30 and 50 and Thiers was no exception. He was too obviously out to make a career and some of his actions, as in February 1831 when he ordered the National Guard not to intervene when the Archbishop's palace was being sacked, were indeed reprehensible or ill-judged. His marriage, too, because of its business-like beginnings, the discrepancy in age between bridegroom and bride and the ostentation with which it was celebrated, lent itself to derogatory and malevolent constructions.

There were other reasons, political and social, which made him vulnerable to attack. Politically he opposed virtually every party at one or another stage of his career. In this he resembled Benjamin Constant, whose ideas were so important for the development of Liberalism, and who regarded himself as an Independent. Like Constant basically moderate as well as independent, Thiers had consistent enemies both in the Legitimists on the Right, except during the Second Republic, and in the extreme

Republicans and Socialists on the Left, whom he treated with verbal and physical harshness before 1871 and then with ruthless repression. Meanwhile, unable to convert Louis-Napoleon and his followers to true parliamentary government, he had become the opponent and victim of the Bonapartists, and by 1871, disillusioned with the Orleanists, he had deserted them for the men he hoped would be conservative Republicans. Thus each party had grievances against him which were aggravated by his habit of insisting that he had always been right and wholly consistent.

Socially, too, he was a target because the abundance of self-made men during the Revolutionary and Napoleonic era had fostered the image of the bourgeois adventurer, and he could too easily be equated with the literary type characterized by Balzac in Rastignac. Nor was he helped socially by his disreputable father and importunate half-brothers. With such relations and an indigent and insecure background it was not surprising that he had aspired to middle-class respectability, to be 'Monsieur Thiers' with a comfortable house and fortune. But this, too, gave him a bad press in certain quarters. He told Nassau Senior, at a time when he was distancing himself from the Orleanists, that he belonged to the people by birth and had no sympathy with the bourgeoisie or with any system under which they were to rule,[14] yet his social and political behaviour made him appear to be their 'most typical representative', as Gambetta once said in a phrase intended to be complimentary.[15] No great innovator, he in many ways mirrored both their fears and aspirations. But the bourgeoisie or middle classes of that era were scorned not only, as is common, by the young but derided by many contemporary reformers and men of letters and artists. Reformers detested them as narrow, harsh and greedy while literary men and caricaturists mocked or rebelled against what they saw as the dullness and complacency of bourgeois conventions and canons of taste. Subsequently they have had an equally poor image in much history written by social and other historians of the twentieth century, themselves generally men and women of the middle classes reacting against the literary and political sterotypes imposed upon them. Because he was in power or exerted influence when 'bourgeois' power and values were in the first phase of their pre-eminence, Thiers, like Guizot and Louis-Philippe, was made to symbolize and so to bear the blame for features in society and politics which have since been widely criticized. Such condemnation may be understandable but it is not necessarily fair.

Politically he was also at something of a disadvantage because he was an outsider. He might tell Senior that, despite his birth, by tastes, habits and associations he was an aristocrat,[16] but he was never wholeheartedly accepted by the Orleanist aristocrats such as the Broglie family, and the ladies of title whom he most often frequented were foreigners like the Comtesse Taverna and the Duchesse d'Albuféra or belonged to an upstart dynasty like Princess Julie Bonaparte. He was unlike most great notables of his day, too, in not having a country house. The young man from Aix had become an urban Parisian: 'I like but one wind', he told Princess Julie in 1859, ' – the one from Paris, and that provided I feel its breath in Paris itself.'[17] He lived on a grand scale there and thought it too expensive to maintain a suitably dignified establishment in the provinces as well, preferring to travel abroad and visit battlefields or frequent some fashionable spa. This lack of a provincial base may have helped to account for his electoral defeat in the Bouches-du-Rhône in 1863, but it clearly made no difference in the 1830s and 1840s even though a high proportion of deputies represented the departments in which they lived. On the other hand the fact that he was never wholly at home in the Orleanist world may have been a reason for his leaving it in the lurch in 1871.[18]

Thiers was of course a conspicuous example of the successful middle-class Frenchman of the nineteenth century. He succeeded as a journalist at the beginning of an era which was to see the multiplicity of newspapers reach its apogee, as an historian at a time when history had never been so popular, and as a professional politician when national, as distinct from local, politics was increasingly left to professionals. At the same time his bourgeois father-in-law's financial connections brought him a directorship of a powerful mining company. Having climbed from obscurity to relative affluence and become a *notable*, he understandably sought to uphold the social and political ascendancy of the circles in which he now moved, and those circles, equally understandably, were all the more tenacious of their hold on power and influence because they were of relatively recent date. They were in no haste to achieve social or political democracy. Like his contemporaries, Gladstone and Disraeli, Thiers was 'an out-and-out inequalitarian'.[19] He did not believe in widening popular education and he and his friends who wanted only limited parliamentary reform were surprised by universal suffrage in 1848 and, to their own undoing, attempted to limit it in 1850. Thereafter he appears to have recognized that universal suffrage, like the railway, was a product of *la force des choses*. But if he made no further attempt to restrict it he made curiously little effort to adapt himself to it.

If Thiers could thus recognize the power of historical change he could also learn from his mistakes. The most conspicuous example of this was in foreign affairs. Just as Louis-Napoleon learnt from his uncle's mistakes that France should never incur the enmity of England, so Thiers learnt from his own rash gamble in the Near Eastern crisis of 1840 that she should never risk war against more than one power at one time. Although he was not a good negotiator, perhaps because he talked too much and listened too little, after 1840 he generally had a shrewd perception of France's true interests. For all his love of military matters he was thenceforward no warmonger and exerted his influence for peace. Recognizing the dangers presented by 'unificatory nationalism' to the balance of power and to France's particular interests, he was, again like Disraeli, opposed to nationalism except in his own country. There, like most Liberals of his generation, he was ready enough to sound the patriotic note.

What would Thiers's reputation have been had he died in 1847 instead of 1877? He would have been remembered for his ability as a journalist and his brilliance as an historian, although his history of the Consulate and Empire was only half done, but his record as a politician would have been more dubious. Men would have recalled his connection with repression, adventurism and devious party politics and forgotten his courage in upholding liberty as well as maintaining order and his contributions to the embellishment of Paris and the improvement of country roads. They would have thought him brilliant but unreliable, a man who had not fulfilled his promise. They might well have agreed with Sainte-Beuve's private verdict in 1845: 'there is an artist in him, a political historian, a statesman when he is at the tribune or has his pen in his hand but he lacks the balance and stability to govern a nation. A reliable pilot is less impulsive and widely inquiring (*curieux*) than this man.'[20]

Had he been able to view his political career as a whole Sainte-Beuve might well have arrived at a different judgement. In Thiers's last thirty years as a politician there is still evidence of southern impulsiveness or impatience or readiness to gamble on a single throw – witness the attempt to recover the cannon in Paris in March 1871 – and during the Second Republic there were grave errors of judgement which weakened his cause. There was still great stubborness. In his attitudes to free trade, short-term military service and decentralization, he was a conspicuous example of what has been called the Frenchman's fantastic capacity to resist change.[21] Accordingly much of his legislative activity was of a negative kind : there is no great Loi Thiers for us to remember. Yet after 1851 the political career is as impressive as it is remarkable. He assumed the role of elder statesman with dignity and effectiveness. His twelve years out of Parliament showed that he was far from being greedy for office at any price. Like Gladstone he could accept change which was distasteful without bitterness and remain *bon enfant* – good-natured. There followed the years in which he was again a statesman at the tribune, eloquently calling for essential freedoms – a call without which, one contemporary thought, France would have resumed her twelve years' slumber[22] – warning of the dangers of Napoleon III's foreign policy and opposing war. After the débâcle in 1870 he was ready, despite his age (73), to tour the European capitals in search of aid and to make tireless efforts to secure an armistice. The elections of February 1871 were held in exceptional circumstances but no man before or since, during the period when multiple candidatures were permissible, was elected by so many constituencies. The ambitious and supposedly untrustworthy politician of the 1830s and 1840s had indeed gained the trust of the nation. He repaid it by negotiating peace, repressing the Commune and liberating the territory from German occupation.

These ends were achieved at immense cost in lives, land and money, and it is arguable that a more apt negotiator should have won a reduction of the indemnity if not of territory and that a better advised and more lenient ruler could both have averted the setback of 18 March, which sparked the Communard insurrection, and have reduced the ultimate slaughter. But the ends were achieved. Thiers's patriotism was universally acknowledged and it was with justifiable pride that he could ask for the words *patriam dilexit* to be engraved upon his tomb. His strength of purpose gave France what she most needed, peace at home and abroad, relative stability and a new confidence. In Livy's succinct phrase, *restituit rem*; thereby he earned a place in the roll of 'saviours' of modern France from Napoleon to Clemenceau and de Gaulle.

Above all, although there were still to be some bumpy passages, France was made safe for representative or parliamentary government. Thiers's persistent aim was thus accomplished and the Third Republic was endowed with an Orleanist type of constitution functioning on a basis of universal suffrage. It would in many ways be the conservative Republic which he had championed in his last election address in 1877. Great social injustices had yet to be remedied – they were not the concern of men like Thiers who had been scared by so many insurrections and lacked the compassionate imagination to investigate possible social reforms that were practical and not utopian : but the way had been paved for the achievement of other 'necessary' freedoms. Moreover, for all its shortcomings, the Third Republic became the most durable of France's nineteenth-century regimes precisely because, as Thiers had foreseen, it divided Frenchmen least. He, its first President and prime architect, was France's strongest President until General de Gaulle. He was also the first and almost the only man of letters to become an elected head of state.[23] This was appropriate in a country in which, as Raymond Aron remarked in 1983, politics would always have a literary flavour.[24] In several ways comparable to Gladstone as well as Disraeli and probably the oldest statesman to exercise a dominant influence in France since Fleury who died in 1743, Thiers was politically 'the Grand Old Man of French history in the nineteenth century'.[25]

Abbreviations

AHG	Archives Historiques de Guerre.
Annales	Published debates of the various parliamentary bodies (*du Parlement Français, du Corps Législatif, de l'Assemblée Nationale*) (Paris, 1830–73).
BN n.a.fr.	Bibliothèque Nationale (manuscripts department): nouvelles acquisitions françaises.
BPP Levant	British Parliamentary Papers: *Correspondence Relative to the Affairs of the Levant* (Accounts and Papers 1841) (Session 1841, vol. 29) (London, 1841).
BT	Bibliothèque Thiers.
Correspondances	*Correspondances de 1841 à 1865: M. Thiers à Mme Thiers et à Mme Dosne; Mme Dosne à M. Thiers* (Paris, 1904).
Courrier	*Le Courrier de M. Thiers: d'après les documents conservés au département des manuscrits de la Bibliothèque Nationale*, ed. D. Halévy. (Paris, 1921)
Discours	*Discours parlementaires de M. Thiers* ed. M. Calmon, 16 vols (Paris, 1879–89).
Dosne	*Mémoires de Mme Dosne, l'Egérie de M. Thiers*, ed. H. Malo, 2 vols (Paris, 1928).
Enquête 18 mars	*Enquête parlementaire sur l'insurrection du 18 mars* 2 vols (Versailles, 1872).
Enquête GND	*Enquête sur les actes du Gouvernement de la Défense Nationale* 7 vols (Paris, 1874).
MAE	Ministère des Affaires Etrangères.
MAE(B)	Ministère des Affaires Etrangères, Belgium.
Malo	H. Malo, *Thiers 1797–1877* (Paris, 1932).
Mignet	Y. Knibiehler, *Naissance des sciences humaines: Mignet et l'histoire philosophique au XIXe siècle* (Paris, 1973).
Rémusat	C. de Rémusat, *Mémoires de ma vie*, ed. C. Pouthas, 5 vols (Paris, 1958–67).

Notes

CHAPTER 1

1 N. W. Senior, *Conversations with M. Thiers, M. Guizot and other Distinguished Persons during the Second Empire*, 2 vols (London, 1878), Vol. 1, p. 137.
2 *Courrier*, p. 256.
3 BT, TMS. 556.
4 E. Baratier, *Histoire de la Provence* (Toulouse, 1971) pp. 437ff.; *Mignet*, p. 21.
5 C. Pomaret, *Monsieur Thiers et son siècle* (Paris, 1948), p. 104.
6 BT, TMS. 556.
7 Some forty years later, Th. Lavallée described Aix as 'encore une ville de noblesse, de magistrature, d'université, solennelle, mais triste, que l'industrie et le commerce ont peine à animer'. Cit. J. Verne and T. Lavallée, *Géographie illustrée de la France* (Paris, 1876), p. 109.
8 The two essays expressed the same point of view in quite different styles.
9 C. A. Sainte-Beuve, *Portraits contemporains*, Vol. 2 (Paris, 1852), p. 458. Sixty years later both Vauvenargues and Thiers had streets named after them in Aix.
10 F. Morin-Pons, 'Thiers avocat aixois', *Provence Historique*, Vol. 9 (Oct–Dec. 1959), pp. 236–9.
11 Undated letter from Adolphe's mother, cit. *Courrier*, p. 18.
12 Morin-Pons, 'Thiers avocat aixois', p. 240, letter of 21 Dec. 1820 to Teulon.
13 ibid., p. 254. It is not clear what the 'brochure' was. Pellenc does not mention the glasses which Adolphe is said to have started wearing when quite young.
14 ibid., p. 255.
15 John M. S. Allison's translation, *Thiers and the French Monarchy* (London, 1926), pp. 16–17.
16 Letter of 29 Aug. 1821 in Morin-Pons, 'Thiers avocat aixois', p. 255. Adolphe's momentary reluctance to be a journalist was probably because journalism was then widely considered a refuge for 'des ratés de la littérature et du théâtre' (M. Martin, 'Journalistes parisiens et notoriété (vers 1830–1870). Pour une histoire sociale du journalisme', *Revue Historique*, July–Sept. 1981, p. 56).
17 *Mignet*, p. 47.
18 C. Ledré, *La Presse à l'assaut de la monarchie, 1815–1848* (Paris, 1960), pp. 16, 242.
19 *Mignet*, p. 67.
20 ibid.
21 Sainte-Beuve, *Portraits contemporains*, Vol. 2, p. 443.
22 'Corinna', i.e. Madame de Staël, was the duchess's mother.
23 See also below, page 153.
24 Pomaret, *Monsieur Thiers*, p. 80.
25 *Les Pyrénées et le Midi de la France* (Paris, 1823), pp. 14–15.
26 *Portraits contemporains*, Vol. 2, p. 447. For the influence of the Pyrenees on

French writers, see Jean Fourcassié, *Le Romantisme et Les Pyrénées* (Paris, 1940).

27 For example, pp. 151, 201–2, 218–20.

28 Rémusat, Vol. 2, p. 91.

29 One of those confounded was presumably Mignet who, in the *Courrier Français*, had strongly opposed the war (*Mignet*, p. 82).

30 For the vicissitudes of the *Tablettes Universelles*, see Rémusat, Vol. 2, p. 84.

31 For Thiers as an historian and his place in French historiography see below, Chapter 8.

32 R. Marquant, *Thiers et le Baron Cotta* (Paris, 1959), p. 99 n.1; Rémusat also wrote for the *Globe* (Rémusat, Vol. 2, p. 147).

33 Pomaret, *Monsieur Thiers*, p. 163. The journalists Chambolle and Léon Faucher were examples.

34 Malo, p. 85.

35 R. Christophe, *Le Siècle de Monsieur Thiers* (Paris, 1966), p. 34.

36 Marquant, *Thiers et le Baron Cotta*, pp. 105–6. According to Martin, 'Journalistes parisiens', p. 54, monthly payment was relatively uncommon. Most journalists were paid by the line or the article.

37 Marquant, *Thiers et le Baron Cotta*, p. 44.

38 ibid., p. 491.

39 P. de Rémusat, *A. Thiers* (Paris, 1889), p. 16. But Marquant, *Thiers et le Baron Cotta*, p. 113 n.1, points out that Stendhal's 'Chroniques anglaises' (1822–9) were very similar in character. Stendhal, too, indulged in occasional art criticism, e.g. his account of the Salon of 1824 in the *Journal de Paris*.

40 19 Dec. 1824, Marquant, *Thiers et le Baron Cotta*, p. 201.

41 For his moving tribute to his grandmother, see *Courrier*, pp. 14–17.

42 Pomaret, *Monsieur Thiers*, p. 84.

43 ibid., p. 85.

44 C. P. T. Laplace, *Voyage autour du Monde par les mers de l'Inde et de Chine exécuté sur la corvette de l'état La Favorite pendant les années 1830, 1831 et 1832, sous le commandement de M. Laplace* (Paris, 1833–9).

CHAPTER 2

1 The Republican *Dictionnaire politique* (1842), edited by Garnier-Pagès jeune, began its entry 'Libéralisme' with the words: 'Il y a peu de mots plus difficiles à définir que celui-là.'

2 *Mignet*, p. 434.

3 Rémusat, Vol. 2 p. 287.

4 P. Bastid, *Benjamin Constant et sa doctrine*, 2 Vols (Paris, 1966), Vol. 1, p. 305. For an excellent more recent analysis, see S. Holmes, *Benjamin Constant and the Making of Modern Liberalism*, (New Haven, 1984), ch. 5.

5 P. Bastid, *Les Institutions politiques de la monarchie parlementaire française, 1814–1848* (Paris, 1954), p. 172.

6 R. Marquant, *Thiers et le Baron Cotta* (Paris, 1959), p. 210. The passage containing this sentence was not printed.

7 ibid., p. 306.

8 ibid., p. 392, 20 Jan. 1827. This passage was watered down in German translation.

9 Letter to F. Benoît, cit. John M. S. Allison, *Thiers and the French Monarchy* (London, 1926), p. 96. A. Chambolle, *Retours sur la vie* (Paris, 1912), p. 67, says Paulin first thought of founding the paper, hoping to divert his friend Sautelet from thoughts of suicide.

10 BT, MS. 1251.

11 Rémusat, Vol. 2 pp. 284–5.

12 P. Reboul, *Le Mythe anglais dans la littérature française* (Lille, 1962), p. 310.

13 According to C. Bellanger *et al.*, *Histoire générale de la presse française*, Vol. 2 (Paris, 1972), p. 94, he took only half of one of the twelve *actions payantes*, but his firm made itself responsible for three-quarters of the 6,000 francs caution money. Chambolle, *Retours sur la vie*, p. 66, said there were ten shares of 20,000 francs.

14 ed. M. Levaillant, Vol. 3 (Paris, 1948), p. 576.

15 *Mignet*, p. 190. The Duc de Dalberg and Baron Louis have also been suggested as possible financial backers.

16 G. Lacour-Gayet, *Talleyrand 1754–1838* (Paris, 1928–34), Vol. 3, p. 219.

17 Chateaubriand, *Mémoires d'outre-tombe*, ed. Levaillant, Vol. 3, pp. 576–7.

18 BT, TMS. 1251. F. L. Lindner was one of the leading journalists on the staff of the *Gazette d'Augsbourg*. Thiers paid him 100 francs a month.

19 E. L. Newman, 'The blouse and the frock coat', *Journal of Modern History*, Vol. 46, no. 1 (March 1974), p. 34 n. 40. Thiers's letter of 11 Dec. 1828 to the *Gazette d'Augsbourg* sheds light on the pattern of newspaper subscriptions: 'Les abonnés d'hiver qui pour chaque journal forment le quart de sa clientèle et . . . ne sont pas encore retournés. Le *Constitutionnel* . . . n'a pas un abonné de plus qu'au mois d'août. C'est au mois de janvier que le zèle se réveillera, par l'effet ordinaire de la session' (i.e. of Parliament) (Marquant, *Thiers et le Baron Cotta*, p. 482).

20 BT, TMS. 1408 lists these articles from 1 February. Two in March are recorded as the joint work of Thiers and Mignet and one on 16 March as that of Thiers, Mignet and Chambolle. For an analysis, see *Mignet*, pp. 191–203. These attributions sometimes differ from those in the annotated copy of the *National* in the Bibliothèque Nationale (BN Réserve, Gr. Fol. Lc^2 1239).

21 Letter to J.-J. Ampère, *André-Marie Ampère et Jean-Jacques Ampère: Correspondance et souvenirs (de 1805 à 1864)*, 2 vols (4th edn, Paris, 1877), Vol. 2, p. 12.

22 A threat of which Thiers wrote: 'C'est là . . . l'article 14 tout entier' (*Le National*, 3 March 1830). Article 14 of the Charter included the following words: 'Le Roi . . . fait les règlements et ordonnances nécessaires pour l'exécution des lois et la sûreté de l'Etat.' Cf. *Le National* 2 and 3 May for articles specifically about Article 14.

23 Articles of 6, 9, 11, 22 Feb., 2, 22 March, 7 May.

24 Articles of 14, 20, 22 July; cf. Mignet's articles on France's role in the Mediterranean (*Mignet*, pp. 192–5).

25 D. Halévy, *Trois épreuves, 1814, 1871, 1940* (*Paris*, 1942), p. 36.

26 Marquant, *Thiers et le Baron Cotta*, pp. 497–8, letter of 22 May.

27 *Journal de Viennet, Pair de France, témoin de trois règnes 1817–1848* (Paris, 1955), p. 99.

28 For this tragedy, see Doris Gunnell, *Sutton Sharpe et ses amis français* (Paris, 1925), Ch. 8.

29 Bellanger *et al.*, *Histoire générale de la presse*, Vol. 2, p. 99. The number of 1,590 quoted by L. Rader, *The Journalists and the July Revolution in France* (The Hague, 1973), p. 213, is based on a list of circulation figures printed in *Le Temps*, 28 May 1830.

30 The poll in the Seine and nineteen other departments had been deferred until 13 and 19 July.

31 That is, those who paid 300 francs or more in direct taxes, an *écu* or crown being a coin worth 3 francs.

32 Bastid, *Les Institutions politiques*, p. 74 n. 2.

33 D. Pinkney, *The French Revolution of 1830* (Princeton, 1972), p. 83, regards the sources for this as dubious. Boulay de la Meurthe, however, in his unpublished 'Souvenirs de 26, 27, 28 et 29 Juillet 1830' which Professor Pinkney does not appear to have seen, states categorically that three printers came to the *National's* offices towards 10 p.m. and reported that, of seventeen who had met, eleven had decided 'fermer leurs ateliers et de renvoyer leurs ouvriers qui s'élevaient à 1500'. This, he was convinced, was an unpremeditated act (BT, TMS. 55, fol. 7). Monday, *Le Saint Lundi*, was incidentally a day workers often took off; 26 July was a Monday.

34 According to L. Rozet, *Chronique de Juillet 1830*, 2 vols (Paris, 1832), Vol. 1, p. 129, only one press was dismantled; 'on le remplaça le soir et la presse travailla la nuit comme à l'ordinaire'.

35 Pinkney, *French Revolution of 1830*, p. 95.

36 Hippolyte Bonnelier, *Mémorial de l'Hôtel de Ville de Paris 1830* (Paris, 1830), p. 11, says the deputation consisted of Thiers, himself and Chevalier, formerly director of a publication called *La Bibliothèque Historique*. Rémusat, Vol. 2, p. 323, adds Goudchaux, an *agent de change*, and Armand Carrel.

37 BT, TMS. 55, fol. 4.

38 *Le National*, 31 July 1830.

39 L. Blanc, *The History of Ten Years 1830–1840*, 2 Vols (London, 1844), Vol. 1, p. 97.

40 Although Rader (*The Journalists*) says that the Prefecture of Police had no records of their home addresses, p. 227.

41 Rozet, *Chronique de Juillet*, Vol. 1, p. 208 and Rémusat, Vol. 2, p. 330, allege that they attended a meeting at Guizot's at or a little before 10 a.m. If so they must have gone to Bessancourt later in the morning.

42 Lacour-Gayet, *Talleyrand*, Vol. 3, p. 227, gives a different version.

43 Marquant, *Thiers et le Baron Cotta*, pp. 175, 273.

44 A. Cauchois-Lemaire, *Lettres politiques, religieuses et historiques*, 2 Vols (Paris, 1828–32), Vol. 2, p. 218.

45 *Mémoires de la Comtesse de Boigne*, Vol. 2, 4 Vols (Paris, 1907), p. 183.

46 According to L. de Viel-Castel, *Histoire de la Restauration*, Vol. 20 (Paris, 1860) p. 638, Dupin had reached Neuilly before Thiers and put the case for the duke to come forward 'aux deux princesses avec plus de rudesse'.

47 The original text is in the Thiers papers, BN n.a.fr. 20601.

48 We do not know what else was said at this first meeting between two men whose relations would be so important for France during the next eighteeen years.
49 G. Weill, *Histoire du parti républicain en France (1814–1870)* (Paris, 1928), p. 25.
50 P. Duvergier de Hauranne, *Histoire du gouvernement parlementaire en France 1814–48*, 10 Vols (Paris, 1857–71), Vol. 10, pp. 651–2, 654.
51 E. L. Newman, 'The blouse and the frock coat'.
52 Printed at the end of his wife's, Lady Morgan's, *France in 1829–30* (London, 1830).
53 Rémusat, Vol. 2, p. 287.
54 *Mignet*, p. 203.
55 Malo, p. 126.
56 Rozet, *Chronique de Juillet*, Vol. 1, pp. 22–3.
57 C. Pomaret, *Monsieur Thiers et son siècle* (Paris, 1948), p. 176.
58 For example in *La Monarchie de 1830* (Paris, 1831), p. 21.
59 Pomaret, *Monsieur Thiers*, p. 171.
60 Rémusat, Vol. 2, p. 287.
61 M. Goldie, 'Historiographical review', *Historical Journal*, Vol 26, 3 (Sept. 1983), p. 733.
62 *Histoire de la Révolution Française*, 10 Vols (Paris, 1823–7), Vol. 1, p. 294.

CHAPTER 3

1 In 1832 the English electorate numbered over 618,000. J. Prest, *Politics in the Age of Cobden* (London, 1972), p. 28.
2 *La Monarchie de 1830* (Paris, 1831), p. 58.
3 P. Thureau-Dangin, *Histoire de la Monarchie de Juillet*, 5 Vols (Paris, 1884–90), Vol. 1, p. 28 n. 1.
4 P. Vigier, *La Monarchie de Juillet* (3rd edn, Paris, 1969), p. 14.
5 David H. Pinkney, *The French Revolution of 1830* (Princeton, 1972), p. 284.
6 Among the most important political histories of the period are P. Thureau-Dangin, *Histoire de la Monarchie de Juillet*, A. -J. Tudesq, *Les Grands Notables en France, (1840–1849): étude historique d'une psychologie sociale*, 2 Vols (Paris, 1964), C. H. Pouthas, 'Les Ministères de Louis-Philippe', *Revue d'Histoire Moderne et Contemporaine*, Vol. 1 (April–June 1954), pp. 102–30, Douglas Johnson, *Guizot: Aspects of French History, 1787–1874* (London, 1963).
7 *Dosne*, Vol. 1, p. iv.
8 For details see Malo pp. 153–4.
9 R. Marquant, *Thiers et le Baron Cotta* (Paris, 1959), pp. 501, 499.
10 ibid., p. 501.
11 Thureau-Dangin, *Histoire*, Vol. 1, p. 174.
12 Letter of 8 April 1831. Marquant, *Thiers et le Baron Cotta*, p. 502.
13 Thureau-Dangin, *Histoire*, Vol. 1, pp. 190–1; Rémusat, Vol. 2, pp. 433–4.
14 Thureau-Dangin, *Histoire*, Vol. 1, pp. 201–2; Marquant, *Thiers et le Baron Cotta*, p. 501.

15 Malo, p. 167; Rémusat, Vol. 2, p. 523.
16 Rémusat, Vol. 2, pp. 526–8.
17 Thureau-Dangin, *Histoire*, Vol. 2, pp. 37, 42.
18 Malo, p. 171.
19 Pouthas, 'Les Ministères', pp. 114–5.
20 A thorough recent study is M. L. Lifka, 'Social order and upheaval: Adolphe Thiers as Minister of the Interior, 1832–1836', Ph.D. thesis, University of Michigan, 1974.
21 A Bourbon prince kidnapped and shot on the orders of Napoleon, whose reputation greatly suffered in consequence.
22 See below, Chapter 7.
23 Malo, pp. 184–9.
24 *Dosne*, Vol. 1, p. ii; *Mignet*, p. 249.
25 *Dosne*, Vol. 1, pp. ii, v.
26 C. Pomaret, *Monsieur Thiers et son siècle* (Paris, 1948), pp. 92, 100.
27 See *Correspondances, passim*.
28 For a full recent account, see R. J. Bezucha, *The Lyon Uprising of 1834: Social and Political Conflict in the Early July Monarchy* (Cambridge, Mass, 1974).
29 Lifka, 'Social order', pp. 264–7.
30 ibid., pp. 269–85; Malo, pp. 219–20.
31 Lifka, 'Social order', pp. 285–6, 293–4.
32 A small but influential group of conservative Liberals who argued that government by an elite was for the general good. Guizot was one of their leaders.
33 Thureau-Dangin, *Histoire*, Vol. 2, pp. 245–6, and Ch. 11, *passim*. See also Malo, pp. 217–8, 223.
34 J. Lucas-Dubreton, *Louis-Philippe et la machine infernale (1830–1835)* (Paris, 1951).
35 Thureau-Dangin, *Histoire*, Vol. 2, p. 394; Vol. 3, pp. 49–50, 104; R. Bullen, 'France and the problem of intervention in Spain, 1834–1836', *Historical Journal*, Vol. 20, no. 2 (1977), pp. 366–7, 376; R. Bullen, 'France and Europe 1815–48: the problem of defeat and recovery', in A. Sked (ed.), *Europe's Balance of Power, 1815–1848* (London, 1979), pp. 122–44.
36 Thureau-Dangin, *Histoire*, Vol. 2, p. 428.
37 Thureau-Dangin, *Histoire*, Vol. 3, Ch. 1, *passim*.; F. Santoni, 'Le Premier Ministère Thiers', unpublished thesis, University of Paris I, 1971, pp. 15–44.
38 ibid., p. 182. Thiers's precise links with the *Constitutionnel* remain obscure, but it seems likely that he or his friends had invested a considerable sum in it during the July Monarchy.
39 Santoni, 'Le Premier Ministère Thiers', pp. 155–80.
40 Johnson, *Guizot*, p. 265; A. Jardin, *Alexis de Tocqueville, 1805–1859* (Paris, 1984), pp. 296–7, 303.
41 See Thiers's diplomatic dispatches, BN n.a.fr. 20607 *passim*.; also Bullen, 'France and Europe', pp. 137–8.
42 Santoni, 'Le Premier Ministère Thiers', part 2, *passim*.
43 BN n.a.fr. 20607, Thiers's dispatches to Sainte-Aulaire of 10 July 1836, fols 209–18 (reprinted in *Courrier*, pp. 17–89) and 8 August, fols 261–2, and to Bresson, 7 August, fols 251–3.
44 Bullen, 'France and the problem of intervention in Spain', p. 388.

45 BN n.a.fr. 20607, Thiers to Gen. Harispe, 3 August, fol. 239, and to Comte de Rayneval, 5 August, fols 246–8.
46 ibid., fols 275–9.
47 ibid., to Bois le Comte, 29 August, fol. 291. See also Santoni, 'Le Premier Ministère Thiers', pp. 250–8.
48 Bullen, 'France and the problem of intervention in Spain', pp. 390–3.
49 Rémusat, Vol. 3, pp. 156, 158. On the general consequences of Thiers's ministry, see Thureau-Dangin, *Histoire*, Vol. 2, pp. 429–30; Vol. 3, p. 28; Pouthas, 'Ministères de Louis-Philippe', p. 119.
50 S. Girard *et al.*, *La Chambre des Députés en 1837–1839* (Paris, 1976), pp. 38, 45.
51 ibid., part 3, *passim*.
52 Thureau-Dangin, *Histoire*, Vol. 3, pp. 362–87, Vol. 4, p. 29; Rémusat, Vol. 3, pp. 249–54.
53 Thureau-Dangin, *Histoire*, Vol. 4, p. 99.

CHAPTER 4

1 C. de Barante (ed.) *Souvenirs du Baron de Barante*, 8 Vols (Paris, 1890–1901), Vol. 6, p. 441.
2 A.-J. Tudesq, *Les Grands Notables en France (1840–1849): étude historique d'une psychologie sociale*, 2 Vols (Paris, 1964), p. 513.
3 P. Thureau-Dangin, *Histoire de la Monarchie de Juillet*, 5 Vols (Paris, 1884–90), Vol. 4, pp. 114–5.
4 *Annales* (session 1840–1), Vol. 3, p. 88 (27 Nov. 1840).
5 Thureau-Dangin, *Histoire*, Vol. 4, pp. 126, 130.
6 Tudesq, *Notables*, Vol. 1, pp. 487–8.
7 Thureau-Dangin, *Histoire*, Vol. 4, p. 128.
8 Tudesq, *Notables*, Vol. 1, p. 514.
9 Thureau-Dangin, *Histoire*, Vol. 4, pp. 143–78.
10 Report of Count Le Hon (the well-informed and gossipy Belgian Minister to Paris), 28 March. MAE(B), France Vol. 10 (1840), no. 29.
11 Barante, *Souvenirs*, Vol. 5, p. 451.
12 *Gazette de France* (21 March) and *Hermine* (6 March), in Tudesq, *Notables*, Vol. 1, p. 487.
13 For the background to the crisis see M. S. Anderson, *The Eastern Question, 1774–1923: A Study in International Relations* (London, 1966); Sir C. Webster, *The Foreign Policy of Palmerston, 1830–41: Britain, the Liberal Movement and the Eastern Question*, 2 Vols (London, 1951); Thureau-Dangin, *Histoire*, Vol. 4, pp. 23–94; Charles Pouthas, 'La Politique de Thiers pendant la crise orientale de 1840', *Revue Historique*, Vol. 182 (Jan–June 1938), pp. 72–96.
14 Thureau-Dangin, *Histoire*, Vol. 4, pp. 70, 73, 76, 199; Kenneth Bourne, *Palmerston: The Early Years, 1784–1841* (London, 1982), p. 584; dispatches of Palmerston and Bulwer, Sept. 1839, in BPP Levant, part 1.
15 Thureau-Dangin, *Histoire*, Vol. 4, p. 139.
16 Rémusat, Vol. 3, p. 449.
17 *Annales* (1840), Vol. 2, p. 129.

18 BN n.a.fr. 20613–14, fol. 323 (also in *Courrier*, p. 149).
19 Sainte-Aulaire to Barante, 27 June, in Barante, *Souvenirs*, p. 455.
20 The term Syria then applied to the whole of the Levant, from Egypt to Turkey.
21 Pouthas, 'La Politique de Thiers', p. 76; and see Granville (British Ambassador) to Palmerston, 13 March, BPP Levant, part 1, pp. 603–4.
22 François Charles-Roux, *Thiers et Méhémet-Ali* (Paris, 1951), pp. 47–50.
23 ibid., pp. 70–1.
24 Sir H. L. Bulwer, *The Life of John Henry Temple, Viscount Palmerston*, 3 Vols (London, 1870), Vol. 2, p. 315.
25 Charles-Roux, *Thiers*, pp. 71–2, 88–90; D. Johnson, *Guizot, Aspects of French History, 1797–1874* (London, 1963), pp. 178, 269.
26 Tudesq, *Notables*, Vol. 1, p. 493.
27 Thureau-Dangin, *Histoire*, Vol. 4, pp. 232–4.
28 L. Faucher, *Biographie et correspondance*, 2 vols (2nd edn, Paris, 1875), Vol. 1, p. 93, letter to Henry Reeve, 2 Aug.
29 Thureau-Dangin, *Histoire*, Vol. 4, pp. 237–40; and see C. I. Hamilton, 'Naval power and diplomacy in the nineteenth century', *Journal of Strategic Studies*, Vol. 3, no. 1 (May 1980), pp. 82–3.
30 Thiers to Consul-General in Alexandria, 30 July and 4 Aug., Charles-Roux, *Thiers*, pp. 114–7, 157–60.
31 Thureau-Dangin, *Histoire*, Vol. 4, pp. 248; Charles-Roux, *Thiers*, p. 46.
32 Thureau-Dangin, *Histoire*, Vol. 4, pp. 242–3; and see Louis-Philippe's letters to Thiers, BN n.a.fr. 20611.
33 Thureau-Dangin, *Histoire*, Vol. 4, pp. 243, 246.
34 See P. O'Brien, '*L'Embastillement de Paris*: the fortification of Paris during the July Monarchy', *French Historical Studies*, vol. 9, no. 1 (1975), 63–82.
35 Webster, *Foreign Policy*, pp. 709–13; Bourne, *Palmerston*, pp. 596–9, 604; Donald Southgate, '*The Most English Minister. . .*' *The Policies and Politics of Palmerston* (London, 1966), p. 129.
36 Rémusat, Vol. 3, p. 474; Le Hon, dispatch 21 September, MAE(B) France Vol. 10, no. 74; Thureau-Dangin, *Histoire*, Vol. 4, pp. 329–30.
37 Bulwer, *Palmerston*, Vol. 2, pp. 324–9.
38 F. Guizot, *Mémoires pour servir à l'histoire de mon temps*, Vol. 5 (Paris, 1862), p. 378.
39 Charles-Roux, *Thiers*, pp. 183, 201.
40 ibid.; Bulwer, *Palmerston*, Vol. 2, p. 351; Bourne, *Palmerston*, p. 576.
41 Rémusat, Vol. 3, pp. 472–3.
42 Bourne, *Palmerston*, p. 606.
43 Thureau-Dangin, *Histoire*, Vol. 4, pp. 300, 305.
44 Charles-Roux, *Thiers*, pp. 215–6.
45 Bourne, *Palmerston*, p. 607.
46 Letter to Consul-General in Alexandria, 9 Oct., Charles-Roux, *Thiers*, pp. 280–1.
47 We are indebted to Dr T. C. W. Blanning for these details.
48 Tudesq, *Notables*, Vol. 1, pp. 495–8, 519, 523–7.
49 Rémusat, Vol. 3, p. 486.
50 *Dosne*, Vol. 1, p. 211.
51 Guizot speech, 26 Nov. 1840, *Annales* (1840–1), Vol. 3, p. 77.

52 For an account that fully reflects that confusion, see Rémusat, Vol. 3, pp. 474–82.

53 *Dosne*, Vol. 1, p. 201; Granville to Palmerston, 8 Oct., BPP Levant, part 2, p. 274.

54 *Dosne*, Vol. 1, p. 202. See also letters from Duvergier de Hauranne to Thiers, 23 Sept. and 11 Oct., BN n.a.fr. 20609, fols 101–5.

55 Thureau-Dangin, *Histoire*, Vol. 4, p. 331; *Dosne*, Vol, p. 207.

56 Granville to Palmerston, 5 October, BPP Levant, part 2, p. 267; Thiers's speech, 25 Nov., *Annales* (1840), Vol. 2, p. 32. There was inconclusive talk among ministers of making a naval demonstration at Alexandria or even against the Balearics.

57 *Dosne*, Vol. 1, p. 208; Thiers to Bresson, 10 October, BN n.a.fr. 20613–14, fol. 306.

58 Substance of text in Charles-Roux, *Thiers*, pp. 225–8.

59 Bulwer, *Palmerston*, Vol. 2, pp. 380–1.

60 *Annales* (1840–1), Vol. 3, p. 214. For British reactions to the Note and to Thiers's verbal explanations, see Granville's dispatches of 8 and 9 Oct., BPP Levant, part 2, pp. 274–5, and A. C. Benson and Lord Esher (eds), *The Letters of Queen Victoria: A Selection from Her Majesty's Correspondence between the Years 1837 and 1861*, 3 vols (London, 1907), Vol. 1, pp. 299–302.

61 Charles-Roux, *Thiers*, pp. 230–3.

62 BPP Levant, part 2, pp. 313, 335.

63 *Dosne*, Vol. 1, p. 218; Guizot, *Mémoires*, Vol. 5, p. 402.

64 See, for example, Louis-Philippe to Thiers, 14, 18, 19, and 20 Oct., BN n.a.fr. 20611; Le Hon dispatch 29 Oct. MAE(B) France Vol. 10, no. 118; Palmerston to Granville, 27 Oct., BPP Levant, part 2, p. 337.

65 Benson and Esher, *Letters of Queen Victoria*, Vol. 1, p. 306; Bourne, *Palmerston*, pp. 611–12. Louis-Philippe got the message in letters from Leopold and the Queen of the Belgians immediately before his break with Thiers.

66 *Dosne*, Vol. 1, pp. 215–17.

67 Rémusat, Vol. 3, pp. 482–4.

68 BN n.a.fr. 20613–14, fol. 317.

69 Duchesse de Dino, *Chronique de 1831 à 1862*, Vol. 1 (5th edn, Paris, 1909), p. 421. Thiers remained as caretaker until 29 October.

70 *Annales* (1840–1), Vol. 3, pp. 105, 195.

71 For example, Rémusat, Vol. 3, p. 485; Faucher, *Biographie*, Vol. 1, p. 96.

72 *Annales* (1840–1), Vol. 3.

73 Tudesq, *Notables*, Vol. 1, pp. 510–11, 531.

74 Rémusat, Vol. 3, p. 513; Tudesq, *Notables*, Vol. 1, p. 510; Faucher, *Biographie*, Vol. 1, p. 101; Guizot to Barante, 13 Dec. in Barante, *Souvenirs*, Vol. 6, p. 546.

75 W. B. Lincoln, *Nicholas I, Emperor and Autocrat of All the Russias* (London, 1978), p. 218.

CHAPTER 5

1 Robert Blake, *Disraeli*, (Paperback edn, London, 1978), p. 243.

2 This theme was pursued by the satirical paper *Charivari* almost to the end of the July Monarchy.

3 A phrase in a letter of 24 July 1841 from Thiers to his friend Chambolle. A. Chambolle. *Retours sur la vie* (Paris, 1912), p. 507.

4 For Thiers as an historian, see Chapter 8 below.

5 For lively accounts of his impressions, see 'Lettres de M. Thiers à la Comtesse Taverna', *Le Correspondant*, vol. 188 (25 Sept. 1906), pp. 1066–9.

6 There had been a terrible accident on the Versailles line one Sunday in 1842.

7 A. J. Tudesq, *L'élection présidentielle de Louis-Napoléon Bonaparte, 10 décembre 1848* (Paris, 1965), p. 17.

8 Aberdeen to Princess Lieven, 5 Feb. 1842, cit. Lady Frances Balfour, *The Life of George Fourth Earl of Aberdeen, K. G., K. T.,* Vol. 2 (London, 1922), p. 116.

9 P. O'Brien, 'L'Embastillement de Paris: the fortification of Paris during the July Monarchy', *French Historical Studies*, vol. 9, no. 1, (1975), pp. 63–82. The fortifications were dismantled between 1920 and 1924.

10 Speech of 25 Feb. 1841, *Discours*, vol. 5, pp. 494–518.

11 'De l'état actuel des partis en France et de la nécessité d'une transaction', *Revue des Deux Mondes*, vol. 28 (1841), pp. 453–502.

12 See above, p. 63.

13 See the analysis in F. Julien-Laferrière, *Les Députés fonctionnaires sous la Monarchie de Juillet* (Paris, 1970), pp. 94–7.

14 See above, p. 46; *Mignet*, p. 246.

15 ibid., p. 247. Cf. Lamartine's influence in securing the establishment of a royal college at Mâcon in 1843 and in ensuring in 1844 that the Paris–Lyons railway passed through the town (W. Fortescue, *Alphonse de Lamartine: A Political Biography* (London, 1983), pp. 97–8).

16 *Archives parlementaires* (21 April 1836), Vol. 102, p. 380.

17 Marcel Bernos *et al.*, *Histoire d'Aix-en-Provence* (Aix-en-Provence, 1977), pp. 274–5.

18 For this speech of 10 May 1842, see *Discours*, Vol 6, pp. 137ff. In a speech on 25 Jan. 1848 (Vol.7, pp. 484–5) Thiers complained that the essential line from Dunkirk to Paris, Lyons and Marseilles was still uncompleted. On 10 June 1840 he had said that it would be a scandal if nothing was done (*Annales* (1840), Vol. 2, pp. 704 ff.).

19 *Dosne*, Vol. 1, p. 219; *Discours*, Vol. 6, pp. 200ff.

20 *Discours*, Vol 6, p. 262.

21 *Correspondance du duc d'Aumale et de Cuvillier-Fleury* 4 Vols (Paris, 1910–14), Vol. 1, p. 325.

22 Speech of 27 May 1846 (*Discours*, Vol. 7, pp. 302–3).

23 Undated letter from Mignet to Thiers after the 1846 elections (BN n.a.fr. 20617. Cf. Thiers's speech of 17 March 1846: 'le règne des opinions a malheureusement cédé au règne des intérêts' (*Discours*, Vol. 7, p. 126).

24 For example, speeches of 21 Jan. 1845, 20 Jan. and 29 May 1846 (*Discours*, Vol. 6, p. 575, Vol. 7, pp. 3 and 356).

25 Speech of 17 March 1846 (*Discours*, Vol. 7, p. 149). The speech was printed and distributed throughout the country.

26 Julien-Laferrière, *Les Députés fonctionnaires*, pp. 98–100.

27 Malo, p. 430.
28 *Mignet*, p. 247.
29 Speeches of 4 April 1842 and 21 Jan. 1845 (*Discours*, Vol. 6, pp. 84–5, 575).
30 Louis Blanc, *The History of Ten Years 1830–1840* 2 Vols (London, 1844), Vol. 2, pp. 483–4; P. Guiral, *Marseille et l'Algérie 1830–1841* (Gap, 1956), pp. 145–6.
31 Speech of 24 March 1840 (*Discours*, Vol. 4, pp. 481–2).
32 Duvergier to Thiers, letter of 23 July 1847 (BN n.a.fr. 20617).
33 The House of Commons at this time contained 658 members.
34 See above, p. 73–4.
35 A. J. Tudesq, *Les Grands Notables en France (1840–1849): étude historique d'une psychologie sociale* (Paris, 1964), Vol. 2, p. 967.
36 O. Barrot, *Mémoires posthumes d'Odilon Barrot*, 4 vols (Paris, 1875–6), Vol. 1, p. 463.
37 John M. S. Allison, *Thiers and the French Monarchy* (London, 1926), pp. 332–3.
38 cit. D. Johnson, *Guizot: Aspects of French History 1797–1874* (London, 1963), p. 254.
39 Letter of 26 June 1841 (Houghton Collection, Trinity College, Cambridge).
40 Thiers to Chambolle, 9 Sept. 1847 (A. Chambolle, *Retours sur la vie* (Paris, 1912), p. 514.
41 *Courrier*, pp. 207–8.
42 Johnson, *Guizot*, p. 256.
43 For example, the Prince de Joinville, cit. P. Vigier, *La Monarchie de Juillet* (3rd edn, Paris, 1969), p. 119.
44 Comte de Montalivet, *Fragments et souvenirs*, Vol. 2 (Paris, 1900), pp.73 and 96.
45 Speeches of 31 Jan. 1848 (*Discours*, Vol. 7, pp. 496–8, 501) and 2 Feb. (ibid., pp. 565 and 570).
46 ibid., pp. 591–2. He intervened briefly on 12 February in a debate on parliamentary reform in which the government had a majority of thirty-three.
47 *Courrier*, p. 214.
48 There was at least one precedent, on 20 March 1821, when General Donnadieu had proposed an address requesting the king to choose another Cabinet (P. Bastid, *Les Institutions politiques de la monarchie parlementaire française, 1814–1848* (Paris, 1954), p. 286). Lord Normanby thought the proposed impeachment very injudicious (Normanby, *A Year of Revolution: From a Journal Kept in Paris in 1848*, 2 Vols (London, 1857), Vol. 1, p. 83). For the suggestion that Thiers torpedoed an offer by some conservative deputies, and Tocqueville and his friends, to vote against the government in return for the opposition's cancelling the banquet, see *Recollections of Alexis de Tocqueville*, ed. J.P. Mayer (London, 1970), pp. 273–5.
49 Comte de Falloux, *Mémoires d'un Royaliste*, 2 Vols (Paris, 1888), Vol. 1, pp. 245–6.
50 Malo, p. 371.
51 L. Girard, *La IIe République (1848–1851)* (Paris, 1968), p. 46.
52 Malo, p. 368.

53 Thiers to Panizzi, 12 Jan. 1847 (L. Fagan, *The Life of Sir Anthony Panizzi, K. C. B.* (London, 1880), Vol. I, p. 223).

54 *Dosne*, Vol. 1, pp. 227–9.

55 ibid., p. 232.

56 Figures from Girard, *La IIe République*, p. 50.

57 See above, p. 53.

58 On 1 Dec. 1848 Apponyi (*Vingt-cinq ans à Paris. Journal du Comte Rodolphe Apponyi*, 4 Vols (4th edn, Paris, 1913), Vol. 4, p. 207) recorded that earlier Thiers had told him that if Louis-Philippe had withdrawn to Saint-Cloud and summoned the Chambers there, Bugeaud 'l'aurait parfaitement défendu' so that if the king could not have returned to Paris at least the dynasty would have been saved. But he does not say that Thiers claimed to have advised the king to go to Saint-Cloud, and Rémusat (Vol. 4, pp. 22–6) doubts whether he did so. So perhaps did Duvergier (see A. Crémieux, *La Révolution de février: étude critique sur les journées des 21, 22, 23 et 24 février 1838* (Paris, 1912), p. 264n.

59 L. Faucher, *Biographie et correspondance*, 2 vols (2nd edn, Paris, 1875), Vol. 1, p. 214.

60 Cf. Thiers to Panizzi, 20 March 1848: 'j'ai failli être égorgé par la populace, qui trois heures auparavant criait: vive Thiers! à tue-tête' (Fagan, *Panizzi*, Vol. 1, p. 241).

61 J. Lucas-Dubreton, *Aspects de Monsieur Thiers* (Paris, 1948), p. 204; C. Pomaret, *Monsieur Thiers et son siècle* (Paris, 1948), p. 193; Duc de Castries, *Monsieur Thiers* (Paris, 1983), pp. 215–16.

62 Duc de Castries, *Monsieur Thiers*, p. 216.

63 J. Bruhat, *Les Journées de février 1848* (Paris, 1948), p. 17.

64 Blake, *Disraeli*, p. 272.

65 In 1848 this influence was surprisingly limited. Indeed one historian has remarked that Thiers and Barrot were then like men 'qui ne disposaient ni du *Constitutionnel* ni du *Siècle*, ni d'aucun journal'. C. Bellanger *et al.*, *Histoire générale de la presse française*, Vol. 2 (Paris, 1972), p. 145.

66 A. Jardin and A.-J. Tudesq, *La France des notables* (Paris, 1973), Vol. 1, p. 156.

67 *Courrier*, pp. 224–6.

68 Crémieux, *La Révolution de février 1848*, pp. 263–4. Crémieux's book provides the fullest examination of the many conflicting accounts of the events of these days.

69 In England, too, the queen and the prince consort had their strong likes and dislikes: 'He has not one particle of the gentleman in his composition', wrote the prince of Disraeli, and the queen referred to Russell and Palmerston as 'those dreadful old men' (Blake, *Disraeli*, p. 277). 'It was still better to have the Court with you than against you' (ibid., p. 278).

70 Tocqueville, *Recollections*, pp. 267–8; Rémusat, Vol. 4, p. 220.

71 See, for example, with variations, that of the Duc de Nemours: R. Bazin, *Le Duc de Nemours* (3rd edn, Paris, 1907), pp. 308–9.

72 Rémusat, Vol. 4, pp. 223–4.

73 'Lettres ... à la Comtesse Taverna', *Le Correspondant*, vol. 188 (25 Sept. 1906), p. 1073.

74 Lucas-Dubreton, *Monsieur Thiers*, p. 204. With his feeble voice, however, he

would have had little chance of dominating an invading crowd. In a later comment Rémusat remarked that no one more than Thiers needed 'délibérer à l'aise' and that he said to the king: 'Je ne suis pas informé, et quand je ne suis pas informé, je n'ai pas d'avis' (Rémusat, Vol. 4, p. 223).

CHAPTER 6

1 Posthumously published in 1902 under the title *Notes et souvenirs de M. Thiers 1848: Révolution du 24 février.*
2 Mme Dosne to Borély (BT, TMS. 1311).
3 Letter to Floret, a friend at Aix (printed in *Le Monde*, 4 March 1948); cf. letter of 20 March to Panizzi (L. Fagan, *The Life of Sir Anthony Panizzi, K. C. B.* (London, 1880), p. 241).
4 *Discours*, Vol. 8, pp. 59–60, speech of 13 Sept. 1848.
5 Letter of 22 March to Borély, BT T MS. 1311.
6 ibid., p. 134.
7 Letter of 31 March to Rémusat, Rémusat, Vol. 4, pp. 286–7.
8 'Lettres de M. Thiers à la Comtesse Taverna' *Le Correspondant*, vol. 188 (25 Sept. 1906), p. 1077; Mme Dosne to Borély, 29 April and 1 May (BT, TMS. 1311, pp. 48, 55–7).
9 For details, see A-J. Tudesq, *Les Grands Notables en France (1840–1849): étude historique d'une psychologie sociale* (Paris, 1964), pp. 1086–92. The four departments were Seine, Seine-Inférieure, Orne and Gironde. A. Robert, E. Bourloton and G. Cougny, *Dictionnaire des parlementaires français*, 5 vols (Paris, 1889–91), substitute Mayenne for Gironde.
10 L. Girard, *La IIe République (1848–1851)* (Paris, 1968), p. 123.
11 Letter from Thiers to Floret, *Le Monde*, 4 March 1948.
12 Rémusat, Vol. 4, pp. 332–3; Malo, p. 386.
13 For Madame Dosne's account of the duel see *Dosne*, Vol. 2, pp. 208–10. According to Rémusat, Vol. 4, p. 371n, he had spoken and even written the words Bixio attributed to him and thought a duel the only means 'retirer le propos de la circulation'.
14 Letter to Chassan (BT, TMS. 24). In fact the Rue de Poitiers meetings normally occurred once or twice a week. After their first meeting it is the practice for the members of French parliaments to divide into a number of bureaux for the preliminary discussion of legislation.
15 *Discours*, Vol. 8, pp. 1–28.
16 ibid., pp. 38–40. Peel and Gladstone had reintroduced the income tax in 1842. Gladstone regarded it as essentially immoral and would later have liked to abolish it.
17 R. Schnerb, 'La Politique fiscale de Thiers', *Revue Historique*, vol. 201 (Jan–June 1949, pp. 196–7); see below p. 214–5.
18 For a review of the bureaux's observations, see P. Bastid, *Doctrines et institutions politiques de la Seconde République* (Paris, 1945), Vol. 2, ch. 3.
19 *Discours*, Vol. 8, pp. 59ff.
20 For a summary of what Thiers told the committee on behalf of the third Bureau, see Bastid, *Doctrines et institutions*, Vol. 2, p. 35.

21 ibid., p. 139; cf. J. Monteilhet, *Les Institutions militaires de la France (1814–1932)* (Paris, 1932), pp. 28–31.

22 *Discours*, Vol. 8, pp. 165ff. Short-term conscripts were the main constituent of the Prussian army.

23 See the letters in *Courrier*, p. 243; Bastid, *Doctrines et institutions*, Vol. 2, p. 53.

24 In a letter of 17 October to Chassan, Thiers claimed to have contributed to the ministerial reshuffle which brought the first Republicans *du lendemain* into the Cabinet (BT, TMS. 24).

25 ibid.

26 D. Johnson, *Guizot: Aspects of French History, 1787–1874*, p. 86.

27 *Courrier*, p. 241.

28 Marquis of Normanby, *A Year of Revolution: From a Journal Kept in Paris in 1848*, 2 Vols (London, 1857) Vol. 2, p. 280.

29 This was a decision on which Thiers, Barrot and Berryer had abstained from voting. Comte de Falloux, *Mémoires d'un Royaliste*, 2 Vols (Paris, 1888), Vol. 1, p. 354.

30 According to P. Albert *et al.*, *Documents pour l'histoire de la presse nationale aux XIXe et XXe siècles* (Paris, 1973), pp. 196–7, propaganda put out by the Rue de Poitiers as early as July indicated Thiers as a future president.

31 Cavaignac on 3 November offered him the vice-presidency (*Dosne*, Vol. 1, p. 265).

32 Tocqueville (letter of 10 Nov. to Beaumont, in *Oeuvres et correspondances inédites*, ed. G. de Beaumont, 8 Vols (Paris, 1861), Vol. 8., p. 90 called Thiers's attitude one of 'neutralité malveillante'.

33 See Thiers to Chassan, 8 Nov. (BT TMS. 24); *Mémoires du Duc de Broglie*, 2 Vols (Paris, 1938), Vol. 1, p. 310.

34 *Dosne*, Vol. 1, pp. 280–300, Vol. 2, pp. 36–43.

35 At a reception at the Elysée on 1 February, Thiers, noted Fortoul, a new representative, 'y était comme le maître de la maison'; *Journal d'Hippolyte Fortoul*, Vol. 1 (Geneva, 1979), p. 19. Cf. Viennet's account of an intimate dinner on 22 January at which Thiers was a guest; *Journal de Viennet, Pair de France, témoin de trois règnes 1817–1848* (Paris, 1955), p. 318.

36 Rémusat, Vol. 4, p. 372; see also A.-J. Tudesq, *L'Election présidentielle de Louis-Napoléon Bonaparte, 10 décembre 1848* (Paris, 1965), pp. 186–7, 192.

37 King Leopold to Thiers, 25 Dec. 1848, BN, n.a.fr. 20617.

38 One who regained a modest position, that of consul at Ancona, was Thiers's half brother, Charles, who had been brusquely dismissed in May 1848. F. Boyer, 'Un demi-frère d'Adolphe Thiers vice-consul de Napoléon III à Girgenti', *Revue d'Histoire Diplomatique* (April–June 1959), pp. 2–3.

39 R. Apponyi, *Vingt-cinq ans à Paris. Journal du Comte Rodolphe Apponyi*, 4 vols (4th edn, Paris, 1913), Vol. 4, pp. 217–8.

40 *Dosne*, Vol. 2, p. 58.

41 'Lettres à la Comtesse Taverna', *Le Correspondant*, vol. 188 (25 Sept. 1906), p. 1079.

42 ibid., p. 1080.

43 Malo, p. 398.

44 P. Magnus, *Gladstone* (paperback edn, London, 1963), p. 188.

45 *Dosne*, Vol. 2, pp. 113–4. Apponyi (*Journal*, Vol. 4, p. 241) noted on 5 February Parisian society's fear of new risings and added that Thiers seldom slept at home. At the end of January Thiers dissuaded Louis-Napoleon from dissolving the Assembly by force as Changarnier, the Commander ot the National Guard, had urged. He said that the deputies should be allowed to go on 'yelling' for some time.

46 *Dosne*, Vol. 2, p. 185.

47 For the text see *Discours*, Vol. 8, pp. 253ff.

48 Speech of 5 Jan. 1850 (ibid., p. 384). Although opposed, he said in 1846, to distant colonies, he had long been concerned to defend French interests on the shores of the River Plate.

49 Lawrence C. Jennings, *France and Europe in 1848: A Study of French Foreign Affairs in Time of Crisis* (Oxford, 1973), p. 162; cf. ibid., p. 238.

50 *Discours*, Vol. 7, pp. 490ff.

51 Rémusat, Vol. 4, p. 272. For some of Thiers's Italian correspondents, see R. Ciampini, *Thiers et le 'Risorgimento' d'après les documents inédits* (Florence, 1948).

52 *Discours*, Vol. 8, pp. 206ff. O. Barrot (*Mémoires posthumes d'Odilon Barrot*, 4 Vols (Paris, 1875–6), Vol. 3, p. 155) said that Thiers's, paroles foudroyantes de vérité écrasaient la Montagne'. Thiers was also involved in a negotiation between the president and the Austrian chargé d'affaires calculated to intimidate Austria while keeping the peace (ibid., pp. 148–9 n.l).

53 Tommaseo to Mignet, *Mignet*, pp. 403–4. He pleaded that Venice should be made 'Une ville anséatique (?)' and asked Mignet to speak to Thiers. As early as 1834 Thiers had asked the Swiss government to repress Mazzinian agitators (Ciampini, *Thiers et le 'Risorgimento'*, p. 58).

54 He more than once argued that while nations had the right to self-government, the Roman states belonged to the whole Catholic world which wished for the Pope's temporal sovereignty and therefore had the right to impose it. P. de Rémusat, *A. Thiers* (Paris, 1889), p. 110.

55 Girard, *La IIe République*, p. 185.

56 *Discours*, Vol. 8, p. 254.

57 For the text of the *Motu Proprio*, see Barrot, *Mémoires*, Vol. 3, pp. 435–8.

58 Letter of 4 Nov. 1849, Tocqueville, *Oeuvres et correspondances*, Vol. 8, pp. 232–3.

CHAPTER 7

1 *Dosne*, Vol. 2, p. 197; BN n.a.fr. 20618, fols 30, 57; Rémusat, Vol. 4, p. 461.

2 Speech of 24 July 1849, *Discours*, Vol. 8, pp. 300–1.

3 Dreyfus, *L'Assistance sous la seconde république (1848–1851)* (Paris, 1907), pp. 134, 140–1, 197–207; *Discours*, Vol. 8, p. 537.

4 For example, the sanitation law did not compel local authorities to act; and the law setting up state-guaranteed pension funds, which ran for more than half a century, by 1903 only covered 2 per cent of the workforce, and half of those received pensions of less than 50 francs per year.

5 Dreyfus, *L'Assistance*, p. 208.
6 ibid., p. 207.
7 Comte de Falloux, *Mémoires d'un Royaliste*, 2 vols (Paris, 1888), Vol. 2, p. 10.
8 Letter of Cardinal de la Tour d'Auvergne, BN n.a.fr. 20617.
9 Elementary schools (*écoles primaires*) provided basic education at minimum cost from the age of 6 onwards to about 3.5 million children. State secondary schools (*écoles secondaires*), which included *lycées*, *collèges* and their preparatory schools, formed a quite separate fee-paying system for about 45,000 boys aged 10 to 18.
10 Georges Chenesseau (ed.), *A l'origine de la liberté d'enseignement: la Commission extraparlementaire de 1849* (Paris, 1937), pp. 31–2, 39–40.
11 R. D. Anderson, *Education in France 1848–1870* (Oxford, 1975), pp. 41–4; Giolitto, *Histoire de l'enseignement primaire au XIXe siècle: L'organisation pédagogique* (Paris, 1983), pp. 119–20.
12 Chenesseau, *A l'origine*, pp. 30, 33, 153–4.
13 ibid., pp. 154, 157, 264–5.
14 ibid., pp. 192, 31.
15 ibid., pp. 191–4.
16 Anderson, *Education*, pp. 47–50; Giolitto, *Histoire*, pp. 122–31.
17 Price, *The French Second Republic: A Social History* (London, 1972), p. 255; Dupanloup, *Le Catéchisme chrétien* (Paris, 1865), p. xxxii.
18 *Histoire du Consulat et de l'Empire*, 20 vols (Paris, 1845–62), Vol. 3, pp. 205, 206, 208.
19 *Discours*, Vol. 8, p. 609 (13 Feb. 1850).
20 *Correspondances*, p. 173; Duvergier to Thiers, 13 March 1850, BN n.a.fr 20618, fol. 22.
21 *Discours*, Vol. 8, p. 685 (23 Feb. 1850); Malo, p. 405.
22 A. Dansette, *Louis-Napoléon à la conquête du pouvoir* (Paris, 1961), pp. 234–5; Rémusat, Vol. 4, pp. 128–9; *Recollections of Alexis de Tocqueville*, ed. J. P. Mayer (London, 1948), p. 266.
23 P. Raphael, 'La Loi du 31 mai 1850', *Revue d'Histoire Moderne et Contemporaine*, vol. 13 (Nov–Dec, 1909), pp. 277–304, vol. 14 (May–Oct. 1910), pp. 44–79, 297–331.
24 Rémusat, Vol. 4, p. 461; Molé to Thiers, BN n.a.fr. 20618, fol. 60.
25 *Discours*, Vol. 9, p. 40; N. W. Senior, *Conversations with M. Thiers, M. Guizot and Other Distinguished Persons during the Second Empire*, 2 vols (London, 1878), Vol. 1, p. 77.
26 N. W. Senior, *Journals Kept in France and Italy from 1848 to 1852*, 2 vols (London, 1871), Vol. 1, pp. 221, 230–1, 233, 243.
27 Raphael, 'La Loi du 31 mai', p. 74.
28 See below, Chapter 11.
29 Quoted in J. Dautry, *1848 et la deuxième république* (3rd edn, Paris, 1977), p. 245.
30 Tocqueville, *Recollections*, p. 89.
31 Chenesseau, *A l'origine*, p. 155. The example of contemporary Spain was not reassuring.
32 ibid., p. 30.
33 Rémusat, Vol. 4, p. 441; Thiers, letter to Count Stroganoff, 8 July 1850, BN

n.a.fr. 20618, fol. 84. In Volume 1 of his *Histoire de la Révolution française* Thiers had written, 'Les princes ne peuvent se résigner, les peuples se modérer.'

34 *Dosne*, Vol. 2, pp. 235–6.

35 Rémusat, Vol. 4, p. 461.

36 Dautry, *1848*, p. 268; Dansette, *Louis-Napoléon*, pp. 337–8; J. Ridley, *Napoleon III and Eugénie* (London, 1979), p. 283.

37 Rémusat, Vol. 4, p. 455.

38 *Discours*, Vol. 9, pp. 63–112.

39 Letter to Orléans family, 2 March 1851, BN n.a.fr. 20618, fol. 134 (also in *Courrier*, p. 267).

40 ibid., fol. 148 (*Courrier*, p. 277).

41 P. D. G. Smith, 'The Orleanists, 1849–1852', Ph. D. thesis, University of Cambridge, 1979, p. 187. This fine study is a most important contribution to understanding the politics of the Second Republic.

42 BN n.a.fr. 20618, fols 132–48 (also in *Courrier*, pp. 268–70, 273–5.)

43 Smith, 'The Orleanists', pp. 143, 145–6, 157–8, 161–2, 187. See also letter from Orléans family to Thiers, March 1851, BN n.a.fr. 20618 fol. 156.

44 *Discours*, Vol 9, pp. 117–32.

45 ibid., Vol. 9, pp. 139–43.

46 Malo, pp. 419–20.

47 Smith, 'The Orleanists', pp. 193–205.

48 BN n.a.fr. 20618, fols 99–102.

49 Smith, 'The Orleanists', p. 240.

50 ibid., p. 278.

51 *Discours*, Vol. 9, pp. 313–25. See comments of Rémusat, Vol. 4, p. 475, and of Duvergier, in N. W. Senior, *Conversations with Distinguished Persons during the Second Empire from 1860 to 1863*, 2 vols (London, 1880), Vol. 1, p. 88.

52 Smith, 'The Orleanists', pp. 291–4, 297–302.

53 R. Apponyi, *De la révolution au coup d'état, 1848–1851* (Geneva, 1948), pp. 183–4; Rémusat, Vol. 4, pp. 479–80.

54 Smith, 'The Orleanists', pp. 315–16. One of the earliest and best accounts of the *coup d'état* is E. Ténot, *Paris en décembre 1851: étude historique sur le coup d'état* (Paris, 1868), and *La Province en décembre 1851: étude historique sur le coup d'état* (Paris, 1865).

55 *Correspondances*, p. 231; *Dosne*, Vol. 2, p. 230.

56 Ténot, *Paris en décembre*, p. 89. Compare, for example, Duc de Castries, *Monsieur Thiers* (Paris, 1983), pp. 253–4.

57 Smith, 'The Orleanists', pp. 323–4.

58 See, for example, Ténot, *Paris en décembre*, pp. 135–41.

59 Smith, 'The Orleanists', p. 348. For accounts of the uprising, see Ténot, *La Province en décembre* and T. W. Margadant, *French Peasants in Revolt: The Insurrection of 1851* (Princeton, 1979), and for the plebiscite, F. Bluche, *Le Bonapartisme: aux origines de la droite autoritaire (1800—1850)* (Paris, 1980), pp. 274–6.

60 Smith, 'The Orleanists', p. 354.

61 BN n.a.fr. 20618, fol. 264 (also in *Courrier*, p. 283).

62 BN n.a.fr. 20618, fol. 176 (letter of 16 Jan. 1852).

63 V. Wright, 'The *coup d'état* of December 1851: repression and the limits to

repression', in R. Price (ed.), *Revolution and Reaction: 1848 and the Second French Republic* (London, 1975), pp. 303–33.

64 Duc de Broglie, *Mémoires du Duc de Broglie*, 2 vols (Paris, 1938), Vol. 1, p. 240.

65 Letter to Orléans family, 2 March 1851, BN n.a.fr. 20618, fol. 135 (also in *Courrier*, p. 268).

66 Smith, 'The Orleanists', pp. 41, 264.

67 BN n.a.fr. 20618, fol. 134.

CHAPTER 8

1 Letters, 1852 (1 Jan., and undated), BN n.a.fr. 20618, fols 262 and 299–30.

2 Letters, Mignet to Thiers, 9 Jan. and 2 April 1852, ibid, fols 213, 219; *Correspondances*, pp. 231, 314–19.

3 ibid., pp. 257, 336–7.

4 A. Chambolle, *Retours sur la vie* (Paris, 1912), p. 356; *Correspondances*, pp. 319, 394; Thiers to Cousin, 1 Jan. 1852, BN n.a.fr. 20618 fols 262–3 (also in *Courrier*, pp. 286–7).

5 ibid.

6 *Correspondances*, p. 241 (18 Dec. 1851).

7 ibid., pp. 263, 365–6; will, BN n.a.fr. 20628, fol. 414.

8 To Cousin, 1 Jan. 1852, BN n.a.fr. 20618, fols 260–1 (also in *Courrier*, p. 285).

9 ibid., fol. 261.

10 Mignet to Thiers, ibid., fol. 224; *Correspondances*, pp. 237, 319.

11 BN n.a.fr. 20618, fol. 228.

12 ibid., fol. 335.

13 D. Johnson, *Guizot: Aspects of French History, 1797–1874* (London, 1963), p. 192.

14 Thiers to Saint-Aulaire, 10 July 1836, BN n.a.fr. 20607, fol. 218 (also in *Courrier*, p. 89).

15 *Annales* (1873), vol. 18, pp. 46–7.

16 BN n.a.fr. 20628. This epitaph, echoing a phrase in his will of 1852, is inscribed on his tomb in the Père Lachaise cemetery.

17 *Mignet*, p. 118; J. McManners, 'The historiography of the French Revolution', in A. Goodwin (ed.), *New Cambridge Modern History*, Vol. 8 (Cambridge, 1971), p. 625.

18 A. Aulard, 'Thiers historien de la Révolution française', *La Révolution Française*, vol. 66 (June 1914), pp. 496, 501.

19 Thiers, *Histoire de la Révolution française*, 10 vols (Paris, 1823–7), Vol. 1, p. 41.

20 *Mignet*, p. 129.

21 F. Mignet, *Histoire de la Révolution française*, 2 vols (Paris, 1824), introduction.

22 C. A. Sainte-Beuve, *Cahiers*, ed. J. Troubat (Paris, 1876), p. 59 (27 Nov. 1847).

23 *Mignet*, p. 118.
24 C. A. Sainte-Beuve, 'Historiens modernes de la France', *Revue des Deux Mondes*, vol. 9 (1845), pp. 266–7.
25 *Mignet*, p. 128.
26 Thiers, *Révolution française*, Vol. 3, pp. 366–7.
27 *Mignet*, p. 174; S. Mellon, *The Political Uses of History: A Study of Historians in the French Restoration* (Stanford, Calif., 1958), pp. 29, 23; Thiers, *Révolution française*, Vol. 6, p. 493.
28 Thiers, *Révolution française*, Vol. 3, pp. viii–ix.
29 *Mignet*, p. 175.
30 Thiers, *Révolution française*, Vol. 3, p. xi.
31 A. Jardin, *Le libéralisme politique en France, pensée et mouvement, de la crise du XVIIe siècle à la Constitution de 1875* (Paris, 1985), pp. 233–7.
32 Aulard, 'Thiers historien', p. 158.
33 Acton Papers (Cambridge University Library), MS Add. 4917 F, card 28.
34 Last lines of Vol. 8 (1826). For sales, see *Mignet*, p. 167n.
35 See above, Chapter 1.
36 BT, TMS. 564.
37 G. Mauguin, 'Thiers et son histoire de la République de Florence', *Annales de L'Université de Grenoble*, vol. 30, no. 2 (1918), pp. 241–94, and Thiers's notes BT, TMS. 564. See also R. Ciampini, *Thiers et le 'Risorgimento' d'après les documents inédits* (Florence, 1948), pp. 8–15.
38 Duc de Castries, *Monsieur Thiers* (Paris, 1983), p. 272.
39 Vol. 20, p. 710.
40 P. Geyl, *Napoleon: For and Against* (new edn, London, 1965), p. 57.
41 Acton Papers (Cambridge University Library), MS Add. 4917, card 95.
42 A. Laya, *Études historiques sur la vie privée, politique et littéraire de M. A. Thiers*, 2 vols (Paris, 1846), Vol. 2, app. 2, p. cxxxv.
43 ibid., p. cxlvi; BN n.a.fr. 20618, fol. 81 (9 Jan. 1850).
44 BN n.a.fr. 20617, fol. 49.
45 BN n.a.fr. 20618, fols 275 (1 Nov. 1853), 334 (1855) and 374 (31 Aug. 1856).
46 BN n.a.fr. 20618 and 20619, *passim*.
47 Vol. 20 (1862), last lines.
48 BN n.a.fr. 20618, fol. 432 (27 Dec. 1857 and in *Courrier*, p. 326).
49 BN n.a.fr. 20617 and 20618, *passim*.
50 Malo, p. 441.
51 For example, V. Chaffour-Kestner, *Sur l'Histoire du Consulat et de L'Empire de M. Thiers* (Paris, 1863).
52 Vol. 20, pp. 794–5. Acton had read Thiers, and it is interesting to speculate on whether his famous dictum on absolute power, written in 1887, might have been inspired by Thiers's words on Napoleon.
53 Vol. 20, pp. 793, 721.
54 'Avertissement de l'auteur', Vol. 8, p. iii.
55 Vol. 3, p. 206.
56 Laya, *Études*, p. cxiv; BN n.a.fr. 20617, fol. 88.
57 Johnson, *Guizot*, p. 23.
58 Vol. 8, pp. ii–iii.
59 ibid, p. xxvi.

60 *Choses vues: souvenirs, journaux, cahiers, 1847–1848*, ed. H. Juin (Paris, 1972), p. 252. Scribe was a successful author of 'well-made' comedies.

61 Sainte-Beuve, 'Historiens modernes de la France', p. 241.

62 Laya, *Études*, p. cxxxviii; BN n.a.fr. 20619, fols 46 and 84.

63 R. Baschet, 'Thiers critique d'art: les salons de 1822 et de 1824', *Les Amis de Saint François*, vol. 12, no 1 (Jan.–Feb. 1971), pp. 11–18, points out that Thiers also praised several third-rate artists in similar terms. For background, see Chapter 1.

64 W. Vaughan, 'The visual arts', in D. G. Charlton (ed), *The French Romantics*, Vol. 2 (Cambridge, 1984), p. 335.

65 We are indebted to Professor Lee Johnson for his comments on Thiers's patronage of Delacroix. See also H. Malo, 'M. Thiers et les artistes de son temps', *Revue de Paris*, vol. 31 part 4 (1924), pp. 141–59; Charles Blanc, *Collection d'objets d'art de M. Thiers léguée au musée du Louvre* (Paris, 1884); H. Michaud, 'L'Exotisme de M. Thiers', *Annuaire-Bulletin de la Société de l'Histoire de France* (1976–7), pp. 157–63. For Thiers's own comments on art, see *Correspondances* and Henriette Bessis, 'Adolphe Thiers et la Duchesse Colonna', unpublished thesis, University of Paris I, 1977, *passim*. The Duchess, the leading woman sculptor of her time, was a close friend.

66 ibid., pp. 18–19.

67 Alfred Kelly, *The Descent of Darwinism: The Popularization of Darwinism in Germany, 1860–1914* (Chapel Hill, North Carolina, 1981), p. 17.

68 Letter to Agassiz, 23 Nov. 1871, BN n.a.fr. 20623, fol. 187 (also in *Courrier*, p. 454).

69 R. Vallery-Radot, *La Vie de Pasteur* (Paris, 1900), p. 128. See also J. Farley and G. L. Geison, 'Science, politics and spontaneous generation in nineteenth-century France: the Pasteur–Pouchet debate', *Bulletin of the History of Medicine*, vol. 48, no. 2 (Summer 1974), pp. 161–98.

70 BN n.a.fr. 20623, fol. 185. See also J. Marcou, *Life, Letters and Works of Louis Agassiz*, 2 vols (London and New York, 1896).

71 Vallery-Radot, *Pasteur*, p. 128, and see Farley and Geison, 'Science, politics', *passim*.

72 E. Jovy, *Autour de M. Thiers pascalisant, d'après des documents inédits* (Clermont-Ferrand, 1928).

73 Pasteur to Thiers, 19 July 1867, BN n.a.fr. 20619, fol. 346; Thiers to Agassiz, 23 Nov. 1871, BN n.a.fr. 20623, fol. 185. See also Vallery-Radot, *Pasteur*, p. 198.

74 See their letters, BN n.a.fr. 20619 and 20628, *passim*.

75 A. Pannekoek, *A History of Astronomy* (London, 1961), p. 363.

76 Jovy, *Autour*, p. 10.

77 Pannekoek, *History*, p. 364.

78 BN n.a.fr. 20623, fol. 159.

79 P. Vallery-Radot (ed.), *Correspondance de Pasteur 1840—1895*, 3 vols (Paris, 1951), Vol. 2, p. 573; letter to Thiers from Academy of Sciences, 26 Jan. 1877, BN n.a.fr. 20628, fol.407.

80 *Plan d'un ouvrage de philosophie* (Paris, 1905), p. 1. For his single-minded work on this project, see Bessis, 'Thiers et Colonna', pp. 320, 322, 344, 346.

81 *Plan*, p. 2.

82 Sainte-Beuve, *Cahiers*, ed. Troubat, pp. 59, 100–1.
83 For a comparison of the attitudes of Thiers and Guizot, see P. Rosanvallon, *Le Moment Guizot* (Paris, 1985), pp. 350–3.
84 *Plan*, pp. 24–5.
85 Letter to Edward Ellice, 25 March 1853, BN n.a.fr. 20618, fol. 298 (and in *Courrier*, p. 313). He expressed the same belief more piously in his will of 14 July 1867, n.a.fr. 20628, fol. 415.
86 Jovy, *Autour*, p. 7.
87 Sainte-Beuve, 'Historiens modernes de la France', p. 213, quoting an article written by Thiers in 1829. Thiers was not alone among nineteenth-century spiritualists in having such ideas; see C. Delacampagne, 'Ravaisson et l'idée d'action', *Le Monde*, 30 June 1984.

CHAPTER 9

1 On 13 April 1868 he told Julie Bonaparte that he would like to write 'a kind of Plutarch' of great men's lives which would be 'L'Histoire de l'esprit humain'. I. D. Basso (ed.), *La Princesse Julie Bonaparte, Marquise de Roccagiovine, et son temps: mémoires inédits (1853–1870)*, 2 vols (Rome, 1975), p. 389.
2 Thiers to Aumale, 5 Jan. 1861, *Courrier*, pp. 343–8.
3 For these soundings, see Malo, pp. 442–7.
4 P. Guiral, *Prévost-Paradol 1829–1870: pensée et action d'un Libéral sous le second Empire* (Paris, 1955), p. 142, n. 336.
5 E. Ollivier, *Journal, 1846–69*, ed. T. Zeldin and A. Troisier de Diaz, 2 vols (Paris, 1961), Vol. 2, p. 88. For the election in the Nord see B. Ménager, *La Vie politique dans le département du Nord de 1851 à 1877*, 3 vols (Lille, 1983), Vol. 2, pp. 572, 589–91.
6 E. Laboulaye, *Le Parti libéral son programme et son avenir*, 2nd edn (Paris, 1868), p. 313; L. Girard, *Les Libéraux Français, 1814–1875* (Paris, 1985), pp. 186–7.
7 H. Welschinger, 'L'élection de Littré à l'Académie française. Lettres inédites', *Revue des Deux Mondes*, vol. 44 (15 March 1918), pp. 394–422, cf. S. Aquarone, *The Life and Works of Emile Littré 1801–1881* (Leyden, 1958), pp. 87–94.
8 Ollivier paid remarkable tribute to her qualities in his *L'Empire libéral: études, récits, souvenirs*, 18 vols (Paris, 1895–1918), Vol. 6, pp. 381–2.
9 Sir Mountstuart Grant Duff, *Notes from a Diary 1851–1872*, Vol. 1 (London, 1897), p. 266.
10 Good accounts or glimpses of Thiers's day are to be found in Basso, (ed.), *Julie Bonaparte*, p. 150, *Courrier*, pp. 344–5, and N. W. Senior, *Conversations with M. Thiers, M. Guizot and other Distinguished Persons during the Second Empire*, 2 vols (London, 1878) especially Vol. 2, p. 152.
11 L. Halévy, *Carnets*, ed. D. Halévy, 2 vols (Paris, 1935), Vol. 1, p. 82.
12 Ollivier, *Journal*, Vol. 2, p. 232.
13 Guiral, *Prévost-Paradol*, *passim*.
14 Halévy, *Carnets*, Vol. 1, pp. 82, 100, 150. For the way in which Thiers prepared his speeches, see P. de Rémusat, *A. Thiers* (Paris, 1889), pp. 144–5,

who also quotes (pp. 66–7) an amusing skit on the didactic character of Thiers's oratory in L. Reybaud's *Jérôme Paturot à la Recherche d'une position sociale*.

15 Halévy, Carnets, Vol. I, p. 102.

16 A well-known caricaturist, in private life Comte Amédée de Noé.

17 L. Halévy, *Notes et souvenirs* (Paris, 1889), p. 137; cf. Allain-Targé, *La République sous l'Empire: Lettres (1864–1870)*, ed. S. de la Porte (Paris, 1939), pp. 26–7, 113.

18 Baron Beyens, *Le Second Empire vu par un diplomate belge*, 2 vols (Bruges, 1924), Vol. 2, p. 82.

19 For the oratorical duel between Thiers and Rouher, see R. Schnerb, *Rouher et le Second Empire* (Paris, 1949), pp. 133–4.

20 Halévy, *Carnets*, Vol. 1, p. 93. His protectionism came out in many speeches on financial and economic affairs.

21 For example, 14 March 1867, *Discours*, Vol. II, p. 22.

22 For the text, see *Discours*, Vol. 9, pp. 357–405.

23 *Discours*, Vol 10, pp. 3–52.

24 For the text, see *Discours*, Vol. 10, pp. 333–94.

25 Beyens, *Le Second Empire*, Vol. 2, p. 362.

26 See J. P. T. Bury, *Napoleon III and the Second Empire* (London, 1964), p. 95.

27 He who gives quickly gives twice.

28 For the texts, see *Discours*, Vol. 11, pp. 361–535; for a good account of the law and its consequences, see I. Collins, *The Government and the Newspaper Press in France 1814–1881* (London, 1959), pp. 147–56

29 Michael S. Smith, *Tariff Reform in France 1860–1900: The Politics of Economic Interest* (Ithaca and London, 1980), pp. 35–6.

30 N. W. Senior, *Conversations with Distinguished Persons during the Second Empire from 1860 to 1863*, 2 vols (London, 1880), Vol. 2, p. 176. France had joined Britain in sending troops to China in 1857–8 and 1860; she had also sent a force to protect Syrian Catholics in 1860. In a letter of 23 July 1860 from Anzin, however, Thiers had written that he was delighted to see the French acting as Europe's missionaries in Syria. I. D. Basso, 'Lettere inedite di Thiers alla Principessa Giulia Bonaparte Roccagiovine', *Trimestre*, vol. 6, nos 1–2 (March–June 1972), p. 37.

31 See above, p. 113.

32 Senior, *Conversations with Distinguished Persons*, Vol. 2, pp. 113–4.

33 For the text, see *Discours*, Vol. 9, pp. 449–517, and for a brief account of the Mexican affair, Bury, *Napoleon III*, pp. 133–9.

34 9 July 1867. For the text, see *Discours*, Vol. 11, pp. 164–248.

35 ibid., Vol. 8, p. 311.

36 Senior, *Conversations with M. Thiers*, Vol. 1, pp. 28–9; cf. R. Ciampini, *Thiers et le 'Risorgimento' d'après les documents inédits* (Florence, 1948), p. 24 for the way in which some of these ideas echoed those of Gioberti.

37 *Courrier*, pp. 337–40; cf. Comte de Hübner, *Neuf ans de souvenirs d'un ambassadeur d'Autriche à Paris sous le Second Empire 1851–1859*, 2 vols (Paris, 1904), Vol. 2, pp. 249–50, 311–12, 323. On 11 June 1859 Thiers had remarked: 'Qu'on reprenne le Rhin, à la bonne heure; mais il est absurde de vouloir rendre l'Italie et l'Allemagne unes … Accroître le Piémont n'est pas non plus sensé' (Ollivier, *Journal*, Vol. 1, p. 387).

38 Bury, *Napoleon III*, pp. 97–8.

39 For the texts, see *Discours*, Vol. 10, pp. 56–171. For the 'levée des journaux démocratiques contre Thiers', see Guiral, *Prévost-Paradol*, p. 389.

40 Odo Russell to Earl Russell, 26 April 1862, Noel Blakiston (ed.) *The Roman Question, Extracts from the Despatches of Odo Russell from Rome 1858–1870* (London, 1962), p, 224.

41 For the whole speech, see *Discours*, Vol. 11, pp. 258–342.

42 Cit. Schnerb, *Rouher*, p. 220.

43 *Discours*, Vol. 10, p. 65.

44 Lynn M. Case, *French Opinion on War and Diplomacy during the Second Empire* (Philadelphia, 1954), pp. 197–9.

45 For the whole speech, see *Discours*, Vol. 10, pp. 574–629.

46 Case, *French Opinion*, p. 199. For Thiers's slight retrospective modification of his advice, see *Discours*, Vol. 11, pp. 62–3.

47 In March 1867 he said he regretted not having spoken earlier, i.e. in February or March 1866 in the debates on the address.

48 For Napoleon's irritation at Thiers's speech, see *Conversations with Napoleon III*, ed. Sir V. Wellesley and R. Sencourt (London, 1934), p. 257, and Case, *French Opinion*, p. 200.

49 For the whole speech, see *Discours*, Vol. 11, pp. 3–91.

50 For these elections, see A. Olivesi, 'Marseille', in L. Girard, *Les Elections de 1869* (Paris, 1960), and Ménager, *La Vie politique dans le département du Nord*, Vol. 2, pp. 834–5, 841–5.

51 For maps showing the alterations, see L. Girard, *Nouvelle histoire de Paris: la Deuxième République et le Second Empire 1848–1870* (Paris, 1982), p. 402.

52 *Le Figaro*, 9 June, cit. R. Dreyfus, *Monsieur Thiers contre l'Empire* (Paris, 1928), pp. 43–4.

53 *Dosne*, Vol. 2, pp. 329–31.

54 Letter of 4 Sept. to Madame Bocher in the authors' possession; Basso (ed.), *Julie Bonaparte*, p. 464. Cf. Rémusat, Vol. 5, p. 253. One who wrote to condole was Guizot with whom he had resumed courteous relations in 1856.

55 Letter of 29 Sept. 1868, Basso (ed.), 'Lettere inedite', p. 65.

56 Rémusat, Vol. 5, p. 250, mentions ten 'parlementaires plus ou moins orléanistes' who were defeated. They included the Ducs Decazes and d'Audiffret-Pasquier, the Duc de Broglie's son, Albert, and Prévost-Paradol.

57 See introduction to Girard, *Les Elections de 1869*, pp. iv, v, and Girard, *Les Libéraux français*, pp. 200–6.

58 Schnerb, *Rouher*, p. 268; Guiral, *Prévost-Paradol*, p. 670. For speculations on whether he would have taken office, see Maxime du Camp, *Souvenirs d'un demi-siècle*, Vol. 1 (24th edn, Paris, 1949), p. 243.

59 *Carnets*, Vol. 2, p. 105. Letters of 23 April, 1 May from Thiers to Heirieis (BN n.a.fr. 24734).

CHAPTER 10

1 T. Zeldin, *Emile Ollivier and the Liberal Empire of Napoleon III* (Oxford, 1963), p. 174; E. Ollivier, *L'Empire libéral: études, récits, souvenirs*, 18 vols (Paris, 1895–1918), Vol. 14, p. 96; Lord Newton, *Lord Lyons: A Record of*

British Diplomacy, 2 vols (London, 1913), Vol. 1, p. 297. For background see L. D. Steefel, *Bismarck, the Hohenzollern Candidacy and the Origins of the Franco-German War of 1870* (Cambridge, Mass. 1962); L. M. Case, *French Opinion on War and Diplomacy during the Second Empire* (Philadelphia, 1954); and A. Sorel, *Histoire diplomatique de la guerre franco-allemande*, 2 vols (Paris, 1875).

2 Ollivier, *Empire libéral*, Vol. 14, p. 93; M. Howard, *The Franco-Prussian War* (London, 1961) p. 51.

3 Ollivier, *Empire libéral*, Vol. 14, pp. 193–4.

4 P. Lehautcourt, *Les Origines de la guerre de 1870: la candidature Hohenzollern 1868–1870* (Paris, 1917), pp. 647–8; speech by Thiers, 30 June, *Annales* (1870), Vol. 5, p. 301.

5 Rémusat, Vol. 5, p. 275.

6 *Annales* (1870), Vol. 5, pp. 302–3, 310–11; *Enquête GDN*, Vol. 4, pp. 9–10, 14.

7 BN n.a.fr. 20620, fol. 203 (and in *Courrier*, pp. 414–15).

8 Letter to Duvergier, 17 July, BN n.a.fr. 20620, fols 197–8 (and in *Courrier*, pp. 410–14). His account is confirmed by P. de La Gorce, *Histoire du Second Empire*, 7 vols (Paris, 1894–1905), Vol. 7, p. 273, and P. Muret, 'Emile Ollivier et le duc de Gramont les 12 et 13 juillet 1870', *Revue d'Histoire Moderne et Contemporaine*, vol. 13 (1909–10), pp. 305–6.

9 La Gorce, *Second Empire*, Vol. 7, pp. 289–99; W. E. Mosse, *The European Powers and the German Question 1848–1871: With Special Reference to England and Russia* (Cambridge, 1958), p. 387; Sorel, *Histoire diplomatique*, Vol. 1, pp. 137–47, 167–79.

10 *Annales* (1870), Vol. 6, pp. 68–9.

11 ibid., pp. 70–1.

12 ibid., pp. 80–2.

13 ibid., pp. 72, 100–5.

14 ibid., pp. 69, 71.

15 BN n.a.fr. 20620, fols 196–201 and 202–3 (and *Courrier*, pp. 410–16).

16 BN n.a.fr,. 20620 fol. 64.

17 ibid., fols 196–203.

18 Ollivier, *Empire libéral*, Vol. 14, pp. 582–97, 553–9.

19 Comte de Chambrun, *Nos historiens: Guizot, Tocqueville, Thiers* (Paris, 1888), p. 37.

20 BN n.a.fr. 20620, fol. 164.

21 Ollivier, *Empire libéral*, Vol. 16, pp. 300–1; *Annales* (Session Extraordinaire 1870), p. 146.

22 Rémusat, Vol. 5, p. 283.

23 ibid., p. 286

24 ibid., pp. 286–7; *Enquête GDN*, Vol. 4, p. 15.

25 Memoranda by Thiers for Committee, and its Minutes, BN n.a.fr. 20620; Rémusat Vol. 5, pp. 287–9; Ollivier, *Empire libéral*, Vol. 16, p. 427.

26 Thiers to *Enquête GDN*, Vol. 4, p. 17. A. W. Raitt, in *Prosper Mérimée* (London, 1970) p. 352, disbelieved Thiers's account of a visit from Mérimée at this time, and doubted that the visit of 18 August was made with the full authority of the Empress. It is significant, however, that two members of the parliamen-

tary Commission of Inquiry into the events of the war (*Enquête GDN*) were aware of these approaches from the Empress after Sedan (Vol. 4, pp. 17, 143–4). Moreover, Ollivier, though hostile, accepted Thiers's account. *Empire libéral*, Vol. 16, pp. 444, 467.

27 Thiers to *Enquête GDN*, Vol. 4, pp. 17–19; Ollivier, *Empire Libéral*, Vol. 16, pp. 469–83.

28 Jules Favre, *Gouvernement de la Défense Nationale*, 3 vols (Paris, 1871), Vol. 1, pp. 374–8.

29 Newton, *Lyons*, Vol. 1, p. 312.

30 Rémusat, Vol. 5, p. 300. See also Thiers to *Enquête GDN*, Vol. 4, p. 18.

31 *Gouvernement de la Défense Nationale: Procès-verbaux des séances du conseil* (Paris, 1906), p. 100; Favre, *Gouvernement*, Vol. 1, p. 128.

32 J. P. T. Bury, *Gambetta and the National Defence: A Republican Dictatorship in France* (London, 1936), p. 79.

33 Rémusat, Vol. 5, p. 287; *Enquête GDN*, Vol. 4, pp. 21–2; Castiglione Papers, BN n.a.fr. 25068; J. H. Rose, *The Mission of M. Thiers to the Neutral Powers in 1870* (London, 1918), p. 40; A. R. Allinson (ed.), *The War Diary of the Emperor Frederick III 1870–1871* (London, 1927), p. 148.

34 Thiers to Favre, 13 Sept., BN n.a.fr. 20629, fols 29–36; Lord Edmund Fitzmaurice, *The Life of Granville George Leveson Gower, Second Earl Granville K. G., 1815–1891*, 2 vols (London, 1905), Vol. 2, pp. 52–5.

35 H. G. G. Matthew (ed.), *The Gladstone Diaries with Cabinet Minutes and Prime-Ministerial Correspondence*, Vol. 7 (Oxford, 1982), p. 359; Thiers to Favre, 13 Sept., BN n.a.fr. 20629, fols 33–4; Fitzmaurice, *Granville*, Vol. 2, pp. 55–7; A. Ramm (ed.), *The Political Correspondence of Mr Gladstone and Lord Granville 1868–1876*, 2 vols (London, 1952), Vol. 1, pp. 135–7.

36 Favre, *Gouvernement*, Vol. 1, pp. 183–6.

37 Thiers to Favre, 13 Sept., BN n.a.fr. 20629, fols 33–5. (This important dispatch is reproduced in Favre, *Gouvernement*, Vol. 1, pp. 134–46, and summarized in *Memoirs of M. Thiers 1870–1873* (London, 1915), pp. 14–16.)

38 Ramm, *Correspondence*, Vol. 1, p. 124; Matthew, *Gladstone Diaries*, Vol. 7, pp. 358–60, 373.

39 Ramm, *Correspondence*, Vol. 1, pp. 129, 132, 135.

40 Matthew, *Gladstone Diaries*, Vol. 7, pp. 359–60, 372–3.

41 Thiers to Favre, 15 and 16 Sept., BN n.a.fr. 20629, fols 53–4 and 81–2.

42 Thiers, *Memoirs*, p. 24.

43 ibid., pp. 33–6, 42–3; Thiers to Chaudordy, 10 Oct., BN n.a.fr. 20629, fols 136–46; and see A. J. P. Taylor, *The Struggle for Mastery in Europe 1848–1918* (Oxford, 1971), pp. 214–5.

44 Rose, *Mission*, p. 51; Thiers to Chaudordy, 10 Oct., BN n.a.fr. 20629, fols 144–6.

45 Taylor, *Struggle*, p. 215; Mosse, *European Powers*, pp. 335–7, 342–4.

46 Thiers to Chaudordy, 10 Oct., BN n.a.fr. 20629, fols 141, 145, 147–8.

47 Mosse, *European Powers*, pp. 341–2; Thiers to Crémieux, 4 Oct., BN n.a.fr. 20629, fol. 105.

48 Thiers to Chaudordy, 10 Oct., BN n.a.fr. 20629, fols 149–50.

49 Taylor, *Struggle*, pp. 208–9; F. R. Bridge, *From Sadowa to Sarajevo: The Foreign Policy of Austria-Hungary, 1866–1914* (London, 1972), pp. 49–52;

J. Decsy, *Prime Minister Gyula Andrássy's Influence on Habsburg Foreign Policy during the Franco-German War of 1870–1871* (New York, 1979), Ch. 6.

50 Rose, *Mission*, pp. 55–6; Thiers, *Memoirs*, pp. 52–3. See also Decsy, *Andrássy*, pp. 102–3.

51 Chaudordy to Thiers, 2 Oct., BN n.a.fr. 20629, fol. 100.

52 Ramm, *Correspondence*, Vol. 1, pp. 139, 140, 146; Rose, *Mission*, p. 54.

53 Thiers to Chaudordy, 16 Oct., BN n.a.fr. 20629, fols 189–90; see also Sénard to Tours delegation, 3 Oct., ibid., fol. 125, and note of military plan, ibid., fol. 129.

54 F. Pichereau, 'M. Visconti-Venosta et la France en 1870', *Le Figaro*, 14 Aug. 1896.

55 Thiers to Chaudordy, 16 Oct., BN n.a.fr. 20629, fols 190–1.

56 Telegram, 16 Oct., BN n.a.fr. 20629, fol. 188; and see Thiers, *Memoirs*, p. 57.

57 Minutes of meetings, 21 Oct., and letter, Gambetta to Thiers, 25 Oct., BN n.a.fr. 20629, fols 193–4, 201; Bury, *Gambetta and the National Defence*, pp. 167–9; Sorel, *Histoire diplomatique*, Vol. 2, p. 46.

58 Bury, *Gambetta and the National Defence*, p. 166; Howard, *Franco-Prussian War*, pp. 294–5.

59 Dupanloup to Thiers, 23 Oct., BN n.a.fr. 20620, fol. 198–9; Castiglione papers, BN n.a.fr. 25068, fols 60, 62.

60 Thiers to Elise and Félicie, 1 Nov., and Favre, instructions to Thiers, 31 Oct., BN n.a.fr. 20629, fols 212 and 209; Thiers, *Memoirs*, pp. 66–72.

61 D. N. Raymond, *British Policy and Opinion during the Franco-Prussian War* (New York, 1921), p. 228.

62 Thiers's account of his mission, to representatives of the Great Powers. *The Times*, 17 Nov. 1870.

63 BN n.a.fr. 20629, fols 235–7.

64 M. Busch, *Bismarck in the Franco-German War 1870–1871*, 2 vols (London, 1879), Vol. 1, pp. 283, 290; Allinson, *War Diary*, pp. 176–8.

65 Thiers, *Memoirs*, pp. 91–4; the draft note to Bismarck, BN n.a.fr. 29529, fol. 235, is annotated by Thiers that it is not to be delivered.

66 Favre, *Gouvernement*, Vol. 2, pp. 23–4; A. Ducrot, *La Défense de Paris* (1870–1871), Vol. 2 (Paris, 1876), pp. 74–7; Thiers, *Memoirs*, pp. 95–7; *Gouvernement de la Défense Nationale*, p. 284.

67 BN n.a.fr. 20629, fols 229–31.

68 *Gouvernement de la Défense Nationale*, pp. 283–4; Bury, *Gambetta and the National Defence*, pp. 167–8, 172–3; Thiers and Gambetta to *Enquête GDN*, Vol. 4, pp. 28 and 482–8.

69 Bury, *Gambetta and the National Defence*, p. 274; Thiers to Mignet, 7 Nov., BN n.a.fr. 20629; Busch, *Bismarck*, Vol. 2, pp. 182–3; Broglie to Thiers, 14 Oct., BN n.a.fr. 20620, fol. 24.

70 Richard Hartshorne, 'The Franco-German boundary of 1871', *World Politics*, vol. 2 (1949–50), p. 211.

71 Thiers, *Memoirs*, pp. 92–3; *Gouvernement de la Défense Nationale*, p. 283.

72 Busch, *Bismarck*, Vol. 2, p. 341; and see Hartshorne, 'Franco-German boundary', pp. 299–31, 244. Neither side considered the iron-ore deposits, the full value of which was not yet realized.

73 Mosse, *European Powers*, p. 354.
74 Except for the Army of the East, which the Germans quickly surrounded.
75 Jules Simon, *The Government of M. Thiers: from 8 February 1871 to 24 May 1873* 2 vols (London, 1879), Vol. 1, pp. 24–43; letters to Thiers, BN n.a.fr. 20620 (e.g. from Broglie, Daru, Casimir-Perier, Rivet).
76 BN n.a.fr. 20620, fol. 142.
77 Thiers to Mignet, 7 Nov. 1870, BN n.a.fr. 20620.
78 Quoted in L. M. Greenberg, *Sisters of Liberty: Marseille, Lyon, Paris and the Reaction to a Centralized State, 1868–1871* (Cambridge, Mass., 1971), p. 314.
79 Speech of 30 June 1870, *Annales* (1870), Vol. 5, p. 301.

CHAPTER 11

1 R. R. Locke, 'A new look at conservative preparations for the French elections of 1871', *French Historical Studies*, vol. 5 (1967–8), pp. 351–8.
2 BN n.a.fr. 20622 (and *Courrier*, p. 424). He was elected in Basses-Alpes, Aude, Bouches-du-Rhône, Charente-Inférieure, Cher, Dordogne, Doubs, Drôme, Finistère, Gard, Gironde, Hérault, Ille-et-Vilaine, Landes, Loire-et-Cher, Loire, Loiret, Lot-et-Garonne, Nord, Orne, Pas-de-Calais, Saône-et-Loire, Seine, Seine-et-Oise, Seine-Inférieure, and Vienne. J. Gouault, *Comment la France est devenue républicaine: les élections générales et partielles à l'Assemblée nationale, 1870–1875* (Paris, 1954), p. 65.
3 BN n.a.fr. 20622 (and *Courrier*, pp. 425–6). For Thiers's election to office, *Annales* (1871), Vol. 1, p. 64.
4 Letter, 3 March, BN n.a.fr. 20621, fol. 166.
5 For Simon's later comments on the significance of this, see *Courrier*, pp. 423f.
6 ibid., p. 426.
7 BN n.a.fr. 20628, fol. 279; *Annales* (1871), Vol. 1, p. 287; BN n.a.fr. 20621 (Duvergier letters, 9 Feb. and 3 March), fols 165–7.
8 A. R. Allinson (ed), *The War Diary of the Emperor Frederick III 1870–1871* (London, 1927), pp. 311, 314, 325. See also R. I. Giesberg, *The Treaty of Frankfort: A Study in Diplomatic History September 1870–September 1873* (Philadelphia, 1966), pp. 108–9.
9 Giesberg, *Treaty*, p. 112; Allinson, *War Diary*, pp. 313–4. On indemnity, see F. Stern, *Gold and Iron: Bismarck, Bleichröder, and the Building of the German Empire* (London, 1977), pp. 150–4. For Thiers's own account, *Memoirs of M. Thiers 1870–1873* (London, 1915), pp. 102–16.
10 Giesberg, *Treaty*, p. 123.
11 Favre to Thiers, 4 March, BN n.a.fr. 20622, fol. 8; Thiers to Favre, 10 March, BN n.a.fr. 20623, fol. 108; Thiers to Favre, 12 March, MAE Papiers Favre, Vol. 5, fol. 13.
12 Favre to Thiers, 8 and 9 March, MAE Papiers Favre, Vol. 5, fols 314, 319–20; *Annales* (1871), Vol. 1, pp. 280–8; Ferry to *Enquête 18 mars*, Vol. 2, p. 64.
13 *Enquête 18 mars*, Vol. 2, p. 9.
14 Thiers to Gen. Susane, 5 March, AHG Li 90.
15 Thiers to *Enquête 18 mars*, Vol. 2, p. 11; Broglie to Thiers, 11 March, BN n.a.fr. 20621, fol. 76 Favre to Thiers, 6 March, BN n.a.fr. 20622, fol. 13.

16 For military aspects, see R. Tombs, *The War against Paris 1871* (Cambridge, 1981), pp. 36–43.
17 ibid., pp. 44–53; and see J. Rougerie, 'Notes pour servir à l'histoire du 18 mars 1871', in *Mélanges d'histoire sociale offerts à Jean Maitron* (Paris, 1976), pp. 229–48.
18 See their statements to *Enquête 18 mars*, especially those of Tirard, Dubail and Vautrin. For general accounts, see L. Fiaux, *Histoire de la guerre civile de 1871* (Paris, 1879), and D. Griffin, 'Adolphe Thiers, the mayors and the coming of the Paris Commune of 1871', Ph.D. thesis, University of California at Santa Barbara, 1971.
19 Tirard to *Enquête 18 mars*, Vol. 2, p. 343.
20 ibid., Vol. 2, pp. 340, 344; *Annales* (1871), Vol. 2, pp. 4–15, 20.
21 Saisset and Schoelcher to *Enquête 18 mars*, Vol. 2, pp. 308, 327.
22 He made no mention of them in the Assembly on 24, 25 and 26 March.
23 *Mémoires du Duc de Broglie*, 2 vols (Paris 1938), Vol. 2, p. 74.
24 Rémusat, Vol. 5, p. 335; and see Lord Newton, *Lord Lyons: A Record of British Diplomacy*, 2 vols (London, 1913), Vol. 1, p. 380; E. B. Washburne, *Recollections of a Minister to France, 1869–1877*, 2 vols (London, 1887), Vol. 2, p. 57; *Le Soir*, 26 March 1871.
25 Tombs, *War against Paris*, pp. 71–90.
26 The major recent contributor to the large historiography of the Commune has been Jacques Rougerie, with *Le Procès des communards* (Paris 1964), and *Paris libre 1871* (Paris, 1971).
27 See J. Gaillard, *Communes de province, Commune de Paris 1870–1871* (Paris, 1971), and 'La ligue d'union républicaine des droits de Paris', *Bulletin de la Société d'Histoire Moderne*, 13th series no. 5 (1966), pp. 8–13; L. M. Greenberg, *Sisters of Liberty: Marseille, Lyon, Paris and the Reaction to a Centralized State, 1868–1871* (Cambridge, Mass, 1971).
28 Rémusat, Vol. 5, p. 337; Thiers, *Memoirs*, p. 128.
29 F. C. Du Barail, *Mes souvenirs*, 3 vols (Paris, 1894–6), Vol. 3, p. 260.
30 Tombs, *War against Paris*, pp. 127–31; Thiers, *Memoirs*, pp. 132–4, 138–9.
31 Thiers, *Memoirs*, p. 129; *Enquête 18 mars*, Vol. 2, p. 14; Tombs, *War against Paris*, pp. 66–7, 104.
32 See, for example, correspondence and dispatches, AHG Lu 95 and Li 118 and 119 *passim*. Thiers's links with Cissey are well illustrated by nine letters written to him by Thiers during April and May, and in the authors' possession.
33 MAE Papiers Favre, Vol. 5, fols 70–1; Giesberg, *Treaty*, pp. 132–65; M. Paz, 'Le Mythe de la Commune: relations avec les Prussiens', *Est et Ouest*, no. 479 (Dec. 1971) pp. 20–4.
34 Thiers to Favre, MAE Papiers Favre, Vol. 6, fol. 119; see also Giesberg, *Treaty*, pp. 159–65.
35 BN n.a.fr. 20622, fol. 123 (25 Aug. 1871), See also Gaillard, *Communes*, pp. 83–4, and 'La Ligue', p. 12; and Greenberg, *Sisters of Liberty*, pp. 270–2, 310–14.
36 Favre to Thiers, 7 May, MAE Papiers Thiers, fol. 6.
37 Tombs, *War against Paris*, pp. 172–3.
38 Fiaux, *Guerre civile*, pp. 430–5; Gaillard, 'La ligue', pp. 11–12.
39 *Annales* (1871), Vol. 2, pp. 914, 918.

40 Greenberg, *Sisters of Liberty*, pp. 296–9.
41 Malo, pp. 509–10; G. Bouniols (ed.), *Thiers au pouvoir (1871–1873)*: *Texte de ses lettres* (Paris, 1921), pp. 68–9.
42 See C. Pelletan, *La Semaine de Mai* (Paris, 1880).
43 *Annales* (1871), Vol. 3, p. 135.
44 Thiers, *Memoirs*, p. 144; MacMahon to *Enquête 18 mars*, Vol. 2, p. 26.
45 Circular, 12 April, and Proclamation, 8 May, AHG Lu 95. (Authors' italics.)
46 Gen. Bruat to Gen. Vinoy, 14 June, AHG Li 125.
47 P. O. Lissagaray, *Histoire de la Commune de 1871* (reprint of 1896 edn, Paris, 1972), p. 497; *Enquête 18 mars*, Vol. 2, p. 468; Tombs, *War against Paris*, p. 178.
48 For discussion of this question, Tombs, *War against Paris*, pp. 174–5, 184–5.
49 Archives Jules Ferry (Bibliothèque Municipale de Saint-Dié).
50 Garcin to *Enquête 18 mars*, Vol. 2, p. 241; Gen. Vinoy, Circular, 29 May, AHG Li 124.
51 Tombs, *War against Paris*, pp. 116, 184–5; letter, Thiers to Cissey, 31 May, in authors' possession.
52 *Annales* (1871), Vol. 3, pp. 110, 117.
53 Broglie, *Mémoires*, Vol. 2, pp. 94–5; H. Rochefort, *Les Aventures de ma vie*, ed. G. Guichard-Meili (Paris, 1980), p. 177; BT, TMS. 1316, fol. 32.
54 Gaillard, 'La Ligue', p. 10.
55 H. Pessard, *Mes petits papiers*, Vol. 2, *1871–1873* (Paris, 1888), p. 152.
56 O. Rudelle, *La République absolue: aux origines de l'instabilité constitutionelle de la France républicaine 1871–1889* (Paris, 1982), p. 22.
57 Comte de Falloux, *Mémoires d'un Royaliste*, 2 vols (Paris, 1888).
58 *Annales* (1871), Vol. 5, pp. 199–201, 273. For stimulating, if diverging, accounts of Thiers's policy, see D. Halévy, *La Fin des notables*, 2 vols (Paris, 1930); P. F. Simon, *Adolphe Thiers, chef du pouvoir exécutif et président de la république française* (Paris, 1911); A. Lajusan, 'Adolphe Thiers et la fondation de la République (1871–1877), *Revue d'Histoire Moderne*, vol. 7 (1932), pp. 451–83, vol. 8 (1933) pp. 36–52; and Rudelle, *République absolue*.
59 Thiers to Cissey, 16 Oct. 1871 (in authors' possession).
60 Rémusat, Vol. 5, pp. 364–5. For Thiers's relations with the press, see P. Albert, *Histoire de la presse politique nationale au début de la Troisième République (1871–1879)*, 2 vols (Paris, 1980), Vol. 1, p. 334, Vol. 2, pp. 1213–14.
61 Rémusat, Vol. 5, p. 365.
62 B. Gille, 'Les Emprunts de la libération en 1871–1872', in *Mélanges offerts à Charles-Hippolyte Pouthas: la France au XIXe siècle* (Paris, 1973), pp. 172–81, 196; Rouland to Thiers, 13 March 1872, BN n.a.fr. 20623, fols 38–41; debate in Assembly (including Thiers's speech), 20 June 1871, *Annales*, Vol. 2, pp. 512–40; Thiers, *Memoirs*, pp. 157–66.
63 Gille, 'Les Emprunts', pp. 184–9; *Annales* (1871), Vol. 3, pp. 528–9; G. O. Kent, *Arnim and Bismarck* (Oxford, 1968), pp. 78–9; D. S. Landes, 'The spoilers foiled: the exclusion of Prussian finance from the French liberation loan of 1871', in C. P. Kindleberger and G. di Tella (eds), *Economics in the Long View: Essays in Honour of W. W. Rostow*, Vol. 2 (London, 1982), pp. 67–110.

64 Landes, 'The spoilers foiled', p. 75. See also P. Mathieu-Bodet, *Les Finances françaises de 1870 à 1878*, 2 vols (Paris, 1881), Vol. 1, pp. 184–5; BN n.a.fr. 20621, fol. 44 (police report).

65 BN n.a.fr. 20621, fols 46–51.

66 ibid., fol. 52. For the importance Thiers placed on hastening evacuation, as opposed to economic advantage, see R. Poidevin, 'Aspects économiques des négociations franco-allemandes, juin–octobre 1871', *Revue d'Histoire Moderne et Contemporaine*, vol. 19 (April–June 1972), pp. 219–34.

67 *Annales* (1871), Vol. 2, pp. 345–6.

68 M. S. Smith, *Tariff Reform in France 1860–1900: The Politics of Economic Interest* (Ithaca and London, 1980), p. 37.

69 R. Schnerb, 'La Politique fiscale de Thiers', *Revue Historique*, vol. 201 (Jan–June 1949), pp. 182–212 and vol. 202 (July–Dec 1949), pp. 184–220.

70 ibid., pp. 210–20; Smith, *Tariff Reform*, pp. 37–8, 145.

71 A. Mitchell, *Victors and Vanquished: The German Influence on Army and Church in France after 1870* (Chapel Hill and London, 1984), pp. 21–8. For Thiers's involvement in the building of new fortifications, see J.-C. Jauffret, 'Monsieur Thiers et le Comité de Défense, 1872–1888', *Cahiers de Montpellier*, no. 5 (1982), pp. 28–40.

72 Mitchell, *Victors*, pp. 33–8; D. Porch, *The March to the Marne: The French Army 1871–1914* (Cambridge, 1981), pp. 27–8.

73 Rémusat, vol. 5, p. 364.

74 Quoted in Lajusan, 'Thiers', p. 455.

75 BN n.a.fr. 20623, fols 98 (6 March 1871) and 107–8 (10 March); BN n.a.fr. 20626, fol. 121 (26 Sept. 1872).

76 ibid., fols 114 and 121 (16 and 26 Sept. 1872).

77 ibid., fol. 143 (4 Nov. 1872),

78 BN n.a.fr. 20626 and 20628, *passim.*, for diplomatic correspondence.

79 To Le Flô (ambassador to Russia), 22 Aug. and 26 Sept. 1872, BN n.a.fr. 20622, fols 62 and 121.

80 Giesberg, *Treaty*, pp. 216–17.

81 Kent, *Arnim*, pp. 104–5; Thiers, *Memoirs*, p. 191; A. Mitchell, *The German Influence in France after 1870* (Chapel Hill, NC, 1979), pp. 67–9; Giesberg, *Treaty*, pp. 219–40.

82 J. Simon, *The Government of M. Thiers: From 8 February 1871 to 24 May 1873* 2 vols (London, 1879), Vol. 2, p. 409.

83 Letter to Schneider, 19 Sept. 1872, BN n.a.fr. 20626, fol. 116 (and in *Courrier*, p. 457).

84 Message of 13 Nov. 1872, *Annales* (1872), Vol. 14, p. 18. For other important expressions of Thiers' advocacy of a Republic, see speech of 24 May 1873, *Annales* (1873), Vol. 18, pp. 45–54; and letters to Casimir-Perier (7 Oct. 1872), BN n.a.fr. 20626, fols 125–6, and Le Flô (4 Nov. 1872), ibid., fols. 139–40 (also in *Courrier*, pp. 466–70).

85 R. Hudemann, *Fraktionsbildung im französischen Parlament* (Munich, 1979), for details of membership of groups.

86 Broglie, *Mémoires*, Vol. 2, p. 114.

87 Halévy, *La Fin des notables*, Vol. 1, Ch. 12. Our account differs from his in

believing that Thiers wanted an alliance with the moderate Right, not with the extreme Left.

88 BN n.a.fr. 20626, fol. 107 (11 Sept. 1872) and in Bouniols, *Thiers au pouvoir: texte de ses lettres*, pp. 239–41.

89 J. P. T. Bury, *Gambetta and the Making of the Third Republic* (London, 1973), p. 108.

90 ibid., pp. 113–16; Thiers, *Memoirs*, pp. 275–7; Broglie, *Mémoires*, Vol. 2 pp. 123–4.

91 *Annales* (1872), Vol. 14, pp. 11–19.

92 Broglie, *Mémoires*, Vol. 2, p. 126; Thiers, *Memoirs*, pp. 282, 292; *Annales* (1872), Vol. 14, p. 20.

93 Broglie, *Mémoires*, Vol. 2, p. 117.

94 *Annales* (1872), Vol. 14, pp. 312–13; Broglie, *Mémoires*, Vol. 2, p. 133.

95 *Journal politique de Charles de Lacombe*, ed. A. Hélot, Vol. 1 (Paris, 1907), p. 160. For prosecution of Radical papers, see Albert, *Histoire de la presse*, Vol. 1, p. 330.

96 *Annales* (1873), Vol. 16, pp. 215, 219, 381–2; Lacombe, *Journal politique*, pp. 146–7.

97 *Annales* (1873), Vol. 16, pp. 277, 287; Broglie, *Mémoires*, Vol. 2, pp 132–3; Lacombe, *Journal Politique*, pp. 164–5.

98 Lajusan, 'Thiers', p. 39; see also Thiers's speech of 4 March, *Annales* (1873), Vol. 16, p. 283.

99 *Annales* (1873), Vol. 16, p. 298.

100 Pessard, *Mes petits papiers*, Vol. 2, p. 296.

101 See letters, Gen. Bourbaki to Thiers, 12 Aug. and 4 Sept. 1871, BN n.a.fr. 20621, fols 59–62. For his policy of general non-interference in local affairs, see P. C. Ali, 'Discretion shall preserve thee: the evolution of the French prefectoral corps under Adolphe Thiers, 1871–1873', Ph.D thesis, University of South Carolina 1983, pp. 214–15.

102 Bury, *Gambetta and the Making of the Third Republic*, pp. 139–45; Bury, 'The Seine and the Rhône. Two French by-elections in 1873', *Historical Journal*, vol. 10 (1967), pp. 391–9; J.-C. Wartelle, 'L'Élection Barodet (avril 1873)', *Revue d'Histoire Moderne et Contemporaine*, vol. 27 (Oct–Dec. 1980), pp. 601–30.

103 BN n.a.fr. 20628, fols 46–7.

104 Broglie, *Mémoires*, Vol. 2, pp. 96, 121.

105 Letter, 27 May 1873, BN n.a.fr. 20628, fol. 40.

106 *Mémoires*, Vol. 2, pp. 180–1.

107 Letter to Jules Simon, 18 May, in Simon, *Government*, Vol. 2, p. 423.

108 Lacombe, *Journal politique*, p. 146.

109 *Mémoires*, Vol. 2, p. 165.

110 Lacombe, *Journal politique*, p. 172; and see Simon, *Government*, Vol. 2, pp. 402, 427.

111 *Annales* (1873), Vol. 18, pp. 46–7, 54.

112 Broglie, *Mémoires*, Vol. 2, p. 139; Thiers to Tréveneuc, 28 May, BN n.a.fr. 20628, fols 42–3 (and in *Courrier*, p. 494).

113 Broglie, *Mémoires*, Vol. 2, pp. 104, 92.

114 *Annales* (1873), Vol. 18, p. 43 (speech of 24 May). For Thiers's ambition to

merit 'half a line' in history, see letter from Montalivet in *Courrier*, p. 440.
115 Message of 13 Nov. 1872, *Annales* (1872), Vol. 14, p. 18.

CHAPTER 12

1 Mary King Waddington, *My First Years as a Frenchwoman, 1876–1879* (London, 1914), p. 302; *Memoirs of Prince Chlodwig of Hohenlohe Schillingsfuerst*, ed. F. Curtius, Vol. 2 (London, 1906), p. 151. For a detailed description of the two houses and their furnishings, see François Fossier, 'La Maison du parricide. Heurs et malheurs de l'hôtel Thiers', *Bulletin de la Société de l'Histoire de Paris et de l'Ile de France* (1982), pp. 279–88.
2 Hohenlohe, *Memoirs*, p. 137.
3 E. L. G. H. de Marcère, *Histoire de la République de 1876 à 1879*, 2 vols (Paris, 1908–10), Vol. 2, p. 89.
4 *The Times*, 8 Sept. 1875.
5 For example, letters from Duvergier, 11 July, 26 Oct. 1874 and Pasteur, 14 May 1874, BN n.a.fr. 20628.
6 Letter of 30 Jan. 1875 to Bonnal (ibid.).
7 C. Bellanger *et al.*, *Histoire générale de la presse française*, 5 vols (Paris, 1969–76), Vol. 3, p. 214.
8 Cit. Malo, p. 581.
9 Cit. C. Pomaret, *Monsieur Thiers et son siècle* (Paris, 1948), p. 275.
10 Cit. J. P. T. Bury, *Gambetta and the Making of the Third Republic* (London, 1973), p. 167.
11 Maxime Du Camp, *Souvenirs d'un demi-siècle*, 2 vols (Paris, 1949), Vol. 2, p. 307.
12 L. Gambetta, *Lettres 1868–1882*, ed. D. Halévy and E. Pillias (Paris, 1938), nos 205 and 213.
13 Probably because of his independent character as well as having been President of the Republic he never formally enrolled as a member of the group in the National Assembly, and it seems unlikely that he did so in the Chamber of 1876–7. We are grateful to Dr Rainer Hudemann for his expert opinion.
14 *Illustrated London News*, 15 Nov. 1873; *Discours*, Vol. 15, p. 639.
15 *Illustrated London News* 10 Oct. 1874; letter from Saint-Hilaire, 13 Oct. 1874, BN n.a.fr. 20628.
16 Cit. Bury, *Gambetta and the Making of the Third Republic* p. 199.
17 F. Goguel, *La Politique des partis sous la III e République (1871–1939)* 2 vols (Paris, 1958), Vol. 1, p. 42. E. Laboulaye was unduly optimistic in 1863 when he wrote in *Le Parti libéral son programme et son avenir*, p. 179, that the division of representatives between two chambers had become an undisputed political axiom.
18 P. de Rémusat, *A. Thiers* (Paris, 1889), p. 213.
19 A. Mitchell, *The German Influence in France after 1870* (Chapel Hill, NC, 1979), p. 134.
20 *Discours*, Vol. 15, pp. 654–5.
21 Bury, *Gambetta and the Making of the Third Republic*, p. 261; P. Bosq, *Souvenirs de l'assemblée nationale 1871–1875*, (Paris, 1908), pp. 334–7.

22 Hohenlohe, *Memoirs*, Vol. 2, p. 171.
23 R. Henrey, *Letters from Paris* (London, 1942), 3 Oct. 1874. Gambetta in a celebrated speech in 1872 had called himself a traveller and salesman of democracy.
24 P. Cambon, *Correspondance 1870–1924*, Vol. 1 (Paris, 1914), p. 66, 15 May 1875.
25 *Discours*, Vol. 15, p. 660.
26 *Courrier*, p. 482; see above, p. 217.
27 In a letter of 10 Nov. 1874 Lord Granville gave Gladstone an amusing account of Thiers wrangling with his hostess at Voltri: 'age', wrote Granville, 'is beginning to have its effect'. A. Ramm (ed.), *The Political Correspondence of Mr Gladstone and Lord Granville 1868–1876*, 2 vols (London, 1952), Vol. 2, p. 549.
28 Madame Thiers survived until 1880, Mademoiselle Dosne until 1906.
29 Cit. E. Ollivier, *L'Empire libéral: études, récits, souvenirs*, 18 vols (Paris, 1895–1918), Vol. 6, pp. 383–5.
30 *The Times*, 8 Sept. 1875.
31 Mitchell, *The German Influence*, p. 184; Marcère, *Histoire de la République*, Vol. 1, p. 194.
32 D. Halévy, *La République des ducs* (Paris, 1937), pp. 278–9.
33 *Courrier*, pp. 502–3.
34 To Princess Julie Bonaparte, 25 June, cit. Ollivier, *L'Empire libéral*, Vol. 6, p. 387.
35 Hohenlohe, *Memoirs*, Vol. 2, pp. 194–5.
36 Bury, *Gambetta and the Making of the Third Republic*, p. 419.
37 One of Gambetta's playful names for Thiers (ibid., p. 425 n.1).
38 J. Adam, *Après l'abandon de la revanche* (Paris, 1910), pp. 39–40. For Hohenlohe's vivid account of his meeting with Gambetta who listened to Thiers's old stories 'with the attentiveness of a son', see his *Memoirs*, Vol. 2, p. 195.
39 Gambetta, *Lettres*, no. 327.
40 E. A. Vizetelly, *Republican France 1870–1912* (London, 1912), p. 215.
41 Mitchell, *The German Influence*, p. 157.
42 Hohenlohe, *Memoirs*, Vol. 2, p. 196; cf. similar words to Francis Charmes quoted by H. Avenel, *Histoire de la presse française depuis 1789 jusqu'à nos jours* (Paris, 1900), p. 729.
43 Hohenlohe, *Memoirs*, Vol 2, p. 197; Waddington, *My First Years*, p. 31.
44 *Lettres de Jules Ferry, 1846–1893* (Paris, 1914), p. 247; Gambetta, *Lettres*, no. 333.
45 Letter of 4 Oct. 1877 (Houghton Papers, Trinity College Library, Cambridge).
46 'Ah! si le Grand vieillard était encore là, quelle revanche!' (Gambetta, *Lettres*, no. 340, 28 Sept.).

CHAPTER 13

1 C. A. Sainte-Beuve, *Cahiers*, ed. J. Troubat (Paris, 1876), p. 59.
2 N. W. Senior, *Conversations with M. Thiers, M. Guizot and Other Distinguish-*

ed Persons during the Second Empire, 2 vols (London, 1878), Vol. 2, p. 341, Vol. 1, p. 118.

3 Sainte-Beuve, *Cahiers*, pp. 66 and 20. Guizot's remark was an instance of the pot calling the kettle black.

4 Senior, *Conversations with M. Thiers*, Vol. 1, p. 135; Sainte-Beuve, *Cahiers*, p. 106.

5 S. Mellon, *The Political Uses of History: A Study of Historians in the French Restoration* (Stanford, Calif., 1958), p. 2.

6 W. Bagehot, *Collected Works* (London, 1965), Vol. 4, p. 437.

7 Senior, *Conversations with M. Thiers*, Vol. 1, p. 407.

8 *Oeuvres de Napoléon III* (Paris, 1856), Vol. 1, p. 342; A. Thiers, *La Monarchie de 1830* (Paris, 1831).

9 A. Thiers, *Plan d'un ouvrage de philosophie* (Paris, 1905), p. 6.

10 P. de Rémusat, *A. Thiers* (Paris, 1889), p. 104.

11 J. Vier, *La Comtesse d'Agoult et son temps* (Paris, 1955–63), Vol. 6, pp. 53–4; Acton MS Add. 4917 F, card 89 (Cambridge University Library).

12 Malo, p. 210.

13 E. Ollivier, *L'Empire libéral: études, récits, souvenirs*, 18 vols (Paris, 1895–1918), Vol. 6, (1864), p. 368; Théophile Silvestre, *La Conspiration des Quarante*.

14 Senior, *Conversations with M. Thiers*, Vol. 1, p. 39.

15 Speech of 15 June 1874, cit. J. P. T. Bury, *Gambetta and the Making of the Third Republic*, p. 199.

16 Senior, *Conversations with M. Thiers*, Vol. 1, p. 39.

17 I. D. Basso, 'Lettere inedite di Thiers alla Principessa Giulia Bonaparte Roccagiovine', *Trimestre*, vol. 6, nos 1–2 (March–June 1972), p. 34.

18 E. Beau de Loménie, *Les Responsabilités des dynasties bourgeoises*, 3 vols (Paris, 1947–63), Vol. 1, p. 103.

19 R. Blake, *Disraeli* (paperback edn, London, 1978), p. 762.

20 C. A. Sainte-Beuve, *Cahiers*, ed. R. Molho, Vol. 1 (Paris, 1973), p. 273.

21 E.g. a main theme in F. Sieburg's *Is God a Frenchman?* (London, 1931).

22 H. Pessard, *Mes petits papiers, 1860–1870* (Paris, 1888), Vol. 1, p. 93.

23 W. Bagehot, *Collected Works*, Vol. 4, p. 437.

24 Interview in *Le Monde*, 11–12 Sept. 1983.

25 A. J. Grant, *Three Speeches of Adolphe Thiers* (London, 1919), p. 18.

Bibliography

MAIN PRIMARY SOURCES

Manuscripts

Bibliothèque Nationale: Papiers Thiers.
    I. Correspondances n.a.fr. 20601–20628.
    II. Documents n.a.fr. 20629–20684.
    'Candidatures de Thiers dans les Bouches-du-Rhône (1831–1870)', n.a.fr. 24734.
Bibliothèque Thiers: Fonds Thiers.
Ministère des Affaires Etrangères: Papiers d'agents.
    Papiers Thiers.
    Papiers Favre, Vols 5 (Feb.—March) and 6 (March–June) 1871.
Archives Historiques de Guerre: 'Guerre de 1870–71'.
    Series Li, 'Armée de Paris', and Lu, 'Armée de Versailles'.
Bibliothèque Municipale de Saint-Dié: Archives Jules Ferry.
Ministère des Affaires Etrangères, Belgium: Correspondance Politique
    Légations: France, Vol. 10 (1840).
Bibliothèque Nationale: Papiers Castiglione, n.a.fr. 25068.
University Library, Cambridge: Acton Papers.
Trinity College Library, Cambridge: Houghton Collection.

Printed Correspondence

Allain-Targé, H., *La République sous l'Empire: Lettres (1864–1870)*, ed. S. de la Porte (Paris, 1939).
Ampère, A. M. and J. J., *Correspondance et souvenirs (de 1805 à 1864)*, 2 vols (4th edn, Paris, 1877).
Aumale, Duc d', *Correspondance du duc d'Aumale et de Cuvillier-Fleury*, 4 vols (Paris, 1910–14).
Cambon, P., *Correspondance 1870–1924*, Vol. 1 (Paris, 1914).
Cauchois-Lemaire, A., *Lettres politiques, religieuses et historiques*, 2 vols (Paris, 1828–32).
Faucher, L., *Biographie et correspondance*, 2 vols (2nd edn, Paris, 1875).
Gambetta, L., *Lettres, 1868–1882*, ed. D. Halévy and E. Pillias (Paris, 1938).
Gladstone, W. E., *The Political Correspondence of Mr Gladstone and Lord Granville 1868–1876*, ed. A. Ramm, 2 vols (London, 1952).
Pasteur, L., *Correspondance de Pasteur 1840–1895*, ed. P. Vallery-Radot, 3 vols (Paris, 1951).

Thiers, A., *Correspondances de 1841 à 1865: M. Thiers à Mme Thiers et à Mme Dosne: Mme Dosne à M. Thiers* (Paris, 1904).

'Adolphe Thiers et la Duchesse Colonna', ed. H. Bessis, unpublished thesis, Université de Paris I, 1977.

Correspondances du siècle dernier: un projet de mariage du duc d'Orléans (1836): lettres de Léopold Ier de Belgique à Adolphe Thiers (1836–64) ed. L. de Lanzac de Laborie (Paris, 1918).

Le Courrier de M. Thiers: d'après les documents conservés au département des manuscrits de la Bibliothèque Nationale ed. D. Halévy (Paris, 1921).

'Lettere inedite di Thiers alla principessa Giulia Bonaparte Roccagiovine', ed. I. Basso, *Trimestre*, vol. 6, nos 1–2 (March–June 1972), pp. 19–71.

Thiers, A., 'Lettres de M. Thiers à la Comtesse Taverna', *Le Correspondant*, vol. 188 (25 Sept. 1906), pp. 1064–99.

'M. Thiers à la conquête de Paris, avec trente-quatre lettres inédites', ed. F. Benoît, *Le Correspondant*, vol. 287 (1922), pp. 786–819.

Thiers au pouvoir (1871–1873): Texte de ses lettres ed G. Bouniols (Paris, 1921).

Tocqueville, A. de, *Oeuvres et correspondances inédites*, ed. G. de Beaumont, 8 vols (Paris, 1861).

Victoria, *The Letters of Queeen Victoria: A Selection from Her Majesty's Correspondence between the Years 1827 and 1861*, ed. A. C. Benson and Lord Esher, 3 vols (London, 1907).

Works by Thiers cited in text

Histoire de Law (Paris, 1826). *Les Pyrénées et le Midi de la France* (Paris, 1823).

Histoire de la Révolution française, 10 vols (Paris, 1823–7) (first two volumes published under names of A. Thiers and F. Bodin).

La Monarchie de 1830 (Paris, 1831).

Histoire du Consulat et de l'Empire, 20 vols (Paris, 1845–62).

Du droit de propriété (Paris, 1848) (also published as *De la propriété*, Paris, 1848).

Plan d'un ouvrage de philosophie (Paris, 1905).

Printed Documents

A l'origine de la liberté de l'enseignement: la Commission extraparlementaire de 1849: texte intégral inédit des procès-verbaux, ed. G. Chenesseau (Paris, 1937).

Annales (du Parlement Français, du Corps Législatif, de l'Assemblée Nationale) (Paris, 1830–73).

Correspondence Relative to the Affairs of the Levant (Accounts and Papers 1841) (Session 1841), Vol. 29 (London, 1841).

Discours parlementaires de M. Thiers, ed. M. Calmon, 16 vols (Paris, 1879–89).

Enquête parlementaire sur l'insurrection du 18 mars, 2 vols (Versailles, 1872).

Enquête sur les actes du Gouvernement de la Défense Nationale, 7 vols (*Annales de l'Assemblée Nationale, Annexes* Vols 20–6) (Paris, 1874).

Gouvernement de la Défense Nationale (4 septembre 1870–6 février 1871): Procès-verbaux des séances du conseil: publiés d'après les manuscrits originaux de M. A. Dréo, ed. H. des Houx (Paris, 1906).

Newspapers

Le Constitutionnel (1822–3).
Le National (1830).
Le Bien Public (1871–3).
Le Soir (1871).

MEMOIRS

Apponyi, R., *Vingt-cinq ans à Paris, Journal du Comte Rodolphe Apponyi*, 4 vols (4th edn, Paris, 1913).

Barante, G. de, *Souvenirs du Baron de Barante*, ed. C. de Barante, 8 vols (Paris, 1890–1901).

Barrot, O.. *Mémoires posthumes d'Odilon Barrot*, 4 vols (Paris, 1875–6).

Beyens, Baron, *Le Second Empire vu par un diplomate belge*, 2 vols (Bruges, 1924).

Blanc, L., *The History of Ten Years 1830–1840*, 2 vols (London, 1844).

Bonaparte, J., *La Princesse Julie Bonaparte, Marquise de Roccagiovine, et son temps: Mémoires inédits (1853–1870)*, ed. I. Dardano Basso, 2 vols (Rome, 1975).

Bonnelier, H., *Mémorial de l'Hôtel de Ville de Paris 1830* (Paris, 1830).

Broglie, C. J. V. A., Duc de, *Mémoires du Duc de Broglie*, 2 vols (Paris, 1938).

Chambolle, A., *Retours sur la vie* (Paris, 1912).

Chateaubriand, F. R. de, *Mémoires d'outre-tombe*, ed. M. Levaillant, Vol. 3 (Paris, 1948).

Darimon, A., *Histoire de douze ans (1857–1869): Notes et souvenirs* (2nd edn, Paris, 1883).

Darimon, A., *Histoire d'un parti: les Irréconciliables sous l'Empire, 1867–1869* (Paris, 1888).

Dino, Duchesse de, *Chronique de 1831 à 1862*, Vol. 2 (5th edn, Paris 1909).

Dosne, S., *Mémoires de Madame Dosne, l'Egérie de M. Thiers*, ed. H. Malo, 2 vols (Paris, 1928).

Du Barail, F. C., *Mes souvenirs*, 3 vols (Paris, 1894–6).

Du Camp, M., *Souvenirs d'un demi-siècle*, Vol. 1 (24th edn, Paris, 1949).

Ducrot, A., *La Défense de Paris (1870–1871)*, Vol. 2 (Paris, 1876).

Falloux, A., Comte de, *Mémoires d'un Royaliste*, 2 vols (Paris, 1888).

Favre, J., *Gouvernement de la Défense Nationale*, 3 vols (Paris, 1871).

Fortoul, H., *Journal d'Hippolyte Fortoul*, Vol 1 (Geneva, 1979).

Frederick (German Emperor), *The War Diary of the Emperor Frederick III 1870–1871*, ed. A. R. Allinson (London, 1927).

Gladstone, W. E., *The Gladstone Diaries with Cabinet Minutes and Prime-Ministerial Correspondence*, ed. H. G. G. Matthew, Vol. 7 (Oxford, 1982).

Guizot, F., *Mémoires pour servir à l'histoire de mon temps*, Vol. 5 (Paris, 1862).

Halévy, L., *Carnets*, ed. D. Halévy, 2 vols (Paris, 1935).

Hohenlohe, *Memoirs of Prince Chlodwig of Hohenlohe-Schillingfuerst*, ed. F. Curtius, Vol. 2 (London, 1906).

Hübner, Comte de, *Neuf ans de souvenirs d'un ambassadeur d'Autriche à Paris sous le Second Empire 1851–1859*, ed. Comte A. de Hübner, 2 vols (Paris, 1904).

Hugo, V., *Choses vues: Souvenirs, journaux, cahiers, 1847–1848*, ed. H. Juin (Paris, 1972).

Lacombe, C. de, *Journal politique de Charles de Lacombe*, ed. A. Hélot, Vol. 1 (Paris, 1907).

Marcère, E. de, *L'Assemblée Nationale de 1871: Gouvernement de M. Thiers* (Paris, 1904).

Marcère, E. de, *Histoire de la République de 1876 à 1879*, 2 vols (Paris, 1908–10).

Montalivet, M. C. B., Comte de, *Fragments et souvenirs*, Vol. 2 (Paris, 1900).

Morgan, S. Lady, *France in 1829–30*, 2 vols (London, 1830).

Normanby, Marquis of, *A Year of Revolution: From a Journal Kept in Paris in 1848*, 2 vols (London, 1857).

Ollivier, E., *L'Empire libéral: études, récits, souvenirs*, 18 vols (Paris, 1895–1918).

Ollivier, E., *Journal 1846–1869*, ed. T. Zeldin and A. Troisier de Diaz, 2 vols (Paris, 1961).

Pessard, H., *Mes petits papiers*, Vol. 2 (*1871–1873*) (Paris, 1888).

Rémusat, C. de, *Mémoires de ma vie*, ed. C. Pouthas, 5 vols (Paris, 1958–67).

Rochefort, H., *Les Aventures de ma vie*, ed. G. Guichard-Meili (Paris, 1980).

Rozet, I.., *Chronique de Juillet 1830*, 2 vols (Paris, 1832).

Sainte-Beuve, C. A., *Portraits contemporains*, Vol. 2 (Paris, 1852).

Sainte-Beuve, C. A., *Cahiers*, ed. R. Molho, Vol. 1 (Paris, 1973).

Sainte-Beuve, C. A., *Cahiers*, ed. J. Troubat (Paris, 1876).

Senior, N. W., *Journals Kept in France and Italy from 1848 to 1852*, 2 vols (London, 1871).

Senior, N. W., *Conversations with M. Thiers, M. Guizot and Other Distinguished Persons during the Second Empire*, 2 vols (London, 1878).

Senior, N. W., *Conversations with Distinguished Persons during the Second Empire from 1860 to 1863*, 2 vols (London, 1880).

Simon, J., *The Government of M. Thiers: From 8 February 1871 to 24 May 1873*, 2 vols (London, 1879).

Spuller, E., *Figures disparues: Portraits contemporains politiques et littéraires* (*Première série*) (Paris, 3rd edn, 1894).

Thiers, A., *Notes et souvenirs de M. Thiers : 1848 : Révolution du 24 février* (Paris, 1902).

Thiers, A., *Memoirs of M. Thiers 1870–1873* (London, 1915).

Tocqueville, A. de, *Recollections of Alexis de Tocqueville*, ed. J. P. Mayer (London, 1948).

Viennet, J. P. G., *Journal de Viennet, Pair de France, témoin de trois règnes 1817–1848* (Paris, 1955).

Waddington, M. K., *My First Years as a Frenchwoman, 1876–1879* (London, 1914).

Washburne, E. B., *Recollections of a Minister to France, 1869–1877*, 2 vols (London, 1887).

PRINCIPAL SECONDARY WORKS

Albert, P., *Histoire de la presse politique nationale au début de la Troisième République* (*1871–1879*), 2 vols (Paris, 1980).

Albert, P., *et al.*, *Documents pour l'histoire de la presse nationale aux XIXe et XXe siècles* (Paris, 1973).

Albrecht-Carrié, R., *Adolphe Thiers or the Triumph of the Bourgeoisie* (Boston, Mass., 1977).

Ali, P. C., 'Discretion shall preserve thee: the evolution of the French prefectoral corps under Adolphe Thiers, 1871–1873', Ph.D. thesis, University of South Carolina, 1983.

Allison, John M. S., *Thiers and the French Monarchy* (London, 1926).

Allison, John M. S., *Monsieur Thiers* (London, 1932).

Anderson, M. S., *The Eastern Question, 1774–1929: A Study in International Relations* (London, 1966).

Anderson, R. D., *Education in France 1848–1870* (Oxford, 1975).

Aubert, J., *De quoi vivait Thiers* (Paris, 1952).

Aulard, A., 'Thiers historien de la Révolution française', *La Révolution Française*, vol. 66 (June 1914), pp. 492–520, and vol. 67 (July 1914), pp. 5–29.

Avenel, H., *Histoire de la presse française depuis 1789 jusqu'à nos jours* (Paris, 1900).

Balfour, Lady F., *The Life of George Fourth Earl of Aberdeen, K. G., K. T.*, Vol. 2 (London, 1922).

Baratier, E., *Histoire de la Provence* (Toulouse, 1971).

Barthou, L., *Thiers et la loi Falloux* (Paris, 1903).

Baschet, R., 'Thiers critique d'art: les salons de 1822 et de 1824', *Les Amis de Saint François*, vol. 12, no. 1 (Jan–Feb. 1971), pp. 11–18.

Bastid, P., *Doctrines et institutions politiques de la Seconde République*, 2 vols (Paris, 1945).

Bastid, P., *Les Institutions politiques de la monarchie parlementaire française, 1814–1848* (Paris, 1954).

Bastid, P., *Benjamin Constant et sa doctrine*, 2 vols (Paris, 1966).

Bazin, R., *Le Duc de Nemours* (3rd edn, Paris, 1907).

Beau de Loménie, E., *Les Responsabilités des dynasties bourgeoises*, 3 vols (Paris, 1947–63).

Bellanger, C., *et al.*, *Histoire générale de la presse française*, Vol. 2 (Paris, 1972).

Bernos, M., *et al.*, *Histoire d'Aix-en-Provence* (Aix-en-Provence, 1977).

Bertier de Sauvigny, G. de, *La Révolution de 1830 en France* (Paris, 1970).

Bertier de Sauvigny, G. de, *Au soir de la monarchie* (Paris, 1974).

Bezucha, R. J., *The Lyon Uprising of 1834: Social and Political Conflict in the Early July Monarchy* (Cambridge, Mass., 1974).

Blake, R., *Disraeli* (Paperback edn, London 1978).

Blanc, C., *Collection d'objets d'art de M. Thiers léguée au musée du Louvre* (Paris, 1884).

Bluche, F., *Le Bonapartisme: aux origines de la droite autoritaire (1800–1850)* (Paris, 1980).

Bourne, K., *Palmerston: The Early Years, 1784–1841* (London, 1982).

Boyer, F., 'Un demi-frère d'Adolphe Thiers vice-consul de Napoléon III à Girgenti', *Revue d'Histoire Diplomatique* vol. 73 (April–June 1959), pp. 129–36.

Bridge, F. R., *From Sadowa to Sarajevo: The Foreign Policy of Austria-Hungary, 1866–1914* (London, 1972).

Bruhat, J., *Les Journées de février 1848* (Paris, 1948).

Bullen, R., 'France and the problem of intervention in Spain, 1834–1836', *Historical Journal*, vol. 20, no. 2 (1977), pp. 363–93.

Bullen, R., 'France and Europe, 1815–48: the problem of defeat and recovery', in A. Sked (ed.), *Europe's Balance of Power, 1815–1848* (London, 1979), pp. 122–44.

Bulwer, Sir H. L., *The Life of Henry John Temple, Viscount Palmerston*, 3 vols (London, 1870).

Bury, J. P. T., *Napoleon III and the Second Empire* (London, 1964).

Bury, J. P. T., *Gambetta and the National Defence: A Republican Dictatorship in France* (London, 1936).

Bury, J. P. T., *Gambetta and the Making of the Third Republic* (London, 1973).

Bury, J. P. T., 'The Seine and the Rhône. Two French by-elections in 1873', *Historical Journal*, vol. 10 (1967), pp. 391–9.

Busch, M., *Bismarck in the Franco-German War 1870–1871*, 2 vols (London, 1879).

Case, Lynn M., *French Opinion on War and Diplomacy during the Second Empire* (Philadelphia, 1954).

Castries, R., Duc de, *Monsieur Thiers* (Paris, 1983).

Chambrun, J., Comte de, *Nos historiens: Guizot, Tocqueville, Thiers* (Paris, 1888).

Charles-Roux, F., *Thiers et Méhémet-Ali* (Paris, 1951).

Chauffour-Kestner, V., *Sur l'Histoire du Consulat et de l'Empire de M. Thiers* (Paris, 1863).

Christophe, R., *Le siècle de Monsieur Thiers* (Paris, 1966).

Ciampini, R., *Thiers et le 'Risorgimento' d'après les documents inédits* (Florence, 1948).

Collins, I., *The Government and the Newspaper Press in France 1814–1881* (London, 1959).

Crémieux, A., *La Révolution de février: étude critique sur les journées des 21, 22, 23 et 24 février 1848* (Paris, 1912).

Dansette, A., *Louis-Napoléon à la conquête du pouvoir* (Paris, 1961).

Dautry, J., *1848 et la deuxième république* (3rd edn, Paris, 1977).

Decsy, J., *Prime Minister Gyula Andrássy's influence on Habsburg Foreign Policy during the Franco-German War of 1870–1871* (New York, 1979).

Delacampagne, C., 'Ravaisson et l'idée d'action', *Le Monde*, 30 June 1984.

Dreyfus, F., *L'Assistance sous la seconde république (1848–1851)* (Paris, 1907).

Dreyfus, R., *La République de M. Thiers (1871–1873)* (Paris, 1930).

Dupanloup. F., *Le Catéchisme chrétien* (Paris, 1865).

Duvergier de Hauranne, P., *Histoire du gouvernement parlementaire en France, 1814–1848*, 10 vols (Paris, 1857–71).

Fagan, L., *The Life of Sir Anthony Panizzi, K. C. B.* 2 vols (London, 1880).

Farley, J., and Geison, G. L., 'Science, politics and spontaneous generation in nineteenth-century France: the Pasteur-Pouchet debate', *Bulletin of the History of Medicine*, vol. 48, no. 2 (Summer 1974), pp. 161–98.

Fiaux, L., *Histoire de la guerre civile de 1871* (Paris, 1879).

Fitzmaurice, Lord E., *The Life of Granville George Leveson Gower, Second Earl Granville K. G., 1815–1891*, 2 vols (London, 1905).

Fossier, F., 'La Maison du parricide. Heurs et malheurs de l'hôtel Thiers', *Bulletin de la Société de l'Histoire de Paris et de l'Île de France* (1982).

Gaillard, J., 'La Presse de province et la question du régime au début de la IIIe République', *Revue d'Histoire Moderne et Contemporaine*, vol. 6 (1959), pp. 295–310.

Gaillard, J., 'La Ligue d'union républicaine des droits de Paris', *Bulletin de la Société d'Histoire Moderne*, 13th series no. 5 (1966), pp. 8–13.

Gaillard, J., *Communes de province, Commune de Paris 1870–1871* (Paris, 1971).

Gastaldy, A., *Adolphe Thiers: origine, naissance, jeunesse du premier Président de la République française* (Paris, 1878).

Geyl, P., *Napoleon: For and Against* (new edn, London, 1965).

Giesberg, R. I., *The Treaty of Frankfort: A Study in Diplomatic History, September 1870 – September 1873* (Philadelphia, 1966).

Gille, B., 'Les Emprunts de la libération en 1871–1872', in *Mélanges offerts à Charles-Hippolyte Pouthas: la France au XIXe siècle* (Paris, 1973), pp. 166–98.

Giolitto, P., *Histoire de l'enseignement primaire au XIXe siècle: l'organisation pédagogique* (Paris, 1983).

Girard, L., *La Politique des travaux publics du Second Empire* (Paris, 1952).

Girard, L., *La IIe République (1848–1851)* (Paris, 1968).

Girard, L., *Nouvelle histoire de Paris: la Deuxième République et le Second Empire 1848–1870* (Paris, 1981).

Girard, L., *Les Libéraux français, 1814–1875* (Paris, 1985).

Girard, L. (ed.) *Les Élections de 1869* (Paris, 1960).

Girard, L. et al., *La Chambre des Députés en 1837–1839* (Paris, 1976).

Goguel, F., *La Politique des partis sous la IIIe République, 1871–1939* (Paris, 1958).

Gouault, J., *Comment la France est devenue républicaine: les élections générales et partielles à l'Assemblée nationale, 1870–1875* (Paris, 1954).

Grant, A. J., *Three Speeches of Adolphe Thiers* (London, 1919).

Greenberg, L. M., *Sisters of Liberty: Marseille, Lyon, Paris and the Reaction to a Centralized State, 1868–1871* (Cambridge, Mass., 1971).

Griffin, D., 'Adolphe Thiers, the mayors and the coming of the Paris Commune of 1871' Ph.D thesis, University of California at Santa Barbara, 1971.

Guiral, P., *Marseille et l'Algérie 1830–1841* (Gap, 1956).

Guiral, P., *Prévost-Paradol 1829–1870: pensée et action d'un Libéral sous le Second Empire* (Paris, 1955).

Halévy, D., *La fin des notables*, 2 vols (Paris, 1930).

Hamilton, C. I., 'Naval power and diplomacy in the nineteenth century', *Journal of Strategic Studies*, vol. 3, no. 2 (May 1980), pp. 74–88.

Hartshorne, R., 'The Franco-German boundary of 1871', *World Politics*, vol. 2 (1949–50), pp. 209–50.

Howard, M., *The Franco-Prussian War (London, 1961)*.

Howarth, T. E. B., *Citizen-King: The Life of Louis-Philippe King of the French* (London, 1961).

Hudemann, R., *Fraktionsbildung im französischen Parlament: Zur Entwicklung des Parteiensystems in der frühen Dritten Republik (1871–1873)* (Munich, 1979).

Jardin, A., *Alexis de Tocqueville, 1805–1859* (Paris, 1984).

Jardin, A, *Le Libéralisme politique en France, pensée et mouvement, de la crise du XVIIIe siècle à la Constitution de 1875* (Paris, 1985).

Jardin, A., and Tudesq, A.-J., *La France des notables* 2 vols (Paris, 1973).

Jauffret, J.-C., 'Monsieur Thiers et le Comité de Défense, 1872–1888', *Cahiers de Montpellier*, no. 5 (1982), 28–40.

Jennings, L. C., *France and Europe in 1848: A Study of French Foreign Affairs in Time of Crisis* (Oxford, 1973).

Johnson, D., *Guizot: Aspects of French History, 1787–1874* (London, 1963).

Jovy, E., *Autour de M. Thiers pascalisant, d'après des documents inédits* (Clermont-Ferrand, 1928).

Julien-Laferrière, F., *Les Députés fonctionnaires sous la Monarchie de Juillet* (Paris, 1970).

Kelly, A., *The Descent of Darwin: The Popularization of Darwinism in Germany, 1860–1914* (Chapel Hill, North Carolina, 1981).

Kent, G. O., *Arnim and Bismarck* (Oxford, 1968).

Knibiehler, Y., *Naissance des sciences humaines: Mignet et l'histoire philosophique au XIXe siècle* (Paris, 1973).

Lacour-Gayet, G., *Talleyrand 1754–1838*, 4 vols (Paris, 1928–34).

La Gorce, P. de, *Histoire de la Seconde République française*, 2 vols (Paris, 1887).

La Gorce, P. de, *Histoire du Second Empire*, 7 vols (Paris, 1894–1905).

La Gorce, P. de, 'M. Thiers, un bourgeois français du 19e siècle', *Revue des Deux Mondes*, vol 23 (1934), pp. 296–328.

Lajusan, A., 'Adolphe Thiers et la fondation de la République (1871–1877)', *Revue d'Histoire Moderne*, vol. 7 (1932), pp. 451–83 and vol 8 (1933), pp. 36–52.

Landes, D. S., 'The spoilers foiled: the exclusion of Prussian finance from the French liberation loan of 1871', in C. P. Kindleberger and G. di Tella (eds), *Economics in the Long View: Essays in Honour of W. W. Rostow*, Vol. 2 (London, 1982), pp. 67–110.

Laya, A., *Études historiques sur la vie privée, politique et littéraire de M. A. Thiers*, 2 vols (Paris, 1846).

Ledré, C., *La Presse à l'assaut de la monarchie*, 1815–1848 (Paris, 1960).

Lehautcourt, P., *Histoire de la guerre de 1870–1871*, Vol. 1 (Paris, 1901).

Lehautcourt, P., *Les Origines de la guerre de 1870: la candidature Hohenzollern 1868–1870* (Paris, 1917).

Lifka, M. L., 'Social order and upheaval: Adolphe Thiers as Minister of the Interior, 1832–1836', Ph.D. thesis, University of Michigan, 1974.

Lincoln, W. B., *Nicholas I, Emperor and Autocrat of All the Russias* (London, 1978).

Lissagaray, P.-O., *Histoire de la Commune de 1871* (reprint of 1896 edn, Paris, 1972).

Locke, R. R., 'A new look at conservative preparations for the French elections of 1871', *French Historical Studies*, vol. 5 (1967–8), pp. 351–8.

Lucas-Dubreton, J., *Aspects de Monsieur Thiers* (Paris, 1948).

Lucas-Dubreton, J., *Louis-Philippe et la machine infernale (1830–1835)* (Paris, 1951).

McManners, J., 'The historiography of the French Revolution', in A. Goodwin (ed.), *The New Cambridge Modern History*, Vol. 8 (Cambridge, 1971), pp. 618–52.

Magnus, P., *Gladstone* (paperback edn, London, 1963).

Malo, H., 'M. Thiers et les artistes de son temps', *Revue de Paris*, vol 31, part 4 (1924), pp. 141–59.

Malo, H., 'Madame Thiers', *Le Figaro*, 7 June 1924.

Malo, H., *Thiers 1797–1877* (Paris, 1932).

Marcou, J., *Life, Letters and works of Louis Agassiz*, 2 vols (London and New York, 1896).

Margadant, T. W., *French Peasants in Revolt: The Insurrection of 1851* (Princeton, 1979).

Marquant, R., *Thiers et le Baron Cotta* (Paris, 1959).

Mathieu-Bodet, P., *Les Finances françaises de 1870 à 1878*, 2 vols (Paris, 1881).

Mauguin, G., 'Thiers et son histoire de la république de Florence', *Annales de l'Université de Grenoble*, vol. 30, no. 2 (1918), pp. 241–94.

Mellon, S., *The Political Uses of History: A Study of Historians in the French Restoration* (Stanford, Calif., 1958).

Michaud, H., 'L'Exotisme de M. Thiers', *Annuaire-Bulletin de la Société de l'Histoire de France* (1976–7), pp. 157–63.

Mignet, F., *Histoire de la Révolution française*, 2 vols (Paris, 1824).

Mitchell, A., *The German Influence in France after 1870* (Chapel Hill, NC, 1979).

Mitchell, A., *Victors and Vanquished: The German Influence on Army and Church in France after 1870* (Chapel Hill and London, 1984).

Monteilhet, J., *Les Institutions militaires de la France (1814–1932)* (Paris, 1932).

Morin-Pons, F., 'Thiers avocat aixois', *Provence Historique*, vol. 9 (Oct–Dec. 1959), pp. 226–57.

Mosse, W. E., *The European Powers and the German Question, 1848–1871: With Special Reference to England and Russia* (Cambridge, 1958).

Muret, P., 'Emile Ollivier et le duc de Gramont les 12 et 13 juillet 1870', *Revue d'Histoire Moderne et Contemporaine*, vol. 13 (1909–10), pp. 305–28, and vol. 14 (1910), pp. 178–213.

Newman, E., 'The blouse and the frock coat', *Journal of Modern History*, vol. 46, no. 1 (March 1974), pp. 26–59.

Newton, T. W. L., Lord, *Lord Lyons: A Record of British Diplomacy*, 2 vols (London, 1913).

O'Brien, P., 'L'Embastillement de Paris: the fortification of Paris during the July Monarchy', *French Historical Studies*, vol. 9, no. 1 (1975), pp. 63–82.

Pannekoek, A., *A History of Astronomy* (London, 1961).

Pernoud, R., *Histoire de la bourgeoisie en France*, Vol. 2 (Paris, 1962).

Paz, M., 'Le Mythe de la Commune: relations avec les Prussiens', *Est et Ouest*, no. 479 (Dec. 1971), pp. 20–4.

Pelletan, C., *La Semaine de Mai* (Paris, 1880).

Pichereau, 'M. Visconti-Venosta et la France en 1870', *Le Figaro*, 14 Aug. 1896.

Pinkney, D., *The French Revolution of 1830* (Princeton, 1972).

Poidevin, R., 'Aspects économiques des négociations franco-allemandes, juin–octobre 1871', *Revue d'Histoire Moderne et Contemporaine*, vol. 19 (April–June 1972), pp. 219–34.

Pomaret, C., *Monsieur Thiers et son siècle* (Paris, 1948).

Porch, D., *The March to the Marne: The French Army 1871–1914* (Cambridge, 1981).

Pouthas, C., 'La Politique de Thiers pendant la crise orientale de 1840', *Revue Historique*, vol. 182 (Jan–June 1938), pp. 72–96.

Pouthas, C., 'Les Ministères de Louis-Philippe', *Revue d'Histoire Moderne et Contemporaine*, vol. 1 (April–June 1954), pp. 102–30.

Prest, J., *Politics in the Age of Cobden* (London, 1972).

Price, R., *The French Second Republic: A Social History* (London, 1972).

Rader, D. L., *The Journalists and the July Revolution in France* (The Hague, 1973).

Raitt, A. W., *Prosper Mérimée* (London, 1970).

Raphael, P., 'La Loi du 31 mai 1850', *Revue d'Histoire Moderne et Contemporaine*, vol. 13 (Nov.-Dec. 1909), pp. 277–304, vol. 14 (May–Oct. 1910), pp. 44–79 and 297–331.

Raymond, D. N., *British Policy and Opinion during the Franco-Prussian War* (New York, 1921).

Reboul, P., *Le Mythe anglais dans la littérature française* (Lille, 1962).

Réau, L., *M. Thiers, critique d'art et collectionneur* (Paris, 1921).

Reclus, M., *Monsieur Thiers* (Paris, 1929).

Rémusat, P. de, *A. Thiers* (Paris, 1889).

Ridley, J., *Napoleon III and Eugénie* (London, 1979).

Robert, A., Bourloton, E., and Cougny, G., *Dictionnaire des parlementaires français*, 5 vols (Paris, 1889–91).

Rosanvallon, P., *Le Moment Guizot* (Paris, 1985).

Rose, J. H., *The Mission of M. Thiers to the Neutral Powers in 1870* (London, 1918).

Rougerie, J., *Le Procès des communards* (Paris, 1964).

Rougerie, J., *Paris libre 1871* (Paris, 1971).

Rougerie, J., 'Notes pour servir à l'histoire du 18 mars 1871', in *Mélanges d'histoire sociale offerts à Jean Maitron* (Paris, 1976), pp. 229–248.

Rudelle, O., *La République absolue: aux origines de l'instabilité constitutionnelle de la France républicaine 1871–1889* (Paris, 1982).

Sainte-Beuve, C. A., 'Historiens modernes de la France: M. Thiers', *Revue des Deux Mondes*, vol. 9 (Jan. 1845), pp. 209–46.

Santoni, F., 'Le Premier Ministère Thiers', unpublished thesis, University of Paris I, 1971.

Schnerb, R., *Rouher et le Second Empire* (Paris, 1949).

Schnerb, R., 'La Politique fiscale de Thiers', *Revue Historique*, vol. 201 (Jan–June 1949), pp. 182–212, and vol. 202 (July–Dec. 1949), pp. 184–220.

Simon, P. F., *Adolphe Thiers, chef du pouvoir exécutif et président de la république française* (Paris, 1911).

Smith, M. S., *Tariff Reform in France 1860–1900: The Politics of Economic Interest* (Ithaca and London, 1980).

Smith P. D. G., 'The Orleanists, 1849–1852', Ph.D. thesis, University of Cambridge, 1979.

Sorel, A., *Histoire diplomatique de la guerre franco-allemande*, 2 vols (Paris, 1875).

Southgate, D., *'The Most English Minister ...' The Policies and Politics of Palmerston* (London, 1966).

Steefel, L. D., *Bismarck, the Hohenzollern Candidacy, and the Origins of the Franco-German War of 1870* (Cambridge, Mass., 1962).

Stern, F., *Gold and Iron: Bismarck, Bleichröder, and the Building of the German Empire* (London, 1977).

Taylor, A. J. P., *The Struggle for Mastery in Europe 1848–1918* (Oxford, 1971).

Ténot, E., *Paris en décembre 1851: étude historique sur le coup d'état* (Paris, 1868).

Ténot, E., *La Province en décembre 1851: étude historique sur le coup d'état* (Paris, 1865).

Thureau-Dangin, P., *Histoire de la Monarchie de Juillet*, 5 vols (Paris, 1884–90).

Tombs, R., *The War against Paris 1871* (Cambridge, 1981).

Tudesq, A.-J., *Les Grands Notables en France (1840–1849): étude historique d'une psychologie sociale* 2 vols (Paris, 1964).

Tudesq, A.-J., *L'Election présidentielle de Louis-Napoléon Bonaparte, 1. décembre 1848* (Paris, 1965).

Vallery-Radot, R., *La Vie de Pasteur* (Paris, 1900).

Vaughan, W., 'The visual arts', in D. G. Charlton (ed.), *The French Romantics*, Vol. 2 (Cambridge 1984), pp. 308–52.

Vidalenc, J., *La Restauration (1814–1830)* (Paris, 1966).

Vigier, P., *La Monarchie de Juillet* (3rd edn. Paris, 1969).

Wartelle, J.-C., 'L'Election Barodet (avril 1873)', *Revue d'Histoire Moderne et Contemporaine*, vol. 27 (Oct.–Dec. 1980), pp. 601–30.

Webster, Sir C., *The Foreign Policy of Palmerston, 1830–1841: Britain, the Liberal Movement and the Eastern Question*, 2 vols (London, 1951).

Weill, G., *Histoire du parti républicain en France (1814–1870)* (Paris, 1928).

Wright, V., 'The *coup d'état* of December 1851: repression and the limits to repression', in R. Price (ed.), *Revolution and Reaction: 1848 and the Second French Republic* (London, 1975), pp. 303–33.

Zeldin, T., *The Political System of Napoleon III* (London, 1958).

Zeldin, T., *Émile Ollivier and the Liberal Empire of Napoleon III* (Oxford, 1963).

Index

305